CW01574474

PRIVATE INTERNATIONAL LAW

INDIAN AND ENGLISH

PRIVATE INTERNATIONAL LAW

INDIAN AND ENGLISH

FOURTH REVISED AND ENLARGED EDITION

PARAS DIWAN

LL.M., Ph.D.

Former Director
Indian Institute of Comparative and Family Law
Formerly
Professor and Chairman
Department of Law, Panjab University, Chandigarh

and

PEEYUSHI DIWAN

B.A., LL.B., Advocate

DEEP & DEEP PUBLICATIONS
F-159, Rajouri Garden, New Delhi-110027

First Edition	:	1977
Second Revised and Updated Edition	:	1988
Third Revised and Updated Edition	:	1993
Fourth Revised and Updated Edition	:	1998

ISBN 81-7629-078-5

Typeset by Ashish Technographics, 3190, Mohindra Park, Shakur Basti, Delhi-110034.

Printed in India at Efficient Offset Printers, Plot-215, Shahzada Bagh, Delhi.

Published by DEEP & DEEP PUBLICATIONS, F-159, Rajouri Garden, New Delhi-110027. Phones : 5435369, 5440916

Dedicated

to

G.C. CHESHIRE

CONTENTS

PART IV

Law of Persons

PART V

Law of Property

PART VII

Procedure

PART VIII

Foreign Judgments

PREFACE TO THE FOURTH EDITION

We have, indeed great pleasure in presenting this updated fourth edition of our work on Private International Law.

The purpose of the book continues to be of providing to the practitioners and the students of law with a complete account of the entire gamut of Private International Law, English and Indian, with comparative reference to other systems.

We are very happy to record over appreciation to our Publishers, particularly to Shri G.S. Bhatia for taking meticulous care in the production of this work.

PARAS DIWAN
PEEYUSHI DIWAN

PREFACE TO THE THIRD EDITION

We are, indeed, very happy to present this third edition to our readers, both practioners and students of law from whom we are having encouraging response. In most of the Universities it is a prescribed book both for L.L.B. and L.L.M. courses.

This third edition of the work has been prepared by the original author in collaboration with his daughter Peeyushi Diwan, B.A., LL.B., Advocate.

In preparing the present edition, we have taken care to revise, update, and wherever necessary, to rewrite the text.

The purpose of this work continues to be of providing to the practitioners and the students of law with a short yet complete and up-to-date account of the entire gamut of Private International Law. We have tried to see that in the process of updating, the bulk of the work does not increase tangibly.

When the first edition of the work was published, it was hoped that by the time the other editions of the work go to the press sufficient Indian precedents would be available as some areas of Indian Private International Law would be codified so that our own rules of Private International Law would have some certainty. But that has not happened, and our reliance on English precedents to be as heavy as it was a decade or two earlier. Baldev Kohli, while reviewing this work, rightly said:

> Though attained its adulthood in the United Kingdom and other western countries, the subject of Private International Law is still in its infancy in our country. Literature, textual, judicial and legislative, is rather scanty and litigation under this head is minimal and less diversified than in western countries. Therefore, whenever the judges or lawyers are called upon to deal with disputes in this branch of law, they have almost always relied upon the exposition of the principles of law as laid down in England.

Kohli further observes:

The author seems to have borrowed extensively from the foreign authors especially Dicey and Cheshire, but then it is natural for any one writing on Private International Law to follow these authors who have covered different aspects of the subject in great details. It goes to the credit of the author, who, by his hard work, has brought together the scattered rules of Indian Private International Law and put them in a systematic manner.

Quite a few review of the work appeared in journals, and most of them were encouraging. All the reviewers welcomed the work and considered it as pioneering one. In the words of Arsad Masood, " In this perspective Prof. Paras Diwan's book under review comes as a pioneering work and they first in depth study of this precedent-ridden subject."

Apart from the reviewers, we received a number of communications from readers, both student and practitioners of law, containing some very useful suggestions. We have tried to benefit from them. Most of the suggestions we have incorporated in the work.

The Private International Law is yet a developing branch of law, and pace of development is slow; the pace development of Indian law has been particularly very slow. We had tried to note all the important developments in Indian and English Private International Law that took place between the two editions.

During the year 1991, the Supreme Court rendered two important judgments. In *Louis De Readt* v. *Union of India*, AIR 1991 SC 1886, the Supreme Court reiterated the well established proposition of law that, howsoever, long may be the residence of a person at a place, if he has no intention to reside there permanently he cannot acquire a domicile of choice at that place. Thus, where certain foreigners preferred to stay in India after independence on the basis of their passports issued by other countries after obtaining permission from time to time from Indian authorities for their stay in India for specific periods, such persons did not acquire a domicile of choice in India howsoever, long might have been their stay in India.

In *P.Y. Narasimha Rao* v. *Y. Venkata Lakshmi* (1991) 2 Scale 1. a case of recognition of foreign judgment of divorce, the Supreme Court has propounded the doctrine of contextual interpretation. The Supreme Court advancing this thesis observed that section 13(a) of Civil Procedure Code dealing with the competence of the foreign court's jurisdiction to pronounce a judgment which could be recognized by the Indian court said that this clause should be interpreted to mean that only that court would be of competent jurisdiction under which parties were married, i.e., the personal law. The court added that any other court would not be the court of competent jurisdiction unless the respondent had unconditionally submitted to the jurisdiction. In this case the basic question was whether judgment dissolving the marriage passed by court of the domicile of the parties could be recognized in India. Further, the judgment was passed on a ground not recognized under the personal law of the parties. We have seen in Chapter 9 under the title "Recognition of Foreign Divorces" that foreign divorces are recognized in England if the judgment is pronounced by the courts of the country where parties habitually reside, if either spouse is the national of country which pronounced divorce. Similarly, other clauses of section 13 have been given "contextual interpretation." But these interpretations do not help in the advancement of rules of private international law on progressive lines. In our submission this judgment does not also go to solve the problem of limping marriages. In this case the second marriage of the husband was valid in the United States but was a bigamous marriage in India.

The English Law stated in this work is up to December 1991 and the Indian Law is up to December 1992.

I also record my appreciation of Shri G.S. Bhatia of Deep and Deep Publications who has given his constant attention to the production of this work.

Chandigarh

PARAS DIWAN
PEEYUSHI DIWAN

PREFACE TO THE SECOND EDITION

I am happy to present the second edition of this work. The first edition was reasonably well received both by the lawyers and students, In most of the Universities it is a prescribed book both for LL.B. and LL.M. courses. The practitioner of law, too, have found the book useful.

In preparing the present edition. I have taken care to revise, update, and wherever necessary, to rewrite the text.

The purpose of this work continues to be of providing to the practitioner and the student of law with a short yet complete and up-to-date account of the entire gamut of private international law. I have tried to see that in the process of updating, the bulk of the work does not increase tangibly.

When the first edition of the work was published, I thought that by the time the second edition of the work goes to the press, sufficient Indian precedents would be available and some areas of Indian Private International Law would be codified so that our own rules of Private International Law would have some certainty. But that has not happened, and our reliance on English precedents continue to be as heavy as it was a decade or two earlier. Baldev Kohli, while reviewing this work, rightly says:

> Though attained its adulthood in the United Kingdom and other western countries, the subject of Private International Law is still in its infancy in our country. Literature, textual, judicial and legislative, is rather scanty and litigation under this head is minimal and less diversified than in western countries. Therefore, whenever the judges or lawyers are called upon to deal with disputes in this branch of law, they have almost always relied upon the exposition of the principles of law as laid down in England.

Kohli further observes:

> The author seems to have borrowed extensively from the foreign authors especially Dicey and Cheshire, but then it is natural for

any one writing on private international law to follow these authors who have covered different aspects of the subject in great details. It goes to the credit of the author, who, by his hard work, has brought together the scattered rules of Indian Private International Law and put them in a systematic manner.

Quite a few reviews of the work appeared in journals, and most of them were encouraging. All the reviewers welcomed the work and considered it as pioneering one. In the words of Arsad Masood, "In this perspective Prof. Paras Diwan's book under review comes as a pioneering work and the first in-depth study of this precedent-ridden subject."

Apart from the reviewers, I received a number of communications from readers, both students and practitioners of law, containing some very useful suggestions. I have tries to benefit from them. Most of the suggestions I have incorporated in the work. Wherever I have not been able to accept a suggestion, I have tried to give my reasons.

I have cited the provision of the Indian Succession Act, 1925 on domicile and had submitted that if our courts would have looked into them they would not have aped the provision of English law which, before the statutory reforms, adhered rigidly to the doctrine that domicile of married women is the same as and changes with the domicile of the husband. The Indian Succession Act recognizes that in some cases a married woman can have her own independent domicile and I submitted that our courts should have taken their cue from these provisions. One of the reviewers says that " the Indian courts were not wrong in ignoring the provision of the Indian Succession Act because the Act provides for domicile for the purpose of succession and it is doubtful if the said provision would apply to other matters involving question of domicile." That is the technical position, no one would doubt. But, if our courts are free to borrow English precedents—which are of persuasive value, and no more—should they be prevented from looking at the relevant provisions of Indian Law? I think it is their first duty to seek guidance from the existing analogous provisions of the Indian law.

One of the reviewers, in his review article, has mildly and in a friendly manner rebuked me from ignoring certain Indian precedents. After observing that Prof. Diwan is to be congratulated for making a very complicated and intricate subject so easy and understandable for his readers, for example, characterization and renvoi, which are considered as two of the most complicated areas of private international law, have been explained by Prof. Diwan in such a simple language, interspersed with lucid illustrations, that even a beginner would find the problem inherent in both the topics within the reach of his comprehension, he advised me that I should strengthen the topic of characterization by adding Indian cases like *Ram Lal* v. *Chaman Dass,* AIR 1938 Lah, 349, *Sukumar Banerjee* v. *Rajeshwari Devi,* AIR 1939 Cal. 237, and *Bhanrao* v. *Laxshmi Bai,* ILR (1986) 2 Bom. 610. Yes. I should have, but I find that these cases are not of much help. The first and the second cases lay down that where probate has been granted by a foreign court and the original will had been deposited there, the Indian court could grant letters of administration on the basis of the copy of the will, under the provision of sections 228 and 276, Indian Succession Act. The third case is also not relevant.

On renvoi, he desires me to consider: (1) *Ram Lal v. Chaman Dass*, AIR 1938 Lah. 349, (2) *Sukumar Banerjee* v. *Rajeshwari Devi* , AIR 1939 Cal. 237, (3) *Smt. Rani Parbati Devi* v. *Jagdish Chandra Bhaba*, (1910) 20 I.A.82, (4) *Balwant Rao* v. *Baji Rao* , AIR 1921 P.C. 59, (5) *Mailathi Ammi* v. *Subharaya Mudaliar* (1901) 24 Mad. 650, (6) *Ratan Shaw* v. *Bamanji,* AIR 1938 Bom. 239, (7) *Govindan* v. *Bharathi*, AIR 1964 Ker. 244, (8) *Md. Koya* v. *Katheesa Bi,* AIR 1945, Mad. 81, (9) *Mittar* v. *A.G. of Bengal* (1875-76) 1 Cal. 412, (10) *Hill* v. *A.G., Bengal* (1896) 23 Cal. 506, (11) *Sophy Averbeck* v. *Shivaprasad,* AIR 1945 Cal. 484. The first three cases do not deal with renvoi even remotely. The fourth case is a Hindu law case which embodies the well established proposition of Hindu Law that when a Hindu migrates from one place to another he carried with him his school, unless he adopts the law of the place to which he had migrated. The fourth and fifth cases are also of no relevance to the subject. The sixth case lays down the well established old rule of private international law that the status is determined according to the law of domicile and such a status will be recognized by the Indian Court, thought for the purpose of succession to immovable property *lex situs* governs. The seventh case deals with domocile of origin and its abandonment, succession to movable property, and recognition of foreign judgments. This case has been discussed at the relevant place in this work. The eighth case lays down that a foreign domiciled Indian has power to dispose of immovable property situated there (if law of domicile permits it) but his power to dispose of immovable property situated in India would be governed by the Indian Law, *lex situs*. The ninth and tenth cases lay down that succession to movables is determined on the basis of domicile of the deceased at the time of his death. The eleventh case lays down the old position of English law that the English courts would not recognize the potentially polygamous marriage of a Hindu with the result that his second marriage with a woman whose law does not recognize polygamy was valid. We have stated at relevant place of this work that this is no longer the position under English law. Thus, I would submit that these cases are not relevant on the topics on which the reviewer thought that I had omitted them to consider.

On commercial contracts the learned reviewer recommends me to consider *State aided Bank of Travancore Ltd.* v. *Dhrit Ram*, AIR 1942 P.C. 6; *Shankar Vishnu* v. *Meneklal Haridas Gujrathi,* AIR 1940 Bom. 362, *Brij Lal* v. *Ananat Prasad,* AIR 1942 Cal. 509, *Raman Chittiar* v. *Raman Chattiar*, AIR 1954 Mad. 97. The first two cases propound the doctrine of proper law of contract. The third case lays down that the general rule is that all the rights and incidents arising under the contract are governed by the proper law of contract, and the law of contract is the place where the contract is made. Obviously, this is an outmoded view. The fourth case lays down that law of contract depends upon the intention of parties. At relevant places I had discussed all these cases in the first edition itself.

Some of the reviewers and readers have suggested to me that I should also dwell on rules of private international law of other system also, such as those of continental Europe and East European countries including the Soviet Union. Although the suggestion is very good, I have not been able to accept the same for various reasons, the most cogent of which is that if I would do that I would stray away from the basic objective of the book.

The private international law is yet a developing branch of law, where pace of development is very slow; the Indian law moves with a snail's pace. I had tried to note all the important developments in Indian and English private international law that took place between the two editions.

The English law stated in this work is up to March 1987 and the Indian law is up to May 1987.

My thanks are due to Shri Vijai Nagpal, Lecturer in law, who helped me to update the work. I also record my appreciation of Shri G.S. Bhatia of Deep & Deep Publications who has given his constant attention to the production of this work.

Chandigarh PARAS DIWAN

PREFACE TO THE FIRST EDITION

The last two decades have been very fruitful in the development of private international law though international conferences and convention. English Private International Law, too, has made great strides in these two decades. The judicial legislation is having its due share. But the parliamentary legislation, mostly as a sequel to England's acceding to international convention, is also making its contribution.

Boys v. *Chaplin* has made important (and welcome) change in the law of torts. *Coast Lines Ltd.* v. *Huding and Veder Chartering N.V* rightly deprecates the hitherto existing tendency of placing too much reliance on the presumption in favour of the *lex loci contractus and lex loci solution is* in determining the proper law of the contract. With *Travers* v. *Holley, Indyka* v. *Indyka, Mather* v. *Mahoney* the English law of recognition of foreign divorces reached a stage which, some thought, was a deviation from sound legal principle. In this ara the English statutory law has not merely corrected the deviation but has changed the law considerably, though some of the changes are the result of England's acceptance of international conventions. The recognition of Divorces and Legal Separation Act, 1971, has apart from retaining the liberality of *Indyka* v. *Indyka,* made the law certain. It also recognizes by some new bases of recognition of foreign divorces and legal separations. The Domicile and Matrimonial Proceedings Act, 1973, overrules *Qureshi* v. *Qureshi,* and lays down the bases of recognition of non-judicial divorces.

The important statutes which modify certain areas of English Private International Law include the Adoption Act, 1968, the Nuclear Installation Act, 1965, Carriage of Goods by Sea Act, 1971, Merchant Shipping (Oil Pollution) Act, 1971, Maintenance Orders (Reciprocal Enforcement) Act, 1972, Civil Evidence Act, 1972, Carriage of Passengers by Road Act, 1974, Evidence (Proceedings in other jurisdictions) Act, 1975. Mention may also be made of two consolidating statutes, the Legitimacy Act, 1976, and the Adoption Act, 1976, which consolidate all the previous statutes on the subject without making any change in the law.

Private international law "is perhaps the one considerable department in which the formation of a coherent body of law is in course of process; it is at the moment, fluid not static, elusive not obvious; it repels any tendency to dogmatism; and, above all, the possible permutations of the questions that it raises are so numerous that the diligent investigator can seldom rest content with the solution that he proposes". This is what Cheshire said in 1935 about English Private International Law, but this holds good of the Indian Private International Law even in the year 1977. The rules of Indian Private International Law are still in a nascent stage. They are a strange amalgam of statutory law and judicial legislation.

Despite its value as subject of academic interest, private international law is a curiously neglected subject in the legal education of this country. Abroad, on the continent of Europe, including the United Kingdom and the Soviet Union, in the United States and in the Old Commonwealth countries, it is a major subject of study at the universities and law schools, but in India it cannot claim even a professorship of its own, and forms only an insignificant part of the curriculum of law examinations.

In India the process of codification began as early as 1835, and when a particular branch of law was codified, the legislature, sometimes, codified (partially or totally) connected rules of private international law. Thus, to take a few examples, the Civil Procedure Code contains rules for recognition and enforcement of foreign judgments and decrees; the Indian Succession Act, 1925, contains rules relating to domicile; and the Negotiable Instrument Act, 1881, contains a chapter on the relevant rules of private international law. These conflictual rules were codified at a time when even in England the rules of private international law were at a formative stage. Another feature—and remarkably curious—of Indian Private International Law is our heavy reliance (rather dependence) on English precedents, so much so that in their zeal of following English law, our courts have even ignored the statutory law. For instance, on the basis of provision relating to domicile in the Indian Succession Act, it was quite possible for our courts to lay down that in certain circumstances (at least) the wife can have her independent domicile, but at late as 1975 (*Satya* v. *Teja Singh*), we apishly followed the English precedent and insisted on saying that the domicile of the wife is the same as, and changes with, the domicile of her husband. Our love of English precedent is colossal, our dependence upon them total, and at times English precedents are discussed in a manner that one is apt to get a feeling that one is going through a judgment of a English court. At times our judges discuss English precedents for the sheer love of them. Thus, in *Harnam Singh* v. *Delhi Cloth Mills Ltd.*, a case of involuntary assignment, there is a lengthy discussion of most of the English precedents and authorities on proper law of contract. Happily, lately a trend has become manifest where our judges are taking advantage of precedents of other jurisdictions too.

What is here submitted is not that we should not take advantage of comparative jurisprudence—we should do so by all means—but that our reliance on them should not be total or apish. In the words of Sinha, J., our judges should now feel "at liberty to lay down and follow their own rules with regards to private international law, and in this regard we are in a very fortunate position since we can adopt the rules laid down in various countries as accord best with our sense of justice, equity and good conscience. We can profit by their experience and avoid their errors." (*Indian and General Investment Trust Ltd.* v. *Shri Ram Chandra Maharaja Deo*).

The present state of Indian Private International Law is this: in some areas there is a total dearth of rules; in some areas rules are so few and scanty that no generalization is possible; in some areas the statutory rules and rules laid down by the courts are at variance and no symbiosis can be made; and a large part of private international law is based (rather, mutated duplication of) on English law. In this context, the task of a writer on private international law is not easy. No study of Indian Private International Law can profitably be made in isolation of English Private International Law. In view of this, the present study has to be a comparative study of two systems. Here and there, I have made references to other systems, but primarily the study is confined to English and Indian private international law.

Apart from a few articles (some of them very good and scholarly), and a students' handbook by Ram Jethmalani, *Lectures on Conflict of Laws* published in 1955 (no other edition has come out thereafter), in India not much work has been done on Private International Law.

The work examines in a systematic and critical manner the entire gamut of Indian and English private international laws. I would feel amply rewarded if this work satisfies the need of the practitioner and the student of law for a book which deals with the rules of English and Indian private international laws side by side, helps our courts in evolving rules of Indian private international law which are in consonance with the need of our contemporary society and modern thought, thereby laying down a firm foundation of Indian private international law, and stimulates further studies in private international law.

This work is dedicated to Prof. G.C. Cheshire who has been a constant source of inspiration to me; his works on real property, contract and private international law, are a perpetual source of inspiration to students of law all over India.

I wish to express my appreciation to those who assisted me, through suggestions and criticism, in the preparation of the MSS of this work. I particularly wish to record my thanks to Mrs. Nomita Aggarwal, Lecturer, Department of Laws, Panjab University, Chandigarh, who went through the MSS and made many useful suggestions and to Mrs. Nirmal Yadav, B.A., LL.M., who helped me in the preparation of indexes.

Chandigarh PARAS DIWAN

TABLE OF CASES

Part I

INTRODUCTORY

SUMMARY

1

APPLICATION, SUBJECT-MATTER, DENOMINATION AND UNIFICATION OF PRIVATE INTERNATIONAL LAW

Application of Private International Law

Usually the cases that come for trial before the municipal courts are those whose elements are internal. Thus, the usual cases that come for trial before Indian courts are those in which cause of action arises in India, whose parties are Indians or domiciled in India and the other elements of which are also of domestic character. Occasionally, Indian courts are also seized of cases having foreign elements, i.e. one or the other element of the suits is connected with some foreign country. It may happen that an Indian court is called upon to try the question of succession to the property of a person who died in India (domiciled in India or abroad), who has left movable and immovable properties both in India and abroad ; to decide a petition of divorce presented by an Indian domiciled in India who had married an English woman in England, or who had married a French woman in Berlin; or to determine a petition presented by an English domiciled parent for the custody of his child who came to India with its mother as a tourist ; or to try a suit for breach of contract filed by a New York domiciled plaintiff against a defendant domiciled in England in respect of a contract entered into in Paris for the supply of goods to India; to determine a claim of a Pakistani domiciled plaintiff against an Indian domiciled defendant for a tort committed by the latter in Pakistan while he was there on a short visit; or to try a suit of an Indian domiciled plaintiff against an Indian resident in India for the recovery of a debt taken by the latter in Bangladesh and payable there. It is evident that all these cases have some foreign element.

Sometimes, yet another question arises in a municipal court. It is the question of recognition of a foreign judgment or enforcement of a foreign decree. Suppose, an Indian wife files a petition for maintenance under s. 125 of the Indian Criminal Procedure Code in an Indian court against her Indian husband domiciled in New York. The husband takes the plea that the marriage had already been dissolved by a decree of a New York court and therefore the applicant's claim is not maintainable.[1] The question is whether the Indian court will recognize the New York decree and give effect to it. Or, A obtains a money decree against B from a Dacca court and files an execution application of that decree in an Indian court against the Indian situated assets of the judgment-debtor. The question here is, can a foreign decree be executed in India ? Or, P an English mother who had married B an Indian domiciled person at a London registry office files an application in an Indian court for the custody of her child who had been brought to India earlier by the father in defiance of custody order of the London court committing the custody of the child to her. The question before the court is whether an order of the foreign court will be given effect to in India, and if so to what extent ?

Thus in respect of cases having foreign element, a domestic court may be called upon to determine the following three questions :

(i) In what circumstances the court will assume jurisdiction over cases having foreign elements;

(ii) If the court answers the first question in affirmative, then whether it will determine the case entirely under the Indian law, or will it apply the appropriate foreign law; and

(iii) In what circumstances it will recognize a foreign judgment or when it will order the execution of a foreign decree.

So long as international relations are based on the sovereign equality of nations, the municipal courts are not bound to recognize or to give effect to a foreign law or foreign judgment. They will be, strictly speaking within their rights and acting in accordance with the principle if they decide every case in accordance with their domestic law, and ignore all foreign judgments. The doctrine of sovereignty imposes no obligation on municipal courts to apply any other law. But such are the facts of international life that hardly there is a country which claims to decide cases having foreign elements entirely on the basis of its domestic law. Practically every country of the world decides cases having foreign elements with reference to concerned foreign law. Similarly, courts of most countries do accord recognition to foreign judgments. But there is no uniformity in the laws of the countries of the world as to in what circumstances municipal courts assume jurisdiction over cases having foreign element or in what circumstances and in which cases foreign law is to be applied or foreign judgments are to be given recognition.

1. Under s. 125, Cr. P.C. the obligation exists only in respect of wife. Children (legitimate or illegitimate) and parents, the form wife includes a divorced wife who has not remarried.

It is the function and province of private international law to provide solution to these problems. In the words of Cheshire : "Private international law, then, is that part of law which comes into play when the issue before the court affects some facts, events or transaction that is so closely connected with a foreign system of law as to necessitate recourse to that system."[2] In the words of Dicey and Morris, English private international law is that branch of law of England which "consists of rules which do not directly determine the rights and liabilities of particular persons but which determines the limit of the jurisdiction to be exercised by the English courts and also the choice of the body of law, whether domestic law of England or the law of any foreign country by reference to which English courts are to determine different matters brought before them for decision."[3]

Private international law, though has an international aspect, is essentially a branch of municipal law. This is why every country has its own private international law. However, private international law though a branch of municipal law, does not deal with any one branch of law, but is concerned practically with every branch of law and thus has a very wide ambit.

The need for private international law arises because different countries have different systems of law. Every country makes laws regarding marriage, matrimonial causes, adoption, succession, contract, debts, torts and like matters. But, more often than not, laws of different countries have different rules in respect of these matters. Sometimes even within a country laws are different. For instance, laws of different states of the United States differ from each other. Had it not been so, there would not have been any need for private international law. Thus, if marriage means the same thing all over the world and the rules of capacity and ceremonies of marriage are the same in all countries, the question of conflict between the laws of two countries would not arise. And if there is no conflict between the laws of different countries, there would be no need for private international law. Since the laws of different countries differ, it becomes necessary in every country that there should be a branch of law which resolves these conflicts. It is this branch of law which is given the name of private international law or conflict of laws.

Broadly speaking, conflict of laws may arise in the following two cases :

(i) When the laws of two or more countries with which the case is connected differ from each other.

(ii) The conflict may arise between the laws of the same country. This may happen :

2. Cheshire, Private International Law (8th ed.), p. 5.
3. Dicey and Morris, Conflit of Laws (8th ed.), p. 5. See also, Graveson, Conflit of Laws (6th ed.), p. 41; Szaszy, Private International Law, (1964), p. 13.

(a) When laws of different states or provinces of a country differ from each other, just as the laws of states of the U.S.A. or of the Soviet Union or of the provinces of Canada differ from each other. This is a case of conflict of territorial laws, or

(b) When the laws of different communities in a country differ from each other. For instance, in personal matters laws of Hindus, Muslims, Christians and Parsis differ from each other in India. This is a case of conflict between the personal laws of communities.

Whenever municipal courts are called upon to adjudicate upon a dispute, they render decisions on the basis of their internal laws. Thus, an Indian court adjudicating upon a case will decide it in accordance with Indian law. But then the question is : What do we mean by internal law or Indian law ? From the point of view of private international law, the internal law of a country may be divided under two heads.

First, by internal law, or Indian law (i.e. internal law of India), we mean that body of rules by which all matters relating to the rights and obligations of persons residing or domiciled in India, and all disputes arising from contracts and transactions entered into in India between such persons are decided. To distinguish it from the second type of law it may be called "internal law". This internal law is obviously very important. However, howsoever important this law may be, it has, from the point of view of private international law, directly no significance.

Secondly, the second branch of Indian law is that which, though does not decide the rights and obligations of parties, determines the territorial limit of Indian courts and lays down as to whether a given case will be decided by reference to the internal law of India or by reference to relevant foreign law. This branch of law, which fixes the territorial limits of the jurisdiction of Indian courts, comes into operation when a case has some foreign elements. This is known as private international law.

In a very wide and broad sense Indian law means all rules of law which Indian courts apply when they adjudicate upon a case, and in this sense it also includes rules of private international law, under which the courts determine the questions of jurisdiction and choice of law. In a narrow sense, Indian law means all such rules excluding the rules of private international law. The distinction between the broad and narrow meaning of the internal law of a country must always be kept in view. Sometimes even lawyers tend to forget this distinction. From the point of view of private international law, it is absolutely necessary to keep in mind this distinction. Thus, when we refer to the law of a country, i.e. law of India, law of Bangladesh, or law of England, we should keep in view whether we are referring to it in a broad sense or in a narrow sense.

It is, therefore, evident that private international law is a branch of internal law of every country.[4] But private international law is that branch of law by reference to which no adjudication can be finally determined. Private international law, by its very nature, merely indicates the governing law under which a case is to be decided. For example, a court is called upon to determine the validity of a marriage performed between an Indian domiciled man and an English domiciled woman, the ceremonies of marriage were performed in Paris. The private international law merely informs us that the question as to capacity to marriage is to be determined by the law of the domicile of the parties and the question of the performance of ceremonies is to be determined by the law of the place where the marriage was solemnized. On knowing this, the court will decide the case accordingly : if the question is of capacity the matter will be determined by reference to Indian law or English law; or, if the question is whether requisite ceremonies were performed or not, the court will decide it by reference to French law.

Then, when it is said that cases having foreign elements are to be determined by reference to relevant fereign law, the question is what is meant by 'foreign law'. In common parlance, foreign law means the law of a foreign country. But in private international law foreign law has a technical meaning. When a case is decided by a court with reference to a system of law which is different from a system of law which the court will apply to a purely domestic case, such law is called foreign law. This may be the law of a country; or it may be the law of a part of a country. For instance, a Quebec court may decide that the law applicable to the case is the law of India or the law of Ontario. From the point of view of private international law, for the court of Quebec, the law of Ontario is as much a foreign law as the law of India.

Subject-matter of Private International Law

The two major systems of law, the common law and the civil law, differ from each other as to the subject-matter of private international law. Germany, Switzerland and Scandinavian countries restrict the scope of private international law to problems of conflict of laws, and matters relating to status of foreigners fall under a separate branch called the law of foreigners. Private international law of Soviet Union and of the People's Democracies of Eastern Europe include within its ambit the rules of choice of law along with all the connecting factors such as nationality or domicile, the place where the contract was entered into or is to be performed. However, the rules relating to resolving of conflicts of jurisdiction are not included within the rules of private international law. They are considered to relate to procedural law. Similarly, the regulation of legal status of foreigners is not considered to fall within the scope of private international law as

4. See *R. Vishvanatha* v. *Runuk-ul Mulk Syed Abdul Wazid*, AIR 1963 S.C. 1, at p. 14, per Shah, J., *Satya* v. *Tejasingh*, 1975, S.C. 105 at p. 108.

the majority of the rules relating to legal status of foreigners is considered, by these countries, as a branch of administrative law, and not of civil law. According to Szaszy: "Problems connected with conflicts of jurisdiction cannot be included in private international Law, either because the subject of regulating the competence of courts for exercising jurisdiction belongs to the law of civil procedure, more precisely, to the international law of civil procedure."[5] In the Soviet Union and the people's democratic countries of East Europe the object of private international law is constituted by legal relationships that have an international bearing, or an international character, which in other words, contain a foreign, international element and which are tied up with the legal system of several states.[6]

On the other hand, the countries of the common law system include the rules of jurisdiction as well as rules of choice of law within the scope of private international law. Although in India rules relating to jurisdiction of court and rules relating to recognition and enforcement of foreign judgments are laid down in the Indian Civil Procedure Code, yet Indian courts have all along considered the jurisdiction of court and rules of choice of law as falling within the ambit of private international law. Thus India as well as the countries of the common law system consider the following as the subject-matter of private international law:

(i) Rules relating to jurisdiction of courts,

(ii) Rules of choice of law, and

(iii) Rules relating to recognition and enforcement of foreign judgments and decrees.

Of these the first two are of great importance as whenever a case with a foreign element comes before the court usually both matters, or at least one of them, arise for determination of the court. Both these matters are separate and independent of each other. It may happen that in a case the question of jurisdiction is decided in favour of one system of law, and the question of choice of law is decided in favour of another system of law. For example, in a suit for damages for breach of contract an Indian court may hold that it has jurisdiction to adjudicate upon the matter, but then it may come to the conclusion that to various aspects of the contract the law of some foreign country or countries applies. However, it is not necessary that both the questions may arise in the same case. Yet, it should be clearly understood that sometimes they are interdependent upon each other, such as the characterization of principles and bases of characterization;[7] in the determination of domicile[8] and *situs* of property, both questions

5. Szaszy, p. 22.
6. *Ibid.*
7. See Chapter 3 of this work.
8. See Chapter 6 of this work.

are interdependent on each other. Similarly, in adjudication relating to land[9] and dissolution of marriage[10] choice of law depends upon the question of jurisdiction.

Jurisdiction of the Court : Even where all the elements of a suit are internal the question whether the court has jurisdiction to try it often arises. The law of procedure of every country lays down that in what matters which court will have jurisdiction. The procedural law also lays down rules for other matters of procedure and in some systems of law these rules apply to all types of suits, to suits having foreign elements as well as to suits having no foreign elements. For instance, the Indian Civil Procedure Code (so also the law of civil procedure of many other countries) lays down that the court shall not proceed with the case unless the service of summons is made on the defendant. This rule applies to all defendants, including those who are living abroad. Looked at from this aspect, the question of jurisdiction is a fundamental question in all suits and legal actions. However, for the following two reasons it has special significance in private international law.

First, in certain circumstances the court exercises jurisdiction in a case even when the defendant is absent. In a suit whose all elements are internal, the judgment rendered in the absence of the defendant[11] is as much enforceable as a judgment rendered in the presence of the defendant. Such a judgment may also be enforceable when it has some foreign elements so far as the court that rendered the judgment is concerned. But, then, such a judgment may not be recognized elsewhere.

Secondly, there are certain matters in which the court cannot exercise jurisdiction even though the defendant is present, such as in a petition for dissolution of marriage or in a suit relating to immovable property situated abroad. The question of jurisdiction may arise before the court in the following two circumstances : (a) when a suit is filed before the court the question arises whether the court has jurisdiction, or (b) when the question before the court is of the recognition of a foreign judgment or its enforcement, the court may be called upon to determine whether the foreign court that rendered the judgment was a court of competent jurisdiction.

Normally the rules of jurisdiction are based on the principle that the court rendering judgment must be able to enforce it. Ordinarily, a court of law will not like to pronounce a judgment which it has no power to enforce. Today most of the countries of the world are unanimous on the view that in respect of immovables the court of that place has jurisdiction where the property is situated.

9. See Chapter 14 of this work.
10. See Chapter 9 of this work.
11. This happens when substituted service is made on the defendant. The Indian provision for subtituted service is contained in 0.5, r.20, Code of Civil Procedure.

But in respect of movables there is no such unanimity. Similarly, in suits relating to personal matters there is no uniformity. And thus it can happen that in respect of certain matters the courts of more than one place or more than one country may claim jurisdiction. For example, in adjudication in respect of a contract, the court of that place may claim jurisdiction where the contract was entered into, or where the contract is to be performed or where the breach took place. As to suits relating to personal status, India and the countries of common law system take the view that courts of domicile have jurisdiction, while most of the countries of the civil law system, including the Soviet Union and the people's democracies of East Europe take the view that courts of nationality have jurisdiction. Now some countries, including Great Britain, confer jurisdiction on the courts of habitual residence. In most cases the question of jurisdiction is a fundamental question without deciding which the court cannot proceed with the case. Sometimes the rules relating to jurisdiction of court are bound up with facts and circumstances of the case and the court can determine the question of jurisdiction only after considering all these facts and circumstances. Further, the question of jurisdiction is not always connected with the jurisdiction of local courts. Sometimes, questions arise relating to the jurisdiction of foreign courts. For instance, in a suit before the Indian court a foreign judgment is pleaded as *res judicata* then it will be the duty of the Indian courts to find out whether the foreign court which rendered the judgment has jurisdiction in the international sense.

Choice of Law: In case the court comes to the conclusion that it has jurisdiction, then in a conflict of law case (i.e. cases having foreign element), the question that arises is : under which law the suit should be decided ? Whether the law of the forum (i.e. internal law) will apply or whether some foreign law or foreign laws will apply. This is known as the question of choice of law. The problem of choice of law may be illustrated by an example : Suppose the Indian court comes to the conclusion that it has jurisdiction to try the suit, then the question before it would be as to reference to the law of which country or place the suit should be decided, if the suit was filed for damages for breach of a contract entered into between a Burmese resident trader and a Chinese resident trader in Dacca for the supply of certain quantity of rice to be shipped to Calcutta. Now presume that the suit was filed in a Calcutta court. The question before the Calcutta court then is : which law is to be applied : law of Burma, law of China, law of Bangladesh or law of India ? Take another example, a wife files a petition for judicial separation in an Indian court under s. 10, Hindu Marriage Act on the ground of desertion. Both parties are Indian domiciled Hindus married in England, and while they went to Japan the husband deserted her there. The Indian court has jurisdiction to try the suit. Now the question is, which law should be applied : English, Japanese or Indian ? The question of choice of law is to be determined in all such cases by Indian private international law. As has been seen above, it is not the province of private international law to say which rules of foreign law are to be applied, once that law is indicated by its choice of law rules. Private international law merely informs as to which system of law, foreign or domestic, will govern the matter. For instance, it is an established rule of private international law that immovables are governed by the *lex situs.* The function of private international law ends once it has indicated that the law of the place where the immovables are situated governs the matter. From now onward the law of the place where property is situated will take over the charge of the matter.

At the same time it should also be noted that it is not necessary that suit will be governed only by one system of law. It can happen that on different aspects of the suit, different systems of law apply. Thus, in an adjudication in respect of a marriage, questions of formal validity (ceremonies and rites of marriage) are regulated by *lex loci celebrationis* (the law of the place where the marriage was solemnized), questions of capacity to marry by the *lex domicilii* (law of the domicile of parties) and all matters relating to procedure by the *lex fori* (the law of the place where the trial takes place).

Recognition of Foreign Judgments : Recognition and enforcement of foreign judgments and decrees is also the matter which comes under the province of private international law. The private international law has to determine circumstances in which and the basis on which foreign judgments are to be recognized. In some countries including India[12] civil procedure law lays down detailed rule regarding the recognition and enforcement of foreign judgments. Broadly speaking, if the foreign judgment is a judgment of a court of competent jurisdiction, it will be accorded recognition.[13] However, once the court comes to the conclusion that the foreign judgment is a judgment of competent court, it would not take into account the question whether the foreign law made a mistake on matters of law or facts. But if the foreign judgment is not a judgment of a court of competent jurisdiction it would be given no effect, even if the foreign court correctly chose the applicable law and correctly determined the facts of the case. The question of the competency of the foreign court is determined by the rules of private international law.

Reasons for Application of Foreign Law

Various reasons have been given from time to time to explain as to why municipal courts apply foreign law. Comity of Nations was the earliest. Dutch jurist, John Voet, its earliest protagonist,

12. See S. 13, Code of Civil Procedure.
13. A foreign judgment may also be impeached on the ground that it has been obtained by fraud or in violation of the principles of natural justice. These grounds in Indian law are laid down in s. 13, Code of Civil Procedure. See Chapter 25 of this work.

said that one nation applies the law of another to show its regard towards it. Along with some jurists the English and Indian courts have taken the view that international law, both public and private, as well as relations among nations are based on comity.[14] That comity could be the basis of international law could be understood at an age when this view held the sway that international law is a law *between* the sovereign states, but that it could also be the basis of private international law was, even then, hardly tenable. Happily, in modern times this theory had hardly any protagonist and it stands repudiated. For one thing, the question of comity arises in respect of relations among nations; no court of law enforces the rights of private parties on account of comity. Suppose, a nation does not accord recognition to the laws of another nation, then does it mean that the courts of the latter would not apply the law of former to a private international law case even when it is applicable ? Further, if comity were the basis, then during the war the courts of one belligerent country should not apply the law of another belligerent country to a dispute between private parties even when it is applicable. Then, if comity means merely this that "no foreign law is applicable in England except with the permission of the sovereign, it is nothing more than truism."[15] The fact is, Cheshire says, "that the application of foreign law implies no act of courtesy, no sacrifice of sovereignty."[16] The reality is that the function of courts is to do justice between the parties and, in doing so, if they feel that a foreign law is applicable and consequently apply it, then they do so irrespective of the fact whether the other countries reciprocate or not and irrespective of the fact whether the other country is at war with the country whose law is applied. Therefore, when a court applies foreign law, it applies it because it has been directed to do so by its own internal law.[17]

Another basis for the application of foreign law that has been propounded is that foreign law is applied because it is necessary for the determination of the rights of parties. In our contemporary world laws of most countries accept that municipal courts have jurisdiction to try suits having foreign elements. Then it follows that in such cases the courts should apply the relevant foreign law. Thus, if an Indian court is called upon to adjudicate the rights of parties arising out of a contract entered into in Singapore, the performance of which was to be made in Karachi, then for arriving at a complete and just decision, it is incumbent upon the Indian court that it should decide under the law of Singapore or Pakistan,

14. *The Tolten, L.R.* (1946) p. 135; *Theophile* v. *Solicitor-General,* (1950) A.C. 186 : these are border-line cases between private and public international law.

15. See Cheshire, p. 5.

16. *Ibid.* at p. 15.

17. See also M. Ancel, Travaux rela Commission de Reform e du Code Civile, (1951), p. 578, cited and translated in 1952 American Journal of Comparative Law, p. 412.

whichever is considered to be applicable. It can happen that the rights arising under that contract resemble the rights arising under an analogous contract falling under the Indian law. But they can be otherwise as well. Therefore, the questions whether the parties are entitled to any relief and to what relief, can be adequately or justly determined only when the law of Singapore or law of Pakistan, whichever is found applicable, is applied. Otherwise, if Indian courts were to apply only Indian law, it can happen, that rights arising under a contract may be totally frustrated. This may be illustrated by two examples. Suppose, a question arises in a court at Cairo as to whether a son adopted by an Indian Hindu in India is his legitimate child. If the Cairo court was to apply the Egyptian law, then it would come to the conclusion that the child is not the legitimate child, since the Egyptian law does not recognize adoption. Under Italian law a contract without consideration is valid. Suppose, an Italian contract comes for adjudication before an Indian court, if the Indian court was to apply the Indian law, it would come to the conclusion that the contract is void being without consideration. But in the former case if Indian law is applied, the child will be legitimate and if in the latter case the Italian law is applied the contract will be valid. Thus it is said that basis of the application of foreign law is that the application of foreign law is necessary for determining rights of parties.[18]

The third basis for the application of the foreign law is said to be the demand of justice—demand of justice requires that the foreign law should be applied. This is, it is submitted, the other way of looking at the problem (one way of looking at the problem is, as we have seen earlier, that application of foreign law is necessary for determining rights of parties). The protagonists of this view say that invariable application of the *lex fori* (domestic law of the place where the action is tried) would often lead to injustice. Suppose an Indian marriage between two members of the self-respectors' cult[19] comes for consideration before an English court and its validity is challenged on the ground of lack of proper formalities of marriage. If English law is applied the marriage will be void as among self-respector Hindus only ceremony of marriage that is required is exchange of garlands and rings between the bride and bridegroom. The two other illustrations given earlier, one relating to Hindu adoption and the other relating to Italian contract, may also be quoted here. The protagonists of this theory say that the demand of justice requires that in the first case the English court should apply the Hindu law, in the second case

18. Bigelow has explained this remarkably by an illustration; See his note to the eighth edition of Story's Commentaries on Conflict of Laws, p. 38.

19. See *Rajothi* v. *Selliah*, (1966) 2 M.L.J. 46, (where such a marriage was not recognized even by the Indian court. Consequent to which the Madras Legislature inserted another section, section 7A, to the Hindu Marriage Act under which such marriages were validated.

the Egyptian court should apply the Indian law and in the third case the Indian court should apply the Italian law.

The greatest difficulty that one faces in the application of this theory is as to what is the meaning of 'justice'. 'Justice' is a term which is not amenable to precise definition. According to Graveson : "It is to a great extent a legal reflection of ethical and moral values conditioned by time, place and circumstances, much as the concept of reasonableness in common law is a reflection of contemporary social values."[20] Some judicial reflection on the term may also be quoted. Viscount Simonds observed : "In the end and in the absence of authority binding the House, the question is simply : 'What does justice demand in such a case as this'? If I have to base my opinion on any principle, I would venture to say it was the principle of rational justice."[21] Lord Read said : "To my mind the best way of approaching this question is to consider the consequences of a decision in either sense. The circumstances are such that no decision can avoid creating some possible hard cases, but if a decision in one sense will, on the whole, lead to much more just and reasonable results, that appears to me a strong argument in its favour."[22] Recently, Chandrachud, J. said that recognition is accorded "not as an act of courtesy but on considerations of justice."[23] But, then, does it mean that if the court finds that application of an applicable foreign law will result in injustice, it is not bound to apply the foreign law ?

Graveson has propounded a subsidiary principle to the principle of demand of justice. He says that the court applies the foreign law, because its application is convenient. He says : "Some of the subsidiary principles of English law, as of any other legal system, contain no moral quality whatever. They are merely rules of convenience. Of two or more possible courses of legal action, English law selects one and adheres to it. Much of the law of procedure is of this nature. It is neither just nor unjust, but of possible alternatives, the English courts follow the most convenient. . . ."[24] Graveson admits this cannot be an independent basis, but only as supplementary to the principle of justice.[25] It is submitted that to say that rules of law are rules of convenience is rather making matters too simple. Graveson's formulation may explain some marginal cases, where question of justice or injustice is not involved, but, it is submitted, as a basis of application of foreign law it is inadequate.[26]

20. Graveson, p. 7.

21. *National Bank of Greece and Athens* v. *Metliss*, (1958) A.C. 509 at p. 525.

22. *Starkowski* v. *Attorney General*, (1954) A.C. 155.

23. *Satya* v. *Teja Singh*, 1975 S.C. 105 at p. 107.

24. Graveson, p. 12.

25. *Ibid.*

26. Two more theories may also be noted : the theory of vested rights. Protagonists of this theory hold that rights acquired in country must be

Whatever may be considered to be the basis of the application of foreign law, it is now an accepted principle that in a case having foreign elements, some appropriate foreign law is applicable.

Denomination of this Branch of Law

In our contemporary world the question of correct denomination of this branch of law is not so controversial as it used to be sometime back. However, for any author of a work on this subject, it is still considered necessary to advert to this aspect. The private international law and conflict of laws are the two names by which this subject is widely named. English jurist Story first denominated this branch of law as private international law in 1834. Subsequently this nomenclature was adopted by the Continental writers. The most common criticism of this name is that it is likely to create confusion with public international law. The public international law is mostly concerned with nations and not individuals, while the private international law is concerned with disputes between the individuals or between individuals and states. Secondly, the rules of public international law are uniform for all states, while each state has its own private international law.[27] Thirdly, under private international law a dispute can arise between the nations of the same state (just as a matrimonial dispute between two Indians who celebrated their marriage in London), while the public international law is concerned with the dispute between two separate states or a national of one state and another state. The Soviet jurists disapprove of the name for another reason too.[28] According to them, in the Soviet Union there is nothing like private law, and then, they argue, this branch of law "does not contain the substantive rules required to adjudicate the legal relations but only those which indicate the law of which state should be applied when adjudicating the facts bearing on the case."[29] All these criticisms, as far as they go, are correct on their own premises. Westlake supports this nomenclature by saying that the subject-matter of this branch of law falls within the purview of international law as the courts are required to choose one of the several foreign laws, and jurisdictions of one of the several foreign courts.[30] One thing is certain that it cannot

recognized and legally protected in other. For its criticism, see Martin Wolf, Private International Law (2nd edition), pp. 3-4. The second theory maintains that foreign law is applied with a desire of establishing 'harmony of laws all over be world'. It is asserted that decision in a claim should be the same wherever it might be brought.

27. It was for this reason that the Permanent Court of International Justice found it difficult to entertain the dispute between France and Serbia, see *Serbian Loans Case*, 1929 Publication of the Court of International Justice, Series A, no. 20.

28. Lunz (1959); Reczei (1959); Popescu (1955) are some of the important writers of the Soviet bloc who have expressed this view.

29. See Szaszy, p. 14.

30. Westlake, A Treatise on Private International Law (7th Ed. 1925), p. 5.

be said that there is no link between private international law and public international law. There are certain rules of law which are common between the two. Public international law accepts some of the rules of private international law and the private international law accepts some of the rules of public international law.[31]

Nomenclature of 'conflict of laws' for this branch of law is also defective from many aspects. This name includes within its ambit the rules of choice of law, but it leaves out the rules of jurisdiction. So far as the name indicates that there can be conflict between internal laws of two countries, this name may be unobjectionable. Cheshire says that on balance, this title is preferable since it is "little unrealistic to speak in terms of international law if the facts of the case are concerned with England and some other country under English flag."[32] But the serious objection against this name is that in fact there is no conflict of laws; the very purpose of this branch of law is to avoid conflict.[33] Morris very aptly says that so far as the question of conflict of laws arises it may be in the mind of the judge adjudicating a case having foreign element, but if it indicates that there is a conflict between the internal laws of two countries, each trying to have domination over the suit, then the name is misleading.[34] As has been seen, the function of private international law is to indicate the applicable foreign law, with a view to do justice in the case.

There are several other names that have been suggested for this branch of law.[35] Some of them are : international private law,[36] inter-municipal law,[36a] comity,[37] and extra-territorial recognition of rights,[38] Szaszy suggests that it could be named as 'civil, family and labour law', but he himself rightly says that "this would be not only unfamiliar, but rather clumsy and too long; moreover, this would not be quite accurate either, because private international law comprises also the rules governing legal relations which contain foreign elements and which are encountered, quite exceptionally, in other branches of the legal system, e.g. land or farmer's co-operative law."[39]

31. For instance the sovereign immunity is accepted both in public international law and private international law.
32. Cheshire, p. 15. This should not imply that Cheshire is in favour of this name. He, in fact, favours the name, Private International Law, pp. 14-15.
33. Cheshire, p. 15.
34. See Dicey and Morris, p. 5.
35. *Re Queensland*, L.R. (1892) I Ch. 219. This name has also been criticised by Holland, Jurisprudence (13th ed.), p. 421.
36. Fredric Harrison, Jurisprudence and the Conflict of Laws (1919), p. 130, *et. seq.*
36a. *Ibid.*
37. Phillimore, Commentaries on Private International Law or Comity (3rd Ed.), p. 11.
38. Holland, Jurisprudence (23th Ed.), p. 398.
39. Private International Law, p. 15.

It is submitted that of all the names current and suggested, the most appropriate seems to be private international law as it denotes the two essential aspects of the subject, viz., international character of the subject and the relation of the subject with private law as distinguished from public law. And, above all, this is the most current and internationally accepted name.

Unification of Private International Law

It has been said earlier that the need for private international law arises because the internal laws of different countries differ from each other. If the internal laws of the countries of the world lay down uniform rules, probably there will not be any need for private international law. But then, difference is not only in the internal laws of the different countries, but also in the private international laws of different countries, on account of which sometimes conflicting decisions are pronounced by the courts of different countries on the same matter. Thus the need for the unification of rules of private international law arises.

There are two modes for the unification of private international law :

(a) Unification of the internal laws of the countries of the world, and

(b) Unification of the rules of private international law.

Unification of Internal Laws : The first step in the direction of the unification of internal laws was taken by the Bern Convention of 1886 under which an international union for the protection of the rights of authors over their literary and artistic works was formed.[40] After the First World War an International Institute for the Unification of Private Law was established at Rome.[41] The Institute has achieved some success in the field of unification of civil laws of different countries of the world. The Warsaw Convention of 1929 which has been amended by the Hague Convention of 1955 is a very important landmark in this direction. This Convention privides for uniform rules relating to carriage of goods and persons by air. In the Brussels Convention of 1922-23 the unification of rules relating to carriage of goods and persons by sea came into existence. Then came in this series the Geneva Convention on International Carriage of Goods by Road of 1956. The Geneva Conference of 1930 resulted in a Convention on the Uniform Law of Bills of Exchange. An important contribution has been made by the Rome Institute in conjugation with the Hague Conference in arriving at a Convention in 1964 which establishes a uniform set of rules on international sales of goods and also on the formation of contracts for such sales.

40. Since then the Convention has been amended several times.

41. The Institute is now closely linked with the United Nations and the Council of Europe.

If looked at in the background of fundamental differences in the various systems of law in the world, this achievement is not very poor, though looked at in the overall perspective, it is quite insignificant.

Some successful attempts at the unification of internal law at regional level have also been made. Of these mention must be made of the four Scandinavian countries, Finland, Denmark, Norway and Sweden who have signed conventions unifying several branches of law, such as relating to Bankruptcy, *res judicata*, and recognition of judgments and enforcement of decrees. In the United States of America, since every state has its own private law, acute problems of conflict of laws often arise. One way of solving this difficulty has been found in the form of Restatement of Private International Law. It should be noticed that the Restatement is not a codification of rules of private international law and the American states are not bound by it. It merely contains simple and reasonable analysis of the accepted rules of private international law. In this sense it may be considered as a praiseworthy work at the unification of the rules of private international law of the constituent states of the United States.

There has also been attempts at the unification of civil law between the Soviet Union and the Peoples' Democracies of Eastern Europe.[42] These countries are also attempting to unify certain laws with the West European countries.[43]

Unification of the Rules of Private International Law: On account of basic ideological differences among the countries of the world, it is not possible to achieve unification of all private laws. Therefore, another method of avoiding the situation where courts in different countries may arrive at different results on the same matter is the unification of the rules of private international law. Considering the importance of the unification of rules of private international law, several serious international efforts have been made in this direction, some with success. Before 1951 the main effort was directed at the unification of rules of private international law of the European continental countries, since most of them follow civil law system. On the other hand, nothing could be done towards the unification of the rules of private international law of the countries of the Commonwealth and the states of the United States and the continental countries on account of fundamental differences between the two systems of law. However, it is heartening to note that after 1951 some serious attempts have been made with some success at the unification of rules of private international law of all countries of the world. In 1951, a permanent bureau of Hague Conference was constituted. This has been done under a Charter which has been accepted by many countries. Assistant secretaries belonging to different countries have been set up

42. Szaszy, pp. 17-19.
43. For instance Convention on Economic Assistance, 1956.

at The Hague. Its main functions are : to keep in contact with the official and unofficial bodies, such as international law•association, which are engaged in the direction of unification of the rules of private international law and to examine and prepare proposals for the unification of private international law. The Bureau works under the general direction of the Standing Governmental Commission of the Netherlands which was established by a Royal decree in 1897 with the object of promoting codification of private international law. The Bureau has done some commendable work in the direction of the unification of the rules of family law. Thus in the unification of law of divorce, legal separation, guardianship, international validity of marriages some success has been achieved. In 1964 proposals for the unification of rules of private international law relating to adoption were accepted. In 1964 came the Convention on Uniform Law of International Sale of Goods and Uniform Law on the Formation of Contract for the International Sale of Goods. On June 9, 1967 was adopted the Convention on the Recognition of Divorces and Legal Separations. Then came the Convention on the Recognition and Enforcement of Foreign Judgments in Civil and Commercial Matters. Mention may also be made of the following other conventions : the United Nations Convention on the Recovery Abroad of Maintenance, New York, dated June 20, 1956; Convention on Choice of Court, dated November 25, 1965 (not in force); Convention on the Service Abroad of Judicial and Extra-judicial Documents in Commercial and Civil Matters, dated November 15, 1965; Convention on Jurisdiction, Applicable Law and Recognition of Decrees Relating to Adoptions, dated November 15, 1965; Convention Abolishing the Requirement of Legalization of Foreign Public Documents, dated October 5, 1961; Convention on the Conflicts of Law Relating to the Forms of Testamentary Dispositions, dated October 5, 1961; Convention on the Jurisdiction of the Authorities and the Law Applicable in the Matter of Protection of Minors, dated October 5, 1961; Convention Concerning the Recognition and Enforcement of Decisions involving Obligations to Support Minor Children, dated April 15, 1958; Convention on the Law Applicable to Obligations to Support Minor Children, dated October 24, 1956; Convention concerning Recognition of the Legal Personality of Foreign Corporation, June 1, 1956 (not in force); Convention to Regulate Conflicts between the Law of Nationality and the Law of the Domicile, dated June 15, 1955 (not in force); and the Convention on Civil Procedure, dated March 1, 1954.

Regional and Bilateral Convention : Attempts at regional and bilateral level towards unification of rules of Conflicts of Laws have also been made. The outstanding example is again provided by the Scandinavian countries. The Inter-Scandinavian Conventions of 1929-1933, between Sweden, Norway, Denmark, Finland and Iceland, unify the rules of private international law relating to marriage, adoption and guardianship. The importance of these conventions lie in another direction also : Denmark and Norway follow the rule that in personal matters law of domicile is the determining law, while Sweden and Finland law down that personal matters are regulated by the law of nationality. The difficulty has been resolved by laying down that as regards to these countries *inter se*, the law of domicile will govern, but as regards to other countries each signatory country is free to adopt their individual attitudes. Another example is provided by the 1951 Convention between Benelux countries, the Netherlands, Luxembourg and Belgium. The Convention unifies the rules of private international law in personal matters, such as status, capacity, divorce, succession and essential validity of contracts. In the United States and Canada attempts have been made for uniformity of law in all states of the United States and all the provinces of the Canadian Dominion. It has endeavoured to draft a number of model laws on various topics in the hope that the national uniformity would be attained in those matters by each state incorporating such draft laws into its own law. But these efforts have achieved only limited success. The Uniform Commercial Code may be cited as a landmark in this direction. Regional attempts at the unification of rules of private international law have been made with some success between the Soviet Union and the people's democracies of Eastern Europe. Success has been achieved in such fields as family law and succession. The 1951 Convention of the Carriage of Goods by Rail is another instance.

But international Conventions can be part of municipal law only when the same have been recoginzed or incorporated in the municipal law.[44]

44. See *Jolly George* v. *Bank of Cochin*, 1980, S.C. 470.

2

HISTORICAL DEVELOPMENTS AND THEORIES OF PRIVATE INTERNATIONAL LAW

In our contemporary world there is hardly any country which can boast of having fully developed private international law. Indian private international law is yet in its formative stage. Most of the rules of Indian private international law have been borrowed from, or are based on, English private international law. Probably, before August 15, 1947 nothing else was possible. But, now our courts have an opportunity to develop their own rules of private international law.

Among the laws, private international law is perhaps the youngest. The history of the development of English private international law does not go beyond two hundred years. The private international law of the Continental countries has an earlier history. We would briefly survey of historical antecedents of the private international law of the Continental Europe, England and India.

Historical Antecedents of Europe

Era of Territorial Law : All the conditions that could be said to be essential for the development of the rules of private international law were present during the Roman Empire. Each province of the Roman Empire has its own law. To the Roman citizens the Roman law applied and to the citizens of provinces, the provincial law applied. Disputes between Romans were decided under Roman law. But the disputes between citizens of provinces (who were aliens for Romans) were decided by a different law, called law of nations.[1] This seems to be the reason that, despite ideal conditions for the development of private international law, there was practically nothing like private international law during the Roman Empire. Thus, the *Corpus Juris Civilis* does not contain even a word on the application of foreign law in any situation.

It was incidentally, some concepts of private international law

1. The law of nations was a body of rules different and distinct from provincial laws of either party.

such a domicile[2] or the rule that the *lex situs* governs all matters relating to immovables[3] found their place in Roman law, but, it is submitted, to build any structure of private international law from these rules would be an exercise in futility.

The Era of Personal Laws : With the fall of Roman Empire, begins the era of personal laws, which covers roughly a period of four centuries, from sixth century to tenth century. This ended the territoriality of Roman law.[4] The implication of law becoming personal was that wherever a person went, he carried his law with him. Thus a Saxon was governed by Saxon law and Sabian was governed by Sabian law, wherever he might go. Only a few exceptions were admitted. Two of these exceptions were that the same criminal law and canon law applied to all persons. Sometimes parties themselves specified the law by which their transactions would be governed. Thus, in a country like Italy which had a huge mixed population, it was usual for the parties to state the law by which they chose their contract or transaction to be governed. It is likely that in such a situation some cases of conflict of personal laws might have arisen.[5] But no coherent picture is discernible.

Era of Feudalism and City States : Eleventh and Twelfth centuries witness the exit of the era of personal law and its replacement by the era of feudalism in the North of Alps and of city states to South of Alps. It is a remarkable historical development that two diverse tendencies put the era of personal laws to an end. During this period in France, Germany, Spain, England and other countries, North of the Alps, feudalism came into existence. And with this was ushered in the era of territorial laws. In feudalism there is no place for personal laws. Feudalism does not tolerate the application of any foreign law. Thus, again, there was no scope for the development of rules of private international law.

In the South of Alps also territorial law emerged, but for different reasons. The city states of Italy came into existence and it was laid down that all persons living in a city were governed uniformly by the law of the city. At this period of history, there

2. Under Roman law domicile meant connection of a person to a place which he had made his permanent abode.
3. In Digest the rule is stated thus : if a piece of land is sold, the question whether and how the settler should *cavere pro evinctine* should be determined by the law of the place where contract was entered into. One may derive from this that sale of immovable property is governed by the *lex loci actus* and not *lex situs*. From this was derived by the writers of the middle ages the rule that the *locus actus* applies to construction of contracts. (See Dig. 21.2.6).
4. It may be noted that in 212 A.D. Roman law was made the law of the entire Roman Empire.
5. For instance, the rule that capacity to contract is governed by personal law, succession by personal law of the deceased, transfer of property by the law of the transferor and the validity of marriage by personal law of the husband.

rose many prosperous city states, such as Milan, Genoa, Pisa, Bologna, Venice. Each of these states had their own laws and these laws differed from each other. There was a progressively developing trade and commerce among these states. This seems to be one important reason as to why one city state could not ignore the law of other city states. In this background the emergence of rules of private international law becomes imminent.

Era of Statutists : The credit of witnessing the emergence of rules of private international law goes to the thirteenth century. In this century trade and commerce between the city states had reached its zenith. Pursuant to these activities citizens of one city state went to another practically every day and thus inter-city intercourse was the normal phase of the city-life. It was in the interest of trade and commerce that city states recognized each other's laws.

This was also the age of revival of Roman law. The eleventh century glossators of the *corpus juris* had already done much preliminary work in this direction. However, it was left to post-glossators to make systematic and scientific study of rules of private international law. They hung the rules of private international law on certain doubtful rules of *corpus juris*. These rules hardly existed in the *corpus juris*, but such high was the authority of *corpus juris* that these doubtful pegs held firmly the rules of private international law. One such peg was the Justinian rule that the Catholic religion applied to all citizens. Howsoever illusory these pegs might be, an entire network of rules of private international law was made to hung on them. And they held. Among the authors of this age the name of Bartolus[6] is perhaps the greatest name. He had influenced the legal thought of European countries for several centuries. With Bartolus came the Statute theory.

In the middle ages the word 'statute' meant any law or custom which prevailed in any city of Italy contrary to Italian law. Originally the theory was conceived to provide solution to the conflict among the laws of Italian city states and between the laws of Italy and other city states. The protagonists of the statute theory classified statutes under three heads : (a) Statutes relating to person, (b) Statutes relating to things, and (c) mixed Statutes. It is for this reason that the theory is nomenclatured as statute theory. Apparently under this theory it seems to be very easy to provide a solution to any problem conflict of laws, but in practice it is not so easy. The greatest difficulty is of characterization : which matters, transactions, legal relations, things, etc. would fall under which statute ?

In the sixteenth century the credit of developing the statute theory goes to French jurists. Foremost among them are : Dumoulin and D'Argentre. Although both accept the division of

6. His full name is Bartolus de Saxoferrato, (1314-1357).

statute into two, yet we find that Dumoulin exaggerated the scope of personal statutes, while D'Argentre, being the protagonist of territoriality of laws, was not in favour of giving extended meaning to personal statutes. According to him if there was any doubt about a matter as to which category a subject should fall, it should be treated to fall in statutes pertaining to things.[7]

In the seventeenth century the Dutch jurists attempted to give a new twist to statute theory. According to them it depended upon the will of the sovereign as to what solution should be provided to any problem, including the problems of conflict of laws. This led to the emergence of doctrine of territoriality of laws.[8]

Modern Era : The nineteenth century may be regarded as the beginning of the modern era. Friedrich Carl von Savigny, the famous German jurist, propagated a new theory.[9] According to him, for the entire civilized world there can be developed one uniform system of private international law. Rejecting the statute theory, Savigny said that to classify law with its object in view is not correct. The object of private international law is, he says, to establish the co-relation of a legal relationship with some territorial law. According to him every legal relationship must belong to some law and therefore the object of private international law is to find out the 'seat' of every legal relationship. In the event there being a conflict between the territorial law and the law of the place to which legal relationship belongs, the latter should be applied.[10]

When we come to our century, we find that initially the development of private international law was influenced by the Napoleonic Civil Code and nationalism.[11] On the European continent this led to the acceptance of the principle that personal law of an individual is the law of his nationality. Mancini is the top brass of nationalism.

On the Continental Europe, and perhaps elsewhere also, the emergence of the Soviet Union after the First World War and its allies, the East European contries, after the Second World War, has influenced the development of private international law. According to Szaszy the Great October Socialist Revolution accomplished at the end of the First World War, and the socialist revolution that took place in the people's democracies after the Second World War have change the aspect of the world. "Parallel to the capitalist system

7. For a discussion of the view of both the jurists see Part II of this Chapter.
8. The most famous Dutch jurists are : Huber (1636-1694), John Voet (1647-1714), Nicolaus Burgundus (d. 1649) and Christian Rodenburg (d. 1668).
9. C.G. Von Watcher, a predecessor of Savigny had already torn this theory to bits.
10. In our times Jessup of the United States has propounded this theory in his book, Transnational Law.
11. Mancini held the field for quite some time.

founded on private property, the socialist legal system founded on the social property of the means of production came into being. Accordingly, contacts of a completely new type were established as regards the relationship between capitalist and socialist states, and between socialist states themselves, and the nature of these contacts was substantially different from that of international relations which had been previously prevailing. Economic and other contacts of a new type were created between the organizations of the socialist states too, and the nature of these contacts is also essentially differing from international contacts existing between the citizens and organizations of the socialist and capitalist states."[12] But the road to the uniformity of rules of international law is a long one with many detours, since ideological differences do affect the development of law.

Evolution of English Private International Law

Although from very beginning England had several systems of law and hence the possibility of conflict of laws and need for their resolution could have existed, but for several historical reasons, the rules of private international law could not develop before the seventeenth century. The dominant reason for this state of affairs was the steam-rolling rule that to all suits before the English courts, the rules of English law applied. Thus in the middle ages there never arose a case of conflict of laws, but only of conflict of jurisdiction.

When in 1863, James I became the king of England and Scotland, the question arose as to whether English law should be recognized in Scotland. Another question that arose was whether the rule of English law which prevented foreigners from becoming owners of land would apply to Scots also. In *Calvin's case*,[13] the latter question was answered in the negative. In some cases English courts showed their willingness to take evidence of foreign law.[14] In seventeenth century English courts also showed their willingness to recognize foreign judgments.[15] Beyond these stray cases, the seventeeth century drew blank in the development of private international law. In the seventeenth century a rule of English law also laid down that English courts had no competence to take cognizance of foreign suits. At that time England had some special courts which entertained the complaints of foreigners[16] or to hear disputes relating to trade and commerce.[17] In the latter

12. Szaszy, pp. 9-10.
13. (1608) 7 Rep. 2a.
14. Professor Sack in his work, Conflict of Laws in the History of English Law, in 'Law, a Century of Progress' III, 342-454 had cited *Anon*, (1611) 2 *Browne* and *Golds*, 123 E.R. 786. 789 and *Slany* v. *Cotton*, (1625) 2 Rolls 486 = 81 E.R. 922.
15. *Weir's case*, (1607) I Rolls Abridgement, 530, p. 12 = 84 E.R. 320.
16. For instance, there were special courts to hear complaints from the foreigners invited by the King.
17. Such as Staple and Pie Power courts.

case, courts applied the law of merchants which was a universal law and not the law of any country.

Even in the sixteenth century when England had a flourishing overseas trade and commerce, there was a possibility of development of rules of conflict of laws. A question often arose before the courts: whether English courts would not provide any relief in respect of foreign contracts. But again the application of foreign law was evaded by establishing court of admiralty which alone could entertain foreign suits. The problem of conflict of laws that could have arisen in such suits was solved by applying the law of merchants. At the close of the sixteenth century the common law courts also started entertaining foreign suits, or suits having foreign elements.[18] In the beginning the courts entertained only mixed cases, i.e. such of which some facts occurred in England and some abroad. The final step in this direction was taken by the division of legal actions into local and transitory actions. In the latter case the cause of action might arise anywhere, there was no necessity of summoning the jury from the place of occurrence.[19] The plaintiff had the right to sue the defendant wherever he could be found. By the time of Coke, it was finally established that courts at Westminster could entertain all transitory actions.[20] But, it is remarkable, that English courts refused to apply foreign law to such cases. They took recourse to the law of merchants.

Thus in the beginning of the seventeenth century, although the English courts could entertain suits having foreign elements, they were reluctance to entertain them.[21] At this time they showed their willingness to enforce foreign judgments.

In the seventeenth century a state is reached when English courts are, by social necessity, compelled to take cognizance of private international law situations.

In the eighteenth century the British Empire had reached the dimensions on which, 'sun never sets'. The various constituent parts of the Empire had different laws. With the ever-growing trade, commerce and intercourse among the peoples of the Empire, there was a spate of cases having foreign element. But, as usual, English courts took time to face the realities squarely. In

18. Originally, one of the reasons why the common law courts could not entertain such suits was the rule that the jury must come from the place where the act took place. Later on this rule was changed and it was laid down that jury could give its verdict by hearing witnesses also. With this change, the basic objection against the entertaining of foreign suits by the common law courts disappeared.

19. In a transitory action all facts could be foreign.

20. For details see Sack, cited earlier.

21. In 1960 in *Robinson* v. *Bland*, (1760) 2 Burr 1077 the question whether a suit on a contract which is valid under the French law and void under English law could be filed was left open. In 1775 in *Mostyn* v. *Fabrigas*, (1774) I Cowp. 161 = 98 E.R. 1021, some discussion took place on the subject, but again no decision was rendered on this matter.

Robinson v. *Bland*[22] Mansfield L.J. said, *obiter*, "The general rule. . . is that the place where the contract is made, and not the place where action is brought, is to be considered in expounding and enforcing the contract. But this rule admits of an exception when the parties at the time of the making of the contract had a view to a different kingdom." Then Mansfield, L.J. propounded the notion of what is today known, as proper law of contract. In *Mostyn* v. *Fabrigos*[23] Lord Mansfield also propounded rules governing a foreign tort. But these were the stray attempts by individual judges.[24]

As the years rolled by, it become evident that cases having foreign elements could not be decided purely by the application of English law. Gradually and slowly, but surely rules of private international law began to emerge such as of contracts, torts, legitimacy, etc. were thus developed.[25-26] In the words of Cheshire the eighteenth century may be termed as "the embryonic period" of private international law[27]—a period which extended to at least the middle of the next century.[28]

The nineteenth century can justly take the credit for a period in which rules of private international law start taking shape.

Evolution of Indian Private International Law

In what form, if any, private international law existed in ancient India, it is difficult to say. It is well-known that much before the advent of the Mughal rule in India, particularly during the Gupta and Mauryian Empires, India had a flourishing trade and commerce with countries far and beyond, across the high seas and through the inland routes. It seems to be evident that many suits

22. (1760) 2 Burr. 1077.
23. (1774) Cowp. 161.
24. The other important cases are : *Scrimshire* v. *Scrimshire*, (1752) 2 Hag. Con. 395 (*lex loci celebrations* governs the formal validity of a marriage); *Pipon* v. *Pipon*, (1744) Amb, 25 (movables are subject to *lex domicilii* for the purpose of succession): *Solomon* v. *Ross*, (1964) I Hy. Bl. 131n = 126 E.R. 79 (movables are subject to the *lex domicilii* of the owner in bankcruptcy distribution); *Shelling* v. *Farmer*, (1726) 1 Strange 646 (an action in respect of foreign situated immovables in not maintainable in England).
25. Cheshire rightly cautions : an important fact that should never be overlooked either by the student or the practitioner is that many of the older decisions are faulty and dangerous guides, and especially so when the point at issue has been the subject of more recent adjudication. This is one sphere, he says, in which the wisdom of our elders is less sacrosanct than usual (p. 39).
26. In this regard the contribution of the American jurist Story is noteworthy. Story attempted to knit into some principles the American and English decisions and propounded some new principles. See his work, Commentaries on Conflict of Laws.
27. See Cheshire, p. 37.
28. Even in 1825 an English Judge said that questions of private international law do not often occur : *Arnot* v. *Redfern*, (1825) 2 C. & P. 88 = 130 ER 549, por, Best, L.J.

pertaining to contracts and transactions relating to trade, commerce and other matters must have come before Indian courts. The Indian courts did not decide there matters entirely by reference to Indian law: India has a fairly developed law and custom of merchants and suits were decided thereunder. It is also evident that during the Gupta Empire and Mauryian Empire, law in India was territorial, though usage and custom too had their place, sometimes supplementing law, sometimes even overriding it.

With the establishment of the Mughal Empire in India on many matters rules of Muslim law came to be applicable. However, in most matters, if both the parties were Hindus, Hindu law applied and if both the parties were Muslims Muslim law applied. In personal matters—in the entire area of family law—it was the personal law of the parties that applied: Hindus were governed by Hindu law and Muslims were governed by Muslim law. Thus emerged the era of personal laws in India.

During the British period, from its very beginning to its end, various communities in India were governed by their personal law in personal matters. Thus Hindus were governed by Hindu law, Muslims by Muslim law, Christians by Christian law, Parsis by Parsi law and Jews by Jewish law.[29] Thus there was a possibility of conflict in personal laws. However, occasions of such conflicts were very few.[30] It was because a Hindu could not marry a non-Hindu, under Hindu law and so on.[31] In short intercommunity relations were not possible.[32] Inder-community or inter-religious marriages could be performed in civil marriage from under a separate statute, the Special Marriage Acts, 1872-1928.[33] Once a marriage was performed under the Special Marriage Acts, parties ceased to be governed in most matters by the law of their respective community. In all matrimonial matters, including

29. Regulating Act of 1773 had such a provision.

30. See Ved Prakash Verma, "Conflict of Personal Laws in Divorce Cases in India," (1969) Law Review, 78-93 : most of the Indian cases have been discussed.

31. Muslims of Sunni school can marry a non-Muslim who is *Kitabia*, but not an idol-worshipper or fire-worshipper.

32. Most of these cases are such in which one of the parties is a Muslim: *Khambatta* v. *Khambatta*, 1935 Bom. 5, an Indian domiciled Hindu married a Scot lady; in *Noor Jahan* v. *Tiscenko*, 45 C.W.N. 1047, where both the parties were Russian Christians; *Ayesha Bibi* v. *Subodh Chandra*, 49 C.W.N. 439, where both the parties were Hindus. In the latter two cases wife had converted to Islam and offered Islam to her husband, on his refusal to accept it she divorced him. The same is true in *Sayeeda Khatun* v. *Obadiah*, 49 C.W.N. 745.

33. Inter-caste and inter-religious marriages were made possible under the Act by an amendment of 1923. This statute has been now repealed and replaced by the Special Marriage Act, 1954 under which on the satisfaction of certain requirements as to capacity 'any two persons' can perform a civil marriage.

matrimonial causes, they were governed by the Special Marriage Act and succession to their properties was regulated by the Indian Succession Act, 1925. Thus in the most potential areas of conflict of communal laws, the conflict was avoided. This continues to be the situation even now. In personal matters laws in India are not territorial but personal. The situation is something like this : a Hindu living in any area is governed by the personal Hindu law prevailing in that area. Thus, a Hindu living in Bengal is governed by the Dayabhaga school of Hindu law.[34] He will be continued to be governed by Dayabhaga school wherever he goes in India.

During the British period, India developed contacts not merely with the countries of the British Empire but also with other countries. The result was cases with foreign elements did come for adjudication before the Indian courts. Just as in other matters, so in the cases having foreign elements, Indian court decided them mostly by applying rules propounded in English decisions. Thus, basically the rules of Indian private international law are based (sometimes bodily borrowed) on the rules of English private international law. Indian courts have almost blindly, apishly, followed and adhered to English precedents. Probably in a dependent India nothing else was possible.

But now after independence it is not at all necessary or logical to ape any country and follow its rules. Now we are in a position to develop the rules of private international law in accordance with the social needs and circumstances of our contemporary society and in accordance with the ideas and notions of world justice. In this context the following observation of Sinha, J. is noteworthy :

"Circumstances, however, have now altered, and in my opinion it is no longer incumbent upon us to follow the English rules, or for the matter of that, any rules excepting our own. . . .

"The net result is that the courts in India are now at liberty to lay down and follow their own rules with regard to private international law; and in this regard we are in a very fortunate position since we can adopt the rules laid down in various countries as accord best with our sense of justice, equity and good conscience. We can profit by their experience and avoid their errors."[35]

34. In respect of uncodified Hindu law, Hindus are still governed by their schools. The two main schools of Hindu law are : Mitakshara school and the Dayabhaga school. The Mitakshara school has four sub-schools : the Mithila, the Mayukha, the Dravida and the Varanashi. In respect of codified Hindu law, schools have no relevance and all Hindus are governed by the codified Hindu law.

35. *Indian and General Investment Trust Ltd.* v. *Shri Ramchandra Maharaja Deo*, 1952 Cal. 508, at pp. 516-17.

Mostly we are still following rules of English private international law.[36]

Theories of Private International Law

The existence of private international law has been justified on several doctrinal grounds. Thus several theories have come into existence. The important ones are the following :

(1) Statute theory,

(2) International theory,

(3) Territorial theory and the theory of acquired rights,

(4) Local law theory, and

(5) Theory of justice.

Statute Theory

In Its Original Form : The statute theory is probably the most ancient theory. In its original version, it is a product of the thirteenth century Italian theories. At that time Italian universities were flocked by scholars of the entire Europe. These scholars and jurists commanded such respect as no scholars and jurists had commanded elsewhere. This was also the period of Renaissance of Roman law. The glossators of the eleventh century had done much work for the revival of Roman law. Thus the field was wide open for the post-glossators. As in many other fields so in the field of private international law some scholarly works were done. The statute theory of private international law was propounded by Bartolus who may be called the father of this theory.[37] Originally the theory aimed at solving the conflict between the laws of various city states on the one side and the law of city states and the Italian law on the other side. At that time the law of Italian city states, such as Genoa, Pisa, Milan, Bologna, Venice, Florence, Parma, Siena, Amalfi, was contained in statutes.[38] A statute was a declaratory re-statement of older customary law of the city and its commercial community.[39] Statutes contained new legal rules also. At this period of history the Italian city states had flourishing trade and commerce not merely with each other, but also with other countries such as Syria, Arabia, Spain and Southern France. Thus, the social conditions were ripe for the

36. *Sankaran Govindan* v. *Lakshmi Bharti*, A.I.R. 1974 S.C. 1764 is an exception.

37. Some hold the view that the contribution of Bartolus to private international law has been somewhat overestimated, as his forerunners have done good deal of spadework.

38. In the middle ages 'statute' indicated any law, legislative or customary, in an Italian city state which was peculiar to it and contrary to general law prevailing in Italy.

39. See Wolff, pp. 21-22.

breeding of rules of choice of law.[40]

Considering the object of law, statutes were classified under two heads: (i) statutes concerning person (*statuta personalia*), and (ii) statutes concerning things (*statuta realia*). Bartolus classified them into three, by adding another type, the mixed statutes (*statuta mixta*). A personal statute was the one which mainly concerned persons, real statute was the one which concerned things, and the mixed statute was the one which concerned acts, such as formation of a contract, rather than a person or things. The real statutes were essentially territorial. Personal statutes applied to persons domiciled within the territories of the state enacting those statutes and they continued to govern such persons when they went to another state or territories. For instance, a Milan domiciled person who went to Pisa and lived there, continued to be governed by the personal statutes of Milan. Mixed statutes applied to all acts done in the country enacting such statutes, even when litigation in respect of such acts was filed in another jurisdiction.

Apparently the theory appears to be very simple. But in its practical application it presents great difficulties. The greatest difficulty lies in the determination as to which statute is personal, real or mixed. For instance, the English rule of primogeniture: is it real or personal? Cheshire rightly says: "The truth is, of course, that the problem is insoluble. Should, for instance, a law which regulates one's capacity to transfer land be classified as personal because it concerns persons, or as real because it affects land?"[41] It is interesting to note that Bartolus made the distinction between the two to turn upon the grammatical construction of the enactment. A statute is real, if things are mentioned first, it is personal if persons are mentioned first. Then some of the protagonists of this theory dealing with capacity made a distinction between favourable onerous statutes: the incapacity on account of age, which might he regarded favourable, was to follow the person affected thereby on matter where he went. On the other hand, a law which disqualified a person from succeeding property was classified as onerous and belonged to real statute.

French Version of the Theory: Such was the political organization of France at this period of history that a study of rules of choice of law became imperative. Different French provinces had different systems of laws, called *coutume*. Provincial laws differed from each other, and, owing to inter-provincial trade and intercourse between the people of different provinces, the provincial laws were in constant conflict with each other. Thus emergence of the

40. It is interesting to note that at the beginning of the thirteenth century the following principles were fully developed: (a) laws promulgated by a city-state were binding on its citizens alone, (b) a distinction was made between substantive law and procedural law, and (c) *lex situs* determined all matters relating to immovables.

41. See Cheshire, p. 22.

rules of choice of law became inevitable.

In the sixteenth century France, scholars undertook to develop the statute theory further. They tried to mould it in such a manner that it suited French social conditions. The arch protagonists of the French version of statute theory are Charles Dumoulin and Bertrand D'Argentre.[42] Broadly speaking the endeavour of the French jurists was to make the statute theory applicable to each and every legal relations. Dumoulin was the first to propound the doctrine that the governing law of a contract was the one intended by the parties to be applicable.[43] He thus emphasised the volition of parties as the deciding factor. On the other hand, D'Argentre, protagonist of feudalistic views as he was, propounded the theory of territoriality of law. According to him whenever there was a doubt as to whether a rule was real or personal or mixed, it should be treated as real. He held the view that personal statutes were those that dealt with the status, capacity of parties or with property in chattels. Contracts and torts were not discussed by him. It is remarkable that though he accepted that there were mixed statutes, D'Argentre said that such statutes which dealt both with person and things must belong to real statute. He further maintained that a statute though personal might in fact be real. For instance, legitimation would mean that the child would inherit the property of his father. This means that though the statute appears to be personal, in fact it is real.[44] Thus were sown the seeds of the territorial theory which were to bloom into a full-grown tree later.

Dutch Version of the Theory : In the seventeenth century new strides were made in the statute theory. For this credit goes to the Dutch jurists of whom the most notable was Frisian Ulric Huber.[45] Huber sought a solution to the problem of conflict of laws in the following three principles which he propounded :

(a) The laws of each state operate within its territory and are applicable to all its subjects, but beyond its territorial boundaries, they have no operative force.

(b) Laws of a state are applicable to all those persons who are within the realm irrespective of the fact whether they are permanent residents or casual visitors.

(c) By comity every sovereign accepts that a law which had come into operation in its country of origin shall retain

42. Along with these, name of Gui Coquille may also be mentioned.
43. This is also the modern view.
44. D'Argentre propounded the view that if a person dies leaving immovable property in various countries, the law of each country where immovable property is situated will apply. This is now known as the *lex situs*. This rule is now accepted by most of the countries as governing immovables.
45. Other important Dutch jurists were: Nicolaus Burgundus, Christian Rodenburg, Paul Voet and John Voet.

its force everywhere, provided it does not cause any prejudice to the subjects of the sovereign by whom its recognition is sought.

The first two principles embody the doctrine of territoriality. Under the third principle an extraterritorial effect is given to the law by the application of *comitas gentium*. It seems that Huber affirmed the principle that all acts and transactions validly effected according to the law of a particular place were to be recognized as valid even in a country whose law would consider them as void; on the other hand (as a corollary to the former), acts and transactions which were void according to the law of the place where they were entered into would continue to be void everywhere.[46] In other words, comity and the pressure of the international commerce required that acts and transactions entered into validly in one jurisdiction should be upheld in all other jurisdictions. Huber, ultimately, became the protagonist of the theory of acquired or vested rights, which was later on adopted and developed by Dicey and other English jurists.

John Voet, another Dutch jurist who easily ranks next to Huber, expressed similar views. He emphasized that the principle of territoriality applied to personal and mixed statutes.

The contribution of Dutch jurists to the science of private international law was considerable and far reaching. They laid down the rule—which is valid till this day—that every state was free to lay down its own rules of private international law. Every state is free to lay down that its courts will not apply any foreign law or will apply certain rules of foreign law under the conditions laid down by it. This freedom of states is in no way hampered by rules of inter-state law. However, in reality no state would exercise this freedom arbitrarily. In fact, each state by comity applies foreign law. Thus were laid down the well built foundations for the building up of a sound structure of private international law.

Seventeenth and Eighteenth Century Development of the Theory: In the seventeenth and eighteenth centuries the statute theory was developed by French and German Jurists.[47] It may be noted that by this time statute theory was not one single theory with single contents, but of several parts and with varied contents. One 'statutist' differed from another; they differed in terminology, in method, in the questions they raised, and in answers they gave. The scholastic method of the fourteenth century became an alien, out-moded instrument in the hands of the sixteenth century statutist. The political opinions and contemporary events brought about many modifications in the theory. Development of public international law, Grotious's doctrines in particular, contributed largely in the formation of the new Dutch theory. The doctrine of

46. Beale, iii, 1903-1904.
47. Henry de Coceji, John Nicholas Hert, L. Froland, Boullenois and Boulier are some notable names.

law of nature and other philosophic concepts of the time could not but influence the theory.[48]

Whatever differences there might be in the form and contents of the statute theory as it has been propounded from time to time and in different countries, two things seems to be common to all statutists : (i) They all examine the individual legal rule itself and consider the question whether it is restricted in its application to the state which enacted it, or whether it is equally valid extra-territorially, (ii) They all try to evolve principles which are meant to apply super-nationally, super-provincially, super-locally.[49] Cheshire very aptly says : "It is not a flattering epitaph upon a doctrine that had been developed by a series of eminent jurists with ingenuity and enthusiasm over a period of five hundred years."[50]

International Theory

Founder-father of the Theory : *Savigny* : In 1849 Fridrich Carl Von Savigny published the eighth volume of his work "System of Modern Roman Law". The volume intituled as book on Conflict of Laws rejected the statute theory as well as the territorial theory. Rejecting the statute theory, Savigny said that the solution of the problem did not lie in classifying the laws on the basis of their object, but in the ability to find out the seat of each legal relationship, as each legal relationship has its natural seat in some local law. Therefore, even if the law of the forum is the law of the place which is the seat of legal relationship, it will be the latter which will be applicable. Savigny maintained that in a case having foreign element "the same legal relations have to expect the same decision whether the judgment is pronounced in this state or that state." Savigny says that it is essential to keep in mind that there exists an international community of nations. He says that the application of foreign law is not based on comity but on the benefit that it brings to all concerned.[51]

The main postulate of Savigny's formulation is that every legal relation has a seat. The task of the jurist is to find this out. On this assumption he developed many rules to enable one to find out the seat of legal relation. Thus, he said that the seat of a thing was the place where it was situated; the seat of the legal relationship of the capacity of a person was the place where he was domiciled.

Other Protagonists of International Theory : Savigny's theory was further developed in Germany by Von Bar, in England by Westlake and in the United States by Wharton. In modern times its protagonists are Holland's Jitta, and Germany's Zitelmann. Accordingly to the latter private international law is a complete

48. See Wolff, p. 29.
49. Wolff, pp. 29-30.
50. Cheshire, (8th Ed.), p. 25.
51. Savigny, pp. 68-69.

system capable of resolving every possible case of conflict. In recent times Dr. Rabel has given this theory a moderate and realistic form.[52]

The international theory has been criticised on many counts. The most damaging criticism of this theory is that it starts on the assumption that there is uniformity in the laws of the countries on characterization of legal relations, while in fact it is not so. For instance, breach of marriage promise is regarded as breach of contract in some countries, while in some it is regarded as a tort. In such a situation it may be difficult to find out the natural seat of the legal relationship.[53] Then, in our contemporary world there are still more than one international systems, of which the important ones are, the common law system and the civil law system.

The merit of the theory lies in this that protagonists of the theory attempt to decide each case, in the light of all relevant circumstances, according to the legal system to which it seems most naturally to belong.[54] The theory has been dubbed as pure metaphor. It is said that it leads to juristic impressionism. Wolff answers this criticism. He says : "It is not always possible for the jurists to argue without making use of metaphors, and a good metaphor often enables the reader to attain the mental attitude necessary to observe and weigh the phenomena he is studying. True the word, 'seat' is possibly too vague."[55] Realizing the vagueness of the term, Gierke, who in the main adopts Savigny's formulation, substituted it with the term 'centre of gravity'. Further, Westlake, who also subscribes to this theory, spoke of the law with which the relationship is most closely connected. Westlake obviously ignored all the territorial implications of the theory. In a sense, none of these terms are precise. But, as Wolff put it, "jurist are not mathematicians; they are often bound to operate with concepts that are less than absolutely clear cut . . . . Be that as it may, Savigny showed the way as far as one can do so by a general formula."[56] The merit of this theory lies, as Cheshire says, "in the light of all relevant circumstances, they attempt to decide each case according to the legal system to which it seems most naturally to belong."[57]

Territorial Theory or Theory of Acquired Rights

As has been seen earlier some Dutch jurists, particularly D'Argentre, placed undue emphasis on the real statutes and thereby gave birth to the territorial theory. Courts of a country,

52. Conflict of Laws (1945-1950).
53. See Harrison, Jurisprudence and Conflict of Laws, p. 123.
54. Cheshire, p. 27.
55. Wolff, p. 37.
56. Wolff, p. 38.
57. Cheshire, p. 27.

according to them, apply foreign law only to the extent to which they are permitted to do so by the sovereign. This aspect of theory makes it resemble the theory of comity. By some jurists the territorial theory was also named as the theory of acquired rights. Apart from the Dutch jurists, Dicey in England and Beale in the United States are its main protagonists. According to them courts of a country are ordinarily bound to apply the law of their own country. The courts can neither recognize nor apply the foreign law. They cannot enforce the foreign judgments either. This principle applies to private international law and, the protagonists of this theory assert that under private international law courts do not apply foreign law or enforce foreign judgments, but they merely recognize and enforce the rights acquired under foreign law. Thus foreign acquired rights are protected and given effect to, and not the foreign law. Dicey puts it thus : "English judges never in strictness enforce the law of any country but their own, and when they are popularly said to enforce foreign law, what they enforce is not a foreign law, but a right acquired under the law of a foreign country."[58]

This theory has been vigorously criticised and had been effectively demolished by French jurist, P. Arminjon. The criticism of the theory may be summarised under the following three heads :

(1) The very meaning of the term 'territorial law' has been misconceived by the protagonists of the acquired right theory. They give it a very narrow meaning. But, the fact is that the term 'territorial law' is not confined to the laws of a sovereign state having operation within its territory, but they also include the rules of choice of law. For instance the rules of choice of law under Indian law are part of Indian territorial law. Looked at from this angle, when an Indian court enforces a contract entered into by an Indian and a Pakistani in Colombo by reference to French law or Pakistani law, it does so because it has been directed to do so by the Indian private international law. Thus it would appear that the theory of acquired rights is nothing but the invocation of a fiction which is unnecessary and useless.

Beale's exposition of the theory presents a difficulty of a slightly different order. According to him foreign law under which rights are acquired does not include within its ambit rules of choice of law. This may be correct as a general principle but in its practical application it is likely to result in the enforcement of rights of an entirely different nature, rights which may not exist under the foreign law. In the logic of the vested right theory (as Beale calls it) the foreign law under which rights are acquired would include the rules of choice of law.

58. Dicey, Conflict of Laws (5th Ed.), p. 18. See also Holland, Jurisprudence (9th ed.), pp. 398-99. See also *Dalrymple* v. *Dalrymple*, (1811) 2 Hag. Con. 54.

(2) It has been said that the theory begs the question and produces a vicious circle. Cheshire says, "The theory is futile if its supposed object is to indicate what legal system governs each legal relation."[59] It may then be revealed that it is under more than one foreign law that the right has been acquired. Cook very aptly said that there are no fundamental and logical principles which infallibly indicate in any given situation which court has jurisdiction and what law is applicable.[60]

(3) It is possible that under the rules of choice of law of a country it may happen that a right which is unrecognized or repudiated by a foreign law may be enforced by the court of the forum. For instance, a French widow claims a share of her husband's English land. This claim raises a question either of succession or of mutual property rights of hasband and wife (recognized under French law). Suppose, the English court before which this question comes classifies the matter as one concerned with mutual property rights of spouses, then he must enforce whatever rights are granted to a widow by the French law. But, had the question come before the French court, it would have been classified as one relating to succession. This means that the English court would be enforcing a right which is not recognised by French law.[61] Or, we may take another example : under the Pakistani law a Muslim wife is not entitled to maintenance after divorce.[62] Yet English courts have power to pass a maintenance order against a Pakistani domiciled husband residing in England who had divorced his wife. Cheshire assesses the theory thus : "The theory of vested rights is analytically defective and inadequate as an explanation of the pattern of rules of private international law. On the other hand, it may have performed a useful role in the development of the subject. . . . The theory stresses one of the primary objects of private international law. It serves to emphasise the need to find solutions with an international flavour. The notion that a foreign right is vested and as such requires respect, although analytically a fiction, tends to induce the correct psychological background for the formulation of conflict rules. The fiction of vested rights is a fiction inimicable to insular prejudices."[63]

Local Law Theory

The Local law theory is an offset of jurists of the realist school of jurisprudence. In a sense it is the extreme application of the doctrine of territoriality. In the words of its American propounder, Walter Wheeler Cook : "No court even enforces foreign right as such. Under our system of the conflict of laws, an

59. Cheshire, p. 28.
60. Logical and Legal Bases of Conflict of Laws, pp. 18-19.
61. This illustration is taken from Cheshire, p. 29.
62. A Muslim wife can claim maintenance against her husband after divorce only till the completion of the period of *iddat*.
63. Cheshire, pp. 29-30.

American court when asked to give damages for an alleged foreign tort (wholly committed on some other state) will 'apply' the 'substantive' law of the other state in question. Although it is often said that the substantive law of the other state 'governs' the case, the word 'governs' is misleading: an American court does not hand over the case to the law of the foreign state for decision. If it allows recovery, it merely decides, on the ground of social convenience, to give a right to damages 'as nearly homologous as possible' to the right given by the foreign law."[64] Cook maintains that no court applies any other law but its own, nor enforces any right or obligation other than that created by its own law. Cook regards law in pragmatic sense of being little more than predictions of what judge would do. In the words of another protagonist of this theory, Kelson: "The true meaning of the rules of so called private international law is that the law of a state directs its organs to certain cases norms which are norms of the state's own law, but which have the same contents as corresponding norms of another state's law."[65]

The propounders of this theory maintain that when the courts of forum have to decide a case having foreign elements, they always apply their own law, though in doing so they adopt and enforce as their own law a rule of decision identical, or at least highly similar though not identical, in scope with a rule of decision found in the system of law in force in another state or country with which some or all of the foreign elements are connected, the rule so selected being in many groups of cases, and the rule of decision which the given foreign state or country would apply, not to the very group of facts now before the courts of the forum, but to a similar but purely domestic group of facts involving for the foreign court no foreign element; the rule thus incorporated into the law of the forum may, for convenience, be called the 'domestic rule' of the foreign state, as distinguished from its rule applicable to cases involving foreign elements. The forum thus enforces, not a foreign right but a right created by its own law.[66]

The local law theory, it is submitted, is a futile exercise in pure intellectualism. Yntema very aptly said that this theory is little more than a sterile truth, sterile because it affords no basis for the systematic development of private international law.[67] "To remind an English judge, about to try a case containing foreign element, that whatever decision he gives he must enforce only the *lex fori*, is a technical quibble that explains nothing and solves nothing. It provides no guidance whatever upon the limits within

64. Cook, p. 223.
65. General Theory of Law and State, p. 245. See also the observations of Lord Parker in *Dynamit Actien-Gesellschaft* v. *Rio Tinto Co.*, (1918) A.C. 292, at p. 302.
66. Cook, pp. 20-21.
67. 2 American Journal of Comparative Law 297 at p. 317.

which he must have regard to the foreign law. The theory, indeed, marks a retrogression from the more scientific and more satisfying thesis of Savigny."[68]

Theory of Justice

In the words of Graveson, this theory is "one of English legislative and judicial justice, based on a consideration of what English statutes say and what English judges do in cases to which the conflict of law applies. It is thus both pragmatic and ethical."[69] According to him its premises are threefold: sociological ethical and legal. Sociologically it rests on the international need for fair treatment in the private transactions of individuals. Ethically it reflects the traditions and training of English lawyers, judges and legislators as expounders of the justice of their day and age. Legally it rests on the terms of the judges' oath.[70] Graveson admits that this theory is not a perfectly valid theory in every case, for one cannot explain in terms of absolutes an empirically developed system like our own. "The application of generally sound principles in this, as in other branches of law, may lead at times to hard individual cases."[71]

Then it seems that no one theory can possibly answer adequately the question as to what are the theoretical bases of private international law. In the twelfth century the principle of territoriality of laws came into existence and in the 'entire Italy the doctrine of territoriality had its sway. In the twentieth century the same theory was propounded in different garbs. Then should it be accepted that the basis of private international law is the doctrine of territoriality? Cook maintains that courts do not apply any other law but their own. The theory of acquired rights or vested rights puts the same thing in a different form. The fact of the matter is that in private international law cases the courts of forum have to apply foreign law. But no one is willing to concede that it is so, as direct admission of this would mean that one sovereign subordinates his sovereignty to the other. To avoid this direct answer, all sorts of indirect answers are provided. Cheshire and others say that the question of subordinating one's sovereignty does not arise as the sovereign enforces foreign law by its own free choice.[72] But has he really much of a choice in the matter ? In the present submission the question should not be looked at from the point of view of subordinating or abdicating the sovereignty. For one thing, the age of absolute sovereignty has been buried in the pages of history. Secondly, today nations of the world in the interest of mutual intercourse, trade and commerce are not in a position to

68. Cheshire, p. 31.
69. Conflict of Laws (6th ed.), p. 53.
70. *Ibid.*
71. *Ibid.*, at pp. 44-45.
72. Cheshire, p. 31.

assert their individual sovereignty. Nations in our contemporary world are so much inter-dependent that they have got to co-operate mutually. Then, it need not be said that the contact of peoples of the world with each at international level has grown so much that the wheel of clock cannot be put back. In short, it is the international social need which has given birth to private international law and so long as this need exists the private international law will stay whatever exercises may be made to find out its theoretical base.

3

CHARACTERIZATION

Characterization[1] or classification of a given factual situation is one of the necessary steps in the decision of a case having some foreign elements. Yet, despite a voluminous literature existing on the subject,[2] the problem of characterization is one of the most complicated problems of private international law. Such is the diversity in the laws of various countries of the world that at times characterization appears to be an unsolvable problem.

The subject may be discussed under the following heads : (a) the nature of problem involved in characterization, (b) theories of characterization, and (c) process of characterization.

I

THE PROBLEM

The problem of characterization may be understood with the help of a few examples : (i) An Indian court is called upon to

1. The alternative word for characterization is classification. The word 'classification' is preferred by some English writers. Here the word 'characterization' is used as, it is submitted, it is more expressive of The problem. In French law it is called 'qualification'.
2. In the West the first author to work on this problem was Franz Kahn who 'discovered' the problem in 1851. In 1897 it was more amply discussed by French writer, Bartin in a monograph entitled, "The impossibility of Arriving at a Definite Suppression of the Conflict of Laws", which has, since then been considered as a classic statement on the problem. In the Soviet Union and the countries of the Eastern Europe the problem was discussed by Lunz in 1949, Reczei in 1959, Bystricky in 1958, Lundwiczak in 1958. Beckett drew the attention of English readers in 1934 in his article, "Classification in Conflict of Laws" 15 B.Y.B.I.L. 46-81. Lorenzen was the first to draw the attention of Americans to the problem : 20 Columbia Law Review 247 [Selected Articles on Conflict of Laws, (1947) Chapters IV and V]. Since then much has been written on the subject : Dicey (5th ed.), p. 62; Dicey and Morris (8th ed.) Chapter 3; Cheshire (2nd ed.), p. 88, (8th ed.) Chapter III, pp. 40-73; Falconbridge, Characterization in Conflict of Laws, 1937 Law Quarterly Review, p. 235; Martin Wolff, Private International Law, p. 146; Robertson, Characterization in Conflict of Laws; Schmitoff, English Conflict of Laws, p. 31. In England it was the *Maltese Marriage* case *Anton* v. *Bartolo*, Clunet (1891), 1171 which made this a fashionable subject of study.

adjudicate the question of inheritance to the immovable property situated in India of a married woman domiciled in Tibet. The female had married in polyandrous form of marriage—polyandry being recognized in the Tibetan tribe to which she belonged. The property is claimed by her two husbands and three children on the one side, and by her two brothers on the other. Much will depend the way the Indian court characterizes the polyandrous union of the deceased woman. If this union is characterized as valid marriage her husbands and children would inherit the property. On the other hand, if this union is characterized as no-marriage, then the brothers of the deceased woman will inherit the property. (ii) An Indian domiciled Muslim goes to England and marries there in a registry office a German domiciled woman. Later on the German wife files a petition for a declaration that her marriage is null and void, her husband being already a married person. Suppose the petition is filed in an English or German court. Much will depend on the question whether the English or the German court will recognize the polygamous marriage performed in India. If they do so, the declaration will be made, otherwise not.[3] But if the petition is filed in India, the petition will not succeed, since in India polygamous unions are recognized as valid marriages under Muslim law. (iii) An Indian enters into a contract with a Frenchman in Paris. The performance of the contract is to be made in India. The contract is not supported by consideration. The Frenchman commits a breach of contract. The Indian files a suit for damages for the breach of contract in an Indian court. The entire matter would depend upon the question whether this transaction will be characterized as contract by the Indian court. (iv) An Englishman domiciled in England enters into a contract of marriage with a French lady domiciled in France. Later on he refuses to perform the marriage. Much would depend as to where the action is brought. If action is brought in England and the English court characterizes the breach of marriage promise as breach of contract (as it is under the English domestic law), it might award compensation, but if it characterizes it as tort (as it is under the French domestic law), the result would be different.

Thus, any court, which assumes jurisdiction over a case involving some foreign element, has, at the first instance, to determine whether a given factual situation gives rise to rights, or imposes obligations, or creates a legal relation or an institution or an interest in a thing.[4] The basic question is : in reference to which law the court is going to characterize the factual situation so that

3. In *Warrander* v. *Warrander*, (1835) 2 Cl. & Fin. 488 and *Hyde* v. *Hyde*, (1866) L. R. 1 P. & D. 130 the English courts refused to recognize polygamous unions as marriage. But in *Baindail* v. *Baindail*, (1946), p. 122 the English court recognized the polygamous marriage in such a situation and passed a decree annulling the second marriage, being a bigamous marriage.

4. See Falconbridge, Characterization in the Conflict of Laws, 1937 Law Quarterly Review, p. 235.

it is able to reach a socially desirable and just result? This is the cardinal question as without answering this question the court can proceed no further. For instance, the following are some of the well recognized rules of private international law : capacity is governed by the *lex domicilii* (this is the predominant view in the common law countries); the formalities are governed by the *lex loci celebrationis* or *lex loci contractus*[5] and immovables are governed by the *lex situs.*[6] Unless the court determines what is meant by capacity, formalities or immovable property, it would be almost impossible for the court to proceed with the case.

In many cases the problem of characterization does not present much difficulty. But in some cases it becomes very complicated and acute. It is because a particular relationship, a situation or an institution is characterized in one way in one country and in a different way in another country. For example, the statute of fraud[7] and law of limitation[8] are characterized as procedural law; the rule that marriage revokes the will is characterized as part of matrimonial law and not of testamentary law; the rule of French law prohibiting the marriage of minor relates to formalities;[9] whether things or interest in things are movables or immovables are to be determined by the *lex situs*:[10] the formalities of marriage are determined by the *lex loci celebrationis*;[11] capacity to marry is governed by the law of the domicile of parties;[12] whether the marriage is void or voidable is to be determined by the *lex fori*;[13] the Argentinian rule permitting marriage by proxy is a matter

5. This is one of those rules of private international law which have found almost universal acceptance.
6. This rule was propounded at the earliest period of history of private international law and is now universally accepted by all the countries of the world.
7. See *Leroux* v. *Brown*, (1852) 22 L.J.C.P. 1. Doubts were expressed as to the correctness of this decision by Willis, J. in *Williams* v. *Wheeler*, (1860) 8 C.B. (N.S.) 299 and also in *Gibson* v. *Holland*, (1865) 35 L.J.C.P. 5. This view has been condemned by almost all writers of private international law : Cheshire 76-78; Beckett, 69; Falconbridge, 285; Lorenzen, the Statute of Fraud and the Conflict of Laws selected articles on Conflict of Laws, p. 322.
8. This is considered to be the established rule of Anglo-American system and also all other countries including India which follow the common law system. However, correctness of this has been doubted by some : see Lorenzen, The Statute of Fraud and the Conflict of Laws, cited above, at p. 352.
9. *Simonin* v. *Mallac*, (1860) 2 Sw. & Tr. 67; *Ogden* v. *Ogden*, L.R. (1908) p. 48.
10. *Re Hoyles*, (1911) 1 Ch. 179.
11. *Scrimshire* v. *Scrimshire*, (1752) 2 Hag. Con. 395; *Dalrymple* v. *Dalrymple*, (1811) 2 Hag. Con. 54; *Warrender* v. *Warrender*, (1835) 2 Cl. & Fin. 488; *Harvey* v. *Fernie*, (1880) 5 P.D. 152; *Berthiaume* v. *Dastous*, (1930) A.C. 79 (P.C.).
12. *Sottomayor* v. *De Barros*, No. 1 (1877) L.R. 3 P.D. 1; No. 2, (1879) L.R. 5 P.D. 94; *Cheni* v. *Cheni*, (1965), p. 85.
13. *De Reneville* v. *De Reneville*, (1948), p. 100. In this case the Court of Appeal has reviewed all the earlier decisions.

relating to formalities;[14] etc. are the accepted norms of characterization under English private international law. On the other hand, the statute of fraud is considered to be relating to substance and not to form under the German and French private international laws;[15] the rule prohibiting the marriage of minors is considered to be the matter of the capacity under the French law;[16] the rule that marriage revokes the will is considered to be relating to testamentary succession by French law;[17] and so on. This tendency of the courts of different countries of characterizing the same factual situation, the same legal relationship or the same institution in diverse categories has often led to grotesque results.[18]

II

THEORIES OF CHARACTERIZATION

The following four theories of characterization have been propounded : (a) Characterization should be governed by the *lex fori*, (b) characterization should be made under the *lex causae*, (c) characterization should be made in two stages: primary characterization and secondary characterization; the former should be governed by the *lex fori* and the latter by the *lex causae*;[19] and (d) characterization should be based on comparative law and analytical jurisprudence.

Characterization on the basis of the lex fori

When Bartin wrote his famous monograph it was the heyday of law of nations theory in private international law. After elaborately discussing the problem, he came to the conclusion that in this field it is almost impossible to arrive at any conclusion on the basis of rules of law of nations for the simple reason that there are no such rules, and, therefore, in all cases (he recognized only a few exceptions) characterization is to be made on the basis of the *lex fori*. Bartin's formulation not only gave a heavy blow to internationalists in private international law, but also brought the problem of characterization to the fore.[20]

14. *Apt* v. *Apt*, (1948), p. 83.
15. See the French case *Benton* v. *Harean* : the case has been discussed by Lorenzen in Marriage by Proxy, p. 379 where the German and the French law has also been discussed.
16. Articles 144, 148, 151 and 170 of the French Civil Code. Beckett has discussed this at pp. 76-79 (cited above).
17. See the *Maltese Marriage* case discussed in subsequent pages.
18. See pages 87, 88, 89 and 90 where some of these cases have been discussed.
19. In some cases it has been advocated, the *lex fori* may be applied even at the stage of secondary characterization.
20. Arminjon, M.M. Pillet and Noboyet are the writers who have adopted Bartin's formulation.

Bartin suggests that the problem of characterization can be solved on the basis of the following two rules :

(i) A court dealing with the question of characterization, must invariably (subject to a few exceptions) apply and decide the issue on the basis of internal law. When a court is called upon to characterize a rule of foreign law, an institution, a legal relationship or some factual situation of a foreign country, it must determine it on the basis of characterization made in its internal law, provided there exists a corresponding rule, institution, legal relationship in the internal law. In case no such corresponding rule, legal relationship or institution exists in the domestic law, it should be determined on the basis of the closest analogy available in its internal law.

(ii) Once the court has determined that the law applicable is of a particular country or place, then the court should apply that law as it is applied in that country or place, and it should also adopt any subsidiary characterization as might be suggested by the law of that country or place.[21]

In his formulation Bartin starts on the fundamental assumption that the basis for the application of foreign law is the sovereign's willingness to restrict its own sovereignty. Thus, when a domestic court is seized of a case having foreign element, the extent of the limitation on the application of domestic law, by its very nature, has to be determined on the basis of the internal law of the forum. Obviously, if the limitation on the application of internal law is voluntary willingness, no foreign law can determine, much less dictate, this limitation; nor can the foreign law determine or suggest that a factual situation, or juridical relationship belongs to, or does not belong to, a particular category. If this will not be so, then it will be the foreign law which will rule, and the law of the sovereign would be relegated to an inferior status. It may also result in imposing a wider obligation which the forum may not like to accept in case the foreign law gives a wider meaning to a given factual situation or juridical relationship.

It would appear that on the basis of Bartin's formulation, the law of the forum will be applicable even in those cases in which the suit has no relationship with the forum except that it is being adjudicated upon in the court of the forum. The situation will not change even if the characterization by the foreign law is entirely different than that made by the courts of the forum. Why Bartin should have reached that conclusion has been very ably summed up by Lorenzen : The system of the characterization by the law of the forum is the necessary compliment of the system of private international law which the law of the forum has adopted. Both are the expression of its ideas concerning its own sovereignty and the limitation thereon which it feels bound to admit. As there is

21. See the illustrations given by Beckett at, p. 52.

no authority other than that of the state which has power to define the sovereignty of such state and the extent to which the international community of nations limits its sovereignty and its law enacted thereunder, each state is invested in the nature of things with the power to fix the extent of limitation itself, and in doing so it draws its inspiration not necessarily from the arbitrary counsels of comity but from the idea it entertains of sovereignty in general, including its own sovereignty. This notion of sovereignty on which the system of private international law rests together with its system of characterization, which is a necessary compliment thereto, is the expression of its conception of the requirement of international justice. It follows, therefore, that it must apply the same notion of, and everything depending thereon, to other states also as to itself.[22] Since in Bartin's formulation, the rules of private international law and rules of internal law are parts of the same system, there is a definite inter-relation between the two, both are to be interpreted in relation to each other.

Bartin supports his theory on practical reason also. He says, when a judge is called upon to determine a particular issue, he, being trained in the laws of the forum, cannot but decide the issue on the basis of the rules of the forum; for him determination of the issue on the basis of some other law would mean groping in darkness. Therefore, he says that before the determination of the question as to which foreign law is applicable, the question of characterization has to be answered, by its very nature, in reference to the law of the forum.

To the rule that characterization is to be made on the basis of *lex fori*, Bartin admits two exceptions : (a) Whether the property is movable or immovable is to be characterized on the basis of the *lex situs* : this is because, he says, this rule would best subserve the security of transactions affecting property. This should not mean, he asserts, that the law of *situs* is given sovereign authority. (b) When a contract is entered into by correspondence the governing law would be determined by reference to that law which postpones its formation longest. The basis of this exception is also the same as of the first.

Some writers have accepted Bartin's theory with some modifications.[23] The theory has many flaws and it has been vigorously

22. Lorenzen, p. 92.

23. The other writers are, Buzzatti, Diena and Kahn. Lorenzen has brilliantly summed up their views : "Originally Buzzatti agreed with Bartin only to the extent of holding that the determination of domicile and perhaps certain other points of contact must be governed by the law of the forum. As regards the other problems he felt that cases discussed by Bartin resulted not so much from a difference in the laws of the different countries as from erroneous interpretation and application of such laws. Buzzatti has, however, modified his opinion since the time of the publication of his original article on the subject, so that his views coincide today more nearly with those expressed by Bartin." (p. 93.)

criticised. Of all the criticisms that of Wolff and Beckett are most cogent.

A universal application of this theory would result in the application of neither the law of the forum nor of *lex causae*, but of the law which is of neither. "A logical application of the theory would result in an English court, through classifying a French rule in a manner different from that in which it is classified in its country of origin, not merely refusing to apply French law when according to French ideas it should be applied, but also applying French law in cases where, according to French ideas, that law is not applicable at all."[24] This is supportable on the basis of pure logic, otherwise it is so repugnant to commonsense that few courts have ever consistently applied it. Whenever courts have applied it, they have, to avoid the absurd position to which it leads, fallen back on the doctrine of *renvoi.* But the application of *renvoi* goes against the logical basis of the theory.

The theory sometimes fails even when an analogy between a foreign rule and internal rule is available and leads to absurd results. The theory leads to most undesirable results where there is no close analogy between the rules of foreign country and the rule of forum. In those cases where there is no similar or identical rule to the foreign rule calling for characterization, the theory entirely fails both on theoretical and practical grounds. In some countries of the world there are certain rules, institutions and legal relationship which do not exist in other countries. For instance, to the French *regime des biens* there is no close analogy either under the English law or Indian law. The nearest possible English institution to the French *regime des biens* (regime between husband and wife) is the one under which whole of the property of the wife is vested in the husband and none of it is vested in the wife;[25] but the fact

He sums up the views of Diena thus: "Where the conflict in qualification is between the law of the forum and that of a foreign system Diena would agree with Bartin's conclusion. But where the only connection of the case with the law of forum is the fact that the suit is brought there Diena would not apply the qualification of the law of forum whenever the foreign systems agree among themselves on the qualification of the legal transaction. In this case he would accept the common foreign qualification." (p. 93)

About Kahn he says: "Kahn dealt with most of the problems . . . a considerable time before Bartin advanced his theory of qualification. Under the head 'Collusions in the Point of Contact,' he included nationality, domicile, *lex loci contractus*, *lex loci solutions*, *lex loci delicti*, and the question of movable and immovable property. Other cases in which there is a difference in the qualification of juridical relations or institutions he discussed under the heading of 'Latent Conflict of Laws'. With respect to both classes of problems Kahn held that the law of forum was alone competent to define the particular institution, relationship, or legal concept. He found it impossible, however, to apply this principle to the case of double nationality when the law of forum is disinterested. In this case he would abandon the rule of nationality and substitute for it that of domicile." (p. 94.)

24. Beckett, p. 54. See also Wolff, p. 152.

25. This was the position prior to the Married Women's Property Act, 1882.

of the matter is that there is no analogy between the two, rather they are diametrically opposite to each other—the French rule recognizes community of property between husband and wife, while the English rule vests all the property of the wife in the husband and gives her nothing in return. Then, should the French *regime des biens* be judged on the analogy of the English rule ? Could a determination be really made on the basis of English analogy ? To this Bartin gives the following answer : when the foreign rule or institution is so alien to the idea of the forum as to deny any analogy with any rule or institution of the forum, then the judge would have to refuse to apply it on the ground of public policy. It is true that sometimes a foreign rule is not applied on the basis of public policy, but the ambit of public policy is not, and should not be, as wide as Bartin seems to suggest. Were it so, many an institution of foreign origin would not be recognized just because there is no analogous institution recognized under the domestic law, thus resulting not merely in denial of justice but also to the repudiation of the very purpose of private international law.

Then, in some cases the analogy to the internal law is more apparent than real. For instance, both the French rule and English rule provide that for the marriage of a minor consent of the parent is necessary. But the analogy ends here. Under English rule the marriage of a minor performed without the consent of the parent is valid, but under the French law such a marriage is void, and can be declared null and void by a court on appropriate proceedings being filed. The English law characterizes this rule as referring to extrinsic or formal validity of marriage, while the French law considers it as of intrinsic or material validity of the marriage. This means that under the English law the matter is governed by the *lex loci celebrationis*, while under the French law, by the law of nationality. If the question of validity of such a marriage would come before the English court, the matter would be characterized according to Bartin, as one pertaining to formalities, since this is how the matter is characterized under the English internal law. This would result in socially undesirable results as is amply illustrated by *Ogden* v. *Ogden*.[26]

Thus, Bartin's theory not merely leads to the indulgences in mechanical jurisprudence but also to socially most undesirable results. It not merely distorts foreign rules and institution, but breaks down completely where there is no analogy between the internal rule or institution and the foreign rule or institution. It is fortunate that no country has accepted Bartin's formulation literally.

Characterization on the basis of lex causae

In opposition to Bartin's theory, Despagnet and Martin Wolff have propounded the theory of *lex causae*. According to Wolff

26. L.R. (1908) p. 48. Happily, the decision in this case has found all round condemnation.

". . .every legal rule takes its classification from the legal system *to which it belongs*. French law classifies French legal rules, Italian law Italian rules, and an English court examining the applicability of French rules will have to take the French classification into consideration. Of course, of English rule on conflict of laws can either expressly or implicitly forbid the court to accept the foreign classification. Such exclusion may be based, for example, on principles of justice of morality. But this will be a rare exception. To examine the applicability of foreign law without reference to its classification is to fail to look at foreign law at all. Bartin and his followers shut their eyes to good portraits and rest satisfied with a collection of caricatures."[27]

Despagnet says that when a judge, drawing inspiration from his own law and the principles of private international law, decides that a foreign law should be applied to a particular judicial relationship, he must be understood as applying such law so far as it organizes and regulates such relationship. The first thing that attracts the legislator and the first thing determined by him is the nature or qualification of the relationship which he regulates. To disregard his decision in this respect will tantamount to non-application of the law to which the juridical relationship in question was, on principle, subject. If the national law has made a certain question one of capacity, can it be said that if the question is covered into one form by the law of the forum, the law which should govern the capacity of the individual has been applied ? Obviously not, the very principle has been violated. What is of capital importance and which produces all subsequent juridical consequences is precisely the qualification to be given to a juridical relationship and it would be flagrant contradiction to import the qualification of the forum and at the same time to pretend that one is following the foreign law.[28] This theory has been adopted by some other writers also with some modification.[29]

This theory also bristles with difficulties. Cheshire, speaking of this theory, says : "If the law which is finally to regulate the matter (i.e. the *lex causae*) depends upon classification, how can a classification be made according to that law ?"[30] Wolff has thus answered

27. Wolff, p. 155.

28. See Lorenzen, p. 94, where he has summed up the views of Despagnet.

29. See Lorenzen, p. 95. The other writers are Gamma and Jitta. Lorenzen has summed up their views, pp. 95-96.

30. Cheshire (2nd ed.), p. 34; (3rd ed.), p. 64. Dicey has thus summed up the criticism : "In the first place, it is arguing in a circle to say that the foreign law governs the process of characterization before the process of characterization has led to the selection of the appropriate law. Secondly, if there are two potentially applicable foreign laws, why should the forum adopt the characterization of one rather than that of the other ?" (Conflict of Laws, sixth edition, p. 67.)

the criticism : "In my opinion the criticism does not hold good, but is based merely on the peculiar way in which conflict rules are framed. To give examples : 'The effect of marriage on the property of spouses is governed by the law of their matrimonial domicile'. More correctly phrased this rule will run thus : 'If two persons are married to each other the court has to apply all those rules operative at their first matrimonial domicile which according to the law there prevailing regulate the effect of marriage on the property of spouses.'[31] This is true in so far as it goes, but still it does not refute the criticism that characterization on the basis of *lex causae* leads into a vicious circle, and that in many cases on the basis of this theory one cannot arrive at a socially just result. Then, in those cases where two foreign laws are equally applicable, the theory fails to explain why one law should be preferred over the other.[32] Lorenzen rightly says : "It (Despagnet's theory) manifestly begs the entire question. The qualification of a legal transaction cannot, in the nature of things, be determined by the law governing the transaction itself, inasmuch as the problem of qualifications, . . . is limited to cases where the application of the foreign law depends upon determination of the preliminary question. Under these circumstances it is impossible. . . to decide the preliminary question by the law governing the transaction itself."[33]

Theory of two-fold Characterization

Some writers maintain that problem of characterization can be best solved by dividing the process of characterization into primary characterization and secondary characterization. The former is for the *lex fori* and latter for the *lex causae*.

According to Cheshire (till recently he had been the main protagonist of this view) the primary characterization is 'that process by which the juridical nature of the question requiring a decision is determined.'[34] According to Robertson (another protagonist of this theory) it is the 'allocation of the factual situation to its correct legal category' or the 'subsumption of facts under categories of law'.[35] Both Cheshire and Robertson maintain that primary classification should be made on the basis of *lex fori* for the *lex causae* is unknown until the process of primary classification is complete."[36] The term *lex fori* is used in its wider meaning by the protagonists of this theory. It does not mean the domestic rules of the forum alone but it includes the rules of private international law also. In the words of Robertson : "The various

31. Wolff, p. 156. See also illustrations given by him on pp. 156-60.
32. See Beckett, p. 58, where he gives some examples to illustrate the unworkability of the theory.
33. Lorenzen, p. 113.
34. Cheshire (4th ed.), p. 63.
35. Robertson, pp. 63-64.
36. Cheshire (4th ed.), p. 64.

legal categories, into one of which the judge must decide that the question falls before he can select his conflict rule, must be wider than the categories of the internal law, because otherwise the judge in a conflict question will be unable to make provision for any rule or institution of foreign law which does not find its counterpart in his own internal law, and thus one of the reasons for the existence of the science of conflict of laws will be defeated."[37]

The protagonist of this theory recognize two exceptions to the rule that primary characterization is to be governed by the *lex fori,* viz., (a) whether things or interest in things are movable or immovable is a question for the *lex situs,* and (b) where there are two potentially applicable foreign laws and their characterization is the same, then the forum should adopt their common characterization.

The secondary characterization is the 'delimitation and application of the proper law', as Robertson puts it.[38] According to Cheshire the difference between the primary characterization and the secondary characterization is that the former precedes and the latter follows.[39] This theory maintains that secondary characterization is governed by the *lex causae.* However, the conflict of procedural rules is governed by the *lex fori.* At the secondary stage of characterization whether a matter is procedural or not, according to Cheshire, is to be governed by the *lex causae,* though, as in the case of primary characterization so here, it is not necessary that the domestic characterization should be followed, rather it should be the classification of private international law.[40]

Cheshire sub-divides the characterization at this stage into two cases : where there is only one *lex causae,* and cases where there are more than one *lex causae.* In the former case characterization is governed by the *lex causae.* Cheshire says, "Once it has been established that by the private international law of England a foreign legal system is the appropriate law to govern the whole of a particular transaction, it seems only rational to admit that the particular view which that law holds with regard to the character of its own domestic rules must also be applied."[41] But Cheshire says that in the latter case, i.e. where there are more than one *lex causae,* the characterization is governed by *lex fori.*[42] Robertson says that 'secondary characterization should be performed by the proper law already shown as applicable to the question

37. Robertson, p. 33.
38. Robertson, p. 118.
39. Cheshire (4th ed.), pp. 72-85.
40. This has been illustrated by Cheshire from the construction given by courts to the Statute of Fraud and Statute of Limitation.
41. Cheshire (2nd ed.), p. 79.
42. *Ibid.*

which has to be characterized.[43] Cheshire says that it comes "perilously near to a *petitio principii*." He further says, "The question to be classified is whether a certain rule is substantial or formal. If the rule is classified as substantial, French law is the proper law, otherwise English law governs. Why, therefore, should the actual classification be left to the one rather than to the other ?"[44]

The theory of two-fold characterization has been criticised as artificial, unreal and too mechanical. Dicey rightly says that not only is there difference of opinion between the protagonists of this theory as to where the line between the primary and secondary characterization is to be drawn—Cheshire for instance characterizes parental consent as a matter to be governed by the primary classification, while Robertson maintains that it is to be governed by the secondary characterization—but it also leads to, by expanding the sphere of secondary characterization, 'all difficulties inherent in the doctrine of *renvoi*.'[45] Morris illustrates the unworkableness of this theory by the following illustration : suppose the validity of a marriage performed at a London Registry Office between an English woman and a Greek national domiciled in Greece is challenged before an English court. Now suppose that the Greek law does not recognize a marriage where one of the parties is a Greek, unless an Orthodox priest is present at the ceremony. If according to this theory, both the formalities and the capacity to marry are considered to be matters for secondary characterization, then both would be governed by the Greek law. If the Greek law characterizes them as matters relating to intrinsic validity of marriage, then the English court will be obliged to hold the marriage as null and void, notwithstanding the English rule of private international law that formalities of marriage are governed by the *lex loci celebrationis*. However, Morris says, "It is inconceivable that an English court would come to any such conclusion."[46]

Criticising the theory, Lorenzen says that by the application of theory of two-fold characterization it can happen that a transaction which is not valid either under the *lax fori* or the *lex causae* will be held valid. He explains this by the following example : suppose, as the protagonists of this school maintain, if the law of the forum has decided that a contract or tort is governed by the law of state X and no rule of the procedure of the forum is involved, such questions as to whether a writing required by the law of the state X affects the formation and validity of the contract or relates to evidence, whether by the law of X the running of the statute of limitation discharges a contract or merely bar the remedy for its breach, whether the failure to give notice to the wrong-doer required by the law of state X will discharge the cause of action or whether it is merely procedural requirement for the bringing of

43. Robertson, p. 34
44. Cheshire, p. 82.
45. Dicey (sixth edition), p. 69.
46. *Ibid.*

the suit, should be governed by the law of state X. What are the consequences of this view? Lorenzen asks and answers by saying that according to the protagonists of the secondary classification theory, if the law of forum says that the statute of limitation is substantive and the law governing the contract says it is procedural, the action will be maintainable, even though it is not brought within the period of limitation prescribed by either law.[47] Cheshire has answered this criticism by saying that the court of forum "is not necessarily precluded from saying that the statute in question should be characterized as 'substantive' for the purpose of its own conflict of laws rule."[48] Upon this Morris remarks, "This suggestion admits that the *lex fori* controls the characterization of the statute of X (*lex causae*), and this involves complete abandonment of the principle that the secondary characterization is a matter for the *lex causae*."[49] As to the sub-division made by Cheshire of the secondary characterization, Morris observes: "This distinction needlessly adds to the complexities of the problem, and is based upon a misconception. Cases in the conflict of laws always involve more than one *lex causae* and if these are the only cases dealt with by the conflict of laws, it follows, that Cheshire in substance abandoned the principle that secondary characterization is a matter for the *lax causae*. It would seem to follow that the distinction between the primary and secondary characterization should also be abandoned because it no longer has any significance."[50]

For the fourth edition onward of his book, Cheshire has abandoned his theory of two-fold characterization.[51]

Characterization on the basis of Comparative Law

Rabel and Beckett have propounded the view that characterization should be governed by the analytical jurisprudence on the basis of comparative study of laws. Starting on the assumption that "rules of private international law are rules to enable the judges to decide questions as between different systems of international law—either between his own internal law and a given foreign law or between two foreign systems of law," and therefore these rules "if they are to perform the function for which they are designed, must be such, and must be applied in such a manner, as to render them suitable for appreciating the character of rules and institutions of all legal systems" and as the "classification is simply an interpretation or application of the rules of private international law in a concrete case and the conception of these rules must, therefore, be conception of an absolutely general character." Thus, "these conceptions are borrowed from analytical jurisprudence,

47. Lorenzen, p. 133.
48. Cheshire (second edition), p. 84, quoting Cook.
49. Dicey, p. 70.
50. Dicey, pp. 70-71.
51. Cheshire (8th ed.), pp. 40-73.

that general science of law, based on the results of the study of comparative law, which extracts from this essential general principles of professedly universal application—not principles based on, or applicable to, the legal system of one country only."[52] Beckett thus asserts that characterization must be based on analytical jurisprudence.

For the purpose of characterization, Beckett divides the cases into the following three classes : (i) cases not involving characterization of a rule or institution of internal law, (ii) cases involving characterization of rules or institutions of internal law, and (iii) cases involving characterization of rules or institutions of foreign internal law.

The characterization of the first class of cases, according to Beckett is governed by the *lex fori*. "The only exception which can be made is where it is clear that upon the application of any conception the courts of law of one of two foreign countries must be competent and the two foreign laws are in agreement in following a conception different from that of the *lex fori*, and in these circumstances a court might in effect, if not in form, adopt foreign conception by the application of a principle analogous to that of the *renvoi*."[53] As regards to the second class of cases, he says, "In most cases the court will simply by applying the rule—statutory or common law—of its internal law, in order to determine its application, its ordinary principles of private international law which can in this connection only be interpreted in the light of general jurisprudence."[54] In respect of the third class of cases he observes that it is essential that "the court should not merely ascertain the purport of this rule as a rule of internal law, but also that it should ascertain in what circumstances it is applied by the courts of the country of whose legal system it forms part. . . . It is only when in possession of this information that a court is in a position to classify the foreign rules or institutions. On the basis of this information the court should classify it according to the conception of analytical jurisprudence.[55]

This theory has been criticised by many. The most apt criticism of the theory is that it is impracticable. Morris rightly says that, "This view is superficially attractive, because judicial technique in conflict cases should be more cosmopolitan and less insular than in domestic cases."[56] The criticism of the theory may be summarized as follows : (i) This theory is vague and impracticable, as there are very 'few principles of universal application'

52. Beckett, p. 59 : see also Rabel, Conflict of Laws, A Comparative Study, Volume I.
53. Beckett, pp. 63-64.
54. Beckett, p 65.
55. Beckett, p. 72.
56. Dicey (6th ed.), p. 67.

and very little measure of agreement as what they are.[57] Thus it is more a theoretical than a practical basis of characterization.[58] (ii) "Characterization on the basis of comparative law would seem to require a supernatural class of judges, deeply learned in comparative law, capable of dissociating problems before them from the law of the forum, and willing to adopt in conflict problems a technique which is entirely foreign to the technique applied by them to other problems."[59] (iii) The study of comparative law is capable of revealing differences between domestic laws, but of hardly of resolving them.[60] There are acute differences in certain areas in the laws of many countries. Then "how could the most learned 'analysing jurists' remove such differences of classification without thereby altering the law ? For such divergence of classifications is not jurisprudential in character, it connotes a difference in the law."[61]

III

PROCESS OF CHARACTERIZATION IN PRACTICE

Before proceeding with the process of characterization in practice, it would help in grappling the problem, if we look into a few decided cases which have posed the problem in most acute from : Two English cases, a German case and a French case are examined here.

Ogden v. *Ogden*[62] amply illustrates the complications involved in characterization. In September, 1898, an English domiciled woman and a Frenchman domiciled in France married in London without the knowledge of their parents. At this time the Frenchman was below the age of twenty-five. When the father of the Frenchman came to know of the marriage he took him to France and got his marriage annulled from a French court as under French law the marriage of a person below the age of twenty-five without the consent of the parent is null and void. Subsequently, the Frenchman contracted another marriage in France. Upon hearing this, the Englishwoman brought proceedings in the High Court of England for the dissolution of her marriage on the ground of husband's desertion and adultery. The petition was dismissed for want of jurisdiction. In October 1906 she married an Englishman, William Ogden with whom she lived for some time. Then Ogden filed a suit asking for a decree of nullity on the ground that at the time of marriage she was already a married woman. The court passed a decree annulling the marriage. The English

57. Dicey (6th ed.), p. 67; (8th ed.), p. 25. See also Wolff, p. 154, Cheshire (2nd ed.), p. 65.
58. *Ibid.*
59. Falconbridge, p. 245.
60. Dicey and Morris (8th ed.), p. 25; Wolff, p. 154.
61. Wolff, p. 154.
62. L.R. (1908) p. 46.

court said that her marriage with the Frenchman was valid as the court would not recognize the nullity decree pronounced by the French court and therefore it held that her marriage with William Ogden was a nullity. The result of the decision is obvious. The parental consent was characterized by the English court as a matter relating to formalities and as formalities are governed by the *lex loci celebrationis*, i.e. the English law, the first marriage was valid under that law and since the first marriage was valid the second marriage was invalid being a bigamous union. In the result, this Englishwoman remained a married woman in the eyes of English law, but unmarried in the eyes of French law !

In *Re Cohn*[63] Mrs. Cohn and Mrs. Oppenheimer, mother and daughter, who were German nationals domiciled in Germany though resident in England, died in air-raid in London. It could not be established who survived the other, or who died first. Mrs. Oppenheimer was entitled to the property under Mrs. Cohn's will provided she survived her. The English and German laws differ as to the presumption in such a case. Under the former the presumption is that the junior in age survives the senior, while under the latter the presumption is that they died simultaneously. Upon counsel for the persons interested in Mrs. Oppenheimer's property arguing that the first question to be determined by the court was whether or not Mrs. Oppenheimer survived Mrs. Cohn and that since that was not certain and since matter of proof is determined by the *lex fori*, the English rule of presumption applied. Mrs. Justice Uthwatt said that the question was not "did or did not Mrs. Oppenheimer survive Mrs. Cohn but was the administration of Mrs. Cohn's estate to proceed on the footing that Mrs. Oppenheimer survived Mrs. Cohn or on the footing that she did not ?" On this basis the learned judge said that the law of the domicile applied, under which Mrs. Cohn's relatives were entitled to her estate.

In the German case[64] a Tunisian promissory note was sued upon in a German court. At the time of the suit the German period of limitation had expired, though the Tunisian period had not. The Reichsgericht held that neither of the period was applicable : the Tunisian period was held not applicable because the Tunisian law characterize limitation as procedural and since under the German private international law no rule of procedural law can be applied by the German law, the Tunisian law was applicable. The German period of limitation was not held applicable as the limitation was characterized by the German law as substantive law—the substantive law applicable to the case was the Tunisian law. In the result the promissory note escaped from the application of the law of the limitation of both countries.

In the French case,[65] commonly known as *Maltese Marriage*

63. *In re Cohn*, L.R. (1945) Ch. 5.

64. Reichsgericht 21st November 1910, quoted by Nussbaum, p. 83.

65. *Anton* v. *Bartolo*, Clunet (1891) 1171.

case, a widow claimed a share in her husband's property situated in Algiers. The husband also died domiciled there. The husband and wife, at the time of their marriage were domiciled in Malta. Under the French private international law succession to immovables is governed by the *lex rei situs*; and the right of husband and wife to property arising out of what is known as '*regime des biens entre epoux*' is governed by the matrimonial domicile, i.e., in the absence of a contract, the law of the country where the couple intended to establish themselves at the time of marriage. Under the French Municipal law, as then existing, the wife was not entitled to any share in her husband's property, though she was, under it, entitled to half a share in the property acquired in common by husband and wife, i.e. *regime des biens*. In this case *regime des biens* was governed by the Maltese law. Under the Maltese law the widow was entitled to half of the *regime des biens*, and a right of survivorship in one quarter of the assets left by the husband. It should be noticed that the difference of characterization between the two laws was : that according to French law the widow's claim to land raised a question of succession, while under the Maltese law it raised the question of matrimonial property. The question before the court was whether the widow was entitled to a quarter share in the immovable and movable assets left by her husband. The French court held that Maltese law applied and therefore the widow's claim was upheld.

These cases bring to the fore the complications involved in characterization. It is submitted that usually characterization in its practical application is made in three stages : (i) the first stage is the stage of characterization of the factual situation, (ii) in the second stage connecting factor is characterized, and (iii) in the third stage the characterization of proper law is made.

First Stage : Characterization of Factual Situation

When a court has determined that it has jurisdiction to entertain the case, it has to decide, before it can select proper law applicable to the situation, whether the factual situation before it constitutes a contract, tort, succession to property, etc. Sometimes it is very easy to place the factual situation in a proper category, but sometimes it is not easy at all. The difficulty arises on account of the fact that different systems of law characterize the same factual situation, institution or legal relationship differently. Thus the main question at this stage that arises before the court is: categorization of which system it should accept. On what basis it should accept one categorization and reject the other.

Different suggestions have been made by different writers and theorists. Ugner holds the view that it is sufficient if the case falls within the analytical framework of the legal system of the forum: this he illustrates from two English decisions, *Re Bonacina*[66] and

66. L.R. (1912) 2 Ch. 394.

Nachimson v. *Nachimson*.[67] In the former case a contract unsupported by consideration was held enforceable, while in the latter a Russian marriage, not falling within the definition of English marriage as it was dissoluble at will, was given recognition.[68] Robertson considers Ugner's formulation rather too narrow, as under it those institutions which are not known to English law would not receive recognition. This he illustrates by citing *DeNicols* v. *Curilier*,[69] where a French institution unkown to English law was recognized and held enforceable by the House of Lords. Therefore according to Robertson, in so far as the characterization of foreign legal situation is determined by the *lex fori*, the term does not mean strictly the internal law of the forum, but a wider concept which needs to be worked out for the purpose of conflict of laws.[70] Lorenzen also holds similar view.[71]

This aspect of the problem has been more fully discussed by Falconbridge. After elaborately discussing the controversial case, *Ogden* v. *Ogden*,[72] Falconbridge said that the English courts might have held that the requirement of English law should be characterized as part of the formalities, and that it was, therefore, inapplicable to marriage of English persons celebrated in Scotland or elsewhere, outside England; and quite consistently they might have held that a requirement of French law as to parental consent should be characterized as a matter of capacity, and that it was, therefore, applicable to a marriage celebrated in England of persons domiciled in France.[73] He thinks that the failure of English courts to maintain this distinction has resulted in arriving at wrong conclusions in *Ogden* v. *Ogden*[74] and *Simonin* v. *Mallac*.[75] A marriage in order to be valid must be extrinsically valid according to the proper law governing formalities and must be a marriage between parties who are capable of marrying each other and must be in other respects intrinsically valid according to proper law governing capacity and other matters of intrinsic validity. He maintains that if this formulation is applied to Bartin's hypothetical problem of Hollander's will, a socially desirable result would have been arrived at.[76] After discussing cases relating to distinction between formalities of contract and

67. L.R. (1930) p. 217.
68. (1937) 19 Bell yard 3.
69. L.R. (1900) A.C. 21.
70. Characterization in Conflict of Laws, p. 63.
71. Lorenzen, p. 122.
72. L.R. (1908) p. 46.
73. Falconbridge, p. 543. Falconbridge observes that the latter situation came before the court in *Simonin* v. *Mallac*, (1860) 2 Sw. & Tr. 67 and *Ogden* v. *Ogden*, L.R. (1908), p. 46.
74. (1908) p. 46.
75. (1860) 2 Sw. & Tr. 67
76. Falconbridge, p. 543.

capacity, between substance (right or obligation) and procedure (remedy), between proprietary rights acquired by the parties to marriage on the occasion of marriage or as a result of the marriage and the right of surviving party on the death of the other and between administration of the property of a deceased person and succession to his property. Falconbridge says that in this class of cases there would appear no reason for departing from the general rule that the question before the court should be characterized in accordance with the *lex fori*, and that any provision or rule of a foreign law which may be the proper law under the conflict of laws of the forum should be characterized, in its context of the foreign law, in accordance with the *lex fori*.[77]

This would appear also to be the view taken in most systems. One should agree with Lorenzen when he says that characterization of the same factual situation, legal relationship and institution may be classified differently in a private international law case from an entirely domestic case. "... as regards the qualification of legal transaction the classification or characterization may have to be upon a broader or narrower basis than the internal law of the forum if it is to be suitable for the need of conflict of laws."[78]

It is remarkable that even though there may be some difference on this proposition that characterization in the first stage should be on the basis of the *lex fori*, there is unanimity or near unanimity as to the following exceptional cases where the characterization even at the first stage by the *lex fori* may be abandoned in favour of some other law. These exceptional situations are the following :

(i) Proprietary rights in respect of property and rights in property give rise to several situations which can lead to different characterization. It is now almost universally accepted that proprietary rights in a thing are characterized by reference to the *lex situs*. Falconbridge says, "... proprietary rights in things, as distinguished from rights relating to things, are, as a general rule, governed by the *lex rei sitae*, and that in many situations this general rule imposes itself imperatively as affording the only practical solution of questions of proprietary rights."[79]

(ii) The second exception relates to status. The question whether a person has got certain status is to be characterized on the basis of the *lex domicilii*. But a distinction is to be made between status and incidence of status and between status and capacity. While status is usually governed by the *lex domicilii*, the same cannot be said about capacity. Whether a person possesses a particular capacity cannot be answered simply be reference to the law that governs status. Then, capacity in one transaction

77. *Ibid.*

78. Lorenzen, p. 123. In support of his argument he quotes two decisions : *Huntington* v. *Attrill*, 146 U.S. 657 and L.R. (1893) A.C. 150 (P.C.).

79. Falconbridge, p. 543.

may differ from another, for example, the question of capacity to marry is to be characterized as a matter of intrinsic validity of marriage, the capacity to succeed to property is to be characterized as a matter of succession, the capacity to make an ordinary commercial contract is to be characterized as a matter of intrinsic validity of the contract, and so on. In short, in every case the question of capacity has to be characterized in connection with the kind of transaction into which a given person enters or intends to enter.

(iii) The third exception arises in those cases where the characterization of the factual situation by the two foreign laws applicable to the situation is the same, then the characterization at the first stage by reference to the *lex fori* may be abandoned.

In summary, it may be said that in the countries of common law, including India and in most countries of civil law system including the Soviet Union and most of the East European people's democracies, the characterization at the first stage of the factual situation, legal relationship, institution, etc. is made by reference to the *lex fori*. In this regard there is some difference as to the meaning of the *lex fori*. Some take the view that the *lex fori* means here the internal law in the narrow sense, while others hold the view that it should mean internal law in the wider sense including the rules of private international law. It is submitted that the latter view is preferable. The former view would result in injustice in some cases. This may be illustrated from two English cases. In *Re Martin*[80a] an unmarried woman made a will. Subsequently she married an English domiciled person. When she died she was domiciled in France. Under Eaglish internal law, a will is revoked on marriage, while under French law it remains valid. To reach to the conclusion whether the will stands revoked or not characterization of the factual situation is necessary. The answer to this question will depend on the question of choice of law between the English law and the French law. The English court characterized the factual situation as pertaining to marriage and not to succession and therefore choice of law fell on English law. In *Re Wilks*[80a] an Ontario domiciled person died leaving behind a will. The deceased was an owner of majority shares in an English corporation. The question before the court was whether the executors of the will should dispose of the shares immediately (law of Ontario required this) or whether they should sell the shares later on when they are able to fetch a good price for them (English law required this). The question before the court was whether the factual situation should be characterized as question of succession or of administration of estate. On the first the law of the domicile of the deceased will apply, on the latter the law of *situs* of the property will apply.

80. (1900) p. 211.

80a. (1935) Ch. 645.

The English court characterized the situation as one of administration of property and applied English law.

Second Stage : Characterization of Connecting Factor

The inquiry at the second stage of characterization precedes the inquiry as to the proper law applicable to the given situation or question. On the ascertainment of this, the factual situation, legal relationship or institution is connected to the law of the country which is to be applied. The inquiry at the second stage therefore is the inquiry of the 'connecting factor' or of 'localizer'.[81] For instance, when the court at the first stage comes to the conclusion that the factual situation or question at issue relates to succession, contract, tort, marriage, etc. then the court is directed by the choice of law rules of the forum to apply the *lex domicilii, lex loci contractus* or the *lex loci delicti* of some such law, then these are called the connecting factors or localizers. In some cases the determination of the connecting factors may be very easy, but in others it may present complications. The complications arise because laws of countries of the world differ as to the precise meaning of these terms. The English law recognizes the doctrine of reverter in cases of domicile, while the American law does not. Under the American law a married woman can have a separate domicile, under English law, till recently, she could not. In English and Indian laws a contract is deemed to be completed when the letter of acceptance is posted, while under the Russian law it is deemed to be concluded only when the letter of acceptance reaches the offeror, and so on.[82] Thus a conflict of conflict rules may arise in, at least, three different ways. If in two given countries the conflict rules on their face are the same in as much as the same connecting factor is specified in respect of a particular matter, but in a given factual situation the question before the court is characterized in one way in one country, in another way in another country. Thus there may be a latent conflict of conflict rules, and the difference in the characterization of the question may result in the use of different connecting factors and consequently the election of different proper laws as applied to the same factual situation. If, on the other hand, different connecting factors are specified in the corresponding conflict rules of two countries with respect to the same type of question, there may be a patent conflict of conflict rules applied to the same factual situation, notwithstanding that the question before the court is characterized in the same way in both countries.[83] The third class of cases are those where conflict rules of two countries are in terms the same

81. See Seziszy, pp. 119-27.

82. Falconbridge says, "The selection of the appropriate connecting factor is equivalent to the selection or formulation of the specific conflict rule of the forum appropriate to the subject or question as already characterized." (p. 547)

83. Falconbridge, pp. 350-51.

in that they both use normally the same connecting factor with respect to a question which is characterized in the same way in both countries, but nevertheless there may be a latent conflict of conflict rules, because the place element specified as the appropriate connecting factor in the conflict rule of one country may be characterized differently from the place element specified in the corresponding conflict rule of the other country.

Most of the writers favour characterization of the connecting factor with reference to the *lex fori*,[84] as, in the words of Cheshire, "an English court must assign to the conception, say domicile, that meaning which it has always borne in English law. To follow any other course would be to abandon the English rule for the choice of law."[85] This view is also supported by the practice of English and American courts.[86] Lorenzen who favours application of the *lex fori* at the second stage of characterization suggests that in those cases where the forum has no connection with them except as a place of trial and if the characterization of the two foreign countries with which the cases have connection is the same then the characterization made by the *lex. causae* should be accepted as it would be conducive to international harmony and there is no inescapable necessity of applying the law of the forum.[87]

The problem of characterization of the connecting factor is given a different dimension by those authors who, though accept the application of the *lex fori*, are yet inclined to accept the doctrine of *renvoi*.[88] This means that they would accept the foreign characterization as far as it is indicated by the application of the doctrine of *renvoi*. Robertson who takes this view explains it by an example : an American citizen, having a domicile of choice in England and domicile of origin in Iowa, after deciding to give up his English domicile and to settle down in the United States in his remaining days, sails for the United States, but dies on the way. An English court is called upon to administer his estate. According to the English doctrine of reverter of domicile, the deceased died domiciled in Iowa, while according to the law of Iowa he died domiciled in England as under it domicile of choice continues till a new domicile is acquired. He says, under the doctrine of *renvoi* as

84 Falconbridge Cheshire, Morris and others. Robertson has elaborately discussed the English and American cases on the point. (See also Schmithoff, English Conflict of Laws where he has discussd some English cases on connecting factor and the conflicting views of Story and Westlake on capacity as a problem of connection, pp. 46-49. See also C.K. Allen, Status and Capacity, 46 Law Quarterly Review, p. 277. Martin Wolff is one of the few writers who favour application of *lex causae*.

85. Cheshire (6th ed.), p. 71. See also *re Martin*, (1900) p. 211.

86. See Robertson for an elaborate discussion of English and American cases.

87. Lorenzen, pp. 126-27.

88. Such as Robertson.

established in *Re Annesley*[89] the English court is to decide the case in the same way as the judge sitting in the court of domicile would decide. This means that the English court would accept back the reference from Iowa court and thus the characterization will be made on the basis of English law.[90]

The difficulty involved in the characterization of the connecting factor may be illustrated by the following examples: (i) Suppose an Indian court at the second stage of characterization comes to the conclusion that the domicile of the plaintiff is French. The question still remains: what is the meaning of French domicile? Is it to be decided on basis of Indian law or French law? (ii) In respect of a contract an Indian court comes to the conclusion that the *lex loci contractus* is the connecting factor. But then which is the *lex loci contractus*? Under the Indian law the place from where the acceptance of an offer is sent is the place where the contract is formed, while according to the Soviet law a contract is formed at the place where acceptance is received. (iii) A Spanish domiciled person dies heirless leaving behind some movable property in England. According to Spanish law the state inherits the property of person who dies heirless. Under English law succession to movables is governed by the *lex domicilii* of the deceased. There is almost a unanimity in the laws of the countries of the world that the property of a person dying heirless goes to state. However, there is a difference of opinion in the laws of countries of the world as to whether state takes the property as an heir—this is the law in Italy, Germany, Spain and India—or whether state takes it by forfeiture (such is the law in Turkey). An English court before which the question of succession of the property of the deceased arises is called upon to decide whether it would accept the characterization of Spanish law. The predominant view is that the characterization of the *lex fori* governs the matter. However, in the last situation, *In the Estate of Maldonado*[91] the English court took the view that the Spanish characterization will be recognized, as the law of domicile regulates all aspects of succession to movables.

Third Stage : Characterization of Proper Law

In the third and the last stage the court is called upon to apply the law indicated by the connecting factor. Robertson calls it, "the delimitation and application of proper law". Apparently, it would appear that once the first two stages have been passed, the application of proper law should follow almost automatically and there should be no difficulty or complication at the third stage. However, in reality it is not so, though in some cases it may happen that there is no difficulty. In the words of Falconbridge the

89. L.R. (1926) Ch. 692.
90. The doctrine of *renvoi* has been discussed in the next chapter.
91. (1954) p. 223.

difficulty arises because the thing which is characterized is not the factual situation; but the juridical question raised by the factual situation, including the various place element. It is true that once the court has chosen the connecting factor, the link joins the situation in question with some country, and this link also directs the selection of the law of some place as the proper law, and in the third stage of characterization the proper law should be applied to the issue before the court and decision should be rendered accordingly. Looked at from this angle, the inquiry at this stage is : which provisions of proper law will exactly be applicable ? For instance, an Indian court has to decide a case involving the distribution of personal property of a deceased person. Suppose it comes to the conclusion that the domicile of the deceased at the time of his death is the connecting factor, and then, characterizing it on the basis of *lex fori* it comes to the conclusion that the deceased died domiciled in France. Or, suppose in an adjudication in respect of a contract it comes to the conclusion that the *lex loci contractus* is the connecting factor and again it finds that the place of connection is France. The question that still remains to be solved before the court is: which French law will be applicable : internal French law or French private international law ? The complications arise, and question becomes vital when the French rules of conflict differ from the Indian rules, the *lex fori*. Here again it may involve the application of doctrine of *renvoi*.

Here the matter is discussed leaving aside the problem of the application of the doctrine of *renvoi* (discussed in the next chapter of this book).

Robertson who discusses the problem under the head 'secondary characterization' holds the view that on principle the characterization of proper law should be on the basis of *lex causae*. It is because, once the proper law is indicated by the rules of the forum, the *lex causae* will determine the question.[92] Cheshire also takes the same view.[93] A brief reference to *Dutch will case*[94] and of *Ogden* v. *Ogden*[95] will amply make the problem clear. In the former case a Hollander made a holographic will in france. The Dutch law prohibits Hollanders from making holographic will either at home or abroad. Assuming that the Dutch law considers the question as one of capacity while the French law considers it as one of formalities, Bartin is of the view that the case is one where no uniformity of decision could be arrived at.[96] Cheshire considers it to be a problem of primary characterization and hence holds that the *lex fori* governs the matter.[97] On the other hand,

92. Robertson, p. 94.
93. Cheshire, p. 36.
94. Cited earlier.
95. (1908), p. 48.
96. The Impossibility of Arriving at a Definite Suppression of the Conflict of Laws.
97. Cheshire, p. 37.

Robertson who considers it to be a matter of secondary characterization, says that if such a will disposing of movables is executed in England, the English court has to enquire as to what is the meaning of capacity under the French law and of formalities under the English law: the English private international law lays down that capacity is governed by the *lex domicilii* and formalities by the *lex actus*.[98] It is interesting to note that Lorenzen summarily disposes of this case by saying that, from the standpoint of Dutch law, the will be invalid without any need of characterization of capacity or form. According to him the case does not pose any problem of difference in characterization.[99]

As to *Ogden* v. *Ogden*[100] all opinions are in agreement that in this case a socially most undesirable result was arrived at by the court. Writers have suggested various solutions to the problem involved in *Ogden* v. *Ogden*.[101] Beckett suggests that full effect should be given to all French provisions, including those relating to formalities abroad as they are matters pertaining to family law and intended for the protection of family interests.[102] But Cheshire[103] and Falconbridge[104] think that the characterization of the French requirement must be according to the law of the forum. Lorenzen[105] thinks that the English rule that capacity to contract marriage is governed by the *lex domicilii* is a general rule, and therefore, if the *lex fori* governs the characterization, then the ultimate question is whether the French law or the English law is to be applied in the matter of parental consent. "The answer to the question depends upon whether the consent of parents is to be characterized as appertaining to capacity or to form. This question, the law of forum must decide for itself. If the English judge were to submit to the French view and regard a French provision as one of capacity when from English point of view it is a matter of form, he would. . . apply a law which is considered inappropriate by the law of the forum. As well the English judge might prefer French to English rules for the choice of law, i.e. accept the *renvoi*."

Thus the problem remains: whether or not the question, and the subsidiary questions that might arise after the foreign law has been chosen by the *lex fori*, should invariably be referred to the *lex causae*. The answer to the question would be simple if the characterization of the problem at this stage merely involves the application of foreign internal law—the answer would be that, that

98. Robertson, p. 94.
99. Lorenzen, p. 130.
100. L.R. (1908), p. 46.
101. *Ibid.*
102. Beckett, p. 46.
103. Cheshire (2nd edition), p. 36.
104. 53 Law Quarterly Review 235 at p. 249.
105. Lorenzen, p. 131.

foreign law should govern. Thus, if the proper law to be applied is directed to be, say, French law, then if the case is, say, of contract or tort, all subsidiary questions, as for instance, whether the contract is to be regarded as a loan or deposit, or whether master is responsible for the tort of the servant, should be governed by the *lex causae*. But since the question cannot be answered that simply, complications arise. The complications arise because some countries take the view that the doctrine of *renvoi* is applicable; complications arise because sometimes it is said that the *lex causae* means the law which would be applied if the judge of the country of the *lex causae* would be seized of the matter. This aspect of the matter is discussed in the next Chapter.

4

RENVOI

In the last stage of characterization, it has been seen in the last chapter, the court is required to apply the law of a particular country or place. The question therefore is what is the meaning of this express 'law of a country'? This brings us to the problem of *renvoi* which has more than one connotation. Sometimes it is used in a wider sense, sometimes it is used in a narrower sense. Despite its controversial nature and despite the fact that most of the decisions in which the doctrine has been applied are far from satisfactory, it has received recognition in many countries, in one form or another.[1] Some have advocated that the theory should have no place in private international law, while some are in favour of its retention. Yet, there are some who advocate that it should be applied only in some exceptional cases.

The problem of *renvoi* arises in connection with the application of 'law of a country'. The crux of the matter is that what do we mean by the 'law of a country'? It has been seen in Chapter 1 of this work that the law of a country may mean the internal law of a country in a narrow sense, i.e. excluding the rules of private international law or in a broader sense including the rules of private international law. We may illustrate the problem thus :

The law of a country or place means :

(a) internal law of that country, or

(b) the whole law of that country, i.e. including the rules of private international law. (If the rules of private international law of a country direct that its municipal law, or internal law, applies, then that law would apply.) It

1. The subject has voluminous literature. Westlake, Chapter II; Cheshire, pp. 53-72; Wolff, ss. 178-195; Falconbridge, Chapters VI-X; Restatement, s. 8; Dicey and Morris, Chapter VI; Lorenzen, Chapters II, III and V; Rabel, Vol. I, pp. 75-90; *Seziszy*, pp. 138-42.

The English decisions mainly adopt the foreign court theory. The main decisions are : *Collier* v. *Rivaz*, (1841) 2 Curt. 855; *Frere* v. *Frere*, (1847) 5 Notes on cases in the Ecclesiastical and Maritime Courts, 593; *Re Annesley*, (1926) Ch. 692 ; *Re Ross*, (1930) 1 Ch. 377; *Re Askew*, (1930) 2 Ch. 259; *Kotia* v. *Nahas* (1941) A.C. 403 (P.C.); *Re Duke of Wellington*, (1847) Ch. 506; *In the Estate of Fuld* (no. 3), (1968), p. 675.

often happens that the rules of private international law of that country, either

(i) refer back to the law of the forum, or

(ii) refer forward to a third country.

The problem of *renvoi* arises in those cases where the rules of private international law either refer back to the law of the forum or refer to law of a third country. For the former situation, the French word is '*renvoi*,' the German word is '*Ruckverweisung*' and the English, 'remission'. For the latter situation, the German term is '*Weiterverweisung*' and the English word is 'transmission'. In the sixth edition of Dicey's Conflict of Laws the former was called, 'a patent conflict of conflict rules involving a reference back to the forum' and the latter, 'a patent conflict of conflict rules involving reference to a third country'[2].

Schreiber puts the problem thus : "When the conflict of laws rule of the forum refer a jural matter to a foreign law for decision, then is the reference to the corresponding rule of the conflict of laws of that foreign country, or is it the reference to the purely internal rules of law of the foreign system, i.e. to the totality of the foreign law, minus its conflict of law rules ?"[3] The problem may be explained by few examples.[4] A, a British subject, domiciled in Italy dies intestate leaving behind movable property in England. C and B, two relatives of A claim the property. The matter is adjudicated upon in an English court. C bases his claim under Italian law of inheritance, while B bases his claim under English law, the Administration of Estate Act. Under the English private international law the law of domicile of the deceased, i.e. Italian law, governs the matter. If the English law rejects the doctrine of *renvoi* it simply applies the Italian internal law and decides in favour of A. On the other hand, if it accepts the doctrine, it would first ascertain the Italian rule of private international law concerning succession and as Italian law lays down that the law of nationality governs succession to movables, it would accept back the reference and decide the matter in favour of B. This is an example of remission. Suppose, in this case the deceased A is a German citizen domiciled in Italy. Now when the English court ~~would~~ refer the matter to the Italian law, the law of domicile and there it would be referred forward to German law, then it would apply the German law. This is an example of transmission.

Take another example : A, a British subject, domiciled in

2. Conflict of Laws, p. 49.
3. 31 Harward Law Review, p. 525.
4. See Martin Wolff, at pp. 187-90 where he gives several illustrations and also Dicey's (sixth edition), pp. 51-54 where the leading cases on the doctrine have been summarized. See also Cheshire (8th ed.), pp. 64-71, where all important English decisions of the theory have been discussed.

Copenhagen from birth, had his ordinary residence (his domicile, in the Danish law) in England, but without losing all his ties binding him with Denmark. In a suit concerning succession to movables of A, the English court will apply English law, as the English conflict rules lay down that the law of the last domicile (in the English sense of the term), i.e. the law of Denmark is decisive and since the Danish conflict rules lay down that law of ordinary residence (what Danish law calls domicile) governs succession, the English court accepts back the reference.

Two more examples may be taken from decided English cases. In *Re Ross*[5] an English woman, whose domicile of choice was in Italy, by a will, left all her property to her distant relatives to the exclusion of her only son. After her death, in an action field in an English court the son claimed his share, i.e. to what he would have been entitled under the Italian law. The beneficiaries under the will resisted the claim of son on the ground that under English internal law, which they contended was applicable, they were entitled to the property. Since under the English rules of private international law succession to movables is governed by the *lex domicilii* and succession to immovables by the *lex situs*, the English court proceeded to determine the *lex domicilii* and the *lex situs*. Since the deceased died domiciled in Italy, the English court proceeded to determine the question as the Italian court would have determined it had the issue been before it. Since the Italian conflict rules lay down that succession to movables is governed by the law of nationality—the Italian law refers the matter to the law of nationality and refuses to take back the remitter—the English court applied the English law. The same process was followed in respect of the succession to immovables. In *Re Duke of Wellington*[6] a British testator domiciled in England under his will gave lands situated in Spain to the person who on his death would become the Duke of Wellington and Ciudad Rodrigo. The testator was killed in action in 1943. At that time he was unmarried. In 1813 the Spanish Duckedom of Ciudad Rodrigo was given to the first Duke of Wellington and his male and female issues, while the British Dukedom was limited in tail male. In 1943, after the death of the testator, the two Dukedoms became separated : to the Spanish Dukedom the sister of the testator succeeded and to the English Dukedom his uncle succeeded. The testator had made two wills : under the Spanish will he bequeathed his Spanish estate to the person who would become Duke of Wellington and under the English will also he bequeathed all his residue properties to the same person. Since after his death in 1943 the two dukedoms had separated because of his dying intestate and because of the requirement that English Dukedom could go only to the male heir, the question of interpretation of Spanish will came before the English court. After holding that the devolution to Spanish estate

5. (1930) Ch. 377.
6. (1947) Ch. 506.

would be governed by the *lex situs*, i.e. the Spanish law, the court proceeded to examine whether the Spanish law would accept the *renvoi*. Since it found that it would not, the English internal law was applied.

Possessing a voluminous literature, the doctrine, of *renvoi* can be traced back to the year 1652[7] and even today many countries have adopted it. Several theories of *renvoi* have been propounded. The principal theories of *Renvoi* are the following :[8]

(a) The mutual disclaimer theory,

(b) The theory of *Renvoi* proper, and

(c) The foreign court theory.

(a) The Mutual Disclaimer Theory

The two main proponents of this theory, Von Bar and Westlake, start on the assumption that all rules of private international law are in reality rules by which one state, for the purpose of administration of private law, defines its own jurisdiction and the jurisdiction of foreign states. Von Bar propounded his views in the following propositions[9] :

"(1) Every country shall observe the law of its own as regards the application of foreign laws.

(2) Provided that no express povision to the contrary exists, the court shall respect :

(a) the provisions of a foreign law which disclaims the right to bind its nationals abroad as regards their personal statute and desires that the said personal statute shall be determined by the law of the domicile, or by the law of the place where the act in question occurred;

(b) the decision of the two or more foreign systems of law, provided it be certain that one of them is necessarily competant, which agrees in attributing the determination of a question to the same system of law."

Starting on the assumption that the distinction between internal law and international law belongs to the science of law alone

7. See the decisions of Parliament of Roness of 1652 and 1863. The English decision in *Collier* v. *Revaz*, (1841) 2 Court. 855, is the fountain-head authority on the English doctrine. See also *Frere* v. *Frere*, cited above; *Goods of Laxroix*, (1877) 2 P.D. 94.

8. Falconbridge who has discussed the problem of *renvoi* very elaborately, discusses three theories : Ping-Pong theory, foreign court theory and vested right theory in Chapter 8.5. In Chapter 9.1 he discusses the theory of partial *renvoi* and the theory of total *renvoi*. Morris in Dicey's sixth edition discusses the following theories : *internal* theory, the partial *renvoi* theory and the total *renvoi* theory. Lorenzen discusses two theories : mutual disclaimer theory and theory of *renvoi* proper. Cheshire discusses doctrine of *renvoi* and foreign court theory, pp. 56-64 (8th ed.).

9. He propounded his theory at the meeting of the Institute of International Law held at Neuchatel in 1900.

and does not exist actually. Westlake illustrates his point of view thus : Suppose, a legislature provides : (A) that the capacity to make a will shall be acquired at the age of nineteen and that (B) the capacity of persons shall be governed by their national law. Westlake says that the Rule (A) will have no meaning without Rule (B) for the question is : whose testamentary capacity is acquired at nineteen ? And this cannot be answered without the aid of Rule (B), which fixed the category of persons whose capacity the legislature thinks it has right to fix. According to Rule (B) Rule (A) provides that the capacity of the subjects of the legislature is acquired at nineteen, but it provides nothing regarding the capacity of foreigners domiciled within the territory. And had the Rule (B) said that the capacity will be governed by the law of domicile, Rule (A) would have enacted that the capacity of persons domiciled within territory of the legislature is aquired at nineteen, but then would have provided no hint regarding the capacity of its own subjects domiciled abroad. Therefore, Westlake says in whatever terms Rule (B) may be expressed its true sense will be limited to cases which, according to the ideas of the legislature fall within its authority; there is certain class of cases which are deemed by a legislature as belonging to it and with regard to which it intends to legislate. This he illustrates as follows : The Danish Parliament, attaching decisive importance to domicile, will regard as the normal case, in matters under discussion, a person domiciled in Denmark for whom it fixes the age say, of twenty-one. While Italian Parliament attaching importance to nationality, will regard as the normal case, in the matter under discussion, an Italian subject, and for him fixes the age at nineteen. Further, according to Westlake a legislature which regards a certain case as normal will regard analogous cases as being normal for other legislatures and as belonging to them. On this principle the Danish Parliament will direct its judges to recognize person domiciled in a foreign country as capable or incapable of making wills in accordance with the law of their domicile. Since the Italian legislature gives importance to nationality it will direct its judges to recognize foreign nationals as capable or incapable of making will in accordance with the law of their nationality. Developing his argument, Westlake says that on the basis of the second step, although the legislatures, like that of Italy, can provide for persons domiciled in a country whose law in the matter is also based on domicile, the Danish legislature cannot provide a rule for persons domiciled in countries like Italy, whose laws are silent as to capacity of persons domiciled in such jurisdictions; likewise the reverse is also true. Therefore, Westlake holds the view that in such situations a third step for the solution of the problem would be necessary : to direct the judge to apply, in the absence of another law, the normal law. This would mean that a Dane domiciled in Italy will be, in Denmark, deemed to have come of age at 21, while, in Italy, he will be deemed to have become major at the age of 19. This formulation is relating to 'remission'.

As regards 'transmission' Westlake holds that the Rule (B) does not require the English judge to follow the direction of transmission, instead he should apply the rule of his own country, i.e. Rule (A). Or, to put it in other words, it is the duty of the judge to determine, in the first instance, to which country 'the legal relationship' presented to it belongs; if the law of the country to which the legal relationship belongs says that the case does not belong to it, there is no further reference to the law of the third country, the law of the forum should be applied.[10]

In its net result the mutual disclaimer theory of von Bar and Westlake is, in all cases where there is a conflict between the law of forum and the law of foreign country, invariably for the application of the law of forum. In other words, whenever the rules of conflict of laws of two countries are different the presumption is that there is no rule of internal law of either country applicable to the 'legal relationship', rather there is a gap, a vacuum, which has to be filled up and the best way to fill it is to apply the internal law of the forum, or what Westlake calls, ordinary law of forum. The theory rejects transmission. Under the theory the judge does not decide the case as if sitting in a court of foreign country.

The only difference between von Bar and Westlake is that Westlake seems to apply his theory to all cases where the difference in the rules of two countries amounts to mutual disclaimer, von Bar seems to restrict his theory to cases where personal statutes are involved.

Buzzati has summed up the criticism of this theory under the following three heads : (a) The starting point, namely, that a legislature adopting the law of domicile to determine capacity, is not interested in its subjects abroad and does not legislate in respect of them, and that a legislature adopting the law of nationality in its system of the conflict of laws is not interested in foreigners domiciled within its territory and does not legislate with respect to them, rest upon an erroneous assumption. It is absurd to say that provisions of the Italian Civil Code do not apply to an Englishman who is domiciled in Italy. (b) Neither von Bar nor Westlake denies the competency of a state to extend its jurisdiction over a matter which another state claims for itself. And yet their theory rest upon the fundamental proposition that due to its respect for state of X, state Y considers it improper to assign to state X a jurisdiction which state X declines; just as if it were not a greater offence to deprive the state X of a jurisdiction which it claims than it would be to assign to it a jurisdiction which it does not claim. (c) The fundamental error of the theory consists in the assumption that it is possible for state Y to bring its own jurisdiction into perfect accord

10. Westlake first propounded his theory in a note to the Institute of International Law. The statements of his theory was somewhat modified by him in his book on Private International Law.

with that of other states so that there will be no infringement upon their jurisdiction. But this is impossible and will remain so as long as the states have different rules relating to the conflict of laws. Each state is, therefore, obliged to adopt its own rules without referring to those of other states.[11] Lorenzen rightly says that this theory lacks support from a historical point of view also.[12]

(b) The Theory of Renvoi Proper

The doctrine of *renvoi* as has been seen earlier, has two aspects, remission, this is sometimes called *renvoi* in its narrow sense or *renvoi* proper, and transmission, which is called *renvoi* in its wider sense. *Renvoi* in its both senses has been thus explained by Schmithoff:

A, a British subject dies intestate in Brussels. He leaves movables in both England and Belgium. An English court is called upon to decide whether movables are to be distributed according to English law or Belgian law. Under the *renvoi* in narrow sense the position would be :

English law *referred* to the Belgian law of domicile,

and

Belgian law *remitted* to English law of nationality.

But if English courts imagine (which they do) that they take the place of Belgian courts, the correct terminology would be :

Belgian law refers to English law (as the law of nationality)

and

English law remits to Belgian law (as law of domicile).

At this stage the answer depends upon whether the Belgian private international law accepts or rejects the remitter (*renvoi*) from English law. Since Belgian law refuses to accept the remitter, English internal law applies.

If the foreign law accepts the remitter, as German law does (now suppose that A had died domiciled in Hamburg) the position would be :

German law (as applied by the English court) refers to English law (as the law of nationality)

and

English law remits to German law (as the law of domicile). German law accepts remitter, consequently German internal law applies.[13]

11. He summed up this criticism as a rapporteur before the Institute of International Law.
12. See Lorenzen, The *Renvoi* Theory and the Application of Foreign Law, p. 19.
13. Schmithoff, English Conflict of Laws, p. 93.

Bentwitch who accepts the theory of *renvoi* in its narrow sense advances the following arguments in its favour. "The *renvoi* is, in principle, a reference back not to the whole law of the foreign country including its different rules of private international law, but simply to its internal law. Suppose a case where the *lex fori* (hereinafter called A) submits the matter to the *lex domicilii* (hereinafter called B), and B refers the matter back to A as the law of nationality, A accepts the *renvoi*, and applies its own law. If we regard first principle, we see that what happened is this : Law is primarily sovereign over all matters occurring within the territory, and so A would ordinarily apply to succession. A, from motives of international comity and to secure a single system of succession, resigns its ordinary jurisdiction to B. But B, by reason of its special juristic conceptions, does not take advantage of the sacrifice by accepting jurisdiction. A's primary jurisdiction consequently is properly exercised and there is no ground for A to decline to accept the renunciation of B, since it thereby puts into operation its fundamental principle of regulating every matter within the territory."[14]

The application of *renvoi* in its proper or narrow form would always, like the mutual disclaimer theory, lead to the application of the law of the forum, wherever there is a conflict between the two foreign laws. However bases of two are different. The theory of *renvoi* in its proper sense is based on the assumption that the rules of private international law in each country are based on the principle of comity which implies a mutual agreement among the states for the application of each other's laws. In other words, the basis is reciprocity. If there is no reciprocity the law of forum will apply. It is submitted that here lies the fallacy of the theory. As we have seen in Chapter 2 of this work rules of private international law are not based on reciprocity.[15] Lorenzen rightly remarks that the *renvoi* in this form is nothing else than a return *pro tanto* to the doctrine of exclusive prevalence of the internal law of the forum.[16] It is submitted the theory is also illogical. No logical reason could be given as to why in one case law of A is to be taken to refer to the rules of private international law of country B, while the latter should not in turn be held to refer back again to the private international law of country A, and so on *ad infinitum*.[17]

(c) The Foreign Court Theory

In 1841 an English judge, Sir Herbert Jenner, formulated the foreign court theory thus : "The court sitting here decides from the persons skilled in that law, and decides as it would if sitting

14. See Bentwitch : the Law of Domicile in its Relation to Succession and the Doctrine of *Renvoi*.
15. See Chapter 3.
16. Lorenzen, p. 66.
17. Schreiber, 31 Harward Law Review, p. 533.

in Belgium."[18] The question before the learned judge was concerning power of testamentary disposition of a British subject who died domiciled in Belgium. It is obvious that the statement of the judge is not to be taken literally. What it means is something like this : In this case the English law will direct the judge that Belgian law, being the law of the domicile of the deceased, should be applied. Then looking to Belgian law the English judge would find that under Belgian law the property of deceased is to be distributed according to the law of nationality, i.e. English law and he would also find that Belgian law follows *renvoi*. Thus informed, the judge would decide the case in accordance with the Belgian law, i.e. the judge would apply the English law since he has been directed to do so by the Belgian law. It is in this sense that the English judge decides the case as if "sitting in Belgium". In this case, the English judge would obviously ignore the existence of doctrine of *renvoi* in Belgian law. The reason for this is that if the doctrine of *renvoi* is recognized, no decision can ever be arrived at the case resulting in endless series of references from Belgian law to English law and from English law to Belgian law. To escape from this, the return reference is understood as reference to internal law alone.

But then, is it also the position in respect of transmission ? Lorenzen thinks that this is doubtful. The doctrine of *renvoi* is an expedient to which court resort in order to justify the application of their own law; it is probable that in the case of transmission the courts might interpret a reference to the law of a third country as a reference to the rules of conflict of laws of that country.

The doctrine of *renvoi* has been criticised not only on historical and logical grounds but also on the ground of principle.[19] The criticism of the theory may be summed as under :

(i) If the foreign country also adopts the doctrine of *renvoi*, then logically no solution is possible, as a perpetual *circulus inextricabilis* would be the result. Therefore, it has been rightly remarked that it is difficult to approve a doctrine which is workable only if other countries reject it.

(ii) "It would be difficult to imagine a harder task than that which faces me", Wynn-Perry, J. observed, "of expounding for the first time either in this country or in Spain the relevant law of Spain as it would be expounded by the Supreme Court of Spain, which, up to the present time, has made no pronouncement on the subject, and having to base that exposition on evidence that satisfies me that on this subject there exists a profound cleavage of legal opinion in Spain and two conflicting decisions of courts of inferior jurisdiction."[20]

18. *Collier* v. *Revaz*, (1841) 2 Curt. 855.
19. See Falconbridge, p. 167.
20. *In re Duke of Wellington*, (1947) Ch. 506.

(iii) The doctrine is hardly conducive to the aim of private international law, viz., to bring uniformity of laws.

(iv) The doctrine of *renvoi* is not only an expedient for the application of the *lex fori*, but it may result in the application of as many laws as there are states before the courts of which the matter might be agitated. This may be illustrated by a few examples.[21] An Englishman who is domiciled in Italy makes a contract there, for the breach of which a suit is brought in India. The defence is lack of capacity. It may also be assumed that in English law capacity is governed by the *lex domicilii*, in Italian law by the *lex patrie* and in Indian law by *lex loci contractus*. According to Westlake and von Bar the law of India, being the law of forum, will apply, though Indian law has no connection with the contract except that the suit is brought in India. Take another example : A suit is brought in India for the execution of Frenchman's testamentary trust of immovable property situated in New York. According to the law of the forum the *lex situs* governs the matter, but according to the law of Germany, the law of nationality of the testator governs the matter. Under the above theories the law of India will determine the case. Lorenzen says : "The extent that this theory is applied, it means a return reference to the exclusive application of the ordinary or internal law of the forum, and a sacrifice of all that has been gained during the last century in the development of the rules of conflict of laws."[22]

The foreign court theory is no better. So far as the remission aspect is concerned, it suffers from the same disadvantage as the other theories, in so far as the transmission aspect is concerned the theory may be manipulated in such a way that the law of the forum may be again applicable. For example, two Indians domiciled in New York enter into a contract in Italy. For the breach of this contract a suit is brought in a New York court. The defence is lack of capacity. Which of the three laws, Indian, New Yorkian or Italian should apply ? Suppose that *renvoi* is not accepted. It may happen that the New York court may apply the Italian law as the *lex loci contractus*, the Indian court may apply the law of New York as *lex domicilii* and the Italian court, the law of India, as the *lex patrie*. Now assume that these countries accept the foreign court theory. In such a case the New York

21. Bentwitch has answered this criticism thus : "The objection, however, is a figment of theory, and is not based on a solid practical difficulty. Even if no rules were established by international convention for the application of the *renvoi*, in any particular case the English court or the French court would know whether the other had already dealt with succession. If this was so, it would adopt the principle already applied to succession, and apply either its own rules of private international law or the doctrine of *renvoi* so as to subject the whole movable succession to one law. Thus in the case supposed, if the English court, being seized of the matter had accepted the *renvoi* and applied English law to English assets of the deceased, a French court would naturally apply English law to French assets according to its own rules."

22. Lorenzen, p. 72.

court would refer the matter to the entire law of Italy, it being the *lex loci contractus* and would find that the conflict of laws rule of Italy directs it to apply the Indian law, the *lex patrie*. The New York court may thus ultimately apply the Indian law. Now suppose the matter is agitated before an Indian court. The Indian judge would refer the matter to the law of New York, being the law of domicile, and there being directed to apply the *lex loci contractus*, would apply the Italian law. Now suppose, the suit is brought in an Italian court. The Italian judge applying the whole of Indian law would find that it is directed to apply the law of New York, the *lex domicilii*. Thus we find that no uniformity results from the application of the foreign court theory.[23]

(v) The foreign court theory suffers from ambiguity. Cheshire says, "The theory must be regarded as untenable unless it formulates with precision the exact enquiry that is to be addressed to the hypothetical foreign court. Its most ardent exponents, however, hold opposite views upon the appropriate formula."[24] Cheshire then explains the ambiguity of both schools of this theory with the help of an illustration. An English court is concerned with the mode of distribution of goods situated in England and belonging to X domiciled in Russia. It is well established rule that the *lex domicilii* governs the matter. The foreign court theory directs that the English court should give the same decision as the court of domicile will give. Sir Herbert Jenner, who is propounder of one school of foreign court theory, holds that actual circumstances and facts of the case must be envisaged. The second school, represented by Dicey, enunciates a formula that ignores the actual facts and circumstances. This school is prepared to presume that the property is situated in Russia. Application of these two formulas would yield different results. According to the law of Russia the property which is situated in Russia is governed by its internal law, irrespective of the nationality or domicile of the deceased. On the other hand, if the property is situated outside Russia then under the Russian law, the Russian law is not applicable, irrespective of the fact whether the deceased was a Russian national or domiciled in Russia. The first school will decide the case by saying that the Russian law has no say in the matter, while the second school will apply the Russian internal law.[25]

Morris rightly says that "as a purely practical matter, it would seem that a court should not undertake the onerous task of trying to ascertain as to how a foreign court would decide the question, unless the situation is an exceptional one and the advantages of doing so clearly outweigh the disadvantages. In most situations,

23. See Lorenzen, p. 75; Dicey (6th ed.), p. 58.
24. Cheshire (2nd ed.), p. 27.
25. Some have tried to answer this criticism : see Dorbin, The English Doctrine and the Soviet Law of Succession, 15 BYBIL, p. 36; See also Wolff, p. 201; Schmithoff, pp. 96-97.

the balance of convenience surely lies in interpreting the reference to foreign law to mean its domestic rules."[26] In our submission this should be the position.

The exceptional cases in which the doctrine of *renvoi* has been considered to be useful are the following:

(1) *Title to Foreign Land*: The country in which immovable property is situated has, by the very nature of things, a permanent and exclusive physical control over it. It would, therefore, be a realistic approach to determine the title to such property by the application of the whole of the law of the *situs* of the property. "The reason for applying the *lex situs* is that any adjudication which ignores the *lex situs* would be a *brutum fulmen*, since in the last resort the land can only be dealt with in a manner permitted by the *lex situs*."[27] It would follow that if the law of *situs* recognizes a will or deed to be valid which is executed in accordance with the law of the place of execution,[28] or if it recognizes the capacity of *de cujus* to execute such a will or deed in accordance with the law of nationality or law of domicile,[29] or if there is return reference to the law of forum or if there is forward reference to the law of a third country, this should be applied by courts of all countries.[30]

(2) *Title to Foreign Movables*: It has been suggested that the doctrine of *renvoi* should be equally applicable to movable property situated abroad. But since the *situs* of movables can always be changed, the argument is not so strong as in the case of foreign immovables.[31]

(3) *Status*: As to the status of marriage it has been suggested that the status of marriage which is recognized by the *lex domicilii* should be recognized everywhere. In view of special favour shown all the world over to the institution of marriage and for the sake of uniformity in the rules of private international law, a view has been propounded that, that a change in the status of parties to marriage effected outside the country of domicile of

26. Dicey and Morris, (8th ed.), p. 68.
27. *Ibid.*, p. 64.
28. See sections 7 and 8 of Restatement of Conflict of laws.
29. *Re Ross*, L.R. (1930) 1 Ch. 377; *In re Duke of Wellington*, L.R. (1947) Ch. 506.
30. Dorbin, *Loc. op. cit.* Lorenzen suggests an alternative rule: "Uniformity might be reached without recourse to the *renvoi* doctrine if all countries would adopt alternative rules in their systems of the conflict of laws. As regards the formal execution of a deed or will, the general acceptance of the rule *locus regit actum* as an alternative rule would be sufficient. With respect to capacity and substantive validity of wills and deeds, international uniformity could be brought about only in case all countries were willing to sustain such instruments if they satisfied either the law of *situs* or the national law of the owner" (pp. 78-79).
31. See Dicey and Morris, p. 64; Cheshire, pp. 72-73, (8th ed.)

parties should also be recognized everywhere else if it is recognized by the country of the domicile of the parties.[32] Then, should this rule be restricted to recognition of status of marriage, or should it be extended to all cases of status ? This has been answered differently. The American Restatement of Conflict of Laws favours the application of the rule to all matters of status, while the decision in *Re Askew*[33] seems to suggest a restricted application of the rule. It is submitted that the former view is preferable. As to the status of marriage, Lorenzen has suggested that a marriage status should be recognized if it satisfies either the law of the place where it was entered into or the law of the domicile of the parties.[34]

(4) *Formalities of a Will* : The doctrine of a *renvoi* has been advocated in respect of formalities of a will. Cheshire suggests that a grant of probate to wills should not be denied 'on the ground of formal invalidity if the instrument if formally valid according to the private international law, though not according to the internal law, of the governing legal system.'[35] Lorenzen seems to support this view.[36] Morris has doubted the expediency of this indulgence.[37] The Wills Act, 1963 excludes the application of the doctrine of *renvoi* to the formal validity of wills, even in respect of immovable property. It leans very favourably in respect of formal validity of will by making a will formally valid if it complies with the formalities of the internal law of the place of execution, of the domicile of the testator, of the habitual residence of the testator, or nationality of the testator.[38]

(5) *International Conventions* : Sometime back, the doctrine of *renvoi* was an expedient through which the nations of the world could come together for framing international convention.[39] This importance of *renvoi* has been lost in our contemporary world.

(6) *Transmission* : Morris advocates the application of the doctrine to certain cases of 'transmission'. He says : "Where the foreign law referred to by the English court refers to a second foreign law, and the second foreign law would agree that it was applicable, the case for applying the second foreign law is strong."[40] Morris proceeds to say that if the second foreign law would not agree that it is applicable, then there seems to be no reason why it

32. This view finds favour in *Armitage* v. *A.G.*, (1906), p. 135. For the criticism of the case, see Morris, 24 Canadian Bar Review, p. 73 at p. 74, and for its defence see Tuck, 25 Canadian Bar Review, p. 226.
33. L.R. (1930) 2 Ch. 259, Cheshire, (8th ed.), p. 68.
34. Lorenzen, pp. 77-78.
35. Cheshire (8th ed.), p. 72. See also *Collier* v. *Rivaz*, (1841) 2 Curt. 855; *Frere* v. *Frere*, (1847) 5 Notes on Cases in Ecclesiastical and Maritime Court, 593; *Re Ross* (1930) 1 Ch. 377.
36. Lorenzen, p. 78.
37. Dicey and Morris (8th ed.), pp. 63-64.
38. Section 1, Wills Act, 1963.
39. For instance see the Hague Convention of June 12, 1912.
40. Dicey and Morris (8th ed.), p. 65.

should be applied. Thus, if a German national domiciled in Italy died leaving behind movables in England, and the Italian and German laws agree that German domestic law is applicable because the *propositus* at the time of his death was a German national, then English court should apply the German internal law. On the other hand, if a Danish national domiciled in Italy dies leaving behind movables in England and if the Italian law will apply the law of nationality and the Danish law would apply the law of domicile, neither law recognizing any *renvoi* from the other, it seems that the English court should apply Italian domestic law.[41]

One would agree with the observation of Morris that the doctrine is of no practical utility.[42] One would be most heartily inclined to agree with Lorenzen when he says, "... it may reasonably be hoped that, when the doctrine with all its consequences is squarely presented to the higher English court, they will not hesitate to reject the decisions of the courts that have lent colour to *renvoi* in English law."[43] Happily, there is no Indian case which directly supports the doctrine of *renvoi* and it may be hoped that our courts would not be tempted to apply the doctrine just because it has found favour in certain decisions of English court and with some eminent English writers like Dicey and Westlake.

At the end of this Chapter a reference to the Hague Draft Convention of 1951[44] may be made, the object of which is to eliminate conflict between the law of domicile and law of nationality. The first three articles of the Convention run as under :

> *Article* 1. When the state where the person concerned is domiciled prescribes the application of the law of his nationality, but the state of which such person is a citizen prescribes the application of the law of his domicile, each contracting state shall apply the provisions of internal law of his domicile.
>
> *Article* 2. When the state where the person concerned is domiciled and the state of which such person is a citizen each prescribes the application of the law of his domicile, each contracting state shall apply the provisions of the internal law of his domicile.
>
> *Article* 3. When the state where the person concerned is domiciled and the state of which such person is a citizen each prescribes the application of his national law, each contracting state shall apply the provisions of the internal law of his nationality.

41. Dicey and Morris (8th ed.), p. 65.
42. *Ibid.* at p. 62.
43. Lornzen, p. 53. It may be recalled that both Dicey (See 5th ed. Appendix I) and Westlake (Chapter II) have been the ardent supporters of the doctrine.
44. The Draft Convention was approved in the International Conference on Private International Law held in October 1951.

Part II

PRELIMINARY TOPICS

SUMMARY

5

APPLICATION AND EXCLUSION OF FOREIGN LAW

A Municipal court adjudicating upon a purely internal case, is usually required to determine two sets of questions : question of fact and question of law. On the former the parties adduce evidence, oral and documentary, on the basis of which the question is determined. In the latter the court takes judicial notice of the law of land and parties are not required to prove it. In a case having some foreign element the same set of questions usually arise. As to question of facts the same procedure is followed, viz., the parties adduce evidence on the basis of which the court determines the issues. When it comes to the question of application to foreign law, the question is looked at from a different angle. Private international laws of the various countries of the world differ on this issue. The courts cannot refuse to apply the internal law, but when it comes to the question of application of foreign law, in certain circumstances, they are free to exclude its application. Thus in a case having foreign elements, a domestic court may be required :

(a) to apply foreign law, or

(b) to exclude the otherwise applicable foreign law.

I

APPLICATION OF FOREIGN LAW

In respect of the application of foreign law the inquiry is : whether the question of application of foreign law is a question of law or a question of fact. On this matter at least five views prevail.

1. Italy is one of very few countries which takes the view that the question of application of foreign law is a question of law exactly the same way as it is in a purely internal case. The Italian view starts on the assumption that when the court is required to apply foreign law under private international law, the rules of private international law are part of domestic legislation, and therefore, the courts decide the case having foreign elements the

same way as they decide a purely internal case. This means that under the Italian private international law, the courts are obliged to know foreign law: the principle of *jura novit curia, memo censetur ignorare ius* applies. According to Italian law if the court is not familiar with foreign law, then it is its duty to find it out.

2. The German law,[1] and law of some other continental countries,[2] take the view that question of foreign law is a question of law, 'but not in the same way as the internal law is the question of law. The German view starts on the assumption that source of foreign law is not domestic legislation and therefore its binding character is of secondary nature: it is binding in so far as it has been made binding by the internal law. In view of this, although the court has obligation to establish the contents of foreign law *ex officio*, it can seek the assistance of parties to find out the foreign law and may call upon them to prove the foreign law. It also implies that the court is not bound by the evidence of foreign law adduced by the parties. It is free to obtain information of foreign law from any source.

3. The French law takes the view that the question of foreign law is a question of fact, but it is not like any other question of fact. It is a question of fact in the sense that the court has no obligation to know foreign law; nor is it the duty of the court to ascertain it *ex officio*. The burden of proving the foreign law and its contents are on the party relying on it. It is different from other questions of fact in the sense that if the court is familiar with foreign law, it may apply it by itself. The court is also free to take steps independently of parties to verify the contents of foreign law.

4. In the Soviet Union and the People's Democracies of East Europe the matter is looked at yet from a different angle. The view that is propounded there is: keeping in mind the interest of society, it is the duty of the court to discover objective truth. Thus, it is true that the parties in a trial are required to prove facts, but the court is 'not the personification of justitia blindfolded', it is not a passive observant of the dispute between the parties and therefore it can take initiative in ascertaining facts. According to Seziszy: (i) when rules of foreign law are considered as simple facts, the parties are required to prove the purport of the rules of law, but the court may also co-operate with parties in verifying the contents of law; (ii) when rules of foreign law have been incorporated into the domestic legislation, then the court will take judicial notice of them (principles of *jura novit curia*); and (iii) when foreign law is applied on the strength of the domestic rules

1. German Code of Civil Procedure, s. 293.
2. Austrian Code of Civil Procedure, s. 293; Danish Law of Bill of Exchange of 1932, s. 87; Finnish Family Act, 1929, s. 56; Polish Act on Private International Law, s. 39. This view also prevails in some of the Latin American states. For instance, see Industry Law of Civil Code of Brazil, 1942, s. 14; Civil Code of Peru, ss. 11, 12.

for the choice of law, then a combination of the principle of trial and the principle of *jura novit curia* is applied. "The court is obliged to strive to establish *ex officio* the substance of the foreign rules of law, for this purpose it may, through the Ministry of Justice, ask information from foreign governments, but may also constrain the parties to prove the contents of foreign rules of law."[3]

5. The common law countries, Spain, Portugal, India and some Latin American states[4] take the view that the question of foreign law is a question of fact in the same manner as any other question of fact. This implies that the burden of proving the foreign law and its contents lies exclusively on the parties. Parties may prove it by evidence, oral, documentary or of expert witnesses.

FOREIGN LAW AS QUESTION OF FACT

English Law

When it is said that the proof of foreign law and its contents is a question of fact it means that the knowledge of foreign law cannot be imputed to judges : a party relying on foreign law must prove it as other facts are proved, by appropriate evidence, i.e. the evidence of experts, unless both the parties agree to leave investigation to the judge and forego the right of adducing evidence.[5] Unless the case is covered by any of the exceptions listed below, English law insists that foreign law must be proved by expert witness, though if a party is called upon to prove foreign usage or custom it may prove it by any evidence; the witnesses called may be experts or otherwise.[6]

Before 1972 it was an established rule of English private international law that a rule of foreign law could not be proved by citing a previous decision of an English court where the same foreign rule was at issue,[7] or by production of books in which it was contained, or presenting a copy of the text of foreign law.[8] It is also an established rule that foreign law cannot be proved by

3. Private International Law in European People's Democracies (1964), p.155.
4. Such as Mexico (Civil Code of Mexico, Puebla, s. 17) and Guatemala (Code of 1926, Ch. 26) and Costa Rica (Civil Code, s. 11).
5. *Jabbour (F. & K.)* v. *Custodian of Israel Absentee Property*, (1954) I All E.R. 145; *Parkaso* v. *Singh* (1968) p. 233.
6. *Sussex Peerage case*, 11 Cl. & Fin. 85; *Doncket* v. *Thelluson*, 8 C.B. 812.
7. *Lazard Bros. & Co. Ltd.* v. *Midland Bank*, (1933) A.C. 289; *McCormick* v. *Garnett*, (1854) 23 L.J. Ch. 777. But see *Re Sebba*, (1959) Ch. 166 and *Simons* v. *Simons*, (1939) 1 K.B. 490 where this rule was departed from. Dicey and Morris's construction is that in these cases the rule was lost sight of, p. 1112 (8th ed.).
8. *Buerger* v. *New York Life Assurance Co.*, (1927) 96 L.J. K.B. 930.

referring to a judgment of foreign court[9] or by referring to a foreign judgment in which the meaning and effect of foreign law is explained.[10] This position has now been substantially altered by the Civil Evidence Act, 1972. Section 4 of the Act lays down that if any question of foreign law has been determined in civil or criminal proceedings at the first instance in the High Court, the Crown Court, a court of quarter sessions or the county palatine courts of Chancery of Lancaster or Durham, or in any appeal therefrom, or in Privy Council on appeal from any court outside the United Kingdom, then any decision rendered or finding given on that question is admissible in evidence in any civil proceedings, and the foreign law shall be taken to be what it has been determined or laid down in the decision or finding, unless the contrary is proved. The decision of any of the aforesaid courts to be admissible in evidence as to the foreign law must be reported or recorded in citable form. This means that it must be reported or recorded in writing in a report, transcript or other document in a citable form in the same manner as if the question has been of English law. Unless the court can take judicial notice of the foreign law, sub-section (3) of s. 4 lays down that except with the leave of the court, a party may not adduce such decision or finding as evidence of foreign law, unless he had notified the other party of his intention to do so. As in the case of other facts so in the case of foreign law, the English law requires that it must be proved to the satisfaction of the judge.[11]

The following exceptions are recognized under English law to the rule that foreign law is to be proved as a question of fact :

(a) Foreign law need not be proved when a statute expressly provides that it shall be judicially noticed.[12]

(b) Foreign law is sometimes noticed as a notorious fact. For instance, English courts have taken judicial notice that roulette is not unlawful in Monte Carlo.[13] It is essential that the foreign law should be sufficiently notorious.[14]

(c) The English courts may take judicial notice of foreign law if its contents are, at least in part, determined by a rule of English law, and if, according to English law, the foreign law is the same as, or substantially similar to, English law. For example, it is a rule of English law that settlers

9. *Callwood* v. *Callwood*, (1960) A.C. 659.

10. *Beatty* v. *Beatty*, (1924) I K.B. 807; *Guaranty Trust Co. of New York* v. *Hannay & Co.* (1918) 2 K.B. 623.

11. Adminstration of Justice Act, 1920, s. 15; the statute has been repealed and replaced by the Supreme Court of Judicature (Consolidation) Act, 1925, s. 102, in respect of the High Court and by the County Courts Acts, 1959, s. 9, in respect of county courts.

12. For instance, Maintenance Order Act, 1950, s. 22(2).

13. *Saxby* v. *Foulton*, (1909) 2 K.B. 208.

14. *Hartmann* v. *Koning* (1933) 50 T.L.R. 114 (H.L.).

from the United Kingdom carry with them to colonies English law so far as it is applicable to the conditions prevailing in the colony; the court can thus take judicial notice of the common law of the colony.[15]

(d) When the English courts hear appeal from colonies and dominions, they take judicial notice of the law of these countries. Similarly, when the House of Lords hears an English appeal it takes judicial notice of Scot law and conversely when it hears a Scottish appeal, it takes judicial notice of English law.[16]

(e) Foreign law need not be proved when it is admitted.[17]

(f) Foreign law need not be proved when both the parties request the court to decide the matter without the proof of foreign law. However, courts have shown some reluctance to take this course unless it is a question of interpretation of foreign law.[18]

(g) Sometimes in very exceptional cases the court may apply foreign law without proof.[19]

Mode of Proof—Expert Evidence : English law takes the view that the foreign law can be proved only by expert evidence.[20] Yet, there is no precise answer to the question : who is an expert witness ? It has been held that a judge and a legal practitioner of the country the foreign law of which is to be proved are competent witnesses.[21] It has also been held that a person, who by virtue of his calling or profession, has acquired knowledge of foreign law, is a competent witness.[22] But the mere academic knowledge has been

15. *Limeric* v. *Limeric*, (1863) 4 Sw. & Tr. 252.
16. It seems that the same principle applies to the Judicial Committee of the Privy Council : see British Law Ascertainment Act, 1859, s. 4.
17. *The Torni* (1932) p. 27; *Moulis* v. *Owen* (1907) 1 K.B. 746; *Lloyd* v. *Guibert*, (1865) L.R. 1 Q.B. 115; *Prowse* v. *European and American Steam Shipping Co.*, (1860) 13 Moo. P.C. 484.
18. *Beatty* v. *Beatty*, (1924) 1 K.B. 807; *F. & K. Jabbour* v. *Custodian of Israeli Absentee Property*, (1954) 1 W.L.R. 139; *Re Marshall*, (1957) Ch. 507; *Re Sebba*, (1959) Ch. 166.
19. *Re Cohn*, (1945) Ch. 5.
20. *Baron de Bode's case*, (1845) 8 Q.B. 208 seems to be the oldest reported case.
21. *Baron de Bode's case* (1845) 8 Q.B. 208; *Wilson* v. *Wilson*, (1903) p. 157; *Brailey* v. *Rhodesia Consolidated Ltd.*, (1910) 2 Ch. 95; *Barford* v. *Barford*, (1918) p. 140.
22. *Cooper-King* v. *Cooper-King*, (1900), p. 65 (a Governor General of a Colony); *The Goods of Oldenburg*, (1884) 9 P.D. 234 (an ambassador); *In the Goods of Dost Aly Khan*, (1880) 6 P.D. 6 (an embassy official); *Lacon* v. *Higgins*, (1822) Dow & Ry. N.P. 38 (a Vice Consul); *In the Goods of Whitelegg*, (1899) p. 267 (a Notary public); *Brailey* v. *Rhodesia Consolidated Ltd.* (1910) 2 Ch. 95 (reader in Roman-Dutch Law in the Council of Legal Education); *Dalrymple* v. *Dalrymple*, (1811) 2 Hag. Con. 54 (learned professor); *Vander Donkt* v. *Thellussion*, (1849) 8 C.B. 812 (a merchant); *Sussex Peerage case*, (1844) 11 Cl. & F. 85 (a bishop); *De Beeche* v. *South American Stones Ltd.*; (1935) A.C. 148 (a Bank manager). In these cases the persons put in brackets were held to be competent.

held not to be sufficient to make a person a competent witness.[23] This no longer seems to be true, if it was, at any time. In some decisions the English judges expressed an opinion that only that person can be an expert witness who has professional knowledge of the foreign law, in the sense that he has been practising law in the foreign country. Now s. 4(1) of the Civil Evidence Act, 1972 lays down that "in civil proceedings a person who is suitably qualified to do so on account of his knowledge or experience is competent to give expert evidence irrespective of whether he has acted or is entitled to act as a legal practitioner" in the foreign country. Thus, those English decisions which hold that a scholar or academician cannot give evidence of foreign law are no longer good law and stand overruled.

Although English courts cannot take judicial notice of the foreign law or make their own research in foreign law or *suo motu* look into the foreign law,[24] when an expert witness is called by either party and he in his testimony tenders a copy of foreign statute, rules or decisions of court or refer to a book of law, then such material becomes part of evidence, and the court is free to pursue it. However, the court is entitled to look into such documents only to the extent it has been cited by the party or his witness.[25] The uncontroverted testimony of an expert witness is usually accepted by the court,[26] though the court is not bound to do so. The court is free to reject the opinion of the expert witness and may reach its own conclusion after perusing the material submitted by the expert witness.[27] In case the testimony of experts is contradictory, the court would look into the entire evidence and is free to form its own opinion of foreign law.[28] Evidence of foreign law includes evidence as to its interpretation.[29] but ths court is free to place its own interpretation and in such a case the English rules of construction of statute are applicable.[30]

23. *Bristow* v. *Sequeville*, (1850) 19 L.J. Ex. 289; *In the Goods of Bonelli* (1875) L.R. 1 P.D. 69; but see *Brailey* v. *Rhodesia Consolidated Ltd.* (cited above); *Baron de Bode's case* (cited above).
24. *Di Sora* v. *Phillipps*, (1863) 10 H.L.C. 624.
25. *Nelson* v. *Bridpatt*, (1854) 8 Beav. 527.
26. *Buerger* v. *New York Life Assurance Co*. (1926) 96 L.J. K.B. 930; *Re Banque de Merchands de Moscou*, (1958) Ch. 182.
27. *O'Callaghan* v. *O'Sullivan*, (1925) 1 Ir. Rep. 90 (obviously false evidence); *Buerger* v. *New York Life Assurance Co.*, (cited above) (Extravagant evidence); *Sharif* v. *Azad*, (1966) 3 All E.R. 788.
28. *Guaranty Trust Corporation of New York* v. *Hannay*, (1918) 2 K.B. 623; *The Russian Commercial and Industrial Bank* v. *Comptoir d'Escompte de Mulhouse*, (1923) 2 K.B. 631, but see (1925) A.C. 112; *Princess Paley Olga* v. *Weizz*, (1929) 1 K.B. 718; *Re Duke of Wellington*, (1947) Ch. 506.
29. *Baron de Bode's case*, cited above.
30. *Papadopoulos* v. *Papadopoulos*, (1930), p. 55; *The Torni*, (1932) p. 78; *Jasiewicz* v. *Jasiewicz*, (1962) 1 W.L.R. 1426 *Mahadervan* v. *Mahadervan*, (1964) p. 233.

A decision of foreign court is ordinarily a weighty evidence of foreign law and is usually given effect to.[31] But if the court is of the opinion that the foreign judgment does not embody the foreign law correctly, it may disregard it.[32] Similarly, when there are conflicting foreign decisions, the court is free to give decision in acccordance with its own views as to foreign law, even though the foreign law is in an unsettled state in the foreign country.[33]

If a question of law involves a political decision, the court will not look into the expert testimony but will be guided by the view taken by the foreign office of its own government. Similarly, no evidence of the motive behind a particular foreign law would be entertained.[33a] For instance, a country has been partitioned or divided on account of insurrection, civil war or revolution, the court will recognize and give effect to the laws of that part of the foreign country whose government is recognized by its country.[34]

Proof of Colonial Law : Under the Evidence (Colonial Statutes) Act, 1907 copies of law made by the legislature of any "British possession" and purported to be printed officially by the Government of that British possession can be received in evidence as proof of foreign law. The text of such law can be proved without calling for the evidence of an expert witness.[35] However, the court has power to call for expert evidence to prove that the law is still in force.

The Act still applies to most legislatures of the Commonwealth countries, which are no longer part of Her Majesty's dominions.[36] The Act empowers the British Government to extend it to a protectorate by an Order in Council.

Judicial Ascertainment of Foreign Law : Under the British Law Ascertainment Act, 1859 a court in any part of Her Majesty's dominions may, if it thinks it necessary or expedient for the proper disposal of an action, state a case for the opinion of a court in any other part of Her Majesty's dominions in order to ascertain the view of that court as to the law applicable to the facts of the case stated.[37] The provisions of the Act apply to 'territories over which Her Majesty has jurisdiction under the Foreign Jurisdiction Act, 1890'. Under the Act the courts have very wide discretion. A court may state a case *suo motu* or it may refuse to state a case

31. *Beatty* v. *Beatty*, (1924) 1 K.B. 807; *Re Annesley*, (1926) Ch. 692.
32. *Guaranty Trust Corporation of New York* v. *Hannay*, (1918) 2 K.B. 623.
33. *Breen* v. *Breen*, (1964) p. 144; *Re Duke of Wellington*, (1947) Ch. 506.
33a. *Bittes Gas and Oil Co.* v. *Hammer* (1982) A.C. 888.
34. *Carl Zeiss Stiftung* v. *Reyur & Keeler Ltd.* (1966) 3 W.L.R. 125 (H.L.)
35. *Papadopoulos* v. *Papadopoulos*, (1930), p. 55.
36. Most of them have now become independent states and have declared themselves as Republics.
37. Section 1.

even when requested to do so by a party to the case. The opinion of the foreign court is binding on the English court.[38]

Under the Foreign Ascertainment Act, 1861 a similar provision exists for the ascertainment of the law of a foreign country. However, under the Act, the opinion of the foreign court is not binding on the English court.[39] The act applies only on the basis of reciprocity.[40]

Indian Law

The Indian law closely follows English law inasmuch as it lays down that, that the foreign law is a question of fact, though it differs from English law in some details. The general provision is laid down in s. 45 of the Evidence Act, 1872. The section provides, "When the court has to form an opinion upon a point of foreign law, . . . the opinion upon that point of persons specially skilled in such foreign law . . . are relevant facts." In the Indian law the burden of proof is on the party setting the plea of foreign law.[41]

The Bombay High Court has taken the view that a judgment of the highest court of the foreign country is best evidence as to the law of that foreign country.[42] In *Palaniappa Chetty* v. *Nagappa Chettiar*,[43] where the court was concerned with a provision of Ceylon Civil Procedure Code, the court said that although the evidence of an expert on a point of law of a foreign country is the usual mode of proving foreign law, the court should itself interpret the provision of foreign law and should not rely on the interpretation of expert howsoever eminent he may be.

Section 57 of the Evidence Act contains a provision under which the Indian courts will take judicial notice of certain laws. Under the section the court shall take judicial notice of the following :

(1) . . . .

(2) All public Acts passed or hereafter to be passed by Parliament of the United Kingdom, and all local and personal Acts directed by Parliament of the United Kingdom to be judicially noticed.

(3) . . . .

38. Section 3.

39. Section 1.

40. Section 1. Before India become free, both the statutes, the Acts of 1859 and 1861, applied to India in the sense that Indian Courts could use these statutes for the ascertainment of law of any part of the United Kingdom as well as of the foreign country. See the Indian Law Commission's V Report, 1957.

41. *Khonday Gangaram Saha* v. *Swaminadha Mudaliar*, 1926 Mad. 218.

42. *Suganchand Bhinkimchand* v. *Mangibai Gulabchand*, 1942 Bom. 185.

43. 1930 Mad. 146

(4) The course of proceedings of Parliament of the United Kingdom . . . .

(5) The accession and the Sign Manual of the Sovereign for the time being of the United Kingdom of Great Britain and Ireland.

(6) All seals of which English courts take judicial notice. . . .

(7) The accession to office, names, titles, functions and signatures of the person filling for the time being any public office in any state, if the fact of their appointment is notified in any official gazette.

(8) The existence of title and national flag of every state or sovereign recognized by the Government of India.

The last but one paragraph of s. 57 lays down that in these cases 'the court may resort for its aid to appropriate books or documents of reference.' The last paragraph of the section lays down that if the court is called upon by any party 'to take judicial notice of any fact, it may refuse to do so unless and until such person produces any such book or document it may consider necessary to enable it to do so'.

The Indian law makes a departure from English law inasmuch as s. 38 of the Evidence Act lays down that a record of law published under the authority of the government is a relevant fact in respect of proof of law of that country. Under s. 84 the court may presume the genuineness of every such record. Then s. 38 provides: "When the court has to form an opinion as to a law of any country, any statement of such law contained in a book purporting to be printed or published under the authority of government of such country and to contain any such law, and any report of a ruling of the court of such country contained in a book purporting to be a report of such ruling is relevant." In the same connection s. 84 provides: "The court shall presume the genuineness of every book purporting to be printed or published under the authority of government of any country, and to contain any law of that country, and of every book purporting to contain reports of decisions of the court of such country." The combined effect of ss. 38 and 84 is that the court may take judicial notice of a publication relating to foreign law, provided it is published under the authority of the foreign government concerned and the court may accept the law contained in such publication as the law in force in that country.

The Evidence Act also defines public documents and lay down a mode of proof of such documents. The public documents may be either Indian or foreign. Section 74(1) defines the public documents. It says that the following documents are public documents: documents forming the act or record of the acts: (a) of the sovereign authority, (b) of official bodies and tribunals, and (c) of public officers, legislative, judicial and executive, of any part of India or of Commonwealth or of any other foreign country. Under this definition, the record of proceedings of a foreign court is a public document.[44] Thus it has been held that a copy of probate granted by the Australian court is admissible in Indian courts.[45] Similarly, the passport obtained from a foreign government is a public document and is admissible in evidence as a *prima facie* evidence that the holder has acquired foreign citizenship.[46] It seems that record of confession of an accused person recorded by a foreign magistrate is public document.[47]

Section 78 of the Evidence Act lays down the mode of proof of public documents. The Acts, orders or notification of the Crown's Representatives or any state government or any department of any state government may be proved by the record of the department certified by the head of the department concerned or by any document purporting to be printed by the order of any such government, or, as the case may be, of the Crown's representative. The proceedings of a legislature may be proved by the journal of the legislature concerned, or by published Acts or abstracts, or by copies purporting to be printed by the order of the government concerned. Proclamations, orders or regulations issued by Her Majesty or by the Privy Council or by any department of Her Majesty's Government may be proved by the copies and extracts contained in the London Gazette or purporting to be printed by the Queen's printer. The Acts of the executive or the proceedings of the legislature of a foreign country may be proved by journals published under its authority, or commonly received in that country as such, or by a copy certified under the seal of the country or sovereign, or by a recognition thereof in some central Act.[48] Public documents of any other class may be proved by the original or by a copy certified by the legal keeper thereof, with a certificate under the seal of a Notary Public or of any Indian Consul or diplomatic agent, that the copy is duly certified by the officer having the legal custody of the original, and upon proof of the character of the document according to the law of the foreign country.

Section 82 of the Evidence Act contains a special provision relating to presumption of documents admitted in England without proof of seal or signatures. The section lays down ; "When any document is produced before any court purporting to be document which by the law in force for the time being in England and Ireland, would be admissible in proof of any particular in any court of justice in England or Ireland, without proof or seal or stamp or signature authenticating it or of the judicial or official character claimed by the person by whom it purports to be signed,

44. *Haranund Chettrugia* v. *Ramgopal Chettrugia* (1899) 27 Cal. 639.
45. *In the matter of Adija*, 11 I.C. 261.
46. *State* v. *Abdul Rashid*, 1961 Pat. 112.
47. *R.* v. *Sunder*, (1890) 12 All. 595.
48. Sub-section (4) of s. 78.

the court shall presume that such seal, stamp or signature is genuine and that the person signing it held, at the time when he signed it, the judicial or official character which he claims, and the document shall be admissible for the same purpose for which it would be admissible in England or Ireland."[49] This section lays down a rule both of admissibility and presumption relating to documents which by the law of England and Ireland are admissible in proof of any particular in any court of justice in England and Ireland. The question for determination under this section is whether the document is one which is admissible in England in proof of that fact without proof of its authentication? If it is, then the document is admissible in India to prove that fact and gives rise to presumption as to its authenticity. Under the section such documents shall be admissible in India for the purpose for which they are admissible in England or Ireland. There are several enactments in England under which documents are admissible in England without the proof of seal, stamp or signature.[50] In England most of the public documents can be proved by certified or examined copies. It is only in exceptional cases that the court examines the original entry.[51]

Thus under the Indian law the position is this : (i) the foreign law may be proved by expert evidence under s. 45 of the Indian Evidence Act, or (ii) the court may take judicial notice of a publication containing foreign law provided it is published under the authority of the government. The court may accept the law as set out in such publication. It should be noted that when such a publication is relied on in evidence of foreign law, then the publication is not the evidence that it contains the whole of law and in such cases expert testimony may still be necessary.[52]

49. This section reproduces provisions of ss. 9 and 10 of Act no. 14 & 15 Vict. c. 99.

50. However, a certificate issued by the Manchester Chamber of Commerce testifying 25 & 26 Vict. c. 89; 40 & 41 Vict. c. 26 (documents relating to companies); 5 & 6 Vict. c. 45; 7 & 8 Vict. c. 12; 25 & 26 Vict. c. 68 (copyright registers); 53, 253. The cases in which certificated copies were held admissible may be noted : *In the Goods of Henderson*, ILR (1895) 22 Cal. 491 (power of attorney augisters); 57 & 58 Vict. c. 60 (documents under the Marchant Shipping Act, 1894).

51. However, a certificate issued by the Manchester Chamber of Commerce testifying a coal strike is not admissible : *Girdhardas* v. *Kerawala*, AIR 1926 Bom. 253. The cases in which certificated copies were held admissible may be noted. *In the Goods of Henderson*, ILR (1895) 22 Cal. 491 (power of attorney authenticated by Chief Magistrate of the city of Glasgow); *In Re Sladen* ILR (1898) 21 Mad. 492 (certified copy of power of attorney); *Blackwood & Sons* v. *A.N. Parsurama*, AIR 1959 Mad. 410 (certified copy of probate granted by the Probate division of the High Court of England).

52. *Jagdish Chandra* v. *Commissioner of Income Tax, West Bengal*, AIR 1956 Cal. 48. Similarly under clauses (4) and (5) of s. 57, course of proceedings of Parliament may be proved by the Journals of Parliament or House or reports purported to be prepared by order of the Government : *Englishman Ltd* v. *Lajpatrai*, (1910) 37 Cal. 760. However, they can be evidence

II

EXCLUSION OF FOREIGN LAW

Private international law of practically every country recognizes certain circumstances in which the application of the foreign law that would otherwise be applicable is excluded. The doctrine on the basis of which the otherwise applicable foreign law is excluded goes by the name of *Ordre Public* on the continental Europe and by the name of public policy in the common law countries including India. The doctrine of *Ordre Public* or public policy in its essence is a virtual repudiation of the policy of international co-operation; it is a negation of private international law. It is a victory of nationalism over internationalism, of policy over unity. Even then, most of the countries adhere to the doctrine. What precisely is the meaning and scope of the doctrine there is no unanimity in the state practice or law. At least four views prevail :

(a) Most of the Latin-American states are committed to the view that there are certain laws of forum which are unconditionally applicable to all situations and thus a foreign law opposed to these internal laws cannot be applied.

(b) The prevailing view in Germany is that all rules of foreign law which are contrary to moral bases, fundamental provisions of the legal system of the forum or to basic notions and principles of its social and economic life are precluded from application.

(c) In the Soviet Union and some of the countries of East Europe the broad principle is that all those rules of foreign law which are at variance with basic values of the forum or are against the fundamental principles of its law and society are precluded from application.

(d) The countries belonging to common law system and India take the view that courts will not apply any rule of foreign law, nor will they recognize any foreign law or judgment which is contrary to public policy. Similarly, the foreign penal and revenue laws are also precluded from application.

Thus, under the English and Indian private international laws, the application of otherwise applipcable foreign law may be excluded under the following three heads :

(i) Foreign law is against the public policy,
(ii) Foreign law is penal law, and
(iii) Foreign law is revenue law.

only of what was stated by speakers in the legislature and are not evidence of any fact contained in the speeches : *Gerlad Lord Strikland* v. *Carmelo Mifsud Bonnici*, AIR 1935 P.C. 34; *Emperor* v. *Chowdhry Mohemmed Hassan*, 1943 Lah. 298.

In *William and Humbert Ltd.* v. *W. & H. Trade Marks (Jersey) Ltd.* (Dry Sack Sherry trade mark case)[52a] the law regarding recognition and exclusion of foreign law has been stated thus :

Class I laws, which the English courts will not recognise : (A) Foreign confiscatory laws which, by reason of their being discriminatory on grounds of race, religion or the like, constitute so grave an infringement of human rights that they ought not to be recognised as laws at all. (B) Foreign laws which discriminate against nationals of this country in time of war by purporting to confiscate their movable property situated in the foreign state.

Class 2 laws, which will be recognised, but to which effect will not be given : (A) Foreign laws confiscating property situated in the foreign state, if they are penal. (B) Foreign laws which purport to confiscate property situated in this country.

Class 3 laws, to which effect will be given provided that they do not fall within class 1 : Foreign laws which confiscate property in the foreign state and where title has been perfected there.

On this matter the Indian law is still in its formative stages and decided cases are very few.

Public Policy

So far no attempt has been made for a precise definition of 'public policy' and it is submitted that it is not possible to give any precise meaning to the term.[53] Graveson says that "public policy is an indefinite concept which indicates those matters regarded by Parliament or the court as clearly of fundamental concern to the state and society at large."[54] Most English authors do not attempt to give any definition to public policy and taking it for granted discuss the scope of its application.[55] It is submitted that the states have used the doctrine as a device under which otherwise applicable foreign law is precluded. Already there are many devices under which courts tend to apply the law of forum. The public policy is used as something like a residual head for the exclusion of application of foreign law. The stock justification for the doctrine is that no country will give effect to laws which are 'repugnant to its ideas of social justice'. Looked at in this perspective, the doctrine becomes a question of values. The Western countries may still consider private ownership as sacrosanct, while the communist countries may consider themselves to

52a. (1085) 3 W.L.R 501; See also *Setteballa Ltd.* v. *Bauco Totta* (1985) 1 W.L.R. 1050.

53. See Upjohn, J. Observations in *re Claim by Helbert Wagg & Co. Ltd.* (1956) Ch. 323.

54. Graveson, p. 563.

55. For instance, Dicey, Chapter VII; and Cheshire, Chapter VI do not attempt any definition, while early writers have given it different names: Wharton calls it 'distinctive policy' (3rd ed., Vol. I, s. 4a), Westlake call it 'stringent domestic policy' (7th ed., p. 51).

be committed to the socialization of means of production. This conflict of values is well illustrated by cases[56] relating to 'nationalization' or 'confiscation' of private property in the Soviet Union and in some other countries.

The English law relating to preclusion of foreign law by operation of doctrine of public policy is thus formulated by Dicey and Morris :

> "The court will not enforce or recognize a right, power, capacity, disability, or legal relationship arising under the law of a foreign country, if the enforcement or recognition of such right, power, capacity, disability or legal relationship would be inconsistent with the fundamental public policy of English law."[57]

At times the English courts have given a very wide application to the doctrine of public policy, at times they have given it restricted interpretation. *Kaufman* v. *Gerson*[58] is an example of the former tendency. In this case the husband of the defendant misappropriated certain amounts entrusted to him by the plaintiff. The defendant entered into a contract with the plaintiff that she would pay him the entire amount of the misappropriated money by instalments in consideration that the plaintiff would refrain from prosecuting her husband. Misappropriation of funds under the circumstances of the case constituted a penal offence under English law, but the contract was valid by the French law. Both the parties were French nationals domiciled in France. Misappropriation of funds occurred in France. Plaintiff's action in the English court for the recovery of the instalments due was dismissed on the ground that "to enforce a contract so procured would contravene, what by the law of this country is deemed, 'an essential moral interest'."[59] The illustrative cases of the latter tendency are, *Santos* v. *Illidge*,[60] where a foreign contract for the sale of slaves was given effect to, at a time when English national policy was against slavery, *Robinson* v. *Bland*[61] where a foreign gaming contract was enforced at a time when domestic contracts of this nature were void; and *Re Bonacina*[62] where a foreign contract without consideration was given effect to.[63]

56. These cases are discussed in subsequent pages.
57. Conflict of Laws, (8th ed.) Rule 2, at 72.
58. (1904) 1 K.B. 591.
59. This case was criticised by Dicey (5th ed.), pp. 828-30. Other examples of this tendency are : *Grell* v. *Levy*, (1864) 16 C.B. (N.S.) 73; *Hope* v. *Hope*, (1857) 8 De G.H. & G. 731. In the latter case the court when very far when it said that a foreign contract to be enforceable here must be consistent with the law and policy of England.
60. (1860) 8 C.B. (N.S.) 861.
61. (1760) 2 Burr. 1077.
62. (1912) 2 Ch. 394.
63. See also *Re Goodman's Trust*, (1881) 17 Ch. D. 266, where foreign legitimacy by subsequent marriage was recognized at a time when

The modern tendency of English courts appears to be to give restrictive interpretation to the doctrine of public policy. In respect of the application of the doctrine to the domestic cases, the House of Lords observed in 1938 that the doctrine of public policy should 'only be invoked in clear cases in which the harm to the public is substantially uncontestable, and does not depend upon the idiocy-cratic inferences of a few judicial minds.'[64] The same may be said about the application of the doctrine to conflict of laws cases. Cheshire very pertinently said : "The conception of public policy is, or should be, narrower and more limited in private international law than in the internal law. A transaction that is valid by its foreign *lex causae* should not be nullified on this ground unless its enforcement would offend some moral, social and economic principle so sacrosanct in English eyes as to require its maintenance at all costs and without exceptions."[65]

Most English authors discuss the doctrine in relation to the areas in which it has been applied.[66] In the present state of law, that seems to be the best course. Thus, what is attempted here is to discuss some illustrative areas where the doctrine has been applied. The earliest cases in which the doctrine has been applied belong mainly to two areas : (i) English ideas of justice and morality, and (ii) the relations of the United Kingdom with foreign countries. When by application of foreign law these are going to be affected prejudicially, the application of foreign law has been excluded. To these two areas we may add two more : (iii) the enforcement of contract resulting in violation of public policy, and (iv) recognition or enforcement of foreign requisition, expropriation and nationalization laws, decrees and orders resulting in the violation of public policy.

English Ideas of Justice and Morality : Justice and morality are subjective and relative notions. They vary from time to time and from society to society. When the question comes before the English court it is mostly the English notions of morality and justice which are invoked and applied. Thus, it has been held that a foreign judgment violative of the principle of natural justice will not be enforced or given effect to.[67] Similarly, foreign contract, transaction, law or judgment violative of English ideas of morality

law of legitimation by subsequent marriage did not exist in England. In *Crowe* v. *Crowe*, (1937) 2 All E.R. 723, foreign collusive divorce decree was recognized.

64. *Fender* v. *St. John-Mildmay*, (1938) A.C. 1 at p. 12.

65. Cheshire (8th ed.), pp. 143-44. In this context see the observation of Cardozo, J. made in *Loucks* v. *Standard Oil Co. of New York*, (1918) 224 N.Y. 99 at. p. 11.

66. See Dicey and Morris, p. 74 : the public policy is also discussed along with specific topics. Cheshire discusses it in one Chapter, viz, Chapter VI, part 3.

67. *Rudd* v. *Rudd*, (1924), p. 72; *Igra* v. *Igra*, (1951), p. 404 (adequate opportunity to defend was not given); *Kaufman* v. *Gerson*, (1904) 1 K.B. 591 (consent was obtained by coercion).

will not be given effect to.[68]

Another class of cases where a foreign contract, transaction, status, legal relationship, law or judgment will not be given effect to are those which may compadiously be covered under English notion of 'individual or human liberty'.[69] English courts will also not recognize status or disqualification, in the words of Cheshire, "arising from slavery, excommunication, heresy, infamy, civil death, popish recusancy and non-conformity".[70] The extreme example under this head is provided by those early cases in which the English courts refused to recognize status arising out of polygamous marriage.[71] Another example of the same is provided by *Re Macartney*[72] where the English court refused to enforce a foreign order awarding an amount of maintenance for indefinite period to an illegitimate child out of the estate of his putative father. It appears that the English courts have now abandoned this extreme approach. They now take the view that a status arising under foreign law has to be recognized, though the courts may not give effect to all legal incidents of that status. Thus status of husband and wife arising out of a polygamous marriage is recognized, though English courts will not yet entertain a divorce petition in respect of such marriage.[73] Now the Matrimonial Proceedings (Polygamous Marriages) Act, 1972 empowers courts in the United Kingdom to grant matrimonial relief to parties to polygamous marriages, provided the parties belong to a system which recognizes polygamous marriages. It is immaterial whether the marriage is in fact polygamous or potentially polygamous. However, the ban on celebrations of polygamous marriages in the United Kingdom continues. Similarly, a person who is domiciled in England and Wales or Scotland or Northern Ireland cannot contract a polygamous marriage overseas, and if he does, the marriage will be null and void; this is now a specific ground of nullity. For the purpose of giving relief to the wife of second marriage of a foreign domiciled and polygamously married person, the marriage being performed in England, the English court has recognized the first polygamous marriage.[74] It has also been held that the offspring of a polygamous marriage is legitimate and entitled to inheritance.[75]

Recently, a tendency is surfacing among the English judges to circumvent this head of public policy which is a hangover of

68. *Pearce* v. *Brooks*, (1866) L.R 1 Ex. 213; *Toylor* v. *Chester*, (1869) L.R. 4 Q.B. 309 (sexual immorality); *Grell* v. *Levy*, (1864) 16 C.B. (N.S.) 73 (champertous contract).
69. Some writers discuss them under separate heads. For instance, see Cheshire, (8th Ed.), pp. 148-52.
70. Cheshire, p. 148.
71. *Warrender* v. *Warrender*, (1835) 2 Cl. & Fin. 488; *Harvey* v. *Farnie*, (1881) 6. P.D. 35; *Re Bethell* (1887) 38 Ch. D. 220.
72. (1921) 1 Ch. 522.
73. *Hyde* v. *Hyde* (1866) 1 P. & D. 130; *Sowa* v. *Sowa*, (1961), p. 70.
74. *Baindail* v. *Baindail*, (1945), p. 122.
75. *Bambose* v. *Daniel*, (1955) A.C. 107.

bygone ages. This has resulted in the emergence of certain exceptions. For instance, in *Cheni* v. *Cheni*[76] the English court said that if an initially polygamous marriage becomes a monogamous marriage, such as by change of domicile, then the English matrimonial jurisdiction is available to parties of such marriage. In *Shahnaz* v. *Rizwan*[77] the English court was concerned with the enforcement of a contract arising under a polygamous marriage performed in India between two Indian domiciled Muslims under which the wife was entitled to her entire dower (*mahr*) or dissolution of marriage. The court held that the contract could be enforced in England.

Yet, another question has come before English courts to test their ability of moulding the law in accordance with the new changing social needs arising out of ever-increasing intercourse between the peoples of the world. To some extent the English judges have well stood the test. At one time the English courts took the view that non-judicial divorces could not be recognized,[78] but later on such divorces were recognized and the courts went to the extent of laying down that a *talak* pronounced in England would validly dissolve a marriage, if such divorce was valid by the law of the domicile of parties.[79] The Recognition of Divorces and Legal Separations Act, 1972 statutorily confirmed this position. But now this position has been modified by the Domicile and Matrimonial Proceedings Act, 1973. Section 16 of the Act lays down : (i) No marriage can now be dissolved by *talak* in the United Kingdom, the Channel Island and the Isle of Man. (ii) A *talak* pronounced by the husband in a country where this dissolves the marriage will not be recognized in England if immediately preceding the pronouncement of the *talak* parties were habitually resident in England for a period of one year.

In *Chenni* v. *Chenni*[80] a marriage between uncle and niece was recognized. The English court has refused to recognize foreign disability arising out of foreign law if such recognition would be contrary to public policy. For instance, the English court refused to give effect to the disability imposed by the Portuguese law that first cousins cannot marry in the absence of a Papal dispensation.[81] Similarly, the court refused to give effect to a disability laid down by the South African law, under which the guilty party could not remarry as long as the other party remained unmarried.[82] But if

76. (1965) p. 85.
77. (1965) 1 Q.B. 390.
78. *Maher* v. *Maher* (1951), p. 342.
79. *Har-Shefi* v. *Har-Shefi* (No. 1), (1953), p. 161 (administratively pronounced divorce); *Manning* v. *Manning*, (1958), p. 112 (divorce by mutual consent); *Lee* v. *Lau*, (1964) 2 All E.R. 248; *Qureshi*, v. *Qureshi*, (1971) 1 All E.R. 325.
80. (1965) p. 85.
81. *Sottomayor* v. *De Barros* (no. 2), (1879), 5 P.D. 94.
82. *Scott* v. *A.G.*, (1886) 11 P.D. 128.

the prohibition is for a shorter period, the English court recognizes it.[83] Recently, the English courts have also held that a foreign status or relationship unknown to English domestic law may be recognized.[84]

Prejudicial to International Relations : From very early times English courts have considered that trading with enemy is prejudicial to the interest of the United Kingdom and therefore any contract or transaction relating to such trade cannot be enforced. In *Dynamit* v. *Rio Tinto Co.*[85] the House of Lords said that English courts will not give effect to any act or transaction which will result in giving comfort or assistance to the enemy in times of war. Lord Dunedin observed : "It is illegal for a British subject to become bound in a manner which sins against the public policy of the King's realm."[86] Prohibition of intercourse with an alien enemy is another instance under this head of public policy.[87]

The other leg of this head of public policy is that any act or transaction will not be given effect to if it prejudices the international relations of the United Kingdom. Thus no person in England, subject or alien, can enter into an engagement which would cause prejudice to a friendly government.[88] The obvious illustrations of this are : raising of loan in England with a view to use the fund to further revolution in another country,[89] to export liquor to a friendly state contrary to its prohibition laws,[90] to export a prohibited commodity,[91] or to commit a crime in a foreign country.[92] In *Foster* v. *Driscoll*[93] Lawrence, L.J. observed : "A partnership formed for the main purpose of deriving profit from the commission of criminal offence in a foreign friendly country is illegal, even though . . . no such criminal offence has in fact been committed."[94]

Contracts and Public Policy : "It seems to me almost absurd to suppose that the courts of this country should enforce a contract which they consider to be against public policy, simply because it

83. *Warter* v. *Warter*, (1890) 15 P.D. 152: in this case parties were prohibited from remarrying for a period of six months under the Indian Divorce Act, 1869.
84. *Re Goodmans Trust*, (1881) 17 Ch. D. 266; *Phrantzes* v. *Argenti*, (1960) 2 Q.B. 19; *Shahnaz* v. *Rizwan*, (1965) 1 Q.B. 390.
85. (1918) A.C. 292.
86. *Ibid.* at p. 294.
87. See *Robson* v. *Premier Oil and Pipe Lines Co.*, (1915) 2 Ch. 124; *Arab Bank Ltd.* v. *Barclays Bank* (1954) A.C. 495.
88. *British Nylon Spinners Ltd.* v. *I.C.I. Ltd.*, (1955) Ch. 37.
89. *De Wutz* v. *Hendricks*, (1824) 2 Bing. 314.
90. *Foster* v. *Driscoll*, (1929) 1 K.B. 470.
91. *Ragazzoni* v. *K.C. Sethia*, (1958) A.C. 301; see also *Re Emery's Investments Trust*, (1959) Ch. 410.
92. *British Nylon Spinners Ltd.* v. *I.C.I. Ltd.*, (1955) Ch. 37.
93. (1929) 1 K.B. 470.
94. *Ibid.* at p. 510.

happens to have been made somewhere else," thus observed Fry, J. in *Rousillon* v. *Rousillon*.[95] This sums up the attitude of English courts. Thus, contracts in restraint of trade,[96] contracts involving trading with the enemy,[97] champertous contracts,[98] the stifling of criminal prosecution,[99] corrupt and collusive arrangements for divorce,[100] a contract obtained by coercion,[101] or duress[102] or contracts that are prejudicial to the relations of the United Kingdom with foreign states,[103] are some of the instances of the operation of the doctrine of public policy under this head. The limits of operation of the doctrine were expressed in *Addison* v. *Brown*[104] in these words : "Although it may be contrary to public policy to oust the jurisdiction of English courts, I cannot think that it is the public policy of England to oust a plaintiff in the English courts from suing on an agreement, assuming that it is otherwise actionable, on the ground that the agreement purports to oust the jurisdiction of a foreign court." Thus English courts have enforced those foreign contracts which would be void under English statute or common law had they been governed by English law.[105] In the words of Kahn-Freund, "Only if the court regards a common law principle as one expressing a basic public policy, will it enforce it in a case in which otherwise foreign law applies."[106] Sometimes a curious situation arises on account of the operation of this head of public policy. In *Wolff* v. *Oxholm*[107] English court enforced a contract which was void by its proper law. It is because English courts disregard foreign discriminatory legislation rendering a contract void.[108] Under s. 72(1), proviso (a) to the Bills of Exchange Act, 1882 a bill of exchange subject to foreign law can be enforced in England even if it is void under the foreign law on the ground that it is not properly stamped.

95. *Rousillon* v. *Rousillon*, (1880) 14 Ch. D. 351 at p. 369.
96. *Ibid.*
97. *Dynamit* v. *Rio Tinto Co. Ltd.* (1918) A.C. 292.
98. *Grell* v. *Levy*, (1864) 16 C.B. (N.S.) 73.
99. *Kaufman* v. *Gerson*, (1904) 1 K.B. 591.
100. *Hope* v. *Hope* , (1857) 8 De G.M. & G. 731.
101. *Kaufman* v. *Gerson*, (1904) 1 K.B. 591.
102. *Kahler* v. *Midland Bank Ltd.*, (1950) A.C. 24.
103 This aspect of the matter has already been dealt with earlier.
104. (1954) 1 W.L.R. 779 at p. 784
105. *Saxby* v. *Fulton*, (1909) 2 K.B. 208; *Re Bonacina*, (1912) 2 Ch. 394 (foreign contract without consideration was held enforceable) : *Shahnaz* v. *Rizwan*, (1965) 1 Q.B. 390 (an ancillary agreement to marriage which was considered to be void by English law was held enforceable).
106. Dicey & Morris, p. 728.
107. (1817) 6 M. & S. 92.
108. *Re Friedrick Krupp Aktien-Gesellschaft*, (1917) 2 Ch. 188; *Re Claim Helbert Wagg & Co.*, (1956) Ch. 323 (if foreign exchange regulation operates as an instrument of oppression and discrimination, it will not be recognized).

Requisition, Expropriation and Nationalization of Property and Public Policy : Under this head the broad question is : whether English courts will give effect to requisition, expropriation and nationalization of private property under the foreign law or decree ? Recognition of such acts has been denied sometimes on the basis that the foreign law requisitioning, nationalizing and expropriating private property is penal in character,[109] sometimes on the ground that such laws are contrary to English ideas of justice and morality,[110] sometimes on the ground that contracts violative of public policy cannot be enforced.[111] It is submitted that it should be treated as a separate head and the matter should be looked at from the angle of private international law. What appears to have happened is this that the trend-setting decisions of English courts have been those in which sloganish approach has been made : "no English court would give effect to foreign confiscatory or expropriatory laws of a foreign state." With this approach it was easy to equate foreign confiscatory or expropriatory and even foreign nationalization with nominal compensation with penal laws and to hold them unenforceable. In this perspective it seems logical that English courts took a subjective view of the matter. It is heartening to note that the English courts have started abandoning this approach and taking a practical view of the matter, though the matter is still not free from complications as English courts get bogged down on account of such ancillary and allied matters as to whether or not the foreign government whose laws are in question is a recognized government or not, or on account of coming into operation the doctrine of immunity of foreign sovereign when property is in his possession. It is submitted that if two well settled rules of law are kept in view, it would not be so difficult to grapple with the matter and much fog shrouding the subject would be cleared. Of these two rules, one is a general rule, viz., no law can ordinarily be given extraterritorial effect, and the other rule is of private international law, viz., the *lex situs* governs the immovable property.

The problem arising under this head may be explained by an example : Suppose country X passes a law under which government takes over the entire textile industry. If for such taking away of the property, due compensation is paid it goes by the name of nationalization under English law; if no compensation (or no proper compensation) is paid, then it goes by the name of confiscation or expropriation. In case only the management of a mill is taken over, then it goes by the name of requisition. Here also the question may arise whether compensation has been paid or not. When any of the above cases come for adjudication before an English court in an action brought by a British subject or English domiciled person or by a foreigner or foreign domiciled person, the English court may be concerned with the matter in several

109. See Cheshire (7th ed.), pp. 124-31.
110. Graveson, pp. 570-72.
111. Dicey & Morris, pp. 725-30.

ways. If the textile mills or their produce remain in the foreign country, there is nothing much the English court can do. But suppose, some cloth manufactured by these mills is brought to England and the owner of the mills which manufactured the cloth claims the ownership in the cloth on the plea that no recognition could be given to foreign confiscatory and expropriatory legislation. More or less it is in this form that the question has arisen in English courts.

Before proceeding further, it is submitted that some preliminary matters may be kept in view :

(a) The question whether the foreign government the law of which is involved is recognized one or not should be immaterial.[112]

(b) If the law affects immovable property situated in a foreign country, the question can hardly arise in English courts as the courts will not have jurisdiction.

(c) The question whether compensation (adequate or otherwise) was paid or not should not overweigh in the mind of the judge, rather, it is submitted it should not figure at all.

(d) If the property is movable but is situated in a foreign country, then also the English court should not exercise jurisdiction over it unless it is brought to England.

In the subsequent pages we would use only one word, namely nationalization, for all types of taking over of property.

It is submitted that in view of the above the question will come before the court in the following two situations : (A) When the property situated in the foreign country at the time of nationalization is brought to England, and (B) when, at the time of nationalization, the property was situated outside the jurisdiction of the foreign country.

A. *When property situated in the foreign country at the time of nationalization is brought to England* : This now appears to be a simple case. The English courts take the view that the nationalization law will be conclusive on the matter even if the property is subsequently brought to England. *Luther* v. *Sagor*[113] is an authority for this proposition. This case is concerned with the nationalization of timber industry in the Soviet Union after the revolution. Under this law was covered a private incorporated company in which this plaintiff has substantial interest. Some timber belonging to the nationalized private company was brought to England. *Luther* v. *Sagor*[114] is an authority for this proposition,

112. *See Luther* v. *Sagor*, (1921) 2 K.B. 532; *Karl Joyice* v. *Reman*, (1966) 2 All E.R. 536. In the latter case Lord Reid said that it is difficult to accept the proposition that recognition would not be given to marriage, decree of divorce or contracts of trade and commerce of an unrecognized foreign state.

113. (1921) 3 K.B. 532.

filed an action to recover this timber. The suit was dismissed. Warrington, L.J. said : "No sovereign state should sit in judgment upon the acts of another foreign state affecting property in its own territory." It is submitted that Bankes, L.J. has taken more rational view. According to him it is impossible to ignore the law of the Soviet Union, the *lex situs*, at the time of nationalization decree. Accepting this reasoning, Cheshire adds, "unless the rule of that law under which the title has been acquired is so immoral or so alien to the principles of justice as understood in England that it must be disregarded as contrary to public policy."[114] It is submitted this need not be so. So far there is no reported English decision in which foreign law of nationalization of property situated within the country has not been recognized or given effect to.[115]

It is also now settled that it would make no difference even if the property nationalized belongs to an alien.[116] In *Re Claim Herbert Wagg & Co. Ltd.*[117] Upjohn, J. said that neither the nationality of the dispossessed owner nor the payment or non-payment of compensation to him affect the general principle laid down in *Luther* v. *Sagor*.[118] The proposition may be thus formulated : under English private international law effect will be given to foreign nationalization law in respect of property situated in that country at the time of passing of nationalization law.[119] Only one probable exception that appears to this general proposition is : if the foreign nationalization law is discriminatory, it may not be given effect to.[120]

B. *When at the time of nationalization property was situated outside the jurisdiction* : When at time of passing of nationalization law, the property is outside the jurisdiction, either in England or in some other country or on the high seas, the first question is : whether the property so situated has been covered by the nationalization law. If the answer is in the negative, the matter ends there.[121] But if the answer is in the affirmative the difficulties begin

114. Cheshire (8th ed.), 135.

115. See *A.G.* v. *Ortiz* (1984) A.C. I.

116. In *Anglo-Iranian Oil Co.* v. *Jaffrate*, (1953) 1 W.L.R. 246. Campbell, J. said that foreign confiscatory decrees do not affect the property of aliens. This view has been dissented by an Italian court : *Anglo-Iranian Oil Co.* v. *S.P.O.R.* (1955) I.L.R. 23 and Japanese court in *Anglo-Iranian Oil Co.* v. *Kabuski*, (1953) I.L.R. 305.

117. (1956) Ch. 323.

118. (1921) 3 K.B. 532.

119. *Willian & Hubert* v. *W.H. Toode Mark* (1985) 3 W.L.R. 501 (C.C.A.) approved by the House of Lords in (1986) 2 W.L.R. 24.

120. Cheshire, p. 136 (8th ed.).

121. *Lecouturier* v. *Rey*, (1910) A.C. 262, where the French law prohibiting manufacture of certain type of liquor was held to have not extra-territorial effect. Similarly, in *The Jupiter*, (No. 3) (1927), p. 122, the court said that the Soviet nationalization law is not applicable to movables situated outside the Soviet Union.

to crop up. The matter could be summarily disposed of if we apply the territorial principle under which no law has extra-territorial effect. However, the matter cannot be so summarily disposed of. The complication arise on account of the following two questions : (i) does the principle of territoriality apply to the property which is in the hands of the national of that state or any other person ? (ii) does the principle apply when the property is in the hands of the foreign sovereign or his agent ? In the latter case the principle of sovereign immunity comes into operation.

On the former question, viz. when the property is in the hands of the nationals of the nationalizing state, the English decisions are conflicting. Dicey maintained the view that a state has power to legislate in respect of its nationals outside the jurisdiction.[122] Predominant authority is against this view. The only recent decision which favours Dicey's view is *Lorentzen* v. *Lydden & Co.*,[123] a war-time decision. In this case the Norwegian government shortly before their escape to England in 1940 passed a law under which they requisitioned all Norwegian ships lying outside the German occupied harbours. Before the outbreak of war, a British firm had agreed to charter a Norwegian ship, but subsequently it repudiated the contract. Norwegian Government filed a suit for damages for the breach of the contract. Atkinson, J. said that the Norwegian law would be given effect to; since under it the ownership of the property situated in England passed to the Norwegian Government, together with the right to sue for breach of contract, the Norwegian Government's action was maintainable in the English court. The learned judge also added that the enforcement of the Norwegian law was demanded by public policy. It is submitted that this may be considered to be the rationale of this war-time decision. Earlier English decisions have taken the view that the Soviet law of nationalization was inapplicable to the property situated in England, even though its owner, at the time of the nationalization decree, was a Russian citizen. This view has been maintained by English courts even after the decision in *Lorentzen's case.*[124] In *Bank voor Handel en Scheepvaart* v. *Statford*[125] Devlin, J. observed : "There seems to me to be every reason, if the authorities permit it, for giving effect to the simple rule that generally property in England is subject to English law and to no other." If the owner or the person possessing property is not the national of the nationalizing state, then, *a fortiori*, the nationalization law does not cover the property outside the jurisdiction.[126]

122. Conflict of Laws, (6th ed.) p. 20.
123. (1942) 2 K.B. 202.
124. *Ibid.*
125. (1953) 1 Q.B. 248.
126. *Tallina Leevauhisus (A/S)* v. *Estonian State S.S. Line*, (1947) 80 Ll.L. Rep. 99; *Cheshire & Another* v. *Frederick Huth & Co.*, (1928) 79 Ll.L. Rep. 262; *Novello* v. *Hinrichsen Edition Ltd.*, (1951) 1 Ch. 595; *Frankfurter* v. *W.L. Exner Ltd.*, (1947) Ch. 629.

When the property nationalized is outside the jurisdiction but in the possession of the sovereign or its agent then the principle of sovereign immunity comes into play. Thus, if the property situated in England is in the possession of the foreign government or its agent, then the dispossessed owner has no remedy as the foreign sovereign cannot be impleaded in any action in any English court.[127] This is also the position when relief *in rem* is sought in his absence against the property owned by him or in his possession or control, though the sovereign is not directly impleaded.[128] This rule applies even when the sovereign obtains possession of the property forcibly.[129]

Public Policy and Judicial Trends : In *Fender* v. *St. John-Mildmay*[130] the House of Lords said that courts are not free to invent new heads of public policy, they may expound what public policy is, but they cannot expand it. This appears to be substantially true in respect to English domestic law, but the courts have not shown the same restraint in cases coming under private international law. In some cases, on the other hand, judges have said that they have a 'residual discretion' to refuse to recognize a foreign status arising under the law of domicile or a foreign decree of nullity of marriage passed by the court of domicile, if they consider that recognition of status or decree would be against the English ideas of justice and morality.[131] Morris takes the view that in *Re Langley's Settlement*[132] "It is probable that the court intended to do no more than call attention to the distinction between recognition of status and recognition of its incidents. . . . In the latter cases[133] it may be that the courts intended to do no more than refer to the doctrine of public policy and to the analogous doctrine that foreign decrees of divorce and nullity will not be recognized in England if recognition would be contrary to natural justice."[134] Despite Morris's apology for this trend, Cheshire condemns it. He says : " . . . the proposition that a judge has a free discretion to exclude a foreign status or its incidents if he considers that in the particular circumstances it will adversely

127. *The Cristina*, (1938) A.C. 485; *The Arantzazu Mendi*, (1939) A.C. 256: *Dollfus Mieg et Compagnie S.A.* v. *Bank of England*, (1949) Ch. 369.

128. *Dollfus Mieg et Compagnie S.A.* v. *Bank of England*, cited above.

129. *The Cristina*, (1938) A.C. 485 : the case belongs to the Spanish Civil War era. The Republican Government of Spain requisitioned all ships registered at Balbao. One such ship berthed at Cardiff. The Spanish consul boarded it, and took control of it. The owners issued a writ *in rem* and claimed possession of the ship. The English court declined to exercise jurisdiction.

130. (1938) A.C. 1.

131. *Re Langley's Settlements Trusts*, (1962) Ch. 541; see also *Russ* v. *Russ*, (1964), p. 315; *Cheni* v. *Cheni*, (1965) p. 85; *Gray* v. *Formosa*, (1963) p. 259. Some earlier cases representing this tendency may also be noted : *Worms* v. *De Valdor*, (1880) 49 L.J. Ch. 261; *Re Scot's Trust*, (1902) 1 Ch. 488.

132. (1962) Ch. 541.

133. Cited in footnote no. 31.

134. Dicey and Morris, p. 76.

affect a person's right to deal with his property cannot be accepted with any degree of complacency. Its impact upon the doctrine of public policy may be disastrous, for what has been laboriously shaped into a reasonably ordered form is once more amorphous and indeterminate."[135] Some of the English judges are also aware of the pitfalls in this trend. Sir Jocelyn Simon observed: "The refusal to recognize an otherwise binding judgment or rule of law on the ground that it is manifestly unjust is now-a-days put as a matter of discretion." But, as Lord Mansfield said in *R.* v. *Wilkies*,[136] "discretion when applied to a court of justice, means sound discretion guided by law. It must be governed by rule, not by humour; it must not be arbitrary, vague and fanciful, but legal and regular. In short, there must be a reasonable consistency in its exercise."[137]

Foreign Revenue Laws

English courts have not yet defined 'revenue law' but it woulc appear to be a law requiring a non-contractual payment of mone: or kind in favour of the state or some department or subdivisioı thereof.[138] Thus laws imposing income-tax,[139] custom duty,[140] stamı duty,[141] succession duty,[142] municipal contribution,[143] capital gain: tax,[144] compulsory contribution to the state insurance scheme[145] anc a profit levy[146] have been held to be revenue laws. On the otheı hand, those laws which do not provide for the collection of mone} but are meant to protect its value have been held to be not revenuc laws, such as exchange control laws,[147] rules abrogating gold clauses[148] and moratorium laws.[149]

The matter may be considered under two heads: (a) enforce-

135. Cheshire (8th ed.), 157.
136. (1870) 4 Burr. 25.
137. *Lepre* v. *Lepre*, (1965) p. 52 at p. 63; see also *Boys* v. *Chaplin*, (1971) A.C. 356, where Lord Hodson said: "Rules of law should be defined and adhered to as closely as possible lest they lose themselves in a field of judicial discretion where no secure foothold is to be found by litigants or their advisers" (at p. 378).
138. *Indian and General Investment Trust Co. Ltd.* v. *Borax Consolidated Ltd.*, (1920) 1 K.B. 539.
139. *Ibid.*
140. *Holman* v. *Johnson*, (1775) 1 Cowp. 341.
141. *James* v. *Catherwood*, (1823) 3 Dowl. & Ry. (K.B.) 190.
142. *Cotton* v. *R.*, (1914) A.C. 176.
143. *Municipal Council of Sydney* v. *Bull*, (1909) 1 K.B. 7.
144. *Government of India* v. *Taylor*, (1955) A.C. 491.
145. *Metal Industries (Salvage) Ltd.* v. *Owners of S.T. Harle*, (1962) S.L.T. 114.
146. *Peter Buchanan Ltd.* v. *McVey* (1955) A.C. 516.
147. *Frankman* v. *Prague Credit Bank*, (1950) A.C. 57; *Kahler* v. *Midland Bank*, (1950) A.C. 24.
148. *R.* v. *International Trustee*, (1937) A.C. 500.
149. *Re Claim by Helbert Wagg & Co. Ltd.*, (1956) Ch. 323.

ment of foreign revenue laws, and (b) recognition of foreign revenue laws.

Enforcement of Revenue Laws : It is a well established principle of English private international law that English courts do not enforce foreign revenue laws.[150] In *Government of India* v. *Taylor*[151] the House of Lords observed : "Tax gathering is not a matter of contract but of authority and administration as between the state and those within its jurisdiction." In this case the Government of India had purchased the business of one Delhi Electricity Supply and Traction Co., a company registered in England but carrying on business in India. Immediately on the receipt of the purchase money the company remitted it to England. The company then went into voluntary liquidation. The Indian commissioner of income-tax claimed income-tax in respect of capital gains derived from the sale of business. The Indian commissioner of income-tax tried to prove the claim in English liquidation proceedings. The claim was rejected. When the case came before the House of Lords several arguments were addressed including the one that this rule is not applicable, to a member of the Commonwealth. Rejecting all the arguments, the House of Lords said that the rule that foreign revenue laws cannot be enforced is based on authority and convenience and that the duty of a liquidator in winding up proceedings is confined to the discharge of such liabilities as are legally enforceable.[152]

It has been held by the English courts that even an indirect evasion of the rule will not be permitted. In *Rossano* v. *Manufacturers Life Insurance Co.*[153] this question came in a curious manner. The plantiff, an Egyptian national residing in Alexandria, filed an action in an English court against the defendants, an insurance company with head office at Toronto and branches in many other countries including Egypt, for the recovery of money due under three insurance policies. The main defence of the defendant company was that garnishee orders had been served on three of their branches in Cairo in respect of certain taxes alleged to be due from the plaintiff to the Egyptian government and if the plaintiff did not pay them, the defendant company would be liable. This plea was rejected, as the court came to the conclusion that it would amount to indirect enforcement of revenue laws of a foreign country.[154]

150. *Government of India* v. *Taylor*, (1955) A.C. 491 (H.L.). Earlier authorities are *Holman* v. *Johnson*, (1775) 1 Cowp. 341; *Sydney Municipal Council* v. *Bull*, (1909) 1 K.B. 7; *Re Visser*, (1928) 1 Ch. 877; *Metal Industries (Salvage)* v. *Owners of S.T. Harle*, 1962, S.L.T. 114.

151. (1955) A.C. 491 at p. 514.

152. Lord Keith dissenting, this decision has been followed in *Brokaw* v. *Scatrain U.N. Ltd.*, (1987) 2 Q.B. 476 and *In re Lord Cable* (1977) 1 W.L.R. 7.

153. (1963) 2 Q.B. 352.

154. Cheshire, 130.

Recognition of Foreign Revenue Laws : "No country ever takes notice of the revenue laws of another." Thus observed Lord Mansfield in his characteristic manner.[155] For a considerable time this dictum had its sway over the judicial thinking. But gradually it came to be eroded and today, it seems, it stands totally washed away. In *Ragazzoni* v. *Sethia*[156] the Court of Appeal said : "It is wrong to say that one shall take no notice of laws of this kind, as distinct from saying that one shall not enforce such laws." It now appears to be established that English courts do take 'notice' of foreign revenue law,[157] and they will not enforce a contract made with an object of breaking them. The recognition of foreign currency regulations constitutes a very good example of this trend. Thus a transaction which is subject to the law of a foreign country, or a contract the proper law of which is the law of a foreign country[158] will be subject to currency regulation of that country. However, if the law of the foreign country is not its proper law, then the foreign currency regulations cannot be recognized.[159] In *Kahler* v. *Midland Bank*[160] the question before the House of Lords was whether the currency regulations of Czechoslovakia could be recognized. The plantiff, a Czechoslovakian national, bought certain Canadian bearer shares. His bank, the Z bank, at Prague deposited these shares with the Midland Bank in London to be held in safe custody for him. In March 1939, Germans occupied Czechoslovakia. The plantiff was allowed to leave Czechoslovakia on his transferring these shares along with other securities to another Bank in Prague, the B Bank. In April 1939 Z bank instructed the Midland Bank to transfer these shares to B Bank. The plantiff subsequently became a naturalized American citizen. He brought an action in detenue in an English court for delivering up of the shares to him against the Midland Bank. The Midland Bank took the plea that it was the bailee of B bank and that by currency regulations of Czechoslovakia it was illegal for B Bank to part with the shares to "currency foreigner", such as the plantiff, without the consent of the National Bank of Czechoslovakia, which consent has been refused. The court accepted this plea. The House of Lords said that the proper law of the original as well as the substituted contract of bailment was Czech law. This decision has been criticised by many. It is submitted that the most valid criticism of this decision is this : since at all material times the *situs* of the chattel, i.e. shares, was England, and shares were redeliverable in London, it was wrong to consider them to be

155. *Halman* v. *Johnson*, (1775) 1 Cowp. 341.

156. (1956) 2 Q.B. 490 at p. 520.

157. *Re Emery's Investments Trusts*, (1959) Ch. 40.

158. *Ralli Brothers* v. *Compania Naviera*, (1920) 2 K.B. 287.

159. *Trinidad Shipping & Trading Co. Ltd.* v. *Alston*, (1920) A.C. 888; *Kleinworth Sons & Co.* v. *Ungarische Baumwolle Industries Aktiengesellschaft*, (1939) 2 K.B. 678.

160. (1950) A.C. 24.

subject to Czechoslovakian law.[161]

In *Re Claim by Helbert Wag & Co. Ltd.*[162] an English company agreed to lend to a German company £ 3,50,000 with interest at 7½ per cent. The loan was secured by the mortgage of certain coal-fields in Germany. Under the terms of agreement the loan was to be repaid with interest by January 1945. Payment was to be made in sterling in London. The German company continued to fulfil its obligations till 1933 when a German moratorium law required it to make all payments to a Government agency in Berlin in Marks. Thence onward the German company paid the amount to the German governmental agency in Berlin and by January 1945 paid in the entire amount of the principal and interest in that manner. The company was discharged of all its future liabilities under the German moratorium law. After the cessation of hostilities the English company filed a claim for £ 1,74,142 in England to be paid out of the German assets held by the Administrator of German Enemy Property. Upjohn, J. not only found that the debt was situated in Germany, the place where the debtor resided, but also found that the proper law of the debt was also German law, as, according to him, the true test whether the moratorium law applied was not the local situation of the debt, but the proper law of the debt. Accordingly, the learned judge held that the claim of the plantiff must fail. Setting the limit of recognition of foreign revenue law, the learned judge said : "This court must be entitled to consider whether looking at all the circumstances, the law is so far-reaching in its scope and effect as really to offend against considerations of public policy of this country." Revenue laws cannot now be viewed in isolation, says Kahn-Freund, from the remainder of the legislation of a country. They often serve economic as well as financial purposes. Abuses can always be checked by the doctrine of public policy.[163]

Foreign Penal Laws

Just as English courts do not enforce foreign revenue laws, they do not enforce foreign penal laws. For the present purpose penal law may be defined as a law which imposes punishment for an offence against the state or some division thereof.[164] A penal law is thus equivalent to criminal law. The Privy Council said that proper test for ascertaining whether an action was penal is that proceedings must be in a nature of a suit in favour of the state whose law has been infringed.[165] From very beginning the English courts have taken the view that the foreign penal law cannot be

161. The House of Lords ignored this aspect of the matter that the plaintiff was made to transfer the shares under duress : see F.A. Mann, 11 M.L.R. 479; 13 M.L.R. 206-12.

162. (1956) Ch. 323.

163. Dicey and Morris, 765.

164. *Huntington* v. *Attrill*, (1893) A.C. 150.

165. *Ibid.*

enforced. The common law has always considered crimes as entirely local and cognizable and punishable exclusively in the country where they are committed. Thus this has been a well established rule that "the courts of no country execute the penal laws of another."[166] Similarly, a judgment in a criminal action cannot be enforced in England.[167]

This rule of private international law may be illustrated from *Banco de Vizcaya* v. *Don Alfonso de Borbony Austria*,[168] where the Spanish King bought certain securities out of his own money and deposited them in a London bank to the order of his agents, the Banco de Vizcaya, a Spanish concern. The Spanish Republican Government decreed that all properties of the king should be confiscated and that all his properties with the Spanish banks should be delivered to the Treasury. The Banco de Vizcaya, exercising original authorities given to them by the King, claimed the securities deposited in the London bank. On the bank's refusal, they filed an action for the recovery of the same. The action failed as English court felt that the plantiffs were acting on instruction from the Republican Government and conceding to their claim would mean giving effect to the confiscatory law (which was regarded as penal law) of a foreign country.[169]

The word 'penal' is equivalent to criminal and therefore does not include all penalties such as the ones that are included in commercial contracts, the purpose of which is the speedy performance of the contractual obligations. *Huntington* v. *Attrill*[170] illustrates this distinction. A New York statute laid down that the directors of an incorporated company would be personally liable for its debts upon proof that false reports as to its financial condition had been published. Sums thus recovered were, under the statute, payable to the creditors in satisfaction *pro tanto* of their claims. Under this statute a creditor of the company instituted a suit and obtained judgment for large amounts against the company from a New York court. He then brought an action on his judgment in an Ontario court. The Privy Council held that the law was not penal but remedial, as it permitted a subject to enforce a liability in his own interest and for the protection of his own private rights.

Huntington v. *Attrill*[171] also answers the question which court should characterize whether the law is penal or remedial. In this case the New York court had characterized it as penal and Ontario law as remedial. The Privy Council said that it is for the court of forum to characterize whether the foreign law is penal or otherwise.

166. Story, ss. 620-621 quoting from *The Antelope*, (1825) 10 Wheat. 66, 123.
167. *Huntington* v. *Attrill*, (1893) A.C. 150.
168. (1935) 1 K.B. 140.
169. *Folliott* v. *Ogden*, (1790) 8 T.R. 726 is an old authority on this view.
170. (1893) A.C. 150.
171. *Ibid.*

Thus a law to be penal need not be a part of the criminal code of foreign country; the right sought to be enforced may be a right which arises under legislation which is essentially designed to regulate commercial activities such as company legislation which may contain a penal provision. A forfeiture law may, in certain circumstances, be a penal law.[172] A suit to enforce forfeiture provisions of a statute will amount to enforcing a penal law. This is very well illustrated by *A.G. of New Zealand* v. *Ortis*,[173] where the New Zealand Historic Articles Act, 1962 prohibited taking out of any 'historic article' from New Zealand without a permit, and s. 12(2) of the Act provided that articles exported in breach of the Act "shall be forfeited to Her Majesty". The court of Appeal held that enforcement of this provision would amount to giving effect to foreign penal law. Lord Denning, M.R. was of the view that there was a third category of laws, namely public law of a foreign state, which, like penal and revenue laws are not enforceable. He thought that Historic Articles Act was not a penal statute but a public law.

It may also be taken as settled law that such as in the case of revenue laws so also in the case of penal laws, English courts are not precluded from taking notice of foreign penal laws.[174] Recently, the question of recognition of confiscatory or political legislation arose in *Oppenheimer* v. *Cattermole*[175] in some peculiar circumstances. A fascist German decree of 1941 deprived all those Germans who had immigrated to England in 1939 of the German nationality. A German who had migrated to England in 1939 became nationalized British subject. From 1953 onward he received a pension from Federal German Republic. He was assessed to income-tax in respect of that pension from 1953-68. Then he sought double taxation relief under Article 9 of the Double Taxation Relief (Taxes on Income) Order, 1955 on the plea that German decree of 1941 had clearly deprived him of his nationality. The court held that the German decree of 1941 should be disregarded for purposes of English municipal law as English courts would not recognize confiscatory political legislation.[176]

172. *R.* v. *Nat Bell Liquors Ltd.* (1922) 2 A.C. 128 ; *Banco de Vizcaya* v. *Don Alfonso de Borbon Y* Austria (1935) 1 K.B. 140.

173. (1982) 3 W.L.R. 570 ; on appeal the House of Lord declined to express any opinion of this aspect : (1983) 2 W.L.R. 801.

174. *Folliott* v. *Ogden*, (1790) 3 Term. Rep. 726; *Reggazzoni* v. *K.C. Setthia*, (1958) A.C. 301.

175. (1972) 2 W.L.R. 1045.

176. See also *Lowenthal* v. *A.G.*, (1948) 1 All E.R. 295; *R.* v. *Home Secretary*, Ex parte L , (1945) 1 K.B. 7. See also Wolff, (2nd ed.) p. 129.

6

DOMICILE

I

INTRODUCTION

In personal matters the *lex patrie* is the governing law in the civil law countries and the *lex domicilii* is the governing law in the common law countries. This fundamental difference between the two major systems of the world has been not only an obstacle in the unification of the rules of private international law, but, at times, has resulted in bizarre results. On account of this difference, more often than not, the result of a suit depends on the fact as to in which country the suit has been filed. For instance, a suit is filed in an Italian court for the succession to the property of an Indian who died domiciled in Italy. In accordance with the rules of Italian private international law, the Italian court will decide the matter on the basis of nationality of the deceased. On the other hand, if the suit will be filed in the Indian court, the Indian court will decide the case on the basis of the Italian law, the law of domicile of the deceased.[1] To what absurdities this tangle of *lex patrie* and *lex domicilii* can lead to may be illustrated from two cases, an Italian, *Re Samara*,[2] and an English, *Re O'Keefe*.[3]

In the Italian case, one Samara, a rich Tunisian Jew, had died domiciled in Liborno, Italy. In 1864, after leaving Tunisia, he first settled down in Paris till 1871 and then in Liborno, and he died so settled there. While in Paris he had made a will which was valid by the French law, but was invalid by the Jewish law, i.e. the law of his nationality. Those relations of Samara who would have succeeded to his property had the will been invalid challenged the validity of the will in an Italian court, on the ground that Samara died a

1. In the law of some countries this problem is solved by the application of the doctrine of *renvoi*, see Chapter 3 of this work.
2. The facts of this case have been narrated by Neddleman in his article, "Nationality *versus* Domicile", 1966, *American Journal of Comparative Law*, 432-33.
3. (1940) Ch. 124.

national of Tunisia and therefore the law of nationality governed succession to his property. The defendants, on the other hand, contended that the Tunisian nationality of Samara was lost the moment he left Tunisia in 1864 ; since Samara did not have any nationality at the time of his death, he was governed by the *lex domicilii*. On this basis the defendants contended that under the Italian private international law any act which was valid by the *lex loci actus* was valid, and since the will was valid by the French law, they were entitled to succeed to his property. The first trial court gave the decision in favour of the defendants. The first appellate court affirmed it, but the second appellate court reversed it on the ground that it has not been satisfactorily proved that Samara had ceased to be the national of Tunisia.

In the English case, one English woman, O'Keefe, died intestate in Naples. Her domicile of origin was Eire. She had been living in Naples for the last 47 years. The question of succession to her movable property arose in an English court. Under the English private international law the matter is governed by the law of domicile. Since English law applied the foreign court theory, it proceeded to decide the matter as Italian court would decide it. On this matter the Italian court applies the law of nationality. Since there is no 'British' law relating to succession, the court applied the law of Eire, the law of her domicile of origin. It is true that the father of O'Keefe was born in Eire in 1835, but at the age of 22 he had left Eire for India and thereafter he lived in India. He died in Calcutta in 1885. O'Keefe was born to him in India in 1860. From 1867 to 1890 she lived in various places in England, France and Spain. In 1890 she settled down in Naples and lived there continuously till her death—a continuous period of 47 years. Except that in 1878 she had made a short tour of Eire with her father, she had no other links with Eire. She had never lost her British nationality, though she had acquired a domicile of choice in Italy.

If these decisions have been criticized all over the world, it should not surprise any one. Even if it was possible for the Italian and English courts to have rendered more rational and just judgments, these decisions do bring to the fore the problem of dual system : so long as this tangle of *lex patrie* and *lex domicilii* continues, complications are bound to arise.

The post-Glossators have no difficulty in saying that the law of domicile will determine the question whenever a conflict between personal laws arose. At that time the question of conflict of laws between the citizens of two states hardly arose. Then the cases of conflict of laws arose between the residents of different parts of the same state. At that time European countries like France, Germany and the Netherlands were divided into different provinces and each province had its own legal system. The question of nationality could not arise as the residents of all the provinces had the same nationality. Thus the acceptance of the *lex domicilii* as the governing law was natural.

The 19th century witnessed the rise of nationalism on the European continent and soon it began to be propagated that law of nationality should govern all personal matters. The arch protagonist of this view was Italy's P.S. Mansini. In his famous speach of 1851 delivered at the University of Turin he propounded his thesis and spoke with vigour and conviction in favour of law of nationality. According to his thesis laws are made for an ascertained number of people and not for a specified area. The greatest responsibility of a sovereign are his subjects. When laws are made, then not only the moral and material qualities and needs of subjects but also the climate and fertility of the land is taken into consideration. Obviously, the Italian legal system will make ideal laws for Italians, as it would take into account the characteristics of Italians. In this perspective, it is natural to lay down that wherever an Italian may be, in whichever country he may become domiciled, he will continue to be governed by Italian law. And we find that under the Italian Civil Code of 1866 all matters relating to personal status and capacity are governed by the law of nationality.[4]

On the other hand, the law of nationality could not have been chosen to be the governing law in personal matters in the common law system, for the simple reason that no country of the common law system has anything like a national law. Every province or a part of the country has its own law. For instance, the family laws and personal laws of every province in Canada, every state in Australia and the United States differ from each other. In United Kingdom laws of different parts are different. Thus Scotland, England and Northern Ireland have different and separate laws. India too has no national law in these matters ; every community has its own personal law. In these circumstances, the law of nationality has no meaning for the common law countries. They have thus no choice but to opt for law of domicile.

The resultant injustice of this dual system in conflict of laws cases has prompted many to make an effort to resolve this controversy. Mansini was aware of the controversy. He was conscious that this conflict between 'nationality' and 'domicile' was the greatest hurdle in the path of international co-operation and unification of laws. He spearheaded the movement for resolving this controversy. He was in favour of unification of laws by international conventions and agreements. In 1873 in Ghant, an institute of international law was established under the chairmanship of Mansini. In the same year another international conference was held at Brussels where an international organization for the unification and codification of international law was established,

4. Under the Code Napolean of 1803 and under the Italian Code of 1941, it is the law of nationality which regulates these matters. In most of the countries of continental Europe even now it is the law of nationality which governs all matters relating to personal status, capacity and family relation. Only Norway and Denmark adhere to the law of domicile.

under the chairmanship of America's David Dudley Field. It was resolved that both the public and private international laws are within the purview of the institute. It was also decided that private international law would be on the agenda of next year's conference. In the 1874 conference Mansini presented his report in which it was suggested to achieve unification of private international law by international treaties and conventions. "Special Part" of the Report was devoted to personal status, capacity, family relations, succession to immovable and movable property. In the schedule to the Special Part, certain guidelines were suggested. The guidelines stipulated that in respect of status, capacity, family relations, rights and duties of dependants, the law of nationality would be applicable, but in case an individual had no nationality, if he had double nationality or if the country of which he was the national was devided into states or provinces having different personal laws, it would be the law of domicile which would govern these matters. It was also stipulated that in case the personal law of an individual was against the public policy of the forum, it would not be given effect to. In the 1875 Conference at The Hague, though the "Guidelines" of Mansini were on the agenda, no discussion took place on account of Mansini's absence. In the 1879 Conference a paper was presented by Westlake and Arntiz in which only one change was suggested in Mansini's Guidelines, namely, domicile was substituted with domicile of origin. No discussion could take place on the paper. The paper was discussed in the 1880 Conference at Oxford but it could not be passed. Then Arntiz submitted a resolution which was passed. The following suggestions were made in the Resolution :

(1) Personal status and capacity of an individual would be governed by law of his nationality ;

(2) In case an individual has no nationality, then his personal status and capacity would be determined on the basis of law of his domicile ;

(3) In case in a country several legal systems prevail, then his personal status and capacity will be determined by the law of his domicile.

In the 1893 Hague Conference one more modification was accepted, viz. in a case where there are several legal systems prevalent in a country, then the law of that part of the country would apply to him with which he has closest connection.

We skip over the first half of the twentieth century. The 1951 Hague Conference was an important step in this direction of resolving the conflict between nationality and domicile. At the Conference the following three principles were accepted :

(1) If in any suit there is a conflict between the laws of two countries, one of which adheres to nationality and the other to domicile, then the court would apply the domestic law of the domicile of the person concerned.

(2) If in a suit there is a conflict between the laws of two countries both of which adhere to principle of domicile, then the domestic law of the country of the domicile of the person concerned would apply.

(3) If in a suit there is a conflict between the laws of two countries both of which adhere to the principle of nationality then the law of the nationality of the person concerned would apply.

The 1956 Hague Conference considered the problem again. Great Britain suggested that consideration be given to resolve the controversy relating to conflict of laws in respect of testamentary succession. The matter was considered in the 1960 Hague Conference and a suggestion was made by Great Britain that the law of nationality of the deceased would mean the law of that part of that country with which the deceased had closest contact. This suggestion was accepted in the 1960 Convention on Guardianship and in the 1964 Convention on Adoption.

II
DOMICILE : MEANING

Based as domicile is on the principle of individual liberty, an individual is free to establish his domicile at any place in the world. The national boundaries are not a hindrance in his choice of domicile. This implies that a person may have his nationality in one country and domicile in another. This also implies that though a person may be stateless he cannot be without a domicile. He must be domiciled at some place.[5] It seems to be natural to lay down that in all those matters which are intimately connected with his personal life, such as marriage, dissolution of marriage, children, adoption, guardianship, succession, capacity and all other matters relating to his family life should be determined by the law of the place with which he is most intimately connected. This can be only the law of his domicile.[6]

In the countries of common law system as well as in some of continental Europe, domicile is a connecting factor in personal matters. It is a jural concept used for the purpose of establishing the connection of a person with the law of the country with which he or she is most intimately connected. It is also used to establish the connection of a dependant with the *lex domicilii* of the person on whom he or she is dependant. This may be explained by an example : A marries B and establishes his matrimonial home at Jaipur. After sometime a son C is born to him. Jaipur is the domicile of A Jaipur is also the domicile of B as in Indian law the domicile of wife is her husband's domicile. Jaipur is also the domicile

5. *Mychel* v. *State*, 1956 Bom. 729.
6. Or the law of nationality according to the prevalent view among the countries of civil law system.

of C, as C is dependent upon A. The domicile of B will remain Jaipur so long as she remains A's wife and it will not change even if she leaves Jaipur for good. Similarly C's domicile will remain Jaipur so long as he remains a minor. If A changes his domicile, the domicile of B and C also changes.

Since domicile is concerned with personal matters, originally it was natural to seek its definition in relation to home. In 1958 Lord Cranworth said : "By domicile we mean home, the permanent home."[7] But then what is home ? Lord Cranworth's retort then was " . . . if you do not understand your permanent home, I'm afraid that no illustrations drawn from foreign writers will very much help you to it". However, five years, later in 1863, Lord Cranworth condescended and observed : "The present intention of making a place a person's permanent home can exist only where he has no other idea than to continue there, without looking forward to any event, certain or uncertain, which might induce him to change his residence. If he has in his contemplation some event upon the happening of which his residence will cease, it is not correct to call this event a present intention of making it a permanent home. It is rather a present intention of making it a temporary home, though for a period indefinite and contingent."[8]

A technical meaning is thus given to home. It is not necessarily a place where a man is living with his wife and children for many many years. If it can be shown that an intention was always lurking in his mind not to make it a permanent home and to return to his original place, howsoever faint and insignificant this lurking intention might be, he would not be deemed to have established his domicile there and his original domicile would continue to cling to him, though he had severed all his connections with it. Thus permanent home has become an 'everlasting' home.[9] This is well illustrated by the decisions of the House of Lords. In *Ramsay* v. *Liverpool Royal Infirmary*[10] a person died leaving behind a will which formally was valid under Scottish law, though invalid by law of England. The testator was born in Glasgow in 1845 and thus had a Scottish domicile of origin. From 1892, till his death in 1927 he lived in Liverpool, England. During these 37 years he never went to Scotland. Only fact that still 'connected him with Scotland was that he often said that he was very proud to be a Glasgow man.' As against this he, on several occasions, refused to go to Glasgow. He did not go to attend the funeral of his mother at Glasgow and arranged for his own burial at Liverpool. The House of Lords unanimously held that it was not proved that he made Liverpool his permanent home and therefore he continued to have his Scottish domicile of origin.

7. *Whicker* v. *Hume*, (1858) 7 H.L. Cas. 124 at p. 160.
8. *Moorhouse* v. *Lord*, (1863) 10 H.L. Cas. 272 at pp. 285-86.
9. Cheshire, 155.
10. (1930) A.C. 588.

The decision of the House of Lords in *Winas* v. *A.G.*[11] is equally startling. Winas was born in 1823 in the United States. In 1850 he left the United States and since then he lived in several other countries till he died in England in 1897. During this period he lived in Russia, Germany and England. In 1859 he established his winter residence in Brighton, England. In 1883 he ceased to visit Russia and lived in Brighton or Germany. From 1893 onward till his death he lived in England. Certain legacy-duties were claimed by the Crown which were recoverable if Winas died domiciled in England. All his life Winas remained a staunch pro-United States and his life mission was the construction in Baltimore of a large fleet of spindle-shaped vessels which could give the United States supremacy on sea over England. On these facts the House of Lords came to the conclusion that it could not be established that Winas ever formed a fixed and settled purpose of abandoning his American domicile and settling finally in England. Thus he died domiciled in the United States. Cheshire's apt comments[12] on this state of English law are : "In the result, therefore, the English courts in the present context have succeeded in giving a strained and unnatural meaning to the word 'permanent'. Now-a-days, an intention of indefinite residence is not equivalent to an intention of permanent residence, if it is contingent upon an uncertain event. Thus the English conception of domicile corresponds neither with what ordinary man understands by his permanent home nor with the continental criterion of habitual residence."[13]

This means that in the English private international law the concept of domicile is different from the notion of permanent home. A person can acquire a domicile at a place only if he resides there permanently or indefinitely with an intention to live there permanently and indefinitely. If a person goes to a place with a fixed intention of residing there, say 20 years, and then to come back, he will not be domiciled there even if he is not able to return and even if he had set up a home there. On the other hand, a person may be considered to be domiciled at a place even if he has not established his home there, such as where a person is a permanent vagrant or he has abandoned one home and has not acquired another.

It should be clearly noticed that domicile connects a person with a system of law and his connection with the place is only in this sense that his *lex domicilii* prevails there. That system of law may be of a country or of a part of a country. For instance, to be domiciled in the United Kingdom has no meaning as the United

11. (1904) A.C. 287.
12. Cheshire, (7th Ed.) 148.
13. Dicey and Morris in their eighth edition define domicile in relation to home. Their formulation runs : "(1) A person, in general, is domiciled in the country in which he is considered by English law to leave his permanent home : (2) A person may sometimes he domiciled in a country although he does not have his permanent home there." (Rule 3, p. 78).

Kingdom is a country of composite legal system. Thus, a person can be domiciled in England, Eire or Scotland. The same applies to the United States, Canada and Australia. In the United States and Australia every state has its own system of law; so have the provinces of Canada. In India the situation is different. In India the states do not have different systems of law, but each community has its own law. Thus for the purpose of private international law a person may have Indian domicile, but then to know which system of law applies to him we will have to find out to which community he belongs.

Under both Indian and English private international law there are four general rules in respect of domicile :

(1) No person can be without a domicile;

(2) No person can have simultaneously two domiciles;

(3) Domicile denotes the connection of a person with a territorial system of law; and

(4) The presumption is in favour of continuance of an existing domicile.

No person can be without a domicile : This is well established rule that no person can be without a domicile; every person must have a domicile.[14] This is based on the practical necessity of connecting every individual with a system of law so that his legal relations may be regulated. A person has freedom to change his domicile but he has no freedom to be without a domicile. Even when a person is actually homeless the law nonetheless attributes a domicile to him. Thus every person has a legal domicile. The domicile of a person is determined on his birth. On his birth a person acquires the domicile of his father in case he is a legitimate child and domicile of his mother in case he is illegitimate.[15] This domicile will stick to him till he adopts another domicile so much so that if a person leaves his country of origin with an intention to live in another, nevertheless, his domicile of origin adheres to him until he actually acquires another. Once he acquires another domicile, his domicile—the domicile of choice—sticks to him, unless he again acquires another domicile. And if he abandons his domicile of choice, his domicile of origin revives till he acquires another domicile. Thus every independent person must have a domicile, either of origin or of choice. Similarly, every dependent person has his domicile, it is either that of the person on whom he is dependent or it is fixed by law. In English law this position stands modified. (See below)

No person can have simultaneously two domiciles : Just as no

14. *Udny* v. *Udny*, (1869) L.R. 1 Sc. and Div. 441 ; *Re Craignish*, (1892) 3 Ch. 180.

15. *Udny* v. *Udny*, cited above; *Kedar Pandey* v. *Narayan Vikram*, 1966 S.C. 160 at p. 163. See also ss. 7 and 8 of Succession Act, 1925 (Indian Statute).

person can be without a domicile, no person can have simultaneously more than one domicile. It is because law in fixing domicile of a person connects him with a system of law and if a person is allowed to have more than one domicile that purpose will be frustrated.[16] The Indian Constitution recognizes only one domicile.[16a] It is exceptionally possible for a person to have two domiciles, such as when a person may retain his domicile of origin and may also acquire a domicile of choice. Similarly, a person may have two houses in two different countries, but he will be domiciled in that country in which he has his principal home.

However, recently a view is maintained that a person may have two domiciles simultaneously but for different purposes. This is possible in a country where its different parts have different systems of law. For instance, in federal systems of Government, there are two sets of governments—one federal government and the other state or regional government. For the purpose of federal laws a person may have federal domicile and for the purpose of regional laws he may have a regional domicile. A very good illustration of this is provided in India in respect of Hindu matrimonial laws. The Hindu Marriage Act, 1955 applies to all Hindus. Under the Indian Constitution matrimonial matters are in the Concurrent List in respect of which both Union and State governments can legislate. The U.P. State Legislature passed an amendment to Hindu Marriage Act under which, *inter alia*, it made cruelty as a ground for divorce. This ground is available to those persons who are domiciled in Uttar Pradesh at the time of the marriage. This means that a person who has an Indian domicile will have to have a state domicile for the purpose of the application of the U.P. law.[17]

"The recognition of such domicile (state domicile) may become imperative where the higher Indian domicile does not and can't regulate a matter governed by a state law. . . . The concept of an Indian domicile does not do away with the concept of subsidiary domicile such as the domicile of the states. The latter may prevail for certain purposes, notwithstanding that there is a larger and the more comprehensive Indian domicile."[18] The learned judge called the higher domicile as "primary domicile" and the state domicile as "secondary domicile". In Australia the Commonwealth Matrimonial Causes Act, 1959, provides that divorce proceedings in the state courts shall not be instituted "except by a

16. *Udny* v. *Udny*, cited above. See also s. 6, Indian Succession Act, 1925, which lays down that a person can have one domicile for the purpose of succession.

16a. *Pradeep Jain* v. *Union of India*, 1984 S.C. 1420.

17. In a different connection the Supreme Court of India also said that in a federal system a person can have more than one domicile. *D. D. Joshi* v. *State of Madhya Pradesh*, 1955 S.C. 334.

18. *Parwatawwa* v. *Channawwa*, 1966 Mys. 100 at p. 103.

person domiciled in Australia".[19] In *Lloyd* v. *Lloyd*[20] it was held that this provision enables a New South Wales domiciled person to institute a matrimonial action in Victoria. For the purpose of divorce jurisdiction parties were domiciled in Australia, while for other purposes they were domiciled in New South Wales. Some statutes of the United Kingdom also speak of "domiciled in the United Kingdom".[21] Thus, in some countries dual domicile has come to be recognised.

Domicile denotes connection with a territorial system of law: "Domicile has reference to the system of law by which a person is governed, and when we speak of the domicile of a country, we assume that the same system of law prevails all over that country. But it might well happen that laws relating to succession and marriage might not be the same all over the country, and that different areas in the state might have different laws in respect of these matters. In that case, each area having a distinct set of laws would itself be regarded as a country for the purpose of domicile."[22] Thus in a country like United Kingdom, domicile of United Kingdom has no meaning. A person is either domiciled in England, Wales or Scotland. The same is true about the United States, Canada, Australia. In India the position is different. A person may be domiciled in India. But that would not be enough. It would also be necessary to find to which community he belongs, as in India personal laws differ from community to community.

Presumption is in favour of continuance of an existing domicile: In both the Indian and English private international laws there is a presumption in favour of the continuance of an existing domicile. Unless conclusively proved, a person continues to have his existing domicile. The burden of proving change in domicile lies on the person who alleges it.[23] This seems to be the reason why the House of Lords in *Winas* v. *A.G.*[24] took the view that the domicile of origin continued to exist till the end. It came to the conclusion that there was no conclusive evidence in favour of a change of domicile. The presumption in favour of continuance of an existing domicile may be rebutted in the same manner as a presumption can be rebutted in a civil action.[25] Scarman, J. very aptly sums up the position thus: "Two things are clear—first that unless the judicial conscience is satisfied by evidence of change, the domicile of origin persists; and secondly, that the acquisition

19. S. 23(4).

20. (1962) V.R. 70.

21. Income Tax Act, 1952, s. 132(2); Finance Act, 1956, s. 10(1).

22. *D.P. Joshi* v. *State of Madhya Pradesh*, A.I.R. 1955 S.C. 334, per Venkatarama Iyyar, J. See also *Casdagli* v. *Casdagli*, (1919) A.C. 145.

23. *Casdagli* v. *Casdagli*, (1919) A.C. 145, *Re Lloyd Evans*, (1947) Ch. 695, *Abdus Samad* v. *State of West Bengal*, 1963 S.C. 505.

24. Cited above.

25. *Winas* v. *A.G.*, (1904) A.C. 287.

of a domicile of choice is a serious matter not to be lightly inferred from slight indications or casual words."[26]

III

DOMICILE OF INDEPENDENT PERSON

Domicile of an independent natural person falls under the following two categories :

A. Domicile of Origin, and

B. Domicile of Choice.

A Domicile of Origin

It has been seen in Part II of this Chapter that no person can be without a domicile. To give this principle practical shape, the law confers a domicile on every person on birth. This is known as domicile of origin. It continues to exist so long as he or she does not acquire another domicile. Even if a person, with a view to acquire another domicile, gives up his domicile of origin, it will continue to exist so long as he does not acquire a new domicile.[27] The moment a person gives up his domicile of choice, his domicile of origin revives.[28]

Since domicile of origin is attributed to every person at birth by operation of law, the basis of domicile of origin is paternity or maternity. According to English private international law a legitimate child born during the lifetime of father has his domicile in the country in which his father was domiciled at the time of his birth. A legitimate child born after the death of his father has domicile in the country in which the mother was domiciled at the time of his birth.[29] An illegitimate child has the domicile in the country in which his mother was domiciled at the time of his birth.[30] This is also the position in the Indian law except that the legitimate child born after the death of his father has his domicile in the country in which the father was domiciled at the time of his death.[31] Thus, the domicile of origin is not dependent upon the place where a child is born, nor on the place where its father or mother, reside, but on the domicile of the father or mother, as the case may be. There is only one exception to his rule, viz., the

26. *In the estate of Fuld* (No. 3), (1966) 2 W.L.R. 717.
27. *Central Bank of India* v. *Ram Narayan* 1954, S.C. 36; *Thomas* v. *Morgas*, (1935) 62 Cal. 869; *Somerville* v. *Somerville*, (1801) 5 Ves. 750; *Winas* v. *A.G.*, (1904) A.C. 287; *Huntley* v. *Gaskell*, (1906) A.C. 56.
28. *Udny* v. *Udny*, (1869) L.R. 1 Sc. & Div. 441 ; *Harrison* v. *Harrison*, (1953) 1 W.L.R. 865. See also Indian cases cited in the preceding footnote.
29. *Udny* v. *Udny*, cited above, *Somerville* v. *Somerville*, (1801) 5 Ves. 750.
30. *Udny* v. *Udny*, cited above ; *Re Grove*, (1888) 40 Ch. D. 216.
31. Indian Succession Act, ss. 7 & 8.

domicile of foundling is the domicile of the country in which he is found.[32]

Domicile of origin is a creature of law and no person can give it up totally.[33] Every person must have a domicile and the domicile of origin continues to exist till a person acquires a new domicile. When a person acquires a domicile of choice, his domicile of origin remains in abeyance and revives immediately on his giving up the domicile of choice.[34] For the revival of the domicile of origin it is necessary that the domicile of choice should be abandoned voluntarily. If one is forced to leave the country of his domicile, even then the domicile continues to exist. *Re Lloyd-Evans*[35] is a good illustration of this rule. A person having his domicile of origin in England established his domicile of choice first in Java, then in Belgium. In 1940, at the time of German invasion, he came to England where he made a will and died. The question was : did he die domiciled in England ? The court held that since he had not abandoned Belgium voluntarily, rather he fled to England on account of German invasion, and would have returned there on the circumstances becoming favourable, he died domiciled in Belgium. Thus the domicile of origin continues until domicile of choice is acquired. The Indian case, *Sankaran Horindan* v. *Lakshmi Bharti*,[36] is a good illustration of this rule. One Krishnan, domiciled in India (Kerala) went to England for higher education in 1925. After some time his parents declined to give him any further financial support. With the help of an English friend, Miss Hopeworth, he completed his studies in 1939 and set up his private practice in medicine in Sheffield. He earned a fortune. He purchased a mansion in Sheffield where he shifted his practice. During this time he was living with Miss Hopeworth in a rented house. He then joined the British Health Service. In 1950 Krishnan died in England. Krishnan lived in England for 30 years and during this period not for once he came to India. But in letters that Krishnan wrote to his friends and relations in India, he always expressed his intention of returning to India. He also wrote to say that on earning sufficient fortune and on his insurance policy maturing he would return to India. On these facts the Kerala High Court came to the conclusion that Krishnan did not abandon his domicile of origin.[37] The extreme application of this

32. Dicey-Morris, Rule 6(3), pp. 84-85.
33. See s. 9, Indian Succession Act, 1925.
34. See cases cited in footnote 28.
35. (1947) Ch. 695.
36. 1964 Ker. 244.
37. It is interesting to note that on appeal, A.I.R. 1974 S.C. 1774, the Supreme Court had reversed this finding of the Kerala High Court. The Supreme Court says : "It would appear that till 1939, Krishnan has the intention to return to India. But when he acquired a comfortable practice, and purchased a house in Sheffield, his intention changed." (page 1774).

rule is found in *Winas* v. *A.G.*[38] and in *Ramsay* v. *Liverpool Royal Infirmary.*[39]

Another important aspect of the domicile of origin is that it automatically revives by operation of law on the abandonment of the domicile of choice, whatever time might have elapsed after its abandonment.[40] That this rule may sometimes result in absurdities and injustice is well illustrated by *Re O'Keefe* facts of which have been discussed earlier.[41] Graveson gives another illustration : A has a domicile of origin in Scotland. At the age of 22 he went to New York and settled there. He lived there until he was sixty, when he decided to establish a domicile in California. After severing all connections with New York A left for California, but died on the way. His domicile of origin revived the moment he left New York and since he could not acquire another domicile of choice, he died domiciled in Scotland. It would be immaterial even if at no time he had sat foot in Scotland. It can so happen. Suppose, in this case at the time of A's birth his father though domiciled in Scotland was residing in Paris and continued to reside there till A was 25 and then A left for New York. This rule has been criticized[42] since it may result in a person being domiciled in a country with which his connections are stale or tenuous or which, indeed, he may never have visited.[43] Indian law does not follow English law in this regard. The Indian Succession Act, section 13 provides : 'A new domicile continues until the former domicile has been resumed or another has been acquired.' Thus under Indian law domicile of choice continues until a new domicile is acquired or the domicile of origin is resumed *amino et facto*. In the United States also the rule is different : the previous domicile, whether of origin or choice, is retained till a new one is acquired.[44]

B. Domicile of Choice

Any independent person may acquire a domicile of choice. Whether a person has capacity to acquire a domicile of choice is determined by the law of his existing domicile. Under English law, before the coming into force of the Domicile and Matrimonial Proceedings Act, 1973, a minor, lunatic and married woman had no capacity to acquire a domicile of choice, while under the Indian law a married woman can acquire a domicile of choice under certain circumstances.[45]

38. (1904) A.G. 287 ; Graveson (6th Ed.), pp. 200-01.
39. Cited above. The facts of these cases have been already discussed at pp. 150-51 of this work.
40. *Udny* v. *Udny* (1869) L.R. 1 Sc. & Div. 451; *King* v. *Foxwell*, (1876) 3 Ch. D. 518 ; *Harrison* v. *Harrison*, (1954) 1 W.I .R. 865.
41. See p. 146 of this work.
42. See Cheshire, p. 175 ; Wolf, p. 112.
43. See also Dices and Morris, p. 106.
44. Restatement of Law : Conflict of Laws, para. 23. This is also the recommendation of the English Committee on Private International Law, 1951.
45. Exception to s. 16, Indian Succession Act, 1925.

For the acquisition of domicile of choice the following two conditions must be satisfied : (1) Residence in the country of domicile of choice, and (2) intention to live in the country of domicile of choice permanently.[45a] The Indian Succession Act, 1925, section 10 lays down, "A man acquires a new domicile by taking up his fixed habitation in a country which is not that of his domicile of origin." In other words, *factum et animus* must concur. At the moment when they concur domicile of choice is acquired. Intention may precede the residence, such as the case of an emigrant who leaves his country of domicile of origin with an intention to settle in another country, or it may be formed after years of residence just as in the case of a fugitive. But the co-existence of intention and residence is essential for acquiring domicile of choice. The residence of a person is a tangible fact, from which intention may be inferred, while intention is an intangible fact which can be gathered from certain tangible facts in which it is manifested.

Recently, after a review and case law, The Supreme Court in *Loicis De Raedt* v. *VOI*,[45b] said that a person who claims to have established his domicile of choice must establish that he had formed an intention of making permanent home in the country of residence and of residing there permanently. A foreigner who continued to stay in India on the strength of his foreign passport by seeking permission of the Government of India for further stay for specified periods, this does not indicate that he intended to make India his domicile of choice.

Residence : "Residence" is an elastic term of which no exhaustive definition is possible. It is differently construed in accordance with the purpose and the context in which it is used. The meaning of the term and the sense in which it is used are controlled by reference to the object.[46] In *Kumud* v. *Jotindranath*,[47] the Calcutta High Court said that it means 'the place where a person eats, drinks and sleeps, or where his family or servants eat, drink and sleep.'[48] It has also been construed to mean 'dwell permanently or for a considerable time'.[49]

The word 'residence' has a time element in it, but it does not necessarily mean that a person must have been residing in the same home or at the same place for a considerably long period. If it is not a temporary stay, as a visitor, tourist or traveller, then such a residence

45a. *Gour Gopal* v. *Sipra Roy*, 1978 Cal. 163.

45b. AIR 1991 S.C. 1886.

46. *Anil Bala* v. *Dhirendra*, (1921) 48 Cal. 577; *Goswami Shri* v. *Govardhan Lalji* (1890) 14 Bom. 541; *Mahomed Shuffli* v. *Laldin Abdula*, (1873) 3 Bom. 227.

47. (1911) 38 Cal. 394.

48. This was in the context of the word 'residence' O. 5, rr. 9 & 17, C.P.C. and is based on *R.* v. *North Corry*, 107 E.R. 1313.

49. *Anil Bala* v. *Dhirendra*, (1921) 48 Cal. 577.

will be sufficient for acquiring domicile. It means 'bodily presence as an inhabitant'.[50] No duration of residence is necessary for acquiring domicile. Residence in a country is *prima facie* evidence of domicile, the presumption of domicile in favour of residence becomes stronger with the length of residence. However, mere long residence is not enough for acquisition of domicile, nor does the brief residence negative domicile. The residence must answer "a qualitative as well as a quantitative test."[51] In the English case, *Jopp* v. *Wood*[52] twenty-five years' residence in India and in the Indian case, *S.P. Ghose* v. *Deputy Collector*[53] ten years' residence in England was not considered enough. In the English case, Turner, L.J. said, "He may have taken up and continued his residence there for some purposes, or he may have elected to make the place his temporary home. But domicile, although in some cases spoken as 'home' imparts an abiding and permanent home, and not merely a temporary one." In *Central Bank of India* v. *Ram Narayan*,[54] before partition of India, one Ram Narayan carried on business in Multan where he was then domiciled. After partition Multan became part of Pakistan. During disturbance that followed in the wake of partition, Ram Narayan sent away his family to India but he himself continued to reside there with a view to wind up his business. Thereafter he also migrated to India. The question before the court was whether before migration he continued to be domiciled in Pakistan, or whether he acquired an Indian domicile the moment he had sent his family to India. Mahajan, J. of the Supreme Court of India said that his domicile cannot be determined by his family coming to India, without any finding that he had established a home for himself in India. Even if *animus* could be ascribed to him, the *factum* of residence is wanting, and therefore, he continued to be domiciled in Pakistan. In *Michael Anthony Rodrigues* v. *State of Bombay*[55] one Michael, born in 1918 in Goa of parents having Goan nationality came to Bombay in 1927 where his father had established a tailoring business for the last forty years. Since then Michael never went back to Goa. He was educated in Bombay and in 1936 he joined his father's business. In 1946, during the war, he joined the Royal Indian Armed Forces. After his discharge from the army he gave Bombay as his permanent address. Thereafter he lived in Bombay and in 1948 he reverted back to his father's business. His name was also entered in the municipal rolls as voter. On these facts, the Bombay High Court held that he had acquired a domicile of choice in Bombay and had abandoned his Goan domicile of origin. On the other hand, howsoever short the duration of residence may be, it is enough

50. *Re Newcomb*, (1908) 192 N.Y. 238.
51. *Ramsay* v. *Liverpool Infirmary*, (1930) A.C. 588 at p. 598.
52. (1865) 4 De G.J. & Sm. 616; see also *A.G.* v. *Yule*, (1931), 145 L.T. 9.
53. 1964 All. 422; see also *Stouds* v. *Stouds*, 1932 Cal. 161.
54. 1955 S.C. 36.
55. 1956 Bom. 729.

for acquiring a domicile of choice.[56] For instance, if a person leaves the place of his present domicile with a view to settle in another country, then the moment he sets his foot in that country he acquires a domicile there.[57] This is well illustrated from the American case, *White* v. *Tennant*.[58] After abandoning his home in state P, a man took his family to a house in state R, about a mile from state P. After depositing his belongings there, he returned to state P with a view to spend the night with a relative. He fell ill and died on that very night. It was held that he died domiciled in state R.

A question arises in a situation where a person has not abandoned his domicile of origin but has clearly indicated his intention to have his domicile of choice in another country and for part of the year he goes to stay there. It was held in *Plummer* v. *IRC*[58a] that since the place of his new domicile is not yet his chief residence, he had not acquired his new domicile of choice.

Intention : Intention is an intangible fact. It is an act of mind and like other mental acts, it is difficult to prove. For the purpose of acquisition of domicile the intention to reside at a place or in a country should be to reside there permanently or for an unlimited time. The intention must be fixed and not fickle and must be directed towards one particular place or country. For instance, a person P who leaves the country of his domicile of origin with a view to settle in country X, Y or Z, does not have an intention to acquire domicile in any one of these countries. But a person who decides to spend the rest of his life in a country X is the person who intends to acquire domicile in that country.

Intention can be gathered from all events and circumstances of the life of a person. This may be illustrated from the Indian case, *Kedar Pande* v. *Narayan Bikram Shah*.[59] The question before the Supreme Court was whether Narayan Bikram Shah was domiciled in India in 1949. Since his father was domiciled in Nepal, Narayan Shah had his domicile of origin there. Born in Benaras, Narayan Shah received his education from 1934 to 1938 in India. After 1938 he lived in Ram Nagar and continued to live there even after the death of his father. His father, Ram Raja, had built a palace in Ram Nagar in 1938-41. Subsequently Narayan Shah also built a mansion there. In 1982 there was a partition suit between

56. *Fasbender* v. *A.G.*, (1922) 2 Ch. 850 (residence of a few days); *Miller* v. *Teale*, (1954) 92 C.L.R. (Australian case); *Bell* v. *Kennedy*, (1868) L.R. 1 Sc. & Div. 307, H.L.
57. A person may be resident in a country even though he is living in hotel and staying there for a particular purpose, *I.R.C.* v. *Lysaght*, (1928) A.C. 234 (for conducting business); *Matalon* v. *Matalon*, (1952), p. 233 (taking part in legal proceedings). However, this residence is not enough for the purpose of domicile.
58. (1888) 31 West Virginia 790.
58a. (1988) 1 WLR 292.
59. 1966 S.C. 160.

Narayan Shah and his brother. During the suit and subsequently also he continued to manage properties. After partition, he and his wife acquired immovable property, including land, in Patna and several other places. On March 23, 1949 he got issued an Indian passport in which he described himself an Indian citizen and domicile and resident of Ram Nagar. He went to Nepal only once when he was 10 or 12 years old. After 1953 he never went to Nepal. He had married an Indian girl. All his children were educated in India. Before the establishment of *Gram Panchayat*, he was the president of the Union Board. His name was entered into the voters' list of the Ram Nagar *Gram Panchayat*. In the 1952 election his name was in the voters' list of Ram Nagar constituency. In 1957 general elections he contested from the Ram Nagar constituency. The Supreme Court said that taking into account all the events and circumstances of Narayan Shah's life, it was clearly established that long before 1949, Narayan Shah had acquired a domicile of choice in India.

The English courts also take this view. Every conceivable event and incident in a man's life is a relevant and an admissible indication of the state of mind.[59a] Eady, L.J. observed : "There is no act, no circumstance in a man's life, however trivial it may be in itself, which ought to be left out of consideration in trying the question whether there was an intention to change the domicile. A trivial act might possibly be of more weight with regard to determining this question than an act which was of more importance to a man in his lifetime."[60]

It may be emphasized that no single fact is necessarily decisive. It is the cumulative effect of facts and events which is indicative of the intention. How difficult it is to find out the 'intention' is well illustrated by the Indian decision, *Sankaran Govindan* v. *Lakshmi Bharathi*[61] whereby emphasizing certain facts the Kerala High Court came to one conclusion and by emphasizing certain other facts the Supreme Court came to another. The facts of the case have been summarised earlier.[62] The Supreme Court emphasized a letter written by Miss Hopeworth to a relative of Krishnan after Krishnan's death, where she said that all that she could say was that Krishnan repeatedly said that he would not go back to India. Mathew, J. found that after 1939, when he had built up comfortable practice and purchased a house in Sheffield, Krishnan had no intention to go back to India.

Declaration of intention and motive may also be considered but by

59a. *Scappaticci* v. *A.G.*, (1955) P. 47; *Re Craignish*, (1892) 3 Ch. 180.

60. *Casdagli* v. *Casdagli*, (1918) P. 89 at P. 99. See also *Winas* v. *A.G.*, (1904) A.C. 287; *Hoskins* v. *Mathews*, (1856) 8 De G.M. & G. 13. See *Wahl* v. *A.G.*, (1932) 147 L.T. 382, where the House of Lords has reviewed earlier cases in which criteria of intention have been laid down.

61. 1974 S.C. 1764; *Govindan* v. *Bharti*, 1964 Ker. 244 (High Court).

62. See page 156 of this work.

themselves they are not of much value. The court has to take into consideration all facts and circumstances in which declaration of intention was made. Its veracity has to be checked. In *Ross* v. *Ross*[63] Lord Brickmaster observed : "Declarations as to intention are rightly regarded in determining the question of a change of domicile, but they must be examined by considering the person to whom, the purposes for which and the circumstances in which they are made and they must further be fortified and carried into effect by conduct and action consistent with the declared expression." Motive, on the other hand, stands on a little higher place. Motive gives direction to a person's intention; motive may indicate as to whether a man really intended to settle down in a particular place. For instance, a criminal runs away from his country and settles down in another country, or a retired person goes to another country and settles down there. The motive in both cases is different. Motives help in judging the sincerity of the declaration of intention. The motive to settle down in another country can be to escape from one's creditors or to take advantage of liberal law of divorce of another country. This is well illustrated by the Indian case, *Satya* v. *Teja Singh.*[64] One Teja Singh, a domiciled Indian national, went to New York in 1959 and spent a year in a University in New York. Then he, joined Utah State University where he studied for four years for his doctorate. In 1964 on the completion of his studies he secured a job in Utah. Before Teja Singh left India he had married an Indian domiciled woman, whom he had left in India. In December 1964 he obtained a decree of divorce from a Nevada court dissolving his Indian marriage. He made a false representation to the Nevada court that he was residing there (he had merely fulfilled the requirement of 30 days residence there). Immediately after securing the decree of divorce he left Nevada. All along he had set up his residence in Utah. Chandrachud, J. of the Indian Supreme Court had no difficulty in holding that Teja Singh was not domiciled in Nevada and therefore the Nevada decree of divorce cannot be recognized.

Intention to settle down in another country must be free and voluntary. In certain circumstances it may not be so. The Indian Succession Act, 1925, Explanation to s. 10 expresses this thus : "A man is not deemed to have taken up his fixed habitation in India merely by reason of his residing there in his Majesty's civil, military, naval or air force service in the exercise of any profession or calling." These are cases which cast doubt as to the freeness of the intention. We may take up some illustrative cases.

Refugees : In our contemporary world the phenomenon of people leaving their country to escape persecution, murder, genocide has become

63. (1930) A.C. 1, at 6.
64. 1975 S.C. 105.

common. When a person flees from his country to escape persecution or plunder and goes to another, the question is, does he lose his original domicile and acquire new domicile ? In case of large scale movement of this nature, such as in the case of Bangladesh refugees to India, the answer is in the negative. The position may be different in case of individual refugees. A person at the first instance may go to another country by force of circumstances and not voluntarily, but later on may choose to settle down there : "what is dictated in the first instance may afterwards become a matter of choice."[65] If that happens, a refugee may acquire the domicile of the country of his refuge. In the Indian case, *Mandal* v. *Mandal*[66] two Austrian domiciled persons were married in Vienna in 1936. In 1939, on the invasion of Austria by Nazi Germany, they fled to India. Since then they lived in India and had no intention of returning to Austria. A full Bench of the Punjab High Court held that they had acquired a domicile of choice in India.

Fugitives : The fugitives fall under two categories : those who go to another country to escape from the consequences of their crime and those who escape from their civil liabilities. In the former category are criminals who flee from their country and take refuge in another to escape justice. In the latter category are debtors who flee the country to avoid their creditors. In such cases one may draw the inference that they had left their country for good and therefore a presumption arises in their favour that they had acquired a domicile of choice in the country of their refuge; although their departure is not voluntary, yet it can't be said that they intended to settle there temporarily. If the stay is long—it was 20 years in *Re Martin*[67]—it may be taken as established that fugitive intended to make that place his home. Similarly, if there is no possibility of the fugitive escaping the punishment in case he returns to his country, then it would be a natural inference that he intended to acquire a domicile of choice in the country which has given him refuge. This equally applies to a fugitive who runs away from his civil liability.[68]

Invalids : Invalids who go to other countries fall under two categories : those who go there for convalescence or for a temporary stay to improve their health and those who go there and settle down as they find the climate more congenial. It is obvious that question of acquiring domicile of choice does not arise in the case of the former.[69] In the latter case the natural inference will be that he has acquired a domicile of choice in that country. In *Hoskins* v. *Mathews*,[70] a 60-year old English domiciled

65. *Winas* v. *A.G.*, (1904) A.C. 287.
66. I.L.R. (1956) Punj. 215.
67. (1990) P. 211.
68. *Briggs* v. *Briggs* (1880) 5 P.D. 163.
69. See *Moorhouse* v. *Lord*, (1863) 10 H.L. Cas. 272; *Johnstone* v. *Beattie*, (1843) 10 Cl. & Fin. 42. See also Cheshire (8th Ed.), 160-70.
70. (1856) 8 De G.M. & G. 13.

person had an injury in his spine and he went to Florence solely because he thought the warmer climate of Italy might benefit his health. He lived there throughout the rest of his life. He died there at the age of seventy-two. The court held that he died domiciled in Florence. Turner, C.J. said, "... in settling there he was exercising a preference, and not acting upon a necessity."

Public Servants : There are several categories of public servants who are posted by their governments in foreign countries. Among these categories are included ambassadors, consuls, staff in embassies, legations or governmental news agencies and the like. The natural inference is that they do not acquire domicile of choice in such countries and retain their existing domicile. This has been specifically laid down in s. 12, Indian Succession Act, 1925.[71] But if a public servant continues to live in that country after he has been discharged from his job, he may acquire a domicile of choice in that country. Similarly, a public servant who goes to work as well as to settle in a foreign country, can acquire a domicile of choice there.[72] In this respect there is no distinction between a private service or public service or a diplomatic service or other service. *Stone* v. *Stone*[73] is an illustration of this : S, a member of the U.S. Armed Forces was stationed in Europe. He used to spend all his holidays in England and wanted to settle there on retirement from his post. The court held that he acquired a domicile of choice in England. Thus a member of armed forces may, while in his service, acquire domicile of choice either in the country in which he is stationed[74] or elsewhere provided he has established there *animo et facto*.[75]

Prisoners : It would appear to be evident that howsoever long the term of imprisonment may be, it will not be enough to confer domicile of choice on the prisoner. He retains his existing domicile.[76] But it seems a prisoner who has been transported for life does not retain his domicile of choice. Thus in all those cases where people reside in foreign countries not by their own free volition but by some force of circumstances, they cannot be said to have acquired a domicile of choice in those countries. Any constraint on the free volition of a person to choose his place of residence would be preclusive of free intention and negative the establishment of a domicile of choice.

Abandonment of Domicile of Choice : *Animo et facto* go to establish

71. The section runs, 'A person who is appointed by the Government of one country to be its ambassador, consul, or other representative in another country does not acquire domicile in the latter's country by reason only of residing there in pursuance of his appointment, nor does any other person acquire such domicile by reason only of residing with such first mentioned person as part of his family or as servant.'
72. *In the goods of James Smith,* (1850) 2 Rob. Ecc. 332.
73. (1959) 1 All. E.R. 194.
74. *Donaldson* v. *Donaldson,* (1949) P. 363.
75. *Stone* v. *Stone,* cited above.
76. *Cruh* v. *Cruh,* (1945) 2 All. E.R. 545; *Zanelli* v. *Zanelli,* (1948) 64 T.L.R. 556.

a domicile of choice. When both these conditions, *factum* and *animus* cease to exist, the domicile of choice is abandoned. Just as mere intention to settle or mere residence in another country is not enough to acquire domicile, similarly mere intention to abandon or mere residence in another country is not enough for abandonment of domicile of choice. Thus the domicile of choice is abandoned when a person gives up residing in the country of the domicile of choice and he has no intention to reside there indefinitely.

The case of the *Goods of Raffenel*[77] is a good illustration of the operation of these two factors. One Madame Raffenel, widow of a French Naval Officer, had her domicile of origin in England. She had her domicile of choice in France. She embarked at Calais on a cross-channel steamer, with the intention of leaving France for good. But she was taken ill before the steamer could sail and had to spend several months in Calais, where she died. The court held that she died domiciled in France, as at the date of her death she had not abandoned her French domicile, though she had an intention to do so. However, had she sailed off the French territorial waters, her English domicile of origin would have revived.[78] In *Zanelli* v. *Zanelli*,[79] the Court of Appeal said that residence is given up by "leaving this country or perhaps more accurately, arriving at another." Dicey and Morris rightly observe that residence can simply be given up; the view that residence in one country can only be given by arriving in another seems to be a relic of the discarded doctrine that a domicile of choice cannot be lost by mere abandonment.[80] On the abandonment of domicile of choice either a new domicile of choice is acquired or the domicile of origin revives.[81]

Domicile of Origin and Domicile of Choice : Comparison

There are some fundamental differences between the domicile of origin and domicile of choice. These are :

(1) The domicile of origin comes into existence by operation of law, independently of the volition of a person and every person gets it on birth. On the other hand, the domicile of choice is a domicile which is acquired by the free volition of the person concerned. For its acquisition the existence of *animo et facto* is necessary.

(2) There is a very strong presumption in favour of the continuance

77. (1863) 3 S.W. & Tr. 49.
78. See also *Zanelli* v. *Zanelli* (1948) 64 T.L.R. 556; *Bardford* v. *Young*, (1885) 29 Ch. D. 617; *Phillip* v. *I.R.C.*, (1971) 1 W.L.R. 684 (for the converse situation).
79. (1948) 64 T.L.R. 556.
80. Conflicts of Laws, 106.
81. English courts have held that for the abandonment of domicile of origin stronger evidence is required than for the abandonment of domicile of choice: *Re Mitchell*, (1884) 13 Q.B.D. 418; *Forbes* v. *Forbes*, (1854) Kay 341.

of the domicile of origin. In comparison with domicile of choice, domicile of origin, in the words of Lord Macnaghten, "is more enduring, its hold is stronger and less easily shaken of."[82] An extreme application of this rule was made in *Ramsay* v. *Liverpool Royal Infirmary* (the case has been discussed earlier at page 150 of this work).

(3) Domicile of origin cannot be abandoned easily. Since it is a creature of law and not of free will, domicile of origin cannot be lost by mere abandonment. Until a domicile of choice is acquired, the domicile of origin continues. *Bell* v. *Kennedy*[83] is a good example of this. One Bell, who had his domicile of origin in Jamaica, with a view to acquire a domicile of choice in Scotland, left Jamaica. He reached Scotland and lived there with his mother-in-law and was looking for an estate to purchase. Yet he had not firmly made up his mind to settle in Scotland. Then his wife died. The court held that till then he had not lost his domicile of origin. On the other hand, the domicile of choice is lost by the moment it is abandoned. If a new domicile of choice is not acquired the domicile of origin revives.

(4) Another outstanding feature of domicile of origin is that it is never lost; when a domicile of choice is acquired, it remains in abeyance. As soon as the domicile of choice is abandoned or lost, it immediately revives, even if all contacts with the country of the domicile of origin have been lost. For instance, D is born in India of parents domiciled in England. In his infancy D is taken to Italy, where he resides and is domicile for the next 50 years. He then leaves Italy, with the intention of settling in New York but dies in mid-Atlantic. He is domiciled in England at his death.[84] On the other hand, there is no question of revival of domicile of choice, once it is abandoned or lost, it does not revive, though it may be acquired once again by *animo et facto*.

IV
DOMICILE OF DEPENDENTS

Minors, married women and mentally disordered persons, such as idiots and lunatics, fall in the category of dependents. In respect of domicile, the term "dependent" is applied to a person who is incapable of having a domicile of choice. The general rule is that a dependent person has the domicile of the person on whom he is dependent. The domicile of dependency, as it is sometimes called, is an imposed domicile

82. *Winas* v. *A.G.*, (1904) A.C. 287. An extreme application of this rule was made in *Ramsay* v. *Liverpool Royal Infirmary*, (1930) A.C. 588; these cases have been discussed in this work at pp. 150-51.
83. (1868) L.R. 1 Sc. & Div. 307.
84. This illustration is taken from Dicey and Morris, 107.

and it changes only when the person on whom the dependent is dependent changes his domicile. A dependent person cannot abandon his domicile of dependency. Thus a wife who lives separate from her husband, a minor who has his own separate home from his parents, and a lunatic who lives in another country cannot acquire a domicile of their own. It is only in one case that a dependent person may get a new domicile. This happens when a female minor marries. But then, what she acquires is not her own domicile but the domicile of her husband. Where the person on whom a minor or a lunatic is dependent dies or when he has no person on whom he is dependent, then the domicile of dependent person cannot change at all. These statements of law in respect of English law have to be read subject to certain qualifications, since the Domicile and Matrimonial Proceedings Act, 1973 had made some changes relating to domicile of married women and minor children. (See below at pp. 170 and 178).

Under English private international law the capacity to acquire a new domicile is governed by English law and not by the law of his previous domicile or by the law of the intended new domicile.[85] We would discuss three classes of dependents, viz., minors, married women and mentally disordered persons, separately.

Married Women

". . . The last barbarous relict of wife's servitude" was the epithet given to the principle of unity of domicile of the wife and husband by Lord Denning in *Gray* v. *Formosa.*[86] Underlying the rule that "domicile of a married woman is, during coverture, the same as, and changes with the domicile of her husband"[87] is the common law principle of unity of the person of husband and wife. In 1765 Blackstone observed : "By marriage, the husband and wife are one person in law, i.e., the very being or legal existence of a woman is suspended during the marriage, or at least is incorporated and consolidated into that of the husband, under whose wing of protection and cover she performs everything . . . . Upon this principle of union of person in husband and wife, depends almost all the legal rights, duties and disabilities that either of them acquire by the marriage."[88] This rule is also expressed by saying that the husband's

85. See *Re Beaumont,* (1893) 3 Ch. 490. Graveson has opined (without any authority to support) that it is governed by his previous domicile or his alleged new domicile : (1950) 3 I.L.Q. 149.
86. (1963), P. 259. Simon, P. called it "Completely outmoded legal concept." *Adams* v. *Adams,* (1971), P. 188 at P. 216.
87. Dicey, Rule 9(2).
88. Commentaries, Vol. 1, Ch. 15, P. 442. Bacon was more apt : "So long as the marriage subsits the law looks upon the husband and wife but one person, and therefore allows but one will between them, which is placed in the husband, as the fullest and ablest to provide for and govern the family and consequently the husband 'hath by law power and dominion over his wife'." (7th Ed.) B. & F. C. (1).

actual and the wife's legal domicile are one, wherever the wife may be personally residing. By a valid marriage, the domicile of the wife becomes that of the husband, and the fact that married couple are living apart under a separation agreement, or a husband has deserted the wife, does not render her free to choose a domicile apart from his.

In *Lord Advocate* v. *Jaffery*,[89] one Mrs. Mackinon was married on June 26, 1876 to one Robert Mackinon who was born in Campbeltown, Argyllshire and at the time of his marriage was a Chief Quartermaster in the Navy. On retiring from the Navy in 1886 till 1893, he lived with his wife in Aberdeen. In 1893, owing to his drunken and dissipated habits, it was arranged, at the instance of the wife that Mackinon should leave Scotland for Australia and his passage out was paid by Mrs. Mackinon's mother. He landed in Sydney and for some time remained in New South Wales. Sometime before June 1902, he went to Queensland and resided in Brisbane where he died on January 1, 1918. On June 2, 1902, he went through a form of bigamous marriage with one Willhemina, with whom he lived until his death, and from whom he had two children. After his departure from Scotland no communication passed between him and his wife. In 1915 Mrs. Mackinon, who continued to live in Aberdeen filed a petition for divorce on the ground of her husband's desertion and adultery. The two main questions before the court were: (a) whether at the date of Mrs. Mackinon's petition Robert Mackinon had acquired a domicile in Queensland, (b) if so, whether Mrs. Mackinon had acquired a derivative domicile in Queensland, by virtue of the marriage then subsisting between them. The trial court was of the opinion that Robert Mackinon acquired a domicile in Queensland, but that, in the special circumstances of the case, wife's domicile remained Scottish; on the latter point the first appellate court reversed the judgment. The House of Lords affirmed the judgment of first appellate court. Lord Dunedin, pronouncing the opinion of House of Lords, quoted the following passage from the opinion of Sir Cresswell in *Yelverton* v. *Yelverton*.[90] "The domicile of the husband is the domicile of wife; and even supposing him to have been guilty of such misconduct as would furnish her with a defence to a suit by him for restitution of conjugal rights, she could not on that ground acquire another domicile for herself."

In *A.G. for Alberta* v. *Cook*[91] the respondent had obtained a decree for judicial separation from a court of Alberta, where both parties resided, in November 1921. The domicile of the husband was Ontario. In 1922 respondent instituted in an Alberta court a suit for divorce on the ground of her husband's adultery and cruelty. The suit was dismissed for want of jurisdiction, as the husband was domiciled in Ontario. On wife's appeal,

89. (1921) 1 A.C. 146.
90. (1859) 1 S.W. & Tr. 574.
91. (1926) A.C. 444.

the first appelate court reversed the judgment as it held that after a decree of judicial separation wife could acquire her own independent domicile. Accepting the appeal against the order, the Privy Council observed : "The contention that the husband and wife may be domiciled apart and may resort to different codes of law to seek thereunder dissolution of marriage between them appear to challenge directly the rule . . . that matrimonial status is governed by the law of the domicile of parties. . . . The contention that a wife judicially separated from her husband is given the choice of a new domicile is contrary to the general principle on which the unity of domicile of the married pair depends."[92] The present position is that so long as coverture continues the wife's domicile is husband's domicile.[93] Even the desertion of husband, his infidelity or separation by private agreement or by decree of court does not entitle her to acquire a domicile of her own. She can get rid of her domicile only on the termination of coverture, by death of the husband or by decree absolute of dissolution or nullity of marriage. Even then she has to acquire a new domicile, otherwise even on the termination of coverture, her domicile will remain that of her husband.[94] But it is not necessary that she should make a declaration. If by her act or conduct, it is evident that she has acquired a new domicile that is enough. In *Re Scullard*[95] the wife had left her husband in 1908 and in 1946 she settled in Gurne. Her husband was resident and domiciled in England. In 1955 she died. A short while earlier her husband had also died. In between the death of her husband and her own she had not made any declaration in respect of her domicile. The court held that by her conduct her intention to make Gurne her home was evident. No declaration was necessary.

If the marriage is void, the wife does not acquire the domicile of her husband.[96] But if she goes to another country and lives with her putative husband, she may acquire a domicile of choice there.[97] But if the marriage is void on the ground that she was already a wife of someone she cannot acquire a new domicile. Then her domicile will remain that of her lawful husband.[98]

The rule that wife's domicile is tagged with that of her husband has been severely criticized.[99] It is evident that in our contemporary world this is socially most undesirable. Attempt to round off its sharpest corners has been made statutory. Under the Law Reforms (Misc. Provisions)

92. *Ibid.* at 447.
93. See also *Harvey* v. *Farnie,* (1880) 5 P.D. 153 : on appeal (1882) 8 A.C. 43.
94. *In the estate of Wallach,* (1950) 1 All. E.R. 199.
95. (1957) Ch. 107.
96. *White* v. *White,* (1937), P. 111; *Mehta* v. *Mehta,* (1945) 2 All. E.R. 690; *De Reneville* v. *De Reneville,* (1948), P. 100 (C.A.).
97. *Von Lorang* v. *Adm. of Austrian Property,* (1927) A.C. 641.
98. *Shaw* v. *Gould,* (1868) L.R. 3 H.L. 55.
99. Graveson, 176-77; Wolff, 122; Cheshire, 167.

Act, 1949, the Matrimonial Çauses Act, 1950 and the Matrimonial Causes (War Marriage) Act, 1944 it has been laid down that if (i) the wife has been deserted by her husband, or (ii) the husband has been deported from the United Kingdom and the husband was immediately before the desertion or deportation domiciled in England, the court will have jurisdiction to entertain a petition in a matrimonial cause. It is further laid down that in case the proceedings are for divorce or nullity, the English Court will have jurisdiction, if (i) the wife is resident in England and has been ordinarily resident there for a period of three years immediately preceding the commencement of the proceedings, and (ii) the husband is not domiciled in any part of the United Kingdom or in the Channel Islands or the Isle of Man.[100] The Domicile and Matrimonial Proceedings Act, 1973 has now repealed this provision, and the wife is now allowed to have her own separate domicile. New jurisdictional rules have been laid down. (See Chapter 9 of this work.) Thus the English law had gone much ahead of the suggession of the Private International Law Committee that a wife who is living separate under a decree of judicial separation should be allowed to acquire an independent domicile.

The Domicile and Matrimonial Proceedings Act, 1973 makes fundamental changes in the domicile of wife. The rule of unity of domicile of husband and wife stands abolished. The Act lays down that the wife does not acquire the domicile of her husband merely by virtue of her marriage. Now her domicile is to be ascertained the same way as the domicile of an independent person is ascertained. Section1(1) lays down: ". . . the domicile of a married woman as at any time after the coming into force of this section shall, instead of being the same as her husband's by virtue only of marriage, be ascertained by reference to the same factors as in the case of any other individual capable of having an independent domicile." The Act came into force on January 1, 1974. A woman already married on January 1, 1974 retains her husband's domicile of dependency (but she retains it not as a dependent's domicile, but as of choice or origin), till she acquires another domicile. Sub-section (2) provides, "Where immediately before this section came into force a woman was married and then had her husband's domicile by dependence, she is to be treated as retaining that domicile (as a domicile of choice, if it is not also her domicile of origin) unless and until it is changed by acquisition or revival of another domicile either on or after the coming into force of this section." This provision came for interpretation in *IRC* v. *Dichess of Portland*[101] in the following circumstances : A Canadian domiciled woman married a person domiciled in England before the

100. S. 40, the Matrimonial Causes Act, 1965 consolidated these provisions. The Act has been replaced by the Act of 1973. The provisions have been repealed by the Domicile and Matrimonial Proceedings Act, 1973, s. 5.

101. (1982) 2 W.L.R. 367.

coming into force of the Act, and thus acquired an English domicile of dependency, which will now in terms of the sub-section called domicile of choice. Throughout her marriage she maintained close links with Canada: She retained her Canadian passport, had a bank account in Quebec and spent some 10 to 12 weeks there. In 1975 her husband agreed that on his retirement they would leave England and live permanently in Quebec where the wife had a house. She was assessed to income-tax for the years from 1973 to 1978 on the basis of being domiciled in England throughout those years. The main question before the court was whether in terms of sub-section (2), her Canadian domicile revived on the coming into force of the Act. The Chancery Division held that only change the sub-section had effected is that wife's domicile of dependency is now called her domicile of choice, and she could not acquire her domicile of origin unless it revived, nor could she get a new domicile unless it was acquired, and, therefore, notwithstanding her continuing intention to return eventually to Canada, she had, since the coming into force of the Act not ceased to reside in England and had not therefore abandoned the domicile of choice imposed on her by the sub-section. In conclusion it was held that she did not reacquire her Canadian domicile of origin.

In the United State the rule of unity of domicile of husband and wife is not taken to the logical end to which it was taken in English law. There, a wife living separate from her husband, separation not amounting to desertion, can acquire her own independent domicile; separation may be by agreement or by a decree of court.[102]

The Indian statutory law also does not follow English law. The Indian Succession Act, 1925, ss. 15 and 16 incorporate the general rule: on marriage the wife acquires the domicile of her husband and during coverture her domicile is the domicile of her husband. Then it is laid down that wife can acquire her own domicile in the following two cases : (1) If the wife is living separate under a decree of the court, or (2) If the husband is undergoing a life sentence.[103]

Indian courts have been called to dwell upon the matter in the several different situations.

In *Prem Pratap* v. *Jagat Pratap*,[104] a German domiciled woman married a domiciled Indian and set up the matrimonial home in India.

102. Restatement s. 28. See also *William* v. *Osenton*, 232 U.S. 619. The New Zealand Matrimonial Causes Act, 1963 also the rule has been modified (s. 3).

103. Exceptions to s. 16. It seems the Indian rule is based on the observation of Lord Crainworth made in an 1859 case, *R. Dolphin* v. *Robins*, (1859) 7 H.L.C. 390, wherein he said that the wife should be permitted to acquire a separate domicile in certain exceptional cases, such as, when husband and wife are living separate, or the husband is undergoing a life sentence or he is living permanently in another country. The Indian law had incorporated the first two exceptional cases.

104. 1944 All. 97.

After some time the husband left the wife. The wife filed a suit for maintenance in an Indian court—the main defence of the husband was that on abandonment of the wife by him, the wife's pre-marriage domicile had revived and therefore the Indian court has no jurisdiction to entertain the petition. Rejecting this plea, the court observed that during coverture the domicile of wife remains that of the husband. The question came before the Punjab and Haryana High Court in a different form.[105] A husband deserted his wife and established a domicile in the United States. He obtained a decree of dissolution of marriage from a Nevada court. Subsequently the wife filed an application for maintenance under s. 488, Criminal Procedure Code. The main plea of the husband was that the applicant had, in view of the decree of dissolution of marriage by the court of the domicile, ceased to be his wife and hence her claim was not maintainable. The Punjab High Court held that since the decree of the Nevada court dissolving the marriage was the decree of the court of the domicile, the Indian court would recognize it. In view of this wife's application was rejected. In the course of the judgment Sandhawalia, J. observed, *obiter*, that the wife's domicile remains that of the husband, even if she is deserted by her husband.

Then we pass on to two cases which came before our courts in the peculiar circumstances arising in the wake of partition of India. In *Rani Saeeda Khatun* v. *State of Bihar*,[106] soon after the partition, one Rani Saeeda Khatun, wife of Capt. Kumar Gopal Narayan Singh, domiciled in India, left with her mother for Pakistan. On 14th May 1950 she visited India on a permit issued by the Indian High Commission for Pakistan. On 23rd July 1950 she was served with a notice of the Government of India to quit India. In a petition for a writ of *mandamus* it was argued on behalf of Rani Saeeda Khatun that she, being a wife of Indian domiciled person, was domiciled in India and therefore cannot be asked to quit India, since by going to another country or by any other act of her she could not, during the subsistence of marriage, acquire any domicile of her own. Her plea was accepted by the Patna High Court.[107] Substantially on similar facts the Allahabad High Court also accepted the plea of the wife. Mr. Justice Mallick, referring to s. 16, Indian Succession Act, 1925 said that during the subsistence of coverture the domicile of the wife is the domicile of her husband.[108]

105. *Teja Singh* v. *Satya*, (1970) 72 P.L.R. 225. The decision has been overruled by the Supreme Court on a different point : the Supreme Court found that the husband did not acquire a domicile of choice in Nevada (see *Supra*). *Satya* v. *Teja Singh*, 1975 S.C. 105.
106. 1951 Pat. 454.
107. On appeal by the State of Bihar, the Supreme Court reversed the judgment on the basis of Article 7 of the Constitution and not on the basis that wife's domicile can be different from her husband : *State of Bihar* v. *Kumar Amar Singh*, 1955 S.C. 282.
108. *Smt. Allabandi* v. *Union of India*, 1954 All. 457.

It is very unfortunate that Indian courts have blindly followed the English decisions on the unity of the domicile of husband and wife. The courts of free India were not bound to do so. If persuasive decisions were considered to be so very necessary they could have easily looked to decisions of other jurisdictions. American precedents are as handy to us as English precedents. Above all, our judges have available to them all the learning of the world and they could have easily taken a socially just view and could have easily taken into account the peculiar and most undesirable results of adhering to the principle of unity of domicile.[109] The social facts of our times clearly indicate that there is a need to give up this principle, at least in those cases where the husband and wife are living separate. It is very curious that in their zeal to follow English precedent, our judges even ignored the specific provisions of the Indian Succession Act, 1925. Had they looked to the Explanation to s. 16 it was possible for them to reach a different conclusion. The Supreme Court of the United States very pertinently observed, "The only reason that could be offered for not recognizing the fact of plaintiff's actual change, if justified, is the now vanishing fiction of identity of persons. But that fiction does not prevail over the facts in relation for which the fiction was created, there is no reason in the world which should be given effect to in any other."[110] But it seems we want to cling to the foreign fiction even in the face of specific provision in Explanation to s. 16 which lays down that wife's domicile does not follow husband's if wife has been judicially separated, or her husband is undergoing a sentence of transportation. Our courts could have easily extended this principle at least to those cases where husband and wife are living separate, or the husband has deserted the wife.

Minor Children

For the purpose of domicile the minority in Indian law continues till a person attains the age of 18 years, while in English law, under s. 3 of the Domicile and Matrimonial Proceedings Act, 1973, minority terminates on the attainment of 16 years or on marriage. This means that under Indian law a child who had completed the age of eighteen years and under English law a child who had completed the age of sixteen or had married has capacity to acquire an independent domicile. Till then they have to domicile of dependency.

Domicile of natural children : In respect of the domicile of natural minor children the established rules of private international law are : (a) the domicile of legitimate minor children, if parents have not separated, during minority (i.e. up to 16 years), (i) is the domicile of the father so long as the father is alive and it changes with the domicile of the

109. *Teja* v. *Satya,* (1970) 72 P.L.R. 225.
110. *William* v. *Osenton,* 232 U.S. 619.

father, (ii) after the death of the father it is the domicile of the mother so long as the mother is alive and changes with the domicile of the mother; (b) the domicile of an illegitimate minor child during minority is the same as that of the mother and changes with the domicile of the mother; (c) the domicile of the minor orphan (i.e. whose both parents are dead) cannot be changed; and (d) when the minor attains majority he can change his domicile.[111]

On the domicile of legitimated children there is no English authority yet available. On the analogy of legitimate child it seems that the domicile of the legitimated child from the time of legitimation and till the minority, is the same as, and changes with, the domicile of the father so long as the father is alive.[112]

Indian law is slightly different from English law. In respect of legitimate child, s. 7, Indian Succession Act provides : "The domicile of origin of every person of legitimate birth, is in the country in which at the time of his birth his father was domiciled; or if he is posthumous child, in the country in which his father was domiciled at the time of father's death."[113] As to domicile of illegitimate child, s. 8, Indian Succession Act provides : "The domicile of origin of an illegitimate child is in the country in which at the time of his birth, his mother was domiciled." Then s. 14 lays down : "The domicile of a minor follows the domicile of the parent from whom he derived his domicile of origin." Indian law recognizes three exceptions when minor's domicile does not follows that of his parent : (1) If the minor is married, (2) if the minor holds any office or employment in the service of Her Majesty, or (3) if the minor has set up, with the consent of the parent, any distinct business.[114]

Both under the English and Indian private international law a child on attaining majority can acquire his own domicile.[115] This proposition came for interpretation in *Handerson* v. *Handerson*[116] in some peculiar circumstances. P whose domicile of origin was England acquired a domicile of dependency in South Australia. At the age of 20 he married a New Zealand domiciled woman. With his wife he came to England and just then he completed the age of 21 (at that time under English law a person who had not completed the age of 21 years was regarded an infant). His wife presented a petition for dissolution of marriage in an English court. The court could have jurisdiction only if it could be established that the husband had regained his domicile of origin. To

111. See Dicey and Morris, Rule 12, p. 110; Cheshire, 176.
112. Dicey and Morris, Rule 12(2), 110; see also Wolff, 118-19.
113. See also *Santos* v. *Pinto*, 41 Bom. 687.
114. Exception to s. 14, Succession Act, 1925.
115. *Michael Anthony Rodrigues* v. *State of Bombay*, 1956 Bom. 729.
116. (1965) 2 W.L.R. 218.

establish this it was argued that her husband had decided to give up the South Australian domicile of dependency and he did not acquire a domicile of choice in New Zealand since on attaining majority he had not lived in New Zealand. Thus in the circumstances when he had given up the domicile of dependency and had not acquired a domicile of choice, his domicile of origin revived and thus he was domiciled in England. The argument was accepted. This cannot be so under the Indian law, as in Indian law existing domicile continues until the former has been resumed or another has been acquired.

The question of minor's domicile of dependency has come before Indian courts in several post-partition cases. In *Sharafat Ali* v. *State of U.P.*[117] the petitioner was born in a village of Raipur district, M.P. India. In 1953 he went to Karachi, Pakistan with his maternal uncle. In 1956, his father died domiciled in India. At that time he was eighteen years and a few months old. On 27th March 1956 on a permit issued by the Indian High Commissioner for Pakistan he came back to India to look after his mother. On 31st August 1957, he was served with a notice to leave India within thirty days as the permit was cancelled by the High Commission of India in Pakistan. In a writ petition, he argued before the Allahabad High Court that during minority he could not acquire a domicile of his own and therefore he continued to have his father's domicile. On attaining majority he could attain a domicile of choice by his act, conduct or declaration. Nothing of this sort was shown and thus his domicile remained Indian. This argument was accepted by the court. The question again came before the Allahabad High Court in *Mukhtar Ahmed* v. *State of U.P.*[118] in slightly different circumstances. Petitioner, when he was a minor, went to Pakistan with his relatives. His father remained in India. Before attaining majority he obtained a Pakistan passport and an Indian *visa* on the averment that he was Pakistani national. On the expiry of his *visa*, the Government of India served him with a notice to quit India. It was argued that he could not acquire an independent domicile during the minority and since his father was domiciled in India, he too had an Indian domicile. The argument was again accepted.[119] But if the father acquires a foreign domicile then the domicile of the child may also change.[120]

Rasheed Hasan v. *Union of India*,[121] gives a new direction to Indian law. While the petitioner was still a minor, his father, leaving him behind

117. 1960 All. 637.
118. 1965 All. 191.
119. In *Mohammad Yusuf* v. *Union of India*, 1967 Pat. 266, the Court took a different view on the basis of Article 7, Indian Constitution.
120. *Karimulla* v. *State of M.P.*, 1955 Nag. 1; *State* v. *Abdul Hameed*, 1957 Punj. 86; *Mohammed Umar* v. *State of Orissa*, 1961 Orissa 150.
121. 1967 All. 154. See also *Sham Raj* v. *Addl. Supt. of Police*, 1978 Cal. 252.

in India, went to Pakistan, acquired a Pakistani domicile and became a Pakistani citizen. The petitioner remained in India. He was in the voter's list and fought elections and became Chairman of Town Area Committee. The Court observed that it is true that the domicile of minor is the same, and changes with, domicile of the father even though the father and the child might be living in two different countries, but this rule cannot be applied to those cases where the father abandons the child in the country of the domicile of origin, goes to another country and acquires a domicile there. It is submitted that this is sound rule and accords well with social facts of modern life.

Adopted children : In English private international law there is yet no authority on the domicile of adopted child. Dicey and Morris have suggested : "The domicile of an adopted infant is during the lifetime of the adopting parent the same as, and changes with, the domicile of that parent."[122] The editor's comment is that this rule is the law in America and should be followed in England as it seems to be eminently reasonable.[123] This is also the suggestion of the Private International Law Committee. In Indian law, we have the authority of Madras High Court that the domicile of the adopted child is the domicile of the adoptive parent.[124] It is submitted that the domicile of adopted child should be the domicile of adopter and should change with the domicile of adopter.[125] A problem may arise when an unmarried woman marries after she has adopted a child. The question is : what will be the domicile of the adopted child ? On marriage the adoptive mother acquires the domicile of her husband. It is submitted that if the mother does not take the child with her, then the child retains its domicile that it had before the marriage of his mother. In case the child is taken care of by the step-father and goes to live with his adoptive mother and step-father, domicile of the adopted child changes with that of the mother.

Domicile of minor children after the death of parents : In English private international law the domicile of a legitimate child, after the death of the father is the domicile of mother and changes with the domicile of the mother, provided the child is living with the mother. However, this change of domicile is not automatic. It may be that in certain circumstances, it does not change. For instance, if the mother marries a person of different domicile, then the domicile of the child will not change. In *Re Beaumont*[126] the court observed : "The change in the domicile of an infant child which may follow from a change of domicile

122. Rule 12(5), 110.
123. *Ibid.*, at 112.
124. (1929) 30 M.L.W. 691.
125. Under the Indian law adopted child is considered just like a natural born (*Aurasa*) child for all intents and purposes : s. 12, Hindu Adoptions and Maintenance Act, 1956.
126. *Re Beaumont*, (1893) 3 Ch. 490.

on the part of the mother, is not to be regarded as a necessary consequence of a change of the mother's domicile, but as the result of the exercise by her of a power vested in her for the welfare of the infants, which, in their interest, she may abstain from exercising, even when she changes her own domicile."[127]

Under the Indian law the domicile of the legitimate minor posthumous child is in the country in which his father was domiciled at the time of his death. The Indian law does not say that the domicile of a legitimate child whose father is dead will be that of the mother. It seems that Indian law fixes the domicile of legitimate child with its father and the domicile of an illegitimate child with the mother. If father or the mother, as the case may be, dies then the domicile of the child remains the same as it was at the death of the parent. This is what Dicey and Morris also seem to suggest. According to them : "The domicile of a legitimate or legitimated infant without living parents, or of an illegitimate infant without a living mother, probably cannot be changed."[128] In his comments the learned editor adds, "It is an open question whether the domicile of an infant without living parents can be changed by his guardian. There is no English authority on this point." Then after referring to certain views[129] he opines that the best view is that which is stated in the rule.[130]

The question whether a guardian can change the domicile of his ward arose in respect of refugee-children of Europe who came to England. These children had come all alone and it was not known who were their parents. England tided over the difficulties by passing the Guardianship (Refugee Children) Act, 1944 under which it was laid down that such children will be considered to be domiciled in England and Scotland.

In our contemporary world every act of guardianship is weighed on the scales of welfare of children. It is submitted that the rule should be that the domicile of an orphan child may be changed by his guardian with the prior permission of the court in the country in which the child is domiciled and further that no court will accord such permission unless it comes to the conclusion that the change would be for the welfare of the child.

Domicile of a child when parents have separated : If parents are living separate, legally or otherwise have obtained a decree of judicial

127. (1893) 3 Ch. 490 at 496-97.
128. Rule 12(4), 110.
129. Goodrich, s. 41: A distinction should be made between a natural guardian who has the power to change the infant's domicile, and others who do not have any such power. There is another view also : guardian should have the power to change the domicile of the child to the country in which he is recognized as guardian.
130. Dicey and Morris, 112.

separation, then the question arises: what is the domicile of the child, of the mother or of the father, and which of the parents have the right to change the domicile of the child ? The answer to this question has now been provided by the Domicile and Matrimonial Proceedings Act, 1973. The domicile of the child in this situation will continue to be the domicile of the father, but in the following cases it will be the domicile of the mother : (i) when the child is living with his mother and is not living with his father [Sec. 4(2)(a) uses the words, "child has his home with her and has no home with his father"], (ii) if he has acquired the domicile of the mother by virtue of his having lived with her, then he will continue to have his mother's domicile, even when he leaves his mother, provided he is not living with his father, and (iii) the child will continue to have his mother's domicile even after the death of the mother, if he acquired his mother's domicile by virtue of his having home with his mother, provided that he did not have his home with his father.[131] It is apparent that in the latter two cases, if the child lives with his father, i.e. makes a home with him, the child will again acquire the domicile of the father. In this regard the position of the adopted son is the same as that of the natural son. It seems to be also the inference that in the event of parents living separate, the child acquires the domicile of the mother only if he lives with her; if he does not live with her, he continues to have the domicile of the father, even if he is living with a relative or with a local authority, or even in those cases where the whereabouts of the father are not known.

In Indian law we have no answer to this question. It is submitted that the child should have the domicile of the parent in whose custody he is living, either under an order of the court or *de facto*, and it should be that parent who should have the right to change the domicile of the child. In case the other parent disputes this, the matter may be decided by the court, keeping this in view that the interest of the child is the paramount consideration.

Domicile of married minor child : Does the domicile of a minor child changes on his marriage ? Before January 1, 1974, the position in English law seems to have been this : a minor male child on marriage retained the domicile of his father or mother, i.e., its original domicile of dependency, while the minor female child acquired the domicile of her husband. Now under the Domicile and Matrimonial Proceedings Act, 1973, the position is that a person 'becomes capable of having an independent domicile when he attains the age of sixteen or marries under that age.'[132] This means that a minor child now attains capacity to acquire an independent domicile on marriage. This applies to both male and

131. See s. 4.
132. Section 3(1).

female minor children. The Indian law retains the position of English law as it was before January 1, 1974. Explanation to s. 14, Indian Succession Act, 1925, lays down : "The domicile of a minor does not change with that of his parents if the minor is married. . . ." The domicile of a minor female married child, under the Indian law, changes on her marriage, as on marriage she acquires the domicile of her husband.[133] It seems that if the husband is minor and therefore, has a domicile of dependency of either the father or mother, then the domicile of the minor married female child will be the same as that of her husband and will change with her husband's domicile. Even when she becomes a widow while a minor, her domicile will be that which her husband had when he died. She cannot acquire back her premarriage domicile of origin. Even when the minor widow becomes a major she would continue to have the domicile of her deceased husband, unless she acquires a domicile of choice.

Domicile of lunatics : In English private international law there is no direct authority on the domicile of lunatics. It seems that an independent person who becomes insane cannot change his domicile, as he is incapable of exercising any will. It seems that even his guardian cannot change it. Thus it seems that the lunatic will retain the domicile which he had when he became lunatic (i.e. when he began to be legally treated as insane) even if he goes to another country and settles there.[134] In the modern English law lunacy is categorized on the basis of degrees of mental disorder : some are treated informally, some are kept under guardianship, some are detained or liable to be detained compulsorily.[135] Should all these categories of lunatics be treated as 'dependent person' incapable of acquiring a new domicile ? It is submitted that if they have sufficient ability to form the necessary intention, they should be able to change their domicile. It is also submitted that those who are kept under guardianship should also be able to acquire a new domicile, if their guardian thinks it proper to do so. The guardian court or the court of protection should be able to accord permission to the guardian to do so whenever it is thought to be in the interest of the child.[136]

In Indian law we have a statutory provision in s. 18, Indian Succession Act, 1925 which runs : "An insane person cannot acquire a new domicile in any other way than by his domicile following the domicile of another person." The Act does not specify who this "another person" is. But it seems clear that if the lunatic is a minor then it is the parent on whom

133. Section 15, Succession Act, 1925.
134. *Urquhart* v. *Butterfield,* (1887) 37 Ch. D. 357; ***Hepburn*** v. ***Skirving,*** (1861) 9 W.R. 764.
135. See Mental Health Act, 1959.
136. This is also the suggestion of the Private International Law Committee : lunatic's domicile may be changed with the prior permission of the court of the domicile of the lunatic.

he is dependent and if lunatic is a married woman, then it is her husband. It is submitted that if the lunatic is a major and has a guardian, then this "another person" should be the guardian of the lunatic. There is no reason why Indian courts should follow the old English decision in *Urquhart* v. *Butterfield*[137] which lays down that a major lunatic's domicile remains static, i.e., it remains the same as it was at the time when he legally began to be treated as insane.

Commercial Domicile

The term "commercial domicile" is a misconception and is in no sense akin to domicile. It is a legal conception used in wartime as a test of enemy character. Foote called it "quasi domicile."[138] It denotes any person, natural or artificial, who resides voluntarily or carries on business in an enemy territory.[139] It includes a firm carrying on business in an enemy territory. It has nothing to do with the nationality of the person who resides there or trades there. He may be an Indian national or a national of a friendly country, or of neutral country or of enemy country. Sometimes even the property is attributed to have a commercial domicile so that it is made liable to seizure.

The distinguishing features of the two domiciles, viz., the domicile and the so-called commercial domicile are : (i) domicile attaches to a person all throughout his life, while the commercial domicile comes into effect only during war-time, (ii) *animo et facto* is essential in the case of domicile, while in the case of commercial domicile neither residence nor intention is necessary. A person may not reside in enemy territory, but if he trades there commercial domicile attaches to him, (iii) no person can have more than one domicile for one and the same purpose, but a person may have any number of commercial domiciles, and (iv) the commercial domicile is *sine animo revertendi* but a domicile is not lost unless a new one acquired.

137. (1887) 37 Ch. D. 357.
138. Foote, (5th ed.) 94.
139. *Porter* v. *Freudenberg*, (1915) 1 K.B. 857.

7

JURISDICTION OF COURTS

In its broadest sense jurisdiction connotes constitutional, legislative, executive and judicial jurisdiction. Jurisdiction is one of those areas where constitutional law, public international law and private international law converge. The legislative and executive aspects of jurisdiction fall more appropriately in the realm of private international law, as these relate to limitations on the territorial jurisdiction of states. The territorial jurisdiction of states and the jurisdictional limits of the municipal courts are still based on the territorial theory. According to this theory every state has jurisdiction over everything situated within and over every person present within the territories : *quid quid est in territorio es estian de territoria.*[1] In the oft-quoted words of Ellenbourgh, C.J., "Can the island of Tobago pass a law to bind the rights of the whole world ? Would the world submit to such an assumed jurisdiction."[2] To the rule that the municipal courts have jurisdiction over every person and every thing present within the jurisdiction, one exception is recognized, viz. foreign sovereigns, personnel of the diplomatic missions and international organizations and their personnel, enjoy jurisdictional immunity.

Sometimes, states purport to give extra-territorial effect to their laws and orders. To what extent effect can be given to them in public or private international law is difficult to say.[3] It is certain, as we have seen, the penal and revenue laws of foreign states having extra-territorial effect are not given effect to.[4] Another manifestation of the territorial theory is found in the principle of allegiance. This principle means that all citizens owe allegiance to their state and it is their duty to obey its laws and orders wherever they might be. This principle also means that all those persons who are present within the jurisdiction owe allegiance to the state.

1. *Sagoon Jayade Dhond* v. *Sociedade Civile e Particular da Taris de Volvvi*, 1966 Goa 38; *Buchanan* v. *Rucker*, (1800) 9 East 192.
2. *Buchanan* v. *Rucker*, (1800) 9 East 192.
3. For instance jurisdiction over continental shelfs. (The United Kingdom's Continental Shelf Act, 1964 extends the jurisdiction of English Courts over continental shelfs.)
4. See Chapter 6 of the work.

Nationality is a basis of jurisdiction in most of the countries of civil law system. Domicile has been the basis of jurisdiction in the common law system. The modern tendency is to substitute ordinary residence or habitual residence as basis of jurisdiction for domicile and nationality. In modern international conventions, habitual residence is being accepted as and alternative basis of jurisdiction.

The question of jurisdiction in private international law is different from the question of jurisdiction in public international law. In private international law jurisdiction means competency of the domestic courts to hear actions and render decisions in matters in which they are called upon to do so. In private international law most of the countries consider the question of jurisdiction as pertaining to procedural law. In an entirely internal suit the question of jurisdiction arises in a different manner. Ordinarily, a suit is to be filed in that court within whose jurisdiction the cause of action arose. This is the place element of jurisdiction. Another question that arises is as to which court, among the hierarchy of courts, can entertain a suit of that nature. This is the valuation element of the jurisdiction. For instance, for a claim amounting to Rs. 50,000 for a breach of contract committed in Chandigarh, the suit has to be filed in a Chandigarh Court and in a court which has jurisdiction to entertain suit of that valuation—this is the district court. In other words, the suit has to be filed in the court of District Judge, Chandigarh. On the other hand, if a suit has some foreign element, then another preliminary question arises : has the Indian Court jurisdiction to try the suit ? If the answer is in affirmative, then the further questions relating to jurisdiction will arise the same way as they arise in an internal suit. The question of jurisdiction in any action, much more in a case pertaining to conflicts of laws, is a primary question, without the determination of which the court cannot proceed further.

Two sets of questions arise. First, against whom an action can be filed, and who can file an action. Secondly, what types of actions may be filed. The actions that may be filed in a court of law may be, broadly, divided under three heads : (a) actions *inter partes* or personal actions, (b) actions relating to property, and (c) actions relating to status. In the last category of actions are included suits and petitions in matrimonial causes, guardianship, custody, adoption and legitimacy. The jurisdictional question in these matters would be discussed in the chapters dealing with these matters respectively.

I

AGAINST WHOM ACTIONS MAY BE FILED

Actions inter partes

A personal action or an action *in personam* or an action *inter partes* (the latter, it is submitted, is the most suitable term in respect of international actions of this type) is one by which rights of parties between themselves are adjudicated. The suit, in such actions may relate to obligations, such as payment of damages for breach of contract, or for a tort, or an action for recovery of debt. It also includes proceedings in equity.[5] The outstanding feature of an action *inter partes* is that it is binding on the parties to the action alone.

English Law

Under English law the courts have jurisdiction in an action *inter partes* if the defendant is served with process, irrespective of the fact that he is a foreigner or was casually present in England, such as a tourist or a person who is in transit. Once the process is served on the defendant the court has the jurisdiction to try the suit, even if the subject-matter of the suit is in no way connected with England. On the other hand, if process cannot be served on the defendant or the defendant evades it, then howsoever closely connected the subject-matter of the suit may be with England, English court cannot try the suit.

In respect of actions *inter partes* the court may have jurisdiction in the following situations :

(1) When the defendant is present within the jurisdiction.

(2) When the court assumes jurisdiction against an absentee defendant.

(3) When the defendant submits to the jurisdiction.

The Presence of the Defendant within the Jurisdiction

If the defendant is present within the jurisdiction the summons can be served on him. Once the summons are served on him the court undisputedly has the jurisdiction over the suit. But if the defendant is brought within jurisdiction by fraud or force, then the service of summon on him is not valid and will be quashed.[6]

The rule is based on the principle that whosoever is present within the realm, citizen or foreigner, owes allegiance to the sovereign. Allegiance denotes that all those persons who are within the frontiers of a state are required to obey all orders and are bound by the laws of the state. If a citizen or foreigner successfully evades the service of the process the court cannot exercise jurisdiction in the suit.

It may be emphasized that under this rule mere presence of the

5. In *Tayler* v. *Judges of the Court of Registration*, (1900), 175 Mass 171, Holmes, J. defined thus : "If the technical object of the suit is to establish a claim against some particular person . . . or to bar some individual claim or objection, so that only certain persons are entitled to be heard in defence, the action is *in personam*, although it may concern the right to, or the possession of, a tangible thing."

6. *Watkins* v. *North American Land Co.*, (1904) 20 T.L.R. 534 (H.L.).

defendant is enough.[7] His residence within the jurisdiction is not required. Even if he leaves the country after the process is served on him, the court will continue to have jurisdiction in that suit.[7a] For instance, in respect of some money-lending transactions between an American and a Russian some dispute arose in Paris. The American filed a suit in an English court. While the Russian was going to New Delhi, his plane stopped over in London, the American got the process served on him. The court will have jurisdiction.[8]

Under English law it is necessary that process must be served personally on each defendant by the plaintiff or his agent.[9] In certain circumstances a substituted service may be enough. In 1915 Lord Reading adverted to two sets of such circumstances : (a) when the court is satisfied that the defendant went outside the jurisdiction before the issue of the writ in order to evade it, and (b) if the defendant went out of jurisdiction after the issue of the writ although not for the purpose of evading the service, and the court is satisfied that the issue of the writ came to his knowledge before he went out of jurisdiction and special circumstances show that such substituted service will be just.[10]

Can English courts exercise jurisdiction over a natural person, who, though not personally present within the jurisdiction, carries on business or trade in England ? Rules 2 to 9, Order 81, of the Rules of the Supreme Court suggest an answer in affirmative. However, Morris takes the view that the answer must be in the negative. "If the defendant is not in England, whether he is, e.g. an American, a domiciled Scotman or (it is submitted) an Englishman, the jurisdiction of the court is not extended by his use in England of a trade name."[11]

The position of firms and corporations is different. In respect of firms Order 81, rule 1 lays down, "Any two or more persons claiming to be entitled, or alleged to be liable, as partners in respect of a cause of action and carrying on business [in England] may sue or be sued in the name of the firm (if any) of which they were partners at the time when the cause of action accrued." This rule applies to all partners, Englishmen or foreigners, etc. resident or non-resident. The rule applies only to partners who are carrying on business in England, and are carrying it in a firm name. Under rule 3 of Order 81 process may be served on any one or more of the partners, or at the principal place of business of the partnership in England on any person having the control or management of

7. *Colt Industries Incorporated* v. *Sarlie*, (1966) 1 W.L.R. 440; *Maharanee of Baroda* v. *Wildenestein*, (1972) 2 All E.R. 689 (These cases are discussed in Chapter 24, "Stay of Actions").

7a. *Razelos* v. *Razelos* (No. 2), (1970) 1 All E.R. 386.

8. For criticism, see Cheshire, p. 76.

9. Order 10, rr, 1(1), 5.

10. For criticism, see Dicey and Morris, p. 172.

11. Dicey and Morris, p. 171. He suggests that in such a case one may proceed under Order 11.

the firm's business; and in such a case the process is deemed to have been duly served on the firm, whether or not any member of the firm is outside England. But the execution of an order or decree can be made only against the property of the firm which is in England or against the property in England of partners who are served in England, or who submit to court's jurisdiction or who are served abroad under Order 11.[12] As to the service of process on corporations, see Chapter 13.

Assumed Jurisdiction of English Courts

In the middle of nineteenth century it was felt that the common law rules relating to jurisdiction were insufficient to meet the need of the times. In many matters the common law courts were helpless as they had no jurisdiction over them. For instance, if a person committed a breach of English contract or committed a tort in England, the courts were helpless and could not entertain any action if the defendant was outside the jurisdiction. To meet such situation rules were made from time to time. Ultimately these rules were consolidated in, what is known as, Order 11 of the Supreme Court Rules. Under Order 11, no court is bound to entertain an action even if it is covered under it. The court has discretion to accord or refuse to accord permission to entertain an action. Clauses (a) to (i) of rule 1 of Order 11 embody some of the exceptional cases where the English court may order service out of jurisdiction, i.e. out of England, of a writ of summons, or notice of a writ of summons on a defendant who is neither present within the jurisdiction nor has submitted to it. Thus, jurisdiction may be assumed :

(1) Where the whole of subject-matter is land situated within the jurisdiction.[13] An action for recovery of land is an obvious illustration of this rule.[14]

(2) Where any act, deed, will, contract, obligation or liability affecting land within the jurisdiction is sought to be construed, rectified, set aside or enforced in an action.[15] This rule has caused some difficulties as to its precise scope. It seems this rule will apply only when something directly affects the land itself and not its value.[16]

(3) Where any relief is sought against any person or corporation domiciled or ordinarily resident within the

12. See O. 81, r. 5.
13. Rule 1(a).
14. *Agnew* v. *Usher*, (1884) 14 Q.B.D. 78.
15. Rule 1(b).
16. *Casey* v. *Arnott*, (1876) 2 C.P.D. 24; *Tassel* v. *Hallen*, (1892) 1 Q.B. 321 (action against the assignee of a lease for breach of covenant to repair is included); *Kaye* v. *Sutherland*, (1887) 20 Q.B.D. 147 (so also a claim by tenant of a farm to recover compensation for improvement). But the claim does not include an action for recovery of rent : *Agnew* v. *Usher*, (1884) 14 Q.B.D. 78.

jurisdiction.[17] Residence here means habitual as distinct from temporary or casual.[18] This is an exception of very wide ambit.[19]

(4) Where the action begun by the writ is for the administration of the estate of a person who died domiciled in England, or if the action begun by the writ is for any relief or remedy which might be obtained in any such action as aforesaid.[20]

(5) Where the action begun by writ is for the execution as to property situate in England, of the trusts of a written instrument, being trusts that ought to be executed according to English law and of which the person to be served with the writ is a trustee or if the action begun by the writ is for any relief or remedy which might be obtained in any such action as aforesaid.[21] For the application of the rule some property subject to trust must be situated in England ; if the trustee had sold out the property situated in England and departed abroad, the rule does not apply.[22]

(6) Where the action is one brought against a defendant not domiciled or ordinarily resident in Scotland to enforce, rescind, dissolve, annul, or otherwise affect a contract, or to recover damages or obtain other relief for, or in respect of, the breach of a contract which was either (i) made in England, or (ii) made by or through an agent trading or residing in England on behalf of a principal trading or residing out of England, or (iii) by its terms or by implication is to be governed by English law.[23]

(7) Where the action is one brought against a defendant not domiciled or ordinarily resident in Scotland or Northern Ireland in respect of a breach committed in England of a contract made in or out of England, even though such breach was preceded or accompanied by a breach out of England which rendered impossible the performance of the part of the contract which ought to have been performed in England [Rule 1(f)]. This rule applies to four types of cases : (a) where the contract is made in England

17. Rule 1(c).
18. *Levene* v. *Inland Revenue Commissioner*, (1928) A.C. 217.
19. In *re Liddel's Settlement Trusts*, (1936) Ch. 365. See also *Jones* v. *Scottish Insurance Co.*, (1886) 17 Q.B.D. 421; *Watkins* v. *Scottish Imperial Co.*, (1889) 23 Q.B.D. 285. A company registered in Scotland and carrying on business in England, is not covered by the rule, though process may be served on it at its place of business in England; Companies Act, 1948, s. 437(2), (3).
20. Rule 1(d).
21. Rule 1(e).
22. *Winter* v. *Winter*, (1894) 1 Ch. 421.
23. Rule 1(b); See *B.P. Exploration Co.* v. *Hunt* (1976) 1 W.L.R. 788.

and where the defendant is neither domiciled nor ordinarily resident in Scotland. This includes quasi-contract.[24] A contract made in England for employment abroad is an obvious example. An action for breach of contract or an action in tort will lie under this rule;[25] (b) where the contract is made by or through an agent trading or residing in England, provided that the defendant is neither domiciled nor ordinarily resident in Scotland;[26] (c) where the contract is by its terms or by implication to be governed by English law, provided that the defendant is neither domiciled nor ordinarily resident in Scotland. In other words, where the proper law of contract is English law, this rule is applicable;[27] (d) where the action is in respect of a breach which has in fact been committed in England of a contract wherever made, even though the English breach has been preceded by breach abroad which rendered that part of the contract which ought to have been performed in England impossible of performance.[28]

(8) Where the action is based on a tort committed in England.[29]

(9) Where an injunction is sought ordering the defendant to do or refrain from doing something in England, whether damages are or are not sought in respect thereof.[30] The main relief should be injunction and injunction should not be incidental to main relief.[31] If another court can deal with it more conveniently, then leave will not be granted.[32]

(10) Where in an action, begun by the writ, properly brought against a person duly served in England, a person out of

24. *Rousou's Trustee* v. *Rousou*, (1955) 3 All E.R. 486.
25. *Matthews* v. *Kuwait Bechtel Corporation*, (1959) 2 Q.B. 57; *Bermer Oeltransport* v. *Drewry*, (1933) 1 K.B. 753 (an action to enforce foreign arbitration award in respect of a contract made in England).
26. *National Mortgage & Agency Co. of New Zealand* v. *Gosselin*. (1922) 38 T.L.R. 832 (rule is applicable even if the agent has no authority to effect a completed contract).
27. *N.V. Kwik Hoo Tong Handel Maatschappij* v. *Finlay & Co.*, (1927) A.C. 604; *Ocean Steamship Co.* v. *Queensland State Wheat Board*, (1941) 1 K.B. 402.
28. See *Vitkovice Horni a Hutni Tezirstvo* v. *Korner*, (1951) A.C. 869. Three conditions must be satisfied : there must be a contract, it must be broken, and breach must occur in England. See also *International Corporation Ltd.* v. *Besser Manufacturing Co.*, (1950) 1 K.B. 488.
29. Rule 1(b), *Kroch* v. *Rossell et Cie*, (1937) 1 All E.R. 725 (tort must have substantial connection with England). See also *George Monro & Co. Ltd.* v. *American Cyanamid Corp.*, (1944) 1 K.B. 432.
30. Rule 1(i).
31. *Rosler* v. *Hilbery*, (1925) 1 Ch. 250.
32. *Societe Generale de Paris* v. *Dreyfus*, (1887) 37 Ch. D. 215.

England is a necessary or proper party thereto.[33] The defendant in England must not be a mere dummy.[34] The following three conditions are necessary for the application of the rule : (i) there must be an action properly brought against the defendant who is the main party to the suit,[35] (ii) the main defendant must be duly served, and (iii) the second defendant who is out of England must be either a necessary or a proper party.[36]

(11) Where an action begun by the writ is either (a) by a mortgagee of property (other than land) situated in England and seeks the sale of the property, or the foreclosure of the mortgage or delivery by the mortgagor of possession of the property but not an order for payment of money due under the mortgage, or (b) by a mortgagor of property (other than land) so situated and seeks redemption of the mortgage or reconveyance of property or delivery by the mortgagee of possession of the property, but not a personal judgment.[37]

(12) Where an action is brought under the Carriage by Air Act, 1961,[38] the Carriage of Goods by Road Act, 1965, the Merchant Shipping (Oil Pollution) Act, 1971 or the Nuclear Installation Act, 1965.

The Carriage by Air Act, 1961 (originally it was the Carriage by Air Act, 1931 which incorporated provisions of the Warsaw Convention, 1929—the convention was amended at The Hague in 1955—relating to uniform rules for international carriage of persons or goods by air for reward), *inter alia*, relates to claims of damages in international carriage of goods and passengers. Under the Act an action for damages may be brought at the option of the plaintiff in the territory of one of the high contracting parties to the Warsaw Convention at any one of the following places (and at nowhere else) : (a) before the court at the place of the destination, or (b) before the court of the place where the carrier ordinarily resides or has his principal place of business or has an establishment by which the contract has been made.[39] The Carriage by Air (Supplementary Provisions) Act, 1962 was enacted to implement the Guadalajara Convention of 1961 which is a supplemental convention to the main Warsaw Convention. Under the original convention only the airline which made the contract could

33. 1(i)(g).
34. *Witted* v. *Gallbraith*, (1893) 1 K.B. 577.
35. *Tyne Improvement Commissioners* v. *Armement Anversois S.A.* (1949) A.C. 326.
36. *Williams* v. *Cartwright*, (1895) 1 Q.B. 142 (C.A.).
37. Rule 1(i)(k).
38. As well as under the Carriage by Air (Supplementary Provisions) Act, 1962.
39. Rule 1(i)(l).

be sued, but now the "actual carrier" can also be sued. In addition to the places where the action can be brought against the original airline, an action against "actual carrier" can also be brought where the actual carrier is ordinarily resident or has his principal place of business.[40]

The Carriage of Goods by Road Act, 1965 gives effect to the International Convention on the Carriage of Goods by Road signed at Geneva in 1956. An action in respect of international carriage of goods and passengers can be filed in any court or tribunal of any country within whose territory (a) the defendant is ordinarily resident, or has his principal place of business, or a branch or agency through which the contract of carriage was entered into is situated, or (b) the place where the goods were taken over by the carrier or the place designated for delivery is situated. Leave to serve the carrier out of jurisdiction has to be obtained. In addition to these places, an action may be brought in the tribunals and courts of the country (which is party to the Convention) which is designated by agreement between the parties.

The Merchant Shipping (Oil Pollution) Act, 1971 has been enacted to give effect to the Brussels Convention on Civil Liability for Oil Pollution Damage, 1969. Under the Convention action for damages can be filed in the courts of contracting state in which damage occurred. Under the Act civil liability is imposed on owner of a ship from which oil has been persistently discharged or escaped. It provides for compulsory insurance against liability for oil pollution damage, and lays down for a direct action against the insurer.

In connection with carriage by rail three international conventions exist, viz., the Berne Convention Concerning the Carriage of Goods by Rail, 1961, the Berne Convention Concerning the Carriage of Passengers and Luggage by Rail, 1961 and the Additional Convention relating to Liability for Death of and Personal Injury to Passengers, 1966. The last Convention deals with : (i) liability for loss, damage or delay to goods, (ii) liability for loss, damage or delay to registered luggage, and (iii) liability for death of or personal injury to passengers and for loss of their hand luggage. Obviously the Conventions apply to international carriages. The English statute, the Carriage by Rail Act, 1972, gives effect to the third Convention, and s. 6(1) lays down that no action of any kind in respect of liability arising under the first two Conventions can be brought except in accordance with the Conventions. Under the Conventions jurisdiction is conferred on the courts of the state to which the defendant railway belongs. Under the third Convention the railway operating the line on which the accident occurs is liable. If the rail is operated by two or more railways, both of them are liable.

40. Article VIII of the Schedule to the Act.

The Nuclear Installation Act, 1965 gives effect to the Paris Convention on the Third Party Liability in the field of Nuclear Energy, 1960, the Brussels Convention, 1963, the Vienna Convention, 1963. The Act imposes absolute liability on the operators (including certain foreign operators) of nuclear installations for "nuclear occurrences" causing injury to any person or damage to any property of any person other than the operator. Under the Convention jurisdiction, *prima facie*, vests only in the courts of the contracting party within whose territory the nuclear incident occurred. However, if the nuclear incident occurred outside the territory of any contracting party, if the place of the nuclear incident cannot be determined with certainty, jurisdiction vests in the courts of the contracting party in whose territory the nuclear installation of the operator liable is situated. In case the jurisdiction lies with more than one contracting parties, then if incident occurred partly within the territory of a single contracting party and partly outside the territory of any contracting party, then jurisdiction lies with the courts of the former. In any other case the jurisdiction lies with the courts of that contracting party which is determined by agreement between contracting parties whose courts will be competent.

Under both the statutes if the defendant-carrier or the defendant-nuclear-operator is a foreign government, and if the foreign government is a party to the convention concerned, it shall be deemed that the foreign government has submitted to the jurisdiction of the court.

(13) Where an action begun by the writ is in respect of a contract which contains a term to the effect that the court shall have jurisdiction to hear and determine any action in respect of the contract.[41]

(14) Where a claim for damages, loss of life or personal injury arising out of collision or like navigational incident involving two or more ships, if (but only if), (a) the defendant has his habitual residence or a place of business within England, or (b) the cause of action arose within inland waters of England or within the limits of an English port, or (c) an action arising out of the same incident is proceeding in the court or has been heard and determined in the court, or (d) the defendant has submitted or agreed to submit to the jurisdiction of the court.[42]

Since the United Kingdom is now party to many international conventions and since it has enacted several statutes to give them effect, it seems to be obvious that no English court can exercise

41. Order 11, r. 2.

42. Order 75, r. 4 which is based on s. 4, Administration of Justice Act, 1956 which was enacted to give effect to the International Convention on Certain Rules Concerning Civil Jurisdiction in Matters of Collusion; see *The World Harmony*, (1967) p. 341.

jurisdiction in respect of any matter arising under them unless the jurisdictional requirement of the statute concerned are satisfied. Thus no English court will have jurisdiction to entertain an action brought under the carriage by Air Act, 1961, the Carriage by Air (Supplementary Provisions) Act, 1962, the Carriage of Goods by Road Act, 1965, the Merchant Shipping (Oil Pollution) Act, 1971 or the Carriage by Rail Act, 1972 unless the jurisdiction requirements of statute concerned are satisfied. The Administration of Justice Act, 1956, s. 6 lays down that no English court will have jurisdiction to entertain an action in respect of a claim or question which is certified under statutory powers by Minister to be a claim or question which under an international convention falls to be determined by a court in some foreign country.

Civil Jurisdiction and Judgment Act, 1982

When in an International Contract, the contract is found to be void, while court would have jurisdiction. This question arose in *Bardays Bank* v. *Glassgow City Council* etc.[42a] The matter related to the new type of financial transaction known as swap contracts. These were found to be void. A claim was made for the return of money on the basis of the doctrine of unjust enrichment. A claim was quasi-contractual. The English Court held that it had jurisdiction of decide the matter in terms of EEC Treaty so as to ensure uniformity of interpretation. *Trade Indemnity* v. *Forsakringatle Bololaget Nirorad*,[42b] has also reference to Act of 1982. The dispute was whether in the case of breach of contract, the court is bound to take jurisdiction on the basis of place of performance or on the basis of *forum conventions*. The Court decided in favour of the latter view.

The suit should be tried in the forum which is more suitable for parties interest and end of justice.[42c]

Indian Law

In India rules relating to jurisdiction in action *inter partes* are laid down in ss. 19 and 20 of the Civil Procedure Code. Section 19 is confined to suit for compensation for wrongs to person or movables. That section runs as under:

> "Where a suit is for compensation for wrong done to the person or to movable property, if the wrong was done within the local limits of the jurisdiction of one court and the defendant resides or carries on business, or personally work for gain within the local limits of the jurisdiction of another court, the suit may be instituted at the option of the plantiff in either of the said courts."

This section is confined to torts committed in India and to defendants residing in India. It does not include within its ambit the suits in respect of foreign torts.[43] Such cases are covered by s. 20 which overlaps this section. Section 20 deals with all other *inter partes* suits. That section runs:

> "Subject to the limitations aforesaid, every suit shall be instituted in a court within the local limits of whose jurisdiction
>
> (a) the defendant, or each of the defendants where there are more than one,

42a. (1994) 4 All ER 865.
42b. (1995) 1 All ER 796.
42c. *Trade Indemnity etc.* v. *Forsakringsa Ktiebolaget Nijod*, (1995) All ER 798.
43. *Govindan Nair* v. *Achutha Menon*, (1916) 39 Mad. 433.

at the time of commencement of the suit, actually and voluntarily resides, or carries on business, or personally works for gain; or

(b) any of the defendants, where there are more than one, at the time of commencement of suit, actually and voluntarily resides, or carries on business, or personally work for gain, provided that in such case either the leave of the court is given, or the defendant who do not reside, or carry on business, or personally work for gain, as aforesaid, acquiesce in such institution; or

(c) the cause of action, wholly or in part, arises.

Explanation—Where a person has a permanent dwelling at one place and also a temporary residence at another place, he shall be deemed to reside at both places in respect of any cause of action arising at the place where he has such temporary residence."

Under s. 20, the Indian courts can exercise jurisdiction in *inter partes* actions in the following four circumstances:

(1) when the permanent or temporary residence of the defendant is within the jurisdiction,
(2) If the defendant is engaged in some business within the jurisdiction,
(3) If the defendant is working for gain within the jurisdiction,
(4) if the cause of action, wholly or in part, arises within the jurisdiction.[43a]

It is submitted that the Indian court should not construe strictly the requirement of residence in private international law cases, nor should it exercise jurisdiction over persons on whom process has not been served just because cause of action arises within jurisdiction. It may be interesting to note that these provisions have been so interpreted by the Indian courts that rules of Indian Private International Law are almost identical with the rules of English Private International Law.

In 1894 the Privy Council got its first opportunity to expound the rules of Indian private international law with respect to jurisdiction in *inter partes actions*.[44] Their Lordships of the Privy Council said that jurisdiction, "being properly territorial and attaching, with certain restrictions, upon every person permanently or temporarily resident within the territory, does not follow a foreigner, after his withdrawal thence, and living in another state. Nor to the courts of state in which the cause of action has arisen, nor in cases of contract to those of the *locus solutionis*, should resort be had by the plantiff, but to the courts of the state in which the defendant resides, *the courts of the latter state having jurisdiction in all personal actions*" (emphasis author's). The case related to recognition and enforcement of foreign judgment against a defendant who was neither resident of the state the court of which rendered the judgment nor did he submit to jurisdiction of the court. From very beginning the Indian courts have adhered to the doctrine of territoriality. Time and again they have said that the power to determine the place at which a particular class of action should be tried vests exclusively in the legislature.

Residence or presence within the jurisdiction: It is a well established rule of Indian law, both of international law and international

43a. *Md. Abdulla* v. *P.M. Abdul Rahim*, 1985 Mad. 375.

44. *Gurdial Singh* v. *Raja of Faridkot*, (1894) 22 Cal. 222.

law, that if the defendant is resident within the jurisdiction the court will have jurisdiction to entertain the suit. But the question is whether the presence of the defendant within the jurisdiction will be enough to confer jurisdiction? In 1899, in *Kasinath* v. *Anant*[45] the question came before the Bombay High Court. Under a contract and usage the plaintiff and the defendant were entitled to share the income of the property situated outside the jurisdiction. The defendant was collecting the income of the property. On defendant's refusal to give the share, the plantiff filed a suit for the recovery of the same. The defendant was not residing within the jurisdiction, though he was present there at the time of the suit. The Bombay High Court said that though under the provisions of the Civil Procedure Code, the court has no jurisdiction, but since Indian courts in such matters follow English law and since English courts have jurisdiction in such a case, Indian courts too have jurisdiction. This rule of English private international law was again followed in *Fernandes* v. *Ray*.[46] The defendant was a political agent in the then Kolhapur State. As he was proceeding on one month's leave to London, he reached Bombay on March 3 and was waiting there to leave for London. On March 8, the plantiff filed a suit for damages and compensation in respect of some tort and got the service done on him. The defendant left Bombay on March 10 on his way to England. The question was : would five days' stay of defendant in Bombay, confer jurisdiction on the Court? Tyabji, J. said that 'residence' may be used in a very wide sense or in a very narrow sense, depending upon the intention of the legislature. As far as court's jurisdiction is concerned, it is a settled law that if a person has no settled abode or residence, then he is deemed to be resident at the place where he is. The learned judge then observed that the defendant had left his Kolhapur residence and had not established residence anywhere else. At the time of the suit he was in Bombay and therefore he would be deemed to be resident of Bombay for the purpose of court's jurisdiction.

Clause 12 of the Letters Patent also confer jurisdiction on the High Courts on the basis of residence of the defendant within the jurisdiction. This clause has come for interpretation in several cases and the courts have said that temporary residence or mere presence of the defendant is enough to confer jurisdiction. In *Srinivas* v. *Venkata Varda Ayyangar*[47] the defendant had come to Madras for one year as an apprentice to a Vakil of the High Court with a view to becoming a Vakil. At the time of the suit he was within the jurisdiction. The Madras High Court said that the court had jurisdiction to try the suit. Again, following English law, a full Bench of the Madras High Court said that the court will have jurisdiction if the defendant was resident or present in

45. (1899) Bom. 407.
46. 21 Bom. 373.
47. (1906) 29 Mad. 239.

the country at the time of the suit.[48] In *T.H.P. De Silva* v. *S. Soosai Pillai Morais*[49] the defendant had gone to Trivandrum voluntarily for the purpose of business and proposed to stay there for three months. A suit was filed and service was got affected on him when he was so staying there. The court held that it had jurisdiction to try the suit. In *Seth Chand Mull* v. *Purushothamdoss*[50] the court observed that when the jurisdiction of the court is invoked against a subject of a foreign state on the ground that by coming within the physical boundaries of jurisdiction of the court, he is liable to be sued as if he were a subject, a duty is cast upon the court to be as zealous in safeguarding his liberties as if he were for all purposes a subject of His Majesty.[51] The High Courts have, in their Letters Patent jurisdiction, exercised jurisdiction on the basis of mere presence of the defendant within the jurisdiction.

Defendant being engaged in some business within the jurisdiction

This has been the consistent view of Indian courts that if the defendant is carrying on business personally or through an agent, then the Indian courts have jurisdiction, irrespective of the fact whether cause of action did not arise within the jurisdiction or that the defendant was not present within the jurisdiction. In *Sriniwas* v. *Venkata Varda Ayyangar*[52] the court said that the actual presence of a person who had come on business within the jurisdiction of a court is enough to invest the court with jurisdiction.[53] In *Chunnilal Kasturchand* v. *Dundappa Danappa*[54] the Bombay High Court said that the right of resorting to the court of one country for the enforcement of the cause of action arising in another country depends upon municipal law of the country where the suit is brought. Sections 15 to 20 of the Civil Procedure Code regulate the forum for the institution of suits in his country. In respect of suits *inter partes* s. 20 clearly confers jurisdiction on the court in cases where the defendant carries on business within the jurisdiction even if the cause of action arises outside it. In *Haveli Shah* v. *Khan Sahib Shaikh Painda Khan*,[55] where the cause of action against the defendant residing in Punjab arose in Perisa but the defendant carried on business in Quetta (then in India), the Privy Council held that the defendant could be sued in Quetta. This case was followed by the Punjab High Court in *Frontier Bank Ltd.* v. *Shrimati Prakash Wati Bahl*,[56] where one Prakash Wati Bahl, the plaintiff, deposited a sum of Rs. 2,050 with the Frontier

48. *Muthukammi Mudaliar* v. *Andappa Pillai* 1955 Mad. 96.
49. 1954 T.C. 141.
50. 1926 Mad. 584.
51. See also *John Baptist D'Souza* v. *Lizzie Jane Lobo*, 1940 Mad. 584.
52. (1906) 29 Mad. 239.
53. This case was followed by the Travancore-Cochin High Court in *T.P.H. De Silva* v. *S. Soosai Pillai Morasis*, 1954 T.C. 141.
54. 1951 Bom. 190.
55. 1926 P.C. 88.
56. I.L.R. (1950) Punjab 635.

Bank at Dera Ismail Khan, a limited company with its headquarters at Dera Ismail Khan. When, on the wake of partition of India, communal disturbances broke out in 1947, she asked the bank to transfer her account to New Delhi. The Bank failed to comply with her request and on January 10, 1950, she brought the present suit for the recovery of a sum of Rs. 4,000 against the Frontier Bank at Delhi. Rejecting the objection of the defendant bank that the court has no jurisdiction, the Delhi Bench of the Punjab High Court said that the case was already covered by Explanation II to s. 20, C.P.C. A full Bench of the Andhra Pradesh High Court also took this view.[57] It has also been held that if the defendant is carrying on business through an agent within the jurisdiction then the court has jurisdiction to entertain the suit.[58]

If cause of action wholly in part arises within the jurisdiction: the Privy Council in *Gurudayal Singh* v. *Raja of Faridkot*[59] said that the action lies in the court within whose jurisdiction the defendant resides and if the defendant has left the jurisdiction the court cannot try the suit even if the cause of action arose within the jurisdiction. Our High Courts have distinguished this case and have held that if cause of action arises within the jurisdiction the courts have jurisdiction to entertain the suit. As early as 1901 the Bombay High Court said that under the Civil Procedure Code[60] courts are empowered to pass judgment against a non-resident foreigner provided that the cause of action arose within the jurisdiction.[61] The Patna High Court rightly observed that according to the principle of private international law a court has no jurisdiction to entertain a suit against a foreigner who did not permanently or temporarily reside within its jurisdiction or who had not submitted to its jurisdiction. But, the court added, if the legislature confers jurisdiction upon the court situated in a particular territory to entertain suit against foreigners, where cause of action, wholly or partly, arises within its jurisdiction,

57. *H. Ahmed & Co.* v. *Kohinoor Glass Factory Ltd.* 1961 A.P. 470 (F.B.).
58. *Girdhar Damodar* v. *Kassigar Hiragar*, (1893) 17 Bom. 662; *Janoo Hassan* v. *Ahmad Esa*, 1924 Mad. 158.
59. (1894) 22 Cal. 222.
60. Then Act XIV of 1882.
61. *Ram Bhat* v. *Shankar Baswant*, (1902) 25 Bom. 528; the same view was expressed in earlier cases, *Kessowji* v. *Khimji*, (1888) 12 Bom. 507; *Hargopal* v. *Abdul*, (1872) 9 Bom. H.C.R. 429; *Rambhat* v. *Shankar Baswant*, (1901) 25 Bom. 528; *Girdhar Damodar* v. *Kassigar Hiragar*, (1893) 17 Bom. 662; cases under clause 12 of the Letters Patent, where the words are substantially the same. The Bombay High Court expressed this view later on also in *Chunni Lal* v. *Dundappa Damappa*, 1951 Bom. 190. The Allahabad High Court has also taken this view : *V.E. Smith* v. *Indian Textile Co.*, 1927 All. 413; *Gaekwar Baroda State Railway* v. *Sheikh Habib Ullah*, 1934 All. 740; *K.E.P. Venkatachalam Pillai* v. *Rajaballi*, 1935 Mad. 663; *Swaminathan Chettier* v. *V.E.N. K.R.M.V.R.M. Somasundaram*, 1938 Mad. 731; *Rajabai Narain* v. *Haji Karim* 35 M.L.J. 189; *Annamalai Chetty* v. *Murugasa Chetty*, (1903) 26 Mad. 544 (P.C.). She also, *Patel Kala Bechar* v. *Patel Mohan Bhagwan*, 1953 Sau. 16.

then such a court has jurisdiction.[62] It is a different matter that the foreign courts may refuse to enforce the judgments passed in such actions.[63]

Thus, we find that under Indian law the courts have power to assume jurisdiction even when the defendant is outside the jurisdiction if cause of action partly or wholly arises in India.

In respect of sevice of summons on defendants who are outside India, the Civil Procedure Code makes several rules. These are : (1) Service of summons may be made on the agent of the defendant appointed to accept service of process. Rule 6 of Order 3 provides that any person residing within the jurisdiction of the court may be appointed an agent to accept service of process. Such appointment may be special or general and shall be made by an instrument in writing signed by the principal, and such instrument or, if the appointment is general, a certified copy thereof, shall be filed in court. Service of process may also be made on 'recognized agent' of the defendant. Recognized agents of the party are : "(a) persons holding power-of-attorney, authorizing them to make and do such appearance, applications and acts on behalf of such parties, and (b) persons carrying on trade or business for and in the names of parties not resident within the local limits of the jurisdiction of the court within whose limits appearance, application or act is made or done, in matters connected with such trade or business only where no other agent is expressly authorised to make any and do such appearance, application and acts."[64] Rule 12 of Order 5 lays down : "Wherever it is practicable, service shall be made on the defendant in person unless has an agent empowered to accept service, in which case service on such agent shall be sufficient." Rule 13 of Order 5 provides : "In a suit relating to any business or work against a person who does not reside within the local limits of the jurisdiction of the court from which summon is issued, service on any manager or agent, who, at the time of service, personally carries on such business or work for such person within such limits, shall be deemed good service." "For the purpose of this rule the master of a ship shall be deemed to be agent of the owner or charterer." Rule 14 of Order 5 relates to the service of summons when suit is in respect of immovable property. The Rule runs : "Where in a suit to obtain relief respecting, or compensation for wrong to, immovable property, service cannot be made on the defendant in person, and

62. *Suresh Narayan Sinha* v. *Akhauri Balbhadra Prasad*, 1957 Pat. 256. Similar observations were made : *Gaekwar Baroda State Railway* v. *Sheikh Habib Ullah*, 1934 All. 740.

63. *Brajmohan Bose* v. *Kishori Lal Kishan Lal*, 1958 M.B. 1. Similar observations were made by the Madras High Court in *Rajabai Narayan* v. *Haji Karim*, 35 M.L.J. 189, the court observed that whether its decree could be enforced against him in the foreign state is a question for disposal of that state. See also *Neelakanda Pillai* v. *Kisuju Pillai*, 68 M.L.J. 506.

64. Order 3, r. 2.

the defendant has no agent empowered to accept service, it may be made on any agent of the defendant in charge of the property." Rule 15 lays down that where the defendant cannot be found or is absent from his residence,[65] and has no agent empowered to accept service of the summons on his behalf, service may be made on any adult male member of the family of the defendant who is residing with him.

Rule 20 provides for substituted service. It runs : "Where the court is satisfied that there is reason to believe that the defendant is keeping out of the way for the purpose of avoiding servive, or that for any other reason the summons cannot be served in the ordinary way, the court shall order the summons to be served by affixing a copy thereof in some conspicuous place in the court house, and also upon some conspicuous part of the house (if any) in which the defendant is known to have last resided or carried on business or personally worked for gain, or in such other manner as the court thinks fit." Rule 20A provides for service of summons by post. The Rule runs : "Where, for any reason whatsoever, the summon is returned unserved, the court may, either in lieu of, or in addition to the manner provided for service of summons in the foregoing rules, direct the summons to be served by registered post addressed to the defendant or his agent empowered to accept service at the place where the defendant or his agent ordinarily resides or carries on business or personally works for gain."

The aforesaid rules are mainly made in regard to domestic suits, but in the given circumstances they can also be used in respect of foreigners. For instance, if a foreigner has been living in India, or has been doing business in India or has been personally working for gain, or his family has been living in India or his immovable property is situated in India, then any one of the above rules can come into application. In case a foreigner is not covered by any one of the above cases, then Rule 25 provides for service of summons on him. First paragraph, Rule 25 runs as under : "Where the defendant resides out of India and has no agent in India empowered to accept service, the summons shall be addressed to the defendant at the place where he is residing and sent to him by post, if there is a postal communication between such place and the place where the court is situate." Two provisos to Rule 25 contain special rules in respect of foreigners residing in Pakistan. They are : (a) Where any defendant resides in Pakistan, the summons, together with a copy thereof, may be sent for service on the defendant, to any court in that country, not being the High Court, having jurisdiction in the place where the defendant resides; (b) where any defendant is a public officer in Pakistan not belonging to the Pakistan military, naval or air force, or is a servant of a railway company or local authority in that country, the summons together with a copy thereof, may be

65. Punjab, Himachal Pradesh and Madras.

sent for service on the defendant, to such officer or authority in that country as the Central Government may, by notification in the Official Gazette, specify in this behalf.

Rule 26 provides for service in foreign territory through political agent or court. The rule runs : (a) where in the exercise of any foreign jurisdiction vested in the Central Government, a Political Agent has been appointed, or court has been established or continued, with power to serve a summon issued by a court under this code in any foreign territory in which the defendant resides, or (b) the State Government has, by notification in the Official Gazette, declared in respect of any court situate in any such territory and not established or continued in the exercise of any such jurisdiction as aforesaid, that service by such court of any summons issued under this code by a court of the state shall be deemed to be valid service. The summons may be sent to such Political Agent or court, by post or otherwise, for the purpose of being served upon the defendant ; and, if the Political Agent or court returns the summons with endorsement signed by such Political Agent or by Judge or other officer of the court that the summon has been served on the defendant in manner hereinbefore directed, such endorsement shall be deemed to be the evidence of service.

SUBMISSION TO JURISDICTION

English Law

A person may submit to the jurisdiction of the court either under an express agreement or by conduct. If a person who is outside the jurisdiction of the court submits to the jurisdiction then the court gets the jurisdiction to try the action and a decree or order passed in such an action will be valid internationally. To constitute submission to the jurisdiction, it is not necessary that the defendant should be personally present before the court. However, the rule that submission confers jurisdiction applies to legal actions only and then submission to jurisdiction will meet only those objections to jurisdiction which are of personal nature, such as the objection that the summons were not served on the defendant. The submission to jurisdiction cannot bring those cases within the jurisdiction which are otherwise outside the jurisdiction. For instance, no amount of submission would confer jurisdiction to entertain a suit for divorce if the court to which submission is made is not a court of domicile of parties. Similarly, the court would have no jurisdiction to entertain an action in respect of immovable property situated outside the jurisdiction, even though the defendant has submitted to the jurisdiction. In certain circumstances, the court may not assume jurisdiction even when the defendant submits to jurisdiction. Ordinarily, a court does not assume jurisdiction if it is convinced that the order or decree passed by it would not be effective. For example, the court may decline to assume jurisdiction despite defendant's submission in a suit in respect of a tort committed on land situated outside the jurisdiction.

Submission to jurisdiction by conduct : The submission to jurisdiction by conduct may assume various forms. Some of the illustrative cases are as under :

(1) A person who voluntarily appears as a defendant submits to the jurisdiction of court, even if he is out of jurisdiction at the time of issue of service of writ. For instance, when a foreigner who is outside England instructs his solicitor to accept service on his behalf. In such a case when the solicitor endorses on the writ or originating summons that he had accepted the service on behalf of the defendant, then the writ or originating summons are deemed to have been duly served on the foreign defendant.[66] The defendant may enter an unconditional appearance, then the writ or the originating summons are deemed to have been duly served on him.[67]

(2) It is a long established rule of English law that if a foreigner comes before the court as a plaintiff, the court has jurisdiction to entertain counter-claim against him. However, an action on an independent ground cannot be entertained against the plaintiff.[68] Similarly appearance as a claimant in an inter-pleader suit does not amount to submission to jurisdiction.[69]

(3) When a foreigner-defendant files an affidavit and appears through counsel to argue the case on merit, it amounts to submission to the jurisdiction.[70] But if he appears merely to contest the jurisdiction of the court, it does not amount to submission.[71]

(4) When a foreigner-defendant moves to set aside a default judgment and at the same time applies for an order that the plaintiff deliver a statement of claim then it amounts to submission to jurisdiction.[72] Similarly, it amounts to submission when he applies for security of costs.[73]

(5) It has been suggested that carrying on business in England may amount to submission of jurisdiction. In

66. Order 10, r. 1(2).
67. Order 10, r. 1(3).
68. *Factories Insurance Co.* v. *Anglo-Scottish Insurance Co.* (1913) 29 T.L.R. 312 (C.A.); *High Commissioner for India* v. *Ghosh*, (1960) 1 Q.B. 134 (C.A.).
69. *Eschger & Co.* v. *Morrison, Kekewich & Co.* (1890) 6 T.L.R. 145 (C.A.).
70. *Boyle* v. *Sacker* (1888) 39 Ch. D. 249; *Re Dulles Settlement*, (2) (1951) Ch. 842.
71. *Re Dulles Settlement* (No. 2), (1951) Ch. 842.
72. *Fry* v. *Moore*, (1889) 23 Q.B.D. 395.
73. *Lloneux Limon & Co.* v. *Hong Kong Banking Corporation*, (1886) 33 Ch. D. 446.

Employer's Liability Assurance Corporation v. *Sedgwick Collins & Co.*,[74] three judges had suggested this in connection with what is now s. 407(1)(c) of the Companies Act, 1948. Dicey and Morris comment to say that a corporation which under the threat of heavy fine, files with the Registrar of Companies the name of a person authorized to accept service of process on its behalf thereby submits to the jurisdiction seems even more artificial than saying that a corporation which establishes a place of business in England is deemed to be present in England.[75]

Submission by contract : The parties may in advance, under a contract, agree to submit to the jurisdiction of the court. However, submission to jurisdiction must be made by way of an express stipulation in the contract. It cannot be implied.[76] At common law the view was that the English courts could not have jurisdiction just because the parties in their agreement stipulated to confer jurisdiction on English courts as the difficulty that the defendant could not be served with a writ if out of jurisdiction still remained.[77] However, if under the agreement or otherwise a party nominates an agent resident in England to accept service of process on his behalf, he is deemed to submit to the jurisdiction.[78] The common law rule is now embodied in Order 10, rule 3, which runs : Where "(1)(a) a contract contains a term to the effect that the High Court shall have jurisdiction to hear and determine any action in respect of a contract or, apart from any such term, the High Court has jurisdiction to hear and determine any such action, and (b) the contract provides that, in the event of any action in respect of the contract being begun, the process by which it is begun may be served on the defendant or on such other person on his behalf as may be specified in the contract, in such manner, or at such place (whether within or out of the jurisdiction) as may be so specified, then if any action in respect of the contract is begun in the High Court and the writ by which it is begun is served in accordance with the contract, the writ shall, subject to paragraph (2), be deemed to have been duly served on the defendant; (2) a writ which is served out of the jurisdiction in accordance with a contract shall not be deemed to have been duly served on the defendant by virtue of paragraph (1) unless leave to serve the writ, or notice thereof, out of the jurisdiction has been granted under Order 11, rule 1 or 2".[79] Thus if the defendant is

74. (1927) A.C. 95.
75. Dicey and Morris (8th ed.), pp. 181-82. The matter has been discussed in Chapter 13 of this work.
76. *Vogal* v. *R. & A. Kohnstamm Ltd.* (1971) 2 All E.R. 1428. Ashworth, J. said that assuming there could be implied agreement to submit to the jurisdiction, in fact there was none.
77. *British Wagon & Co.* v. *Gray*, (1896) 1 Q.B. 35.
78. *Tharsis Sulpher Co.* v. *Societe des Metaux*, (1889) 58 L.J.Q.B. 435.
79. That is now rule 25.

outside jurisdiction, the plaintiff will have to obtain the leave of the court to serve the writ or notice thereof out of the jurisdiction, even though the contract stipulates to confer jurisdiction on the court.

Indian Law

The Indian law of submission closely follows English law. If a person is outside the jurisdiction, the court will have jurisdiction on him only if he submits to the jurisdiction of the court. In case the defendant does not submit to the jurisdiction of the court, then the judgment delivered in his absence would be null and void.[80] There is a long line of cases of the Madras High Court which take the view that if a foreign defendant submits to the jurisdiction of the court by pleading the merits of the case, the court has jurisdiction.[81] If the defendant puts up appearance in the court, then the appearance to amount to submission, must be unconditional; he must unequivocally submit to the jurisdiction of the court.[82] Only full participation by the defendant in the proceedings amounts to submission to jurisdiction. The waiver of objection to the jurisdiction of the court also amounts to submission to jurisdiction. In *Hiralal* v. *Kali Nath*[83] the Supreme Court said that "an objection as to the local jurisdiction of a court can be waived . . . Having consented to have the controversy between the parties resolved by reference to arbitration through court, the defendant deprived himself of the right to question the authority of the court to refer the matter to arbitration, to render the award. It is clear, therefore, that the defendant is estopped from challenging the jurisdiction of the Bombay High Court to entertain the suit and to make the reference to the arbitrator. He is equally estopped from challenging the authority of the arbitrator to render the award."[84] This judgment was reaffirmed by the Supreme Court in *Bahrein Petroleum Co. Ltd.* v. *P.J. Pappu.*[85] Bachawat, J. observed that it is even possible to say that long and continued participation by the defendant in the proceedings without any protest may, in an appropriate case, amount to a waiver of objection to jurisdiction. In this case the plaintiff was in the employment of the Bahrein Petroleum Co. Ltd., the defendant No. 2. The contract of service was signed in Bombay, but the zone of operation under the contract

80. *Shaik Athama Sahib* v. *Davud Sahib*, (1909) 32 Mad. 469; *Raj Rajendra Sardar Maloji Narsingh Rao* v. *Shankar Saran*, 1958 All. 775; *Royal Nepal Airlines Corpn* v. *Manorama Mehar Singh Legha*, 1966 Cal. 319 ; *Kukadap Krishna Murty* v. *Godmatla Venkata Rao*, 1962 A.P. 400.

81. *Ramanathan Chethar* v. *Kali-Mutu Pillai*, (1914) 37 Mad. 163; *Rama Ayyar* v. *Krishna Pattar*, (1916) 39 Mad. 733; *Anant Narayan* v. *Massey Ferguson Ltd.*, (1965) 1 M.L.J. 550; *Wheels India Ltd.* v. *Khem Chand Raj Kumar* (1970) 2 M.L.J. 648.

82. *United Arab Republic* v. *Mirza Ali Akbar Kashmi*, 1962 Cal. 387.

83. 1962 S.C. 199.

84. *Ibid.*, at p. 2001.

85. 1966 S C. 634.

was Bahrein Island, outside India. The plaintiff instituted a suit for the recovery of gratuity and arrears of salary against the defendant company in the court of the subordinate judge at Cochin. In their written statement the defendants contested the jurisdiction of the court and also pleaded on merits. The Cochin Court on the preliminary issue of jurisdiction decided against the plaintiff. Ultimately the matter went in appeal to the Supreme Court. The Supreme Court observed that since the defendants had objected to the jurisdiction of the court at the earliest opportunity, it could not be said that they waived their objection to jurisdiction. Section 21, C.P.C. embodies the rule thus : "No objection as to the place of suing shall be allowed by any appellate or revisional court unless such objection was taken in the court of first instance at the earliest possible opportunity and in all cases where issues are settled at or before such settlement, and unless there has been consequent failure of justice." The waiver under s. 21, C.P.C. is limited to objections in the appellate and revisional courts. Independently of s. 21, the defendant may waive the objection and may be precluded from objecting to it.[86]

Against whom suit may not be filed : Jurisdictional immunity

Although as a general rule an action can be filed against any person who is present within the jurisdiction, there are certain persons who enjoy jurisdictional immunity and therefore suits cannot be filed against them. The following enjoy jurisdictional immunity :

1. Foreign state, its head and its departments;
2. Persons entitled to diplomatic immunity; and
3. Officials of international organizations including United Nations and its organs.

Since no action can be brought against the above categories of persons, no action ordinarily lies against their property.

Foreign State and the Foreign Sovereign : The rule of immunity of foreign state and its head has been derived from the English law maxim *par in parem non habet imperium* and from the rules of public international law. The House of Lords observed, "The principle of sovereign immunity is not founded on any technical rules of law; it is founded on broad considerations of public policy, international law and comity."[87]

The principle of sovereign immunity is now an internationally recognized principle and whatever differences that exist among the states are in matters of detail. So deeply ingrained this principle is in English law that English courts have never tested it on the

86. *Hira Lal* v. *Sri Kali Nath*, cited above and *Bahrein Petroleum Co. Ltd.* v. *P.J. Papp.*, cited above.
87. *Rahimtoola* v. *Nizam of Hyderabad*, (1958) A.C. 397 at p. 499.

touchstone of reciprocity. In an 1880 case[88] the Court of Appeal said that the foreign state has immunity from jurisdiction as the exercise of such jurisdiction "would be incompatible with his regal dignity, that is to say, with the absolute independence of every superior authority." In *The Cristina*,[89] Lord Atkin observed : "The courts of a country will not impeach a foreign sovereign that is, they will not by their process make him against his will a party to the proceedings, whether the proceedings involve process against his person or seek to recover from him specific property or damages . . . they will not by their process, whether the sovereign is a party to proceedings or not, seize or detain property which is his or of which he is in possession or control." The immunity exists even if the foreign sovereign happens to be a British subject.[90]

Foreign Sovereign : The immunity from jurisdiction of the foreign sovereign exists in respect of his person and property. The personal immunity of the sovereign is almost unlimited. *Mighell* v. *The Sultan of Johore*[91] is oft-quoted case for this proposition. The Sultan of Johore lived in England *incognito* and as a private citizen. In that capacity he entered into a contract of marriage with an English woman of which he committed a breach. On being sued for breach of contract, he disclosed his identity and claimed immunity from jurisdiction. The court accepted his plea. *Re C. (An infant)*[92] is a recent example of this principle. The court held that the Crown's prerogative jurisdiction over infants in England was also excluded if the infant was entitled to diplomatic immunity. The former case also illustrates another proposition, viz. jurisdictional immunity of the foreign sovereign is not limited to action arising out of his official acts but also out of his private activities. It extends to his commercial acts also. In English private international law, no distinction is made between *acta imperii and acta gestionis*. Sometimes the sovereign of a particular state is so well known that the court can take judicial notice of it. Sometimes doubts may arise on account of the obscurity of a state. Doubts may also arise in the case of a state which is amidst a revolution,[93] civil war[94] or hostile occupation[95]. In such cases the court will act on the statement of the foreign office or Commonwealth office,[96] as the case may be.

88. *The Parlement Belge*, (1880) 5 P.D. 197.
89. (1938) A.C. 485.
90. *Duke of Brunswick* v. *King of Hanovar*, (1844) 6 Beav. 1.
91. (1894) 1 K.B. 149.
92. (1959) 1 Ch. 363.
93. *The Gagara*, (1919), p. 95.
94. *Compania Naviera Vascougado* v. *The Cristina*, (1930) A.C. 485.
95. *Haile Selassie* v. *Cable and Wireless Ltd.*, (1938) Ch. 839.
96. *Sayce* v. *Ameer Ruler Sadig Md. Abbasi*, *Bahawalpur State*, (1952) 2 Q.B. 390.

It is interesting to note that if the question before the court is not of the jurisdictional immunity of the sovereign but of the existence of sovereignty in some other connection, the court is not bound by the statement of the foreign office or Commonwealth office that the foreign government concerned is not recognized by the Crown. In such a situation actual facts are decisive.[97] *Carl Zeiss Stiftung* v. *Rayner and Keeler Ltd.*[98] is a good illustration of this. At a time when the German Democratic Republic was not recognized by Her Majesty's Government (and was so stated by the certificate of the Foreign Office) the House of Lords said that since Her Majesty's Government did recognize the Soviet Union as having authority on that part of Germany which was called the German Democratic Republic, the acts of the subordinate authority were also valid.

The jurisdictional immunity does not extend to the sovereign of a state which is not recognized by the Crown.[99] However, if the foreign state is recognized provisionally[100] or *de facto*[101] that is enough to confer immunity. The immunity does not exist when the foreign soverein has ceased to be such. The defendant must be sovereign at a time when action is filed and not when cause of action arise.[102]

The jurisdictional immunity is available to the foreign sovereign in respect of his property whether the property is in his or his agent's possession or control. The immunity exists even in those cases where the action is not brought against him directly. Whatever be the nature of sovereign's interest, proprietary, possessive or even of lesser nature, in the property situated within the jurisdiction, an action in respect of such property cannot be proceeded with. Thus it has been held that an action *in rem* against a ship[103] or an action against his agent[104] will not lie in respect of sovereign's property. Lord Wright observed : "The rule is not limited to ownership. It applies to cases where what [the foreign sovereign] has is a lesser interest, which may be not merely not proprietary

97. *Kawasaki Kisen Kabushiki Kaisha of Kobe* v. *Bantham S.S. Co. Ltd.* (1939) 2 K.B. 544 (C.A.); *Luigi Monta of Genoa* v. *Cechofrachat Co. Ltd.* (1956) 2 K.B. 552.

98. (1967) 1 A.C. 853.

99. *Statham* v. *Statham and the Gaekwar of Baroda*, (1912), p. 92; *Duff Development Co.* v. *Government of Kelantan* (1924) A.C. 797.

100. *The Gagara*, (1919), p. 93.

101. *The Arantzazu Mendi*, (1939) A.C. 256.

102. *Munden* v. *Duke of Brunswick*, (1847) 10 K.B. 656; *New Chile Gold Mining Co.* v. *Blanco*, (1888) 4 T.L.R. 346.

103. *The Parlement Belge* (1880) 5 P.D. 197 (C.A.); *The Cristina* (1930) A.C. 485, *The Arantzazu Mendi* ,(1939) A.C. 256.

104. *Morgan* v. *Loriviere*, (1875) L.R. 7 H.L. 423; *Rahimtoola* v. *Nizam of Hyderabad*, (1958) A.C. 379; *U.S.A. & Republic of France* v. *Dollfus Mieg et cie. S.A. and Bank of England*, (1952) A.C. 582.

but not even possessory,"[105] *The Cristina*[105a] lays down the proposition that property is considered to be under the control of the sovereign if he re-questions it and the persons in control of it hold it for him. During the Spanish Civil War, the Republican Government of Spain requisitioned a Spanish ship, *The Cristina,* registered at Bilbo, which was on the high seas at the time of requisition. On arrival of the ship at Cardiff, the Republican Consul took possession of the ship by dismissing the nationalist master and put a republican master in control. The owner's writ *in rem* against the ship claiming possession was dismissed by the English court on the ground that the principle of jurisdictional immunity extended to the property if it was under the control of the agent of the sovereign or in the hands of his bailee of which he is entitled to immediate possession.[106] However, it is submitted that *Rahimtoola* v. *Nizam of Hyderabad*[107] is an illegitimate extension of this principle. Nizam of Hyderabad had an amount of £10,00,000 deposited in his name in a London Bank. During the police action by Indian Government the then Finance Minister of Nizam, Moin, successfully persuaded the then High Commissioner of Pakistan, Rahimtoola to take the transfer of this amount in his name. It appears that the then Foreign Minister of Pakistan had also consented to the transfer. Moin did not obtain any instructions from Nizam to do so. However, he had the authority to operate the account. Subsequently, the Nizam filed a suit in an English Court against the English Bank, Moin and Rahimtoola for the recovery of this amount. The House of Lords posed the question in this form : Did Rahimtoola agree to take the transfer in his personal capacity or as agent of Pakistan ? The House of Lords by majority decided that he did so as agent of Pakistan and as such Pakistan can claim jurisdictional immunity, as the amount belongs to Pakistan government. It was forgotten that the position of Rahimtoola was that of trustee. In *Duke of Brunswick* v. *King of Hanovar,*[108] Lord Campbell observed : "If he (the foreign sovereign) has been a trustee of a marriage settlement, while he resided within the realm, and has become liable, in execution of the trust which he had undertaken and which he was not properly executing, I am by no means prepared to say that the court of Chancery would not have had jurisdiction over him." The learned editor of the eighth edition of Dicey's Conflict of Laws[109] holds the view that after the decision in Rahimtoola's case this observation may not be correct. It is submitted that whenever the House of Lords would get another opportunity to state the law, Lord Campbell's view should be resurrected as it accords well with the English notion of equity and justice.

It has been argued before the English courts as to whether

105. *The Cristina,* (1938) A.C. 485 at p. 507.

105a. (1938) A.C. 485.

106. *Ibid.*

107. (1958) A.C. 379.

108. (1948) 2 H.L.C. 1.

109. Dicey and Morris, p. 129.

the jurisdictional immunity will be available to a foreign sovereign who claims an interest in the property or whether it is necessary for him to prove his title. In *The Cristina*[110] case the former view was passed while in *Juan Ysmael & Co. Inc.* v. *Indonesian Government*,[111] the latter view was pressed. In *Rahimtoola's case*[111a] it appears that the House of Lords took an intermediate view. The foreign sovereign need not prove his title (as that was impossible in this case), but may produce evidence that the claim is not illusory. He must establish a *prima facie* case. The House of Lords said that the claim will not be illusory even if it is established that the foreign sovereign claims no beneficial interest in the property but only the legal title. This leads to a curious situation where the foreign sovereign by claiming jurisdictional immunity succeeds in preventing the plaintiff (the rightful owner) from claiming the property, though he himself cannot obtain possession or delivery of property, as he can do so only when he appears as plaintiff and if he does so it would imply that he had waived his immunity.

Then the question is : are there any limitations on the doctrine of jurisdictional immunity, apart from the waiver of the immunity? In *Sultan of Johore* v. *Abubaker Tunku Aris Bendahar*[112] the Privy Council observed : " . . . there has not been finally established in England any absolute rule that a foreign independent sovereign cannot be impeached in our courts in any circumstances. Thus what precisely are the exceptional cases, it is difficult to state. In the eighth edition of Dicey's Conflict of Laws[113] six possible exceptions were stated : (i) An action *in rem* against a ship owned or requisitioned by a sovereign should be stayed even if the ship is used for ordinary commercial purposes.[114] (ii) Trust funds may be distributed among beneficiaries even if a foreign sovereign is entitled to an interest therein.[115] (iii) The foreign sovereign may be made liable if he were himself a trustee. As to this exception the learned editor comments that the question whether a foreign sovereign could be made liable if he were a trustee is now doubtfull.[116] (iv) No court has yet held that a foreign sovereign can object to an action

110. (1938) A.C. 485.

111. (1955) A.C. 72 (P.C.)

111a. (1958) A.C. 379.

112. (1952) A.C. 318.

113. Dicey and Morris, pp. 128-29.

114. *The Pesto Alexandre*, (1920) P. 30 (C.A.); the correctness of this view was doubted by the House of Lords in *The Cristina* (1930) A.C. 485.

115. The earliest reported case is *Duke of Brunswick* v. *King of Hanovar*, (1844) 6 Beav. 1. The recent cases are : *Sultan of Johore* v. *Abubaker Tunku Aris Bendahar*, (1952) A.C. 318; *U.S.A. & Republic of France* v. *Dollfus Mieg et cie. and Bank of England*, (1952) A.C. 582; and *Rahimtoola* v. *Nizam of Hyderabad*, (1958) A.C. 379. The Court will also not refuse to make an order for the winding up of a company, even though a foreign sovereign may be interested in any surplus assets : *Re Russian Bank for Foreign Trade*, (1933) Ch. 745.

116. The authority is *Duke of Brunswick* v. *King of Hanovar*, (1848) 2 H.L.C. 1 and the case casting doubt on this authority is *Rahimtoola* v. *Nizam of Hyderabad*, (1958) A.C. 379.

against a company in which he owns a share.[117] (v) It is possible that the court might assume jurisdiction to entertain an action against a foreign sovereign in respect of immovable property situated in England and owned by him in private capacity.[118] (vi) The doctrine of waiver may be considered as an exception to the rule.[119]

Foreign Government and its Departments and Public Corporations

The doctrine of jurisdictional immunity applies to the foreign government,[120] its departments[121] and foreign public corporations.[122] Here foreign government includes an independent country of the Commonwealth,[123] as well as a state under British protection.[124] Whether or not a particular body is a department of Government is a question of foreign law on which best evidence is that of foreign ambassador.[125] In any case the certificate of Foreign Office or Commonwealth Relations Office is conclusive.[126]

Definè Head of *de facto* government has no such immunity and its representative cannot sue in English Court.[127]

Is a foreign corporate body which claims to be a department of government entitled to the immunity? Apart from being a department of government, a corporation may also have independent existence. It is obvious that the status of such a corporation is not such that the court may take judicial notice of it. It is also not one of the entities about which the Secretary of State has, so far, given a certificate. Whether or not a foreign corporation is a government department has to be decided by evidence. The burden of proof lies on the defendant corporation. Affidavit or certificate given by the ambassador of the concerned foreign state is considered to be best evidence, though a rebuttable evidence.

The question has come before the court in two cases : *Krajina*

117. See also *Haile Selassie* v. *Cable and Wireless Ltd.* (No. 1), (1938) Ch. 839 (C.A.); No. 2 (1939) Ch. 182 (C.A.); *Government of India* v. *Taylor* (1955) A.C. 491.
118. This is based on *Obiter dicta* in *The Charkieh*, (1873) L.R. 4 Adm. & Ecc. 59. *Sultan of Johore* v. *Bendahar*, (1952) A.C. 318 (P.C.) where the matter was fully argued.
119. This is discussed in the subsequent pages.
120. *Duff Development Co.* v. *Government of Kelantan*, (1924) A.C. 797; *Kahan* v. *Pakistan Federation*, (1951) 2 K.B. 1003 (C.A.).
121. *Compania Mercantil Argentina* v. *U.S. Shipping Board*, (1924) 93 L.J.K.B. 816 (C.A.).
122. *Krajina* v. *Tass Agency*, (1949) 2 All E.R. 274; *Baccus S.R.L.* v. *Servicio Nacional del Trigo*, (1957) 1 Q.B. 438.
123. *Khan* v. *Pakistan Federation*, (1951) 2 K.B. 1003 (C.A.).
124. *Mighell* v. *Sultan of Johore*, (1894) 1 K.B. 149; *Statham* v. *Statham & the Gaekwar of Baroda*, (1912) P. 92; *Duff Development Co.* v. *Government of Kelantan*, (1924) A.C. 797.
125. *Krajina* v. *Tass Agency*, cited above.
126. *Mighell* v. *Sultan of Johore*, cited above; *The Ganga* (1919) P. 95; *Duff Development Co.* v. *Government of Kelantan*, cited above.
127. *Republic of Somania* v. *Woodhouse etc.* (1993); All E.R. 371.

v. *Tass Agency*[127] and *Baccus S.R.L.* v. *Servicio National del Trigo.*[128] In the former case an action was brought to recover damages for a libel published in a magazine called the "Soviet Monitor" of the Tass Agency. The Soviet Ambassador certified that the Agency was statutorily entitled to "all rights of a judicial person and that it was a department of Soviet State". It was proved that it was an independent corporation. The court held that the Tass Agency was entitled to immunity. In the latter case also a similar certificate was given by the Italian ambassador in respect of Servicio Nacional del Trigo. In this case the plaintiff were a company carrying on business in Italy. The defendants, Servicio Nacional del Trigo, were a public corporation carrying on business of buying and selling of grain and other cereals. The defendants under a contract agreed to sell 26,000 tons of rye to the plaintiffs. The contract also stipulated that all disputes arising under the contract between the parties will be referred to "the jurisdiction of the technical courts at London". When sued for breach of contract in the High Court at London, the Italian Government claimed immunity. It was proved that the corporation had a separate existence. But the majority held that the defendants were a department of Italian Government.

Cheshire considers this state of English law unsatisfactory. He holds the view that the rule is open to the following three objections : (1) There is no reason why solicitude should be shown for the dignity of an independent corporation created by a sovereign. The question of preservation of dignity of foreign sovereign is different. (2) It appears to be a little illogical that a corporation can be simultaneously an organ of the state as well as a juristic person separate from the state. (3) It is a doubtful policy to extend the doctrine of immunity to a trading corporation to avoid legal proceedings to which its rivals are exposed.[129] Recently the question again came for consideration before the court of appeal in *Mellenger* v. *New Brunswick Development Corporation.*[130] The plaintiff, a Canadian citizen, applied to serve out of the jurisdiction a writ on the defendants in respect of his claim for commission for introducing a commercial enterprise into New Brunswick. The defendants claimed jurisdictional immunity in the following circumstances : The defendant corporation was established by the New Brunswick Development Corporation Act, 1959 which constituted the corporation "on behalf of Her Majesty in right of New Brunswick." The provision of the Act showed that there was a close connection between the corporation and the government of New Brunswick : the Minister of Industry was the ex-Officio director and other directors were also appointed by the Lieutenant-Governor in Council. The main object of the Corporation was to assist, promote, encourage and advance the industrial development,

127. (1949) 2 All E.R. 274.
128. (1957) 1 Q.B. 438.
129. Private International Law (7th Ed.), p. 101.
130. (1971) 2 All E.R. 593.

prosperity and economic welfare of the Province of New Brunswick. The Corporation had also power to engage in trade and business, though, the court found that it did not in fact engage in trade or business (probably an unseen influence of Cheshire's views). It was argued that the Corporation was not entitled to sovereign immunity; the body that created it was itself not sovereign. Repelling both the contentions, the Court of Appeal (Lord Denning, M.R., Salmond, Philimore, JJ.) held that under British North America Act, 1867, the Province of New Brunswick retained within its own sphere its independence and autonomy and was thus a sovereign state in its own right entitled to claim sovereign immunity.[131] It was also held that the defendant corporation was also entitled to sovereign immunity since, by the express provisions of the 1959 Act which set it up, it was in the same position as a government department; and, even apart from the Act, the corporation's functions, as carried out in practice showed that it was carrying out the policy of the government of New Brunswick and was its *alter ego*.

State Immunity Act, 1978 : In the domestic law of many countries of the world, including India, a distinction is made between the sovereign functions and the commercial activities of the State. In international sphere also, from the point of state immunity, this distinction came to be made in several countries of Europe as well as the United States. Thus it was opined that when states were engaged in commercial and trading transanctions either directly or through separate entities with private citizens in other countries, the doctrine of state immunity did not apply to such transanctions. This came to be known as restrictive theory of sovereign immunity which meant that the national court can exercise jurisdiction over foreign states if claims against them arose out of commercial or trading transanctions that they have entered into with private individuals. But England continued to adhere to the "absolute theory" of sovereign immunity under which the court decline to exercise jurisdiction or entertain claims against foreign states even where these arose out of the commercial and trading transantions. In 1972 that the United States adopted the restrictive theory, and presently, the matter is regulated by the Foreign Sovereign Immunities Act, 1976.

In England the restrictive theory was first recognized by the Privy Council in *The Phillippine Admiral*.[132] Then came Lord Denning's pronoucement in *Trend Lex Trading Corporation* v. *Central Bank of Nigeria*[133] where the doctrine was adopted. Finally the House of Lords puts its seal on the doctrine in *I. Congne so*

131. See *Maritime Bank of Canada* v. *Receiver General of New Brunswick*, (1892) A.C. 437; *Trevel Tax* v. *Central Bank of Nigeria* (1977) 2 W.L.R. 356; *Congneso del Fertido* (1981) 2 All E.R. 1064 (restrictive theory of immunity).

132. (1977) A.C. 373.

133. (1977) Q.B. 529.

del Partido.[134] Presently, the matter is regulated by the State Immunity Act, 1978.

The provisions of the Act 1978 came for consideration before the House of Lords in *Alcomb Ltd.* v. *Republic of Colombia,*[135] where the plaintiffs obtained a default judgment for £ 41,690 for goods sold and delivered against the defendant, Republic of Colombia, a foreign sovereign. Subsequently garnishee orders nisi were granted to the plaintiffs as the judgment-creditors for attaching sums covering the judgment-debt and costs, in the defendant's embassy bank accounts with the garnishees. The defendant ambassador certified that the funds in the bank accounts were intended to be used only in the day to day running of the diplomatic mission. The House of Lords held that, in terms of sections 3(1) and (3) and 13(3) of the State Immunity Act, 1978, a bank account used for an embassy was *prima facie* non-commercial and set aside the garnishee order.

It seems that diplomatic immunity will not apply to a building which has ceased to be the embassy of the foreign state such as when foreign state breaks of diplomatic relations.[136]

In the end we may refer to the summary of law given by Mitter, J. who exhaustively considered all the English authorities as well as some American authorities.[137]

(1) A foreign sovereign cannot be impeached directly in respect of his person and property; a suit will not lie where damages are claimed against the sovereign personally. A foreign sovereign cannot even be impleaded indirectly, viz. by a proceedings *in rem* against a public vessel which would include a vessel which was also used for commercial purposes.

(2) A proceeding with the object of seizing or detaining property in the possession and control of a foreign sovereign will not be allowed to go on. A foreign sovereign will be allowed to intervene in such an action. So far as property used only for commercial purposes of the sovereign is concerned, although there is some difference in the practice of nations, immunity is granted by the English Court.

(3) A suit will not lie against the agent of a foreign state where the act complained of is purported to be done as such agent.

(4) A suit will not lie against a department of a state. It is doubtful whether immunity can be claimed when the

134. (1983) 1 A.C. 244.

135. (1984) 2 W.L.R. 750.

136. *Westminster City Council* v. *Government of the Islamic Republic of Iran* (1986) 1 W.L.R. see also Intro *Properties (U.K.) Ltd.* v. *Sauvel* (1983) 2 W.L.R. 908.

137. *Royal Nepal Airlines Corpn.* v. *Manorama* 1966 Cal. 319.

department is a corporation solely with power to hold and acquire property, and the right to sue and liability to be sued. So far as the English courts are concerned, the mere incorporation of a body will not deprive it of immunity, if it is a department of state. An incorporated body which is a juristic personality carrying on business in the country where proceedings are started against it, will be outside the "protective umbrella" of immunity.

(5) As immunity can be claimed even when foreign sovereign does not figure as a defendant. A notice of motion to set aside the writ based on the certificate or affidavit of the ambassador of the foreign state to the effect that the defendant is a department of state and is not a corporation will be disposed of in its favour. The effect of incorporation under a foreign law will have to be considered by the court on the materials presented.

(6) If the title to property, the subject-matter of the suit, is in dispute, the claim to immunity will not be given effect to before the court is satisfied that the claim is not illusory nor founded on the title manifestedly defective.[138]

Diplomatic representatives and their staff: In the modern English law the question of jurisdictional immunity of the diplomatic representatives and their staff is regulated by the Diplomatic Privileges Act, 1964[139] passed as a sequel to the Vienna Convention on Diplomatic Relations, 1961. The act came into force on October 1, 1964. The Act covers actions commenced before that date. The jurisdictional privileges extend to the properly accredited diplomatic representatives. Before 1964 the English law was committed to the principle of absolute diplomatic immunity, now under the Act the jurisdictional immunity is qualified one. In this connection the State Immunity Act, 1978 is also relevant. However, no foreign state can confer diplomatic immunity on its representative by appointing him as a diplomatic agent, until the receiving state accepts him as a *persona grata*.[140] Such a diplomatic agent is not immune from proceedings in English courts.

The persons entitled to diplomatic immunity under the Diplomatic Privileges Act, 1964 fall under the following three categories :

138. *Ibid.* at p. 344.

139. Previously it was regulated by the Diplomatic Privileges Act, 1708, which was declaratory of common law. See also the United Nations Convention on the Prevention and Punishment of Crimes against Internationally Protected Persons, including Diplomatic Agents adopted on December 14, 1973.

140. *Reg.* v. *Governor of Pentonville, Ex Parte Teja*, (1971) 2 W.L.R. 816, the Costa Rican Government appointed one Dharma Singh Teja, who was wanted by the Indian government in connection with criminal proceedings for misappropriation pending against him, as an economic adviser and he was issued with a diplomatic passport and a letter of credence.

(a) Diplomatic agent, that is, the head of the mission and members of his diplomatic staff;

(b) Members of the administrative and technical staff, that is persons employed in secretariat, clerical, communications and public relations duties, e.g. typist, translators, coding clerks and cultural and public relations staff; and

(c) Members of the service staff, that is members of the domestic staff of the mission, such as chauffeurs, porters, cooks and cleaners.

(a) Diplomatic agents enjoy jurisdictional immunity from criminal, civil and administrative action or other proceedings, including execution proceedings, except in the following three cases :

(i) A real action relating to private immovable property in the United Kingdom unless the property is held for the purpose of the mission.

(ii) An action relating to succession wherein the diplomatic agent is involved as executor, administrator or beneficiary as a private individual.

(iii) An action in respect of any professional or commercial activity of the diplomatic agent outside his official function. The jurisdictional immunity to the diplomatic agent who is a citizen of or permanently resident in the United Kingdom extends only in respect of his official acts performed in the exercise of his function, though the receiving state is free to grant him any additional immunities. The jurisdictional immunity is available to the members of the family of the diplomatic agent forming part of his household, unless they are British citizens.

(b) The persons falling under category (b) above as well as members of their families constituting their respective households, if they are not citizens of the United Kingdom, enjoy like immunity though they can claim jurisdictional immunity only in respect of their official acts.

(c) The persons falling under category (c) above enjoy jurisdictional immunity only in respect of acts performed in the course of their duties and provided they are not citizens of the United Kingdom. The private servants of members of the missions who are not employees of the sending state, enjoy immunity only to the extent admitted by the receiving state.[141]

The United Kingdom have entered into reciprocal arrangements with certain states under which diplomatic missions are

141. Diplomatic Privileges Act, 1964, Sched. 1, Art. 37(4) and Art. 1(b).

granted more extensive immunities and privileges. The Diplomatic Privileges Act, 1964 makes provisions for continuing these arrangements. Before 1964 the question of jurisdictional immunity of the countries of the Commonwealth and of the Republic of Ireland were regulated by s. 1(1) of the Diplomatic Immunities (Commonwealth Countries and the Republic of Ireland) Act, 1952. But now the matter is governed by the Diplomatic Privileges Act, 1964. However, Orders in Council provide that a person who is a member of the diplomatic mission of an independent country or Commonwealth, or of the Republic of Ireland or of Southern Rhodesia, or who is a private servant of such a member, and is a citizen of that country and also of the United Kingdom and colonies shall be entitled to the same privileges and immunities as he would have been entitled to if he were not a citizen of the United Kingdom and colonies.

The Vienna Convention does not cover foreign consuls. But it seems to be an accepted position in England (as well as elsewhere) that they are entitled to jurisdictional immunity in regard to their official acts, though not in respect of their private acts.[142] The immunity of consuls is not of the same quality as that of the diplomatic representatives.

The jurisdictional immunity commences from the moment the diplomatic representative enters the territory of the receiving state to take up his post or, if he is already there, the moment his appointment is notified to the receiving state.[143] The immunity can be claimed even if the diplomatic representative becomes entitled to it only after the issue of the writ.[144] The jurisdictional immunity comes to an end when his functions come to an end and he leaves the country or if he does not do so immediately, on the expiry of a reasonable period.[145] The same applies to members of his family. However, immunity continues to exist in respect of acts performed in exercise of his functions.[146] In case he dies while still holding the post, members of his family enjoy immunity until the expiry of a reasonable period to enable them to leave the country.

Whether or not a person is entitled to jurisdictional immunity, the certificate issued by the Secretary of State concerned to that effect is conclusive evidence.[147] The usual diplomatic practice is that Ambassador or the High Commissioner submits a list of the members of the diplomatic mission for whom diplomatic status is claimed to the Foreign Office or the Commonwealth Relations Office. The latter has the power to refuse to recognize any person

142. See Oppenheim, International Law, 8th Ed., Vol. 1, at 841. See also s. 1(2), the Diplomatic Immunities (Commonwealth Countries and Republic of Ireland) Act, 1952; for the latter proposition see *Engelke* v. *Musmann*, (1928) A.C. 438.

143. Sched. I, Art. 39(1) & s. 2(2) of the Act of 1964.

144. *Ghosh* v. *D'Rozario*, (1963) 1 Q.B. 106.

145. Article 39(2).

146. Sched. I, Art. 39(2). *Zoernsch* v. *Waldock*, (1964) 1 W.L.R. 675.

147. *Engelke* v. *Musmann*, (1928) A.C. 433.

if his diplomatic status is in doubt, or the list is too excessive. But once recognition is conceded, a statement to that effect is conclusive.

Under the Diplomatic Privileges Act, 1964 jurisdictional immunity can be withdrawn from the diplomatic mission of a state which fails to accord reciprocal immunity to Her Majesty's mission.

Thus, after coming into force of the Act of 1964, the diplomatic immunity is not absolute. The immunity from civil and administrative jurisdiction exists in respects of official acts as well as acts done in private capacity, but in respect of the latter action can be launched once the immunity terminates. That this is so is well illustrated by *Empson* v. *Smith*[148] (action related to lease of premises) and *Shaw* v. *Shaw*[148a] (petition for divorce). In the latter case the wife had filed a petition for dissolution of marriage (the jurisdiction was claimed on the basis of spouse's habitual residence in England throughout the period of one year ending with the date of the presentation of the petition) and on that date the husband possessed diplomatic immunity, and therefore the court issued summons for the dismissal of the petition. However, on the date when the summons came for hearing the husband has ceased be a diplomatic agent. The court observed that since a fresh petition could be filed by the wife, there was no reason for dismissing the present petition.

International Organizations and their Representatives: Under the International Organization Act, 1968, English law confers jurisdictional immunity on several international organizations and their representatives. The International Organisations Act empowers the Crown by Order in Council to confer complete jurisdictional immunity upon any international organisation of which the United Kingdom is a member and to confer jurisdictional immunity, as is conferred on an envoy of a foreign state, upon representatives of any organ of the organization or members of its organs or committees, upon specified high officers of the organization and specified persons employed in missions on its behalf.[149]

The official staff of such representative and his wife or husband and child may also be conferred like immunity. The Act also empowers the Crown to confer in the like manner upon specified subordinate officers and servants of the organisation immunity in respect of their official acts and functions.[150]

The Act also empowers the Crown to confer immunity on Judges and registrars of the International Court of Justice and to suitors to that court.[151] Jurisdictional immunity can also be

148. (1966) 1 Q.B. 426.
148a. (1979) 3 W.L.R. 24.
149. Diplomatic and Other Privileges Act, 1971.
150. Section 1.
151. Section 3.

conferred on representatives of foreign states and their staff attending conferences in the United Kingdom.[152] The Diplomatic Immunities (Conferences with Commonwealth Countries and Republic of Ireland) Act, 1961 empowers the government to confer immunity on representatives of the countries of Commonwealth and of the Republic of Ireland and their staff attending the conferences. The Commonwealth Secretariat Act, 1966 confers immunity from suit and legal action on the Commonwealth Secretariat, except in regard to a civil action for damages caused by a motor vehicle belonging to or operated on behalf of the Secretariat or in regard to motor vehicle offences involving such a motor vehicle. Similarly, arbitration proceedings relating to any written contract entered into by or on behalf of the Secretariat are excepted from the immunity. Like immunity with like exception can be conferred on the officer and servants of the Secretariat in regard to acts and omissions in the course of the performances of official duties.[153]

Waiver of immunity : If the jurisdictional immunity enjoyed by the sovereign or the diplomatic representative is waived by the person who has the authority to do so, then the English courts have jurisdiction to entertain the action against such sovereign or diplomatic representative.

Waiver may also be inferred from conduct. Thus if a foreign sovereign or ambassador brings an action in an English court, then the defendant can bring a counter-claim as a defence to action, e.g. something in the nature of a set-off. But he cannot make a counter-claim wholly unconnected with the subject-matter of the suit. In *High Commissioner of India* v. *Ghosh*[154] the High Commissioner of India brought an action against the defendant claiming damages for breach of contract. The defendant brought a counter-claim for damages for slander. It was held that the court has no jurisdiction to hear counter-claim. The defendant can prefer an appeal. Waiver of jurisdiction may also take place when the sovereign or the diplomatic representative appears before the court without protests or objection to jurisdiction and fights the case on its merits.

For the operation of the doctrine of waiver two conditions must be satisfied : (i) Waiver of immunity can be made only with the full knowledge of the right and with the authority of the foreign sovereign or ambassador. (ii) Waiver of immunity must be made at a time when the court is called upon to exercise jurisdiction. *Baccus S.R.L.* v. *Servicio Nacional del Trigo*[155] is a good

152. Section 4, as amended by the Diplomatic Privileges Act, 1964, s. 8(4) and Sched. 2.

153. Section 1(2) and Schedules to the Act.

154. (1960) 1 Q.B. 134 (C.A.).

155. (1957) 1 Q.B. 438; see also *Sultan of Johore* v. *Abubaker Tunku Aris Bendahar*, (1952) A.C. 318 (P.C.).

illustration of the former rule. The plaintiffs, an Italian company made a contract for the purchase of rye from the defendants, a department of Spain as well as a separate corporation. The solicitor of the defendants made an unconditional appearance. After the submission of the statement of claim it applied and obtained an order for the security of cost. The defendants subsequently claimed immunity. It was held that the defendants had not waived its immunity as the interlocutory steps were taken on the instructions of the person who had neither the authority on behalf of, nor the consent of his superior, the Spanish Minister of Agriculture. *R.* v. *Madan*[156] is a good illustration of both the above rules. P, a member of the administrative and technical staff of the High Commission for India was prosecuted for obtaining a railway ticket by the false pretence. At the committal proceedings P's solicitor waived his immunity and P was subsequently convicted. Three months after the conviction, the High Commissioner for India wrote a letter to the Commonwealth Relations Office waiving P's immunity. P appealed against his conviction. The court accepting the appeal said that P's solicitor has no authority to waive the immunity and the waiver by the High Commissioner for India was not made at the time when the court was called upon to exercise jurisdiction.

There are several other good cases illustrative of the second rule. In *Kahan* v. *Pakistan Federation*[157] P, a resident of England, entered into a contract with the Federation of Pakistan for the supply of tanks. One of the terms of the contract stipulated that all disputes arising under the contract would be referred to English court and the process could be served on the High Commissioner for Pakistan in London. A brought an action for breach of contract in an English court. It was held that stipulation in the contract cannot amount to waiver of immunity; waiver has to be made at the time of action. Similarly, the jurisdiction cannot be inferred from an agreement to submit to arbitration.[158] The claim of immunity must be made at a time when the immunity exist. If the claim of immunity is made at a time when it does not exist, then the claim is not sustainable. In *Empson* v. *Smith*[159] the defendant was entitled to immunity when action was filed against him. But he did not claim it then. Subsequently, when the action was still pending, he claimed immunity, but by this time the Diplomatic Privileges Act, 1964 came into force which resulted in the termination of immunity. It was held that he was not entitled to claim immunity.

So far as it concerns the immunity of diplomatic representatives, the Diplomatic Privileges Act, 1964 had made modification

156. (1961) 2 K.B. 1 (C.A.).
157. (1951) 2 K.B. 1003 (C.A.).
158. *Duff Development Co.* v. *Government of Kelantan*, (1924) A.C. 797.
159. (1966) 1 Q.B. 426.

in the law. The immunity can now be waived by the sending state.[160] Section 2(3) of the Act lays down that waiver by the head or acting head of the mission amounts to a waiver by the state. Although waiver under the Act must be express, the Act does not lay down that it must be made at a time when the court is called upon to exercise jurisdiction. Article 32 lays down that waiver of jurisdictional immunity does not imply waiver of immunity in regard to execution of judgment or decree, for which a separate waiver is necessary.

The English doctrine of waiver of immunity is very limited in its operation. The effect of waiver is that the court is enabled to do justice in the case before it. It does not amount to submission to jurisdiction generally. Nor does it amount to submission to the execution of judgment.[161]

Indian Law : Jurisdictional Immunity

Foreign Sovereign, Government and its Departments and Corporations

Indian law of jurisdictional immunity is primarily based on English law, though in some minor details it makes some departure from it. Sections 84 to 87A of the Civil Procedure Code deal with this matter. Section 87A(1)(a) defines "Foreign state" as "any state outside India which has been recognized by the Central Government." Clause (b) of s. 87A(1) defines "Ruler" in relation to a foreign state as "the person who is for the time being recognized by the Central Government to be the Head of that State." Then sub-section (2) of s. 87A lays down :

> Every court shall take judicial notice of the fact :
>
> (a) that a state has or has not been recognized by the Central Government;
>
> (b) that a person has or has not been recognized by the Central Government to be the head of a state.

The recognition, *de facto* or *de jure*, has the same effect.[162] In international law of the Head of a State represents the State as such and not as an individual representing his own rights. In that

160. Art. 32 of Schedule.

161. This is the view held by Cheshire, p. 103. This is also what Article 32, Diplomatic Privileges Act, 1964 lays down. The *obiter* observations to this effect are in *Re Suarez*, (1917) 2 Ch. 131; affirmed in (1918) 1 Ch. 176; *Duff Development Co.* v. *Government of Kelantan*, (1923) 1 Ch. 385, (C.A.), affirmed in (1924) A.C. 797. Morris takes the view that point is not finally settled. Dicey. p. 140.

162. ***German Democratic Republic*** v. ***Dynamic Industrial Undertaking Ltd.***, 1972 Bom. 27. The Court, before which the suit is filed, should obtain necessary information about recognition of a foreign action from the Government of India and the information supplied by the Government of India is conclusive on the matter.

capacity he enjoys certain extra-territorial privileges in other states which are friendly, and in peace are known as the receiving states, with the state he represents. These are ceremonial honours for himself, the members of his family, and his retinue; special protection to his person and exemption from criminal jurisdiction; the grant of extra-territoriality, on the basis that one sovereign does not have any power over the other, such as filing of suits against him, except where he is himself a plantiff, and from other legal process; exemption from taxation, rating and other fiscal enactments and the inviolability of immovable property (house) in which he or the representatives of the state accorded diplomatic immunity resides.[163] The jurisdictional immunity of the foreign sovereign exists not merely in respect of his person but also in regard to his property. In this respect no distinction is made between public property or private property of the sovereign.[164]

The Indian Law has been codified. Section 86, Civil Procedure Code confers jurisdictional immunity to (a) ruler or head of a foreign state, (b) ambassador or envoy of a foreign state, (c) High Commissioners of the Commonwealth States, and (d) members of the staff or retinue of the head or ruler of the foreign state, ambassador, envoy or High Commissioner, as the Central Government may, by general or special order specify in this behalf. These persons cannot be sued in any court in India except with the consent of the Central Government certified in writing by a Secretary to the Government. The jurisdictional immunity extends to all civil actions as well as to execution proceedings. For filing execution proceedings fresh consent of the Central Government is needed. The aforesaid persons cannot also be arrested under any provision of the Code of Civil Procedure. The Central Government will give consent only in the following cases :

(a) when the foreign state, etc. has instituted a suit in the court against the person desiring to sue,

(b) when the foreign state by itself or with another trades within the local limits of the jurisdiction of the court,

(c) when the foreign state is in possession of immovable property situate within those limits and is to be sued with reference to such property or for money charged thereon, or

(d) when the foreign state has expressly or impliedly waived the privilege accorded to it.

In *Gaekwar-Baroda State Railway* v. *Hafiz*,[165] the Privy Council held the requirement of consent under s. 86 as an important matter of policy and therefore cannot be waived by the defendant.

163. *Harinder Singh* v. *C.I.T., Punjab*, 1972 S.C. 202.
164. *Mirza Ali Akbar* v. *United Arab Republic*, 1966 S.C. 230.
165. 1938 P.C. 165.

Consent to sue must be obtained before the institution of suit. Consent given after the institution of the suit is not valid. A suit filed without the consent of the Government of India is not maintainable and must be dismissed.[166] In *Mohanlal* v. *Swami Mansinghji*[167] a suit was filed by the plantiff against the defendant, ruler of Jaipur state, at a time when s. 86B granting jurisdictional immunity was not enacted in the Civil Procedure Code. While the suit was pending, s. 86B came into force and the defendant claimed immunity. The Supreme Court held that the Ruler could claim immunity as s. 86 applied to all stages of the action.

The Indian law lays down that even when a foreign Ruler is sued, the suit is to be in the name of the foreign state whose ruler he is, though the Government of India may direct that the Ruler may be sued in the name of an agent or in any other name.[168] The provisions of s. 86 were considered by the Supreme Court in *Mirza Ali Akbar* v. *United Arab Republic*.[169] The court observed : "The effect of the provisions of s. 86(1) appears to be that it makes a statutory provision covering a field which would otherwise be covered by the doctrine of immunity under international law." According to their Lordships the effect of s. 86(1) is : (a) The doctrine of immunity recognized by international law is to a certain extent modified by it. (b) A foreign state cannot rely on the doctrine of immunity when the Central Government gives consent to institute suit against it. (c) The municipal courts of India are bound to give effect to the provisions of the law which modifies the doctrine of immunity under international law.[170]

It was a suit for damages filed by an Indian against the UER for breach of contract. It was cogently argued on behalf of Mirza Ali that in recent years there had been an enormous increase in the trading activities of States and therefore when a State engaged in commercial activities, it should not enjoy any immunity, as in such a case no legitimate claim of sovereignty was violated if the municipal courts exercised jurisdiction over foreign states in regard to their commercial or trading activities. Thus the argument of Mirza Ali was for the application of the restrictive theory of sovereign immunity which lays down that the national courts have power to exercise jurisdiction over foreign states if the claim against them arose out of the commercial or trading transactions. But the Supreme Court following English precedents, refused to accept this argument and adhered to absolute theory of sovereign immunity. The Supreme Court further opined that jurisdictional

166. *Mirza Ali Akbar* v. *United Arab Republic*, 1966 S.C. 230.
167. 1962 S.C. 73.
168. Section 87, C.P.C.
169. 1966 S.C. 230.
170. See *Bengal River Service* v. *G-G in Council*, (1969) 73 C.W.N. 125; *German Democratic Republic* v. *Dynamic Industrial Undertaking Ltd.*, 1972 Bom. 27.

immunity existed under private international law independently of section 86.

It seems that section 86 does not apply to suits against the department of a State and it would be for the Department to establish its claim for immunity. The question came for consideration before the Calcutta High Court in *New Central Jute Mills. Co. Ltd.* v.*VED Dentfracht Sureedarci Rostock*,[171] where an Indian Company sued the defendants, a DSR lines, a career and supplier of goods, an East German Company. In their defence, the defendants averred that since they were a nationalized company of German Democratic Republic, they, as department, agent, or instrumentality of the Government enjoyed jurisdictional immunity under private international law independently of section 86. A suit did not lie against them without the prior permission of Indian Government, the defendants further argued. The trial court took the view that section 86 had no application to the present case, since it was *ex facie* not a suit against a foreign state. The court observed, "it is quite apparent on a plain reading of the expressions used whereas consent is required to institute suits against foreign states as such it does not appear that such restriction applied to organs of foreign state or against a body or an organ which is even part of the foreign state." On appeal, the Calcutta High Court held that jurisdictional immunity did not exist outside section 86. And, since under section 86 only foreign state could claim immunity, the defendants were not covered. The learned judge, in our submission rightly observed." Speaking for myself I would like to hold that foreign state do not enjoy such immunity. That would be in consonance with justice, equity and good conscience having regard to the various trading or non-governmental activities carried on by the Government." Thus the learned judge favoured the restrictive theory of jurisdictional immunity. But unfortunately the learned judge hesitated to accept it. He opined, "it is yet to be established as a definite proposition of law in India as to whether the present accepted trend of international law is that the foreign states do not enjoy immunity in respect of commercial transactions.) One wishes that the Calcutta High Court should have followed the majority view propounded in *Trendtex Trading Corporation* (we have reviewed the case earlier), since we have been adhering to English precedents and this one was really the one our courts should have followed. Let us hope that our courts will not miss the opportunity of incorporating the restrictive theory of jurisdictional immunity in our law. It should not be necessary for us to have a statute like the one England passed in 1978—State Immunity Act. Let us hope that when cases reaches the Supreme Court, the Supreme Court would benefit from *Trendtex Trading Co*. The matter is also under the consideration of International Law Commission under the title "Jurisdictional Immunities of States and their property."

1983 Cal. 225.

If we examine the aforesaid four cases in which the Government of India may give its consent to enable a plantiff to sue the head of a foreign state, ambassador, high commissioner etc., then it becomes evident that these are also the cases in which, under the English Private International Law, an action or other proceedings lie against the head of foreign state, etc. Section 86, Civil Procedure Code does modify the rule of private international law in the sense that even in those cases where a plantiff can file a suit against a diplomatic representative he cannot do so in India, unless he obtains consent of the Government of India. This means that under the Indian law diplomatic reprentatives are granted additional immunity, in the sense, that even though a diplomatic representative waives his privilege, he cannot be sued unless the Government of India consents to such a suit. Section 86 applies to all stages of proceedings.[172]

There are certain exceptional cases where a diplomatic representative may be sued without the consent of the Government of India. These exceptions are : (a) A person may, as a tenant of immovable property, sue a diplomatic representative from whom he holds or claims to hold the property.[173] (b) When a person sets up a claim of set-off in his defence to a suit by the diplomatic representative, no consent of the Government of India is necessary.[174] (c) If the proceedings in a court of law are not a suit, consent of the Government of India is not necessary. Thus, proceedings under s. 14 read with s. 17, Arbitration Act, 1940 for obtaining a judgment and decree on an award is not a suit within the meaning of s. 86(1) and therefore no prior permission is necessary.[175] Similarly, s. 86 does not apply to proceedings for adjudication of an industrial dispute[176] as the proceedings are not initiated by a suit : thus an Industrial Tribunal is not a court. Section 86(1) does not apply to the insolvency proceedings wherein the diplomatic representative is one of the creditors of the insolvent.[177] But if the proceedings are a suit, then in whatever capacity the diplomatic representative is sued, compliance with s. 86 is necessary.[178]

Immunity in execution proceedings : It has been seen that under English law even when a diplomatic representative waives his immunity or submits to the jurisdiction, this waiver does not extend to execution proceedings.[179] The Indian law also gives effect

172. *Mohan Lal* v. *Sawai Mansinghji*, 1962 S.C. 73
173. Proviso to s. 86(1).
174. *Sukhdev Singh* v. *Hazuramal*, (1921) 62 I.C. 778.
175. *Nawab Usman Ali Khan* v. *Sagarmal*, 1965 S.C. 1798.
176. *Bhagwat Singh* v. *State of Rajasthan*, 1964 S.C. 144 Section 86 does not apply to proceedings for letters of administration (1956 Bom. 45).
177. *Madanlal* v. *H.H. the Nawab Sayed Raja Ali Khan*, 1940 Cal. 244.
178. *Dulerai & Co.* v. *Pokardas*, 1952 Bom. 335.
179. This is also the position maintained under the English statute, the Diplomatic Privileges Act, 1964.

to this principle in a different form. Sub-section (3) of s. 86 runs : "No Ruler of a foreign state shall be arrested under this Code, and except with the consent of the Central Government certified in writing by a Secretary to that Government, no decree shall be executed against the property of the Ruler." Thus, it would appear that under Indian law the question of waiver of immunity or submission to jurisdiction in the execution proceedings by a diplomatic representative is essential. What as required is the consent of the Government of India. It seems that consent of Government of India will also be necessary in execution proceedings when the decree-holder is a tenant and as such covered under the proviso to s. 86(1), under which no consent of the Government of India is required for filing a suit.

Government departments and public corporations : Section 86 of the Civil Procedure Code does not speak of the jurisdictional immunity of the departments and corporations of the foreign governments. This does not mean that under Indian Private International Law, government departments and public corporations do not enjoy jurisdictional immunity. Our courts have taken the view that government departments and public corporations enjoy like jurisdictional immunity as is enjoyed by the foreign Ruler. The question was considered in some details by the Calcutta High Court in *Royal Nepal Airlines Corporation* v. *Manorama*[180] wherein the wife of one Mehar Singh Legha, who was employed by the Royal Nepal Airlines Corporation as an aircraft pilot and who died in an air crash, sued the defendants, Royal Nepal Airlines Corporation, for damages. The defendant corporation claimed jurisdictional immunity on the ground that the Royal Nepal Airlines Corporation was established by the Royal State the Royal Nepal Airlines Corporation Act. The Corporation was owned by his Majesty's government of Nepal and was functioning as its department. The trial court was requested by the defendants to try the preliminary issue of jurisdiction first. But the trial court felt that the jurisdictional issue was connected with the facts of the case and therefore listed the case for hearing. An appeal was made against this order. In the appeal the Nepalese ambassador intervened and claimed sovereign immunity, on behalf of His Majesty the King of Nepal. He also stated that the defendants were a government enterprise and the Airline was operated on commercial basis. Bose, C.J., after an exhaustive review of all the English authorities, observed that even if the defendant corporation was a separate corporate body, it would not prevent the Nepal Government from claiming sovereign immunity provided the defendant can be regarded as a department of the Government of Nepal. The learned judge found that the defendant was a department of the government and therefore held that it was entitled to immunity.[181] Thus a department

180. 1966 Cal. 319.

181. See also, *Mirza Ali Akbar* v. *United Arab Republic*, 1966 S.C. 230.

of the foreign state or a foreign corporation which is a department of the government is entiled to jurisdictional immunity. The Indian law recognizes two exceptions :

(1) When the foreign Ruler or diplomatic representative by himself or another trades within the local limits of the jurisdiction of the court, he can be sued with the consent of the Government of India.[182]

(2) The Government Trading Taxation Act, 1926 applies to the trading activities of foreign sovereigns and diplomatic representatives. The question came for consideration before the federal court in *A.H. Wadia* v. *C.I.T.*[183] The Gwalior Durbar (the Gwalior State, one of the Indian states, was then entitled to sovereign immunity as under private international law it came within the definition of a foreign state) gave some money by way of loan to one corporation which was incorporated in British India. The corporation brought that money to British India and invested it in business. The interest on that amount was payable at Gwalior and it was paid at Gwalior. The loan that the Gwalior Durbar gave was part and parcel of its trading activities. Under the Act of 1926 the tax was payable not only on the income of interests arising in British India but also on the income of all interests arising directly or indirectly in British India. The Federal Court held that the income of the Gwalior Durbar on the funds invested in British India was part of income arising in India and the Gwalior Durbar could not claim immunity from taxation of this income. The statute of 1926 is a state enactment and no rule of international law contrary to it can be given effect to. The Bombay High Court also held that any foreign state while engaged in business and trade in India is liable under the Act of 1926 topay tax on income arising directly or indirectly out of that business or trade.[184]

Diplomatic representatives and their staff : The Indian Law relating to the jurisdictional immunity of the diplomatic representatives and their staff has been codified by the Diplomatic Relations (Vienna Convention) Act, 1972 which has been passed to give effect to the Vienna Convention on Diplomatic Intercourse and Immunities of the year 1961. The unique aspect of the Act is the Vienna Convention of 1967 has been made part of the Act by putting it in the Schedule to the Act. The Act lays down that the Convention shall have the force of law. The

182. Section 86(2)(b).

183. 1949 F.C. 18.

184. *Income Tax Commissioner* v. *Wadia,* 1948 Bom. 87. See also *Patiala State Bank* v. *Commissioner of Income Tax*, 1943 P.C. 181 ; *Rani Amrit Kunwar* v. *Commissioner of Income Tax*, 1946 All. 306; *A.H. Wadia* v. *Commissioner of Income Tax, Bombay,* 1949 F.C. 18.

Government of India has also the power to apply the provisions of the Act to the members of a diplomatic mission of the state which is not a party to the Convention, subject to such modifications, as the Government of India deem necessary or expedient. Similarly, provisions of the Act can be made applicable to special missions also. Wherever any doubt arises whether a person is entitled to privilege, it will be settled conclusively by a certificate given by or under the Authority of the Secretary to the Government of India (Section 9). The immunity on the diplomatic representative is conferred when he has been accepted or received by India. The persons granted immunities and privileges, fall under the following three categories :

(a) Diplomatic agents,

(b) Members of the administrative and technical staff, and

(c) Members of the service staff.

Diplomatic agents : Under this category are heads of the diplomatic missions and members of the mission, such a secretaries, attaches and counsellers.

Such persons are exempt from the civil and criminal jurisdiction of the courts in regard to both official and private acts. They are not liable to any form of arrest or detention. Even though he may institute proceedings, no remedy is enforceable against him in India either at the instance of the State or private individual. But if such a person is Indian citizen, then immunity extends only to official acts. However, Article 31 lays down that the following three exceptions to the exemption from civil jurisdiction :

(a) A real estate action relating to private immovable property situated in the territory of the receiving state, unless he holds it on behalf of the sending State for the purpose of the mission,

(b) An action relating to succession in which the diplomatic agent is involved as executor, administrator, heir, or legatee in his capacity as a private person, and not on behalf of the sending state, and

(c) An action relating to any professional or commercial activity exercised by the diplomatic agent in the receiving state outside his official functions.

No execution proceedings can be filed against the diplomatic agent except in cases coming under the aforesaid three exceptions. But in no case the inviolability of his person or his residence can be impinged. He can also not be obliged to give evidence.

The diplomatic agents are also exempt from all dues and taxes, personal or real national, regional or municipal. But this exemption does not apply to :

(a) indirect taxes of a kind which are normally incorporated in the price of goods or services ;

(b) dues and taxes on private immovable property situated in the territory of the receiving State, unless he holds it on behalf of the sending State for the purposes of the mission ;

(c) estate, succession or inheritance duties levied by the receiving State ;

(d) dues and taxes on private income having its source in the receiving State and capital taxes on investments made in commercial undertakings in the receiving State ;

(e) charges levied for specific services rendered ;

(f) registration, court or record fees, mortgage dues and stamp duty, with respect to immovable property.

The aforesaid privileges granted to a diplomatic agents also extend to the members of his family forming part of his household provided they are not Indian nationals.

Members of the administrative and technical Staff: Under this head are included such persons as clerks, typists, archivists, and wireless and telephone operators. Such persons together with the members of their family are immune from civil jurisdiction in respect of their official acts but not in regard to their private acts. It is also necessary that such members are not Indian citizens. They have the same immunity to taxes and dues as the members of the diplomatic mission.

Members of the service staff : In this category are included domestic staff of the members of the mission, such as butlers, cooks, maids and chauffeurs. These persons have no immunities and privileges if they are Indian nationals, or are permanent residents of India. Otherwise they enjoy immunity from the civil jurisdiction in respect of acts performed in the course of their duties. They are also exempt from income tax and other dues. In other respect they would enjoy only such privileges and immunities as granted by the Government of India.

Premises of mission and residences of the members of the mission : The premises of mission as well as residences of the members of the mission are inviolable and no agent of the Indian Government or any other person can enter the premises without the prior permission of the head of the mission. Similarly, premises of the mission, their furnishing and other property, thereon and the means of the transport of the mission are immune from search, requisition, attachment or execution. Similarly no national, regional and municipal taxes can be levied on such premises.

The archies and documents of the mission are also inviolable.

Communications : Protection is also accorded to free communications for all official purposes such a communication with the Government and other missions and consulates of the sending State. This also means that the mission has the freedom to employ all appropriate means, including diplomatic couriers and messages in code or ciphur. But wireless transmitters can be installed only with the permission of the Government of India. All official correspondence of the mission is also inviolable Diplomatic bags and packages cannot be opened but then they must bear visible external mark of their character. The protection extends to diplomatic curiers, including inviolability of their person.

The inviolability of communication extends to the private correspondence of the members of the mission.

Articles and Goods : The mission has freedom to import articles for official use, for personal use of diplomatic agent or members of his family including articles intended for his establishment (Article 36). But the members of the mission cannot so imports goods in India as to sell them in India and claim exemption from duty of custom. In case they sell these goods in India all duty of custom and other dues will be payable (Section 6). Similarly, the personal baggage of the diplomatic agent is exempt from inspection, unless there are serious grounds for presuming that it contains articles not covered under exemption or contain articles of import or export of which is prohibited by law.

Duration of the Immunities : The immunities and privileges enjoyed by the members of the diplomatic mission normally cease at the moment when they leave India, or when their functions come to an end or within the reasonable time of relinquishing his position. But immunities continues to endure in respect of acts already done by him in exercise of his official functions and duties, but immunity does not extend in regard to private acts already done. In case of the death of members of the mission, the members of his family shall continue to enjoy privileges and immunities until the expiry of a reasonable period in which to leave the country.

Waiver of Immunity : The sending state may waive the jurisdictional immunity of its agent. But waiver should be express. Further, the initiation of proceedings by a diplomatic agent enjoying jurisdictional immunity shall preclude him from invoking immunity from jurisdiction in respect of any counter-claim directly connected with the principal claim. But in execution proceedings a separate waiver would be needed. A waiver by the head of the mission amounts to waiver by the State (Section 5).

It has been seen that under English private international law a diplomatic representative or a foreign sovereign can waive his immunity and submit to the jurisdiction of the court. Under s. 86(2)(d), Indian Civil Procedure Code it has been laid down that if a Ruler of state or diplomatic representative expressly or impliedly waives his privilege, then the Central Government can accord permission to sue him. In Indian law the provision was introduced by the amendment of Civil Procedure Code in 1951. The Indian law of waiver of immunity is substantially the same as English law. In *United Arab Republic* v. *Mirza Ali Akbar*[185] the Calcutta High Court considered the question. Lahiri, C.J. observed : "Under the law of our country . . . whatever may be the purpose for which the defendant enters appearance must necessarily be unconditional. From such an appearance therefore there can be no inference of an unequivocal intention to submit to the jurisdiction of court." The court held that making of an application under Order 7, Rule 11, Civil Procedure Code did not amount to submission to jurisdiction. Similarly, the *Royal Nepal Airlines Corporation* v. *Manorama*,[186] where a written statement was filed before the court in which along with the claim of jurisdictional immunity, the submissions were also made on merit of the case and where all along the proceedings the claim of jurisdictional immunity was pressed, the court held that this did not amount to waiver of immunity, as there was nothing to show that there was an unmistakable election to submit to court's jurisdiction.[187] In *Indian National Steamship Co. Ltd.* v. *Maux Faulbaun*[188] the court held that the conduct of the defendant amounted to submission to jurisdiction. In this case the Republic of Indonesia applied for leave to be examined *pro inter se suo*, as against the adverse claim of the plaintiff in the suit and also asked the court to investigate into the question of the title of the Republic (and the court ordered an inquiry as asked for), and also applied for issue of Letters of Request to examine witnesses in Holland to prove its title, the court held that this amounted to waiver of privilege.

Rules of former Indian states : The Civil Procedure Code confers some jurisdictional immunity on the Rulers of the Indian states.[189] The jurisdictional immunity can be enjoyed only on the fulfilment of the following two conditions :

(1) Former Indian state must be such Indian state as is specified by notification in the official gazette by Government of India, and

(2) Ruler must be a person who, for the time being, is recognised by the President as the Ruler of that state for the purpose of the constitution.

With the merger of Indian states and their integration with the various states of India, the former princely states lost their separate entity. However, with a view to implement the assurances given to Indian princes that they would continue to be entitled to personal privileges enjoyed by them, whether within or outside the territories of their respective states, the present provision in s. 87B was

185. 1962 Cal. 387.
186. 1966 Cal. 319.
187. See *Ibid*. at p. 345 where Mitter, J. has considered the matter in detail.
188. 1955 Cal. 491.
189. Section 87B, C.P.C.

enacted. It should be kept in view that the privilege or immunity conferred by s. 87B applies not to all former princes but only those who have signed an agreement under Article 291(1), Constitution of India, who have been recognized by the President of India and who have been guaranteed a privy purse. With the derecognition of Indian princes by the President, the provision is now only of academic interest.

Reviewing the position of Indian states before independence of India, Mr. Justice Jaganmohan Reddy of the Supreme Court observed : "It is clear from the very nature of native states in India that they were subject to the sovereignty and protection of the British Crown, while their relations with the Crown were governed by treaties, though initially on terms of equality, as time went by and the British Crown in India became paramount the relationship between it and the rulers became unequal with the result that these treaties become subject to the reservation that they could be disregarded where the interest of the British Empire or those of subjects of the native states were concerned."[190]

Thus the former Indian states were not full international persons. However, their rulers were recognized as being at par with rulers of full sovereign states in respect of their jurisdictional immunity. In full Bench pre-independent judgment, the Allahabad High Court observed that there was considerable authority for the view that a ruling prince was not normally capable of being sued in a court of British India or a court in England.[191] Before independence the immunity of princely states was partly gevern-ed by statutes and partly by notifications of the Government of India.[192]

In *Commissioner of Income Tax, A.P.* v. *Mir Usman Ali Khan Bahadur*[193] the question was : whether the Ruler of Hyderabad state prior to January 26, 1950, could claim immunity from taxation under international law. The Supreme Court said that the Nizam being under the sovereignty of the British Crown, had never enjoyed the status of a sovereign as understood in international law and therefore was not governed by that law and that any event, on January 26, 1950, the date on which he became liable to taxation

190. *Harinder Singh* v. *I. T. Commissioner, Punjab,* 1972 S.C. 202 at p. 206. The learned judge also referred to the correspondence between Nizam and Lord Reading in which Nizam's claim of equality was rejected.

191. *Rani Amrit Kunwar* v. *Commissioner of Income Tax,* 1946 All. 306 at p. 316. See also, *The Accountant General, Baroda State* v. *The Commissioner of Income Tax, Bombay City,* 1948 Bombay 409 : The ruler of Baroda is not subject to municipal law of India ; *Maharaja Bikram Kishore of Tripura* v. *Province of Assam* (1949) 17 I.T.R. 78 : The ruler of Indian State is not amenable to taxation in British India in respect of property held by him in his capacity as a ruler.

192. *Chandulal Khushalji* v. *Awad Bir Umer Sultan,* (1897) 21 Bombay 351.

193. 1966 S.C. 1260.

he was no longer a sovereign and therefore could not claim exemption under international law. The court held that the personal property of the ruler was not exempt from taxation.[194] It has also been held that if at the time when suit was filed the state of defendant had merged in the dominion of India, he ceased to be the sovereign prince and therefore s. 86 did not apply to him.[195]

The present position is that there are no rulers of former Indian states as none is recognized by the President of India and therefore there would be no occasion for invoking s. 87B of the Civil Procedure Code.

WHO MAY FILE A SUIT

Under English law, except the alien enemy, any person can file an action or other proceedings in any English court. Whether a person is an alien enemy depends on the fact that the United Kingdom is at war with another country. At common law, 'alien enemy' means any person who voluntarily resides or who carries on business in an enemy or enemy-occupied territory during a war in which the United Kingdom is engaged.[196] A prisoner of war does not come within the meaning of the term 'alien enemy'.[197] The test of enemy character is a territorial test and not a national one. Thus an enemy subject who resides and carries on business in the United Kingdom or in an allied or neutral country is not an alien enemy. He is treated as an alien friend.[198] On the other hand, if a British subject or citizen of an allied or neutral country adheres to enemy, by giving them aid and comfort will be an alien; enemy, even if he resides in United Kingdom or in an allied or neutral country.[199] A company may be also invested the character of alien enemy if it is incorporated in an enemy country or if its directors come within the meaning of the term alien enemy. The

194. The same view was taken in *Harinder Singh* v. *Income Tax Commissioner*, 1972, S.C. 202.

195. *Ibid.*

196. *Porter* v. *Freudenberg*, (1915) 1 K.B. 857.

197. *Vandyke* v. *Adams*, (1942) Ch. 155.

198. *Sovrachat* v. *Van Udens*, (1943) A.C. 203; the test is objective one and is not guided by prejudices, passions or patriotism.

199. *Porter* v. *Freudenberg*, (1915) 1 K.B. 857; *Daimler Co. Ltd.* v. *Continental Tyre & Rubber Co. Ltd.*, (1916) 2 A.C. 307; *Sovrachat* v. *Van Udens*, (1943) A.C. 203 : a company incorporated in Holland and having its principal place of business at Rotterdam; became an alien enemy after the occupation of Holland and Germany in the II World War. See also *Janson* v. *Driefontein Consolidated Mines*, (1920) A.C. 484. See *The Pamila* (1943) 1 All E.R. 269 : if its office is shifted to a country not occupied by enemy, it will not be an alien enemy. See also *Re Hilckes*, (1917) 1 K.B. 48. The Trading with the Enemy Act, 1939 contains a statutory definition of an 'enemy'. But that definition is limited to the purpose of the Act and does not affect the common law definition of alien enemy.

situs of property of a company does not affect its character.[200]

Except under a royal licence, an alien enemy cannot file an action or any other proceedings in an English Court.[201] Even if he had begun an action before he had the character of enemy alien, he cannot continue the action once he acquires that character;[202] nor can he file an appeal;[203] he cannot also appear as a claimant in an interpleader suit.[204] The royal licence given to the alien enemy to sue in a court of law may be express or implied.[205] The licence can also be revoked.[206]

An alien enemy can defend himself if an action is brought against him and can also claim set-off,[207] but not a counter-claim.[208] He can also file an appeal.[209] Dicey and Morris give two or possibly three exceptions to the rule.[210]

(1) Alien enemy can be joined as co-plaintiff in an action by a firm of partners of which he was formerly a member to recover a pre-war debt due to the firm, on somewhat spacious ground that the rule should not be applied if to do would inflict hardship not on the enemy but on British or neutral partners.[211]

(2) An alien enemy can be heard without licence in the Prize Court if the claim is based on an international treaty or convention but not otherwise.[212]

(3) There is an ancient authority for the proposition that an alien enemy can sue *en autre droit*, e.g. as executor or administrator of a deceased person.[213]

Indian Law

In India, except the alien enemies, all others can file a suit or other proceedings in an Indian Court. The same is the position of

200. *Jansen* v. *Driefontein Consolidated Mines*, (1920) A.C. 484.
201. *Porter* v. *Freudenberg*, (1915) 1 K.B. 857; *Sovrachat* v. *Van Udens*, cited above.
202. *Fibrosa* v. *Fairbairn* (1943) A.C. 32.
203. *Porter* v. *Freudenberg*, cited above.
204. *Geiringer* v. *Swiss Bank Corporation*, (1940) 1 All E.R. 406.
205. *Princess Thurn and Texis* v. *Moffitt*, (1915) 1 Ch. 58.
206. *Netz* v. *Ede*, (1946) Ch. 224.
207. *Re Stahlwerk Becker's Patent*, (1917) 2 Ch. 272.
208. *Ibid.*
209. *Porter* v. *Freudenberg*, cited above.
210. Dicey & Morris, p. 145.
211. This is based on *Rodrigues* v. *Speyer Brothers*, (1919) A.C. 59. In *Sovrachat* v. *Von Udens*, (1943) A.C. 203, Lord Wright said that this rule must be limited to the special facts of the case.
212. Based on *The Mowe* (1915) p. 1; *The Glessoy* (1943) p. 109.
213. Based on *Brocks* v. *Philips*, (1599) Cro. Eliz. 683; *Richfield* v. *Udell*, (1667) Carter 48; *Villa* v. *Dimock*, (1694) Skin 370. It is, however, an open question whether this authority would be followed.

a foreign corporation.[214] The law is codified and is contained in s. 83, Civil Procedure Code. The section lays down an alien friend may sue in any Indian Court and an alien enemy may also do so with the prior permission of the Government of India. Explanation to s. 83 defines an alien enemy as under : "Every person residing in a foreign country, the Government of which is at war with India and carrying on business in that country without a licence in that behalf granted by the Central Government, shall, for the purpose of this section, be deemed to be an alien enemy residing in a foreign country." It is necessary that India must be at war with that country.[215]

The term alien enemy includes not only the citizens of the enemy country but also citizens of India as well as of neutral countries who are voluntrily residing in the enemy country.[216] The test of 'alien enemy' under Indian law is that either a person has his residence in an enemy country or that he carries on business in enemy country; nationality is of no consequence. The residence must be voluntary a prisoner of war cannot be called alien enemy.[217] Residenceneed not be permanent one though it should not be fleeting or casual residence. Similarly, just because a person has been interned by the Government of India, he does not become an alien enemy.[218]

An alien enemy residing in a foreign country cannot sue in Indian courts.[219] An alien enemy residing in India can sue in Indian courts if he is residing here with the permission of the Government of India.[220] Such permission may be express or implied. It may be presumed from circumstances. The Madras High Court held that when an alien enemy had been allowed to reside in India even after the outbreak of war without being ordered to remove himself, the permission to continue to reside in India might be presumed.[221] If a suit is filed against an alien enemy, he has the right of defence.[222]

In *Angelina* v. *Joseph*[223] the plaintiff who was a German residing in India, with the permission of the Government of India, filed a

214. *Singer Manufacturing Co.* v. *Baijnath*, (1902) 3 Cal. 103.
215. *Chen Abbheorg* v. *M.A. Pachiri Mohamed*, 1946 Mad. 328; In this case the territory (Federated States of Malay) was occupied by the enemy : but the government of Malay was not at war with India. It was held that person carrying on business there is not an alien enemy.
216. *Ali Jan* v. *Abdul Zallil Khan*, 1920 Lah. 4.
217. *Ibid.*
218. *Prem Pratap Singh* v. *Jagat Pratap Kunwar*, 1944 All. 97.
219. *Ali Jan* v. *Abdul Zallil Khan*, 1920 Lah. 4; *The Karadeniz*, 1920 Bom. 285.
220. *Angelina* v. *Joseph George Reittsteck*, 1917 All. 374.
221. *O. Wuthrik* v. *David*, 1918 Mad. 1294.
222. *Prem Pratap Singh* v. *Jagat Pratap Kunwar*, 1944 All. 97; *Angelina* v. *Joseph George Reittsteck*, 1917 All. 374; *Abdul Kader Khalifa* v. *Fritiza Kapp*, 1917 Cal. 838.
223. 1917 All. 374.

suit for judicial separation in an Indian court against the defendant who was residing in Germany. At that time England was at war with Germany. The plaintiff also filed an application for orders directing the summons to be sent to the Probate etc. Division of the High Court of England for transmission to the foreign office and service upon the respondent. The Allahabad High Court held that suit was maintainable and ordered that summons be sent to the High Court of England. A Pakistani on visit to India on a permit though an alien, can file a suit for restitution of conjugal rights.[224]

Though it was not necessary to provide so, but nonetheless s. 84 lays down that a foreign state may sue in any competent court, provided that the object of the suit is to enforce a private right vested in the Ruler of such state or in any officer of such state in his private capacity. This is obvious. No political rights can be enforced by a suit. Section 85 provides facilities to foreign Ruler who files a suit in an Indian court. At the request of such foreign Ruler, the Government of India may appoint any person to prosecute or defend any suit on behalf of such Ruler. The section runs as under :

"(1) The Central Government may, at the request of the Ruler of a foreign state or at the request of any person competent in the opinion of the Central Government to act on behalf of such Ruler, by order, appoint any person to prosecute or defend any suit on bahalf of such Ruler, and any person so appointed shall be deemed to be the recognized agent by whom appearances, acts and applications under this Code may be made or done on behalf of such Ruler.

(2) An appointment under this section may be made for the purpose of a specified suit or of several specified suits, or for the purpose of all such suits as it may from time to time be necessary to prosecute or defend on behalf of such Ruler.

(3) A person appointed under this section may authorize or appoint any other person to make appearances and applications and do acts in any such suit or suits as if he were himself a party thereto."

II

ACTIONS IN RESPECT OF PROPERTY

Broadly speaking actions in respect of property may be of the following three types :

(1) action *in rem*;

(2) action in respect of immovable property; and

224. *Nizamuddin* v. *Husseni*, 1960 M.P. 212. See also *Anil Chandra* v. *Ravum Chandra Saha*, 1958 Tripura 25.

(3) action in respect of movable property.

Jurisdiction in action in rem : Broadly speaking actions *in rem* are of three kinds, those which determine the title or right to possession of property, admiralty actions relating to ships within English territorial waters, and actions affecting personal states. However, technically speaking after the passing of Common Law Procedure Act, 1852 all actions in the Queen's Bench Division of the High Court are actions *in personam* and the only action *in rem* that no survives is the action in the Admiralty Division of the High Court, against a ship or other *res*, such as cargo or freight, connected with a ship or against an aircraft. The primary object of an action *in rem* is to satisfy the plaintiff's claim out of the *res*. In the words of Morris, "the essence of the procedure *in rem* is that the *res* may be arrested and sold by the court to meet the plaintiff's claim, provided it is proved to the satisfaction of the court."[225] An action *in rem* should not be confused with judgment *in rem*. In an admiralty action *in rem*, the court passes a decree which determines the status of the ship after its sale and this decree is binding on all persons in the world, as it is, sometimes loosely said, binding against the whole world. In the words of Gorrel Barnes, J., "The admiralty action is an action *in rem*, that being, as I understand the term, a proceedings against a ship or other chattel in which the plaintiff seeks either to have the *res* adjudicated to him, the property or possession or to have it sold under the authority of the court, and the proceeds or part thereof, adjudicated to him in satisfaction of his pecuniary claim."[226] In such an action the party is the ship and therefore the jurisdiction can be exercised only if the ship is in territorial waters.[227]

Important changes in this branch of law have been made by the Administration of Justice Act, 1956 which has been enacted to give effect to the Brussels Convention of 1952 on the arrest of sea-going ships. The admiralty jurisdiction *in rem* as well as *in personam* of the court has been defined in s. 1(1) which lists eighteen "claims" of maritime nature. Admiralty actions *in rem* can be filed against the following *res* : ships, cargo in or landed from a ship and identifiable as cargo, freight, aircraft and their cargo, the proceeds of sale of ships, cargo or aircraft. Rules of the Supreme Court provide for service of writs and warrants of arrest. Section 3 of the Act lays down cases in which admiralty jurisdiction of the court may be exercised, in action *in rem*. Section 4 of the Act defines the jurisdiction of the court in actions *in personam* for damage, loss of life or personal injury arising out of a collision between two ships. Section 6 lays down the power of the Secretary of State to certify the cases in which neither jurisdiction *in rem* nor *in personam* can be exercised.

Actions *in rem* should not be confused with judgments *in rem*.

225. Dicey & Morris, p. 214.
226. *The Ripon City*, (1897) p. 226.
227. *Castrique* v. *Imrie*, (1870) L.R. 4 H.L. 414.

In an admiralty action *in rem*, the court passes a decree which determines the status of the ship after its sale and this decree is binding on all persons in the world, as sometimes it is loosely said, binding against the whole world. Proceedings in marriage are proceedings *in personam*, but when the court adjudicates that a marriage is dissolved or annulled, the judgment is a judgment *in rem* in the sense that it is binding on all persons, as it affects the status of parties. Similarly, a suit against immovable property is an action *in personam*, but the judgment delivered therein is a judgment *in rem*.

The jurisdiction rules in actions in respect of property, movable and immovable are discussed in the respective chapters dealing with these topics.

Indian Law

In Indian law strictly speaking there is nothing like an action *in rem*. Section 41 of the Indian Evidence Act defines judgments *in rem*. The section runs as under :

"A final judgment, order or decree of a competent court, in the exercise of probate, matrimonial, admiralty or insolvency jurisdiction which confers upon or takes away from any person any legal character, or which declares any person to be entitled to any such character or to be entitled to any specific thing not as against any specified person but absolutely is relvant when the existence of any such legal character, or the title of any such person to any such thing is relevant."[228]

The question of jurisdiction in respect of an action relating to property, movable and immovable, will be discussed later on along with specific topics. Similarly, the question relating to jurisdiction of courts in matrimonial causes,[229] guardianship, custody,[230] and maintenance of children,[231] legitimacy[232] and adoption,[233] the winding up of companies,[234] the administration of estate of deceased persons,[235] succession,[236] insolvency[237] are not dealt with here but will be dealt with in Chapters respectively dealing with the topics. The jurisdiction of foreign courts in actions *in personam* and *in rem* would be dealt with in a separate chapter dealing with the recognition and enforcement of foreign judgments.[238]

228. See Para. 1 of s. 41.
229. See Chapter 9 of this work.
230. See Chapter 12 of this work.
231. See Chapter 10 of this work.
232. *Ibid.*
233. See Chapter 11 of this work.
234. See Chapter 13 of this work.
235. See Chapter 19 of this work.
236. *Ibid.*
237. See Chapter 18 of this work.
238. See Chapter 25 of this work.

Part III

FAMILY LAW

SUMMARY

8

MARRIAGE

All over the civilized world, marriage is a very important social institution. Whether considered as a sacrament or a contract marriage gives rise to status. It confers a status of husband and wife on the parties to marriage and it confers a status of legitimacy on the children of marriage. The basic difference between the marriage and any other contract is that a commercial or mercantile contract does not give rise to any status, while marriage does. Then, once the marriage is performed, the contract of marriage has no utility in respect of the marriage or in regard to any rights and liabilities arising under it.

I

CONCEPT OF MARRIAGE

Practically all the countries of the world agree that marriage is a union between man and woman. Beyond this there are differences. In the Western countries marriage is considered as a contract, and a monogamous union, though Roman Catholic church (despite the recent Italian legislation conferring power of dissolving marriage on civil courts) still insists that marriage is a sacrament and an indissoluble union. The Muslim world has all along considered marriage as a civil contract, though has, at the same time, recognized limited polygamy.[1] At one time in the East—among Hindus and Buddhists—marriage was considered as a sacrament and indissoluble union; among both the people unlimited polygamy was recognized. Today the Buddhists and Hindus no longer recognize polygamy. The Chinese Buddhists consider their marriage as a contract.[2] Among Hindus marriage is something in between

1. A Muslim can have four wives simultaneously, and even when he takes a fifth or more, the marriage is not void but merely irregular (*fasid*). Some Muslim countries like Turkey, have abolished polygamy, while some, like Pakistan have placed restriction on its practice. On the other hand, in countries, like India, Muslims are allowed to practice polygamy limited to four wives.
2. See the Chinese Family Law of 1931 and 1949.

a sacrament and a contract.[3]

English Law

Under the English domestic law marriage is defined as a voluntary union for life between one man and one woman to the exclusion of all others. English courts have adopted this very concept of marriage to the conflict of laws cases, and this has led to much hardship and injustice in respect of polygamous marriages. In *Hyde* v. *Hyde*[4] Lord Penzence observed : "I conceive that marriage, as understood in Christiandom, may for this purpose be defined as the voluntary union for life of one man and one woman to the exclusion of all others." Then, it seemed logical for him to express the following view : "Now, it is obvious that the matrimonial law of this country is adapted to the Christian marriage, and is wholly inapplicable to polygamy."[5] In this case a husband of a potentially polygamous Mormon morriage, performed at Utah, petitioned for divorce in an English court. After renouncing his faith the husband became a Minister of a dissenting chapel at Derby and the wife remarried. The petition was dismissed because the English courts were not prepared to accord recognition to polygamous unions, and they considered that their matrimonial jurisdiction could not be made available to such marriages. In *Harvey* v. *Farnie*[6] the court of Appeal took the extreme position that polygamous marriages could not be recognized for any purpose. Taking the view that nature and incidents of marriage are determined by the *lex loci celebrationis* and the characterzation of marriage as to whether it is monogamous or polygamous is determined by the *lex fori*, the English court maintained that even if there was a possibility of converting a polygamous marriage into a monogamous marriage, the potentially polygamous marriage remained a polygamous union and cannot thus be recognized.[7] In *Sowa* v. *Sowa*[8], before the solemnization of his polygamous marriage a Ghanian promised his wife that he would, after the marriage, undergo another ceremony (which he was allowed to do under the law of Ghana) converting his potentially polygamous marriage into a monogamous marriage. But he did not fulfil his promise. The English court held that the marriage remained a polygamous union. In a case where personal law permitted only monogamy, though allowed concubines, the English court characterized such marriage as a polygamous union.[9] In those cases where a person had actually married more than one wife, the English courts have refused to recognize any 'wife' of such

3. See Hindu Marriage Act, 1955. See also author's work, Modern Hindu Law, Codified and Uncodified, (1984) pp. 67-69.
4. L.R. (1866) 1 P. M. 130 at p. 133.
5. *Ibid.* at p. 135.
6. L.R. (1880) 6 P. & D. 35; on appeal, (1882) 8 A.C. 43.
7. *Lee* v. *Lau*, (1967), p. 14.
8. (1961) p. 70.
9. *Lee* v. *Lau*, (1964) 2 All E.R. 248.

marriage.[10] On the other hand, if the personal law of a person does not permit him to practise polygamy, then a polygamous marriage contracted by such a person at a place where polygamy is allowed, will not be recognized in England.[11] This seems to be the only explanation of the decision in *Re Bethell*,[12] where a marriage solemnized in Bechuanaland in a polygamous form between the domiciled Englishman and a woman of Barlong tribe was held void.[13] In *Re Ullee*[14] an English court said that a marriage celebrated in polygamous form in England between an English woman and a Mohammedan domiciled in India is not binding on the former.[15] In *Ali* v. *Ali*[16] the court said that a person whose personal law permits polygamy cannot validly take a second wife if he changes his domicile to England. The Matrimonial Proceedings (Polygamous Marriage) Act, 1972 now lays down that a polygamous marriage entered into outside England and Wales between parties either of which is domiciled in England, will be void. It is immaterial that the marriage is only potentially polygamous.[17]

Today it is not necessary that a marriage to be recognized in England must conform to the definition of marriage laid down in *Hyde* v. *Hyde*.[18]

It is an established proposition of law that despite the distinction between Christian and non-Christian marriages made in *Hyde* v. *Hyde*[19] English courts recognize all monogamous marriages, Christian as well as non-Christian. Thus Chinese,[20] Japanese,[21] Jewish[22] and Hindu marriages[23] are recognized as valid monogamous marriages. Similarly, a marriage need not be a 'permanent marriage'. What is necessary is that at the time when it is entered into it must be indefinite in duration. The fact that

10. *Hyde* v. *Hyde*, L.R. (1966) 1 P. & M. 130; *Risk* v. *Risk*, (1951), p. 50.
11. Dicey and Morris, Rule 35, p. 283.
12. (1887) 38 Ch. D. 220.
13. This decision may be contrasted with *Kenward* v. *Kenward*, (1951), p. 124 where Denning, L.J. said that a marriage solemnized in polygamous form in a country where polygamy is lawful between a domiciled Englishman and a woman domiciled there belonging to the community which recognizes polygamy, should be regarded for many purposes as valid in England.
14. (1985) 53 L.T. 711.
15. On the other hand, in *Lendrum* v. *Chakravarti*, 1929 S.L.T. 96 (Scottish case) a marriage solemnized in Glasgow Church between a Hindu belonging to a monogamous sect and domiciled in India with a Scot woman domiciled in Scotland was held valid.
16. (1966) 2 W.L.R. 620.
17. Section 4. Now s. 11(d) of Matrimonial Causes Act, 1973.
18. (1866) L.R. 1 P. & M, 130.
19. *Ibid.*
20. After the abolition of polygamy in 1931.
21. *Brinkley* v. *A.G.*, (1890) 15 P.D. 76.
22. *Penhas* v. *Ten Soo Eng*, (1953) A.C. 304 (P.C.).
23. After the Hindu Marrige Act, 1955.

in future it is dissoluble at the instance of one of the parties or both the parties is immaterial.[24] In *Nachimson* v. *Nachimson*[25] the Court of Appeal said that the dissolubility cannot affect the original character of marriage. It also seems to be settled that whether the marriage is indefinite in duration, or definite in duration, (such as Mutta marriages among Shia Muslims), is governed by the *lex loci celebrationis*.[26]

The most vexed question in private international law is : under which law should marriage be characterized as monogamous or polygamous ? Should it be the personal law of either party or pre-marriage domicile or by the law of matrimonial home or should it be the *lex loci celebrationsis* ? In *Lee* v. *Lau*[27] the court said that it is for the latter to determine the nature and incidents of the union, and then it is for the *lex fori* to decide whether the marriage is polygamous or monogamous. Thus if a Pakistani domiciled Muslim marries in England at a Registry Office (not in a private house) he contracts a monogamous marriage.[28] The converse is also true. If a domiciled Englishman goes through a polygamous ceremony of marriage recognized in a country where polygamy is recognized, he contracts a polygamous union.[29] Cheshire suggests that the character of marriage, whether polygamous or monogamous, should be determined by the law of the matrimonial domicile.[30] This seems to be a sensible suggestion. The only possible criticism of this rule is that it would deny English matrimonial relief to English girls marrying Muslims (or other persons whose personal law or law of matrimonial home recognizes polygamy) in monogamous form in England.[31]

The modern English law has now taken a full circle—from the position of non-recognition of polygamous marriages, it has come to almost full recognition of such unions.[32] The Matrimonial

24. *Nachimson* v. *Nachimson*, (1930), p. 217.
25. *Ibid.*
26. *Ibid.*
27. (1964) 2 All. E.R. 248.
28. There is a long line of cases, beginning with *R.* v. *Hammersmith Superintendent Registrar of Marriages, Ex parte, Miranwarruddin* (1917) 1 K.B. 634; *R.* v. *Naguib*, (1917) 1 K.B. 359; *Maher* v. *Maher*, (1951) p. 342; *Chetti* v. *Chetti*, (1909), p. 67; *Srinivasan* v. *Srinivasan* (1946) p. 67; *Baindail* v. *Baindail*, (1946), p. 122; *Russ* v. *Russ*, (1964) p. 315; *Ohochuku*, v. *Ohochuku*, (1960) 1 W.L.R. 183.
29. *Re Bethel*, (1887) 38 Ch. D. 290 *Risk* v. *Risk*, (1951) p. 50.
30. Cheshire, p. 269 (all references to Cheshire in this Chapter are from the Seventh edition of his work on private international law). In support of his view Cheshire quotes the following case : *Harvey* v. *Fernie*, (1882) 8 A.C. 43, observation of Lord Brougham; *Yousuf* v. *Yousuf*, (1957); *The Times*, August 1; *El-Riyami* v. *El-Riyami*, (1958), *The Times*, April 1; and *Ross* v. *Ross*, (1964) p. 315.
31. Dicey and Morris, p. 277 (All reference to Dicey and Morris are from the eighth edition).
32. For instance, *Mehta* v. *Mehta*, (1945) 2 All E.R. 690 where it was observed that a marriage monogamous in its inception cannot be regarded as potentially polygamous because the husband is free to join a poly-

Proceedings (Polygamous Marriages) Act, 1972 is the culmination.

It may be recalled that in *Harvey* v. *Fernie*[33] Lord Rush observed (*obiter*) that if any one of the two wives of a Muslim came to England and took another husband, then she could not be prosecuted for bigamy. And an Indian court, following English precedents, carried this proposition to its logical end in *Sofia* v. *Shive Prasad*,[34] where an Indian domiciled Hindu already having a Hindu wife, married a Jewess in Paris. The parties came to India. After some time the wife filed a petition in an Indian court for a decree of nullity on the ground that at the time of her marriage the respondent already had a wife living. The Calcutta court held that since the first marriage of the respondent being a polygamous marriage would not be recognized under the French law—the *lex loci celebrationis*—, his second marriage with the petitioner was valid. In *Baindail* v. *Baindail*[35] an Indian domiciled Hindu already having a wife underwent a ceremony of marriage with an England domiciled English girl. When the English girl petitioned for nullity of marriage on the same ground on which Sofia had done, the English court had no hesitation in granting the petition. The English court observed thal recognition of marital status being universal, it would recognize the marital status of even a polygamously married person. However, the court made it clear that polygamous unions cannot be recognized for all purposes.

Then for what purposes do the English courts accord recognition to polygamous unions ? In *Sinha Peerage Claim*[36] the Children of potentially polygamous marriage of an Indian domiciled Hindu were recognized as legitimate and were held to be entitled to inherit the English peerage. *Ali* v. *Ali*[37] goes a little further. Two Indian domiciled Muslims whose marriage was potentially polygamous, acquired a domicile of choice in England, though parties continued to adhere to Islam. The court observed that since the law of domicile did not permit polygamy, the potentially polygamous marriage has got converted into a monogamous union so much so that it was competent for the English court to dissolve it or to provide any other matrimonial relief. In *Cheni* v. *Cheni*[38] two Jews domiciled in Egypt and related to each other as uncle and

gamous sect. On the other hand, in *Sinha Peerage Claim*, (1946) 1 All E.R. 348n (decided in 1939) the court observed that a marriage which at its inception is polygamous may become monogamous if the husband joins a sect which subscribes to strict monogamy. It is submitted that in the latter case the court was called upon to meet a different situation than in the former case.

33. (1880) 6 P.D. 35.
34. (1946) Cal. 484.
35. (1946) p. 122.
36. (1946) 1 All E.R. 348.
37. (1966) 2 W.L.R. 620. The court passed a decree on the ground of husband's adulttry.
38. (1965) p. 85.

niece got married in Cairo. Five years after the marriage the parties acquired English domicile. Subsequently, the wife petitioned for a decree of nullity on the ground that parties were related to each other within degrees of prohibited relationship. The court assuming the jurisdiction said that at the date of proceedings the marriage has ceased to be a polygamous union and since the parties were within the degrees of prohibited relationship at the time of the marriage by their law of domicile, the English court could pass a decree of nulity.[39] These decisions lay down that the decisive date for considering whether a marriage is polygamous or monogamous is not the date of marriage, but the date on which proceedings for matrimonial relief are filed.[40] Before 1972, i.e. before the coming into force of the Matrimonial Proceedings (Polygamous Marriages) Act, 1972, it was also the settled position at English law that the English matrimonial jurisdiction was not available to parties of polygamous marriages.[41]

The Matrimonial Proceedings (Polygamous Marriages) Act, 1972[42] empowers courts in England, Wales, Northern Ireland and Scotland to grant matrimonial relief to parties of marriage whose legal system permits polygamy, irrespective of the fact whether the marriage is in fact polygamous or merely potentially polygamous.[43] Section 1(i) of the Act runs : "A court in England and Wales [similar provision is made in s. 2 in respect of Scotland and in s. 3 in respect of Northern Ireland] shall not be precluded from granting matrimonial relief[44] or making a declaration[45] concerning the

39. See also *Parkasho* v. *Singh*, (1966) 110 S.J. 864=(1968) p. 233.

40. See also *Kenwrad* v. *Kenwrad* (1951) p. 124, where Lord Denning L.J. discusses as to which law governs capacity to marry.

41. *Hyde* v. *Hyde*, (1866) 1 p. & M. 130; *Baindail* v. *Baindail*, (1946) p. 122 (C.A.); *Muhammad* v. *Suna*, (1956) S.C. 366; *Ohochuku* v. *Ohochuku*, (1960) 1 W.L.R. 183; *Ali* v. *Ali*, (1966) 2 W.L.R. 620; *Risk* v. *Risk*, (1951) p. 50.

42. The Act implements the Law Commission's proposal on polygamous marriages (No. 42).

43. Sections 1, 2 & 3 : Now s. 47, Matrimonial Causes Act, 1973.

44. The 'matrimonial relief' is defined in sub-section (2) as :

"(a) a decree of divorce, nullity of marriage or judicial separation; (b) a decree under s. 14 of the Matrimonial Causes Act, 1965 (dissolution of marriage on the basis of presumption of death); (c) an order under s. 8 of the Matrimonial Proceedings for Property Act, 1970 (wilful neglect to maintain); (d) an order under s. 14 of the said Act of 1970 (alteration of maintenance agreements); (e) an order under any provision of the said Act of 1965 and 1970 or the Divorce Reform Act, 1969 which confers a power exercisable in connection with, or in connection with proceedings for, any such decree or order as is mentioned in the foregoing paragraphs; (f) an order under the Matrimonial Proceedings (Magistrates Courts) Act, 1960". This is now s. 47(2) of the Act of 1973.

45. "A declaration concerning the validity of marriage" is defined in sub-section (3) as :

"(a) a declaration that a marriage is valid or invalid; and (b) any other declaration involving a determination as to the validity of a marriage, being a declaration in a degree granted under s. 39 of the said

validity of a marriage by reason only that the marriage was entered into under a law which permits polygamy." The provisions of s. 1 will apply whether or not either party to marriage in question has for the time any spouse additional to the other party.[46]

The next question that arises is : whether a valid polygamous marriage is a sufficient first marriage to support an indictment for bigamy.[47] This question was left undecided in *Baindail* v. *Baindail*.[48] In *R*. v. *Sarwan Singh*,[49] the court answered the question in the negative.[50]

The next question is : how far do English courts accord recognition to the wife of a polygamous union ? Morris thinks that she would be treated as wife unless there is some reason to the contrary.[51] *Alhaji Mohammed* v. *Knott*[52] is a very instructive case in this connection. This may now be treated as settled that the husband-wife status of polygamously married persons would be recognized in English law. English decisions also appear to lay down that spouses of a potentially polygamous marriage cannot be guilty of criminal conspiracy[53] and the wife or wives of a citizen of the United Kingdom and Colonies are entitled to claim citizenship thereof.[54] It is now also settled law that wife of a polygamous marriage is entitled to maternity benefit and a widow of such marriage will be entitled to benefits under the national insurance schemes.[55]

Act of 1965 or a declaration made in proceedings brought by virtue of rules of court relating to declaratory judgments." This is now s. 47(3) of the Act of 1973.

46. Sub-section (4) further lays down : "This section has effect whether or not either party to the marriage in question has for the time being any spouse additional to the other party." This is now s. 47(4) of the Act of 1973.

The Act further lays down that "provisions may be made by rules of the court (a) for requiring notice of proceedings brought by virtue of this section to be served on any such other spouse; and (b) for conferring on any such spouse the right to be heard in any such proceedings." Section 1(4), (a) & (b).

47. Section 57, Offences Against the Person Act, 1861 lays down that the offence of bigamy is committed by any person who 'being married, shall marry any other person during the lifetime of the former husband or wife'. It will not be an offence of bigamy if the first marriage has been annulled or dissolved or if the first spouse has been continuously absent for seven years.
48. (1946) p. 122.
49. (1962) 3 All. E.R. 612.
50. Court of Appeal has approved this view in *R*. v *Sagoo*, (1975) P. 885.
51. Dicey and Morris, p. 290.
52. (1968) 2 W.L.R .1446.
53. *Mawji* v. *The Queen*, (1957) A.C. 126 (P.C.).
54. By registration under s. 6(2), British Nationality Act, 1948.
55. See, The National Insurance Act, 1965, s. 113(1); The National Insurance (Industrial Injuries) Act, 1965, s. 86(5); The Family Allowances Act, 1965, s. 17(c); under these enactments a marriage performed outside the

Then, the question is: how far the children of polygamous marriages are entitled to succeed to the property of their parents situated in England? In *Sinha Peerage Claim*[56] Lord Maugham observed: "a Hindu marriage between persons domiciled in India is recognized by our courts, that issues are regarded as legitimate, and that such issues can succeed to property in this country, with a possible exception which will be referred to later." The high watermark was reached in *Bamgbose* v. *Daniel*[57] where the children of a Nigerian from nine polygamous marriages were held to be entitled to succeed to his property situated in England. This continues to be the trend.[58] This also appears to be clear that a child of polygamous marriage cannot succeed to (a) real estate in England (this is the exception to which Lord Maugham referred to in *Sinha Peerage case*), and (b) to a title of honour and to property limited to devolve therewith.[59] The reason for this distinction appears to be the Englishman's lingering attachment to the notion that English heirship is incompatible with polygamous system of law which makes no distinction of status or between the various wives and their respective childern.[60]

The last question that remains is relating to mutual rights of succession of the spouses of polygamous unions. It appears to be the position in English law that the surviving spouse of a polygamous marriage can succeed to the property of the other spouse in case of intestacy, irrespective of the fact whether the marriage was potentially polygamous or factually polygamous, and irrespective of the fact whether the intestate died domiciled in England or abroad.[61]

Indian Law

In India each religious or quasi-religious community has its

United Kingdom is treated as valid marriage for the purposes of the Acts provided that the marriage has been at all time in fact monogamous. See also, *Imandin* v. *National Assistance Board*, (1967) 2 Q.B. 213.

56. (1946) 1 All E.R. 348n.
57. (1955) A.C. 107 (P.C.).
58. In *Hashmi* v. *Hashmi* (1971) 3 W.L.R. 918, a Pakistani domiciled Muslim who already has undergone a polygamous marriage in 1948, again underwent a ceremony of marriage in England with a domiciled English woman from whóm be had three children. The main question before the court was whether children were legitimate. The court held that though for the purpose of English law the second marriage was void, yet, since the marriage is recognized as valid by the husband's law of domicile, the English courts would recognize the children of such a marriage as legitimate.
59. *Birtwhistle* v. *Vardill*, (1840) 7 Cl. & F. 895.
60. Cheshire at pp. 275-76 relying on *Baindail* v. *Baindail*, (1946), p. 122, at p. 128.
61. *Coleman* v. *Shang*, (1961) A.C. 481 (P.C.), where a Ghana domiciled person married a Ghanian domiciled woman in the polygamous form of marriage. On his death his widow applied for a grant of letters of administration of the estate of the deceased. The court granted her the letters of administration.

own personal law. In personal matters or matters pertaining to family, India has no national or regional (i.e. state law) law. The majority community, the Hindus, have their own family law, so has the biggest minority community the Muslims. Other minorities like Christians, Parsis and Jews too have their own separate personal laws. Besides some differences in fundamentals and some variations in details, Hindus all over India are governed by Hindu law.[62] The Muslims, the largest of them belong to the Sunni sect, and minorities include Shias, Malikis, Shafis and Hanabalis (the last are almost extinct), are governed by Muslim law.[63] Similarly, the Parsis are governed by Parsi law, the Christians by Christian law and Jews by the Jewish law.[64]

The differences and variations in Hindu law are mainly between the two schools of Hindu law, the Dayabhaga which prevails in Bengal, Assam, Tripura and Manipur, and the Mitakshara which prevails in rest of India. There are also some differences in the Mitakshara jurisdiction represented by its four sub-schools, the Benaras, the Bombay, the Mithila and the Dravida. The modern Hindu raw is in two parts, codified and uncodified. Differences and variations exist only in respect of the uncodified law. The codified Hindu law applies to all Hindus uniformly.

Some differences also exist among the different sects of Muslims. The Sunnis, who represent the majority of Muslims, mostly belong to the Hanafi legal system. The Shias, who represent the largest minority sect among Muslims, mostly belong to the Ithna Ashari system. The Shafai and the Ismaili are the other minority Muslim sects. Mention should also be made of the three commercial communities of Muslims, the Khojas, the Bohras and the Memons who, before the Sharait Act, 1937, were not governed by Muslim law, but partly by Hindu law and partly by custom. Now, they are mostly governed by Muslim law, though to some extent custom still governs them. The former two belong to the Shiate Ismaili sect and the last to the Sunnite Hanafi sect. The Mapilla Muslims of South India, another minority community of Muslims, were at one time entirely governed by custom. Today also they are governed in some matters, such as *tarvard*, by custom and in others by Muslim law. The other communities, the Christians, the Parsis and the Jews have no schools or sub-schools, though the urban Parsis are governed by a slightly different law than the rural Parsis. Similarly, some minor differences exist between the European Christians and the native Christians.[65]

62. See Mayne, Hindu Law and Usage (11th ed.), Chapter II; see this author's work, Modern Hindu Law, Codified and Uncodified (IV ed.), Chapter IV; Mulla Hindu Law, (14th Ed.) Chapter II.

63. See Paras Diwan, *Muslim Law in Modern India*, Chapter I. Mulla, Mohammedan Law, Chapter III.

64. See Kumud Desai, Indian Law of Marriage and Divorce, (II ed.) Part IV; Paras Diwan, *Family Law*, Chapter I.

65. *Ibid.*, Part V.

In personal matters, in India, apart from law, custom has always played an important role. It has been an established rule of Hindu law that custom overrides sacred law.[66]

In the context that the personal law in India differs from community to community, it seems inevitable that in India there is no one concept of marriage. India is also a country where different types of marriages prevail and where personal law of a person is not determined by his domicile or his nationality but by his membership of the community to which he belongs.

Muslims are allowed four wives, though if a Muslim took more than four wives the subsequent marriages were not void but merely irregular. Law of no other community recognizes polygamy. Then it was also the country where a very limited number of people were allowed to practise polyandry.[67] After May 18, 1955 (when the Hindu Marriage Act came into force) bigamy is not allowed to Hindus and it has been made a penal offence.[68] Thus in modern India, Muslims are the only people who have the privilege of practising polygamy (limited to four wives).

Hindus have always considered their marriage as a sacrament which has the implication that it is permanent, indissoluble and eternal.[69] In modern Hindu law marriage has become not only monogamous[70] but also a dissoluble union.[71] To a great extent it has ceased to be a sacramental union,[72] though it is doubtful whether it has become a full-fledged contract.[73] It may be noted that under the Hindu Marriage Act, 1955, 'any two Hindus', whether domiciled in India or not, whether Indian nationals or foreigners, can perform their marriage.

Hindus can still perform their marriage in customary modes.[74]

66. *Collector of Madura* v. *Mootoo Ramalinga*, (1868) 12 M.I.A. 397.
67. In Lahaul Valley bordering Tibet in some tribes, whose number is not more than a few thousand people, and a few people in South India practise polyandry.
68. Section 17, Hindu Marriage Act, 1955.
69. See this author's work, Modern Hindu Law, Codified and Uncodified, Chapter V.
70. Section 5(1), Hindu Marriage Act, 1955.
71. Section 13, Hindu Marriage Act, 1955.
72. It is sacramental in the sense that a sacramental ceremony is still necessary; see this author's work, Modern Hindu Law, Chapter VII.
73. *Ibid.*
74. Section 7, Hindu Marriage Act, 1955, for instance Jats in Punjab and Haryana can still perform their marriage by *chadar andazi*. In this form a person marries his brother's widow; what happens is this : He puts a *Chadar* on the head of the widow (or puts it around her shoulders) and if the widow accepts it (which usually she does), then parties become husband and wife. Among some lower caste Hindus *Koreva* form of marriage is still solemnized. In this marriage a man and woman agree to live together as husband and wife and when they actually live as such, they become husband and wife. Among Jati Vaishnavas a marriage can be performed by exchange of garlands between the bride and bridegroom. See Paras Diwan, Customary law (1990); Rattingam's Digest of Customary Law.

A Muslim marriage in India has always been considered as a contract. Muslim marriage (*nikah*) has been defined as "a civil contract which has for its object the procreation and legalizing of children."[75] The Shia Muslims recognize two types of marriages : permanent marriage, and temporary marriages (*muta* marriages). In the latter case the duration of marriage is fixed under the contract of marriage. The duration of marriage may be any, a day, a week, a year or number of days, weeks, or years.[76] A Shia male can contract a valid *muta* marriage with a female who is Muslim, Christian, Jew or even with a fire-worshipper, but with follower of no other religion. On the other hand, a Shia female cannot enter into a valid *muta* marriage with a non-Muslim.[77] The incidents of a *muta* marriage are : it stands dissolved automatically, *ipso facto*, on the expiry of the term; no divorce is recognized, though the husband has the option of terminating it earlier by making a 'gift' of the remaining term of marriage at any time. The children of *muta* marriage are legitimate, and they have the right to inherit the property of both the parents. The wife of *muta* marriage can neither claim maintenance from her husband, nor can she inherit his property. Sunnis do not recognize *muta* marriage. A *Sunni* male has capacity to marry a female of any sect of Muslims as well as a Christian or Jewess, but not with a fire-worshipper or idol-worshipper. However, his marriage with a fire-worshipper or idolatress is not void or voidable but irregular.[78] A *Sunni* female cannot contract a valid marriage with a non-Muslim. But the marriage of a *Sunni* female with a *Kitabia* (i.e. Christian or Jew) is not void but irregular. A Shia Muslim cannot contract a valid permanent marriage with a non-Muslim.[79]

Among the Christians the concept of the marriage is the same as under English law. In India, the Christian marriages are performed under the Christian Marriage Act, 1872. Under the Act a marriage may be performed before a marriage registrar[80] or it may be solemnized by a minister of religion licensed under the Act.[81] The Act contains separate provisions for the solemnization of marriage among Indian Christians.[82] The peculiar feature of the Act (in the Indian context) is that if a Christian, male or female, wants to perform a marriage with a non-Christian, the marriage can be performed only under the Christian Marriage Act, otherwise such a

75. Mulla, Mohammedan law, (17th ed.), p. 255; Paras Diwan, Muslim law in Modern India (1984) Chapter V.
76. In *muta* marriage dower should also be specified. When both term and the dower are fixed, it is a valid *muta* marriage.
77. See Baillie, II, 29, 40; Mulla, p. 265.
78. Hadaya, 30; Baillie, 40-42; Mulla, p. 259.
79. *Ibid.*
80. Part V of the Act.
81. Part III of the Act.
82. Part VI of the Act.

marriage will be void.[83] Whether the marriage of a Muslim female with a Christian male can be validly performed under the Act, it seems, is doubtful.[84] Section 88 of the Act lays down, "Nothing in this Act shall be deemed to validate any marriage which the personal law applicable either of the parties forbids him or her to enter." Mulla thinks that such a marriage cannot be performed under the Act.[85] It has been held that a marriage between a Roman Catholic woman and a Jew under the Act is void as the personal law of the Roman Catholics forbids such marriage.[86] On the other hand, a marriage, between a Roman Catholic male and a Protestant female solemnized in a Protestant Church by a Protestant Pastor but without the dispensation of Roman Church as required under the canon law, was held valid.[87] It is submitted that this appears to be the sound view. Thus, whenever the marriage of a Muslim with a non-Muslim will be irregular under Muslim law, it will be valid under the Christian Marriage Act, but where such a marriage will be void under Muslim law, it will also be void under the Act.

The Parsis also consider their marriage as a contract. The Parsis are those who profess Zoroastrian religion.[88] The Parsis marriage is a monogamous union, so much so that a Parsi by changing his domicile or religion cannot contract another marriage under the Parsi law or under any other law in the life time of his or her, wife or husband, whether a Parsi or not.[89] If such a marriage is performed it will be void.[90] The marriage and matrimonial causes among Parsis are regulated by the Parsi Marriage and Divorce Act, 1936 as amended by the Act of 1988. Under the Act a marriage can be performed only between two Parsis and for every such marriage the religious ceremony of 'ashirbad' is necessary.[91] Parsis also recognize divorce.[92]

The marriage among the Indian Jews is a monogamous union and a contract. A written contract called *katuba* between the parties to marriage is essential. A religious ceremony is also required. Divorce is also allowed among the Indian Jews.

Then, in India, we have the Special Marriage Act, 1954 under which 'civil marriage' can be performed between 'any two persons'.

83. Section 4.
84. There is no judicial authority for the proposition either way.
85. Mulla, p. 259.
86. *Jude* v. *Jude*, 1949 Cal. 563.
87. *Ganansoundari* v. *Nallathambi*, 1945 Mad. 516. See also *Saldanha* v. *Saldanha*, 1930 Bom. 105.
88. Section 2(7), Parsi Marriage and Divorce Act, 1936; see also *Sir Dinshaw M. Petit* v. *Sir Jamsetji Jijibhai*, 11 Bom. L.R. 89; *Jamshed Irani* v. *Banu Irani*, 68 Bom. L.R. 794; The Iranian followers of Zoroastrian religion are also Parsis under the Act.
89. Section 4(1), Parsi Marriage and Divorce Act, 1936.
90. Section 4(2).
91. Section 3(b).
92. Part IV of the Parsi Marriage and Divorce Act, 1936.

In fact, in India, inter-caste, inter-communal and inter-religious marriages can be performed only under the Act.[93] (Provisions of the Act have been summarized in subsequent pages.)

Since in India ordinarily inter-communal and inter-religious marriages are not possible, there is no possibility of direct conflict arising between the laws of various communities. However, there is a possibility of the conflict of inter-communal laws arising indirectly. The situation in which this is possible is when one of the spouses of a marriage converts to another religion. Then the question that arises is : whether it is the law as applicable at the time of the marriage which governs or the law applicable after conversion. In the latter case, whether it would be the law of the spouse who has converted or the law of the non-convert spouse. This question has come before our courts in several cases. In all these cases the non-Muslim spouse has converted to Islam.

The question first arose in *Khambatta* v. *Khambatta*,[94] where in 1905 an Indian domiciled Muslim male married a Scot domiciled woman in Scotland before a Marriage Registrar. Subsequently parties came to India and the wife embraced Islam. In 1922, the husband pronounced divorce on his wife. The wife also obtained a declaration from the civil court that the marriage stood dissolved. Then she underwent a ceremony of civil marriage with one Khambatta under the Special Marriage Act, 1872. After ten years of marriage, the wife petitioned for a declaration of nullity of her marriage with Khambatta on the averment that since her Scottish marriage has not been dissolved by any court of law, her second marriage being bigamous was void. The main question before the court was whether her first marriage was validly dissolved. The court was called upon to decide whether the marriage was governed by the law applicable at the time of the marriage or was governed by the law applicable after conversion (or the law of the matrimonial domicile as Cheshire would put it). The court held that it would be law after conversion that would govern the marriage. Therefore, the court came to the conclusion that the first marriage was validly dissolved. Blackwell, J. observed that if change of domicile can effect a change in status then there is no reason why the change of religion should not do the same thing. In *Nurjahan* v. *Tisanco*[95] two Russians solemnized their marriage in Berlin. Both the parties were Christians at that time. They lived together in several European countries till 1938 when the wife came to India and the husband went to Scotland. In 1940, the wife converted to Islam and assumed the name of Nurjahan and thrice

93. This statement is subject to the limited freedom allowed for inter-religious marriages under Mohammedan law and Christian law (this has already been stated earlier). But even in such cases the marriage is known as either the Muslim marriage or the Christian marriage, as the case may be.

94. 1935 Bom. 5.

95. 45 C.W.N. 1047.

offered Islam to her husband (under Muslim law if a Muslim spouse offers to his non-Muslim spouse Islam thrice and if the latter refuses to accept it, then the marriage stands terminated). On the husband's refusal to accept it, the wife filed proceedings in an Indian court for dissolution of marriage. The court dismissed the petition on the short ground that since the parties were not domiciled in India, the court has no jurisdiction. However, the court observed that no spouse can, on converting to another religion, impose his new religion on the other spouse. In *Aiyasabibi* v. *Subodh Chandra*[96] parties were at the time of marriage Hindus domiciled in India. The marriage was solemnized with Hindu ceremonies and rites. After sometime, the wife converted to Islam, and offered Islam thrice to her husband. On his refusal to do so, she launched proceedings for dissolution of marriage in an Indian court. She also averred that her husband had treated her with cruelty. The court passed a decree in favour of the wife dissolving the marriage. It seems that in granting the decree the cruelty of the husband loomed large in the mind of the judge. The learned judge also observed that in such cases the law applicable will be the law of the wife after conversion. This is the only case where this view has been propounded. Subsequent cases do not subscribe to this view.

In *Saeeda Khatun* v. *Ovedia*[97] two Jews domiciled in India performed their marriage in India in 1943 by Jewish ceremony. In 1945 the wife embraced Islam and offered it to her husband. On his refusal to accept it, she launched divorce proceedings. Dismissing the petition, the court observed that there was no law under which a marriage performed under one personal law could be dissolved under another personal law, just because one of the parties has converted to another religion. This is also the view taken by the Calcutta High Court in another case[98] and by the Bombay High Court.[99]

On the basis of the above decisions two propositions may be formulated : (a) If both parties change their religion, then they will be governed by the new personal law.[100] (b) If one of the spouses alone changes his religion, then no matrimonial relief can be granted to the convert-spouse on the basis of his new personal law.[101] The first view appears to be just but there is a possibility of its abuse. May be, a couple, to whom no matrimonial relief is available under its personal law, may conveniently convert to a religion under which desired matrimonial relief can be obtained.

96. (1945) 2 Cal. 405.
97. (1945) 49 C.W.N. 754.
98. *Rakeya Bibi* v. *Anil Kumar*, (1948) 2 Cal. 119.
99. *Rabav Khanan* v. *Khodadad Jomanji Irani*, (1948) 48 Bom. L.R. 864=1947 Bom. 272.
100. See *Khambatta* v. *Khambatta*, 1935 Bom. 5.
101. See decisions noted in footnotes 97, 98, 99.

The second proposition does not provide a solution to the problem : it is merely its negative disposal. Then does it mean that parties can claim only that matrimonial relief which is available to them under their original personal law ? It may be noticed that under the Hindu Marriage Act, 1955, s. 13(1)(ii), if one of the spouses ceases to be a Hindu by converting to some other religion, then the other spouse can seek divorce on that ground. Under Muslim law apostasy from Islam operates as a complete and immediate dissolution of marriage.[102] But, it is submitted, it is one-sided solution of the problem. The question still remains : should the convert spouse not be entitled to any relief ?

In this connection the provisions of the Native Converts' Dissolution of Marriage Act, 1986 – a master-piece "missionary legislation" by the British rulers of India—may be looked at. Under the Act, if one of the native spouses converts to Christianity, and on account of this if the other abandons him or deserts him for six months or more, then a decree of divorce can be passed on the petition of the convert-spouse. If the respondent is wife, then the court would postpone the consideration of the petition for one year to enable her to accept the new religion of her husband and to cohabit wiih him. If she does not do so during that period, then the decree of divorce would be pronounced. However, the provisions of the Act apply only when both husband and wife are Hindus or Parsis. If parties are Christians, Muslims or Jews the Act does not apply. It is submitted that if a similar law is made available to people of all communities in India, it would provide a socially desirable solution to a problem which arises on account of the change of religion by one spouse and non-accommodation by the other spouse to this changed situation. It is submitted that a provision applicable to the members of all communities should also be enacted on the lines of s. 13(1)(ii) of the Hindu Marriage Act, 1955. So long as India does not have a uniform family law, such a solution of the inter-communal conflict of laws is necessary.

In India we have another branch of matrimonial law which comes into application only when parties choose to be governed by it. This law is enacted in the Special Marriage Act, 1954. Under the Act, 'any two persons' may opt to perform a civil marriage. If they do so, then neither of them is governed by the law of the community to which he or she belongs. Once the parties choose to marry under the Act, all matrimonial matters are regulated by the Act. Marriage under the Act is strictly monogamous, and divorce and other matrimonial reliefs are also available under the Act. Apart from the fact that the Special Marriage Act, 1954 permits civil marriage between 'any two persons', there are two other outstanding features of the Act : (a) Any marriage, which is monogamous in fact (it includes a potentially polygamous marriage also), whether performed in India or abroad, whether

102. In respect of married Muslim woman this has now been modified by s. 4, Dissolution of Muslim Marriage Act, 1939.

performed as civil marriage or as a religious marriage, and irrespective of the fact as to which community or religion parties belong, can be registered under the Act.[103] The effect of registration is that from the date on which a certificate of marriage has been finally entered into in the Marriage Certificate Book, the marriage is deemed to be a marriage solemnized under the Act, with the result that all provisions of the Act become applicable to the parties. (b) The Act also contains a provision under which marriage can be dissolved by the mutual consent of the parties.[104] The foreign married couples and the foreign domiciled couples can also take advantage of this provision. The outstanding, aspect of the Act is that it avoids the conflict of inter-communal and inter-religious laws which is bound to arise when parties to marriage belong to different communities or different religions.[105]

In the end, mention may be made of the Foreign Marriages Act, 1969. The Act provides facility for an Indian national to marry abroad with another Indian national or a national of another country or with a person domiciled in another country.[106] Marriage under the Act is a monogamous union and can be performed only as a civil marriage.[107] Any marriage performed abroad may also be registered under the Act, providedo ne of the parties to the marriage is an Indian national and provided further that the marriage is valid under the *lex loci celebrationis*.[108] Marriages thus registered under the Act are at par with the marriages performed under the Act. The provisions of the Special Marriages Act, 1954 relating to matrimonial causes apply to marriages performed or registered under the Act.[109]

In sum, the position in India is that, with the exception of Muslims, polygamy is not allowed to any people. In the laws of all communities of India the marriage is a contract. It is submitted that in whatever form the marriage may be performed or whatever concept of marriage may prevail anywhere, the status and obligations arising out of marriage should be accorded recognition all over the world, unless it is repugnant to some pronounced principles of public policy.

103. See Chapter III of the Act.
104. Section 28.
105. Succession to the property of such persons is also not governed by their personal law, i.e. by the law of the community to which party belongs, but by the Succession Act, 1925. This is so, even when both the parties belong to the same community.
106. Section 4.
107. Section 13, though parties are free to perform any additional ceremonies, religious or otherwise.
108. Section 17.
109. Section 18.

II
VALIDITY OF MARRIAGE

In any system of law for the validity of a marriage the fulfilment of two conditions is essential : (i) Parties to marriage must have capacity to marry. This is, in private international law, called the question of essential or material validity of marriage. (ii) Parties must have performed necessary ceremonies and rites of marriage. This is, in private international law, called the question of formal validity of marriage. A marriage to be valid must be valid formally and materially. If any of the two requirements is not fulfilled the marriage is void.

Problem of Characterization : The most difficult problem in regard to validity of marriage is the problem of characterization : by reference to which law the formal and the material validity of the marriage is to be judged ? The problem gets complicated as the domestic laws of countries of the world display such diversity as they display in no other area. Thus, it happens, the courts of one country consider a matter relating to marriage as a matter of formal validity, while the courts of another country consider the same matter as of material validity. This is precisely what happened in *Ogden* v. *Ogden*,[110] where the parental consent was characterized by French law as relating to material validity, while the English law as relating to formal validity, with the unhappy consequence that the lady was considered as married in England and divorced in France. "In distinguishing between matters regarded as essential and those of pure formality" Graveson very aptly says, "we must . . . resort to a functional test, namely, what is the reason or purpose of a particular legal system in imposing any requirement for marriage ? Applying this test, it will be found that whether or not any requirement of marriage is an essential or a formality depends on the degree or intensity of the public or social interest which it embodies and expresses. Those matters which are regarded as vital to the maintenance of an accepted standard in the matrimonial or family relation of any given society, whether on ground of consanguinity, religion or otherwise, will be regarded as essentials of the marriage, to be governed by the personal law of each party; while matters of less vital social interest, e.g., the length of public notice to be given before celebration of a marriage, or the number of witnesses whose presence is required at a ceremony, will be treated as pure formalities, to be determined exclusively by the law of the place of celebration."[111]

The vital question, then, is : under which law the classification of any requirement of marriage is to be made. Graveson says

110. (1908) p. 46.
111. Graveson, p. 262; *Apt* v. *Apt* (1947) p. 127.

that 'in justice and logic' it should be made by the law of each party's domicile, "since it is on a basis of control by the personal law that essentials are established".[112] Cheshire says that it should be determined by the matrimonial home of the parties.[113] The predominant English authority is that the characterization of a marriage solemnized in England will be made under English law, irrespective of the fact whether the parties are domiciled in England or elsewhere. If the marriage is solemnized abroad and one of the parties to the marriage is domiciled in England, then also, it seems, English courts characterize the marriage in reference to English law.[114] On the other hand, when both the parties are domiciled abroad and the marriage is solemnized abroad, then, it seems (there is no authority for the proposition) characterization will be made by reference to the law of the country where the marriage was solemnized. The English attitude is well illustrated by *Ogden* v. *Ogden*[115] and *Apt* v. *Apt*.[116] In the latter case an Argentina domiciled and resident German married a Jewess domiciled and resident in England. During the Second World War, the gentleman in Argentina had proposed marriage through correspondence to the lady in England. She accepted the proposal. The ceremony of marriage was performed by proxy which is recognized by Argentina law. When the validity of marriage was questioned in an English court, the court characterized the ceremony as a matter of form governed by the *lex loci celebrationis*, and held the marriage as valid. In this case, since the wife was domiciled in England, the nature of requirement of law was determined by English law.

The fact of the matter is that in early English decisions, the courts did not make much of a distinction between material validity and formal validity of marriage and both were determined by the *lex loci celebrationis*.[117] It appears that in **Brook** v. **Brook**[118] a distinction was made for the first time.[119]

It seems to be established that the material validity of a marriage in private international law is determined by law of the domicile of each party at the time of marriage, i.e. by the pre-marriage domicile, and the formal validity of the marriage is

112. Graveson, p. 265.
113. Cheshire, p. 277.
114. *Ogden* v. *Ogden*, (1908), p. 46. This case has been discussed in Chapter III of this work; *Apt* v. *Apt* (1947), p. 127; on appeal, (1948), p. 83.
115. (1908), p. 46.
116. (1947), p. 127.
117. For instance, see ***Scrimshire*** v. ***Scrimshire***, (1752) 2 Hagg. Con. 395; *Dalrymple* v. *Dalrymple*, (1811) 2 Hagg. Con. 54; ***Jones*** v. ***Robinson***, (1815) 2 Phill. 285.
118. (1858) 3 Sm. & G. 481; on appeal, (1861) 9 H.L.C. 193.
119. It was though adumbrated as early as 1831 in *Gronway* v. *Beazley*, (1831) 3 Hagg. Ecc. 639 by Dr. Lushington. Now this distinction is made in English law.

determined by the *lex loci celebrationis*. It is submitted that the policy of law of every country should be to lean in favour of the validity of every marriage, and courts of every country should be very slow to apply a law which renders the marriage invalid.

Material Validity of Marriage

English Law

As a general rule, capacity to marry is governed by the ante-nuptial domicile of each party. This rule has been laid down by the House of Lords in *Brook* v. *Brook*[120] and by the Court of Appeal in *Sottomayor* v. *De Barros*.[121] In the former case, parties were domiciled in England, and under English law they were within the degrees of prohibited relationship. They solemnized their marriage in Denmark where such marriages were valid. The House of Lords held the marriage as void because the parties lacked capacity to marry under their common ante-nuptial domicile. In the latter case, both the parties were domiciled in Portugal under the law of which they had no capacity to marry since they were related to each other within the degrees of prohibited relationship. They performed their marriage in England where such marriages were valid. On the same test, the Court of Appeal held the marriage as invalid.

Consent of Parties: Consent of parties to marriage has been characterized as a matter of essential validity of marriage, and therefore governed by the ante-nuptial domicile of parties.[122] *H.* v. *H.*[123] is an interesting illustration. A Hungarian domiciled girl underwent a ceremony of marriage in Hungary with her cousin who was domiciled in France with the sole purpose (which was known to the other party) of getting out of Hungary. Parties never lived together. Eventually the husband left for France and the wife for England. The wife petitioned in an English court for a decree of nullity on the ground that marriage was void for lack of consent. The court passed a decree in her favour apparently on the basis that she lacked capacity under her pre-nuptial domicile. It is submitted that the same would be the position in respect of effect of mistake on marriage (English domestic law is not well settled on this matter), if it affects the marriage fundamentally. In *Mehta* v. *Mehta*[124] the marriage was held void since the ceremony that the woman underwent was in fact a ceremony of marriage though she thought it was of betrothal. On the other hand, in *Kassim* v. *Kassim*[125] the court refused to pass a decree of

120. (1861) 9 H.L.C. 193.
121. (No. 1) (1877) 3 P.D. 1.
122. *Way* v. *Way* (1950), p. 71; *Kenward* v. *Kenward*, (1950) 2 All E.R. 297 (C.A.).
123. (1954), p. 258.
124. (1945) 2 All E.R. 690.
125. (1962), p. 224.

nullity on the petition of the husband on the averment that what he underwent was a ceremony of monogamous marriage while he thought it was of polygamous marriage (polygamy was allowed by his personal law).

Non-Age : At what age a person acquires capacity to marry differs from country to country. The Marriage Act, 1949 laysdown that a marriage between persons either of whom is under the age of sixteen shall be void. In *Pugh* v. *Pugh*[126] where a marriage was solemnized in Austria between a domiciled Englishman and a domiciled Hungarian girl who was then fifteen years old. The marriage was valid both by the Austrian and Hungarian laws. The English court, before whom the matter was agitated, held the marriage void. This decision appears to lay down that the English court will consider no marriage as valid if one of the parties to the marriage is domiciled abroad where such a marriage is valid, if such marriage is invalid under the English domicile of the other party.

Prohibited Degree : Every country lays down the degrees of prohibited relationship, and a marriage in violation of them is invalid. There is a great variation in these degrees in the various countries of the world. Since 1839 (now s. 1, Marriage Act, 1949) marriages within prohibited degrees of consanguinity and affinity have been considered void under English law.[127] Here also the general rule applies, i.e. parties must not be within the prohibited degrees of relationship by their ante-nuptial domicile. In *Brook* v. *Brook*[128] and *Sottomayor* v. *De Barros*[129] (as seen above) the marriage was held void on this basis. The English courts have applied this rule even when one of the parties to the marriage is domiciled in England. In *Mette* v. *Mette*[130] a German, domiciled in England, married in Germany, after the death of his wife, his wife's half sister who was domiciled in Germany. The marriage was valid by German law, but void by English law. The English court held the marriage as void.[131] The English courts have applied the rule in the converse situation also. Even when both the parties are domiciled abroad, and their marriage is void by the ante-nuptial domicile of either party, the English courts have held the marriage void in a situation where the marriage has been solemnized in England where such marriages are valid.[132]

To the general rule that capacity to marry is governed by the

126. (1951) p. 482.

127. Although the Marriage (Enabling) Act, 1960 now allows marriages within certain degrees of prohibited relationship, yet the basic principle remains the same.

128. (1861) 9 H.L.C. 193.

129. (No. 1) (1877) 3 P.D. 1.

130. (1859) 1 Sw. & Tr. 416.

131. See also *Re Paine*, (1940) Ch. 46.

132. *Sottomayor* v. *De Barros* (No. 1), (1877) 3 P.D. 1.

law of each party's pre-marriage domicile. Dicey and Morris state the following four exceptions :

(1) A marriage is not valid if either of the parties, being a descendant of George II, marries in contravention of the Royal Marriage Act, 1772.[133] This exception owes it existence to the peculiar English situation of monarchy.

(2) A marriage is possibly not valid if either party is, according to the law of the country where the marriage is celebrated, under an incapacity to marry the other.[134] This exception for which there is no direct authority, has been retained, it seems, in deference to Westlake who first propounded it,[135] to Dicey[136] who adopted it considering it to be "essentially" reasonable, and to its statutory existence in Australia.[137] It is submitted that this exception is not necessary despite its commendation by Westlake and Dicey and its retention by Morris.[138] The *lex loci celebrationis* should have nothing to do with the material validity of the marriage.

(3) The validity of a marriage celebrated in England between persons of whom the one has an English, and the other a foreign, domicile is not affected by any incapacity which though existing under the law of such foreign domicile, does not exist under the law of England.[139] This exception is suggested by the decision in *Sottomayor* v. *De Barros* (No. 2),[140] and is the outcome of the rationalization of, otherwise socially most undesirable, decision in *Ogden* v. *Ogden*.[141] At the second hearing in *Sottomayor* v. *De Barros*[142] (No. 2), (the case was re-opened at the istance of Queen's Proctor) it was established that both the parties were not domiciled in Portugal at the time of the marriage, but only the wife was domiciled there and the husband was domiciled in England.[143] Since the

133. Dicey and Morris, p. 265. This exception has been necessitated on account of the fact that England still recognizes monarchy and lays down certain rules which must be complied with when a member of the Royal family marries.

134. *Ibid.*, at p. 267.

135. Westlake, s. 19. Westlake cites some old English decisions.

136. Dicey (3rd ed.), p. 677.

137. Marriage Act, 1961, ss. 10, 22(1).

138. Dicey and Morris, p. 268. Morris adds that presumably this exception will not apply to marriages validated by the Marriage (Enabling) Act, 1960.

139. *Ibid.*, at p. 269.

140. (1879) 5 P.D. 94.

141. (1908) p. 46.

142. (1879) 5 P.D. 94.

143. *Ibid.*

marriage was valid under English law, though invalid under the Portuguese law, the English court held the marriage as valid. Graveson also justifies this exception.[144] Despite this rationalization, one is apt to agree with Morris that this exception is of 'illogical' character.[145]

(4) A marriage (celebrated in England ?) is not invalid on account of any incapacity which, though imposed by the law of the domicile of both or of either of the parties, is penal.[146] Morris is of the view that this exception should not be limited to marriages celebrated in England (Dicey favoured its limitation to marriages celebrated in England), but should extend to all marriages, otherwise it is likely to lead to socially undesirable results.[147] This exception is a specific application of the rule of private international law that penal laws of another country cannot be given effect.

Under this exception are covered several types of cases. In *Chetti* v. *Chetti*[148] an Indian domiciled Hindu married an English woman domiciled in England in London. When the wife petitioned for judicial separation on the ground of husband's cruelty, the husband argued before the court that the marriage was void, since by his personal law he was forbidden to marry a non-Hindu. The court refused to give effect to this disability.[149] Similarly, an incapacity imposed by the foreign *lex domicilii* has not been given effect to by English courts. In *Scott* v. *A.G.*[150] a marriage was dissolved by a Cape Colony court on the ground of wife's adultery. A law of Cape Colony provides that on a decree of divorce being passed on the ground of adultery, the respondent cannot remarry so long as the petitioner remained unmarried. Soon after the decree of divorce wife came to England and acquired a domicile of choice there and remarried. The court disregarded the disability under Cape law on the ground that it was penal and discriminatory. In *Walter* v. *Walter*[151] an English domiciled and Indian resident husband obtained a decree of divorce from an Indian court. Under the Indian law (Divorce Act, 1969) no party could remarry unless a period of six months elapsed since the date of passing of the decree. The wife came to England and remarried after three months of the decree. The English court held the marriage void as it felt that incapacity

144. Graveson (6th ed.), p. 273.
145. Dicey and Morris, p. 269.
146. *Ibid.*, at p. 271.
147. *Ibid.*
148. (1909) p. 67.
149. *Papadopoulos* v. *Papadopoulos*, (1930) p. 55 (the requirement was that the orthodox Greek priest should be present at the ceremony); *Chapelle* v. *Chapelle*, (1950) p. 134; *Gray* v. *Formosa*, (1963) p. 259.
150. (1886) 11 P.D. 128.
151. (1890) 15 P.D. 512.

imposed by the Indian law was an integral part of the proceedings by which alone both the parties could be released from this incapacity to contract a fresh marriage.[152]

Ante-nuptial Domicile versus *Matrimonial Domicile* : It has been seen that some English authorities and some English writers[153] take the view that material validity of the marriage is governed by the ante-nuptial domicile of parties. On the other hand, Cheshire maintains that the capacity to marry, and all other questions of essential validity of marriage, should be governed by the law of matrimonial domicile.[154] According to him : "The basic presumption is that capacity to marry is governed by the law of the husband's domicile at the time of the marriage, for normally it is in the country of that domicile that the parties intend to establish their permanent home. This presumption, however, is rebutted if it can be inferred that parties at the time of marriage intended to establish their home in a certain country and they did in fact establish it there within a reasonable time."[155] In *Padolecehia* v. *Padolecehia*[156] that Sir Jocelyn Simon, J. unhesitatingly approved the rule as propounded by Dicey and Morris.[157] On the other hand, in *Radwan* v. *Radwan*[158] Cumming-Bruce, J. gave his approval and adopted the rule as propounded by Cheshire in respect of capacity to enter into a polygamous marriage.

The most interesting aspect of the controversy is that the protagonists of both views rely almost on the same authorities and try to distinguish some authorities not favourable to their view. Cumming-Bruce, J. observed that since the matter has not been directly argued in any case, it was his duty to return to examine the foundations as laid down in *Brook* v. *Brook*[159] and *Warrender* v. *Warrender*[160] and the other cases which follow them. What has to be noticed about these authorities is that in most of them the prenuptial domicile of the parties and the intended matrimonial home,

152. This decision is of no value after the passing of the Indian and Colonial Divorce Jurisdiction Act, 1926. These decisions lay down that if the disability imposed by the foreign *lex domicilii* is discriminatory or penal it would be disregarded, but if it is an integral part of the proceedings imposing equal disabilities on both parties. it will be given effect to. These decisions also lay down that in both cases the domicile of the divorced spouse at the date of remarriage is irrelevant. In *Scott* v. *A.G.*, cited above, the court did consider the domicile of the divorced party at the time of the marriage but this aspect of the decision was repudiated by the court (the judge was the same in both cases); *Walter* v. *Walter*, cited above.

153. Such as Dicey and Morris, see Rule 31.

154. Cheshire, pp. 277-78.

155. *Ibid.*, p. 288.

156. (1967) 3 All E R. 863.

157. Rule 31.

158. (No. 2) (1972) 3 All E.R. 1026.

159. (1861) 9 H.L.C. 193.

160. (1835) 2 Cl. & Fin. 488.

was the same, therefore, it is possible to quote them in favour of either view. In *Brook* v. *Brook*[161] (facts have already been stated earlier) ante-nuptial domicile of parties was England and they wanted to establish their matrimonial home there. Lord Campbell observed : "... the essentials of the marriage depend upon the domicile, the law of the country in which parties are domiciled at the time of marriage and in which matrimonial residence is contemplated." Quoting more extensively the observations of Lord Campbell, both Cheshire and Cumming-Bruce, J. rely on this sentence in support of their matrimonial home theory. *Sottomayor* v. *De Barros*[162] and *Re De Wilton*[163] are the other two decisions relied on by Cheshire. In both the cases the ante-nuptial domicile of the parties was the same and it was there they wanted to establish their matrimonial home. These are also the cases relied upon in favour of ante-nuptial theory. Of *Brook* v. *Brook*[164] and *Sottomayor* v. *De Barros*[165] Dicey and Morris's simple observation is that these two cases are generally regarded as laying down the general principle that capacity to marry is governed by the law of each party's ante-nuptial domicile.[166]

In *Warrender* v. *Warrender*[167] parties had a different pre-marriage domicile, and they established their home in the country of husband's domicile. The case was concerned with the effectiveness of Scottish divorce and no question of material validity was involved. But in course of his judgment Lord Brougham, J. observed that the husband at the time of his marriage was domiciled in Scotland and "Scotland was to be the conjugal residence of the married couple" and that "essentials of the contract were to be regulated by the law of Scotland". These observations are relied upon in favour of matrimonial home theory both by Cheshire and Cumming-Bruce, J. (who quotes from the judgment more extensively). *Mette* v. *Mette*[168] was also a case where the parties were domiciled in two different countries; the marriage was performed between a domiciled Englishman and a domiciled German woman at Frankfurt (facts have already been stated). Both parties contemplated to establish their matrimonial home in England. Cheshire is of the view, and it is submitted rightly so, that the *ratio decidendi* of the case is rather doubtful. In this case Sir Cresswell observed that the husband "remained domiciled in this country, and the marriage was with a view to subsequent residence in this country." He also added that "there could be no valid contract unless each was competent to contract with the other". This

161. (1861) 9 H.L.C. 193.
162. (No. 2) (1879) 5 P.D. 94.
163. (1900) 2 Ch. 481.
164. (1861) 9 H.L.C. 193.
165. (No. 1) (1877) 3 P.D.I.
166. Dicey and Morris, 255.
167. (1835) 2 Cl. & F. 488.
168. (1859) 1 Sw. & Tr. 416.

decision also does not conclude the controversy and can be profitably quoted by either side.[169] *Re Paine*,[170] on the other hand, is in favour of the ante-nuptial or dual domicile theory. In this case a domiciled English woman had married a domiciled German who was her deceased sister's husband. The parties established their matrimonial home in England. The marriage was void under English law but valid under German law. Bennett, J. held the marriage void since by her ante-nuptial domicile the English woman had no capacity to marry. On this case Cheshire's comment is that since the matrimonial home was England, even according to his theory marriage was void.[171] *Pugh* v. *Pugh*,[172] on the other hand, appears to favour Cheshire's theory. In this case a domiciled Englishman married a Hungarian domiciled woman aged fifteen years in Austria. By Hungarian law the marriage was valid but by English law it was void. The court held the marriage void. Pearce, J. said that the English statute, the Marriage Act, was intended to apply to "all persons domiciled in the United Kingdom wherever the marriage might be celebrated", and that since by the law of husband's domicile it was a marriage into which he could not lawfully enter into. This seems to indicate that the judge applied husband's pre-nuptial *lex domicilii*, and this case may be taken to support the double domicile theory.

Cheshire is conscious that "none of these decisions is conclusive in favour of the law of the matrimonial home, since each one is open to the construction that the *lex domicilii* referred to was the *lex domicilii* of each party", but he adds that this also implies that they are not conclusive in favour of the dual domicile theory either.[173] Cheshire cites most forcefully *Sottomayor* v. *De Barros*[174] in favour of his theory. In this case (facts have already been stated earlier), the fact that *lex loci celebrationis* was English weighed heavily with the judge, Sir James Hanner observed : "Injustice might be caused to our own subjects if a marriage were declared invalid on the ground that it was forbidden by the law of domicile of one of the parties." It has been seen earlier that on the basis of this decision, Dicey and Morris have framed an exception to the general principle propounded by them.[175] Cheshire very happily observes : "What is equally true is that it makes nonsense of the dual domicile theory."[176]

Cheshire finds some direct support for his view from the *obiter*

169. Cheshire, p. 283.
170. (1940) Ch. 46.
171. Cheshire, p. 277.
172. (1951) p. 482.
173. Cheshire, p. 284.
174. (No. 2) (1879) 5 P.D. 94.
175. Exception 3, see page 269. Graveson also supports this exception, p. 273.
176. Cheshire, p. 285.

observations of the Court of Appeal in *De Reneville* v. *De Reneville*[177] and *Kenward* v. *Kenward*.[178] In the former case, Lord Greene observed : "It is a case of essential validity. By what law is that to be decided ? In my opinion by the law of France, either because that is the law of husband's domicile at the date of the marriage or (preferably, in my view) because at that date it was the law of the matrimonial domicile in reference to which the parties may have supposed to enter into the bonds of marriage." Bucknill, L.J. spoke most nearly to Cheshire's theory. His Lordship observed : "I think it essential that the law of one country should prevail, and that it is reasonable that the law of the country where the ceremony of marriage took place and where the parties intended to live together and where they in fact live together should be regarded . . ."[179] Cheshire draws further support for his views from the observations of Denning. L.J. in *Kenward* v. *Kenward*.[180] His Lordship observes that essential validity of marriage contracted between persons having different pre-nuptial domicile is governed by the law of the country where they intended to live and on the basis of which they agreed to marry.[181]

It was in this state of judicial opinion that the eighth edition of Dicey and Morris's Conflict of Laws was published. After observing that Cheshire's views can be adjusted with *Re Paine*[182] by ignoring judge's finding as to domicile and it is supported by some *dicta*.[183] Morris said : "Any rule under which it is impossible to predicate at the date of the marriage with knowledge of all material facts whether it is valid or invalid is, it is submitted, undesirable, especially in view of the fact that the destination of interests in property may depend on the validity of marriage. Any rule which gives preference in matters of capacity to the law of husband's domicile is, . . . dubious on general principles. . ."[184]

After the publication of eighth edition of Dicey and Morris's Conflict of Laws came the decision in *Padolecehia* v. *Padolecehia*.[185] In this case, in 1953 a marriage was performed in Italy between two Italian domiciled persons. Marriage, then by Italian law, was indissoluble. In 1956 a decree of legal separation was made

177. (1948) p. 100.
178. (1951) p. 124=(1950) 2 All E.R. 297.
179. Cumming-Bruce, J. quotes these passages more fully at pp. 1035-36 of (1972) 3 All E.R. 1026.
180. (1950) 2 All E.R. 297.
181. Cumming-Bruce, J. also quoted Denning, L.J.
182. (1940) 1 Ch. 46.
183. The cases cited are : *Brook* v. *Brook*, cited above; *Warrender* v. *Warrender*, cited above; *De Reneville* v. *De Reneville*, cited above, *Kenward* v. *Kenward*. cited above, although the reference to matrimonial home in the House of Lords' decision in *Brook* v. *Brook* seems to be incidental.
184. Dicey and Morris, p. 258. Graveson is also critical of Cheshire's views more or less on these grounds (6th ed.), pp. 278-281.
185. (1967) 3 All E.R. 863.

by a Roman court. In 1958, claiming to have a Venezuelan domicile, the husband obtained by proxy a decree of divorce against his wife from a Mexican court. The Italian courts would not recognize the Mexican decree. In 1963 the husband met a woman in Copenhagen, and in February 1964, when they were on a day's visit to England, they underwent a ceremony of marriage there. At that time his former wife was alive. In 1966 the husband presented a petition for nullity of marriage on the ground that at the time of his second marriage his first marriage had subsisted. He alleged that he was domiciled in Luxembourg. The court found that at all material time he had retained his Italian domicile of origin. Sir Jocelyn Simons, P. observed: "Each party must be capable of marrying by the law of his or her respective ante-nuptial domicile." And the learned judge added: "see Dicey and Morris, Conflict of Laws (8th edition), p. 254." On this reasoning the second marriage was held void. Then came *R.* v. *Brentwood Superintendent Registrar for Marriages, Ex parte Arias*[186] in which Sachis, L.J. observed: "The fact that the parties to a proposed marriage cannot marry according to the law of the country in which they are domiciled is, as a normal rule, a lawful impediment to their being married in this country. That follows, of course, from what in Dicey and Morris is stated as: Capacity to marry is governed by the law of each party's ante-nuptial domicile."[187]

Then, reviewing practically every decision from *Warrender* v. *Warrender*[188] to *Ex parte Arias*[189] Cumming-Bruce, J. in *Radwan* v. *Radwan*[190] observed: "But that may well be because the matter has never been argued until today, and I have to consider whether the assumption that has been made, as a result of the expression of view in cases to which I have referred, is solidly founded on the common law foundations that are supposed to lie beneath them, and I have come to the conclusion that counsel for the husband is right in his submission that it is my duty to return to examine the foundation in *Brook* v. *Brook*[191] and *Warrender* v. *Warrender*[192] of the propositions that have since been founded on them." The learned judge after examining all the authorities, said: "And my conclusion is that the wife had the capacity to enter into a polygamous union by virtue of her prenuptial dicision to separate herself from the land of her domicile and to make her life with her husband in his country, where the Mohammedan law of polygamous marriage was the normal institution of marriage." In this case an Egyptain domiciled

186. (1968) 3 All E.R. 279.
187. *Ibid.*, at p. 282.
188. Cited above.
189. Cited above.
190. (1972) 3 All E.R. 1026.
191. Cited above.
192. Cited above.

Muslim married an Egyptain domiciled woman in Cairo. Personal law of bcth parties allowed polygamy. Subequently, he married an English domiciled woman in Paris in the Egyptain Consulate General and parties clearly intended to enter into a polygamous union according to Muslim law. It was also clear that at that time parties wanted to make Egypt their matrimonial home. After a short stay in England parties went to Cairo where the husband divorced his former wife. In 1956 parties went to England where they wanted to establish their permanent home, and the husband acquired a domicile of choice there. In 1970 the wife started proceedings for divorce and the question of validity of the marriage arose. At that time parties had eight children of the marriage. The learned judge added : "Nothing in this judgment bears on the capacity of minors, the law of affinity, or the effect of bigamy on capacity to enter into a monogamous marriage." One may be inclined to agree with the learned judge that this branch of law "relating to capacity for marriage is not quite as tidy as some very learned authors would have liked me to believe."[193] It appears to the present writer that the present trend in English law is in favour of the formulation of Dicey and Morris. Certain statutes specifically lean in favour of this view. The Marriage (Enabling) Act, 1960 which enables certain persons within the prohibited degrees (under the law as it existed at the time of the passing of the Act) to marry each other lays down two rules : (i) In case both parties are domiciled in England the marriage is valid whether solemnized in England or abroad.[194] (ii) But if one of the parties is not domiciled in England and if under the law of the foreign country where one of the parties is domiciled the marriage is invalid, then such a marriage will not be valid under the Act.[195] The learned judge in *Radwan* v. *Radwan*[196] did not recognize that his decision may make it necessary for Parliament to consider a further amendment to the Nullity of Marriage Act, 1971.

In the submission of the present writer, Cheshire's formulation accords well with the social facts. Cheshire justifies his theory on (a) sociological grounds, (b) principle, and (c) on the ground of effectiveness,[196] to which the present writer refers *passim*. Cheshire says that hardship that arises under the dual domicile test may be mitigated by introducing an alternative test, though it is regrettable that the mitigation should be confined to the case where the marriage is celebrated abroad.[197] Cheshire is also conscious that several objections of a practical nature may, no doubt, be advanced against his theory of matrimonial home. But he says, "this is true of any particular rule, for an ingenious mind can always suggest circumstances in which its

193. *Ibid.*, at p. 1048.
194. Section 1.
195. Section 3.
196. Cheshire, pp. 278-80.
197. *Ibid.*, at p. 281.

application will be difficult or its operation unfair.[198] *Lawrence* v. *Lawrence*[199] Sir Davis Cairns' referring to the conflict between two views observed, "I should not be bold enough to seek to resolve the conflict unless campelled to do so my own inclination would be to hold that either basis of recognition would suffice.

Indian Law

The present writer is not aware of any direct Indian authority having bearing on the material validity of marriage. It would appear that when marriages are performed in India among the members of any community the capacity would be governed by the personal law of the parties. From the present state of Indian law, it is discernible that, we have displayed adherence to the old approach of English law whereunder both the material and formal validity depended upon the *lex loci celebrationis*.

As we have seen, under the Hindu Marriage Act, 1955, 'any two Hindus' can perform their marriage, provided the conditions laid down under the Act are fulfilled.[200] The Indian courts would accord recognition to such marriages even if one of the parties or both the parties have no capacity to enter into the marriage under their ante-nuptial domicile or the law of their matrimonial home. This is also true in respect of Muslim, Christian, Parsi or Jew marriages performed in India under the law of the respective communities. This is because in India, law of marriage is essentially a personal law—personal law in the sense that the governing law of marriage is not the Indian law or the state law but the law of the community to which parties belong. The most remarkable feature of Indian law is that the Special Marriage Act, 1954, which permits civil marriage between 'any two persons', also gives birth to a separate personal law. If any two persons perform their marriage under the Act[201] then the validity of the marriage is determined under the Act, even when both the parties are domiciled elsewhere.

Thus, it seems that if a marriage is performed in India between "two Hindus", "two Muslims", "two Christians", "two Parsis", "two Jews", or if a civil marriage is performed between "any two persons", the marriage will be valid in India, even if one or both parties are not domiciled in India.

The next question is : what view Indian courts will take of marriages solemnized abroad. One type of marriage, i.e. where one of the parties (or both the parties) is an Indian national and the marriage is performed or registered under the Foreign Marriage Act, 1969,[202] the validity of marriage is governed by the

198. *Ibid.*, at pp. 280-81.
199. (1985) 3 W.L.R. 125 at 140.
200. Section 5.
201. Parties should satisfy conditions laid down in s. 5.
202. Conditions laid down in s. 4 should be satisfied.

Foreign Marriage Act, 1969. Section 11 of the Act contains a provision which has bearing on the conflict of laws problem. It lays down that in the following cases the Marriage Officer will refuse to solemnize the marriage : (a) If *lex loci celebrationis* prohibits such marriage, or (b) if the solemnization of the marriage will be inconsistent with international law or the comity of nations. Section 23 of the Act lays down provisions for the recognition of marriages solemnized under the laws of other countries.

As to the marriages solemnized abroad and not covered by the provisions of the Foreign Marriage Act, 1969, the Act lays down (though it was not necessary to do so) that they will come under the purview of the general rules of private international law.[203] It is submitted that in such cases Indian courts should judge the material validity by reference to the law of matrimonial home of the parties.

III
FORMAL VALIDITY OF MARRIAGE

Formal validity of marriages is one of those few areas of private international law where there is almost unanimity in the laws of all countries of the world. The accepted view is that the formal validity of marriage is governed by the *lex loci celebrationis*. However, in working out the details of this principle some differences are discernible. Barring aside a few exceptions, in English private international law, the requirement that a marriage must be formally valid by the *lex loci celebrationis* is imperative, which admits of no alternative test. On the continental Europe the test is facultative : the requirement is that the marriage should be formally valid either by the *lex loci celebrationis* or by the personal law of the parties. Under French law a marriage which is solemnized outside France should be formally valid either under the law of the place where it is celebrated or by the personal law of the parties. The same is the position under German law. Countries like Greece and Malta lay down that compliance with the personal law is obligatory, if parties belong to Orthodox church in the former case, and to Roman Catholic church in the latter case. In the countries of Eastern Europe the principle of *locus regit actum* is imperative if marriage is performed there. But if the marriage is performed elsewhere, then, under Polish and Czech law, if the marriage is formally valid under the personal law of the parties then the marriage is valid, irrespective of the fact whether it complies with the *lex loci celebrationis*. Under Albanian law the principle of *locus regit actum* is imperative in respect of foreigner, but if the parties are Albanian nationals domiciled in Albania, then compliance with Albanian law would be enough.[204]

203. Section 27.
204. Szeszy, p. 348.

It is a well established rule of English private international law that a marriage to be formally valid must comply with the local law—*locus regit actum*.[205] A marriage which does not comply with the formalities of the local law is not valid.[206] Both the positive and negative requirements of this rule are imperative.[207] The rule means that if the marriage is formally valid in accordance with the law of the place where it took place then the marriage would be valid everywhere. If the law of the place where the marriage is solemnized lays down that a marriage which complies with the requirements of the personal law of the parties (such is the position under the Italian law) is valid, then a marriage performed accordingly will be valid.

What ceremonies should be performed is entirely for the local law to indicate.[208] Thus, if local law recognizes marriage by cohabitation or repute,[209] or if it is constituted *per verba de praesenti*, or by proxy,[210] or if religious ceremony is essential,[211] then a marriage performed according will be recognized as valid. English law goes a step further and lays down that a marriage which is initially invalid by local law will be recognized if it is subsequently validated by local legislation.[212] In *Starkowski* v. *A.G.*[213] two domiciled nationals of Poland got married in Austria in a Roman Catholic church on May 19, 1945. They did not perform the civil ceremony as required by the Austrian law and at that time Austrian law did not recognize any other ceremony. On June 30, 1945 an Austrian law was passed which validated such marriages restrospectively, provided the marriage was registered under the law. The marriage was duly registered in 1945, but without the consent or knowledge of the wife. Parties went to England in 1946 and acquired English domicile. In 1950, the wife underwent another ceremony of marriage with another man in England. On her prosecution for bigamy, the English court held that the Austrian marriage was valid.[214] Similarly, the marriage will be valid even if it is performed in a foreign country with a specific view to avoid some irksome ceremony under

205. *Scrimshire* v. *Scrimshire*, (1752) 2 Hagg. Con. 395; *Dalrymple* v. *Dalrymple*, (1811) 2 Hagg. Con. 54; *Warrender* v. *Warrender*, (1835) 2 Cl. & Fin. 488; *Harvey* v. *Fernie*, (1882) 8 A.C. 43; *Berthiume* v. *Dastous*, (1930) A.C. 79; *Kenward* v. *Kenward*, (1951) p. 124.
206. *Berthiume* v. *Dastous*, (1930) A.C. 79 at p. 83, per Lord Dunedin.
207. Dicey and Morris, pp. 235-36.
208. *Rooker* v. *Rooker*, (1864) 3 Sw. & Tr. 526; *Re Green*, (1909) 25 T.L.R. 222.
209. *Compton* v. *Bearcroft*, (1769) 2 Hagg. Con. 430; *Beamish* v. *Beamish*, (1861) 9 H.L.C. 274.
210. *Apt* v. *Apt*, (1948) p. 83; *Ponticelli* v. *Ponticelli*, (1958) p. 204.
211. *Swifte* v. *A.G.*, (1912) A.C. 276; *Despatie* v. *Tremblay*, (1921) 1 A.C. 702 (P.C.).
212. *Starkowski* v. *A.G.*, (1954) A.C. 155.
213. *Ibid.*
214. See for the criticism of the judgment, Cheshire, p. 291.

the law of domicile. In *Simonin* v. *Mallac*[215] two domiciled French persons performed their marriage in London, as the parties wanted to avoid the French requirement of parental consent. When later on the wife petitioned for nullity on the ground of non-compliance with the formalities of their personal law, the English court held the marriage valid.[216] In England such marriages are valid even if they are held null and void in the country of the domicile of parties.[217] However, if such a marriage is later on annulled by the courts of domicile, then English courts will recognize the decree of nullity.[218]

To the maxim *locus regit actum* some exceptions are recognized under the common law as well as the statutory law. In the initial stages of Empire building, it was recognized that the English settler in colonies such as Canada or Australia, took so much of common law with them as was suitable to the local conditions.[219] This gave rise to the first common law exception that a common law marriage performed abroad was valid.

Common Law Marriages Performed Abroad: The concept of common law marriages has not been the same. In the initial stages of colonialism the requirement the persence of an episcopally ordained priest or deacon could not be fulfilled.[220] In *Catterall* v. *Catterall*[221] it was observed : "Where there has been a fact of consent between two parties to become man and wife the marriage will be treated as validly performed." Thus a marriage may also be validly performed without bans or licence.[222] Similarly, requirement of the presence of witnesses is also not necessary.

A further extension of this exception is that a common law marriage performed abroad would be valid where compliance with the local form was impossible. Thus, marriages in heathen countries if performed in common law form are valid. Similarly, in a country where Roman Catholic priests are not allowed to officiate at Protestant marriages and Prctestants are not allowed to enter into Roman Catholic marriages, a marriage performed by a

215. (1860) 2 Sw. & Tr. 67.
216. See also *Scrimshire* v. *Scrimshire*, (1752) 2 Hagg. Con. 395; *Stathatos* v. *Stathatos*, (1913) P. 46; *De Montaigu* v. *De Montaigu*, (1913) p. 154.
217. *Ogden* v. *Ogden*, (1908) p. 46; *Simonin* v. *Mallac*, (1860) 2 Sw. & Tr. 67.
218. *Salvesen* v. *Administrator of Austrian Property*, (1927) A.C. 641; *De Massa* v. *De Massa*, (1939) 2 All E.R. 150n; *Merker* v. *Merker*, (1963) p. 283. But see *Formosa* v. *Formosa*, (1963) p. 259 and *Lepre* v. *Lepre*, (1965) p. 52, where the Court of Appeal declined to accord recognition to such a decree on the ground that it violated the English notion of substantial justice.
219. Dicey and Morris take the view that this may not be the real exception as it may mean that Her Majesty exercised extra-territorial jurisdiction, p. 241.
220. See *R.* v. *Millis*, (1843-1844) 10 Cl. & Fin. 534.
221. (1847) 1. Rob- Ecc. 580.
222. *Phillips* v. *Phillips*, (1921) 38 T.L.R. 150.

Protestant priest will be valid.[223] For the application of this exception, it is necessary that compliance with the local form is impossible.[224] *Wolfenden* v. *Wolfenden*[225] is a modern case which illustrates this principle. The marriage was held valid as the presence of the episcopally ordained priest was impossible.[226]

On the other hand, if difficulties are not unsurmountable; compliance with the local form is essential. This proposition seems to have become somewhat doubtful after the decision in *Taczanowska* v. *Taczanowska*.[227] But there is a possibility of rationalizing this case by putting it under a different head: "Marriages in countries under belligerent occupation."[228] In this case two domiciled Polish nationals went through a ceremony of marriage in Italy. The ceremony of marriage was performed by a Polish army chaplain, as episcopally ordained priest. The husband was serving in the Polish II Corps in belligerent occupation of Italy. The marriage was neither formally valid under Italian law, the *lex loci celebrationis* nor under Polish law, the *lex domicilii*, but was valid as a common law marriage. There were no unsurmountable difficulties in complying with the local form. The Court of Appeal said that the presumption that the parties intended to submit to the Italian law was rebutted as a member of conquering force can scarcely be expected to subject himself to the law of the vanquished country. It was further observed that it did not matter that both the parties were not British subject as "the common law conception of marriage knows no distinction of race or nationality."[229] Similarly, in *Preston* v. *Preston*[230] two domiciled Polish nationals solemnized their marriage in Germany which was invalid by German law but valid as common law marriage. At the time of marriage the husband was a resident in an English reception camp for military personnel and was not a member of armed forces. This camp was held to be a military camp. Dicey and Morris are of the view that the proposition should be confined to the marriages of members of belligerent occupying forces celebrated in the occupied country, or to the marriages of members of forces associated with such forces or (perhaps) of persons in strictly

223. *Lord Cloncurry's* case, (1811) Cruise on Dignities, p. 276.
224. *Starkowaski* v. *A.G.*, (1952) p. 135; on appeal, (1953) 2 All E.R. 1272 (H.L.).
225. (1946) p. 61.
226. See also *Penhas* v. *Tan soo Eng.* (1953) A.C. 304, where a marriage was solemnized in Singapore between a Jew and a Chinese woman, both British subjects domiciled in Singapore. At the marriage both Chinese and Jewish ceremony of marriage was performed and this composite ceremony was meant to express the wish of parties that they took each other as man and wife. The marriage was held valid.
227. (1957) p. 301.
228. Dicey and Morris, p. 242.
229. This decision was followed in *Merker* v. *Merker*, (1763) p. 283 and *Preston* v. *Preston*, (1963) p. 411.
230. **Cited in the last foot-note.**

analogous situations, such as members of an organized body of escaped prisoners of war.[231] This principle does not extend, Morris maintains, to marriages of ordinary civilians who are present in a belligerent country from necessity and not from choice.[232]

The decision in *Taczanowska's case* was not followed in *Lazarewicz* v. *Lazarewicz*.[233] In the latter case a Polish corporal, serving with the Polish Army in Italy was married in Italy to an Italian girl. The ceremony did not comply with Italian law, though marriage was valid as common law marriage. Phillimore, J. said that from the circumstances the inference was clear that parties intended to submit to Italian law and therefore non-compliance with Italian form was fatal to the marriage. These decisions are obviously difficult to reconcile and do not represent a healthy trend.[234]

Marriages celebrated on Merchant Ships: Since in public international law the theory is that the ship is a floating portion of the country whose flag it carries, it has been thought that a marriage solemnized on a merchant ship on the high seas to be formally valid must comply with the law of the ship's port of registry: the law of the ship's port of registry would be sufficient to indicate the law of that portion of the country the flag of which it flies. It seems that it would suffice if parties took each other for man and wife *per verba de praesenti*, provided the court is satisfied that it was impracticable for them to wait until the ship reached a port where sufficient facilities were available either by the *lex loci* or under the Foreign Marriage Act.[235] If the ship is berthing at a port, then compliance with the local form is necessary unless there are insuperable difficulties in marrying in local forms.[236]

Marriages of Members of His Majesty's Forces Serving Abroad: This matter is regulated by the Foreign Marriage Acts, 1892-1947. The Acts lay down:

> "A marriage solemnized in any foreign territory by a chaplain serving with any part of naval, military, or air force of His Majesty serving in that territory or by a person authorized. . . by the commanding officer of any part of those forces serving in that territory shall, subject as hereinafter provided, be as valid in law as if the marriage had been

231. *Merker* v. *Merker*, cited above and *Kochanski* v. *Kochanski*, (1958), p. 147.

232. Dicey and Morris, p. 244.

233. (1962) p. 171.

234. Sec Dicey and Morris, p. 244; see for criticism of Taczanowska's case, Cheshire, pp. 300-04, and Andrews, (1959) 22 Modern Law Review, 403-07.

235. Dicey and Morris, p. 242.

236. But see *Culling* v. *Culling*, (1896), p. 116, where marriage was performed in the common law form on a warship lying off Cyprus.

solmenized in the United Kingdom with a due observance of all forms required by law :

Provided that this sub-section shall not apply if—

(a) one at least of the parties to the marriage is a member of the said forces serving in that territory or a person employed in that territory in such other capacity as may be prescribed by Order-in-Council; and

(b) such other conditions as may be so prescribed are compiled with."[237]

Foreign territory under the Act includes, *inter alia*, ships which are in waters of any foreign territory. A marriage performed in compliance with the above requirements will be valid whether the armed forces are on active service or in the occupation of foreign territory after conclusion of hostilities.

Consular Marriages : The Foreign Marriage Acts, 1892-1947 lay down that a marriage between parties, one of whom at least is a British subject, solemnized before a marriage officer in a foreign country in the manner prescribed by the Act, shall be valid as if it has been solemnized in the United Kingdom with due observance of formalities as required by law.[238] A British ambassador, high commissioner, consul, governor or any member of the ambassador's diplomatic staff may be appointed as a marriage officer under the Act. A marriage under the Act must be performed at the official residence of the marriage officer, with open doors, in the presence of at least two witnesses. The ceremony may be in accordance with the rites of Church of England or in such other form as the parties see fit to adopt.[239] In the latter case a declaration at some stage of ceremony to the following effect is necessary : "I call upon these persons here present to witness, that I, AB. take thee, CD, to be my lawfully wedded wife (or husband)."

A consular marriage is valid as regards the form (though not necessarily in other respects) even though it may be invalid under the local law.[240] The possibility of such marriage being invalid by local law has been eliminated by the Foreign Marriage Order, 1964 under which it had been laid down that a marriage officer must not solemnize a marriage in a foreign country unless he is satisfied, (a) that at least one of the parties is a British subject; (b) that the authorities of that country will not object to the solemnization of the marriage; (c) either (i) that insufficeint facilities exist for the marriage of the parties under the law of that country, or (ii) that the marriage will be recognized as valid in form by the law of that country; and (d) that the marriage will be recognized

237. Section 2.
238. Section 1.
239. Section 8(2).
240. *Hay* v. *Northcote*, (1900) 2 Ch. 262.

as a valid form of marriage by the law of the country to which each party belongs. The Acts further lay down that the Marriage Officer need not solemnize a marriage, if in his opinion the solemnization thereof would be inconsistent with international law or the comity of nations.[241] The Acts also lay down that nothing in them is to confirm or impair or affect the validity of any marriage solemnized abroad otherwise than as therein provided.[242]

Indian Law

In India two forms of marriages are available : If both the parties are Hindus, Muslims, Christians, Parsis or Jews, then they may perform their marriage under (i) the personal law of the community to which both the parties belong, or (ii) under the Special Marriage Act, 1954. In the latter case the marriage has to be a civil marriage though parties are free to append any other ceremonies.[243] In the former case the marriage may be performed in accordance with the ceremonies laid down by the personal law of the parties. If parties belong to different communities then they can perform their marriage only in the civil marriage form. Whenever a marriage is performed in India compliance with one of the above formalities is essential ; non-compliance will render the marriage null and void.

Among Hindus, i.e. when both parties are Hindus (irrespective of their domicile or nationality), a marriage may be solemnized in accordance with the customary rites and ceremonies of either party thereto.[244] These ceremonies and rites fall under two heads : the *Sastric* ceremonies and rites as prescribed under Hindu law, or (b) the customary ceremonies and rites recognized by custom in the caste or community to which either party belongs. In the modern Hindu law the former are, though still religious ceremonies, very few and simple.[245] The customary ceremonies may be religious ceremonies or purely non-religious ceremonies. They may be very elaborate or very simple. It is also possible that custom of a particular community may not provide for any ceremony of marriage; living together as husband and wife may be enough.[246]

Muslim marriage being primarily a contract, the only essential ceremonies that are required are that there must be a proposal and

241. Section 39.
242. Section 23.
243. Section 12.
244. Section 7(1), Hindu Marriage Act, 1955, see also author's work, Modern Hindu Law. Codified and Uncodified, (1990) Chapter VII.
245. See author's work, Modern Hindu Law, Codified and Uncodified, (1990) Chapter VII; Paras Diwan, Law of Marriage and Divorce (Indian Personal Laws), Vol. I, Chapter II.
246. *Ibid.* For instance, in *Chadar Andazi* marriage among the Jats no ceremony of marriage is required : In *Kerawa* marriage also no ceremonies are required : see Sohan Singh v. Kabla Singh, 1928 Lah. 706 (for *Karewa* marriage); *Charan Singh* v. *Gurdial Singh,* 1961 Punj. 301 (F.B.) (for *Chadar Andazi* marriage). Among the Buddhists also no ceremony is required : *Mi Me* v. *Mish We,* (1915) 39 Cal. 492.

acceptance made in one and the same meeting. Among the Sunnis presence of sane and adult witnesses—two males or one male and two females—is required at the time when proposal and acceptance of marriage are made. But the absence of witnesses does not render the marriage void but only irregular.[247] Among the Shias presence of witnesses is not necessary. No religious ceremony is needed. Even writing is not required.[248] Among Christians two forms of marriages are provided, (a) marriage may be solemnized by a Minister of Church,[249] or (b) it may be solemnized by, or in the presence of, a Marriage Registrar. In the former case, it may be solemnized in such form as the Minister thinks fit to adopt, though presence of two witnesses besides the Minister is essential.[250] In the latter case the marriage is to be solemnized according to such form and ceremonies as parties think fit to adopt, but every such marriage shall be solemnized in the presence of a marriage registrar and in some part of the ceremony parties must say to each other, "I do solemnly declare that I know not of any lawful impediment why I, AB, may not be joined in matrimony to CD" and further each party must say to the other, "I call upon these persons here present to witness that I, AB, do take thee, CD, to be my lawful wedded wife (or husband)."[251] In case the marriage is solemnized among the Indian Christians, the formality of notice is not necessary. The Indian Christians can perform their marriage in the presence of a person licensed to perform such marriages and, at least, two credible witnesses, by saying to each other, "I call upon these persons present here to witness that I, AB, in the presence of Almighty God, and in the name of our Lord Jesus Christ, do take thee, CD to be my lawfully wedded wife (or husband)."[252]

A Parsi marriage must be solemnized in the "Ashirbad" form by a Parsi priest in the presence of two Parsi witnesses other than the priest.[253] Among the Jews a written contract called *Katuba* between the parties is essential. Presence of witness is also required. A civil marriage may be solemnized at the office of the Marriage Officer at such other place within a reasonable distance therefrom as the parties may desire, in any form the parties may choose to adopt. But a civil marriage shall not be complete and binding on the parties unless each party says to the other in the presence of the Marriage Officer and at least three witnesses in any language understood by the parties : "I, A, take thee, B, to be my lawful wife (husband)."[254]

247. Mulla's Mohammedan Law, (14th Ed.), p. 257.
248. *Ibid.*, at p. 256.
249. Part III, Christian Marriage Act.
250. Section 25.
251. Section 51.
252. Section 60.
253. Section 3(b), Parsi Marriage and Divorce Act, 1936.
254. Section 12, Special Marriage Act, 1954.

It is an established principle of Indian private international law that a marriage to be formally valid must comply with the *lex loci celebrationis.*[255]

Consular Marriages: The Foreign Marriage Act, 1969, modelled on the English statutes of that name and the Foreign Marriage Order, 1964 provides for consular marriages if one of the parties to the marriage is an Indian national. The Act lays down that a consular marriage may be performed abroad when one of the parties to the marriage is an Indian national (the other party may be an Indian national or a foreigner) at the official house of the marriage officer appointed under the Act with open doors between the prescribed hours, in the presence of at least three witnesses in any form which the parties may choose to adopt, but in no case a marriage will be complete and binding on the parties unless each party declares to the other in the presence of the marriage officer and witnesses, in any language understood by the parties, "I, A, take thee, B, to be my lawful wife (or husband)."[256] The marriage officer has power to refuse to solemnize or register a marriage which, in his opinion, is inconsistent with international law or the comity of nations.[257] A marriage solemnized abroad in accordance with the *lex loci celebrationis* between parties one of whom at least is an Indian national, may also be registered under the Act and once it is so registered it shall be deemed to be a marriage under the Act.[258] But if a marriage has not been registered under the Act, a petition for devorce cannot be filed in India.[259] A marriage solemnized by an Indian with a foreigner even before the comity into force of the Foreign Marriage Act can be registered under the Act.[260] A marriage solemnized or registered under the Act[261] shall be good and valid in law and will be recognized as such in India. Section 23 of the Act lays down that if the Government of India is satisfied that the law in force in any foreign country for the solemnization of marriages contains provisions similar to those contained in this Act, it may by notification in the Official Gazette declare that marriages thus solemnized shall be recognized by Indian courts as valid. Section 27 lays down that the provisions of the Act in no way affect the validity of the marriages solemnized abroad which are neither celebrated nor registered under the Act.

255. *Sainapati* v. *Sainapati*, 1932 Lah. 116; *Ma Twe* v. *Lwe Hain*, 1919 L.B. 14; *Mandakini Pundalik Salkar* v. *Chandrastin Paikar*, 1986 Bom. 172.
256. Section 13.
257. Sections 11(2) and 17(3).
258. Chapter III of the Act.
259. *Joyce* v. *Robert*, 1982 A.P. 385.
260. *Abdul* v. *Padma*, 1982 Bom. 341.
261. Sections 15 and 17(6).

9

MATRIMONIAL CAUSES

I

INTRODUCTORY

In England, before 1857, the jurisdiction over matrimonial causes was exercised by the ecclesiastical courts. Then divorce was unknown. In those days actions in matrimonial causes did not involve any problem of conflict of laws as the jurisdiction of the ecclesiastical courts extended to all Christians. The church was not concerned with the domicile or nationality of the parties.[1] The basis of the exercise of jurisdiction by the ecclesiastical courts was the residence of the parties within the jurisdiction.[2] And, as has been seen in the preceding Chapter of this work, the jurisdiction was available to those marriages alone which fell within the definition of the Christian marriage.[3]

In the rapidly advancing English society of eighteenth and nineteenth centuries the need for divorce was so pressing that its recognition became imperative. All the ingenuity of the Church failed to avert its reception in English law. In 1857 the first Matrimonial Causes Act was passed which not only repudiated the doctrine of indissolubility of marriage, but also transferred the entire jurisdiction in matrimonial causes from ecclesiastical courts to civil court.[4] Subsequently, bit by bit, many reforms

1. *Niboyet* v. *Niboyet*, (1878) 4 P.D. 1.
2. *Ross-Smith* v. *Ross-Smith*, (1963) A.C. 280.
3. It is interesting to note the development of law of nullity in the ecclesiastical courts. At the ecclesiastical law consent and coitus were essential for the validity of the marriage; absence of either rendered the marriage void. The former was called *impedimentum dirimens* which rendered the marriage void *ab initio,* and the latter was called *impedimentum impeditivum* which rendered the marriage voidable. The ecclesiastical courts showed such ingenuity in adapting these to individual cases that they served the same need which divorce could have served. However, soon the doctrine of indissolubility proved too irksome to people, and demand for divorce was voiced more loudly. Initially the sovereignty of Parliament was also used to persuade parliament to pass an Act of divorce in individual cases. But this was an expensive and complicated remedy which only rich could afford.
4. The Act also set up a court of "divorce and matrimonial causes"—this

were made. The same have now been consolidated in the Matrimonial Causes Act, 1973, and which has been supplemented by the Domicile and Matrimonial Proceedings Act, 1973.[5]

The matrimonial causes were statutorily defined in England in 1925 by the Supreme Court of Judicature Act, 1925. They are defined as actions for nullity of marriage, divorce, judicial separation, restitution of conjugal rights (which has been now abolished),[6] and jactitation of marriage.[7]

In India these have always been treated to include the first four matrimonial causes, though jactitation of marriage does not find any place in any of the Indian matrimonial statutes. However, a civil suit for such a declaration is maintainable under the Specific Relief Act, 1963.

In India the matrimonial causes are comparatively of recent growth. Muslim law has all along recognized divorce, but it never had anything akin to matrimonial causes. Divorce has been recognized in some Hindu communities by custom, otherwise Hindu marriage has been a sacramental (i.e. essentially indissoluble, apart from other aspects) union. Thus, among Hindus the question of existence of matrimonial causes could not have arisen, and, broadly speaking, India did not have anything like matrimonial causes before the advent of British rule. In 1869, the Indian Divorce Act was passed which for the first time introduced matrimonial actions of divorce, nullity of marriage, judicial separation and restitution of conjugal rights,[8] and ancillary reliefs of alimony, and custody, etc. of children. But then the Act applies to very limited persons : to Christians alone.[9] Four years earlier, the Parsi Marriage and Divorce Act, 1865 was also passed which recognized matrimonial causes for Parsis[10] and which was modelled on the Matrimonial Causes Act, 1857. This and its successor statute, the Parsi Marriage and Divorce Act, 1936 make provision for divorce, nullity of marriage, judicial separation and restitution of conjugal rights. However, till 1869, Christian and Parsis were in very small and insignificant (so far as concerned with the present subject) number.

The Dissolution of Muslim Marriages Act, 1939 was passed to

later on became the divorce division of the High Court and now has been renamed as the Family Division.

5. See Reports "Putting As under" and of the Law Commission.
6. See the Matrimonial Proceedings and Property Act, 1970, s. 20.
7. Section 225 of the Judicature Act, 1925.
8. The remedy of restitution of conjugal rights was made available to all people in India, i.e. to members of all the Indian communities under the general law.
9. Section 2. *Mary Geraldine Rooke* v. *John William Rooke*, 1934 Bom. 230. Under the Act the court has jurisdiction if one of the parties is a Christian : *Sasivaranam* v. *Gnanasundari*, 1954 Mad. 1018; *Dalal* v. *Dalal*, 1930 Bom. 385.
10. It also made Parsi marriage monogamous.

enable the Muslim wife to obtain divorce on certain grounds, as before 1939 there was hardly any ground on which the Muslim wife could ask for divorce.[11] This enactment enables the Muslim wife alone to file a suit for divorce. This is the only aspect of the Muslim matrimonial causes where a suit for divorce can be filed in a court of law. Of course, under general law a suit for restitution of conjugal rights can be filed by any Muslim husband or Muslim wife.

The Special Marriage Act, 1954[12] makes provision for all the four matrimonial causes. It also provides for ancillary reliefs.

The Hindu Marriage Act, 1955 introduced all the four matrimonial causes for Hindus.[13]

Thus, in 1955 India reaches a stage when it recognizes all the four matrimonial causes for all its people except the Muslims. Among Muslims, the position is that a wife can file a suit for divorce under the Dissolution of Muslim Marriages Act, 1939 and a Muslim (male or female) can ask for restitution of conjugal rights by filing a suit in a civil court. Just as in India we do not have a uniform law of marriage, so also we do not have a uniform law of matrimonial causes; every community has its own personal law. The question of conflict of inter-communal law hardly arise in India, though conflict of laws situation in personal laws do arise at an international level.

II

DISSOLUTION OF MARRIAGE

The modern English law accords recognition to both the consent theory and the breakdown theory, though in its own way.

11. In the *Khula* and the *Mubaarat* forms of divorce consent of the husband is imperative. It is only in *lian*, i.e. when her husband falsely accuses her of adultery that wife could sue for divorce. Before 1939 apostasy of either party led to automatic and complete and immediate dissolution of marriage. The law has been changed in this regard, see *infra*.

12. Its predecessor, the Special Marriage Act, 1872-1923 was defective in many respects.

13. Some efforts at regional level to introduce matrimonial causes were made. Earliest was made in 1930 when the Baroda state introduced divorce for Hindus. The Bombay state did it in 1947 by the Hindu Divorce Act. Earlier in 1946 it had passed the Prevention of Hindu Bigamous Marriage Act. The province of Madras did it in 1949 by enacting similar statutes. Saurashtra state did it in 1952. In the erstwhile states of Travancore and Cochin statutes reforming the law of marriage and divorce were passed some of which recognized divorce by mutual consent, such as under the Travancore Nayar Act. The Hindu Code Bill, 1948, which was drafted by a Hindu Law Committee under the Chairmanship of Sir Benegal Narsingh Rau, for the first time stipulated to introduce matrimonial causes for all Hindus. But the measure could not make much headway, mainly on account of opposition from a conservative section of Hindus. Ultimately the Indian Parliament passed the Hindu Marriage Act, 1955 which recognized all the four matrimonial causes for all Hindus.

The modern English law of matrimonial causes is contained in the Matrimonial Causes Act, 1973 and the Domicile and the Matrimonial Proceedings Act, 1973.[14]

Grounds of Divorce

The modern English law recognizes only one ground of divorce, viz. the marriage has broken down irretrievably.[15] What constitutes such breakdown is laid down in sub-section (2) of s. 1, Matrimonial Causes Act, 1973; the following facts will constitute such breakdown :

(a) that the respondent has committed adultery and the petitioner finds it intolerable to live with the respondent;

(b) that the respondent has behaved in such a way that the petitioner cannot reasonably be expected to live with the respondent;

(c) that the respondent has deserted the petitioner for a continuous period of at least two years immediately preceding the presentation of the petition;

(d) that the parties to the marriage have lived apart for a continuous period of at least two years immediately preceding the presentation of the petition and the respondent consents to a decree being granted;

(e) that the parties to the marriage have lived apart for a continuous period of at least five years immediately preceding the presentation of the petition.

These grounds appear to be a fair blending of the three traditional fault grounds, viz., adultery, cruelty, desertion, with the modern theories of consent and breakdown of marriage.

In contrast to English law, the Indian Divorce Act, 1869 stands as a reminder of the 19th century English matrimonial law, while the Special Marriage Act, 1954 presents a spectacle where guilt grounds of divorce are put side by side with divorce by mutual consent and divorce on the ground of breakdown of marriage. In between them stand the Parsi Marriage and Divorce Act, 1936

14. From 1857 onward several statutes on matrimonial causes were passed which were consolidated in the Matrimonial Causes Act, 1950. Again in the sixth decade of the twentieth century several peacemeal reforms were made and they were then consolidated in the Matrimonial Causes Act, 1965. But the process continued and again another instalment of piecemeal legislation came of which mention may be made of the Divorce Reform Act, 1969. All these reforms together with some fresh ones have been consolidated in the Matrimonial Causes Act, 1973. But again, some more vital changes were made in the same year and so came the Domicile and Matrimonial Proceedings Act, 1973. Now these two statutes are the main foundations of the English matrimonial law which also contain provisions for conflictual problems and for recognition of foreign divorces.

15. Section 1(1) of the Matrimonial Causes Act, 1973.

which is though an outcome of the late nineteenth century outlook of English matrimonial law has some linings of modernity, and the Hindu Marriage Act, 1955 which is a remarkable blending of traditional Hindu conservatism with the modern and not-so-modern notions of matrimonial law.

The Indian Divorce Act, 1869 recognizes only one ground of divorce. A husband can seek divorce on the ground that his wife has been guilty of adultery; a wife can seek divorce on the ground that her husband has converted to another religion and married a second wife, or has been guilty of incestuous adultery, or of bigamy with adultery, or of marriage with another woman with adultery, or of rape, sodomy or bestiality or adultery coupled with such cruelty as without adultery would have entitled her to a divorce *mensa et toro*, or of adultery coupled with desertion, without any reasonable excuse for two years or upward.[16]

The Parsi Marriage and Divorce Act passed in 1936. The Act gives no place to voidable marriages. Some grounds of voidable marriages have been made grounds of divorce. Of the eleven grounds of divorce that the Act recognized two relates to pre-marriage faults and test to post marriage faults. Under the former are : pre-marriage pregnancy and the pre-marriage insanity of the respondent. Under the latter are : wilful refusal to consummate the marriage, unsoundness of bind for two or more years, cruelty, adultery, fornication, bigamy, rape or unnatural offence; physical cruelty (amounting to grievous hurt), infecting of the plaintiff with venereal disease, or compelling the wife to submit to prostitution; sentence of imprisonment for a term of seven years or more; two years desertion non-resumption of cohabitation for two years or more after an order awarding maintenance, and conversion of some other religion. These grounds are hedged with usual safeguards and conditions.[17]

The Special Marriage Act, 1954 has the unique feature of enacting all the three theories of divorce side by side, in ss. 27 and 28. The eight fault grounds are : adultery; two years desertion; seven years' sentence of imprisonment; cruelty; incurable insanity or mental disorder of such a kind and to such an extent that the petitioner cannot reasonably be expected to live with the respondent; venereal diseases in a communicable form; leprosy; and presumption of death (i.e. seven years' unheard absence). Two grounds on which the wife alone can sue for divorce are : (i) the respondent has been guilty of rape, sodomy and bestiality; and (ii) cohabitation between the parties has not taken place for one year or upwards after the passing of an order awarding maintenance in favour of the petitioner under section 125. Criminal Procedure Code, 1973, or section 18, Hindu Maintenance and

16. Section 10.
17. Section 32.

Adoptions Act, 1956. The two breakdown grounds are: non-resumption of cohabitation for a period of one year or more after the passing of a decree for judicial separation, and non-compliance with the decree of restitution of conjugal rights for a period of one year or more give a right to either party (irrespective of the fact as to who is guilty) to present a petition for divorce.[18] Section 28 allows the parties to present a petition for divorce on the basis of mutual consent of parties. The provision is hedged with adequate safeguards.

Under the Hindu Marriage Act, 1955 the nine fault grounds are: adultery; desertion, cruelty; conversion to another religion; incurable insanity or mental disorder; virulent leprosy; venereal disease in a communicable form; renunciation of the world; and presumption of death (i.e. seven years' unheard absence). These are four additional grounds of divorce on which wife alone can sue are: (a) another wife of the husband's pre-Act polygamous marriage being alive; (b) the husband has been guilty of rape, sodomy or bestiality; (c) cohabitation between the parties has not taken place for one year or upwards after the passing of an order awarding maintenance to the wife under section 125, Criminal Procedure Code, 1973, or under section 18, Hindu Maintenance and Adoptions Act, 1956; and (d) the marriage of the wife (whether consummated or not) was solemnized before she attained the age of fifteen years and she had repudiated the marriage after attaining that age but before attaining the age of eighteen years. The break-down grounds are the same as under the Special Marriage Act, 1954,[19] and so is the provision for divorce by mutual consent.

Divorce under Muslim law is largely non-judicial. This may be divided under two heads: (a) unilateral divorce by husband, and (b) divorce at the instance of the wife but with the consent of the husband. The former is called *Talak*. No particular form is required. It may be oral or in writing. The intention to divorce must be clear and unequivocal. The presence of the wife is not required; nor need it be addressed to wife. It may be in approved form (*Talak-i-sunna*)[20] or it may be in unapproved form (*Talak-ul-Biddait*).[21] While pronouncing divorce on his wife, the

18. Section 27(2).

19. Section 13(1) deals with fault grounds, s. 13(2) deals with two additional fault grounds, and s. 13(1A) with breakdown grounds.

20. It has two forms, *hasan* and *ahsan*. In *hasan* form, it consists of three pronouncements of divorce (I divorce thee three times) made during successive periods of *tuhr* (it is a period when the wife is free from menstruation, the period of purity), no marital intercourse taking place during all the three periods of purity. In *ahsan* form it is made by a single pronouncement of divorce made during a period of *tuhr* followed by abstinence from marital intercourse during the period of *iddat*.

21. *Talak-ul-biddat* consists of three pronouncements of divorce made during a single *tuhr*, either in one sentence, 'I divorce thee thrice' or in separate three sentences: I divorce thee, I divorce thee, I divorce thee. It may also

Muslim husband need not mention any reason or cause; none is necessary under Muslim law. Muslim law also recognized *talak* in delegated form. It is called *Talak-i-Tafweez.*[22] Muslim law also recognizes two other forms of divorce (*talak*), *Ila* and *Zihar*,[23] which are no longer in vogue. The most curious feature of Muslim matrimonial law is that it holds valid a divorce which a husband may pronounce under compulsion, in a state of voluntary intoxication or to satisfy his father or someone else.[24]

Muslim marriage may also be dissolved at the instance of the wife, provided the husband consents to it.[25] When wife alone is desirous of divorce it is called *Khula*, when aversion to marriage is mutual then it is known as *Mubaarat*. *Khula* divorce is effected by an offer from the wife to compensate the husband, if he releases her from marital rights, and its acceptance by the husband. Once the offer is accepted, it operates as a single irrevocable divorce.[26] In the *Mubaarat* form wife has to offer something by way of compensation to the husband, which is usually her forbearance to claim her entire, or part of, dower. *Lian* or imprecation gives right to the wife to sue her husband for divorce. Before the coming into force of the Dissolution of Muslim Marriages Act, 1939, apostasy from Islam of either party to a marriage operated as dissolution of marriage automatically. This has been altered by the Dissolution of Muslim Marriages Act, 1939. Now apostasy of the wife does not automatically operate as divorce.[27] Apostasy of the husband still does.

be made by a single pronouncement of divorce during a period of *tuhr* clearly indicating an intention irrevocably to dissolve the marriage. See Mulla (17th ed.), p. 297.

22. Under Muslim law the husband has power to delegate his power of pronouncing divorce to any other person, including the wife. When the person to whom the power is delegated exercises that power and pronounces divorce, it is known as *Talak-i-Tafweez*.
23. In *ila* form of divorce the husband swears not to have intercourse with his wife and if he abstains for four months, it amounts to divorce. In *zihar* form the husband compares his wife to his mother or any other female within the prohibited degrees of relationship. If he intends to revoke this as operating divorce, he can do so on payment of money to his wife by way of expiration or by fasting for a certain period. In case he does not revoke it, the wife has the right to go to the court to obtain divorce.
24. This, it seems, was an effort on the part of later Muslim law givers to overcome the rigidity of Muslim law which did not allow Muslim wife divorces under these conditions she could make her husband pronounce divorce on her. *Ibrahim Moola* v. *Enayetur Ruhman*, (1869) 4 Beng. L.R. A.C. 13; *Rashid Ahmed* v. *Anisa Khatun*, (1921) 59 I.A. 21. See also Mulla, pp. 301-302.
25. Tyabji, Mohammedan law (4th ed.), p. 176.
26. Mulla, p 303.
27. Section 4 of the Dissolution of Muslim Marriages Act, 1939. But this provision does not apply to a wife who before her marriage was a non-Muslim and converted to Islam either at the time of the marriage or subsequently. If such a wife reconverts to her original faith, then it still amounts to an automatic and immediate dissolution of marriage.

The right to obtain judicial divorce is available to the wife alone. A Muslim wife can obtain a decree of divorce from a court of law by filing a suit on any of the following grounds : the whereabouts of the husband had not been known to her for a period of four years; two years' (or more) neglect; or failure to provide maintenance for two years or more; sentence of imprisonment for a period of seven years or more; failure to perform marital obligations without any reasonable cause for a period of three years or more; impotence at the time of marriage; insanity for a period of two years or more, or leprosy or virulent venereal disease; repudiation of marriage before the attainment of the age of eighteen years; cruelty; or any other ground recognized under Muslim law.[28]

Jurisdiction

English Law

In respect of jurisdiction of English courts, some fundamental changes have been effected by the Domicile and Matrimonial Proceedings Act, 1973. Now English court can assume jurisdiction only on two grounds : domicile, and habitual residence of the parties.[29] All other bases of jurisdiction have been abolished.[30] Domicile as a basis of jurisdiction has to be understood in the light of s. 1, Domicile and Matrimonial Proceedings Act, 1973 which abolishes wife's dependent domicile.

Domicile : Since the Privy Council decision in *Le Mesurier* v. *Le Mesurier*,[31] which was confirmed by the House of Lords in *Indyka* v. *Indyka*[32] it has been the settled proposition of English law that the English court has jurisdiction to entertain a petition for divorce if parties are domiciled in England at the time of commencement of the proceedings.[33] The Domicile and the Matrimonial Proceedings Act, 1973 now lays down that the court will have jurisdiction to entertain a petition for divorce if either of the parties to the marriage is domiciled in England on the date when proceedings are begun.[34] Now that the wife can have her own separate

28. Section 2.
29. Section 5(2).
30. The section uses the words, "if (and only if) . . ."
31. (1895) A.C. 517.
32. (1969) 1 A.C. 33.
33. Before the Privy Council decision, the tendency was to base 'jurisdiction on residence', probably a hangover of the ecclesiastical jurisdiction : See *Niboyet* v. *Niboyet*, (1878) 4 P.D. 1. At one time probably under the influence of 'contractual theory' the *lex loci celebrationis* was also preached as a basis of jurisdiction : *R* v. *Lockey*, (1812) 2 Cl. & F. 567; *Tovey* v. *Lindsay*, (1813) 1 Dow. 117. Then, the 'penal theory' propagated the conferment of jurisdiction on the court of the place where the matrimonial offence was committed : *Ginesi* v. *Ginesi*, (1948) p. 179, but see *Preston-Jones* v. *Preston-Jones*, (1951) A.C. 391. In Scotland it has some influence, though in England it did not make much of headway.
34. Section 5(2).

domicile, the Act effects a basic change inasmuch as it lays down that a petition can be filed for divorce if either the petitioner or the respondent is domiciled in England at the date when proceedings are commenced.

Once the court has jurisdiction to entertain the petition its jurisdiction cannot be defeated by a subsequent change of husband's domicile.[35] Under the Act, not only the petition already filed will not be affected by the subsequent change of domicile by the party on the basis of whose domicile the petition was filed, but the court will retain jurisdiction to entertain any cross petition that may be filed subsequently for a different form of relief (suppose, the petition is filed for divorce, the respondent may cross petition for judicial separation, or *vice versa*.[36])

Habitual Residence : With the Hague Conventions adopting "habitual residence" as a basis of jurisdiction, the English law is now giving it full reception.[37] The Domicile and Matrimonial Proceedings Act, 1973 adopts it as the second basis of jurisdiction : if either party to the marriage was habitually resident in England throughout the period of one year ending on the date when the proceedings are begun, the English court has jurisdiction to entertain a petition for divorce. What is the meaning of "habitual residence" has, however, not been defined either statutorily or judicially. According to the Law Commission it can be proved, "by evidence of a course of conduct which tends to show substantial links between a person and his country of residence."[38] "The factual element" of habitual residence has been emphasised by the Council of Europe on Fundamental Legal Concepts thus : "In determining whether a residence is habitual, account is to be taken of the duration and the continuity of the residence as well as other factors of a personal or professional nature which point to durable ties between a person and his residence."[39] The term habitual residence has been judicially used in at least two cases.[40] Probably it is the same thing as "ordinary residence" which term

35. *Leon* v. *Leon*, (1966) 3 W.L.R. 1164. The English courts have rejected all other bases of jurisdiction, such as nationality of parties, *Uhling* v. *Uhling*, (1916) 86 L.J.R. 90; their residence, *Le Mesurier* v. *Le Mesurier*, cited above; their submission to jurisdiction, *Harriman* v. *Harriman*, (1909) p. 123; commission of matrimonial offence in a country different from their domicile *Wilson* v. *Wilson*, (1872) 2 P & D. 435; their domicile at the time of marriage, *Goulder* v. *Goulder*, (1892) p. 240 or place of marriage, *Ratcliff* v. *Ratcliff*, (1859) 1 Sw. & Tr. 467; *Goulder* v. *Goulder*, cited above.

36. Section 5(5).

37. For instance, see Administration of Justice Act, 1956, ss. 3(8), 4(1)(a); Wills Act, 1963, s. 1; Adoption Act, 1968, s. 11(1); Recognition of Divorces and Legal Separations Act, 1971, s. 3(1)(a).

38. Report, para. 42.

39. "Current Law", Statutes, 45/5.

40. *Indyka* v. *Indyka*, (1969) 1 A.C. 33, at p. 68, per Lord Reid and *Angelo* v. *Angelo*, (1968) 1 W.L.R. 401 at p. 403, per Lord Reid.

has been defined by Lord Denning in connection with ordinary residence of a minor child.[41] It is submitted it means the same thing as "residence" means under Indian matrimonial law (see *supra*), though somewhat flexible meaning has been given to it in some English decisions.[42]

The above two basis of jurisdiction are applicable to all the grounds of divorce including the dissolution of marriage on the basis of presumption of death.[43]

Indian Law

Although the matrimonial law in India differs from community to community, the jurisdictional rules differ only slightly. The matrimonial laws of all communities, except the Muslims and the Jews, is now statutory laws. The peculiar feature of all these statutes, except the Divorce Act, 1869, is that the domicile or nationality of either party is not relevant for the purpose of jurisdiction in any matrimonial cause. The outstanding feature of all statutes is that in all causes the jurisdictional basis is the same.[44]

Under the Indian Divorce Act, 1869[45] a petition is in any matrimonial cause may be present to the District Court or the High Court,[46] in any matrimonial cause on the basis of the residence of the parties within the jurisdiction or that the parties last resided together within the jurisdiction of the court,[47] or for dissolution of marriage, the parties are domiciled in India at the time of the presentation of the petition.[48]

A further jurisdictional requirements in a petition for nullity are that such a petition can be presented only if the marriage was solemnized in India, and further that the petitioner was resident in India at the time of the presentation of the petition.[49] In respect of a petition for judicial separation or restitution of conjugal rights, the additional requirement is that at the time of the presentation of the petition the petitioner must be residing in India.[50]

41. *Re P.* (G.E.), (1965) Ch. 568: See Chapter XII of this work.
42. See *Matalon* v. *Matalon*, (1952) p. 223; *Sinclair* v. *Sinclair*, (1868) p. 189.
43. See s. 19, Matrimonial Causes Act, 1973, sub-sections (2) and (5) of which have been repealed by the Domicile and Matrimonial Proceedings Act, 1973.
44. For instance, see section 19, Hindu Marriage Act, 1955.
45. Section 2. See also, *Mary Geraldine Rooke* v. *John William Rooke*, 1934 Bom. 230; *Sasivaranam* v. *Gnanasundari*, 1954 Mad. 1018 (where one party alone was Christian); *Dalal* v. *Dalal*, 1930 Bom. 385 (where the petitioner was a Russian lady of Christian faith.
46. See ss. 10, 18, 23 and 32.
47. Section 3(3).
48. Section 2, para. 2.
49. Section 2, para. 3; see also *Taylor* v. *Wenkenbasch* (1937) Cal, 417; *Agnes* v. *Paul*, 59 Mad. 509.
50. Section 2, para. 4.

The Parsi Marriage and Divorce Act, 1936[51] stipulates for the establishment of special courts known as Parsi Chief Matrimonial Courts at Calcutta, Bombay and Madras and at such other places as the state governments may think fit. The courts established at any place other than at Bombay, Calcutta and Madras are known as the Parsi District Matrimonial Courts. The Parsi matrimonial courts are assisted by seven delegates all of which must be Parsis.[52] The jurisdictional requirements in respect of all the matrimonial causes are the same. The Act lays down that a suit in a matrimonial cause may be filed :

(i) in the Parsi matrimonial court within the limits of whose jurisdiction the defendant resides at the time of the institution of the suit,

(ii) (if the defendant is not residing in India), in the Parsis matrimonial court within whose jurisdiction parties last resided together,[53]

(iii) (with the permission of the court) at a place where the plaintiff is residing or at a place where the parties last resided together irrespective of the fact whether the defandant resides in India or nct.[54]

Thus, the main basis of jurisdiction is 'residence' which has been used in a broad sense.[55] The domicile or the nationality of either party does not figure anywhere. The Act applies not merely to Indian Parsis but also to all Zoroastrians[56] (including from Iran) who are either temporarily or permanently residing in India.[57]

The Hindu Marriage Act, 1955 applies to all Hindus. It is also not necessary that they should be Indian nationals.[58] The domicile has significance in respect of those Hindus who are outside India.[59] Hindu Marriage Act, 1955 too makes no distinction from the jurisdictional point of view between any of the matrimonial causes. Under the Special Marriage Act, 1954, domicile is important only in respect of those Indian citizens who are outside India.[60] Again, in the jurisdictional rules no difference is made between the matrimonial causes. The jurisdictional grounds under

51. In s. 2(5) husband is defined to mean "Parsi husband" and in s. 2(9) wife is defined to mean "Parsi wife".
52. Section 18.
53. A delegate is like a juror, *Dinbai* v. *Framroz*, 1918 Nag. 77.
54. Section 29.
55. *Panthaky* v. *Panthaky*, 1941 Bom. 330.
56. Section 2(7).
57. *Sir Jamsedji* v. *Jijabhai*, 11 Bom. L.R. 85; *Jamsed Irani* v. *Bani Irani*, (1967) 68 Bom. L.R. 749; See also the article by Phiroz K. Irani. The Personal Law of Parsis in India, *Family Law in Asia and Africa*, pp. 273, at p. 286.
58. Section 2, Hindu Marriage Act, 1955.
59. Section 1(2).
60. See s. 4 and Part III.

both the statutes are the same.[61,62] Under the Acts a petition for dissolution of marriage, nullity of marriage, judicial separation or restitution of conjugal rights may be presented to the District court within the local limits of whose jurisdiction—

(a) the marriage was solemnized,

(b) the parties last resided together,[63]

(c) the respondent, at the time of presentation of petition resides, and

(d) the petitioner is residing at the time of presentation of petition, in a case where the respondent is, at the time, residing outside the territories to which the Act extends has not been heard of being alive for seven years.

The Special Marriage Act, 1954 contains a special jurisdictional rule in respect of the wife's petition. It runs : ". . . the District court may . . . entertain a petition by a wife domiciled in the territories to which this Act extends for nullity of marriage or for divorce if she is resident in the said territories and has been ordinarily resident therein for a period of three years immediately preceding the presentation of the petition and the husband is not resident in the said territories."[64] It is submitted that the last provision would apply to those cases where two Indian domiciled persons solemnize their marriage abroad, but after sometime their marriage fails and wife alone comes to India. In such a case, she cannot file the petition under the main jurisdictional rules, but she can do under this special provision. It is in this context that one can understand the significance of the words, 'husband is not resident' in India.

Under Muslim law, as has been seen earlier, a legal action for divorce can be filed by the wife alone on any one of the grounds laid down in the Dissolution of Muslim Marriages Act, 1939. The Act does not contain any juridictional rule and the matter is therefore regulated by the general provisions of the Civil Procedure Code. A suit for restitution of conjugal rights[65], can also be filed by any wife or husband. Similarly, a suit for a declaration that the marriage is null and void or a suit for jactitation of marriage, can

61. Section 19.

62. Section 31.

63. Some of the cases under the Indian Divorce Act on 'residing together' may be noted : *Murphy* v. *Murphy*, 1951 All. 180; *Robey* v. *Robey*, 1931 Cal. 121; *Leadon* v. *Leadon*, 1926 Oudh 319; *Borgonah* v. *Borgonah*, 22 Bom. L.R. 361; *Heneritta* v. *James*, 47 P.R. 1911; *Walsh* v. *Walsh*, 29 Bom. L.R. 308. Cases on 'parties are residing' are : *Murphy* v. *Murphy*, 1951 All. 180, *Premlatika* v. *Provash*, 1953 Cal. 242; *Morton* v. *Morton*, 1916 Lah. 256.

64. Section 31(2)

65. Under this category will come people like Jews. The High Courts under their Letters Patent jurisdiction and all other courts of original jurisdiction can entertain a suit for divorce: *Benjamin* v. *Benjamin*, 50 Bom. 369; *Engel* v. *Engel*, 1944 Bom. 15.

be filed under the Specific Relief Act, 1963. Two such suits provisions of s. 20, Civil Procedure Code apply.[66'67] This means that the suit can be filed in a court within whose jurisdiction the defendant is residing at the time of the filing of the suit, or the cause of action arose. Since a Muslim marriage is a contract, the cause of action arises, it has been held, at the place where the marriage was solemnized.[68] It has also been held that a suit can be filed at a place where the parties are residing[69] or where the matrimonial misconduct was committed.[70] In most of the cases the courts have assumed jurisdiction on the basis of the residence of the defendant or on the basis of accrual of the cause of action. Thus, it has been held that a suit for restitution of conjugal rights can be filed at a place where their violation occurred,[71] or at a place where the defendant is residing.[72] The same is the position of the suit for jactitation of marriage,[73] or for a suit for a declaration that the marriage is null and void.[74]

Residence : Time and again courts have said that residence is a question of fact ; whether or not a person is residing at a particular place would depend upon the facts of each case.[75] The word 'residence' is obviously capable of a narrow as well as a broad meaning. In the former sense it usually means a permanent home or abode, in the latter sense it means any place where a person is living, permanently or temporarily.

In its narrow meaning (or natural meaning, as it is sometimes said), the term means "the abiding or dwelling" in a place for some continuous time ;[76] it means the place where a person "eats, drinks and sleeps" or where "his family and servants eat, drink and sleep".[77] In short, in its natural and ordinary meaning (which is

66. Under the Sharait Act, 1937 a suit could be filed only in the District court, but that provision has been repealed by s. 6, Dissolution of Muslim Marriage Act.
67. These provisions have already been discussed in Chapter 7.
68. *Nizamuddin* v. *Hussani*, 1960 M.P. 212; suit was for restitution of conjugal rights.
69. *Jahoor Ahmed* v. *Tehrabi*, 1954 Nag. 51.
70. See Chapter 7 of this work.
71. *Smt. Chandanwant Kaur* v. *Sukhdev Singh*, 1956 Pepsu 49; *Chhitar* v. *Harju*, 1919 All. 96; *Venu Gopal Naidu* v. *Lakshmi*, 1936 Mad. 288.
72. *Nusserwanjee* v. *Eleonora*, 1914 Bom. 211 (where both parties are residing); *Zahoor* v. *Mst. Tehrabi*, 1954 Nag. 51.
73. *Bhagwan Ghanshayandas* v. *Charlotte*, (1959) 1 Cal. 84; *Beham* v. *Allabux*, (1903) P.R. 1882.
74. *Ajaintadasi* v. *Prahalad Chandra*, (1871) 6 Bom. L.R. 243; *Bhagwan Ghamshyandas* v. *Charlotte*, (1959) 1 Cal. 84; *Sophy* v. *Shiva Prosad*, 1945 Cal. 484.
75. *Jagir Kaur* v. *Jaswant Singh*, 1963 S.C. 1521.
76. *Anilbala* v. *Dhirendra*, (1921) 48 Cal. 577; *Goswami* v. *Govardhanlalji*, (1890) 14 Bom. 541.
77. *Kumud Nath* v. *Jotindranath*, (1911) 38 Cal. 394, per Mukerji and Teunion, JJ. while interpreting the term 'residence' in Order 5, rules 9 and 17 of the Civil Procedure Code.

called the narrow meaning), residence means "permanent abode or home" or a permanent place where a person lives, and does not include a temporary residence.[78] It has also been expressed by saying, "to dwell permanently or for a considerable time" or "to have a settled abode for a time" or "to remain for a long time".[79] It seems to be obvious that if a person has a permanent abode or home and from here he goes out and lives at another place temporarily, on account of business, pleasure, health, education or for any other reason, then the former would continue to be the place of residence and not the latter.[80] Thus, in *Robey* v. *Robey*,[81] a case under the Divorce Act, 1869, a husband was living in Delhi with his wife for a period of six years. Thereafter he went to Calcutta for launching criminal proceedings and stayed there for sometime with his brother. He was a government servant liable to transfer. Subsequently, he filed matrimonial proceedings in a Calcutta court. It was held that since he resided at Delhi and not Calcutta, the petition was not maintainable for want of jurisdiction.[82] In *Arthur Flowers* v. *Minnie Flowers*[83] the parties were residing at Hyderabad, where the husband also worked. The husband used to go to Meerut for official visits, on some of which the wife also accompanied. Subsequently, he filed a petition for judicial separation at a Meerut court on the ground of adultery of his wife. Declining to exercise the jurisdiction, a Full Bench of the Allahabad High Court said : " . . . a mere casual visit to a place for a temporary purpose with no intention of remaining is not dwelling, and where a party has a fixed residence out of jurisdiction, an occasional visit within jurisdiction will not suffice to confer jurisdiction by reason of residence." Similarly, when a person goes abroad temporarily for some job or business, he continues to reside in India and the Indian courts will have jurisdiction on the basis of his residence.[84]

The words 'reside' and 'last resided' together have not only been used in the Indian matrimonial statutes, but s. 488 (s. 225 of the new Code) of the Criminal Procedure Code also uses these words. The latter provision came for interpretation before the Supreme Court in *Jagir Kaur* v. *Jaswant Singh*.[85] Subba Rao, J. said that the word 'residence' includes both permanent dwelling and temporary living at a place, but it does not include "a casual

78. *David* v. *Dennis* 1954 Nag. 248; *Robo* v. *Robo*, 1931 Cal. 121; *Kershaw* v. *Kershaw*, 1930 Lah. 916 (cases under the Indian Divorce Act); *Panthaky* v. *Panthaky*, 1941 Bom. 330 (case under the Parsi Marriage and Divorce Act, 1936); *Saraswati* v. *Keshwan*, 1961 Ker. L.J. 1247.
79. *Anil Bala* v *Dhirendra*, (1921) 48 Cal. 577.
80. *Carol* v. *Carol*, 1933 All. 39; *Walsh* v. *Walsh*, 1927 Bom. 230.
81. 1931 Cal. 121.
82. Similar view was expressed in *D'Souza* v. *Lobo*, 1940 Mad. 584; *Dulari* v. *Narayan*, 1959 Punj. 50 (case is under Hindu Marriage Act); *Flowers* v. *Flowers*, 32 All. 203.
83. 32 All. 203.
84. *Hary* v. *Joseph* 1980 Ker. 131.
85. 1963 S.C. 1521.

stay in, or a flying visit to, a particular place." His Lordship ventured to define residence thus : "A person resides in a place, if he through choice makes it his abode permanently or even temporarily, whether a person has chosen to make a particular place his abode depends upon the facts of each case."[86] Subba Rao, J. emphasises that there must be an intention to stay for a period, the length of period depending upon particular circumstances of each case, but what is essential is that he must make the place his abode, though it need not be for enjoyment of marital relationship.[87]

But there may be situations where the parties have not been able to establish a matrimonial home at all. It may be that during the period their marriage was going well, they were moving from place to place, may be looking for a nice place to establish a matrimonial home, or may be looking for nothing. A situation something of this nature came before the court in *Murphy* v. *Murphy*,[88] a case under the Divorce Act, 1869. After the marriage, parties lived together in a Bombay hotel for the greater portion of a month; then the husband was on leave from the active service in Mesopotamia. After that he left Bombay to join his service. Parties had not established a matrimonial home at any place whatever, and the living at the Bombay hotel was all the living together that the parties had. On these facts, the Bombay High Court said that since parties have no residence anywhere else, their stay together in Bombay, howsoever temporary, was the place where they resided together. In *Tara* v. *Jaipal Singh*[89] also parties did not set up any permanent residence and lived at various places for short periods, and in this manner when they were living at Darjeeling for a week, the marriage broke down. It was held that they last resided together at Darjeeling.[90] *Clarance* v. *Raicheal*[91] presents a rather peculiar situation. Soon after the solemnization of marriage in a place in Bangalore District which was also the home of wife's father, the wife told the husband that she had sexual connection with the co-respondent. Whereupon the husband left the wife at her parent's home and filed a petition in a Bangalore court for judicial separation. The Mysore High Court held that the court had jurisdiction as parties last resided together at Bangalore, even though only for a few hours. The full Bench decision in *T.J. Poonen* v. *Rathi Varghese*[92] discounted that the place where parties stay for some casual visit

86. His Lordships gave four examples to illustrate this definition.
87. *Madhvi Sirothia* v. *N.M. Sirothia*, 1974 All. 36.
88. 1921 Bom. 211.
89. (1946) 1 Cal. 604
90. See also *Ritchson* v. *Ritchson*, 1934 Cal. 570; *Bright* v. *Bright*, (1909) 36 Cal. 964; *Berrett* v. *Berrett*, 1950 All. 193; *Murphy* v. *Murphy*, 1951 All. 180; *D'Souza* v. *Lobo*, 1940 Mad. 584.
91. 1964 Mys. 67.
92. 1967 Ker. 1 (F.B.).

could be called residence.[93]

Despite the decision in *Poonen's case,* there is clear line of cases which hold the view that in those cases where parties have not set up a matrimonial home nor have they any dwelling place or abode, the place where they stayed together—whatever be the duration, a few hours or a few days—is the place where they would be considered to have last resided together for the purpose of conferring jurisdiction on the matrimonial court. Thus, in *Saroja* v. *Emmanual*[94] parties did not establish any matrimonial home, as both the husband and wife were employed and posted at different places. The wife used to go for short periods in her vacations to the place where the husband was living. The Mysore High Court held that the place where the husband was living was the place where the parties last resided together. This case and others taking this view[95] have been followed in *Lalithamma* v. *Kannan,*[96] a case under the Hindu Marriage Act, 1955. This way of looking at residence, it is submitted, would go a long way to solve the problem inherent in the type of cases in which this approach has been taken, and give residence the desired flexibility.

Thus, it is submitted that the "residence" for the purpose of matrimonial jurisdiction of the Indian courts means :

(i) The place where the parties have set up a matrimonial home or the place where parties already have a permanent home or abode where they live (or lived together) is the place where they have their residence.

(ii) In cases where the parties have not set up any matrimonial home, nor do they have any permanent abode or home, it will be the place where they stay (or stayed together), however short the duration of stay might be (or might have been).[97]

Residence or Domicile of Petitioner as a basis of Jurisdiction : In some cases under the Divorce Act, 1896, a view has been expressed that the court has jurisdiction to entertain a petition in a matrimonial case on the basis of petitioner's residence, even though the defendant is not residing in India. It appears that these decisions have been rendered on the basis of the last two paras of s. 2 of the Act without looking at s. 3(3) of the Act. However, it is submitted that in some cases it would be desirable to confer jurisdiction on the basis of petitioner's residence, residence here taken in its natural meaning. In *Christopher Neelkantam* v. *Annie Neelkantam,*[98] where an Indian domiciled

93. *Ibid.*, at p. 13.
94. 1965 Mys. 12.
95. See cases cited in footnotes 88 to 91.
96. 1966 Mys. 178.
97. See author's work, Modern Hindu Law, Codified and Uncodified, p. 189.
98. 1959 Raj. 133.

Christian solemnized his marriage with an English domiciled woman in London. His wife refused to accompany him to India, when he left England for India. On arriving in India, the husband instituted devorce proceedings against his wife in a Rajasthan court under the Special Marriage Act, 1954. Tne Rajasthan High Court said that the court has jurisdiction since the petitioner was domiciled in India. In *Hariram* v. *Jasoti*[99] the problem was tackled on a different plane. In this case, before the partition of India, parties were married in that part of the country which now forms part of Pakistan. After partition, the parties came to India, but in India parties did not reside together at any place, nor were they residing at the same place. Parties were Hindus. The court did not consider the case as posing any problem of conflict of laws and tackled it purely as a domestic case. The court said that it would have jurisdiction under s. 20, Civil Procedure Code if the cause of action arose in India or if the defendant resided within jurisdiction. The Madras High Court has also taken this view.[100] The jurisdictional rules have been enacted in Section 19(iv) of the Hindu Marriage Act and section 31(iv) of the special Marriage Act.

Choice of Law

English Law

Once English court decides that it has jurisdiction in the case, it has never felt any difficulty as to the choice of law. They have invariably applied the English domestic law. This is a typical corollary of the English attitude towards divorce decrees of foreign courts. Once English court has found that the foreign court has jurisdiction, it has never bothered to look at the ground on which the foreign court pronounced the decree of divorce. Thus, it has been immaterial that the matrimonial offence or fault, i.e. the ground on the basis of which divorce was granted, was committed abroad in the country where the parties were domiciled or resident.[101] It has been irrelevant that the matrimonial misconduct complained of does not constitute a ground for divorce in the country where it was committed or in the country of domicile of parties. Wolff supporting this state of English law said that the question whether the marriage would be dissolved or not "touches fundamental English concept of morality, religion and public policy" and therefore is a matter which should be exclusively decided by English law.[102] This may be justified on the ground that since under common law, jurisdiction is assumed on the basis of domicile of the parties and therefore the law that is applied is that of domicile. But what is remarkable is that even in those

99. 1963 Bom. 176.
100. *M. Gomathi* v. *S. Natrajan*, (1973) I M.L.J. 246.
101. *Czepek* v. *Czepek*, (1962) 3 All. E.R. 990.
102. Private International Law, p. 374.

cases where the jurisdiction was assumed on the basis of residence of parties (under the statutory exceptions), the English private international law took the view that the English domestic law was applicable. In *Zanelli* v. *Zanelli*[103] an Italian national domiciled in England married an English woman. Subsequently, he was deported from England. On deportation he assumed his Italian domicile. The English court assumed jurisdiction on the basis of special statutory provision and granted divorce to the wife by applying English domestic law—by the law of domicile divorce was not permitted then. This rule was given statutory recognition.[104] Although the special statutory jurisdiction has been abolished,[105] the choice of law rule that in all those cases where the court has jurisdiction, it applies English domestic law is still valid. This follows from the status theory adopted by English courts. Thus, it seems clear that when an English court determines that it has jurisdiction to entertain the petition for divorce, and applies English law, then English law is applied not as the *lex domicilii* but as the *lex fori*.[106]

Indian Law

Although there is not much authority, it seems clear that once the Indian court decides that it has jurisdiction to entertain the petition for divorce, then it will apply the personal law of the parties, i.e. the law of the community to which parties belong. Thus, if parties are Christians the Indian Divorce Act, 1869, if parties are Hindus the Hindu Marriage Act, 1955, if parties are Parsis, the Parsi Marriage and Divorce Act, 1936, or if parties are Muslims (when wife had filed a suit for divorce), the Dissolution of Muslim Marriage Act, 1939, will apply, being the *lex fori*. It seems that if marriage is performed abroad, or it has some foreign elements, the court will apply the provisions of the Special Marriage Act, 1954, even if both the parties are Hindus, Christians or Parsis. Thus in the submission of the present writer the Special Marriage Act, 1954 will apply not merely to civil marriages performed in India, but to all marriages which have some foreign element. Some support for this view is derived from *Christopher Neelkantam* v. *Annie Neelkantam*,[107] where both the parties were Christians and the court could have easily applied the Christian law, i.e. the Indian Divorce Act, 1869, but it chose to apply the Special Marriage Act, 1954. If the courts would not do so, then

103. (1948) 64 T.L.R. 556.

104. Section 18(3), Matrimonial Causes Act, 1950. It was re-enacted in s. 40(2) of the Matrimonial Causes Act, 1965 and in s. 46(2), Matrimonial Causes Act, 1973. Now this has been repealed by the Domicile and Matrimonial Proceedings Act, 1973.

105. See the Domicile and Matrimonial Proceedings Act, 1973.

106. Graveson, p. 306; See also Graveson's article in 28 B.Y.B.I.L. 273 at pp. 278-279.

107. 1959 Raj 133.

they would be involved in the insoluble problem of conflict of personal laws. An Indian domiciled Hindu, Christian, Muslim, Parsi or Jew can perform a marriage abroad in accordance with the *lex loci celebrationis* with any person who may not belong to the religious community to which he or she belongs. If such people come to India, and seek a matrimonial relief from an Indian court, then the court would be faced with the difficult question as to which of the communal laws it should apply, of the petitioner, or of the respondent ? But if the court takes the view that to such marriages law of the community of neither party is applicable and applies the provisions of the Special Marriage Act, 1954, all difficulties will be solved. The question is not of applying the *lex domicilii* of the parties, but of *lex fori*. In respect of foreign marriages solemnized under the Foreign Marriages Act, 1969, the specific provision in the Act is that to such marriages the provisions of the Special Marriage Act, 1954 apply.[108]

Recognition of Foreign Divorces

English Law

The English law of recognition of foreign divorces has been codified and reformed by the Recognition of Divorces and Legal Separations Act, 1971.[109] Even before the codification of law, the English law had travelled far and wide away from the doctrinal view that only the decrees of the court of domicile would be recognized, so much so that in 1970 Webb[110] could remark that it appeared that the honour of being the only case reported where English court refused to accord recognition to a foreign divorce since the decision in *Indyka* v. *Indyka*[111] went to *Peters* v. *Peters*[112]; in some cases probably it travelled too far.[113]

In view of the codification and reform of English law of recognition of foreign divorces, a brief survey of the pre-1971 law would suffice. The rule that was laid down in early cases was that English courts would not recognize a foreign divorce decree unless pronounced by the courts of the country where the parties were domiciled at the time of the suit.[114] This basis was extended by

108. Section 18.

109. The Act was passed as a sequel to the Hague Convention on the Recognition of Divorces and Legal Separations. The matter was referred to the Law Commission as well as to the Scottish Law Commission, on whose recommendations (No. 34 for the former and No. 16 of the latter) the present Act is based.

110. 1970 I.C.L.Q. 697.

111. (1969) 1 A.C. 33=(1967) 2 All E.R. 689.

112. (1967) 3 All E.R. 318.

113. For instance see *Qureshi* v. *Qureshi*, (1971) 2 W.L.R. 518. The case has been repealed by the Domicile and Matrimonial Proceedings Act, 1973.

114. *Le Mesurier* v. *Le Mesurier*. (1895) A.C. 517, where the court said : "The principle of recognizing the validity of a decree pronounced by the court of the domicile has been long established and forms an essential part of the comity of nations." See also *Bater* v. *Bater*, (1906), p. 209; *Ogden* v. *Ogden*, (1908) p. 46.

laying down that English courts would recognize a foreign decree of divorce (even though not pronounced by the court of domicile) if it is recognized as valid by the court of the domicile of parties.[115] Then came the turning point. *Travers* v. *Holley*[116] laid down that if the foreign court exercised jurisdiction on a basis on which English courts would exercise jurisdiction (the reference was to the statutory jurisdiction where the court exercised jurisdiction on the basis of ordinary residence), then the English courts would recognize the foreign decree of divorce.[117] Then came the most radical (or startling) decision of the House of Lords in *Indyka* v. *Indyka.*[118]

The *Indyka* test may be formulated thus : If there is a real and substantial connection between the party obtaining divorce and the country of the court which dissolved the marriage, then the foreign decree of divorce would be recognized. In this case two persons domiciled in Czechoslovakia got married in 1938. In 1946 the husband acquired a domicile of choice in England. In 1949 the wife, who had remained in Czechoslovakia, and was resident there, obtained a decree of divorce from a Czech court.[119] In *Mather* v. *Mahoney*[120] a further extension of this rule was made by laying down that if the court of the place where one of the parties has a substantial connection recognizes a decree of divorce passed by a foreign court, then the English courts too would recognize it.

In another direction too the pre-1971 law of recognition of foreign divorces had gone much away from the orthodox approach. This relates to the recognition of non-judicial divorces. In *R.* v. *Hammersmith, Superintendent Registrar of Marriages*[121] the English

115. *Armitage* v. *A.G.* (1906), p. 135.
116. (1953), p. 246.
117. In this case Hodson, L.J. very pertinently said : "It must surely be that what entitled an English court to assume jurisdiction, must be equally effective in the case of a foreign court. . . it would be contrary to principle and inconsistent with comity if the courts of this country were to refuse to recognize a jurisdiction which *mutatis mutandis* they claim for themselves." (p. 256). Its further extension was made in *Robinson-Scott* v. *Robinson-Scott*, (1958) p. 71. For the restrictive application of the rule, see *Mountbatten* v. *Mountbatten*, (1959) p. 43.
118. (1967) 2 All E.R. 689.
119. This decision was followed in *Angelo* v. *Angelo*, (1967) 3 All E.R. 314; *Welsby* v. *Welsby* (1970) 2 All E.R. 467 and *Munt* v. *Munt*, (1970) 2 All E.R. 516 (in all the three cases the husband was domiciled in England). Indyka decision was not rightly followed in *Peters* v. *Peters*, (1967) 3 All E.R. 318 as the only connection the petitioner had with the country which pronounced the divorce was that the marriage was solemnized there. It may be recalled that both under the Hindu Marriage Act, 1955 and the Special Marriage Act, 1954 the courts of country where marriage was solemnized have jurisdiction.
120. (1968) 3 All E.R. 223.
121. (1917) 1 K.B. 634

court said that the non-judicial divorce in the Muslim form of *talak* could not effectively dissolve an English marriage. English law then veered round to the position that non-judicial divorces in any form would be recognized in England if parties were domiciled in a country which recognized such mode of dissolution of marriage.[122]

The modern English law on recognition of foreign divorces is contained in ss. 3 and 6 of the Recognition of Divorces and Legal Separations Act, 1971 and s. 16, Domicile and Matrimonial Proceedings Act, 1973 and the Act of 1984. Section 6 of the Recognition of Divorces and Legal Separations Act, 1971 which has been modified and substituted by s. 2(2) of the Domicile and Matrimonial Proceedings Act, 1973, saves pre-Act grounds of recognition of foreign divorces, with some modifications; s. 3 introduces two new grounds and s. 16, Domicile and Matrimonial Proceedings Act, 1973 deals with non-judicial divorces.

Old grounds : (a) The English courts will recognize a foreign decree of divorce if it has been passed by the court of the country where the parties were domiciled at the time of the filing of the proceedings.[123] It would be immaterial if the parties changed their domicile after the date of the institution of the petition. (b) The English courts recognize a foreign divorce if it is recognized as valid by the domicile of the parties.[124] This was the position maintained by s. 6 of the Act of 1971. Since the Domicile and Matrimonial Proceedings Act, 1973 allows the wife to have her separate domicile, s. 6 of the Act of 1971 has been reconstituted. Sub-section (1) of the reconstituted s. 6 states the position as it has been stated in (a) and (b) above. Then sub-section (2) proceeds to provide a solution to those cases where the domicile of the parties at the institution of suit is different. This position may be stated in three propositions. The English court would recognize a foreign divorce if : (i) both the parties were domiciled in the country where divorce was obtained at the time of the institution of the suit, (ii) one of them was domiciled there and the divorce is recognized as valid in the country where the other is domiciled, (iii) the divorce is recognized as valid in the country of the common domicile of the parties, or where the parties have different domicile in the country of domicile of each party. (This covers the case where both the parties are not domiciled in the country

122. *Nachimson* v. *Nichimson*, (1930) p. 217 (administrative decree dissolving the marriage); *Qureshi* v. *Qureshi*, (1971) 2 W.L.R. 51 (Muslim divorce in *talak* form), *Russ* v. *Russ*, (1963) p. 87, on appeal (1964) p. 315 (divorce by mutual consent); *Her-Shefi* v. *Her-Shefi*, (No. 1.) (1953) 1 All E.R. 793 (Jewish divorce by relgious decree of Rabbinical court); *Joseph* v. *Joseph*, (1953) 2 All E.R. 710.

123. *Le Mesurier* v. *Le Mesurier*, (1895) A.C. 517.

124. *Armitage* v. *A.G.*, (1906) p. 135.

where the divorce was granted).[125] It should be noted that the Act also makes it clear that the date that is material is the date of institution of suit.[126]

The third old ground of recognition of foreign divorce that is retained is found in certain statutes which provide for the recognition of certain Colonial divorces. These statutes are, the Colonial and other Territories (Divorce Jurisdiction) Act, 1926-1950, the Indian Divorce (Validity) Act, 1921, Kenya Divorces (Validity) Act, 1922 and the Matrimonial Causes (War Marriages) Act, 1944. The former three Acts no longer apply to Burma, India, Pakistan, Bangladesh, Kenya and Sri Lanka (Ceylon), except in relation to proceedings pending in the court before these countries became independent. The former Act has now relevance only in respect of Hongkong.

New grounds : The two new grounds of divorce that have been added by the Act of 1971 are : A foreign divorce will be recognized in England : if (a) at the time of the institution of proceedings either spouse was habitually resident in the country where divorce was obtained,[127] (b) at the time of the institution of proceedings either spouse was a national of the country where divorce was obtained.[128] In ground number (a) in respect of a country which uses the concept of domicile as a ground of jurisdiction in the matter of divorce, the words "habitual residence" should be substituted with "domicile". This may be formulated thus : English courts will recognize a foreign divorce if obtained in a country where either party was domiciled at the time of the institution of proceedings.[129]

Speaking of these provisions from the floor of Parliament Lord Chancellor said that the greater liberality of *Indyka* v. *Indyka*[130] led to "greater uncertainty"; this section retains liberality but injects more certainty.[131] These new grounds would cover cases like *Mayfield* v. *Mayfield*[132] where a domiciled English husband permanently residing in England obtained a decree of

125. Sub-sections (2) & (3) of s. 6.
126. Sub-section (4) of s. 6.
127. Section 3(a).
128. Section 3(b).
129. Section 3(2).
130. (1969) 1 A.C. 33.
131. Hansard, House of Lords, Vol. 315, Col. 485. However, the decisions like *Blair* v. *Blair*, (1968) 3 All E.R. 639, (where a domiciled Englishman married a Norwegian woman in Norway and acquired Norwegian domicile of choice. While he was receiving a training course in England, he heard that his wife had become pregnant from someone else. He remained in England and reverted back to his domicile of origin. Then he went to Norway and divorced his wife there. This divorce was recognized as "just and appropriate") would no longer be recognized.
132. (1969) 2 All E.R. 219.

divorce from a court of Germany where the wife was permanently residing and of which she was a national. At that time this divorce was recognized on the basis of *Indyka* doctrine, but now it cannot be recognized on that basis, but on the basis of the nationality or habitual residence of the respondent.

The term "habitual residence" has not been defined either in the Act or in the Convention; nor is there any judicial definition of the term. The draft recommendations of the Council of Europe's sub-committee on Fundamental Legal Concepts has defined the term thus : "In determining whether a resident is habitual, account is to be taken of the duration and the continuity of the residence as well as of other facts of a personal or professional nature which point to durable ties between a person and his residence. The voluntary establishment of a residence and a person's intention to maintain it are not conditions of the existence of a residence or an habitual residence, but a person's intentions may be taken into account in determining whether he possesses a residence or the character of that residence." It is submitted that the habitual residence means the same thing which Indian courts have given to "residence" in its natural or limited sense.

In matters of status the continental countries have always adhered to nationality. Since the decision of *Indyka* v. *Indyka*[133] the English courts have emphasised nationality as an additional and important factor in establishing real and substantial connection.[134] "Nationality" has now been recognized as an independent basis of jurisdiction. Now a Muslim of Indian or Pakistani nationality can divorce his wife by *Talak* even though he was domiciled in England. (This was the natural consequence of the provision as it was worded in s. 3 of the Act of 1971; now this cannot be so after its amendment by the Domicile and Matrimonial Proceedings Act, 1973.)

The problem of countries whose different territories have different laws, such as the United States, is solved by laying down that in such cases the provisions relating to habitual residence or domicile shall have effect as if each territory were a separate country.[135] This provision does not apply to nationality. This would mean that the Nevada decrees cannot be recognized on the basis of nationality, but the Canadian or Australian would be, as they have one national law of divorce, while the United States does not have one national law of divorce.

If there are cross-petitions, then a divorce pronounced in the original petition or in the cross-proceedings will be recognized in the United Kingdom if the foreign court has jurisdiction in either

133. (1969) 1 A.C. 33.

134. Lord Peace. In this regard **Peters** v. **Peters**, (1968) p. 275 is a high watermark. See also *Mayfield* v. *Mayfield*, (1969) 2 All E.R. 219; *Angelo* v. *Angelo*, (1967) 3 All E.R. 314; **Brown** v. **Brown**, (1968) p. 518.

135. Section 3(3).

of the two proceedings.[136] Under some systems of law a decree of judicial separation can be converted into a decree of divorce after the expiry of prescribed period.[137] If this happens, then the Act lays down that such divorce would be recognized in the United Kingdom, irrespective of the fact that the basis of jurisdiction disappeared when the legal separation was converted into divorce.[138]

In *Lawrence* v. *Lawrence*,[139] the wife, a national of Brazil had married in that country H, whose domicile of choice was Brazil. In 1970 she obtained a divorce from H, in proceedings in Nevada in which H was represented by his attorney. Divorce was not recognized in Brazil and under the Brazilian law the wife was not free to re-marry. On the day following the divorce, the wife married in Nevada an American who was living in England and has acquired a domicile of choice there. He intended to establish matrimonial house in England. After marriage, the parties lived in England, but in 1972, the wife left the matrimonial home and returned to live permanently in Brazil. The husband sought a declaration that the marriage celebrated in Nevada was valid and subsisting marriage. The trial judge held that as the matrimonial house was established in England, the marriage has a real and substantial connection with England and applying English law, gave the declaration as sought by the husband. Upholding the judgment, the court of Appeal (per Ackner, L.J.) observed that the essential function of decree of divorce was to dissolve the marriage hitherto existing between the parties. It is, he added, plainly inconsistent with recognizing a divorce to say that the marriage which it purports to dissolve still continues in existence. Thus the inevitable consequence of recognizing the Nevada divorce is to recognize that it dissolved the Brazilian marriage. Thereafter, that dissolved marriage could no longer be a bar to the wife's remarriage. This is in accordance with section 3, Recognition of Divorces and Legal Separations Act, 1971.

Section 1 of the Act of 1971 lays down that a decree of divorce granted after the coming into force of the Act (i.e. December 31, 1971) in Scotland, Northern Ireland, the Channel Islands or the Isle of Man will be recognized in England.

Non-Judicial Divorces : Section 2 of the Act of 1971 lays down that in case the aforesaid grounds of divorce exist (i.e. under s. 3 and s. 6) then the foreign divorce will be recognized whether it is obtained in "judicial proceedings or other proceedings". This

136. Section 4(1).
137. This is so under the Indian law. Under the Special Marriage Act, 1954 after the expiry of one year or more and under the Hindu Marriage Act, 1955 after an expiry of two years from the date of the decree of judicial separation, if parties do not resume cohabitation, either party can file a petition for divorce.
138. Section 4(2).
139. (1985) 3 W.L.R. 125.

provision of s. 2 read with s. 6 of the Act merely codified the existing law, i.e. the non-judicial divorces will be recognized in England if they were valid under the law of the country where they were granted; they would also be recognized in England if they were recognized under the personal law of parties.[140] In *Qureshi* v. *Qureshi*[141] it was held that a *talak* pronounced in England, even if pronounced in respect of a marriage celebrated in England will be recognized if under the law of domicile of the parties this mode of divorce was valid. This position has now been substantially changed by s. 16, Domicile and Matrimonial Proceedings Act, 1973. Now (i.e. after January 1, 1974) an extra-judicial divorce obtained or pronounced in British Isles[142] will not be recognized in England. Further, an extra-judicial divorce obtained or pronounced outside the British Isles (after January 1, 1974) will not be recognized in England, if both parties were habitually resident in the United Kingdom throughout the period of one year immediately preceding the institution of the proceedings. With these qualifications the non-judicial divorces will be continued to be recognized as they were before the coming into force of the Act.[143] Non-judicial divorces will also be recognized if they fall under the two new grounds of recognition, viz. the habitual residence and nationality.[144]

It remains to be seen that what is the meaning of "other proceedings" in s. 2 in the context of non-judicial divorces. It is clear that these words were used in the Hague Convention in connection with non-judicial divorces. It should be noticed that in the laws of many countries which recognize non-judicial divorces some public proceedings are necessary, though more often than not they are nothing more than a public record or public seal on such divorces. Thus, a *ghet* divorce among Jews even when it is granted by the rabbinical court does not involve any investigation[145]; in Egypt, *talak* needs registration, though non-registration does not render it invalid,[146] again no investigation is made; in Pakistan parties are required to undergo conciliation proceedings before an arbitration council.[147] These may be termed as 'other proceedings' in the terms of s. 2.[148] It is submitted that the words 'other proceedings' in s. 2 are used in contradistinction to 'judicial proceedings' and therefore would include all and every type of proceedings,

140. See cases cited in footnote 22.
141. (1971) 2 W.L.R. 518.
142. The diplomatic premises of foreign or Commonwealth state are part of the British Isles: *Radwan* v. *Radwan*, (No. 1), (1972) 3 W.L.R. 735.
143. Section 16(2)(c).
144. Section 3(1) of the Act of 1971.
145. *Her-Shefi* v. *Her-Shefi*, (No. 2), (1953) p. 220.
146. *Russ* v. *Russ*, (1963) p. 87, on appeal (1964) p. 315.
147. Pakistani Muslim Family Law Ordinance, 1961.
148. See *Quazi* v. *Quazi*, (1980) A.C. 744.

howsoever minimal they may be. After all no divorce (howsoever unilateral it may be) can be pronounced without some proceedings. Thus, in the *talak-ul-Biddaat* when a husband says to his wife "I divorce thee thrice," he has initiated and concluded these proceedings. 'Other proceedings' in the context of non-judicial divorce cannot mean 'proceedings' in which both parties have participated. If this meaning would be given to 'proceedings' then most non-judicial divorces would not qualify for recognition under the Act. Further, the requirement of 'notice' in s. 8(2)(a)(i) has to be construed in this context. Too strict a construction of this provision would, it is submitted, lead to non-recognition of such divorces. The object of the Recognition of Divorces and Legal Separations Act, 1971 and of the Hague Convention is to accord recognition to extra-judicial divorces howsoever one's conscience may feel about them or howsoever abhorent they may appear to one. Any other construction would go to frustrate that object. It seems that English courts are not got prepared to take this in the view.

The term "other proceeding" has come for interpretation in several cases. In *Quazi* v. *Quazi*,[149] the House of Lords took the view that a divorce obtained in Pakistan by *talaq* followed by compliance with the procedural requirements of the Pakistani Muslim Family Laws Ordinance, 1961 was a divorce obtained by "other proceedings" within the intendment of section 2(a) of the Recognition and Divorces and Legal Separation Act as supplemented by section 16 of the Domicile and Matrimonial Proceedings Act, 1973. But the House of Lords did not express its opinion or to the recognition of foreign bare *talaqs* which it is effective without any further procedure. In *Sharif* v. *Sharif* [150] the family division took the view that bare talak would not fall within the phrase "judicial or other proceedings" in section 2(a) of the Act of 1971. But a contrary view was expressed in *Zaal* v. *Zaal*.[151] In the latter case Bush, J. said that where a bare *talak* was recognized by the local law as effective to end the marriage it was divorce within the phrase. In *R.G. Immigration Appeal Tribunal*[152], Tylor, J. was inclined to agree with Bush, J.

Obviously, the purpose of Act of 1971 was to reduce or prevent the continuance of "Limping Marriages". In *Chaudhary* v. *Chaudhary*,[153] Cumming-Bruce L.J. observed that if the use of the phrase "Judicial and other proceedings" was meant to restrict recognition to narrow category of divorce, then all the divorces obtained by any means whatsoever which are effective by the law of the country in which divorce was obtained should be recognized. If the legislature wanted to give it that wide meaning it would have used

149. (1980) A.C. 744.
150. (1980) 10 Fam. 216.
151. (1982) 4 F.L.R. 284.
152. (1984) 2 W.L.R. 36.
153. (1985) 2 W.L.R. 350.

the words as used in the convention "officially recognised" in the country where divorce was obtained. Thus, it is necessary that divorce must be obtained in "some proceedings" and pronouncement of bare *talaq* in not such proceedings.

The question come for consideration before the court in *Regina* v. *Secretary of State for the Home Department, Ex parte Ghulam Fatima*[154] indifferent circumstances. One Pakistani pronounced *talak* in England against his wife, who was resident in Pakistan. In compliance with the Pakistan Muslim Family Laws Ordinance, 1961 he sent a written notice that he had pronounced the *talak* on his wife to the Chairman of his local union council in Pakistan as well as to his wife. Under the provisions of the Ordinance, his marriage was dissolved 90 days after the receipt of the notice by the chairman of the local union council. He then acted as sponsor to his Pakistani fiancee's application for leave to enter the United Kingdom. On arrival of Ghulam Fatima, the immigration officer refused her leave to enter the country on the ground that he was not satisfied that the intended marriage could take place within the reasonable time as her sponsors' divorce was not recognized in the United Kingdom. The applicant filed an appeal with the House of Lords. Dismissing the appeal the House of Lords observed that the pronouncement of a *talak* was initiated in England and was followed by a written notice to the Chairman of the Pakistan local union and it is, therefore, formed part of preceedings for divorce under Pakistani law, and constituted the institution of proceedings for the purpose of sections 2 and 3(1) of the Recognition of Divorces and Legal Separations Act, 1971. This means that the sponsor's divorce had been obtained by proceedings partly in England and partly in Pakistan. The House of Lords further observed that on the true construction of the aforesaid sections of the Act, "the proceedings" under section 2(a) meant a single set of proceedings that had to be instituted in the same country as that in which the divorce was ultimately obtained, and since the institution of the sponsor's divorce proceedings had taken place in the United Kingdom as well as in Pakistan, the requirements of section 3(1) had not been compiled with and the immigration officer was right in taking the view that he took.

Under the Family Law Act, 1986, the court will recognize for foreign *gat* decree of divorce as recognized among the Jews.[154a]

When Foreign Divorces need not be recognized

Before 1971, the English courts developed some criteria on the basis of which foreign divorces pronounced by the courts of competent jurisdiction could be refused recognition in England. Broadly speaking, it was laid down that a foreign decree which was offensive to English notions of justice would not be recognized. In 1899, Lindley, M.R. observed that where substantial justice, according to English notions, is not offended, all that the English courts look to is the finality of the judgment and the jurisdiction of the court, in this sense and to this extent, namely, its competence

154. (1986) 2 W.L.R. 693.
154a. *Berkovits* v. *Grinberg* etc., (1995) 2 All E.R. 681.

to entertain the sort of case which it did and its competence to require the defendant to appear before it. If the foreign court has jurisdiction in this sense and to this extent, His Lordship said, this country (England) never requires whether the jurisdiction has been properly or improperly exercised, provided always that no substantial injustice, according to English notions, has been committed.[155] In *Indyka* v. *Indyka*[156] Lord Pearce observed : "Our courts should reserve to themselves the right to refuse recognition of those decrees which offend our notions of genuine divorce. They have done so when decrees offend against substantial justice, and this, of course, includes a decree obtained by fraud. But I think it also includes, or should include, decrees where a wife has gone abroad in order to obtain divorce and where divorce can be said not to be genuine." In the same case, Lord Morris said : "Recognition should, however, always be subject to the proviso that foreign decree is not vitiated by fraud or is not contrary to natural justice."[157] The law has now been codified in s. 8, Recognition of Divorces and Legal Separations Act, 1971.

The Act of 1971 lays down that foreign divorces will be refused recognition on any one of the following grounds (and for none else) :

(a) When there is violation of principles of natural justice,[158] or

(b) When recognition would manifestly be contrary to public policy.[159]

Natural Justice : This is a very old head of English law on the basis of which foreign decrees and judgments have been refused recognition. This has been formulated by the Recognition of Divorces and Legal Separations Act, 1971 thus : an English court may refuse to recognize a foreign divorce if it was obtained by one spouse, (i) without such steps having been taken for giving notice of the proceedings to the other spouse as, having regard to the nature of the proceedings and all the circumstances, should reasonably have been taken ; or (ii) without the other spouse having been given (for any reason other than lack of notice) such opportunity to take part in the proceedings as, having regard to the matters aforesaid, he should reasonably have been given. Before 1971, the courts have taken the view that a foreign divorce will be recognized, (a) if the foreign court took the view that its rules of service have been duly complied with[160], or (b) lack of notice was

155. *Pemberton* v. *Hughes*, (1899) 1 Ch. 781 at p. 790.
156. (1969) 1 A.C. 33.
157. Graveson says that the concept of evasion propounded in Indyka decision is somewhat new, it represents an unheralded innovation: Graveson, p. 327.
158. Section 8(2)(a).
159. Section 8(2)(b).
160. *Igra* v. *Igra*, (1951) p. 404.

not consequent to petitioner's fraud.[161] However, it has been held that a foreign judgment cannot be refused recognition merely on the ground that it was obtained by fraud of one of the parties.[162] The rule seems to be this that if fraud affects the merit of the case it is not material, but if its affects jurisdiction it is.[163] The local incompetence of the jurisdiction is of no consequence. Sir N. Lindley, M.R. observed : "The jurisdiction which alone is important in these matters is the competence of the court in an international sense . . . Its competence or jurisdiction in any other sense is not regarded as material by the courts of this country."[164] The English court interfere in those cases where (though the foreign court takes the view that the service has been sufficient) it considers the foreign rules of service contrary to natural justice.[165] It would appear that mere want of notice is no ground for refusing a foreign divorce decree,[166] unless it is proved that the respondent had no notice of the proceedings.[167]

Public Policy: This has been a general head of English law under which English courts have refused to recognize foreign judgments.[168] However, as Dicey and Morris observe : "There is no case in which foreign divorce granted by a court of the parties' domicile has been denied recognition in England on the ground that to recognize it would be contrary to public policy."[169] This statement is no longer true, the English Courts have refused to recognize a foreign divorce on this basis.[170] *Ordre public* looms large in the continental law and its ambit is larger than that of its English counterpart, public policy. In comparison to *ordre public*, the English horse of public policy has not been so unruly, but the Recognition of Divorces and Judicial Separations Act, 1971 nonetheless qualifies 'public policy' with the word "menifestly" and the Solicitor-General said that this word has been used to make the horse of public policy trifly less unruly.[171] It is submitted that this is not going to make much of a difference. The Law Commission said that the word "is probably redundant because our courts would never invoke the doctrine of public policy unless they were

161. *Middleton* v. *Middleton*, (1967) p. 62.
162. *Vardy* v. *Vardy*, (1932) 48 T.L.R. 661.
163. *Bater* v. *Bater*, (1909) p. 209; *Middleton* v. *Middleton*, (1961) p. 62.
164. *Pemberton* v. *Hughes*, (1899) 1 Ch. 781 at p. 791.
165. *Macalpine* v. *Macalpine*, (1958) p. 35.
166. *Igra* v. *Igra*, (1951) p. 404; *Maher* v. *Maher*, (1951), p. 342; *Arnold* v. *Arnold*, (1957) p. 237; *Wood* v. *Wood*, (1957), p. 254.
167. *Macalpine* v. *Macalpine*, (1958), p. 35.
168. See Chapter 25 of this work.
169. Dicey and Morris, p. 317. However, some of the borderline cases may be noted : *Re Meyer*, (1971) 2 W.L.R. 401; *Szechter* v. *Szechter*, (1970) 3 All E.R. 905; *Macalpine* v. *Macalpine*, (cited above); *Igra* v. *Igra*, (1951) p. 404.
170. *New March* v. *New March*, (1978) Fam. 79; *Joyee* v. *Joyee*, (1979) Fam. 79; *Choudhary* v. *Choudhary*, (1985) 2 W.L.R. 350.
171. Hansard, Vol. 315, Col. 1553.

quite clear that it was right to do so."[172] Section 8 makes it evidently clear that foreign divorces cannot be refused recognition in Great Britain on any other ground. This means that the doctrine of evasion of law developed in *Indyka* v. *Indyka*[173] has no place under s. 8. The same should apply to the residuary discretion of the court under which it could refuse to recognize a foreign divorce if doing so would result in grave injustice.

Section 8(1)(b) also states what appears to be obvious. The English court will not recognize a foreign decree of divorce if at the time when the divorce was obtained there was no subsisting valid marriage between the parties.

Indian Law

Apart from the general provisions contained in s. 13, Civil Procedure Code, the Indian law of recognition of foreign divorces is still not well developed. The general provisions relating to recognition of foreign judgments and decrees are discussed in Chapter 25. Whatever little case law that exists in India there is a clear tendency to follow English law.

We have only a few decisions on the subject. In *Joao Gloria Pires* v. *Ana Joaquina Pires*[174] two persons of Roman Catholic faith underwent a ceremony of marriage in Goa in the Church April 27, 1957. Parties were resident and evidently domiciled in Goa at the time of the marriage. The husband obtained a decree of divorce from Uganda court, where he was residing. (The report does not say whether he acquired a domicile of choice there.) Subsequently, he made a petition in a Goa court that the decree of divorce obtained by him from the Uganda court be confirmed. Wife opposed the petition on the grounds, *inter alia*, that under Goan law a Roman Catholic marriage is a sacrament and an indissoluble union, and, therefore, the Ugandan decree of divorce cannot be confirmed Clause (6) of s. 1102 of the Civil Code of Goa lays down that a foreign decree or judgment which is against public policy cannot be recognized Bindra, A.C.J. felt that the law of indissolubility of Roman Catholic marriage was a matter pertaining to public policy (and not of substance or material validity) and, therefore the Ugandan divorce decree being against public policy cannot be confirmed, or accorded recognition, in Goa. It is indeed very curious that neither any arguments were addressed nor did the court consider the question whether the husband acquired a domicile in Uganda and therefore the decree of Uganda was the decree of the court of the domicile, nor did the court consider whether it was the decree of the court where the husband was residing and therefore could or could not be recognized. The fact of the matter is that the court did not at all consider the question as to whether the decree of the Uganda court was a

172. Law Commission's Report, p. 43.

173. (1969) 1 A.C. 33. *Kendall* v. *Kendall* (1977) Fam. 208.

174. 1967 Goa 113.

decree of competent court. Or, one may say that the court started on the assumption that the decree was valid but could not be recognized being contrary to public policy. If one is permitted to put that construction on the judgment, then it would mean that the court would recognize a decree on the basis of residence of the petitioner. This will be welcome as this is near to one of the grounds laid down in the Hague Convention on the basis of which a foreign divorce could be recognized. The Convention uses the words 'habitual residence', which, as has been submitted, means, more or less, what 'residence' means in Indian law.

The second case is *Teja Singh* v. *Smt. Satya.*[175] A Hindu wife filed a petition for maintenance of herself and her two children under s. 488 (s. 225 of the new Code) of the old Criminal Procedure Code against her husband. The main defence of the husband was that his marriage with the petitioner had been validly dissolved by a court of Nevada where he was domiciled at the time of the decree. After quoting some English writers[176] and *Le Mesurier* v. *Le Mesurier*,[177] Sandhawalia, J. gave the finding on facts that the husband acquired a domicile of choice at Nevada and since the divorce decree was the decree of the *lex domicilii* of the husband, it would be recognized in India. Again, after quoting several English authorities[178] His Lordship observed: ". . . it now seems to be beyond all dispute that the domicile of the husband at the time of the suit for divorce is the sole test for the purpose of giving jurisdiction to the matrimonial court. Whatever doubts existed had long been laid to rest by the decision of the Privy Council in *Le Mesurier* v. *Le Mesurier* . . ."[179] Towards the end, after quoting another instalment of English authorities,[180] the learned judge said that a decree of divorce pronounced by the court of domicile will be accorded recognition universally and would be recognized in India. So far as it goes the judgment states the English law as stated in *Le Mesurier* v. *Mesurier*. It is a pity that the learned judge did not discuss the more recent English decisions,[181] nor did he try to give any direction to Indian law. This judgment could have been rendered in any British colony in the first decade of the twentieth century. The judgment

175. (1970) 72 P.L.R. 235.

176. Latey on Divorce and Matrimonial Causes (14th ed.), p. 50; Cheshire, (7th ed.) 332.

177. (1895) A.C. 517.

178. *Le Mesurier* v. *Le Mesurier*, (cited above), *Lord Advacate* v. *Jaffrey*, (1921) 1 A.C. 146; *A.G. for Alberta* v. *Cook*, (1926) A.C. 444; *Selveson* v. *Administrator of Austrian Property*, (1927) A.C. 641.

179. Then followed the citation of English authorities cited in footnote 69.

180. *Breen* v. *Breen*, (1961) 3 All E.R. 225; *Mezger* v. *Mezger*, (1936) 3 All E.R. 130.

181. In the next step the learned judge inevitably said that the law applicable would be the law of the domicile, and again he quoted from Cheshire and *Bater* v. *Bater*, (1906) P.D. 209, *Mezger* v. *Mezger* (cited above) and *Harvey* v. *Fernie*, (1880) 6 P.D. 35; on appeal, (1882) A.C. 43.

has since been reversed by the Supreme Court on the finding of fact. The Supreme Court came to the conclusion that the husband was not domiciled in Nevada.[182] In *Hogan Bhai* v. *Hariben*,[183] the indian court refused to recognize a foreign judgment obtained by the husband who falsely represented to the foreign court about his domicile and residence.

It is submitted that the Indian courts will still have ample opportunities to develop the law of recognition of foreign divorces and, without the aid of any legislation, the Indian court can develop the law on the modern lines. Already in the domestic Indian matrimonial law, residence is a basis of jurisdiction. If the Indian courts assume jurisdiction on the basis of residence, there is no reason why they should refuse to recognize foreign divorces based on the same jurisdictional rules. Thus, it is submitted that there is ample scope for our courts to develop law on the lines of the Hague Convention on the Recognition of Divorces and Legal Separations.

The Law Commission in its 65th report recommended that :—

(1) The practice of recognition of divorce granted in the country of domicile of the parties should continue.

(2) The divorce or legal separation though not granted in the country of domicile, if recognised as valid in the country of domicile should be recognised in India and this should be expressly provided for.

(3) There should be a general provision to save the provisions of any other enactment which provide for recognition.

(4) Non-recognition of a divorce by a third country should not be a bar to the recognition of divorce in India.

(5) It is desirable to provide for the recognition of foreign divorces or legal separations granted by countries where both parties were habitually resident or by countries of which both are a national, in addition to the current test of domicile.

(6) It is desirable to provide that the rule that on marriage the wife acquires the domicile or the nationality of the husband shall not apply in relation to the recognition of foreign divorces and separations.

(7) A foreign judgment will not be recognised :—

(i) If the other party had no reasonable notice of proceedings, or

(ii) If the party had no opportunity of hearing depending on the nature of the proceedings and all circumstances of the case, or

182. *Satya* v. *Teja Singh*, 1975 S.C. 105. The Supreme Court said that the judgment was also vitiated by fraud.

183. 1985 Guj. 187.

(iii) If contrary to public policy, or

(iv) If obtained by fraud.

(8) Any anciliary order (concerning the custody of children and other allied questions) should not be treated as binding by Indian courts even though the foreign decree of divorce is recognised.

(9) The proposed bill should apply to non-judicial divorces as well. To avoid any ambiguity, the term "proceeding" was defined as including any act which might be sufficient to effectuate a dissolution of marriage, however, informal that act might be, and whether or not any formalities or legal process is required.

Pursuant to the recommendation of the Law Commission, no law has yet been passed.

III

NULLITY OF MARRIAGE

Traditionally, the law of nullity of marriage is concerned with the impediments to marriages. As has been seen earlier in this Chapter, on the basis of impediments, destructive impediments and obstructive impediments, the notion of void and voidable marriages was developed in the Ecclesiastical law. This distinction was carried over to Common law even after the ecclesiastical courts ceased to have jurisdiction in matrimonial matters. This distinction has been carried over all throughout and now into the latest statute in the series, the Matrimonial Causes Act, 1973. From English law this distinction was received by the colonies, including India.[184] A remarkable development that has taken place in India in the law of marriages is that violation of some of the obstructive impediments does not render the marriage voidable or void; if solemnized, the marriage is perfectly valid. Thus, under the Hindu Marriage Act, 1955 a boy below the age of eighteen and a girl below the age of fifteen cannot marry,[185] but if marriage is performed in violation of condition, the marriage is valid, though some punishment can be imposed on the party guilty of violating the same.[186]

A void marriage is void *ab initio*, i.e. from its inception; no legal consequences flow from it. On the other hand, a voidable

184. But the remarkable thing is that this distinction has been accorded reception in free India. The Indian Divorce Act, 1869 and the Parsi Marriage and Divorce Act, 1936 (the two statutes passed during British period) do not make this distinction. The Hindu Marriage Act, 1955 and the Special Marriage Act, 1954 do make this distinction.

185. Section 5(iii).

186. Under s. 18(a), a term of simple imprisonment which may extend to fifteen days or a fine which may extend to Rs. 1000 or both for violating the requirement of age, and a fine which may extend to Rs. 1000 for violating the condition of parental consent, may be imposed on the guilty party.

marriage is valid till it is avoided on the petiton of one of the parties to the marriage.[187] A void marriage is called a marriage because two persons have undergone the ceremony of marriage. But since the marriage between the two was impossible because of destructive impediments two persons could not become husband and wife just by undergoing the ceremony of marriage. This implies that a void marriage does neither confer the status of husband and wife on the parties to the marriage, - nor does it confer a status of legitimacy on the children of such marriage.[188] In fact, in the case of a void marriage, no decree of court is necessary.[189] When a court passes a decree of nullity it merely declares the marriage as void; it is not the decree which renders the marriage void, but the decree is merely a judicial declaration of an existing fact. A void marriage can neither be approbated nor can it be ratified.

A voidable marriage, on the other hand, is a perfectly valid marriage so long as it is not avoided (and it can be avoided only by one of the parties to the marriage). On the death of either party the marriage becomes unimpeachable.[190] So long as a voidable marriage is not avoided all legal consequences flow from it. But such has been the historical development of the nullity of marriage that once a voidable marriage is annulled it is given retrospective effect : the marriage is deemed to have never taken place and parties are deemed to have never been husband and wife and children to have never been legitimate. The rule has its origin in the doctrine of ecclesiastical law of indissolubility of marriage—either marriage exists for ever or never. The modern English law still retains the distinction, though gradually some of its sharp corners have been rounded of. The process began with Matrimonial Causes Act, 1950 under which status of legitimacy was conferred on the children of annulled voidable marriages.[191] Since then the process has continued and with the passing of Nullity of Marriage Act, 1971 most of these corners have been totally rounded of, so much so that the modern English law of nullity no longer could be said to "perpetuate a cannonial fiction."[192] The effect of a decree of nullity of marriage has now been almost equated with the effect of a decree of divorce.[193] Section 16, Matrimonial Causes Act, 1973 practically obliterates

187. *Ross Smith* v. *Ross Smith*, (1963) A.C. 280 at p. 314.

188. *De Reneville* v. *De Reneville*, (1948) p. 100 at p. 111.

189. *Lila* v. *Laxmi*, 1968 All. L.J. 683.

190. *De Reneville* v. *De Reneville*, (1948) p. 100 at p. 111.

191. Section 9; this was then s. 11 of the Matrimonial Causes Act, 1965.

192. *R* v. *Algar*, (1954) 1 Q.B. 279 at p. 288.

193. This Section clarifies the position and confirms the trend set in *De Reneville* v. *De Reneville*, (1948) p. 100, to treat the decree of annulment at par with the decree of divorce so far as the consequences of such decree are concerned. But this trend was upset by *Re D'Altroy's Wills Trust*, (1968) 1 All E.R. 181 and *Re Rodwell* (1969) 3 All E.R. 1863. The rule as laid down in these cases is now repealed by this section.

the distinction between a decree of annulment of voidable marriage and a decree of nullity of a void marriage. It also obliterates virtually the distinction between a decree of divorce and a decree of nullity. In some respects the latter is more advantageous : a decree of divorce cannot ordinarily be obtained before the expiry of a period of three years from the date of the solemnization of the marriage,[194] on the other hand, a petition for annulment of marriage (i.e. when marriage is voidable) must be filed within three years of the solemnization of the marriage.[195] However, the children of void marriage are legitimate only if at the time of the act of intercourse resulting in the birth of the child or at the time of the celebration of marriage, if later, both or either party reasonably believed that the marriage was valid.[196]

This distinction between the effect of the void and voidable marriage led to some controversy in conflict of laws for the purpose of jurisdiction. In *Inverclyde* v. *Inverclyde*[197] and *De Reneville* v. *De Reneville*[198] this distinction was considered material.[199] This distinction is no longer valid in the modern English law.[200]

Indian Law

It is interesting to note that the early matrimonial statutes, the Divorce Act, 1869 and the Parsi Marriage and Divorce Act, 1936, did not adopt the English law distinction between void and voidable marriages. But the distinction was adopted in the two statutes, the Special Marriage Act, 1954 and the Hindu Marriage Act, 1955 which were passed by India after attaining independence. It is equally interesting to note that the Indian Divorce Act, 1869, which otherwise follows the English Matrimonial Causes Act, 1857 also contains a unique provision in respect to legitimacy of children of certain void marriages. Section 21 lays : "Where a marriage is annulled on the ground that a former husband or wife was living and it is adjudged that the subsequent marriage was contracted in good faith and with full belief of the parties that the former husband or wife was dead, or when a marriage is annulled on the ground of insanity, children begotten before the decree is made shall be specified in the decree and shall be entitled to succeed, in the same manner as legitimate children, to the estate of the parent who at the time of the marriage was competent to contract." The Parsi Marriage and Divorce Act, 1936 contains no provision relating to legitimacy of the children

194. Now s. 3 of the Matrimonial Causes Act, 1973.
195. Section 13(2) Matrimonial Causes Act, 1973.
196. Legitimacy Act, 1959, s. 2(1).
197. (1931) p. 29.
198. (1948) p. 100.
199. See also *Easterbrook* v. *Easterbrook*, (1944) p. 10; *Hutter* v. *Hutter*, (1944), p. 95; *Ramsay-Fairfax* v. *Ramsay-Fairfax*, (1956) p. 115.
200. See s. 1 and s. 5, respectively of the Domicile and Matrimonial Proceedings Act, 1973.

of void marriages and therefore children of void marriages are illegitimate.

The Hindu Marriage Act, 1955[201] and the Special Marriage Act, 1954[202] adopt the distinction between void and voidable marriages. Under both the statutes when a voidable marriage is annulled[203] or void marriage is declared null and void,[204] the children remain legitimate though they can inherit[205] to their parents alone.[206]

Characterization of Marriage as Void and Voidable

It is submitted that the characterization of marriages into void or voidable marriages has lost all its utility after the coming into force of the new jurisdictional rules under the Domicile and Matrimonial Proceedings Act, 1973.[207,208,209]

It may be still of some importance to the Indian private international law. It is submitted that in those cases where the parties have in fact established a matrimonial home, the matter should be determined by the law of the matrimonial home; where parties have not established a matrimonial home, but are residing (residence, as it is used in Indian law in its natural meaning) at a place then by the law of that place. If the parties have established neither, then it may be determined by the law of the individual domicile (now that in English law wife can have her separate domicile) or by the law of individual residence (i.e. where the party alleged to have the defect or impediment has it or not by the law of his or her domicile or residence). All formal defects should be determined by the *lex loci celebrationis*.

Grounds of Void and Voidable Marriages

English Law

English law of nullity of marriage has been codified, consolidated and reformed by the Nullity of Marriage Act, 1971, provisions of which with some minor modifications have been re-enacted in the Matrimonial Causes Act, 1973. The grounds laid down in the Act apply to those marriages which take place after 31st July 1971.

201. Section 16.
202. Section 26.
203. Section 16(1) of the former statute and s. 26(1) of the latter.
204. Section 16(2) of the former statute and s. 26(2) of the latter.
205. Section 16(3) of the former statute and s. 26(3) of the latter.
206. For details, see Paras Diwan, *Modern Hindu Law,* (1990) 119.
207. See for the old law, Dicey and Morris, Rule 44(3).
208. For old law, see Cheshire, 312.
209. See also *White* v. *White* (1937) p. 111; *De Renville* v. *De Renville* (1948), p. 100.

Void Marriages : Under the modern English law grounds of void marriages are :[210] (i) the parties are within the degrees of prohibited relationship [as laid down in the Marriage Act, 1949 read with Marriage (Enabling) Act, 1960]; (ii) either party is under the age of sixteen (s. 2, Marriage Act, 1949); (iii) the parties have intermarried in disregard of certain requirements as to the formation of the marriage (s. 49, Marriage Act, 1949); (iv) at the time of the marriage either party was already lawfully married; (v) the parties are not respectively male or female[211] (vi) a polygamous marriage was entered into outside England and Wales, between parties, either of which was, at the time of the marriage, domiciled in England and Wales.[212]

Voidable Marriages : Under the modern English law the grounds of voidable marriages are[213] (a) the marriage has not been consummated owing to the incapacity of either party to consummate it; (b) the marriage has not been consummated owing to the wilful refusal of the respondent to consummate it; (c) either party to the marriage did not validly consent to it, whether in consequence of duress, mistake, unsoundness of mind or otherwise; (d) at the time of the marriage either party, though capable of giving a valid consent, was suffering (whether continuously or intermittently) from mental disorder within the meaning of the Mental Health Act, 1959 of such kind or to such an extent as to be unfit for marriage; (e) at the time of marriage the respondent was suffering from venereal disease in a communicable form; and (f) at the time of marriage the respondent was pregnant by some person other than the petitioner.[214]

Indian Law

Various Indian matrimonial statutes lay down different grounds of void and voidable marriages, though some of the grounds in the statutes are common. The Divorce Act, 1869[215] and the Parsi Marriage and Divorce Act, 1936[216] contain only grounds of void marriage and do not lay down any grounds of voidable marriage (since under these statutes concepts of voidable marriages are not recognized).

210. Section 11 of the Act of 1973.
211. This codified the rule laid down in *Corbett* v. *Corbett*, (1970) 2 All E.R. 33.
212. This was formerly s. 4 of the Matrimonial Proceedings (Polygamous Marriages) Act, 1972.
213. Section 12 of the Act of 1973.
214. With these grounds s. 13 should also be read, which lays down some restrictive conditions for filing a petition for annulment of marriage on any one of the grounds of voidable marriage.
215. Section 19.
216. Section 3.

Void Marriages : The Indian Divorce Act lays down the following grounds of void marriage[217] : (i) respondent was impotent at the time of the marriage and at the time of the institution of the suit; (ii) parties are within the prohibited degrees of consanguinity or affinity[218]; (iii) either party was a lunatic or idiot at the time of the marriage; and (iv) the former husband or wife of either party was living at the time of the marriage and the marriage with such former husband or wife was then in force. The scheme of matrimonial causes in the Parsi Marriage and Divorce Act, 1936 is different. Part IV calls them matrimonial suits. Section 30, which is in Part IV, lays down only one ground of void marriage, viz. impotency. Section 3, which is in Part I, intituted as "Preliminary Matters", deals with requisites of marriage in the negative form, viz., "no marriage shall be valid . . ." From s. 3 following three more grounds of void marriage could be deduced : (a) the parties are within the prohibited degrees of consanguinity or affinity (Schedule I to the Act deals with the degrees of consanguinity and affinity); (b) the proper Parsi ceremony of marriage has not been performed [s. 3 (b) : it is the ceremony of *ashirbad* which is performed by a Parsi priest in the presence of two Parsi witnesses]; (c) the bride has not completed the age of 18 years and bridegroom has not completed the age of twenty-one years.

Under the Special Marriage Act, 1954 grounds of void marriges are :[219] (i) respondent had a spouse living at the time of the marriage, (ii) respondent was, at the time of the marriage, incapable of giving a valid consent to the marriage in consequence of unsoundness of mind, or though capable of giving a valid consent to marriage has been suffering from mental disorder of such a kind as to be unfit for marriage and the procreation of children, or has been subject to recurrent attacks of insanity or epilepsy; (iii) respondent, at the time of the marriage, had not completed the age of twenty-one years (if bridegroom) or of eighteen years (if bride); (iv) the parties are within the degrees of prohibited relationship (Schedule I to the Act); and (v) respondent was important at the time of marriage and at the time of the institution of the petition. Under the Hindu Marriage Act, 1955 there are only three grounds of void marriage,[220] *viz.*, (a) respondent had a spouse living at the time of the marriage; (b) respondent is sapinda to the petitioner [sapinda relationship is defined in s. 3(f)] and (c) the respondent and the petitioner are within the degrees of prohibited relationship [these are defined in s. 3(g)].[221]

Muslim law classifies marriages into valid (*sahib*), void (*batil*)

217. Section 19.

218. Section 88 lays down that the prohibited degrees of relationship are to be determined in accordance with the personal law of parties.

219. Section 24.

220. Section 11.

221. See Paras Diwan, *Family Law*, Chapter 8, for detailed discussion.

and irregular (*fasid*). Whenever essential conditions of marriage, i.e. degrees of prohibited relationship (on the basis of consanguinity, affinity, fosterage) or proper ceremonies are violated the marriage is void. When some restrictive conditions of marriage, such as taking a fifth wife, marrying a woman while she is undergoing *iddat* or marrying two sisters, are violated, the marriage is neither valid nor void, it is irregular. Such a marriage can be made valid by doing certain things, such as when a Muslim husband takes a fifth wife, he may make his fifth marriage valid by divorcing any one of the first four wives. It is a peculiar features of Muslim law that it gives a person a right to repudiate his or her marriage. This is when a minor is married by his or her guardian, he or she has the option to repudiate it on attaining majority. In this regard Muslim law makes a distinction between the guardianship of the father and grandfather, on one side, and the guardianship of others on the other. In the former case the marriage can be repudiated only if the guardian has acted fraudulently, negligently or the marriage is manifestly to the disadvantages of the minor. In the latter case the minor can repudiate the marriage on attaining majority without assigning any reason. This is known as the option of puberty.[222] Repudiation of marriage to be valid in law has to be confirmed by the court.[223] This aspect of the matter relating to minor females has been codified in the Dissolution of Muslim Marriage Act, 1939 which makes it a ground of divorce. It is laid down that the Muslim wife may seek divorce on the ground that she (wife), having been given marriage by her father or other guardian before she attained the age of fifteen years, repudiated the marriage before attaining the age of eighteen years, and that the marriage has not been consummated.[224]

Voidable Marriages : Under the Special Marriage Act, 1954 the grounds of voidable marriages are :[225] (a) Since the solemnization of the marriage it has not been consummated owing to the wilful refusal of the respondent to consummate it; (b) the respondent was at the time of the marriage pregnant by some person other than the petitioner, provided that the petitioner was, at the time of the marriage, ignorant of the respondent's pregnancy, the marital intercourse with the consent of the petitioner has not taken place since the discovery of the respondent's pregnancy by the petitioner, and the petition is presented within one year of the solemnization of the marriage; and (c) the consent of either party to the marriage was obtained by coercion or fraud as defined in

222. See *Hadaya*, 37-38; Baillie, 50-52; Ameer Ali, *Muhammedan Law*, Vol. II, p. 370; Mulla, *Mohammedan Law* (17th ed.), pp. 268-270. Under *Shia Law* when the marriage of a minor is performed by a gurdian other than the father and grandfather, it is ineffective unless ratified by the minor, on attaining majority. See also Paras Diwan, *Muslim Law in Modern India* (1987), p. 102-103.

223. The matter is yet not free from doubt.

224. Section 2(vii).

225. Section 25.

the Indian Contract Act, 1872, provided that the proceedings have been instituted within one year after the coercion had ceased or, as the case may be, the fraud had been discovered and the petitioner had not with his or her free consent lived with the other party to the marriage as husband and wife after the coercion had ceased or, as the case may be, fraud had been discovered. The Hindu Marriage Act, 1955 lays down four grounds of voidable marriages, viz.[226] (a) that the marriage has not been consummated owing to the importence of the respondent,[227] (b) that at the time of marriage the respondent was incapable of giving valid consent to the marriage in consequence of unsoundness of mind or though capable of giving a valid consent, has been suffering from mental disorder or such a kind or to such an extent as to be unfit for marriage and procreation of children or has been subject to recurrent attacks of insanity or epilepsy, (c) that the consent of the petitioner was obtained by force or fraud as to the nature of the ceremony or as to any material fact concerning the respondent, provided the petition shoud be presented within one year after the force has ceased to operate or, as the case may be, the fraud had been discovered and the petitioner has not with his or her consent lived with the respondent as husband or wife after the force had ceased to operate or the fraud has been discovered, and (d) that the respondent was at the time of marriage pregnant by some person other than the petitioner, provided the petitioner was at the time of his marriage with the respondent was ignorant of respondent's pregnancy, the marital intercourse had not taken place with the consent of the petitioner since the discovery of respondent pregnancy, and the petition has been presented within one year of the marriage. Under Parsi Law there is only one ground, namely, consummation of Marriage for natural causes is impossible.[227a]

Jurisdiction of the Court

English Law

Before the coming into force of the Domicile and Matrimonial Proceedings Act, 1973, it had become fashionable to make a distinction between void and voidable marriages from the point of view of jurisdiction also.[228] In respect of void marriages, domicile[229] residence[230] and solemnization of marriage[231] within the jurisdic-

226. Section 12.
227. For a discussion of eunuch's marriage under Hindu law, see author's work, Modern Hindu Law Codified and Uncodified, pp. 109-112.
227a. Section 30.
228. See Dicey and Morris (8th ed.) Rule 44, pp. 344-345.
229. *White* v. *White,* (1937) p. 111; *De Reneville* v. *De Reneville,* (1948) p. 100 (Petitioner's domicile); *Von Lorang's* case, cited above (common domicile).
230. *Ramsay-Fairfax* v. *Ramsay-Fairfax,* (1956) p. 115; *Garthwaite* v. *Garthwaite,* (1964), p. 356.
231. *Simonin* v. *Mallac,* (1860) 2 Sw. & Tr. 67; *Sottomayer* v. *De Barros* (1977) 3 P.D. 1; *Cooper* v. *Crane,* (1891), p. 369; *Simons* v. *Simons,* (1939) 1 K.B. 490; *Hutter* v. *Hutter,* (1944), p. 95.

tion were considered to be the basis of jurisdiction. Common domicile[232] of parties and residence of both the parties[233] in England were considered to be the basis of court's jurisdiction in respect of voidable marriages.[234] Certain statutory grounds were also recognized on the basis of which the wife alone could petition.[235]

The Domicile and Matrimonial Proceedings Act, 1973 has made radical changes in the jurisdiction of court regarding petitions for nullity of marriage. The jurisdictional rules in respect of void and voidable marriages are now the same. The difference in the jurisdictional rules between divorce and nullity has been reduced to to a bare minimum. Now, under the Act, the English court will have jurisdiction to entertain a petition for nullity of marriage (in both cases of void and voidable marriages) on the ground that.[236]

(a) either of the parties to the marriage is domiciled in England on the date when proceedings are begun, or

(b) either of the parties to the marriage was habitually resident in England throughout the period of one year preceding the presentation of the petition.

The Act also makes an innovation as it enables a party to petition for nullity after the death of the other party to the marriage.[237] The surviving party to a void marriage may petition to the court for nullity of marriage if

(i) either party was domiciled in England at the time of the death of the respondent, or

(ii) either party was habitually resident in England throughout the period of one year ending with the date of death of the respondent.

Section 5(5) applies to nullity proceedings as much as it applies to petitions of divorce. This means that if the court has jurisdiction in the main petition, then it will have jurisdiction to entertain and decide cross-petitions and supplemental proceedings.

The first two jurisdictional grounds of the nullity are the same as of divorce, therefore, reference may be made thereto.

232. *De Reneville* v. *De Reneville*, (1948) p. 100.
233. *Inverclyde* v. *Inverclyde*, (1931), p. 29; *Ramsay-Fairfax* v. *Ramsay-Fairfax*, (1956) p. 115; *Casey* v. *Casey*, (1949) p. 420.
234. *Ross Smith* v. *Ross Smith*, (1963) A.C. 280, laid down that the jurisdiction cannot be assumed on the basis of celebration of marrige within the jurisdiction.
235. Reference to these had already been made in connection with divorce.
236. Section 5(3).
237. Section 5(3)(c).

Indian Law

Since under the Hindu Marriage, Act,1955 and the Special Marriage Act, 1954, a declaration of nullity of marriage of a void marriage confers a status of legitimacy on the children, some of our High Courts have expressed a view that a petition for nullity of marriage under s. 11, Hindu Marriage Act, 1955 can be presented to a court of law even after the death of one of the parties to the marriage.[238] In *Thulsai Ammal* v. *Gowri Ammal*,[239] it was observed, *obiter*, "Since the decree of nullity appears, in our opinion, to be a declaration of status of a person, we are unable to see why the death one of the spouses should put an end to the right of the other surviving spouse to seek for such a declaration."[240] Earlier in this case a single judge of the Madras High Court has expressed, *obiter*, that such a petition is not maintainable.[238] This *obiter* observation of Srinivasan, J. in *Thusai Ammal* v. *Gowri Ammal*[242] has been relied upon first by a single judge[241] and then by a Division Bench[244] of the Punjab High Court. The Law Commission has expressed a disagreement with the Punjab view,[245] and the Marriage Laws (Amendment Act, 1976 has overruled these cases by laying down that any marriage solemnized after the commencement of this Act shall be null and void and may, on a petition presented by either party thereto, against the other party be so declared by a decree of nullity.

Choice of Law

The ecclesiastical courts applied the law of celebrations of marriage to all questions affecting the validity of a marriage. When jurisdiction was transferred to civil courts, the civil courts, after initial adherence to the *lex loci celebrationis*, made a distinction between the formal validity and essential validity of a marriage. Subsequent development has been such that annulment of marriage on the grounds of impotency and wilful refusal to consumate the marriage has been made a category by itself. In two cases the English court took the view that English law determined the matter.[246] For the first time an attempt to apply foreign law

238. Section 16 of the former and section 26 of the latter.
239. *Tulsan* v. *Krishni*, 1973 P. & H. 442; *Lakshmamma* v. *Thayamma*, 1974, A.P. 255.
240. 1964 Mad. 118.
241. *Ibid.* at p. 119.
242. *Gowri Ammal* v. *Thulasi Ammal*, 1962 Mad. 510.
243. **Smt. Krishni Devi v. Smt. Tulsan, 1972 P. & H. 305, per Manmohan Singh Gujral, J. *Lakshmamma* v. *Thayamma*, 1974 A.P. 255 also takes this view.**
244. *Smt. Tulsan* v. *Smt. Krishni*, 1973 P. & H. 442.
245. Law Commission's Report, no. 59, para. 6.1A.
246. *Easterbrook* v. *Easterbrook*, (1944) p. 10; *Hutter* v. *Hutter*, (1944) p. 95.

was made in *Robert* v. *Robert*.[247] This was a petition for annulment of the marriage on the ground of wilful refusal to consummate the marriage. Parties at all material time were domiciled in Guernsey and the marriage was also solemnized there. The court applies the law of domicile.

Then came *De Reneville* v. *De Reneville*[248] where a marriage was solemnized between a domiciled Frenchman and a woman domiciled in England. After living with her husband for some time in France, the wife returned to England and petitioned for annulment of marriage on the ground of impotency and wilful refusal to consummate the marriage. The husband appealed and protested that the English court has no jurisdiction to entertain the petition. The Court of Appeal expressed the view that the court will have jurisdiction only if she was domiciled in England and whether or not she was domiciled in England depended upon the question whether the marriage was void or voidable, a question which should be decided under the French law. Since no evidence of French law was given, the Court of Appeal determined the question of jurisdiction on two alternatives : if marriage was void the court will have jurisdiction as the wife will continue to have her English domicile, if the marriage was voidable the English court will have no jurisdiction. On the basis of this decision Chesire takes the view that the material validity (he calls them personal defects) should be determined by the proper law of marriage, i.e. the law of the intended matrimonial home.[249] Dicey and Morris are critical of this judgment.[250] Now that the wife does not take the domicile of her husband on her marriage (i.e., if she desires she can retain her pre-marriage domicile), the capacity to marry in the sense of material validity of the marriage should be determined by the pre-marriage domicile of each party.

It seems clear that the English court can pass a decree of nullity of a foreign marriage. Section 14(1) of the Matrimonial Causes Act, 1973 lays down that where any matter affecting the validity of a marriage would fall to be determined in accordance with rules of private international law by reference to the law of a foreign country, nothing in the Act preclude the determination of that matter by the relevant foreign law, nor does anything in the Act require the application to such marriage any of the bars[251] laid down in the Act. This means that a foreign marriage can be annulled on any ground recognized by the proper foreign law, such as degrees of prohibited relationship (even though such a marriage is valid by English law) or on grounds which are not known to English law such as conversion from one religion to

247. (1947) p. 164.
248. (1948) p. 100.
249. Cheshire, pp. 319-320.
250. Dicey and Morris, pp. 361-362.
251. Sections 1 to 3.

another, or exercise of option of puberty under Mohammedan law.[252]

Section 14(2) of the Act lays down that if a marriage has been celebrated under the Foreign Marriages Acts, 1892-1947, or a common law marriage has been solemnized abroad, the nothing in s. 11 (ground of void marriages) will prejudice then grounds of void marriages available under the Foreign Marriages Acts or under the law governing common law marriages solemnized abroad.

Indian Law

No Indian decision is available on the choice of law in nullity cases. As has been seen, the Indian courts exercise jurisdiction in nullity cases on the basis of domicile as well as residence; the same difficulties are likely to arise (particulary in respect of domicile) which arose in English cases at the time when the rule was that the wife took the domicile of husband, if the marriage was voidable. It is submitted that in Indian law the door is still open to our courts to say that the Indian courts exercise jurisdiction on the basis of residence of either party as well as on the basis of domicile. If they are able to take that view, the road to choice of law in nullity cases need not be full of detours and potholes. It seems that the Indian courts will determine formal validity of marriage by the *lex loci celebrationis* and the material validity by the personal law of parties at the time of the marriage.

Recognition of Foreign Nullity Decrees

It appears to be established rule that English courts recognize a decree passed by the court of the common domicile or residence of the parties. They will also recognize a foreign nullity decree if it is recognized by the country of the common domicile or common residence of the parties.

Domicile : This may be treated as a well settled rule of English law that the court of the country of the common domicile of the parties at the time of the institution of the proceedings has the jurisdiction to entertain the proceedings, and a decree passed in such proceedings will be recognized in England. It is immaterial whether or not parties were then resident in that country. In *Von Lorang* v. *Administrator of Austrian Property*[253] one Miss Salveseen, a British subject domiciled in Scotland, married an Austrian subject in 1897 at Paris. For most of the time parties lived at Wiesbaden and acquired German domicile. In 1923, the English Administrator of Austrian property claimed movables of the wife on the ground that by the marriage she had become an Austrian citizen. To get rid of her Austrian nationality she filed proceedings in a Wiesbaden

252. See *supra*, grounds of nullity under Indian law at pp. 280-281.
253. (1927) A.C. 641.

court for nullity of marriage on the plea that proper French ceremonies of marriage were not performed. The German court granted the decree. According recognition to the decree, the House of Lords said that the court of common domicile of the parties is internationally competent to determine conclusively and finally all questions relating to status of parties. In *De Massa* v. *De Massa*[254] and *Galene* v. *Galene*[255] the decree pronounced by the court of common domicile was recognized; in both cases the marriage was formally valid under the *lex loci celebrationis*, though not under the law of the common domicile. The reason for this was succinctly explained in *Corbett* v. *Corbett*[256] thus : "It is well established that if the English courts recognize the jurisdiction of a foreign court to annul a marriage, then the ground on which that marriage was annulled by the foreign court is wholly immaterial."[257]

It may now be treated to be established (after some controversy[258]) that in a case where the marriage is void, the English court will recognize a decree passed by the court of the country where the petitioner alone is domiciled.[259]

The English courts will recognize a decree of court of the common domicile irrespective of the fact whether the marriage was solemnized in England or abroad,[260] and whether it is annulled for lack of form or for anything else.

Residence : This also now appears to be settled rule of English private international law that a decree pronounced by the court of the country where the parties have their common residence will also be recognized in England,[261] wherever the parties might be domiciled. Whether the courts will recognize the decree passed by the court of the country where the petitioner alone is resident seems to be doubtful.

Whether the English court will recognize a decree passed by

254. (1939) 2 All E.R. 150n.
255. (1939), p. 237.
256. (1957) 1 W.L.R. 486.
257. *Ibid.* at 490.
258. See *Chapelle* v. *Chapelle*, (1950) p. 134 and *Lepre* v. *Lepre*, (1963) 2 All E.R. 49. The former is a much criticized judgment and has been overruled by *Gray* v. *Formosa*, (1963) p. 259. See also Dicey and Morris, 373-374; Cheshire, 348-350.
259. *Gray* v. *Formosa*, (1963) p. 259. Now that the wife can have her own separate domicile any controversy relating to voidable marriages whether or not wife takes her husband's domicile is purely academic.
260. See cases cited in footnotes 46 and 47. This implies that the decisions in *Simonin* v. *Mallac*, (1860) 2 Sw. & Tr. 67 and *Ogden* v. *Ogden*, (1908) p. 46 stand overruled.
261. *Travers* v. *Holley*, (1953) p. 246; *Mitford* v. *Mitford*, (1923) p. 130; *Corbett* v. *Corbett*, (1957) 1 W.L.R. 486; *Merker* v. *Merker*, (1963) p. 283.

the courts of the country where the marriage was solemnized seems to be doubtful, though in *Mitford* v. *Mitford*,[262] *Corbett* v. *Corbett*[263] and *Merker* v. *Merker*[264] the *lex loci celebrationis* and the common residence of the parties were the same. It should be noted that in *Ross Smith* v. *Ross Smith*[265] the House of Lords expressed a view against the recognition of a decree passed by the courts of the place where the marriage was solemnized. However, this was a case relating to voidable marriage. It is submitted that this should make no difference.

Decree effective in the courts of common domicile : In *Abate* v. *Abate*[266] it was held that the English courts will recognize a decree of nullity passed by any court if it is recognized as valid by the courts of common domicile of the parties. This is on the analogy of recognition of foreign divorce decrees, which was the rule in English law before the passing of the Recognition of Divorces and Legal Separations Act, 1971. There is no authority for the proposition that the English court will also recognize a decree of nullity passed by any court provided it is recognized by the courts of the common residence. It is submitted that there is no reason why such decrees of nullity should not be recognized. A problem can also arise if such a decree is recognized only by the court of the country where only one party is domiciled (now this is possible not only in respect of void marriages but also in respect of voidable marriages) or resident.

Towards the further development of the law of recognition, the following observation of Sir Jocelyn Simon, P. can provide a masterkey to all problems : "If we ourselves claim a ground of jurisdiction we must concede a similar ground of jurisdiction to foreign courts."[267] Now that the English court assumes jurisdiction on the basis of the domicile or habitual residence of either party, it is submitted that the English court should also recognize a decree passed by the court of the country where either of the party is domiciled or habitually residing. In *Perrini* v. *Perrini*,[268] the court observed, once recoginsed it must be taken to have declared the pretended marriage a nullity, with each party free to marry again.

Where these exists a decree of English court refusing to pass a decree of nullity, a subsequent decree of foreign court declaring the marriage as null and void will not be recognized by English courts.[269]

262. (1923) p. 130.
263. (1957) 1 W.L.R. 486.
264. (1963) p. 283.
265. (1963) A.C. 280.
266. *Abate* v. *Abate*, (1961) p. 29.
267. *Lepre* v. *Lepre*, (1965) p. 52.
268. (1979) Fam. 84.
269. *Virvalka* v. *Smith* (1981) 1 All E.R. 55.

Choice of law : The question as to what choice of law was made (rightly or wrongly) by a foreign court of competent jurisdiction seems to be entirely irrelevant in relation to recognition of foreign divorce decrees. It may be treated as an established proposition of English private international law that if the foreign court that passed the decree of nullity is of competent jurisdiction, then that decree will be recognized even if the foreign court made a wrong or faulty choice of law. In *De Massa* v. *De Massa*[270] Lord Merrivale observed : "A French tribunal of competent jurisdiction has annulled the marriage and that declaration of nullity comes into operation."[271] This principle has also been applied to the decrees passed by the courts of common residence. In *Mitford* v. *Mitford*[272] one Mitford, domiciled in England underwent a ceremony of marriage in Berlin with a German domiciled woman. After marriage parties lived together in Berlin; while they were so living the wife obtained a decree of nullity from a Berlin court on a ground (masculine indolence and unbearable selfishness) which was not recognized by the law of the common domicile of the parties. Recognizing the Berlin decree of nullity, the English court observed that judgment being that of a competent court it was a conclusive judgment like any other judgment in a civil suit and it did not worry the court that this would mean an alteration of status inadmissible by the law of domicile. This, of course, does not mean that such a judgment cannot be impeached on any ground. Like any other judgment it can be impeached on the ground of violation of principles of natural justice and other grounds on which foreign judgments can be impeached.[273]

Indian Law

So far as the present writer is aware there is no reported Indian case on the recognition of foreign nullity decrees. It may be hoped that the Indian courts will recognize the jurisdiction of foreign courts to pronounce the decrees of nullity on the same basis on which they assume jurisdiction. Since in Indian law there is no distinction whatever in any matrimonial cause regarding jurisdiction, the Indian law of recognition of foreign nullity decrees should be the same as of recognition of divorce decrees.

IV

JUDICIAL SEPARATION

Judicial separation, like its predecessor, divorce *a mensa et thoro*, is a separation from bed and board. It does not bring the marital tie to an end. It merely leads to the suspension of marital obligations; parties, after the decree of judicial separation, are no

270. (1939) 2 All E.R. 150n.
271. This decision has been followed in *Galene* v. *Galene*, (1939) p. 237.
272. (1923) p. 130.
273. See Chapter 25 of this work; see also *Gray* v. *Formosa*, (1963) p. 259.

longer bound to cohabit with each other. But parties remain husband and wife. If any one of them takes another spouse, he or she will be guilty of bigamy. While the decree of separation subsists, if one of the parties dies intestate, the other would succeed to his or her property. A decree of judicial separation is a decree *in rem*, and, if parties want to resume cohabitation, it would be necessary to get the decree rescinded.

Does the decree of judicial separation affect status ? In the words of Cheshire, the problem is : "Whether such a decree affects the status of parties or whether in the interest of internal order and social decency, it merely protects the petitioner from some of the consequences of that status. The answer is important, at any rate on principle, for both as regards jurisdiction and choice of law, the predominant factor should be the domicile of the parties if their status is affected, otherwise it should be their place of residence."[274] On this matter there is conflict of opinion. *Le Mesurier* v. *Le Mesurier*[275] and *Anghinelli* v. *Anghinelli*[276] take the view that a decree of judicial separation does not affect status. The unity in the law of husband and wife is affected by such decree only marginally, as marital obligations remain suspended so long as decree subsists; the moment the decree is rescinded the parties once again become full-fledged husband and wife. On the other hand, Atkin, L.J. said that a decree of judicial separation does affect status.[277] Cheshire also favours this view.[278] It is submitted that the former view is better and correct view. The moment we subscribe to the latter view, the inevitable conclusion is that the domicile should be the basis of jurisdiction.

Law of judicial separation varies from country to country. Thus in most Roman Catholic countries (such as Spain and, till recently, Italy) divorce is still not recognized, and therefore in these countries nullity of marriage and judicial separation alone have been the basic matrimonial remedies. In some countries like Norway and Sweden, separation may lead to divorce. In some countries, like India, if cohabitation is not resumed for a certain period after the decree of judicial separation, it gives a right to either party to obtain divorce. Similarly, in France, *separation de corps* may be converted into divorce after three years at the instance of either party.

Grounds of Judicial Separation

English Law

In the modern English law the grounds of judicial separation

274. Cheshire, p. 351.
275. (1895) A.C. 517.
276. (1918) p. 247.
277. *Eustace* v. *Eustace*, (1924) p. 45; see also *Niboyet* v. *Niboyet*, (1878) 4 P.D. 1, per Bret, L.J. at p. 12.
278. Cheshire, p. 352.

are embodied in s. 17, Matrimonial Causes Act, 1973.[279] Sub-section (1) of the section lays down that the facts which constitute breakdown of marriage under s. 1 of the Act are grounds on which a petition for judical separation may be filed. These are : that the respondent had committed adultery and the petitioner finds it intolerable to live with the respondent; that the respondent has behaved in such a way that the petitioner cannot reasonably be expected to live with the respondent; that the respondent has deserted the petitioner for a continuous period of two years immediately preceding the presentation of the petition; that the parties to the marriage have lived apart for a continuous period of at least two years immediately preceding the presentation of petition and the respondent consents to a decree being granted; and that the parties to the marriage have lived apart for a continuous period of at least five years immediately preceding the presentation of petition. On any one of these set of facts being established the court will grant a decree of judicial separation. In a petition for judicial separation the court is not concerned to consider whether or not marriage has broken down[280] (as it is concerned in a petition for divorce).

Indian Law

Under the Indian law the grounds of judicial separation are laid down in various matrimonial statuses. Under the Divorce Act, 1869 the grounds of judicial separation are a few. Section 22 of the Act lays down : "No decree shall hereafter be made a divorce *a mensa et thoro* but the husband or wife may obtain a decree of judicial separation on the ground of adultery or cruelty or desertion without reasonable excuse for two years or upwards and such a decree shall have effect of a divorce *a mensa et thoro* under the existing law and such other legal effect as hereinafter mentioned." The Parsi Marriage and Divorce Act, also contains a simple provision. The Act lays down[281] that a Parsi husband or wife can obtain a decree of judicial separation on any one or more grounds on which he or she can obtain divorce.[282]

The Special Marriage Act, 1954 also contains a very simple provision relating to grounds of judicial separation. Section 23 lays down that either party to the marriage may present a petition

279. This reproduces s. 12(1) of the Matrimonial Causes Act, 1965 and s. 8(1) & (3) of the Divorce Law Reform Act, 1969
280. Section 17(2).
281. First part of s. 34.
282. Last portion of s. 34, has been omitted by the Act of 1988.

for judicial separation on any ground on which he may present a petition for divorce under s. 27(1). A petition for judicial separation may also be presented on the ground of failure to comply with a decree for restitution of conjugal rights.[283] Under the Hindu Marriage Act, 1955 the grounds of judicial separation are the same as the fault grounds of divorce.[284]

The Muslim law does not recognize judicial separation

Jurisdiction of the Court

English Law

Before the abolition of the remedy of restitution of conjugal rights[285] and before the coming into force of the Domicile and Matrimonial Proceeding Act, 1973, the English jurisdictional rules relating to judicial separation and restitution of conjugal rights were the same, irrespective of the fact whether a decree in these matrimonial causes affected the status or not. The domicile of both parties in England was enough to confer jurisdiction on English court from very beginning.[286] It was immaterial that one of the parties or both were resident abroad.[287] The second jurisdictional ground was the residence of the parties in England at the time of the commencement of the proceedings.[288] This has been a very old jurisdictional basis; it had existed in English law from the ecclesiastical times.[289] However, the petitioner's residence alone was not recognized as a basis of jurisdiction.[290] No other ground

283. Section 23(1)(b).
284. Section 10.
285. The Matrimonial Proceedings and Property Act, 1970, s. 20, had abolished the matrimonial cause of restitution of conjugal rights.
286. *Eustace* v. *Eustace*, (1924) p. 45.
287. *Ibid.*
288. The jurisdictional basis of residence in all matrimonial causes that prevailed at the ecclesiastical courts was retained by the first Matrimonial Causes Act (of 1857, s. 22). This provision was subsequently re-enacted with the modification that it would be confined to procedure and practice: Supreme Court of Judicature (Consolidation) Act, 1925, s. 32. This change was considered of not much consequence in *White* v. *White*, (1937) p. 111; *Hutter* v. *Hutter*, (1944), 95; *Baxter*, v. *Baxter*, (1948) A.C. 274; *Ramsay-Fairfax* v. *Ramsay-Fairfax*, (1956), p. 115; and *Ross Smith* v. *Ross Smith*, (1963) A.C 280 (a case of nullity of marriage). The ecclesiastical courts always considered an unseparated wife to be residing with her husband, even though she was in fact living at a different place. Similarly, seamen who are mostly outside the country on their navigational duties, are regarded to be residing at a place where they have provided a home for their wife and children. The same was the position of those businessmen who were on business away from home most of the time : *Raeburn* v. *Raeburn*, (1928) 44 T.L.R. 384.
289. See *Armytage* v. *Armytage*, (1898) p. 178; *Anghinelli* v. *Anghinelli*, (1918) p. 241.
290. *Raeburn* v. *Raeburn*, (1928) 44 T.L.R. 384; *Ward* v. *Ward*, (1923) 39 T.L.R. 440.

was considered to be sufficient to confer jurisdiction.[291] Apart from these grounds certain statutory grounds also existed.[292]

The Domicile and Matrimonial Proceedings Act, 1973 now repeals old grounds and lays down new grounds of jurisdiction which are the same as for divorce. Thus the English court will have jurisdiction to entertain a petition for judicial separation if:[293]

(a) at the date of the institution of proceedings either party is domiciled in England, or

(b) at the date of the institution of the proceedings either party was habitually resident in England throughout the period of one year preceeding the presentation of the petition.

A petition for judicial separation cannot be filed on any other basis. However, if a cross-petition is filed or some supplemental proceedings are filed, then the court will exercise jurisdiction if it has jurisdiction in the main petition, though it has no jurisdiction in the cross-petition or supplemental proceedings.[294]

Indian Law

The unique aspect of Indian matrimonial jurisdiction has been that it makes no distinction from the point of view of jurisdiction between the matrimonial causes. Except under the Indian Divorce Act, 1869, where, for a petition for divorce, Indian domicile of the parties is essential, in all the matrimonial causes and under all other matrimonial laws the juridictional rules are the same as for divorce and nullity.

Choice of Law

English Law

Once English courts decide in favour of jurisdiction, they have been invariably applying English law, even if the parties are domiciled abroad. When the English courts exercised jurisdiction on statutory grounds, they were statutorily required to apply English

291. But see *Sinclair* v. *Sinclair*, (1968) p. 189; Scarman, J. observed : "The court must take into account the respondent's whole situation, matrimonial as well as personal, in determining whether he was resident within the jurisdiction at that time. The matrimonial home, the last place of cohabitation, the events leading up to the suit, and events occurring after, his personal movements, location and way of life, the situation of wife and children—all are facts to which the court will have to have regard. Residence in this context is not merely a personal, or property presence, with some degree of permanence, but a state of affairs which connects a man and his family sufficiently clearly with England to make it just that the court should intervene."

292. Section 40(1)(a) of the Matrimonial Causes Act, 1965.

293. Section 5(2).

294. Section 5(5).

law.[295] No change in the law has been effected by the recent legislation. Nor did the Law Commission recommend any change.[296]

Indian Law

There is a total dearth of authority on the choice of law in connection with a petition for judicial separation. What has been stated earlier in connection with divorce should apply here also.

Recognition of Foreign Decrees of Judicial Separation

Under the Recognition of Divorces and Legal Separations Act, 1971[297] the basis for the recognition of judicial separation and divorces are the same, and therefore what has been stated in connection with divorces applies here also.[298]

In India we have no reported case where the question of recognition of any foreign legal separation came before the Indian courts. So far Indian courts have applied the general provisions of recognition laid down in s. 13, Civil Procedure Code to foreign decrees in matrimonial causes and that seems to be the view that our courts are taking. This means that if a decree in a matrimonial cause has been passed by a court of competent jurisdiction, the Indian court will recognize it, unless it is impeached on any one of the grounds laid down in s. 13, Civil Procedure Code.[299] This is what our Supreme Court has said with respect to divorce decrees.[300]

V

RESTITUTION OF CONJUGAL RIGHTS

In modern times the remedy of restitution of conjugal rights is a much criticised remedy. In its essence the decree of restitution of conjugal rights means that the respondent is asked to live with the petitioner. It has been said that the restitution of conjugal rights is worst form of tyranny, it is worst form of slavery.

In countries where it still prevails most of its stings have been removed. In most countries, a decree of restitution of conjugal rights can be executed neither by the arrest of the respondent nor by the attachment of his property.[301] It has now been abolished in English law.[302] In Indian law it still exists.

In the Indian Divorce Act, 1869 the provisions are contained in ss. 32 and 33. The former section provides : "When either the

295. Section 40(2), Matrimonial Causes Act, 1965.
296. Law Commission's Report No. 48, para. 105.
297. *Tursi* v. *Tursi*, (1958) p. 54, states the old Law.
298. Section 3.
299. See Chapter 25 of this work and also *Satya* v. *Teja Singh*, 1975 S.C. 105.
300. *Satya* v. *Teja Singh*, 1975, S.C. 105.
301. In Indian law it is still possible : Order 22, C.P.C.
302. The Matrimonial Proceedings and Property Act, 1970, s. 28.

husband or the wife has, without reasonable excuse, withdrawn from the society of the other, either wife or husband may apply by petition to the District Court or the High Court for restitution of conjugal rights, and the court on being satisfied of the truth of the statements made in such petition and that there is no legal ground why the application should not be granted, may decree restitution of conjugal rights accordingly." Then, s. 33 provides : "Nothing shall be pleaded in answer to a petition for restitution of conjugal rights which would not be a ground for a suit for judical separation or for a decree of nullity of marriage." In the Parsi Marriage and Divorce Act, 1936 the provision (equivalent to s. 32 of the Divorce Act, 1869) runs thus : "Where a husband shall have deserted or without a lawful cause ceased to cohabit with his wife, or where a wife shall have deserted or without lawful cause ceased to cohabit with her husband, the party so deserted or with whom cohabitation shall have so ceased may sue for restitution of conjugal rights and the court, if satisfied of the truth of the allegations contained in the plaint and that there is no just ground why relief should not be granted, may proceed to decree such restitution of conjugal rights accordingly."[303] The Act does not contain any provision equivalent to s. 33 of the Divorce Act, 1869. The Special Marriage Act, 1954 contains a provision equivalent to s. 32, Divorce Act, 1869 and to s. 36, Parsi Marriage and Divorce Act, 1936, but nothing equivalent to s. 33 of the Divorce Act, 1869.[304] The provision in the Special Marriage Act, 1954[305] and the Hindu Marriage Act[306] in non-identical runs thus : "When either the husband or the wife has, without reasonable excuse, withdrawn from the society of the other, the aggrieved party may apply by petition to the District Court for restitution of conjugal rights, and the court, on being satisfied of the truth of the statements made in such petition, and that there is no legal ground why the application should not be granted, may decree restitution of conjugal rights accordingly." The provision under the original Act was different[307] and it led to some judical controversy.[308, 309]

Thus, the provision of restitution of conjugal rights exists in India for all people including Muslims.[310] In India such a decree can be executed by attachment of the property of the respondent.[311] When the decree of Restitution is not complied with by

303. Section 36.

304. See Paras Diwan, *Family Law*, Chapter VII.

305. Section 22.

306. Section 9.

307. Section 9.

308. See author's work, Modern Hindu Law, Codified and Uncodified, pp 165-67.

309. See author's article, "Restitution of Conjugal Rights through the Punjab High Court, (1967) 1 Law Review 207-224.

310. Muslim law also recognizes the remedy of restitution of conjugal rights. See Tyabji's formulation in s. 87, p. 103 (17th ed.).

311. Order 21, r. 32, Civil Procedure Code.

the husband, the wife can claim maintenance under the Parsi Marriage and Divorce Act, 1936,[312] Divorce Act, 1869[313] and the Special Marriage Act, 1954.[314] Under the Hindu Marriage Act, 1955[315] the petitioner (whether wife or husband) can claim maintenance if the respondent does not comply with it. Under the Parsi Marriage and Divorce Act, 1936, if the respondent does not comply with the decree, the petitioner has a right to petition for divorce on that ground[316] If a decree for restitution of conjugal rights is not complied with for one year, under the Special Marriage Act, 1954,[317] under the Hindu Marriage Act, 1955,[318] and Parsi Marriage and Divorce Act,[318a] either party may file petition for divorce.[319]

Jurisdiction and Choice of Law

The jurisdictional requirements in the matrimonial laws of every community are practically the same in all the matrimonial causes; so are the rules of choice of law. The same have been discussed in connection with divorce, reference may be made to the same.[320]

VI

MATRIMONIAL RELIEFS IN RESPECT OF POLYGAMOUS MARRIAGES

It has been seen in Chapter 8 of this work that the modern English law not merely recognizes polygamous marriages validly performed overseas between parties who are not domiciled in the United Kingdom, but English courts also grant matrimonial reliefs in respect of them. The Matrimonial Proceedings (Polygamous Marriages) Act, 1972 codified and reformed the law in this respect. The provision has now been re-enacted in s. 47, Matrimonial Causes Act, 1973. Under sub-section (3) certain declaratory reliefs can be claimed in respect of a polygamous marriage. The declarations that may be obtained are: (i) a declaration that the marriage is valid or invalid; (ii) a declaration that the applicant is legitimate child of his parents or that the marriage of his father and mother or of his grandfather and grandmother was a valid marriage, or (iii) a declaration that the

312. Sections 39 & 40.
313. Sections 36 & 37.
314. *Ibid.*
315. Sections 24 & 25.
316. Section 32(i).
317. See Paras Diwan, *Family Law* (1983), Chapter VII.
318. Section 22(2)(ii).
318a. Section 32A(1)(ii).
319. Section 13(1A)(ii).
320. See pp. 366-321.

applicant became or his parent, or remoter ancestor, became or has become a legitimated person.

A party to a polygamous marriage may seek and obtain any one of the following matrimonial relief under sub-section (2) of s. 47 : (a) a decree of divorce, nullity of marriage or judicial separation, (b) a decree for presumption of death and dissolution of marriage, (c) an order for financial provision in the case of wilful neglect under s. 27, Matrimonial Causes Act, 1973, (d) an order for alteration of maintenance agreements under s. 35, Matrimonial Causes Act, 1973, (e) an order under the Matrimonial Proceedings (Magistrate's Courts) Act, 1960, and (f) an order under any provision of the Matrimonial Causes Act, 1973 which confers a power exercisable in connection with, or in connection with proceedings for, any such decree or order as mentioned in (a) to (d).

The provisions of s. 47, Matrimonial Causes Act, 1973 apply to a polygamous marriage which is potentially polygamous or in fact polygamous.

VII

ANCILLARY RELIEFS[321]

Once the court assumes the jurisdiction in a petition[321a] in any matrimonial cause, it may be called upon to pass orders, in supplemental proceedings, for, broadly speaking, financial provisions for the parties and their children (or for the children of the family, this has now come to be the expression used in respect of children, since it includes not merely the children of the parties but also the children of either party which have been accepted as of family) and for custody, education, access, etc. of children. The Indian matrimonial law of all communities still recognize only two types of ancillary proceedings:[322] (a) proceedings for maintenance and alimony of spouses (under Hindu law either party can claim it), and (b) proceedings relating to custody, maintenance, etc. of children. The modern English law has now been consolidated in Matrimonial Causes Act, 1973. Of the 44 substantive sections, 24 sections are devoted to these matters. The Act has four parts : the

321. The title "ancillary relief" is still retained for the subject discussed under this part of the Chapter, though this title is no longer in vogue. This title is retained as it is still indicative of the supplemental reliefs that may be claimed consequent to proceedings in a matrimonial cause. Then under the Indian law the reliefs are substantially the same as used to be claimed under this head under English law when these reliefs were tagged to the main proceedings; if main proceedings are dismissed these reliefs too could not be claimed. This continues to be the position in Indian law.

321a. *Ibid.*

322. See ss. 36, 37 & 38 of the Special Marriage Act, 1954 : these matters are dealt with under Chapter VII which is entitled, Jurisdiction and Procedure."

fourth part deals with miscellaneous and supplemental provisions; Parts II and III deal with these matters. Part II is intituted as, "financial relief for the parties to marriage and children of the family" and Part III is entitled as, "Protection, custody, etc. of children." Thus English matrimonial law has travelled far to meet the social needs of our contemporary society. Adequate protection is accorded to those persons who are worst sufferers and who are the most innocent persons in the entire matrimonial strife and proceedings leading to the social solution of that strife, i.e. children, so much so that courts have power to refuse to pass a decree of divorce, separation of nullity, if they feel that doing so would serve the interest of children.[323] The court has power to keep the children under the supervision of any person, if it thinks proper to do so.[324] Similarly, the court now exercises very wide powers for making financial provision for the parties and children.[325]

Jurisdiction of the Court

From very beginning the English courts have maintained that it has jurisdiction to pass orders in ancillary proceedings if it has jurisdiction in the main proceedings.[326] However, in these matters the court exercises a discretion, and, if in a given case it feels that an order passed by it would not be effective, it may decline to make an order.[327] In an early case, Lord Chancellor Cranworth observed : "There might be cases in which it would be improper to exercise it, as for example where both parties may be abroad and there should be no property here . . . . I should probably make no order, because the parties should feel that I was doing no good but incurring a sort of scandal, as every court does, if it attempts to make an order which it has no power to enforce."[328] None-theless, the court may exercise jurisdiction in an exceptional case, even if it knows that it may not be possible for it to enforce the order. Thus, in *Harten* v. *Harten*[329] an English domiciled man married an Irish domiciled woman. The husband and wife settled down in Eire and had three children of the marriage. In 1956, he parted company with the wife leaving the children in wife's custody. Subsequently, he asked for access to children which wife allowed him. Thereupon he immediately took the children to Jersey in a privately chartered aircraft. The wife filed a petition for divorce on the ground of husband's cruelty in the High Court.

323. Section 41.
324. Section 44.
325. Part II. In English law their scope is now much wide : See Matrimonial Causes Act, 1973.
326. See author's work, Parental Control, Guardianship and Custody of Minor Children, Chapter XXXII, pp. 600-607.
327. *Tallak* v. *Tallak* (1927) p. 211 ; *Goff* v. *Goff*, (1934) p. 107.
328. *Hope* v. *Hope*, 43 E.R. 534.
329. (1957) 1 All E.R. 379.

She made two interlocutory applications, one for an injunction restraining the husband from removing the children from Jersey and the other for an order that he should deliver up the children to her in England. The court said that it would exercise jurisdiction over the children who were abroad, as it considered this to be an exceptional case. In *Re P.*[330] the question again came for consideration before the court whether it would exercise jurisdiction over a child who was abroad. The court again exercised the jurisdiction.[331]

In a series of cases,[332] it has been held that the court has power to vary a settlement *inter parties*, even though it comprises property situated abroad, is governed by foreign law and the trustees also reside abroad. In such a case service made on the trustees would be set aside if they protest against the jurisdiction, and there is no possibility of any order made against them to be effective.[333] The English courts have expressed a view that they can exercise jurisdiction to order settlement of a guilty wife's English property, even though she is domiciled and resident abroad.[334] The courts have also passed orders for payment of maintenance to the wife against a husband who is domiciled and resident abroad and had no property within the jurisdiction.[335] The English courts have now jurisdiction to make an order for varying or revoking any financial arrangements made under a maintenance agreement or inserting financial arrangements therein "if each of the parties to the agreement is for the time being either domiciled or resident in England and Wales."[336]

It has now been statutorily laid down that the court can make any order for the benefit of any child of the family if proceedings in a matrimonial cause are dismissed after their institution on the ground that the marriage has been validly dissolved by a foreign court.[337]

Since 1949,[338] the English courts have exercised jurisdiction to order a husband who has been guilty of wilfully neglecting his wife to provide reasonable maintenance to her as well as for the minor children of the marriage, to make periodical payments to the wife wherever it has jurisdiction to entertain proceedings for

330. (1965) 2 W.L.R. 1.
331. *Ibid.* at p. 9.
332. *Nunneley* v. *Nunneley*, (1890) 15. D. 186; *Forsyth* v. *Forsyth*, (1891) p. 363; *Goff* v. *Goff*, (1934) p. 107.
333. *Goff* v. *Goff*, (1934) P. 107; *Wyler* v. *Lyons*, (1963) p. 274.
334. *Hunter* v. *Hunter*, (1962) p. 1.
335. *Cammel* v. *Cammel*, (1965) p. 467.
336. Section 35(1) of the Matrimonial Causes Act, 1973. Section 35(2) lays down the grounds on the basis on which such revocation or variation may be made.
337. See s. 23(2)(b), Matrimonial Causes Act, 1973; *P.* v. *P.* (1971) p. 318.
338. Law Reforms (Miscellaneous Provisions) Act, 1949, s. 5. The Matrimonial Proceedings and Property Act, 1970, s. 6.

judicial separation by the wife. This provision had undergone several modifications.[339] Now, under the Matrimonial Causes Act, 1973 not merely the wife but the husband also can claim maintenance for wilful neglect to maintain the applicant or any child of the family.[340] The jurisdictional rule has been modified by the Domicile and Matrimonial Proceedings Act, 1973.[341] The English court can now exercise jurisdiction on an application for an order for financial provisions on the ground of wilful neglect to maintain on any of the following grounds (and on no other) :

(a) On the date of the application the applicant on the respondent was domiciled in England,

(b) the applicant has been habitually resident in England throughout the period of one year immediately preceding the presentation of the application, or

(c) the respondent is resident in England on the date on which application is filed.

Choice of Law

It is an established role of English private international law that in ancillary proceedings the court applies the English law, whatever may be the domicile of parties.[342] However, it appears that under the Maintenance Orders (Facilities for Enforcement) Act, 1920 and the Maintenance (Reciprocal Enforcement) Act, 1972, application of foreign law may be necessary in some situations. Thus, a provisional maintenance order in another country (to which Act extends) cannot be confirmed in England if the defendant is successful in raising any defence available to him under the law of the country the court of which passed the original order,[343] then maintenance order is defined under the Act as an order for periodical payment of sum of money towards the maintenance of any person whom the person against whom order is made is liable to maintain under the law of the country where the order was made. Similarly, when the English court revokes a foreign order of maintenance, it should apply the law of the country which made the order, unless both the parties are residents of the United Kingdom.[344] The English court is also required to apply foreign law when it makes a maintenance order against a person who is subject to the jurisdiction of a convention country.[345]

339. See Matrimonial Causes Act, 1950, s. 23; the Matrimonial Causes Act, 1965, s. 22; s. 6 of the Matrimonial Proceedings and Property Act, 1970 replaced these provisions. Now this is s. 27, Matrimonial Causes Act, 1973.

340. Section 27.

341. Section 6(1).

342. *Sealey* v. *Callan* (1953) P. 138; *Cammell* v. *Cammell*, (1965) p. 467.

343. Section 10 of the Act of 1920 and s. 21(1) of the Act of 1972.

344. Section 9(4) of the Act of 1972.

345. Section 26(3) & (4) of the Act of 1972.

Enforcement of Foreign Maintenance Orders

At common law foreign maintenance orders were enforced if they were final and conclusive.[346] But the common law provisions were not sufficient to meet all situations and therefore these rules have been supplemented by several statutes. The Maintenance Orders (Facilities for Enforcement) Act, 1920 makes provisions for the reciprocal enforcement of maintenance orders made in England and Northern Ireland and the countries of Commonwealth overseas, as well as in those countries to which the Act may be extended. Under the Act overseas maintenance orders may be registered in England or Northern Ireland. Such orders may be of superior courts or of inferior courts of the Commonwealth countries. A procedure for registration is provided. On their registration these orders have the same effect as if made by the courts in England or Northern Ireland. Once the Commonwealth maintenance orders are received of through the proper channels as laid down in the Act, the English courts have to register them, they have no discretion whatever even if they think that the order had been made by a court which had no jurisdiction;[347] nor can it hear any objection from the person against whom the order has been made.[348] Similarly, the English court cannot vary or alter the maintenance order,[349] though it seems that it has power to remit arrears.[350]

The Colonial and Other Territories (Divorce Jurisdiction) Acts, 1920-1950 provide facility for the execution in England and Northern Ireland of orders of alimony, maintenance, custody etc. of children, costs in the suit or damages against the co-respondent, made by the courts of colonies or other countries to which these statutes extend, in matrimonial proceedings between the parties domiciled in England or Northern Ireland and resident in the colony or the country concerned. Such orders may be registered under the Acts in the courts of England or Northern Ireland, wherever the parties are domiciled, and on such registration these orders will be treated as if they have been made by the court in which they have been registered.[351] These orders can be registered only in the High Court or the Court of Session.[352] The registering court has power to modify or discharge any of these orders but it will not exercise the power so long as the petitioner in the matrimonial proceedings continues to reside in the country, the court of which made the order.

346. *Harrop* v. *Harrop*, (1920) 3 K.B. 386; *Re Macartney*, (1921) 1 Ch. 522, *Beatty* v. *Beatty*, (1924) 1 K.B. 807.
347. Section 1.
348. *Pilcher* v. *Pilcher*, (1955) P. 318.
349. Section 1.
350. *Pilcher* v. *Pilcher* (No. 2), (1956) 1 W.L.R. 298.
351. Section 1(3).
352. Section 1(2).

The third statute in this series, the Maintenance Order Act, 1950 is designed to facilitate the enforcement of maintenance orders, made in other parts of the United Kingdom, in England, Scotland or Northern Ireland.[353] The usual mode is by registration of orders in the court where enforcement is desired. The requirement of registration of maintenance orders made in one part of the United Kingdom in another part is that the person against whom order is made is residing in that part of the United Kingdom where execution of the order is sought.[354] It is also necessary to show that it would be convenient to execute the order there. The procedure for registration of orders is discretionary, but the discretion vests not in the registering court but in the court which made the order. Once an order is registered, it is enforceable there as if it is an order made in that part of the United Kingdom.[355] The power to vary or discharge such orders does not belong to the registering court but to the court which made the order,[356] though if the orders are of a Magistrate's court or a sheriff's court then variation in the rate of payments due under the order may be made by registering court; but the registering court cannot increase the liability.[357]

In the end we pass on to the Maintenance Orders (Reciprocal Enforcement) Act, 1972 which is of great international significance and has been passed to give effect to the United Nations Convention on the Recovery Abroad of Maintenance to which the United Kingdom has acceded. Part I of the Act provides for the designation of the reciprocating countries for the purpose of transmission of maintenance orders made in the United Kingdom for enforcement in the reciprocating countries, for variation and revocation of orders made by the courts in the United Kingdom; for registration, confirmation, enforcement, variation or cancellation of orders made by the courts in reciprocating countries and like, and consequential and supplemental provisions. Part II of the Act deals with the reciprocal enforcement of claims for the recovery of maintenance and makes provisions for application by persons in the United Kingdom for recovry, etc. of maintenance in convention countries (the convention country under the Act is that country to which the Act of 1972 extends), for appllcation for recovery of maintenance in England, Wales and Northern Ireland, for complaints by a spouse in convention country for recovery in England, Wales, Northern Ireland and Scotland of maintenance from other spouse, for transfer of orders, for enforcement of orders, and for consequential and supplemental matters.[358]

353. Part II of the Act.
354. Section 17(2).
355. Section 18(1).
356. Section 21(4) and s. 22(4).
357. *Ibid.* But see Maintenance Order Act, 1968.
358. Sections 6, 7, 8 & 9.

This Act replaces the Maintenance Orders (Facilities for Enforcement) Act, 1920.

The Act of 1972 can be extended to any country in the world by an Order in Council which accords reciprocal treatment to the United Kingdom.[359] Under the Act "maintenance order" is defined to mean : (a) an order (including an affiliation order or order consequent upon an affiliation order) which provides for the periodical payment of sums of money towards the maintenance of any person, being a person whom the person liable to make payment under the order is, according to the law applied in the place where the order was made, liable to maintain; and (b) an affiliation order or order consequent upon an affiliation order, being an order which provides for the payment by a person adjudged, found or declared to be child's father, of expenses incidental to the child's birth or, where the child has died, of his funeral expenses. "Maintenance Order" also includes a maintenance order which has been varied.[360] Under the Act, maintenance orders made in a reciprocating country can be registered in the United Kingdom : orders which are confirmed in a reciprocating country can also be registered.[361] Before registering an order, an officer of the registering court shall ascertain whether the payer under the maintenance order is residing within the jurisdiction of the court.[362] If the payer is not resident within the jurisdiction of the court, the order is returned to the Secretary of State through whom such orders are received. Under s. 7 "provisional maintenance orders" can also be registered in the United Kingdom. Otherwise, the court to whom the order is sent for registration has no discretion to refuse to register even if the court considers that the order has been passed by a court without jurisdiction.[363] Payer under the order too has no right to be heard to show cause against the registration. The orders of reciprocating country whose registration is sought may be any court, superior, subordinate or courts of summary jurisdiction. Once a maintenance order is registered in a court in the United Kingdom, it is enforceable in the same manner as if it is an order of the registering court.[364] The registering court has also the power of variation and revocation of such maintenance orders.[365] Registered order can be varied or revoked in the same manner as if it is an order of the registering court, but it can be varied or revoked only by a provisional order. It can be finally varied or revoked if both the payer and the payee under the registered order are for the time being resident in the United Kingdom, or the application is made

359. Section 1.
360. Section 21(1) and s. 24.
361. Section 6(1).
362. Section 6(4).
363. Section 8(1).
364. Section 8.
365. Section 9.

by the payee under the registered order, or the variation consists of a reduction in the rate of payments under the registered order and is made solely on the ground that there has been a change in the financial circumstances of the payer since the registered order was made. The provisional order, registered in the United Kingdom, may be varied if "since the registered order was confirmed and the courts in the reciprocating country in which the maintenance order in question was made do not have power, according to the law in force in that country, to confirm provisional orders varying maintenance orders."[366] The Act also makes provisions for the transfer of registered orders to a court in another part of the United Kingdom or to another reciprocating country.[367] Section 16 makes provision for the conversion of sums mentioned in foreign currency into the currency of the United Kingdom.

Foreign Custody Orders

The question often come, before the courts regarding recognition and enforcement of foreign custody orders. In *Mrs. Kuldeep Sidhu* v. *Charan Singh,*[368] the Punjab and Haryana High Court said that foreign custody should be given the regard. In this parties were married in India but settled in Canada, having acquired a domicile there the father brought the two children of marriage to India. It seems that marriage broken down and mother obtained a custody order in her favour from a Canada Court. Armed with the Canadian order, mother came to India and wanted the custody of children from the grandfather. On their refusing to do so, she filed proceeding the India. Mother was given custody of children by the order of the Court.

366. Section 9(1)(c).

367. Section 10.

368. AIR 1989, Punjab and Haryana 103. See also *Marilynn* v. *Mergaret,* ILR (1984) Punjab and Haryana.

10

LEGITIMACY AND LEGITIMATION

I

LEGITIMACY

Although distinction between legitimate and illegitimate children is still maintained, there is a tendency in most of the countries of the world, including the communist countries, to blur this distinction. In this regard two trends are discernible. One is to confer the status of legitimacy on some type of illegitimate children. The other is to confer rights of legitimate children on illegitimate children.

The English common law (like Roman law) started by openly declaring an illegitimate child as *filius nullius*.[1] England gradually modified its stand on illegitimate children till in 1969, by the Family Law Reform Act, 1969,[2] it has almost obliterated the distinction between an illegitimate child and a legitimate child; in respect of property rights the illegitimate child has been put almost at par with legitimate child.[3] In regard to guardianship and custody his position is at par with legitimate child.[4] Thus what Cheshire said in his seventh and earlier editions (to stress the importance of the subject of "legitimacy and legitimation") that the first importance of the subject is that the expression "gift to children" in the will of a domiciled Englishman *prima facie* means gift to legitimate children and that the same rule applies in case of intestacy, seems to be no longer tenable.[5] Some other

1. As late as 1955 Viscount Simonds said that common law of England did not contemplate illegitimacy and, shutting its eyes to the facts of life, described an illegitimate child as *filius nullius* : *Galloway* v. *Galloway*, (1953) 3 All E.R. 429. In 1841 Maule, J., said : "How does the mother of an illegitimate child differs from a stranger ?" *Re Lloyds*, (1841) 3 Man. & G. 547.
2. Part II of the Act.
3. See Paras Diwan, The Law of Parental Control, Guardianship and Custody of Minor Children, Chapter IX, pp. 175-182.
4. Guardianship of Minors Act, 1971.
5. Cheshire (7th ed.), p. 359. This statement is continued in the eighth edition also, p. 424. See the Family Law Reforms Act, 1969, ss. 14-16. Section 18 of the Act provides that an illegitimate child shall count as a dependent under the Inheritance (Family Provisions) Act, 1938.

Western countries too have undergone this process of eroding the distinction between the two. In some countries this process was complete in the first half of the twentieth century. Some states of the United States have the most radical law in this regard. For instance, an Arizonian law of 1921 provides : "Every child is hereby declared to be the legitimate child of its natural parents and as such is entitled to support and education to the same extent as if it has been born in lawful wedlock. It shall inherit from its natural parents and from their kindred heirs lineal and collateral in the same manner as children born in lawful wedlock."[6] Probably, the most radical law in the communist countries is that of People's Republic of China. Article 15 of the marriage law runs: "Children born out of wedlock shall enjoy the same rights as children born in lawful wedlock. No person shall be allowed to harm or discriminate against children born out of wedlock."[7]

Muslim law is one of those few systems of law of the world, which still subscribes to the notion that a child born out of wedlock is *filius nullius*. According to Muslim law it owes no *nasab* to either parent; neither parent has an obligation towards it. The Shias still rigidly adhere to this view. The Hanafis, on the other hand, have modified their stand to this extent that an illegitimate child for its nurture should be left in the care of the mother till it is seven years old. After that age, even the mother has no obligation towards it.[8]

The most remarkable feature of Hindu law in this regard has been that an illegitimate child has never been considered as *filius nullius*. His relationship with both parents was recognized. Father's obligation to maintain every type of illegitimate child has been recognized from an early period. One species of an illegitimate child, called *dasiputra* (son born to a permanently and exclusively kept concubine) was accorded a definite status in his father's family, although along the first three classes his status was inferior to the *aurasa* (natural) son, inasmuch as he had no right of inheritance or survivorship, his position among the *Sudras* was much better. In the absense of a natural born son, he had the right of survivorship and inheritance almost like that of a natural born son. When he as well as the *aurasa* son existed side by side, his rights of inheritance and survivorship and of partition were slightly inferior.[9] This appears to be rather curious that in the modern Hindu law, the rights of illegitimate children have suffered diminution. Under the Hindu Succession Act, 1956, no illegitimate

6. See Paras Diwan, The Illegitimate Child in the Modern Law, 1969, Allahabad Law Review, pp. 5-24.
7. See *Ibid.* The laws of the East European Communist countries do not go that far. For instance, see the Polish Family Code of 1964.
8. See author's work referred to in footnote 3, pp. 182-183.
9. See author's work referred to in footnote 3, Chapter IX, 168-173; *Gur Narain Das* v. *Gur Tehal Das,* 1952 S.C. 225.

child (not even of a *sudra*) can inherit the property of his father.[10] He has been totally excluded from the agnatic succession, though it seems that he can succeed to the property of his mother and other relations through her.[11] His rights are slightly better under the modern Hindu law in respect of maintenance, since he can claim now from both parents.[12]

On account of this diversity of laws in the countries of the world on the status of legitimate and illegitimate children, at the outset of our enquiry, the private international law is concerned with the question : under which law a child is to be determined as legitimate or illegitimate ?

Broadly speaking, a child born within lawful wedlock has been considered to be a legitimate child,[13] and a child who is born outside the lawful wedlock has been considered to be an illegitimate child. These traditional definitions of illegitimate and legitimate children have undergone some modifications. This has been on account of the recent trend of conferring a status of legitimacy on certain illegitimate children. Thus in modern English law[14] as well as Indian law[15] the children of annulled voidable marriages[16] and of certain void marriages[17] are regarded as legitimate children. It seems clear that whether a child is legitimate or illegitimate is to be characterized by the *lex domicilii* of the child.[18]

10. Section 3(j).
11. This is how the term 'related' is defined in s. 3(j), Hindu Succession Act, 1956.
12. Section 6, Hindu Minority and Guardianship Act, 1956; see also Paras Diwan, Modern Hindu Law, Codified and Uncodified, Chapter IX, pp. 216-232.
13. Under English common law the rule was that only that child was legitimate who was conceived and born during the lawful wedlock. This is no longer the position in English law : birth alone in lawful wedlock is sufficient.
14. The Matrimonial Causes Act, 1973, s. 16 and Sch. 1, para 12; see also the Legitimacy Act, 1976.
15. Hindu Marriage Act, 1955, s. 16; Special Marriage Act, 1954, s. 26.
16. See footnotes 14 and 15.
17. Section 2, Legitimacy Act. 1959, lays down that children of void marriages will be legitimate if the parties at the time of the act of intercourse resulting in the birth of the child or at the time of celebration of marriage, if later, believed that their marriage was valid. This is a rule of English domestic law and sub-section (22) of s. 1 lays down the limitation : this section applies, and applies only, where the father of the child was domiciled in England at the time of the birth, or if he died before the birth, was so domiciled immediately before his death. See also the Legitimacy Act, 1976. Under the Hindu Marriage Act, 1955 and the Special Marriage Act, 1954, the children of void marriages which are declared void are legitimate. See *Krishni* v. *Tulsan*, (1972) P. & H. 305; *Gowri Ammal* v. *Thulsai Ammal*, 1962 Mad. 510.

    The *Shastric* Hindu law tried to solve this problem by conferring a status of legitimacy on as many types of sons as possible and in that process Hindu law recognized as many as thirteen types of sons : See author's work, Law of Parental Control, Guardianship and Custody of Minor Children, Chapter I, pp. 13-14.
18. This matter is discussed under the next head.

JURISDICTION OF COURT

English Law

The question of jurisdiction in respect of legitimacy of children may arise before the court in any one of the following two ways : (a) It may arise incidentally, as an ancillay or collateral matter to the main issue of succession, intestate or testamentary, or to a claim of person under a settlement. In such cases the question is simple enough : if the court has jurisdiction in the main issue, it has also jurisdiction on the ancillary or collateral matter.[19] (b) A person may file proceedings for a declaration of his legitimacy. In the later case, the matter, under English law, is governed by the Matrimonial Causes Act, 1973.[20] Section 45(1) of the Act runs : "Any person who is a British subject, or whose right to be deemed a British subject depends wholly or in part on his legitimacy or on the validity of any marriage, may, if he is domiciled in England and Wales or in Northern Ireland or claims any real or personal estate situate in England and Wales, apply by petition to the High Court for a decree declaring that he is the legitimate child of his parents, or that the marriage of his father and mother or his grandfather and grandmother was a valid marriage or that his own marriage was a valid marriage." Under this provision the petitioner can ask for a declaration : (a) of his legitimacy or (b) of the validity of his own marriage or the marriage of his parents or grandparents. Under this provision the petitioner cannot ask for a declaration of legitimacy or illegitimacy of some one else, or of the validity or otherwise of somebody else's marriage. When a decree is passed in proceedings under s. 45 of the Matrimonial Causes Act, 1973, it is binding on the Crown and on all other persons. However, if certain persons interested in the decree are not given notice of the proceedings or made parties to them, then it cannot affect them adversely. A copy of every application under this section and of any affidavit accompanying it is to be given to the Attorney-General.[21] A decree obtained by fraud or collusion is ineffective.[22]

Choice of Law

The English law has now gone a long way in blurring the distinction between legitimacy and illegitimacy.[23] However, the picture of choice of law in the present English law appears to be

19. *Brook* v. *Brook*, (1861) 9 H.L.C. 193; *Skinner* v. *Carter*, (1948) Ch. 387 : such decisions do not amount to judgments *in rem*. They are binding only on the parties or the persons claiming through them.
20. Formerly, s. 181 of the Supreme Court of Judicature (Consolidation) Act, 1925, then s. 39(1), Matrimonial Causes Act, 1965, now s. 45(1) of the MCA, 1973.
21. Section 45(6), Matrimonial Causes Act, 1973.
22. Matrimonial Causes Act, 1973. s. 45(5)(9).
23. Family Law Reform Act, 1969; see also the Legitimacy Act, 1976, section 5(3).

somewhat distorted. In most cases the question has come before English courts in connection with succession. Thus, when under a will property is bequeathed to children of X, then two questions may be involved. One, of construction : what was the intention of the testator in using these words ? The second question is : whether the children are in fact legitimate or illegitimate ? It seems that former being the question of construction will be determined by the English domestic law. The second question relates to status and should, like all questions of status, be determined by the *lex domicilii*.[24] When one looks at the case law one is at once confronted with two conflicting decisions : one of House of Lords in *Shaw* v. *Gould*[25] and the other of the High Court in *Re Bischoffsheim*[26] which has been approved by Privy Council in *Bamgbose* v. *Daniel*.[27]

In *Shaw* v. *Gould*[28] under the will of an English domiciled testator certain funds were bequeathed in trust on Elizabeth Hikson for life and after her death in trust for her children and certain English land was also devised after her death to 'her first and other sons lawfully begotten.' Elizabeth underwent a ceremony of marriage with one Buxton from whom she separated immediately after marriage. Subsequently, she got engaged with one Shaw, a domiciled Englishman. A scheme for obtaining divorce from Buxton was devised under which Shaw acquired a domicile in Scotland and Buxton was persuaded to go to Scotland for forty days. The marriage was dissolved by a Scottish court. Elizabeth and Shaw were married in Edinburgh. From this marriage Elizabeth had two daughters and a son. At the time of present action Elizabeth was dead. The marriage of Elizabeth and Shaw was valid by Scot law. But the question that English court considered was : was it valid under English law ? It may be noted that at the time of the second marriage of Elizabeth, she and her former husband remained domiciled in England. The House of Lords held that the second marriage of Elizabeth was invalid by English law as her first marriage was not dissolved by the court of her domicile. In view of this, it was held that all her three children were not born within the lawful wedlock and therefore were not entitled under the will. Another authority on the same line is *Re Paine*[29] where the children of a marriage which was void by the *lex domicilii* were held to be illegitimate.[30]

24. Cheshire, p. 434.
25. (1868) 3 H.L. 55.
26. (1948) Ch. 79.
27. (1955) A.C. 107 which lays down two conflicting rules. See Cheshire (8th ed.) pp. 426-436; Dicey and Morris, pp. 421-425.
28. (1868) 3 H.L. 55.
29. (1940) Ch. 46.
30. Cheshire says that in this case the possibility that the children may be legitimate though the marriage was void was not canvassed before the court and the arguments were addressed solely on the basis of the validity of the marriage, (8th ed.), p. 430.

In *Re Bischoffsheim*,[31] a testator domiciled in England gave a share of residue to his granddaughter Nesta for life with remainder to her children. In 1917 Nesta had married one George, her deceased husband's brother in New York. Subsequently, George acquired a domicile in New York, and while Nesta and George were so domiciled a son was born to them. In 1917 the marriage of a woman with her deceased husband's brother was invalid by the law of England, but valid by the law of New York. Thus, if the question of legitimacy of children is tagged with the validity of the marriage, then Nesta's son was illegitimate, but if it is not so tagged, then Nesta's son was legitimate when it was born; since the law of New York, *lex domicilii*, conferred a status of legitimacy on him when he was born. Romer, J., it is submitted rightly, refused to be dragged into the question of validity of marriage and held Nesta's son as a legitimate child.[32]

It is submitted that the difficulty of the House of Lords in *Shaw* v. *Gould*[33] was its inability to make this distinction. Accepting the social realities, the modern English decisions have abandoned the doctrinaire approach in other spheres.[33] Cheshire suggests that legitimacy of a person should be determined by the law of his domicile of origin.[34] Cheshire is using the same language which Romer, J., used.[35] Graveson puts it thus : "... the status of legitimacy, like that of any other family status, must be determined by the law of domicile—in the case of legitimacy, by the law of the domicile of the father at the time of the birth—of the person whose status is in question."[35] Graveson further said : "Despite the English rule that the domicile of an illegitimate child is that of its mother, the determination of whether or not a child is legitimate or otherwise is always governed by the law of the father's domicile."[36] It is submitted that Cheshire offers a better solution to the problem inherent in the rule that it is the law of the domicile of the father at the time of the birth of the child which determines the legitimacy of the child. Cheshire agrees with Wolf[37] that 'legitimacy is concerned with the relationship between a child and father,' and therefore the domicile of the natural father should be decisive."[38]

31. (1948) Ch. 79.
32. *Ibid.*, at p. 92.
33. For instance the development of law in respect of children of polygamous marriages. *Khoo Hooi Leong* v. *Khoo Hean Kwee*, (1926) A.C. 529, where the Privy Council said : "In deciding a case where the custom and the law are so different from British ideas a court may do well to recollect that it is a possible jural conception that a child may be legitimate, though its parents were not and could not be legitimately married at p. 543. See also *Bamgbose* v. *Daniel*, (1955) A.C. 107.
34. Cheshire (8th ed.) p. 433.
35. *Re Bischoffsheim*, (1948) Ch. 79 at p. 92.
36. Graveson, (6th ed.) p. 381.
37. *Ibid.* He quotes *Re Grove*, (1888) 40 Ch. D. 216 (C.A.).
38. Cheshire (10th ed.) p. 454. See also Dicey and Morris for the contrary view, pp. 419-420.

There are some cases which may not be covered under the rule. For instance, the father has a different domicile at the time of the conception of the child than at the time of the birth, and the child is legitimate under the former but illegitimate under the latter. Cheshire, it is submitted rightly, suggests the principle of most favourable law.[39] Then, there is the problem of the posthumous child, whose mother has changed her domicile after the death of the father. Two solutions are possible : one is the domicile of the father at the time of his death (as we have seen in Chapter 6, this is domicile attributed to such a child under the Indian Succession Act, 1925), the other is the domicile of the mother at the time of the birth of the child. It is submitted that here also the principle of most favourable law should be applied.[40] The third problem arises in those cases where a child, who is born within a lawful wedlock, is not regarded as legitimate by the law of the domicile of the father, because the law of domicile takes the view that the child would not be legitimate unless it was conceived within the lawful wedlock.

It is submitted that the rule of choice of law may be formulated thus :

(i) A child born anywhere is lawful if born within lawful wedlock. (This is in accordance with Dicey and Morris, except that the words in parenthesis, viz., or may be presumed to be, are omitted.)

(ii) A child is legitimate if the law of his father's domicile (or nationality, in countries where nationality is still a test) or habitual residence regards him as legitimate.

(iii) In those cases where the legitimacy of a child is determinable under two systems of law, then the principle of most favourable law should be applied.

Indian Law

The Indian law of legitimacy in this regard is entirely undeveloped. Under the Indian domestic law a child born during the lawful wedlock or born within 280 days of the death of the father or of the dissolution of the marriage is presumed to be the legitimate child.[41]

Jurisdiction : The question of jurisdiction can come before the Indian courts in the same way as it can come before an English court (or, for that matter, any court), it may arise as a collateral issue when a court is called upon to determine questions relating to succession, or claims under a settlement, or it may arise directly when a person files proceedings for a declaration of the legitimacy of himself or some other person. In the former case, the Indian court will have

39. Cheshire, p. 454.

40. Cheshire favour mother's domicile, p. 455.

41. Indian Evidence Act, 1872, s. 112.

jurisdiction on the collateral issue if it has jurisdiction on the main matter. In the latter case, in the absence of any specific provison (just as there is one in s. 39, Matrimonial Causes Act, 1965, in English law), a declaratory suit has to be filed under the provisions of the Specific Relief Act, 1963. When such a suit is filed, the general provisions of the jurisdiction laid down in the Civil Procedure Code will apply.[42] It may be noted that under the Specific Relief Act, 1963, a person can file a declaratory suit not only for his own legitimacy but also for the illegitimacy (or legitimacy) of some one else.

Choice of law: It is submitted that the Indian courts will profit by the controversy and conflict of English decisions and will ferry clear of them. Suggestions made here may help them to formulate some of their own rules of choice of law which are socially just and internationally acceptable.

II
LEGITIMATION

In the past when distinction between a legitimate child and an illegitimate child was very pronounced, and bastardly attached a great social stigma and legal disability, there was a tendency in some countries to confer a status of legitimacy on some illegitimate children. Such children were known as legitimated children. Legitimation is a legal process by which status of legitimacy is conferred on the children born outside the lawful wedlock.

It appears that the law of legitimacy was first developed by Romans. Before the adoption of the Christian faith, the marriage among Romans was not a sacrament. It was essentially a private act of parties, for which no formalities were required. Marriage was as free as divorce. Concubinage was rampant with its concomitant, the illegitimate children. Constantine took it to be his mission to do away with concubinage and reduce the number of illegitimate children to the minimum. In 335 A.D. he introduced the rule of legitimation by *Subsequence matrimonium*. Under this rule a child born outside the lawful wedlock could be legitimated (in other words, became legitimate) by the subsequent marriage of its parents. Justinian laid down that for the legitimation of a child under this rule it was necessary that the mother of the child has the capacity to marry the father of the child at the time of the conception of the child or at the time of the birth of the child, though she might be *ingenua* or *libertina*.[43] From the Roman law the institution of legitimation by subsequent marriage of parents descended and spread to the countries of civil law system. It spread to some states of the United States and some Latin American countries. In the Scottish law also it was received at an early date, but England could have it only in

42. See Chapter 7 of this work.
43. Code, 5.27.

1926 when it was introduced by an Act of Parliament, the Legitimacy Act, 1926. The provision did not apply to chiidren born of adulterous unions.[44]

In India, neither under the general law or the law of any community, legitimation by subsequent marriage of parents is known. In fact, institution of legitimation is unknown in India.

Another form of legitimation also came into vogue on the pattern of Roman *legitimatio per rescriptum principis*, i.e. legitimation by acknowledgment or recognition. In this form of legitimation the putative father recognizes or acknowledges his illegitimate child as his own child. Upon this, a status of legitimacy is conferred on the child. In several countries of continental Europe, in some states of the United States and in some Latin American states this mode of legitimation exists, though its form differs from country to country.[45] Muslim law also recognizes a mode by which status of legitimacy may be conferred on a child. This is something akin to acknowledgment, but differs in one fundamental, namely, under Muslim law a bastard cannot be legitimated. Under Muslim law a status of legitimacy is conferred by acknowledgment on a child whose paternity is doubtful. Thus, an offspring of *zina* (adultery), incest or fornication cannot be acknowledged. In short, it applies to those cases where either the fact or exact time of marriage is a matter of doubt or uncertainty, that is, marriage is neither proved nor disproved. The other requirements are that the child acknowledged should be of such a age as to admit of the acknowledger being the father of the child, the child should not be known to be somebody else's child, and the child should not repudiate the acknowledger. The result of acknowledgment under Muslim law is that not only the child is acknowledged as legitimate child, but the mother is also acknowledged as the lawfully wedded wife of the acknowledger.[46]

Jurisdiction

Just as in the case of legitimacy so in the case of legitimation the question of legitimation may come before the court in two situations : in collateral proceedings, as the question may arise in

44. Section 1(1). But now this disability has been removed by s. 1(1) of the Legitimacy Act, 1959.

45. In French law either parent or both parents can acknowledge the child. But an adulterine or incestuous child cannot be acknowledged. (See Articles 332-336 of the Civil Code.) Under the German Civil Code a governmental declaration that the acknowledger acknowledges the child as his own may also be obtained. Under the Code it is immaterial that the acknowledger is not in fact the father of the child. But such a declaration cannot be made if at the time of the conception of the child the marriage of its parents could not legally take place. (Sections 1735-1737). In the Family Code of Poland the provision is the same as under the German Code. See the English statute, the Legitimacy Act, 1976.

46. Baillie, 406; Hadaya, 439; *Alladad* v. *Muhammed,* (1888) 10 All. 289; *Habibul Rehman* v. *Altaf*, (1921) 48 I.A. 114.

connection with succession or settlement, or in a declaratory suit filed by a person for a declaration of himself as a legitimated child. In the former case the court would have jurisdiction, if it has jurisdiction in the main proceedings, while in the latter case the matter is now governed by the Matrimonial Causes Act, 1973. Sub-section (2) of s. 45 lays down : "Any person claiming that he or his parents or any remoter ancestor became or has become a legitimate person may apply by petition to the High Court, or may apply to a country court in the manner prescribed by the country court rules, for a decree declaring that he or his parent or remoter ancestor, as the case may be, became or has become a legitimated person." For the purpose of this sub-section, "legitimate person" is defined as "a person legitimated by the Legitimacy Act, 1926, and includes a person recognized under s. 8 of the Act as legitimated."[47] This provision applies to two types of cases of legitimation : (a) domestic legitimation, and (b) foreign legitimation. For the domestic legitimation provision is contained in s. 1 of the Legitimacy Act, 1926 which lays down, " . . . where the parents of an illegitimate person marry or have married one another, whether before or after the commencement of this Act, the marriage shall, if domiciled in England or Wales, render that person, if living, legitimate from the commencement of this Act, or from the date of the marriage whichever last happens." The jurisdiction of the court for this purpose can be invoked by any person whether he is domiciled in England or not, or whether he is a British subject or not. In respect of foreign legitimation the provision is enacted in s. 8 of the Act. (This is discussed later in connection with recognition of foreign legitimation.) What should be noted is that a declaration of legitimation in regard to such persons can also be obtained under s. 45(2), Matrimonial Causes Act, 1973.

Just as decree in proceedings for a declaration of legitimacy is a decree binding on the Crown and all other persons so is a decree in legitimation proceedings. If persons who are interested in the proceedings are not made parties in, or given notice of, proceedings, then the decree is not binding on them. Similarly, a decree obtained by fraud or collusion is ineffective. It is also necessary that the attorney-general is supplied with a copy of the petition and any affidavit accompanying it.

Choice of Law and Recognition of Foreign Legitimations

Although legitimation by any method was not recognized under English law, English courts were quite early called upon to adjudicate upon the foreign legitimations. The law relating to this matter got crystallized at common law in 1888. In *Re Grove*,[48] one Sarah was born to an English domiciled woman from a man who was

47. Para. 2 of sub-section (2). This was formerly s. 39(2), Matrimonial Causes Act, 1965.

48. (1888) 40 Ch. D. 216.

originally domiciled in Geneva, but at the time of the birth of Sarah had acquired an English domicile of choice. After the birth of the child both parents married in England. By Swiss law the effect of this marriage would have been to legitimate Sarah had her father continued to have the Swiss domicile. However, the English court held Sarah to be illegitimate. Thus, the common law propounds a double test : father must be domiciled at the time of the birth of the child in a country which allows legitimation by subsequent marriage and he must also be domiciled at the time of his marriage in a country which permits legitimation by this mode.[49] In *Re Goodman's Trust*[50] the question before the court was whether all the five children of a man and a woman were illegitimate ? The father of the children while domiciled in England had three children from a woman whom he had not married. He then acquired a Dutch domicile and had fourth child from the same woman. After the birth of the fourth child he underwent a ceremony of marriage with this woman and subsequently the fifth child was born to him. The Dutch law recognized legitimation by subsequent marriage of the parents. The court held that only the fourth and fifth child were legitimated as they alone fulfilled the twin test.

This common law rule has been criticised by both jurists and judges. The jurists have criticised the first requirement as pre-eminently illogical.[51] Of this twin test, Scott, L.J. observed : "I confess that the very idea of attributing to a newly born child, to a *filius nullius*, a sort of latent capacity for legitimation at the hands of the natural father to whom he is denied any legal relation, seems to me an even more absurd legal fiction and even less convincing than the mythical contract of marriage supposed by the cannonists to have been entered into at the moment of procreation."[52]

However, this criticism did not prevent English courts from extending this principle to legitimation by acknowledgment. The question has come only in one case : *Re Luck's Settlement Trusts*,[53] where an English domiciled man went to California and there he had a child from a woman in 1906. Then he acquired a domicile of choice in California and in 1920 he married the woman. He then publicly acknowledged the child as his own. This conferred a status of legitimacy on the child by the Californian law. If the child was held legitimate he was entitled to take certain funds under an English trust as well as under a will. The court held the child illegitimate since at the time of its birth, his father was domiciled in England where this mode of legitimation was not recognized.

49. *Re Wright's Trust*, (1856) K. & J. 595; *Re Andros*, (1883) 24 Ch. D. 637; In *re Goodman's Trusts*, (1881) 17 Ch. D. 266.
50. (1881) 17 Ch. D. 266.
51. Graveson, 389; Dicey and Morris, 438-39; Cheshire (8th ed.) 437-38.
52. *Re Luck's Settlement Trusts*, (1940) Ch. 864 at p. 912.
53. (1940) Ch. 864.

The decision has been criticized.[54]

Fortunately, the operation of the common law rule has been much restricted by the Legitimacy Act, 1926 which makes the legitimation by subsequent marriage of parents as part of English law. The Act lays down (as a domestic rule) that a child is legitimated by the subsequent marriage of his parent if *at the date of marriage* the father was or is domiciled in England.[55] Then, s. 8(1) lays down a rule of conflict of laws: "Where the parents of an illegitimate person marry or have married one another, whether before or after the commencement of this Act, and the father of the illegitimate person was or is, at the time of marriage, domiciled in a country other than England or Wales, by the law of which the illegitimate person became legitimated by virtue of such subsequent marriage, that person, if living, shall in England and Wales be recognized as having been so legitimated from the commencement of this Act or from the date of the marriage, whichever last happens, notwithstanding that his father was not at the time of the birth of such person domiciled in a country in which legitimation by subsequent marriage was permitted by law." It is evident that the sub-section lays down only one test: the *lex domicilii* of the father at the time of the marriage is the sole test both in the case of domestic as well as foreign legitimation. It seems to be clear that all the reguirement of legitimation by subsequent marriage laid down by the father's *lex domicilii* should be satisfied. The rights of a child legitimated under the Act are limited by s. 3 of the Act. It is also clear that the Legitimacy Act does not abrogate the common law rule but is in addition to it.[56]

The rights of a legitimated person (by the subsequent marriage of his parents) are governed by the common law, the Legitimcay Act, 1926, and the Family Law Reforms Act, 1969, and the Legitimacy Act, 1976.[57]

The common law rule will still apply to those cases where it is desired to prove that the person was legitimated before the date of the commencement of the Act and to those cases where legitimated person claims under a will or other instrument that came into operation before the date of his legitimation.[58] Under the Legitimacy Act, 1926, the legitimated person, his spouse, children and more remote issues are entitled to take any interest in the estate of an intestate dying after the date of legitimation, or under any disposition coming into operation after that date or by descent under an entailed interest created after the date of his legitimation.[59] On

54. See Cheshire (10th ed.) 454.
55. Section 1(1).
56. *Re Hurll*, (1952) Ch. 722.
57. Under section 5(3), a legitimated person and any other person, shell be entitled to take any interest as if legitimated person had been born legitimate.
58. *Ibid.*
59. Section 3(1).

the death of the legitimated person, his spouse or children, the order of succession is what it would have been, had he been born as legitimate.[60] Under the Family Law Reforms Act, 1969, since illegitimate children are entitled to inherit as if they were legitimate children, the legitimated person too will inherit the property as legitimate child even if he is not able to inherit under the common law or under the Legitimacy Act, 1926.[61]

Once the court determines that the child is legitimate or legitimated, the attributes of the status of legitimacy, its effect and consequences, are determined by the law of his domicile of origin, whatever the event might be (his birth, marriage of his parents after his birth or his acknowlegment by his father) which conferred on him this status. Thus, such a person qualifies to be a legatee, next of kin or devisee of English immovables under the English law of succession, with one exception, *viz.* he cannot claim to succeed an heir to an English entailed interest.[62] The effect of this common law rule in the modern English law has been limited to a bare minimum by the Administration of Estate Act, 1925 and, more particularly, by the Legitimacy Act, 1926, which, as has been seen, lays down that where a person has been legitimated by the subsequent marriage of his parents, he, his spouse, children and more remote issue shall be entitled to take by descent under an entailed interest created after the date of legitimation, in like manner as if the legitimated person had been born legitimate.[63]

60. Section 4.
61. See Part II of the Act.
62. This is because at common law no one could succeed to entailed estate unless he was a person born within the lawful wedlock. Statute of Merton, 1235; *Birtwhistle* v. *Vardill*, (1826) 5 B. & C. 438.
63. Section 3(1). See also s. 8(1) which extends the provision to a person recognized legitimate under his foreign *lex domicilii*.

11

ADOPTION

When Hindus and Romans conceived the idea of adoption, they did not contemplate it as a mode of conferring a state of legitimacy on illegitimate children. The sole object of adoption then was to provide a child to childless. It was a means by which the family line was prevented from extinction and made to continue. Among the Hindus its object was also to confer spiritual benefit on the adopter and his ancestors.[1] It was then natural for Hindus and Romans to consider adoption as part of private law. In most systems of law adoption is still meant to provide consolation and relief to childless. In the modern laws of some countries, its object, sometimes dominant,[2] is considered to rescue the helpless, the unwanted, the destitute or the parentless child and provide it with parents and a home. Sometimes its purpose is also considered to provide richer family life—a person who has only one or two children can make his family life richer by adopting a few more children.[3]

Under the old Hindu law adoption was hedged with many conditions.[4] Under the modern Hindu law every Hindu, male or female, has the capacity to make an adoption if he or she is a major and of sound mind.[5] A married Hindu male can adopt only with the consent of his wife.[6] A married woman cannot adopt even with the consent of her husband. It is because when both husband and wife are alive primarily it is for the husband to exercise the right of adoption.[7] A married male can adopt without the consent of his wife, and a married woman can adopt a child,

1. Manu Smriti, IX, 168, 141, 142; Vasistha, XV, 1-6.
2. This is the claim made by the framers of the Adoption Bill, 1972.
3. In the modern Hindu law one cannot adopt more than one son and one daughter : Hindu Adoptions and Maintenance Act, 1956, s. 11, clauses (i) and (ii).
4. See Paras Diwan, Modern Hindu Law, Codified and Uncodified, (1985) Chapter VIII.
5. The Hindu Adoptions and Maintenance Act, 1956.
6. See ss. 7, 8(a) and (b).
7. Proviso to s. 7.

if the other spouse has ceased to be a Hindu by converting to some other religion, or has finally and completely renounced the world or has been adjudicated upon as of unsound mind by a court of law.[8] A Hindu can adopt a male child if the adopter has no Hindu son, son's son or son's son's son.[9] Similarly, an adoption of a female child can be made only when an adopter has no daughter or son's daughter.[10] When a child of opposite sex is proposed to be adopted, then adopter must be senior to it by at least twenty-one years.[11] So long as the father is alive he alone can give the child in adoption, though the consent of the mother of the child is necessary.[12] During the lifetime of the father, the mother can give the child in adoption only when he has ceased to be a Hindu by converting to another religion, or has finally and completely renounced the world, or has been adjudicated to be of unsound mind by a court of competent jurisdiction.[13] The mother can give the child in adoption after the death of the father.[14] After the death of the parents, or (if alive) if they have finally and completely renounced the world or have been judicially declared to be of unsound mind, or have abandoned the child, or where the parentage of the child is not known, child's guardian, *de jure* or *de facto*, may give the child in adoption with the prior permission of the court.[15] The guardian can also give the child to himself.[16] The court will not accord permission if the proposed adoption is not for the welfare of the child.[17] It is interesting to note that if parents give the child in adoption, neither the prior permission of the court nor an adoption order is necessary. The adopters cannot give the adopted child in adoption.[18] Only a Hindu child can be adopted[19] and an already adopted child cannot be again taken or given in adoption.[20] The child must be below fifteen years in age and must not be a married child.[21] The same child cannot be simultaneously adopted by more than one person,[22] unless they happen to be husband and wife. Consent of the child is not necessary.

8. Proviso to s. 7 and s. 8(c).
9. Section 11(i).
10. Section 11(ii).
11. Section 11, Clauses (iii) and (iv).
12. Section 9(2).
13. Section 9(3).
14. *Ibid.*
15. Section 9(4).
16. *Ibid.*
17. Section 9(5).
18. Section 10(ii).
19. Section 10(i).
20. Section 10(ii), and s. 13(iv).
21. Clauses (iii) & (v) of s. 10. If a custom permits the adoption a child of fifteen or above, or of a married person, then the adoption will be valid.
22. Section 11(v).

Under Roman law also the adoption was meant primarily to perpetuate one's line by creating artificial relationship. Initially, adoption was a source of power. From Roman law the institution of adoption descended on the Continental countries from where it was taken by the immigrants to the countries of both Americans. Most of the civil codes which accord recognition to adoption basically follow Roman law pattern.

England had known *de facto* adoptions in the latter half of the nineteenth century, though a formal law of adoption was enacted for the first time in 1926. A comprehensive statute of adoption was passed in 1950, which was further modified and consolidated by the Adoption Act, 1958. Then came the Adoption Act of 1968 whose main purpose was to give effect to the Hague Convention on Adoption of Children, 1965, to which England is a party.

Under the English Adoption Acts no adoption can be made without an adoption order from a competent court (i.e. the High Court, the country court or Magistrates' court). A child cannot be simultaneously adopted by more than two persons unless they are husband and wife.[23] An adoption can be made by the father or mother or any other relative of the child only if he or she is at least twenty-one years old.[24] When adoption is made by any other person he or she must be at least twenty-five years old.[25] When husband and wife jointly make an adoption, then each one of them should be at least twenty-one years old.[26] Before an application for adoption is made the child must have been in the care and possession of the adopter continuously at least for a period of three months.[27] The consent of the parent or guardian of the child is necessary,[28] and if one of the spouses is an applicant, the consent of the other spouse is necessary.[29] If the adoption is made in Scotland, then the consent of the child is also necessary.[30] In certain cases the consent may be dispensed with. The consent of the parent or guardian may be dispensed with if he has persistently failed without reasonable cause to discharge the obligation of a parent or gaurdian, or has abandoned, neglected or persistently illtreated the child or cannot be found or is incapable of giving consent or is withholding the consent unreasonably,[31] or that the spouses have separated and are living apart.[32] No adoption can

23. Section 2.
24. Section s. 2(1)(a).
25. Section 2(1)(b).
26. Section 2(2).
27. Section 3.
28. Section 4(1)(a).
29. Section 4(1)(b).
30. Section 4(1).
31. Section 5.
32. *Ibid.*

be made unless the court finds that the proposed adoption is for the welfare of the child.[33]

Jurisdiction

English Law

Ordinarily, an English court has jurisdiction to make an adoption order only if :

(i) the applicant is domiciled in England or Scotland,[34] and

(ii) the applicant and the child reside in England.[35]

In exceptional circumstances the court can make an adoption order even when the applicant and the child are not resident in Great Britain.[36]

Ordinary Jurisdiction : In a normal case the jurisdiction of the court exits only on the satisfaction of twin conditions that the applicant is domiciled in England (this has been considered to be the 'essential foundation of adoption order'[37]) and the child and the applicant are resident in England.[38] It may be noted that the adoption Acts do not require that the child should be domiciled in England. Cheshire feels that this omission may lead to limping adoptions : a child is considered adopted in England. but he may not be so considered in the country of his domicile.[39] The most formidable argument against including the domiciliary test is that it would lead to practical difficulties in making an adoption order. Then, in some cases it may be difficult to find out the domicile of the child, such as in the case of orphans, refugee-children, foundlings or abandoned children. If the court embarks on making enquiries as to child's domicile in many cases it may reach a deadlock. Dicey and Morris very aptly observe : "That does not seem a practical proposition, because . . . an enquiry in the domicile of an infant prior to adoption may often be very difficult and expensive."[40]

In *Re B(S) (an infant)*,[41] where the mother of a Spanish

33. Section 7(i)(b). The factor that the court has to take into account are, health of the applicant, wishes of the child. The court can also make an interim order of adoption giving custody of the child to the applicant for a period of not exceeding two years by way of a probationary period upon such terms and conditions as it may deem fit in the interest of the child; s. 1.
34. Section 1(1).
35. Section 1(5).
36. Section 12.
37. *Re R. (An Infant)*, (1967) 3 All E.R. 629 at p. 652.
38. The meaning of the term 'residence' had already been considered in another context in this work, reference may please be made to the same (See Chapter 9).
39. Cheshire (8th ed.) 449; see also Graveson, pp. 401-402.
40. Dicey and Morris, p. 458.
41. (1968) Ch. 204.

domiciled child wanted to give it in adoption to an English domiciled couple to whom she had entrusted the custody and possession of the child when it was eight days old. For the proposed adoption consent of the father of the child was not obtained. The applicant prayed that the requirement of the consent of the father may be dispensed with as he had not cared for the child at all from its birth. The court considered the views of Dicey and Morris, Cheshire and Graveson. Goff, J., said that the view of Morris is too narrow and that of Cheshire too rigid. While making an adoption order, the learned judge observed that the court is free to take into account the effect of adoption order in Spain. However, the consideration of domiciliary law of the child is purely one of the factors, may be an important one, in determining overall welfare of the child. (In this case there was evidence before the court that the Spanish law will recognize such adoption.) Thus, it seems the proposition that emerges is that in a given case the court is free to take into account the domicile of the child (as it is free to take into consideration many other matters), but the domicile of the child is not a precondition to the exercise of the jurisdiction. This is, it is submitted, a sound view.[42]

Exceptional Jurisdiction: In exceptional cases the English courts may make an adoption order on the application of an English domiciled person who is not resident in England. This concession is given to persons such as colonial civil servants domiciled in England but resident abroad.[43] In terms of s. 12(1), it is not necessary either for the adopter or for the child to reside in England or Scotland. However, it seems that since s. 3(1) requires that the child must have been continuously in the care and possession of the applicant for at least three months immediately before the date of order (unless the child is over the upper age limit of compulsory school age), the care and possession should be in Great Britain. But if the child is over the upper limit of compulsory school age, its three months' residence with the applicant is enough, though out of these three months, one month's residence of the child with the applicant must be in Great Britain.[44]

Provisional Adoption Orders: A unique feature of the Adoption Act, 1958, is that it confers on the court power to make a provisional order of adoption. With the exception of the applicant's domicile, all other conditions relating to adoption laid down in the Act must be satisfied. It should be noted that it is a criminal offence under English law for any person other than a parent, guardian or relative to take or send a child who is a

42. See Cheshire (8th ed.) pp. 450-451. See also *Re R. (Adoption)*, (1966) 3 All E.R. 613; *Re A. (An Infant)*, (1963) 1 All E.R. 531.
43. See *Re Adoption Application* 52/1951, (1952) Ch. 16.
44. But see *Re M. (An infant)*, (1973) Fam. 66 where it has assumed that the care and possession need not be in England, even if the child is very young. See J.D. McClean and K.W. Patchett, English Jurisdiction in Adoptions, 1970 I.C.L.Q. 6-7.

British subject out of Great Britan to any place outside the British Isles with a view to his adoption, whether *de facto* or *de jure*.[45]

Effect of an Adoption Order : Whenever an adoption order is made in respect of a child, its effect is (a) to extinguish all rights, duties and obligations and liabilities of the parents or guardians of the child in relation to its future custody, maintenance and education, and (b) to vest all such rights, duties, obligations and liabilites in the adopter as if the child were a child born to the adopter in lawful wedlock.[46] He becomes a child in his adoptive family or parent and ceases to be a child of his natural family or parent, the same way as under Hindu law.[46a] If the adopter is a citizen of the United Kingdom and Colonies and the child is not, then the child becomes a citizen of the United Kingdom and Colonies from the date of adoption order.[47]

Jurisdictional Rules under Adoption Act, 1968 : An adoption order cannot be made under the Adoption Act, 1968, if the applicant or applicants and the child are United Kingdom nationals and habitually resident in Great Britain or a specified country.[48] In such a case adoption has to be made under the Adoption Act, 1958.

Section 1 of the Adoption Act, 1968, creates a new and additional jurisdictional rule. Under the section a qualified person who is defined as a person who either resides in Great Britain and is a United Kingdom national or a national of a convention country[49] or resides in a convention country or specified country[50] and is a United Kingdom national or a qualified spouse[51] may obtain an adoption order upon an application made in the prescribed manner for the adoption of a qualified infant.[52] It is necessary that the applicant should be a qualified person or a

45. Section 52. See *Re M. (An infant)*, (1973) Fam. 66.
46. Section 13(1). See also the Children Act, 1975.
46a. The Children Act, 1975.
47. Section 19(1).
48. Section 3(2).
49. A convention country means any country where the Convention on Adoption of Children is in force. A declaration by the Secretary of State to that effect is necessary : s. 11(1).
50. A specified country is defined to mean Northern Ireland, Channel Islands, the Isle of Man and a Colony being a country designated by the order of the Secretary of State : s. 11(1).
51. Qualified spouses mean two persons married to each other in a case where (a) both reside in Great Britain and each is a United Kingdom national, or a national of a convention country, or (b) both are United Kingdom nationals and each resides in the United Kingdom, a specified country or a convention country : s. 11(1).
52. The term qualified infant is defined as a person (a) who is under eighteen years of age on such date as the Secretary of State may by order specify and is not and has not been married, and (b) if a United Kingdom national or a national of a convention country resides in Great Britain, specified country or a convention country.

qualified spouse not merely at the time when the application is made but also at the time when adoption is made.[53] Such an adoption order can also be made in respect of a child who is already an adopted child under an adoption order or otherwise.[54]

Thus under the Act adoption can be made by a person who is not a national of the United Kingdom (though in that case he must be a national of a convention country) and not domiciled in any part of the United Kingdom merely on the basis of his residence in the United Kingdom. An adoption can be made merely on the basis of British nationality, even if a person is not resident in England, though in such a case he must be resident in a convention country or specified country. Thus, it would appear, the domicile has lost its importance in English law in respect of adoptions.

The Adoption Act, 1968, further lays down that if the adopter is not a United Kingdom national, then an adoption order shall not be made if the proposed adoption is prohibited by the internal law of the country of which the applicant is a national.[55] A similar restriction has been laid down in respect of a child who is not a national of the United Kingdom. An adoption order cannot be made in respect of a child (a) except in accordance with the provisions, if any, relating to consents or consultations of the internal law relating to adoption of which the infant is national, (b) where the application for adoption is made by one of the two spouses, unless the other spouse consents to the application or the court dispenses with his or her consent.[56] In such cases provisions of consent contained in ss. 4 to 6 of the Act of 1958 do not apply.[57]

Indian Law

Jurisdiction of the Court : In India adoption is recognized among Hindus alone. The Hindu Adoptions and Maintenance Act, 1956, lays down that the adopter as well as the child should be Hindus. Thus, if one of the parent ceases to be a Hindu, then the other parent, or, in case the other parent is dead, the guardian may give the child in adoption. When a parent gives the child in adoption

53. Section 3(5).
54. Section 1(2).
55. Section 3(1); the sub-section further lays down that the provision of the internal law of the country of the nationality of the applicant should be one which is specified in order of the Secretary of State as one notified to the Government of the United Kingdom in pursuance of the provisions of the convention relating to prohibition on an adoption order contained in the national law of the adoptee.
56. Section 3(3) : the consent may be dispensed with if the court is satisfied that the person whose consent is dispensed with cannot be found or is incapable of giving consent or that the spouses have separated and are living apart and that the separation is likely to be permanent : Section 5(4), Adoption Act, 1958.
57. Section 2(4).

no adoption order is necessary. The necessary ceremonies of adoption must be satisfied.[58] The Act does not lay down any requirement of residence, domicile or nationality. A parent who is a Hindu can give the child who is also a Hindu to *any person* if he is a Hindu, irrespective of the fact whether he is an Indian national or alien, or domiciled in India or abroad.

It is only when the child is given in adoption by the guardian, that a court of law comes into picture. A guardian, whether *de jure* or *de facto*, cannot give the child in adoption without the prior permission of the court.[59] The permission can be accorded only by that court within whose jurisdiction the child 'ordinarily resides'.[60] The court will not accord permission for the proposed adoption unless it comes to the conclusion that the adoption will be for the welfare of the child, 'due consideration being for this purpose given to the wishes of the child having regard to the age and understanding of the child'.[61] In no other case the 'residence' or 'ordinary residence' of the child in India is necessary. If all the parties concerned, the natural parent, the child and the adopter, are Hindus then an adoption can take place in India under Hindu law. No other condition as to residence, nationality or domicile is required. Of course, compliance with other provisions of the Hindu Adoptions and Maintenance Act, 1956, is necessary.

Provisional Adoption Orders : Under the Hindu Adoptions and Maintenance Act, 1956, there is no specific provision for making provisional orders of adoption. However, the Madras High Court exercised such a power in *Re Sister Gemma*,[63] under the Guardians and Wards Act, 1890. An unclaimed, destitute and orphan child was sent to one Mercy Home when it was one year old. A French lady domiciled and resident in France expressed a wish to take care of, educate and look after the child and ultimately to adopt it. With this object in view, sister Gemma, in-charge of the Mercy Home, applied for her appointment as guardian of the person of the child and for permission to her to transfer the child to France to be taken care of by the French lady. Making the order, Ismail, J., observed that the most striking feature of the case was that the child was destitute and there was nobody to take care of it or claim it. The learned judge said that under the circumstances it would obviously be for the welfare of the child to make the order as prayed for.

Effect of Adoption : Under Hindu law for all intents and purposes an adopted child is like a natural child. It is removed from its natural family and is transplanted in the adoptive family,

58. Section 11(vi).
59. The court here means the city civil court or a district court : section 9, explanation (ii).
60. Section 9, explanation (ii).
61. Section 9(5).
62. 1970 Mad. 263.

so much so that all its ties with the natural family are severed, except that it cannot marry any female in its natural family whom it could not have married before its adoption. On the other hand, all ties in the adoptive family come into existence as if he is a natural child. He is related not merely to his adoptive parents, he also becomes a brother of the daughter (natural or adopted) of his adoptive parents.[63] He is related to all the relations on the side of his adoptive mother and to all the relations on the side of his adoptive father, to whom he would have been related had he been a natural child.[64] He is prohibited from marrying any relation on his maternal and paternal side whom he could not have married had he been a natural child.[64a] In short, in Hindu law the fiction of adoption is taken to its logical end, so much so that on him are conferred all the rights and privileges of a natural born child in the adoptive family. The same is the position of the adopted daughter. Under Hindu law once an adoption is made it is final and irrevocable. It cannot be cancelled by the adopter or the natural parent. Nor can the adopted child renounce his adoptive parents and return to his natural family.[65]

Recognition of Foreign Adoptions

It appears to be clear that adoption orders made in Scotland under the Adoption Act, 1958, will be recognized in England, as the law of adoption in both countries is regulated by the same statute, under which the jurisdictional requirements in both the countries are the same. The Adoption Act, 1964 makes provisions for recognition of adoptions made in Northern Ireland, Channel Islands and the Isle of Man, and lays down that adoptions made there would be recognized in England and Scotland.

Recognition of Foreign Adoptions under Common Law : Despite the fact that England did not recognize adoptions in its domestic law till 1926, it has accorded recognition to foreign adoptions if the adopter and the child were domiciled in the same country, the law of which permits adoptions. English court have recognized such adoptions without any hesitation since English law has been wedded to the doctrine under which personal status is governed by the *lex domicilii*, only reservation has been that of public policy. It is interesting to note that in *Re Wilby*[66] an English court refused to recognize an adoption valid by the common domocile on the ground that a foreign adoption might be recognized for some purposes but cannot be recognized in respect of English intestacy. The later English decisions[67] have expressed the view

63. Section 12.

64. Section 12(a).

64a. *Ibid.*

65. Section 15. See also author's work, Modern Hindu Law, Codified and Uncodified, Chapter VIII.

66. (1956) p. 174.

67. *Re Marshall*, (1957) Ch. 263, on appeal (1957) Ch. 507, *Re Valentine's Settlement*, (1965) Ch. 831 (C.A.).

that *Re Wilby*[67a] has been wrongly decided.

Some difficulties that have crept up in English law are on account of the tendency to equate adoption with legitimation. Once one succumbs to the temptation one naturally looks for the satisfaction of the twin-test of common law : that is, to the domicile of the adopter and adoptee not merely at the time of the adoption but also at the time of the birth of the child. The fallacy of the argument is obvious. Even then, the difficulty that English law is facing is this : suppose the adopter and adopted child belong to different domicile, then is it necessary that the adoption to be valid in England must be valid by the *lex domicilii* of both ? Or, should it not be enough if it is valid by the *lex domicilii* of the adopter ?

This question came for consideration in Re *Valentine's Settlement*.[68] A South Rhodesian domiciled couple adopted a boy and a girl in South Africa, under an adoption order from South African court. The children were domiciled in South Africa. There was evidence that these adoptions would not be recognized in Rhodesia. The Court of appeal held that the adoptions were not valid. This case lays down that if the adoption is valid by the law of adopter's domicile, then adoption is valid, whatever might be the position at the *lex domicilii* of the child. But, then, is it necessary that the child should be resident of the place where adoption took place. Lord Denning, M.R., in the aforesaid case answered the question in affirmative (*obiter*).[69] This has been approved in a later case.[70] One wonders whether the English courts would be prepared to extend the 'real and substantial connection', test propounded by them in connection with the recognition of foreign divorces, to foreign adoptions.

Recognition under Statute : The Adoption Act, 1968, lays down rules for the recognition of foreign adoptions. These provisions are very complicated.[71] Before we proceed further, meaning of certain terms is necessary to be noted. "Convention adoption" means an overseas adoption of a description as the Secretary of State may by order specify, being a description of adoptions of infants appearing to him to be effected under the law of any country outside Great Britain. "Convention country" means any country (excluding Great Britain and a specified country) for the time being designated by an order of the Secretary of State as a country in which, in his opinion, the Convention is in force. "Nationality" and "habitual residence" are the connecting factors under the Act. In English private international law, nationality

67a. (1956) p. 174.

68. (1965) Ch. 831 (C.A.).

69. *Ibid.* at p. 842.

70. *Re B. (S.)*, (1968) Ch. 204.

71. This legislation is not at all easy to interpret and there are a number of points of very great difficulty : J.D. McClean and K.W. Patchett; English Jurisdiction in Adoption, 1970 I.C.L.Q.R. 1.

as a connecting factor has been full of difficulties. Now that the Act accepts "nationality" as a connecting factor, s. 9 tries to avoid some difficulties. Wherever a person has dual nationality, one of the United Kingdom and the other of another country, he will be treated as a United Kingdom national; if he is a national of a convention country as well as of a non-convention country, then he will be treated as a national of convention country; in other cases he will be treated to be the national of a country with which he is most closely connected; stateless person or persons of doubtful nationality are to be treated as nationals of a country of their habitual residence. "United Kingdom national" is defined as a citizen of the United Kingdom and Colonies satisfying such conditions, if any, as the Secretary of State by order may specify. The term "habitual residence" has not been defined. The Act throughout uses the term "residence", but in interpreting the section it says that residence means "habitual residence".[72] "Specified order" means an adoption order made under any enactment in force in a specified country and corresponding to s. 1 of the Act.[73] "Specified country" means Northern Ireland, Channels Islands, the Isle of Man and a Colony. "Internal law" is defined, in relation to any country, as the law applicable in a case where no question arises as to the law in force in any other country. These definitions are obviously for the purpose of the Act.

If an authority of a convention country or specified country having power to do so under the law of that country passes any order in respect of a convention adoption or specified adoption, of effecting, confirming or terminating it or confirming its termination, then such a determination by the authority concerned shall be effective in England. If the adopter (or adopters, in case of husband and wife) and the adopted child are residing in Great Britain,[74] then the court has power to annul a convention adoption on any one of the following grounds :[75] (a) that at the time when adoption became effective, it was prohibited by the internal law of the country of which the adopter was national (or adopters were nationals); (b) that at the time when the adoption became effective, it contravened the provisions relating to consents to adoption of the internal law of the country of which the adopted person was then a national, if under that law the adoption could then have been impugned on that ground; and (c) that the adoption was invalid on any ground under the law in force in the country where adoption was made.

The High Court or the Court of Session has the power to pass orders that an overseas adoption or a determination of it shall cease to be valid in Great Britain on the ground that the adoption

72. Section 11(1).
73. *Ibid.*
74. Section 7(2).
75. Section 6(1).

or determination is contrary to public policy or that the authority, which purported to authorize adoption or make determination, was not competent to entertain the case.[76] The courts in Great Britain have power to decide the extent, if any, to which a determination has been effected by a subsequent determination.[77] An application for either of the two aforesaid orders must be made in a prescribed manner and within such period as may be prescribed.[78] In no other case can the validity of overseas adoption or determination be challenged in any proceedings before any court in Great Britain.[79]

Any finding of fact made by an authority of a convention country and stated by that authority to be so made for the purpose of determining whether the authority was competent to entertain the case is binding on English court.[80]

When an adopted child whose adoption is made in a convention country becomes legitimated subsequently on account of the marriage of its parents, the court has power, upon the application of the parties concerned, to revoke the adoption.[81] It is necessary that all the concerned must be resident in England at the time an application for revocation of the adoption is made.[82]

Provision for the registration of adoptions is made. The Registrar General is required to register adoption in the Adopted Childern's Register under the Adoption Act, 1958.[83] In the case of a convention adoption he is required to make an entry to that effect.[84]

Indian Law

The Indian law of recognition of foreign adoptions is yet to develop. There is only one reported case in which question has come before Indian courts. In *C.S. Natraja* v. *C.S. Subbaraya*[85] one Shadashive Chettiar died domiciled in Pondichery. His wife Vassavambal who continued to be domiciled there made an adoption to herself and to her husband of a male child aged three years. The question of validity of this adoption came before the Madras High Court. From the decision of the Madras High Court an appeal was preferred to the Privy Council. It was established that

76. Section 6(3)(a).
77. Section 6(3)(b).
78. Section 7(1).
79. Section 6(5).
80. Section 7(3).
81. Section 6(2).
82. Section 7(2).
83. Section 21.
84. Section 8(1).
85. (1949) 54 C.W.N. 200 (P.C.).

under Hindu law as it prevailed in Madras province such an adoption was not valid as the widow had no capacity to adopt to herself. It was also established that under Hindu law as obtaining in Pondicherry a Hindu widow had capacity to make an adoption to herself as well as to her husband. On these facts, the Privy Council observed: "Vassavambal was domiciled in Pondicherry and her capacity to adopt a son to herself and the status of the child so adopted as her adoptive son were matters to be determined in accordance with the law of her domicile, i.e. French law." Thus, the Indian law appears to take the view that an adoption valid by the *lex domicilii* of the adopter will be recognized in India. It seems, the Indian law takes the simple view that an adoption (wherever made) is valid if it is recognized to be valid by the *lex domicilii* of the adopter, whether the adoption is made in the country of the adopter's domicile or in some other country.

Adoption by Foreign Parents

In *Laxmi Kant* v. *Union of India (1)(2)(3)*,[86] the Supreme Court formulated and laid down guidelines for inter-country adoptions. Subsequently, the Government of India laid down guidelines for inter-country adoption in 1995. In *K.S. Council for Child Welfare* v. *Society of Sisters of C.S.G. Convent*,[87] the validity of adoptions was challenged as the same was given to foreign parents in violation of the guidelines. The Supreme Court held that the guidelines should have been followed, but it said that since the children were already abroad and were doing well, the non-observance of guidelines could not be a ground to open the matter and cancel the adoptions.

86. AIR 1984 SC 468; AIR 1986 SC 272; AIR 1987 SC 23.
87. AIR 1994 SC 658.

12

GUARDIANSHIP AND CUSTODY OF MINOR CHILDREN

Introductory

The modern law all over the world is now veering around the proposition that there is a social interest in the protection of childhood; a child is to be accorded protection just because it is a child—its birth within or without the lawful wedlock is hardly a factor to be taken into consideration. The modern world is also accepting, now more readily, that there is a social responsibility to see that every child grows into adulthood as a normal human being without any drawbacks or inhibitions. Guardianship laws of most countries now accept that in all adjudication in respect of children, the uppermost consideration is the welfare of children so much so that even parental rights are subordinated to it.[1]

Guardianship and Custody

Both under the Indian law and English law a natural person below the age of eighteen years is known as minor.[2] The law of guardianship and custody is concerned with minors. Law of guardianship implies the exercise of parental control and care over children by parents or, in their absence or when they are incapable of exercising it, by the guardian. The law of guardianship includes all matters relating to guardianship, such as appointment of guardians, custody, maintenance and education of children, including their care and control as well as access to them. In short, it includes all aspects of upbringing of children. Broadly speaking, the entire law of guardianship may be divided into guardianship and custody. In the English domestic and Indian domestic law,

1. Section 1, Guardianship of Minors Act, 1971, Section 13, Hindu Minority and Guardianship Act, 1956; Kvartshav *v.* Redkova, No. 36/677, (1946) 9 Sud. Park, USSR 4.
2. See Indian Majority Act, 1875, s. 3, para (2). Before 1969 in English law such a person was known as infant and the age of infancy was below twenty-one years. But under the Family Law Reform Act, 1969, such a person is now known as minor and the age of majority has been reduced to eighteen years: s. 1. The English domestic law of guardianship and custody is contained in two Statutes, the Guardianship of Minors Act, 1971 and the Guardianship Act, 1973. In India each community has its own law of guardianship subject to the Guardians and Wards Act, 1869. The Hindu laws of guardianship has been codified in the Hindu Minority and Guardianship Act, 1956.

particularly under the domestic Muslim law,[3] there exists a clear-cut distinction between guardianship and custody. But in private international law this distinction is not yet recognized, either in respect of jurisdiction or in respect of choice of law.[4]

The question of custody can be agitated both in the matrimonial proceedings as well as guardianship proceedings. In the former, as we have seen earlier,[5] the court exercises jurisdiction over children if it has jurisdiction in the petition for matrimonial relief irrespective of the fact whether the child is within the jurisdiction or not, though the court has discretion to decline to exercise jurisdiction. In matrimonial proceedings the question of guardianship does not arise. In guardianship proceedings all matters relating to guardianship and custody can be agitated. This chapter is confined to guardianship and custody proceedings.[6]

It seems to be clear that parental control can be exercised only in accordance with the law of the place where it is purported to be exercised. Thus, a foreign parent desiring to exercise his parental control over the child in India can do so only in accordance with the Indian law. On the other hand, whether or not parent-child relationship exists will be determined by the law of domicile of the parent. It is an established rule of English private international law that a parent domiciled abroad can exercise his parental control over a child in England, whether born of polygamous or monogamous marriage, only in accordance with English law, whenever the English courts have jurisdiction to pass an order in respect of a child.[7]

Domestic laws of India and England enunciate the principle that the sovereign as *parens patriae* is bound to look to the welfare of all children within the jurisdiction. English law extends this principle to all its subjects whether within or without the jurisdiction. This principle of domestic law has undergone some modification in respect of jurisdiction of the court in private international law cases. Therefore, the question that arises is : on what basis the court would assume jurisdiction ? We would proceed to examine the claim of nationality, domicile and residence.

Jurisdiction

Nationality : The continental countries recognize nationality as

3. In Muslim law custody is usually termed as *hizanat*. See *Rudd-ul-Muhtar*, Vol. 11, 1041. See also authors' work, *Parental Control, Guardianship and Custody of Minor Children*, Chapter VII, Guardianship and *Hizanat* under Mohammedan Law, pp. 128-150.
4. In Dicey's seventh edition comments were made separately under two heads, Guardianship and Custody, but this approach has been abandoned in the eighth edition.
5. Chapter 10 of this work.
6. The question of custody, etc. of children has already been discussed in Chapter 9, Part VI.
7. *Re Ullee*, (1886) 54 L.T. 286; *Johnstone* v. *Beatie*, (1843) 10 Cl. & F. 42.

a basis of jurisdiction in family law matters including guardianship and custody. In English common law guardianship has been one of those exceptional cases where domicile as a basis of jurisdiction was substituted by nationality.[8] In 1854, in *Hope* v. *Hope*[9] the court exercised jurisdiction over a minor child who was a British subject and who was removed outside the jurisdiction without the consent of the guardian. In 1965 nationality as a basis of jurisdiction was reiterated by the court in *Re P. (G, E.)*.[10] The English courts have also assumed jurisdiction to appoint a guardian, and make orders for custody, on the basis of nationality of child.[11]

In India the chartered High Courts have all along exercised the same jurisdiction as English courts in respect of guardianship.[12] Clause 37 of the Charter of the Supreme Court at Bombay and Clause 25 of the Charter of the Supreme Court at Calcutta authorized the courts to appoint guardians and keepers for infants and their estates, according to the order and course observed in that part of Great Britain called England. In the same terms the jurisdiction was conferred on the Supreme Court of Madras. The Indian High Courts Act, 1861, which stipulated to establish High Courts at Calcutta, Bombay and Madras, perpetuated this jurisdiction. The Presidency High Courts have all along exercised the jurisdiction in matters of appointing guardians or committing custody of minor children on the basis of the nationality of the minor, irrespective of the fact whether the child or his property was outside jurisdiction.[13] Beaumont, J., said that the jurisdiction of the court was the same as that of the court of Chancery and there were no territorial limits.[14]

The Letters Patent of non-chartered High Courts which were also established by the Indian High Courts Act, 1861, though have no ordinary original jurisdiction, were given extraordinary original jurisdiction in some matters, including guardianship of minors. Most of these High Courts were given same jurisdiction in respect of guardianship and custody of minors as that exercised by the chartered High Courts. For instance, Clause 12 of the Letters Patent of the Allahabad High Court said "shall have like powers

8. Dicey's Conflict of Laws, 8th edn., p. 385.
9. (1854) 4 De G.M. & G. 328.
10. (1965) Ch. 568 (C.A.).
11. *Re Willoughby*, (1885) 30 Ch. D. 324 (C.A.); *Harben* v. *Harben*, (1957) 1 W.L.R. 261; *Hope* v. *Hope*, cited earlier.
12. The High Courts also have inherent jurisdiction, which has been preserved by s. 3, Guardians and Wards Act, 1890.
13. *In re Tarunchandra Ghose*, (1930) 57 Cal. 533; *In re Lovejoy Patel*, 1944 Cal. 433; *In the matter of Kamal Rudra* (1949) 2 Cal. 375; *In re Meakin*, 21 Bom. 137; *In re Ratanji Ramji*, 1941 Bom. 397; *Rajah Vizianagram* v. *Secretary of State*, 1937 Mad. 51; *Annie Beasant* v. *Naryaniah*, 1913 Mad. 159; *Pamela Williams* v. *P.C. Martin* 1970 Mad. 427.
14. *In re Ratanji Ramji*, 1941 Bom. 397.

and authority with respect to the persons and estates of infants, idiots, and lunatics" as that which "is exercised in the Bengal Division of the Presidency of Fort Williams by the High Court of Judicature at Fort Williams in Bengal."[15]

This jurisdiction of these High Courts (the Presidency High Courts and others) has been retained by the Constitution of India.[16]

It is submitted that nationality as a basis of jurisdiction still has some practical utility. The main objection of passing orders on the basis of nationality is that they may not be effective in those cases where the child is outside the jurisdiction. However, in certain circumstances such orders are very useful. For instance if the child comes within the jurisdiction, even on a transitory visit, the order may become enforceable. May be, the courts of the country where the child is residing may recognize such orders and give effect to them.

Domicile : The learned editor of the seventh edition observed, "The English Court will have jurisdiction in regard to British subjects resident abroad only if the infant is domiciled in England. . . this shows that domicile and not nationality is the relevant factor determining this jurisdiction."[17] The only support that the learned editor derives is from certain Scottish decisions,[18] and an *obiter dictum* of Key, J.[19] The matter came for consideration directly in *In re P*: (*G.E.*)[20] and the Court of Appeal unanimously rejected domicile as a basis of jurisdiction. Lord Denning, M.R., said that enquiry in these cases would invariably be that of father's domicile, and it all depends on his intention. "Goodness knows how you are to find that out. . .when did domicile change ? Are you to take his words for it ? If so, he could always defeat the jurisdiction of the court by saying that from the very outset, he intended never to return to England and abandoned his English domicile." In matters relating to minor's domicile, this, his Lordship said, is the most unsatisfactory test.

Fortunately, there is not a single judgment where Indian courts have assumed jurisdiction on the basis of domicile.[21]

15. *Ellen Ram* v. *Charlos Spencer*, 1903 2 A.L.J. 709; *Mst. Haidari Begum* v. *Jwad Ali*, 1934 All. 722.
16. Article 225.
17. Dicey's Conflict of Laws, 7th ed., p. 390.
18. *Ponder* v. *Ponder*, 1932 Scot. Cas. 233; *Kiston* v. *Kiston*, Scot. Cas. 434; *Mc Lean* v. *Mc Lean*, 1947 Scot. Cas. 79. In the United States domicile is a basis of jurisdiction : *Corpus Juris Secundum*, Vol. 15, para 14, p. 912; Beale, Vol. I, p. 115. However, in the United States a clear tendency is discernible to interpret domicile as almost equivalent to ordinary residence.
19. *Brown* v. *Collins*, (1883) 25 Ch. D. 56.
20. (1965) 2 W.L.R. 1.
21. Though in some cases courts have interpreted ordinary residence as meaning domicile, for instance in *Kamla* v. *Bhanumal*, 1956 All. 328 Bhargava, J. said that question of ordinary residence depends upon the intention.

Presence and Residence : The English courts have exercised jurisdiction over minors present within the jurisdiction,[22] even though they were foreign nationals or ordinarily resident abroad. This is because every person present within the realm owes allegiance to the Crown and the Crown as *parens patriae* of all children present within the realm owes a duty to protect them and to look after their welfare.[23] In *re D.*[24] a minor of German nationality, whose parents were believed to be in a Nazi concentration camp, was brought to England and kept in a hostel. From the hostel it was removed and detained by some of the relatives of the child. The court exercise jurisdiction in appointing the guardian on the basis of the presence of the child within the jurisdiction. *Re G.*[25] illustrates the extent to which sometimes English courts have gone in exercising jurisdiction on the basis of mere presence. In this case an illegitimate child born in the United States was made a ward of the court at the instance of mother when the child was passing through England with its putative father to the Soviet Union. However, this was an exceptional case, otherwise it is unusual for the court to exercise jurisdiction[26] on the basis of temporarily or transitory presence of the child within the jurisdiction.

The courts will also not assume jurisdiction if the minor has been brought to England by stealth in violation of the right of a person abroad to have custody or guardianship or in violation of order of a foreign court not to remove the child outside the jurisdiction.[27] It may once again be emphasized that this is not a hard and fast rule and if the welfare of the child requires the court may assume jurisdiction. In *Mckee* v. *Mckee*[28] a child was brought to Ontario in violation of the order of a California court under which custody was committed to mother. In the welfare of the child the Ontario court exercised jurisdiction and committed custody to the father. This decision was upheld by the Privy Council.

The English courts now exercise jurisdiction over a child who is ordinarily resident, though not present, in England. In *re P.*

22. *Johnstone* v. *Beattie* (1843) 10 Cl. & F. 42; *Stuart* v. *Bute*, (1861) 9 H.L.C. 440; *Nugent* v. *Vetzera*, (1866) L.R. 2 Eq. 704; *Re D.*, (1943) Ch. 305; *McKee* v. *McKee*, (1951) A.C. 352 (P.C.). In the countries of continental Europe, courts in some cases exercise jurisdiction on the basis of residence. Most of these countries are members of the Hague Convention on Guardianship of August 12, 1902.
23. *Hope* v. *Hope*, cited above; *In re P.*, (1965) 2 W.L.R. 1, per Denning, M.R.
24. (1943) Ch. 305.
25. *The Times*, December 14, 1956.
26. *Re P.* (G.E.), (1965) 2 W.L.R. 1.
27. *Re H.*, (1969) 1 W.L.R. 381.
28. (1951) 1 All E.R. 942.

(G.E.)[29] a child who was ordinarily resident in England was removed, or rather kidnapped, from England. The child was not a British subject. Exercising the jurisdiction, Lord Denning, M.R., said: "The Crown protects every child who has his home here and will protect him in respect of his home. It will not permit anyone to kidnap the child and spirit it out of the realm. Not even its father or mother can be allowed to do so without the consent of the other. The kidnapper cannot escape the jurisdiction of the court by such strategem."[30] In the context, what will be the ordinary residence of the minor? Lord Denning M.R. said: "So long as the father and mother are *living together in the matrimonial home*, the child's ordinary residence is the home, and it is still his ordinary residence, even while he is away at the boarding school. It is his base, from whence he goes out and to which he returns. When father and mother are at variance and living separate and apart and by arrangement the child resides in the house of one of them—then that home is his ordinary residence, even though the other parent has access and the child goes to him from time to time. I do not see that a child's ordinary residence, so found, can be changed by kidnapping him and taking him away from his home, even if one of the parents is the kidnapper. Quite generally I do not think a child's ordinary residence can be changed by one parent without the consent of the other. It will not be changed until the parent who is left at home childless, acquiesces in the change, or delays so long in bringing proceedings that he or she must be taken to acquiesce. Six months' delay would, I should have thought, go far to show acquiescence. Even three months might be enough in some circumstances. But not less."

In the Report of the Committee on Conflict of Jurisdiction affecting children the test of 'pre-eminent jurisdiction' has been propounded. The 'pre-eminent jurisdiction' does not mean exclusive jurisdiction; the court may have jurisdiction on other basis also. Thus, in some cases jurisdiction, may be assumed on the basis of presence or nationality. But in cases of conflict of jurisdiction, the order passed by the court of pre-eminent jurisdiction must be given due respect. The majority of the Committee was of the view that the court within whose jurisdiction the child 'ordinarily resides' is the court of pre-eminent jurisdiction. The Committee was further of the view that except in a case of emergency, the courts elsewhere should decline to exercise the jurisdiction. The Committee was also of the view that the parties should be permitted to establish jurisdiction by consent. The meaning that the Committee gives to ordinary residence is the same that which is given to it by Lord Denning.[31]

In Custody of Abducted Child

In *Re A and another (Minors) No. 2*[31a] the mother had abducted the children with aquiscence of the father from Australia to England. In English court father applied for the return of the child to Australia. The Court held that after considering all facts and circumstances of the case and welfare of children, it would not be proper for the court to order the return of the children.[31b] *B.* v. *B*[31c] is a

29. Cited above.
30. (1965) 2 W.L.R. 1 at p. 10.
31. Cited above.
31a. (1993) All ER 272.
31b. The Court considered the Convention on Civil Aspects of International Child Abduction 1980 and the Child Abduction and Custody Act, 1985.
31c. (1993) 2 All ER 144 the Court said that it sees no reason not to comply with the mandatory requirement of Article 13 of the Convention.

case where child was abducted by the mother to England from Canada while it was ward of the Canadian Court. The court ordered return of the child to Canada on father's application.[31d]

In *Re G,*[31e] the English Court gave access to the father to the children living in England as per order of Ontario Court. The children were removed to England with consent of Ontario Court.

The Indian High Courts in their ordinary and extraordinary jurisdiction have been exercising jurisdiction over children on the basis of mere presence.[32] This jurisdiction of our High Courts has been preserved by Article 225 of the Constitution. Such jurisdiction was statutorily conferred on some of the High Courts. Thus s. 30 of the Rajasthan High Court Ordinance lays down, "The High Court shall have power and authority with respect to the persons and estate of infants, idiots and lunatics within the state." This jurisdiction was exercised by the Rajasthan High Court in respect of a child who was lodged in the Rajasthan Central jail.[33] The basis on which the District Courts exercise jurisdiction is "ordinary residence" of the minor. In respect of guardianship of person sub-section (1) of s. 9 of the Guardians and Wards Act, 1890 runs as under: "If the application is with respect to the guardianship of the person of the minor, it shall be made to the District Court having jurisdiction in the place where the minor ordinarily resides." The same is the position with respect to custody of minor children.[34] Our courts have often said that the term 'residence' being an elastic word is capable of different construction depending upon the purpose for which and the context in which it is used; its meaning is usually controlled with reference to its object.[35] In *Mst. Lalita* v. *Pramatma Prasad*[36] where the mother of two illegitimate children removed the children from Benares where they were living with their putative father to Shadiabad, Ganganath, J., said, "the fact that a minor is found actually residing at a place at the time of the application is made does not determine the jurisdiction." The learned judge held that the Benares was the place where the children had their ordinary residence. Our courts appear to be clear that ordinary residence is not equivalent to actual residence.[37] But our courts seem to take the view that as between the father and mother, the father has a right to change the ordinary residence of the child, even without the permission or consent of the mother, and if he does so, the new residence will be the ordinary residence of the child.[38] And this has sometimes led them to say that the ordinary residence of the child is the place where the legal guardian resides.[39] In the absence of the father the mother can change the residence of the child.[40] If this means that after the death of the

31d. See also Re 5 (1993) 2 All ER 683: Re T (1993) 3 All ER 127.

31e. (1993) 3 All ER 657.

32. For instance Clause 37 of the Charter of the Supreme Court at Bombay and Clause 25 of the Charter of the Supreme Court at Calcutta authorized the respective courts to appoint guardians and keepers of minors on this basis.

33. *Keswanand* v. *Afrozabegum*, 1958 Raj. 221.

34. *Chimanlal* v. *Rajaram*, 1937 Bom. 158.

35. *Anilbala* v. *Dhirendra*, (1921) 48 Cal. 577.

36. 1940 All. 329.

37. *Chandrakishore* v. *Hemlata*, 1955 All. 611; *Smt. Vimlabai* v. *Babooram*, 1951 Nag. 179.

38. *Ramswaroop* v. *Chimanlal*, 1952 All. 79; *Chandrakishore* v. *Hemlata*, cited above.

39. *Vimlabai* v. *Babooram*, 1951 Nag. 179.

40. *Smt. Kamla* v. *Bhanumal*, 1956. All. 328; *Jamuna Prasad* v. *Mst. Panna*, 1960 All. 285.

father, the place where mother ordinarily resides is the place of the child's ordinary residence, then the proposition is sound. In *Nazir Begum* v. *Ghulam Quadi*[41] till the death of the father the child was residing with its parents at Multan. After the death of the father a relation of the mother with her permission took the child to Bhawalpur and refused to return it. The court rightly held that Multan was the place where the child ordinarily resided. Our courts have also rightly taken the view that if under a separation agreement the custody of the child is entrusted to one of the parents, then the child is ordinarily residing with the parent who has been entrusted with the custody of the child.[42] Our courts have also taken the view that if one of the parents removes the child and the other parent acquiesces in it, then the ordinary residence of the child is the place where the parent had removed the child. In *Bholanath* v. *Shardadevi*[43] where on account of differences between the parties, the wife left her husband's house at Benares with her child to her parent's house at Buxtar. There the child remained for some months, then the father removed it stealthily to Benares. The court held that the child's ordinary residence was at Buxtar. Similarly, if the child is living with a third person, with the acquiescence of the parent, then the ordinary residence of the child will be the place where the child is living with the third person.[44] The removal of the child to another place shortly before an application for guardianship or custody is moved, will not make any difference and the child's ordinary residence will be the place where it was residing before its removal.[45] The Privy Council decision in *Annie Beasant* v. *Narayaniah*[46] can be explained only on the basis of parent's acquiescence in the change of minor's residence. In this case two minors were residing in Chingleput District with their father. With a view to giving good education, the father entrusted their custody to Mrs. Annie Beasant. Mrs. Beasant sent them to Oxford for education. Subsequently, the father filed an application in the District Court of Chingleput for the recovery of the custody. The Privy Council held that it could not be said that the children were ordinarily residing in Chingleput. It is submitted that, if we apply the test propounded by Lord Denning the children's ordinary residence continued to be at Chingleput.

In some cases our courts have taken the view that the ordinary

41. 1937 Lah. 793.

42. *Goman* v. *Munsiram*, (1938) 40 P.L.R. 708; *Harbans Singh* v. *Vidhyawanti*, 1960 Punj. 372; *Jhala Harpal Singh* v. *Bau Arunkunwar*, 1954 Saurashtra 13 (in this case the court expressly negatived the proposition that the ordinary residence of the child is the place where its legal guardian resides). *Mst. Froza* v. *Akhtaruddin*, 1963 Assam 193, *Virbala* v. *Harichand*, 1973 Guj. 1.

43. 1954 Pat. 489.

44. *Sardar Nayar* v. *Vayankara Amma*, Kar. 158; *In re Lovejoy Patel*, 1944 Cal. 158.

45. *Ibid.*

46. 1914 P.C. 41.

residence of the minor is the place where he is found.[47] These are the cases where minor being parentless has no residence at all. After the death of the parents, if the child is brought up by some-one of its relations or in an orphanage or mission, and some one removes it from that place, it would be right to say that the place where the child was living before its removal, is the place of its ordinary residence. In *Robert* v. *Velchand*,[48] after the death of parents, a child along with his brother embraced Christianity and lived for three years in an American Mission at Baroda. Then the brother left the Mission and came to Allahabad to which place he removed the child. Subsequently, the child was brought back to Baroda. On the brother's application for appointment of himself as guardian at the District Court of Ahmedabad, the court held that the ordinary residence of the minor was at Baroda. In *Chimanlal* v. *Rajaram*[49] where an orphan child was living at Kolhapur with its paternal uncle and was later on removed by the maternal uncle to Poona, and lived there for eight months, the court held that the ordinary residence of the minor was Poona. This case can be explained on the basis of acquiescence of the paternal uncle in the removal of the child to Poona.

Then the question arises : as to which place may be treated as a place of ordinary residence of the child in those cases where the child has not lived at any one place but has been living for short durations at several places. In such a case the Bombay High Court has held that the place where the child lived longest may be treated as a place of its ordinary residence.[50] It is submitted that this is an exceptional case. It can also happen that by agreement between parents or under an order of court a child lived for six months with one parent and for six months with another parent. In such cases, the child will have a shifting residence. The parent who is entitled to the custody at the time the proceedings are filed will be the place, it is submitted, where the minor may be deemed to have his ordinary residence. It is submitted that in such cases the place where the person who is entitled to custody of the child resides may be treated to be the residence of the child, provided, of course, the child has been living with him before its removal.

It is submitted that ordinary residence of the minor may be accepted as a basis of jurisdiction internationally, though in exceptional cases, in cases of emergency, jurisdiction may be assumed on the basis of presence or nationality of the child. It should also be accepted that in matters relating to minors the court exercises a large amount of discretion and in a given case it may choose to exercise jurisdiction or it may decline to do so—the welfare of the minor being the paramount consideration.

47. *Robert* v. *Velchand*, (1909) 34 Bom. 121.
48. Cited above.
49. 1937 Bom. 158.
50. *Lakshman* v. *Gangaram*, 1932 Bom. 592.

The Supreme Court in *Surinder Kaur Sandhu* v. *Harbux Singh Sandhu*[51] reiterates the principle that welfare of the children is of the paramount consideration. The parents of the child, a boy, were married in India but went to England which country they made their home. The child was born to them in England. The father tried to get the mother of the child murdered for which offence he was convicted by an English Court. The mother obtained a probation order for him, but he abused her magnanimity and ran away to India with the boy. The mother obtained a custody order from the Family Division of the High Court under which the father was ordered to handover the custody of the child to mother or her agent forthwith. Armed with this order, the mother filed a writ petition in the Punjab and Haryana High Court, which came to the conclusion, it would be for the welfare of the child if he were allowed to live in India which was his own country; in this way the child would grow in an atmosphere of self-confidence and self-respect. The court also observed that the paternal grandparents of the child were in affluent circumstances and the traumatic experience of the father in a criminal charge must have chastened him. The Supreme Court reversed these findings and held that under the circumstances it would be in the interest of the child to be committed to the custody of the mother. The Court felt that the traumatic experience of the father of a conviction on a criminal charge was not a factor in his favour especially when his conduct following immediately upon his release on probation showed that experience had not chastened him. Further, the affluence of the grandfather, the court observed, could not be a factor of such importance as to tilt the balance in favour of the father on the question of what was truly for the welfare of the minor.

On the question of jurisdiction of the English court over the matter, Chandrachud, C.J. observed (and in our submission these are very important observations) :

> The modern theory of conflict of Laws and, in any event, prefers the jurisdiction of the State which has the most intimate contract with the issues arising in the case . . . . That is to say, for example, that in matters relating to matrimony and custody, the law of that place must govern which has the closest concern with the well being of the spouses and the welfare of the offsprings of the marriage.

In this case, the parties have clearly established their matrimonial house in England, and the fact that the child was not in England (in fact the child was deceitfully taken away from the jurisdiction) would not deprive the court of its jurisdiction. On the other hand, the mere presence of the child in India would not give jurisdiction to the Indian Court.

51. 1984 S.C. 1224 : this case was followed in *Isabell* v. *Ram Singh*, 1985 Raj. 30.

Choice of Law

So far the English courts have taken the position that whenever they have jurisdiction in matters relating to guardianship and custody, they apply the English domestic law.[51a] They have declined to apply the law of domicile,[52] and it seems that they would also not apply the law of nationality.

In Indian law there is no direct decision on the question of choice of law, but it seems to be clear that our courts have been applying *lex fori.* In India the *lex fori* is, apart from the Guardians and Wards Act, 1890, the personal law of the child. It is submitted that if we should accept ordinary residence as the basis of jurisdiction, unless its application is not in the welfare of child.

II

RECOGNITION AND ENFORCEMENT OF FOREIGN GUARDIANSHIP AND CUSTODY ORDERS

At one time English courts held the view that a foreign order of appointment of guardian in regard to a minor residing in England would not be given any effect.[53] Although English courts still adhere to the principle that welfare of children is paramount consideration and although they still adhere to the rule that orders relating to children are not final and can be changed at the discretion of court on change of circumstances, they have abandoned the extreme position of not giving effect to any foreign order of gua rdianship or custody. However, this does not mean that foreign orders will be given effect without scrutiny. The essential and paramount fact before the court is still the promotion of the welfare of children which is the uppermost consideration, to which consideration all others yield. In *Staurt* v. *Bute*,[54] where recognition to foreign guardianship order was given, the court said: "There is but one object which ought to be kept strictly in view and that is the interest of the infant."[55]

The present position in English law seems to be that English courts ordinarily give effect to foreign guardianship orders, though foreign custody orders are scrutinized more closely and examined on the touchstone of welfare of children more rigourously.

Foreign Guardianship Orders: Explaining the decision of *Johnstone* v. *Beattie*,[56] House of Lords in *Stuart* v. *Bute*[57] said that

51a. *Johnstone* v. *Beattie*, (1843) 10 Cl. & F. 42; *Re R.'s Settlement*, (1940) Ch. 54; *McKee* v. *McKee*, (1951) A.C. 352 (P.C.).

52. *Johnstone* v. *Beattie*, cited above.

53. *Ibid.*, where an order of Scottish court appointing a guardian was ignored by the English court.

54. (1861) 9 H.L.C. 440.

55. *Ibid.*, at p. 469.

56. (1843) 10 Cl. & F. 42.

57. (1861) 9 H.L.C. 440.

decision does not imply that foreign guardians would be totally ignored in England and would be regarded as strangers who could not do anything even if their ward was kidnapped. In the absence of a guardian appointed by English courts, foreign guardians would be recognized in England. In case the position of a foreign guardian is not contested in England, he would be allowed to exercise his powers.[58] English courts still take this position that if an application for appointment of a guardian is moved in an English court, the English court would not recognize or appoint a foreign guardian as a matter of course, though would take into account his claim for appointment of guardian.[59] This is because of the adherence to the principle that "the welfare of children is the paramount consideration . . . the benefit of the infant, which is the foundation of jurisdiction, must be the test of its right exercise."[60]

In *Nugent* v. *Vetzera*[61] an Austrian court had appointed one Vetzera as guardian of ten children whose both parents were dead. Mother of the children was an English woman and father was an Austrian. The Austrian court had ordered that all children should be educated and brought up in the father's religion and they should be educated in Vienna. At that time five of them were receiving education in England in various schools. In pursuance of the order of the Austrian court Vetzera wanted to remove these children to Vienna. A sister of the children who had married an Englishman and who was living in England being against the removal of children to Vienna moved the English court and applied for the children to be made ward of court. In these proceedings the English court appointed two Englishmen as guardians of these children. Vetzera filed an appeal and prayed that English guardians be ordered to deliver the custody of children to him. Passing the orders in favour of Vetzera as prayed for the court observed that it would not interfere with the discretion of duly appointed foreign guardian who wanted to take the children to Vienna in order to complete their education. The court further said that it was not abandoning its own jurisdiction but it had no desire to interfere in the discretion of foreign guardian on the basis of any supposed benefit to children.

The English courts have non-abandoned their hesitation of giving effect to foreign guardianship orders. In *Monaco* v. *Monaco*,[62] the only question that court considered was as to who was the guardian of the child under the Monegasque law, the law of the nationality of the child. In this case there was no guardian of the child appointed by an English court, nor was the child ward of

58. *Nugent* v. *Vetzera*, (1866) L.R. 2 Eq. 704.
59. *Johnstone* v. *Beattie*, cited above.
60. *Ibid.*, at p. 463.
61. *Nugent* v. *Vetzera*, cited above.
62. (1937) 157 L.T. 231.

the court. In *Re H.*[63] a New York court had passed custody orders in respect of a child. The mother of the child removed the child to England without the permission of father or of the New York court. The New York court had already passed orders asking mother to return the child to the father. In proceedings before an English court, the court said that in our contemporary world kidnapping of the child from one jurisdiction to another has became very common and it was the duty of the courts in every country not to allow the kidnapper to reap the benefit of his misdeeds. The court passed orders in favour of the father allowed him to remove the child to New York. Affirming this view in *Re E.*[64], the Court of Appeal said that in the welfare of children the court is not bound to honour and give effect to every order of the foreign court. In *Re T.*[65] the court again expressed the same view.

It may also be treated to be the established rule of English private international law that foreign guardian can exercise those powers which are allowed to him to exercise under English domestic law.[66]

As regards the foreign guardian's powers over the ward's property situated in England, it appears that the guardian's power of disposal should be regulated by the law of the country to which he owes his appointment as guardian.[67] "However, where there is a fund in court, the court need not order payment out of it to a foreign guardian as a matter of right but may, if it thinks fit, require proof that the fund will be duly applied by the guardian."[68] As in other matters here also the English courts adhere to the principle of welfare of children.

Foreign Custody Orders : It seems that the position of the persons in whose favour a custody order has been made by a foreign court and whose position is not challenged before an English court is the same as that of the foreign guardian, *viz.*, they can exercise their right in the same manner and with the same limitations as foreign guardians. But in case their position is challenged in English courts, then the courts have invariably exercised the wide powers conferred on them under s. 1, Guardianship of Minors Act, 1971. In other words, they have not hesitated in the least in passing new orders on the basis that the welfare of the child is the paramount consideration; they have done so even if the order

63. (1966) 1 W.L.R. 381.
64. (1967) 2 All E.R. 881.
65. (1968) 2 All E.R. 441.
66. *Johnstone* v. *Beattie*, cited above.
67. Dicey and Morris, p. 396. This observation has been made on the basis of *Mackie* v. *Darling*, (1871) L.R. 12 Eq. 319; *Re Crichton's Trust*, (1855) 24 L.T. O.S. 267. See also, *Re Brow'n Trust*, (1865) 12 L.T. 488.
68. Dicey and Morris, p. 396; see also Cheshire, (7th ed.) p. 391. *Mackie* v. *Darling*, (1871) L.R. 12 Eq. 319; *Re Crichton's Trust*, (1855) 24 L.T. O.S. 267. See also, *Re Brown's Trust*, (1865) 12 L.T. 488.

of the foreign court is an order of competent court.[69] The Privy Council in *McKee* v. *McKee*[70] observed : "Such an order (foreign custody order) has not the force of foreign judgment. Comity demands not its enforcement, but its grave consideration. This distinction . . . rests on the peculiar character of jurisdiction and the fact that an order providing for custody of an infant cannot be in its nature final."[71]

Such a grave consideration to a foreign order was given by the English court in *Re H.*[72] where a child of foreign nationality was removed to England in defiance of a foreign order; the court gave effect to the foreign order.[73] The circumstances under which the court deemed it fit to do so were : the injustice done to the parent who was entrusted with the custody in consequence of the removal of the child, England was not the *forum conveniens*, and the danger of proceedings being protracted as the witnesses and other evidence may be called from abroad and consequent danger of the child being rooted in England.

There is yet no direct authority as to which foreign court has jurisdiction to appoint guardians. The guardians appointed by the country of which the minor is a national has been given effect to in England and therefore it seems that the courts of the nationality of the minor have jurisdiction to appoint guardian internationally. Since the Court of Appeal has propounded the test of ordinary residence of the child as a basis of jurisdiction of English courts, it is submitted the English private international law would recognize the orders of the courts of the country where the child is ordinarily residing. If the courts of the country of the nationality or ordinary residence of the minor would recognize the orders passed by the courts of any other country, then, (as elsewhere) the English courts would accord recognition to the orders of such courts.

There is another question also : should the foreign courts have jurisdiction at the time when the proceedings are begun or should it have jurisdiction when the order is passed ? It is submitted that it should have jurisdiction all throughout the proceedings.

Indian Law

In respect of recognition of foreign custody and guardianship orders the Indian law is in its formative stage. These are few Indian precedents and in practically of all them the decision has been rendered on

69. *Re B's Settlement*, (1940) Ch. 54; *Re Kernot*, (1965) Ch. 217. The Privy Council took this view in *McKee* v. *McKee*, (1951) A.C. 352.
70. (1951) A.C. 352.
71. *Ibid.*, at p. 365.
72. (1966) 2 All E.R. 886.
73. Detailed facts of the case have been given earlier.

the basis of English precedent. In *Margrett* v. *Chakoo*[74] the Kerala High Court rendered the decision on the basis of *Re H.*,[75] *Re E.*,[76] and *Re T.*[77] An Indian Christian domiciled in India went to West Germany for higher studies and married there a German domiciled woman. Two children, a boy and a girl, were born of this marriage. But the marriage broke down and the mother obtained a decree of divorce from a German court and also an order of custody of children in her favour. Subsequently, defying the order of the German court, he flew to India with the children. He did not inform the mother of the children either before leaving Germany or after arriving in India. However, the mother was able to trace the whereabouts of the children and came to India and filed an application for custody of children and for permission to take the children out of India. Nair, J. of the Kerala High Court said the court would recognize the German order of custody and give effect to it, as to do so would be in the welfare of children. In *Elizabeth Dinshow* v. *Arvind*,[78] on similar facts the Supreme Court took the same view. The Supreme Court quoted with approval Willmer L.J. join *Re H Infants*:[79] the sudden and authorized removal of children from one country to another is far too frequent these days, if and as if seems to me, it is the duty of all Courts in all countries to do all that they can to ensure that the wrongdoer does not gain an advantage by their wrongdoing. The same view Punjab and Haryana High Court took in *Mrs. Kuldeep Sidhu* v. *Charan Singh*.[80]

This writer would submit that courts should accord recognition and give effect to a foreign custody or guardianship order passed by a court of competent jurisdiction, i.e., the court of minor's nationality or ordinary residence, unless it is found manifestly to the disadvantage of the minor.[81]

74. 1970 Ker. 1. See also *Surinder Kaur* v. *Harbax Singh*, AIR 1984 S.C. 1224.
75. (1966) 2 All. E.R. 886.
76. (1967) 2 All. E.R. 881.
77. (1968) 3 All. E.R. 441.
78. ILR (1984) 1 P. & H. 1.
79. AIR 1987 S.C. 3.
80. AIR 1985 P. & H. 103.
81. See author's work, Law of Parental Control, Guardianship and Custody of Minor Children, Chapter XXXII, pp. 611-12.

Part IV
LAW OF PERSONS

SUMMARY

13

CORPORATIONS

Most domestic systems of law confer artificial or legal personality on certain entities, of which the corporations are the most obvious and common instance. Once an entity is considered to be a legal person, it is natural and logical to attribute it the most of the characteristics of a natural person. The private international law too is as much concerned with artificial persons as with natural persons. It may appear somewhat forced and strained to talk of birth, death, rights, obligations, liabilities, etc. of an artificial person, but all this has to be talked and (more important) determined. Just as to determine the status, capacity. etc. of a natural person, his connection with a particular system of law has to be known, similarly to determine the status, capacity, rights, liabilities and obligations of an artificial person, it is necessary to know its connection with a particular system of law. It is also necessary to know the domicile, nationality and residence of a company as they are as much connecting factors in its case as they are in the case of a natural person.

Domicile

Under private international law, status, capacity, etc., of a company are determined by the law of its domicile. Just as a natural person gets, by operation of law, a domicile by birth, similary an artificial person gets a domicile at the time of its birth. This domicile of origin in the case of a company is the country where it has been created, i.e. the place or country of its incorporation. Thus, a company formed under the English Companies Act, 1948, has an English domicile if it is registered in England, and a Scottish domicile, if registered in Scotland. Similarly, a company incorporated under the Indian Companies Act, 1956, will have an Indian domicile. Conversely, the Indian and English private international laws take the view that a company (even if the predominant shareholders in it are Indians and Englishmen) incorporated under a foreign law, such as under the law of Bangladesh, Pakistan or France, will have a Bangladesh, Pakistani or French domicile, irrespective of the fact as to where it is regarded to be domiciled by Bangladesh, Pakistan and France. In

Lazard Bros. v. *Midland Bank Ltd.*[1] Lord Wright observed : "English courts have long since recognized as juristic persons, corporations established by foreign law in virtue of the fact of their creation and continuance under and by that law . . . . But if the creation depends on the act of the foreign state which created them, the annulment of the act of creation by the same power will involve the dissolution and non-existence of the corporation in the eyes of English law. The will of the sovereign power which created it can also destroy it."[2] In *Re Travancore National etc. Bank Ltd.*[3] Rao, J., on the other hand, said that the domicile of a company is the place considered by the law to be the centre of its affairs which in the case of (i) a trading company is its principal place of business, i.e. the place where the administrative business of the corporation is carried, and (ii) in the case of other corporations, it is the place where its functions are discharged. This is based on the old edition of Dicey's Conflict of Laws, and, it is submitted, no longer considered to be the test of domicile.[4] This is in fact a criterion of residence. The test of domicile of a company is the same under the Indian law as it is under the English law. The basic distinction between the domicile of a natural person and domicile of a corporation is that the domicile of origin or the domicile of birth in respect of a company clings to it all throughout, and it cannot have a domicile of choice.[5] It should be kept in mind that the domicile of the company is entirely distinct and independent of the domicile of its members or shareholders. The fact that majority of shareholders of a company are Indians will not make it an Indian domiciled company, if it has been incorporated elsewhere.

Apart from the companies, in some countries certain institutions, foundations and bodies are regarded as juristic persons. For example, in some European countries unincorporated partnerships are clothed with legal personality. In Indian law Hindu idols,[6] Hindu *maths* and certain religious and charitable institutions[7] and foundations are regarded as juristic persons. It is submitted for the purpose of private international law such bodies and foundations and institutions should also be recognized as juristic persons.[8]

Capacity and Internal Matters of a Corporation : Ordinarily every company functions subject to the following two limitations

1. (1933) A.C. 289.
2. *Ibid.* at p. 297.
3. (1939) Mad. 318.
4. Conflict of Laws (Third edition).
5. *Gasque* v. *Inland Revenue Commissioner*, (1940) 2 K.B. 80.
6. *Pramath Nath* v. *Pradyumaya Kumar*, (1925) I.A. 245.
7. See *Manohar* v. *Lakhiram*, (1888) 12 Bom. 247; *D.A.V. College* v. *S.N.A.S. Higher Secondary School*, 1972 P. & H. 245 (F.B.). See also Mukherjea, Hindu Law of Religious and Charitable Trusts, (2nd Ed.) p. 265.
8. *Von Hellfeld* v. *Rechnitzer & Mayer Freres & Co.*, (1914) 1 Ch. 748.

on its capacity : (a) The limits of the capacity of a company are laid down in its constitution. No company has capacity to go beyond these limitations and in case it does something in access of its powers, the doctrine of *ultra vires* applies. For instance, if a corporation has come into being for purchase of land, for making housing plots and for selling them, then the corporation has no power to construct houses. (b) The limits on the capacity of a company may also be imposed by the laws of the place where it is functioning. For example, the law of the country where the company is operating may fix land ceiling, then a land-holding corporation cannot hold land in access of the ceiling, even though the corporation was established with the avowed purpose of establishing big agricultural farms. Subject to these limitations, the law of the domicile of the company governs not only matters relating to its constitution and dissolution and but also all other internal matters. Thus, the extent and limitations of the liability of its members, as distinct from its own liability, what transactions are *ultra vires* or *intra vires* of its powers, whether the director or someone else would represent it in legal proceedings, its internal constitution, its relationship with its members and relationship of members *inter se*, powers of alienation of its property, its merger with another company, and like matters are governed by the law of domicile.[9] *National Bank of Greece and Athens* v. *Metliss*[10] provides a good illustration of this. The National Mortgage Bank of Greece and Athens issued some sterling mortgage bonds in 1927. The principal amount of bonds was payable in 1957. The National Bank of Greece stood guarantee for the bonds. It was also stipulated that all questions arising between the Bank and the bond-holders were to be settled by arbitration in London in accordance with English law. The bank did not pay any interest after 1941. A 1949 decree of the Greek Government imposed moratorium suspending all obligations and right of action on bonds. In 1953 another decree dissolved the guarantor bank and amalgamated it and the Bank of Athens into a new banking company called the National Bank of Greece and Athens. The decree also made this Bank as the "universal successor" to the rights and obligations of the amalgamated banks. A bond-holder brought an action in an English court for the recovery of interest due on bonds after 1941 against the Bank of Athens which had traded in England before its amalgamation and had acquired assets which were still in England. The main contention of the plaintiff was that the defendant was the successor to the obligations of the now defunct guarantor bank. It was the admitted position that the English court was bound to recognize the Greek dissolution of the banks as well as the coming into

9. *Carl Zeiss Stiftung* v. *Rayner & Keeler Ltd.*, (No. 2) (1966) 3 W.L.R. 125; and (No. 3) (1970) Ch. 506; *A.G. der Manufacturen etc.* v. *Fredrick Huth & Co.*, (1928) 79 L.I.L.R. 262n; *C.H. Dreyfus* v. *Commr. of Inland Revenue*, (1959) Ch. 672.

10. (1958) A.C. 509.

existence of the new amalgamated bank. The only arguable question was whether the English court would recognize the doctrine of "universal successor" as there is nothing similar to it in English domestic law? The court held that it would recognize the liability of the successor bank, since the same is recognized by the law of domicile of the defendant bank.

It appears to be settled law that just as company's incorporation is determined by the law of its domicile so also its dissolution and winding up[12] as well as the amalgamation of companies.[13]

Winding up of the Company: Under the Companies Act, 1948, an English court has jurisdiction to wind up (i) any company registered in England, and (ii) any unregistered company which has some commercial subject-matter connected therewith situated in England.[14]

In respect of companies registered in England, the English court has jurisdiction to wind it up, even though the company is formed to carry on business abroad, or consists of entirely or dominantly of foreigners.[15] But if a company is registered in Scotland, the jurisdiction to wind it up vests exclusively in the appropriate Scottish courts.[16] If a company is registered in Northern Ireland, the English courts may have jurisdiction to wind it up in one case, *viz.*, when it had carried on business in Great Britain which it had ceased to carry on at the time of its winding up. Under the Companies Act, 1948, an unregistered company includes a company incorporated outside the United Kingdom.[17] Like any other unregistered company it may be wound up in the following circumstances:[18] (a) if the company is dissolved, (b) if the company has ceased to carry on business, (c) if the company is carrying on business only for the purpose of winding up its affairs, (d) if company is unable to pay its debts, and (e) if the court is of the opinion that it is just and equitable that the company should be wound up. Until 1951, the English court took the view that for the exercise of jurisdiction over the foreign companies another condition was also necessary, namely, the company must also have a place of business in England. In 1951, the Court of appeal held that the existence of place of business in England for the exercise of jurisdiction was not necessary, but, the English court may decline to exercise it for the winding up of a foreign company,

11. See also, *Metliss* v. *National Bank of Greece and Athens*, (1957) 2 Q.B. 33 at p. 46; see also *Adams* v. *National Bank of Greece and Athens*, (1961) A.C. 255.
12. *Lazard Bros.* v. *Midland Bank*, (1933) A.C. 289.
13. *National Bank of Greece and Athens* v. *Metliss*, (1958) A.C. 509.
14. Chapter 21.
15. *Reuss* v. *Bos.*, (1871) L.R. 5 H.L. 176.
16. Section 220(1), Companies Act.
17. Section 398.
18. Section 399(5).

if it does not have in England 'some commercial subject-matter', upon which order could operate.[19] No precise definition of 'commercial subject-matter' has yet been given. It is submitted that if the foreign company has some assets—whatever be their value—situated in England, it would amount to its having 'commercial subject-matter' situated in England.[20] It is immaterial that claimants or potential claimants are foreigners or English.[21]

In the exercise of this jurisdiction, the court has a discretion and in a given case it may decline to exercise jurisdiction. Thus, if winding up proceedings are already going on in the court of the domicile of the company, the English court would decline to exercise jurisdiction.[22]

If a foreign company had already been dissolved in the country of its domicile, the question is: Whether winding up proceedings could be filed in respect of it in England? It seems that English courts have jurisdiction to do so under s. 399(5), Companies Act, 1948. Under s. 400 of the Companies Act, 1948, the court has discretion to make a winding up order where a foreign company "has been carrying on business in Great Britain... notwithstanding that it has been dissolved or otherwise ceased to exist as company". There is no reported case in which an order has been made under this section. The reason seems to be the very wide ambit of s. 399(5) (a). Section 400, it seems, has been added by Parliament as *ex abundanti cautela*.[23]

On dissolution of a foreign company its assets vest in the Crown as *bona vacantia*. When this happens, the legal requirement that the foreign company should have some 'commercial subject-matter' upon which the order can operate is satisfied by treating the title of the Crown as a defeasible one which is defeated when the order is passed. Then the assets revest in the revivified company.[24] A creditor whose debt has been abrogated on account of dissolution of the company has been allowed to petition for an order of winding up of the company,[25] even though in consequent liquidation of the company it might be shown that the debt was irrecoverable for reasons which are legally independent of the dissolution.[26]

The winding up of a company is governed by the English law.

19. *Banque des Marchands de Moscou* v. *Kindersley*, (1951) Ch. 112 (C.A.).
20. See *Ibid.*
21. *Re Azoff-Don Commercial Bank*, (1954) Ch. 315.
22. *Re Matheson Bros.*, (1884) 27 Ch. D. 225.
23. *Banques Des Merchands de Moscou* v. *Kindersley*, (1951) Ch. 112.
24. *Re Azoff-Don Commercial Bank*, (1954) Ch. 315; *Russian & English Bank* v. *Barling Bros.*, (1936) A.C. 405; *Re Banque Industrielle de Moscou*, (1952) Ch. 919.
25. *Re Russian and English Bank*, (1932) 1 Ch. 663.
26. See Dicey and Morris, pp. 490-491; See also cases cited in the preceding footnote.

The result of the winding up order is the termination of company's beneficial interest in its property. It is incumbent on the liquidator to take into his custody or control all the properties to which the company is or appears to be entitled to,[27] though the order may provide that the liquidator is not to take into his custody or control assets situated outside England. The foreign winding up order has no effect except that the liquidator duly appointed by the foreign order can act on behalf of the corporation in England. Once a winding up order is made, no action or proceeding against the company can be continued or filed without leave of the court.[28]

Indian Law

Under the Indian Companies Act, 1956, the Indian courts have jurisdiction to entertain winding up proceedings in respect of the following two categories of companies : (a) when the company has been incorporated in India, and (b) when it is an unregistered company.[29] In respect of the former the Indian courts have jurisdiction irrespective of the fact that the entire business of the company is carried on abroad, or that all its members are foreigners. In such winding up proceedings, Indian as well as foreign creditors can prove their debts.[30] Part X of the Indian Companies Act deals with the winding up of the unregistered companies. Under the Act, an unregistered company is defined as ; "For the purpose of this Part, the expression 'unregistered company' (a) shall include (i) a railway company incorporated by any act of Parliament or other Indian law or any act of Parliament of the United Kingdom; (ii) a company registered under this Act; or a company registered under any previous company law and not being a company the registered office whereof was in Burma, Aden, or Pakistan immediately before the separation of that country from India, and (b) save as aforesaid, shall include any partnership, association or company consisting of more than seven members at the time when the petition for winding up the partnership, association or company, as the case may be, is presented before the court."[31] Section 584 of the Act relates to dissolved foreign companies. That section runs : "Where a body corporate incorporated outside India which has been carrying on business in India ceases to carry on business in India, it may be wound up as an unregistered company under this Part, notwithstanding that the body corporate has been dissolved or otherwise ceased to exist as such under or by virtue of the law of the country under which it was incorporated."

27. Section 243(1).
28. Section 231. See also *Re Dynamics Corporation of America*, (1973) 1 W.L.R. 63. See also s. 226.
29. Part X of the Indian Companies Act.
30. *Rajah of Vizianagram* v. *Official Receiver and Liquidator*, 1962 S.C. 500.
31. Section 582.

The foreign companies fall within the meaning of unregistered companies. A bank incorporated in a foreign country is an unregistered company and winding up proceedings can be filed in India.[32] Winding up proceedings in respect of a foreign company not falling under section 584 of the Companies Act can be filed under s. 582 as an unregistered company. In *Mohan Lal* v. *Chawla Bank Ltd.*,[33] before partition of India, a company incorporated under the Indian Companies Act, 1913, had its registered office in North Western Frontier Province and a branch office in the United Provinces. After partition it got itself registered as a foreign company. It was obvious, and it was so held, that for the purpose of s. 582 its position was that of an unregistered company. A foreign company carrying on business in India can be wound up as an unregistered company under s. 582 of the Act.[34] And the Indian courts have jurisdiction to wind up a foreign company whatever be the number of its members, provided it has assets and an office in India.[35] It would make no difference, even if an order for its winding up has been made by a court of competent jurisdiction of the place of the company's domicile.[36] However, just because a winding up order has been made by the court of domicile of a foreign company, it does not mean that the Indian courts are bound to entertain its winding up proceedings. The court may decline to exercise jurisdiction on practical considerations.[37]

Sub-section (4) of s. 588 lays down the circumstances in which a foreign company may be wound up. These are : (i) if the company is dissolved, or has ceased to carry on business, or is carrying on business only for the purpose of winding up its affairs; (ii) if the company is unable to pay its debts, (iii) if the court is of the opinion that it is just and equitable that the company should be wound up.[38] It appears that the Indian court will have jurisdiction to entertain a petition for the winding up of an unregistered company only if it has "place of business" in India.[38a] Part XI of the Company Act, 1956 lays down provisions for the establishment of place or places of business in India by a foreign company. These provisions are made to regulate the activities of foreign companies operating in India.

32. *Re Travancore National Bank Ltd.*, 1939 Mad. 318; *Raghubardayal* v. *The Sarafa Chambers*, 1954 All. 555.

33. 1949 All. 778.

34. *Rajah of Vizianagram* v. *Official Receiver*, 1962 S.C. 500; *Re River Steam and Navigation Co. Ltd.*, (1967) 71 Cal. W.N. 854.

35. *Re Travancore National Bank Ltd.*, 1939 Mad. 318; *In re Frontier Bank Ltd.*, 1951 Punj. 145; *In the matter of Indian Companies Act*, 1913, 1949 Lah. 48 (for contrary view).

36. *Ibid.*

37. *Re Travancore National etc. Bank*, 1939 Mad. 318.

38. *In the Matter of Equitable Assurance Society*, 2 I.C. 164.

38a. Section 583(2).

It appears that an Indian court may decline to exercise jurisdiction over a foreign company if it has no assets situated in India.

Application for winding up can be made not only by any creditor and contributor but also by the company itself.[39] Section 583(3), Indian Companies Act, however, lays down that no unregistered company shall be wound up under the Act voluntarily or subject to the supervision of the court. Winding up of the company can be initiated at the instance of Indian as well as foreign creditors.[40]

The winding up of the company under the Indian Companies Act is entirely governed by the Indian law. The court has power by the winding up order or by any subsequent orders to direct that 'all or any part of property, movable or immovable, belonging to the company or held by trustees on its behalf shall vest in the official liquidator by his official name and thereupon the property or part thereof specified in the order shall vest accordingly'.[41]

Nationality

The nationality of a corporation is seldom relevant in cases of conflict of laws. A company is regarded as the national of the country in which it is incorporated.[42] Under the law of most of the Continental countries a corporation is national of the country where its centre of management exists.[43]

Residence

Residence of an artificial person is important, mostly, for the income-tax purposes. Both under the Indian law and the English law, income-tax is levied on a person who is 'resident in India or the United Kingdom respectively.'[44] A person who is a resident of India has the liability to pay income tax, whether the income is derived from the Indian source or foreign sources. The same is the position under English law.

The question of residence of a natural person probably does not present so much of a problem as does the question of the

39. *State of Madras* v. *Madras Electric Tram. Co.*, 1956 Mad. 131; *Rajah of Vizianagram* v. *Official Receiver*, 1962 S.C. 500.

40. *Rajah of Vizianagram* v. *Official Receiver*, 1952 Mad. 136, confirmed in 1962 S.C. 500.

41. Section 588(1).

42. See *Janson* v. *Driefontein Consolidated Mines Ltd.*, (1902) A.C. 484 (for English law) and *Dickie & Co.* v. *Municipal Board*, 1956 Cal. 216 (for Indian law).

43. See Wolff, p. 308.

44. There seems to be no difference in this respect between 'residence' and 'ordinary residence'; *Levene* v. *I.R.C.*, (1928) A.C. 217; *Union Corporation* v. *I.R.C.*, (1953) A.C. 483. See also s. 468 of the English Income Tax Act, 1952 and s. 6, Indian Income Tax Act, 1961.

residence of an artificial person like company. It is because a company may be doing business in more than one country and consequently it may have business offices in several countries It should be noted that in the case of a company, domicile and residence are not the same things. There may be a corporation which is incorporated in India but which is doing business exclusively abroad and may not be resident in India. Conversely, a company may be incorporated in a foreign country but might be doing its entire business in India.

English Law

Under the English private international law a company is resident in the country where its central management and control is exercised. For determining the central place of management and control of a company, neither the place of its incorporation[45] nor the place where central management and control ought to be exercised are of any importance.[46] In *Cesena Sulphur Co.* v. *Nicholson*[47] a company was incorporated in England with a view to operate sulphur mines in Italy. The practical business of manufacturing and selling the sulphur was done in Italy by an Italian delegation. Its managing director was also permanently resident in Italy. In short, company's entire business was carried on in Italy and not even an once of sulphur was sent to England, except that its Memorandum of Association had set up a Board of Directors in London which 'controlled the sale, order, direction and management' of the working of the company's mines, 'the mode of disposal thereof and the general business of the company'. The shareholders' meetings were also held in London and dividends were also declared there. On these facts the court held that the central place of management and control was located in London. We may contrast this case with *Egyptian Delta Land and Investment Co.* v. *Todd*,[48] where a company was incorporated in England with the object of acquiring and disposing of land served by the Egyptian Delta Railway Company. The entire business of the company was located and controlled in Egypt. The only contact that the company had with England was that it kept a registered office in London to satisfy the requirement of the Companies Act. On these facts the House of Lords held that the central place of business and control was located in Egypt. *Swedish Central Railway* v. *Thompson*[49] is also an instructive case. A company was incorporated in England with the object of constructing and running a railway in Sweden. Its registered office was situated in London. It leased the railways in Sweden to a traffic company at an annual rent of £ 33,500 payable in England.

45. *Egyptian Delta Land and Investment Co.* v. *Todd*, (1929) A.C. 1.
46. *Unit Construction Co. Ltd.* v. *Bullock*, (1960) A.C. 351.
47. (1876) 1 Ex. D. 428.
48. (1929) A.C. 1.
49. (1925) A.C. 495.

Simultaneously with this lease by a change in the articles of association, the control and management was shifted to Sweden. The meetings of directors and of shareholders were held in Sweden, dividends were declared in Sweden. At the same time a Committee was also set up in London which dealt with share transfers, which drafted and attached seals to share certificates, and which signed cheques on the London banking account. The annual accounts were made and audited in London and the company's secretary also resided there. On these facts, the House of Lords held that the company resided at both places, in London as well as Sweden.

M. Mann rightly observed that at first sight it appears logically inconsistent that a company should have two places or central management and control.[50] But as has been explained by the Court of Appeal 'central management and control' should not be equated with 'the power of final arbitrament, the latter must invariably be in one place, while the former may be divided.'[51] However, M. Mann considers this solution as unsound as the House of Lords has itself said that central management and control is the place of paramount authority. Sometimes in the circumstances of a company it may not be possible to identify one country as the place of central management and control since paramount authority "may be divided or even, at any rate in theory, peripatetic".[52] It is submitted, since life is not logic, such inconsistencies do occur in fact and law cannot but reflect these inconsistencies.

In conclusion, it may be said that under English private international law a corporation resides (or has its residence) in the country where it has its central management and control. It is possible that a company may have its residence at more than one place : this will happen in those cases where its central management and control is exercised from more than one country.

Indian Law

The Indian private international law closely follows English private international law in the matter of test of residence of a company. In *Guardian Assurance Co. Ltd.* v. *Thakur Shive Mangal Singh*[53] an insurance company incorporated outside India carried on insurance business in India through agent. The company paid the rent for the office and licence fee to the municipal corporation, kept a sign-board and maintained a separate account of its business in India. On these facts, the Allahabad High Court held that

50. Dicey and Morris, p. 483.

51. *Union Corporation* v. *I.R.C.* (1952) 1 All E.R. 646 : on appeal, (1953) A.C. 482.

52. *Unit Construction Co. Ltd.*, v. *Bullock*, (1960) A.C. 351.

53. *Guardian Assurance Co. Ltd.* v. *The Shiva Mangal Singh*, 1937 All. 208.

since the company's business was carried on in India, it was resident here.[54]

The Indian Income Tax Act, 1961, lays down that if a corporation has the control and management of its affairs located in India, then for the purpose of income tax it is resident in India.[55] Under Part XI of the Indian Companies Act, 1956, all foreign companies who establish a place of business in India are required to get themselves resistered with the Registrar of Companies.[56] One of the information that the foreign company is required to furnish under s. 592 is to give 'full address of the officer of the company in India which is to be deemed its principal place of business in India'.[57] Thus, the Indian law uses the expression "principal place of business" instead of "central management and control" as used in English law. Clause (d) of s. 592 lays down that service of summons will be complete and sufficient if made on any person whose name has been given by the company to the Registrar of Companies. In *P.S. Anant Narayan* v. *Massey Ferguson Ltd.*[58] the Madras High Court held that if a foreign company furnishes address to the Registrar of Companies under s. 592, then it is sufficient to confer jurisdiction on the court in private international law sense. (In this case the defendant company has given its address as "12 Mclean Street, Broadway, Madras-1"). In *Baboolal Choukani* v. *Caltex* (*India*) *Ltd.*[59] the defendant company has a 'general office' at Bombay and a District office at Calcutta. The suit was filed against the company in the Calcutta High Court. The question was : did the defendant company carry on business in Calcutta so as to confer jurisdiction on the Calcutta court ? The Calcutta High Court held that the company carried on business in Calcutta subject to general supervision of the Bombay office. The court emphasised the fact of company's carrying on business in Calcutta, and said that the fact that the business at Calcutta was carried on subject to general supervision of the Bombay office, all the more showed that business was carried on at Calcutta of their own and through an agent.

English Law

Presence

It is a well established rule of private international law that wherever a suit is filed against a defendant, process should be served on him. Ordinarily, a person can be served with the process

54. See also, *Anant Narayan* v. *Messy Ferguson Ltd.*, (1965) 1 M.L.J. 550; *Baboolal Choukhani* v. *Caltex* (*India*) *Ltd.*, 1967 Cal. 205; See also *Union of India* v. *Ladoolal*, 1963 S.C. 1681.
55. Section 6(3)(2).
56. Section 592.
57. Clause (e) of s. 592(1).
58. (1965) 1 M.L.J. 550.
59. 1967 Cal. 205.

when he is within the jurisdiction of the court. However, requirement of 'residence' for the purpose of service of process is different from the requirement of residence for the purpose of income-tax. For the purpose of service of process mere presence of the defendant within the jurisdiction of the court is enough. Thus, it is in respect of service of process that the location of the place of presence of the company is required.

In this respect the rules of Indian and English private international laws are the same. The Supreme Court Rules (English), Order 65, Rule 3 lays down: "Personal service of a document on a body corporate may, in cases for which provision is not otherwise made by any enactment, be effected by serving it . . . . on the mayor, chairman or president of the body, or the town clerk, clerk, secretary, treasurer or other similar officer thereof." It is a well-established rule of common law that exercise of jurisdiction depends upon service and if the defendant is 'found' within the jurisdiction he can be served with the process. This equally applies to companies. In *Re La Bourgogne*[60] a French shipping company has an office and an agent in London. Lord Halsbury observed : "They are here, and if they are here they may be served." For the service of process two conditions are necessary : (a) the business must be done in England and not with England. If an agent, clerk or servant is employed to do business in England, the foreign company is doing business in England. (b) The agent, servant or clerk must operate at a fixed place of business for some definite period of time. Morris summarises the law under six points, *viz.*, foreign company must be doing business in England, business must be done for some substantial period, business must be carried on at some fixed place, business must be that of the corporation and not of the agent, the summons must be served on the person who is in the position of a head officer of the corporation.[61] However, the brevity of time during which business was done or the impermanency of the place is not sufficient to render the corporation immune from jurisdiction.[62] In *Dunlop Pneumatic Co.* v. *Action Gesellschaft Motor etc. Co.*[63] a stand was occupied by a foreign motor-car company at a nine-day cycle show. It was held that the company was present in England. It should be noted that it is immaterial whether the cause of action arose in England or elsewhere.[64] The Companies Act, 1948, s. 407 makes it obligatory for foreign corporation to file with the Registrar of Companies the name and address of a person authorized to accept service of process on behalf of the company. It is submitted that with the

60. (1899) A.C. 431.
61. Dicey and Morris, pp. 175-176.
62. *Dunlop Pneumatic Co.* v. *Action Gesellschaft Motor, etc. Co.*, (1902) 1 K.B. 342.
63. (1902) 1 K.B. 342.
64. *Re La Bourgogne*, (1899) A.C. 431; *A/S Damskip Hercules* v. *Grand Trunk Pacific Railway of Canada*, (1912) 1 K.B. 222.

coming into force of this provision the common rule becomes obsolete.[64a]

Indian Law

Order 29, Civil Procedure Code deals with suits by and against companies. Rule 2 of the Order lays down the method of effecting service on corporations. It runs : "Subject to any statutory provision regulating service of process, where the suit is against a corporation, the summons may be served—(a) on the secretary, or any director, or other principal officer of the corporation, or (b) by leaving it or sending it by post addressed to the corporation at the registered office, or if there is no resistered office, then at the place where the corporation carries on business." In *Hyderabad Municipality* v. *Hakumal*[65] it was held that in Rule 2(b) of Order 29, the place where the corporation carries on business is the principal place of business of the company. The mode of service and on whom it may be effected has now been laid down in the Companies Act, 1956, in the same terms as it exists under the English Companies Act. Part XI of the Companies Act lays down provisions for the establishment of place of business in India. Section 592 provides that the foreign corporations which establish a place of business in India shall, within thirty days of the establishment of the place of business, deliver to the Registrar of Companies for registration', *inter alia*, 'the name and address or the names and addresses of one or more persons resident in India, authorized to accept on behalf of the company service of process and any notices or other documents required to be served on the company',[66] and the 'full address of the office of the company in India which is to be deemed its principal place of business.'[67]

Section 596 deals with the mode of service on foreign companies. The section runs : "Any process, notice, or other document required to be served on a foreign company shall be deemed to be sufficiently served, if addressed to any person whose name has been delivered to the Registrar under the foregoing provisions of this Part [i.e., s. 592(i)(d)] and left at, or sent by post to, address which has been so delivered. Provided that—(a) where any such company makes a default in delivering to the Registrar the name and address of a person resident in India who is authorized to accept on behalf of the company service of process, notice, or other document; or (b) if at any time all the persons whose names and addresses have been so delivered are dead or have ceased so to reside, or refuse to accept service on behalf of the company, or for

64a. *The Theodotios* (1977) 2 Loyds Rep. 428. In case of overseas corporation, the only procedure to be followed is as laid down in the Companies Act, 1948.

65. 1928 Sind 111.

66. Section 592(1)(d).

67. Section 592(1)(e).

any reason, cannot be served, a document may be served on the company by leaving it at, or sending it by post to, any place of business established by the company in India." It has been held that service is effective if it is addressed and delivered to any person within clause (d) or (e) of s. 592(1) of the Companies Act, 1956.[68]

The English courts take the view that the office of the foreign company should be in existence at the time of the service. If the office has been closed at the time of service, then the service of summons at such an office will not be enough.[69] On the other hand, under Rule 28 of the Indian Companies Rules, it has been laid down that service of the summons can be made on the last known principal place of business of the company.[70]

Recommendations of the Institute of International Law

On September 10, 1965, the Institute of International Law adopted rules on the system of law governing corporations and recommended to all states to adopt the rules in order to resolve the conflicts of law with regard to companies formed under a municipal law. The summary of these rules is as follows :

Rules on the law Governing Companies : Article 1 provides : "A company is governed by the law under which it has been incorporated." Articles 7 and 8 lay down the particular application of this rule. The law governing the company also applies to the form and to the substance of its constitution. It applies, in particular, to the requirements concerning its capital, both at the time of its incorporation and in the course of its existence.[71] The law governing the company determines what organs the company must have in order to operate, the powers of those organs, the rights and obligations of the persons serving as organs of the company and of the shareholders, both among each other and in relation to the company, including in particular the protection of minority shareholders and replacement of lost or stolen share documents.[72]

Recognition of Corporation and Rights of a Recognized Corporation : Article 2 sets out the general principle of recognition thus : "Any company established in accordance with the law mentioned in the first article will be recognized in all other states as a

68. *Anant Narayan* v. *Messy Ferguson Ltd.*, (1965) 1 M.L.J, 550.
69. *Deverall* v. *Grand Advertising Inc.*, (1955) Ch. 111.
70. Rule 28(2) runs : Every petition and . . . every application shall, unless presented by the company, be served on the company at its registered office, or if there is no registered office at its principal place of business by leaving a copy thereof with an officer or employee of the company, and in case no such person is available, in such manner, as the judge or the Registrar may direct or by sending a copy thereof by pre-paid registered post addressed to the company at its registered office, or if there is no registered office, at its principal or last known principal place of business, or to such person and at such address as the judge or Registrar may direct."
71. Article 7.
72. Article 8.

corporate person" Then Article 5 sets out the rules relating to "actual seat of company." The Article provides : "The actual seat of a company is the place at which it has its principal centre of control and management, even if the decisions which are taken at that place follow directions given by shareholders who reside elsewhere." This definition of "actual seat of company" is similar to the definition adopted of "residence" under English private international law.[73] Articles 3 and 4 deal with non-recognition of companies. Non-recognition of a company depends upon the "actual seat of the company". If a company's actual seat is situated outside the territory in which the law of its incorporation is in force and if the principal business activities of the company take place outside that territory,[74] or if the company has no real connection with that territory, the recognition of the company as a corporate person may be refused if its constitution is not in accordance with the law of the place where it has actual seat. The real connection must be established by facts other than the mere indication of a registered office, and may in particular consist of a place of business in the territory of the origin of the share or loan capital of the company, of the nationality, or habitual residence of the shareholders or of those in control of the company.

Rights of a recognized corporation are set out in Article 6 in the following terms : A company which is recognized in accordance with the preceding provisions enjoys all rights which are conferred upon it by the law by which it is governed, except rights which the state by which it is recognized refuses to grant either to foreign nationals in general or to companies of a corresponding type governed by its own law. However, a recognized company can carry on its business only under the conditions which are imposed by the local laws concerning the carrying on business in that country.

Place of Business : Article 9 deals with the place of business. It provides : "If a company has a place of business in a state other than the state of its incorporation, the state in which that place of business is situated may impose upon the company obligations with regard to : (a) the publication of the registration of its constitution, its annual accounts, and the powers conferred upon its organs; (b) the appointment of a representative in charge of the management of the place of business and, if required, the application to this representative of the local laws concerning the powers and duties of members of organs of management; (c) the application of the local provisions concerning the representation of the employees within the enterprise, but only on those which operate at the level of the plant or place of business; and (d) the protection of creditors through the creation of financial securities." It is further laid down, "The state in which the place of business is situated may also, in the interest of creditors and under the

73. See cases cited under the head Residence.

74. Article 3.

conditions laid down in its own law, liqudate the place of business and the other assets belonging to company situated in its territory."

Miscellaneous Matters : Articles 10 to 14 deal with miscellaneous matters, such as governing law for the issue of shares, powers of the organs of the company, governing law of the liabilities and obligations of the company, etc. Article 10 provides : "The public issue of shares is governed by the provisions of the law which governs the company as well as by the law of the country in which the issue takes place. The public issue of debentures is governed by the provisions of the proper law of the contract of loan as well as by the law of the country in which the issue takes place."

Articles 11 and 12 deal with the *ultra vires* rule and the liabilities of the organs of the company acting on its behalf. Article 11 provides : "The powers of the organ of the company to act on its behalf are governed by the law which governs the company. The liability of a person who has entered into a transaction by which the company is not bound is governed by the law of the place at which he has entered into that transaction." Article 12 lays down : "If a contract has been concluded in a country other than in which the company is incorporated, the company cannot rely on any limitations of the power to act on behalf of the company which the law governing the company imposes upon the organs of the company that has concluded the contract if such limitations do not exist under the law of the place where the contract was concluded, and if the other party to the contract did not have reasonable notice of the provisions of the law governing the company." Then the second para of the Article adds : "For the purpose of the preceding provision a contract is deemed to have been concluded in a given country only if it has been concluded there *inter praesentes* or, in the case of contracts by correspondence, if both the offer and acceptance have taken place in that country."

Article 13 provides : "Any liability incurred by reason of a violation of the law governing the country are governed by that law." Article 14 provides : "Any law which would be applicable by virtue of the preceding articles can be excluded if in a given case its application would lead to result clearly incompatible with the public policy of the forum."

Part V

LAW OF PROPERTY

SUMMARY

14

LAW OF PROPERTY : CHARACTERIZATION

English internal law continues to be wedded to the historical and technical classification of property into reality and personality. However, the English private international law abandoned this classification at an early date and recognized the universally accepted classification of property into movables and immovables.[1] In *Re Hoyles*[2] the Court observed : "In order to arrive at a common basis on which to determine questions between the inhabitants of two countries living under different systems of jurisprudence, our courts recognize and act on a division otherwise unknown to our law into movables and immovables." The classification of property into movables and immovables is not co-extensive with the internal law classification between reality and personality. It is a broader classification. Morris very aptly remarks, "The importance of the distinction between movables and immovables is most apparent in the field of succession, because succession to movables is (in general) governed by the *lex domicilii* of the deceased whereas succession to immovables is (in general) governed by the *lex situs*. But the distinction may also be important in transaction *inter vivos*, because such transactions are (in general) governed by the *lex situs* so far as immovables are concerned, whereas they are not necessarily governed by the *lex situs* so far as movables are concerned."[3]

Luckily Indian law escaped the reception of this English internal classification of property into reality and personality and all along classified property into movables and immovables. The Indian private international law also classifies property into movables and immovables. Thus both the English and Indian private international law accept the universally accepted classification of property into, (a) movables, and (b) immovables.

Movables are further classified into tangibles and intangibles.

1. Farwell, L. J.'s formulation in *Re Hoyles*, (1911) 1 Ch. 179, that the classification of English internal law should be retained in respect of those countries which recognize this classification was not adopted by the English courts : See *Re Cutcliffe*, (1940) Ch. 565.
2. Cited above.
3. Dicey and Morris, Conflict of Laws, (8th edition) pp. 78-79.

This classification is more easily accepted by international lawyers than any other. The English internal law classified movables into *choses in possession choses and in action*. Examples, of the former are, car, horses, television, etc. Examples of the latter are debts, patents, copyright, goodwill, stock and shares. Cheshire advocates the retention of this classification in English private international law.[4] It is submitted that if any one is bent upon ascribing *situs* to all types of properties, one would do so in whatever manner movables are classified. But the classification of property into tangibles and intangibles has the merit of universal acceptance.

Chacterization

Whenever a court is called upon in a conflict of laws case to adjudicate any question relating to ownership, possession or any other right in a property, its first task is to determine whether the property in question is movable property or immovable property. It is now an accepted principle of private international law the only law that can effectively answer this question is the law of the country where the property is in fact situate. According to Morris, "Law . . . deals in reality with rights; and the law of the country where a given tangible thing is in fact located can determine whether the rights over such things, e.g., land, or obligations connected with it, or the documents which embody such rights or obligations, shall be treated as interests in movables or immovables."[5]

Ordinarily, the determination of the question as to whether a particular property is movable or immovable should present no difficulty. But the difficulties arise because different systems of law characterize property differently. For instance, title-deeds, fixtures, fish in a pond or the key of a house would appear to everybody to be movables but English law classifies them as interests in land. Similiarly, buildings erected for holding an exhibition and which cannot be removed without losing their identity would appear to everybody as immovables, but in some American states and Germany their owner is deemed to hold an interest in movables- Thus arises the question : if one system of law characterizes property as movable, while the other characterizes it as immovable, which system of law should have the final say ? This is one area of private international law where we have near uniformity. English, Indian and most other private international laws take the view that the final decision should be left to the law of the country where the property is situate, or to the *lex situs* of property. If the *lex situs* characterizes it as immovable it should be treated as immovable, and it should be so treated in every country in which any adjudication with respect to them arises.[6] In English private international law it is well settled that if there is a conflict betweer

4. Private International Law (Seventh edition), p. 403.
5. Dicey's Conflict of Laws, p. 501.
6. **See Story, Commentaries on Conflict of Laws, 8th ed., s. 447.**

the *lex situs* and the *lex fori* as to whether a particular property is movable or immovable it is the *lex situs* which determines the issue.[7] The same seems to be the position in Indian law. It is because, in the last resort, it is the *lex situs* which has effective control over the property. As to the question at what point of time *situs* of property is important, Morris says that '*lex situs*' at the decisive moment must control.[8] As to what is the 'decisive moment' he explains it by an example : T, domiciled in England, owns a farm in country X, and that by the law of X (but not by English law) horses of the plough are regarded as immovables for the purpose of succession. T dies intestate leaving A and B. B is entitled to the horse, because by the *lex situs* they are regarded as immovables and that it should make no difference if A chanced to remove the horses to England without B's consent after the death of T. But if T has removed the horses to England before his death, then A would be entitled to them; in other words, in a case of succession the decisive moment is the death of the tesator or intestate.[9]

Thus, in conflict of laws cases, abandoning their demoestic classification, the English courts have classified properties as movables and immovables. For instance, leaseholds in England are interests in immovables, despite the fact that the domestic law regards them as personal estate;[10] a rent charge on land in England is an interest in an immovable, though domestic law for some purposes it is considered as personal estate; mortgagee's interest in land situated in England is considered as interest in immovable, though in internal English law it is regarded as personality.[11] How sometimes the matter may become confusing is illustrated by *Re Berchtold*,[12] where a domiciled Hungarian who was entitled to an interest in an English freehold land subject for sale but yet not sold, died intestate. The English rule of conflict of laws is that intestate succession to immovables is governed by *lex situs*, and to movables by the *lex domicilii*. Thus the question for determination before the court was whether the freehold interest is to be characterized as movable or immovable. The English equitable doctrine of convension lays down that under such circumstances it is regarded as personal estate. And it was, therefore, argued on behalf of the next-of-kin who was entitled to his interest under the Hungarian law that freehold interest of the deceased may be regarded, by application of doctrine of convension, as personality. Rejecting the argument, the English court held that the freehold

7. *Re Hoyles*, cited above; *Re Berchtold*, (1923) 1 Ch. 192; *Re Cutcliffe*, (1940) Ch. 565.
8. Dicey, 8th ed., p. 504.
9. *Ibid.*
10. *Duncan* v. *Lawson*, (1889) 41 Ch. D. 394; *Pepin* v. *Bruyere*. (1900), 2 Ch 504 on appeal, (1902) 1 Ch. 24.
11. *Re Hoyles*, cited above.
12. (1923) 1 Ch. 192.

interest was immovable property.[13] The question came in a converse form in *Re Cutliffe*,[14] where A made a claim to a reversionary interest in certain stock which represented the reinvestment of the proceeds of sale of settled freehold land situated in England. The stock, being that of a British company and being held by English trustees of an English settlement, was obviously situated in England. After the death of A, the question before the court was whether A's interest in the stock passed to his next-of-kin under the law of Ontario which was *lex domicilii* or whether it passed to heirs at law under English law which was *lex situs* ? The English Settled Land Act, 1925, provides that the stock be treated as land *for all purposes* of devolution, disposition and transmission. The court held that the English statutes applied and the stock was characterized as immovable property. This decision has been criticised.[15] Cheshire, it is submitted rightly, supports the decision by saying that the stock was physically situated in England and English law, therefore, had to determine whether it was to be treated as movable or immovable; since English statute peremptorily demand that stock was to be treated as land, the decision of English court was correct.[16]

The question that remains is : should every property, immovable or movable, tangible or intangible, have a *situs* ? M. Mann seems to take the view that it is possible to ascribe a *situs* to every thing. Rule 79 in Dicey's Conflict of Laws is accordingly framed as under :[17]

"The *situs* of things is determined as follows :

(1) Choses in action generally are situate in the country where they are properly recoverable or can be enforced

(2) Land is situate in the country where it lies.

(3) Subject to the Exceptions here-in-after mentioned, a chattel is situate in the country where it can be found at any given time."

The two Exceptions mentioned are :

Exception 1. A merchant ship may at some time be deemed to be situate at her port of registry.[18]

Exception 2. A civil aircraft may at some time be deemed to be situate in its country of registration.[19]

13. *Ibid.*, at p. 206; see also Cheshire, p. 401, for the analysis of the case.
14. (1940) Ch. 565.
15. Falconbridge, Chap. 28, p. 589.
16. Cheshire, p. 402; see also Dicey and Morris, p. 506. See also *Re Midleton's Settlement*, (1947) Ch. 583 (C.A.).
17. Conflict of Laws, p. 508.
18. *Ibid.* at p. 516.
19. *Ibid.*, at p. 517.

Cheshire is of the opinion that tendency of ascribing *situs* even to *choses in action* is fraught with danger.[20] It is submitted that it is true that in every situation it is not necessary to view the question from the angle of the *situs* of property, particularly in respect of intangibles. But in some situations even intangibles may need to be ascribed a *situs*. It is submitted that each matter should be viewed in its own situation.

At the first stage of characterization once the *lex situs* of property characterizes it as movable or immovable, it is possible in the next stage to apply any further distinction of internal law. For instance, if the law chosen is one which recognizes distinction between reality and personality then this will be given effect. *In Re Berchtold*[21] once it was determined that the deceased died entitled to an immovable property, in the next stage, the English domestic law doctrine of conversion was allowed to operate under which such immovable property, being considered as personality, was allowed to devolve as personality.

In the private international law of most of the countries, it is an established rule that in respect of practically every transaction relating to immovable property, the *lex situs* governs. The rules of private international law relating to transactions in respect of immovable property are, therefore, simple and uncomplicated. On the other hand, rules of private international law relating to transactions in respect of movable property are still not fully developed. There is a conflict in the laws of various countries. Most of the difficulties arise because the *situs* of movables can be changed easily. Then, it may be difficult to determine the *situs* of intangibles. A view is propounded that we need not bother about the *situs* of intangibles. Most of the difficulties relating to movables arise relating to their transfer.

20. Cheshire, 8th ed., p. 473,

21. Cited above.

15

IMMOVABLE PROPERTY

I

GENERAL RULES

In the private international law of most countries including England, India, the United States and most countries of the European continent, it is an established rule that in respect of all transactions relating to immovable property, and all right over, or in relation to, immovable property are ordinarily governed by the law of the *situs* of the immovables.[1] The reason for this rule is obvious : convenience and expediency; any other rule would be ineffective as in the last resort the only effective order that can be passed has to be in accordance with the *lex situs* of the property. English law recognized this rule as early as 1845. In *Nelson* v. *Bridport*,[2] the court observed : "The incidents to real estate, the right of alienating or limiting it, and the course of succession to it, depends entirely on the law of the country where the estate is situated." The same is the position in Indian law.[3]

Meaning of Lex Situs : The most vital question relating to the present discussion is : what is the meaning of *lex situs* ? Does it mean the domestic law or does it mean the entire law including the rules of conflicts of laws of the country where the property is situate ? It is fortunate that most writers on private international law are unanimous on this point and take the view that *lex situs* in this context means the entire law of the country where the property is situate.[4] In the words of Morris, "The sovereign of the country where land is situate has absolute control over the land within his dominions : he alone can bestow effective rights over it; his courts alone are, as a rule, entitled to exercise jurisdiction over such land. Consequently, any decision by an English

1. Under the law of Italy, Spain, Sweden, Finland and Germany succession to immovables is also regulated by the law of the nationality of the deceased.
2. (1845) 8 Beav. 547.
3. Section 16, Civil Procedure Code.
4. See Dicey's Conflict of Laws, p. 520; Cheshire, p. 502; Beale, p. 97; Falconbridge, pp. 216-217; Cook, pp. 264, 279-280.

court which ran counter to what the *lex situs* had decided or would decide would be in most cases a *brutum fulmen*."[5] For instance, an Indian domiciled Hindu dies leaving behind immovables in Spain. Under the internal law of Spain A is the heir to the property of the deceased, while under Hindu law B is the heir. The Spanish courts would apply the law of the nationality of the deceased, i.e. Hindu law; thus if the matter was decided by the Spanish court, B would be considered to be the heir. If the matter is agitated in an Indian court and if Indian courts applying the *lex situs* as meaning domestic law of Spain, would declare A as the heir to the property of the deceased, then this decision would be *brutum fulmen*. Thus, *lex situs* mean that law which the court of *lex situs* would apply; in other words, here the foreign court theory is applied most appropriately.[6] Thus in *Proctor* v. *Frost*,[7] a New Hampshire law provided that a wife is incapable of becoming surety for her husband. A Massachusetts domiciled married woman became surety for her husband and mortgaged her lands in New Hampshire. Under the law of New Hampshire there was no such prohibition for married women. Then, what does *lex situs* here means ? Cheshire poses the question : was the purpose of New Hampshire law to regulate conveyance of New Hampshire land, or was it to protect wives against the importunities of embarrassed husband ? If it was the latter, "it would be unseemly and inexpedient to extend this paternal solicitude to wives domiciled in foreign jurisdictions". Cheshire nods approvingly at the decision of the court which held that the purpose of the statute being to protect the New Hampshirian married woman, it would not apply in the instant case. The court held the conveyance valid.[8] Further, Cheshire holds that the narrow meaning to *lex situs* may be adopted when a dispute concerns the legal effect of conveyance, as, for example, when the question is whether there has been an infringement of the rule against perpetuities or whether the interest created is legally possible.[9]

The English courts have held that they have no jurisdiction to adjudicate in respect of any matter relating to immovable property situated abroad, even though the parties may be resident or nationals of England or domiciled there.[10] The House of Lords, in *British South Africa Co.* v. *Companhia de Mocambique*,[11] where an action of trespass was brought against the defandants for having broken into and taken possession of large tracts of lands and mines in South Africa, said that an English court has no

5. Dicey, p. 520.
6. Cheshire, (8th ed), p. 476.
7. (1938) 89 N.H. 304.
8. *Ibid.*, pp. 502-503.
9. *Ibid.*, at p. 503.
10. *British South Africa Co.* v. *Companhia de Mocamlique*, (1893) A.C. 602; *Deschamps* v. *Miller* (1903) 1 Ch. 856.
11. Cited above.

jurisdiction to entertain an action relating to foreign immovables. In *Deschamps* v. *Miller*[12] the father of the plaintiff had made a settlement of some immovable situated abroad in favour of his wife and others. When the plaintiff challenged the validity of this settlement in an English court, the court declined to exercise jurisdiction. That this continues to be the law was reiterated by the House of Lords recently in *Hesperides Hotels Ltd* v. *Muftizade.*[13]

This is also the position under the Indian law. Section 16, Indian Civil Procedure Code incorporates this principle.[14] The Privy Council in *Neelkant* v. *Vidhya*[15] said the British Indian courts have no jurisdiction to entertain an action in respect of a mortgage of immovable property situated in a foreign State. The same view has been taken in other cases also.[16]

To the general rule that the *lex situs* of immovable property regulates all right in, and all relations to it, there are certain exceptions which would be discussed in Part II of this Chapter.

Capacity

This is a settled rule of both English and Indian private international laws that capacity to give or take immovable property is governed by the *lex situs* of property. Thus, if the law of the *lex situs* imposes restrictions on foreigners or on a class of persons to take property, then any conveyance made to such persons anywhere else in the world would not be valid. The same is true of the capacity to convey property; the transfer of property, then, may be in any form. For instance, under the law of the United States a person has capacity to convey property when he completes the age of twenty-one years, while under the Indian law a person has capacity to convey property when he attains the age of eighteen years. Thus, if an Indian domiciled person who had attained the age of eighteen years conveys land situated in the state of New York, then such a conveyance would not be valid, as he had no capacity to convey immovables under the *lex situs*. On the other hand, if a New York domiciled person who had attained the age of eighteen (but not of twentyone) conveys land situated in India, then the conveyance would be valid, as under the law of the *situs* of the land, he had the capacity to convey the land.

12. Cited above.
13. (1978) 3 W.L.R. 378.
14. See for details Chapters 8 of this work.
15. 1930 A.C. 188.
16. *Krishna D. Iyyar* v. *Subbarama Aiyer* 1932 Mad. 462; *Upendranath.* v. *Het Lal*, 1933 All. 380 : this was an Application to file an award in respect of immovable property suited abroad. *Keshav* v *Vinayak*, (1889) 23 Bom. 22; (his was a suit for declaration of share in property situated in Hyderabad state); *Krishan Swami* v. *Benugopal*, 1942 Mad. 614; (suit was for possession of immovable properry situated in Burma).

There is no direct authority for this proposition in English law, but it has never been doubted, and in *Bank of Africa Ltd.* v. *Cohen*[16a] this was stated to be so.[17] The Court observed "...that a person's capacity to make a contract with regard to an immovable is governed by the *lex situs*."[18]

The Indian courts have expressed the same view. In *Nachiappa Chettiar* v. *Muthu Karuppan Chettiar*[19] Rajamannar, J. said "...a person's capacity to alienate an immovable by sale or mortgage, *inter vivos*, or to devise an immovable or to acquire, or to succeed to an immovable is governed by the *lex situs*.[20] The same view was taken by the Punjab High Court in *Labh Singh* v. *Chief Settlement Commissioner*.[21] The *lex situs* must determine whether an effective and lawful transfer of title has taken place.

Formal Validity

It is an established rule of English and Indian private international laws that formal validity of the conveyance or any other transaction relating to immovables is governed by the *lex situs*. Here, as elsewhere, the meaning of the *lex situs* is the same as suggested earlier in this Chapter. For instance, if the formal validity of a conveyance of immovable property situated in India is before the Indian court, then it would mean the Indian internal law, and if the formal validity of a conveyance of immovable property situated abroad is before the Indian court, then it would mean whether system of law the *lex situs* would apply.

A distinction is to be made between conveyance and a contract to transfer. In the former case the formal validity of the transaction must be in accordance with the *lex situs* of the property, but in the latter case it need not be. For instance, if two Indians enter into a contract for the conveyance of a house situated in London, it is not necessary that the formalities of contract should be in accordance with English law. Morris takes the view that such a contract is formally valid "if it complies with the formalities prescribed by the proper law of the contract or (semble) by the *lex loci contractus*. The proper law of the contract is usually, but not necessarily, the *lex situs*."[22] Cheshire also takes this view. "A contract is binding so far as it relates to form, if it satisfies the

16a. (1909) 2 Ch. 129.
17. Cheshire thinks that the case related to form and not capacity : Cheshire p. 508: Morris thinks that the case was wrongly decided.
18. (1909) 2 Ch. 129 at p. 143.
19. 1946 Mad. 398 at p. 406.
20. The learned judge relied on Dicey and Story's formulations, see p. 406.
21. 1959 Punj. 575.
22. Dicey, p. 523.

requirement of the *lex loci contractus* or of its proper law."[23]

Thus, if a contract to convey land or other immovable property is valid by the proper law of the contract, then contractual rights and liabilities of the parties can be adjudicated upon and an action in courts of proper law of contract for breach of contract would be maintainable. This adjudication may relate to an action for damages for breach of contract or for specific performance of the contact.[24]

Material Validity

The general rule that in respect of all transactions regarding immovables, *lex situs* governs applies to material or essential validity of the conveyance of immovables. Thus no disposition or transaction can create an interest in or right over immovable property which is not valid by the *lex situs*, even though it is valid by the law of the country where it is made. It is the *lex situs* which exclusively governs the tenure, title and descent to immovables, as well as the nature of estates that can be created and what are the incidents of those estates,[25] whether the interests created infringe the rule against perpetuities or accumulations,[26] whether gifts to charities are valid[27] and like matters.

The material validity of a contract retating to immovables, is governed by the proper law of the contract.[28]

Indian law is also substantially the same. It is the *lex situs* which determines the essential validity of any transaction or conveyance in respect to immovables.[29]

II
PERSONAL JURISDICTION IN RESPECT OF FOREIGN IMMOVABLES

To the general rule is that the *lex situs* governs all matters relating to immovable property, certain exceptions are recognized to this rule. One of the exceptions that courts of equity have recognized from earliest times is relating to actions *in personam*. The reason for this rule was thus explained in *Ewing* v. *Orr-Ewing* :[30] "The English courts of equity are, and always have been,

23. Cheshire, p. 510. Cheshire in his support quotes Westlake, s. 26; and *British South Africa Company* v. *De Bears Consolidated Mines Ltd.*, (1910) 2 Ch. 502 on appeal (1912) A.C. 52, *Re Smith, Lawrence* v. *Kitson*, (1916) 2 Ch. 206.
24. *Re Smith, Lawrence* v. *Kitson*, (1916) 2 Ch. 206.
25. *Nelson* v. *Bridport*, (1846) 8 Beav. 547; *Re Miller*, (1914) 1 Ch. 511.
26. *Re Grassi* (1905) 1 Ch. 584.
27. *Duncan* v. *Lawson*, (1889) 41 Ch. D. 394; *Re Hoyles*, (1911) 1 Ch. 179 (C.A.).
28. See Dicey's Conflict of Laws, p. 524.
29. *Labh Singh* v. *Chief Settlement Commissioner*, 1959 Punj. 575.
30. (1883) 9 A.C. 34.

courts of conscience operating *in personam* and not *in rem*, and in the exercise of this personal jurisdiction they have always been accustomed to compel the performance of contracts and trusts as to subjects which were not either locally or *rations domicilii* within their jurisdiction."[31] The peculiarity of this jurisdiction is that the courts cannot act upon the immovables directly but act upon the conscience of the defendant. The essential of this jurisdiction is that the defendant must be amenable to the jurisdiction of the court. In short, it is based on the presence of the defendant within the jurisdiction. Service of notice of a writ under Order 11 is necessary.

We would proceed to illustrate this jurisdiction in regards to :

(a) Contracts relating to foreign land,

(b) Fraud and other unconscionable conduct, and

(c) Fiduciary relationship.

Contracts relating to Foreign Land : The Courts of Equity have exercised this jurisdiction of ordering specific performance of contracts relating to foreign land whenever the defendant has been present within the jurisdiction. In *Archer* v. *Preston*[32] the defendant who refused to perform a contract for sale of land situated in Ireland was ordered to perform the contract specifically while he was on visit to England. The leading case on the subject is *Penn* v. *Baltimore*[33] where a contract was entered into in England between the plaintiff and the defendant for fixing the boundaries of Pennsylvania and Maryland. On the plaintiff's suit for specific performance of the contract the defendant contended that the court had no jurisdiction since it could neither make an effective decree nor had it means to execute it. The court granted the decree of specific performance on the ground that the court of equity always acts *in personam.*[34] In *Re Smith, Lawrence* v. *Kitson*,[35] a decree for specific performance of the contract to execute a legal mortgage for valuable consideration of land situated in Dominica was passed. An action for conversion of foreign situated movables is also maintainable against a defendent present within the jurisdiction.[35a]

Fraud and other Unconscionable Conduct : In *Crabstown* v. *Johnston*,[36] the leading case of the subject, the plaintiff was liable

31. *Deschamps* v. *Miller* (1908) 1 Ch. 856 at p. 863.
32. The case has been cited in *Arglasse* v. *Muschamp*, (1682) 1 Vern. 75 at p. 77.
33. (1750) 1 Ves Sen. 444.
34. *British South Africa Co.* v. *Companhia de Mocambique*, (1892) 2 Q.B. 358; on appeal (1893) A.C. 602.
35. (1916) 2 Ch. 206.
35a. *Harpindes Hotels* v. *Muftizade*, (1978) 3 W.L.R. 378.
36. (1796) 3 Ves. 170.

under an award to pay to the defendant a certain sum in London. He was also entitled to a plantation of great value in St. Christopher. Under the law of St. Christopher a creditor could proceed against an absent debtor after leaving a summon at the freehold of the debtor and by nailing another on the court-house door. On the plaintiff's failure to pay the sum owing to his absence abroad, the defendant took advantage of the law of St. Christopher and obtained a decree against the plaintiff and got his plantation sold to himself far less of its value. The plaintiff filed a bill of relief in the English Court of Equity. The court assuming jurisdiction did not deny the jurisdiction of the courts of the *situs*, but observed that this was a gross injustice to obtain the estate of the plaintiff at an inadequate price and this justified the court acting upon the conscience of the defendant. Consequently, the court passed a decree that upon the receipt of the amount due under the award together with interest, the defendant should reconvey the plantation to the plaintiff. As early as 1682 the court of equity rejected the argument that the English courts had no jurisdiction to hear a suit founded on fraud which solely related to the foreign land. The Chancellor said that it was 'only a jest put upon the jurisdiction of this court by the common law lawyer.'[37] Fraud is an extrinsic, collateral act violating all proceedings, even those of court of justice, and it always creates a right in the injured party to sue the defendant *in personam* wherever he can find him, no matter where the cause of action has arisen or where the subject-matter of the action is situate.[38]

Fiduciary relationship : The Court of Equity has also exercised jurisdiction to enforce fiduciary relations in respect of land situated abroad. Thus a trust attached to foreign land may be enforced by the court provided that the trustee is present within the jurisdiction, even though the trustor is not subject to the jurisdiction.[39] Similarly, personal equities arising from mortgages of foreign land have been enforced by the court.[40] It is for the court to determine whether a personal obligation is such as to affect the defendant's conscience and it is not concerned whether such personal relationship is not recognized by the *lex situs*.[41]

There are two main limitations on the exercise of the personal jurisdiction in respect to foreign immovables: (a) If it is not possible for the English decree to be carried into effect under the *lex situs*, such as when such an act is forbidden by the *lex situs*;[42] and (b) when there is no privity of obligation between the parties to the action.[43]

37. *Arglasse* v. *Muschamp*, (1682) 1 Vern. 75.
38. Cheshire, p. 526.
39. *Ewing* v. *Orr-Ewing*, (1882) 9 A.C. 34.
40. *Beckford* v. *Kebble*, (1882) 1 Sim. & St. 7; *Toller* v. *Carteret*, (1705) 2 Vern. 494; *Paget* v. *Ede*, (1874) L.R. 18 Eq. 118.
41. *Re Courtney*, (1840) Mont. & Ch. 239; *Re Anchor Line*, (1937) 1 Ch. 483.
42. *Re Courtney*, cited above.
43. *Re Hawthorne*, (1883) 23 Ch. D. 743; *Norris* v. *Chambers*, (1861) 29 Beav. 246; *Deschamps* v. *Miller*, (1908) 1 Ch. 856.

The doctrine of personal jurisdiction regarding immovable situated abroad has been criticised.[44]

Indian Law

The equitable doctrine of actions *in personam* regarding immovables situated in foreign countries has been exercised by the Indian courts. Proviso to s. 16, Civil Procedure Code runs :

> Provided that a suit to obtain relief respecting, or compensation for wrong to immovable property held by or on behalf of the defendant may, where the relief sought can be entirely obtained through his personal obedience, be instituted either in the court within the local limits of whose jurisdiction the property is situate, or in the court within the local limits of whose jurisdiction the defendant actually and voluntarily resides, or carries on business or personally works for gain.

It is not clear whether the provision of this proviso applies to immovables situate outside India. One view is that the provision does not apply to property situated outside India.[45] However, the Bombay High Court in *Mahadev* v. *Ramchandra*[46] said that even if the Proviso to s. 16, C.P.C. is considered to be not applicable to cases where land is situated outside India, the English law rule relating to jurisdiction *in personam* applies in India if relief can be obtained entirely through the personal obedience of the defendant. This was a suit for mesne profits of land situated in another country against the defendant who was amenable to the jurisdiction. Earlier, the Bombay High Court in *Kashinath* v. *Anant*,[47] following the English decisions in *Ex parte Pollard*[48] and *Ewing* v. *Orr-Ewing*[49] said that the law in India is the same as in England.[50] In this case the plaintiff had claimed his share of the income of the immovable property situated in a foreign country. The defendant was residing within the jurisdiction and it was here that he was receiving the income of the property. The court passed a decree in favour of the plaintiff.[51] But this is a discretionary jurisdiction and it will act in compliance with limitations on its discretion. One of such limitations is that the court will not pass a decree unless the decree can effectively be enforced by the personal obedience of the defendant within the jurisdiction.[52]

In *Girdhari* v. *Sheoraj*[53] the question before the court was

44. Cheshire, pp. 530-531.
45. *Krishnaji* v. *Gajanan*, (1909) 33 Bom. 373.
46. 1922 Bom. 188.
47. (1899) 34 Bom. 407.
48. (1840) Mont. & Chit. 239.
49. (1883) 9 A.C. 34.
50. *Ex parte* v. *Polland* was relied upon.
51. See also, *Yadoo* v. *Krishnaji*, 1928 Nag. 56; *Gokuldas* v. *Chaganlal*, 1927 Cal. 768.
52. *Gokuldas* v. *Chaganlal* 1927 Cal. 768.
53. (1877) 1 All. 431.

whether a suit for redemption of a mortgage could be maintainable in respect of properties which were outside the jurisdiction, though the defendant was amenable to court's jurisdiction ? The court said that it had jurisdiction and the court was competent to take account for the purpose of deciding whether the entire mortgage debt had been satisfied and might give the plantiff a decree for redemption of the property, notwithstanding that in doing so it would have incidentally to determine questions relating to lands lying within the domains of a foreign country.[54] In *Prithvi Singh* v. *Ganesh Prasad Singh*[55] a suit for accounts and possession of immovable property (subject to a usufructuary mortgage) partly situated within the jurisdiction of the court and partly outside the jurisdiction, was filed against the defendant within the jurisdiction. The court said that it had jurisdiction to decree for the possession of that property, though it could pass a decree for possession of that property, alone which was within its jurisdiction.

The Indian courts have also exercised jurisdiction to declare that a will relating to properties situated outside the jurisdiction is a forgery,[56] or for a declaration that an adoption is null and void.[57] Similarly, jurisdiction has been exercised for a dissolution of partnership in a factory situated outside the jurisdiction[58] or for settlement of accounts of factory situated outside the jurisdiction of the court.[59] Speaking of the limitations of the jurisdiction in *Durgadas* v. *Jainarayan*[60] the Allahabad High Court said that in such actions *in personam* there was no question involved relating to title or ownership of the property situated outside the jurisdiction and in *Nihal Chand* v. *Jairamdas*[61] the Lahore High Court said that the question before the court did not relate to any interest in the property situated outside the jurisdiction of the court.

For the exercise of jurisdiction *in personam* it is essential that defendant must be within the jurisdiction of the court,[62] and if there are more than one defendant, all must be amenable to court's jurisdiction.[63]

54. See also *Prithi Singh* v. *Ganesh Prasad Singh*, 1951 All. 462, where most of the Indian decisions on jurisdiction *in personam* have been discussed.
55. Cited above.
56. *Niyyala Chayya* v. *Nittala Yellama*, 1923 Mad. 109; also *Hadjee Ismael* v. *Hadjee Mohmad*, 13 B.L.R. 91.
57. *Ramkrishyya* v. *Mahalakhamma*, 30 M.L.W. 691.
58. *Durgadas* v. *Jainarayan*, 1919 All. 350.
59. *Nihalchand* v. *Jairamdas*, 1931 Lah. 673.
60. 1919 All. 350.
61. 1931 Cal. 673.
62. *Mohamad Yashin* v. *Bimola Prasad*, 1924 Cal 443.
63. *Ibid.* See also *Hadjee Ismael* v. *Hadjee Mohmad*, 13 B.L.R. 91.

16

TRANSFER OF TANGIBLE MOVABLES

This chapter is concerned with transfer of movables, which is often called particular assignment of movables, as distinguished from general assignment, such as devolution of property on the death of a person, i.e. succession, or distribution of assets in bankruptcy. Transfer of tangible movables, or particular assignment of movable, means transfers *inter vivos*, such as sale, gift, pledge.

While there appears to be almost a universal acceptance of the principle that the *lex situs* governs all or almost all matters relating to immovables, there is no such acceptance of any one principle relating to movables, tangibles and intangibles. In fact, at the outset of our enquiry we are confronted with conflicting theories and confusing judicial pronouncements, from which it is well nigh impossible to deduce anything. The vital question is whether one system of law should be allowed to determine all questions that arise in respect of movables, or whether different laws should apply to different aspects of transfer, such as to assignability of movables, to formal validity, to material validity, to priorities, etc.

I
THEORIES

There exist as many as four theories, viz. the *lex domicilii*, the *lex situs*, the *lex loci actus* and the theory of proper law of transfer. The oldest of these theories is that of *lex domicilii* and newest, it seems, is the proper law theory.

The Domicile Theory : This is the oldest theory. The argument has been : the movables have no fixed *situs*; their *situs* can be shifted at any time by its owner. Therefore, the medieval Italian statutists propounded the principle of *mobila sequuntur personam.* This doctrine had wide acceptance not merely on the continent of Europe but also in England and the United States.[1] Judicially, it

1. Von Bar, p. 488, see note 1, where he had collected all the authorities of his time. See also the learned contribution of Chesterman (1973) 22 I.C.L.Q. 213.

was accepted in several cases between 1750-1830. In *Sill* v. *Worswick*,[2] Lord Loughborough said, "With respect to the disposition of it, with respect to the transmission of it either by succession or the act of the party, it follows the law of the person."[3] Originally, this principle was applied to the universal assignment and, it seems, judges and jurists without giving much thought to it, applied it to particular assignments also.

In the contemporary world, the theory have few advocates. It has been judicially abandoned both in England and the United States.

Cheshire says,[4] " . . . It is now generally agreed that to allow either party to invoke his *lex domicilii* in the case of a dispute arising out of a transfer of a chattles would be commercially impracticable and contrary both to natural justice and to the normal expectation of the parties themselves."[5] Graveson very aptly says : " . . . the chief defect of the domicile principle in this connection is its complete unpredictability in a world where men of commerce call, not always with success, for certainly."[6] However, Graveson favours the application of the theory to two situations : (i) when the movable is in the course of transit from one country to another at the date of assignment (e.g., goods delivered by post), so that it has no fixed *situs* between the place of dispatch and that of its ultimate destination.[7] Another illustration of this situation is when a ship is sold in the course of its voyage on the high seas. "In such a case reference cannot be reasonably made to the actual *situs* of the movable, and resort may be had to the law of domicile of the assignor or the *lex actus* of the assignment."[8] Graveson himself admits the limited application of the theory by saying that if movable came to rest through some interruption in transit, then the theory would not apply. (ii) The second case advocated by Graveson relates to non-commercial assignments, such as assignment of property to trustees of a settlement. He says that in such a case 'domicile may still be one of several relevant factors.'[9] It is submitted that the application of the domiciliary principle to any type of particular assignment of movables is going to serve no useful purpose and it is better to abandon the theory entirely.

The lex actus theory : The *lex actus* or *lex loci actus* theory is also a rejected theory in our contemporary world, though judicially it has been advocated in some cases and there are some writers

2. (1791) 1 Hy. Bl. 665.
3. *Ibid.*
4. Cheshire, p. 406.
5. *Ibid.*
6. Graveson, p. 472.
7. *Ibid.*, at p. 471.
8. *Ibid.*, at p. 473.
9. *Ibid.*, at p. 473 : reliance was made on Upjohn, J.'s observation in *Iveagh* v. *I.R.C.*, (1954) Ch. 364.

who also advocate it. In *Alcock* v. *Smith*[10] Kay, L.J. observed : "as to personal chattles, it is settled that the validity of a transfer depends, not upon the law of the domicile of the owner, but upon the law of the country in which transfer takes place."[11] Most of the writers of private international law have criticised this theory. Cheshire says that the mere fact that a transaction is completed in a particular place is no adequate reason for admitting the control of the local law. "If, for instance, an Englishman executes a document in Edinburgh granting a lien over his furniture in London to another Englishman, it is unthinkable that this slight and perhaps accidental connection with Scotland should require the possessory rights of the parties to be determined by Scot law."[12] Graveson gives another example to illustrate this :[13] A and B are flying from London to Prague.[13a] During the flight A sells to B his wife's jewellery in England. By English law he cannot do so, even though assuming he can do so under the law of any of the countries he is flying. He advances the illustration by saying that suppose at the very time A's wife in England sells her jewellery to X and, under English law, sale confers valid title on X. The *lex loci actus* theory fails.[14] In support of the theory Graveson says (and possibly nothing else can be said in its favour). "It is not unreasonable to suppose that the validity of an act should be governed by the law of the place where it is performed, for reasonable men expect to comply with the law of any country in which they may carry out their transaction."[15] The predominant English authority is against this theory.

The lex situs theory : In our times the *lex situs* is the most favoured theory. It has been accepted in English judicial pronouncements and by a majority of writers. In *Re Anzinani*[16] Maugham, J. said : "I do not think anybody can doubt that with regard to the transfer of goods, the law applicable must be the law of the country where movable is situate. Business could not be carried on if that were not so." Another English judge, Devlin, J. said : "There is little doubt that it is the *lex situs* which, as a general rule, governs the transfer of movables when effected contractually."[17] The writers like Savignly, Westlake, Dicey, Foote, Schminthoff and Wolff support this theory. Westlake said, "Questions as to transfer or acquisition of property in corporeal movables, or of any less extensive real rights in them as pledges

10. (1892) 1 Ch. 238.
11. *Ibid.*, at p. 267.
12. Cheshire, p. 408.
13. Graveson, p. 475.
13a. Graveson, pp. 475-76.
14. Wolff is also critical of this thing : Private International Law, pp. 517-18.
15. Graveson, p. 475.
16. (1930) 1 Ch. 407.
17. *Bank Voor Handel* v. *Slatford*, (1953) 1 Q.B. 248.

or lien, are generally to be decided by the *lex situs*."[18] In *Wickworth* v. *Christe, Mason and Woods Ltds.*[18a] the Chancery Division took for granted that under English private international law title the goods is determined by the *lex situs* of the goods. Dicey's Rule 152 was to the same effect.[19] In Dicey's eighth edition, Morris has retained this theory, though the rule has been worded differently.[20]

The *lex situs* theory obviously has its advantages, chief of which is that in most of the cases it provides a single and easily ascertainable system of law based on the focal point of transaction, namely, the goods with which the transaction deals.[21] "Moreover, its right of control satisfies the expectations of the reasonable man for a party to transfer naturally concludes that the transaction will be subject to the law of the country in which the subject-matter is at present situated."[22]

Morris who supports the *lex situs* theory and is critical of proper law theory says that a distinction has to be drawn between the contractual effects of transfer and its proprietary effects. The former depends upon the proper law of the contract but the latter on the *lex situs*. He says that in connection with transfer of property the proprietary effects of the transfer are more important than the contractual effects and gives three reasons for this : first the transferor may fraudulently deliver the goods to a third party. instead of to the other party to the contract. It is true that in this case transferor is liable in damages for breach of contract, but then, that does not conclude the question of title. In whom does the title in the transferred goods vests ? Secondly, in a case a transferor becomes insolvent before the delivery of the goods to the transferee, according to the proper law the property in good would vest in the transferee, but according to the *lex situs* in the transferor's trustee in bankruptcy. Thirdly, in case of gifts, the transferor is not under any contractual obligation to perfect the transferee's title.[23] The strongest argument in favour of the *lex situs* is that under no other system, the adjudication may be effective.[24] Morris maintains that in the converse case i.e., when the court is sitting at the *situs* of good, also the court should apply the conflicts rules and not the domestic law.[25]

The *lex situs* theory break down totally in one case, *viz*. when the goods are in transit. Graveson says that this situation is met

18. Westlake, s. 150.
18a. (1980) 1 All E.R. 1121.
19. Dicey, 9th Edition, p. 534.
20. Rule 81 Dicey and Morris, p. 544.
21. Graveson, p. 477.
22. Cheshire, p. 408.
23. Dicey and Morris, pp. 546-47.
24. *Ibid*, pp. 457-58.
25. *Ibid*.

by the mercantile practice of treating the normal documents of title to such goods; such as, bills of landing, as reprensenting the good themselves, so that in effect the relevant *situs* is generally that of the document of title.[26] In those cases where no such title deeds exist, the *lex situs* theory cannot work and to meet such a situation Morris admits of an exception : "If goods are in transit, and their *situs* is casual or not known, a transfer which is valid and effective by its proper law will (semble) be valid and effective."[27]

The Proper Law Theory : Admitting the virtues of the *lex situs* theory, Cheshire says, ". . . It is going too far to say that every type of question must be submitted to the law of the *situs* and to that law alone." On this premises, he propounds the theory of proper law thus : the law "that may be chosen to govern questions arising out of the transfer of movables is the law of the country with which the transfer has the most real connection or more shortly, the *lex actus*, i.e., the proper law of the transfer, analogous to the proper law of the contract."[28] The ascertainment of the proper law would not present any difficulty, if the proper law and the *lex situs* is the same. But the difficult case will be where it is not so. Cheshire himself gives the following example: A, resident and domiciled in England, sells goods lying in a Naples warehouse to B, a resident and domiciled in Holland. From these facts alone we cannot say what will be the proper law of the transfer "Before it could reach a decision the court would require to know, *inter alia* : where was the transfer effected ? If reduced to writing, was it drafted in terms peculiar to English or Dutch law ? Were the goods only temporarily in Italy ?[29] Cheshire does not give any answer. Probably, the proper law theory cannot give an answer to a situatibn like this. Cheshire himself admits that the *lex situs* governs questions between one of the original parties to a transfer and a third person who has obtained derivative title from the other party, but he maintains that the proper law of the transfer, and not the *lex situs*, governs the validity and effect of transfer when the question arises between the original parties thereto.[30] Morris who is critical of proper law theory (his criticism we have noted in connection with the *lex situs* theory) is in favour of applying it to goods in transit.[31]

II

TRANSFER OF PROPERTY

The rules of English and Indian private international law relating to transfer of tangible movables are still in the formative

26. Graveson, p. 477.
27. Diecy and Morris, p. 550.
28. Cheshire, p. 408.
29. *Ibid.*, p. 409.
30. *Ibid.*
31. Dicey and Morris, p. 550.

stage. The controversy among writers, as we have already seen, is still raging as to which law should govern, though the main contest is between the protagonist of the *lex situs* theory and the proper law theory. We may discuss the present law under the following three heads :

(a) matters arising between parties to the transfer,

(b) matters arising from the transfer which affect third parties, and

(c) certain special types of transfer.

Matters arising between the Parties to Transfer

As has been seen earlier in respect of transfer of property, two main questions may arise between the parties to the transfer : (a) contractual question, and (b) proprietary questions. The former is obviously governed by the proper law of the contract and we are not concerned with it here. It is the latter question with which we are concerned. The question is : if a dispute arises between the parties as to title to property or as to possessory rights to property, which law should govern the matter ? In *Inglis* v. *Usherwood*,[32] an English merchant purchased some goods in Russia through his factor and ordered him to ship the goods to England. The goods were loaded on a vessel which the English merchant had chartered and of which the defendant was the captain. When the goods were on the board of the ship, the Russian factor came to know of the bankruptcy of the English merchant and consequently ordered the captain to deliver up the cargo, which the captain complied. Under the Russian law the action of the factor was proper, but it was not so under English law, as under English law property in goods passed to the merchant on being slipped abroad his own charatered vessel. This is also the Indian law.[33] The English court held that the Russian law applied. It is interesting to note that both the *lex situs* and proper law were Russian. Therefore, the judgment can be marshalled in support of both theories. In *Cammell* v. *Sewell*[34] on the order of an English merchant, residing in England, his Russian agent shipped a cargo of deals on board a Prussian vessel owned and commanded by a Prussian captain. The goods were consigned to the English merchant under an ordinary bill of lading and were to be carried to Hull. On the coast of Norway the vessel was wrecked, but the cargo was safely brought to the shore of Norway. Under the law of Norway the captain of the vessel in such circumstances was responsible to the owners if he sold goods improperly, but nonetheless he had power to sell the cargo so as to pass good title to a *bona fide* purchaser. The goods were in fact sold by the captain to a *bona fide* purchaser who brought the goods to England. In

32. (1801) 1 East 515.

33. See s. 23(2), Sale of Goods Act, 1980.

34. (1858) 3 H. & N. 617, on appeal, (1860) 5 H. & N. 728.

England, the English merchant brought an action of trover for them. The court said that law of Norway applied and therefore the action of trover failed. It was observed, "If personal property is disposed of in a manner binding according to the law of the country where it is, that disposition is binding everywhere; and we do not think that it makes any difference that the goods were wrecked, and not intended to be sent to the country where they were sold."

Cheshire favours the application of proper law.[35] As has been seen earlier Morris propagates the application of the *lex situs*, though he is for the application of the total *renvoi* theory.[36]

Question affecting Third Parties

The problem that arise under this head is : Suppose A an Englishman purchases a Chinese made car in Pakistan and brings it to India. Now suppose, by Indian law such a purchase is not valid. Nonetheless, A's title in the car will be recognized as it is recognized under the *lex situs*. Now suppose, A takes the car from B, the dealer in Pakistan, for a trial run, and brings it to India and despite several demands, does not return it to B. At this stage the title of B will be recognized in India. But suppose A sells it to C, an Indian who is a *bona fide* purchaser, under the circumstances that are covered under s. 30, Indian Sales of Goods Act, 1930 (or s. 25, English Sales of Goods Act, 1893 or ss. 2, 8 or 9, English Factor Act, 1889), then the title acquired by C will be respected and given effect to over the title of B, if the *lex situs* is to govern the matter. There seems to be least controversy on this matter and the judges and writers appear to be unanimous that the *lex situs* is the governing law. We had already discussed the English authority, *Cammell* v. *Sewell*.[37] The rule obviously causes hardship to the original owner, but it cannot be helped.[38]

Cheshire also holds the view that in such cases the *lex situs* should govern. He says, ". . . in this type of case logic and principle must certainly yield to expediency. The *lex situs* must prevail on practical grounds."[39] Wolff says, "As the place a thing is situate is the natural centre of rights over it, everybody concerned with the things may be expected to reckon with the law of such place."[40] Cheshire sums up the position by saying that it is now established that the effect of a particular assignment of movables is governed exclusively by the law of the country where they are situated at the time of assignment. An owner would be divested

35. Cheshire, p. 410.
36. Dicey and Morris, pp. 544-48.
37. Cited above.
38. *Cammell* v. *Sewell*, cited above.
39. Cheshire, 412.
40. Private International Law (second edition), p. 520.

of his title to movables if they are taken to a foreign country and there assigned in circumstances sufficient by the local law to pass a valid title to the assignee. The title recognized by the foreign *lex situs* overrides earlier and inconsistent titles, no matter by what law they have been reated.[41] Cheshire says that this applies to derivative title also. Cheshire[42] and Dicey and Morris[43] are for the application of the doctrine of *convoi*, i.e. the *lex situs* here means the law that the court at the *situs* will apply to the case before it.[44]

Special Types of Transfers

Gifts : In Indian law gifts *inter vivos* of movables may be effected by a registered instrument signed by or on behalf of the donor and attested by at least to witnesses or by delivery.[45] Under English law gift of chattels must be confirmed by delivery or executed under seal. An oral gift which has not been followed by delivery of possession cannot be enforced as contract. The question is : which law applies to gifts ? *Lex situs* or proper law. Or, in other words, when does the property pass to the transferee, and if so, under which law ? Cheshire gives an illustration to explain the problem. "If merely by words of present gift spoken in London, an Englishman purports to pass to another the ownership of a horse kept at the stables in Paris, no title whatsover will pass to the donee. He will be frustrated by the English rule that a gift of chattels is nullity unless confirmed by delivery or executed under seal.. Even if the French law were to have a less rigorous rule, it would not avail the donee."[46] These are the facts of *Cochrane* v. *Moore*.[47] The case was decided according to English law, but then the French law was not pleaded.[48] Dicey and Morris say that by the French law, the law of the *situs* of the horse; words of the gift pass the title to the donee. Thus, Cheshire favours the application of proper law to such gifts, as he insists that as between the parties the proper law determines whether the property in goods has passed to the other party. Morris, on the other hand, favours the application of the *lex situs*. Cheshire too would favour application of the *lex situs* if the donor sells the horse to a third party.

Donationes Mortis Causa : *Donationes Mortis Causa* are recognized both in the Indian and English law. Section 191 of the Indian Succession Act, 1925 lays down that a person may dispose,

41. Cheshire, p. 412.
42. *Ibid.*, p. 414.
43. Dicey and Morris, p. 548.
44. Cheshire cites *Dulaney* v. *Merry and Sons*, (1901) 1 K.B. 536 in support of this proposition.
45. Section 123, Transfer of Porperty Act, 1882.
46. Cheshire, p. 411.
47. (1890) 25 Q.B.D. 57.
48. The facts of this case are also given in Dicey's Conflict of Laws under Rule 81, in illustration 4 and the learned editor's comments are, "B (i.e. donee) is (semble) the owner of the horse," Dicey, p. 549.

by gift made in contemplation of death, of any movable property which he could dispose of by will. Delivery of possession is necessary. Such gifts do not take effect if the donor recovered from the illness during which it was made or if the donor survived the donee. Such gifts are regarded as gifts *inter vivos* and not testamentary disposition. *Donationes mortis causa*, gift *muraz-ul-maut* are also recognized in Muslim law, but they are considered part of testamentary disposition. In English law also *donationes mortis causa* are regarded as gifts *inter vivos*. The English law applies the *lex situs* to determine the nature of the transaction in *donationes mortis causa*. In *Re Korvine's Trusts*,[49] a person, domiciled in the Soviet Union and resident in England, made a gift of his movables situated in England to take affect on his death. By the law of the Soviet Union, the *lex domicilii*, the gift was void, but the English court applied the *lex situs* (or *lex actus*) and held the gift valid. From this case inference seems to be that the capacity to make a *donationes mortis causa*, the form of the gift and the material validity are all to be governed by the *lex situs*. In this case, incidentally the proper law of the gift was also English law. On the other hand, in *Re Carven's Estate*[50] a different approach was made. In this case a testarix who died domiciled in England made a *donationes morits causa* of moneys situated in Monaco. Russell, J. considered the matter as of testamentary disposition and applied English law, being the *lex domicilli* of the testarix at the time of her death. But the learned judge further held that what was the necessary to pass the dominion must be determined by the law of Monaco, the *lex situs* of moneys, and he was satisfied that the domination in the moneys has been validly transferred to the donee according to the *lex situs*.

Goods in Transit : The difficulty about the goods in transit is that they have no fixed *situs*; they have a shifting *situs* and therefore the *lex situs* cannot govern. The problem may be stated thus : A and B enter into a contract in Bangladesh for the sale of certain goods lying in a Calcutta warehouse to be transported through the road. While the goods are in transit, they are sold to someone else. Which law should govern. The *lex situs* is out of the question. The *lex domicilii* has been almost unanimously rejected as a test in commercial transactions, even when the domicile of the seller and purchaser is the same; and in case it is different, then the further question would be : whose domicile, vendor's or vendee's ? The law of the stipulated place of destination has also been suggested. Objecting to this test, Lord Watson very pertinently said : "I am not prepared to hold that whenever the cargo of a ship is destined to a port in one country, the dealings of the owner of the cargo with the bill of lading which represents and carries the property of the goods must in every other country be governed by the law of the *locus* where the ship

49. (1921) 1 Ch. 343.
50. (1937) Ch. 423.

is to unload."[51] So far the question has not arisen directly in any case. The reason seems to be that the bill of lading or other documents which symbolize the ownership are capable of independent dealings. Morris treats this case as an exception to the general principle that the *lex situs* governs the transfer of movables and advocates the application of proper law. The learned editor propounds this rule very reservedly. He says: "It should be noted that this Exception has a somewhat limited scope. It is expressed in positive terms only, and does not assert that a transfer which is invalid or ineffective by its proper law will necessarily be treated as invalid or ineffective in England. Nor does it apply when the goods have come to a rest a definite state in the transit, as when a ship is wrecked and the cargo is saved."[52] To the situation contemplated in the last sentence, the *lex situs*, it seems, would apply.[53] Cheshire says: "The proper law is, no doubt, suitable to govern questions dependent upon the effect of a particular transaction, but scarcely apposite to every question. The truth again is that no one law can be made the exclusive arbiter of disputes arising out of a transfer of goods *in itinere*. The problem must be broken down. A dispute between the parties to a particular transaction, as, for example, a mortage of the goods granted by the assignee, will be governed by the proper law of the transaction. If the movables comes to rest sufficiently to admit of a dealing with them, as where they are seized by creditors in accordance with the local law or wrongfully sold by the carrier, the question of title must be clearly determined by the *lex situs*. If the transit is by sea in one ship, there is much to be said for applying the law of the flag."[54]

The Ship: If a ship on high seas is transferred, the question is which law is to govern? It should be noted that the ship is a very movable object. The same question is likely to arise in respect of air-crafts which are sold or transferred in any other mode. In Dicey's Conflicts of Laws, fifth edition, the law of the flag of the ship was advocated.[55] The difficulty in this test lies in respect of composite states. Therefore, the law of flag would indeed mean—if it has any meaning—the law in force at the port of the ship's registration. It should be noted that the employment of the law of ship's flag is a fiction of law—a means of ascertaining of fixing *situs* of an otherwise very movable thing. Therefore, if the ship acquires a *situs* in territorial waters or at some port the fiction no longer remains necessary, and the law of the actual *situs* of the ship should be applied. This is the view taken by the English courts. In *Liverpool Marine Credit Co.* v. *Hunter*,[56] A, an

51. *Inglis* v. *Robertson*, (1898) A.C. 616 at p. 627.
52. Dicey, p. 550.
53. *Cammell* v. *Sewell*, (1860) 5 H. & N. 728.
54. Cheshire, p. 419.
55. Dicey, Conflict of Laws, 5th ed., p. 996.
56. (1867) L.R. 2 Ch. App. 282.

Englishman, mortgaged a ship to B, another Englishman, in London. When the ship was in New Orleans, then P, a creditor of A got it attached for his debt. Under the law of New Orleans the mortgage of the ship was invalid. To prevent the ship being sold in execution, B gave a bond to P. Later on B filed a suit for injuction to prevent P from getting the bonds enforced. The House of Lords applied the *lex situs* of the ship and held that the bond was enforceable.[57]

Negotiable Instruments : In the modern law negotiable instruments, such as bills of exchange, cheque, etc. are regarded for the purpose of assignment as tangible movables. They are subject to numerous successive assignments. The intangible nature of right to payment of money inherent in them has been merged into the tangible nature of the document which has come to represent the title to such right. We shall discuss them in Chapter 21.

57. See also *Hooper* v. *Gumm*, (1867) L.R. 2 Ch. App. 282.

17

ASSIGNMENT OF INTANGIBLE MOVABLES

At one time when the maxim *mobilia sequuntur personam* ruled the day, the *lex domicilii* was suggested to be the law applicable to all aspects of assignment of intangible movables. At that time it was thought that intangibles have no *situs*. But later on an artificial *situs* or quasi-*situs* was ascribed to the intangible movables for different legal purposes. This led to the propagation of the *lex situs* theory. When the theory of proper law of contract came to be established, a theory of proper law of assignment was propounded by some. In between these theories, the theory of *lex loci actus* has also been propounded. Thus, there have been four theories of assignment of intangible movables. They are : (a) The *lex domicilii* theory, (b) the *lex situs* theory, (c) the *lex loci actus* theory, and (d) the proper law theory.

I

THEORIES

The lex domicilii theory : This theory was propounded in the hey day of the maxim, *mobilia sequuntur personam*. In our contemporary world, it has practically no advocates, though at one time it has a galaxy of some prominent advocates of which Story and Phillimore were at the top. Phillimore spoke of the theory succinctly thus : "Debts and rights and causes of action are universally treated by jurists as attached to the person of the creditors and governed by the law of his domicile. They may be subject to assignment either absolutely or conditionally, with or without notice to the debtor, according to that law."[1] Morris rightly says : "Domicile is of great importance in family law, but has little significance in commercial matters, except perhaps as an element in determining the proper law of the transaction."[2] The fact of the matter is that the *lex domicilii* cannot be applied in many cases. It has been abandoned even in the countries of

1. Phillimore, IV, 544.
2. Dicey and Morris, p. 559.

continental Europe. There is no English authority in favour of this theory.

The lex situs theory : Those who have advocated the application of the *lex situs* to the tangible movables, also advocates its application to the assignment of intangible movables : Westlake and Dicey were its main protagonists. Dicey said :[3] "An assignment of a movable which cannot be touched, i.e. of a debt, giving a good title thereto according to the *lex situs* of the debt (in so far as by analogy a *situs* can be attributed to a debt) is valid."[4] The most elaborate statement on the theory is that of Lord Justice Atkin. His Lordship observed : "The question as to the locality, the situation of a debt or *chose in action* is obviously difficult, because it involves consideration of what must be considered to be legal fictions. A debt or *chose in action*, as a matter of fact, is not a matter of which you can predicate position; nevertheless for a great many purposes it has to be ascertained where the debt or *chose in action* is situated. . . . The test in respect of simple contract was where was the debtor residing ? No one knows that, ordinarily speaking, accordingly to our law, a debtor has to seek out his creditor and pay him; but it seems plain that the reason why the residence of the debtor was adopted as that which determines where the debt was situated was because it was in that place where the creditor could, in fact, enforce payment of the debt . . . that being the place where under the ordinary circumstances the debt is enforceable."[5]

The modern advocates of the theory are Falconbridge[6] and Schmitthoff.[7] This theory has many difficulties in its practical application. Morris rightly says : While this theory 'avoids problems of priorities as between conflicting transfers' it 'involves the difficulty that only an artificial *situs* or quasi-*situs* can be ascribed to an intangible thing.'[8] Since the situs of the debt is the place where the debtor resides, the theory would fail if the debtor resides at several places, such as in the case of corporations which may be doing business at several places. In fact, this was the difficulty with which Lord Atkin was faced in *New York Life Insurance Co.* v. *Public Trustee*,[9] and his Lordship were forced to evolve another test : the place where the payment would be exigible is the place of the *situs* of the debt. But if the debtor has only one residence, than the *situs* of the debt is that place even if the debt is payable at a different place. Cheshire says rightly : "The fact, however, that debt possesses a definite, though artificial,

3. Dicey, 5th ed., Rule 154.
4. See also Westlake, s. 152.
5. *New York Life Insurance Co.* v. *Public Trustee*, (1924) 2 Ch. 101, at p. 119.
6. Falconbridge, p. 274.
7. English Conflict of Laws, (3rd Ed.) p. 211.
8. Dicey and Morris, p. 559.
9. Cited above.

situation for certain purposes does not necessarily imply that its assignment should be governed by the *lex situs*."[10] Bose, J. has been also critical of the theory in *Delhi Cloth and General Mills Ltd.* v. *Harnam Singh.*[11]

The lex loci actus theory: According to protagonists of this view, the place, where the assignment is made, or where the document assigning the debts is executed, is the governing factor and the assignment is governed by the law of that place. This theory has been advocated by English judges in several cases.[12] This theory was applied to formal validity and capacity of assignment in *Republic de Guatemala* v. *Nunez.*[13] Graveson seems to support the application of this theory to certain aspect of assignment, particularly as to the validity and effect of the assignment between the assignor and the assignee. But Graveson admits, that the theory cannot be applied as to the validity and effect of an assignment as between the assignor and the original debtor; it can also not be applied to questions of priorities of competing assignments if the law of each of the various assignments renders valid the assignment subject to it.[14] Justice Bose also to some extent supported this theory in the *Delhi Cloth and General Mills Ltd.* v. *Harnam Singh.*[15] This theory is obviously unworkable and can be applied only to one aspect of assignment.

The proper law theory: The modern theory is the theory of proper law. Cheshire explains the theory thus: "The clue is furnished by Foote, when he says that the assignment of a *chose in action* arising out of a contract is governed by the proper law of contract. If we understand him correctly, the appropriate law is not the proper law of (using that expression in the contractual sense) of the assignment, but the proper law of the original transaction out of which the *chose in action* arose. It is reasonable and logical to refer most questions relating to a debt to the transaction in which it has source and the legal system which governs that transaction . . . This is not to deny that certain questions are determined by the proper law of the assignment itself, as for example those concerned with formal validity of a particular assignment . . . .One undeniable merit of this is that, where there has been assignment in different countries, no confusion can arise from a conflict of laws, since all questions are referred to one single system."[16] Bose, J. supports Cheshire's formulation of the proper law theory. He said that 'driven to a choice, we would prefer this

10. Cheshire, p. 422.
11. (1955) S.C.J. 645 at p. 652.
12. *Lee* v. *Adby* (1886) 17 Q.B.D. 309; *Alcock* v. *Smith*, (1892) 1 Ch. 238; *Embricos* v. *Anglo Austrian Bank*, (1905) 1 K.B. 677; *Republic de Guatemala* v. *Nunez*, (1927) 1 K.D. 669; *Re Anziani*, (1930) 1 Ch. 407.
13. Cited above.
14. Graveson, pp. 491-92.
15. Cited above, at p. 652.
16. Cheshire, p. 422.

way of stating the law.'[17] The merit of this theory is that it avoids problems of priorities between competing assignments, and also avoids conflicts between the rights and obligations of the debtor and creditor on the one hand, and those of the assignor and assignee on the other.[18]

Morris very rightly says that in most cases the proper law of the debt coincides with its artificial *situs*, and therefore this test, like the *lex situs* test, in inconsistent with the most recent authorities.[19] Graveson says that this theory would not apply to assignment of intangible movables other than *chose in action*, such as patents, in which the *lex situs* would always be decisive.[20] Morris holds the view that the key to the problem of application of governing law to the assignments of intangible movables lies in not applying the same law to all aspect of assignments. Thus he suggests that questions relating to assignability and of the intrinsic validity of the assignment should be governed by the proper law of the debt, and questions of attachment or garnishment should be governed by the *lex situs* of the debt.[21]

II

ASSIGNMENT OF INTANGIBLE

The rules of English and Indian Private International laws relating to assignment of intangible movables are far from satisfactory. It would help in the understanding of the subject if we divide the assignment of intangible movables under the following two heads :

A. Those intangible movables which are represented by the right itself, i.e. right of action. Debt is a very common instance of this type of intangible movable property. The debt may arise from a loan or it may arise out of mercantile transactions.

The assignment of debts may be :

(a) Voluntary, i.e. when a creditor assign the debt by his own free will to some one; or

(b) Involuntary, when the rights of a creditor are assigned to some one against his will, such as when the debt is attached in execution of a money decree against the creditor.

B. The other type of intangible movable property is that which is represented by a document or writing which is capable of

17. *Delhi Cloth and General Mills Ltd.* v. *Harnam Singh*, cited above, at p. 654.
18. See Dicey and Morris, p. 559; Graveson, p. 493.
19. Dicey and Morris, p. 559.
20. Graveson, p. 493.
21. Dicey and Morris, p. 559.

delivery and which is also negotiable as a separate entity. Under this head the most common examples are :

(a) Negotiable instruments, such as bills of exchange and cheques, and

(b) Shares.

Tangible Movables which are mere Rights of Action

It is submitted that the key to the problem lies, as Morris says, in treating different aspects of assignment separately and in not insisting that all aspects of assignment should be governed by the same system of law.[22]

Voluntary Assignment

The state of judicial confusion that exists in English law is evident from the opinions expressed in the leading English case, *Republica de Guatemala* v. *Nunez*.[23] In this case, Cabrera, at a time when he was President of Guatemala had deposited large sums of money with a London bank. He assigned this sum of money to his son, who was then a minor. Cabrera was then deposed, and, while he was in prison, assigned this very sum of money to the Republic. The first assignment was valid by English law, but was invalid by the law of Guatemala. In an action before the English court the validity of the assignment to the son of Cabrera arose. The Republic of Guatemala also presented its claim. Both the claims were dismissed by the court. The debt was obviously situated in England. The only question of importance was whether the validity of the assignment was governed by the Guatemalan law or by English law. The trial judge, Greer, J. dismissed the claim of the son on the basis that the formalities required under *lex actus*, i.e. law of Guatemala were not complied with. The Court of Appeal also dismissed the claim of both parties, but for different reasons. Scrutton, L.J. said that the capacity of the parties and the validity and effect of assignment in form and results must be determined by the *lex domicilii* or the *lex actus* (which were in this case the same). Lawrence, L.J. held the assignment to the son invalid as, according to him, son has no capacity to accept the gift both by the assignee's personal law and by the *lex actus*. However, he supported the theory of the *lex situs*. The third judge, Bankes, L.J., got involved in the question of priorities. He then said that the validity of the assignments must be judged by the law of the domicile of the parties.

This being the state of judicial opinion, expressed in the leading case, one can visualize the state of the present law. We

22. *Ibid.*
23. Cited above.

would proceed to discuss various aspects of assignments of intangible movables.

Assignability : Which law should govern the assignability of debt or other intangible movables falling in this category ? Jurists seem to be predominantly of the view that the assignability of the debt depends on the law under which it arose or was created,[24] or on the proper law of the debt (so far as it affects the debtor).[25] In other words, the assignability of intangible movables is governed by the law which created it or the proper law of the original transaction out of which it arose. Morris rightly says that the liability of the debtor ought not to be increased by an assignment, whatever might be its proper law.[26] Thus if notice to the debtor is required by the proper law of the debt, or if by that law the assignee takes subject to equities, or if by that law the debt is not assignable (such as claims for damages in tort and certain military pensions are not assignable under English law), it would hardly be material if a different view of the matter is taken by the proper law of the assignment. The only relevant English case on this subject is *Campbell Connelly and Co. Ltd.* v. *Noble*,[27] where a composer of a popular tune and the owner of the English and American copyright therein assigned the copyright in the tune to a company 'in all countries . . . so far as it is assignable by law. together with all rights which the composer now has or may hereafter become entitled to'. By virtue of international conventions the copyright can exist by operation of law in many countries simultaneously. The American copyright law provides two periods of copyright : first period of twenty-eight years commences from the date of the publication; the second, the renewal period, of twenty-eight years commences, if the composer is still living, at the end of the first period of the copyright. This was not so under English law. In respect of the assignment of the copyright operative in the United States, the English court said : "The disputed subject-matter is the creation of the law of the United States of America, and I must look at the law in order to ascertain whether it is assignable at all, and if so in what conditions it is assignable ?"

Thus, it is submitted that so far as the question of relationship of debtor and creditor, the assignability of the debt should be governed by the proper law of the debt, but so far as the relationship of assignor and assignee is concerned, its validity should be judged by the proper law of assignment. For instance, if consideration is not necessary for the validity of the assignment by the proper law of the debt, then the proper law of the debt should have no say on the matter. It should be the proper law of the assignment which should govern the matter.

24. See Graveson, 496.
25. Dicey and Morris, p. 558.
26. *Ibid.*, p. 560.
27. (1963) 1 W.L.R. 252.

Capacity : There is an utter confusion in the English authorities on the subject of capacity to assign an intangible movable property. In *Lee* v. *Adby*[28] a husband assigned a policy of insurance issued by an English company to his wife at the Cape, where parties were domiciled. The assignment was valid by English law, but was invalid by the law of the Cape colony as there a person could not assign the policy of insurance to his own wife. On the suit of the wife against the English insurance company, the latter pleaded that the assignment was invalid. The court applied the law of the Cape colony, probably as the law of the domicile, and held the assignment void. It may be noted that the *lex actus* was also the Cape. Therefore, it may be that the *lex actus* was in the mind of the court. We have already noted the leading case of *Republica de Guatemala* v. *Nunez*[29] where four judges expressed four views on the question of capacity.

Although the judicial opinion is confusing and conflicting, it is heartening to note that the jurists are almost unanimous that the capacity of assignment should be governed by the proper law of assignment. Cheshire rightly says : "The assignment of the debt, so far as concerns the capacity of the parties, stands on the same footing as a mercantile contract in which case the question is governed by the proper of the contract."[30] Morris also takes the same view, and says that the language of the judges should be interpreted broadly as meaning the proper law of assignment.[31]

Intrinsic Validity : The same confusion of judicial opinion prevails here also. In the *Guatemala case*, Scrutton, L.J. observed, *obiter* : "In my opinion both the capacity of the parties to enter into such a transaction and the validity and effect of such a transaction in form and results must be determined by one or other of those laws (i.e. . . . . *lex actus* and *lex domicilii*) . . ."[32] The leading case on the matter is *Re Anziana*.[33] Under a settlement, drafted in English language and form, the trustees of which were persons resident in the United Kingdom, a married woman domiciled in Italy was entitled to certain moneys. She made an assignment of part of these moneys to two trustees, both of whom resided in London. The assignment was invalid by Italian law since it did not comply with the requirement of the Civil Code. The Italian law regarded the requirement of Civil Code as a matter of essential validity. The English court applied the Italian law as the *lex loci actus* (following the above quoted observation of Scrutton, L.J.). Cheshire says that this decision is right as the proper law of the assignment was Italian law.[34]

28. (1886) 17 Q.B.D. 309.
29. (1927) 1 K.B. 669.
30. Cheshire, p. 425.
31. Dicey and Morris, pp. 562-63.
32. (1927) 1 K.B. 669 at p. 693.
33. (1930) 1 Ch. 407.
34. Cheshire, p. 427.

It is submitted that matter of intrinsic validity of assignment should be looked into from two angles :

(a) as regards the relationship of debtor and creditor and matters between them, such as whether the debt is assignable. This, as we have already seen, is to be determined by the proper law of the debt.

(b) As regards matters between the assignor and assignee, it is submitted, the matters including the intrinsic or material validity of the transaction should be governed by the proper law of the assignment.[35] Morris is in favour of the application of the same principles which apply to contracts.[36]

Formalities : The judicial observations as to formal validity of an assignment made in the *Guatemala case* have already been noted. In that case the court expressed itself in favour of the *lex actus*. In *Dulaney* v. *Merry and Sons*[37] it was thought that an assignment would be formally ineffective unless it complied with and special form prescribed by the *lex situs*. Morris holds the view that the formalities should ordinarily be governed by the proper law of assignment, but if the assignment is valid by the law of the place where it is made, then it will be valid, even if it is not formally valid by its proper law.[38] Morris makes the following comment : "The scope of the Exception is necessarily limited, because in the great majority of cases the law of the place where the assignment was made is the same as the proper law of assignment. But cases are conceivable in which they may differ."[39] Cheshire also takes this view that an assignment which is valid either by its proper law or by its *lex loci actus* will be formally valid.[40]

Priorities : The question of priorities arises when there are successive valid assignment of the same property or debt. The question came before the English court in *Keppy* v. *Selwyn*.[41] In this case two valid assignments were made of a certain trust fund. The first assignment was executed in New York, where, at that time, assignor was domiciled. Since the law of New York did not require any notice of assignment, no notice was given to the trustees. The second assignment was made thirteen years later by a deed executed in England. As required by English law, immediate notice of this assignment was given to the trustees. In a dispute arising in respect of these assignments before the English

35. See Dicey and Morris, pp. 562-563.
36. *Ibid.*, at p. 562.
37. (1901) 1 K.B. 536 at p. 542.
38. Dicey and Morris, pp. 562-565.
39. *Ibid.*, at p. 564.
40. Cheshire, p. 426.
41. (1905) 2 Ch. 117.

court, decision was given in favour of the second assignee. Warrington, J. observed : "The ground upon which I decide it is that the fund is here, being an English trust fund and this being the court which would have administered that trust fund, the order in which the parties are to be held entitled to the trust must be regulated by the law of the court which is administering that fund."[42] Scrutton, L.J. said that Warrington, J. treated the issue as one for the *lex fori*.[43] However, nothing is clear, the learned judge might have applied English law as the *lex situs* or as the proper law as much as the *lex fori*. Cheshire seems to support Morris who says that if the language of the judge is considered as a whole the inference can be drawn that he meant to apply the proper law of the trust fund.[44] Morris, it is submitted rightly, says : "It is obvious that question of priorities cannot be governed by the *lex loci actus* of the assignment or by its proper law, because the assignments may have been made in different countries or may be governed by different proper laws, and there is no reason why one law should govern rather than the other. It appears that the only possible laws which can govern priorities are the proper law of the debt or other intangible thing, the *lex situs* of the debt, or the *lex fori*. It is submitted that the first of these laws accord best with principle and authority."[45]

Indian Law

On voluntary assignment of intangible movables, only one decision of Indian courts is available. As is the usual practice of our courts most of the English authorities have been quoted extensively and reliance has been placed on them.[46] The case is : *Rabindra N. Maitra* v. *Life-Insurance Corporation of India*.[47] Where the father assigned his life insurance policy to his son. The assignment deed was made in Bombay and due notice of assignment of the policy was given to the insurance company's office at Bombay. Under the terms of the policy the sum assured was payable in Bombay. The insurance policy was taken before partition of India in Rajshahi and premiums were paid in the Dacca office of the company. Rajshahi and Dacca became part of Pakistan after partition. The insurance company alleged that the insurance policy

42. *Ibid.*, at p. 122.

43. *Republica Guatemala* v. *Nunez*, (1927) 1 K.B. 669; Westlake also held the same view : s. 152.

44. Cheshire, 429 supporting Morris's view expressed in Cases on Private International Law, (3rd. ed.) pp. 341-42.

45. Dicey and Morris, p. 565; *Le Feuvre* v. *Sullivan*, (1855) 10 Moo. P.C. 1 is the authority quoted in support. Another authority in support of this view is ; *Compania de Colomiana de Seguros* v. *Pacific Steam Navigation Co.*, (1965) 1 Q.B. 101 at pp. 128-29; most of the English authors who support this view : Cheshire, pp. 429-30; Graveson, pp. 499-500; Wolff, p. 538; Schmithoff, pp. 209-10.

46. Cheshire and Halisbury's Law of England have also been quoted.

47. 1964 Cal. 141.

has been confiscated by the Government of Pakistan, and therefore, they were not liable to make payment to the assignee. On evidence the court found that the proposal for the insurance policy was received and accepted in Bombay and the policy was executed and issued at Bombay and it was also payable in Bombay in Indian rupees. The mere fact that the premiums were paid at the Dacca branch hardly matters. On these facts the court came to the conclusion that the proper law of the contract of insurance is Indian law and it is this law which governs the contract. Relying on Dicey,[48] Cheshire[49] and Halsbury's Laws of England,[50] U.C. Law, J. observed : "Thus it is clear that the assignment of a chose in action arising out of a contract is governed by the proper law of the contract. It is reasonable and logical to refer most questions relating to a debt to the transaction in which it has its source and to the legal system which governs the transaction. One undeniable merit of this is that where there have been assignments in different countries, no confusion can arise from a conflict of laws since all questions are referred to a single legal system."[51] In the result Indian law was applied and the assignment was held valid.

Involuntary Alienation

English Law

Garnishment under English law (which is called attachment under Indian law) is an instance of involuntary assignment. Another instance of involuntary assignment is when a customer's credit at a bank or at the hands of another individual or person is vested by legislation in some authority or government. Garnishment is a process whereunder a judgment-creditor is allowed to attach a sum of money (usually it is a liquidated sum, though in some cases it may be an unliquidated amount) owed to his judgment-debtor which is in the hands of a third party called garnishee. The involuntary assignment may fall under the following two heads :

(1) When the debt of a private individual, whether national or otherwise, whether domiciled or not, is attached by an individual in execution of his decree by the ordinary process of law, and

(2) When a debt or credit is vested in an authority or governmental agency by legislation.

As far as the question of assignment is concerned, the considerations in both the cases are the same. The law in respect of involuntary assignment may be taken to be well settled; the predominant authority is in favour of the *lex situs*.

48. Conflict of Laws, 7th ed., Rules 89-90.
49. Private International Law, 5th ed., pp. 461-64.
50. Third Editian, Vol. VII.
51. *Rabindra Nath Maitra* v. *L.I.C.*, 1964 Cal. 141 at p. 152.

The question has come in a number of cases before the English courts. We may begin with, *Swiss Bank Corporation* v. *Boehmische Industrial Bank*.[52] The plantiffs, having obtained a judgment for a sum of money against the defendants, a company carrying on business exclusively in Czechoslovakia, applied for the issue of garnishment orders against a London bank, where the defendant company kept an account. At that time the account showed a credit balance of over £ 9,000. The main objection against the issuance of garnishment order was : if the Bank was sued in Czechoslovakia, it would probably be asked to make payment there over again to the defendants, and thus any garnishment orders passed by the English court would be inequitable and cause hardship to the Bank. Overruling the objection, the court said: "Does this debt arise in this country ? It is a debt held by a banker who is resident in this country ? In my view this is a debt arising in this country and situate in this country."[53] The decision clearly lays down that the *situs* of the debt governs the assignment of the debt. The court said that the *situs* of the debt is at the place where the debt is properly recoverable : obviously this debt was with a bank situated in England and the amount was recoverable in London since it was not payable unless a demand was made on the Bank.

Sometimes it has been said that a debt is properly recoverable at the place where the debtor resides. It is submitted that the residence of debtor, permanent or temporary, should have no consideration in determining the *situs* of the debt. It is possible that the debtor may reside in more than one place or his residence may be shifting. This was the situation in *New York Life Insurance Co.* v. *Public Trustees*[54] and the court said that the debt is properly recoverable at the place where the debt has arisen under the contract and where the payment would normally be exigible.

In this series, we may review an earlier decision. In *Re Queensland Mercantile Agency Co.*[55] the Union Bank of Australia, having its domicile in England, held debentures issued by the Queensland Company, having its residence in Queensland, charging the shares of that company which were not fully paid up. The company called upon its shareholders, resident in Scotland, to pay up the balance of amount due on the shares. Before the payment was made by the shareholders, a company resident in Scotland commenced proceedings in a Scotland court, claiming damages from the Queensland Company on an alleged act of its negligence and got issued orders of attachment before judgment. It was primarily a question of priorities before the court : which of the two, the Union Bank or the Scottish Company, should have

52. (1923) 1 K.B. 673.
53. *Ibid.*, at p. 681.
54. (1924) 2 Ch. 101.
55. (1891) 1 Ch. 536.

priority? North, J had no difficulty in applying the law of Scotland, since the debtors were resident in Scotland and the debt (unpaid calls) were situated in Scotland. It seems that the residence of the debtors was a prime consideration before the court, but, then the *situs* of the debt was also Scotland.

We would now pass on to the second type of involuntary assignments, *viz.*, when the debt is vested in some authority or agency by legislation.

In *Re Banque Des Merchants De Moscou*[56] a Russian Bank which carried on business exclusively in Russia had, in 1917, an account, which was then in credit, with Midland Bank situated in London. On December 19, 1917, the Russian Bank was nationalized by a decree of the Soviet Government, and was subsequently dissolved by a Soviet decree of January 1919 and all the liabilities of the Bank were extinguished. On September 21, 1932, one A, domiciled in France, lodged a proof in the winding up of the company in respect of an alleged debt of £ 12,000 A's case was that on December 16, 1917, two documents were signed, purporting to be orders from the Russian Bank to the Midland Bank in London, directing it to pay to the order of A two sums of £ 10,000 and £ 2,000. Before fleeing from Russia, he alleged, after the outbreak of the revolution, he got all his properties sold to the Russian Bank and in consideration of the same he obtained the aforesaid two orders. The claim of A was rejected by the liquidator and he appealed. Rejecting the appeal, the court observed that the debt was situated in Russia where the Russian Bank had resided, and that even if the debt could have been recovered in England by an action instituted in England, that fact alone would not have made England the *situs* of the debt. The debt was subject to the nationalization decree of the Soviet Government and it has been liquidated by a decree of that government.

Then came *Fouad Bishara Jabbour* v. *Custodian of Absentee Property of State of Israel*[57] and the *Arab Bank* v. *Barclays Bank*.[58] In the former case one Y and Co., an Insurance Co., having its head office in England, constituted one M & Co. Ltd. their agents in Palestine under a power-of-attorney, giving them wide powers to carry on the insurance business on their behalf, in Palestine and to issue, within certain limits, new policies without reference to them. Under a policy of insurance issued in Palestine by Y and Co. to the plaintiffs, it agreed to indemnify the plaintiffs against loss or damage caused through fire or riot up to an amount of £ 6,000 in respect of a garage and its contents owned by the plaintiffs and situated in Haifa, Palestine. On January 18, 1948 the garage was mined and blown up. On March 26, 1948, the plaintiffs

56. (1954) 2 All E.R. 246.
57. (1954) 1 All E.R. 145.
58. (1954) 2 All E.R. 226.

left Haifa and arrived in Egypt and coutinued to live there. Y and Co., admitted the claim of the plaintiff on the insurance policy, but pleaded that the said claim of the plaintiffs had already vested in the Custodian General of Absentees' Property of the Government of Israel under a law of Israel and consequently they were not liable to pay it. When on November 17, 1950 the plaintiffs issued a writ against Y and Co., the latter paid the amount in the court and by an inter-pleader order the Custodian General of Israel was made defendant. Parson, J. discussed the matter elaborately and after discussing some proper law authorities said that there was considerable weight of authority in favour of the view that the *lex situs* alone can alter title to debts and other *choses in action*. According to the learned judge the debt was situated where the damages were recoverable. Since the insurance amount was payable in Palestine, the debt was situated in Palestine and therefore Palestine was the *situs* of the debt.

In the second case, the *Arab Bank* v. *Barclays Bank*[59] the appellants, the Arab Bank Ltd., were a company incorporated in Palestine in 1930 and their head office remained in Jerusalem till July 1, 1948, when it was shifted to Jordan, where they got themselves registered. The respondents, Barclays Bank Ltd., were a company incorporated in England, having branches overseas. In 1939 the appellant opened a current account with the respondents' Jerusalem branch. On the termination of British mandate over Palestine, war broke out between Israel and Arabs in Palestine and at the time of action a state of war existed there. The head office of the appellants was situated in that part of Jerusalem which was controlled by Arabs; while the respondents' branch office was situated in that part of Jerusalem which was controlled by Jews. Appellants subsequently moved out their head office from Jerusalem. After the termination of the mandate they had no branch in Israel territory. By a regulation of Iseral it was made illegal to make any payment to, or place any sum to the credit of, any person resident outside Israel. By another regulation properties of absentees vested in the Custodian-General of absentees' properties. It was also laid down by the regulation that it was the duty of every person having in his possession any property of an absentee to deliver such property to the Custodian-General, and, where the property was in the form of a debt to the absentee, to pay the same to the Custodian-General. Further, making of payment to any one else was made an offence. The appellants in terms of the above regulation became absentees and the respondents in compliance with an order of the Israel government made over the amount to the Custodian-General. The House of Lords have no difficulty in saying the debt was situated in Jerusalem, where alone it was payable.

Thus, the English authorities seems to lay down that the validity and effect of an involuntary assignment of intangible

59. Cited above.

movables, including the question of priorities, are governed by the *lex situs* of the debt or other intangible property, debtor's absence from the jurisdiction is immaterial. However, the making of an order is discretionary and the court would refuse to make it if there is a risk that the garnishee will be compelled to pay it again abroad.[60] The *lex situs* of the debt governs the involuntarily assignment of the debt, irrespective of the fact as to where the debtor is residing, within or without the jurisdiction.[61] The procedural aspect of the voluntary assignment is governed by the *lex fori*.[62]

Recognition of Foreign Garnishment Orders : There is not much English authority on the question as to on what basis effect would be given to a foreign garnishment order. In *Rossano* v. *Manufacturers Life Insurance Corporation*[63] the court refused to give effect to an Egyptian garnishment order on the following grounds : (a) the claim of the creditor was for taxes and its recognition would mean indirectly giving effect to the foreign revenue laws, (b) the *situs* of the debt was not Egypt, (c) the Egyptian garnishment proceedings were administrative and not judicial, and (d) that the debtor was not subject to the jurisdiction of the Egyptian court. It is submitted that the ground (b) was enough. It seems that the English court would give recognition to foreign garnishment orders if these are the orders of the court of the *lex situs*, since to do otherwise would mean that the garnishee might be compelled to pay his debt twice.

Indian Law

On the involuntary assignment of intangible movables, four Indian authorities are available. Two of them were decided before and two after Independence.

In Chaturbhuj Piramal v. *Chunni Lal*,[64] one Shankar Rao was a resident at Indore and an employee of the Government of Indore (then an Indian State). In 1924 he was arrested and charged, *inter alia*, with misappropriation of huge amounts of the Government of Indore. Shankar Rao had large dealings with one Onkarmal whose main place of business was Indore, though he was also carrying on business at Bombay. Shankar Rao had two accounts with Onkarmal, at Bombay and Indore. He also had an account in the name of his wife. In 1924 the Indore account showed even, though the Bombay account showed a credit balance of Rs. 2,00,000. The Government of Indore by an executive

60. *Employer's Liability Assurance Co.* v. *Sedwick Collins & Co.*, (1927) A.C. 95.
61. Dicey, Rule 86, p. 566; Cheshire, pp. 430-32. Graveson appears to take the view that the *lex fori* should govern the matter, p. 500.
62. See Cheshire, p. 432; Graveson, p. 501.
63. (1963) 2 Q. B. 352.
64. 1933 P.C. 150.

order attached the properties of Shankar Rao and served a notice upon Onkarmal to hand over the amount due in Shankar Rao's account. On May 15, 1924 Onkarmal made an entry crediting the Government of Indore with an amount of Rs. 1,98,497. On May 19, 1924 the plaintiffs had filed a suit against Shankar Rao for the recovery of a sum amounting to over two lakh rupees alleged due in connection with some forward transactions in a court at Bombay, and on that very day obtained an order for attachment before judgment of Shankar Rao's properties including the account with Onkarmal. Onkarmal replied that no sum was due and the account has been squared up. On September 3, 1924 the plaintiffs obtained a decree against Shankar Rao and on September 25 obtained an order from the court prohibiting Onkarmal from giving over the debt to Shankar Rao and obtained leave to file a suit against Onkarmal for declaration that the alleged payment by Onkarmal was collusive, and fraudulent and that debt still remained payable to Shankar Rao. Pursuant to that, the plaintiffs filed the suit against the defendant and the present appeal to the Privy Council arose out of this suit. Their Lordships of the Privy Council rightly said that unless it was shown that the debt was expressly or impliedly made payable in Bombay, they could not but hold that the *situs* of the debt was Indore. His Lordship observed : "On examination of the contract it appears that the principal Shankar Rao employed the agent, Onkarmal to enter into executory contracts of purchase and sale for him both in Indore and Bombay. The agent's head office of business was Indore, and while separate accounts were kept in Indore and Bombay, and the transactions were kept distinct, it is plain from the evidence and from the nature of things that Shankar Rao, who was employed at the Court of Indore, was in the habit of giving orders for his Bombay account in Indore where they were transmitted, if necessary at his expense by telegram to Bombay, and made and received payments in respect of Bombay account in Indore. . . .The accounting would in ordinary circumstances take place in Indore where the head office of the agent was, and where both parties resided."[65] Undoubtedly, the residence of the debtor at Indore weighed with their Lordships in coming to the conclusion that the *situs* of ~~the~~ debt was Indore, but their formulation as to the *situs* of the debt in correct, as they very clearly said that the debt was payable at Indore and therefore *situs* of the debt was Indore.

In *State Aided Bank of Travancore Ltd.* v. *Dhirit Ram*,[66] on being told by the Travancore Bank, having its registered Office at Alleppey, that he could make deposit with the National City Bank at Bombay and if he did so the same would be accepted by it and the interest would be allowed from the date the amount was deposited in the Bombay Bank, the plantiff deposited a sum of

65. *Ibid.*, at p. 151.
66. (1942) Bom. 318 (P.C.)=(1941) I. A. 1.

amount with the National City Bank at Bombay. The defendant bank, i.e. the Travancore Bank, paid the interest at Bombay. Later on, on creditor's application winding up proceedings of the Travancore Bank were taken up and a scheme was settled. Before the winding up proceedings had commenced the plantiff had asked for the repayment of the deposit since the same became due. On the Bank's failure to do so, the plantiff brought an action against the defendant Bank for the recovery of the amount in a Bombay court, on the averment that since the contract was made in Bombay, and was to be performed in Bombay, the law applicable was the law of Bombay and not of Travancore State. When the case ultimately went to the Privy Council, it was decided on the basis of proper law of contract. Their Lordships said that since the contract was made in Travancore and it was to be performed in Travancore, the proper law of contract was Travancore and therefore the law applicable was the Travancore law. It is submitted that the case may be looked at from the angle of the *situs* of the debt : the Bank was incorporated under the law of Travancore, its head office was at Travancore, the deposit was made at Travancore (the fact that it was remitted through the National City Bank of Bombay was of no consequence, it might as well have been remitted through the post office) and it was recoverable there, therefore the *situs* of the debt was Travancore.

Then, we pass on to the two decisions of the Supreme Court.

In *Delhi Cloth and General Mills Ltd.* v. *Harnam Singh*[67] the plantiffs filed a suit against the defendants in a Delhi Court to recover a sum amounting to Rs. 11,496 on the averment that the said amount was due against the defendants in respect of their cloth dealing in Lyallpur (now in Pakistan) before partition of India. The defendants admitted the claim of the plantiffs but averred that, since the plantiffs migrated to India, they became evacuees within the meaning of the Pakistan Evacuees Property Ordinance, their (defendants) assets, including the said amount in their hands, were frozen by the Government of Pakistan, and, therefore, they had no liability to pay the amount over again. Vivian Bose, J. made a distinction between the following two types of cases of assignment : (a) those where the defendant has garnishable assets within the jurisdiction of the court and payment, pursuant to the law of garishment, is in fact made to the person concerned, and (b) those where the defendant has no garnishable assets in the foreign country and no payment is made in fact. It is not clear why this distinction was sought to be made. The matter was disposed of by the learned judge by saying that since that was not the issue before him he would not express any opinion on it, "but different conclusions might possibly arise in such a case" It is submitted on such distinction need be made.

67. (1955) S.C.J. 645.

It is submitted that the simple question before their Lordships of the Supreme Court was : where was the *situs* of the debt ? If *situs* of the debt was Pakistan, then the said amount of the plantiffs in the hands of the defendants was validly taken over by the Custodian of the Evacuees Properties of Pakistan and the defendants were absolved of all their responsibilities towards the plantiffs. But Bose, J. discussed at length the doctrine of proper law as applicable to contracts and quoted English authorities profusely and came to the following conclusion : "On these facts we hold that the elements of this contract, that is to say, the contract out of which the obligation to pay arose, were most densely grouped at Lyallpur and that was its natural seat and the place with which the transaction had its closest and most real connection. It follows from this that the 'proper law of contract', in so far as that is material, was Lyallpur law." The contract out of which obligation arose was not disputed by the parties, but it seems that the proper law doctrine was so overpowering that the learned judge could not extricate himself from it. Since the *lex situs* of the debt was also Pakistan, he reached the right conclusion, but nonetheless observed : "If driven to a choice, we would prefer this way (i.e., proper law governs assignment) of stating the law but we need not decide this, for, so far as, the present case is concerned, the result is the same, whether we apply the proper law of the contract or the English rules about the *lex situs*."[68]

In similar circumstances the question again came before the Supreme Court in *State Bank of India* v. *Ghamandi Ram*.[69] A Hindu joint family firm was having a cash credit account in the Bhavalpur (now in Pakistan) branch of the Imperial Bank of India before partition of India. The firm had pledged its goods with the Bank as security for the repayment of the advances made to it. After partition of India the entire family migrated to India and thus became evacuees within the meaning of the Pakistan (Administration of Evacuees Property) Ordinance, 1949. The Bank sold the goods of the firm for the realization of its dues in the cash credit account and credited a sum of about Rs. 2,541 left as surplus balance after the adjustment of its dues in the said account. This balance vested in the Custodian of evacuees property under the aforesaid Ordinance. The plantiffs claimed this amount from the State Bank of India (which succeeded the Imperial Bank of India). The main question before the court was (so far as we are concerned) whether the liability of the Bank to the firm be deemed to be extinguished on account of the operation of the Pakistan Ordinance under which the said amount became vested in the Pakistani Custodian ? Ramaswami, J., it is interesting to note, did not refer to any of the aforesaid three Indian decisions, but relied on two English decisions, in *Arab Bank Ltd.* v.

68. *Ibid.*, at p. 654.
69. 1969 S.C. 1330.

Barclays Bank Ltd.[70] and *Re Queensland Mercantile and Agency Co.*,[71] and came to the conclusion that the *lex situs* of the debt governs the matter. His Lordship rightly said that the question whether a given contractual right, e.g. debt was transferred under such legislation and whether therefore payment to a custodian or administrator had the effect of discharging the debtor, depends on the *situs* of that right and not so much on the proper law of the contract from which the right arose. Thus, the Supreme Court of India applied the almost internationally accepted principle that the involuntary assignment of the debt or any other intangible property is governed by the *lex situs* of the debt or the other intangible property. The distressing aspect of the decision is that the learned judge, it is submitted without any relevance, quoted Morris's observation[72] under Rule 83 (which relates to the voluntary assignment of debt), *viz.*, the key lies in distinguishing between (1) questions of assignability, which are governed by the proper law of debt, and (2) [which is in fact number four in the observation] questions of attachment or garnishment, which are governed by the *lex situs* of the debt.[73] This does not add to clarity of law, rather it adds to confusion. His Lordship were concerned with a simple case of involuntary assignment of debt.

III

INTANGIBLE MOVABLES WHICH ARE REPRESENTED BY A DOCUMENT

Under this head the most common types of properties are : (a) negotiable instruments, and (b) shares. The former are dealt with in a separate chapter.[74] Here 'shares' alone are discussed as an illustrative case.

Shares

English Law

Shares are a species of intangible movables which are represented by a document. The share-certificate can be pledged and otherwise dealt with as a document of value. However, in English and Indian law, the entry on the company's register alone constitutes legal ownership. In view of this, a share of stock is connected with the place of the issuing, the general rule is that it can be effectively transferred only by an entry in the register of shares, by

70. (1954) A.C. 495.
71. (1891) 1 Ch. 536, on appeal (1892) 1 Ch. 219.
72. Dicey and Morris, p. 559. The learned judge quoted these lines without acknowledging their source.
73. 1969 S.C. 1330 at p. 1334.
74. *Simons* v. *London Joint Stock Bank*, (1891) 1 Ch. 270, on appeal (1892) A.C. 201.

which the name of transferee is substituted for the transferor. Thus, shares are situate in the country where, as between the company and the shareholder, it can be dealt with effectively, i.e. the place of the company's principal business where normally the register of shares is kept. If a company keeps registers at more than one place, then that place will be considered to be the *situs* of shares where the share can be effectively dealt with.

The rule of transfer of shares in English private international is that the *situs* of the shares is the place where they can be effectively dealt with as between the owner of the share for the time being and the company, i.e. the place where the register of share is kept by an entry into which alone a transfer can be effectively made.[75] In those cases where a company keeps the register of shares in several places, then the *situs* of the share is the country where an entry relating to the shares in question can be effectively made.[76] Where a shareholder purports to transfer his share by blank signatures and makes the delivery of the share to the transferee, this may give the transferee a right of registration against the company, but this does not, and cannot, effect a transfer.

Sometimes companies issue share-certificates which, according to the legal system which governs the incorporation of the company entitles the owner of the share to transfer the legal and equitable ownership to the transferee even prior to registration. In such a case the question is : the law of which country will govern the transfer, when transfer is made in a country where the register is not kept ? The question has two aspects : (a) its effect against the company, and (b) its effect between the transferor and transferee and the parties claiming under them.

The effect of the transfer against the company is governed by the *lex situs* of the share. This is ordinarily the law of the country where the company has been incorporated. Thus, if share-certificates of a company incorporated in Bangladesh have been transferred in India, the law of Bangladesh would determine whether an effective transfer has been made in favour of the transferee. Shares which are transferable as against the company under the law of the country of incorporation by delivery, with or without endorsement, i.e. bearer or order shares, according to Mann, must be held situate where the instrument of title (i.e. the share warrant) is from time to time situate.[77]

75. *London & South American Investment Trust* v. *British Tobacco Co.*, (1927) 1 Ch. 107; *Brassard* v. *Smith*, (1925) A.C. 371; *Erie Beach Co.* v. *A.G. for Ontario*, (1930) A.C. 161; *R.* v. *Williams*, (1942) 2 All E.R. 95.

76. *R.* v. *Williams*, cited above; *Treasurer of Ontario* v. *Blonde and others*, (1947) A.C. 24.

77. Dicey and Morris, p. 513. This proposition has been propounded on the basis of the decision in *Winas* v. *A.G.* (No. 2), (1910) A.C. 27 and the Canadian decision in *Secretary of State of Canada* v. *Alien Property Custodian*, (1931) 1 D.L.R. 890.

As to the effect of the transfer on the transferor and transferee, the governing law is the proper law of the transaction, i.e. the law of place where the share-certificate has been delivered. In *Colonial Bank* v. *Cady*[78] an Englishman died owning shares in a certain American company. His executors wanted the share-certificates to be registered in their name and consequently sent the certificates signed in blank to be London brokers to be sent to America. The brokers instead of transmitting the shares to America deposited them with the Colonial bank as a security for a debt. Subsequently, they became bankrupt. The question before the court was whether the deposit of shares conferred on them a valid title ? Under English law no title passed to the Bank, but under the American law the delivery of the shares vested both legal and equitable title in the Bank. The court held that since the proper law of the transaction, the deposit of shares being made in England, was English law, it governed the transaction. Lord Herschell observed : " . . . the question what is necessary or effectual to transfer the shares in such a company, or to perfect the title to them, must be answered by a reference to the law of the state of New York. But I think that the rights arising out of a transaction entered into by the parties in this country, whether, for example, it operated to effect a binding sale or pledge as against the owner of the shares, must be determined by the law prevailing here."[79]

Indian Law

The Indian Companies Act, 1956, s. 82 lays down, "The shares or other interest of any member in a company shall be movable praperty, transferable in the manner provided by the articles of the company." The procedure for the transfer of share-certificates is laid down in ss. 108, 109, 110 and 111. Briefly, the procedure is : every instrument of transfer of share should be in the prescribed form,[80] should be presented for stamping or endorsing the date of presentation to Registrar (or some other authority prescribed by the central government). It should be executed by or on behalf of the transferor and transferee and then should be delivered to the company. The transfer would be complete only on the registration of the transfer in the name of the transferee in their Register. In *Re Indian Speci Bank*[81] a share-holder transferred the shares that he held of a company in the name of several transferees and an application was made to the company for the registration of their names. But before registration could be effected the company became insolvent. The court held that so far as the share-holder and the company are concerned the ownership in the shares continued to vest in the share-holder.

78. (1890) 15 A.C. 267.
79. Ibid., at p. 283.
80. Form 7B in Annexure A of the General Rules and Forms of Companies, 1966.
81. (1915) 17 Bom. L.R. 342.

It is evident that under the Indian Private International law also so far the effect of the transfer is concerned between the company and the shareholder, it will be determined by the *lex situs* of the share-certificate which is the place where the register for the registration of shares is kept. Sub-section (1) of s. 112 of the Companies Act lays down : "The certification by a company of any instrument of transfer of shares in, or debentures of, the company, shall be taken as a representation by the company to any person acting on the faith of the certification that there have been produced to the company such documents as on the face of them show a *prima facie* title to the shares or debentures in the transferor named in the instrument of transfer, but not as a representation that the transferor has any title to the shares or debentures."

It appears so far as the effect of transfer as between the transferor and transferee or persons claiming through them is concerned the proper law of the transaction governs.

18

INSOLVENCY

Adjudication of a person as insolvent or bankrupt confers a status of bankruptcy or insolvency on him and accords him protection from his creditors. When a person is unable to pay his debts, proceedings may be filed in a court of law by that person himself or by his creditors for his adjudication as insolvent or bankrupt. Once a person is adjudicated as insolvent, a disabling status is conferred on him : he cannot thenceforth deal with his property till he is discharged by the court. From the date of his adjudication as an insolvent and till his discharge, his entire property vests in the administrator (the term is used in a very wide sense so as to include all categories of officials who administer or manage insolvent's property). The legal concept of insolvency serves threefold interests : The individual interest of the debtor, the interest of the community of creditors, and the social interest of according protection to trade and commerce. On the adjudication of a person insolvent, all his assets are distributed equitably among his creditors. On this being done, the debtor is discharged from the disabling status and is allowed to start life afresh. In private international law, insolvency is referred to as a general or universal assignment of property, since insolvency implies disposal of entire assets of the insolvent among his creditors.

The concept of insolvency is recognized practically all the world over. All systems of law agree that the purpose of insolvency proceedings is the appointment of administrator for the benefit of creditors of the insolvent. Apart from this, there is no agreement in the laws of bankruptcy of the countries of the world. In the common law system any person can be adjudicated as insolvent, but in the countries like France, only merchants can be declared insolvent. In the common law system the property of the insolvent vests in the administrator, while under the civil law system, only the management of properties is entrusted to the administrator.

English Law

English law uses the term 'bankruptcy', though in its concept and meaning it does not differ from the term 'insolvency' which is used in the Indian law. The modern English law of bankruptcy is statutory law and is contained in the Bankruptcy Acts, 1914-1926; most of the conflictual matters are covered by the Acts. Some of the provisions of the Acts have been given a fairly wide interpretation.

Jurisdiction

Under the Bankruptcy Acts a petition for bankruptcy may be filed by the debtor himself or by any of his creditors. When the former files a petition, the jurisdiction of the court is much wider. When a creditor files a petition for adjudicating the debtor as insolvent, the jurisdictional rules are somewhat narrow. An English court can exercise jurisdiction when the following two preliminary conditions are satisfied :

(i) There must be an act of bankruptcy, and

(ii) There must be a debtor.

Act of Bankruptcy : Under the Acts the following circumstances constitute acts of bankruptcy :[1]

(i) if the debtor, in England or elsewhere, makes a conveyance or assignment of his property to a trustee or trustees for the benefit of his creditors generally,

(ii) if the debtor, in England or elsewhere, makes a fraudulent conveyance, gift, delivery, or transfer of his property or any part thereof,

(iii) if the debtor, in England or elsewhere, makes any conveyance or transfer of his property or any part thereof or creates any charge thereon, which would, under the Bankruptcy Act, 1914 or any other Act, be void as fraudulent preference, if he was adjudged bankrupt,

(iv) if the debtor, with intent to defeat or delay his creditors departs out of England, or being out of England remains out of England or departs from his dwelling house, or otherwise absents himself, or begins to keep house,

(v) if an execution against the debtor has been levied by seizure of his goods under process in an action in any court, or in any civil proceeding in the High Court, and the goods have been either sold or held by the sheriff for twenty-one days,

(vi) if the debtor files in the court a declaration of his inability to pay his debts or presents a bankruptcy petition against himself.

(vii) if the debtor fails to comply with a bankruptcy notice issued by a judgment-creditor requiring him to pay the judgment debt, or

(viii) if the debtor gives notice to any of his creditors that he

1. - Section 1(1).

has suspended, or that he is about to suspend, payment of his debts.

Of the above eight acts of bankruptcy, ordinarily only the first four relate to conflictual problems. Acts (i), (ii) and (iii) may be committed in England or abroad. In the fourth case, the act of bankruptcy is committed by departing out of England or by remaining out of England if already out of England. Acts (v), (vi) and (vii) must be committed in England, though it is not necessary that the debtor should be present in England. Of these, the first four acts have given rise to some controversies and difficulties, and divergent views have been expressed.

Before the enactment of the Bankruptcy Act, 1914, the jurisdictional rules were somewhat obscure.[2,3] In *Theophile* v. *Solicitor-General*[4] the House of Lords had suggested that the rule laid down in *Cook* v. *Chas. A. Vogeler Co.*[5] may no longer be applicable as s. 1(2) of the Act of 1914 now defines jurisdiction in bankruptcy by reference to the person of the debtor. Morris and Lipstein are in favour of acceptance of this suggestion and according to them the rule should be : a universal assignment affecting property in England made by a person domiciled abroad will constitute an act of bankruptcy for the purpose of assuming jurisdiction in England provided the assignor is a debtor within the definition of the Act.[6]

The acts of bankruptcy Nos. (ii) and (iii) postulate that the conveyance must be fradulent or must create fraudulent preference. It seems that the terms 'fraudulent' or 'fradulent preference' should be interpreted in accordance with English law whether the conveyance is one which is made in England or abroad. On the act of bankruptcy No. (iv), the House of Lords decision in *Theophile* v. *Solicitor-General*[7] has thrown some new light. According to the House of Lords a person, who has been carrying on business in England personally, has given up business and has gone abroad is deemed to continue to carry on business for the purpose of this act of bankruptcy, if he leaves behind unpaid trading debts.

Hitherto accepted view has been that an act of bankruptcy must be a personal act, and it cannot be committed by an agent. unless the agent is authorized to do the particular act. This view has now been thrown open by the House of Lords' decision in *Theophile* v. *Solicitor-General*,[8] which seems to take the view that a person, who has never been in England and who carries on business in England through an agent or manager or was a member

2. *Cook* v. *Chas. A. Vogeler & Co.*, (1901) A.C. 102.
3. Dicey and Morris, (8th ed)., 656.
4. (1950) A.C. 186.
5. (1901) A.C. 102.
6. Dicey and Morris, p. 656.
7. (1950) A.C. 186.
8. *Ibid.*

of a firm or partnership which carried on business in England, may commit an act of bankruptcy within the meaning of No. (iv) by remaining out of England with intent to defeat or delay his creditors.[9]

Debtor : Before the Bankruptcy Act, 1914 the English court gave a narrow definition to the term 'debtor'. Under the Bankruptcy Act, 1914, the term debtor has been widened to include any person, whether British subject or not, whether domiciled in England or not, who, at the time of the commission of any of the aforesaid acts of bankruptcy :

(a) was personally present in England,

(b) ordinarily resided or had a place of residence in England, or

(c) was carrying on business in England, personally or by means of an agent or manager, or

(d) was member of a firm or partnership which carried on business in England.[10]

The aforesaid definition of the 'debtor' for the purposes of bankruptcy proceedings is an exhaustive definition. The court has given wide meaning to clause (c) : a debtor who has traded in England is deemed to be 'carrying on business in England' even if after selling his business he departs the country, provided he had left behind unpaid trading debts.[11]

Debtor's Petition : The jurisdiction of the court is wider when the debtor files a petition for his adjudication as bankrupt than the jurisdiction of the court when a creditor files a petition. Thus, any person who is a debtor within the meaning of the term may file a petition for adjudication of himself as bankrupt. The second condition is automatically satisfied since the filing of petition for adjudication of himself as bankrupt is by itself an act of bankruptcy. On the other hand, when a creditor wants to file a petition for getting his debtor adjudicated as an insolvent, there are further conditions which must be satisfied. Was it not so laid down, it would be possible for bankruptcy proceedings to be filed against a foreigner who committed an act of bankruptcy while on a casual visit to England or against a foreigner who committed an act of bankruptcy abroad, but happened to have a place of residence in England.

Creditor's petition : Section (1) of the Bankruptcy Act lays down : a creditor shall not be entitled to present a petition against the debtor unless :

(a) the debt owing by a debtor to the petitioning creditor, or if two or more creditors j oin the petition, the aggregate

9. Dicey & Morris, p. 658.
10. Section 1(2).
11. *Theophile* v. *Solicitor General*, cited above.

amount of debts owing to the several petitioning creditors, amounts to fifty pounds, and

(b) the debt is a liquidated sum, payable either immediately or at some certain future time, and

(c) the act of bankruptcy on which the petition is based has occurred within three months before the presentation of the petition, and

(d) the debtor is domiciled in England, or within a year before the date of the presentation of the petition has ordinarily resided, or had a dwelling-house or place of business, in England, or (except in the case of a person domiciled in Scotland or Ireland or a firm or partnership having its principal place of business in Scotland or Ireland) has carried on business in England, personally or by means of an agent or manager, or (except as aforesaid) is or within the said period has been a member of a firm or partnership of persons which has carried on business in England by means of a partner or manager.

The effect of this provision is that no creditor can file a petition for the adjudication of his debtor as bankrupt unless the debtor either is domiciled in England and comes under the definition of debtor or has within a year before the date of the presentation of the petition, fulfilled one or the other conditions necessary for constituting him a debtor under clause (b), (c) or (d) of the definition of the debtor.

Jurisdiction is Discretionary : Court's jurisdiction to adjudicate a debtor bankrupt being equitable jurisdiction is, in its very nature, discretionary. Thus, even when all the conditions for the exercise of jurisdiction are fulfilled, it may nevertheless refuse to exercise the jurisdiction. The court has declined to exercise the jurisdiction when the debtor has been made bankrupt in another country.[12] Ordinarily, the English court does not decline to exercise jurisdiction merely on the basis that proceedings have been started abroad, unless it is shown that the debtor has no assets in England,[13] or other equitable ground. The English court has not declined to exercise jurisdiction on the ground that the petition-creditor's debt was not contracted in England[14] or that the debtor was absent from England at the time when the petition was presented[15] or that the creditor or debtor is an alien.

Choice of Law

Whenever English court exercises jurisdiction in a petition for adjudication of a person as bankrupt, it applies English law

12. *Re McColloch*, (1880) 14 Ch. D. 716.
13. *Re Robinson*, (1883) 22 Ch. D. 816.
14. *Ex parte Pascal*, (1876) 1 Ch. D. 509.
15. *Ex parte Crispin*, (1873) L.R. 8 Ch. App. 374.

concerning the administration of assets of the bankrupt, such as distribution of assets among the creditors, the priorities among the creditors *inter se*, the rules of double proof in case of partnerships, set-off and every matter of procedure including limitation.[17] All creditors, English or otherwise, must prove their debts in accordance with English law, irrespective of the fact whether the debt is governed by English law or foreign law, though it may be necessary to refer to foreign law, if the proper law of a debt is foreign law, to determine its validity. The mode of dealing with the assets of the debtor by the administrator or trustee is governed by the English law, but what property has passed to the administrator or trustee and subject to what limitations and encumbrances it has passed are to be determined by the proper law. For instance, if the right is to immovable property situated abroad, then the *lex situs* will determine as to what property the administrator has got in it. Beyond this, it would appear, all matters are to be governed by English law.

Effect of English Bankruptcy

Administration of Property : The result of an English adjudication of bankruptcy of a debtor is that all his properties vest in the administrator known as trustee in bankruptcy. The term 'property' has been very widely defined under the Bankruptcy Act : "Property inclues money, goods, things in action, land, and every description of property, whether real or personal and whether situate in England or elsewhere; also obligations, easements, and every description of estate, interest, and profit, present or future, vested or contingent, arising out of or incidental to property as above defined."[18] The Act lays down that an order of English court in bankruptcy proceedings is given universal effect so far as it concerns the vesting of properties in, and their administration by, the trustee in bankruptcy. In other words, an order in bankruptcy proceeding amounts to universal assignment of all properties of debtor in the trustee in bankruptcy. The properties of the bankrupt which vest in the trustee include those which were owned by the bankrupt at or since the first act of bankruptcy by him and within three months of the presentation of the petition.[19]

So far as the question relates to a purely domestic situation, there is no difficulty : all properties of a bankrupt situated in England vest in the trustee; but so far as the question is concerned with the vesting of properties situated abroad, the position is not simple.

As regards Scotland and Ireland, the Act provides that the English bankruptcy order shall be enforced there in the same

16. *Ex parte Pascal*, (1876) 1 Ch. D. 509.
17. *Ex parte Melbourn*, (1870) 6 Ch. App. 64.
18. Section 167.
19. Section 45 of the Act.

manner and in all respects as if it is an order passed by a court there.[20] The same is true of countries foming part of the dominions of the Crown.[21] It is submitted that that is no longer true regarding countries of the Commonwealth.

In fact, whether or not the property situated abroad would pass to the English trustee in bankruptcy, would ultimately depend upon the view the local law takes of the English bankruptcy order, despite the fact that in theory the property situated there also vests in the English trustee. The beauty of this provision is that it can be utilized in aid of coercive English action *in personam* against the debtor as well as creditors. In this regard the Bankruptcy Act, 1914 itself contains certain provisions :

(i) *The debtor is present within the jurisdiction* : The act specifically lays down that the debtor "shall execute such power of attorney, conveyances, deeds, and instruments, and generally do all such acts and things in relation to his property. . .as may be reasonably required by" the trustee in bankruptcy.[22] The provision in s. 53(4) may also help the trustee to some extent as it lays that a certificate of appointment of a trustee is deemed to be a conveyance or assignment of property for purposes of any law in force in any part of the British dominions.

(ii) *When the creditor is present within the jurisdiction* : The English court can restrain a creditor resident in England from suing the bankrupt abroad, from recovering his debt.[23] It can also restrain a creditor resident abroad, if he seeks to prove his debt in English bankruptcy. This procedure is helped by the English rule of hotchpot, *viz.*, creditor, whether a British subject or alien, will not be allowed to prove his debt in the English bankruptcy unless he brings in the commonpool what had been recovered by him already in England or abroad.[24]

(iii) *The difficult question is* : Can a creditor, who has obtained payment abroad under a judgment of the foreign court or otherwise and who does not seek to participate in the English bankruptcy, be made to pool the property obtained by him in the hotchpot ? There are three old decisions[25] from which no clear rule can be deduced. Cheshire[26] and Morris[27] also make different formulations. Morris and Lipstein suggest that the rule should be : "A creditor who obtains property of the bankrupt situated

20. Section 121.
21. *Callender Sykes & Co.* v. *Colonial Secretary af Lagos*, (1891) A.C. 460.
22. Section 22(2).
23. *Re Distin, ex parte Ormiston*, (1871) 24 L.T. 197.
24. *Banco de Portugal* v. *Waddel*, (1880) L.R. 5 A.C. 161.
25. *Sill* v. *Worwick*, (1791) 1 H.B.L. 665; *Hunter* v. *Potts*, (1791) 4 Term Repo. 182; *Phillips* v. *Hunter*, (1795) 2 H.B.L. 402.
26. Cheshire (6th ed.), 556.
27. Dicey and Morris, 672.

abroad can be thus compelled to refund it to the trustee if, at the time when he received payment, he was resident in England."[28]

Discharge in Bankruptcy : It has been seen earlier that the adjudication of a debtor as bankrupt confers on him disabling and privative status. The discharge in bankruptcy removes that disabling and privative status and restores the bankrupt to the position of a normal person. The court which has power to adjudicate a person bankrupt has also the power to discharge him from bankruptcy.

Another aspect of discharge in bankruptcy is the effect of discharge on the outstanding obligation of the bankrupt. Does a discharge extinguish all outstanding obligations of the bankrupt ? The effect of a discharge in bankruptcy is to extinguish all the outstanding obligations of the debtor incurred prior to the order of discharge—wherever the obligation might have been incurred. This is because of the specific statutory provision in the Bankruptcy Act. The order of discharge of an English court in English bankruptcy is thus effective in England in respect of all outstanding obligations of the bankrupt.[29]

II

FOREIGN BANKRUPTCY

In respect of foreign bankruptcies two main questions that arise are : (a) While bankruptcy proceedings are pending in an English court, bankruptcy proceedings are initiated in another country or when English proceedings are filed bankruptcy proceeding are already pending in some foreign court, then will an application to English court for the stay of English proceedings lie ? (b) When a person has been adjudicated bankrupt by a foreign court, what effect is to be given to the foreign bankruptcy order? It is obvious that bankruptcy proceedings can be filed in more than one country. This happens in those cases where a debtor has assets and business in several countries. The rule of English law is that foreign adjudication in bankruptcy does not in any way hamper the jurisdiction of English court to adjudicate a debtor bankrupt provided it has jurisdiction to entertain the petition. But since the jurisdiction is discretionary, the court may refuse to exercise it on the ground that the debtor had already been adjudicated bankrupt by the foreign court.[30]

There is a school of thought which propagates the theory of unity of bankruptcy. It postulates that the adjudication of bankruptcy should be in one jurisdiction and adjudication by that jurisdiction should be respected all the world over. In this regard

28. Dicey aud Morris, 672.
29. Section 28(2).
30. *Ex parte McColloch*, (1880) 14 Ch. D. 716.

two main theories that are propounded are : (a) theory of debtor's domicile, and (b) theory of priority.

Theories of Unity of Bankruptcy

Domicile of Debtor : Savigny said : "As the bankruptcy has in view an adjustment of the claims of a number of creditors, it is possible only one place, namely, at the domicile of the debtor."[31] English Judge, Fry, L.J., thus spoke of the theory : "Another rule which has been suggested in this, that every other forum shall yield to the forum of the domicile, that the forum of every foreign country, every country not of the domicile, shall act only as accessary and in aid of the forum of the domicile. That, it is said, is *forum concursus*, to which all persons interested in the administration of the estate are bound to have recourse."[32]

This theory of unity of bankruptcy was founded on the mid-nineteenth century practice of the Continental countries of mutual assistance in bankruptcy. Under this practice, the administrator appointed by the court of the debtor's domicile was entitled to seek the help of the courts of other countries wherever the assets of the debtor were situated. On the continental Europe this practice did not last long. Nor did it find favour with English courts. The only advantage—and this was the one which appealed most to the protagonist of this theory—of this theory is that it provides a single ascertainable law, since exclusive jurisdiction conferred on the court of domicile for adjudicating the debtor bankrupt or discharging him from bankruptcy. But the greatest disadvantage of this theory—and it is this which knocks out the entire foundations of the bankruptcy jurisdiction—is that the domicile of the debtor may not be the place where he carried on business or where he has assets. This defeats the fundamental aim of bankruptcy jurisdiction of making available the assets of debtor to his creditors.[33]

This theory has never been recognized in England.

Priority of Proceedings : The theory of priority of proceedings visualizes that the forum where the bankruptcy proceedings are first started has the exclusive jurisdiction, and all the courts where proceedings are started later on should use their proceedings in assisting the distribution of assets in accordance with the law of the country where the proceedings were first started and trustee in bankruptcy appointed. Again, the only advantage of this theory is that it provides for a single jurisdiction in bankruptcy proceedings. Fry, L.J., said : "The theory of priority appears to me to be entirely unreasonable one."[34] Cheshire rightly says that if there is

31. Savigny, s. 374.
32. *Re Artola Hermanos*, (1890) 24 Q.B.D. 640.
33. Cheshire (8th ed.), 548; Graveson, (6th ed.) pp. 584-585.
34. *Re Artola Hermanos*, (1890) 24 Q.B.D. 640 at p. 649.

to be one principal of administration, it ought to be either in the place where the assets are chiefly situated, or, in the case of a trader, in the place where the debtor has his chief business establishment, neither of which facts may be true of the country in which proceedings are first started.[35]

Doctrine of Plurality : In opposition to the theory of unity of bankruptcy, there is a school of thought which holds that there is no harm if proceedings are started and concluded in several jurisdictions. Once the proceedings for adjudication of a debtor as bankrupt are commenced, the administrator may administer assets situated within his jurisdiction. Similarly, the administrators in other countries may administer assets of the debtor situated within their respective jurisdictions. This theory is supported by the practice of English courts. In an English bankruptcy, the English trustee in bankruptcy administers such assets as are situated in England in accordance with the rules laid down in the Bankruptcy Act, though, as has been already seen, in such proceedings both English and foreign creditors can prove their claims. This does not imply, as we would see, that English courts totally disregard the status of the foreign trustee in bankruptcy.[36] The jurisdiction of the English court is unaffected by prior or subsequent bankruptcy proceedings in other countries.

Jurisdiction of Foreign Courts

There is not much English authority on the question as to on what basis English courts would recognize the jurisdiction of the foreign courts. Morris and Lipstein have formulated the rule thus :

"The court will recognize that courts of any other (i.e., other than a Scottish or Northern Irish court) foreign country have jurisdiction over a debtor if—

(a) he was domiciled in that country at the time of the presentation of the petition, or

(b) he submitted to the jurisdiction of its courts, whether by himself presenting the petition or by appearing in the proceedings."[37]

The learned editors in their comments on these propositions say that these propositions "must be regarded as somewhat speculative, because the question is a vexed and controversial one which English courts have had few opportunities of considering." They further comment : "It is not possible to assert that the jurisdiction of foreign courts will be recognized only in circumstances which are identical with those in which English courts will assume jurisdiction. For neither the domicile of the debtor in England,

35. Cheshire, p. 444.
36. Sections 121, 122.
37. Dicey and Morris (8th ed.), Rule 120(2), p. 674.

or his submission to the jurisdiction is a sufficient ground for exercising jurisdiction."[38] The learned editors also do not rule out the possibility of English courts recognizing the jurisdiction of the foreign courts on any other basis.[39]

Effect of Foreign Adjudication in England

Administration of Property situated in England: Northern Ireland and Scotland are not considered to be foreign countries in bankruptcy adjudication inasmuch as the title of trustee in bankruptcy appointed in England, Scotland and Nothern Ireland extend to all movables and immovables of the debtors wherever situated in any one of these parts of Great Britain.

With respect to adjudications of bankruptcy in other countries, the question is: whether the properties situated in England vest in the foreign trustee in bankruptcy? Will the order of the foreign court be enough to vest English assets in foreign trustee or will separate proceedings, such as in the case of administration of the property of a deceased, would be necessary in England?

Since English courts recognize the principle of universality of bankruptcy adjudication, the recognize foreign adjudication in bankruptcy, if the debtor was a party to the foreign proceedings and subject to the jurisdication of the foreign court.[40] But the difficult question remains: when the debtor may be considered to be subject to the jurisdiction of the foreign court? To this no straight answer is possible. Maximum that can be said is that the debtor must be a party to the foreign proceedings. In *Re Anderson*[41] a domiciled Englishman was declared insolvent by a New Zealand court in proceedings to which he was a party. The debtor was entitled to a reversionary interest in some English money, but by some oversight the reversionary interest was not disclosed in the New Zealand proceedings. Six years later the debtor was adjudged bankrupt in English proceedings. The English court held that the New Zealand trustee was entitled to the reversionary interest in preference to the English trustee. The court observed: ". . . .The adjudication in New Zealand, being a valid adjudcation according to the law of New Zealand, passed the right to movable property of the bankrupt in any country to his official assignee in bankruptcy in New Zealand. If he had not been a party to the adjudication, if it has been made against him in his absence, other considerations might very well have applied."

Thus the trustee is bankruptcy appointed in a foreign adjudication is recognizad in England. The English law, making a distinction between movables and immovables, recognizes that debtor's movables situated in England vest in the foreign trustees. The English court recognizes foreign trustee's right to sue in his

38. *Ibid.*, at pp. 675-676.
39. *Ibid.*, at p. 676.
40. *Re Davidson's Settlement*, (1873) L.R. 15 Eq. 383.
41. (1911) 1 K.B. 896.

own name to recover debts of the debtor situated in England, provided that he has the right so to sue by the law of the country of his appointment.[42] However, this vesting of English movables in the foreign trustees is subject to certain limitations : (a) the foreign adjudication order should purport to have extraterritorial effect. If it is an order effective only locally then English movable asset will not vest in the foreign trustee. (b) The English assets vest in the trustee subject to all prior charges and encumbrances, irrespective of the fact as to what view the foreign law takes of such English charges and encumbrances. But it is necessary that such charges and encumbrances should be prior to the declaration of the debtor as a bankrupt in the foreign country. Subsequent encumbrances will not affect the title of the foreign trustee. Thus in *Solomons* v. *Ross*[43] it was held that if a creditor of the debtor attaches property of the debtor in England after the commencement of foreign bankruptcy proceedings, the foreign trustee will be entitled to the attached property. This decision has not been followed by the House of Lords[44] which held that the Scottish trustee was not entitled to debtor's debt situated in England which an English judgment creditor was in process of garnishing at the time of judgment-debtor's adjudication as bankrupt in Scottish proceedings. It is interesting to note that the title of the trustee would have prevailed over the judgment-creditor had the garnishee proceedings been commended in Scotland or had the bankruptcy proceeding been commenced in England. But the House of Lords took the view that neither Scottish nor the English doctrine of relating back applied. Lord Loreburn propounded the test thus. "Could the bankrupt have assigned to the trustee, at the date when the trustee's title accrued, the debt or assets in question situated in England ?" If the foreign bankruptcy order has been made prior to attachment of the debt, then the foreign trustee in bankruptcy would be entitled to the attached property. In both the cases, *Solomons* v. *Ross*[45] and in *Galbraith* v. *Grimshaw*,[46] the bankruptcy proceedings were pending in the foreign court when the assets were attached in England.

The recognition of the title of the foreign trustee over English movables does not preclude the English court from adjudicating the debtor once again a bankrupt in English proceedings, though English court would not ordinarily exercise jurisdiction in such a case.

The principle of universality does not apply to immovables, and immovable property of the bankrupt situated in England does not vest in the foreign trustee in bankruptcy. However, the

42. *Macaulay* v. *Guarantee Trust Co. of New York*, (1927) 44 T.L.R. 99.
43. (1764) 1 Hy. Bl. 131.
44. *Galbraith* v. *Grimshaw*, (1910) A.C. 508.
45. Cited above.
46. (1910) A.C. 508.

English court may authorise the appointment of a receiver of the rents and profits of immovables situated in England,[47] for the benefit of the bankrupt's creditors.

Foreign Discharge in Bankruptcy : Apart from the orders of discharge passed in the Scottish and Northern Irish bankruptcy proeedings which are recognized and given effect to in England, the position of foreign orders of discharge in bankruptcy is different. The doctrine adhered to is that a foreign discharge in bankruptcy is neither an order nor a judgment and therefore the question of according it recognition as an order or judgment of the court does not arise. The English courts take the view that if the discharge is valid by the proper law of the debt or obligation, then the discharge is effective in England; if discharge is not effective by proper law it will be ineffective in England. In *Gardiner* v. *Houghton*[48] an action was brought for the recovery of debt the proper law of which was Victoria. Prior to the action the debtor was adjudged bankrupt and subsequently discharged by a court in Victoria. It was held that since the defendant was discharged from the debt by the court of the proper law of the debt, the discharge is valid and will be given effect to in England. On the other hand, in *Gibbs and Son* v. *Societe Industrielle*[49] the proper law of the debt was not the law of the country where the debtor was adjudicated and discharged in bankruptcy proceedings. It was held that no effect would be given to this discharge in England. Lipstein and Morris hold the view that a discharge should be recognized as effective in England if the courts of the country whose law governs the contract recognise the discharge as valid.[50]

It is obvious that a foreign discharge in bankruptcy cannot be given a greater extra-territorial effect than it has in the country where it has been pronounced. Similarly, a foreign discharge will not be effective in England unless it amounts to extinction of debt in the foreign country; if the foreign discharge merely bars the remedy and does not extinguish it, then it will not be a discharge effective in England.[51]

III

INDIAN LAW

The Indian law of insolvency is contained in two statutes : the Presidency Town Insolvency Act, 1909 and the Provincial Insolvency Act, 1920. The Indian law is primarily based on English law. The former statute is applicable only in the towns of

47. *Re Levy's Trusts*, (1885) 30 Ch. D. 119; see also s. 112, Bankruptcy Act, 1914.
48. (1862) 2 B. & S. 743.
49. (1890) 25 Q.B.D. 399.
50. Dicey and Morris, pp. 687-688.
51. *Gibbs* v. *Societe Industrielle de Metaux*, (1890) 25 Q.B.D. 390.

Bombay, Calcutta and Madras, while the latter applies to the rest of the country.

Jurisdiction of the Indian Court

Just as under the English law so under the Indian law, the following two conditions are necessary for the exercise of the jurisdiction by the court :

(a) act of insolvency, and
(b) debtor.

Act of Insolvency : In both the statutes, the Presidency Towns Insolvency Act, 1909 and the the Provincial Insolvency Act, 1920, eight acts of insolvency are listed and, with verbal differences of no significance, they are identical. Both the statutes lay down that the 'act of an agent may be the act of the principal'[52] with this difference that under the Act of 1919 following clause is also added : 'even though the agent has no specific authority to commit the act'. Under both the Acts,[53] a debtor commits an act of insolvency in each of the following cases :

(i) If in India (under the Act of 1919 the word in place of India is 'States') or elsewhere, he makes a transfer of all or substantially all his property to a third person for the benefit of his creditors generally,

(ii) If in India or elsewhere, he makes a transfer of his property or of any part thereof, with intent to defeat or delay his creditors,

(iii) If, in India or elsewhere, he makes a transfer of his property, or of any part thereof, which would, under this or any other enactment for the time being in force, be void as fraudulent preference if he was adjudged an insolvent,

(iv) If, with intent to defeat or delay his creditor,—

(a) he departs or remains out of the territories to which this act extends,

(b) he departs from his dwelling-house or usual place of business or otherwise absents himself,

(c) he secludes so as to deprive his creditor of the means of communication with him,

(v) If any of his property has been sold in execution of the decree of any court for the payment of the money, (under the Act of 1919 this clause is worded thus : if any of his property has been sold or attached for a period of not less than twenty-one days in execution of the decree of any court for the payment of money),

52. Explanation to s. 6 of the Act of 1920 and explanation to s. 9 of the Act of 1919.

53. Section 6 of the Act of 1920 and s. 9 of the Act of 1909.

(vi) if he petitions to be adjudged as insolvent,

(vii) if he gives notice to any of his creditors that he has suspended, or that he is about to suspend, payment of his debt, or

(viii) if he is imprisoned in execution of the decree of any court for the payment of money.

Of the above eight acts of insolvency acts mentioned in clauses (v) and (viii) are involuntary acts, while the rest are voluntary. The involuntary acts are of a kind by which a creditor is able to compel a debtor to disclose his insolvent condition even if the insolvent is careful enough not to commit a voluntary act of insolvency.[54] The acts of insolvency mentioned in clauses (i), (ii), (iii) and (iv)(a) are the cases which may cause conflictual problem. In the first three clauses the acts of insolvency may be committed in India or abroad, under the fourth case departure out of India constitutes an act of insolvency. The rest of the acts constituting insolvency must be committed in India; if they are committed outside India, they do not constitute acts of insolvency under either of the two statutes. It seems that a transfer of assets made abroad under first three clauses to constitute an act of insolvency should include Indian assets. It also seems clear that such expressions as 'fraudulent' or 'fraudulent preference' should be interpreted under the Indian law, as choice of law in all cases will be the Indian law. Mere delay in payment to creditor is not *per se* an act of insolvency.[55]

The Indian statutes specifically lay down that an act of insolvency committed by an agent may constitute an act of insolvency of the principal.[56] Obviously every act of the agent cannot be imputed to the principal; it will depend upon the circumstances of each case.

Debtor : The second condition for the exercise of the jurisdiction by the court is that there must be a debtor who, under the Provincial Insolvency Act :

(i) Ordinarily resides within the jurisdiction of the court, or

(ii) carries on business within the jurisdiction of the court, or

(iii) personally works for gain within the jurisdiction of the court, or

(iv) is, on being arrested or imprisoned, in custody within the jurisdiction of the court.[57]

Under the Presidency Towns Insolvency Act, 1909 the court has jurisdiction :[58]

54. *Yenumula Malludora* v. *Peruri Seetharathnam*, 1966 S.C. 918.
55. *K. Maranaichen* v. *R.S. Saradhambal*, 1982 Mad. 117.
56. *Theophile* v. *Solicitor General*, (1950) A.C. 186, the House of Lords made this suggestion.
57. Section 11 of the Act.
58. Section 11.

(v) (a) if the debtor is, at the time of the presentation of the insolvency petition, imprisoned in execution of the decree of a court for the payment of money in any prison to which debtors are ordinarily committed by the court in the exercise of its ordinary original jurisdiction, or

(b) if the debtor, within a year before the date of the presentation of the insolvency petition, has ordinarily resided or had a dwelling house or had carried on business either in person or through an agent within the limits of the ordinary original civil jurisdiction of the court, or

(c) if the debtor personally works for gain within those limits, or

(d) if in the case of a petition by or against a firm of debtors, the firm has carried on business within a year before the date of the presentation of the insolvency petition within those limits.

Under the Provincial Insolvency Act, a petition for insolvency can be filed only in the District court, though the State Governments have power to entrust jurisdiction to any court subordinate to be District court, provided, of course, the aforesaid two conditions of the exercise of the jurisdiction are satisfied.[59] The Presidency Towns Insolvency Act confers jurisdiction on the High Courts of Calcutta, Bombay and Madras.[60] A single judge of the High Court is competent to hear the petition. Here also the aforesaid two conditions for the assumption of jurisdiction should be satisfied.

Debtor's Petition : Just as under the English law, so under the Indian law (both the statutes) the court's jurisdiction is much wider when a debtor files a petition for his adjudication as insolvent than when a creditor files such a petition, inasmuch as, in the former case, the filing of a petition by itself amounts to an act of insolvency. The other condition of debtor's residence, etc. within the jurisdiction applies only when creditors file the petition. However, before a debtor is allowed to file a petition the following conditions should also be satisfied :

(a) his debts should amount to five hundred rupees, or

(b) he should underarrest or imprisonment in execution of the decree of any court for the payment of money, or

(c) an order of attachment in execution of such decree should have been made, and should be subsisting against his property.[61]

A further requirement is also laid down in the sub-section (2)

59. Section 3.
60. *Ibid.*
61. Section 10 of the Act of 1920 and s. 14 of the Act of 1909.

of both the sections in respect of a debtor who had earlier filed a petition under any of the two statutes.

Creditor's Petition : Whenever a creditor wants to file a petition in addition to the aforesaid two conditions for the assumption of the juisdiction, the following requirements should also be satisfied :

(i) the debt owning by the debtor to the creditor, or if two or more creditors join in the petition, the aggregate amount of debts owning to such creditors, amounts to five hundred rupees, and

(ii) the debt is liquidated some payable either immediately or at some certain future time, and

(iii) the act of insolvency on which the petition is grounded has occurred within three months before the presentation of the petition.[62]

It has been further laid down that if the petitioning creditor is a secured creditor, he shall in his petition either state that he is willing to relinquish his security for the benefit of the creditors in the event of the debtor being adjudged insolvent, or give an estimate of the value of the security. In the latter case, he may be admitted as a petitioning creditor to the extent of the balance of the debt due to him after deducting the value so estimated in the same way as if he was an unsecured creditor.[63]

Under both the Acts, the debtor's domicile or nationality is of no consequence; if a person comes under the definition of debtor, a petition can be filed against him by his creditors on the fulfilment of the above stated requirements. The jurisdiction of the insolvency court under Indian law is discretionary.

Choice of Law

In all proceedings for adjudication of a debtor insolvent the Indian courts apply *lex fori*. Sub-section (1) of s. 4 of the Provincial Insolvency Act lays down :

"Subject to the provisions of the Act, the court shall have full powers to decide all questions whether of title or priority, or of any nature whatsoever, and whether involving matters of law or of fact, which may arise in any case of insolvency coming within cognizance of the court, of which the court may deem it expedient or necessary to decide for the purpose of doing complete justice or making a complete distribution of property in any such case.[64]

62. Section 9(1) of the Act of 1920 and s. 12(1) of the Act of 1909.

63. Sub-section (2) of each of ss. 9 and 12 respectively of the Acts of 1920 and 1909.

64. Section 7 of the Act of 1909 is to the same effect.

Effect of Indian Insolvency

Administration of Property : In regards to the vesting of the property in the administration in insolvency, there is a slight difference between the provisions of the Presidency. Towns Insolvency Act and the Provincial Insolvency Act. Under the former, "On the making of order of adjudication, the property of the insolvent wherever situate shall vest in the official assignee and shall become divisible among the creditors and thereafter except as directed by this Act, no creditor to whom the insolvent is indebted in respect of any debt probable in insolvency shall, during the pendency of the insolvency proceedings, have any remedy against the property of the insolvent in respect of the debt or shall commence any suit or other legal proceedings except with the leave of the court and on such terms as the court may impose."[65] Under the Provincial Insolvency Act the property of the insolvent vests in the court or in the receiver.[66] It has further been laid down :

> Any property which is acquired by or devolves on the insolvent after the date of an order of adjudication and before his discharge shall forthwith vest in the court of receiver. . . .[67]

The term property has been widely defined in both the Acts. Under s. 2(1)(d) of the Provincial Insolvency Act, 1920 property is defined as including 'any property over which or the profits of which any person has a disposing power which he may exercise for his own benefits'.[68] Then, under sub-section (3) of section 3 of the Act of 1920 the following properties are also deemed to be the property of the insolvent : "all goods being at the date of the presentation of the petition are . . . in the possession, order or disposition of the insolvent in his trade or business, by the consent and permission of the true owner, under such circumstances that he is the reputed owner thereof." Then section 28A further lays down :

> The property of the insolvent shall comprise and shall always be deemed to have comprised also the capacity to exercise and to take proceedings for exercising all such powers in or over or in respect of property as might have been exercised by the insolvent for his own benefit at the commencement of his insolvency or before his discharge.

An order of adjudication of insolvency relates back and takes effect from the date of the presentation of the petition.[69] It is obvious that under both the statutes all the properties of the insolvent, wherever situated, in India or abroad, vest in the Official

65. Section 17.
66. Section 28(2).
67. Section 28(4).
68. In s. 2(e) of the Presidency Towns Insolvency Act, the definition is in identical language.
69. Sub-section (7) of s. 28 of the Act of 1920.

assignee or the receiver with effect from the date of the presentation of the petition. So far as the question relates to assets situated in India there is no difficulty : all properties, movables as well as immovables vest in the official assignee (under the Provincial Insolvency Act, as we have seen, the properties vest in the court or the receiver; but, for the sake of convenience, we would use in these pages only one word, the official assignee). But in respect of assets situated abroad, the position is the same as under English law : movables situated abroad vest in the official assignee, while the immovable properties vest in him only ideally.[70] *In B.N. Lang* v. *Jasvantlal*[71] the Bombay High Court said that all the properties of the insolvent, wherever situate, vest in the official assignee, though it is a different matter whether he will be able to take possession of them, particularly when properties are situated in a foreign country. In this case in execution of a decree passed by a foreign court one of the creditors has got attached certain properties of the insolvent by the order of the court. The official assignee applied for the vacation of the attachment order on the plea that this property should be set free so that it is also available for rateable distribution among all creditors. The court accepted the prayer and released the property from attachment. It was observed that all the properties of the insolvent vest in the official assignee and the court should not bother itself as to how the official assignee would be able to get possession of the foreign situated assets. The position was clarified by the Bombay, High Court in *Jayantilal Keshavlal* v. *Kantilal Jesinghbhai*.[72] Their Lordships observed : "Even if the land situate in a foreign state be regarded as vested on adjudication in the Receiver insolvency in an ideal sense, unless the law of the foreign state recognises the vesting as a transfer of the property to the receiver, the vesting cannot operate, to confer title upon the receiver in insolvency and the property situate in the foreign state would continue to be liable for the satisfaction of the claims against the debtor according to the law of that state and unaffected by the insolvency."

Thus, the question is : how can the official assignee bring foreign situated assets under his control so as to make them available for distribution among all the creditors of the insolvent ? He may do so in any of the following manners : (a) the most effective way of bringing the assets is to use the compulsive machinery of the court to force the insolvent to assist the official assignee to collect the assets, (b) to some extent, i.e. when he is amenable to

70. *Anantapadmanabhaswami* v. *Official Receiver* 1933 P.C. 134; *Re Jeewandas*, (1912) 40 Cal. 78; *Official Assignee* v. *Ghanshyamdas*, 1934 Sind 44; *B. Veeranna Sha* v. *Official Assignee*, 1940 Mad. 47; *Sumermull Surana* v. *Bansilal Abirchand*, 1932 Cal. 310; *In re Sumermull Surana*, 1932 Cal. 124; *N.A. Aiyaswami* v. *Official Assignee*, 1934 Mad. 344; *In the Matter of Motilal Presukhdas*, 1938 Rang. 324; *Yokohama Specie Bank* v. *Curlender & Co.* 1926, Cal. 898; *Patel Jeshbhai Revendas* v. *Patel Narsinghbhai Girdharibhai*, 1968 Guj. 101.

71. 1926 Bom. 271.

72. 1955 Bom. 170.

court's jurisdiction, a creditor may be forced to bring the assets of the insolvent in the common-pool which he had recovered abroad, and (c) the official assignee may himself file legal actions in foreign countries for the recovery of insolvent's property situate there, so far as he is permitted to do under the foreign law.

Debtor's Duty : The Provincial Insolvency Act and the Presidency Towns Insolvency Act contain certain specific provisions under which an insolvent may be compelled to assist the official receiver in the realization of foreign assets. The general provision is enacted in sub-section (1) of s. 28 of the Act of 1920 : "On the making of an order of adjudication, the insolvent shall aid to the utmost of his power in the realization of his property and the distribution of the proceeds among his creditors." It is the duty of the insolvent to "execute such powers-of-attorney, transfers and instruments, and generally to all such acts and things in relation to his property . . . as may be required by the official assignee . . . ."[73] If the insolvent assigns his foreign situated immovable property to the official assignee, the latter may proceed to recover that property by legal action or otherwise in the foreign country, but only so far as he permitted to do under the law of that country.[74]

Action Against Creditors : This appears to be an established position in Indian law that if a creditor is amenable to court's jurisdiction he may be forced to hand over to the assignee the assets of the insolvent that he had recovered abroad, after debtor's adjudication. In *Official Receiver* v. *Ghanshyamdas*[75] a creditor of the insolvent recovered some of his debts from the property of the debtor situated in Bahrain. He also wanted to participate in the distribution of the Indian assets of the insolvent. The court said that he could do so only if he handed over the money that he had recovered in Bahrain to the official assignee so as to form part of the common-pool. The question came for consideration before the Calcutta High Court in some peculiar circumstances in *Yokohama Specie Bank* v. *Curlender & Co.*[76] One Mogi & Co. carried on extensive business in Japan as well as in several parts of the world. They banked with the Yokohama Specie Bank Ltd., which has its head-office in Japan and several branch offices all over the world. One S. Curlender & Co., obtained a money decree for Rs. 1,84,000 against Mogi & Co. from a Calcutta Court and got attached before judgment their Calcutta situated assets. The Yokohama Bank claimed a lien on the attached goods under a deed of hypothecation dated 14th July, 1920. Curlender & Co. got Mogi & Co. adjudicated insolvent from a Calcutta court. The official assignee also obtained a declaration that the deed of hypothecation obtained

73 Section 33(2), Clasues (d) and (e) of the Act of 1909 and s. 22 of the Act of 1920.

74. *N.A. Aiyaswami Chetty* v. *Official Assignee*, 1934 Mad. 344.

75. 1934 Sind 44.

76. 1926 Cal. 898.

by Yokohama Bank on the goods of Mogi & Co. was invalid. Before adjudication, the general creditors of Mogi & Co. in Japan appointed a re-adjustment committee consisting of several creditors including the Yokohama Bank. Under a circular letter issued by them to all the creditors, they got themselves appointed as trustees. The committee carried on liquidation proceedings of Mogi & Co. and paid certain dividends to creditors. The Yokohama Bank got an amount of fifteen lakhs of rupees as dividends. Curlender & Co. did not join in the proceedings; nor did it receive any dividends. In the Calcutta insolvency proceedings the Yokohama Bank lodged a proof of debt, claiming that after the realization of all securities, an amount of over one crore and fifty-two lakhs of rupees was still due to it. Curlender & Co. applied to the court for several orders, one of which was that the bank should deposit in the court all the money that it had recovered from the assets of Mogi & Co. in Japan and only then it could participate in the Indian assets. It also asserted that the dividends paid to the Bank and the other creditors by the Japanese Committee were in full satisfaction of their claim. The trial court held, *inter alia*, that the Bank was entitled to participate in the Indian insolvency of Mogi & Co. only if it handed over the dividends received by it in Japan. It is submitted that the court stated the law correctly. But on appeal, the High Court did not agree with the trial court. Chatterjea, A.C., J. said the provision in the Presidency-Towns Insolvency Act relating to vesting of the insolvent's property anywhere situated in the official assignee has operation 'only with respect to property affected by our law'. Then, the learned judge proceeded to lay down the position of the property under private international law. Quoting English authorities and writers he said that so far as it concerns movables, they are subject to the law 'which governs the person of the owner' and so far as it concerns immovables, they are governed by their *lex situs*. Since both Mogi & Co. and the Yokohama Bank were incorporated in Japan, Japanese law applied to movables. Unless it was shown that the Indian Official assignee could successfully sue the Bank in Japan for the recovery of the money received by it in Japan, the Bank could not be asked to hand over the money it had received in Japan. Similarly, the other Judge, Rankin, J., after stating that the Indian statute applies to Indian assets only, embarked on the exercise of stating the rules of private international law relating to movables and immovables. It is submitted that both the judges got confused and muddled up in the rules relating to right to movables and immovables, while the simple question before the court was whether a creditor (Indian or foreign, hardly mattered) could participate in the distribution of assets of an insolvent in the Indian adjudication without bringing into the hotchpot the assets he has received elsewhere? The English law (which the learned judges claimed to follow) is crystal clear (as we have already discussed in Part I of this Chapter) and answers the question in the affirmative without any qualification. There is no reason why the Indian law should be different. In fact, on this matter there is marked similarity in the laws of most of the countries of the world.

The next question is : can the Indian court restrain a party amenable to its jurisdiction from prosecuting a suit against the property of the debtor in a foreign court if it considers that the action of the party is contrary to its notions of equity and justice ? The Indian courts have answered the question in the affirmative, though they have stated, time and again, that as to whether they would issue an injunction would depend upon the facts of each case.[77] In *Re Sumermull Surana*,[78] Pankridge, J. said that the court has power of granting an injunction restraining a creditor of the insolvent who is amenable to court's jurisdiction because he is residing or carrying on business within the jurisdiction. In this case, a firm by the name and style of Sumermull Surana was adjudicated insolvent on its own petition by a Calcutta court and a scheme of composition was also approved by the creditors as well as the court. A day earlier to debtor's petition for adjudication, a creditor of the debtor-firm filed a suit in the court of Bikaner State (then an Indian state and hence a foreign state for the purposes of private international law) for recovery of certain debts due to him got the Bikaner situated immovable attached before judgment. This creditor has not taken part in the Calcutta insolvency proceedings and was also not a party to the composition scheme. Refusing to grant the injunction on these facts, the court said that the immovable property situated in a foreign country did not in fact vest in the assignee and since the creditor had not taken part in the Calcutta insolvency of the debtor-firm, there is no reason why he should be prevented from seeking the aid of the court of their own country for recovering their dues from the property that had never been the subject-matter of the insolvency proceedings.[79]

The Indian courts have taken the view that if foreign properties of the insolvent have been attached in a foreign country before his adjudication as invsolent, then the insolvency of the petitioner does not in any way affect the creditor's right in respect of those properties. In *Jayantilal Kashavlal* v. *Kantilal Jesingbhai*[80] G, a creditor, got the properties of the insolvent situated in Baroda state (then an Indian state, hence a foreign country for the purposes of private international law) attached and sold in execution of his decree against the insvolent on 21-9-1947. G had got the properties attached on 3-3-1946. M, a creditor of A, had filed an insolvency petition on 27-2-1946 and got him adjudicated as insolvent and appointed a receiver on 28-2-1946 by the insolvency court at Ahmedabad. A had properties both within the jurisdiction of the court as well as in Baroda state. The main question before

77. *Lakshmiram Kevalram Bhatt* v. *Poonam Chand*, 1921 Bom. 128; *Venaichand* v. *Laxmichand* (1920) 21 Bom. L.R. 955; *Re Sumermull Surana*, 1932 Cal. 124, on appeal, 1932 Cal. 310.
78. 1932 Cal. 310.
79. On Appeal the decision was affirmed, 1932 Cal. 310.
80. 1955 Bom. 170.

the court was whether the receiver could recover the sale proceeds of the immovable property situated in Baroda state from G? The receiver had filed a suit in a court in Ahmedabad against G for the recovery of this amount. The trial court held that the suit was maintainable against G. On appeal the Bombay High Court said: "The assumption made by the learned trial judge that a receiver in insolvency in whom the estate vested by order of the court in British India was entitled to ignore proceedings competently entertained by a foreign court in respect of immovable property of the insolvent and the order passed therein to claim the amount received by a creditor of the insolvent to which the receiver was entitled to by reason of the order of adjudication, is my judgment fallacious." Then, the court said that since the Baroda court had jurisdiction to entertain the suit against the insolvent when it was filed and to pass a decree and execute it against the property situated there, the order of the Ahmedabad court vesting insolvent's property in the receiver could not operate in respect of those property.[81] Although the court has put the argument this way, it is submitted that at the time when the adjudication order was made the property was already under an attachment order and the creditor had not asked for the participation in the distribution of the assets of the debtor in the insolvency proceedings. This also seems to be the reason why the Calcutta High Court declined to pass the injunction order in *Sumermull Surana* v. *Bansilal*.[82] It is submitted that the reasoning given by the Madras High Court in *Aiyaswami* v. *Official Assignee, Madras*[83] is correct: The test is whether at the date of the adjudication, the insvolent was free to dispose of this property? Did this property form part of his free assets on that date or was there anything which affected his power of disposal over that property? This question, *viz.* whether the adjudication of a debtor as insolvent affect the properties under attachment before the adjudication order is passed, has come up before Indian Courts in connection with the foreign official assignee's power in respect of such properties.[84] (These cases are discussed in the subsequent pages).

Discharge in Insolvency

The direct purpose of the order of discharge is to enable the insolvent to once again start his normal activities free from the liability to pay his pre-insolvency debts. Section 44(2) of the Provincial Insolvency Act lays down, "...an order of discharge shall release the insolvent from all debts provable under this Act."[85] As far as the effect of the order of the Indian insolvency court is concerned, it amounts to the discharge of all debts and

81. This reasoning has been adopted by the Gujarat High Court in *Jeshbhai* v. *Narsingh Bhai*, 1868 Guj. 101.
82. 1932 Cal. 310.
83. 1934 Mad. 344.
84. See s. 51 of the Act of 1920 and s. 53 of the Act of 1909.
85. Section 44(2); s. 45 of the Act of 1909 is also to the same effect.

outstanding liabilities of the debtor provable in insolvency. This order would be effective throughout India.

The question that remains is : what will be the position of undisposed of assets of the insolvent after an order of his absolute discharge has been passed ? Such assets may be those which are surplus or those which could not be utilized by his creditors being considered worthless. This appears to be the established position that an insolvent is entitled to get back all undisposed of assets as surplus when an absolute order of discharge is made in his favour.[86] The same is the position of property which is considered to be of no value by the official assignee and hence abandoned.[87] The authority for this proposition at that time was *Sheonandan* v. *Kashi*.[88] This proposition has been supported by decision *in C.D. Deshikachari* v. *Official-Receiver*,[89] *Mutha Sarbaravudu* v. *Vammi Kondalaravudu*,[90] *Jeshbhai* v. *Narsinghbhai*.[91] The cases taking contrary view are : *Tarakdas Dhar* v. *Santosh Kumar*[92] and *Vijirangam Naidu* v. *Narayanappa*.[93] In view of the observations of the Supreme Court in *Raghunath Keshava* v. *Ganesh*,[94] these cases no longer represent good law. Mr. Justice Shelat, it is submitted rightly, said that where the property in insolvency remains undisposed of being found useless by every one concerned in an insolvency proceeding and an absolute order of discharge is given, a sale thereafter of his right, title and interest in the property by the insolvent cannot be held invalid in law. As to *Jeshbhai* v. *Narsinghbhai*,[95] his Lordship said that this is a case different from the surplus mentioned in s. 67 of the Provincial Insolvency Act, 1920. In this case some immovable property of the insolvent was situated in a foreign country and the receiver felt that there was no use in getting a transfer of this property executed in his favour by the insolvent since the property was subject to a mortgage and no one was willing to pay for it an amount more than for what it was mortgaged. It was in these circumstances that the claim to this property was abandoned in the insolvency proceedings.

FOREIGN INSOLVENCY ORDERS

In regard to foreign insolvency orders, two main questions that have come before the Indian courts are : what effect is to be given to a foreign insolvency order in respect of properties of the

86. *Raghunath Keshav* v. *Ganesh*, 1964 S.C. 234.
87. See Mulla's Law of Insolvency, p. 346.
88. 1917 All. 302.
89. 1943 Mad. 26.
90. 1961 A.P. 219.
91. 1968 Guj. 101.
92. (1937) 2 Cal. 386.
93. 1946 Mad. 371.
94. 1964 S.C. 234.
95. 1968 Guj. 101.

insolvent situated in India ? Should the Indian court stay execution proceedings pending before it in respect of property situated in India, after an order of adjudication had been passed by a foreign court ?

In *Anantpadmanabhswami* v. *Official Receiver, Secunderabad*[96] a creditor of the insolvent got a preliminary decree passed in the latter's suit for partition in the Madras High Court in execution or his money decree obtained by him from a Bombay court in 1926. In 1928, the debtor was adjudged insolvent by a Secunderabad court.[97] At that time execution proceedings were pending in the Madras High Court. When the creditor sought to proceed further with the execution of attachment proceedings, the official receiver of Secunderabad opposed them. The Privy Council following the decision in *Galbraith* v. *Grimshaw*[98] observed that an adjudication order of a foreign court could not be recognized as having the effect of vesting in the receiver any immovable property of insolvent situated in India. Their Lordship further said that since the creditor had attached the properties before adjudication, he was entitled to the benefit of his prior attachment and could not be restrained from doing so. It was observed : ". . . a the date when the foreign adjudication order was made, the appellant (creditor) was entitled to the benefit of his prior attachment of the decree in the Madras partition suit."[99] This very case came up before the Madras High Court again in 1940.[100] The further fact that may be added are : before the orders for adjudication of the debtors as insolvent were made there were as many as nine other creditors who had attached the preliminary decree in the Madras partition suit. Three creditors attached the preliminary decree after the adjudication. The partition suit was compromised in 1937 and pursuant to that an amount of Rs. 1,31,231 in cash and Goverement securities was paid in the court. The official receiver of Secunderabad compromised the claim of seven creditors who had attached the decree before adjudication; two of the creditors allowed their claim to lapse and one sought to prove his claim in insolvency proceedings. After this settlement an amount of Rs. 64,305 of the debtors remained in the court and the official receiver asked that this amount should be paid to him. This was objected. Overruling the objection the court said that when a foreign court adjudicates a person insolvent the only property that vests in the receiver is the movable property situated in India which the insolvent was free to assign at the date of adjudication and such property vested in the receiver. If a creditor has attached the property before adjudication, he remains entitled to

96. 1933 P.C. 134.
97. The Hyderabad state was then an Indian State and hence a foreign state for the purpose of private international law.
98. (1874) 2 E.R. 150.
99. 1933 P.C. 134 at p. 135.
100. *Verranna* v. *Official Assignee*, 1940 Mad. 47.

the benefit of his attachment. But the creditor who attaches after the adjudication is not entitled to anything by virtue of his attachment, and he is left with the only remedy of proving his debt in his insolvency.

This is also the position taken by other High Courts, *viz.* the immovable property situated in India of the debtor who has been adjudicated insolvent by a foreign court does not in fact vest in the foreign assignee in bankruptcy, and therefore a decree-holder can execute his decree against debtor's immovable property situated in India.[101]

The question of concurrent bankruptcy has come before the Indian courts in two cases. In the matter of *William Watson*[102] one William Watson Co. of England failed and was declared insolvent by an English court in England on February 1, 1904, and a trustee in bankruptcy was appointed on February 14, 1904. On the application of firm's constituted attorney, a Bombay court passed a vesting order. The manager of the Calcutta Office of the firm also closed down the Calcutta business, and, on the petition of a friendly creditor, the firm was adjudicated insolvent by a Calcutta court on February 2, 1904. On April 13, 1904 vesting order made by the Bombay High Court was discharged, and the adjudication was set aside. The Calcutta assets of the insolvent firm vested in the official assignee appointed by the Calcutta High Court. The English trustee in bankruptcy made an application in the Calcutta High Court for setting aside the adjudication and vesting orders. Rejecting the application, the court observed that insolvency courts in India have a discretion in making an adjudication order notwithstanding the existence of a prior adjudicating order in another country, provided the conditions of insolvency as laid down in the Indian statute are satisfied and there is no valid reason to the contrary; the presence of large assets within the jurisdiction is a valid ground in favour of making an adjudicating order by the Indian court. The court further observed that the order of the court in England adjudicating the debtors as bankrupt with the result of vesting of their property by operation law in the trustee in bankruptcy does not extend to personal assets of the debtors in this country in such sense that this court would be powerless to interfere with Indian assets; Indian assets will vest in the official assignee appointed by the Indian court in Indian insolvency adjudication. Thus, the English trustee in bankruptcy has no *locus standi* to ask the Indian court to rescind the adjudication order passed by it. *In the matter of Motilal Prem Sukdas*[103] a firm was adjudicated insolvent in Calcutta and then in Rangoon. On application being made for the

101. *Lakhpat Rai* v. *Atma Singh*, 1962 Punj. 228; *Yokohama Specie Bank Ltd.* v. *Curlender & Co.*, 1926 Cal. 898; *In re Sumermull Surana*, 1932 Cal. 124.

102. (1904) 31 Cal. 761.

103. 1938 Rang. 324.

stay of Burma adjudication proceedings the court said that though under s. 22, Presidency Towns Insolvency Act, 1909 the court has power to stay adjudication pending before it, the proceedings in the Rangoon court should not be stayed as the insolvent's assets within the jurisdiction were not inconsiderable, nor were the liabilities inconsiderable.

Foreign Discharge in Insolvency

There is not much Indian authority on the question as to what would be the effect of a foreign discharge order. In *Magadhu Pillai* v. *Asan Muhammadhu*[104] under a contract entered into between two persons resident in Colombo it was stipulated that both the parties would go to India and execute a registered deed in respect of land situated in India in consideration of Rs. 2,000. The defendant did not perform his part of the contract and no deed was registered. Subsequently, he was adjudicated insolvent by the Colombo court. The Colombo court also gave him discharge. Subsequently, the plantiff filed a suit for the recovery of their debts for damages for the breach of contract in an Indian court. The Madras High Court said that the cause of action arose in Ceylon and the discharge granted by the Ceylon court was a valid discharge of every debt everywhere, including India. So far as it related to trace debts arising out of the trade transactions between the parties entered into in Ceylon, the proper law of the debt being Ceylon, a discharge by the proper' law is a valid discharge everywhere. But the proper law of the contract was not Ceylonese law, but Indian law. On this aspect of the matter court observed that even if the performance of the contract was to be in India, that fact did not affect the validity of discharge given by the Colombo insolvency court. It is submitted that this may not be treated as good law, and, whenever in future the question comes before the Indian court, it should be free to say that discharge which is valid by proper law of the debt or contract alone will be valid and recognized by the Indian courts.

104. 1920 Mad. 934.

19

SUCCESSION

In the countries of continental Europe and other civil law countries all matters relating to succession are governed by one single system of law, *viz.*, the law of the nationality of the deceased. This is because these countries follow the principle of unity of succession (France and Belgium are two exceptions) under which succession, testamentary as well as intestate, and all matters relating to succession are regulated by one single system of law, *viz.* the personal law of the deceased which most countries take to be the law of the nationality of the deceased at the time of his death. In the civic law countries, as well as under the personal law of Hindus and Muslims in India, the property vests in the heirs immediately on the death of the deceased.

India, England and other countries which follow the common law traditions adopt the principle of succession under which movables and immovables do not devolve under one single system of law. In English law this distinction seems to be on account of historical reasons. In England, freehold land could not be devised by will until 1540,[1] while movables could be bequeathed and were governed by the principle of *mobilia sequuntur personam.* Although the historical reasons have disappeared, the distinction still exist in English Private International Law under which succession to immovables is regulated by the *lex situs* and not by the personal law of the deceased, while succession to movables is regulated by the *lex domicilii* of the deceased. Thus, if a person dies intestate leaving behind immovables in England, then devolution to his property would be in accordance with English internal law, whatever might have been his nationality or domicile. On the other hand, a British national or a person domiciled in England dies leaving behind immovable properties in India, then devolution to his property would be governed by the Indian law, i.e. the way an Indian court would determine the question. Section 5, Indian Succession Act, 1925 statutorily recognizes this principle. The Section runs as under :

"(1) Succession to the immovable property in India of a person

1. Wills Act, 1540.

deceased shall be regulated by the law of India, wherever such person may have had his domicile at the time of his death.

(2) Succession to the movable property of a person deceased shall be regulated by the law of the country in which such person had his domicile at the time of his death."

The differences between the private international laws of the civil law countries and common law countries are not merely in respect of the appointment of heirs or personal representatives or executors and administrators, but also in the basic concept of will. The civil law countries, though with some modifications, still regard will as a public document the chief object of which is the appointment of heir. On the other hand, English common law considers will as a private and secret document, the purpose of which is the disposal of properties on death. The Indian law, particularly the Hindu law and Muslim law, does not require appointment of any administrator in case of intestacy, as Hindus have not known anything like testamentary disposition, and whatever modern Hindu law of wills exists it is essentially modelled on English law. Muslims, on the other hand, have always recognized the testamentary power, though a Muslim is not allowed to dispose off his entire property; the concept of executors and administrators too has been different.

The rules of English and Indian Private International Law could hardly be considered as satisfactory. The Will Act, 1963 has tried to solve some of the difficulties. The Act applies to form and construction, but as Graveson suggests, it is submitted rightly, by analogy it can be applied to other branches of testamentary succession.

We would proceed to discuss the subject under the following three heads :

(a) Administration of Estates,
(b) Succession to immovables, and
(c) Succession to movables.

I

ADMINISTRATION OF ESTATES

In English law administration and succession are two different concepts. In English law no one is entitled to deal with or distribute the property of a deceased person unless he has obtained authorization from the court.[2] If a person dies intestate, or where a will has been made, but the appointment of executor has failed for any reason, then the next-of-kin (husband, wife or child of the

2. There are some statutory exceptions to the rule, such as under the Small Payment (Administration of Estates) Act, 1950.

deceased) can acquire the necessary authority for dealing with the property by obtaining letters of administration. In case a person has appointed an executor under the will who consents to act, then the executor may obtain necessary authority by obtaining probate of the will. In such administrator or executor the property vests immediately on the death of the deceased. Executors and administrators are together referred to as personal representatives. In the countries of Continental Europe such persons are known as heirs or universal legatee. For all these persons here it is proposed to use the term administrators'.[3] The administrators under English law have three main functions : (a) collection of assets of the deceased, (b) payment of debts, and (c) distribution of residue among the heirs.

Jurisdiction of the Court

In the following three situations the question of administration of estate of the deceased may arise before the English court :

(a) When the deceased has made a will and had also appointed an executor who consents, then the executor may obtain probate of the will,

(b) When the deceased has made a will, but has either not appointed an executor or the appointment of executor has failed, then the court may appoint an administrator, and

(c) When the deceased had died intestate, then the court may grant letters of administration.

Until 1932 the English court wedded as it was to the ecclesiastical doctrine of presence of property within the jurisdiction, exercised the jurisdiction only if some property of the deceased was within the jurisdiction; it was of no consequence that the deceased was domiciled in England or was a British subject. This led to injustice. A person who died domiciled in England leaving behind property abroad faced this difficulty : English court would not appoint an administrator as he had left no property in England, and the foreign court would not appoint one as he was not domiciled there at the time of his death. To obviate this difficulty, the Administration of Justice Act, 1932, laid down that the court has jurisdiction to make a grant of administration in regard to the property of any deceased person, 'notwithstanding that the deceased person left no estate' in England.[4] English court granted probate of foreign will dealing purely with foreign assets when a testator had left properties not merely abroad but also in England which he disposed off under an English will.[5] Under the Probate Registrar's direction, in the absence of special circumstances, administration is not ordinarily granted unless

3. See Graveson, 538.
4. Section 2(1). See also *In the Estate of Wayland*, (1951) 2 All E.R. 1041.
5. *In the Estate of Wayland*, (1951) 2 All E.R. 1041.

there is property in England.[6] The English courts have always granted administration in respect of not only property that is in England at the time of the death of the deceased but also of any of his property which is brought to England after his death at any time before a third party had acquired a good title under the *lex situs*. The domicile of the deceased, whether English or foreign, does not have any effect on the jurisdiction of the court.[7]

Thus English courts generally exercise jurisdiction in granting administration on the basis of presence of assets in England. In respect of intangible movables sometimes it is difficult to establish their situation. However, in respect of the grant of administration, English courts have evolved certain rules as to the *situs* of movable intangibles : judgment debts are situated where the judgment is recorded; leases where land lies; speciality debts, where the instrument happens to be; simple contract debts, where the debtor resides at the time of testator's death; a share or stock, transferable only by registration, is situated in the country where registration must be effected; and securities, such as bonds, promissory notes and bills of exchange, are assets in England if situated there.[8]

A person sometimes makes separate wills disposing of his property in England and abroad. When one will confirm the other, both of them together constitute the will of that person and probate of both has to be obtained.[9] But if the several wills made by a testator are independent of each other, then probate of any one of them may be obtained.

Choice of Law

Here the main question is : who are the persons entitled to a grant of administration ? If a person dies domiciled abroad, then the general rule is that the English court will appoint that person as administrator who is considered to be the personal representative of the deceased by his *lex domicilii*. For instance, a person died domiciled abroad leaving behind bulk of his assets there and a small amount in England. In such a case, the English court has followed the practice of either appointing the person selected in the domicile as administrator of English assets or to appoint a person who is entitled to act as such by the *lex domicilii*.[10] The general principle was thus stated by Lord Penzance in *In the Goods of Hill* :[11] ". . . where the court of the country of the domicile of the deceased makes a grant to

6. Direction of November 30, 1932.

7. See Cheshire, 473-74.

8. *A.G.* v. *Bouwens*, (1838) 4 M. & W. 171; *Brassard* v. *Smith*, (1925) A.C. 371; *Erie Beach Co.* v. *A.G.*, (1930) A.C. 161, *R.* v. *Williams*, (1942) A.C. 451; *Winnas* v. *A.G.*, (No. 2) (1910) A.C. 27.

9. *In the Goods of Lockhart*, (1893) 69 L.T. 21.

10. *In the Goods of Smith*, (1868) 16 W.R. 1130; *In the Estate of Yahuda*, (1956) 3 W.L.R. 20.

11. (1870) 2 P. & D. 89.

a party, who then comes to this country and satisfies it that, by the proper authority of his country, he has been authorized to administer the estate of the deceased, I ought, without further consideration, to grant power to that person to administer the English assets." (In this case a domiciliary administrator who applied for an English grant was appointed administrator of English assets also.) The domiciliary administrator may derive authority from an appointment of foreign court or he may automatically become an administrator by the operation of foreign law such as under the law of several Continental countries a person becomes an heir or universal successor by virtue of close relationship with the deceased. Such a foreign administrator can be appointed as an English administrator.[12] In this regard *Re Yahuda*[13] is very instructive. In this case a testatrix had made four wills relating to her properties situated in four countries; each will contained a general revocation clause. She died domiciled in Connecticut, where probate of all the four wills was obtained. The executors of her will relating to property situated in England applied to the English court for probate, and necessary orders were made by the court on the basis of grant of probate by the courts of *lex domicilii*, despite the fact that the will appeared to have been revoked by one of the later wills. In such a case usually the English court does not go into the question of validity of will which has been accepted to be valid by the *lex domicilii* in case of movables and by the *lex situs* in the case of immovables. It should be noted that grant of probate or letters of administrator to the domiciliary administrator is made as a matter of course, but it is not automatic; it cannot be claimed as of right. The court has a discretion. For instance, if a foreign administrator is incompetent to act as administrator, such as a minor, then no grant will be made to him.[14] The court also has a discretion to make a grant to some other person such as a creditor of the deceased.[15] If the domiciliary administrator takes no steps to obtain probate or letters of administration, the grant of administration may be given to the foreign administrator himself or to any attorney who has been authorized to apply for such a grant. The domiciliary administrator is called the principal administrator and the English administrator is called 'ancillary' administrator.

The position of grant of administration in respect of immovables situated in England is not so clear. The Non-Contentious Probate Rules, 1954 provide : "Where the whole of the estate in England consists of immovable property a grant limited thereto may be made in accordance with the law which would have been applicable, if the deceased had died domiciled in England." The practice of English courts is to make a grant to the foreign

12. *In the Estate of Weiss*, (1962) 1 All E.R. 308.
13. (1956) 5 W.L.R. 20.
14. *In the Goods of D'Orleans*, (1859) 1 Sw. Tr. 253.
15. *In the Estate of Leguia*, (1934) p. 80.

administrator, except in those cases where the English estate consists wholly of immovables. In the latter case a grant limited thereto may be made to the person who would have been entiled 'if the deceased had died domiciled in England.'

Functions of the Administrator

As soon as probate or letters of administration are granted to a person, all properties of the deceased which at the time of his death are situated in England vest in him; so does any movables of the deceased which are brought into England after the death of the deceased before any person has by the *lex situs* obtained a good title to them. Administration in the broad sense insludes the discharge of all the three functions mentioned above, *viz.*, collection of assets, payment of debts, and distribution of the residue among the heirs. As a general rule the first two functions are governed by the *lex fori* and the last by the *lex domicilii* in regards to movables, and the *lex situs* in regards to immovables. In its narrow sense it includes only the first two functions. In the private international law, it is submitted that it is better to use administration in the narrow sense and to use the term 'succession' for the third function of the administrator. It is this meaning of administration which is followed in these pages.

In brief, under English private international law grant of administration and all matters connected with it up to the time that distribution of the residue assets is made are governed by the *lex fori*. *In Re Lorrilard*[16] Warringkton, L.J. observed : "The principle is that the administration of the estate of the deceased person is governed by *lex fori*, and it is only when the administration is over that the law of his domicile comes in."

Collection of Assets : The first duty of the administrator is to collect the assets of the deceased person with due diligence. He must collect all assets locally situated as well as the assets situated outside the jurisdiction, but the latter duty is conditioned by several factors. Ordinarily, he would not be able to collect foreign assets unless he obtains a foreign grant of administration. Or, it may be that a foreign administrator had already been appointed who had taken control of assets. It seems that an English administrator would be concerned with the foreign assets of the deceased only if the deceased died domiciled in England, as only then he can obtain a grant of administration from the court of foreign country.[17]

An administrator is liable to account for assets collected byhim under the English grant in the character of an English administrator. If he has obtained a grant from a foreign court and had collected assets in that capacity, then he is not accountable in

16. (1922) 2 Ch. 638.

17. *Ewing* v. *Orr-Ewing* (1885) 10 A.C. 453.

England in the capacity of English administrator. When the English administrator holds assets in foreign country or in England in the capacity of a foreign administrator, then, he must administer them according to foreign law, but once he had done so, the English court can compel him to carry out the trusts upon which the surplus is held.[18]

Payment of Debts : The second duty of the administrator is to make payment of the debts of the deceased. This duty extends to all debts of the deceased wherever incurred and it covers all assets of the deceased in the hands of the administrator wherever collected. This is done in accordance with the *lex fori*, and the *lex domicilii* of the deceased at the time of his death has nothing to do with it. English and foreign creditors rank equally. The English private international law follows the general principle that every question relating to debts, their admissibility as well as priorities, are matters of procedure and hence are governed by the *lex fori.*

Proof of debt, extinction of debts by limitation and priorities of debt are regulated by *lex fori*. *Re Kloebe*[19] was a case of priorities. This related to the administration of estate of deceased person who had died domiciled in Greece. All the assets under administration were in England. On the dispute having arisen as to priorities between the English creditors and foreign creditors, the court said that "no distinction could be made on the basis of nationality . . . the law of England has always been that you must enforce claims in this country according to the practice and the rules of our courts, and according to them a creditor, whether from the furtherest north or furtherest south, is entitled to be paid equally with other creditors in the same class." The same is true of debts barred by limitation.[20] *In the Estate of Goenaga*[21] the court held that a rule of the *lex domicilii* restricting the authority of an executor to a period of one year from the death of the testator is to be disregarded in the English administration as it was a rule of foreign procedural law.

The distinction that exists between the position of a foreign creditor and English creditor is in the ancillary administration. An English ancillary administrator has no duty of advertising for foreign creditors or to give notice of their claim. But if he has received notice of foreign debts, he is not excused from making payment.[22]

After the debts have been paid, the surplus assets are to be distributed among the beneficiaries. But in the case of an ancillary administrator the normal procedure is to remit the surplus assets to the principal administrator, so that these may be distributed

18. Dicey and Morris, 580.
19. (1884) 28 Ch. D. 175.
20. *Re Lorillard*, (1922) 28 Ch. D. 638.
21. (1949) p. 367.
22. *Re Achillopoulos*, (1928) Ch. 433.

among the heirs. However, the remission of assets is not a matter of course, and the administrator should seek guidance of the court. It is for the court to decide whether surplus assets should be remitted to the principal administrator or should they be distributed among the beneficiaries from England. *In Re Lorrilard*[23] a testator died domiciled in New York leaving behind assets and creditors both in England and New York. On administration proceedings being taken in both countries and on New York assets being exhausted, the question arose whether the New York creditors could claim satisfaction of their debts from the English assets which were found surplus. The debt of the creditors was time-barred by the English law of limitation, though it was not so barred by the law of New York. The English court ordered that if the New York creditors did not, within two months, establish that their debts were payable under English law, the administrator should distribute them among the beneficiaries.[24] The converse of *Re Lorrilard*[25] is *Re Northcote's Will Trusts*.[26] In this case the English assets were insolvent but foreign assets were solvent. The English grant was made on the condition that the administrator would obtain a foreign grant in the country where most of the assets were situated.

Position of Foreign Administrator

Just as the English courts have jurisdiction to appoint administrators of assets situated in England, similarly foreign courts have power to appoint administrators of assets situated there. This jurisdiction of English court or of the foreign court is not affected by the domicile or nationality of the deceased : it is entirely based on the *situs* of assets within the jurisdiction. The English law takes the position that a foreign administrator is not recognized in England for any purpose, nor does he enjoy any rights in England. He is entitled to the property that lies within the jurisdiction of the court which appointed him. Neither he can lay his hand on, nor has he any right to, English assets without obtaining an English grant. He cannot sue in his capacity as a foreign administrator in England either. If he meddles with the English assets of the deceased he is liable as an inter-meddler. He has no privileges as a foreign administrator.[26]

From the English rule that status of foreign administrator is not recognized in England for any purpose, it follows that an English debtor who makes payment to a foreign administrator cannot claim to be discharged from the debt. The debtor is under

23. Cited above.
24. This case has been criticised. See Cheshire, 477. See also *Re Manifold* (1962) Ch. 1, which followed the decision in *Re Lorrilard*, cited above.
25. (1949) 1 All E.R. 442.
26. *New York Breweries* v. *A.G.*, (1899) A.C. 62.

no compulsion to make payment to the foreign debtor.[27] Cheshire opines that if an English debtor had reasonable grounds for believing that the foreign administrator was the *bona fide* representative of the deceased, 'it would seem justifiable to depart from strict principle and to regard the payment as a valid discharge.'[28] The question whether payment to the foreign administrator under compulsion, such as in satisfaction of a judgment, discharges the debtor is equally unsettled, though, Leonard Hoffmann says, the argument that it should do so is of course much stronger.[29]

It is settled law that a foreign administrator is not entitled to sue in England in the capacity of a foreign administrator. But this does not debar him from establishing by legal action a right or claim to which he is entitled in his individual capacity. This right or claim may as well be connected with the estate that he is administering. Thus, in his capacity as administrator if he had obtained a judgment on a debt against a debtor, he can file a suit on judgment in England.[30]

Converse of the above rule is that a foreign administrator is not liable to be sued in England for property held or acts done by him in the capacity of foreign administrator, even if he enters an unconditional appearance, because he had no power to submit the assets of the deceased to the judgment of the English court.[31] But it seems that if a foreign administrator sends or brings assets into England which have not been so appropriated as to lose their character as part of the assets of the deceased, then he may be made to account for them by an action for their judicial administration. The foreign administrator can also be sued in England upon a claim that is sustainable against him in his individual capacity. In this manner he would be liable upon any contract that he makes in England in connection with the winding-up of the estate, or where he places himself in a position of a debtor or trustee and incurs liabilities in that capacity.

Indian Law

Indian law closely follows English law. The provision relating to grant of probate and letters of administration are contained in the Succession Act, 1925. In the matter of grant of letters of administration or probate, the jurisdiction is conferred on the District Judge.[32] The High Courts also have concurrent jurisdiction with the District Judge.[33]

27. There is no direct authority for the proposition, but it follows from the general rule. See also the case cited in the preceding footnote.
28. Cheshire, 479.
29. Dicey, 585.
30. *Re Macnichol*, (1874) L.R. 19 Eq. 81; *Vanquelin* v. *Bouard*, (1863) 15 C.B. (N.S.) 341.
31. Dicey, 587.
32. *Ibid.*
33. Section 270.

Jurisdiction

Under s. 270 of the Succession Act, 1925 the basis of jurisdiction are two : (a) if at the time of his death the deceased had a fixed place of abode within the jurisdiction, or (b) if movable or immovable property of the deceased is situated within the jurisdiction of the District Judge. In a purely domestic case, any of these two are alternative bases of jurisdiction, but it seems that in a conflict of laws case Indian court may decline to grant a probate or letters of administration merely on the basis that the deceased had 'a fixed place of abode' in India. The grant will be made only if the deceased had left some movable or immovable property within the jurisdiction.[34] From an early date Indian courts have taken the view that a grant of probate can be made of a will executed abroad by a person who is neither domiciled here nor a national of India, if the testator had left some immovable or movable property in India.[35] though the court has discretion to decline to exercise jurisdiction, if only a very small portion of property is situated within the jurisdiction.[36] Indian courts still do not have any jurisdiction to appoint an administrator on the basis that the deceased was domiciled in India, though under S. 270, Succession, they have power to grant administration on the basis that at the time of his death he had a fixed place of abode in India. If a will has been executed by an Indian outside India and if a probate of that will has been obtained from the court of that country an ancillary probate of his will way be obtained in India for the administration of his Indian situated property.[37]

Choice of Law

In the matter of grant of letters of administrations Indian law makes a distinction between Hindus, Muslims. Buddhists, Sikhs and Jains on the one side, and other persons on the other. In the former case, letters of administration are not required and, therefore, it is optional for them to obtain letters of administration. In case some one desires to obtain letters of administration, then s. 218, Succession Act lays down that grant may be made 'to any person, who accordingly to the rules for the distribution of the estate applicable in the case of such deceased, would be entitled to the whole or any part of such deceased's estate.' When several such persons apply for grant, the court has discretion to grant it to any one or more of them. Sub-section (3) of s. 218 lays down that if heirs do not apply, the creditor of the deceased may apply for administration of the estate. The domicile or nationality of

34. Section 300.
35. *Kalyantkutty Padaji* v. *Gaurikutty*, 1953 T.C. 352.
36. *Bhaurao* v. *Lakshmi Bai*, (1896) 20 Bom. 607.
37. *Algammal* v. *Rakkammal*, 1982 Mad. 354 (case law reviewed); See also *Umasashi* v. *Daribala*, 1984 Cal. 409.

deceased is immaterial. The heir of the deceased would be determined on the basis whether he died as a Hindu or as a Muslim. In case the decased was not a Hindu or Muslim, then those who are connected with him by marriage or by consanguinity are entitled to obtain letters of administration. The order in which they may apply is laid down in s. 219 of the Succession Act, 1925 which is as under :

(a) If the deceased has left a widow, administration shall be granted to the widow, unless the court sees cause to exclude her, either on the ground of some personal disqualification, or because she has no interest in the estate of the deceased.

(b) If the judge thinks proper, he may associate any person or persons with the widow in the administration who would be entitled solely to the administration if there were no widow.

(c) If there is no widow, or if the court sees cause to exclude the widow, it shall commit the administration to the person or persons who would be beneficially entitled to the estate according to the rules for the distribution of an intestate's estate :

Provided that, when the mother of the deceased is one of the class of persons so entitled, she shall be solely entitled to administration.

(d) Those who stand in equal degree of kindred to the deceased are equally entitled to administration.

(e) The husband surviving his wife has the same right of administration of her estate as the widow has in respect of the estate of her husband.

Clause (f) of s. 219 then lays down that in case there is no person connected with the deceased by marriage or consanguinity who is entitled to letters of administration or, in case there is no one, willing to act, the letters of administration may be granted to a creditor. These provisions relate to domestic situations. Then clause (g) provides for conflict of laws case. The clause runs as under :

> "Where the deceased has left property in India letters of administration shall be granted according to the foregoing rule, notwithstanding that he had his domicile in a country in which the law relating to testate and intestate succession differs from the law of India."

Thus, it seems clear that in respect of property situated in India the *lex fori* applies to all matters of administration.

As to grant of probate, s. 222 of the Succession Act, 1925 lays down that probate 'shall be granted only to an executor appointed by the will.' When no executor has been appointed by the will or when the executor so appointed is incapable of acting or refuses to act or has died, "a universal or a residuary legatee may be admitted to prove the will, and letters of administration with the will annexed may be granted to him of the whole estate, or of so much thereof as may be unadministered."[38] In case there is a failure of residuary legatee and his representative, then any person who would have been entitled to administer the estate, had the deceased died intestate, or any other legatee having a beneficial interest, or a creditor, may be admitted to prove the will and letters of administration may be granted to him.

In respect of foreign wills which have been proved abroad by a court, an ancillary grant may be obtained from an Indian court on the production of authenticated copy of the will. This grant may be made to the foreign administrator or to his representative in India. This section has come for interpretation in several cases.[39] In *Re Wilfred*[40] a testator died in England leaving a will, the probate of which was obtained from an English court. The executor granted a power-of-attorney to an Indian who applied for an ancillary grant. The court ordered grant of letters of administration to the attorney-general.

Functions of the Administrator

Here also the Indian private international law closely follows the English private international law. The *lex fori* governs all matters relating to administration. On getting the grant, all properties of the deceased which are situated in India or which are brought into India after his death vest in the administrator.[41]

The first duty of the administrator is to collect the assets of the deceased wherever situated.[42] He may or may not succeed in collecting foreign assets, as it would depend upon the foreign law, but he must collect all assets situated in India. Under s. 317, Succession Act, 1925 the administrator is required to exhibit in the court an inventory 'containing a full and true estimate of all the properties in his possession, and all the credits, and also all the debts owing by any person to which the executor or administrator is entitled in that character."[43]

After making payment for certain expenses and wages,[44] the executor is required to make payment for the debts. Section 323 of the Succession Act provides, ". . . no creditor shall have a right of priority over another; but the executor or administrator shall

38. *Babu Devi Bakhs Singh* v. *Smt. Ashtbhuja Ratan Kunwar*, 1937 All. 670. See also s. 271, Succession Act 1925.
39. Section 232, Succession Act, 1925.
40. 1940 Mad. 680.
41. See also *In the Goods of Ashton*, (1905) A.W.N. 551
42. Sections 220 and 227, Succession Act.
43. Section 319, Succession Act.
44. See also ss. 305-307 of the Successtion Act on the administrators' powers, the causes of action that survive the deceased, and of right of action.

pay all such debts as he knows of, including his own, equally and rateably as far as the assets of the deceased will extend." Then section 324 provides for conflict of laws cases and lays down that the *lex fori* will govern the matter. That section runs :

"(1) If the domicile of the deceased is not in India, the application of his movable property to the payment of his debts is to be regulated by the law of India."

Then sub-section (2) runs :

"No creditor who has received payment of a part of his debt by virtue of sub-section (1) shall be entitled to share in the proceeds of the immovable estate of the deceased unless he brings such payment into account for the benefit of the other creditors."

The application of the principle embodied in the section is explained by an illustration appended to the section : A dies, having his domicile in a country where instruments under seal have priority over instruments not under seal, leaving movable property to the value of 5,000 rupees, and immovable property to the value of 10,000 rupees, and debts on instrument under seal to the value of 10,000 rupees, and debts not under seal to the same amount. The creditors holding instruments under seal receive half of their debts out of the proceeds of movable estate. The proceeds of the movable estate are to be applied in payment of the debts on instruments not under seal until one-half of such debts has been discharged. This will leave 5,000 rupees which are to be distributed rateably amongst all the creditors without distinction, in proportion to the amount which may remain due to them.

The Indian law lays down a clear provision regarding the transfer of surplus asset when the Indian administration is ancillary to the foreign administration. Section 367 of the Succession Act provides that whatever surplus are left with the Indian administrator who is acting as an ancillary administrator, after administration of estate, are to be transferred to the principle administrator. The section runs as under :

"Where a person not having his domicile in India has died leaving assets both in India and the country in which he had his domicile at the time of his death, and there has been a grant of probate or letters of administration in India with respect to the assets there and a grant of administration in the country of domicile with respect to the assets in that country, the executor or administrator, the case may be, in India, after having given such notices as are mentioned in s. 360, and after having discharged, at the expiration of the time therein named, such lawful claims as he knows of, may, instead of himself distributing any surplus or residue of the deceased's property to persons residing out of India who are entitled thereto, transfer, with the consent of the executor or administrator, as the case may be, in the country of domicile, the surplus or residue to him for distribution to those persons."

The section does not make it obligatory on the part of the ancillary Indian administrator to remit the surplus to the principal administrator abroad. If he choses to do so he may distribute the same from India. It seems that in case he decides to remit the surplus to the principle administrator, prior permission of the court would be necessary.

Position of a Foreign Administrator

The Indian courts do not recognize a foreign administrator for any purpose of administration of assets of the deceased situated in India. The foreign administrator cannot file any suit in an Indian court, unless he has obtained grant from an Indian court.[45]

II

SUCCESSION TO IMMOVABLE PROPERTY

As has been seen earlier in this Chapter, the English and Indian Private International laws follow the principle that succession to immovables is governed by the *lex situs*.

English Law

Under English law the general rule is that all aspects of succession, intestate or testamentary, are regulated by the *lex situs*.

When a person dies leaving immovable properties, then it is the *lex situs* and the *lex situs* alone which decides matters relating to capacity to make will, revocation of will, power of disposition, the validity of disposition and like matters. The law of domicile or nationality of the testator has absolutely nothing to do with any of these matters.[46] The Wills Act, 1963 giving effect to the Fourth Report of the Private International Law Committee and to the Draft Convention on the Formal Validity of Wills made at the Hague in 1961, lays down that will be formally valid if it conforms to the internal law in force in the country where it was executed, or in the country where, at the time of its execution or of the testator's death, he was domiciled or had his habitual residence, or in a state of which, at either of those times, he was a national.[47] The Act applies to wills executed on or after January 1, 1964. Thus, under the modern English Private International law most wills are saved from formal invalidity, as a testator has now a choice of about seven systems of law, and if a will is formally valid under any one of them, then it is formally valid.

45. Section 320 (funeral expenses), s. 321 (expenses for obtaining probate or letters of administration) and s. 327 (wages due to services rendered to the deceased within three months next preceding his death).

46. *Pepin* v. *Bruyere*, (1900) 2 Ch. 504, on appeal (1902) 1 Ch. 24.

47. Section 1.

There is some controversy as to which law governs the construction of wills. Should it also be regulated by the *lex situs* or should it be regulated by the *lex domicilii* of the deceased as is the rule in respect of wills of movables ?[48] Or, should it be governed by some other system of law ? Cheshire suggests that a will should be construed in accordance with the system of law intended by the testator.[49] Cheshire fortifies his formulation with the following argument : The adoption of this principle does not infringe any local rule of the *lex situs*, nor does it derogate from the sovereign power of the country in which the land is situated. All courts in administering private international law, desire to give effect to expressed intentions, provided that this does not conflict with the public policy of the forum or of the *situs*. If the rules of the *lex situs* make it illegal or impossible to give effect to the will as construed by the system of law intended by the testator, the general principle must perforce give way, and the construction adopted must be that of the *lex situs*. Or again, if the interest arising from a will that has been so construed possesses incidents different in the *situs* from those recognized by the *lex domicilli*, the *lex situs*, must prevail, for it is that law which determines the nature and extent of estates and intestate of immovable.[50] In the end Cheshire observes : "The testator may, indeed, make his own dictionary, but the *lex situs*, has the last word."[51] It is submitted that the will should be construed in accordance with the *lex situs* though for words and phrases used by the testator which are not tangible under the *lex situs* reference may be made to the law in contemplation of which the testator made the will.

Another question that arises relating to wills is of election. Take in example : It is a settled rule of English private international law that whenever a beneficiary is put to his election the matter is governed by the law of testator's domicile.[52] The rule will not apply if the intended device is illegal by the foreign *lex situs*.[53] The rule is applicable to English heirs only; it is not applicable to heirs to foreign immovable property. Further, the question of election by a foreign heir, as a matter of English law, can arise only when the distribution, as distinguished from the administration, of the testator's property falls to be determined by the English law, or when the testator dies domiciled in England leaving

48. See Dicey, 535. This is treated as an exception to general rule.

49. Cheshire, 518.

50. *Ibid.* at 518.

51. *Ibid.* at 518. In support Cheshire cites *Studd* v. *Cook*, (1883) 8 A.C. 577, but agrees that it is in conflict with Re *Miller*, *Bailie* v. *Miller* (1914) 1 Ch. 511.

52. The rule was established at a fairly early time. The earliest reported case is, *Trotter* v. *Trotter*, (1828) 4 Bli. (N.S.) 502. Some other cases are : *Maxwell* v. *Maxwell*, (1852) 2 D. G.M. & G. 705; *Re Ogilvie*, (1918) 1 Ch. 492.

53. *Brown* v. *Gregson*, (1920) A.C. 860.

movables either in England or elsewhere, whose distribution depends on the *lex domicilii*.[54]

Indian Law

The Indian Private international law is substantially the same. Section 5(1), Indian Succession Act, 1925 runs as under :

> "Succession to the immovable property in India of a person deceased shall be regulated by the law of India, wherever such person may have had his domicile at the time of his death."

In *Vishvanathan* v. *Syed Abdul Wazid*[55] the Supreme Court observed that succession to immovables is governed by the *lex situs* of the immovable property. The question came for consideration before the Kerala High Court in *Sankaran Govindan* v. *Lakshmi Bharti*.[56] One Dr. Krishnan lived in England from 1920 to 1950. He died intestate in England in 1950. He built a comfortable practice at Sheffield. He also got in employment in the National Health Scheme. He purchased a building there in which he housed his evening surgery. At the time of his death he left his house in England and some properties. movables as well as immovables in India. The court found that he died domiciled in India. In respect of his Sheffield situated properties letters of administration were obtained by Miss Woodliff, Dr. Krishnan's private secretary, and Arksey, an attorney. The entire assets of Dr. Krishnan, both movables and immovables, were sold by the administrators, and sale proceeds were divided half and half between a brother and a sister of Dr. Shankaran who survived him. Before the Kerala High Court the main question was : whether the heirs of late Dr. Shankaran in respect of his Sheffield situated immovable property were to be reckoned under the English law, the *lex situs*, or the Indian law, the *lex domicilli* ? Raghavan, J., has no difficulty in holding that succession to immovables is governed by the *lex situs* and therefore English law of succession applied. The learned judge also rightly observed that whether a particular property is movable or immovable is to be determined by the *lex situs*. Since the assets of the deceased were converted into cash, it was argued before the English court that the property being converted into movables the *lex domicilli* should govern succession. The court followed the decision of the English case, *Re Berchtold*[57] and held that since the interest left by the deceased was immovable, the succession to it would be governed by the *lex situs* even if the property is converted by the administrators into cash.[58]

54. Dicey, 540-541.
55. 1963 S.C. 1.
56. 1964 Ker. 244.
57. (1923) 1 Ch. 192.
58. On appeal, this aspect of the decision has been confirmed by the Supreme Court in A.I.R. 1974 S.C. 1764, though on the question of finding of domicile of the deceased the decision of Kerala High Court has been overruled. See also *Chettiar* v. *Chettiar*, 1946 Mad. 398.

Under the Indian private international law also, it seems, all matters relating to capacity to make will, revocation of will, power of disposition and the validity of disposition and like are governed by the *lex situs*.

Provisions relating to construction of wills are laid down in ss. 74 to 111, Succession Act, 1925 and relating to election is ss. 180-190, Succession Act, 1925. It appears that whenever a will of deceased person in respect of immovables situated in India comes for construction before an Indian court, the Indian court is bound to apply the *lex fori*; i.e., rules of construction as laid down in ss. 74 to 111 of the Succession Act, 1925. This follows not merely from the provisions contained in these sections but also from the general rule laid down in sub-section (1) of s. 5 of the Act. The *lex fori* would apply whether the will was executed in India or elsewhere. The Indian courts have all along taken the view that intention of the testator is to be carried out. But clear and unambiguous dispositive words are to be given effect to, and not to be controlled by the so-called intention of the testator.

III

SUCCESSION TO MOVABLE PROPERTY

English Law

Jurisdiction of the English Court: In English law succssion is usually termed as benefical distribution of property. Theoretically, if the English court has jurisdication to grant administration, it has also jurisdiction to determine beneficial distribution of property. But, as has been earlier,[59] in the absence of the local assets the English court exercises jurisdiction only when the foreign country where assets are situated requires a grant of administration from the court of the country of the domicile of the deceased. But if he died leaving behind property in England, the English court has jurisdiction to determine the validity of his will, the construction and effect of the will, persons entitled to succeed to property and all matters connected with succession, even though the deceased died domiciled abroad.

Jurisdiction of Foreign Courts: The court of the country where the deceased died domiciled have jurisdiction to determine succession to all movables whether situated, though courts do not recognize that the courts of domicile have exclusive jurisdiction. However, "while title has been adjudicated upon by the courts of the domicile, such adjudication is binding upon, and must be followed by, the courts of this country."[60] It may be conjectured that the English law would concede jurisdiction to courts of the country where movables are situated even if the deceased is not

59. Part I of this Chapter.

60. *Re Trufort*, (1887) 36 Ch. D. 600.

domiciled there, as English courts also exercise Jurisdiction on this basis.[61]

Choice of Law

Intestate Succession

Intestate succession to movable is governed by the law of the domicile of the deceased person at the time of his death, irrispective of the fact as to the place where he was born, or died, or of the situation of movables at the time of his death.[62] It is the *lex domicilii* which determines the heirs who are entitled to take the relative proportion to which they are entitled to, the right of representation, the rights of a surviving spouse, the liability of the distributes for unpaid debts, the relationship of the claimant with the deceased, and like matters.

Testamentary Succession

Testamentary succession to movables is also governed by the law of the country where the deceased was domiciled at the time of his death. If a deceased person domiciled elsewhere dies leaving behind assets in England, then a grant of probate in England is essential and so far as the administration is concerned it is governed by the *lex fori*, but then all questions relating to beneficial succession must be decided in accordance with the law of the domicile of the deceased. In other words, the executor must ascertain as to who are the persons entitled to succeed and in what proportion they would take the property under the law of the domicile.

Capacity to Make Will : The testamentary capacity, i.e. personal capacity to make will, is determined by the *lex domicilii* of the testator. If the testator's domicile is the same at the time of making of the will as well as at the time of the death, there is no difficulty. The *lex fori* is immaterial.[63] But if the domicile of the testator at the time of death has changed and he died domiciled at a different place, then, whether the domicile at the time that he made the will would apply or whether the domicile that he had at the time of death would apply ? So far there is no English decision on the matter. The majority of jurists[64] are in favour of the view

61. See Dicey, Rule 29, 592.
62. *Pipon* v. *Pipon*, (1744) Amb. 25. Practically all the writers of international law are unanimous on this point: Westlake, ss. 59-120; Story s. 481; Dicey, 592, Rule 98; Cheshire, 481.
63. *In the Goods Maraver*, (1828) 1 Hagg., Ecc. 498.
64. Story, s. 465; Savigny, s. 377; Dicey, 595 Cheshire, 482; and Wolff, s. 557 favour this view. Those who take the view that domicile at the death governs capacity are: Westlake, s. 86, Goodrich, s. 168. Thomas suggests that the testator should have capacity at both times; Private International Law (1955), 130-31. Graveson seems now to suggest that if the will is valid under either law it should be treated as valid : Conflict of laws, 6th ed. (paperback) 507-508.

that it is the domicile of the testator at the time of making of the will which governs the capacity.[65] The rule applies to personal capacity of the testator, such as age, mental or physical capacity, but it does not apply to proprietary capacity, such as whether the testator can bequeath his entire property or not. Such questions may be regarded as questions of material validity.[66]

As to the legatee's capacity to receive legacy under the will, the view, on principle, is that it is governed by *lex domicilii* of the legatee.[67] But the English courts[68] have taken somewhat liberal view and have laid down that a legatee has capacity to take a legacy of movables if he has capacity either by his own *lex domicilii* or by the *lex domicilii* of the testator.[69]

Formal Validity : Under the English common law the rule has been that the will of movables to be formally valid must comply with the law of the domicile of the testator at the time of his death. This rule led to much inconvenience and hardship[70] and led to the passing to the Will Act, 1861 which was not only unsatisfactory but discriminatory between the British subject and foreigners. This Act was repealed and replaced by the Wills Act, 1963 which has been passed to incorporating the recommendations of the Private International Law Committee of 1958 and of the international convention. The Act lays down that a will 'shall be treated as properly executed' if it formally conforms to the internal law of the country where it was executed, or to the law of the country where at the time of its execution or at the time of testator's death, the testator was domiciled or habitually resided or to the law of the country of which, at either of those times, the testator was a national.[71] This is a very welcome provision. When the testator is a national of a composite state like the U.S.A. or the United Kingdom, the Act provides this solution : (a) If there is in force throughout the sovereign state a rule indicating which of the various systems can properly be applied to the case in question, that rule shall be followed; or (b) failing such a rule, the governing system shall be the one with which the testator was most closely connected at the relevant time.[72] In case of double nationality the solution seems to be to select either the nationality of the country in which the testator "is habitually and principally

65. Dicey, 595.

66. *Ibid. In the Estate of Fuld* (No. 3), (1966), 2 W.L.R. 717, Scarman, J. seems to take the view that capacity to make a will of movables is governed by the law of the domicile of the testator at the date of making the will.

67. *Re Hellmann's Will*, (1866) L.R. 2 Eq. 363; *Re Schnavper*, (1928) Ch. 420.

68. *Re Hellmann's Will*, cited above.

69 Cited above.

70 For instance see *Bremer v. Freeman*, (1857) 10 Moo. P.C. 306.

71. Section 1.

72. Section 6(2).

resident, or the nationality of the country with which in the circumstances he appears, to be in fact most closely connected."[73]

Under the Wills Act, 1963, there is no possibility of application of the doctrine of *renvoi*, as the validity of the will under any of the alternative laws is to be tested under the internal law of that country. The internal law is defined as the 'law which would apply in a case where no question of the law in force in any other territory or state arise."[74]

How much the Wills Act, 1963 leans in favour of the formal validity of wills is clear from the position it takes in the case of alteration of relevant law after the execution of the will. If a later alteration in the will validates the will then regards must be had to be changed law, but not if it invalidates a will.[75] The place of execution of wills is given extended meaning in case of wills made on board of a vessel or aircraft of any description, if at the time of the execution of the will the aircraft is grounded in a particular territory or the vessel is within the territorial waters, the testator may comply with the internal law of that territory, or he may comply with the internal law of the territory with which, having regard to its registration and other relevant circumstances, the vessel or aircraft, whether in course of transit or not, has the closest connection.[76] In the latter case the law will be the law of the flag, or the law in force at the port of registration (this will be so in the case of a composite state).

The Wills Act, 1963 also provides a solution to a difficult problem of characterization of certain requirement of internal law; such as, whether a requirement is formal requirement or material requirement ? For instance, Article 992 of the Dutch Civil Code lays down that Dutch nationals cannot make wills in Holland or outside except in 'the authentic form prescribed by Dutch law'. Now section 3 of the Wills Act, 1963 lays down that where a law in force outside the United Kingdom falls to be applied any requirement of that law whereby special formalities are to be observed by the testator answering a particular description, or witnesses to the execution of a will are to possess certain qualifications, shall be treated as a formal requirement, notwithstanding any rule of that law to the contrary. For instance, A, German national, aged seventeen, domiciled and habitually resident in Germany, makes a will in holograph form in Bonn. The German law lays down that any person under twenty-one years and over sixteen can make a will only in notarial form. A's will is not valid, as under the relevant law, i.e. German law,

73. This is the test laid down by the Hague Convention on Conflict of Nationality Laws, 1930.

74. Section 6(1), Wills Act, 1963. See also the Washington Convention of 1973 on the formal validities of Wills. It establishes an additional form of will, called "International Will".

75. Section 6(3), Wills Act.

76. Section 2(1)(a), Wills Act.

formalities have not been complied with. But, if the same person makes a will in holograph form in France where such forms are valid, then the will be valid.[77]

Material Validity : The English Private International Law lays down that the material validity of a will is governed by the *lex domicilii* of the testator at the time of his death. It may happen that a will which is made by a person who has full capacity and which is formally valid, may nevertheless be invalid, as it is violative of certain essential provisions of law. Thus, a bequeath which violates the rule against perpetuity as laid down under the English law or Indian law, or which violates the rule of Muslim law or Scot law that the entire property cannot be bequeathed, will be invalid, if, in the former case, the deceased died domiciled in England or India or, in the latter case, in Scotland or India, since these are the matters of essential validity of the will. Under this head also come questions such as whether the testator is bound to leave a certain proportion of his estate to his wife and children, whether legacies to charities are valid, to what extent a gift is invalid as infringing the rule against perpetuities or accumulations, whether substitutionary wills are valid, whether gifts to attesting witnesses are valid, and like. We may illustrate the rule by *Re Groos*, *Groos v. Groos*,[78] a Dutch lady domiciled in England at the time of her death made a will under which she gave all her movable property to her husband except for the 'legitimate portion to which her descendants were entitled'. On her death she was survived by her husband and five children. Under Dutch law 'legitimate portion' of the children was three-fourth of the estate. But under English law there was no such rule. It was held that children were entitled to nothing, since the English law was the *lex domicilii* at the time of the death of the testator.[79] It is sometimes difficult to make a distinction between the formal validity and material validity of a will as is illustrated by the much criticised decision in *Re Priest*.[80]

Should all questions relating to the material validity of the will be subjected to the *lex domicilii* of the testator ? Cheshire says that affirmative answer to this question would be neither consonant with principle nor warranted by authorities. It entirely ignores the essential difference between the right to give and the right to receive. The two are not necessarily *in pari materia*." Cheshire says that the right to give is to be governed by the *lex domicilii* of the deceased, but there is no reason why this law should restrict the right of foreign legatee to enjoy a gift in accordance with the terms of the will provided that the legacy is valid according to his personal law.[81] Illustrating this, Cheshire says that

77. The illustrations have been adopted from Dicey, 601, Illustrations 3 and 4.
78. (1915) 1 Ch. 572.
79. See also *In re Colin*, (1945) Ch. 5.
80. (1944) Ch. 58.
81. Cheshire, 491.

a bequeath for charity, to be valid must satisfy the following three conditions : (a) the charitable bequest must be valid according to the law of the country where it is to be administered, (b) there must be persons in that country willing and competent to undertake the task of administration, and (c) the purposes for which bequest is to be employed must not conflict with some rule of English public policy intended to operate extra-territorially.[82] This view has been supported by Morris.[83] It is submitted that Cheshire's views are in consonance with the principle of international justice.

Construction of Wills : The writers of English law and some English decisions take the view that construction of will should be made under the law of the domicile of the testator at the time when the will is made In Dicey's Conflict of laws[84] the rule is formulated thus : "A will of movables is to be interpreted and will receive effect in accordance with the law intended by the testator. Is the absence of indication to the contrary, this is presumed to be the law of his domicile at the time when the will is made."[85] Cheshire rightly says, "It is merely a *prima facie* rule that is displaced if the testator has manifestly contemplated and intended that his will should be construed accordingly to some other system of law."[86] Thus, if the will is expressed in the technical terms of the law of the country where the testator was resident (but not domiciled) at the time of execution, or, in the technical terms, of the law of the country where the trusts of the will are to be carried out, then it should be construed in accordance with that law.[87] The majority of the House of Lords in *Re Philipson-Stow* v. *I.R.C.*[88] observed that construction of the will should be in accordance with 'proper law'. In the case of will of immovables, the proper law will be the *lex situs* of property. But it seems that, in view of the majority of the House of Lords, this proper law may change from *lex situs* to *lex domicilii* if immovables were converted to movables.[89]

The question as to which law apply when a legatee is put to election, sometimes becomes difficult because of the characterization of election as a matter of essential validity or as a matter of construction. Morris says that it should be regarded as a matter of essential validity of the will.[90] The judicial support for this view is derived from Buckley, J. who said : "The doctrine of election

82. Cheshire, 492-93.
83. Dicey, 602-603.
84. Rule 102, 605.
85. Rc *Philipson Stow* v. *I.R.C.*, (1961) A.C. 727 at 761.
86. Cheshire, 497.
87. Dicey & Morris, 606.
88. Cited above.
89. This view was affirmed in *Levick's Will Trusts,* (1963) 1 W.L.R. 311.
90. Dicey and Morris, 610.

has nothing to do with intention, and, consequently, nothing to do with construction of the testator's will."[91] Most of the writers of the private international law take this view.[92]

Revocation of Wills : The rules relating to revocation of will differ from country to country. Ordinarily, a person who has capacity to make a will, will also have the capacity to revoke it. A will may stand revoked by (a) the act of the testator, or (b) by operation of law. The Wills Act provides for one case of revocation when a will is revoked by another will. Under the Act, a revocation by will shall be valid if it complies with any system by which the revoked will could be valid under the Act. In other words, revocation of the will, will be valid if it is valid under any system of law which applies to formal validity of the earlier will.[93] The Act applies to revocation of will by a 'testamentary act'. The Act does not apply to non-testamentary revocation of wills.

The other, and the most usual, mode of revocation of a will by the act of testator is by destruction of the will such as by tearing of or by burning. It may be noted that the question of choice of law arises only if the testators's domicile has not remained the same throughout. When the domicile of the testator is not the same at the time when the two events took place, Graveson suggest that the matter should be governed by the law of the domicile of the testator at the time of his death.[94] Cheshire[95] and Morris[96] take the view that revocation in such case is governed by the law of the testator's domicile at the time of the alleged act of revocation.[97]

The most usual case of revocation by operation of law is the revocation of the will by the subsequent marriage of the testator. But this is the rule of English law. In some countries, such as India (except in those cases where s. 69, Indian Succession Act, 1925 applies) or France, marriage does not revoke the will. Thus an English ,domiciled person made a will and then got married while still domiciled there. Later on, he changed his domicile and died domiciled in India. The question is : does his will stand revoked ? Which law should govern, English law or Indian law ?

The English courts have taken the view that the law of testator's domicile at the time of marriage will govern the question. If the will stands revoked by that law it would be deemed to be revoked, but not otherwise.[98] This virtually means the law of the

91. *Re Mengel*, (1962) Ch. 791.
92. Cheshire 520; Westlake, s. 125; Beale, s. 306, 5; Goodrich, s. 170,
93. Section 2(1)(c).
94. Graveson, 524 (6th ed.), paperback.
95. Cheshire, 499.
96. Dicey, 611-12.
97. Cheshire, 499.
98. *In Re Reid*, (1866) 1 P. & D. 74; *Re Morten* (1900), p. 211 (C.A.); In *re Gross*, P. (1904) 269.

country where the husband is domiciled at the time of the marriage.[99] *In Re Martin*[100] an opinion was expressed that the English rule that marriage revokes a will is part of matrimonial law and not part of testamentary law. Cheshire, supporting this, takes the view that revocation of the will by marriage should be governed by the law of the matrimonial domicile.[101] Cheshire's view is in accordance with his central theme that all matrimonial matters must be governed by the matrimonial domicile.[102]

Power of Appointment

English law empowers a person to give, by an instrument, such as will, to some other person or to himself a power to appoint by will the person or persons who would succeed to the property on the death of the person to whom the power is given. The person who thus gives the power is known as the 'the donor of the power' of 'the appointor' and the person to whom the power is given is known as 'the donor of the power' or 'the appointee'. The power of appointment may be either general or special. In the former case the donee can appoint any one, including himself, and in the latter case his choice is limited to specified persons or classes as indicated by the donor. In both cases, the donee is dealing with the property which is not his but of the donor. Now, it can happen that the donor, the donee and the appointee, each may have a different domicile or each one of them may change his domicile after the creation of the power of the appointment. Superficially, it might be thought that the matter being analogous to wills, it need not be treated differently. But different considerations apply here. The reasons seem to be .wo : The power of appointment is unknown to laws of most of the countries; secondly, the donee in exercising the power of appointment is not dealing with his own property but with the property of the donor, and thus he is to be regarded in some sense not as a testator making his own will, but as a mandatory or agent carrying out the wishes of the donor.[103]

Capacity : It has been held that if the donee has the capacity by the law of his own domicile, then it is enough even though he is incapable by the law that governs the instrument by which the power was created.[104] But suppose, the donee has no capacity by his own domicile, but he has capacity by the law governing the creation of power, can the donee validly exercise the power ?

99. This may not be the situation now after the coming into force of the domicile and Matrimonial Proceedings Act, 1973, which allows wife to have a separate domicile.

100. Cited above.

101. Cheshire, 99. Some have criticised this opinion : Falconbridge, 112-17; Wolff, s. 570, Morris supports the opinion; Dicey and Morris, 613.

102. See also Graveson 526-27, who has discussed the matter in some detail.

103. Dicey & Morris, 616-17.

104. *Re Lewal's Settlement Trusts* (1918) 2 Ch. 391.

Affirmative answer[105] has been criticized.[106] Cheshire[107] takes the view that "the testimentary exercise of general power is invalid for want of capacity, unless the appointor is capable by his *lex domicilii*; but that in the case of a special power, the exercise is valid if he is capable by his *lex domicilii* or by the law that governs the instrument of creation."[108]

Formal Validity : The matter is now regulated by the Wills Act, 1963. Before January 1, 1964, the testamentary exercise of power of appointment was valid if it satisfied the formal requirement of the foreign legal system governing the appointor's will, or the internal English law.[109] Under the Will Act, 1963 exercise of power of appointment is formally valid if it is valid under the internal law in force in the country where, at the time of its execution or of the appointor's death, he was domiciled or had his habitual residence, or in a state of which, at either of those times he was a national, or if it was formally valid under the law which governs the material validity of the power.[110] Further, no such will be treated as improperly executed by reason only that its execution was not in accordance with any formal requirements contained in the instrument creating the power.[111]

Material or Essential Validity : The distinction between the general power of appointment and special power of appointment seems to be more pertinent here than anywhere else. There is no difference of opinion that the material validity of a special power of appointment is regulated by the law which governs the operation of the will.[112] In *Pouey* v. *Hordern*[113] a special power of appointment was given under an English settlement to a domiciled French woman. She was incapable of exercising power under the French law, though capable under English law.[114]

But when the donee exercises general power of appointment, different considerations operate. Under the general power, the donee is entitled to treat the property as his own and can dispose it of as such. The Court of Appeal said that the operation and effect of his appointment must be determined by the law of his last domicile.[115] In *Re Pryce*[116] an English domiciled person gave a

105. Dicey's Conflict of Laws (3rd Ed.), Rule 198.
106. Dicey and Morris, 8th ed., 617.
107. Cheshire, 483.
108. *Ibid.*
109. Section 2
110. Section 2(1)(d).
111. Section 2(2), Wills Act.
112. See Dicey & Morris, 622; Cheshire, 496.
113. (1900) 1 Ch. 492.
114. Per Farwell J., *Ibid.* at 494
115. *Re Pryce*, (1911) 2 Ch. 286.
116. Cited above.

general power of appointment to his daughter over funds in England. The daughter married a Dutchman and became domiciled in Holland. By her will, she appointed her husband as the sole heir of these funds. Under the Dutch law, to which her will was subject, she could dispose of only seven-eighth of her property, and one-eighth has to be reserved for the mother. The court held that the Dutch law applied and the husband was entitled to only seven-eighth. A different view was pronounced in *Re Waite's Settlement Trusts*.[117] It was held that restrictions imposed by the law of the donee's domicile did not matter if the exercise of power was valid by the law which created the power. This decision has been criticised[118] and has not been followed in *Re Khan's Settlement*.[119]

Construction : The rule relating to the construction or interpretation of a will made in exercise of a power of appointment by will is the same as of the will which has already been discussed.[120] In short, it should be interpreted in accordance with the law intended by the testator (whatever system of law he might have indicated); in the absence of any indication, it will be presumed to be the law of his domicile at the time when the will was made.

Revocation : If power of appointment has been exercised by a will and it has been revoked by a will, then the Wills Act, 1968 applies.[121] This we have already discussed in connection with the revocation of wills. The exercise of power may also be revoked in a manner which is sufficient by the law of the donee's domicile.[122]

Indian Law

So far as the testamentary succession is concerned, in India, members of all communities are governed wholly or partly by one law, *viz.*, the Succession Act, 1925, though different rules of succession apply to members of each community in the case of intestate succession. Law of testamentary succession in India is contained in Part VI of the Succession Act, 1925, and constitutes the law of testamentary succession in India, and applies to all communities, except the Muslims. To the Hindus it applies with some modifications. As to the other communities, such as Christians and Parsis, it applies fully.

Section 5(2) of the Succession Act, 1925, as has already been noted, contains a rule of conflict of laws. It lays down that succession to the movables of a deceased person is to be regulated by the law of the country in which such person had his domicile at the time of his death. But the application of this provision has been excluded in case the deceased is a Hindu, Mohammedan, Buddhist,

117. (1958) Ch. 100.
118. Dicey and Morris, 624-25, Cheshire, 494-96.
119. (1966) Ch. 567.
120. Dicey and Morris 621.
121. Section 1(a).
122. *Velasco* v. *Coney*, (1934), p. 143.

Sikh or Jain. This provision was enacted at a time when the British Government in India was least inclined to interfere, directly or indirectly, with the personal laws of Hindus and Muslims. In the modern context, this provision would mean that the succession to the property, movable as well as immovable, situated in India will be regulated by the personal law of Hindus and Muslims, as the case may be. But this provision cannot be construed to mean that the immovable property of a Hindu or Muslim situated abroad would also be governed by the personal law, and not by the *lex situs* of the property. Similarly, if a Hindu or Muslim had died domiciled abroad, then succession to his movables will be regulated by his *lex domicilii* at the time of his death. In short, this provision cannot affect the rules of private international law.

Jurisdiction of the Court

Jurisdiction of the Indian Court : It has been seen in Part I of this Chapter that under the Succession Act, 1925 letters of administration or probate can be obtained in respect of the estate or will of any person, including a Hindu and a Muslim. The Indian courts exercise jurisdiction either on the basis of presence of assets within the jurisdiction, or that the deceased had a fixed place of abode at the time of his death within the jurisdiction. We have seen that in a conflict of laws case, the Indian courts have declined to exercise jurisdiction purely on the basis of 'fixed place of abode' of the deceased within the jurisdiction. It seems clear that if the Indian court would exercise jurisdiction in granting administration, it would also exercise jurisdiction in respect of succession. The Indian court does not have as wide a jurisdiction as the English court has under the Act of 1932 to grant administration in respect of 'any deceased person'. But it seems, in view of the generality of the provision of s. 5(2), in respect of movables, the court may exercise jurisdiction on the basis that the deceased died domiciled in India whenever it is called upon to exercise jurisdiction in the interest of justice, such as when the courts of the country where assets are situated requires a grant of administration from the court of domicile of the deceased. It is clear that the Indian court would not assume jurisdiction to determine succession to the movables of the deceased who died domiciled elsewhere and left no assets in India. But in case he died leaving behind assets in India, then Indian courts have jurisdiction to determine the validity of his will and allied matters relating to testamentary succession.

Jurisdiction of Foreign Court : There is no reported decision of Indian court as to on what basis the Indian courts would recognize the jurisdiction of foreign courts to determine succession to movables. In this connection the main question is : suppose, an Indian Hindu dies domiciled in England leaving behind assets in India, will the Indian courts accept the determination of succession in accordance with the *lex domicilii* of the deceased ? The question becomes complicated as for Hindus and Muslims, strictly speaking, there is nothing like *lex domicilii*, they are governed by their personal law, which is the law of their community. When the English court determines succession on the basis of the *lex domicilii* of the deceased, then it should apply the personal law of the deceased Hindu, as in his case, broadly construed, that will be the law of his domicile. If the English court applies any other law, then the Indian courts will not accord recognition to such assumption of jurisdiction.

It it submitted that the Indian court should accept the assumption of jurisdiction by the foreign court on the same basis on which it assumes jurisdiction.

Choice of Law

Intestate Succession

It seems to be clear that intestate succession to movables is governed by the *lex domicilii* of the deceased at the time of the death.[123] But will it equally apply to Hindus and Muslims? Under the influence of English private international law it is often forgotton that nationality is an important connecting link in personal matters in India. Suppose, a Burmese Buddhist dies in Burma leaving behind movable in India. The Buddhist are included in the definition of the term 'Hindu.'[124] Will succession to his property be regulated under Hindu law? The answer will be in affirmative, if we ignore his nationality. In the converse case, an Indian Hindu who dies domiciled in New York leaving behind his assets in India, then succession to his property should be regulated not by his *lex domicilii* at the time of the death but by the law of his nationality i.e. Hindu law. The same would be true of an Indian Muslim.

It should not be ignored that in India intestate succession differs from community to community. Hindus are governed by their own law of succession,[125] Muslims by Muslim law of succession,[126] Parsis by the Parsi law of succession,[127] and Christians and others by their own laws of intestate succession.[128]

Testamentary Succession

As has been seen earlier, with minor exceptions, there is one law of testamentary succession in India. Muslims are governed by their own law of testamentary succession, and provisions relating to testamentary succession in the Succession Act, 1925[129] do not apply

123. Section 5(2), Succession Act, 1925, *Shankeran* v. *Lakskmi*, 1974 S.C. 1964.
124. See s. 2(1)(b) Hindu Succession Act, 1956.
125. Hindu Succession Act, 1956.
126. Which is different among Shias and Sunnis and other sects of Muslims.
127. Chapter III, Succession Act, 1925.
128. Chapter II, Succession Act, 1925.
129. Part VI of the Act.

to them. However, provisions relating to grant of probate and letter of administration apply to them also.[130] Provisions of the testamentary succession in the Succession Act, 1925 applies to all other communities with minor modifications in respect of Hindus.

Capacity : The Indian law lays down the broad rule that succession to movables is governed by the law of the domicile of the deceased at the time of his death. The question is : does this general principle apply to capacity to make will ? It is submitted as far it concerns the personal capacity, it should be governed by the law of the domicile of the deceased at the time of making of the will, as the same arguments apply here as they apply under English private international law. In the case of a Muslim or Hindu the capacity to make will is regulated by his personal law at the time of making the will.

Formal validity : India has not enacted anything like the English statutes of 1861 and 1963. Therefore, it seems that the general rule enacted in s. 5(2), Succession Act, 1925 would apply to formal validity of wills. It appears that wills executed in India in respect of movables situated in India will be valid, if they comply with the *lex fori*. An Indian Muslim has power to make an oral will and if a will is made in respect of movables situated in India, then its formal validity will be judges under Muslim law, i.e. the personal law of the deceased (the law of his nationality), even if he died domiciled abroad. But in respect of a will of foreigners domiciled abroad, the formal validity would be determined by the *lex domicilii* of the testator at the time of his death—this is because of the provision in s. 5(2), Succession Act, 1925.

Material or Essential Validity : It seems that under India private international law the same rules apply to material validity as they apply to formal validity. The material validity of the will of a foreigner will be governed by the law of his domicile at the time of his death. Under Muslim law, a Muslim cannot bequeath more than one-third of his property;[131] if an Indian Muslim bequeaths one-half of movables situated in India and if the validity of his will comes into question before an Indian court, then such a bequeath will not be valid, even if the Muslim died domiciled in England. Similarly, whether an Indian Hindu can bequeath his coparcenary interest will be determined by Hindu law if the question of validity of his will in respect of Indian assets comes before an Indian court.[132]

Construction of the Will : It seems that the same consideration apply to the interpretation or construction of will of movables under Indian law as they apply under English law. The Succession

130. Part IX of the Act.

131. Mulla : Mohammadan Law (16th Ed.) 127.

132. Before 1956, a Hindu could not bequeath his undivided interest in the Mitakashara coparcenary property, but now under s. 30 Hindu Succession Act, 1956, he can do so.

Act, 1925, Chapter six contains provisions relating to construction of wills. The cardinal rule of construction of wills is to give effect to the intention of the testator.[133] In case of ambiguity, the court would apply that law with which the deceased has most intimate connection, and this can be the law of the place where he made the will or the law of the country where he was domiciled at the time he made the will. If the testator has indicated some law, then the will, will be interpreted according to that law. The court shall try to give effect to the intention of the testator so far as it is possible.[134]

Revocation of the Will: Under the Indian law a will may be revoked : (a) by another will or codicil of the deceased or by some writing declaring an intention to revoke the same and executed in the manner a will is evecuted, (b) by destroying the will, such as by burning or tearing it,[135] and (c) by marriage of the testator,[136] but this does not apply to the wills of Hindus and Muslims. Again, there is no Indian decision available on the matter. It is submitted that in the case of the former, the law to which the testator was subject to at the time of revocation should apply. In the third case the law of the domicile at the time of marriage should govern the matter.

133. See Chapter VI, particularly, ss. 74, 75, 82, 87.
134. See s. 87, Succession Act, 1925.
135. Section 70, Succession Act.
136. Section 69, Succession Act.

Part VI

LAW OF OBLIGATIONS

SUMMARY

20

COMMERCIAL CONTRACTS

From the dawn of the civilization, the nations of the world have been trading with each other. In the early stages of the international trade and commerce, there came into existence a body of rules, compadiously called the law of merchants, which regulated most of the aspects of international trade and commerce. Since the international trade and commerce give rise to problems of conflict of laws, it was inevitable that a body of conflictual rules should develop and regulate the commercial activities whenever they have a foreign element. Since every commercial activity is ordinarily preceded by a contract, the main problem of private international law is of determining the governing law of contracts. Every contract gives rise to obligation, but only when it is validly formed. Thus, a contract has two aspects :

(a) formation of contract, and

(b) effect of contract.

How a conctract is formed, the laws of the world differ. Laws of the world also differ as to what effect is to be given to the obligation or obligations arising out of a valid contract. In the modern private international law of most of the countries, the mooted point is whether the same law should apply to the formation of the contract as well as to the effect of contract. It is also debated whether all aspects of the formation of contract should be governed by the same law or whether some aspects could be governed by one law and other aspects by another law. The law is still unsettled. The theory that is gaining almost world-wide support and acceptance is the theory of proper law of the contract. It has been increasingly advocated that to all aspects of formation of contract (or at least to most of its aspects) as well as to the effect of the contract the proper law of the contract should be applied.

Along with the development of an appropriate theory of law applicable to international contracts at national level, there have been attempts at developing uniform law applicable to all international contracts at international level, though not with much success. In 1939 the Institute of International Law at Rome prepared a draft relating to the contracts for the sale and purchase of movable property. Again at the Sixth Hague Conference three drafts were prepared on the unification of law relating to sale and purchase of movable property, but none could be adopted. The 1956 Hague Conference considered the question as to the law applicable to international contracts relating to sale and purchase of tangible movables, but again, the conference could not reach to any agreement. In the Ninth Hague Conference held in 1960 some agreements have been arrived at on some aspects of international contracts. In the 1964 Hague Conference a convention relating to international sale and purchase of goods has been passed. These international agreements touch the problem only on the fringe, and therefore solution to the problem of conflict laws in commercial contracts has to be found by the private international law of each individual country.

The most current and acceptable theory all the world over is the theory of proper law of contract.

I

PROPER LAW OF CONTRACT

Since the contract is an agreement enforceable by law, parties enter into it under some law. How far the parties are free to choose the law applicable to their contract cannot be answered *simpliciter*. Generally most countries of the world subscribe to the principle of autonomy of parties;[1] though there is a divergence on the question whether the parties freedom to choose the law applicable to their contract is absolute or limited. The English law has always subscribed to the notion that just as parties are free to stipulate any terms in their contract, they are equally free to lay down the law which would govern the obligations arising out of it. The law by which a contract is intended to be governed is, called 'proper law of contract'.

Lord Wright observed :[2] "The proper law of the contract means that law which the English court is to apply in determining the obligations under the contract. English law in deciding these matters has refused to treat as conclusive any rigid or arbitrary criteria such as *lex loci contractus* or *lex loci solutionis* and has treated the matter as depending on the intention of parties to be ascertained in each case on a consideration of the terms of the contract, the situation of the parties, and generally of all the fact."[3]

1. See Dicey and Morris, 692-93; Cheshire, 185-87, Saziszy, 261-62; Rabel, 368.
2. *Mount Albert Borough Council* v. *Australasian Temperance etc. Society*, (1938) A.C. 224 at 240.
3. See also *Vita Food Products Inc.* v. *Unus Shipping Co. Ltd.*, (1939) A.C. 277 at 290.

Westlake's real connection theory is sometimes said to be in opposition of Dicey's intention theory.[4] It is submitted that the modern proper law theory is in reality the blending of the 'intention theory' of Dicey and 'the most real connection theory' of Westlake. If parties have chosen a law applicable to their contract, then ordinarily that law will apply. When parties have not expressed any intention about the law that will govern the contract, the law of the country with which the contract has most real connection will apply.[5-6]

Dicey formulated the rules thus : "The term 'proper law of a contract' means the law, or laws, by which the parties intended, or may fairly be presumed to have intended, the contract to be governed, or (in other words) the law or laws to which the parties intended or may fairly be presumed to have intended, to submit themselves."[7] Whenever the parties choose their proper law expressly, Dicey's formulation still holds good, but when parties have not expressly chosen the law to govern the contract, Dicey's formulation of 'presumed intention' has given way to concrete test. This test was formulated by Lord Simonds thus : "The system of law by reference to which the contract was made or that with which the transaction has its closest and most real connection."[8] Lord Denning[9] formulated it thus : "With what country the transaction has the closest and most real connection."[10]

Thus it is evident that the modern proper law theory has two legs :

(a) When the parties have chosen the law governing their contract. In other words, when parties have expressed an intention in favour of some law which they contemplate to govern the obligations arising out of the contract, then that law is ordinarily the proper law of contract.

(b) When parties have not chosen any law, in other words, when parties have not expressed their intention, then it is the law of the place with which the contract has most closest contact.

When Parties have Chosen the Proper Law

Some assert that English law accepted the doctrine of the proper of contract as early as 1760 in *Robinson* v. *Bland*[11] or at any rate in 1796 with the decision in *Gienar* v. *Mayer*.[12] However, the

4. Private International Law (7th ed.), 302.
5. See Gutteridge view. 1936 Cambridde Law Journal, 19.
6. See Cheshire, for comment on Gutteridge view, 188.
7. Conflict of Laws, 148.
8. *Bonythan* v. *Commonwealth of Australia*, (1951) A.C. 201, at 219.
9. *In re United Railways of Havana and Regla Warehouses Ltd.*, (1961) A.C. 1007 and 1008.
10. See Conflict of Laws, Rule 127, 691.
11. (1760) 2 Burr. 1078.
12. (1796) 2 Hy. Bl. 603.

fact of matter is that, in the words of Graveson, "until the nineteenth century the idea of proper law was hardly distinguished from that of the proper jurisdiction; the questions of choice of law and choice of jurisdiction were confused."[13] In modern English law it is fully established that if parties have expressly chosen the proper law of their contract, the contract will be governed by that law. In 1937 Singleton, L.J. observed : "The legal principle which are to guide an English court on the question of the proper law of a contract are now well settled. It is the law which the parties intended to apply. Their intention will be ascertained by the intention expressed in the contract, if any, which will be conclusive."[14] Two years later, the Privy Council gave full effect to the autonomy of the parties to choose any proper law of the contract. Lord Wright observed : "It is now well-settled by English law. . . the proper law of the contract is the law which the parties intended to apply."[15] In this case parties agreed to subject to English law their contract for carriage of goods in a Canadian ship from Newfoundland to New York. The contract was made in disregard of the law of Newfoundland. The Privy Council held that the contract was governed by English law and further observed that the Newfoundland law (which laid down that the Hague Rules would be incorporated in every contract of carriage of goods by sea) was merely directory and therefore failure to comply with it did not make the contract illegal.[16] In *The Assunzione*,[17] it was *obiter*, said, "if parties do express in their contract the law by which they desire the contract to be governed, well and good."[18] Again, in *Tzortis* v. *Monark Line*[19] the Court of Appeal said : "It is clear that, if there is an express clause in a contract providing what the proper law is to be, that is conclusive in the absence of some public policy to the contrary."[20] In 1970 in the House of Lords, Lord Morris of Borth-y-Gest said : "The general rule is that the proper law of a contract is that law by which the parties intended that their rights should be governed."[21] Lord Morris of Borth-y-Gest and Lord Diplok also took this view, though they added that assuming that the parties had not so exercised their choice, the proper law would be the system of law with which the contract had its closest association, *viz.*, French law.

13. Graveson, 427
14. *R.* v. *International Trustee for the protection of Bondholders*, (1937) A.C. 500 at 529.
15. *Vita Food Products* v. *Unus Shipping Co.* (1939) A.C. 277.
16. This decision has been criticised by many. For instance, see Chashire, 197.
17. (1954) p. 150.
18. *Ibid.* at 175.
19. (1968) 1 W.L.R. 406.
20. *Ibid.* at 411, per Lord Wright.
21. *Cie. Tunisienne* v. *Cie d'Armement*, (1970) 3 W.L.R. 389 at p 396. See also *In re United Railways of Havana and Regla Warehouses*, (1961) A.C. 1007.

In English private international law it is now well-established that if the parties have chosen the law governing their contract then that would be the proper law of contract.

Lest difficulties may arise and it is possible in a given that a contract may governed partly by one proper law and partly by another. This was held by the House of Lords in *Forsikringsakticselskapet Vesta* v. *Butelur*.[21a]

Indian law also takes this view.[22]

Incorporation of Foreign Law : Just as parties are free to choose the governing law of their contract, they are also free to incorporate in their contract any provision of law. However, incorporation of certain provisions of domestic law of a foreign country in the contract stand on different footing and have different effect from choosing that law as proper law. When parties incorporate a domestic provision of a foreign law, the law so incorporated is just like any term or stipulation of the contract, irrespective of the fact whether the incorporation of foreign law is by verbatim copy of the foreign provision of law or whether by a mere reference to it. Thus, parties who have chosen the proper law of contract as English law, may as well incorporate in their contract that in respect of a particular matter their rights and obligations will be governed by the law of the United States. This reference to the law of the United States does not make the law of the United States as the proper law of the contract.[23] In *Re Helbert Wagg & Co. Ltd.'s Claim*[24] a loan was granted by a company, which carried on business in England, to another company which carried on business in Germany, and the parties agreed that the contract was to be construed under German law, but that the bond was to be issued conforming to the usual text and practice ruling in the city of London. It was held that the latter got incorporated in the contract and became a term of contract, but the proper law of contract remained the law of Germany.[25]

The distinction between the choice of foreign law as proper law and the incorporation of foreign law into the contract comes out of in clear relief in two respects. First, when the foreign law is incorporated in the contract, it is like any term of the contract and has to be established as such; it does not amount to application of foreign law. Secondly, since the foreign law thus incorporated is no more than a term of the contract, the foreign law so incorporated becomes fixed, as it was at the time of incorporation and no subsequent change in the foreign law can have effect on it. On the other hand, when the foreign law is chosen as proper

21a. (1989) 3 W.L.R. 290.
22. See *Rabindra N. Maitra* v. *Life Insurance Corporation of India*, 1964 Cal. 141.
23. *Dobell & Co.* v. *The S.S. Rossmore Co. Ltd.*, (1895) 2 Q.B. 408.
24. (1956) Ch. 323.
25. See also *Compania Colombiana de Seguros* v. *Pacific Steam Navigation Co.*, (1965) 1 Q.B. 101.

law of the contract, it is chosen as 'living and changing body of law.' This means that effect is to be given to any changes occurring in it before performance falls due.[26] Thus, for instance, if a legislation is passed in the country of the proper law by which law is modified, or rescinded, such as in the case of gold value[27] or where the rate of interest is reduced, the contract is correspondingly modified.[28]

Are parties free to choose any law as proper law : Have the parties absolute freedom to choose any law, even if the chosen law has no connection whatever with the contract ? Here we are not considering a situation when the proper law of contract is contrary to any law of the forum. The difficulty that arises in answering this question in a straight way lies in striking a balance between the principle of certainty and principle of commonsense. It is argued in favour of granting unfettered discretion to the parties that this would lead to certainty and puts proper law beyond peradventure. It is also supported on the principle of autonomy of parties. Lord Atkin[29] observed : "Their intention will be ascertained by the intention expressed in the contract, if any, which will be conclusive".[30] Any connection with English law is not as a matter of principle essential. On the other hand, in the words of Cheshire, judged by the standard of commonsense, it is not so attractive, since it may, if capriciously exercised, subject the parties to a law which is unrealistic to the point of absurdity.[31] Upjohn, J. said that the court will not necessarily regard an express choice of law "as being the governing consideration where a system of law is chosen which has no real or substantial connection with the contract looked upon as a whole."[32] Kahn-Feund says that there is no reason why the proper law of a contract which has no real or substantial connection with the contract should not be given effect to, if the choice is "express and reasonable".[33] But if the choice of law is not '*bona fide* and legal' it will not be given effect to.[34] Thus, no court will give effect 'to a choice of law (whether English or foreign) if the parties intended to apply it in order to evade the mandatory provisions of that legal system with which the contract has its most substantial connection and which, for this reason, the court would, in the absence of an express or implied choice of law, have applied.[35]

The Supply of Goods (Implied terms) Act, 1973 lays down

26. *Re Chesterman's Trust*, (1923) 2 Ch. 466; *Re Helbert Wagg & Co. Ltd.*, (1956) Ch. 323.
27. See *R.* v. *International Trustee*, (1937) A.C. 500.
28. See *Jaboour* v. *Custodian of Isreal Absentee Property*, (1954) 1 W.L.R. 139, (there was a change of sovereignty : from the Palestinian State to Israel State).
29. *R.* v. *International Trustee*, (1937) A.C. 500 at 529.
30. *Vita Food Products Inc.* v. *Unus Shipping Co.* (1939) A.C. 277 at 290, per Lord Wright.
31. Cheshire, 194.
32. *Re Helbert Wagg & Co. Ltd.*, (1956) Ch. 323.
33. Dicey and Morris, 700-5.
34. Dicey & Morris, 699.
35. See the Indian decision in *Rabindra N. Maitra* v. *L.I.C.*, 1964 Cal. 141, at 146.

that where proper law of the contract is English law; the parties are not free to stipulate for another law, the purpose of which would be to avoid ss. 12 to 15 and s. 55 of the Sales of Goods Act, 1893. This provision applies only to sale of goods and to hire-purchase agreements. However, this prohibition does not apply to contracts for the international sale of goods.

It is submitted that the problem whether a proper law chosen by the parties which has no real or substantial connection with the contract has got bogged down on account of somewhat confused interpretation placed on those contracts which have arbitration clauses.

Arbitration Cases : In contracts having arbitration clauses it has happened more often than not that parties by a clause in their contract expressly agree to an arbitration in a particular country but do not specify the law applicable to arbitration. Where the proper law coincides with the law of the country to which parties have agreed to refer their disputes to arbitration, there is no difficulty. But in those cases where two laws, proper law of the contract and the law of the country of the arbitration, do not coincide, difficulties arise. The English court in such cases have mostly taken the view that the law of the country which the parties have chosen for their arbitration is also the proper law. The high water-mark of this view was reached in the Court of Appeal decision in *Tzrotzis* v. *Monark Line A/B*,[36] where it was laid down that when a contract contains a London arbitration clause the resulting implication that the parties intended that the proper law applicable should be English law can only be rebuted by an express provision to the contrary. A further step was taken by the Court of Appeal in *Cie. Tunisienne* v. *Cis. d'Armenent*,[37] where it was said : "An express choice of a tribunal is an implied choice of the proper law. . . ." This destination has been reached *via Kwik Hoo Tong Handel Maatschappij* v. *James Finlay & Co. Ltd.*,[38] *Naamlooze Vennotschap Handel Maatschappij 'Vulcan'* v. *A/S Ludwig Mownkels Rederi*,[39] and *Vita Food Products Inc.* v. *Unus Shipping Co.*[40]

That the presence of an arbitration clause, though powerfully persuasive, was not conclusive of an intention to choose that law as proper law of the contract was recognized by the House of Lords in an early case,[41] but somehow or other it was overlooked in later cases. What was not clearly expressed in these cases—and which it is submitted led to this error—was that it is possible that proper law of contract may be different from the law by reference

36. (1968) 1 W.L.R. 406.
37. (1970) 3 W.L.R. 389.
38. (1927) A.C. 604 (H.L.).
39. (1938) 2 All. E.R. 152.
40. (1939) A.C. 227 (P.C.).
41. *Hamlyn & Co.* v. *Taliskar Distillery*, (1894) A.C. 202.

to which parties have agreed to arbitrate their disputes. This distinction exists has been now expressly brought out by the House of Lords in two recent decisions. In *Miller* v. *Whitworth Street Estates*,[42] the House of Lords made the distinction between the two and termed the latter as crucial law of the contract, and observed that two laws may be different. This aspect of the matter was more fully considered by Lord Diplock in *Cie. Tunisienne* v. *Cie. d'Armenent*.[43] His Lordship said : "It is not now open to question that if parties to a commercial contract have agreed expressly upon the system of law of one country as the proper law of their contract and have selected a different crucial law by providing expressly that disputes under the contract shall be submitted to arbitration in another country, the arbitrators must apply as the proper law of the contract that system of law upon which the parties have expressly agreed."[44] But in those cases where the parties have chosen only the crucial law and have not indicated the proper law of the contract, then, according to Lord Diplock, the fact that they have expressly chosen to submit their disputes under the contract to a particular arbitral forum of itself gives rise to a strong inference that they intended that their mutual rights and obligations under the contract should be determined by reference to domestic law of the country in which the arbitration takes place, since this is the law with which arbitrators sitting there may be supposed to be most familiar. But this is an inference only. It may be destroyed by reference to the contrary drawn from other express provisions of the contract or relevant surrounding circumstances, and those inferences may be so compelling as to lead to the identification of another system of law which the parties must have intended to be the proper of contract. It is submitted that this is the perspective in which the problem has to be looked at.

Implied Choice of Law : It has been said, time and again, that "when the intention of the parties to a contract with regard to the law governing the contract is not expressed in words, their intention is to be inferred from the terms and nature of the contract, and from the general circumstances of the case, and such inferred intention determines the proper law of the contract."[45] Recently, this has been repeated by the Court of Appeal and has been approved expressly at least by one of the opinions in the House of Lords.[46] This view was approved by Viscount Dilhorne,[47] though, along

42. (1970) 2 W.L.R. 728.
43. (1970) 3 W.L.R. 389.
44. *Ibid.*, at 412.
45. These are the wordings of sub-rule (2) of Rule 127 in eighth edition of Dicey's Conflict of Laws, 704.
46. See per Lord Widgney, L.J. *Miller* v. *Whiteworth Street Estates*, (1969) 1 W.L.R. 377, at 383, on appeal (1970) 2 W.L.R. 728.
47. *Whiteworth Street Estates* v. *James Miller* (1970) 2 W.L.R. 728 at 740. This overrules (1969) 1 W.L.R. 377.

with other judges in the House of Lords, he expressed the view that conduct subsequent to the contract cannot be taken into consideration. The test of 'inferred intention' has been propounded in several cases. Then, a debate started whether the test for the determination of 'inferred intention' is to be subjective or objective[48] By 1954 the judicial opinion veered around the objective test.[49] This view was reiterated in *R.* v. *International Trustees for the Protections of Bondholders.*[50]

Side by side with the propagation of the objective view, a consistent attempt has been made to erode the test of 'inferred intention' and replace it with the test of 'real and substantial connection with the contract'. And this takes us to what Widgery, L.J. called, the third and final stage or inquiry when the parties have not expressed any intention, and what, in the submission of the present writer, is the second stage of the enquiry in the task of finding out the proper law of the contract.

When parties have not expressed any Intention : *Real and Substantial Connection Theory* : As has been seen earlier, Westlake propounded the test of 'most real connection'. *In Boissevain* v. *Weil,*[51] Lord Denning remarked that the proper law of the contract 'depends not so much on the place where it is made, nor even on the intention of the parties or on the place where it is to be performed, but on the place with which it has the most substantial connection.'[52] Lord Denning repeated this view in two subsequent cases.[53] His Lordship observed that where intention is not expressed, it is a matter of inference and the search should be of the legal system with which the contract has most closest links. In 1972 Lord Denning said that to determine the proper law of the contract 'we have to ask ourselves : what is the system of law with which the transaction has the closest and most real connection ? His Lordship said that to answer this question all circumstances connected with the case are to be studied.[54] It appears that this test was impliedly adopted first in *Bonthoyn* v. *Commonwealth of Australia*[55] by Lord Simonds, then it was accepted explicitly by the House of Lords in *Re United Railways of the Havana and Regla Warehouses Ltd.*[56] This test was recently reiterated unanimously by

48. See *The Assunzione* (1954), p. 150.
49. *Ibid.*
50. (1937) A.C. 500 at 529.
51. (1949) 1 K.B. 482 on appeal (1950) A.C. 327.
52. *Ibid.* at 490.
53. *The Fehmarn*, (1958) 1 W.L.R. 159 and in *Philipson-Stow* v. *I.R.C.*, (1961) A.C. 727 and in *Tzortis* v. *Monark Line A/B*, (1968) W.L.R. 406 at 411.
54. *Coast Line Ltd.* v. *Hudig & Vendor*, (1972) 1 All E.R. 451 at 455.
55. (1951) A.C. 201.
56. (1960) 2 All E.R. 332, per Lord Denning, and Lord Morris of Borth-y-Gest.

the House of Lord in *Miller* v. *Whiteworth Street Estates*[57] and in *Cie. Tunisienne* v. *Cie. d'Armenent*.[58]

But the most complicated aspect of this test lies in the difficulty of its application to the facts of each individual case, and, more often than not, the judges have reached to diametrically opposite conclusions on the same facts. Denning, L.J., observed : "This new test is all very well. It is often easy to apply. But, there are sometimes cases where it is quite indecisive. The circumstances do not point to one country. They point equally to two countries, or even to three."[59] This may be illustrated from three recent cases.

The facts of the House of Lords case, *Miller* v. *Whiteworth Street Estates*[60] are : An English Company which owned premises on Dubarton, Scotland, wanted to convert them into a bounded warehouse. They invited tenders and accepted the tender of a company, which had their registered office in Scotland. The contract was in RIBA form. The contract also contained an arbitration clause under which it was stipulated that any dispute arising under the contract should be referred to arbitration of a person to be agreed upon; or, falling agreement, arbitrator was to be appointed by the President of RIBA. This case had two important facts which could be considered as two important pointers to proper law, *viz.*, the form of contract was English, and therefore had closest connection with the English system of law, and, the other important fact was that the performance of the contract was to be made in Scotland. There were several subsidiary facts, such as the contract referred to English rates being applicable, and the contractor was Scotish. On these facts the five law Lords did not reach to any unanimous conclusion. Lord Reid examined the terms of the contract and said that contract had many connections with the law of England but it also had "very important connections with the law of Scotland"; these very important connections were that the contract was to be performed in Scotland and "apart from the possibility of an arbitration being conducted in England, substantially every question which could arise in the course of carrying out the contract would arise in Scotland." His Lordship thus came to the conclusion that law of Scotland was the proper law of contract.[61] Lord Wilberforce also reached to this conclusion. His Lordship said that the most weighty fact was that the place of performance was Scotland, the work was to be done in Scotland under Scottish regulations and probably by Scottish workers. "If any single factor," His Lordship said, "carries more weight in these matters

57. (1970) 2 W.L.R. 728.
58. (1970) 3 W.L.R. 389.
59. *Re Coast Line Ltd.* v. *Hudig & Vendor*, cited above, at 455.
60. Cited above.
61. (1970) 2 W.L.R. 728, at 733-34.

than others, it is the *lex loci solutionis*, and this factor must particularly be important where whole contract is so visibly localised in one place."[62] On the other hand, Viscount Dilhorne said : "It is to be presumed that the English respondents with their English architect would naturally choose a form of contract with which the architect was familiar, a contract 'in English form' and one governed by English law."[63] His Lordship therefore held that the proper law of the contract was English law. Similarly, Lord Hodson said : "The parties deliberately used the RIBA form which has many connections with English law" and agreeing with Court of Appeal held that the proper law of the contract was English law.[64] Lord Guest said : "There are very strong factors either way and one of the most important is the fact that the place of performance of the contract was Scotland. But equally I recognise that there are persuasive factors in opposite direction, one of them being the RIBA form of contract."[65] His Lordship came to the conclusion that English law was the proper law of contract.[66]

In *Sayers* v. *International Drilling Co.*,[67] the plaintiff, an Englishman, entered into a contract of employment in England with a Dutch company engaged in off-shore oil drilling, under which he was employed as a derrickman on one of company's rigs off Nigerian coast. His salary was to be paid in sterling. The contract was entirely to be performed outside England. The contract written in English was on a printed form of contract drawn up by the company for employing persons from different European countries. The contract did not contain any express clause stating by which law it is to be governed. One of the clauses of the contract excluded the application of workmen's compensation insurance or benefits under the laws of the United Kingdom and made applicable company's compensation programme to the plaintiff. The plaintiff was injured in an accident on account of negligence of the other workers of the company. If the proper law of the contract was English law, the plaintiff would be entitled to benefits of workmen's compensation insurance and other benefits as the Law Reforms (Personal Injuries) Act, 1948 makes such exemption clauses as the one entered into by the plaintiff void. Lord Denning found the following pointers towards English law as proper law : the contract was negotiated and made in England; it was for the service of an Englishman; it was in English language; the salary was payable in sterling; the plaintiff was to return to England; and the contract was administered in England. On the

62. *Ibid.*, at 744.
63. *Ibid.*, at 740.
64. *Ibid.*, at 735.
65. *Ibid.*, at 737.
66. See also *Cie. Tunisienne* v. *Cie. d'Armement*, (1970) 3 W.L.R. 389, where the law Lords displayed the same divergence of opinion in finding out the proper law of the contract.
67. (1971) 3 All E.R. 163.

other hand, Salmond, L.J. came to the conclusion that the Dutch law was the proper law of the contract. According to his Lordship: since the Dutch employers were engaging people of various nationalities in different parts of the world to work abroad together, it certainly gives the greatest business efficacy to such contracts to presume that the parties must have intended to adhere to the law of Holland, as that system of law has the closest and the most real connection with the contract. The learned judge said that another pointer towards Dutch law is that the Dutch law permits such an exclusion of liability under a contract, and, ordinarily, parties intend to be governed by a law under which their contract is valid rather than under a law under which it is invalid. The third judge, Stamp, L.J. also found in favour of Dutch law. None of the three judges for a moment thought that the Nigerian law, the law of the place of the performance of the contract, could have been the proper law of the contract.

In *Coast Lines Ltd.* v. *Hudig & Vendor Chartering NV*[68] the plaintiff shipowners, an English company, chartered their ships to the defendant charterers, whose residence and principal place of business was Rotterdam and who had no place of business or assets in England. The charterparty was signed in Rotterdam following negotiations by telephone and telex between the charterers in Rotterdam and the shipowner's agents in Cardiff. The charterparty, which was in English, in Gencon form, provided for the carriage of the two cargoes from Rotterdam to Ireland. It contained no express provision as to the law governing the contract. The bill of lading was issued in Rotterdam signed by agents on behalf of the master. It contained a clause binding the shipowners to exercise due diligence. On the other hand, the charterparty contained a clause exempting the shipowners from the liability for damage to goods caused by unseaworthiness of the vessel unless unseaworthiness was attributable to want of due diligence on the part of shipowners. Under the law of the Netherlands any clause in charterparty restricting the shipowners liability for damages due to unseaworthiness was rendered null and void and this law applied to all cases of carriage of goods by sea from the Netherlands ports, even if the parties have chosen some other proper law. Lord Denning said that it was one of those difficult cases where it is not easy to apply the test of real connection with the contract. His Lordship said that in such cases law must give some help and it should provide a pointer to a solution, if only as a last resort. "One such pointer is that, in a contract of charterparty, other things being equal, the law of the ship should govern." The difficulty with which the learned judge was faced was, in his words, one important circumstance is that the contract was made in Rotterdam by Dutch charterers for shipment at Rotterdam: that points to Netherland law; another important circumstance is

68. (1972) 1 All E.R. 451; see also *Armer Shipping Co.* v. *Caisse*, (1981) 1 All E.R. 498.

that the contract was for carriage in an English ship owned by English owner for carriage on high seas : that points to English law. "Put those two into scales, one on one side, the other on the other, you find they are equal. Other circumstances point one way, then another. There is nothing to choose. So, as a last resort, you take the law of flag, which is English law."[69] Megaw, L.J. applying the *Bonython* test, or formula as he called it, said that what was significant in the test was the connection sought between the transaction, i.e. the transaction contemplated by the contract, and the system of law and thus more importance is to be attached 'to what is to be done under the contract—its substance—than to considerations of the form and formalities of the contract or considerations of what may, without disrespect, be described as lawyer's point as to inference to be drawn from the terms of the contract."[70] Then, his Lordship said : with which system of law did this transaction have its closest and most real connection? The shipowners were English, the charterers were Dutch. The charterparty which was negotiated across the sea was dated Rotterdam, 13th December 1967. It was only in technical sense that the contract was made there. It was in English language. In the light of the uncontradicted evidence, that was not a matter of great weight in favour of English law. The fact that the freight and demurrage were expressed in sterling deserves slightly greater weight, although, again, in the light of evidence, it is not a strong factor. The loadings of vessel took place in Rotterdam and bills of lading were to be issued there. To that extent the performance of the obligation of the contract was connected with the Netherlands. So far as bills of lading were concerned it might well be that the fact they were issued in Rotterdam in respect of goods loaded there would be conclusive, or at least powerful, indication that the proper law of the contracts to which they might have considered was the law of the Netherlands. But different considerations apply to the two types of contract—charterparty contract and bill of lading contract. As against the connecting factors with the law of the Netherlands, the factors connecting the transaction with English law were : the ship, the principle subject-matter of the charterparty, was English, the flag was British with English registration and English ownership. The judge concluded in favour of English law as proper law on the ground that the subject-matter of the charterparty was an English ship and the whole of the transaction contemplated by the contract concerned the activities of the English ship, in loading, carrying and discharging the cargo and, therefore, viewed as whole and weighing all the relevant factors, the contract has a closer and more real connection with English law than with the law of the Netherlands. The third judge, Stephenson, L.J. would have, if left to himself, decided in favour of the Dutch law but reluctantly agreed with other judges. The most important factor, along with other facts, pointing to the Dutch law was that the Dutch

69. *Ibid.* at 455.
70. *Ibid.* at 457-58.

charterer could never have contracted to transgress the commercial code of their own country as under the Dutch law clauses in a contract excluding shipowners liability were void.[71]

We may also refer to *Mauroux* v. *Sociedale Conmercial Abel Pererira da Fonseca Sarl*,[72] where the Chancery Division has the same sort of difficulty in determining the proper law of the contract by applying the closest connection test. This was an action by the plaintiff, resident in England, against the defendant a Portuguese company, for damages for breach of contract, for account and for payment of commission found to be due. Under the contract the defendants constituted the plaintiff as their agent in the British Isles, i.e. England, Scotland, Ireland and Channel Islands, for the sale of wines, brandies and liquors produced by the defendant company. On the facts, it was conclusively established that the *lex loci contractus* was Portuguese. As to the place of performance, on the plaintiff's side the following important facts emerge ; all the feats of agency that would induce customers to buy from the defendant company would be performed in England, customers would be persons trading in England and it would be in England that the defendant company would have to pay the plaintiff. On the defendant company's side, samples and literature would have to be despatched to the plaintiff from Portugal, goods too would have to be despatched from Portugal. Then the plaintiff has to perform the contract not merely in England but also in Scotland, Ireland and Channel Isles. The same is true about the surrounding circumstances. Much can be said on either side. The agency contract was entered into at the instance of the plaintiff. Megarry, J. came to the conlusion that the proper law of the contract was Portuguese. His conclusion was based on the following facts : in a case of an agency agreement, like the present one, the agent had to seek the principal, and the contract was constituted in principal's country. Whatever claim the English law might have, the learned judge felt, they were weakened by the single fact that the performance of the contract had to be done not only in England but other jurisdictions also.

Presumptions as to Proper Law : At the time when English law adhered to the test of 'inferred intention' of parties, the court developed certain presumption which helped them in inferring the intention of the parties from the terms and nature of the contract.[73] The modern English law has virtually abandoned the test of inferred intention and replaced it with the 'closest and most real connection' test, the presumption are hardly of any utility.[74] The judicial tendency of not giving much weight to presumptions became evident from the decision in *The Assunzione*.[75] This

71. *Ibid.* at 461.
72. (1972) 2 All E.R. 1085.
73. See Dicey, Rule 127, Sub-Rule 3, 712-723; Graveson, 435-441.
74. Cheshire, 190.
75. (1954) 150.

trend continues,[76] and it may be now taken that the courts have abandoned the approach of presumptions.[77] Thus, the position[78] that emerges is that the *lex loci contractus, lex loci solutionis* or the law of the flag are no longer regarded as presumption, but they are, like any other facts (though sometimes more important than others) pointers to the proper law of the contract and should be looked upon as such. For instance, it was in this perspective that the Court of Appeal in *Coast Lines Ltd.* v. *Huding & Vendor*[79] gave importance to the law of the flag, Megarry, J. in *Mauroux* v. *Pereira*[80] to the *lex loci contractus* and the House of Lords to place of performance in *Miller* v. *Whiteworth Street Estate.*[81]

In the case of insurance contracts some significance is attached to the place of performance which is the place of payment, and some significance may also attached to the place where the underwriter carries on business, even if some elements of the contract are to be determined by a specified different law.[82] In *Amin Raseed Shipping Corporation* v. *Kuwait Insurance*,[83] the plaintiffs, a shipping company based on Dubai, owned a cargo vessel which was insured under an insurance policy issued by the defendants, an insurance company incorporated in Kuwait and carried on business there and elsewhere in the Arabian Gulf. The form of policy closely followed the form of Lloyd's standard marine policy but gave Kuwait as the place of issue and provided for claims to be payable in Kuwait. It contained no express provision as to the law that was to govern the contract. Rejecting the argument that since English form of Insurance policy (Lloyd's form) was used, English law was the proper law, Binghan, J. observed that the contract had the most real and closest connection with Kuwait and contract was also to be performed in Kuwait. The Court of appeal agreed with this view. But the House of Lords[84] held that the proper law of contract was English law; since the provisions of the policy taken as a whole by necessary implication led to the inevitable conclusion that it was the parties intention that their mutual rights and obligations under it should be determined in accordance with English law of marine insurance; objectively determined the contract had its closest and most real

76. See House of Lords decisions in *Miller* v. *Whiteworth Street Estates*, (1970) 2 W.L.R. 728; *Cie. Tunisienne* v. *Cie. d'Armement*, (1970) 3 W.L.R. 389.
77. *Ibid.*
78. *Coast Lines Ltd.* v. *Vendor*, (1972) 1 All E.R. 451 at 458.
79. Cited above.
80. Cited above.
81. Cited above.
82. *Rossano* v. *Manufacturers' Life Insurance Co.*, (1963) 2 Q.B. 352; *Gree* v. *Poole* (1880) 5 Q.B.D. 272.
83. (1982) 1 W.L.R. 961.
84. *Amin Raseed Shipping Corporation* v. *Kuwait* Insurance (1983) 3 W.L.R. 241 (Case law has been reviewed).

connection with English law. Lord Diplock also added that by the proper law of a contract was meant the substantive law of the country which the parties have chosen as that by which their mutual legally enforceable rights were to be ascertained, but excluding any renvoi, whether remission or transmission, that the Courts of that country might themselves apply if the matter was litigated before them.

In Indian law precedent is very little, discussion is much less and the tendency to ape English law is in abundance. In *Rabindera v. L.I.C.*[85] the court said that where parties have not expressly chosen the proper law of the contract, then proper law of the contract will be that system of law with which the transaction has its closest and most real connection. It is interesting to note that the court also paid lip-service to imputed or inferred intention test.[86]

Conclusion : It appears to be now well settled that in determining the proper law of a contract containing no express choice of law, the task of the court is to ascertain the intention of the parties from the terms and the nature of the contract and the general circumstances of the case and, if no intention can be inferred, to identify the system of law with which the transaction has its closest and most real connection. Obviously, where parties have expressed a choice of law, ordinarily that is the proper law of contract.[87]

II
FORMATION OF CONTRACT

The question here is : as to which aspects of formations contracts or whether all aspects of the formation of the contract and its effect are governed by the proper law of contract ? It may appear surprising that while English authority on the proper law of contract is copious, it is very scanty on the subject under discussion.

Under the formation of the contract are included matters such as communication of offer and its revocation, acceptance of the

85. 1964 Cal. 141, the Calcutta High Court referred to *Bonython* v. *Commonwealth of Australia*, cited above; *Tomkison* v. *First Pennsylvania Banking and Trust Co.* (1960) 2 W.L.R. 969; *Re United Railways of Havana and Regla Warehouse Ltd.*, (1960) Ch. 52; and the Supreme Court decision in *Delhi Cloth and General Mills* v. *Harnam Singh*, 1955 S.C. 590.

86. Reference was also made to Cheshire, 190-191 (6th ed.).

87. *Bonython* v. *Commonwealth of Australia*, (1951) A.C. 201; *In re United Railways of Havana and Regla Warehouses Ltd.*, (1961) A.C. 1007; and *Amin Rasheed Shipping Corporation* v. *Kuwait Insurance Co.* (1982) 1 W.L.R. 961; *Armadora Accidental S.A.* v. *Haraca Mann Insurance Co.* (1977) 1 W.L.R. 521, in court of appeal, (1977) 1 W.L.R. 1098; *Coupland* v. *Arabian Golf Oil Co.*, (1983) 1 W.L.R. 1136. See also Dicey and Morris, *Conflict of Laws* (10th ed. 1980) Vol. 2, Rule 145.

offer and its communication, and consideration and its reality or otherwise. Here we are also concerned with *consensus ad idem* and reality of consent, questions such as whether the contract is void or voidable for mistake, fraud, misrepresentation, undue influence and like, legality of contract, enforceability of contract (contract otherwise valid many be unenforceable because it violates some statutory law, or its enforcement is contrary to public policy), and the like. With these are linked the questions or formal and material validity of the contract. Matters such as interpretation and discharge of a contract and the obligations arising under contract would also come for consideration.

The tendency that is gaining ground is that all aspects of the contract should be governed by the proper law of the contract.

Formation of the Contract

A valid contract comes into existence when parties reach an agreement : when an offer is made by one party and accepted by another. Some systems of law insist that consideration is also an essential element of the agreement, while some do not subscribe to that view. Then, sometimes, parties have apparently reached an agreement but in reality there is none. This is the case when consent of parties is vitiated by mistake, undue influence, fraud, etc. Thus, the creation of contract may be looked at from two aspects : (a) factum of agreement, and (b) reality of agreement.

Factum of agreement : This relates primarily with offer and acceptance. What constitutes an offer and acceptance is a question of law, but whether an offer has been made and accepted is a question of fact. In the case of an oral contract where offer and acceptance is made instantaneously there is no difficulty. But in those cases where a contract is negotiated by correspondence, the difficulties arise. They arise because different systems of law take different view as to the precise point of time at which acceptance is complete and binding. The common law countries as well as India subscribe to the view that acceptance is complete as soon as it is posted, while most civil law countries take the view that it is not complete and binding until it is received by the offeror. Some continental countries take the view that the moment the acceptance has come to the knowledge of the offeror, it is complete and binding. This diversity in legal systems can lead to divergent results as to the creation of the contract. For instance, a person posts an offer from New Delhi to a person in Bonn. The person in Bonn mails the acceptance. The letter is lost in the transit. According to Indian law a binding agreement has come into being, but accordding to German law, it has not. Thus, the question is which law governs ?

At one time *lex loci contractus* was vigorously advocated. It looked logical that the contract must be valid by law of the place where it has been created. But practical difficulty is in determining the *locus* of the contract. Kahn-Freund rightly says : "Apart from the fact that the place of contracting may be purely fortuitous, there is a danger that by submitting to the *lex loci contractus* the question whether a contract has been concluded at all one may involve oneself in a vicious circle."[88]

In view of the difficulties inherent in the test of *lex loci contractus*, another test, what Cheshire names as 'putative proper law'[89] or what Kahn-Freund calls 'the system of law which would determine the validity of the contract on the assumption that the offer has been made and accepted,"[90] or, in the words of Cheshire, "it seems only rational that the valid *creation* of contract, a matter upon which the parties are not free to choose the governing law, should be determinable in all its aspects by a single legal systems."[91] Support for this proposition is sought by both the writers from the decision in *Albeko Schuhmaschinen* v. *Kamborian Shoe Machine Co. Ltd.*[92]

In respect of the third element of the contract, *viz.* whether consideration is required for the validity of the contract, the same suggestion has been made, i.e. it is governed by the proper law of the contract. There is no English authority for this proposition too. The difficulty here also is of the same character. In some system of law, such as Scottish, German and French, consideration is not regarded as an essential element of the contract, while in most of the countries of the commonwealth, including India and the United States, consideration is considered to be an essential element of the contract. The application of proper law to this aspect of creation of contract is suggested by analogy. It is also justified on principle.[93]

Reality of the Agreement : At one time the personal law of the party concerned was advocated to be the law governing the reality of the agreement.[94] But it did not find favour with courts of the country where it was advocated. The problem here also is of the same nature : different systems of the law in the world have different nations and rules on this matter. What types of mistakes vitiate a contract, Indian law takes one view, German law takes another view.

There is no direct English or Indian authority on the matter. Cheshire, Kahn-Freund and Graveson[95] suggest the application of the proper law. It is argued cogently that the factum and reality

88. Dicey and Morris, 741.
89. Cheshire, 203.
90. Dicey & Morris, 741.
91. Cheshire, 203.
92. (1961) 111 L.J. 519.
93. Dicey and Morris, 129.
94. Bartin in France (Principles de Droit International Prive, I, 175: II, 60) and Leward in Germany (Das Deutsche Internationale Privatrecht, 232-241).
95. Cheshire 204; Dicey and Morris, 741.

of the agreement are two constituent elements of the agreement and there is no reason why they should be separated from each other and therefore their validity should be governed by the same system of law, i.e. proper law.

One of the most valid criticism of this principle has been made by Wolff. He says that certain matters must be reserved for the law of the place of residence or business of the party concerned, particularly in such matters, such as whether silence amounts to acceptance. Thus, say, a person in England receives an offer from another person in Denmark : Under Danish law in certain circumstances offeree's silence amounts to acceptance. Now suppose that there is an express clause in the offer that the contract would be governed by the Danish law. The person in England does not reply. Then does it mean that Englishman's silence amount to acceptance, since the proper law of the contract is Denmark ?[96] It is submitted that despite some apparent reason in this view,[97] it ignores that the proper law advocated here is not the proper law as chosen by the parties, but that system of law with which the contract has closest and most real connection, or what Cheshire calls, 'the law to which the contract naturally belongs.'[98]

Capacity to Contract

There is a lack of authority : the three different tests governing capacity to enter into a contract have been suggested. These are *lex domicilii, lex loci contractus* and proper law. Some judicial dicta exists in favour of *lex loci* too.[99] The *lex loci* has no modern advocates and it is least justified on principle, and therefore it should not detain us any more.

Whatever judicial authority exists in favour of *lex domicilii*, it is in the cases of status—particularly matrimonial status—and it is from them that by analogy it has been applied to commercial contracts.[100] Now it is almost universally accepted that the *lex domicilii* as a test of capacity in commercial contracts is wholly unsatisfactory.[101]

96. Private International Law, 439.
97. Kahn-Freund seems to support this : see Dicey and Morris, p. 742.
98. Cheshire, 204.
99. Lord Greene, per *Baindail* v. *Baindail*, (1946), p. 122.
100. The dictas in favour of *lex domicilii* are in : *Sootomaor* v. *De Barros*, (No. 1) (1877) 3 P.D. 1; *Re Cooke's Trust*, *(1887)* 56 L.J. Ch. 637; *Cooper* v. *Cooper*, (1888) 13 A.C. 88, *Ogden* v. *Ogden*, (1908), p. 46; *Braindail* v. *Baindial*, (1946), p. 122. See also *Republic of Gautemala* v. *Nunez*, (1927) 1 K.B. 669, where Scrutton and Lawrence, L.J. declined to arbitrate between the claim of *lex domicilii* and the *lex actus*. Early Indian decisions also applied the *lex domicilii* : *Rohilkhand* v. *Khumaun Bank* v. *Row Fateh Bahadur* 25 All. 195: *Kashibadin* v. *Sripad*, 19 Bom. 697; Contrary view is expressed in *T.N.S. Firm* v. *Md. Hussain*, 65 M.L.J. 458.
101. Dicey and Morris, 745.

The *lex loci contractus* as a test of capacity to contract is recognized in the continental countries such as France and Germany.[102] In England the *lex loci contractus* has been advocated by some authors and, *obiter*, in some judicial decisions.[103] The *lex loci contractus* as a test exclusively governing capacity has been considered unsatisfactory for various reasons, the prominent of which are: first, it will enable a party to evade his incapacity by the simple device of choosing that forum for his contract where he has capacity. Secondly, in those cases where the place of contract happens to be transitory or fleeting, there is no justification on principle to apply the *lex loci contractus*.[104]

The first two tests thus ruled out, the choice veers round the third test : the capacity of a party to enter into contract is governed by the proper law of the contract, that is to say the law of the country with which the contract has the closest and most real connection. Here the subjective test of the proper law, is not to be applied, for the simple reason that a party cannot be permitted to confer upon himself capacity by choosing a law which is favourable to him.[105] "This would provide, e.g., for the case of a contract entered into in one country where the person contracting had no capacity but to be carried out in another country where he had such capacity. It would make it possible to apply the *lex situs* where it is the proper law of the contract concerning land, and to resort to the *loci contractus* wherever it is the system of law which has the most substantial connection with the contract."[106] It is submitted that this formulation is correct on principle and would be in accordance with justice and convenience.

Formal Validity

At one time on formal validity of a contract the *lex loci contractus* was given the full and undisputed sway. Again, there is dirth of judicial authority both in England and India.

Even now juristic opinion subscribes to the view that compliance with the *lex loci contractus* is sufficient for the formal validity of the contract.[107]

The view that is gaining ground is that, as elsewhere so here, if the contract is formally valid by the proper law of the contract then it will be accepted as valid everywhere, even if it is not valid

102. It has been done by legislation, Law of the Civil Code, Art. 7, s. 30.
103. See *Baindail* v. *Baindail*, (1946), p. 122, at 128. Foote, Private International Law (5th Ed.), 376.
104. Dicey and Morris, 744.
105. See *Male* v. *Roberts*, (1800) 3 Esp. 163, is an authority which is cited both for this proposition (See Cheshire, 201) and also for *lex loci contractus*. In fact this was not decided in the case as decision was rendered on another point.
106. Dicey and Morris, 745.
107. Cheshire, 205.

by the *lex loci contractus*. Cheshire rightly says that there is "neither justification nor authority for the view that the observance of the local form is compulsory. If, for instance, two Englishmen make a contract by which one agrees to act in a play to be produced by the other at a London theatre, the mere fact that they sign a memorandum to this effect in some foreign place scarcely requires that the question of formal validity should be tested exclusively by the *lex loci contractus*. The place may be uncertain."[108]

Thus, it appears that consensus of the view is that a contract will be valid if it complies with the form prescribed either at the *lex loci contractus* or at the proper law of the contract.[109] The utility of this alternative test of the formal validity of the contract can be illustrated from several types of contract. The most cogent illustrations are provided by contracts for the transfer of property. Most matters relating to the transfer of immovable property are governed by the *lex situs*, which may be termed as proper law. Thus, formal validity of contract relating to immovable property depends upon the proper law of the contract which is ordinarily, though not necessarily, the *lex situs* of the property. It is an established rule that conveyance of the immovable property must comply with the form prescribed at the *lex situs*. But the contract for the transfer of the immovable property need not comply with the form laid down by the *lex situs*; if it complies with the *lex loci contractus*, the contract will be valid. More or less the same situation operates in respect of transfer of movables, both tangible and intangible. A contract for the transfer of movable property, as distinguished from actual transfer, will be formally valid if it complies with the formalities laid down by the proper law or the *lex loci contractus*. The distinction between contract to transfer and actual transfer, i.e. conveyance, should be strictly maintained and understood, as in the latter case compliance with the proper law is imperative. In the former case the compliance with the proper law or the *lex situs* is not imperative. Compliance with the *lex loci contractus* will be sufficient. The question of formalities has been of some particular importance in respect of transfer of some species of intangible property, namely, negotiable instruments because of its frequent and successive transferability. The matter is now subject to statutory regulation.[110]

In recent times formal requirements have been laid down in respect of certain transactions with a view to protect the economically weaker party from exploitation by the stronger party. Instances of this type of legislation are hire-purchase and credit sales. The legislation makes it imperative that the local formalities must be complied with, irrespective of the fact whether compliance has or has not been made with the proper law. It is in this regard

108. Cheshire, 205; See also Dicey and Morris, 751.

109. See Rule 131, in Dicey's Conflict of Laws, 749-50; See Cheshire, 205.

110. See Chapter 21 of this work.

that compliance with the *lex loci contractus* as to form is imperative.

Lastly, we may refer to the problem of characterization in regard to formalities. What matters relate to formalities and what do not ? For instance, the law may lay down that a particular contract is to be in writing, signed by the parties, attested by witnesses and stamped; the question is : are all these matters related to form, or only some of them relate to form, while others to procedure ? The English courts have shown a marked tendency to characterize many such matters as of procedure, even when under the foreign law such requirements are characterized as of formalities. The basis of characterization that English courts follow is this : those requirements, the purpose of which is merely to make the contract enforceable by action or to allow it to be given in evidence, are procedural and hence are to be governed by the *lex fori*. On the other hand, those requirements which will prevent the contract from coming into existence or the failure to observe which would render the contract formally void, are characterized as of formalities. Thus, in *Leroux* v. *Brown*[108] a contract validly made in accordance with the formal requirements of the French law was held as unenforceable by the English court as the requirements of writing under the Statute of Fraud, which is characterized as procedural were not complied with. This type of difficulty has come up on the surface, particularly, in respect of foreign requirement of stamping. The English and Indian courts have taken the view that where stamping is classified by the foreign law as part of formalities and the law of the place of the making of the contract renders the contract void on that ground, the courts would not enforce the contract.[112] But if the requirement of stamping is considered to fall into the other category, then English and Indian courts would enforce the contract.[113] Kahn-Freund observes : "In any event, the extended interpretation given by the English courts to the term 'procedural' has diminished the importance, from the point of view of the English conflict of laws, of the rule *locus regit actum* in the law of contract."[114] As to negotiable instruments the matter is regulated by the statute.[115]

Material Validity

It can happen that a valid agreement entered into by parties having capacity may be unenforceable in law. Thus, under the

111. (1852) 12 C.B. 801.

112. *Re Visser, Queen of Holland* v. *Drubber*, (1928) Ch. 877. *In the Goods of McAdam*, 23 Cal. 187 (P.C.); *Dhoudiram* v. *Shadasukh*, 42 Bom. 522.

113. *Bristow* v. *Sequenville*, (1850) 5 Ex. 275, *Venkatraman Reddi* v. *Sri Maharaja Seetharama, Bhupal Rao* (*Raja of Gadwal*), 53 Mad. 968; *Manattil Ali* v. *Vazahapulli Varial*, (1941) 1 M.L.J. 35.

114. Dicey and Morris, p. 754.

115. See Chapter 21 of this work.

English and Indian law a contract to commit criminal offence, a contract in the nature of champerty, a contract in restraint of trade, and a wagering contract, are unenforceable in law. These and like matters relate to material or essential validity of the contract.

The difficulty here as elsewhere arises because laws of different countries differ as to factors which render contract materially invalid. For instance, both under the Indian law and English law, wagering contracts are unenforceable and they create no obligations whatsoever. But in some countries such transactions are valid. Similarly, a contract by a lawyer with his client under which it is stipulated that he would have a share in the damages recovered in the action is illegal under the English and Indian law, but it is perfectly valid in some countries. Therefore, whenever the material validity of such contracts arises, the question is which law governs the matter ?

It seems to be clear that material validity of the contract is governed by proper law of the contract. Thus, whether a wagering contract creates a valid obligation would depend upon the proper law. It has been held that the money won at a game or lent for the game is recoverable by an action in England, if it is recoverable in the country where it is won.[116] On the other hand, a wagering contract will not be enforceable if its proper law is English law, even though it is recoverable in some other country with which it has close contact.[117] The House of Lords observed : "The courts in this country will not compel the performance of a contract if by its proper law performance is illegal."[118]

In regard to material validity of the contract, it appears that the role of *lex loci contractus* has been totally ruled out. A contract which is materially void by its proper law will not be enforced by English courts, even if it is valid under the *lex loci contractus*. A contract which is materially valid by it proper will be held valid in England, even if it is materially invalid by the *lex loci contractus*.[119] After the decision in *The Torni*,[120] a view if propounded[121] that a contract which is invalid by the *lex loci contractus* will not be enforced in England, even if it is valid by its proper law. It is submitted that this view is not correct and has been ruled out, because the *locus* of contract is more often than not a fortuitous place, particularly in the modern conditions of international trade and commerce, of which contracts of international

116. *Quarrier* v. *Colston*, (1842) 1 Ph. 147; *King* v. *Kemp*, (1863) 8 L.T. 255; *Saxby* v. *Fulton*, (1909) 2 K.B. 208.

117. *Kahler* v. *Moulis*, (1907) 1 K.B. 746.

118. *Kahler* v. *Midland Bank Ltd.*, (1950) A.C. 24 at 27; See also *Zivnostenska Banka* v. *Frankman*, (1950) A.C. 57.

119. *Royal Exchange Assurance Corporation* v. *Vega*, (1902) 2 K.B. 384; *Vita Food Products Ltd.* v. *Unus Shipping Co. Ltd.*, (1939) A.C. 277.

120. (1932), p. 78.

121. Per Greer and Slesser, L. JJ. at 88 and 91.

sale of commodities and of international loans are the obvious instances.

The next question is: should the material validity of a contract be tested by the *lex loci solutionis*? At one time this was answered in the affirmative by some.[122] It appears that there is some English authority[123] for the view that if the contract is valid by its proper law, then it will be enforced in England, even if it is invalid by the *lex loci solutionis*. It is submitted that the material validity should exclusively be determined by the proper law of the contract, and neither the *lex loci contractus* nor the *lex loci solutionis* should be allowed to have a say in the matter.

The *lex loci solutionis* is relevant only in one case, *viz*. when the performance of a contract is unlawful under it, then such a contract will not be enforced even if it is valid by its proper law.[121] However, there is no direct English authority for this proposition, and some authors cosider this proposition as doubtful,[125] though *obiter* observation do exist in its support in the observation of Lord Reid in *Kahler* v. *Midland Bank Ltd.*[126] and in *Zivnostenska Banka* v. *Frankman*.[127] Earlier also Lord Wright made a similar statement.[128] The sheet-anchor of this view is the decision in *Ralli Bros*. v. *Compania Naviera Sota y Aznar*,[129] where Scrutton, L.J. observed: "Where a contract requires an act to be done in a foreign country, it is, in the absence of very special circmstances, an implied term of the continuing validity of such a provision that the act to be done in the foreign country shall not be illegal by the law of that country.[130] This was a case where on account of a supervening law of the country of the performance of the contract the maximum freight rate was fixed which was only one-fifth of the agreed rate. *Kahler* v. *Midland Bank*[131] was obviously a case where the Czech exchange control regulation—the proper law of the contract was Czech—made the payment illegal without the prior consent of the Czech National Bank. The same was the position in *Zivnostenska Banka National Corporation* v. *Frankman*.[132] In these cases and all other cases cited in support of this view it

122. See Foote, Private International Law (5th ed.), pp. 399; 413.
123. *Spurrier* v. *La Cloche*, (1902) A.C. 446 (P.C.); *R.* v. *International Trustee*, (1937) A.C. 500; *Vita Food Product Inc.* v. *Unus Shipping Co. Ltd.* (1939) A.C. 277 (P.C.); *Kehler* v. *Midland Bank*, (1950) A.C. 24; *Zivnostenska Banka* v. *Frankman*, (1950) A.C. 57; *Re. Banque des Merchandas de Moscou*, (no. 2) (1957) 3 W.L.R. 637.
124. Dicey and Morris, Exception to Rule 132, 760.
125. See Cheshire, 211-213.
126. (1950) A.C. 24 at 48.
127. (1950) A.C. 57 at 78.
128. *R.* v. *International Trustee*, (1937) A.C. 500 at 519.
129. (1920) 2 K.B. 287.
130. *Ibid.*, at 304.
131. Cited above.
132. Cited above.

is noteworthy that the performance of the contract was illegal or has become illegal by the proper law, or the contract was an English contract. So far no case has arisen in which the proper law of the contract was a foreign law and the performance of the contract was illegal or has become illegal by the law of a third country. It may be noticed that here we are not concerned with the situation when contract is illegal or has become illegal by the *lex fori*. Thus, it is submitted that the *lex loci solutionis* as such should not have any effect on the validity of the contract governed by foreign law and to be performed in a third country, that is a foreign country other than that of the proper law.[133]

Performance of a contract cannot be excused if a party to a contract alleges that by performing the contract he would be infringing the law of the country in which he is residing or in which he is domiciled, or carries on business. But if that is the country of the proper law of the contract, or the contract is subject to the law of that country in other respects,[134] then performance will be excused.

Last question that remains is : whether proper law here means proper law in the broader sense, i.e. including that law which parties have expressly chosen or does it mean only that law which the contract has closest and most real connection ? It is submitted that it should mean the latter. Kahn-Freund suggests that it means the proper law in its broader meaning.[135] It may be noted that doctrine of evasion of law in English private international law is yet in its formative stages. This bizarre situation can be avoided, if by proper law we mean that system of law with which the contract has closest and most real connection.

Thus, legality as an aspect of material validity of the contract is, under English private international law, and, it would seem, also under Indian private international law, is governed by the proper law of the contract, and English and Indian courts would not enforce a contract which is illegal by its proper law, even if it is legal by the *lex loci contractus* or by the *lex loci solutionis* or by the *lex fori*. A contract which is lawful by the proper law will be given effect to even if it is unlawful by the *lex loci solutionis* or the *lex loci contractus*. But it would appear that a contract which is valid by its proper law may not be enforced if its enforcement would violate any rule of public policy of the forum or if its enforcement will be illegal by the law of the forum.

133. See Dicey and Morris, 761-762; for fuller discussion see Mann, 18 British Year Book of International Law, 107-113. See also Cheshire, 210-213.

134. *Kleinwort Sons & Co.* v *Ungarische Baumwolle Industrie*, (1939) 2 K.B. 678.

135. Dicey and Morris, 757-58. He also gives other arguments in favour of his view.

Contract Contrary to Public Policy, Law and Procedure of the Forum

A contract which is valid by its proper law may not be enforced by an English court or Indian court if its enforcement will be contrary to its public policy, or law of procedure. Sometimes the application of proper law is also excluded on balance of convenience.

Public Policy: This compendious head, a creature of judicial legislation, which has been used from the very beginning as a convenient instrument for the exclusion of otherwise applicable foreign law, has already been discussed in Chapter 5 of this work. Here a bare summary is attempted.

(a) The courts have refused to enforce contracts which are opposed to the fundamental principle of public policy or morality.[136] Under this head will fall contract in restraint of trade, contracts involving trading with enemy, champertous contracts, contract for stiffling criminal prosecution, collusive arrangement for divorce.[137]

(b) A contract may not be enforceable if the circumstances in which it was entered into are opposed to or ideas of morality and justice, though in its substance the contract is flawless.[138]

(c) A contract may not be enforceable if its enforcement is opposed to the interests of the state, such as when it is likely to jeopardise the friendly relations between the Government and any other government with which the United Kingdom or India is at peace. Under this head are included those contracts whose object is to further a venture for breaking the laws of foreign states.[139]

As a corollary to the above, the following three principles may also be noted :

(i) A foreign contract will not be held unenforceable on the basis of a rule of public policy unless the contract has some close connection with England. What is relevant is not the character of the foreign contract in the abstract, "but the result of its enforcement in the concrete case. Hence if the performance of the contract does not affect this country the court will not be inclined to apply principles of English public policy."[140]

136. *Rousillon* v. *Rousillon,* (1880) 14 Ch. D. 351.
137. Cases have cited in Chapter 5 of this work.
138. *Kaufman* v. *Gerson,* (1903) 2 K.B. 114 (contract was obtained by coercion); *Kahler* v. *Midland Bank Ltd.,* (1950) A.C. 24 (duress).
139. *Foster* v. *Driscoll,* (1929) 1 K.B. 470; (purpose of the contract was to violate the prohibition law of the United States) *Reggazonni* v. *Sethia,* (1956) 2 Q.B. 190 (contract in violation of the Indian legislation which prohibited shipment of jute to South Africa); *Boissevain* v. *Weil,* (1950) A.C. 327 (contract in violation of exchange control law); *Libyan Arab Bank* v. *Bankers Trust Co.* (1989) 3 W.L.R. 314.
140. Dicey and Morris, 727. See also *Addison* v. *Brown,* (1954) 1 W.L.R. 779.

(ii) Enforcement of foreign contract will be declined only if it violates a common law principle which is one of basic public policy. If it is not a rule of basic policy the contract will be enforced.[141] To use the expressive French expression, only those principles of *ordre public interne* which belong to *ordre public externe* will make a foreign contract unenforceable.

(iii) When the foreign law, the violation of which is the object of the contract, is itself contrary to public policy of the forum then such a contract is not considered to be contrary to public policy. An obvious though an old instance is of those contracts, the purpose of which was the violation of foreign slavery laws. This principle may lead to the enforcement of a contract by English court, although by the law governing it, the contract is void. Thus, the English court will not give effect to a foreign law which deprives the contract its effectiveness.[142]

Contrary to Statutory Law: It is very interesting to note the distinction which English court make between the judicial legislation and the parliamentary legislation. As has been seen earlier, the English courts have held contracts in restraint of trade and champertous contracts as void being against the universal public policy, but they have held contract for the sale of slaves governed by Brazilian law as enforceable in England on the ground that prohibition against slave trading was statutory.[143] This trend is also reflected in wagering contracts and money lending contracts.[144] It is submitted that the following proposition emerges from the Engligh decisions :[145]

(a) Whenever a statute expressly contains a rule governing validity or invalidity, then that rule must be applied by the courts, without considering the effect of foreign law governing the contract. Thus, when a statute lays down that a particular type of contract is to be governed by the *lex fori*, the courts have no option but to apply the *lex fori*.[146]

(b) In the absence of an express rule in the statute the general rule of interpretation applies, i.e. a statute will not have extra-territorial effect unless it is expressly given such operation or is 'inferred

141. *Saxby* v. *Fulton*, (1909) 2 K.B. 208; *Re Bonacina*, (1912) 2 Ch. 394 (contract without consideration); *Godard* v. *Gray*, (1870) 6 Q.B. 139.

142. *Re Friendrich Krupp Aktien-Gesellschaft*, (1917) 2 Ch. 188; *Re Helbert Wagg & Co.'s claim*, (1956) Ch. 323 (foreign exchange control law was found to be an 'instrument of oppression and discrimination').

143. *Santos* v. *Illidge*, (1860) 8 C.B. (N.S.) 861; *Madrazo* v. *Willes*, (1820) 3 B. & A. 353.

144. *Saxby* v. *Fulton*, cited earlier; *Shrichand* v. *Lacon*, (1906) 22 T.L.R. 245. See also Dicey, 735-37 where the matter is fully discussed.

145. See also Dicey and Morris, 731.

146. For instance s. 72 of the Bill of Exchange Act, 1882 and s. 265 of the Merchant Shipping Act, 1894 lay down 'general choice of law clause'.

from its object, subject-matter and history.'[147] Thus, it has been held that the Stamp Acts,[148] the Gaming Acts[149] and statutes regulating interests,[150] or providing for moratoria[151] apply only to contracts the proper law of which is English law. On the other hand, statutes which invalidate contractual provisions as a sanction for the contravention of statutory requirements, e.g., concerning the disclosure of facts or the adequate disclosure of contractual terms by one party to another, such as statutory provisions regulating hire-purchase agreements or deductions from wages under contract of employment. In sūch cases statutory provisions are applicable irrespective of the proper law of the contract, if the act prohibited by the statute takes place within the territory in which it was enacted.[152]

(c) The statutes designed to implement a social policy will normally be applied irrespective of the proper law of the contract and, in particular, an agreement to submit the contract to foreign law can have no effect on the scope of their application.[153]

Contracts contrary to Procedural law : This is a well-established rule of private international law that procedure is governed by the *lex fori*. A contract the enforcement of which will be contrary to a rule of procedural law will not be enforced by the court.[154] A party who opposes the enforcement of the contract on the ground that it would be violative of the procedural law need not prove that the statute has extra-territorial effect.[155]

Balance of Convenience : It is an established rule, as we have seen earlier, if parties choose their forum for determining disputes between them, they are bound by the contract. To this general rule, there is an exception founded not only on balance of convenience but also on considerations of justice. The court has discretion in this matter and will exercise it after weighing the pros and cons of all the circumstances taken together.[156]

147. Maxwell, Interpretation of Statutes (11th ed.), 139.

148. *Norske Atlas Insurance Co. Ltd.* v. *London General Insurance Co. Ltd*, (1927) 43 T.L.R. 541.

149. *Robinson* v. *Bland*, (1760) 2 Burr. 1077; *Saxby* v. *Fulton*, (1909) 2 K.B. 208.

150. *Re Mount Albert B.C.* v. *Australasia etc Assurance Co.*, (1938) A.C. 224.

151. *Re Helbert Wagg & Co. Claim*, cited above.

152. Dicey and Morris 733. See the provision under the Hire-Purchase Act, 1965; s. 17. See *Draber (C.E.B.) & Sons Ltd.* v. *Edward Turner & Sons Ltd.*, (1965) 1 Q.B. 424 where restrictive interpretation was placed on s. 2(2) of the Fertilizers and Feeding Stuffs Act, 1926, which contained a mandatory provision implying a warranty on the sale of articles.

153. Dicey and Morris, 734.

154. The Status of Fraud is an obvious example of this.

155. See also Chapter 22 of this work.

156. *The Eleftheria* (P.D.A.), (1969), 2 W.L.R. 1073; *Messers, Black Sea State Steamship Line* v. *The Mineral and Metals Trading Corporation of India Ltd.*, (1970) I M.L.J. 548; *Far East Steamship Line, Valdivastok* v. *Union of India*, (1972) 2 M.L.J. 578.

Construction or Interpretation of Contract

"The expression 'construction' as applied to documents, at all events as used by English lawyers," said Lindley, L.J., "includes two things : first the meaning of the words; and secondly the legal effect which is to be given to them. The meaning of the words I take to be a question of fact in all cases, whether we are dealing with a poem or a document. The effect of the words is a question of law."[157] It is an established rule of English private international law that the interpretation and the meaning of the terms used in the contract is governed by the proper law.[158] Since the province of interpretation is to discover the true meaning of the words, terms, phrases and clauses used by the parties, no other law but the law chosen by the parties is to govern the contract, i.e. the proper law. If parties have expressly indicated that their contracts is to be interpreted by reference to a particular law that law should be applied. If parties have not expressed a choice, then their intention is to be inferred from the language of the contract and its surrounding circumstances. If the proper law ascribes a particular meaning or peculiar meaning to certain words and terms, the parties using them must be bound by that meaning.[159] If no particular or peculiar meaning is attached to the terms and words by the proper law then the intention of the parties is to be ascertained under the established principles of construction of the particular instrument which forms part of the proper law. Thus, it is for the proper law to determine whether and how far trade usages should be deemed to be part of the contract, or what circumstances can be considered to find out the intention of parties. However, if parties have used certain technical expressions whose meaning is unintelligible under proper law though intelligible by the law of another country, then it is reasonable to infer that when the parties used those expressions their mind was directed to the law of that country.

One exception that is recognized to the application of proper law to the interpretation of the contract is : where reference in a contract is to currency other than that of the proper law, then the meaning of that currency is to be determined by the law of the country to which the currency belongs, i.e. by the *lex monetae*. Thus, the *lex monetae* in such cases would determine the meaning of units of that currency, e.g. pounds, francs or rupees.[160] But whether a creditor has a right to revalorization is to be determined by the proper law.[161]

157. *Chateney* v. *Brazilian Submarine Telegraph Co.*, (1891) 1 Q.B. 79 at 85.

158. *St. Pierre* v. *South American Store Ltd.*, (1937) 3 All E.R. 349 at p. 351.

159. *Di Sora* v. *Phillipps*, (1863) 10 H.L.C. 624.

160. See *Ottoman Bank* v. *Chakarian*, (1938) A.C. 260; *Pyrmount Ltd.* v. *Schott*, (1939) A.C. 145 (P.C.).

161. *Anderson* v. *Equitable Life Insurance Society*, (1926) 134 L.T. 557 (C.A.). See also *Tehran-Europe Co. Ltd.* v. *S.T. Belton (Tractors) Ltd.*,

Effect of the Contract or Obligations arising Under the Contract

Rights and obligations of the parties arising under the contract and their enforcement and their effect (if any) on the rights and obligations of the third parties are to be governed by the proper law of the contract.[162]

When the proper law of the contract and the *lex loci solutionis* are the same there is no difficulty. But in those cases where the proper law of the contract and the *lex loci solutionis* are different a distinction is to be made between the substance of the obligation and the mode of the performance of the obligation. The substance of the obligation is governed by proper law.[163] Thus, the method and manner in which the obligation is to be performed is governed by the *lex loci solutionis.* For instance, the *lex loci solutionis* decides in which unit of currency an obligation is to be discharged. But the effect of such obligation, or to put it in different words, substance of the obligation, wherever it may be performed, is governed by the proper law which may or may not be identical with *lex loci solutionis.* In *Bonython case*[164] a loan was raised in 1895 in 'pound sterling' by the Government of Queensland and was repayable in London in 1945. The Privy Council rightly rejected the argument that if London was chosen as the place of payment, the English law as the *lex loci solutionis* governs the contract and determines the measure of obligation. In this case the proper law of the contract was the law of Queensland. This is also the view taken by English courts.[165] *Mount Albert Borough Council* v. *Australasian Temperence and General Mutual Life Assurance Society*,[166] a Privy Council decision, provides another good illustration of the proposition submitted here. A New Zealand Borough Council raised a loan from a Victorian Company and issued debentures in 1926 repayable in Victoria and bearing interest at the rate of £5 12s. 9d. per centum per annum also payable in Victoria. In 1931 a Victorian statute reduced the rate of interest with the purpose of rectifying financial instability then prevailing there. The Privy Council said that the proper law of the contract being the law of New Zealand, the contractual obligation remained unaffected by the Victorian statute.

It is also necessary to understand the distinction between the substance of the obligation and the remedies that are available for the enforcement of contractual obligations. Kahn-Freund

(1968) 3 W.L.R. 205 where implied warranty of fitness on the sale of certain goods for delivery with a view to resale abroad in the light of purchaser's special knowledge of the foreign market was construed as inapplicable.

162. *Kahler* v. *Midland Bank Ltd.*, (1950) A.C. 24 at 35.
163. *Bonython* v. *Commonwealth of Australia*, (1951) A.C. 201 at 219.
164. Cited above.
165. *Jacobs* v. *Credit Lyonnais*, (1884) 12 Q.B.D. 589.
166. (1938) AC. 224.

says : "Whether a contract gives rise to a claim for performance or to a claim for damages, whether, in the event of a breach of contract, the other party has a right to rescind it, whether interest is payable on a debt, all these are matters which, on a proper analysis, should be regarded as affecting the rights and obligations to which the contract gives rise."[167] The question of remoteness of damages is also a matter of substance of the obligation; so are the heads of damages. Diplock, L.J. said that 'head of damages' as distinct from 'quantification of damages' sustained under each head are matters of substance.[168] On the other hand, the assessment or 'quantification' of damages is a matter of remedies governed by the *lex fori*.

Discharge of Contract

The normal mode of discharge of contractual obligation is the performance of the contract. But the discharge of obligation may also take place by impossibility of performance, by accord and satisfaction, by novation or by change in legislation. By whatever manner the discharge of obligations may take place, it is, as a general rule, governed by the proper law.[169] Therefore, whether or not a contractual obligation has been extinguished by performance or by impossibility of performance or by accord or satisfaction is governed exclusively by the proper law of the contract. In *Jacobs* v. *Credit Lyonnais*[170] the question was whether the contract was discharged by impossibility of performance. The proper law of the contract was English law and the *lex loci solutionis* was French law. The court held that the matter is governed by English law. Similarly, in *Mount Albert* v. *Australasian etc. Assurance Society Ltd.*[171] the contract was governed by the law of New Zealand while the debt was payable in the State of Victoria. By a Victorian law the rate of interest was reduced. It was held that the proper law being that of New Zealand, the obligation was not discharged under the law of Victoria. It should be noted that *lex situs* of the debt has nothing to do with the discharge of the debt which is governed by the proper law of the contract under which it arises.[172]

Discharge of contractual obligation by novation merits separate consideration. Novation consists of two elements : (a) discharge of original debtor, and (b) his substitution by another.

167. Dicey and Morris, 778.
168. *Boys* v. *Chaplin*, (1969) 3 W.L.R. 322. The case has been fully discussed in Chapter 23, "Tort".
169. *Ellis* v. *M'Henry*, (1871) L.R. 6 C.P. 228 at 234
170. (1884) 12 Q.B.D. 589.
171. (1938) A.C. 224 (P.C.).
172. *Adams* v. *National Bank of Greece and Athens*, (1961) A.C. 255; *Re United Railways of the Havana and Warehouses Ltd.* (1960) Ch. 52 (C.A.) on appeal (1961) A.C. 1007; *Rossano* v. *Manufacturers' Life Insurance Co.*, (1963) 2 Q.B. 352; *Libyen Arab Bank* v. *Bankers Trust Co.* (1989) W.L.R. 314.

It does not in any sense mean transfer of property. It is now well-established that the discharge of the original debtor by novation is governed by the proper law, whether the substitution is by legislation,[173] or by a voluntary act. It should be noted that novation is a substitution of one debtor for another and therefore it is different from the replacement of one creditor by another. The latter is a case of assignment of debt and, as we have already seen[174] the governing law in the case of the voluntary assignment is the proper law of the debt and in the case of involuntary assignment in the *lex situs* of the debt. The assignment of debt is different from discharge of debt, and it is well-established that by the operation of the *lex situs* of the debt the contractual obligation cannot be discharged.

The outbreak of war affect certain type of contracts and either abrogates or suspends the obligations and liabilities arising under them. Whether or not a contract has been abrogated or suspended by the outbreak of the war does not depend upon the *situs* of the debt, but, it seems, upon the proper law of the contract.[175] But when contractual rights belonging to the enemies or certain categories of persons are vested in the government of certain public authorities, such as custodians or administrators by legislation, the question whether or not the debt has been transferred to such authorities and whether or not this has the effect of discharging the debtor from his obligation is governed by the *situs* of the debt and not by the proper law of the contract under which the debt or the right arose.[176]

Thus a distinction between the discharge of contractual obligations by legislation has to be distinguished from the assignment of contractual rights, such as debt, under the legislation. In the former case the proper law of the contract governs the discharge. This is illustrated by the *Employees' Liability Assurance Co.* v. *Sedgwick Collins & Co.*[177] where 'annulment' of rights under insurance policy by the Soviet legislation was held valid, the law of the Soviet Union being proper law, and by *R.* v. *International Trustee*[178] where by a joint Resolution of the Congress of the United States, a gold clause attached to a dollar obligation was declared void, the discharge of obligation in this manner (debtor could discharge his obligation by making payment in paper dollars) was held valid, as

173. *Re United Railways of Havana etc.*, cited above. *Tomkinson* v. *First Pennsylvania Banking and Trust Co.*, (1961) A.C. 1007.

174. Chapter 17.

175. See *Ertel Bieber & Co.* v. *Rio Tinto Co. Ltd.*, (1918) A.C. 260 where English law was applied on ground of public policy and not because the debt was situated in England.

176. *New York Life Insurance Co.* v. *Public Trustee*, (1924) 2 Ch. 101 (C.A.); *Jabbour* v. *Custodian of Israel Absentee Property*, (1954) 1 All E.R. 145. These cases have been discussed earlier in this work.

177. (1927) A.C. 95.

178. (1937) A.C. 500.

the law of the New York was the proper law of contract. The legislation of the country of the *locus solutionis* or of the country where debtor resides or carries on business will not have the effect of discharging the contract, unless, that also happens to be the proper law of the contract.[179]

A very good illustration of discharge of contractual obligations is provided by the contracts involving international money obligations. In all contracts involving money obligations, the amount due under the contract is fixed by the contract and is thus a matter of substance. We have already seen that any change in this by the *lex loci solutionis* or the country of payment cannot affect the obligation. But the difficulty arises where the money or the currency is not clearly identified. In such cases the identification of the currency is a matter of deduction and it is done by trying to find out that currency the parties have in their mind at the time of making the contract. This is once again a process of inferring the intention of parties by the terms of the contract and surrounding circumstances. All factors must be taken into account.[180] Once identification of currency is made, the debt is dischargeable in that currency. What is the nominal value of the currency is to be determined by the law of country to which the currency belongs. The payment in that currency discharges the party from the debt or contractual obligation, whatever might be the real value of the currency at the time of payment, that is to say, the depreciation or appreciation of currency from the date of making the contract and payment of money is immaterial.[181] This obviously means that if currency has depreciated the creditor will receive less.[182] With a view to meet cases of currency depreciation some countries adopt a system of revalorization which means that the debt is revalued so that it is brought at par with the depreciated currency. Since revalorization is revaluation of debt, it is determined by the proper law of the contract.[183]

With a view to avoid the consequences of depreciation of currency, the device of including gold clauses in the contract has been used. The gold-clause links the money payable to gold. The gold clauses may lay down the sum of money payable under the contract shall be paid in gold coins (this is known as gold-coin

179. *Mount Albert Borough Council* v. *Australasian, etc. Ltd.*, (1938) A.C. 224; *Adams* v. *National Bank of Greece and Athens*, (1961) A.C. 255.

180. *De Bueger* v. *Ballantyne & Co.*, (1938) A.C. 452 (reference to pound sterling was construed to mean English pound); *Bonython* v. *Commonwealth of Australia*, (1951) A.C. 201 (this inference could not be drawn); *Adelaide Electric Supply Co.* v. *Prudential Assurance Co.*, (1934) A.C. 122 (the place of payment chosen by the parties is important but not conclusive).

181. *Pyrmont Ltd.* v. *Schott*, (1939) A.C. 145; *Marrache* v. *Ashton*, (1943) A.C. 311.

182. This is precisely what happened in *Re Chesterman's Trusts*, (1923) 2 Ch. 466.

183. *Anderson* v. *Equitable Assurance Society of the United States*, (1926) 134 L.T. 557.

clause), of it may lay down that the debtor would pay at the due date a sum equal to the value of the gold-coins specified at the time of the making of the contract (called gold-value clause). In a contract having the gold-clause there are four steps to be taken in determining as to what amounts to effective discharge of the contract.

First, step is the determination of the proper law which governs the contract. This means the usual process of determining proper law of the contract.[184] The second step is to determine the meaning of gold clause, whether it means gold-coin clause or gold-value clause. This is to be determined by considering the terms of the contract and surrounding circumstances.[185] The third step is whether the gold-clause can be implemented. Implementation of gold-clause means that the debt is discharged by payment and this is determined by the proper law of the contract. The proper law of the contract that is to be taken into account is that state of proper law which prevails at the time of repayment of loan and not at the time of taking of the loan. Thus, in *Feist* v. *Societe Intercommunale Belge d'Electricite*,[186] where the gold-clause provided that repayment was to be made in sterling gold-coin of the United Kingdom equal to the standard of weight and fineness existing at the date of loan (it was year 1928). The date of repayment was 1932. The proper law of the contract was English law. Before 1932 the United Kingdom has by statute substituted paper currency for gold as the mode of payment. It was held that though the English statute has substituted paper for gold as mode of payment before the date of repayment and although the paper pound of 1932 was of less value than the 1928 pound, the borrower must pay as many paper pounds as represented the gold value according to the 1928 standard of weight and fineness of the nominal sum due to the creditor.[187] The last step is to find out what is the money of payment. In other words, in what currency should the debtor tender the amount that he has agreed to pay ? Since this is a matter affecting the mode of performance, it is to be determined by the *lex loci solutionis*, the rule being that the debt is dischargeable in the currency of the country where the debt is payable.

183. *R.* v. *International Trustee*, (1937) A.C. 500.

184. *Ibid.* See also *Feist* v. *Societe Intercommunale Belge d'Electricite*, (1934) A.C. 161, and *New Brunswick Railway Co.* v. *British and French Trust Corporation*, (1939) A.C. 1.

186. Cited above.

187. See also *R.* v. *International Trustee* cited above.

21

NEGOTIABLE INSTRUMENTS

The Negotiable instruments, such as bills of exchange, cheques, *hundis* and promissory notes have been of great importance ever since the human beings embarked on trade and commerce. In 1930-31 six international conventions relating to negotiable instruments were signed in Geneva to unify national laws relating to negotiable instruments.

Negotiable instruments are a special type of contracts which, in the days of ever-increasing international trade and commerce and intercourse, are of particular interest and significance to international law. Since a negotiable instrument represents a debt, it is regarded as a species of tangible property. The greatest importance of the negotiable instruments lies in the fact that they are negotiable. The nature and characteristics of a negotiable instrument have been broadly thus summarized : "A negotiable instrument payable to bearer is one which, by custom or trade (or under statute) passes from hand to hand by delivery, and the holder of which for the time being, if he is *bona fide* holder for value, has good title, notwithstanding any defect of title in the person from whom he took it."[1] The outstanding feature of a negotiable instrument is that the series of contracts, which are entered into by the drawer, the acceptor and the endorser of a bill of exchange, or by the maker or endorser of the promissory note, give rise to several rights and liabilities of these several parties, and these rights and obligations of parties are different and distinct from each other. The fundamental question that arises in respect of negotiable instruments is : are these series of contracts to be regarded as a single transaction and therefore governed by "single law", or are these to be regarded as a series of transaction, each of which is governed by a different law, i.e. by "several laws"? Great Britain and India adopt, as a general rule, "the several law" theory. It is this theory which is accepted practically in most of the countries of the world.

The important types of negotiable instruments, for the purpose

1. *Simmons* v. *London Joint Stock Bank*, (1891) 1 Ch. 270 on appeal, (1892 A.C. 201.

of private international law, are : bills of exchange, cheques, which are species of bills of exchange, promissory notes, bank notes, bearer debentures and dividend warrants. It seems to be an established rule that the negotiability of a foreign negotiable instrument depends upon the fact whether it is so recognized by the custom or law of the country where it is sought to be enforced.[2] The conflictual rules relating to negotiable instruments have been codified in the English statute, Bills of Exchanges Act, 1882 and in the Indian statute, Negotiable Instrument Act, 1881. The provisions of both the statutes are comprehensive but not exhaustive. They have been supplemented by some judicial decisions. The law cannot be said as fully developed (particularly the Indian law). It is rather curious that though both the statutes have been enacted with a year's gap (the Indian statute preceding the English statute), they do not contain identical provisions.

The negotiable instruments are a special type of contract to which the proper law doctrine cannot be applied the same way as it is applied to ordinary mercantile contracts. The negotiable instrument has to be in a form which indicates with dead certainty the right and liabilities that it embodies. It seems that the proper law of a negotiable instrument can be either the *lex loci contractus* or the *lex loci solutionis*. It is clear that the English statute does not embody the proper law doctrine of contract in respect of negotiable instruments, but, with a few exceptions, adopts the *lex loci contractus* as the governing law. On the other hand, the Indian statute gives effect to proper law doctrine of contract inasmuch as it lays down : "In the absence of a contract to the contrary . . ."[3]

We would proceed to discuss the several aspects of negotiable instruments separately, first under English law, then under Indian law.

English Law

The Bills of Exchange Act, 1882 defines a bill of exchange as "an unconditional order in writing, addressed by one person to another, signed by the person giving it, requiring the person to whom it is addressed to pay on demand, or at a fixed or determinable future time, a sum certain in money to, or to the order of, a specified person, or to bearer."[4] The bills are classified as "inland bills" and "foreign bills". Section 4 of the Act defines as inland bill as one which is, or on the face of it, purports to be (a) both drawn and payable within the British Islands, or (b) drawn within the British Islands upon some person resident therein. Any other bill is a foreign bill; and the holder of the bill may treat it as inland bill unless contrary appears on the face of it.

2. *Picker* v. *London and County Banking Co.*, (1887) 18 K.B.D. 515.
3. Section 3(1).
4. Section 4. It is interesting to note that both the Indian and the English statutes were drafted by Mr. Chalmers.

Capacity : The Bills of Exchange Act, 1882 does not make any provision relating to capacity. It seems, on general principle, the capacity to take a bill should be governed by the *lex loci contractus*. The same should apply to the capacity of becoming a party to any of its subsequent contracts : capacity to enter into the subsequent contract should be determined by the *lex loci contractus* of the supervening contract.[5]

Formalities : Section 72 contains a specific provision in relation to formalities. The relevant portion of s. 72 runs as under :

> Where a bill drawn in one country is negotiated, accepted, or payable in another, the rights, duties and liabilities of the parties thereto are determined as follow—
>
> (1) The validity of a bill as regards requisites in form is determined by the law of the place of issue, and the validity, as regards requisites in form of the supervening contracts, such as acceptance or endorsement or acceptance *supra protest* is determined by the law of the country where such contract was made.
>
> Provided that—
>
> (a) Where a bill is issued out of the United Kingdom, it is not valid by reason only that it is not stamped in accordance with the law of the place of issue;
>
> (b) Where a bill, issued out of the United Kingdom conforms as regards requisites in form to the law of the United Kingdom, it may, for the purpose of enforcing payment thereof, be treated as valid as between all persons who negotiate, hold, or become parties to it in the United Kingdom.

It is evident that on the formal validity[6] of a negotiable instrument the Bills of Exchange Act, 1882 enacts the principle of *locus regit actum*. The original instrument is formally valid if it complies with the formal requirements of the place of issue and the supervening contracts are formally valid, if they comply with the law of the place where such contracts were made. Thus, acceptance will be formally valid if it complies with the law of the place where it was made; endorsement is formally valid if it complies with the formal requirements of the place where endorsement was done; and acceptance supra protest is valid if it complies with the formal requirements of the place where it was made. The 'place of issue' or 'the country of issue' is the place where the instrument is first handed over to the holder, and not the place where it is written

5. Graveson suggests a qualification : see Graveson, 459.
6. As to what are the matters of form and what are matters of substance, see *Guaranty Trust Co.* v. *Hannay and Co.*, (1918) 1 K.B. 43.

and signed.[7] *Koechlin* v. *Kestenbaum Bros.*[8] provides a good illustration of this rule. In this case a bill was, drawn in Paris to the order of P, signed and endorsed by X's son with his authority, but without any indication on the face of the bill of such authority. This form of endorsement and signature were valid by the French law but not by English law. The English court held that the French law governed the formalities and, therefore, the bill was valid.

The section enacts two exceptions, to the general rule. First, foreign bill (i.e. issued out of the United Kingdom) will not be formally invalid in England for the mere reason that it has not complied with the formal requirement of stamping of the law of the country of issue. It is submitted that it would not make any difference if non-stamping of an instrument in the country of issue makes it merely unenforceable or makes it void. Secondly, the second exception enacted in the statute lays down that a foreign bill which complies with the formalities of English law and therefore is valid under it, will be fornally valid in the United Kingdom even if it is not formally valid by the law of the country of issue, but only for the purpose of enforcing payment. It also seems clear that such an instrument will be treated as valid between persons who hold, negotiate and become parties to it in the United Kingdom.

Interpretation, Material Validity and Assignment : Section 72(2) of the Bills of Exchange Act, 1882 contains a specific provision relating to interpretation, but is silent as to the other two matters discussed under this head. Considering the applicability of 'several law theory' and the advisability of the application of the *lex laci contractus* to each of the transactions embodied in a negotiable instruments, all these matters are grouped and discussed together. Sub-section (2) lays down : "Subject to the provision of this Act, the interpretation of the drawing, endorsement, acceptance, or acceptance supra protest of a bill is determined by the law of the country where such contract is made."[9] The interpretation of each supervening contract will be made by the *lex loci contractus* of each contract. For instance, a bill drawn in India and accepted in England, the interpretation will be governed by English law. Similarly, the endorsement of an instrument is to be interpreted by the law of country where the endorser delivered the instrument to the endorsee.

I can be argued, possibly with convincing reasons that the law of the place where payment is to be made should be the governing

7. Graveson says : The form of the bill must comply with the law of the place where original delivery is made, whatever the law of the place where the bill is drawn." (p. 459). See also Dicey and Morris, 823-825.

8. (1927) 1 K.B. 616, on appeal (1927) 1 K.B. 889.

9. *Koechlin* v. *Kestenbaum*, (1927) 1 K.B. 616, 889.

law. The proviso to sub-section (2) of s. 72 enacts one exception on these lines : "Provided that where an inland bill is endorsed in a foreign country, the endorsement will, as regards the payer, be interpreted according to the law of the United Kingdom." It should be noticed that the exception applies to the payer, i.e. the acceptor of the bill or the maker of the note, only. It will not apply as between endorser and endorsee.

Whether the material validity and the effect of a negotiable instrument are governed by the *lex loci contractus* or *lex loci solutionis* there is no clear English authority. It is possible to argue that the word 'interpretation' as used in the sub-section includes the material validity of the instrument also, and therefore, the governing law is the *lex loci contractus*.[10] But there is no direct English authority for either view. In *Moulis* v. *Owen*[11] in respect of legality of a negotiable instrument, the Court of Appeal has expressed itself in favour of the *lex loci solutionis*. But it seems also equally clear that a contract which is illegal by its proper law is to be considered illegal everywhere, even though it is valid by the *lex loci solutionis*. The principle will equally apply to contracts indicated by the negotiable instruments. It appears (The Bill of Exchange Act, 1882 is silent on the matter) that discharge from liability under a negotiable instrument is also governed by the general rule, *viz.*, the proper law of the contract. However, it should be noted that the discharge of the negotiable instrument under the *lex loci solutionis* will automatically discharge the parties to the supervening contracts.

As to assignment of negotiable instruments the question is whether the general law of transfer of tangible property should be applied to negotiable instruments (since negotiable instruments are considered as tangible property) or whether the matter is governed by the Bills of Exchange Act, 1882 ? On this matter English decisions seem to hold that the matter is governed by the Bills of Exchange Act, 1882.

In *Alcock* v. *Smith*,[12] which was decided ten years after the coming into force of the Bills of the Exchange Act, 1882, not much consideration was given to the provisions of the Act. In this case, a bill of exchange drawn by and upon an English firm and payable in England to the order of A was endorsed and delivered in Norway by A to B. While the bill was with B it was seized by a judgment-creditor and was sold through judicial sale by auction in Norway. The sale was valid by the law of Norway and passed a valid title to the auction-purchaser, but it was not valid by English law. The court of Appeal upheld the validity of the transfer by applying Norwegian law, as the *lex loci actus*. It may be noted that Norway was also the *lex situs* of the bill. In *Embiricos* v. *Anglo-Austrian*

10. *Alcock* v. *Smith*, (1892) 1 Ch. 238.
11. (1907) 1. K.B. 746.
12. (1892) 1 Ch. 238.

Bank,[13] a Roumanian Bank drew a cheque at Bralia in favour of A payable at a London bank. A endorsed the cheque there to a firm in London and placed it in an envelope addressed to the London firm. The cheque was stolen by A's clerk who forged the endorsement of the London bank and gave it to B who got it cashed at a bank in Vienna. The Vienna bank endorsed it in favour of Y their London agent who collected the amount from the London bank. A sued Y in damages for conversion. . Under the Austrian law the Vienna bank acquired good title to the cheque despite theft and forgery. The English court applied the Austrian law, as the *lex situs* of the cheque. Austrian law was also the *lex loci actus*. *Koechlin* v. *Kestenbaum*,[14] relates to a bill of exchange drawn in France by A upon X in England to the order of B who was A's father. It was accepted by X as payable in London. The bill was then endorsed by A and not by B, and was transferred for value to C in France. A had affixed endorsement on behalf of B and under his authority. When the bill was presented to X, he refused to make payment on the ground that it had not been endorsed by B. Under English law an endorsement to be valid must be endorsed by the payee, or by an agent who signs it *per pro* the payee. On the other hand, an endorsement by an agent in his own name is valid under French law, provided he acts under the authority of the payee. Bankes, L.J. observed that the law applicable in such a situation has been laid down in the Bills of Exchange Act, 1882 : the proper law that governs the validity of transfer is the *lex loci actus*. This decision relates to formal validity of an endorsement, upon which depended the validity of the transfer of the instrument. On this view the case falls under sub-section (1) of section 72. But Sargent, L.J. thought that the case was covered by sub-section (2) of s. 72. In that sense it is a matter of 'interpretation'. Thus the matter is not free from doubt as to whether it is the general law of the transfer of tangibles which applies to the transfer of negotiable instruments or it is the provisions of s. 72, Bills of Exchange Act, 1882 which govern the matter. If it is the former then the *lex situs* governs all transfers of negotiable instruments, whether the instrument is inland or foreign. If it is the latter, then whether it is governed by sub-section (1) or sub-section (2) can still be debated. It is submitted that the former view is preferable.

Presentment, Protest and Dishonour : In respect of presentment, protest and dishonour provision is contained in sub-section (3) of s. 72, Bills of Exchange Act, 1882. Under this provision, presentment of a negotiable instrument by the holder to the drawee for acceptance or payment, and in case of dishonour, the sufficiency of protest or notice of dishonour are governed by the "law of the place where the act is done or the bill is dishonoured". It should be noticed that the sub-section deals with three things,

13. (1905) 1 K.B. 677.
14. (1927) 1 K.B. 616, on appeal, (1927) 1 K.B. 889.

presentment, protest and notice of dishonour. It lays down rules of law and indicate two systems of law, *viz.*, the law of the place where the act is done and the law of the place where the bill is dishonoured. The provision of this sub-section is shrouded in heavy mist, or to put it in Cheshire's words, "This obscure section verges perilously on the unintelligible."[15] Westlake with a view to make the provision intelligible suggested that words "or not done" should be interpolated.[16] This would mean that the question of presentment, for instance, will be determined by the law of the place where the bill is dishonoured. Dicey and Morris suggest that to make the section meaningful the words should be construed *reddendo singula singulis*.[17] This would mean that the question of presentment of a bill will be governed by the law of the place where the act is done. Cheshire[18] says that whatever the obscurity of the provision, it is clear beyond any doubt that all these matters which are concerned with the payment of the bill are covered by the principle that the incidents and mode of performance are determinable by the law of the place of performance.[19] Cheshire adds that the rule "that the law of the place where a bill is payable exclusively governs the incidents of payment and non-payment holds good only where the person liable is bound to pay in that place.[20]

Dicey and Morris maintain that the necessity for presentation is governed by the 'several law' principle, and the sufficiency of presentation by 'single law' principle. This is explained by the following illustration : If X in London draws a bill to the order of A in London and Y in Paris accepts it for accommodation of X, A or any other holder for value can charge X, without having presented the bill for payment to Y. If A chooses to present the bill to Y, French law determines the manner in which this must be done.[21] Dicey and Morris take the view that necessity for and sufficiency of a protest or notice of dishonour, on the other hand, are determined by the law of the place where the bill is dishonoured.[22] The law of the place where the bill or not is payable decides whether, how, and when the last holder must protest the instrument and give

15. Cheshire (8th ed.), 254.
16. Westlake, 322.
17. Dicey and Morris, 836. They say : "The language of this sub-section is obscure. It should probably be construed *reddendo singula singulis*. The words "act is done" refer to presentment for acceptance or payment, the words "bill is dishonoured" refer to "protest and notice of dishonour."
18. Cheshire (8th ed.), 254. He quotes Foote extensively in his support : Foote, 460-461.
19. He drew support for *Rothschild* v. *Currie*, (1841) 1 Q.B. 43. He also relies on *Hirschfield* v. *Smith*, (1866) L.R. 1 C.P. 340; *Horne* v. *Rouquette*, (1878) 3 Q.B.D. 514.
20. Cheshire (8th ed.), 255.
21. Dicey and Morris, 836.
22. *Ibid.*

notice of dishonour.[23] This also applies, according to them, to notice of dishonour out to be given by prior holder.[24-25]

Date of Payment : As to the date of payment sub-section (5) of s. 72, Bills of Exchange Act, 1882 lays down : "Where a bill is drawn in one country and is payable in another, the due date thereof is determined according to the law of the place where it is payable." This means that if the country where bill is payable postpones the due date of the bill on account of emergency, then payment cannot be enforced in England till the moratorium is lifted.

In this context the provisions of the Exchange Control Act, 1947 may also be referred to. Under the Act permission of the treasury for payment by any person in the United Kingdom to or for the credit of a person outside the schedule territories is necessary. The Act further provides that it shall be an implied term of any contract requiring treasury consent that performance shall not be made without such consent, unless the parties otherwise intend; but a claim for recovery of debt in a court of law shall not be defeated merely on account of failure to obtain consent of treasury.[26]

Discharge : The Bills of Exchange Act, 1882 does not lay down the law which would govern the validity and effect of a discharge from liability under a negotiable instrument except one aspect of it. It has been submitted earlier that the governing law of the discharge of liability, under the main contract and all the supervening contract is the proper law of each contract. The one aspect of discharge that is dealt with in the Bills of Exchange Act, 1882 relates to currency in which a negotiable instrument payable in the United Kingdom may be discharged. Sub-section (4) of s. 72 runs :

> Where a bill is drawn out, but payable in, the United Kingdom, and the sum payable is not expressed in the currency of the United Kingdom, the amount will, in the absence of some express stipulation, be calculated according to the rate of exchange for sight drafts at the place of payment on the day the bill is payable.

It should be noted that if a legal action is brought on an instrument which stipulates payment in foreign currency, then action has to be brought for the sterling equivalent of the amount mentioned in foreign currency.

Indian Law

Chapter 16, which is entitled "Of International Law", of the Negotiable Instrument Act, 1881 deals with the Indian conflict of

23. *Ibid.*
24. *Ibid.* 837.
25. See also, Graveson, *Conflict of Laws* (6th Edn.), 463.
26. *Contract and Trading Co. Ltd.* v. *Barbey*, (1959) 3 All E.R. 846.

laws rules relating to negotiable instruments. These rules are not exhaustive and have to be supplemented by the general rules of private international law. The other feature of the Act is that the proper law doctrine of commercial contracts is retained since s. 134 begins, "In the absence of a contact to the contrary. . . ."

Capacity : The negotiable Instrument Act, 1881 is silent on the question of capacity to enter into the main and supervening contracts under the negotiable instruments. The Indian courts, after occillating between the *lex domicilii* and the *lex loci contractus*, have settled down, it seems, in favour of the latter.[27] Thus, in Indian law the capacity to enter into the main and supervening contracts under a negotiable instruments is governed by the *lex loci contractus* or *lex loci actus*.[28]

Formalities : The Negotiable Instruments Act, 1881, unlike its English counterpart, is silent on the formalities. However, s. 136 lays down that in instrument made outside India will be valid as to the formal validity if it is valid as to form under the Indian law, even if it is invalid under the foreign law. The section runs :

> If a negotiable instrument is made, drawn, accepted or endorsed out of India, but in accordance with the law of India the circumstance that any agreement evidenced by such instrument is invalid according to the law of the country wherein it was entered into does not invalidate any subsequent acceptance or endorsement made thereon in India.

Under Indian law the governing law of the formalities is the *lex loci actus*, even though there is no direct Indian authority.[29] It seems also to be clear that the place where the instrument is drafted and signed is not the place where it is made, but it is the place where it is delivered. The Indian law does not contain any exception on the lines in which it is contained in proviso (a) to sub-section (1) of s. 72, English Bills of Exchange Act, 1882. The Indian courts follow the law as it prevailed in England before the passing of the Bills of Exchange Act, 1882. A negotiable instrument which is not void but merely unenforceable under the foreign law for want of proper stamping is formally valid under the Indian law if it is valid otherwise.[30] On the other hand, if for want of proper stamp the instrument is void under the foreign law, then no action is maintenable on such an instrument in an Indian court.[31]

27. *Rohilkhand and Kumaun Bank* v. *Row*, (1885) 7 All. 490; *Kashiba* v. *Sripad*, (1894) 19 Bom. 697; *Lachmi Narain* v. *Fateh Bahadur Singh* (1902) 25 All. 195 (*lex domicilii*); *T.N.S. Firm* v. *Mohammed Husain*, 66 M.L.J. 458 (*lex loci actus*).
28. *T.N.S. Firm* v. *Mohammed Husain*, 66 M.L.J. 458. See also the Indian Law Commission's Report on the subject (11th Report), paras. 27 & 29.
29. See s. 134, Negotiable Instrument Act. See also Row's Negotiable Instrument Act (5th ed.), 790.
30. *Amina Begum* v. *The Nawab of Rampur*, (1911) 36 All. 571.
31. *Dhondiram Chaturbhuj* v. *Sadasuk Savatram*, (1918) 42 Bom. 522.

Section 136 of the Negotiable Instruments Act, 1881 lays down the rule that the invalidity of an instrument under foreign law does not render it invalid as to the subsequent contracts entered into in India provided the instrument is formally valid under the Indian law. The provision of the section is confined to persons who become parties to the instrument by acceptance or endorsement in India. It would not cover a case where a person sought to be made liable on the instrument had become party to it in any other country.

Material Validity : Section 134 of the Negotiable Instruments Act, 1881 deal with the material validity of negotiable instruments. It lays down :

> "In the absence of a contract to the contrary, the liability of the maker or drawer of a foreign promissory note, bill of exchange or cheque is regulated in all essential matters by the law of the place where he made the instrument, and the respective liabilities of the acceptor and endorser by the law of the place where the instrument is made payable."

An illustration is also appended to the section. The illustration runs : A bill of exchange was drawn by A in California, where the rate of interest is 25 per cent, and accepted by B, payable in Washington, where the rate of interest is 6 per cent. The bill is endorsed in India and is dishonoured. An action is brought on the bill against B in India. He is liable to pay interest at the rate of 6 per cent only; but if A is charged a drawer, A is liable to pay interest at the rate of 25 per cent.

The Indian law makes a distinction between the liability of the maker or drawer and acceptor and endorser. In the former case it is the *lex loci actus*, that is the law of the place where the instrument is made, which governs the material validity of the instrument, while in the latter case it is the *lex loci solutionis*, i.e. the law of the place where the instrument is made payable, which governs the essential validity. According to Story there is a difference between the liability of the maker and acceptor and the drawer and endorser. The latter do not undertake to make the payment under the instrument at the place where the instrument is payable but only guarantee its acceptance and payment in that place by the drawee, and default of such payment they agree to reimburse the holder at the place where they entered into their respective contracts for the loss sustained by him. The case of a maker or acceptor, on the other hand, is different inasmuch as he undertakes to pay the amount due under the instrument at the place indicated in the instrument.[32] This was also the view held by some others. The Indian law deviates from this formulation and lays down that the liability of the maker of the note is governed by the *lex loci actus*. The same is the position of the drawer, but in his

32. See s. 135 Negotiable Instruments Act. See also *Sukhlal* v. *Eastern Bank Ltd.*, (1919) 46 Cal. 584.

case the place of drawing is also the place where payment is made. As to the liability of the acceptor and endorser, it is governed under the law of the place where the instrument is payable. Thus in *Ardeshir Sorabsha* v. *Khusaldas*,[33] in respect of a bill drawn abroad and payable in India, the Bombay High Court said that the acceptor was liable even if no protest of dishonour had been made.

Presentment, Protest and Dishonour : Section 135, Negotiable Instrument Act, 1881 deals with dishonour and notice of dishonour specifically. The section runs as under :

> Where a promissory note, bill of exchange or cheque is made payable in a different place from that in which it is made or endorsed, the law of the place where it is made payable determines what constitutes dishonour and what notice of dishonour is sufficient.

An illustration is also appended to explain the meaning of the section : A bill of exchange drawn and endorsed in India, but accepted payable in France, is dishonoured. The endorsee causes it to be protested for such dishonour, and gives notice thereof in accordance with the law of France, though not in accordance with the rules herein contained in respect of bills which are foreign. The notice is sufficient. Although the section applies only to a case where the instrument is made payable at a place different from that in which it is made, the rule is the same when the instrument is made payable at the same place where it is made. The section does not cover protest, but it is submitted, the same law applies to protest as applies to dishonour and notice of dishonour. On logic it seems that the presentment too should be governed by the same law by which the dishonour is governed. Thus, the Indian law seems to adopt Cheshire's views that all those matters which are concerned with the payment of the instrument are covered by the principle that the incidents and mode of performance are determinable by the law of the place of performance.[34]

Transfer : The Negotiable Instruments Act, 1881 does not deal with the transfer of negotiable instruments. It is submitted that the *lex situs* principle would apply to the transfer of negotiable instruments.[35]

Definitions : As to the definitions of 'inland instrument' and 'foreign instrument' given under the Indian Negotiable Instrument Act, 1881 and the definition of 'inland bill' and 'foreign bill' given in the English Bills of Exchange Act, 1882, there is marked resemblance. Section II of the Indian statute defines an 'inland instrument' as : "A promissory note, bill of exchange or cheque drawn or made in India and made payable in, or drawn upon any person

33. 10 Bom. L.R. 268.
34. Cheshire, (7th ed.) 238.
35. See Chapter 17 of this work.

resident in India shall be deemed to be an inland instrument."[36] A 'foreign instrument' is defined as : "Any such instrument not so drawn, made or made payable shall be deemed to be a foreign instrument."[37] In *Kidston* v. *Seth Brothers*[38] Buckland, J. expressed the view that a bill drawn upon a resident of India is an inland bill, irrespective of the fact as to where it was drawn. It is submitted that this is not correct. A bill drawn outside India will be a foreign instrument. One of the distinguishing features of inland instruments and foreign instruments is that the latter must be protested for dishonour when so required by the law of the place where they are drawn,[39] while the former need not be.

36. Section 11, Negotiable Instrument Act, 1881.
37. Section 12, Negotiable Instrument Act, 1881.
38. 1930 Cal. 692.
39. Section 104, Negotiable Instrument Act, 1881.

22

TORT

The peculiar feature that tort occupies in private international law is that if the tortious act has been committed entirely locally, then *lex loci delicti* governs it, irrespective of the fact whether it has or has not some foreign element, such as, both or one of the parties is domiciled or resident abroad or national of another country.[1] The foreign law is relevant only in some very exceptional situations. For instance, if defamation is committed in England, it would be governed by English internal law, but if the defence is of qualified privilege on account of the official position of the defendant that he holds as a representative of a foreign government, then whether that plea will be sustained or not depends on the foreign law. Similarly, the defendant may successfully plead a defence available to him under a foreign contract with the plaintiff.[2]

In English private international law, of torts centre round two English decisions of a century apart, one of the year 1869-70 and the other of 1969-70.[3] Before proceeding with the subject it would be helpful in its understanding if we briefly review the theories relating to the application of law to foreign torts.

I
THEORIES

Mainly, the following three theories relating to application of law to foreign torts have been propagated :

(a) The *lex fori*,

(b) The *lex loci delicti*, and

(c) The proper law or social environment theory.

The Lex fori Theory : Savigny, a prominent proponent of the

1. *Szalatnay-Stacho* v. *Fink*, (1947) 1 K.B. 1.
2. *Ibid.* See also, *Zivnostenska Banka* v. *Frankman*, (1950) A.C. 57; *Kahler* v. *Midland Bank Ltd.*, (1950) A.C. 24.
3. *Phillips* v. *Fire*, (1870) L.R. 6 Q.B. 1: and *Chaplin* v. *Boyes*; (1969) 3 W.L.R. 322.

theory of *lex fori*, was of the view that delictual liability was either akin to criminal liability, or else closely connected with the fundamental principles of public policy applicable in the country of the forum, and therefore it should be governed entirely by the *lex fori*.[4] Westlake, said that a plaintiff should not, in an action for tort, obtain damages for which 'the personal law of the defendant' does not provide.[5]

In our contemporary world there are a very few protagonists of this view.[6] The English courts have never followed this view.[6a] Westlake's view could have some relevance if the jurisdiction of the court *in personam* was based not on mere presence of the defendant within the jurisdiction but also on his domicile or ordinary residence. Cockburn, C.J. very rightly said that the application of this doctrine would lead to "the most inconvenient and startling consequences." This doctrine would mean that the plaintiff would be free to choose the forum most favourable to him, provided he succeeds in finding the defendent there. It may also happen that the defendant may be liable for an act which was innocent under the law where it was committed, though a wrong under the law of the country where he was sued. On the other hand, by declining to exercise jurisdiction in favour of the plaintiff simply because the tortious act complained of is not a tort under the *lex fori* though it is a tort by the *lex loci delicti commissi* would not cause any injustice to the plaintiff.[8]

The Lex Loci Commissi Theory. In the leading English case on the subject, Willis, J. observed : "The civil liability arising out of a wrong derives its birth from the law of the place, and its character is determined by that law."[9] Similarly, Lord Haldane said that if the *lex loci delicti* did not confer any right to sue, then the common law action for damages for tort cannot be maintained, even if it is a tort under the *lex fori*.[10] This is also the theory which prevails in the United States.[11] Rabel said : "The principle unanimously established by the canonists and later by the statutists since the 13th century and generally adopted today is that the *lex loci delicti commissi* governs."[12] Holmes, J. has tried to convert this theory into the *obligatio* theory, though the basis

4. Private Internatioal Law (Guthrie's translation) 205-06.
5. Westlake, 282.
6. The modern protagonists of this view are : Ehrenzweig, Treatise on the Conflict of Laws, 211; Currie, Selected Essays on Conflict of Laws, Chapter I.

7a. *Ibid.*

7. *Phillips* v. *Eire*, (1869) L.R. 4 Q.B. 225.
8. Dicey and Morris, 913.
9. *Phillips* v. *Eire*, (1870) L.R. 6 Q.B. 1 at 28.
10. *Canadian Pacific Railway* v. *Parent*, (1917) A.C. 195 (P.C.)
11. *Slater* v. *Mexican National Railway Co.*, 194 U.S. 120; *American Banana Co.* v. *United Fruit Co.*, 213 U.S. 347; *Loucks* v. *Standard Oil Co. of New York*, 224, N.Y. 99.
12. Rabel, Conflict of Laws. A Comparative Study, Vol. II, 235.

remains the same.[13] In support of this theory Westlake said that if the defendant's act disturbed the social order of any country, then it was the law of the country where it was committed, the law of which therefore is the best authority on the subject.[14]

The difficulty of application of this theory arises in those cases where the facts constituting tortious act take place in more than one country. Suppose A standing on the Indian side of the Indo-Pakistan border pushes a boulder which rolls down and dashes against the car of B parked on the Pakistan side of the border. The question : where the tort has been committed, in India or Pakistan ? The question sometimes becomes material as there may be marked difference between the laws of two countries as to whether the act constituted a tort or not, or as to the nature of tortious act. Three possible solutions have been suggested. The governing law should be of the place where the act commenced which constituted the tort. This solution would fail if the act commenced at more than one place, just as a letter containing defamatory material is written in country X and is posted from country Y. The second suggestion is : the tort may be deemed to be complete in the country the law of which is most favourable to the plaintiff.[15] This solution favours the plaintiff unduly. The third solution is : The tort is completed in the country where the harm ensues.[16] Objections to this theory are : harm of non-physical nature, such as harm to reputation, cannot be localized physically except by resort to fiction,[17] and it is possible that damage may occur in more than one country.

There is hardly any English decision on this aspect of the choice of law, though some decisions are available in connection with jurisdiction of the court. The question arises under Order 11, Rule 1(h) of the Supreme Court Rules under which leave may be granted to serve outside the jurisdiction : "if the action begun by the writ is founded on a tort committed within the jurisdiction." In *Monro (George) Ltd.* v. *American Cynamid and Chemical Corporation*[18] a suit was filed with the averments that the defendant company was liable in negligence for selling to the plaintiffs in New York a substance without warning them of its dangerous qualities. The substance was shipped to England where the plaintiffs sold it to a farmer who suffered injury by its use upon his land. Du Parcq and Goddard, L. JJ. observed : "Where was the wrongful act, from which the damages flows, in fact, done ? The question is not where the damage was suffered, even though damage may be

13. *Slater* v. *Maxican National Railway Co.*, cited above, at 120.
14. Private International Law (7th Ed.), 282.
15. Cook, Logical and Legal Bases of Conflict of Laws (1942), 345.
16. See Beale, Conflict of Laws, Vol. II, 287 (Second edition).
17. Cheshire, 255.
18. (1944) 1 K.B. 432.

the gist of the action."[19] On the other hand, in *Bata* v. *Bata*[20] where defamatory letters were written by the defendant in Zurich and posted to certain addresses in London, the court of Appeal said that since the publication is the material element that completes the tort of libel, the cause of action arose in England. In *Distillers Co. (Bio-Chemicals) Ltd.* v. *Thompson*,[21] the plaintiff lodged an action in England on the ground that he suffered deformity and defective vision on account of sale of a drug by the defendants, a company incorporated in England through their New South Wales agents on account of their negligence not to warn the consumer that the drug has harmful effect on the foetus of an unborn child during the first three months of pregnancy. The drug was purchased and consumed by the plaintiff's mother resulting in his deformity and loss of vision. The Privy Council said that it was not necessary that every ingredient of the cause of action should have occurred within the jurisdiction, nor was it necessary, or sufficient, that the last ingredient, i.e., that which completed the cause of action, should have occurred within the jurisdiction; what was necessary was that the act, or omission, on the part of the defendant which gave the plaintiff his cause of complaint should have been performed within the jurisdiction. In the present case, according to Lord Pearson, the act complained of was the failure to give a warning that the drug would be harmful if taken during the first three months of pregnancy. Since this warning was not communicated to the consumers in New South Wales where the drug was taken, the cause of action arose in New South Wales.[22] Lord Pearson was of the view that the cause of action arose within the jurisdiction if the act on the part of the defendant, which gives the plaintiff his cause of complaint, had occurred within the jurisdiction. Lord Pearson admitted that some cases like the following may be difficult ones : if country X is the place where the defendant was negligent and Y is the country where the defendant's negligence caused the plaintiff hurt, but he did not express any views on it.

Cheshire suggests a test by which the theory of *lex loci delicti Commissi* can work in all situations. According to him the *lex loci delicti commissi* is applied partly because it is the law of the country which is most directly affected by the defendant's allegedly tortious activity and partly in order to give effect to the reasonable expectations of the parties. "It would not, therefore, be inappropriate to regard a tort as having occurred in any country which is substantially affected by the defendant's activity or its consequences and the law of which is likely to have been in the reasonable contemplation of the parties. If a man shoots across a frontier, the alleged tort could thus be regarded as having occurred

19. *Ibid.*, at 441. This observation was *obiter*.
20. (1948) W.N. 366.
21. (1971) 1 All E.R. 694.
22. Reliance was placed on *Jacson* v. *Spittali*, (1870) L.R. 5 C.P. 542.

in both countries."[23] Cheshire adds that his test would introduce an element of flexibility into the *lex loci* rule, but this would not be tantamount to latent acceptance of any notion of proper law of tort.[24]

The most valid criticism of the *lex loci delicti* is : if the place where tort was committed happens to be a chance place, then why the law of that place should be held applicable ? This is well illustrated by Kahn-Freund by the following examples : If one Englishman assaults another while both are together on a holiday or a business trip in Italy, little can be urged in favour of application of Italian law by an English court called upon to decide the question of damages.[25]

Proper Law or Social Environment Theory : On the analogy of proper law of contract the 'social environment' theory is propogated. Morris says : "If we adopt the proper law of a tort, we can at least choose the law which, on policy grounds, seems to have the most significant connection with the chain of acts and circumstances in the particular situation before us."[26] In the United States the proper law theory has been judicially accepted.[27] It has now been judicially accepted in England. In *Boys* v. *Chaplin*,[28] following American decisions, Lord Denning, M.R. propounded the theory thus : "After considering the authorities, I am of the opinion that we should apply the proper law of the tort, that is, the law of the country with which the parties and the act done have the most significant connection. And once we have decided which is the correct law to apply, I think that law should be applied, not only to ascertain whether there is a case of action, but also to ascertain the heads of damages that are recoverable and also the measure of damages : for these are matters of substantive law. They are quite distinct from the mere qualification of damages, which is a matter of procedure for the *lex fori*." When this case went in appeal to the House of Lords[29] two of the judges expressed some qualified support for this theory. Wilberforce, L.J. said : "Given the general rule . . . (as laid down in *Phillips* v. *Eire*)[30] as one which will normally apply to foreign torts, I think that the necessary flexibility can be obtained from that principle which represents at least a common denominator of the United

23. Cheshire, (8th Ed.) 281.
24. *Ibid.*
25. Dicey and Morris, 915.
26. 64 Harvad Law Review, 888.
27. *Babcock* v. *Jackson*, (1963) 12 N.Y. 2d. 473; *Kilberg* v. *North East*, (1960) 9 N.Y. 2d. 34; Restatement, 2nd ed., Conflict of Laws, 379(i); See also the Canadian case, *Abbotsmith* v. *Governors of the University of Toronto*, (1964) 45 D.L.R. (2nd) 672.
28. (1968) 2 Q.B. 1
29. (1969) 3 W.L.R. 322.
30. 6 Q.B. 1.

States decisions, namely, through segregation of the relevant issue and consideration whether, in relation to that issue, the relevant foreign rule ought, as a matter of policy or as Westlake said of science, to be applied. For this purpose it is necessary to identify the policy of the rule, to inquire to what situations, with what contracts, it was intended to apply; whether or not to apply it, in the circumstances of the instant case, would serve any interest which the rule was devised to meet."[31] Then His Lordship quoted the general principle as stated in the American Law Institute Restatement (second). Conflict of Laws,[32] and observed : "This states as the general principle that rights and liabilities of the parties with respect to an issue in tort are determined by the local law of the state, which, as to that issue, has the most significant relationship to the occurrence and the parties, and that separate rules apply to different kinds of torts. The importance of respective contracts is to be evaluated according to their relevant importance with respect to the particular issue, the nature of the tort, and the purpose of the tort rules involved."[33]

Probably, the most significant criticism of the theory is that it leads to uncertainty.[34] In the House of Lords, Lord Hodson gave the proper law theory his qualified support along with Lord Wilberforce. The other judges, Lord Guest, Lord Donovan, and Lord Pearson, did not subscribe to the theory. Lord Guest summarily and succinctly dismissed the theory by saying that he was not in favour of this theory; the theory has never been part of English law; and it produces uncertainty.[35] The other judges also rejected the proper law theory as it leads to uncertainty.[36] Among the English writers, Cheshire is not in favour of the theory.[37] Graveson seems to support it.[38] Kahn-Freund says that social environment theory is of special importance in cases where the *locus delicti* is in a country with whose society and civilization the parties are entirely unconnected; of when the tortious act is done in an uninhabited country.[39]

II

THE MODERN ENGLISH LAW

Jurisdiction

Since an action on tort is an action in *personam* the English

31. (1969) 3 W.L.R. 323 at 343.
32. Proposed Official draft of May 1, 1968.
33. *Ibid.*, at 342.
34. *Phillips* v. *Eire*, (1968) 2 Q.B. 1, at 32.
35. *Phillips* v. *Eire*, (1969) 3 W.L.R. at 334.
36. Lord Pearson, though rejected the theory, said that it may help the English courts to deal with the danger of forum-shoping which is inherent in English rule; *Ibid.*, at 356.
37. Cheshire (7th Ed.), 252-54.
38. Graveson, 623.
39. Dicey and Morris, 918.

court acquires jurisdiction by the mere presence of the defendant within the jurisdiction or when under Order 11. Rule 1(h) of the Supreme Court Rules a writ can be served on the defendant out of jurisdiction.

Cause of Action and Locus Dilicti : The *locus delicti* of tort has been discussed in some decisions in the jurisdictional situation contemplated under Order 11, Rule 1(h), Supreme Court Rules under which leave to serve process out of jurisdiction may be given by the court 'if action begun by the writ is founded on a tort committed within the jurisdiction.' In *Monro (George) Ltd.* v. *American Cynamid and Chemical Corporation*[40] (facts have already been stated earlier) it was held that since the alleged tort, i.e. sale of the harmful drug without warning, was committed in the United States the leave to serve the writ out of the jurisdiction could not be given. Following, and further extending, this rule Will, J. in *Cordova Land Co. Ltd.* v. *Black Diamond Steamship Corporation*,[41] (where the alleged fraudulent misrepresentation was made in the United States and acted on in England, thus completing the tort) said : " . . . tort is first complete when the representation is relied on, although it would not become actionable until damage has resulted. But whether one is concentrating upon the moment when the tort becomes actionable or upon the moment when the tort is complete, it does not seem to me that either of those tests is an appropriate one when one is considering proper effect to be given to the words 'founded on a tort committed within the jurisdiction'. *Ex hypothesi*, not the whole of the tort complained of was committed within the English jurisdiction." Earlier in *Bata* v. *Bata*[42] libellous matter had been published abroad from where it was posted to England and was further published. The Court of Appeal distinguished the *Monro case* by saying that the tort was committed in England and leave to serve out of the jurisdiction was granted. The Privy Council considered the question in *Distillers Co. (Bio-Chemicals) Ltd.* v. *Thompson*[43] where a similar provision of the New South Wales law came for interpretation and said that what was necessary was the act, or omission, on the part of the defendant, which gave the plantiff his cause of complaint should have been performed within the jurisdiction (the case has been discussed earlier). In this case the act complained of was the omission of the defendant to give warning that the article was dangerous if taken by an expectant mother in the first three months of pregnancy. Since this warning was not communicated in New South Wales, the omission took place there where the plantiff's mother purchased the drug.

40. (1944) K.B. 432.
41. (1966) 1 W.L.R. 793.
42. (1948) W.N. 366.
43. (1971) 1 All E.R. 694. See also ***Lure Hosplrides Holes Ltd.*** **(1978) 3 W.L.R. 378 (Conspiracy).**

It seems that these cases lay down that if act or omission constituting the wrongful act is committed within the jurisdiction then that is the *locus delicti*, even if the damage was ensued at another place.

Choice of Law

The foundation of the English rule of choice of law is still the following passage in the decision of the Court of Exchequer Chamber in *Phillips* v. *Eire*:[44] "As a general rule, in order to found a suit in England, for a wrong alleged to have been committed abroad, two conditions must be fulfilled. First, the wrong must be of such a character that it would have been actionable if committed in England. . . . Secondly, the act must not have been justifiable by the law of the place where it was done."[45, 46]

First Part of the Rule : Actionable as Tort According to English Law

The brief facts of *Phillips* v. *Eire*[47] are : In 1865 there was an insurrection in Jamaica and the Governor, Edward Eyre, proclaimed martial law and called out the force to suppress it. During these days Phillips was arrested in the house, handcuffed, put on board a ship and taken away. After the insurrection was suppressed, the legislative council of Jamaica passed an Act of Indemnity saving Governor Eyre from any liability for what was done in suppressing the revolt. Governor Eyre returned to England. Phillips had already returned. On an action for assault and false imprisonment by Phillips against Eyre in an English Court, Eyre, *inter alia*, pleaded the Act of Indemnity as an answer to the action. This plea was sustained by the Court of Exchequer Chamber. In sustaining the plea and in meeting plantiff's argument that Jamaican Act cannot have any extra-territorial validity, Wills, J. said that civil liability arising out of a wrong derives its birth from the law of the place and its character is determined by that law. Therefore, an act committed abroad, if valid and unquestionable by the law of the place, cannot so far as civil liability is concerned, be drawn in question elsewhere.[48] Two years earlier the Privy Council had taken the same view in *The Halley*.[49] In this case, on an action of foreign shipowners against a British steamer to recover compensation for a collusion caused by the negligent navigation of the British steamer in Belgian waters, the defendants pleaded that since at the time of the collusion their steamer was under the charge of a compulsory pilot whom they were compelled to employ under

44. (1870) L.R. 6 Q.B. 1.
45. Per Willis, J. *ibid.* at 28. The case decided by seven judges.
46. Dicey in 1968 edition formulated the rule on that basis. But after the decision in *Boys* v. *Chaplin*, (1969) 3 W.L.R. 32 he changed it.
47. (1870) L.R. 6 Q.B. 1.
48. *Ibid.*
49. (1868) L.R. 2 P.C. 193.

the Belgian law, they were not liable for the negligence of the compulsory pilot under English law. But the defendants were liable even for the negligence of compulsory pilot under the Belgian law. The Privy Council was of the view that it was contrary both to principle and authority to give a remedy for that which did not constitute wrong by English law, even though it was a wrong under the *lex loci delicti commissi*. Thus, the double test came to be applied : the wrong complained of must be wrong not only under the *lex loci delicti commissi* but also under the English law, the *lex fori*.

Should this double test be retained : What is the precise meaning of 'actionable' in England ? Some writers have tried to twist the meaning of 'actionable' so as to mitigate the rigour and ill-foundedness of the rule. Cheshire says that position could be alleviated by a liberal construction of the rule itself. "It might, for instance, be taken to mean no more than that the *lex fori* must recognize a type of liability roughly similar to that for which the plaintiff seeks remedy."[50] Professor Yntema[51] says that Wills, J. in formulating the first limb of the rule had in this mind the question of jurisdiction and in that context he used the word 'actionable'; he did not mean to use it in the sense of substantive liability.[52]

Whatever might be the criticism, the House of Lords decision in *Boys* v. *Chaplin*[53] which is mainly concerned with the second part of the rule, has not been critical of the first part of the rule. In fact, Wilberforce, L.J. specifically said : "I am of opinion, therefore, that, as regards the first part of this rule, actionability as a tort under and in accordance with English law is required."[54]

Second Part of the Rule : Not Justifiable According to the lex loci delicti

The formulation of this proposition was made in *Phillips* v. *Eire*. The meaning, or rather the interpretation, of the word 'justifiable' has been giving trouble for now almost a century. It appears that the real mischief was done by the decision in *Machado* v. *Fontes*[55] which has now been overruled by the House of Lords in *Boys* v. *Chaplin*[56] and without a spill-over.

In *Machado* v. *Fontes*[57] the plaintiff Machado sued defendant Fontes in an English court for a pamphlet published in Brazil

50. Cheshire (7th Ed.), 245.
51. 7 Canadian Bar Review, 118.
52. See also Dicey and Morris, 921.
53. Cited above.
54. (1969) 3 W.L.R. 322 at 339.
55. (1897) 2 Q.B. 231.
56. Cited above.
57. Cited above.

containing libellous material against him (plaintiff). Under the then law of Brazil publication was not actionable in civil proceedings, though it was probably subject to criminal proceedings. It was obviously actionable as tort by English law. The main defence of the defendant was that the publication was not actionable by the law of Brazil. Rejecting this plea the court said that the two conditions laid down in *Phillips* v. *Eire* are fulfilled inasmuch as the first condition was fulfilled because the libel was of such a character that it would have been actionable if committed in England, and the second condition was fulfilled because it was not justified by the law of Brazil, since it was not an innocent act there but subject to criminal proceedings. Ever since this decision has been pronounced, it has been subject of criticism.[58]

It would appear that the most valid criticism of *Machado* v. *Fontes*[59] is the equation of 'not justifiable' with 'wrongful' and of 'justifiable' with 'innocent' and the insistence of Righby, L.J. that in *Phillips* v. *Eire*[60] Wills, J. deliberately changed from 'actionable' in the first branch of the rule to 'justifiable' in the second branch, and equated 'justifiable' with 'authorized, or innocent or excusable'. But a plain reading of the judgment of Wills, J. and facts of the case clearly indicates that the attribution of Righby, L.J. is entirely baseless. Willis, J. was concerned with the legal effect attached to the statute of indemnity by the *lex loci delicti* and was not referring to the nature of the act. The acts of Eyre became justifiable by the Act of Indemnity, but thereby they did not become innocent.[61] It is submitted that the word 'justifiable' itself is ambiguous and it is its ambiguity that has led to the mischief not merely in *Machado* v. *Fontes* but also in the other jurisdiction.[62]

The criticism of *Machado* v. *Fontes*[63] is that if a tortious act is not actionable by the *lex loci delicti commissi* it should not be held actionable just because it is actionable under the *lex fori*.

Before proceeding further it would be appropriate to summarise the

58. See Cheshire, 247; Wolff s. 475; Graveson, 612, Falconbridge, Chapter 4; Lorenzen. Chapter xiii; Pillock, 13 L.Q.R. 233-34, 334-35; Willis, 14 Can. Bar Rev. 20-26; Gutteridge, 6 Camb. L.J. 20, 55 L.Q.R. 131; Robertson, 4 M.L.R. 35; Yntema, 27 Can. Bar Rev. 120; Thomas, 3 I.C.L.Q. 653; Cowen, 68 L.Q.R. 322.
59. Cited above.
60. Cited above.
61. The exact passage from the judgment of Righby, L.J. runs as follows : "The innocency of the act in the foreign country is an answer to the action. That is what is meant when it is said that the act must be 'justifiable' by the law of the place where it was done", (1897) 2 Q.B. 231 at 235.
62. Take for instance the Canadian decision in *McLean* v. *Pettigrew,* (1945) S.C.R. 62=(1945) 2 D.L.R. 65.
63. Cited above.

facts of *Boys* v. *Chaplin*.[64] Both the plaintiff, Boys, and the defendant, Chaplin, were members of Her Majesty's Armed Forces and were stationed on duty at Malta.[65] There, in Malta, the plaintiff suffered serious injuries in a road accident on account of the negligence of the defendant. Both parties were normally resident in England and the action was filed in the English court on their return from duty at Malta. The act of the defendant constituted tort both under the Law of Malta and under English law. The question before the court was : What is the law applicable to assessment of damages ? Under English law Boys was not only entitled to receive expenses and money loss, but also to the compensation for pain and suffering and loss of amenities in life, while according to the law of Malta he was entitled to receive only expenses and his money loss and nothing whatever for his pain and suffering and loss of amenities. The main question before the Court of Appeal and the House of Lords was whether Boys could claim damages under the head 'pain and suffering' and loss of expenses and money loss? What, it is submitted, seems to have bothered the English judges was that if the former law was applied, Boys was entitled to damages worth £ 53 only which was nothing considering the seriousness of his injuries, but if the latter was applied he was entitled to damages worth £ 2,250. Some of the judges have approached the matter from the standpoint whether the heads of damages are to be treated as matters of substantive law or of remedial or procedural law. Of the three judges in the Court of Appeal and the five judges of the House of Lords, Diplock, L.J. is the only judge who came to the conclusion that Boys should get only £ 53 as damages, while all other judges, though on different reasoning, came to the conclusion that he should get £ 2,250 as damages. Diplock, L.J., by what Wilberforce, L.J. calls, purely legal analysis, took the view that heads of damages are part of substantive law and are, therefore, governed by the *lex loci delicti commissi*. The learned judge, after lending his support to the proposition that damages should be recoverable for a wrongful act committed out of England only if it is actionable both by the law of England and by the *lex loci delicti commissi*, holding that *Machado* v. *Fontes*[65a] was wrongly decided on that count, and being confronted by the argument that once the double actionability rule was satisfied recovery of damages is merely the remedy granted by the court for the wrong and accordingly all questions of assessment of damages are governed by the *lex fori*, said, "The heads of damages as distinct from the 'quantification of damages' sustained under each head, are matters of substantive law . . ."

64. Cited above.
65. Cited above.
65a. Cited above.

In the House of Lords, Lord Donovan said that once a case was covered under the rule in *Phillip* v. *Eire*[66] (which he supported and expressed the view that the test of double actionability should not be substituted) the English court was competent to award its own remedies.[67] Lord Guest, on the other hand, agreed with the reasoning of the Diplock, L.J. that there was a distinction between questions affecting heads of damages and quantification of damages, but was of the view that compensation for pains and suffering was not a separate head of damges but merely an element in the quantification of the total compensation.[68]

Of the remaining three judges in the House of Lords, two seemed to support the application of the proper law of tort test as a qualification or exception to the general rule and the third judge was also prepared to accept some exception to the general rule in *Phillips* v. *Eire*[69] so as to tackle the problem of 'forum-shopping'.

Pearson, L.J., who dealt with the matter elaborately, said that had the matter been regarded only as a difference of procedural law—between the Maltese law and English law—there would have been an easy solution of the matter. But this was not so. Then the learned judge said that the rule laid down in *Phillip* v. *Eire* was not wrong from the beginning. It was right. It has the advantage of high degree of certainty and it enables the English court to give judgment according to its ideas of justice. The principal disadvantage of the rule is that it might lead to 'forum-shopping'. The question, therefore, is, has the rule become out of date by reason of changes in legal, social or economic conditions ? The only modification that the learned judge suggested was that, with a view to discourage 'forum-shopping' it may be desirable to apply the law of the natural forum.

Wilberforce, L.J. said that the rule in *Phillip* v. *Eire*[70] needed restatement and he restated it thus : a foreign tort should be actionable as tort according to English law, subject to the condition that civil liability in respect of the relevant claim exists as between the actual parties under law of the foreign country where the act was done.

Hodson, L.J. said that the rule in *Phillip* v. *Eire*[71] as stated by Willis, J. was a general rule which need some qualification. He said that, in general, in actions for personal injuries the *lex loci delicti* determines the rights and liabilities of the parties, where in respect of the particular

66. Cited above.
67. (1969) 3 W.L.R. at 336.
68. *Ibid.* at 334-35.
69. Cited above.
70. Cited above.
71. Cited above.

issue some other state had a more significant relationship with the occurrence and the parties, the local law of that state would be applied and, accordingly, English law was applicable here because even though the occurrence took place in Malta that was overshadowed by the indentity of circumstances of the parties, *viz*., Britain subjects temporarily resident in Malta.[72]

In the result the House of Lords decision[73] overrules *Machado* v. *Fontes*[74] and lays down that an action on a foreign tort will be maintainable if the act is tort under English law and it is also actionable in foreign country where it was done. It also seems to lay down that the general rule of choice of law is that the *lex loci delicti commissi* should apply, though in those cases where the tortious act is committed in more than one country that law may be applied with which parties are most intimately connected, what Wilberforce, L.J. prefers to call the contact or interests principle, what Lord Denning, M.R. prefers to call proper law, and what Hodson, L.J., it is submitted, prefers to call something in between the two (*lex loci delicti* may be overshadowed by 'identity and circumstances of the parties' is the phrase he used).

The decision in *Boys* v. *Chaplin* was applied by the Chancery Division in *John Walker & Sons Ltd.* v. *Henry Ost & Co. Ltd.*[75]

The question come for consideration before the court of Appeal in *Coupland* v. *Arabian Gulf Oil Co.*,[76] where the plaintiff, while working in Libya for the defendant oil company as a senior maintenance technician ha an accident, as a result of which his leg was amputated below the knee. The plaintiff sued the defendant company in England for negligence and breach of contract in causing the accident. The court applied the rule propounded in *Boys* v. *Chaplin*, *viz*. the tort should be actionable under English law and that the civil liability in respect of the claim exists as between the actual parties under the law of the foreign country where the act was done.

The importance of these decisions lies in this that it clarifies two things : (a) that the first rule laid down in *Boys* v. *Champlin* is the rule of choice of law and that quantification of damages and all other matters will be governed by *lex delicti*.(b) If there is a contract of servicebetween the parties during the course of which accident took place the contract is only relevant to the claim in tort insofar as it does, on its true

72. *Ibid*. at 342-43.
73. (1969) 3 W.L.R. 323.
74. (1897) 2 Q.B. 231.
75. Cited above.
76. (1983) 1 W.L.R. 1136.

construction in accordance with the proper law of the contract, have the effect of excluding or restricting the claim on tort.

After the judgment in *Boys* v. *Chaplin*, in his 11th edition of Dicey's Comflict of Laws, Morris formulated the rule thus :

> As a general rule, an act done in a foreign country is a tort and actionable as such in England, only if it is both (a) actionable as a tort according to English law, or in other words is an act which, if done in England, would be a tort; and (b) actionable according to the law of the foreign country where it was done. But a particular issue between the parties may be governed by the law of the country which, with respect to that issue, has the most significant relationship with the occurrence and the parties.

The application of the rule should gives rise to no problem in cases where all relevant events, apart from the institution of proceedings, have taken place in one country. But if tort takes place in more than one country, the question is which law will be applicable. Where several acts alleged to form part of one tort have occurred in more than one country or the injury or damage alleged to constitute the tort has occurred in a country different from the place of one or more of the relevant acts. These are double locality cases. This question came for consideration in *Metall & Rohstoff* v. *Donaldson Inc*,[76a] the Court of Appeal said that, first, in deciding whether an alleged tort has been committed in this country or in some other country, our courts will look back over the series of events constituting it and ask themselves "Where in substance did this cause of action arise?" Secondly, in answering this question, the courts will apply exclusively English Law. One suggestion that the "substance test" should be applied to such cases, the Court of Appeal said :

> . . . in double locality cases our courts should first consider whether, by reference exclusively to English law, it can properly be said that a tort has been committed within the jurisdiction of our courts. In answering this question, they should apply the now well familiar "substance" test previously applied in such cases as *Distillers Co. (Biochemicals) Ltd.* v. *Thompson* (1971) A.C. 458. If on the application of this test, they find that the tort was in disregard the rule in *Boys* v. *Chaplin* the fact that some of the relevant events occurred abroad will thenceforth have no bearing on the defendant's liability in tort. On the other hand, if they find that the tort was in substance committed in some foreign country, they should apply the rule and impose liability in tort under English law, only if both

76a. (1985) 3 W.L.R. 563.

(a) the relevant events would have given rise to liability tort in English law if they had all taken place in England, and (b) the alleged tort would be actionable in the country where it was committed.

The Privy Council reviewed and considered the dual actionability test in *Red Sea Insurance Co. v. Bouyagues.*[76b] Their hardship of the Privy Council said: As a general rule an act done in a foreign country was a tort and actionable as such in England only if it was actionable as tort both according to English law and actionable according to the law foreign country where it was done. However, the Privy Council said, the rule of double actionability was not inflexible and it was possible to depart from it on clear and satisfying grounds in order to avoid injustice by holding that a particular issue between the parties to litigation should be governed by the law of the country which, with respect to that issue, had the most significant relationship with the occurrence and with parties.

Defences

In an English action on a foreign tort double defences are available to the defendant: (i) Any defence, whether substantive or procedural under the *lex fori.* (ii) Any defence under the *lex loci delicti* with the exception on purely procedural defences. If we look at *Phillip v. Eire,*[77] apart from the general rule propounded by Willis, J., it is evidently a case of defence available to the defendant under the *lex loci delicti commissi.* The case is an authority for the proposition that if the defendant is excused from his liability for the wrong by a retrospective law passed by the country where the tortious act was committed, then the English action against him would fail. The defendant can also avail of any defence available to him under the *lex loci delicti commissi* at the time of the commission of the act. The *Mary Moxham*[78] and *The Waziristan*[79] are authorities for this proposition.

Sayers v. International Drilling Co.[80] lays down that if the defendant's liability has been excluded or restricted by a valid term in a contract with the plaintiff, then it can be successfully pleaded as a defence to an action in tort. In this case plaintiff, an Englishman, entered into a contract of employment in England with a Dutch company engaged in off-shore oil drilling, under which he was to be employed as a derrickman on one of the company's rigs off the Nigerian coast. One of the terms of the contract specifically provided that by virtue of his employment the plaintiff was not covered "by workmen's compensation insurance or benefits under the laws of the United Kingdom" but could claim compensation out of the fund maintained by the company. Under the contract the plaintiff accepted this "to be the exclusive remedy in lieu of 'any other claims, rights, demands or action', whether at common law or under the statute of the United Kingdom or any other nation." Whilst working on the company's oil rig off the Nigerian coast the plaintiff was injured owing to the alleged negligence of his fellow employees. The plaintiff filed in action in English court against the Dutch company for damages for the injuries caused to him on account of the negligence of its employees. The issue was whether the contract was governed by the English law, in that case the clause excluding the

76b. (1994) 3 ALL ER 794.
77. (1970) 6 Q.B. 1.
78. (1953) 1 P.D. 107.
79. (1953) 1 W.L.R. 1446.
80. (1971) 3 All. ER 163.

company's liability would be void by virtue of s. 1(3) of the Law Reforms (Personal Injuries) Act, 1948. The court held that the contract was governed by Dutch law and not by English law.

III

MARITIME AND AERIAL TORTS

The maritime and aerial torts are, by the nature of their location, different from inland torts. In this respect the question that arises is : How far, if at all, the rule of *Phillips* v. *Eire*[81] applies to them. Here we are not concerned with the torts committed in the territorial waters as, it is submitted, they are governed by the ordinary rule of *Phllip* v. *Eire*,[82] as modified by *Chaplin* v. *Boys*.[83]

Maritime Torts

Here by maritime torts we mean those torts which are committed on high seas. The question is : what law should govern torts committed on high seas ? Tortious acts on high seas may fall under the following two categories :

(i) Those acts which are confined to a single ship. Examples of such torts may be assault by a member of the crew on another or on a passenger or torts committed by a passenger against another or a member of the crew. This appears to be a case which should not present any problem. They are, in a sense like domestic torts and are not the concern of the private international law. They are governed by the law of the flag, as a ship is considered to be part of the territory of the country the flag of which it flies. Thus, if a tort is committed on the board of an Indian ship, the matter will be exclusively governed by Indian law. But if an action is brought on such a tort in an English court, then the rule laid down in *Phillip* v. *Eire*[83a] as modified by the House of Lords' decision in *Boys* v. *Chaplin* would apply. The only difficulty that arises is in respect of the meaning of the law of the flag in the case of a composite country. It has been, it is submitted rightly, suggested that it will be the law of the port of registry.

(ii) Those acts which are external to a ship. These refer to those torts which affect person or property not on board of a ship. Such acts broadly may be of the following two types : (a) negligent navigation resulting in a collusion with another ship, (b) negligent navigation resulting in some damages to the property of another such as when submarine

81. (1870) L.R. 6 Q.B. 1.
82. *Ibid.*
83. (1970) 3 W.L.R. 322.
83a. (1870) L.R. 6 Q.B. 1.

cables are fouled, or when crew of a fishing boat dispute as to the catch of another boat. In such cases it is obvious that the general rule cannot be applied. It is an established rule of English law that in such cases it is general maritime law, as applied and administered by the Admiralty Division of the High Court, applies, whatever might be the law of the flag. In such a case the requirement is that the tortious act must amount to tort by English law and by general maritime law. Only then an action in an English court would be maintainable. In *Chartered Mercantile Bank of India* v. *Netherlands India Steam Navigation Co.*,[84] on plaintiff's action for damages on account of damage caused to their goods due to the negligent navigation of the ship of the defendants, the court said that the question of negligence was to be tried, not indeed by the common law of England, but by maritime law, which is part of the common law of England as administered in this country."[85]

This rule does not apply when a matter is covered by some international convention to which England is a party. In such a case the matter would be governed by the provisions of the Convention. Similarly, matters relating to claims for damages by reason of interference with or damage done to platforms, derricks, etc., installed for exploration or exploitation on the sea bed and sub-soil and their natural resources on the continental shelf, the matter is governed by the Convention on High Seas concluded at Geneva in 1958.

Aerial Torts

There is yet no judicial authority in England or India on aerial torts. Aerial torts include torts committed on board of an aircraft, collusions in the air between two aircrafts, or damage caused to life or property on account of crashing of aircrafts. For the purpose of aerial torts 'aircraft' includes any mechanical device capable of flight.[86]

In the absence of law of aerial torts, the law is sought to be developed either on the analogy of ships or motor cars. Then, under international law the territorial jurisdiction of a state extends to the air-space over land and territorial waters. This implies that an aircraft is within the territorial jurisdiction of one state or the other over the air-space of which it is flying, except when it is flying over high seas or *territorium nullius*. On this basis it is asserted that whenever a tort is committed on an aircraft or whenever a collusion occurs while the ship is flying over thc air-space of a country, then the *locus delicti* of the tort is that country. Therefore, the choice lies between the law of the country which

84. (1883) 10 Q.B.D. 521.
85. *Ibid.*, at 537.
86. See Graveson, 625.

is the *locus delicti* or the law of the country of aircraft's registration. Kahn-Freund suggests that it should be the law of the place where the aircraft is registered, i.e. the law of the nationality of the aircraft, because "the connection of the aircraft and its passengers and crew with the territories of the countries over which it flies is fortuitous and fleeting, and in many cases it will be difficult to prove the precise moment at which the tort was committed and therefore, the precise location of the aircraft at the time of the tort."[87] Graveson doubts whether the general application of the law of the nationality of the aircraft would serve the purpose, though he seems to be in favour of its application on torts committed on the board of an aircraft. In respect of torts committed when the aircraft is on high seas the law applicable to maritime torts seems to be applied to them by analogy. This is what Graveson means. Thus, is a tort is committed on an English aircraft, the *lex loci delicti* would be English common law, and in the case of a collusion taking place between two or more aircrafts, it would be the English maritime law. On the other hand, McNair takes the view that the true analogy is not between an aircraft and a ship but between an aircraft and a motor-car driven across a country with which the driver and passengers may have no connection and which, in the event of a tort being committed in the car, is nevertheless the *locus delicti*. This would mean that in respect in torts committed, whether within or without the aircraft, while the aircraft is over the air-space of a country, the *locus delicti* will be that country and the law of that country would apply; if tort is committed when the air-craft is on high seas, then the general maritime law or English law would apply.[89] The learned writer favours the application of the law of the nationality of the ship ". . . the most satisfactory basis for a solution is to accord to aircraft a 'law of flag' analogous to that of ships."[90]

To some extent the matter is now governed by international conventions, the Warsaw Conventions of 1929-1959 on Air Transport, the Chicago Convention on International Civil Aviation, 1944 to which corresponds the English statutes of Carriage by Air Act, 1961 and the Civil Aviation Act, 1949.

Article 28 of the Convention on Air Transport (which is part of the Carriage by Air Act, 1961 being contained in the Schedule) deals with choice of jurisdiction and lays down that an action for damages can be brought only in the court of the country (the High Contracting Parties)

87. Dicey and Morris, 958.
88. Graveson, 628.
89. McNair, Law of the Air (3rd Ed.), 282-84; See also Dicey and Morris, 598.
90. McNair, 270.

where the carrier ordinarily resides, or has his principal place of business, or has an establishment by which the contract has been made, or at the place of destination of goods. Article 29 provides that the right of damages shall be extinguished if an action is not brought within two years. The period will be calculated under the *lex fori*.[91] Similarly, the Civil Aviation Act, 1949 lays down certain rules relating to aerial torts. Section 40(1) lays down that 'no liability shall be incurred for trespass to the air-space.' Section 40(2) lays down that 'where material loss or damage is caused to any person or property on land or water by, or by a person in, or an article or a person falling from an air-craft while in flight, taking off, or landing, then . . . damages shall be recoverable without proof of negligence or intention, as if caused by wilful act, neglect or default of the owner of the air-craft."

The aforesaid statutory provisions cover only certain aspects of the aerial torts. It is submitted that Lord Denning's "proper law of tort" theory is most suited to the maritime and aerial torts.

IV

INDIAN LAW

The Indian private international law relating to torts is in a nascent stage of development. It seems to be evident that as to the jurisdiction of the court, the rules laid down in the Civil Procedure (which have already been discussed in Chapter 7) will apply. Section 19 of the Civil Procedure Code runs : "Where a suit is for compensation for wrong done to the person or to movable property, if the wrong was done within the local limits of the jurisdiction of one court and the defendant resides or carries on business, or personally works for gain, within the local limits of the jurisdiction of another court, the suit may be instituted at the option of the plaintiff in either of the said courts." It seems that in a case where a suit for compensation is filed for a tort committed abroad, the Indian court will entertain an action against a defendant who resides, carries on business or personally works for gain in India. The residence will also include the presence of the defendant within the jurisdiction of the court. In short, the courts are free here also to give a wide meaning to the word 'residence'. Thus in a pre-independence case[92] the Privy Council held that the court at Quetta has jurisdiction to entertain an action against a defendant who resides in Punjab and carried on business in Quetta in respect of a tort committed by him in Persia.

As to the choice of law, there is only one reported case of 1960

91. See also Sub-sections (1)(b), (2) and (3) of 5.4 and 58, 8.9(1) and 10 of the Carriage by Air Act, 1961.
92. *Haveli Shah* v. *Painda Khan*, (1926) 96 I.C. 887.

which follows English law. In *The Kotah Transport Ltd.* v. *The Jhalawar Bus Service Ltd.*[93] a suit for damages was filed by the plaintiff company against the defendant company for damages caused to the plaintiff but by rash and negligent driving on the part of the defendant's driver. The accident in which the plaintiff's bus was damaged occurred in Jhalawar state (then an Indian state, and hence a foreign state for the purpose of private international law), and the action was brought in a court of Kotah (which was then another Indian state). The main defence of the defendant was that the alleged tortious act should constitute an actional wrong not merely by the law of the Kotah state but also by the law of Jhalawar state, the *lex loci delicti commissi*. S. Prasad, C.J. after an examination of the law of tort of Jhalawar state, found that there was nothing in the law of the state which justified the act of the defendant and thus the case was decided in favour of the plaintiff.

93. 1960 Raj. 224.

Part VII

PROCEDURE

SUMMARY

23

PROCEDURE

Domestic law of practically every country makes a distinction between the substantive law and procedural or adjective law. Broadly speaking, substantive law is that branch of law which is constitutive of rights and obligation and the procedural law is that branch of law which provides methods and ways of enforcing rights and obligations. "The mode of proceeding by which a legal right is enforced, as distinguished from the law which gives or defines the right, and which by means of the proceeding the court is to administer; the machinery as distinguished from the product."[1] This distinction between substance and procedure, between right and remedy has come to be established, but, in its practical application, a clear-cut distinction between the two is too difficult to make. There are no water-tight compartments of rules of substance and rules of procedure; nontheless the distinction exists.

Yet, no other principles are more well-established in private international law than the principle that all matters of procedure are governed by the *lex fori*, and that no rule of procedure of foreign law can be given effect. There are no exceptions to the general principle.[2]

The principle that all matters of procedure are governed by the *lex fori* is justified on the basis that since the law of procedure is the most technical branch of any legal system, the machinery that will work most smoothly in enforcing rights acquired elsewhere can be the one provided by the *lex fori*, and therefore any person who chooses the forum for enforcing his rights must accept the procedure as laid down by the *lex fori*.[3] The greatest merits of this principle is that it establishes certainty and equality.

1. *Poyser* v. *Minors*, (1881) 7 Q.B.D. 329 at 333.
2. *Huber* v. *Steiner*, (1835) 2 Bing. N.C. 207=(1935-42) All E.R. Rep. 159; *British Linen Co.* v. *Drummond*, (1830) 10 B. & C. 903; *De La Vega* v. *Vianna*, (1830) 1 B. & Ad. 284 are some of the early English decisions. This propostion has never been doubted. *Nel Tambi* v *Ponuswami*, 2 Mad. 406; *Ramanathan* v. *Somasundaram*, 1964 Mad. 527; *Dikki & Co.* v. *Municipal Board*, 1956 Cal. 216 are some of the Indian decisions.
3. *De la Vega* v. *Vianna*, above cited.

What matters are procedural and what are substantive is sometimes difficult to discern and the laws of different countries differ on this count. However, the following are usually considered to be the matters of procedure : jurisdictional competence of courts under the domestic law; the question of actionality, which includes the rules of limitation for various causes of action and proceedings; parties to proceedings, the questions relating to necessary and proper parties; the procedure for filing proceedings, pleadings, services of process, method and mode of trial; all matters relating to evidence, such as essential facts and relevant facts, admissibility of evidence, presumption, competence and examination of witnesses, admissibility of documents; priorities; enforcement of remedies and orders; execution of judgments and decrees, proof of foreign law, appeals and the like.

Characterization of Law as Substantive and Procedural

Not merely all matters relating to procedure are governed by the *lex fori* but whether a matter relates to substantive law or procedural law is also characterized by the *lex fori*.[4] The importance of this classification is obvious as matters of substance are governed by the appropriate foreign law as directed by the choice of law rule, while the matters of procedure are governed by the *lex fori*.[5] In the early period of development of private international law, English court tried to give an extended meaning to matters of procedure with a view to evade what they thought to be an unsatisfactory or inconvenient foreign choice of law rule. What injustice can be caused by improper classification is illustrated by the oft-cited English decision in *Leroux* v. *Brown*,[6] where the question before the court was whether an oral agreement of service for more than one year entered into in France was enforceable in England. Under the English statute, the Statute of Fraud, all such agreement for more than one year must be under seal. An action brought in an English court for its breach failed as the court held that the statute imposes a rule of procedure which is binding on parties choosing English forum. The judgment has obviously been widely criticised and English courts no longer give such a wide and extended meaning to matters of procedure.[8]

Sir Jocelyn Simon, P.[9] very pertinently observed : "It is not everything that appears in a treatise on the law of evidence that is to be classified internationally as adjective law, but only provisions

4. *Huber* v. *Stenier*, cited above.
5. *Ibid.*
6. (1852) 12 C.B. 801.
7. See *Mahadervan* v. *Mahadervan*, (1964) P. 233 for the modern judicial trend in English law. See also, *Willims* v. *Wheeler* (1860) 8 C.B. (N.S.) 299 and *Gibson* v. *Holland*, (1865) L.R. 1 C.P. 1 where Willis, J. criticised the judgment in *Leroux* v. *Brown*.
8. Cook Logical and Legal Basis of Conflict of Laws, 154.
9. *Mahadervan* v. *Mahadervan*, (1964), p. 233.

of a technical or procedural character—for example, rules as to the admissibility of heresay evidence or what matters may be noticed judicially".[10] Graveson, it is submitted rightly, says, "It would be appropriate and in line with established developments in many areas of the conflict of laws to apply that system of procedure most closely connected with the proceedings in their substantive aspect." In short, to develop an objective proper law of procedure which may and indeed often will, point to the *lex fori* as the most appropriate system.[11]

We would proceed to discuss some important procedural matters.

Actionability and Proper Parties

Actionability: What type of action may be brought on a particular cause of action is governed by the *lex fori*. This can lead to the situation where an action may be brought in Indian Court which could not be brought under the foreign system under which the cause of action arose. The reverse may also happen. Thus, in *Hansen* v. *Dixon*[12] English court allowed an action for breach of marriage-promise which was governed by the Danish law. The Danish law did not allow an action for breach of marriage-promise. The requirement of Danish law was held procedural and therefore could not affect the English jurisdiction.[13] An interesting illustration is provided by *Phrantzes* v. *Argenti*.[14] Under Greek law, while giving his daughter in marriage, the father has an obligation to provide a dowry for his son-in-law. In case the father failed to fulfil this obligation at the time of the marriage, the daughter has a cause of action to compel him to enter into a dowry contract with her husband. In those cases where the father is abroad the Greek law confers a power on the court to give directions to the father to enter into the contract in the presence of a notary public or the Greek consul. In this case the wife brought an action in an English court to compel her father to enter into a dowry-contract with her husband. The wife, the father and the husband were all living in England. Although the English court observed that such an obligation was enforceable in England, it dismissed the daughter's action on the ground that there was no appropriate common law remedy under which wife's right could be enforced and that wife's claim was for an unascertained sum of money which English court was not in a position to ascertain since it could be ascertained in accordance with the financial position of the father, his liabilities and his social position in the Greek social environment. On the other hand, in *Shahnaz* v. *Rizvan*[15] a claim of divorced wife to claim her dower (under

10. Dicey and Morris, 1090-91.
11. Conflict of Laws, p. 633.
12. (1906) 23 T.L.R. 56.
13. See also *Worms* v. *De Valdor*, (1880) 49 L.J. Ch. 261
14. (1960) 2 Q.B. 19.
15. (1965) 1 Q.B. 390.

a pre-marriage contract) under Muslim law was held enforceable in England by an English court, even though such an obligation did not exist under English law. In this case, the dower was of a specified amount.

The form in which remedy is to be pursued is a matter of procedure and it is no defence to prove that had the action been filed in another country or in the country where the cause of action arose, the form should have been entirely different. The proper law of the transaction does not determine the form of action.

Parties to the action : In this connection the two main questions are : who can sue and who can be sued ? Ordinarily, these questions present no difficulty even in a conflict of laws case, but sometimes problems arise when a title is acquired derivately, such as on assignments, or when a third person claims benefit under a contract, or when the question is whether an agent of a foreign company can be personally sued for wrongful acts committed by him as such agent or when a foreign state brings an action, the question may arise whether an unrecognized state can maintain an action or when it is recognised, is it capable of filing an action. Who are the proper parties to the suit is also a question of substance. Thus, who has a right to sue and who is liable to be sued are questions of substance. But once it is determined by the substantive law that who have a right to sue on whom lies the liability, the question who should actually be parties to the suit, i.e. in whose name suit can be filed and against whom suit can be filed, are matters of procedure to be determined by the *lex fori*. Thus, whether an action can be filed in England or India in the name of the dead man is a question of procedure and therefore has to be determined by the *lex fori*; and if such an action cannot be maintained by the *lex fori*, it would not be maintainable even if the *lex causae* permits such an action.[16] Or, whether a company has been wound up, liquidated or dissolved is to be determined by the law of the place of its incorporation, the matter being of substance, but whether an action is maintainable by or against a dissolved company is to be determined by the *lex fori*.[17]

Some difficulty arises in cases where a person brings an action on the basis of a derivative title or when he sues under a contract to which he is not a party but a beneficiary.[18] In this respect Cheshire remarks : "But on principle it is doubtful whether every rule that regulates the name in which an action must be brought

16. *Banque Internationale de Commerce de Petrograd* v. *Goukassow*, (1925) A.C. 150.

17. *Ibid. See also Russian and English Bank* v. *Baring Bros. & Co. Ltd.*, (1936) A.C. 405. There are certain statutory exceptions under which an action by and against a dissolved company can be filed.

18. *See O'Callagham* v. *Thomond*, (1810) 3 Taunt, 8; *Innes* v. *Dunlop*, (1800) 8 Term. Rep. 595.

is merely procedural in character. It would seem to be an unwarranted extension of the province of procedure, at any rate in cases falling within the sphere of private international law, to regard a rule of procedure if the effect is to deprive the plantiff of a right which he has definitely acquired under the governing legal system.[19]

The difficulty of the same nature arises in respect of the party to be sued. Thus, the question arises whether the foreign rule determining the identity of the party to be sued, or of joinder of parties or prescribing the order in which various parties might be sued is procedural or substantive ? Suppose under the *lex fori* an action is maintainable against the defendant, but by the law governing the transaction liability falls on a person other than the defendant, then can an action be maintained against the defendant ?[20] This is well illustrated by *General Steam Navigation Co.* v. *Guillou*,[21] where an action was brought in an English court to recover damages for injury caused to one of the ships of the plantiffs by the negligent navigation of a French ship. The French ship at the time of the accident was under the direction and control of the servants of the defendant. The defendant was a shareholder and acting director of the French company to which the ship belonged. One of the pleas of the defendant was that under the French law the defendant could not be sued in his individual name : an action could be maintained only against the company. The main question before the English court was whether under the French law the defendant was totally absolved of his liability or whether it merely imposed on him a joint liability ? There was some difference of opinion among the judges as to the construction of the French law. On the main issue, Parke, B., speaking for himself and three other judges; said : "If the defendant was not liable for the acts of that other by that law which is also to govern this case, he had a good defence to the action; and for the defendant, it is contended that the plea means to aver that, by the law of France, he was not liable for those acts, but that a body established by French law, and analogous to an English corporation, were the proprietors of the vessel and alone liable for the acts of the master, who was their servant and not the servant of the individuals composing that body."[22] Thus, whether the defendant is liable or not is to be determined by the proper law of the transaction. Once the existence of liability is determined, then action has to be brought in accordance with the *lex fori*, whatever might be form and procedure prescribed under the proper law of the transaction. This may further be illustrated from partnership cases. In *Bullock* v. *Caird*[23] the proper law of the transaction laid

19. Private International Law (8th Ed.), 673-74.
20. *General Steam Navigation Co.* v. *GullIou*, (1843) 11 M. & W. 877; *Bullock* v. *Caird*, (1875) 10 Q.B. 276.
21. Cited above.
22. (1843) 11 M. & W. 877 at 895.
23. (1875) 10 Q.B. 276.

down that the individual partner can be sued only when in a suit against partnership its assets have been totally exhausted. The English court allowed an action against an individual partner of the firm on the ground that the foreign rule was procedural.[24],[25] These cases[26] also establish that a defendant who is liable under the proper law of the transaction, can be sued in England even if under the foreign mode of procedure he could not the sued alone, or must be sued along with some other or others who are also liable since such foreign rule, being the rule of procedure, cannot be applied.

All routine matters of procedure arising after an action is filed are also governed by the *lex fori*. Thus, matters such as service of summons, interlocutory applications, the title of action and all other matters of procedure leading to the passing of the order or decree as well as execution and appeals, are all governed by the *lex fori*.

Limitation

Practically all the countries of the world provide a period of limitation within which a remedy is to be pursued. Once that period expires the remedy becomes time barred, though right continues to exist. In the Common Law system, the law of limitation is considered to belong to procedural law. Sometimes a statute of limitation is such that not merely the remedy is barred but the right is also extinguished. Such statutes are classified as of substance. The former is governed by the *lex fori*, while the latter by the proper law of the transaction. An example of the latter is found in the law of adverse possession. If A continues to be in adverse possession of P's land for a period of twelve years or more, A becomes the owner of the land and P's ownership is extinguished.[27] Another provision of the Limitation Act, 1939, lays down that where a cause of action in trover or detinue has accrued to a person his title to the chattels shall be extinguished after the lapse of six years from the time of accrual.[28] These are the illustrations when not merely the remedy but also the right is extinguished. An example of the situation when only remedy is extinguished, while right remains is provided by the period of limitation provided for the recovery of loans.[29]

English private international law strictly adheres to the rule that limitation being matter of procedure is governed by the *lex fori*. Strict adherence to this rule has resulted in an action being

24. See also *Re Doetsch*, (1896) 2 Ch. 836.
25. See also Cheshire, Private International Law, (8th Ed.) 674-675.
26. *General Steam Navigation Co.* v. *Guillou*, cited above; *Bullock* v. *Caird*, cited above; and *Re Doetsch*, cited above.
27. Section 11 Limitation Act, 1939.
28. S. 3(2), English Limitation Act.
29. Und[illegible] of Limitation the period is six years.

maintainable in English court when it has become time-barred by the *lex causae* or *vice versa.* In *Huber* v. *Steiner*[30] the proper law of the transaction (the French law) which barred an action on promissory note after a lapse of five years from the date of protest was characterized as rule of procedure and the action in English court was held maintainable (under English law the period of limitation is six years). An extreme illustration of this rule is provided by *Harris* v. *Quine*,[31] where an action for the recovery of fees was filed by the attorneys of the defendant in a Manx Court. The court held the action time barred, being filed beyond three years, the period of limitation laid down under the law of the Isle of Man. The attorneys subsequently filed an action on the same cause of action in an English court which passed a decree in their favour on the ground that the statute of the Isle of Man prescribing the period of limitation being procedural would be ignored.[32] In *British Linen Company* v. *Drummond*[33] the English period of six years limitation to an action on a Scottish contract was applied, though the period of limitation for such action was forty years under Scottish law of limitation.

The Indian law closely follows the English law. The Calcutta High Court, following English decisions, said that the law of limitation is a matter of procedure and a person filing a suit in an Indian court cannot have any advantage conferred on him by the foreign law of procedure or limitation and, at the same time, he cannot be deprived of any benefit or advantage conferred on him by the Indian law.[34] In *Dhanji* v. *Ramji*[35] the court said that even if an action has become time-barred by the foreign *lex causae*, it would be maintainable in the Indian court if it is within the period of limitation under the Indian law. Section 11 of the Indian Limitation Act, 1963 clearly lays down that in any action filed in any Indian court the period of limitation provided by the Act would apply.[36]

Just as under English law so under the Indian law if a foreign statute of limitation bars not merely the remedy but also extinguishes the right, then the foreign law will be accorded recognition. The Indian courts have consistently taken this position.[37] Section 27 of the Indian Limitation Act lays down the principle of

30. (1835) 2 Bing. N.C. 202.
31. (1869) 4 Q.B. 653.
32. See also *Huber* v. *Steiner*, (1835) 2 Bing. N.C. 202, per Tindel, C.J.
33. (1830) 10 B. & C. 903.
34. R.A. *Dikkie & Co.* v. *Municipal Board*, Benaras, 1956 Cal. 216.
35. 1950 Kutch 58.
36. See also *Hukum Chand Aswal* v. *Gyanender Chunder*, 14 Cal. 570; *Nabibhai* v. *Daya Bhai*, 1916 Bom. 200.
37. *Ramanathan* v. *Somasundaram*, 1964 Mad. 527 at 528; See also *Lakhpatrai* v. *Atma Singh*, 1962 Punj. 228; *Sheik Ali* v. *Sheik Mohammed*, 1967 Mad. 45; *Dikkie & Co.* v. *Municipal Board Benaras*, 1956 Cal. 216; *Raman Chettier* v. *Roman Chettier*, 1954 Mad. 97.

adverse possession whereunder a continuous possession of twelve years over immovable property not merely creates a right of ownership in the possessor but also extinguishes the right of true owner. The Indian rule applies to both movable and immovable property. Similarly, s. 11(2) lays down that if a contract has been totally extinguished by the foreign law, then the Indian law would recognise that law provided the parties are domiciled in that foreign country.

Evidence

At one time the general rule of private international law was that evidence is a matter of procedure and governed by the *lex fori*. However, the modern trend is not to regard everything pertaining to evidence as procedural. In *Mahadervan* v. *Mahadervan*[38] the court said : "It is not everything that appears in a treatise on law of evidence that is to be classified internationally as adjective law, but only provisions of technical or procedural character—for instance rule as to the admissibility of hearsay evidence or what matters may be noticed judicially." Graveson rightly says that the *lex fori* in this connection must be interpreted in a wide sense as comprising the rules of private international law of evidence. "In this matter a preliminary distinction should be made between the law applicable to the construction of a document, which is its proper law, and that applicable to the evidence adduced to the court in aid of its construction and its proof, which is always the *lex fori*."[39] Similarly, what are facts in issue is a matter of substance, but how facts in issue are to be proved is a procedural matter. Former are governed by the proper law of the transaction, while the latter are governed by the *lex fori*.

Some of the specific matters pertaining to evidence call for separate treatment.

Admissibility of Evidence : It is a well-established rule that all questions relating to admissibility of evidence are governed by the *lex fori*. If a document is admissible in evidence under English law it will be admissible, irrespective of the fact that it is not admissible by its proper law. The reverse is also true.[40] Under the Evidence (Foreign, Dominion and Colonial Documents) Act, 1933 of official and properly authenticated copies of foreign registers are admissibile in the United Kingdom to prove the contents of such registers.[41] The United Kingdom has ratified the Hague Convention of 1961 for the Abolition for Foreign Public Documents

38. (1964) p. 233 at 243.
39. Conflict of Laws, 642.
40. *Bristow* v. *Sequeville* (1850) 5 Exch. 275; *Clegg* v. *Levy*, (1812) 3 Camp. 166 (where the document was a total nullity by the *lex causae*); *Appleton* v. *Broybrooke*, (1817) 6 M. & S. 34; *Finlay* v. *Finlay*, (1862) 31 L.J. P. 149.
41. Provision can be brought into force by Orders in Council and would be made on the basis of reciprocity.

which dispenses with the formality of authenticating seals and signature on foreign official documents.[42]

The rule of domestic law as to oral evidence in relation to documents applies. Apart from certain exceptions,[43] such as the reception of extrinsic evidence for the construction or interpretation of documents, the English and Indian rule is that oral evidence is not admissible to add to, vary or contradict the terms of the document.[44]

Witnesses : Whether a witness is competent or compellable or whether he can claim privilege are considered to be matters of procedure and are therefore governed by the *lex fori*.[45] It seems that the question whether there should be a trial by jury, and if so, then the respective functions of the judge and the jury are all matters to be governed by the *lex fori*. Lord Brougham said : "Whether a witness is competent or not, whether a certain matter requires to be proved by writing or not whether certain evidence proves a certain fact or not, that is to be determined by the law of the country where the question arises."[46]

Burden of Proof : In the English and Indian private international law of evidence burden of proof is used in several senses. Graveson is of the view that the question as to which party must bear the burden of proof is governed by the *lex fori*.[47] However, the determination of this question exclusively by the *lex fori* may at times lead to injustice. For example, if a person can bring forward no evidence of a right he claims, and though under the proper under which the right arouse the burden of proof would rest on a person denying the existence of the right, under English law the burden of proof would lie on the other way. Graveson says, "Under such circumstances, given that procedure is the means and not the end itself, the application of the *lex fori* appears self-defeating."[48] There is a dirth of authority. Whatever little authority is available, it is conflicting. It is submitted that the following observation of G.H. Treitel seems to state the desirable proposition of law : "Rules governing the incidence of the evidential and legal burdens (which in civil cases, rest almost invariably on the same party) ought to be regarded as substantive. No procedural inconvenience is caused by applying foreign rules which do not regulate the mode of proof but merely designate the

42. Section 14, Civil Procedure Code.
43. See for details, Graveson, The Ninth Hague Conference of Private International Law, (1961) 10 I.C.L.Q. 18.
44. Dicey and Morris, 1098, See also *Vitkovice* v. *Korner*, (1951) A.C. 869; *St. Pierre* v. *S.A. Stores*, (1937) 3 All. E.R. 340.
45. *Bain* v. *Whitehaven & Furness Railway*, (1850) 3 H.L.C. 1; *United States* v. *MacRae*, (1867) L.R. 3 Ch. App. 79.
46. *Bain* v. *Whitehaven Ry. Co.* (1850) 3 H.L.C. 1, at 19; See also *Leroux* v. *Brown*, cited above.
47. Conflict of Laws, 644.
48. *Ibid.*

person who is to bring proof. On the other hand, the forum will probably always apply its own rules as to *quantum* of proof. Similarly, where English law requires corroboration, either as a matter of strict law or a matter of practice, it seems that such a requirement is procedural."[49]

Presumptions : Graveson opines that questions of presumptions of law and fact are generally governed by the *lex fori*,[50] since these have been considered to be matters of procedure. But it is now accepted that this rule does not apply to all types of presumptions. In the English and Indian domestic law presumptions are usually divided under three heads : presumption of facts, rebuttable presumption of law and irrebutable presumption of law. The presumptions falling in the first category are now generally accepted to be rules of substance, even under the domestic law. Rebuttable presumptions of law may be subdivided into particular presumptions and general presumptions. The former are presumptions of advancement, satisfaction and ademption. Treitel suggests that they should be classified as rules of substance.[51] In the second category fall presumptions such as of legitimacy, marriage and death. Treitel observes : "It is uncertain whether such presumptions are rules of substance or rules of procedure. In cases involving presumptions of marriage the courts have applied the *lex causae* whenever the law was proved."[52] But as to other cases of presumption there is uncertainty. Thus it seems certain that the presumptions of facts are as a rule governed by the *lex fori*, since they are treated as procedural matters. It also seems to be clear that irrebutable presumptions of law are matters of substance and not of procedure.

Taking Evidence for Foreign Proceedings : The Foreign Tribunals Evidence Act, 1956 and the Evidence by Commission Act, 1859 lay down provisions under which evidence may be taken in England at the request of a foreign tribunal, in connection with the proceedings pending before it. Under the Act of 1856 application can be made to the English court for the examination of witnesses or the production of documents. For these purposes directions may be given as to time, place and manner of taking evidence as may appear reasonable and just.[53] Under the Act the court could order for the production of ascertained documents but not for unascertained documents. Such directions can be issued to a corporation also.[54] The Act of 1859 applies to recording of evidence in England for the purpose of proceedings in any part of

49. Dicey and Morris, (8th Ed.) p. 100. Cheshire also seems to take the same view : Private Internationl Law, 670.
50. Conflict of Laws, p. 644. He cites *Re Cohn*, (1945) Ch. 5 in support.
51. Dicey and Morris, 1101.
52. Dicey and Morris 1101. See *Mahadervan* v. *Mahadervan*, (1964), p. 233.
53. Section 1.
54. *Penn-Texas Corporation* v. *Murat Anstalt*, (1964) 1 Q.B. 40.

the Commonwealth. Under the Act the court is empowered to issue orders for the attendance of witnesses as well as for the production of documents.[55]

Similar provisions are found in the Indian Civil Procedure Code.[56] Section 78 lays down that "subject to such conditions and limitations as may be prescribed, the provisions as to the execution and return of commissions for the examination of witnesses shall apply to commissions issued by or at the instance of . . . courts of any state or country outside India." Order 26 lays down procedure for the execution and return of commissions. Rules 19 to 22 of or. 24 specifically provide procedure for the execution and return of commission issued by the Indian courts at the request of foreign courts. The commission can be issued by the High Courts only and it will issued when the High Court is satisfied, "(a) that a foreign court situated in a foreign country wishes to obtain evidence of a witness in any proceeding before it, (b) that the proceeding is of a civil nature, and (c) that the witness is residing within the limits of the High Court's appellate jurisdiction. . . ."

A 1968 international Convention lays down rules for taking evidence in foreign countries in respect of disputes relating to commercial matters.

Priorities

The general rule of English and Indian private international law is that priorities are governed by the *lex fori*. However, a distinction is drawn where the claim is considered to be purely personal and when the claim is secured one or is in respect of a right *in rem*. The English courts have consistently taken the position that whenever the property is in possession of the court it is distributable among the creditors in accordance with the domestic rules of English law.[57] For instance, priorities of creditors claiming in bankruptcy or intestacy are regarded purely as matters of procedure and are governed by the *lex fori*. The same applies to aliens.[58] But in those cases where the creditors claims are secured, it is incumbent on the court to first determine by reference to the proper law of the transaction under which the charge arose, and the nature of the right or claim. Once it has so ascertained the claim, the court treats the claim according to its domestic rules in the same manner as a similar English claim would be treated. The decision in *The Colorado*[59] illustrates this position, where the court was called upon to determine priorities between the mortgagee of a ship under a French *hypotheque* and an English firm of ship

55. *Panthalu* v. *Ramnord Research Laboratories*, (1966) 2 Q.B. 173.
56. Section 78 and Or. 24. rr. 19-20.
57. *Pardo* v. *Bingham*, (1868) L.R. 6 Eq. 485; *Re Melbourn*, (1870) L.R. 6 Ch. App. 64. *The Colorado*, (1923) p. 102.
58. *The Colorado*, Supra.
59. (1923), p. 102.

repairers called necessaries men. English law preferred the claim of mortgagee over the claim of necessaries men, but according to the French law the necessaries men have preference over the mortgagee. The court of Appeal determined the right given under the *hypotheque* according to French law and held that the mortgagee claim would have priority over the necessaries men. Thus, the French law determined the substance of the right and English law determined whether a right of that nature had priority over the other.[60]

Set-Off and Counter Claim

A counter claim is a claim made by the defendant which can be conveniently tried together with the plaintiff's claim against the defendant and therefore, is a matter of procedure. It is governed by *the lex fori.*[61] Even if the court of the *lex fori* refuse the counter-claim, the defendant's substantive right is not affected. On the other hand, a set-off may be one which amounts to an equity directly attaching to the plaintiff's claim and thus operates as a partial or total extinction of the plaintiff's claim. Such a set-off is a question of substance and not of procedure and is therefore governed by the proper law of the transaction.[62]

Remedies

Just as what type of action may be brought on a particular cause of action is governed by the *lex fori*, similarly what type of remedy may be available to a plaintiff on a foreign cause of action is governed by the *lex fori*. Thus, the English courts have held that a remedy available under the *lex fori* though not available under the foreign *lex causae*, will be available to a plaintiff who sues in English courts. For instance, by the foreign *lex causae*, the plaintiff is entitled to only damages but under the *lex fori* he is entitled to specific relief, then he may be granted specific performance.[63] Converse is also true. Thus, no injunction can be obtained by a plaintiff suing on a foreign cause of action for a breach of negative condition in a contract of service if granting of injunction would virtually amount to specific performance of the contract.[64] Not only those remedies can be claimed which are recognized by the *lex fori*, but the foreign remedies claimed by a plaintiff must harmonize with the remedies provided by the *lex fori.*[65] G.H. Treitel succinctly summarises the position thus:

60. See *The Tagus*, (1903), p. 44, where a contrary view was taken. See also *The Zigurds* (1932), p. 113.
61. *South African Republic* v. *La Compagnie France-Belge etc.*, (1897) 2 Ch. 487.
62. See Dicey and Morris, 1105.
63. *Baschet* v. *London Illustrated Standards*, (1900) 1 Ch. 73.
64. *Warner Brothers Pictures Incorporated* v. *Nelson*, (1937) 1 K.B. 209. However, this point was not discussed in this case.
65. *Phrantzes* v. *Argenti*, (1960) 2 Q.B. 19, the facts of the case have been discussed earlier in this Chapter.

"Generally speaking the principle that the forum grants it own remedies in respect of wrongs governed by a foreign law only applies if two conditions are satisfied. First, the *lex causae* must give the plaintiff some remedy against the defendant in respect of a wrong similar in character to that alleged in the English proceedings. Secondly, the English remedy sought must harmonize with the right according to its nature and extent as fixed by the foreign law."[66]

Damages: English and Indian authorities on the subject are scanty. Some decisions in tort cases have caused confusion in the matter whether damages are entirely governed by the *lex fori*. However, some recent House of Lords decisions have clarified the position.[67] The English domestic law is based on the principles enunciated in two decisions, *Robinson* v. *Harman*[68] and *Hadley* v. *Baxendale*.[69] The rule of English private international law has been that the damages are generally governed by the *lex fori*. It is submitted that the confusion has arisen because of the failure to make a distinction between remoteness of liability and measure of damages.[70] The failure to make this distinction led to the belief that the entire matter of damages is governed by the *lex fori*. However, now it is clearly recognized that the question of damages is partly a question of substantive law and partly of procedural law. The former question, *viz.*, the remoteness of liability is a question of substance and therefore must be governed by the proper law of the transaction, while the latter question, *viz.* measure of damages and quantification of damages is procedural matter and hence is governed by the *lex fori*.

The question of remoteness of liability in contract cases was considered in *D'Almeida Araujo da.* v. *Becker & Co. Ltd.*[71] The plaintiff, merchants of Lisbon, agreed to sell 500 tons of palm oil to the defendants, a British company carrying on business in London. The contract was governed as to its substantial validity by the Portuguese law. On account of breach of contract by the defendants, the plaintiffs became liable to pay an indemnity amounting to £ 3,500 to a third party from whom plaintiffs have agreed to buy 500 tons of palm oil with a view to fulfil the contract entered into by them with the defendants. Under English law this amount was irrecoverable from the defendants as this liability was remote which could not have been foreseen by the parties, but under the Portuguese law it was not considered remote and was recoverable. Since the question of remoteness of damages is one of substance, the Portuguese law was applied by the court.[72]

66. Dicey and Morris, 1091.
67. See Chapter 22.
68. (1848) 1 Ex. 850.
69. (1854) 9 Ex. 341.
70. *D'Almeida Araujo da.* v. *Becker & Co.*, (1953) 2 Q.B. 329 per Pilcher, J.
71. (1953) 2 Q.B. 329.
72. *Ibid.*, at 338.

Similarly, it seems whether interest is payable upon a contractual debt and at what rate is also a matter of substance. In tort cases also the remoteness of liability is considered to be a question of substance.[73]

It also now seems to be fully established that measure of damages or quantification of damages is governed by the *lex fori.*[74] It is an established rule of English private international law that payment of damages cannot but be in English currency.[75] A question arises in those cases where the amount of damages is fixed by the parties in some foreign currency, as to whether the rate of exchange would be determined at the date when cause of action arose or when the court decreed the suit? The English court has taken the view that the date on which cause of action arose would be governing date.[76] To this rule two statutory exceptions exist which provide the governing date of the rate of exchange is the date of judgment.[77]

Execution

All matters relating to enforcement of judgments and orders and execution of decrees are governed by the *lex fori*. Under this head are included matters such as whether the judgment may be satisfied out of land or goods, whether the debts in the hands of third party can be attached, whether a receiver may be appointed and the like.

73. *Boys* v. *Chaplin*, (1969) 3 W.L.R. 322.
74. *Kohnke* v. *Karger*, (1951) 2 K.B. 670; *Boys* v. *Chaplin*, (1969) 3 W.L.R. 322.
75. *Re United Railways of Havana etc.* v. *First Pennsylvania Banking Co. etc.* (1961) A.C. 1007.
76. Re *United Railways of Havana etc.* v. *First Pennsylvania Co., etc.* cited above; *Madeleine Vionnet* v. *Wills*, (1940) 1 K.B. 72 (case of breach of contract); *Societe des Hotels Le Touguet-Paris-Plage* v. *Cummings*, (1922) 1 K.B. 451; *Graumann* v. *Treital*, (1940) 2 All. E.R. 188; *Re Russian Commercial and Industrial Bank*, (1955) Ch. 148 (cases of account); *Syndic in Bankruptcy of Khoury* v. *Khayat*, (1943) A.C. 507 (payment under a negotiable instrument).
77. Section 1(5), Carriage by Air Act, 1932; Foreign Judgments (Reciprocal Enforcement) Act, 1933, where a foreign judgment expressed in foreign currency is registered in England under s. 2(3).

24

STAY OF ACTIONS

Most countries of the world keep the doors of their courts of justice open to all and sundry litigants. This implies that a litigant is not only free to choose any country as a forum of his action, but can also pursue his remedy in more than one jurisdiction. In actions *in personam* this is very easy, since the service of process on the defendant within the jurisdiction (this may be done sometimes even when he is on casual visit) or without the jurisdiction (under special rules relating to service of summons on the defendant : writ may be served on him when he is outside the jurisdiction; or a substituted service may be effected on him) is enough to confer jurisdiction on the court. In our contemporary world the jurisdictional rules are very simple and very wide either under the internal rules of a country or under the international conventions, so that even in other actions, such as matrimonial proceedings,[1] an action can be filed in more than one country. Thus, in our contemporary world with easy means of communication and intercourse and with very wide and open jurisdictional rules, it has become possible for litigants to file legal proceedings on the same or substantially same subject-matter and between the same parties in more than one jurisdiction. The multiplicity of suits sometimes results in injustice. With a view to avoid injustice and inconvenience in such cases the domestic laws of practically every country lay down rules for stay of actions pending before it or for restraining a party from proceeding further with his action that he had filed in a foreign country.

The general rules for stay of actions have existed from the very beginning under the general law. But under the general rules the courts have exercised very wide discretion; in no case are they bound to stay actions. With the coming into force of the international convention on arbitration, for the first time it was accepted that in certain circumstances the court has no discretion but to stay suits. With the widening of jurisdiction in matrimonial

1. For instance, Schedule 1 to the Domicile and Matrimonial Proceedings Act, 1973 confers jurisdiction on the English courts to stay matrimonial proceedings. See Part III of this Chapter.

causes under the recent international convention, the need for specific provision for stay of legal action arose.[2] Thus, in this Chapter we would discuss the following three types of stays :

(a) Stay of actions under general law,

(b) Stay of action in reference to arbitration agreements, and

(c) Stay in matrimonial proceedings.

I

STAY UNDER GENERAL LAW

English Law

Under English law the matter has three aspects : (i) stay of English proceedings when proceedings are already pending in a foreign court or restraining proceedings in a foreign court when proceedings are pending in an English court; (ii) stay of English proceedings when no proceedings are pending in a foreign court; and (iii) restraining the enforcement of foreign judgments. This first case is covered by what is called, the doctrine of *lis alibi pendens*. The doctrine applies to two situations : (a) when the same plaintiff files two actions, one in English court and the other in a foreign court; and (b) when the plaintiff in the English action is a defendant in a foreign action filed by the defendant or *vice versa*. The doctrine of *lis alibi pendens* comes into application only when two simultaneous actions are pending, one in an English court and the other in a foreign court, when both the actions are between the same parties, and when same or similar issues are involved and the same or similar relief is sought in both actions. In an old English case it was observed : "Where a plaintiff sues the same defendant in respect of the same cause of action in two courts, one in this country and another abroad, there is a jurisdiction in the court of this country to act in one of the three ways—to put the party so suing to his election, to stay all proceedings in this country or to stay all proceedings in the foreign country."[3] In this context, it should be noted that 'staying of foreign proceedings' does not mean the same thing as staying domestic proceedings. It means restraining the plaintiff by an injunction from prosecuting the proceedings in the foreign country. This does not mean that the foreign court is asked to stay proceedings pending before it.

The jurisdiction to stay proceedings in all the aforesaid three cases is exercised reluctantly and sparingly. Just because a person has started two proceedings, one in a domestic court and the other

2. Thus under the Protocol on Arbitration Clauses requires that if there are arbitrations clauses in an agreement that a suit in violation of the same must be stayed.

3. *The Christianburg*, (1885) 10 P.D. 141 at 152.

in a foreign court is no reason to stay the domestic proceedings.[4] It may be that both proceedings are justified. For instance, a plaintiff may be entitled to one remedy in the domestic court, and a different remedy in the foreign court; or the domestic judgment may be enforceable against some defendants, while the foreign judgment may be enforceable against others.[5] The courts are even more reluctant to stay or restrain proceedings when in one court the proceedings are started by the plaintiff and the other by the defendant. In *The Janera*,[6] the court observed : "The Court ought not to stay a plaintiff in the courts of this country on the ground that he happens to be a defendant elsewhere." *Sealay* v. *Callan*,[7] illustrates the extreme reluctance of the court to stay the action. A wife, domiciled in Natal and resident in England filed a petition for divorce in an English court against her husband who was domiciled and resident in Natal. The husband put up appearance in protest before the English Court and later on he launched divorce proceedings in a Natal Court. He then applied to the English Court for stay of English proceedings. Despite the plea of the husband that English divorce would not be recognized in Natal and elsewhere being not a divorce pronounced by the court of domicile and therefore he would be driven to continue his Natal proceedings and thus would have to incur double expenses unnecessarily, the court refused to stay the proceedings, as it felt that the defendant had failed to satisfy the court that the wife would not get any advantage from English proceedings; on the contrary the maintenance that she is entitled to in English proceedings, she would not get in Natal proceedings.

The criterion that English Courts have developed for stay of proceedings of any type—when two simultaneous suits are pending in two courts or only one action is pending which is sought to be stayed—is that it must be proved to be vexatious or oppressive in point of fact. The matter is now governed by S. 41, Supreme Court of Judicature (Consolidation) Act, 1925. In *St. Pierre* v. *South America Stores Ltd.*[8] the following tests have been propounded :

"(1) A mere balance of convenience is not a sufficient ground for depriving a plaintiff of the advantage of prosecuting his action in an English Court if it is otherwise properly brought. The right of action to King's court must not be lightly refused. (2) In order to justify a stay two conditions must be satisfied, one positive and the other negative : (a) the defendant must satisfy the court that the continuance of the action would work an injustice because it would be oppressive or vexatious to him

4. *Peruvian Guano Co.* v. *Bockwoult*, (1883) 23 Ch. D. 225; *Cohen* v. *Rothfield*, (1919) 1 K.B. 410.
5. *McHenry* v. *Lewis*, (1882) 22 Ch. 397.
6. (1928) p. 55.
7. (1953) p. 135.
8. (1936) 1 K.B. 382.

or would be an abuse of the process of the court in some other way; and (b) the stay must not cause an injustice to the plaintiff. On both the burden of proof is on the defendant."[9]

Thus, the defendant must show that that continuance of both actions is oppressive or vexatious or. embarrassing. Each case would depend upon its circumstances. *Egbert* v. *Short*[10] and *Re Norton's Settlement*[11] illustrate how the court exercises jurisdiction in favour of the defendant. In both the cases the defendant was resident in India and had come to England for a short visit. In both the cases summons were served upon them when they were on such visit. In each case action was not brought *bona fide* for the purpose of obtaining justice but for the purpose of annoying and harassing the defendant. In each case it would have been great injustice and inconvenience to the defendant to fight the action in England. A hypothetical case was thus put up by Sir Gorell Bannes, P. in *Logan* v. *Bank of Scotland.*[12] "A dispute of complicated character had arisen between two foreigners in a foreign country, and one of them were made defendant in an action in this country by serving him with a writ while he happens to be here for a few days' visit. I apprehended that, although there would be jurisdiction in the court to entertain the suit, it would have little hesitation in treating the action as vexatious for staying it."[13]

The question came and consideration before the courts of Appeal in *Maharanee of Baroda* v. *Wildenstein.*[14] In 1965 the plaintiff, Maharanee of Baroda bought in Paris from the defendant, an art dealer a painting said to be by French painter, Boncher, for a sum of £ 32,920. The painting was delivered to the plaintiff at her home in Paris. In July 1966, Maharanee of Baroda brought the painting to England, where two art experts expressed the opinion that the paintings was not by Boncher. On September 3, 1969, Maharanee of Baroda issued a writ in England against the defendant claiming rescission of the contract of sale, repayment of the price paid and damage. The writ was served on the detendant while he was on a visit to England in June 1970 to attend Ascot races. The defendant applied for stay of action and for getting the writ set aside on the ground that to continue the England action would be oppressive and vexatious and inconvenient to him. Both the parties lived in Paris. Both had also close association with England and with some other countries. The plaintiff frequently visited England for long periods for social reasons, and horses from her stud in Holland were trained in

9. *Ibid.*, at p. 398.
10. (1907) 2 Ch. 205.
11. (1908) 1 Ch. 471.
12. No. 2, (1906) 1 K.B. 141.
13. *Ibid.*, at 152.
14. (1972) 2 All. E.R. 689.

England. When the action commenced the defendant was the principal director of a firm of art dealers; he also had studs in Ireland from time to time he came over to England for races. Lord Denning said that the main issue in the action was whether the painting was genuine Boucher or not. This issue was one of fact and which was crucial to both under the English law and French law. It was not solely a French issue. "The art world is so international in character today that this issue has itself something of an international character. The parties on either side are citizens of world. . . furthermore, there might be difficulties, if not injustice, in requiring the Maharanee to go to France and to seek redress. We are told that the courts of France appoint their own court experts and might hesitate about receiving the opinion of experts from England. It would be a matter for their discretion. . . .It is true that even in England there may be difficulties. It appears that both experts for the Maharanee are not willing to give evidence and may have to be subpoenaed. But there would be no difficulty in Mr. Wittenstein's expert, such as Professor Ananoff, giving evidence here orally with all the advantages that are carried with it. So there is no injustice in that regard in leaving it tried in England. Apart from the admission of evidence, there is then question of delay."[15] In conclusion His Lordship said that weighing one thing with another, it appears that the case can be tried quickly, fairly and properly in England.

The court also exercises jurisdiction for stay of action in those cases where the parties have under a contract stipulated to confer jurisdiction on the courts of a particular country and in contravention to that stipulation a party file an action in the court of another country. In *The Fehmarn*[16] the court observed : "It is well established that, where there is a provision in a contract for providing that disputes are referred to foreign tribunal, then *prima facie*, this court will stay proceedings instituted in the country in breach of such agreement and will only allow them to proceed when it is satisfied that it is just and proper to do so." It should be kept in view that the ground on which stay is granted is not that the continuance of the suit would be vexatious or oppressive but that courts make people to abide by their contracts. In *The Eleftheria*[17] that defendant prayed for the stay of the plaintiff's suit on the averment that under the terms of the contract, in the event of a dispute between the parties the suit is to be filed in the court of the country which is the principal place of business of the carrier. The central place of business of carrier was Athens. Brandon, J., said that in such matters this court was not bound to grant a stay, but had a discretion whether to do so or not. The learned judge further observed that the discretion should be exercised by granting a stay unless strong cause for not

15. *Ibid.*, at p. 693-694.
16. (1958) 1 W.L.R. 159.
17. (1969) 2 W.L.R. 1073.

doing so is shown, the burden of proving such strong cause being on the plaintiff. Granting the stay, the court said the plaintiffs have not been able to establish a good cause for not staying the suit.[18] In *Law* v. *Garrett*,[19] a partnership agreement for trading in Russia provided that 'all disputes shall be referred to the St. Petersburg Commercial Court' whose decision shall be final. One of the partners brought an action in England. The court stayed the action. On the other hand, the court of Appeal, refused to grant stay in *The Fehmarn*.[20] Under a contract, turpentine was to be shipped from a Russian port to London in a German ship. The contract contained a term under which all disputes were to be judged in the Soviet Union under the Soviet law. One of the consignees filed an action in an English court on the averment that turpentine was contaminated on delivery. All the witnesses of the plaintiff resided in England; the German ship regularly traded in England and most of the witnesses including owners could be conveniently examined in England. The court rejecting the prayer of the defendant for stay said that balance of convenience was in favour of the trial of action in the English court.

In *Mac-Shannon* v. *Rockware Glass Ltd.*[21] the House of Lords has laid down the following two conditions necessary for the stay of action:

(a) The defendant must satisfy the Court that there is another forum to whose jurisdiction he was amenable in which justice could be done at substantially less inconvenience and expenses, and

(b) the say would not deprive the plaintiff of a legitimate personal or juridical advantage which would be available to him in England.

In *Continental Bank* v. *Aeokos Cia Naviera*,[21a] the question was where in a contract there was an exclusive jurisdiction clause, an action filed in a different court should by stayed. The ECE Convention was also referred to. The Court granted in injunction in the matter as it felt that injunction was the only effective remedy in this case.

In *Neste Chemicals* v. *D.K. Lines*,[21b] the court granted stay of proceeding on the principle that the court first seized of the matter will have precedence.

Indian Law

Section 10, Civil Procedure Code deals with stay of suits. The section runs, "No court shall proceed with the trial of any suit in which the matter in issue is also directly and substantially in issue in a previously instituted suit between the same parties, or between parties under whom they or any of them claim litigating under the same time where such suit is pending in the same or any other court in India having jurisdiction to grant the relief claimed, or in any court beyond the limits of India established or continued by the Central Government and having like jurisdiction, or before the Supreme Court." It is evident that S. 10 cannot apply when the final decision in the previous suit would not operate as *res judicata* in the subsequent suit and where the parties

18. See also *Mackender* v. *Feldia*, (1967) 2 Q.B. 590; *Unterweser Reederei* v. *Zapata Off Shore Co.*, (1968) 2 Lloyd's Rep. 158.
19. (1878) 8 Ch. D. 26.
20. (1958) 1 W.L.R. 159.
21. (1886) 1 W.L.R. 286.
21a. (1994) 2 All ER 540. Earlier precidents have been referred.
21b. (1994) 3 All ER 180.

in both the suits are not the same or claiming under the previous parties. The object of this provision is to prevent courts of concurrent jurisdiction from simultaneously entertaining and adjudicating upon two parallel litigations in respect of the same cause of action, the same subject-matter and thc same relief and to obviate the possibility of two contradictory verdicts by one and the same court in respect of the same relief.[22] Suit may also be stayed on the ground of Constructive *res judicata*.[23] Under section 10 it is the second suit which is to be stayed and the court has no power to stay the previous suit. It is also evident that if conditions laid down in section 10 are fulfilled the court has no option but to stay the second suit. In this regard Indian law differs from English law where the court is invested with a very wide discretion.

Section 10, Civil Procedure Code applies to purely domestic suits. In respect to international cases Explanation to Section 10 merely lays down as under : "The pendency of a suit in a foreign court does not preclude the courts in India from trying a suit founded on the same cause of action." Section 10, Civil Procedure Code does not deal with the courts power of staying a domestic suit when a suit is pending in a foreign court or the courts power of restraining by injunction or otherwise a suit pending in foreign court. The Explanation merely lays down that if a suit is pending in a foreign court, the Indian courts can proceed with the subsequently filed suit in the Indian court. However, the Indian courts have exercised the power of staying domestic suit when a suit is pending in a foreign court or of restraining a foreign suit pending there under the inherent powers under s. 151, Civil Procedure Code.[24]

In *Nath Bank Ltd.* v. *Andhar Manick Tea Co. Ltd.*[25] the Calcutta High Court said that where a suit is pending in an Indian Court and a party who is within the jurisdiction is proceeding with another suit on the same cause of action in a foreign country, the court has power of restraining him from continuing his suit in the foreign country, if the prosecution of such action would be contrary to equity. The court said that the principle is that the courts act *in personam* and will not suffer any one within its reach to do what is contrary to its notions of equity, merely because the act to be done may be, in point of locality, beyond its

22. *Balkishan* v. *Kishanlal*, (1889) 11 All. 148; *F.E. Dinshaw* v. *J.C. Galstaun*, 1927 Bom. 245; *Jinnat Bibi* v. *Howrah Jute Mill Co. Ltd.*, 1932 Cal. 751; *Laxmi Bank Ltd.* v. *Harikishan*, 1948 Nag. 297; *Naurati* v. *Mehma Singh*. 1972 P. & H. 421.

23. *Life Pharmaceuticals (Private) Ltd.* v. *Bengal Medical Hall*, 1971 Cal. 345.

24. See *Jethabhai Versey & Co.* v. *Amarchand*, 1924 Bom. 90; *Bhagat Singh* v. *Dewan Jagbir Sawhney*, 1941 Cal, 670,

25. 1960 Cal. 779.

jurisdiction.[26] In a Punjab case, an application for winding up of company was filed in the Lahore High Court before partition. After partition a second application was made before the East Punjab High Court, while the first application was pending. It was held that though under the High Court (Punjab) Order, the Lahore High Court continued to possess jurisdiction over the pending application, the applicant should not be refused relief.[27] In *Jethabhai* v. *Amar Chand*[28] the plaintiff filed a suit for damages for the breach of a contract. The contract was entered into in Rangoon and the instructions in respect of the transaction were issued in Rangoon and the money in respect of these transactions were paid in Rangoon and the goods were delivered in Rangoon. All account books, relating to transactions were also in Rangoon. The court held that stay of suit pending before it could be granted. It was observed that the stay would not result in any injustice to plaintiff but the continuance of suit would result in injustice and inconvenience to the defendant; the suit would be vexatious and oppressive to him, while if the suit is filed in a Rangoon court neither party would suffer any inconvenience or harassment. The court quoted with approval the following passages in *Logan* v. *Bank of Scotland*.[29] The court will stay an action, brought within the jurisdiction, in respect of a cause of action arising out of the jurisdiction if satisfied that no injustice will be done thereby to the plaintiff and that the defendant would be subject to such injustice in defending the action as would amount to a vexation and oppression to which he would not be subjected if an action brought, in another and accessible court, where the cause of action arose."

The Indian courts (just as English Courts do) exercise jurisdiction for stay of action in those cases where under the terms of a contract parties have agreed to refer all their disputes to the courts of a particular country and are the parties in contravention of that term file a legal proceeding in the court of another country.

The question has come before the Indian courts in several cases. In *Moti Bhai Gulal Chand & Co.* v. *Laxmi Cotton Mills Ltd.*,[30] the contract stipulated that disputes arising under the contract would be adjudicated by Bombay Courts. The Bombay High Court said that such a contract was enforceable. In *Marittima Italiana Steamship Co.* v. *Burjor Framroz Rustomji*[31] the contract stipulated that all disputes will be decided by Italian courts. The court held that the stipulation was enforceable and

26. See also *Kn Pr. Periakararuppan Chettiar* v. *R.M.S.R.M. Ramaswami*, 1928 Mad. 491; *V.R. Naik* v. *Balwant Sitaram*, 1927 Bom. 135; *Bhagat Singh* v. *Dewan Jagbir Sawhney*, 1941 Cal. 670 (court has inherent jurisdiction to grant stay).
27. *Ladli Prasad* v. *Karnal Distillery Co. Ltd.*, 1954 Punj. 94.
28. 1924 Bom. 90.
29. (1906) 1 K.B. 141.
30. 91 Cal. L.J. 1.
31. 1930 Bom. 185; *Yadao Ghirnikar* v. *Krishnaji*, 1928 Nag. 56.

granted the stay of the Indian suit. The same question came before the Calcutta High Court in *M/s. Lloyds Triestino Societa Per Azinni di Navigazione Sede in Triesta* v. *M/s. Laxmi Narayan*[32] the court observed that the covenant in the contract conferring jurisdiction on Italian court did not contravene the provision of s. 28, Contract Act, as the Italian Courts have jurisdiction to try the suit in an ordinary manner. The court should in appropriate cases enforce such covenants. On appeal the Calcutta High Court observed : "The court acts upon the principle that in general the court will compel the parties to abide by their contract. And if on a consideration of all the circumstances of the case the court comes to the conclusion that it will be unjust or unfair to stay the suit, it may refuse to grant the stay asked for but not otherwise."[33] In *Dayawhla & Sons Private Ltd.* v. *M/s. Invest Import*,[34] M/s. Ramji Dayawahla & Sons entered into a contract with Invest Import Corporation of Yugoslavia under which they agreed for the erection of two complete radiation type steam-boilers for a thermal power station at Baranni. There was an arbitration agreement between the parties which was to be adjudicated by the International Chamber of Commerce at Paris. It was also one of the stipulations of the contract that all aspects of contract will be governed by the Yugoslavian law. On some disputes arising between the parties, M/s. Ramji Dayawahla filed a suit for damages in a Calcutta Court. The defendants prayed for the stay of suit. Granting the stay, the court observed : "It is, therefore, not only commonsense but also common honesty that no attempt should be made, or if made countenanced, to flee the terms of the contract except in exceptional circumstances which we do not see upon the whole of materials we have had, put before us."[35]

These may be situations when despite the stipulation in the contract conferring jurisdiction in a foreign court, the court may not consider it proper to give it effect and therefore may refuse to stay the suit. An instance of this is provided by *Michael Golodetz* v. *Serajuddin & Co.*[36] Shah, J., enunciated the principle thus : Ordinarily courts require the parties to resort to the forum contemplated by them in their contract for resolving their disputes. This is not because the court regards itself bound to abdicate its jurisdiction over a dispute within its cognizance, but it seeks to promote the sanctity of contracts and for that purpose stays the suit. The jurisdiction of the court to try the dispute remains there, but court's discretion is interposed on grounds of equity. It follows that the court is not bound to grant stay just because a

32. 1959 Cal. 669.
33. *M/s Laxminarayan Ramnivas* v. *Lloyd Triestino etc.*, 1960 Cal. 155.
34. 70 C.W.N. 199.
35. *Ibid.*, at p. 233. *See also* *Rungta Sons Private Ltd.* v. *Jugometal Trg. Republike*, 1959 Cal. 423; *Juggilal Kamlapat* v. *N.V. International Credit-en-Ilandels Vereeninging Rotterdam*, 58 C.W.N. 730.
36. 1963 S.C. 1044.

contract stipulates to confer jurisdiction on another court. In this case an agreement between an Indian firm and an American company for supply of manganese ore contained an arbitration clause under which arbitration of all disputes were to be held at New York according to American Arbitration Association Rules. When a dispute arose the Indian party filed a suit in a Calcutta Court and the American Company sought its stay. The proper law of the contract was Indian law, all evidence was in India. Furthermore, there was difficulty about foreign exchange which practically rendered it impossible for the Indian party to attend or take witnesses to New York. This would result in injustice to the Indian party. The court refused to grant injunction.

Similarly, in *Far East Steamship Line, Vladivostok, U.S.S.R.* v. *The Union of India*[37] the Madras High Court refused to exercise its discretion to grant stay of suit. In this case a contract between the Union of India and a Russian Shipping company provided for determination of disputes by the Russian court. The Madras High Court said the claim being small (of Rs. 5000 only) and the expenses involved in driving the Union of India to the Russian court would far exceed the amount of the claim, the present suit would not cause any prejudice to the Russian party. The court observed : "While normally parties should be bound by their contract, the rule has exceptions founded not merely on balance of convenience, but on considerations to meet the ends of justice in particular circumstances. In our opinion, the Court has the discretion which will, of course, be exercised after weighing the pros and cons of all the circumstances taken together."[38]

II

ARBITRATION AGREEMENT AND STAY OF LEGAL PROCEEDINGS

English law

Section 4 of the Arbitration Act, 1950 deals with stay of legal proceedings when an agreement stipulates for arbitrations. The section contains : (a) Discretionary power of the court to stay actions. This is the common law power of the courts to stay actions when parties have agreed to settle their disputes by arbitration.[39] (b) Mandatory power of the court to stay legal proceedings. This relates to those agreements to which the International Protocol on Arbitration Clauses applies.[40] Here the court has no discretion but to stay proceedings.

37. (1972) 2 M.L.J. 578.
38. *Ibid.*, at 580.
39. Originally the provision was enacted in s. 11 of the Common Law Procedure Act, 1854, from where it was re-enacted in s. 4, Arbitration Act, 1889 and from there to the present Act.
40. Originally this provision was enacted in s. 1, Arbitration Causes (Protocol) Act, 1924 which was passed to carry out the Protocol on Arbitration

Discretionary Power : Sub-section (1) of s. 4, Arbitration Act, 1950 enacts this common law power of the court in the following terms :

> If any party to an arbitration agreement or any person claiming through or under him, commences any legal proceedings in any court against any other party to the agreement, or any person claiming through or under him, in respect of any matter agreed to be referred, any party to those legal proceedings may at any time after appearance and before delivering any pleadings or taking any other step in the proceedings, apply to that court to stay the proceedings, and the court or a judge thereof, if satisfied that there is no sufficient reason why the matter should not be referred in accordance with the agreement and that the applicant was, at the time when proceedings were commenced and still remains, ready and willing to do all things necessary to the proper conduct of the arbitration, may make an order staying the proceedings.

The power under the sub-section is a discretionary power which the court may exercise whenever a legal action is filed in breach of an arbitration agreement. It is immaterial that the agreement to refer disputes to arbitration is governed by English law or foreign law and irrespective of the fact whether the parties are citizens of the United Kingdom or alien. But it is necessary that the arbitration agreement is "a written agreement to submit present and future differences to arbitration."[41]

An application for stay under the sub-section may be made at any time after appearance and before delivery of pleadings or taking any other step in the proceedings; the application cannot be made later. The basic principle is that people must abide by their contracts and the courts should respect the sanctity of agreements. This implies that once an agreement to arbitrate is shown, the burden of proof is on the plantiff to show why proceedings should not be stayed.[42] Whether the arbitration clause is wide enough to include the dispute in respect of which proceedings have been filed is a question of interpretation and must be decided by the proper law of the contract. That law will also determine whether the arbitration clause will apply when one of the parties alleges that the contract is void or voidable or has become void. When the court exercises its power to stay proceedings it is not concerned nor does it enquire whether under the law governing arbitration or under the proper law of the contract, the foreign court has or

Clauses of September 24, 1923. It was then amended by s. 8 Arbitration (Foreign Awards) Act, 1930. From there the provision has been re-enacted in the present section.

41. Section 32, Arbitration Act, 1950.

42. *Bristol Corporation* v. *John Aird & Co.*, (1913) A.C. 241.

has not the power to grant stay.[43]

The discretionary power of stay can be exercised only in respect of an arbitration agreement which does not fall under sub-section (2).[44]

Mandatory Power : Sub-section (2) of s. 4, Arbitration Act, 1950 was inserted to give effect to the Protocol on Arbitration Clauses of September 23, 1923. The provisions runs thus :

"(1) Upon application by any party to the proceedings the court will make an order staying any legal proceedings commenced by any party to a submission to arbitration made in pursuance of an agreement to which the International Protocol on Arbitration Clauses of September 24, 1923, applies, against any other party to the submission in respect of any matter agreed to be referred to arbitration, unless the court is satisfied that the agreement or arbitration has become inoperative or cannot proceed or that there is not in fact any dispute between the parties with regard to the matter agreed to be referred.

(2) The International Protocol on Arbitration Clauses of September 24, 1923 applies when the parties :

(a) are subject to the jurisdiction of different States between which that Protocol is in force; and

(b) have agreed to submit to arbitration present or future differences in connection with a contract relating to commercial or other matters capable of settlement by arbitration, whether or not the arbitration is to take place in a country to whose jurisdiction none of the parties is subject."[45]

Under this sub-section the court has no discretion and is duty bound to stay proceedings if a party relies on 'submission to arbitration made in pursuance of an agreement to which the Protocol applies'. "Submission to arbitration" includes an agreement to refer present or future disputes to arbitration. Even if no arbitrators have been appointed, the court is under a duty to stay proceedings. The submission of a dispute to arbitration is not a condition precedent to the application of sub-section (2). An agreement to submit the dispute or actual submission of the dispute to arbitration is enough.[46] The sub-section applies only to

43. But See *Municipal Council of Johannesburg* v. *D. Stewart & Co.*, (1909) S.C. 53 (H.L.); the decision was explained in *Heyman* v. *Darwins Ltd.*, (1942) A.C. 356.

44. The sub-section also applies to the Washington Convention for settlement of International Investment Disputes, although the Arbitration Act, 1950 does not in general apply to it.

45. This is as formulated by Dicey and Morris in Rule 182, pp. 1073-1074.

46. The Merak, (1965), p. 223. Before this decision there was some controversy on the words used in Article 4 to which effect has been given in

commercial matters or any other matter capable of settlement by arbitration. As under sub-section (1) so also under this sub-section the application for stay should be made at any time after the appearance and before the delivery of pleading or taking any other step in the proceedings, but not later.[47] The sub-section applies to the parties which are subject to the jurisdiction of two different Contracting Parties, i.e. the parties reside or do business in two different states (though both the states should be parties to the Protocol). The stay of proceedings can be refused only on one ground : if the court is satisfied that the agreement or arbitration has become inoperative or cannot proceed or that there is not, in fact, a dispute between the parties.[48]

Indian Law

Under the Indian law the matter is covered under three statutes : the Arbitration Act, 1940, the Arbitration (Protocol and Convention) Act, 1937 (the Act was passed to give effect to the Protocol on Arbitration Clauses of September 24, 1923 to which India is a party), and the Foreign Awards (Recognition and Enforcement) Act, 1961 (which was enacted to give effect to the Convention on the Recognition and Enforcement of Foreign Arbitral Awards passed at New York on June 10, 1958, to which India is a party). Under the Arbitration Act, 1940 the court's power of stay of legal proceedings is discretionary power, while under the latter two statutes the court's power is mandatory : if an agreement to arbitrate exists then the court has no discretion but to grant stay.

Discretionary Power : Section 34 of the Arbitration Act, 1940 deals with the court's power of staying legal proceedings. That section runs as under :

> Where any party to an arbitration agreement or any person claiming under him commences any legal proceedings against any other party to the agreement or any person claiming under him in respect of any matter agreed to be referred, any party to such legal proceedings may, at any time before filing a written statement or taking any other steps in the proceedings, apply to the judicial authority before which the

s. 4(2), Arbitration Act, 1950, 'submission' to arbitration means actual submission of dispute to arbitrators or more agreement to submit will be enough. See *Radio Publicity Ltd.* v. *Compagnie de Luxembourgeoise de Radiodifusion*, (1936) 2 All E.R. 721.

47. First Schedule, Article 1.

48. Here the question may be whether the matter will be governed by the proper law of the arbitration agreement (this is the logical view to take) or the law governing the arbitration proceedings (which is equally logical). But, it seems, if party argues before the English court for refusing stay, then it will be for the English court to determine and it may as well apply the *lex fori*. See *Mavani* v. *Ralli Bros. Ltd.*, (1973) 1 W.L.R. 468 (courts powers to make order for security and costs.)

proceedings are pending to stay the proceedings; and if satisfied that there is no sufficient reason why the matter should not be referred in accordance with the arbitration agreement and that the applicant was, at the time when proceedings were commenced, and still remains, ready and willing to do all things necessary to the proper conduct of the arbitration, such authority may make an order staying the proceedings.

It is obvious that the section modelled on the English statute and almost a verbatim copy of the same. The court's power under s. 34 is discretionary power and a party cannot claim stay of proceedings as a matter of right.[49] The discretion, however, is to be exercised judicially. In *Michael Golodetiz* v. *Serajuddin & Co.*[50] the Supreme Court said that the provision of s. 34 applies even when there is a covenant to refer a matter to foreign arbitration tribunal.[51] Enunciating the principle, Shah, J. observed : "Where a party to an arbitration agreement commences an action for determination of a matter agreed to be referred under an arbitration agreement, the court normally favours stay of action leaving the plantiff to resort to the tribunal chosen by the parties for adjudication. The court in such a case is unwilling to countenance, unless there are sufficient reasons, breach of the solemn obligation to seek resort to the tribunal selected by him, if the other party thereto still remains ready and willing to do all things necessary for the proper conduct of the arbitration. This rule applies to arbitration by tribunals, foreign as well as domestic." His Lordship further observed that this is done not because the court finds itself bound to abdicate its jurisdiction in respect of disputes within its cognizance; it merely seeks to promote the sanctity of contracts and for that purpose stays the suit. The learned judge then said : "The jurisdiction of the court to try the suit remains undisputed : but the discretion of court is on grounds of equity interposed. The court is therefore not obliged to grant a stay merely because the parties have even under a commercial contract agreed to submit their disputes in a matter to an arbitration tribunal." In this case the Supreme Court agreed with the Calcutta High Court and refused to grant stay.[52] In *Rungta Sons Private Ltd.* v. *Jugometal Trg. Republike*[53] the court granted stay of proceedings on these facts : under a contract between an Indian Company and a Yugoslavia Company parties agreed to refer their disputes arising under their contract to arbitration to a Zurich tribunal. On the plantiff arguing that it would be difficult for him

49. *Printers (Mysore) Private Ltd.* v. *Pothan Joseph*, 1960 S.C. 1156.

50. 1963 S.C. 1044.

51. See the earlier cases where the same view was expressed; *Haji Abdulla* v. *George*, 1924 Bom. 381; *Maritime Italiana Steumship Co.* v. *Burjor Framroze, Rustomji* 1930 Bom. 185.

52. It may be interesting to note that the single judge had granted the stay : *Michel Golodetz* v. *Serajuddin & Co.*, 1959 Cal 603.

53. 1959 Cal. 423.

to produce evidence at Zurich, the court said that there was no reason why necessary evidence could not be given at Zurich, the mere fact that parties may have to incur large costs in the arbitration held at Zurich is no sufficient reason for not staying the proceedings filed in India.

The requirements under s. 34 of Arbitration Act, 1940 are the same as under its English counterpart, s. 4(1) Arbitration Act, 1950.

Mandatory Power : Section 3 of the Arbitration (Protocol and Convention) Act, 1937 deals with the stay of proceedings when the Protocol on Arbitration Clauses apply to an agreement. The section runs as under :

> Notwithstanding anything contained in the Indian Arbitration Act, 1899 [which has been replaced by the Act of 1940] or in the Code of Civil Procedure, 1908, if any party to a submission made in pursuance of an agreement to which the Protocol set forth in the First Schedule as modified by the reservation subject to which it was signed by India applies, or any person claiming through or under him, commences any legal proceedings in any court against any other party to the submission or any person claiming through or under him in respect of any matter agreed to be referred, any party to such legal proceedings may, at any time after appearance and before filing written statement or taking any other steps in the proceedings, apply to the court to stay the proceedings; and the court unless satisfied that the agreement or arbitration has become imperative or cannot proceed, or that there is not in fact any dispute between the parties with regard to the matter agreed to be referred, shall make an order staying the proceedings.

This section is almost a verbatim copy of s. 4(2) of the English Arbitration Acts. The International Protocol on Arbitration Clauses applies on the satisfaction of the following two conditions : (i) when parties are subject to the jurisdiction of different states between whom the protocol is in force, and (ii) when parties have agreed to submit to arbitration present or future disputes in connection with a contract relating to commercial matters capable of settlement by arbitration.

Section 3 of the Foreign Awards (Recognition and Enforcement) Act, 1961 also related to stay of proceedings was a verbatim copy of s. 3 of the Arbitration (Protocol and Convention) Act, 1937 before its amendment in 1973.[54] The position under the Indian statutes of 1937 and 1961 and under the English statute of 1950, s. 4(2) relating to stay of action is the same *viz.*, once the requirements of the respective sections are satisfied the court has no discretion in the matter and is bound to stay proceedings. In

54. *CUSID Inc.* v. *Steel Authority of India*, 1986 Del. 8.

Rawsagar Power Co. Ltd. v. *General Electric Co.*,[55] the Supreme Court has held that the provision is mandatory. It may be recalled that in English law, before the decision of the court in *The Merak*[56] in 1965, there was a judicial difference of opinion as to whether under s. 4(2) an actual reference to arbitration was necessary or as to whether mere agreement to arbitration was enough. This difference of opinion was resolved (it is submitted rightly) by the decision in *The Merak*[56a] which laid down that actual reference to arbitration was not necessary, an agreement to refer the dispute to arbitration was enough. However, in 1959 the Calcutta High Court[57] and in 1971 the Supreme Court took a different view. In the Calcutta case[58] Chakravarti, J. observed : "It is arbitration agreement made between parties belonging to jurisdiction of different States that the Protocol recognizes and what s. 3 of the Act contemplates is obviously an actual reference to arbitration made in pursuance of one such agreement. Whatever words may be substituted for the word 'submission' in s. 3, it is impossible to escape the effect of the words 'made in pursuance of an agreement to which the Protocol . . . applies'.[59] If the agreement to which Protocol applies is an agreement for arbitration, there cannot possibly be an agreement in pursuance of that agreement. Section 3 must, therefore, be construed as contemplating a case where not only is there an arbitration agreement in force between the parties, but there has also been an actual reference to arbitration." This decision and these observations are based on the *obiter* opinion expressed by Clanson, J. in *Radio Publicity (Universal) Ltd.* v. *Compagnie Luxembourgeoise de Radiodifusion.*[60] It may be noticed that one of the reasons (and it is submitted the main and very sound reason) which prevailed in *The Merak* was that by construing 'submission to arbitration' as an actual submission of an existing dispute to a particular arbitrator would make 'nonsense of the Protocol'. This has been noted by Grover, J. in the Supreme Court case. Yet, Grover, J. insisted to take the other view, as his Lordship thought that "if statutory enactments are clear in meaning, they must be construed according to their meaning even though they are contrary to the comity of nations or international law."[61] His Lordship went on in this strain : "If the terms of legislative enactments do not suffer from any ambiguity or lack of clarity they must be given effect to even if they do not carry out the treaty obligations."[62] The learned judge showed his awareness

55. 1985 S.C. 1156.
56. (1965) p. 223.
56a. *Ibid.*
57. *W. Wood & Sons Ltd.* v. *Bengal Corporation*, 1959 Cal. 8.
58. *V/O Tractorexport* v. *Tarapore & Co.*, 1971 S.C. 1.
59. But see *Ramji Dayawala & Sons* v. *Invest Import* 1981 S.C. 2085.
60. (1936) 2 All E.R. 721.
61. 1971 S.C. 1 at 8.
62. *Ibid.* 8 and 9.

of the fact that the view propounded by him would hamper (rather frustrate) in carrying out the purpose and object behind the protocol, but such was the attachment of his Lordship to the mechanical jurisprudence that he felt compelled to take the view which, to use the words of Scarman, J., made "nonsense of the Protocol".[63]

Since the Supreme Court judgment made nonsense of the Protocol, section 3 was amended by the Parliament in 1973. The amended section runs :

> Notwithstanding anything contained in the Arbitration Act, 1940 or in the Code of Civil Procedure, 1908, if any party to an agreement to which Article II of the Convention set forth in Schedule applies, or any person claiming through or under him commences any legal proceedings in any court against any other party to the agreement or any person claiming through or under him in respect of any matter agreed to be referred to arbitration in such agreement, any party to such legal proceedings may, at any time after appearance and before filing a written statement or taking any other step in the proceedings, apply to the court to stay the proceedings and the court unless satisfied that the agreement is null and void, inoperative or incapable of being performed or that there is not, in fact, any dispute between the parties with regard to the matter agreed to be referred, shall make an order staying the proceedings.

The other conditions of the application of the provisions of stay are the same as under English law which have already been summarized. But the transaction must be a commercial one. A contract for the supply of technical know-how on payment of fee is not a commercial transaction[64] Charter-party contact for carriage of goods by sea is a commercial contract.[65]

III

STAYING OF MATRIMONIAL PROCEEDINGS

The power of the English court to grant stay in matrimonial proceedings have been very scanty and have been exercised in a very exceptional case. The English matrimonial court has exercised the power of staying English proceedings in a case where the husband plaintiff has failed to make payment under a maintenance order *pedente lite*.[66] As has already been in Part I of this Chapter

63. See for critical analysis of the judgment: Upendra Baxi, *Goodbye to Unification ? The Indian Supreme Court and the United Nations Arbitration Convention*, (1973) Journal of the Indian Law Institute, 358-370.
64. *Josef Meisaurer GMBR & Co.* v. *Kanoria Chemicals*, 1986 Cal. 45.
65. *Union of India* v. *N.V. Hoegh Ordeid*, 1983 Guj. 34.
66. See *Curtis* v. *Curtis*, (1868) 38 L.J.P. & M. 9.

the English courts have power to stay English suit or restrain a party from pursuing his suit filed by him in another country, when the suit is between the same parties, relating to the same subject-matter and claiming the same relief.[67] However, this power has been exercised by English courts only sparingly.[68] This provision applies to matrimonial suits also, but the courts have shown extreme reluctance to exercise it in respect of them.[69]

The Domicile and Matrimonial Proceedings Act, 1973 has now very much extended the jurisdiction of the court to entertain divorce proceedings,[70] giving rise to the possibility of matrimonial suits being filed in several jurisdictions.[71] This has rendered it desirable to confer certain specific powers of staying of proceeding on matrimonial courts. The Schedule I to the Domicile and Matrimonial Proceedings Act, 1973 now confers specific powers of staying matrimonial proceedings between parties. It contains two sets of powers : One called "obligatory stays" and the other "discretionary stay". When there are concurrent proceedings in more than one jurisdiction in respect of the same marriage, then the power of staying proceedings can be exercised. But this new jurisdiction does not require or authorize a stay of proceedings which are pending when this provision came into force, nor does it prejudice any power to stay proceedings which was exercisable by the court before coming into force of this provision.[72] Under para 7 of the Schedule the parties are bound to furnish information of any proceedings which they know are continuing in another jurisdiction and are in respect of that marriage or are capable of affecting its validity or subsistence.

Obligatory stays : Paragraph 8 of the Schedule I deals with obligatory stays. It runs as under :

(1) Where before the beginning of the trial or first trial in any proceedings for divorce which are continuing in the court it appears to the court on the application of a party to the marriage—

(a) that in respect of the same marriage proceedings for divorce or nullity of marriage are continuing in a related jurisdiction; and

67. The principal has been re-stated by the House of Lords in *The Atlantic Star*, (1973) 2 W.L.R. 795 (1974) A.C. 436.

68. See *Thornton* v. *Thornton*, (1886) 11 176; *Orr-Levis* v. *Orr-Levis*, (1949) p. 347; *Sealey* v. *Calln*, (1953) p. 135.

69. *Ibid.*

70. Section 5.

71. The Schedules to the Act have been added to give effect to the Law Commission's recommendation (Report No. 48, paras. 75-102) which said that the existing law was not sufficient to meet the problem of conflict of jurisdictions that could arise on the coming into force of s. 5, Domicle and Matrimonial Proceedings Act, 1973.

72. Section 5(6).

(b) that the parties to the marriage have resided together after its celebration; and

(c) that the place where they resided together when the proceedings in the court were begun or, if they did not then reside together, where they last resided together before those proceedings were begun, is in that jurisdiction; and

(d) that either of the said parties was habitually resident in that jurisdiction throughout the year ending with the date on which they last resided together before the date on which the proceedings in the court were begun.

it shall be the duty of the court . . . to order that the proceedings in the court be stayed.

Under this provision the court cannot stay proceedings at its own motion. One of the parties to the proceedings must move an application. Under this provision a stay as matter of right is available to a party to an English divorce suit. Once a case is made out, the court is bound to stay English divorce proceedings.

Discretionary Stays: Paragraph 9(1) of Schedule 1 to the Domicile and Matrimonial Proceedings Act, 1973 lays down the provision for discretionary stay. It runs as under :

(1) Where before the beginning of the trial or first trial in matrimonial proceedings which are continuing in the court if, it is appears to the court,

(a) that any proceedings in respect of the marriage in question, or capable of affecting its validity or subsistence, are continuing in another jurisdiction; and

(b) that the balance of fairness (including convenience) as between the parties to the marriage is such that it is appropriate for the proceedings in that jurisdiction to be disposed of before further steps are taken in the proceedings in the court or in those proceedings so far as they consist of a particular kind of matrimonial proceedings,

the court may then, if it thinks fit, order that the proceedings in the court be stayed or, as the case may be, those proceedings be stayed so far as they consist of proceedings of that kind.

Under this provision the court has the power to stay proceedings of its own accord even if no application to do so is made to the court. The court's power of granting discretionary stay extends to not only divorce proceedings but "any matrimonial proceedings", which, it seems, would include even non-judicial matrimonial proceedings. "Another jurisdiction" means "any country outside England and Wales".[73]

"Balance of fairness" is elucidated in sub-paragraph (4). Under this head the court can have regard to all factors appearing to be relevant, including the convenience of witnesses and any delay or expenses which may result from the proceedings beings stayed or not stayed. This is nothing but enunciation of basic common law principles.[74]

In *Nacshannon* v. *Rockwase Glass Ltd.*,[75] the House of Lords said that in order to justify stay of proceedings two conditions must be satisfied, one positive and the other negative : (a) the defendant must satisfy the court that there is another forum to whose jurisdiction he is amenable in which justice can be done between the parties at substantially loss inconvenience or expense, and (b) the stay must not deprive the plaintiff of a legitimate advantage which would be available to him if he invoked the jurisdiction of English Court. Further, the exercise of the Court's discretion in any particular case necessarily involves the balancing of all the relevant factors on either side, those favouring the grant of a stay on the one hand, and those militating against it on the other. Such balancing may be difficult process and some cases may be very near the line.

It would appear that in considering the balance of fairness in matrimonial proceedings, the Court should take all relevant circumstances into account, including the loss of any important personal or juridical advantage which the petitioner, in a property constituted English proceeding, might lose if the proceedings were stayed. *Gadd* v. *Gadd*[76], is good illustrative case. Here the parties were British nationals who married in Bahamas in 1967 and lived there until 1973. They then lived in France and Monaco until 1983 when the marriage broke down. The wife returned to England and filed a petition for divorce. The husband commenced divorce proceedings in Monaco and applied for a stay under para 9(1) of Schedule I to the Domicile and Matrimonial Proceedings Act, 1973 : The Court of Appeal refusing the stay of proceedings said that in granting stay the court should consider whether the petitioner would loss an important personal or juridical advantage in the proceedings were stayed. In the present case the England domicile wife would deprived of the advantage of financial provisions available in England which was not available to her in Monaco proceedings and therefore, balance of fairness required that the wife's petition should be allowed to continue.[77]

73. Para. 3(1) of the Schedule.

74. *See, St. Pierre* v. *South American Stores*, (1937) 1 K.B. 382; *The Atlantic Star*, (1973) 2 W.L.R. 795.

75. (1978) A.C. 795, see also *Shemshadford* v. *Shemshadford*, (1981) 1 All E.R. 726.

76. (1984) 1 W.L.R. 1435.

77. See also *Thyssen-Bonemisza* v. *Thyssen* Bornemisza (1985) 2 W.L.R. 715.

Discharge of Stays : Paragraph 10(1) of Schedule 1 deals with discharge of stays. The obligatory stays as well as discretionary stays may be discharged by the court if it thinks fit, on the application of a party to the proceedings, that the other proceedings by reference to which the order was made are stayed or concluded, or that a party to those other proceedings has delayed unreasonably in prosecuting them. Once the obligatory stay is discharged, the same proceedings cannot be stayed over again.

Stay and Ancillary Reliefs : Once the matrimonial proceedings are stayed either under paragraph 8 or 9 the English court's power to pass orders in respect of ancillary relief are restricted. Existing orders for maintenance of a spouse *pendente lite* or for periodical payment for children, or for custody and education of children, or restraining a person from removing the child out of the jurisdiction or out of the custody, care or control of another person ceases to have effect on the expiration of three months beginning with the date on which stay was imposed, unless the stay is removed earlier, or the court orders otherwise on account of some urgency.[78] Not only this, no fresh orders in any of these matters can be made by the court once the stay is granted, unless some urgency impels the court to do otherwise.[79] If a court in other jurisdiction passes an order on any of these matters, then the order passed by the English court on that matter ceases to have any effect.[80] In such a case even in a case of urgency the English court will not pass an order on that matter. But the ancillary orders of the other courts will have no effect on the orders of English court already passed relating to a lumpsum payment to the child or restraining a person from removing the child out of the jurisdiction or out of the custody, care or control of another person.[81]

78. Para 11(2), (a) and (b).
79. Para 11(2), (a) and (c).
80. Para 11(3).
81. Para 11(1) and (3).

Part VIII

FOREIGN JUDGMENTS

SUMMARY

25

FOREIGN JUDGMENTS

A question often arises in the municipal courts : What effect can be given to foreign judgments, or can they be enforced ? The question may assume various forms. For instance, P who had obtained a money decree against D from a court in country X fails to get it satisfied there. On getting the information that D has assets in country Y, P files an application in a court of country Y for the enforcement of the decree ? Can he do so ? If so, in what manner ? Or, P who had instituted a suit against D in the court of country X for damages for a breach of contract and whose suit had been dismissed there, files a fresh suit in a court of country of Y. Can D take the plea *res judicata* ? Or, a decree dissolving the marriage between P and D is passed by a court of competent jurisdiction of country X. P comes to country Y and marries again. P is prosecuted for bigamy there. Can he take the plea that his former marriage had already been dissolved by a court of competent jurisdiction of country X and therefore he cannot be held guilty of bigamy ? Today, the question in all the three illustrations can be answered affirmatively.[1]

The English courts have, from early times, accorded recognition to foreign judgments, though direct effect could not be given to them. Today, most of the countries of the Commonwealth, including India and the United States give recognition to foreign judgments. On the other hand, the position is different in the Continental Countries. The Continental system places much reliance on reciprocity. Foreign judgments are enforced there on the basis of reciprocity. Different continental countries have different rules of conflict of laws.[2] However, the plea that the matter had already been finally litigated upon between the parties can be taken in the courts of many Continental countries. The European countries also recognize foreign judgment relating to status.[3]

1. See Chapter 1 of this work.
2. See Arthur Kuhn, *Comparative Commentaries on Private International Law*, pp. 102-114.
3. *Ibid.*

In this Chapter we would discuss the following matters :

(a) Basis of recognition of foreign judgment.
(b) Recognition of foreign judgments,
(c) The execution of foreign decrees, and
(d) The execution of pre-Partition decrees.

I

BASIS OF RECOGNITION OF FOREIGN JUDGMENTS

On the recognition of foreign judgments, various theories have been propounded, of which the theory of comity is considered to be the oldest theory. Apart from the theory of comity, the obligation theory, the theory of judicial reason or ideas of social value, theory of harmony between judgment and law are some other theories.

The old English cases took the view that foreign judgments are recognized on the basis of comity.[5] The difficulty inherent in the theory of comity is that no foreign judgment can be recognized unless there is reciprocity. If reciprocity is the basis of recognition, then it is difficult to say as to what defences are precisely available to a defendant or a judgment-debtor. Cheshire rightly says that if the English court is compelled by comity to enforce the judgment, logic would seem to exclude all defences, except the want of jurisdiction in the foreign court; but to carry enforcement to these lengths is obviously inconsistent with the most elementary notion of natural justice.[6] It is evident that English private international law does not base the recognition of foreign judgments on the basis of reciprocity.

The obligation theory too was propounded at an early time.[7] Blackburn, J. said : "The judgment of a court of competent jurisdiction over the defendant imposes a duty or obligation on him to say the sum for which judgment given, which the courts in this country are bound to enforce."[8] Thus an adjudication of a competent foreign court becomes a legal obligation which can be enforced in any country as such. The one merit of this theory is that it eliminates the question of reciprocity. If B is under a legal obligation to pay the amount to A under a judgment obtained by the latter from a court in country X, then that is enough for its enforcement in country Y. The question as to what treatment

4. For discussion of theories, see Martin Wolf, *Private International Law*, pp. 252-53. For detailed discussion see, H.E. Reads, *Recognition and Enforcement of Forign Judgments*, p. 52 *et seq.*
5. *Gever* v. *Aguilar*, (1798) 7 Term Rep. 681 at p. 697.
6. *Private International Law*, (8th. Ed.), p. 613.
7 *Russell* v *Smyth*, (1842) 9 M. & W. 810. See also *Willams* v. *Jones*, (1845) 13 M. & W. 628; *Godard* v. *Gray*, (1870) L.R. 6 Q.B. 139.
8. *Schibsby* v. *Westenholz*, (1870) L.R. 6 Q.B. 155 at p. 159.

would be meted to a person under similar circumstances in country X is immaterial. The doctrine of obligation also simplifies the question of defences available to the judgment-debtor against a foreign judgment. All those defences that go to nullify the obligation of B would be available to him.[9] In criticism of the doctrine the most valid argument is that it brings a fictitious contract into play and cannot justify the recognition of divorce decrees and other judgments *in rem*.[10]

H.E. Reads has propounded the view that foreign judgments are recognized on "grounds of judicial reason or ideas of social value or both."[11] Theoretically this view appears to be sound, as every judgment is recognized in the interest of justice.[12] But the most important question is : when would the justice require the recognition and when would it not ? It is difficult to answer this question. This would, in practice, involve the examination of a vast number of cases and thus the principle would be unworkable in practice.

Von Bar has propagated another theory. The basis of recongnition of foreign judgments, according to him, is the doctrine of harmony between law and judgment. Von Bar holds that a judgment is a *lex specialis*, a law regulating one single case. Thus, he maintains, in order to maintain harmony between conflict rules and respect for foreign judgments, the courts of a given country 'should in principle, and as far as possible, decide on such actions as are to be decided under the municipal law of that country.'[13] The doctrine tends to over-simplify the matter and is thus unsatisfactory.[14]

Pillet has propounded a simple theory as a basis of recognition of foreign judgments. He says that courts recognize a foreign judgment only if the judgment has been rendered in accordance with its rules of conflict of laws. Martin Wolf supports this view, though he also recognizes its limitation.[15] The greatest objection to this theory is that 'it reduces the number of enforceable judgments below a reasonable limit.'[16]

The recognition of foreign judgments is also sometimes based on the theory of acquired rights. This theory holds the view that since a foreign judgment implies an acquisition of a right, it should be enforced. Wolf says that the doctrine of acquired rights begs the question by presupposing a right as acquired, while the problem is whether the right has been acquired or not.[17] The criticism has

9. See Cheshire, *Private International Law*, 8th (Ed.), p. 251.
10. Martin Wolf, *Private International Law*, p. 251.
11. *Recognition and Enforcement of Foreign Judgments*, p. 257.
12. *Ibid.*
13. Von Bar, *International* Law, II, p. 413.
14. Martin Wolf, *Private International Law*, pp. 252-53.
15. *Ibid.*, p. 253.
16. *Ibid.*
17. *Ibid.*, p. 252.

been answered thus : as soon as a plaintiff appears in a court on the basis of a foreign judgment, the court presumes that he has acquired a right, though the defendant is free to rebut that presumption by establishing that for one reason or another that judgment cannot be enforced. What the defendant does is not to establish that the right has not been acquired under the judgment, but he asserts that, for some reason, the judgment cannot be enforced. In other words, the defendant can plead defences available to him against the foreign judgment. For instance, A files a suit in a court of country Y on a judgment obtained by him in country X against B. The court of country Y will enforce the judgment unless B takes any one of the pleas available to him under the law on account of which the judgment is made unenforceable, such as want of jurisdiction by the court of country X.

The theory of acquired rights is different from the theory of vested rights propounded by Dicey and Beale. Dicey and Beale were of the view that the private international law was founded on the theory vested rights. The recognition of foreign judgments was based on the same principle. Hardly any one subscribes to this theory in our times. It is because when a municipal court enforces a foreign judgment it enforces a right created by the municipal law and not the one created by the foreign law.[18] It is because when the municipal court enforces a foreign judgment it is necessary that the foreign court should have jurisdiction not under the foreign law but under the municipal law of the country enforcing the judgment and that the defences that are available to a defendant against the foreign judgment are the defences recognized under the municipal law and not under the foreign law.

Basis of Recognition of Foreign Judgments under English law : The English courts have been enforcing foreign judgments from the seventeenth century onwards. As we have seen earlier, the early English decisions have favoured the theory of comity. Later on English courts advocated the theory of obligation. In *Warrender* v. *Warrendor*[19] Lord Brougham said : "The courts of England can hardly be said to act from courtesy *ex comitate* but *ex debito justitiae*." The obligation theory has had held sway in English law for a considerable time and even now it is not lacking its advocates.[20] But the obligation theory fails in those cases where the question is not of enforcement of foreign judgments but of their recognition, i.e. those judgments which impose no obligation. It was in this background that a wider basis of recognition and enforcement of foreign judgments was propounded by Lord Brougham. Whatever may be now considered to be the basis of the enforcement of foreign judgments in the modern English law, foreign judgments have never been directly executable at common law. English law has all along required that the judgment-creditor

18. See Dicey and Morris, p. 968.
19. (1835) 2 Cl. & Fin. 488 at p. 530.
20. For instance see Cheshire (8th Ed.), 614.

should bring an action on foreign judgment. Foreign judgments are directly executable only under certian statute.[21]

This has also been a remarkable development in the English private international law that the domestic doctrine of merger of cause of action in the judgment is not applied to forein judgments.[22] This means that the plaintiff who had obtained a judgment from a foreign court has the option either to bring an action on the foreign judgment or to sue on the original cause of action. There is no rationale for this distinction in private internanal law,[23] but such has been the historical development that alternative remedies were made available to a plaintiff who had obtained a judgment from a foreign court. The reason for this development seems to be the fact that until the later half of the nineteeth century a foreign judgment was not considered to be a final and conclusive adjudication. It was merely treated as a primary evidence of rights and liabilities of the parties. Thus, the original cause of action survived and a suit could be again brought on it. The House of Lords in 1870 held that a foreign judgment of a court of competent jurisdiction was conclusive and could not be re-examined on merits.[24] But the doctrine still survives. In 1967 Lord Wilberforce called it as an 'illogical survival' but other law Lords accepted it as correct.[25] English court still seem to subscribe to the view that a foreign judgment creates merely a simple contract debt between the parties.[26]

Basis of Enforcement of Foreign Judgments in Indian Law : Under the Indian law the foreign judgments are recognized and enforced under the provisions of s. 13 of the Civil Procedure Code. This is a statutory provision. The question is : are Indian courts free to search the principle on which the enforcement of foreign judgments is based in Indian law. The Indian courts have tried to find out the basis of enforcement of foreign judgments and as elsewhere so here too they have read the English decisions into the Indian law. It should not surprise any one that our courts have found both the comity and the obligation theories to be the basis of the enforcement of foreign judgments. And this trend continues in the post-independence judgments also. In 1963, Shah, J. of the Supreme Court said that though the rules of private international law are different in different countries, yet on the basis of comity certain rules are applied practically by all the countries.[27] In a

21. See the next Part of this Chapter.
22. See *Hall* v. *Odber*, (1809) 11 East 118; *Smith* v. *Nicolls*, (1839) 5 Bing. N.C. 208; *Bank of Australasia* v. *Harding*, (1850) 9 C.B. 661; *Bank of Australasia* v. *Nias*, (1851) 16 Q.B. 717; *Re Flynn*, (No. 2) (1969) 2 All E.R. 557.
23. See Read, *Recognition and Enforcement of Foreign Judgments*, pp. 116-121; Piggot, *Foreign Judgments*, Part I, p. 15.
24. *Godard* v. *Grey*, (1870) 6 Q.B. 139.
25. *Carl Zeiss Stiftung* v. *Rayner and Keeler Ltd.* (No. 2), (1967) 1 A.C. 853.
26. For criticism of this doctrine, see Cheshire, (8th Ed.), p. 614.
27. *Vishwanathan* v. *Abdul Wazid*, 1963 S.C. 1.

1963 decision[28] Madholkar, J. of the Supreme Court seems to be in agreement with the obligation theory as propounded by Blackburn, J.[29] Even in earlier decisions this principle has been accepted by the Indian courts.[30] It is submitted that it was not necessary for the Indian courts to find out any basis for the enforcement of the foreign judgments. In India the foreign judgments are recognized and enforced under the statutory provision contained in the Civil Procedure Code. They are not enforced because under the judgment an obligation of the defendant arises and which obligation he is bound to fulfil. Section 13 of the Civil Procedure Code explicitly says that 'a foreign judgment shall be conclusive as to any matter thereby directly adjudicated upon between the same parties . . .' Thus if it is necessary to know the basis of enforcement of foreign judgment under the Indian law, then it is the principle of conclusiveness of a foreign judgment.[31]

Not merely this, the Indian courts have also discovered the doctrine of non-merger of cause of action in respect of foreign judgments. In certain pre-independence judgments this doctrine was considered to be part of Indian law.[32] In a 1964 decision, Subba Rao, J. of the Supreme Court took the view that doctrine of non-merger is an accepted doctrine of Indian law.[33] It is submitted that the doctrine of non-merger should not be read in Indian law. Foreign judgments are enforced in India under s. 13 of the Civil Procedure Code. If the conditions of s. 13 are fulfilled a foreign judgment would be enforceable, otherwise not.

II

RECOGNITION OF FOREIGN JUDGMENTS

Under the Indian and English law a foreign judgment-creditor can bring an action on a foreign judgment. If the defendant has filed a suit on the same cause of action, he can also take the plea of *res judicata*. The English law is now contained in the civil jurisdiction and Judgments Act, 1982. The Indian law on this matter has been enacted in s. 13 of the Indian Code of Civil Procedure. With minor differences on matters of detail, the position in English

28. *Badat & Co.* v. *East India Trading Co.*, 1964 S.C. 538 at p. 554.
29. *Schibsby* v. *Westenholz*, (1870) 6 Q.B. 155. The learned judge has also quoted Schmithoff, *English Conflict of Laws*, p. 459 where the learned author supports the theory of private rights.
30. The earliest reported case is : *Bhavani Shanker* v. *Pursadri*, (1882) 6 Bom. 292. See also *Barkatlal* v. *Devidas*, 1953 Hyd. 29.
31. See *Vishwanathan* v. *Abdul Wazid*, 1963 S.C. 1, p. 20 which supports this view.
32. See *Oppenhemi & Co.* v. *Mohammed Haneef*, 1922 P.C. 120; *Nilratan* v. *Cooch Behar Loan Office*, 1941 Cal. 64 ; *Popatvirli* v. *Damodar*, 1934 Bom. 390.
33. *Badat & Co*. v. *East Indian Trading Co.*, 1964 S.C. 538 at p. 542.

private international law is also the same. Section 13 of the Code runs as under :

A foreign judgment shall be conclusive as to any matter thereby directly adjudicated upon between the same parties or between parties under whom they or any of them claim litigating under the same title except—

(a) where it has not been pronounced by a court of competent jurisdiction;
(b) where it has not been given on the merits of the case;
(c) where it appears on the face of the proceedings to be founded on an incorrect view of international law or a refusal to recognize the law of the States in cases in which such law is applicable;
(d) where the proceedings in which the judgment was obtained are opposed to natural justice;
(e) where it has been obtained by fraud;
(f) where it sustains a claim founded on a breach of any law in force in the States.

Section 14 of the Code lays down, "The court shall presume upon the production of any document purporting to be a certified copy of a foreign judgment, that such judgment was propounded by a court of competent jurisdiction, unless the contrary appears on the record; but such presumption may be displaced by proving want of jurisdiction." It is a well established rule of English private international law as well as of the Indian private international law that a court cannot subject a foreign judgment to a general review. A foreign judgment cannot be impeached on the ground that it is based on an error or internal law or on an error of fact[34] nor can it be impeached on the ground of some procedural error. Whenever an action is brought on a foreign judgment it is for the defendant to establish that for one or the other defence available to him, he is not bound by it. However, no action can be founded on a foreign judgment which is not a final and conclusive adjudication between the parties.

Finality of the Foreign Judgment

It is a settled rule of private international law that no cause of action arises on a foreign judgment in which the matter at issue has not been conclusively and finally determined. In short, what is required is that the judgment should operate as *res judicata* in the country, where it has been delivered.[35] The English cases,

34. The French and some other Continental countries take the opposite view with the result that more often than not a judgment-creditor is compelled to bring the suit *de novo*.

35. *Tyne Improvement Commissioners* v. *Armement Anversors S/A*, (1949) A.C. 326 (H.L.), *Black-Clawson International Ltd.* v. *Papier Werke-Waldhof Ashchaffenburg A.G.* (1974) 2 W.L.R. 789=(1975) A.C. 591; *K.M. Jabbar* v. *Indo-Singapore Traders (P.) Ltd.*, 1981 Mad. 118.

Nouvion v. *Freeman*[36] and *Blohn* v. *Desser*[37], provide good illustration of this. In the former case the plaintiff who had sold certain land in Surville to the defendant, brought an 'executive action' in Spain against the defendant and obtained a 'remate' judgment. Spanish law recognizes two kinds of action : the executive or summary proceedings, and plenary or ordinary proceedings. In the former action, if a *prima facie* case is made out the judge issues attachment order without any notice to the defendant. Then the notice is given to the defendant and he may defend the case. But the defences available to the defendant are few and, above all, he is not permitted to impeach the original transaction upon which he had been sued. The party defeated in the executive action may then bring a plenary action and all defences available to him under the ordinary law may be taken by him. Under the Spanish law the 'remate' judgment cannot be pleaded as *res judicata*. In this case the plaintiff brought an action in an English court on the basis of 'remote judgment' he had obtained from a Spanish judge. The House of Lords refused to enforce the judgment as the rights and liabilities of the parties were not finally determined by the remote judgment; nor did the judgment operated as *res judicata*.

In *Blohn* v. *Desser*,[38] a partnership business, consisting of two sisters and a brother, was carried on in Vienna. One of the sisters resided in England and did not participate in the conduct of its business. The plaintiff obtained a judgment from an Austrian court against the partnership for the amount of a bill of exchange accepted by the brother on behalf of the partnership. Under the Austrian judgment the sister was not personally liable. To make her personally liable under the Austrian law, a separate action against her was necessary. When the plaintiff filed an action against the sister in an English court, the English court held that the judgment, being not final and conclusive against the sister, could not be enforced against her. On the service of summons on the defendant, the decree was passed by taking note of the consent of the defendant, it was held that the judgment was conclusive.[39]

Another illustration of this found in alimony cases : the amount of alimony is subject to modification by the divorce court not only in respect of future amount but also in respect of the amount already fixed by the court. In short, orders relating to alimony are not final and conclusive orders. In *Harrop* v. *Harrop*,[40] where the plaintiff brought an action in England for the recovery of an amount of alimony ordered to be paid to her by a court in Perak, Sankey, J. observed. "In my view a judgment or order cannot be said to be final and conclusive if (i) an order has to be obtained for its enforcement, and (ii) on application such an order or judgment is liable to be abrogated or varied."

36. (1889) 15 A.C. 1
37. (1962) 2 Q.B. 116.
38. (1962) 2 Q.B. 116.
39. *Md. Abdulla* v. *P.M. Abdul Rahim*, 1985 Mad. 379.
40. (1920) 3 K.B. 386.

However, finality of the judgment means that it is final in the court in which the matter is adjudicated. The fact that the judgment is subject to an appeal does not mean that the judgment is not final; it is not even necessary for the court to wait for the expiry of the period of limitation for appeal.[41] Even when an appeal is actually pending it is not necessary for the court to stay the proceedings. But if under the law of the foreign country pendency of appeal means stay of execution, the order will not be enforced till the final disposal of the appeal. The court has equitable jurisdiction to stay the execution in cases where an appeal is actually pending.[42]

When an action on Foreign Judgment may fail

It has been seen earlier that under s. 13 of the Indian Code of Civil Procedure, barring aside the cases listed in clauses (a) to (f), a foreign judgment is considered to be conclusive on any matter that was directly litigated upon between the parties. In other words, if defences laid down in clauses (a) to (f) of s. 13 are available to the defendant an action on foreign judgment will fail.

Foreign Court must be of Competent Jurisdiction

It is a well established rule of both English and Indian international laws that no foreign judgment can be enforced or recognized which has been pronouced by a court having no jurisdiction in the cause. The competency of the foreign court is determined by the rules of private international law and not by the rules of the law of the forum or by the law of the country where the foreign court is situated.[43] The leading Indian case on the matter is *Sirdar Gurdyal Singh* v. *Raja of Faridkote*.[44] One Raja of Faridkote obtained two *ex parte* decrees for sums together amounting to Rs. 76,474-11-3 from a civil court at Faridkote against the defendant who was, five years before the decree, the treasurer of the Raja. In both the cases the defendant had not submitted to the jurisdiction of the Faridkote court. Subsequently, the Raja brought an action on both the judgments of the Faridkote court in a Lahore court, within the jurisdiction of which the defendant was residing. (At that time Faridkote was an Indian state and *vis-a-vis* British India, judgment pronounced by the Faridkote court were judgments of foreign courts.) Ultimately the matter went to the Privy Council. The Privy Council, dismissing the suit of the Raja, observed, "In a personal action . . . a decree passed *in absentem* by a foreign court, to the jurisdiction of which the defendant has not in any way submitted himself is by international law an absolute nullity." The Lordship of the Privy Council observed : "All jurisdiction is purely territorial and extra-territorium *jus dicenti impure non paremur*.

41. *Scott*. v. *Pilkington*, (1862) 2 B. & S. 11.
42. *Nouvion* v. *Freeman*, (1889) 15 A.C. 1.
43. *Pemberton*. v. *Huges*, (1899) 1 Ch. 781.
44. (1894) A.C. 670.

Territorial jurisdiction attaches (with special exceptions) upon all persons either permanently or temporarily resident within the territory, while they are within it; but it does not follow them after they have withdrawn from it and when they are living in another independent country. It exists always as to land within its territory; and, in questions of status or succession governed by the domicile, it may exist as to persons domiciled there, or who when living were domiciled within the territorry." In other words, the foreign court should have jurisdiction in the international sense.

Both the Indian law and English law classifies judgments under two heads, judgments *in personam* and judgments *in rem*. The same principles do not apply to both types of judgments and hence we would proceed to deal with them separately.

Judgments in Personam : It has been seen earlier that the protagonists of the obligation theory take the view that since the foreign judgment imposes an obligation upon the defendant, therefore it is enforceable elsewhere. If no such obligation is imposed on the defendant, then he is not bound. Apart from the theory, it is an established rule of English and Indian law that personal jurisdiction depends upon the right of the court to summon the defendant. Then, in short, the jurisdiction in personal actions depends upon the presence of the defendant within the jurisdiction.[45] If the defendant is not present within the jurisdiction the court has no jurisdiction, unless the defendant submits to the jurisdiction. In *Mallappa Yellappa* v. *Raghavendra Sham Rao*,[46] Rangnekar, J. listed the following six cases in which the foreign court may be said to have jurisdiction :

(a) If the defendant is subject of the foreign country,

(b) If the defendant is a resident in the foreign country when action has begun against him,

(c) If the defendant is served with the process while temporary present within the foreign country,

(d) If the defendant in his character as plaintiff in the foreign action has selected the forum where the judgment was given against him,

(e) If the defendant has voluntarily appeared before the foreign court, and

(f) If the defendant has contracted to submit to the jurisdiction of the foreign court.[47]

In the English decision *Rousillon* v. *Rousillon*,[48] Fry, J. listed all the cases given by Rangnekar, J. except the case (c). Most of

45. See Chapter 7 of this work.

46. I.L.R (1938) Bom. 16.

47. The Calcutta has listed four cases : *Balchand* v. *Kasturi Chand*, (1936) 40 C.W.N. 591.

48. (1880) 14 Ch. D. 351.

the English writers discuss the matter under three to five heads.[49] Cheshire discusses the subject under two heads : residence and submission.[50] He discusses the last three heads of Rangnekar, J., under the head, submission. There is no authority for the third head of Rangnekar, J. There is some English authority against it.

We may discuss the subject under the following heads :

(a) Residence and presence,

(b) Submission, and

(c) Nationalily of the defendant.

Residence and Presence : There is no doubt that the residence of the defendant within the jurisdiction at the time when the action was filed gives the court jurisdiction.[51] Does residence require presence? This leads us to another question : Is temporary presence alone sufficient to confer jurisdiction ? In *Carrick* v. *Hancock*,[52] a writ was served on a domiciled Englishman while he was on a short visit to Sweden. Subsequently, a judgment was passed against him which the plaintiff sought to enforce in an English court. The English court held that the action on judgment was maintenable. Lord Russell observed that the jurisdiction of the court was based upon the principle of territorial dominion, and that all persons within the territorial dominion owe their allegiance to the sovereign power and obedience to all its laws and to the lawful judgments of its courts. So far as this reasoning is applied to the casual presence of the defendant, Dicey and Morris rightly observe : "It may be doubted, however, whether casual presence, as distinct from residence is a desirable basis of jurisdiction if parties are strangers and the cause of action arose outside the country concerned."[53] The reason is that "the court is not convenient one for either of the parties, nor is it in a favourable position to deal intelligently either with the facts or with the law."[54]

In respect of corporations it seems to be an established principle that the foreign court will have jurisdiction over it only if at the time of trial it carries on substantial business there at some definite and more or less permanent place in that country. The court took this view in *Littauer Glove Corporation* v. *F.W. Millington Ltd.*,[55] where a director of an English company, which has no place of business in New York, was on a visit to New

49. In Rule 160 Dicey and Morris, discuss the matter under five heads and three exceptions. See pp. 973-991. Graveson discusses the matter under three heads, see pp. 664-668.
50. *Cheshire* (8th Ed.), pp. 624-631. Cheshire adds another head, 'Nothing else founds jurisdiction', p. 631.
51. *Schibsby* v. *Westenholz*, (1870) 6 Q.B. 155.
52. (1895) 12. T.L.R. 59.
53. *Conflict of Laws*, p. 981. See also Cheshire, p. 625
54. Dodd, (1929) 23 Ill. L. Rev. 427 at pp. 437-38.
55. (1928) 44 T.L.R. 746.

York, was staying in a hotel and was making an occasional use of the office of an important customer of the company. While the director was so staying in the hotel, a writ was served upon him in an action against the company. He did not put up appearance, nor did he take any step to defend the suit. Judgment in default was passed against the company. Subsequently, an action was brought on the judgment in an English court. Dismissing the suit, Salter, J. said that the company was not in any sense of the term carrying on business in New York. He further said that the foreign court will have jurisdiction if the company is engaged in 'carrying on of business at a definite, and, to some reasonable extent, permanent place."[56] Merely maintaining of an agent in a foreign country does not amount to carrying on of business.[57]

A question has also come before English courts as to whether the foreign court could be said to have jurisdiction in a personal action against a defendant who does not reside within the jurisdiction of the court but carries on some business through an agent residing there. This question came in *Blohn* v. *Desser*.[58] In this case the agent was residing there and action was also brought in respect of a transaction effected by the agent. The court held that the foreign court has no jurisdiction.

In a series of cases the Indian courts, too, have taken the view that if the defendant does not reside within the jurisdiction of the court, the court has no jurisdiction unless the defendant submits to the jurisdiction.[59] The Indian courts have also taken the view that the foreign court will not have any jurisdiction on the basis that the defendant carried on business through an agent in the foreign country unless by conduct or otherwise he submits to the jurisdiction.[60] In *Sahib Thambi Matakayar* v. *Hamid Markakayar*[61] a firm was sued in a Singapore court in the firm's name, but only one of the partner's was served, and a decree was passed. The other partners were residing in India. The creditor also obtained personal decrees against all the partners. He filed a suit on the judgment in an Indian court. The High Court of Madras held that the decree was not enforceable against the partners who were

56. *Ibid.*, at p. 747.
57. *Sfeir & Co.* v. *National Insurance Co.*, (1964) 1 Lloyd's Rep. 330.
58. (1962) 2 Q.B. 116.
59. *Jivappa Timmappa* v. *Jeerji Murgappa*, (1916) 40 Bom. 551; *K.N. Guruswami* v. *Md. Khan Sahib*, 1933 Mad. 112; *Wazir Sahu* v. *Musshi Das*, 1941 Pat. 109; *Chunnilal* v. *Dundappa*, 1951 Bom. 190; *A.S. Subramanian Chettiar* v. *M.K. Srinivasa*, 1951 Mad. 289; *Maloji Rao* v. *Shankar Saran* 1955 All. 490; *Ramkishan Janakilal* v. *Seth Harmukharai*, 1955 Nag. 103; *Gena* v. *Birdichand*, 1958 Raj. 189; *Metal Corporation of India Ltd.* v. *P. Colombi*, 1960 Mys. 1; *Raj Rajendra Sardar Maloji Narsingh Rao Shitole* v. *Shankar Saran*, 1962 S.C 1737; *Bharat Nidhi Ltd.* v. *Meghraj Mahajan*, 1967 Del. 22.
60. *Fazal Shau Khan* v. *Gaffar Khan*, (1891) 15 Mad. 82; *Vithal Bhai Shivabna Patel* v. *Lalbhai Bhim Bhai*, 1942 Bom. 199.
61. (1911) 22 M.L.J. 109.

not served and who did not reside within the jurisdiction of the foreign court.

Submission : It is a well established rule of private international law that in a personal action if the defendant puts up appearance before the foreign court, then the foreign court's judgment is a judgment of court of competent jurisdiction. This is known as submission by the defendant to the court's jurisdiction. It is an obvious case of submission where the defendant has entered and appearance and defended the suit on merit.[62] The appearance should be voluntary. Once the defendant submits to the jurisdiction of the court and the judgment goes against him, he cannot turn and say that the court had no jurisdiction.[63] It is because, once the defendant has taken a chance on the judgment it would be unfair to allow him to take exception to it if it goes against him. Now section 33, Civil Jurisdiction and judgment Act, 1982 lays down as to what amount to submission. In *Indian and General Investment Trust Ltd.* v. *Sri Ramchandra Maharaj, Raja of Kalikote*,[64] Sinha J. said : " 'Submission' means a voluntary acceptance of the authority of a court to pass Judgment which authority such a court would not otherwise possess. A submission may be express or implied."

The case of express submission is too obvious to merit any further discussion. But the cases of implied submission present some difficulties. It seems to be clear that submission must be before the passing of judgment; submission after the judgment does not confer jurisdiction on the court.[65] If a defendant proceeds to get an *ex parte* decree set aside, this does not amount to submission.[66] We would proceed to discuss some illustrative cases of implied submisson.

The question has come in some cases as to whether execution of power of attorney in favour of some one residing in the foreign country by the defendant amounts to submission ? In *Ramanathan Chettiar* v. *Kalimuthu Pillai*[67] the defendant gave a general power of attorney to an agent residing in a foreign country. Under the power of attorney the agent had the authority to file and defend suits on behalf of the defendant. The judgment was passed after service of summons on the agent. The court said that the defendant is *prima facie* bound by the judgment.[68] Similar view was taken in *Jannoo Hasan Sait* v. *S.N. Mahamad Ohuthu.*[69] But

62. *Molony* v. *Gibbons*, (1810) 2 Camp. 502; *Guiard* v. *De Clermont*, (1914) 3 K.B. 145; *Israel Discount Bank* v. *Hadjipateras* (1984) I.W.L.R. 137; *Adams* v. *Cape Industries* (1990) 2 W.L.R. 657.
63. *O.P. Verma* v. *Lala Gehrilal*, (1962) Raj. 231.
64. 1952 Cal. 508.
65. *Narappa Naicken* v. *Govindaraja Naicken*, (1934) 57 Mad. 824.
66. *Ibid.* See also *Sheo Tahal Ram* v. *Binaek*, 1931 All. 689.
67. (1914) 37 Mad. 163.
68. See also *K.N.M. Meera* v. *K.M.M. Meera*, 1926 Mad. 259.
69. 1925 Mad. 155.

mere authorization to another person to put up appearance does not amount to submission. In *Ramkisan* v. *Seth Harmukharai*,[70] a suit was brought by the defendant against the plaintiff for breach of contract in a court at Indore (then, an Indian state). The plaintiff authorized a person to put up appearance on his behalf, but the latter did not do so and *ex parte* decree was passed against the plaintiff. The plaintiff was not successful in getting the *ex parte* decree set aside. Subsequently, he filed a suit in a Madhya Pradesh court against the defendant for breach of contract. The defendant pleaded the Indore judgment as res *judicata*. It was held by the Madhya Pradesh High Court that the Indore judgment was without jurisdiction as the facts that the plaintiff instructed someone to put up appearance on his behalf and that he tried to get the *ex parte* decree set aside do not amount to submission. Similarly, if the power of attorney comes to an end by the time the suit is filed, then it cannot be said that the defendant submitted to the jurisdiction.[71]

The question that arises is : when parties agree to submit their disputes to a particular court or to the law of a particular country whenever disputes between the two arise, does it amount to submission ? *Feyerick* v. *Hubbard*,[72] provides a clear illustration. Under contract for sale of patent rights, it was stipulated that all disputes arising under the contract should be submitted to the jurisdiction of Belgian courts. This was held to amount to submission. In *Copin* v. *Adamson*,[73] a domiciled Englishman resident in England purchased certain shares in a French company the article of association of which provided that all disputes arising during the liquidation of the company would be adjudicated upon by the French courts. The French company went in liquidation and the French court gave judgment against the English purchaser of shares to pay up the balance of the amount due on the shares purchased by him. When an action was brought on this judgment in an English court, the English purchaser pleaded, *inter alia*, that the French court had no jurisdiction to pass the judgment as he did not submit to the jurisdiction, nor was any process served upon him. The plea failed. Lord Cairns observed : "It appears to me that to all intends and purposes it is as if there had been an actual and absolute agreement by the defendant." Such an agreement may also be inferred from the circumstances. In *Blohn* v. *Desser*[74] the defendant was a partner with her brother and sister in a family business carried on in Vienna. Although the defendant was registered in the commercial register of Vienna as a partner, she resided in England and did not participate either in the conduct of the business or in the profits. An Austrian

70. 1955 Nag. 103.
71. *Vthalbhai Shivabhai Patel* v. *Lalbhai Bhimbhai*, 1942 Bom. 199.
72. (1902) 71 L.J.K.B. 509.
73. (1874) L.R. 9 Ex. 345.
74. (1962) 2 Q.B. 116.

court passed a judgment in favour of the plaintiff against partnership on a bill of exchange accepted by the brother on behalf of and in the name of the firm. The plaintiff then personally sued the defendant in an English court on the judgment. Diplock, J. held that this amounted to submission.

This decision has been criticised. Cheshire sums up the criticism thus : "The facts, no doubt showed that the defendant had held her brother out to the world as having ostensible authority to make contracts on her behalf in Austria, but they scarcely justified the inference that she had promised the world at large to submit herself personally to the Austrian jurisdiction with regard to such contracts. Thus, it has been objected that what the learned judge did was to impute to the defendant an agreement that was not reasonably inferable from the facts."[75] The decision also conflicts with *Emanuel* v. *Symon*[76] where it was held that the mere fact that the defendant entered into a partnership contract in a foreign country does not mean that he agreed to refer all the disputes regarding partnership to the foreign court.

Indian courts have consistently taken the view that partnership or participation in foreign business does not amount to submission. As early as 1897 the Madras High Court said that merely because the defendant was a partner in a firm carrying on business in a foreign country did not confer any jurisdiction on the foreign court.[77] The Madras High Court has reiterated this view in subsequent cases.[78] Similarly, the Lahore High Court held that the mere fact that the defendant is a partner in a foreign business does not give the foreign court jurisdiction against the defendant in an action *in personam*.[79] On the other hand, if parties agree to submit their disputes to the law of any country, then it would ordinarily amount to submission. Sinha, J. said that the mere fact that the parties agree that the law of a particular country would apply may or may not amount to an implied submission to the jurisdiction of the courts of that country. It will depend on the contract taken as a whole and all the circumstances of the case. What must be gathered therefrom is the intention of the parties. But even such an intention cannot be given effect to if it militates against public policy.[80] The stipulation in a mortgage that money are to be paid in a foreign country does not amount to an implied submission to the jurisdiction of the courts of that country.[81] In *Mathappa*

75. *Private International Law* (8th Ed.), p. 628. See *Vogel* v. *Kohnstamm Ltd.*, (1971) 3 W.L.R. 537.
76. (1908) 1 K.B. 302.
77. *Nallakaruppa* v. *Md. Ihuram Saheb*, (1897) 20 Mad. 112.
78. *K.N. Guruswami* v. *Md. Khan Sahib*, 1933 Mad. 112; *Narappa* v. *Rangaswami*, 1933 Mad. 393.
79. *Hari Singh* v. *Md. Said*, 1927 Lah. 200.
80. *Indian and General Investment Trust Ltd.* v. *Sri Ramchandra*, 1952 Cal. 508.
81. *Ibid.*

Chetti v. *Chellappa Chetti*[82] the Madras High Court said that merely because a contract was entered into a foreign country, it does not mean that the foreign court has jurisdiction in a personal action.

Does the conduct amount to submission ? Whether or not conduct amounts to submission would depend upon the circumstances of each case.

When a defendant appears before the court in protest with a view to saving his property, does it amount to submission ? When an action is filed against a non-resident defendant in respect of his property situated in a foreign country, he is faced with a delemma. If he appears to protect his property (even by way of protest) and if the judgment goes against him, then the judgment can be satisfied not merely against his foreign situated property but also against the property situated wherever he is residing. On the other hand, if he does not appear to protect his property, there is a possibility of the judgment going against him, and, in that event, his foreign property would be seized in the satisfaction of the judgment. The English cases makes a distinction between appearance before and after the property is actually seized by the court. In the latter case, i.e. when his property is actually seized by the court, the appearance would not amount to submission, but it would so amount in the former case.[83] Cheshire says that this distinction is illusory, for the property, even though not seized by the foreign court before the trial of the action, will inevitably be seized in due process of law if the defendant remains quiescent and allows judgment to go against him by default.[84]

The Indian courts have taken the view that appearance before the foreign court with a view to save property does not amount to submission. In *Veeraraghava* v. *Muga Sait*,[85] the defendant put up appearance before the foreign court to save his property. It was held that this did not amount to submission. But if the defendant appears before the court and does not protest against the jurisdiction till the suit reaches the appellate stage, then it cannot be said that he appeared in protest, and it would amount to submission.[86]

When the defendant has no property abroad, but he puts up appearance in protest, does it amount to submission ? It is submitted that if the defendant does nothing else while he appears before the foreign court except that he protest again the jurisdiction, then

82. (1876-78) 1 Mad. 196.

83. *De Cosse Brissac* v. *Rathbone* (1861) 6 H. & N. 301; *Voinet* v. *Barrett*, (1885) 55 L.J. Q.B. 39; *Guiard* v. *De Clermont*, (1914) 3 K.B. 145.

84. *Private International Law*, (8th Ed.) p. 629.

85. 39 Mad. 24.

86. *Kaliyugam Chetti* v. *Chokalinga Pillai*, (1889) 7 Mad. 105. See also *Nalla-Tambi* v. *Poonuswami*, (1879) 2 Mad. 400 and *Hari Singh* v. *Md. Said*, 1927 Lah. 200.

it would not amount to submission.[87] In *Re Dulles' Settlement*,[88] Denning L.J. observed : "I cannot see how anyone can fairly say that a man has voluntarily submitted to the jurisdiction of a court where he has all the time been vigorously protesting that it has no jurisdiction."[89] But, it seems that if a defendant does something more than just protesting the jurisdiction, then it would amount to submission. In *Boissiere* v. *Brockner*[90] where the defendant who protested against the jurisdiction, did not stop there, but proceeded further to defend the suit on merit. This was held to amount to a submission to jurisdiction.

There is long line of Indian cases where conduct has been held to amount to submission. In *Rama Ayyar* v. *Krishna Patter*[91] the defendant appeared before the court and protested against the jurisdiction. On his protest being negatived, he proceeded to defend the case on merit. His reasons for doing so were : (a) the creditors' son to whom he had repaid the suit debt refund the amount unless he defended the suit brought by his father, and (b) that if a decree were passed against him he might be arrested when he went there. The full Bench said that this conduct amounted to submission to jurisdiction.

In *V. Subramania Iyar* v. *Annaswami Iyer*,[92] the defendant did not put up appearance in a suit filed by the plaintiff in a Trivandrum court. The plaintiff got a commission issued to the court at Srivaikuntum to have the defendant summoned and examined as witness. The defendant appeared and pleaded that the court at Trivendrum has no jurisdiction. He, however, engaged a counsel, objected to the questions put to him in the examination and raised a plea in the course of his examination which, if had been accepted by the court, would have resulted in the dismissal of the suit. It was held that this amounted to submission.

It is obvious that if the defendant appears before the court to protest against the assumption of the jurisdiction, but then starts pleading on merits, then it amounts to submission.[93] But mere intention to submit is not tantamount to submission.[94] An application by the defendant for leave to examine witness amount to submission.[95] In *Shalig Ram* v. *Firm Daulatram Kundanmal*[96]

87. *Tallock* v. *Tallock*, (1927), p. 211.
88. (No. 2) (1951) Ch. 842.
89. *Ibid.* at p. 850, See also *N.V. Daarnhouwer & Co.* v. *Boulos*, (1968) 2 Lloyd's Rep. 259. In these decisions the court held that *Harris* v. *Taylor*, (1915) 1 K.B. 580, where, contrary view had been taken, is not correct.
90. (1889) 6 T.L.R. 85.
91. (1916) 39 Mad. 733 (F.B.).
92. 1948 Mad. 203.
93. *Chormal Balchand* v. *Kasturi Chand Seraogi*, (1936) 63 Cal. 1033.
94. *Ram Kishen Jankilal* v. *Harmukhrai*, 1955 Nag. 103.
95. *Indian National Steamship Co. Ltd.* v. *Maux Faulbaum*, 1955 Cal. 491.
96. 1967 S.C. 739.

where in a summary Bombay, High Court, the defendant, a resident of Hyderabad (then an Indian state) appeared in obedience of summons of the court and applied for leave to defend the suit without protesting against the jurisdiction and the same was granted to him on condition of his depositing certain amount in court within the prescribed time. On his default an *ex parte* decree was passed against him. In 1954 the plaintiff filed execution proceedings in a Hyderabad court (by this time Hyderabad state had become part of India and the same Civil Procedure Code was applicable there). The defendant took the plea that the Bombay judgment was without jurisdiction as he did not submit. The Supreme Court held that the defendant's conduct amounted to submission.

Appearance by the defendant as plaintiff in a foreign court : It is obvious that a person who files an action in a foreign court is himself bound by the judgment, if the judgment goes against him. Similarly, when once he invokes the jurisdiction, it would also amount to acceptance of the jurisdiction if any counter-claim of set-off is claimed against him; or if a counter-action is brought against him by the defendant.[97] This is also the view taken by the Indian courts. If the defendant in his character of the plaintiff has selected the forum in which he is afterwards sued, then he cannot be heard of saying subsequently when judgment goes against him that the foreign court has no jurisdiction.[98] Thus, in an early Bombay case where the defandant instituted a suit in a foreign country for damages caused by a collision at sea and the court in its judgment found againt the plaintiff, it was held that he cannot plead that the foreign court has no jurisdiction when an action is brought against him on the judgment.[99] In *A.N. Meera* v. *K.M.M. Meera*[100] the court said that a person who invokes the jurisdiction of the court as plaintiff cannot deny it as defendant. But just because a person has filed a suit in a foreign court having jurisdiction to try it, does not mean that he submitted to the jurisdiction of the court in all the later suits filed against him in that court even when he made no appearance in them.[101],[102]

Nationality as a basis of jurisdiction : Nationality as a basis of jurisdiction has been suggested by several writers.[103] There are certain dicta in English decisions which have suggested nationality

97. *Schibsby* v. *Westenholz*, (1870) L.R. 6. Q.B. 155. See also Westlake, ss. 324-325.
98. *R. Vishvanathan* v. *Rukn-ul-mulk Syed Abdul Wajid*, 1963 S.C. 1.
99. 4 B.H.C.R. 149.
100. 1926 Mad. 259; See also *Sheo Tahal Ram* v. *Binaik Shukul*, (1937) 53 All. 747.
101. *Oomer Hajee Ayoob Sait* v. *Thirunavukkrasu*, (1926) 59 Mad. 918.
102. See also *Thirunavakkaru Pandaram* v. *Parasurama*, 1937 Mad. 97.
103. Westlake, p. 399; Foote, p. 398; Schmitthoff, p. 465. Till the sixth ed, Dicey also supported nationality as a basis of jurisdiction.

as a basis of jurisdiction.[104] In *Rousillon* v. *Rousillon*[105] Fry, J. observed that since the defendant was the national of the foreign country, the foreign court has the jurisdiction. This observation was *obitor*. *Douglas* v. *Forrest*[106] is probably the nearest on this view. These English *obiter* observations have been followed in certain Indian decisions. In *Moazzim Hossein* v. *Raphael Robinson*[107] the Calcutta High Court said that an action in an English court against defendant who were resident in India may not be nullity as they were subjects of the same sovereign as the plaintiff. In *Mathurukovil* v. *Ramaliga Iyer*,[108] the defendant had dual nationality—he was a Cochin subject as well as a British subject. The court held that a decree passed by a Cochin court was binding on the defendant.[109]

If we are not to question the fundamental assumptions of private international law, then nationality cannot be attached any importance either under the English or under the Indian private international law. Dicey and Morris rightly say that it is evident that "nationality is quite inappropriate as a basis of jurisdiction when the defendant is, e.g. a British subject or an American citizen, since in neither case does the political unit (or state) coincide with the law district (or country)."[110] Cheshire says, "The argument usually advanced in its favour, namely, that a subject is bound to obey the command of his sovereign, and, therefore, the judgments of his sovereign courts, is no doubt true, but as Wolff pointed out it is not the duty of another sovereign to aid the enforcement of the obligation."[111]

Just as nationality is not a sufficient basis of jurisdiction in a personal action, similarly the domicile is not an adequate basis.[112]

Cause of action arising within the jurisdiction : It is an established rule both under the Indian and English private international law that just because cause of action arose within the jurisdiction of the foreign court, the foreign court cannot be invested with the jurisdiction.[113] The Indian law is to

104. *Douglas* v. *Forrest*, (1828) 4 Bing. 686; *Schibsby* v. *Westenholz*, (1870) 6 Q.B.155; *Rousillon* v. *Rousillon*, (1880) 14 Ch. D. 351; *Emanuel* v. *Symon*, (1908) 1 K.B. 302; *Gavin Gibson & Co.* v. *Gibson*, (1913) 3 K.B. 379; *Harris* v. *Toylor*, (1915) 2 K.B. 580; *Forsyth* v. *Forsyth*, (1948), p. 125.
105. Cited above.
106. *Ibid.*
107. (1901) 28 Cal. 641.
108. 1941 Mad. 688.
109. See also *Mallappa* v. *Raghavendra*, 1935 Bom. 173.
110. *Conflict of Laws*, p. 984.
112. The *dicta* supporting the view that domicile is sufficient basis of jurisdiction are found in the following cases : *Turnbull* v. *Walker*, (1892) 67 L.T. 767; *Emanuel* v. *Symon*, (1908) 1 K.B. 302; *Jaffer* v. *Williams*, (1908) 25 T.L.R. 12, *Gavin Gibson & Co.* v. *Gibson*, (1913) K.B. 379. But there is no direct authority. The view of jurists is that domicile does not found jurisdiction in a personal action : Read p. 160; Dicey and Morris, p. 160; Cheshire, 633.
113. *Phillips* v. *Batho*, (1913) 3 K.B. 25 at 30.

the same effect. In *Indian and General Investment Trust Co.* v. *Shriramchandra Raja and Colikote*[114] the Calcutta High Court held that mere fact that cause of action arose within the jurisdiction of the foreign court does not invest the foreign court within jurisdiction.[115]

When Property is situated in a foreign country : In some early cases a view was propounded that possession of property by the defendant in a foreign country was sufficient to found jurisdiction in a personal action even if the defendant was outside the jurisdiction.[116] But it seems to be clearly established that the fact that the property of the defendant is situated in a foreign country is not sufficient to invest the foreign court with jurisdiction.[117] Some Indian decisions have followed the view propounded in some early English decisions. In *Chormal Balchand* v. *Kasturi Chand*,[118] the Calcutta High Court observed that if the defendant has real estate within the jurisdiction, the foreign court is competent to exercise jurisdiction over an absent defendant. These observations were *obiter*. In *Hari Singh* v. *Md. Said*[119] the Lahore High Court observed that the fact that defendant has in his possession property does not confer jurisdiction on the foreign court

Actions in Rem : Perhaps the simplest definition of judgment *in rem* is : as adjudication upon the status of some particular subject-matter. In the words of Lord Watson : "The action is *in rem*, that being, as I understand the term, a proceeding against a ship or other chattel in which the plaintiff seeks either to have the *res judicata* to him in property or possession, or to have it sold under the authority of the court, and the proceeds, or part thereof, adjudicated to him, in satisfaction of his pecuniary claims."[120] The judgments *in rem* are not confined to tangibles. They include intangibles also. Thus, a judgment which adjudicates upon a status is a judgment *in rem*. Lord Dunedin observed. "All are agreed that a judgment of divorce is a judgment *in rem* but the whole argument of judges in the court of sessions turns on the distinction between divorce and nullity. The first remark to be made is that neither marriage nor the status of marriage, is, in the strict sense of the word, a *res*, as that word is used when we speak of judgment *in rem*. A *res* is tangible thing within the

114. 1952 Cal. 508.

115. See also *Ram Kishan* v. *Seth Harmukhrai*, 1955 Nag. 103 and *Indian and General Investment Trust Ltd.* v. *Shri Ramchandra*, 1952 Cal. 508.

116. *Becqet* v, *MacCarthy* (1831) 2 B. & Ad. 951; *Douglas* v. *Forrest*, (1828) 4 Bing. 686.

117. *Emanuel* v. *Symon*, (1908) 1 K.B. 302 (C.A.).

118. 1938 Cal. 511.

119. 1927 Lah. 200.

120. *Taylor* v. *Judges of the Court of Registration*, Beale's cases on *Conflict of Laws*, 317.

jurisdiction of the court, such as a ship or other chattel. A metaphysical idea, which is what status of marriage is, is not strictly a *res*, but it, to borrow a phrase, savours of *res*, and has all along been treated as such. Now the learned judges make this distinction. They say that in action of divorce you have to do with a *res*, to wit, the status of marriage, but that in an action for nullity there is no status of marriage to be dealt with, and, therefore, no *res*. Now it seems to me that celibacy is just as much a status as marriage."[121]

A judgment *in rem* is a judgment under (a) possession or property in a thing is adjudicated to a person, (b) the sale of a thing is decreed in satisfaction of a claim against the thing itself, (c) the status is adjudicated upon, such as a decree of nullity or divorce, and (d) property is ordered to be sold by way of administration in bankruptcy or on death.[122] The distinction between the judgment *in rem* and judgment *in personam* is that the former settles the destiny of the *res* itself and binds all persons claiming an interest in the property inconsistent with the judgment even though pronounced in their absence, while the latter, although it may concern a *res*, merely determines the rights of litigants *inter se* to the *res*.[123] Of the four categories of the judgments *in rem* listed above, we have already examined the rules relating to the recognition of the last two. Here we would confine ourselves to the first two.

It is a well established rule of private international law that a judgment pronounced by a court of competent jurisdiction in an action *in rem* is accorded universal recognition, even if the defendant is neither a resident of the foreign country nor has submitted to the jurisdiction of its courts.[124] Foreign judgments *in rem* usually call for their recognition. It is only in a very few cases that the question of their enforcement arises. For instance, a foreign judgment *in rem* which determines title to immovable property would hardly call for its enforcement as the property would be situated within the jurisdiction of the court.[125] *The*

121. *Salveson* v *Administrator of Austrian Property*, (1927) A.C. 641.

122. See Dicey and Morris, p. 992.

123. See Cheshire, p. 636. See also *Dollfus Mieg et Compagnie S.A.* v. *Bank of England*, (1949) Ch. 369; *Castrique* v. *Immrie*, (1870) L.R. 4 H.L. 414.

224. *Castrique* v. *Immrie*, cited above. *Minna Craig Steamship Co.* v. *Chartered Bank of India*, (1897) 1 Q.B. 55.

125. See Dicey and Morris, p. 992. The other instances given by the authors are : If the person entitled under a foreign judgment *in rem* vesting in him the title to some movable thing brings an action for conversion or detinue in England against a person who denies that title, he is in reality relying on his title rather than the source of it—the judgment. So also is the purchaser of a ship sold by foreign judicial sale who sets up the foreign judgment by way of defence to the original owner's action in conversion. All that is involved is, at most recognition of the foreign judgment, and, at that, recognition *qua* an assignment.

City of Mecca[126] is a case in which a foreign judgment *in rem* was sought to be enforced in an English court. A collision had occurred on the high seas between a Spanish ship and a British ship. The owners of the Spanish ship obtained a judgment against the British ship which was then lying in Lisbon from a Portuguese court. The ship returned to England before the judgment was satisfied. The owners of the Portuguese ship filed an action in an English court on the basis of the Portuguese judgment. The action was allowed by the English court.[127] The Indian law is the same.[128]

(ii) Judgment Impeachable on Merits

At a time when English courts thought that the enforcement of foreign judgments was based on the principle of comity, a view was held that a foreign judgment can be impeached on merits. If the foreign judgment was enforced *ex gratia*, the enforcement of a judgment which is assailable on merits would be doing injustice. The other view is that a foreign judgment should not be reopened on merits, because 'the facts can never be inquired into so well as on the spot where they arose, and law never administered so satisfactorily as in the tribunal of the country governed by them.'[129] If this is so, then, it is argued, the rehearing of the case by an English court would in all likelihood result in injustice to parties. This was established to be a correct view later on when the enforcement of foreign judgments was founded on the doctrine of obligation.[130]

It is now a settled rule of English private international law that a foreign judgment cannot be impeached on merits.[131] English private international law has taken the doctrine that a foreign judgment cannot be re-opened on merit to its logical conclusion by laying down that even when the foreign judgment is based on the mistaken notions of English law[132] or that it is based on mistaken notion of its own law.[133] The English court takes the view that there is no difference between one kind of mistake and

126. (1879) 5 P.D. 28.

127. The Court of Appeal reversed this judgment as the defendant produced further evidence that the Portuguse law had abolished action *in rem*. But the principle has been accepted by the writers : see Halsbury's *Laws of England*, (3rd Ed.), Vol. 35, para. 1203.

128. *Menahan* v. *Moses*, 1938 Bom. 394.

129. Smith's *Leading Cases* (13th Ed.) ii, 717-718, quoted by Cheshire, p. 643.

130. See also Cheshire (8th Ed.), pp. 643-44.

131. *Pemberton* v. *Huges*, (1899) 1 Ch. 781; *Messina* v. *Petrococahino*, (1872), L.R. 4 P.C. 144; *Bank of Australasia* v. *Nias*, (1851) 16 Q.B. 717; *Henderson* v. *Henderson*, (1844) 6 Q.B. 188; *Vanquelin* v. *Bouard*, (1863) 15 C.B.N.S. 341; *Godard* v. *Gray*, (1870) 6 Q.B. 139; *Vadala* v. *Lawes*, (1890) 25 Q.B.D. 310; *Merker* v. *Merker*, (1963) p. 283.

132. *Godard* v. *Gray*, cited above.

133. *Henderson* v. *Henderson*, cited above.

any other kind.[134] Thus, in *Henderson* v. *Henderson*.[135] where it was argued by the defendant that the plaintiff brought the original action in representative capacity without establishing that she had such capacity and that the defendant had a right to a set-off against the plaintiffs husband, the court held that neither plea could be entertained. In *Ellis* v. *M'Henry*[136] the defendant put up the defence that there existed a deed which completely nullified the claim of the plaintiff and exonerated him from his liability completely. The Court rejected the plea.

Thus, English law takes the view that if the foreign court is of competent jurisdiction in the international sense, then that is enough. Competence in any other sense is not regarded as material.[137] This means that an action will lie on a foreign judgment even though it is a judgment delivered by a court which, according to its own internal law, has no jurisdiction.[138]

The Indian law is different.

Clause (b) of s. 13, Indian Civil Procedure Code lays down that a foreign judgment shall not be conclusive if it 'has not been given on the merits of the case'. In *Mallappa Yellappa Bonnur* v. *Raghavendra Sham Rao Despande*[139] the question came for consideration before the Bombay High Court. The simplified facts of the case are : Pursuant to a settlement of accounts in respect of money dealings between the parties, the respondent executed a promissory note for Rs. 15,000 in favour of the appellant. The account was subsequently disputed by the respondent and the matter was referred to arbitration. The award was given in favour of the appellant. They were awarded an amount of Rs. 17,000 which included interest. On respondent's failure to pay the amount, the appellant filed a suit on the basis of the award, and obtained a decree from a Savanur court. On failing to get the decree satisfied in Savanur state (then an Indian state), the appellant instituted a suit on the judgment in a Dharwar court. The respondent put up appearance and took all the pleas available to him under s. 13, C.P.C., but subsequently absented himself. Meanwhile the respondent had filed a suit in the Savanur court for getting the decree set aside on the ground that the court had no jurisdiction in the suit as he did not reside within the jurisdiction of the court. The decree was set aside. Thereafter the respondent put up appearance in the Dharwar court and got the *ex parte* proceeding set aside, and sought the leave of the court to amend the written statement, which was allowed. The appellant submitted

134. *Gadard* v. *Gray*, cited above.
135. (1844) 6 Q.B. 288.
136. (1871) L.R. 6 C.P. 228.
137. *Pemberton* v. *Huges*, (1899) 1 Ch. 781; *Papadopoulos* v. *Papadopoulos* (1939), p. 55.
138. *Ibid.* See also *Pemberton* v. *Huges*, (1899) 1 Ch. 781.
139. 1938 Bom. 173.

to the court that the second judgment of the Savanur court was invalid as it contravened clause (b) of s. 13, C.P.C. But the suit was dismissed. On appeal, the Bombay High Court said that the second judgment of the Savanur court is founded on complete disregard of international law in as much as it ignored the principle of submission. Since the respondent had not submitted to the jurisdiction of the court, the judgment was of a competent court. It was held that the second judgment was also invalid as it was not given on merits. Rangnekar, J. said that ordinarily it is not open to the court to sit in appeal over a foreign judgment, and a foreign judgment cannot be ignored just because it proceeds on ground which would not be adequate had the matter been proceeded in an Indian court. However, the Indian courts are competent to ignore a judgment which has not been given on merits, since law in India is different from English law.

In *D.T. Keymer* v. *P. Visvanatham*[140] the plaintiff filed a suit against the defendant in a court in England and the defendant appeared before the court; certain interrogatories were served on him which he refused to answer, whereupon his defence was struck off and a decree was passed against him. The plaintiff sought to enforce this judgment in an Indian court. The defendant took the plea that the judgment was not on merit. Ultimately, the matter came for consideration before the Privy Council. The Privy Council held that the case was not decided on merits, rather the merits of the case were not at all investigated. Their Lordships observed : It refers to those cases where, for one reason or another, the controversy in the action has not, in fact, been the subject of direct adjudication by the court.[141]

The Indian courts have taken the view that if a judgment is given as a matter of penalty or as a matter of mere form based on special or summary procedure inasmuch as such trials does not offer any real or substantial opportunity to the defendant to contest the suit as a matter of right as he would under a regular procedure.[142] Thus a decree passed without recording any evidence is not a judgment on merit. In *Babu Nemi Chand* v. *Y.V. Rao*[143] the plaintiff filed a suit in which the defendant put up appearance on the first day of hearing and submitted his written statement, but subsequently absented himself. Whereupon the court passed a decree without further proceeding in the case. When the plaintiff filed a suit on the judgment, the court accepted the plea of the defendant that the judgment was not on merit where a petition for divorce the husband did not appear in the court, the service of summons was published in official gazette and no evidence was accorded it was held that the judgment was not on merit.[144]

140. 1916 P.C. 121.

141. *Ibid.* at 123; See also *Heera* v. *Promothonath,* (1867) 8 W.R. 32.

142. *O.P. Verma* v. *Lala Gehri Lal,* 1962 Raj. 231.

143. 1946 Mad. 448.

144. *Mangabhai* v. *Maniben,* 1985 Guj. 187.

In *Gajanan Sheshadari* v. *Shantabai*[145] in a mortgagee's suit for foreclosure against a minor in a Osmanabad court her husband was appointed as guardian *ad litem*. On his failure to put up appearance, the court's *Nazir* was appointed as guardian *ad litem*. The *Nazir* put up some defence, but nonetheless the decree was passed against the defendant. The judgment also proceeded to pass a personal decree against the minor in case the mortgaged property was not sufficient to pay off the debt. When a suit was filed in a Bombay court for the enforcement of the judgment, the court held that so far as the personal decree was concerned, it was made in a judgment which was not on merits. Similarly, a decree passed by a foreign court on default of appearance without any trial or evidence is a decree passed in a judgment which is not on merits,[146] or, when a foreign court passes a judgment on default of the defendant in furnishing security without proceeding with the trial, the judgment cannot be said to be on merit.[147] Similarly, a decision rendered by a foreign court in summary proceeding, after refusing leave to defend, is not a judgment on merit.[148]

Guidmetla Chnia v. *Kota Venkata Subba Rao*[149] provides an interesting illustration. Both the parties appeared before a foreign court with a draft of a compromise and submitted to the court that a decree be passed on the basis of compromise. The court passed a decree accordingly. When the parties went to the court they have not taken their dispute to it; they had gone there with a compromise. Therefore, the decree was merely a recognition of an arrangement already arrived at between the parties and there was no dispute between the parties for the decision of the court. When a suit was filed on this judgment, the Indian court rightly said that the judgment was not given on merit. But where the defendant contests the suit by filing the written evidence and takes part in further proceedings, but later on compromises the suit, and a decree is passed on the basis of the compromise, then the judgment made on the basis of compromise is a judgment on merits.[150] Similarly, if the foreign court does not decide some of the issues, it does not mean that the judgment is not on merit.[151] Merely because it is a judgment rendered in *ex parte* proceedings does not mean that the judgment is not on merits. If trial is held, evidence

145. 1939 Bom. 374.
146. *R.E. Mahommed Kassim & Co. Seeni Pakir-bin Ahmed*, 1927 Mad. 265 (F.B.).
147. *M.K. Sivagaminatha Pillai* v. *Natraja Pillai*, 1961 Mad. 385; see also *Trilochan Choudhary* v. *Dayanidhi*, 1961 Or. 158; *Sheo Tahal Ram* v. *Binaik Shukul*, (1931) 53 All. 747.
148. *K.M. Abdul Jabbar* v. *Indo-Singapore Trader P. Ltd.* 1981 Mad. 118.
149. 1946 Mad. 296.
150. *Satya Narayan* v. *Balchand* 1955 Raj. 59; *Md. Abdulla* v. *P.M. Abdul Rahim* 1985 Mad. 379.
151. *Wazir Sahu* v. *Munsi Das*, 1941, Pat. 109. See also *Sheik Abdul Rahim* v *Mohamed Din*, 1943 Cal. 42; *Midnapore Zamidari* v. *Naresh*, 192: P.C. 241.

it taken, arguments are addressed and then the judgment is rendered, then such a judgment is on merit, even though the defendant is absent.[152] Similarly, a wrong view as to the legal liability of a party or as to the onus does not render a foreign judgment to be not on merit.[153] Where the document is registered and the court passes a decree after recording the evidence, the mere absence of the defendant would not render the foreign judgment as one not on merit.[154]

The Rajasthan High Court very aptly said that an *ex parte* judgment *per se* cannot be said to be not on merit. It may well be. It is not the presence or absence of the defendant which can really condition the quality of a judgment as to its having been given on the merits or not. What really matters is whether the procedure according to which the suit has been decreed requires the court to determine the truth or falsity of the contentions raised. Where it so requires and the court applies its mind to the contentions raised on either side, then the adjudication is on merits.[155] In short, the true test is whether the judgment has been given as a penalty for any conduct of the defendant, such as default in appearance, or whether it is based on a consideration of the truth or otherwise of the plaintiff's case.[156]

However, it should be noted that when a court holds that a judgment is not on merit, then it does not mean that it reopens the entire case. Nor do the courts examine as to whether on the basis of the facts before the foreign court, it reached to the right or wrong conclusion.[157] If it can be gathered from the foreign judgment that it did apply its mind, then it is not open to the defendant to say that the foreign court applied its mind wrongly or that it misunderstood the facts or the law.

(iii) Judgment Opposed to Natural Justice

As has been already seen, a foreign judgment cannot be impeached on the ground that it is unjust or that it perpetrates

152. *S. Jayam Sundar* v. *K. Muthuswami*, 1958 Mad. 203; *Dr. Kulwant* v. *Dhan Raj Dutta*, 1935 Lah. 396; *Brijlal Ramjidas* v. *Govindaram Gordhandas*, 1947 P.C. 192; *Ishwari Pd.* v. *Sriram*, 1927 All. 510; *Narayan* v. *Syed Bahadur*, 1918 Nag. 91 ; *Govinda* v. *Laxman*, 1923; Nag. 139; *Govindan Asari* v. *Sankaran* 1958 *Ker.* 203; *Sheikh Abdul Rahim* v. *Mohamed Din*, 1943 Cal. 42; *Ephrayim H. Ephrayim* v. *Turner Morrison & Co.*, 1930 Bom. 511.

153. *R.S. Rama Shenoi* v. *M.A. Hallagna*, (1917) 41 Mad. 205.

154. *George* v. *Gatherine*, 1919 All. 228; *Ishwari Prasad* v. *Sriram*, 1927 All. 510.

155. *O.P. Verma* v. *Lala Gehrilal*, 1962 Raj. 231; See also *R.M.V. Vedlachi* v. *R.M.A. Ramanathan Chettiar*, (1972) 2 M.L.J. 468.

156. *O.P. Verma* v. *Lal Gehrilal*, cited above; *Sheo Tahal Ram* v. *Binaik Shukul*, (1931) 52 All. 747; *Trilochan Choudhury* v. *Dayanidhi*, 1961 Ori. 158.

157. *Mallappa Yellappa Benner* v. *Raghavendra*, 1938 Bom. 173.

injustice on one of the parties. English judge Channell, J. said.[158] "In my view of it, the judgment appears, according to our law, to be clearly wrong, but that of course is not enough . . ., and whatever the expression 'contrary to natural justice', which is used in so many cases, means (and there is really very little authority indeed as to what it does mean), I think that it is not enough, therefore, to say that the result works injustice in the particular case, because a wrong decision always does."[159] Recently, the Indian Supreme Court[160] after observing that it is extremely difficult to fix with precision the exact cases in which the contravention of any rule of procedure is sufficiently serious to justify a refusal of recognition or enforcement of a foreign judgment and that it is difficult to trace a definite gradations of injustice so as to reach a definite point at which it deserves to be called the negation of natural justice, said :[161] "The expression 'contrary to natural justice' has figured so prominently in judicial statements that it is essential to fix its exact scope and meaning. When applied to foreign judgments, it merely relates to the alleged irregularities in procedure adopted by the adjudicating court and has nothing to do with the merits of the case. If the proceedings be in accordance with the practice of the foreign court but that practice is not in accordance with natural justice, this court will not allow it to be concluded by them.[162] In other words, the courts are vigilant to see that the defendant had not been deprived of an opportunity to present his side of the case. The wholesome maxim *audi alteram partem* is deemed to be of universal, not merely of domestic, application."[163]

Whatever the difficulty might be in defining the expression 'contrary to natural justice' with precision, in its actual application to judicial proceedings, it would always be violation of natural justice, (a) if the defendant was not served with any notice of the proceedings, (b) if the defendant was not given adequate opportunity to present his case, or (c) if the judge (or any one of the judges where the case is decided by more than one judge) was personally interested in the subject-matter of the suit.

When the defendant is not served with any notice : This head of natural justice relates to cases where a judgment is pronounced against an absent defendant who has not been served with any notice of the proceedings. Under the Administration of Justice Act, 1920 this rule is laid down thus : no foreign judgment may be registered under the Act, if the defendant (being the judgment

158. *Robinson* v. *Fenner*, (1913) 3 K.B. 835.
159. *Wazir Sahu* v. *Munshi Das*, (1941) 20 Pat. 144.
160. *Sankaran* v. *Lakshmi*, 1974 S.C. 1764.
161. *Ibid.* at pp. 1775-76.
162. This sentence is a reproduction of the observation of Bramwell, B. made in *Crawley* v. *Isaacs*, (1867) 16 L.T. 529 at p. 531.
163. The entire passage is a verbatim reproduction of Cheshire at 656.

debtor in the case) 'was not duly served with the process of the court and did not appear'.[164] The Foreign Judgments (Reciprocal Enforcement) Act, 1933 lays down that the registration of a foreign judgment under the Act will be set aside 'if the judgment-debtor, being the defendant in the proceedings, did not receive notice thereof in sufficient time to enable him to defend and he did not appear'.[165] At common law this question had arisen in respect of the recognition of certain nullity and divorce degrees. The most apt case is *Rudd* v. *Rudd*[166] where a husband who had filed a petition for divorce in a Washington court purported to serve the notice of the petition by sending a copy thereof to an English address where the wife never resided and by publishing a notice in a newspaper which she never was in the habit of reading. Ultimately, a decree of divorce was passed in favour of the husband. When the question came for its recognition in an English court, the court refused to recognize it. Horridge, J. said that the decree was void since it was pronounced in the absence and without the knowledge of the wife. But then, in this case, since the husband was domiciled in England, the decree was also of a court of incompetent jurisdiction. Similarly, in *Macalpine* v. *Macalpine*,[167] though no notice of the proceedings was served on the husband, the husband had obtained the decree of divorce by playing fraud on the court. Recent judicial pronouncement take the view that a foreign judgment cannot be refused recognition merely for want of notice to the respondent.[168] Although in *Gray* v. *Formosa*[169] a foreign decree was refused recognition on the ground that it violated the principle of natural justice, a tendency is discernible not to refuse recognition on the ground of violation of principles of natural justice.[170] Ifa notice is served but the defendant does not appear, the judgment cannot be impeached on that basis.[171]

Before the Indian courts this question has come in several cases, though predominantly the cases are those which do not relate to divorce or nullity.

In *Indian and General Investment Trust Ltd*. v. *Raja of Khalikote*[172] one Raja of Khalikote was in need of money. He conceived of a scheme of raising loan in England upon the security of his

164. Section 9(2)(c).
165. Section 4(1)(a)(iii).
166. (1924) p. 72.
157. (1958) p. 35
168. *Igra* v. *Igra*, (1951) p. 404; *Maher* v. *Maher*, (1951) p. 342; *Arnold* v. *Arnold*, (1957) p. 237; *Wood* v. *Wood*, (1957) p. 254; *Adams* v. *Cape Industries*, (1990) 2 W.L.R. 657.
169. (1963) p. 259; followed (though reluctantly) in *Lepre* v. *Lepre*, (1965) p. 52.
170. See for instance, *Mitford* v. *Mitford*, (1923) p. 130.
171. *S.A. Consortium General Taxtiles* v. *Sun and Sand Agencies*, (1978) 2 W.L.R. 1.
172. **1952 Cal. 508.**

Zamindari. Pursuant to this idea a company was floated. On or about January 24, 1949 an action was instituted in the Chancery division of the High Court for the recovery of the amount. The Raja had died earlier in 1909. While raising the loan in England he had also acted as guardian of his minor son. On January 24, 1949 two writs were issued on the son, who was made the defendant, requiring him to cause appearance to be entered into within 90 days of the service of the writs. The writs were returned as the defendant refused to take them; while doing so he had made an endorsement on the writs that as he had no movable or immovable property in England, the English court had no jurisdiction over him. On November 17, 1949 the plaintiffs took out two jMaster summons addressed to the defendant for passing the final udgment. These summons were not served on the defendant. However, the English court proceeded in the action and passed a decree against the defendant. When an action was filed on the judgment in the Indian court. Sinha, J., held that the judgment violated principle of natural justice inasmuch as no summons were served on him.[173]

Edulji Burjorji v. *Manekji Patel*[174] illustrates this principle very aptly. In the winding up proceedings of an English company in an English court certain notices were issued to the shareholders to pay up the balance of their shares. Such a notice was also issued to the defendant. Since the notice was wrongly and carelessly addressed, it was returned to the addressee by the dead-letter office. On an action being filed against the defendant on the English judgment, the Indian court held that since the notice was not served on the defendant, the defendant was not bound by the judgment. The court observed that Indian court when called upon to give effect to foreign judgments should insist upon a strict proof of the validity of the service of summons and other process alleged to have emanated from a foreign court and made a foundation of a liability to be enforced here. But, the court observed, if the foreign court considers a particular sort of notice enough, the courts in India, in the absence of any evidence to the contrary, should consider that as enough.

No adequate opportunity to represent was given : In *Hari Singh* v. *Mohammed Said*[175] the Lahore High Court said that in those cases where the legal representatives of the deceased defendant are not brought on record, or where proceedings against the minor defendants are without appointing a guardian *ad litem*, then it amounts to violation of principles of natural justice. Similarly, in *Popat Virji* v. *Damodar Jairam*[176] the Bombay High Court said that where guardian *ad litem* of minor defendant is not a fit person to act as such, then there is a violation of principles of natural

173. 1952 Cal. 508 at p. 510.
174. (1887) 11 Bom. 241.
175. 1927 Lah. 200.
176. 1934 Bom 390.

justice. In *Gajanan Sheshadri* v. *Shantabai*[177], the court said that it was wrong to appoint a court's officer as guardian *ad litem* when the minor defendant had a natural guardian who did not express his unwillingness to act as guardian.[178] But where the notice of the proceedings was served on the natural guardian, but the natural guardian did not put up appearance and therefore the court appointed a guardian, it was held by the Supreme Court that this, did not violate the principle of natural justice.[179]

Another interesting case illustrating this principle in *Firm Tijarati Hindu Joint Family Kesardas Rajan Singh* v. *Parmanand*.[180] A suit was instituted in July 1947 on a pro-note for the recovery of money lent in a Bannu court (now in Pakistan). By the time the suit came for hearing the plantiff had to flee to the Indian dominion on account of very disturbed communal situation at Bannu. After coming to India, he sent a telegram seeking an adjournment as under the circumstances it was not possible for him to send the pro-note. The court refused the adjournment and dismissed the suit. Subsequently, the plantiff filed a suit in a Karnal court on the pro-note and the defendant pleaded the judgment of the Bannu court as *res judicata*. The court observed that the summary dismissal of the suit in the manner in which it was done violated the principle of natural justice as in the circumstances of the case refusal to allow an adjournment was extremely harsh and arbitrary.[181]

This principle finds another illustration in the English case, *Jacobson* v. *Frachon*.[182] The plantiffs who were residents in England entered into a contract with the defendant for the purchase of *crepe de chine*. The defendants were residents of France. The plantiffs filed a suit in France for the cancellation of the contract on the ground that the goods supplied were inferior in quality and short in quantity. They also claimed damages. The French court appointed an expert to examine the material supplied to the plaintiff in England. The expert was a relative of the defendants. While the expert was examining the goods in England, he refused to listen to the witnesses of the plantiffs, and ultimately made a report adverse to the plantiffs. On the basis of this report the French court entered a judgment against the plaintiffs. Thereafter, the plaintiffs sued the defendants in an English court on the original cause of action. The defendants took the plea of *res judicata* on the basis of the French judgment. The plaintiffs asserted that the French judgment was invalid being contrary to the principles of natural justice. The Court of Appeal

177. 1939 Bom. 374.
178. *Sankaran* v. *Lakshmi*, 1974. S.C. 1764.
179. *Ibid.* at p. 1776.
180. 1959 Punj. 306.
181. See also *Keymer* v. *Vishwanathan Reddi*, 1916 P.C. 121.
182. (1928) 138 L.T. 386.

held that the French judgment cannot be impeached on that ground as the plaintiffs had not been prevented from presenting their case before the French court even though the expert did not hear their evidence. By the French law, it appeared, the French court was not bound by the report of the expert and could reject it, if found it accurate.

In *Veena Kalia* v. *Dr. Jatindra Nath Kalia*[182a] the husband filed a divorce petition in a foreign court. Since wife had no means to contest the case in a foreign court, she could not do so. An *ex parte* decree of divorce was passed in favour of the husband. It was held that foreign decree was a nullity as it was violative of the rule of natural justice.

If the Judge was interested in the subject-matter of the suit: In domestic law, it is a well established principle that if the judge is himself personally interested in the subject-matter of the suit, then the judgment is void being contrary to the principle of natural justice.[183] There is hardly any reported case relating to foreign judgments in which the question has arisen either before an Indian court or English court.

There is a practical difficulty in the application of this principle to the foreign judgments. Cheshire rightly says that: "it is difficult to trace the delicate gradations of injustice so as to reach a definite point at which it deserves to be called negation of natural justice."[184] Cheshire is also against the extension of the principle of natural justice to, what Cairns, J. called, "substantial justice".[185] He says, "Such a vague general principle would seem to encompass not only judgments contrary to natural justice, but also those where there has been fraud as to the jurisdiction. It merely seems to confuse that which was reasonably clear in a way so as to create undesirable uncertainty in the field of recognition."[186]

(iv) Judgment Vitiated by Fraud

It is a well established rule of Indian and English domestic law that a judgment obtained by fraud may be impeached. Though difficult it is to make out the case, a party is free to bring an independent action to set aside a judgement obtained by fraud. In the leading English case, *Dutchess of Kingston*,[187] court observed: But if it (judgment) was a direct and decisive sentence upon the point, and as it stands to be admitted as conclusive evidence upon the point and not to be impeached from within; yet like all other acts of the highest judicial authority, it is impeachable from without, although it is not permitted to show that the court was mistaken, it may be shown that they were misled. . . Fraud is an extrinsic, collateral act, which vitiates most solemn proceedings of the court of justice." Thus, it seems than an unsuccessful party cannot bring an action to get a judgment set aside on the ground that the court made a mistake of fact or law, but it can bring an independent action on the ground that in passing

182a. AIR 1996 Del 54.

183. See Indain case, 191 P.R. 1888.

184. *Private International Law*, (8th Ed.), p. 65.

185. *Middleton* v. *Middleton*, (1967), p. 62; he defined 'substantial justice', as 'that what strikes an English judge as being fundamentally unfair,' (at p. 70).

186. Cheshire, p. 658.

107. Smith's *Leading Cases*, (13th Ed.) ii, 641 at p. 651.

the judgment the court was tricked or imposed upon. An English domestic action on this ground can be maintained only if the party wanting to get the judgment set aside can succeed in proving some new facts, evidential of fraud, which have been discovered after the judgment was pronounced and which could not have been reasonably discovered at the time of the trial.

A foreign judgment can also be equally impeached on the ground of fraud. But the English private international law makes a significant departure from the domestic rule inasmuch as a foreign judgment can be impeached on the ground of fraud even though no new facts are discovered and the fraud is alleged to be in the foreign proceedings. This has been laid down in series of four cases and seems to be the established rule of English private international law. The earliest case is *Ochsenbein* v. *Papelier*,[188] where a French seller told the English buyer in Paris that he had begun an action to recover the price of goods. Upon being remonstrated as to why he should have gone to the court of law instead of going to arbitration, he burned the writ and agreed to refer the dispute to arbitration in London. But, nonetheless, he proceeded with the action and obtained a judgment in his favour. When he filed an action on the French judgment the English buyer was successful in impeaching the judgment on the ground that the French court was tricked into passing the judgment. The trick was not apparent at that time but was discovered afterwards.[189]

In *Abouloff* v. *Oppenheimer*,[190] the plantiffs filed a suit on a foreign judgment under which the defendant was ordered to return to the plantiff certain goods or to pay their value. The defendant alleged that the judgment was obtained by fraud since the plantiff said before the foreign court that goods were not in her possession, while in fact they were in her possession. The plaintiff countered this averment by saying that the plea was one which the Russian court could, and as a matter of fact did, consider and thus to examine it again would mean the reopening of the case on merit. Overruling this contention, Lord Esher said : "I will assume that in the suit in the Russian court the plantiff's fraud was alleged by the defendants and that they gave evidence in support of the charge; I will assume even that the defendants gave the very same evidence which they propose to adduce in this action, nevertheless the defendants will not be debarred at the trial of this action from making the same charge of fraud and from adducing the same evidence in support of it."[191] This view was reiterated in *Vadala* v.

188. (1873) 8 Ch. App. 695.
189. See also *Israel Discount Bank of New York* v. *Hadjpateras*, (1984) 1 W.L.R. 137 (under influence).
190. (1882) 10 Q.B.D. 295; *House of Spring Lordens Ltd.* v. *Waith*, (1990) 3 W.L.R. 347.
191. *Ibid.* at 306.

Lawes.[192] *Syal* v. *Heyward*[193] takes this trend to its logical conclusion. An Indian moneylender obtained a judgment for Rs. 20,000 against the defendant from an Indian court. The writ was served on the defendant when he was in India, but he failed to appear. The plantiff registered the judgment in England under the Foreign Judgments (Reciprocal Enforcement) Act, 1933. The defendant applied to set aside the registration on the ground of fraud inasmuch as the amount of loan was only Rs. 10,800 and the rest was by way of interest, but the plantiff did not disclose this fact before the Indian court lest the amount he reduced under the Indian Usurious Loans Act. The English court accepted the plea. Thus, this case lays down that it is of no consequence even if fact relied on by the defendant constituting fraud were known to him at all material times and he could have very conveniently taken this defence in proceedings before the Indian court.[194] This was also the view taken in the earlier case, *Ellerman Lines* v. *Read*,[195] where the defence against the enforcement of a foreign judgment was that the plantiff suppressed from the foreign court that there was already an agreement in respect of salvage fee under which an amount had already been deposited in a London Bank. This was an action in a Constantinople Court for the recovery of the salvage fee. The English Court accepted the plea of the defendant.

These decisions establish a distinction between the domestic judgments and foreign judgments : An English domestic judgment can be impeached for fraud on facts discovered subsequently after the trial, but a foreign judgment can be impeached for fraud even for facts known to the defendant at the time of trial and which could have been then taken in defence. Graveson rightly says : "Such a distinction suffers from defects both of its inherent absurdity and of being completely inconsistent with the proposition, which the court accepted, that the same principle apply in respect of both English and foreign judgment."[196]

Clause (e) of s. 13, Civil Procedure Code lays down that a foreign judgment shall not be conclusive if 'it has been obtained by fraud'. But the Indian cases on the subject are few and sparse. In *Sama Rayer* v. *Annamalai*,[197] a decision under the old code, the Madras High Court observed, *obiter*, that a foreign judgment can be impeached for fraud or collusion. In *Popat Virji* v. *Damodar*,[198] after a review of English authorities, Kania, J. said that a foreign judgment cannot be impeached on the ground that the foreign court was mistaken; it can be impeached on the ground that the

192. (1890) 25 Q.B.D. 310.
193. (1948) 2 K.B. 443.
194. *Ibid.*
195. (1928) 2 K.B. 144.
196. Graveson, (1949) 12 M.L.R. 105 at p. 106; See also Cheshire, pp. 653-54; Dicey and Morris Wolff, p. 1009; s. 247; Read, pp. 279-293.
197. (1884) 7 Mad. 164.
198. 1934 Bom. 390.

foreign court was misled or imposed upon. In *Sundaram Pillai* v. *Kandasami Pillai*[199] King J. observed (it is interesting to note that he does not refer to any English or Indian decision) : "It cannot be argued that merely because a plantiff obtains a decree upon evidence which is believed by the court but which in fact is not true, he had obtained a decree by fraud. There must be fraud connected with the procedure in that suit itself to bring the matter within the clause."[200] In *Abdul Wazid* v. *Vishwanathan*[201] the court affirmed that fraud vitiates a judgment. But since, in this case, the plea of fraud was raised for the first time at the appellate court, the court said that the plea could not be taken at that stage. In *Magan Bhai* v. *Maniben*,[202] the Indian court refused to recognized a Mexican decree of divorce which was obtained by fraudulent misrepresentation of his domicile and residence by the husband.

In *Sankaran* v. *Lakshmi*[203] the question has been examined in some detail by the Kerala High[204] and by the Supreme Court.[204a] Once Krishnan went to England for higher studies but ultimately did not return to India and died in England leaving behind some movable and immovable property. On behalf of certain relatives of Krishnan letters of administration of the estate of Krishnan were obtained. As there was a likelihood of dispute relating to the domicile of Krishnan, the administrators took out originating summons in the High Court of Judicature in England for deciding the question. The High Court held that Krishnan died domiciled in England. In this case, *inter alia*, this judgment was impeached as one obtained by fraud. It was alleged that those relatives of Krishnan who instructed the English administrators deliberately withheld those facts from the court which would have established that Krishnan did not acquire any domicile of choice in England. The trial court and the Kerala High Court found that one of the relatives of Krishnan who had in fact instructed the British administrators of the estate of Krishnan 'in spite of his knowledge that Krishnan had no intention to settle down in England permanently, made the administrators believe and thereby imposed upon the English court that Krishnan had an English 'domicile at the time of his death, as a result of which the decision' from the English court was obtained.[205] Thus, it was held that the judgment of English court was vitiated by fraud.

On appeal, the Supreme Court did not agree to the finding of fraud. After reviewing all the English decisions on fraud[206] and

199. 1941 Mad. 387
200. *Ibid.* at 389.
201. 1953 Mad. 261.
202. 1985 Guj. 187.
203. 1974 S.C. 1764.
204. 1964 Ker. 244.
204a. 1974 S.C. 1764.
205. 1964 Ker at p. 249. But see *Md. Mausour* v. *N. Abdul Kadir*, AIR 1970 Mad. 510.
206. The decisions have been already reviewed.

then referring to certain Canadian[207] and the United States decision,[208] Mathew, J., critical of the English decisions, was inclined to agree with the view of Duff, J. in *MacDonald* v. *Pier*[209]: "Such jurisdiction exists but in the exercise of it the court will not permit its process being used for the purpose of obtaining retrial of an issue already determined . . . under the guise of impugning a judgment as procured by fraud. Therefore, the perjury must be in a material matter and therefore it must be established by evidence not known to the parties at the time of the former trial." On this formulation the learned judge found that there was no new material before the Indian court which could go to establish that the English decision was obtained by fraud. His Lordship said that the administrators who obtained the order from the English court did not practice any fraud by adducing evidence which they knew was false or induced any person or witness to give false evidence or file any false affidavit. Nor could it be said that the English court was misled by the evidence of any person. Thus, it seems, the Indian law obliterates the distinction between domestic judgments and foreign judgments : both types of judgments can be impeached for fraud only upon allegations and proof of new and material facts which were not before the court when it adjudicated upon the dispute between the parties and which constituted the fraud. In other words, the Indian law in this respect is akin to Canadian law : the fraud on the basis of which a foreign judgment can be impeached must be something collateral or extreneous and not merely the fraud which is imputed from alleged false statements made at the trial which were met, or could have met by counter-statements of the other party.[210]

Fraud vitiating a judgment may be (i) the fraud of one of the party to the proceedings, or (ii) of the court itself. The former is the usual case. Whenever a foreign judgment is impeached on the basis of the latter, it usually merges into the plea of judgment being contrary to the principles of natural justice.

Practically all the English and Indian cases discussed so far relate to the fraud of the party. In *Ochenbein* v. *Papelier*,[211] fraud was directly exercised on the other party. While *Abouloff* v. *Oppenheimer*,[212] *Vadala* v. *Lawes*,[213] *Syal* v. *Heyward*,[214] *Popat Virji* v. *Damodar*,[215] (where allegation of fraud did not succeed),

207. *Woodruff* v. *McLennan*, (1887) 14 Ont. A.R. 242; *Jocobs* v. *Beaver*, (1908) 17 Ont. L.R. 496.

208. *Hilton* v. *Guyot*, (1895) 159 U.S. 113.

209. 1963 S.C.R. 107.

210. *Jacobs* v. *Beaver*, (1908) 17 Ont. L.R. 496.

211. (1873) 8 Ch. App. 695.

212. (1882) 10 Q.B.D. 295.

213. (1890) 25 Q.B.D. 310.

214. (1948) 2 K.B. 443.

215. 1934 Bom. 390.

Sundaram v. *Kandasami*,[216] (where the allegation of fraud did not succeed) and *Sankaran* v. *Lakshmi*,[217] (where the allegation of fraud also did not succeed) are cases of fraud being practiced on the court.

The cases of court's fraud are rare. A usual illustration is when the foreign court takes bribe or the judge is himself personally interested in any of the parties or in the subject-matter of the suit. For instance, in the English case, *Prince* v. *Dewhurst*,[218] the judges who were to distribute the property were themselves interested in it. *Abdul Wazid* v. *Visvanathan*,[219] is another good illustration of the fraud of the court. In this case it was alleged that the foreign judgment was already prepared and ready before the hearing began and was delivered soon after the hearing, the judges pretending fraudulently that it had been prepared after the hearing. This plea was disallowed by the court since it was for the first time raised at the appellate stage.

(v) Judgment contrary to International law or based on non-recognition of Indian law

It has been seen earlier that a foreign judgment cannot be impeached on the ground that the foreign court was not competent to adjudicate upon it under its own law, since one time it was doubtful whether a foreign judgment contrary to the law of the country where it is sought to be enforced, could be enforced. In *Ellis* v. *M'Henry*[220] the question was left open. But in subsequent cases, when the doctrine of obligation was finally accepted by the English court,[221] it was laid down that even if the judgment is based on a mistaken notion of English law, the defendant should, nonetheless perform the obligation. The leading case is *Gordard* v. *Gray*.[222] The plaintiff sued the defendant in a French court for the breach of a charter-party, the proper law of which was English law. One of the clauses of the charter party ran : "Penalty for non-performance of this agreement is estimated cost of freight." Failing to understand its technical meaning, the French court interpreted it literally and awarded damages on the basis of freight. Under English law this is not the meaning of the clause; the damages are assessed on the basis of exact loss suffered by a party. Subsequently, when the plaintiff sought to enforce the judgment in an English court the defendant impeached the judgment on the ground that it was based on an erroneous view of English law. The English court held the judgment enforceable as it made no difference as to whether the mistake was relating to its own law or English law.

216. 1941 Mad. 387.
217. 1974 S.C. 1764.
218. (1837) 8 Sim. 279.
219. 1953 Mad. 261.
220. (1871) L.R. 6 C.P. 228.
221. See, for instance, *Castrique* v. *Imrie*, (1870) L.R. 4 H.L. 414.
222. (1870) 6 Q.B. 139.

Although no direct authority exists as to whether the English court will recognize a judgment which is contrary to international law,[223] it seems to be clear that if the judgment has been pronounced by a court of competent jurisdiction, then the English court would not decline to recognize it.

The Indian law is different. Clause (c) of s. 13 Indian Civil Procedure Code lays down that a foreign judgment is not conclusive if "it appears on the face of proceedings to be founded on an incorrect view of international law or a refusal to recognize the law of the States in cases in which such law is applicable." This clause is to be distinguished from Clause (f) which lays down that a foreign judgment is not conclusive if "it sustains a claim founded on a breach of any law in force in India," though it is obvious that both the clauses are bound to over-lap.

Clauses (c) and (f) have come for interpretation before our High Courts in several cases.

In *H.H. Bikrama Singh* v. *Sardar Bir Singh*[224] The court observed : " . . . it may be pleaded to an action in our courts upon a foreign judgment pronounced on merits, that it is, upon its face, founded upon an inaccurate view of the law of British India, or of international law." Both the aspects of clause (c) came for interpretation in *Panchapakesa Iyer* v. *K.N. Hussien Muhammad.*[225] A Penang court had granted probate to the defendant of a will executed by one Noor Mohammed who died in Penang leaving behind properties both in Malaya and Tanjore (India). The probate was confined to immovable properties situated in Penang. In 1919 the widow of Noor Mohammed started proceedings for the administration of the estate of her husband and claimed an account against the defendant in a Penang court. The Supreme Court of Penang came to the conclusion that (a) the plaintiff as widow of the deceased Noor Mohammed was entitled to one-third share in the property of her husband, and that (b) she was entitled to certain other assets, the quantum of which was arrived at by adding up together the assets of the deceased in Penang and Tanjore. The Tanjore assets of the deceased consisted of the immovables only. The plaintiff filed a suit on the judgment of the Penang Supreme Court. Mr. Justice Reilly came to the conclusion that the judgment could not be enforced as it offended the principles of international law as well as of Muslim law, inasmuch as no foreign court can adjudicate in respect of immovables situated outside its jurisdiction and "that mistake is patent on the face of the proceedings" and the widow being a Sunni of Hanafi school was entitled to only 1/8 estate of the deceased in the presence of a son under Muslim law. In *Mallappu Vellappa Bennun* v. *Raghavendra Sham*

223. See *Dent* v. *Smith*, (1869) 4 Q.B. 414.
224. (1888) P.R. 191.
225. 1934 Mad. 145.

Rao,[226] the Indian court refused to recognize a foreign judgment as it was violative of the principle of submission to the jurisdiction, and in *Popat Virji* v. *Damodar Jairam*,[227] foreign judgment was not recognized as it was found violative of Indian law. In *Indian and General Investment Trust* v. *Raja of Khalikote*,[228] the court felt that the decision of the English court was based on an incorrect view of international law. It also said that the court did not apply the Orissa Money Lenders Act which was applicable, yet it could not be said that the English court 'refused' to apply the Act, as the court merely accepted the submission of the plaintiff, howsoever erroneous, that the Indian law did not apply. In such circumstances it may be said that the court went wrong but it cannot be said that the court refused to apply the Indian law.

The decision in *Pires* v. *Pires*[229] is an authority on Clause (f) of s. 13 that a foreign judgment which sustains a claim on a breach of any law in force in the states cannot be recognized or enforced by the Indian courts. In this case a confirmation of a foreign decree of divorce was sought from a Goan court. The marriage was a Roman Catholic marriage and the law in force in Goa laid down that a Roman Catholic marriage was an indissoluble union. Confirmation of the foreign decree was refused as it would be violative of Goan law.

There are several other cases where Clause (f) has been invoked but without any success. In *T. Sundaram Pillai* v. *Kandasami*,[230] a foreign judgment was impeached on the ground that it violated the Indian Contract Act. But the court did not accept the contention as it found that the foreign judgment did not violate the Contract Act. It also seems to be clear that the clause applies to substantive law and not to procedural law.[231]

Where a foreign court follows its own law which on a particular matter happens to be different from the law in force in India, it cannot be said that the foreign judgment was founded on a breach of Indian law.[232] If the transaction was not governed by the Indian law and therefore the foreign court applied the proper law of the transaction which was violative of Indian law, the foreign judgment cannot be impeached under the clause.[233]

226. 1938 Bom. 173.
227. 1934 Bom. 390.
228. 1952 Cal. 508.
229. 1967 Goa 113.
230. 1941 Mad. 387.
231. *Ganga Prasad* v. *Ganeshi Lal*, 46 All 119; *Gadodia & Co.* v. *The Great India Penninsula Railway Co.*, 1924 All. 254; *Nallatuambi Mudaliar* v. *Ponnusami* (1878-81) 2 Mad. 400.
232. *Ganga Prasad* v. *Ganeshi Lal*, (1923) 46 All. 119=1924 All. (6).
233. *C.V. Kunhiman* v. *P.M.K. Indrosekutty*, 1988 Ker. 126. *L. & K. Investment Trust Ltd.* v. *Raia of Khalikote*, 1952 Cal. 508.

(vi) Foreign Judgments against Public Policy

It may be taken to be a well established rule of English[234] and Indian private international law that a foreign law which is against the public policy will not be enforced or recognized. The same is true of foreign judgments given in proceedings of a penal or revenue nature.[234a] This matter has already been fully discussed.[235] Section 13, Indian Civil Procedure Code does not recognize this as a separate head, but it seems to be covered under Clause (f).[236]

It is submitted that the matter has already been sufficiently discussed and therefore, here we would discuss only an illustrative case. In *Re Macartney*[237] (and the oft-cited cases) the foreign court awarded perpetual maintenance to the mother of an illegitimate child against the estate of the deceased putative father. The English court refused to enforce the judgment on the ground that "the general recognition of the permanent rights of illegitimate children and their spinster mother is contrary to the established policy of this country." The learned editor of Dicey's sixth edition made the following observation : "It is indeed upon the great authority of Dicey that this exception largely rests."[238] But this has now been recognized statutorily,[239] and a foreign judgment which is contrary to public policy cannot be enforced either in India[240] or in England.

III

DIRECT EXECUTION OF FOREIGN DECREES

Ordinarily foreign decrees cannot be executed directly. If a decree-holder wants to execute a foreign decree he has, as has been seen in Part II of this Chapter, to file a suit on judgment. But in most systems foreign decrees are executable directly on the basis of reciprocity. In the modern law most of the countries allow direct execution of foreign decrees if there are reciprocal agreements between the countries for their direct execution.

In India and England in certain cases direct execution of foreign decrees is possible under certain statutes.

English Law

Under the following statutes, the foreign judgments can be

234. See s. 9(2)(f), Administration of Justice Act, 1920; s. 4(1)(a)(v), Foreign Judgment (Reciprocal Enforcement) Act, 1933.
234a. *USA* v. *Inkley,* (1988) 3 W.L.R. 304.
235. See Chapter 5.
236. *Piros* v. *Pires*, 1967 Goa 113.
237. (1921) 1 Ch. 522; but see *Phrantzes* v. *Argenti,* (1960) 2 Q.B. 19 which repudiates that part of the decision which lays down that a cause of action unknown to English law will not be enforced.
238. Conflict of Laws (sixth edition).
239. See Part IV of this Chapter.
240. *Pires* v. *Pires,* 1967 Goa 113.

directly executed : (a) Judgment Extension Act, 1868, (b) the Administration of Justice Act, 1920, (c) the Foreign Judgments (Reciprocal Enforcement) Act, 1933, (d) Recognition of Divorces and Legal Separation Act, 1971, and (e) Maintenance Orders (Reciprocal Enforcement) Act, 1972. Reference should also be made to the Civil Jurisdiction and Judgment Act, 1982, while lays down the bases of recognition of foreign judgments.

Judgment Extension Act, 1868 : From the point of view of private international law, Scotland and Ireland are considered to be foreign countries, and, prior to 1868, a judgment of a court of Scotland or Ireland could be enforced by a suit on such judgment. By the Judgment Extension Act, 1868 the judgments rendered by the superior courts of England, Ireland and Scotland have been made directly enforceable in any part of the United Kingdom. The Act applies to the judgments of superior courts only. However, the judgments of inferior courts have also been made enforceable all throughout the United Kingdom by the Inferior Courts Judgment Extension Act, 1882. Similarly, s. 121 of the Bankruptcy Act, 1914 makes orders made in bankruptcy, and s. 223 of the Companies Act, 1929 makes orders made in the course of winding up proceedings by the courts of England, Scotland and Ireland enforceable all throughout the United Kingdom.

Under the Judgment Extension Act only the judgments which are for 'any debt, damages or costs,[241] are made enforceable. Other judgments cannot be enforced directly.[242] Then, the control of the executing court was originally limited to execution, but now by an amendment of 1956 it has been laid down that the creditor may either obtain a judgment on summons or may start bankruptcy proceedings against the debtor.[243]

The Act provides that courts in Scotland, Northern Ireland and England keep a register in which a certificate affirming that a judgment has been obtained in either of the two other countries may be entered. By registration a judgment is 'extended' in the country where its execution is sought and the effect of registration is that the decree is treated as if it is decree of the registering court.[244] This implies that judgments so registered cannot be impeached on merit or on any other ground. The enforcing court is also precluded from inquiring as to the validity or otherwise of the registered judgment. If the judgment debtor wants to challenge the validity or otherwise of the judgment, he should file proceedings in the courts of the country in which the judgment was originally pronounced.

A certificate cannot be registered more than twelve months

241. Section 1.

242. Thus judgments in probate or divorce suits or for the recovery of land or decrees of courts of equity are outside the ambit of the Act.

343. Section 40(a), Administration of Justice Act, 1956.

244. Section 1 of the Act.

after the date of the judgment without obtaining the leave of the court.

Administration of Justice Act, 1920 : Like the Judgment Extension Act, the Administration of Justice Act, 1920 provides for the enforcement of judgments of superior courts. The Act applies to the judgments of the superior courts of any part of the Commonwealth.[245] The Act is based on the principle of reciprocity. The Act applies to a Commonwealth country only when it has been extended to that country by an Order in Council. On reciprocal provision being made by a Commonwealth country for the enforcement of judgments of English, Scottish and Irish courts, an order in Council is passed extending the Act to that country.[246]

Any person who has obtained a judgment in a Commonwealth country with which reciprocal arrangments exist may, within twelve months from the date of the judgment or within such time as the court allows, apply for registration of the judgment to the High Court in England or Northern Ireland or to the Court of Session in Scotland for its registration.[247] Issuance of the certificate is in the discretion of the court. The court may register a judgment if it comes to the conclusion that "in all the circumstances of the case it is just and convenient that the judgment should be enforced in the United Kingdom".[248] Only those judgments can be registered which are for a sum of money payable.[249] Further, registration of a judgment would not be allowed if (a) the original court acted without jurisdiction, (b) the judgment debtor did not voluntarily submit to the jurisdiction of the adjudicating court, unless he was carrying on business or was ordinarily resident within that jurisdiction, (c) the judgment debtor was not served and did not appear in the original proceedings, (d) the judgment was obtained by fraud, (e) an appeal is pending, or (f) the original cause of action was one which, for reasons of public policy or for some other similar reason, could not have been entertained in England.[250]

The effect of registration is that the judgment has the same force and effect as if it was judgment of the registering court.[251] Under the Act, just as under the Judgment Extention Act, the original cause of action is not lost. A judgment creditor is also

245. Section 13 of the Act.

246. Section 14 of the Act.
The Act has been extended along with other countries to Jamaica, Kenya, Federated Malay States, New Zealand, New South Wales, Queensland, South Australia, Western Australia, Victoria and Tasmania.

247. Section 9(1).

248. *Ibid.*

249. Section 12.

250. Section 9(2).

251. Section 9(3)(a), (b) as amended by the Administration of Justice Act, 1956.

free to sue on the judgment,[252] but if he sues on a judgment which is registrable under the Act he will not be entitled to the cost of the action unless the registration has been refused or the court otherwise directs.[253]

Foreign Judgment (Reciprocal Enforcement) Act, 1933 : This Act has been enacted with a view to enforce the judgment of other foreign countries with which reciprocal arrangement for the enforcement of the judgments of the courts of the United Kingdom exist. The provisions for registration of foreign judgments in the Act may be extended by an Order in Council to any reciprocating country,[254] including a Commonwealth country. The Act has been made applicable to the Commonwealth countries with a view to end gradually two systems of registration, one for Commonwealth countries and the other for other countries. To achieve this objective it has been laid down that when the Act of 1933 is made applicable to a Commonwealth country, the Act of 1920 will cease to apply to such country.[255]

The judgment creditor of a judgment passed by a superior court of the reciprocating country may apply at any time within the six years[256] from the date of judgment for the registration of judgment in England, provided the judgment has finally and conclusively adjudicated a sum of money to be payable to the applicant, other than a sum in respect of taxes or in respect of fine or some other penalty.[257] Under the Act a judgment is considered to be final and conclusive even if an appeal may be pending against it or that it may still be subject to appeal in the foreign country.[258]

The distinguishing feature of this Act from the others is that the High Court has no discretion in the matter of registration of judgments.[259] However, under the following circumstances the registration must be set aside on the application of the judgment-debtor : (i) if the judgment is not one to which the Act applies; (ii) if the foreign court acted without jurisdiction; (iii) if the judgment debtor, being the defendant in the original proceedings, did not (despite service of process in accordance with the foreign law) receive notice of the proceedings in sufficient time to enable him to defend them and did not appear; (iv) if the judgment was obtained by fraud; (v) if the enforcement of the judgment would be contrary to public policy in England; and (vi) if the rights

252. *Yukon Consolidated Gold Corporation* v. *Clark*, (1938) 2 K.B. 241.
253. Section 9(5).
254. Section 1.
255. S. 4. The Act is applicable to India, Bangladesh, Pakistan, Australian Capital Territory.
256. Section 2.
257. Secion 1(1), (2).
258. Section 1(3).
259. Section 2.

under the judgment are not vested in the applicant.[260] The registration of a foreign judgment may also be set aside if the court is satisfied that the matter adjudicated upon had already been the subject of a final and conclusive judgment by a court of competent jurisdiction in the matter.[261] The Act also specifies the circumstances in which foreign court shall be deemed to have jurisdiction.[262] Judgments in matrimonial causes, or any proceedings connected with matrimonial matters, the administration of the estate of deceased persons, bankruptcy, winding up of the companies, lunacy and guardianship of infants are excluded from the purview of the Act.[263]

No action can be filed on a judgment which is registrable under the Act.[264] The effect of registration is that the judgment registered has the same force and effect as if it was the judgment of the registering court, but only in respect of its execution.[265]

The grounds of jurisdiction recognized under the Act[266] as conferring jurisdiction in action *in personam* do not apply if the subject-matter of the judgment is a contract for the carriage of goods by road where the place of taking over the goods and the place of their delivery are situated in two different countries, and, at least, one of which country is a contracting party to the Geneva Convention on International Carriage of Goods by Road, 1956. In such a situation, the Carriage of Goods by Road Act, 1965 determines the competency of the jurisdiction. In the following cases the foreign court is regarded as court of competent jurisdiction : (a) the court of a country, being a party to the Convention, designated by agreement between the parties, or (b) the court of a country, whether a party to the contract or not, where the defendant is ordinarily resident, or has his principal place of business or a branch or agency through which the contract was made, or (c) the court of the place where the goods were taken over by the carrier, or of the place designated for the delivery.[267]

Recognition of Divorce and Legal Separation Act, 1971 : The provisions of this Act have already been reviewed in this work elsewhere.[268]

Maintenance Orders (Reciprocal Enforcement) Act, 1972 : This

260. Section 4(1) see, *S.A. Consortium General Textiles* v. *Sun and Sand Agencies* (1978) 2 W.L.R. 1.
261. Section 4(2)(a).
262. Clause (a) in respect of actions *in personam* and clause (b) in respect of action *in rem* of section 4(2).
263. Section 1(2).
264. Section 9(3)(b).
265. Section 2(2).
266. Section 4(2).
267. Section 4(2), Schedule . Art. 31 (1), Carriage of Goods by Road Act, 1965.
268. See Chapter 9 of this work.

Act has been passed to give effect to the United Nations Convention on the Recovery Abroad of Maintenance, and replaces the Maintenance Orders (Facilities for Enforcement) Act, 1920. Under the Act the procedure for the registration of maintenance orders of the reciprocating countries is different.[269] On the receipt of a certified copy of a foreign maintenance order from a reciprocating country, the Secretary of State, if it appears to him that the payer under the order is residing in the United Kingdom, shall send the copy of the order to the prescribed officer of the appropriate court. The latter shall register the order unless he is satisfied after enquiry that the payer is not residing in the United Kingdom.[270] Section 7 makes provisions for the registration of provisional orders of maintenance made by any court of a reciprocating country.

The effect of registration of maintenance order is as if the order had been made by the registering court.[271] Under the Act, the registering court can vary or revoke a registered order by a provisional order as if it is an order of the registering court.[272] Payment of sums due under the registered order can also be ordered to be paid to the payee.[273]

Part II of the Act makes provisions for the reciprocal enforcement of claims for the recovery of maintenance. When a person in the United Kindom claims to be entitled to recover in a convention country maintenance from another person, and if that other person is, for the time being subject to the jurisdiction of that country, then such a person may apply to the Secretary of State to have his claim for the recovery of maintenance from that other person transmitted to that country.[274] Similarly, where the Secretary of State receives from the appropriate authority in a convention country an application by a person in that country for the recovery of maintenance from another person who is for the time being residing in the United Kingdom, he shall send the application to the appropriate court within whose jurisdiction the other person is residing.[275] The Act also makes provisions for complaints by a spouse in a convention country for the recovery in England or Wales of maintenance from the other spouse,[276] for recovery of maintenance from husband residing in Northern Ireland,[277] and for recovery of maintenance for children.[278]

269. The Act applies to only reciprocating countries.
270. Section 6.
271. Section 8.
272. Section 9.
273. Section 16.
274. Section 26.
275. Section 27.
276. Section 28.
277. Section 29. In section 31 provisions have been made for the recovery of the amount of maintenance in Scotland.
278. Section 30.

Provisions have also been made for transfer, enforcement, variation and revocation of registered orders.[279]

The Act is extended to a reciprocating country by an Order in Council. The Order may also specify that the Act will apply with exceptions, adaptations or modification.[280]

Civil Jurisdiction and Judgment Act, 1982 : This statutes provides for the recognition and enforcement of judgments of the Courts of the ECC European Community).

Indian Law

At the time of the passing of the Indian Independence Act, 1947, India was divided into two parts : British India and the Indian States (sometimes called Natives States). At that time the Judgments of the courts of the Indian states were considered to the judgments of the foreign court and the Civil Procedure contained certain provisions for their enforcement. They could be enforced by a suit on judgment under section 13, C.P.C. Section 44 of the Code (as it stood before the Adaptation of Laws Order) provided that the Government of India may by notification in the Official Gazette declare that a decree of any civil or revenue court of any Indian State might be executed in British India as if it has been passed by the courts of British India. Just as under the English statute, the Judgment Extention Act, the decree of the courts of the Indian States were treated as if they were the decrees of the court of British India so far as it related to the execution of the decree.[281] All the objections that were open to a foreign judgment could also be taken against such decrees of the courts of the Indian States. By the Adaptation of Law Order, the Indian states were substituted by Part B States and the power of issuing notification were conferred on the State Governments.

From April 1, 1951, the Civil Procedure Code has been made applicable to all the States of the Indian Union. The Indian Constitution also contains a full faith and credit clause, by virtue of which judgment of Part B States could be enforced in Part A States and *vice versa*. Clause (3) of Article 261 of the Indian Constitution provides : "Final judgments or orders delivered or passed by the civil courts in any part of the territory of India shall be capable of execution anywhere within that territory according to law."

The Civil Procedure Code (Amendment) Act, 1951 had changed this position in respect of Part B States. The modified sections 43 and 44 provide for the direct execution of decrees and orders of civil and revenue courts situated in any part of the country. Section 43 runs : "Any decree passed by any civil court established in any part of India to which the provisions of this Code do not extend, or by any court established or continued by the authority of the Central Government outside India, may, if it cannot be executed within the jursidiction of the court by which it was passed, be executed in the manner herein provided within the jurisdiction to

279. Sections 36, 37 and 38.
280. Section 40.
281. See observations of the Madras High Court in 27 M.L.J. 535.

which this Code extends." For the application of this section it is necessary that (a) the transferee court is one which has been established by the authority of the Central Government in such foreign territory,[282] and (b) the State Government has by notification declared this section applicable. Section 45 further provides : "So much of the foregoing sections of this Part as empowers a court to send a decree for execution to another court shall be construed as empowering a court in any State to send a decree for execution to any court established by the authority of the Central Government outside India to which the State Government had by notification in the Official Gazette declared this section to apply."

The combined effect of sections 43, 44 and 45 may be summed as under :

I. *Execution of decrees by Indian Court* : The Indian courts have power to execute : (a) decrees of those Indian courts to which the Civil Procedure Code does not apply, (b) the decrees of civil courts outside India which are established or continued by the authority of the Central Government, and (c) decrees of the Revenue courts situate in India to which the Code of Civil Procedures does not apply.

II. *Execution of Decrees by Courts outside India* : The decrees of Indian courts can also be executed in territories outside India by the courts established or continued by the authority of the Central Government and to which the State Government has notified that section 45 applies.

Decrees which were passed by the courts in India or by the courts of the Indian States before the coming into force of the Constitution of India have given rise to divergence of opinion in our court. This is briefly discussed in Part IV of this Chapter.

Reciprocal Enforcement of Foreign Decrees : Section 44A of the Civil Procedure Code provides for the reciprocal enforcement of foreign judgments.[283] The section has been modelled on the analogous provision in the Foreign Judgments (Reciprocal Enforcement) Act, 1933. Under the section the decrees of the superior courts[284] of the United Kingdom and other foreign countries with which India has reciprocal arrangement have been made enforceable as if they are decrees of the Indian courts. In reference to this section a decree means 'any decree or judgment. . . under which a sum of money is payable, not being a sum payable in respect of taxes or other charges of a like nature or in respect of fine or other penalty,'[285] and it does not include an arbitration

282. Sections 43 and 44 apply to Schedules Districts also. For instance the court of Political Agent at Sikkim is a court established by the authority of the Central Government: I.L.R. 38 Cal. 859. (This was the situation before the accession of Sikkim to the Indian Union.)

283. Section 44A(1).

284. *Ibid.*

285. Explanation (3) to s. 44A.

award, even if such an award is enforceable as a judgment or decree.[286]

When the execution of a foreign decree is sought in an Indian court, then it is necessary that a certified copy of it should be filed in the court together with a certificate as to the extent, if any, to which the decree has been satisfied or adjusted. Such a certificate shall be conclusive proof of such satisfaction or adjustment.[287] Foreign decrees can be executed in District Courts only.[288] Any territory which reciprocates in the execution of decree is a reciprocating territory.[289]

No foreign decree or judgment can be executed or enforced by any court in India if :

(a) it has not been pronounced by a court of competent jurisdiction,

(b) it has not been given on the merits of the case,

(c) it appears on the face of the proceedings to be founded on an incorrect view of international law or a refusal to recognize the law of India in cases where it is applicable,

(d) the proceedings in which it was obtained are opposed to natural justice,

(e) it has been obtained by fraud, or

(f) it sustains a claim founded on a breach of any law in force in India.[290]

IV

DRAFT CONVENTION ON THE RECOGNITION AND ENFORCEMENT OF FOREIGN JUDGMENTS IN CIVIL AND COMMERCIAL MATTERS

The Hague Convention (to which a Protocol has also been appended) on the Recognition and Enforcement of Foreign Judgments in Commercial and Civil matters covers some of those judgments which are not covered under other conventions. The Convention does not apply to status or capacity in family matters, including foreign divorces, existence or constitution of legal persons or the powers of their officers; question of succession; orders and decision in bankruptcy; questions of social security; questions

286. Explanation 3(b) to s. 44A.
287. Sub-section 1 of s. 44A.
288. *Ibid.*
289. Explanation (2) to s. 44a.
290. Even when reciprocal arrangements exists, a foreign decree can be challenged on any one of these grounds: *Sheo Tahal Ram* v. *Binaek Shukul*, 1931 All. 689; *Chunnilal* v. *Dundappa*, 1951 Bom. 190; *Verriarajora* v. *Muga Salt*, 39 Mad. 486.

relating to damage or injury in nuclear matters, as well as to decisions for the payment of custom duty, tax or penalty.[291] A final judgment in civil and commercial matters of a court of competent jurisdiction will be accorded recognition and it may also be enforced.[292] But those foreign judgments which are violative of public policy, or are obtained by fraud or on a matter on which decision has been earlier rendered by a court of competent jurisdiction of some other state, or when a suit on the same subject-matter between the same parties is pending in another court of competent jurisdiction.[293] A judgment made in default will not be enforced if the defendant was not given notice of proceedings.[294] If the foreign court is a court of competent jurisdiction, then its judgment is enforceable even if it made a mistake in the application of proper law to the transaction.[295]

The convention is reproduced in the Appendix to this Chapter.

291. Article 1.
292. Article 4.
293. Article 5.
294. Article 6.
295. Article 7.

APPENDIX I

THE HAGUE DRAFT CONVENTION ON THE RECOGNITION AND ENFORCEMENT OF FOREIGN JUDGMENTS IN CIVIL AND COMMERCIAL MATTERS

The States, signatory to the present Convention Desiring to establish common provisions on mutual recognition and enforcement of judicial decisions rendered in their respective countries,

Have resolved to conclude a Convention to this effect and have agreed on the following provisions :

CHAPTER I : SCOPE OF THE CONVENTION

Article 1

This Convention shall apply to decisions rendered in civil or commercial matters by the courts of Contracting States.

It shall not apply to decisions the main object of which is to determine—

(1) the status or capacity of persons or questions of family law, including personal or financial rights and obligations between parents and children or between spouses;

(2) the existence or constitution of legal persons or the powers of their officers;

(3) maintenance obligations, so far as not included in sub-paragraph (1) of this article;

(4) questions of succession;

(5) questions of bankruptcy, compositions or analogous proceedings; including decisions which may result therefrom and which relate to the validity of the acts of the debtor;

(6) questions of social security;

(7) questions relating to damage or injury in nuclear matters.

The Convention does not apply to decisions for the payment of any customs duty, tax or penalty.

Article 2

This Convention shall apply to all decisions given by the courts of a Contracting State irrespective of the name given by that State to the proceedings which gave rise to the decision or of the name given to the decision itself such as judgment, order or writ of execution.

However, it shall apply neither to decisions which order provisional or protective measures nor to decisions rendered by administrative tribunals.

Article 3

This Convention does not apply to the nationality parties.

CHAPTER II : CONDITIONS OF RECOGNITION AND ENFORCEMENT

Article 4

A decision rendered in one of the contracting States, shall be entitled to recognition and enforcement in another Contracting State under the terms of this Convention.—

(1) if the decision was given by a court considered to have jurisdiction within the meaning of this Convention, and

(2) if it is no longer subject to ordinary forms of review in the State of origin.

In addition, to be enforceable in the State addressed, a decision must be enforceable in the State of origin.

Article 5

Recognition or enforcement of a decision may nevertheless be refused in any of the following cases.—

(1) if recognition or enforcement of the decision is manifestly incompatible with the public policy of the State addressed or with due process of law or if, in the circumstances either party had no adequate opportunity fairly to present his case;

(2) if the decision was obtained by fraud in the procedural sense;

(3) if proceedings between the same parties, based on the same facts and having the same purpose :

(a) are pending before a court of the State addressed and those proceedings were the first to be instituted, or

(b) have resulted in a decision by a court of the State addressed, or

(c) have resulted in a decision by a court of another State which would be entitled to recognition of enforcement under the law of the State addressed.

Article 6

Without prejudice to Article 5, a decision rendered by default shall neither be recognized nor enforced unless the defaulting party received notice of the institution of the proceedings in accordance with the law of the State of origin in sufficient time to enable him to defend the proceedings.

Article 7

Recognition or enforcement may not be refused for the sole reason that the court of the State of origin has applied a law other than that which would have been applicable according to the rules of private international law of the State addressed.

Nevertheless, recognition or enforcement may be refused if, to reach its decision, the court of the State of origin had to decide a question relating either to the status or the capacity of a party to his rights in other matters excluded from this Convention by sub-paragraphs 1-4 of the second paragraph of Article 1, and has reached a result different from that which would have followed from the application to that question of the rules of private international law of the State addressed.

Article 8

Without prejudice to such review as is required by the terms of the preceding Articles, there shall be no review of the merits of the decision rendered by the court of origin.

Article 9

In questions relating to the jurisdiction of the court of the State of origin, the authority addressed shall be bound by the findings of the fact on which that court based its jurisdiction, unless the decision was rendered by default.

Article 10

The court of the State of origin shall be considered to have jurisdiction for the purposes of this Convention—

(1) if the defendant had, at the time when the proceedings were instituted, his habitual residence in the State of origin, or, if the defendant is not a natural person, its seat, its place of incorporation or its principal place of business in that State;

(2) if the defendant had, in the State of origin, at the time when the proceedings were instituted, a commercial, industrial or other business establishment, or a branch office, and was cited there in proceedings arising from business transacted by such establishment or branch office;

(3) If the action had as its object the determination of an issue relating to immovable property situated in the State of origin;

(4) in the case of injuries to the person or damage to tangible property, if the facts which occasioned the damaged occurred in the territory of the State of origin, and if the author of the injury or damage was present in that territory at the time when those facts occurred;

(5) if, by a written agreement or by an oral agreement confirmed in writing within a reasonable time, the parties agreed to submit to the jurisdiction of the court of origin disputes which have arisen or which may arise in respect of a specific legal relationship, unless the law of the State addressed would not permit such an agreement because of the subject-matter of the dispute;

(6) if the defendant has argued the merits without challenging the jurisdiction of the court or marking reservations of the court or making reservations thereon; nevertheless such jurisdiction shall not be recognized if the defendant has argued the merits in order to resist the seizure of property or to obtain its release, or if the recognition of this jurisdiction would be contrary to the law of the State addressed because of the subject matter of the dispute;

(7) if the person against whom recognition or enforcement is sought was the plaintiff in the proceedings in the court of origin and was unsuccessful in those proceedings, unless the recognition of this jurisdiction would be contrary to the law of the State addressed because of the subject-matter of the dispute.

Article 11

The court of the State of origin shall be considered to have jurisdiction for the purposes of this Convention to try a counter-claim—

(1) if that court would have had jurisdiction to try the action as a principal claim under sub-paragraphs 1-6 of Article 10, or

(2) if that court had jurisdiction under Article 10 to try the principal claim and if the counterclaim arose out of the contract or out of the facts on which the principal claim was based.

Article 12

The jurisdiction of the court of the State of origin need not be recognized by the authority addressed in the following cases—

(1) if the law of the State addressed confers upon its courts exclusive jurisdiction, either by reason of the subject-matter of the action or by virtue of an agreement between the parties as to the determination of the claim which gave rise to the foreign decision,

(2) if the law of the State addressed recognizes as a different exclusive jurisdiction by reason of the subject-matter of the action or if the authority addressed considers itself bound to recogniz. such an exclusive jurisdiction by reason of an agreement betwee the parties;

(3) if the authority addressed considers itself bound to recognize an agreement by which exclusive jurisdiction is conferred upon arbitrators.

CHAPTER III : RECOGNITION AND ENFORCEMENT PROCEDURES

Article 13

The party seeking recognition or applying for enforcement shall furnish—

(1) a complete and authenticated copy of the decision;

(2) if the decision was rendered by default, the originals or certified true copies of the documents required to establish that the summons was duly served on the defaulting party;

(3) all documents required to establish that the decision fulfils the conditions of sub-paragraph 2 of paragraph 1 of Article 4, and where appropriate, of paragraph 2 of Article 4;

(4) unless the authority addressed otherwise requires, translations of the documents referred to above, certified consular agent or by a diplomatic or consular agent or by a sworn translator or by any other person so authorized in either State.

If the terms of the decision do not permit the authority addressed to verify whether the conditions of this Convention have been complied with, that authority may require the production of any other necessary documents.

No legislation or other like formality may be required.

Article 14

The procedure for the recognition or enforcement of foreign judgments is governed by the law of the State addressed so far as this Convention does not provide otherwise.

If the decision contains provisions which can be dissociated, any one or more of these may be separately recognised or enforced.

Article 15

Recognition or enforcement of an award of judicial costs or expenses may be accorded by virtue of this Convention only if this Convention is applicable to the decision on the merits.

This Convention shall apply to decisions relating to judicial costs or expenses even if such decisions do not proceed from a court, provided that they derive from a decision which may be recognized or enforced under this Convention and that the decision relating to costs or expenses could have been subject to judicial review.

Article 16

A judgment for costs or expenses given in connection with the granting of refusal of recognition of enforcement of a decision may be enforced under this Convention only if the applicant in the proceedings for recognition or enforcement relied on this Convention.

Article 17

No security, bond or deposit, however termed under the law of the State addressed, shall be required by reason of the nationality or domicile of the applicant, to guarantee the payment of judicial costs or expenses if the applicant, being a natural person, has his habitual residence in or, not being a natural person, has a place of business in a State, which has concluded with the State addressed a Supplementary Agreement in terms of Article 21.

Article 18

A party granted legal aid in the State of origin shall be extended such aid in accordance with the law of the State addressed in any proceedings for the recognition or for the enforcement of a foreign decision.

Article 19

Settlements made in court in the course of a pending proceeding which may be enforced in the State of origin shall be enforceable in the State addressed under the same conditions as decisions falling within this Convention, so far as those conditions apply to settlements.

CHAPTER IV : CONCURRENT ACTIONS

Article 20

If two States have concluded a Supplementary Agreement pursuant to Article 21, the judicial authorities of either State may dismiss an action brought before them or may stay such an action when other proceedings between the same parties, based on the same facts and having the same purpose, are pending in a court of another State and these proceedings may result in a decision which the authorities of the State in which the first mentioned action was brought would be bound to recognize under the terms of this Convention.

The authorities of these States may nevertheless order provisional protective measures regardless of proceedings elsewhere.

CHAPTER V : SUPPLEMENTARY AGREEMENTS

Article 21

Decisions rendered in a Contracting State shall not be recognised or enforced in another Contracting State in accordance with the provisions of the preceding Articles unless the two states being Parties to this Convention, have concluded a Supplementary Agreement to this effect.

Article 22

This Convention shall not apply to decisions rendered before the entry into force of the Supplementary Agreement provided for in Article 21, unless that agreement otherwise provides.

The Supplementary Agreement shall continue to be applicable to decisions in respect of which recognition or enforcement proceedings have been instituted before any denunciation of that agreement takes effect.

Article 23

In the Supplementary Agreements referred to in Article 21 the Contracting States may agree—

(1) to clarify the meaning of the expression "civil and commercial matters," to determine the courts whose decisions shall be recognized and enforced under this Convention, to define the expression "social security" and to define the expression "habitual residence";

(2) to clarify the meaning of the term "law" in States with more than one legal system;

(3) to include within the scope of this Convention questions relating to damage or injury in nuclear matters;

(4) to apply this Convention to decisions ordering provisional or protective measures;

(5) not to apply this Convention to decisions rendered in the course of criminal proceedings;

(6) to specify the cases under which a decision is no longer subject to ordinary forms of review;

(7) to recognize and enforce decisions upon which enforcement could be obtained in the State of origin even if such decisions are still subject to ordinary forms of review and in such a case stay of proceedings for recognition or enforcement is possible;

(8) not to apply Article 6 if the decision rendered by default was notified to the defaulting party and the latter had the opportunity to lodge a timely appeal against such a decision;

(9) to consider the courts of the State in which the defendant has his "domicile" as having jurisdiction under Article 10;

(10) that the court of origin shall be considered as having jurisdiction under the terms of this Convention in cases where its jurisdiction is admitted by another Convention in force between the State of origin and the State addressed if that other Convention contains no special rules relating to the recognition and enforcement of foreign judgments;

(11) that the court of origin shall be considered as having jurisdiction under the terms of this Convention either when its jurisdiction is admitted by the law of the State addressed relating to foreign judgments, or on grounds additional to those in Article 10;

(12) to define, for the purposes of the application of Article 12, the bases of jurisdiction which are exclusive by reason of the subject-matter of the action;

(13) to exclude, in cases where jurisdiction is based on an agreement between the parties, the application of sub-paragraph 1 of Article 12 as well as to exclude that of sub-paragraph 3 of Article 12;

(14) to regulate the procedure for obtaining recognition or enforcement;

(15) to regulate the enforcement of judgments other than those which order the payment of a sum of money;

(16) that the enforcement of a foreign judgment may be refused when a specified period has elapsed from its date;

(17) to fix the rate of interest payable from the date of the judgment in the State of origin;

(18) to adapt to the requirements of their legal systems the list of documents required by Article 13 but with the sole object of enabling the authority addressed to verify whether the conditions of this Convention have been fulfilled;

(19) to subject the documents referred to in Article 13 to legalisation or to a similar formality;

(20) to depart from the provisions of Article 17 and to depart from the provisions of Article 18;

(21) to make the provisions of paragraph 1 of Article 20 obligatory;

(22) to include within the scope of this Convention, "acts authentiques", including documents upon which immediate enforcement can be obtained and to specify those documents.

CHAPTER VI : FINAL CLAUSES

Article 24

This Convention shall not affect other Conventions relating to the recognition and enforcement of judgments to which the Contracting States are already Parties so long as those States have not concluded a Supplementary Agreement under the terms of Article 21.

Unless it is otherwise agreed, the provisions of a Supplementary Agreement concluded under Article 21 prevail over the terms of any prior Conventions in force between the Parties relating to the recognition and enforcement of judgments to the extent that their terms are mutually inconsistent.

Article 25

Whether or not they have concluded a Supplementary Agreement under Article 21, the Contracting States shall not conclude between themselves other Conventions relating to the recognition and enforcement of judgments within the scope of this Convention unless they consider it necessary, in particular because of economic ties or of particular aspects of their legal systems.

Article 26

Notwithstanding the provisions of Articles 24 and 25, this Convention and the Supplementary Agreements made under Article 21 shall not prevail over Conventions to which the Contracting States are or may become Parties in special fields and which contain provisions for the recognition and enforcement of judgments.

Article 27

This present Convention shall be open for signature by the States represented at the Tenth Session of the Hague Conference on Private International Law and Iceland, Cyprus and Malta.

It shall be ratified, and the instruments of ratification shall be deposited with the Ministry of Foreign Affairs of the Netherlands.

Article 28

This Convention shall enter into force on the sixtieth day after the deposit of the second instrument of ratification.

This Convention shall enter into force for each State which ratifies it subsequently on the sixtieth day after the deposit of its instrument of ratification.

Article 29

Any State not falling within the provisions of the first paragraph of article 27 may accede to this Convention after it has entered into force in accordance with the first paragraph of article 28. The instrument of accession shall be deposited with the Ministry of Foreign Affairs of the Netherlands.

This Convention shall enter into force in such a State in the absence of any objection from a State, which has ratified this Convention before such deposit, notified to the Ministry of Foreign Affairs of the Netherlands within a period of six months after the date on which the said Ministry has notified it of such accession.

In the absence of any such objection, this Convention shall enter into force for the acceding State on the first day of the month following the expiration of the last of the periods referred to in the preceding paragraph.

Article 30

Any State may, at the time of signature, ratification or accession, declare that this Convention shall extend to all the territories for the international relations of which it is responsible, or to one or more of them. Such a declaration shall take effect on the date of entry into force of this Convention for the State concerned.

At any time thereafter, such extensions shall be notified to the Ministry of Foreign Affairs of the Netherlands.

This Convention shall enter into force for the territories mentioned in such an extension on the sixtieth day after the notification referred to in the preceding paragraph.

The parties to a Supplementary Agreement concluded under Article 21 shall determine its territorial application.

Article 31

This Convention shall have duration of five years from the date on which it entered into force under the first paragraph of Article 28. even in its application to States which have subsequently ratified or acceded to it.

In the absence of any denunciation, this Convention shall be renewed tacitly every five years.

Any denunciation shall be notified to the Ministry of Foreign Affairs of the Netherlands at least six months before the end of the fiveyear period.

Such denunciation may be limited to any one of the territories to which this Convention applies.

Such denunciation shall affect only the notifying State. This Convention shall remain in force for the other Contracting States.

Article 32

Each Supplementary Agreement concluded under Article 21 shall take effect from the date specified in such Agreement; a certified copy, and if necessary, a translation into French or English, shall be communicated to the Ministry of Foreign Affairs of the Netherlands.

Any Contracting State may, without denouncing this Convention, denounce a Supplementary Agreement either under any provision for denunciation in such Agreement or, if such Agreement contains no such provision, by giving six month's notice to the other State. Any State denouncing a Supplementary Agreement shall so inform the Ministry of Foreign Affairs of the Netherlands.

Notwithstanding the denunciation of this Convention, it shall nevertheless continue to have effect between the denouncing State and any other State with which the former has concluded a Supplementary Agreement under Article 21, unless such Agreement provides otherwise.

Article 33

The Ministry of Foreign Affairs of the Netherlands shall give notice to the States referred to in Article 27 and to the States which have acceded in accordance with Article 29, of the following—

(a) the signatures and ratifications referred to in Article 27;

(b) the date on which the present Convention enters into force in accordance with the first paragraph of Article 28;

(c) the accessions referred to in Article 29 and the dates on which they take effect;

(d) the extensions referred to in Article 30 and the dates on which they take effect;

(e) a translation or a copy of the text in English or French of Supplementary Agreements concluded under Article 21;

(f) the denunciations referred to in the third paragraph of Article 31 and the second paragraph of Article 32.

In witness whereof the undersigned, being duly authorized thereto, have signed this Convention.

Done at The Hague, on the . . . day of . . . 19 . . . . . . in the English and French languages, both texts being equally authentic, in a single copy which shall be deposited in the archives of the Government of the Netherlands, and of which a certified copy shall be sent, through the diplomatic channel, to each of the States represented at the Tenth Session of the Hague Conference on Private International Law, and to Cyprus, Iceland and Malta.

APPENDIX II

GUIDELINES FOR INTER-COUNTRY ADOPTION[1] 1994

CHAPTER 1: AIMS AND OBJECTS

1.1 The objective of the present guidelines is to provide a sound basis for adoption with in the framework of the norms and principles laid down by the Supreme Court of India in the series of judgments delivered in *L.K. Pandev* vs. *Union of India and Others* between 1984 and 1991.

1.2 Adoption undoubtedly offers an important avenue for the care and a protection of an abandoned, destitute or neglected child in a family setting and provides an atmosphere of happiness, love and understanding for the realisation of his/her talents and potentials. It carries with it all the emotional physical and material security necessary for the proper development of the child and also serves as the most reliable means of preventing situations associated with the abuse, exploitation and social maladjustment of abandoned, destitute and neglated children.

1.3 The Government of India, in pursuance of its constitutional mandate, has evolved a National Policy for the welfare of children. The thrust of this policy is summed up in the following words:

> "The nation's children are a supremely important asset. Their nature and solicitude are our responsibility. Children's programme should find a prominent part in our national plans for the development of human resources, so that our children grow up to become robust citizens, physically fit, mentally alert and morally healthy, endowed with the skill's and motivations needed by society. Equal opportunities for development to all children during the period of growth should be our aim, for this would serve our larger purpose of reducing equality and ensuring social justice.

1.4 There has been equally great concern for the welfare of children at the international level culminating in the Declaration of the Rights of the Child, adopted by the General Assembly of the United

1. Issued by The Government of India, Ministry of Welfare: Gazette of Indian, Extraordinary Dated May 29, 1995.

Nations on the 20th November, 1989. Thereafter, in various international fora, conference and seminars, this subject of child welfare has continued to be constantly debated.

1.5 The National Policy for the Welfare of Children also stresses the vital role which the voluntary organisations have to play in the field of education, health, recreation and social welfare services for children and declares that it should be the endeavour of the state to encourage and strengthen such voluntary organisations. Need for Family support for the Development of the children.

1.6 It accepted fact that the balanced development of a child—emotional, physical and intellectual—can be best ensured within the family, or where this is possible, then in familial surroundings. The responsibility for providing care and protection to children including those who are orphaned, abandoned, and abured rests primarily with the family, the community and the society at large. However, since many traditional institutions including the family structure are undergoing vertical as well as horizontal social changes on account of urbanisation, industrialisation and the general process of development, family support to a child is not always available. It, therefore, becomes the responsibility of the community, of the society and of the State to provide both institutional and non-institutional support to destitute children. Government of India considers adoption as the best non-institutional support for rehabilitation of children.

Traditionally, our society has been providing support through charitable institutions and non-institutional activities like adoption, guardianship and foster care. Due to rapid changes in the social structure and other related factors, the number of children who need care, protection and rehabilitation is on the increase. It is, therefore, necessary not only to expand both institutional and non-institutional facilities for the nurture of such children, but also to regulate and monitor all programmes so as to ensure minimum standards in all child welfare activities. Among non-institutional modes, the interest of the child can best be served through adoption in a family. Further, it is also an accepted fact that the child develops best in his or own cultural and social milieu. Thus, placement of a child through adoption in an indigenous setting would be ideal for his or her growth and development, inter-country adoption, i.e. adoption of Indian children by adoptive parents residing abroad, should be resorted to only if all efforts to place the child with adoptive parents residing in India prove unsuccessful. Generally, in all matters concerning adoption whether within the country or abroad, the welfare and interest of the child shall be paramount. Therefore, private adoptions of abandoned, destitute and surrendered relinquished children conducted by unauthorised individuals, agencies or institutions should be discouraged and it should not be open to any individual, agency or institution whether owned or run by the Government or not to process an application from a foreigner for taking a child in adoption. It should be the endeavour of Government to facilitate in-country adoption and to regulate inter-country adoption of Indian children.

Review of Adoption Procedure

1.7. In pursuance of the Supreme Court directives, the Ministry of Welfare vide its resolution dated 4-7-1989 formulated a set of guidelines to repute, monitor and supervise programmes pertaining to adoption. That laid down the existing procedure and practices. The existing procedure and practices followed in the case of inter-country adoption were thoroughly reviewed by the Supreme Court in their subsequent judgments dated 19th September, 1989, 14th August, 1991 29th October 1991, 14th November, 1991 and 20th November 1991 respectively in Writ Petition (CRD) No. 1171/1982 by Shri *L.K. Pandev* vs. *Union of India and others*. The Ministry of Welfare after a careful study of all the judgments of the Supreme Court of India and existing laws of the land and after taking into account the experience of the concerned Governmental as well as voluntary agencies and the changing social realities, decided to moddy these guidelines. In this direction, the Ministry of Welfare constituted a Task Force consisting of members representing various voluntary placement agencies under the chairmanship of Mr. Justice P.N. Bhagwati (The former Chief Justice of India).

1.8 The revised guidelines as contained hereinafter have emerged from the Task Force recommendations.

CHAPTER II: ROLE OF GOVERNMENT OF INDIA

2.1 In the Government of India all matters relating to adoption shall be dealt within the Ministry of Welfare. The Central Adoption Resource Agency (CARA) set up on 28-6-1990 under the aegis of the Ministry of Welfare in pursuance of Cabinet decision dated 9-5-1990 and when the Central Adoption Resource Agency is set up under these guidelines, then such Central Adoption Resource Agency shall deal with all matters concerning adoption as specified hereinafter.

2.2 The Government of India, Ministry of Welfare shall, from time to time, frame rules and guidelines and issue instructions to State Governments, voluntary agencies and voluntary coordinating agencies as well as to scrutinising agencies to facilitate and promote in-country adoption and to regulate inter-country adoption of India children.

List of Recognised Foreign Agencies for Adoption

2.3 The Central Adoption Resource Agency, shall maintain a list of all foreign agencies for adoption enlisted by the Government of India. A copy of the lists of these agencies shall be supplied by the Central Adoption Resource Agency to the various High Courts in India, all the State Governments, all recognised Indian agencies, all voluntary coordinating agencies, all scrutinising agencies and all Indian missions abroad as well as all passport offices once every year.

List of Recognised Indian Agencies for Adoption

2.4 The Central Adoption Resource Agency shall also prepare a list of all recognised Indian agencies for adoption. It shall publish once a year the list of these agencies operating in each State in three leading newspapers having vide circulation in the State, one in the English language, one in the Hindi language and the third in the regional language of that State. The list shall also be sent to all the High Courts in the country for circulation to the District Courts in each State, all the State Governments, all recognised Indian placement agencies, all foreign enlisted agencies, all Indian Missions abroad, all voluntary coordinating agencies, and all scrutinising agencies.

Liaison with Indian Diplomatic Missions

2.5 The Central Adoption Resource Agency shall maintain liaison with Indian diplomatic mission abroad in order to safeguard the interests of children of Indian origin adopted by foreign parents against neglect, maltreatment, exploitation or abuse and to maintain an unobtrusive watch over the welfare and progress of such children. For this purpose, the Central Adoption Resource Agency shall inform every Indian diplomatic missions concerned whenever an Indian child is taken in adoption or for the purpose of adoption, by foreign parents. The names, address and other particulars of such children and their adoptive or prospective adoptive parents shall be supplied to the Indian diplomatic missions as early as possible and in any case before the end of every quarter.

Meeting of Agencies Involved in Adoption

2.6 The Central Adoption Resource Agency shall arrange every year a meeting of all recognised placement agencies, voluntary coordinating agencies and scrutinising bodies for discussing matters of mutual interest and such other matters as are considered necessary and expedient.

Role of the Central Adoption Resource Agency (CARA)

2.7 As per the directions of the Supreme Court of India in Writ Petition (CRL) No. 1171/82 and on the basis on a Cabinet decision dated 9-5-1990, the Government of India in the Ministry of Welfare vide Resolution No. 1-10/88-CH(AC) dated 28th June,1990 published in the Gazette of India No. 166 dated 3rd July, 1990 has set a Central Adoption Resource Agency (CARA) to act as a clearing house of information in regard to children available for in-country and inter-country adoption and to regulate, monitor and develop programmes for the rehabilitation of children through adoption.

Headquarters and Regional Office of CARA

2.8 Central Adoption Resource Agency (CARA) shall have its headquarters in New Delhi. Branches/Regional Offices of Central Adoption Resource Agency (CARA) may, however, be set up at such places as may be considered appropriate.

Central Adoption Resource Agency

2.8A The Central Adoption Resource Agency (CARA) shall function under the overall policy guidance of a Steering Committee consisting of the following—

(i) Chairman (Non-Official).
(ii) Secretary (CARA)—Member Secretary-*cum*-Executive Officer.
(iii) One representative from Indian Council for Child Welfare (parent body).
(iv) One representative from Indian Council from Social Welfare (parent body).
(v) Four representatives of recognised placement agencies, one from each region, doing atleast more than 50 per cent in-country adoption.
(vi) One representative from among voluntary coordinating agencies.
(vii) One representative from the Ministry of External Affairs.
(viii) One representative from the Deptt. of Women and Child Development.
(ix) One representative from the ministry of Information and Broadcasting.

The tenure of the members representing recognised placement agencies and voluntary coordinating agencies shall be for a period of two years on rotational basis. On the expiry of the tenure, the members shall not be eligible for renomination for the next succeeding period of two years.

The appointment of the Chairman would be in an honorary capacity. The Member Secretary-*cum*-Executive Officer of Central Adoption Resource Agency (CARA) would be an official of the rank of Deputy Secretary/Director in the Government of India who would enjoy a reasonable tenure, preferable five years.

2.9 The Central Government may pay to the Central Adoption Resource Agency (CARA) such sums of money as may be considered necessary for the performance of its functions under this Resolution.

2.10 The accounts of the Central Adoption Resource Agency (CARA) shall be maintained and audited in such manner as may, in consultation with Comptroller and Auditor General of India, be specified by the Central Government.

2.11 The Central Adoption Resource Agencies (CARA) shall, subject to the approval of the Central Government, frame its own regulations and by-laws for discharging its functions in consonance wilt its aims and objectives.

2.12 The Central Adoption Resource Agency (CARA) shall have the power to constitute a Committee which will exclusively look into matters pertaining to promotion of in-country adoption at advice CARA on suitable policies and programmes for this purpose.

Functions of CARA

2.13 The functions of the Central Adoption Resource Agency (CARA) shall be as follows

(1) To act as a clearing house of information in regard to children available for in-country adoption as well as for in-country adoption;

(2) To receive application or copies of applications alongwith requisite documents (as prescribed by the Supreme Count of India in CRL (Wp) 1171/1982 in the matter of (*Shri Laxmi Kant Pandev* vs. *Union of India and Others*) of foreigners desirous of taking Indian children in adoption through a recognised social or child welfare agency in the foreign country or through an organisation owned or operated by the Government in that country;

(3) Whenever such applications are received directly by Central Adoption Resource Agency (CARA) to forward such applications to one of the Indian social or child welfare agencies recognised by CARA for processing applications of foreign parents for adoption in the competent court;

(4) To receive names and particulars of children available for adoption who are under the care of Indian social or child welfare agencies recognised by CARA and to maintain a register containing the names and other particulars of such children;

(5) To receive periodical data from all Indian social or child welfare agencies recognised by CARA about the children admitted to their Children's Home and the children given in adoption in-country as well as inter-country in a proforma prescribed by CARA;

(6) To monitor and regulate the working of Indian social or child welfare agencies recognised by CARA consistently with their independent and voluntary functioning;

(7) To inspect Indian social or child welfare agencies recognised by CARA and to report to the Central Government on the working of such agencies;

(8) To call for annual audited statements of account from Indian social or child welfare agencies recognised by CARA;

(9) To receive data from competent courts about children whose guardianship has been awarded in favour of foreign adoptive parents and/or who have been adopted by Indian nationals, both residents and non-residents;

(10) To send periodical data to Indian's Diplomatic Missions abroad in a proforma prescribed by CARA in respect of Indian children taken abroad;

(11) To receive periodical reports about children taken by foreign parents for the purpose of adoption in a proforma prescribed by CARA from all recognised social or child welfare agencies in foreign countries through India's Diplomatic Mission in the country where such agency is located;

(12) To obtain periodical progress reports of children from foreign adoptive parents as well as from recognised social or child welfare agencies in foreign countries, to examine such reports and to take such follow-up action as deemed necessary;

(13) To organise and arrange periodical meetings of VCAs working in the field of adoption for discussing matters of common interest;

(14) To arrange sponsorship of children through community support by means of publicity and awareness programmes;

(15) To mobilise community opinion and community resources in furtherance of adoption of children in the country itself and take all other measures necessary for the promotion of in-country adoption of children as well as welfare of children generally;

(16) To arrange training programmes for social workers and other engaged in child welfare activity specially in the rehabilitation of children by means of adoption, and also to bring about standardisation of training courses conducted by the voluntary agencies;

(17) To assist the courts to cross-check or re-verify the information furnished to them by various sources including the placement agencies and scrutinising agencies or to provide an independent advice in matters relating to adoption of children; and

(18) To initiate action on any other activity relating to adoption of children within the country and abroad.

Procedure to be Followed

2.14 After careful consideration the Supreme Court of India has laid down that the following requirements should be insisted upon so far as a foreigner wishing to take a child in adoption is concerned. Every application from a foreigner desiring to adopt a child must be sponsored by social or child welfare agency recognised or licensed by the Government of the country in which the foreigner is resident and enlisted by CARA, Ministry of Welfare, Government of India. No application by foreigner for taking a child in adoption should be entertained directly by an social child welfare agency in India working in the area of inter-country adoption or by any institution or centre or home to which children are committed by the Juvenile Court.

The original application alongwith original documents as prescribed by the Supreme Court of India would be forwarded by the foreign enlisted agency to a recognised placement agency in India. The foreign enlisted agency shall also send a copy each of the application as well as all the prescribed documents including Home Study Report enclosed with it to the Central Adoption Resource Agency (CARA) duly notiorised by Notary Public whose signature would be duly attested either by an officer of the Ministry of External Affairs or Justice or Social Welfare of the country of a foreigner or by an Officer of the Indian Embassy or High Commission or Consulate in that country. A list of required documents is given at Annexure 'A'. The Home Study report being a crucial document should broadly included the following information:

(a) Social Status and family background;

(b) Description of Home;
(c) Standard of living as it appears in the Home;
(d) Current relationship between husband and wife;
(e) Current relationship between the parents and children (if any children);
(f) Development of already adopted children (if any);
(g) Current relationship between the couple and the members of each other's family;
(h) Employment status of the couple;
(i) Health details such as clinical test, hear condition, past illness etc. (medical certificate etc.);
(j) Economic status of the couple;
(k) Accommodation for the child;
(l) Schooling facilities;
(m) Amenities in the Home;
(n) Reasons for wanting to adopt an Indian child;
(o) Attitude of grant-parent and relatives towards Adoption;
(p) Anticipated plans for the adoptive child; and
(q) Legal status of the prospective adoptive parents.

The sponsoring agency should carefully get the Home Study report prepared by the professional social worker broadly on the basis of the above information.

The receipt of the original application as well as original documents would not entitle the placement agency to proceed with the case. It can proceed only after getting "NO OBJECTION CERTIFICATE" from the Central Adoption Resource Agency (SARA), Ministry of Welfare.

Therefore, no recognised placement agency can process the application in the competent court for inter-country adoption without having "NO OBJECTION CERTIFICATE" issued by the Central Adoption Resource Agency (CARA), Ministry of Welfare. Central Adoption Resource Agency shall however ensure that such certificate should as far as possible be issued within a reasonable period of time, say 5 weeks from the date of receipt of the certified copies of the application and other documents from them. In case Central Adoption Resources Agency (CARA), rejects the application, it may specify the reasons for such refusal to the Indian recognised placement agency.

After the receipt of the original application and original documents from the enlisted foreign agency by the recognised Indian placement agency, the concerned placement agency will register the name of the prospective foreign parents in the register meant for them. The recognised placement agency shall carefully examine the home study report of the prospective foreign adoptive parents and start the exercise in matching the home study report with the child study report. When they arrive at the conclusion that child can be placed with that particular family, they will have to ensure that the concerned child cleared by the VCA for inter-country adoption. Thereafter the recognised placement agency will sent the child study report, the photograph of the child and the medical report to the sponsoring foreign agency for the approval of the prospective adoptive parent. After obtaining the approval of the child by the prospective adoptive parents the concerned recognised placement agency will apply to CARA for getting a clearance of the child. At this stage, Central Adoption Resource Agency (CARA) shall have to ensure that the recognised placement agency has put in adequate efforts for finding an Indian family for the said child, and the clearance by the VCA to that effect is also enclosed. CARA after going through the information furnished by the recognised placement agency and VCA will immediately give the clearance to the agency. The recognised placement agency thereafter will process the case with the competent court for awarding the guardianship of the child to the foreign prospective adoptive parents. At this stage the scrutinising agency has to scrutinise all the documents and advise the competent court that the said inter-country adoption is in the best interest of the child. The competent court within the stipulated time as laid down the Supreme Court of India awards the guardianship of the child to the foreign parents. On the bases of the Guardianship order of the court the recognised placement agency is to apply in the Regional Passport Office for obtaining an Indian Passport in favour of the child. Thereafter the visa issued by the concerned Embassy High Commission of the concern country for the child. The child leaves the country alongwith the prospective adoptive parents or with the escort, whatever the case may be, to the country of prospective adoptive parents, i.e., child's future country of residence.

The requirement of obtaining "NO OBJECTION CERTIFICATE" from Central Adoption Resource Agency will also apply in case of handicapped children, children needing urgent medical attention which the social or child welfare agency looking after the child cannot provide within the country, sibling and also children above the age of 6 years. The recognised placement agency, soon after the admission of such child without waiting for locating foreign prospective adoptive parents, shall make an application alogwith information of such child to CARA for issue of "NO OBJECTION CERTIFICATE". CARA shall ordinarily issue "NO OBJECTION CERTIFICATE" in case of handicapped special needs children etc. within a period of one year from the date of receipt of information of such child from the Indian recognised placement agency. Simultaneously the recognised Indian placement agencies would be allowed to send the refusal of such children to foreign agencies of its choice and after the approval of the child by any foreign parents, the concerned placement agency could follow the procedure as laid down in the judgment of the Supreme Court of India. At this state the scrutinising agency should carefully examine all the documents furnished by the foreign agencies in this regard and advise the competent court in coming to the conclusion whether it would be in the interest of the child to be given in adoption to the foreigner. However, the recognised Indian placement agency shall obtain a certificate in this regard from the concerned Chief Medical Officer of the Government hospital prior to processing the case concerning the handicapped children and the children needing urgent medical attention for record. Details of such children together with a copy (each) of the certificate(s) issued by the CMO, where required, shall be sent at the end of each month to CARA by the concerned Indian placement agency.

2.15 Where there is no recognised foreign agency in any country, the concerned Government Department/Ministry of that country may forward the applications and related documents of the prospective adoptive parents to CARA. CARA will examine and send those papers to the recognised Indian placement agencies indicated in the application or, if there is no such indication, then to any of the recognised Indian placement agencies for further processing the case. The procedure to be adopted thereafter shall be the same as indicated in the foregoing paragraph.

The procedure for inter-country adoption at a glance may be seen at Annexure 'B'.

2.16 The recognised placement agencies should provided to the Central Adoption Resource Agency a list of the enlisted foreign agencies with which they are working or proposing to work. Where any application is originally received by the Central Adoption Resource Agency from a recognised foreign agency, Govt. Department or an Indian agency or Indian parents, the Central Adoption Resource Agency would on the basis of information available to it, send the application to any placement agency for processing it, bearing in mind the operational relationship, if any, between the foreign agency and any particular placement agency. If the placement agency is unable to entertain such case, it shall promptly inform the Central Adoption Resource Agency giving reasons for not accepting the request. The Central Adoption Resource Agency may thereafter either send such case to any other recognised placement agency or even return the application to the forging source.

2.17 The placement agencies must at the end of every quarter provided information on the number of children given in in-country adoption, the number given in inter-country adoption, and the number awaiting adoption, to the Central Adoption Resource Agency.

Requirement Before the Court

2.18 Where no application is made to the Court by the parents proposing to take a child in adoption or by a placement agency on behalf of such parents for appointment of such parents as guardians of the child with a view to taking the child in adoption, the certificate of no objection by the Central Adoption Resource Agency shall be produced alongwith the application and if no response has been made by the Central Adoption Resource Agency to the application for taking the child in adoption, within the time limit specified in these guidelines, the application shall be accompanied by an affidavit to be made by the placement agency stating that the requirements of the guidelines have been fulfilled in regard to obtaining certificate of no objection from the Central Adoption Resource Agency.

CHAPTER III: ROLE OF THE STATE GOVERNMENT/UNION TERRITORY ADMINISTRATION

List of Children's Home

3.1 The State Governments (the terms "State Government" shall include Union Territory Administration wherever applicable) shall maintain a list of all children's homes being run for the maintenance of destitute, abandoned, orphaned, delinquent or neglected children by voluntary/private organisations which are registered, recognised or licensed under various laws.

List of Adoption Agencies

3.2 The State Government shall also separately maintain a list of all agencies for handling in-country and inter-country adoption of children and shall identify those institutions agencies which have children who are legally free for adoptoin.

3.3 The State Governments shall recognise Indian adoption agencies for in-country adoption as per the procedure laid down herein and shall forward applications of Indian agencies seeking recognition for inter-country adoption to the Central Adoption Resource Agency after proper verification according to the criteria laid down in these guidelines.

Each State Government shall also—

(i) monitor the adoption programme within its jurisdiction and coordinate the activities of placement agencies and VCAs and scrutinising agencies;

(ii) encourage and promote placement of eligible children on adoption or guardianship with families within the country;

(iii) enforce the Orphanages and other Charitable Homes (Supervision and Control) Act, 1960 and or formulate suitable alternate rules in order to maintain certain minimum standards for child care and child welfare institution;

(iv) inspect organisations which have applied for recognition for inter-country adoption to the Central Adoption Resource Agency and after considering whether the applicant agency fulfils all the requirements as laid down, forward the application to the Central Adoption Resource Agency with its comments, and this process shall be completed within a period of 60 days. If no response is received from the State Government within this period, the Central Adoption Resource Agency shall immediately take up the matter at an appropriate level in the State and if no response is received within a further period of 30 days, it shall presume that the State Government has no objection to the grant of recognition. If the State government is of the view that the applicant agency should not be recognised, it shall give relevant reasons for taking this view and forward the same to the Central Adoption Resource Agency with its comments;

(v) form an advisory committee on adoption which shall have the following as members:

(a) Secretary, Women & Child Chairman Development/ Social Welfare Panchayat Raj;

(b) Director, Welfare Social Member Welfare/Women & Child Development;

(c) Two representatives of Member placement Agency, VCAs and scrutinising agencies operating under the State; and

(d) Three expert Members in the field of social and child welfare.

The Committee shall meet periodically to discuss child welfare measures, specifically ways and means to promote in-country adoption of children. The State Government may also set up an Adoption Cell in the Directorate of Social Welfare to coordinate, irregulate and develop the work of adoption and render all assistance to the advisory form on adoption. The tenure of such committee shall be three years.

Inspection of Adoption Agencies

3.4 The State Government shall periodically and atlest once a year, inspect or cause to be inspected, all agencies and institutions handling in-country and inter-country adoption as also their papers, document's and activities connected with the service of children, generally, in order to verity:

(i) that adoption as activity is being pursued by the organisation as a welfare measure in the interest of children and not as a commercial activity;

(ii) that proper records are being maintained for children admitted to the homes;

(iii) that the children admitted are provided with basic minimum facilities for their care, at least for education and development;

(iv) that lists of persons interested in adopting a child or taking a child under guardianship are being maintained by the organisation regularly;

(v) that the accounts of the organisation are being maintained and audited annually without delay and that the auditor's reports confirm that the accounts are fair and accurate; that any organisation which is in receipt of foreign funding is duly registered with the Ministry of Home Affairs and has otherwise complied with the provisions of the Foreign Contributions (Regulations) Act, 1976;

(vi) that the organisation is receiving regular progress reports about the well-being of children given in adoption; and

(vii) that qualified staff having social work experience are employed by the agency organisation to take care of the children or they have access to such staff.

Monitoring of Performance

3.5 The State Government shall all for information and data every quarter from all agencies engaged in adoption order to monitor the functioning of these agencies. The data shall be called for in a proforma to be prescribed by the Central Adoption Resource Agency.

3.6 The State Government shall take all such measures as are deemed necessary to actively encourage in-country adoption of children in preference to inter-country adoption. Special care/efforts shall be made for rehabilitation of children in orphanages through placement by adoption.

CHAPTER IV: ROLE OF RECOGNISED INDIAN AGENCIES FOR ADOPTION

Listing with Authorities

4.1 Every institution and child welfare agency engaged in care and custody of children or in adoption work in any other activity related to orphan, abandoned, destitute, neglected or relinquished children shall immediately be listed by the concerned State Government and such list shall be forwarded to CARA.

Only Recognised Agencies could Undertake Adoption.

4.2 (i) No agency shall engage in placement of or promotion of in-country adoption unless it is recognised by the State Government and in case of agency engaged in placement work, it would be a child welfare agency. Any Indian agency desirous of undertaking inter-country adoption work shall apply for recognition to the Central Adoption Resource Agency, the State Government concerned and only such agencies as are recognised by the Central Adoption Resource Agency, shall be entitled to undertake inter-country adoption work. Such agencies shall be termed recognised placement agencies", of adoption. The agencies which are not doing placement work but are involved in promotional work of Indian adoption shall also be recognised by CARA.

(ii) No agencies except those recognised by the State Government concerned shall engage in in-country adoption. Rules and guidelines for this purpose may be formulated by the State Government.

Emphasis on Child Welfare

4.3. Only such voluntary agencies as are primarily engaged in child welfare programmes for the growth and development of children and which undertake adoption as a part of their total activities may apply for recognition for inter-country adoption to the Central Adoption Resource Agency.

List of Prospective Adoptive Parents

4.4 Every social child welfare organisation recognised for placement work in adoption shall regularly maintain a list of all prospective adoptive parents containing their names, address and data on the basis of which they were approached the organisation for taking a child in adoption and other relevant details.

Priority to In-Country Adoption

4.5 When a recognised Indian agency receives a child, its first responsibility is to trace the biological parents and restore the child to them, failing which, as far as possible, to place the child in adoption with Indian families. It would be desirable that an Indian recognised placement agency should place annually more than 50 per cent of the total number of children given in adoption with Indian families. However, the handicapped children, children above 6 years of age and siblings will be excluded from this calculation. The placement agencies are required to adhere the following order of priority while considering the adoption of Indian children:

1. Indian families in India,
2. Indian families abroad,
3. One parent of Indian origin abroad,
4. Totally foreign.

Every recognised placement agency shall also give full details of the child to the prospective adoptive parents except the name and addresses of the biological parents, where known to the agency. It is only when all efforts to place the child within the country fail then the child would be cleared for inter-country adoption. These efforts should include contracting the VCA within the area of operation. A clearance certificate should be taken from VCA in this regard. Such clearance certificate shall be given by VCA. If within 60 days from the date the application to VCA, VCA is unable to find suitable Indian parents who are willing to take the child in adoption, intimation of making of the application to VCA shall be given to the Central Adoption Resource Agency forthwith. The Central Adoption Resource Agency will prepare a uniform proforma for clearance certificate to be issued by all voluntary coordinating agencies.

4.6 Adoption of Indian children placed with Indian living abroad will be treated as in-country placement. However, such Indian would have to follow the same procedure of sending their applications, documents etc. through an enlisted foreign agency in that country as in the case of inter-country adoption.

Record of Promotion Efforts

4.7 Every recognized agency shall keep a complete record in chronological order of the effects made by it for locating an Indian parent for the adoption of a child and shall specifically note the reasons for any case of non-placement of a child in in-country adoption with any particulars of Indian parents.

Case History

4.8 Every recognised Indian placement agency shall maintain a separate the law each child with the child's complete case history.

Quarterly Data to be Furnished to Authorities

4.9 Every recognised Indian placement agency shall furnish quarterly data to the government of the State in which the agency is operating and quarterly statement to the Central Adoption Resource Agency, in such proforma as may be prescribed by Central Adoption Resource Agency in respect of children given to Indians and others for adoption from time to time.

In take of Children

4.10 All children admitted by the recognised agency should be entered in the admission register with all the available information in the format prescribed by the Central Adoption Resource Agency.

4.11 In the case of an abandoned child not received through Juvenile Welfare Board/Juvenile Court as the case may be or through direct relinquishment by biological parents, a first information report (FIR) should be filed by the concerned agency in the local police station within 24 hours of arrival on the child at the recognised agency's children's home. The nearest Juvenile Welfare Board or where it does not operate, the Juvenile Court or the District Collector should also be notified within 24 hours of arrival of the child at the agency's children's home.

4.12 The recognised agency should ensure that medical examination of the child is conducted within 24 hours of its arrival and appropriate treatment given where necessary.

Surrender of a Child

4.13 In the case of surrender of a child, the biological parents/ parent should be counselled and duly informed by the agency concerned of the effect of their consent for adoption and the alternative available for the care and maintenance of the child.

4.14 The surrender documents should be executed at the free will of the biological parents/parent with no compulsion, payment or compensation of any kind on the part of the agency. If the biological parents state a preference for the religious upbringing of the child, their wish should be respected as far as possible. But ultimately the interest of the child alone should be the sole guiding factor before the child is placed in adoption.

4.15 The Parents/parent should be informed by the agency of his/ her/their right to reclaim the child within 90 days from the date of surrender. He/She/They should be made aware that after the period of 90 days relinguishment deed will become irrevocable and the agency will be free for place the child in adoption or guardianship within or outside India.

4.16 Whenever possible the surrender document should be executed on stamped paper in the presence of two responsible witnesses whom the recognised agency should be able to produce, if necessity, arises. The responsibility for the authenticity of the surrender document would be on the agency.

During the surrender process, the recognised Indian placement agency should ensure that:

(i) If a legitimate child is surrendered, both parents sign the relinguishment document and in case of the parents is dead, proof of death is furnished.

(ii) In case of a child born out of wedlock the mother herself, and none else, surrenders the child.

(iii) If the surrender is effected by any person other than the biological parents/parent, the same procedure is followed as far as abandoned child.

Destitute or Abandoned Child

4.17 If a child is found abandoned or is picked up as a destitute then the procedure of going through the Juvenile Wefare Board/Jevenile Count or the Social Welfare Department or the Collector would have to be adopted. As soon as an at abandment on destitute child is found by a social on child welfare agency on a nursing home or hospital or the police to anyone else, a report should immediately be lodged with the local police station alongwith a photograph of the child. The Collector of the District must be informed, who in turn must immediately inform the nearest recognised agency and CARA. The Inspector General of Police or the Commissioner of Police as the case may be, should instruct every police station within his jurisdiction to immediately undertake an inquiry for the purpose of ascertaining and tracing the parents of the child in respect of which the report is made and such inquiry must be completed within one month of the report being lodged with the Police Station. Meanwhile, the social or child welfare agency which has found the abandoned or destitute child may make an application to the Juvenile Welfare Board and where it is not functioning, then the Juvenile Court or to the Social Welfare Department or the Collector, and the case may be for a release order declaring that the child is legally free for adoption. Since the report of the enquiry to is made by the police has to be completed within a period of one month, it should be possible for the Juvenile Court or the Social Welfare Department or the Collector to make a release order declaring the child legally free for adoption within a period of six weeks from the date of making of the application form in the case of children below the age of two years and three months, in the case of children above that age.

Birth Certificate

4.18 Every child must have a birth certificate. For issuing a Birth Certificate in respect of an abandoned or destitute child, the registration of whose birth is not available, the agency concerned shall make an application to the local Magistrate alongwith any other material which the agency considers relevant in the form of an affidavit made by a responsible person to the agency. The local magistrate will then pass an order approving the particulars to be entered in the birth certificate and on the basis of the magistrate order the requisite certificate will be issued by the local birth certificate issuing authority of the city/ townmen where the child has been found. The Magistrate would ordinarily act on the certificate granted by the Chief Medical Officer. This process would be initiated only after the adoption is finalised, so that the particulars of the adoptive parents are available for inclusion in the certificate. In case the child has attained the age of three and the adoption has still not be a finalised, the agency may obtain a birth certificate, if it is found necessary, after informing the court in the form of an affidavit:

(a) That in the best of its knowledge the child has attained the age of three years;
(b) that his/her adoption has not been finalised is likely to take some time or may never be finalised in all probability;
(c) that a certificate is required for educational/medical/legal purposes or any other reasonable purpose which may be specified, and
(d) that person/persons would stand in as local parents to the child this (person/these persons should be responsible person/ responsible persons belonging to the placement agency) till such time as he/she attains majority, or is adopted, whichever is earlier.

In such cases a second birth certificate may be issued after adoption to provide for a change in the name/names of the child and the adoptive parent/parents after obtaining an order that effect from the court which had reposting order for issuing the original birth certificate.

4.19 A quarterly statement on child available for guardianship/ adoption in the format prescribed by CARA should be furnished to the appropriate authority in the State Government/UT Administration and CARA, and every month to the CARA concerned.

Procedure for Adoption

4.20 No child should be offered for adoption:

(a) In the case of abandoned children until the Juvenile Welfare Board/Juvenile Court, the Collector or the District Magistrate or the Department of Social Welfare declares the child legally free for placement.
(b) In the case of surrendered children, till the three months period for reconsideration by the parent is over.
(c) In the case of a child who can understand and express his/ her consent.

Role of the Placement Agencies

4.21 In the case of surrendered children, after 3 months time for reconsideration, the placement agencies should make all efforts within fifteen days to place the child with Indian parents in the country. But in case of destitute or abandoned child, the placement agency after getting a releasing order declaring the child legally free for adoption from the competent authority, should make all the efforts to place the child within the country within a period not exceeding seven weeks from the date of releasing order which includes one week time for reconsideration of the biological parents, if traced.

4.22 If the Recognised Placement Agency is not able to find a suitable Indian family within the country, it will give all the details of the child to the voluntary coordinating agency wherever it exists. The information must include details of admission, medical history legal status, photograph and efforts made to find families in the country. The officers of the CARA shall be permitted to visit and see the child, as and when necessary.

4.23 Where there is a VCA maintaining a register of children available for adoption as also a register of Indian adoptive parent, who want to take a child in adoption, VCA will immediately contact the Indian family which is on its register as prospective adoptive parents and inform them that a particular child is available for adoption. If, within a period of two months, the child is not taken in adoption by an Indian family, it should be regarded as available for inter-country adoption. The possibility of inter-State adoption in India and VCA coordination should also be exhausted before a child is offered for inter-country adoption. The first priority in inter-country adoption should be given to Indians residing abroad and, if no such Indian family is available, then to adoptive couples where atleast one parent is of Indian origin. However, the children placed with parents or one of the parents having Indian origin would be considered as given as in-country adoption.

4.24 It is only where a VCA does not exist or no Indian family comes forward to take a child in adoption within a maximum period of two months, that the child should be regarded as available for inter-country adoption. However, if the child is handicapped or is a sibling or above 6 years of age, the procedure of obtaining VCA clearance need not be followed and the child should be regarded as available for inter-country adoption without the waiting period of two months. In other cases also, if the child is in a bad state of health, needing urgent medical attention which it is not possible for the social or child welfare agency looking after the child to provide within the country, the agency need not wait for the period of two months but after obtaining a medical certificate from a medical specialist in a Government hospital stating the need for urgent treatment and also that the child will be able to withstand the journey, get VCA clearance and process the case for inter-country adoption. However, in the case of surrendered children, the three months time for reconsideration should always be adhered to.

4.25 A child should be offered in inter-country adoption by a recognised Indian agency only on receipt of a no-objection certificate from the VCA except in the cases mentioned in paragraphs 4.5 and 4.24 above. If it has not been possible to find suitable Indian parents for taking a child on adoption within the period of two months, specified in paragraph 4.23 VCA shall issue a no-objection certificate.

4.26 In completing formalities for adoption/guardianship the procedures as laid down by Central Governments/CARA should be followed.

Documentary proof of age, marriage, income, health, property and savings of prospective parents, letter of acceptance accepting a particular child alongwith countersigned child study report, medical report and photograph of the prospective parents/agency, consent and power of Attorney in the name of the functionary of the Indian Agency, should be taken. A Home study report prepared by or under the supervision of a professionally trained social worker should be taken into account. Photographs of prospective parents should also be kept on record.

4.27 Pending completion of formal adoption guardianship proceedings, the child may be placed with prospective adoptive parents in foster caste in the case of Indian parents living in India.

Placement of Handicapped Children

4.28 The placement of handicapped children and children with deficiencies may be considered as a plus point in evaluating the performance.

Transfer of Children

4.29 All children transferred to the recognised placement agency (recognised by Government of India) from an unrecognised agency, whether within the State or from outside, should be in the physical custody of the recognised agency for a period of not less than one month before any act for the placement of the child abroad is taken.

4.30 Transfer of the child should be accompanied by available documents pertaining to its admission, preliminary case history, documentary evidence to prove that the child is legally free for adoption, and a letter of transfer. The recognised placement agency should verify all the facts before accepting the child, as they are legally responsible for its placement.

4.31 Attempts to find adoptive parents for children who are legally free for placement may be made by the child welfare agency which has first received the child, either directly or through an unrecognised agency or through the VCA.

4.32 In the case of inter-State transfer of children may be transferred by the recognised Indian agency to any of its desipitated branches, provided that it is done with the written consent and permission of the Social Welfare Department/Magistrate/Collector, as is relevant to the case. The nearest VCA should also be informed.

Follow-up

4.33 The follow-up of children placed within the country will be as follows:

(i) If any pre-placement foster case is effected, there should be regular monitoring and evaluation of the foster case. A professionally trained social worker should visit the family regularly.

(ii) The follow-up format should be completed and forwarded by the recognised placement agency concerned every six months to VCA, the State Government and the Central Adoption Resources Agency.

(iii) The agency should see that legal adoption is effected at the earliest thereby safeguarding the interest of the child.

(iv) Even after legal adoption, the agency should keep in touch with the family for a period of three years.

(v) Post-adoptive counselling should be provided by the agency to the adoptive parents.

Records

4.34 The following records and registers should be maintained by every recognised Indian placement agency,

(i) Admission register.

(ii) A separate file on each child in the prescribed format, giving full details/history. Relevant, legal documents of every adoption and child's background history should be maintained atleast for a period of 18 years for future reference.

(iii) Register of prospective adoptive parents with details.

(iv) Register of children showing their arrival, departure, admittance into hospitals, return to their parents or death, if any.

(v) Follow-up register of children placed with adoptive family prior to legal placement and after legal placement.

(vi) Quarterly reports in the prescribed format as forwarded to the State Government, Central Adoption Resource Agency and VCA.

(vii) The annual report of the organisation together with the necessary details and statistics in the prescribed format as forwarded to the State Government, the Central Adoption Resource Agency and VCA.

(viii) Audited statement of accounts, together with a copy of CARA account submitted to the Home Ministry, as forwarded to the State Government and CARA.

(ix) Other records stipulated under the Societies Registration Act. ISCO or the relevant State law relating to public trusts.

Recovery of Costs

4.35 The organisation shall pursue only no-profit objectives. Under no circumstances should be derive improper financial gain from any activity related to inter-country or in-country adoption. It may however, receive reimbursement or other payment for direct or indirect costs and actual expenses.

4.36 For in-country adoption, the following charges may be recovered by the agency from the adoptive parents, if the agency deems it necessary:

(i) Maintenance cost as lived by the Court from time to time, from the date the child has been approved and accepted by the Indian parent/parents to the date of departure from the institution.

(ii) Such out of pocket cost, administrative cost and service charges for preparation of child study, medical and IQ reports, legal expenses and conveyance etc. as may be fixed by the court from time to time.

4.37 The maximum amount to be charged by any agency from Indian parents as reimbursement of maintenance expenses shall be fixed by the court.

4.38 For inter-country adoption the following costs may be recovered by the agency from the foreign adoptive parents:

(i) Cost of any surgical or medical treatment of the child against production of bills or vouchers duly certified.

(ii) The Indian placement agency processing the application of a foreigner for being appointed guardian of a child with a view to its eventual adoption, should be entitled to recover from the foreigner, cost incurred in preparing and filing the application and processing it in court including legal expenses, administrative expenses, preparation of child study report, preparation of medical and I.Q. reports, passport and visa expenses, and conveyance expenses and that such expenses may be fixed by the court at a figure not exceeding Rs. 6,000. Any increase in maximum recoverable expenses in this regard would be done only with the approval of the Supreme Court of India. Insofar as the maintenance or medical expenses incurred by the recognised concerned, they are entitled to receive reimbursement of such maintenance or medical expenses from the foreigner taking the child in adoption at a figure not more than Rs.78 per day per child from the date of selection of the child by the adoptive parents until the child is taken by the adoptive parents after they are appointed as guardians. This outer limit of recoverable expenses may be reviewed by the Ministry of Welfare, Government of India once in three years depending on escalation of the expenses including cost of living.

(iii) Cost of travel of the child from India in the receiving country and the cost of an escort if the foreign recognised agency is unable to provide the escort.

(iv) In case of disruption or failure of adoption, the cost of repatriating the child to India, if no alternative placement for the child is effected in the foreigner's country by the recognised foreign agency with the concurrence of the Indian agency.

(v) If it comes to CARA's notice that any recognised Indian agency charges more fees than the prescribed fees or tries to exploit financially the foreign enlisted agency, CARA may, after giving an opportunity to such agency to explain its point of view, suspend or revoke its recognition. Similarly, if any foreign enlisted agency induces an Indian recognised agency by giving or offers more money than the prescribed fees for processing a case of inter-country adoption of an Indian child. CARA may after giving an opportunity to such agency to explain its point of view de-enlist the foreign agency.

CHAPTER V: RECOGNITION OF INDIAN AGENCIES FOR ADOPTION

Proforma for Application

5.1 Any Indian social child welfare agency desirous of obtaining recognition from the Government of India for undertaking intercountry adoption work shall submit an application in the prescribed form to the CARA through the Department dealing with Social Welfare/Women and Child Development in the State in which the agency is located.

Un-Recognised Agencies Barred

5.2 No agency which does not hold a certificate of recognition from the CARA shall give a child to foreign parents for the purpose of adoption nor submit an application to an Indian court under the guardians and Wards Act, 1890, for declaring a foreigner as a guardian of an Indian child.

Recognition for Specified Period

5.3 Recognition to an Indian agency shall be granted initially for a period of three years. Subject to the conditions laid down in these guidelines.

Conditions for Recognition

5.4 Any Indian agency which seeks recognition shall generally fulfil the following conditions:

(a) It shall be a society registered under the Societies Registrations Act, 1860 or a trust created under the Charitable Trust Act, or an organisation registered under an appropriate law or an organisation which has worked for the welfare of children during the proceeding five years;

(b) The organisation shall be duly licensed by the State Government under the provisions either of the Women and Children Institutions (Licensing) Act, 1956 or the Orphanages or Charitable Institutions (Supervision and Control) Act, 1960;

(c) It shall have a duly constituted Executive Committee: the Chief Executive of the organisation as well as the majority of members of the Board/Executive Committee should be Indian Citizens;

(d) It should have appropriate children's home for the protection and up-keep of children including infants;

(e) It should be able to raise funds through donations or Government grants;

(f) It should be running on a non-commercial, non-profitable basis;

(g) It should have atleast one qualified social worker on its staff to carry out the adoption work;

(h) The Chief Executive of the organisation should be willing to sign a written undertaking to follow the guidelines laid down by the Supreme Court of India and those prescribed, from time to time, by the Government of India and the Regulation, if any, made by CARA; and

(i) Recognition of the agency should be recommended by the State Government concerned. Or, if it is not so recommended, the reason for the refusal should be given. CARA may accept or reject the reasons for refusal. The decision of CARA shall be final.

Renewal of Recognition

5.5 The original application should be sent to the appropriate authority of the State Government and a copy of it should simultaneously be forwarded directly to CARA. The State government will forward the original application to CARA alongwith its views within a period of two months from the date of receipt of the application. If the State Government does not send the application to CARA with its views within a period of two months from the date of receipt of the application the concurrence of the State Government will be presumed by CARA and the application will be processed by CARA for grant of recognition within a maximum further period of two months. If there is no response from CARA to the application within such further maximum period of two months, or before the expiry of the recognition of the agency, whichever is later, the renewal shall be deemed to have been granted for a period of two years. Recognition would normally be renewable for a period of three years at a time subject to the following conditions:

(i) Satisfactory performance in in-country adoption. The Authority should ensure that the agencies should abundantly exhibit their involvement in the area of Indian adoption. Therefore, it shall be obligatory on the part of every recognised placement agency to make atleast 25 per cent placement of children in Indian families out of the total placements effected by it by way of adoption/guardianship in the first year of its recognition. This level of in-country adoption/guardianship shall be raised to 50 per cent by the third year of its recognition. The recognition is liable to be suspended or revoked in cases where the recognised agency fails to arrange in-country adoptions upto the figures stipulated also. However, an opportunity would be given to the placement agency to show cause against such suspention or revocation, as the case may be and such suspension or revocation, as the case may be and such suspention or revocation shall be made by a written order giving reasons for such suspension or revocation.

(ii) Regular submission of reports and return.

(iii) No instance of proved malpractice against the placement agency.

(iv) Recommendation of the concerned State Government provided that the refusal to recommend is not based on any inadequate, irrelevant or inacceptable reasons.

Agencies to Maintain Accounts

5.7 (i) Every agency shall maintain proper accounts to be audited by a Chartered Accountant every year.

(ii) A photostat copy of audited accounts together with audit report shall be furnished by every agency within one months from the date accounts have been audited by the Chartered Accountant, to the Social Welfare Department of the State Government concerned and to the CARA.

(iii) A photostat copy of the CARA accounts submitted to the Home Ministry should be furnished to CARA together with the audited accounts, by the agency.

Application to be Processed only by Recognised Agencies

5.8 An application for declaring a foreigner or an Indian to be the guardian of an Indian child as a prelude to adoption in a foreign country shall be processed only by a recognised Indian agency after following the procedure set out in these guidelines.

Application to be Sponsored by Enlisted Foreign Agencies

5.9 A recognised Indian agency may submit an application of a foreign adoptive parent to an Indian court for awarding the guardianship of an Indian child to a foreigner provided the application of such foreigner has been forwarded by a foreign voluntary agency enlisted by the Government of India and the application is made in accordance with these guidelines. However, if there is an agency owned or operated by the Government in a foreign country, the foreign adoptive parents can approach a recognised Indian agency in India through such agency operated or owned by the foreign Government.

Indian Agencies Recognised to Deal who Enlisted Agencies Abroad

5.10 No recognised Indian agency shall entertain any application directly for adoption of an Indian child from a foreigner or sponsored by a foreign enlisted agency unless the prescribed documents alongwith the application are cleared by CARA.

Inspection of Agencies

5.11 The premises of the recognised Indian agencies including their children homes, and their records shall open to inspection by officials of the CARA and for official of the State Government at any time.

CHAPTER VI: ROLE OF ENLISTED FOREIGN AGENCIES FOR ADOPTION

Foreign Agencies to Apply to India's Diplomatic Missions

6.1 A foreign social/child welfare agency desirous of sponsoring applications of foreign adoptive parents for adopting an Indian child shall make an application for enlistment with CARA in the office of India's diplomatic mission in that country and only such foreign agencies enlisted for this purpose by CARA shall undertake this activity.

Criteria or Enlistment of Foreign Agencies

6.2 The criteria for enlistment of foreign agencies by CARA for the purpose of inter-country adoption are as under:

(i) It shall be either a part of the Government of the country or a duly registered voluntary agency registered under the relevant law of the concerned country and should be recognised by the appropriate authority of that country.

(ii) It shall be a child welfare agency having an established standing in this field and it must be staffed with qualified social workers who have experience in the field of adoption.

(iii) The agency in question shall be run on non-commercial and non-profitable basis. The foreign agency should be asked to submit a report and audited statement of accounts of their operations in India.

(iv) Undertaking by the enlisted foreign agency that in case of disruption of the foreigner's family before adoption is effected or in case the child is not properly looked after or is mal-treated or abused in the adoptive family, it will take care of the child under intimation to the Indian Diplomatic Mission, the Central Adoption Resource Agency, Ministry of Welfare and the concerned Indian recognised placement agency and try to find suitable alternative placement for the child with the concurrence of the recognised placement agency which processed the case and report such alternative placement to the Indian Court which made the order for guardianship and also to CARA.

(v) The Head/Chief Executive of the Organisation should be willing to sign a written undertaking to follow the guidelines laid down by the CARA for observance by the enlisted foreign agencies. The enlisted foreign agencies should send to CARA a list of the Indian agencies with whom they have contacts and working relations or with whom they are prepared to have working relations.

Procedure for Enlistment

6.3 (i) A Foreign Social/child welfare agency desirous of sponsoring applications of foreign adoptive parents for adopting Indian children shall apply for enlistment by CARA, though the office of India's Diplomatic Mission and the Government of the country where it is located.

(ii) On the recommendation of India's Diplomatic Mission in the country concerned, CARA shall examined the application and consider the agency concerned for recognition provided it fulfils the criteria stated in paragraph 6.2 above.

Renewal of Enlistment

6.4 (i) A foreign agency engaged in inter-country adoption would be enlisted by CARA initially for a period of five years. Enlistment would be renewal for five years at a time in case of satisfactory performance subject to conditions laid down in these guidelines.

(ii) CARA will take the following factors into consideration while granting renewal of enlistment provided an application for renewal is received through proper channel atleast six months before the expiry of the previous recognition.

(a) Whether the agency is still recognised by the appropriate authority of the country in which it is based.

(b) Whether the agency has been regular in the submission of process reports of the children placed by them in adoption.

(c) Whether the general performance of the agency is satisfactory and whether the children placed by them are making satisfactory progress.

(d) Whether Government of India's Diplomatic Mission in the country concerned has recommended the case for renewal.

De-enlistment

6.5 The Central Adoption Resource Agency, Ministry of Welfare, Government of India, may at any time de-enlist any enlisted foreign agency for adoption for valid or legitimate reasons and shall not be bound to disclose the same. However, it at the time of de-enlistment there is any case under process that would be allowed to be completed.

6.6 When the Court makes an order appointing adoptive parents as the guardian of the child, the order shall contain an undertaking of the adoptive parents that they shall protect and safeguard the best interests of the child and that the child would be legally adopted in the receiving State not later than two years from the date of the order and that on such adoption in the receiving State, subject to the laws of the country the child would have all the rights of a natural born child.

Rights of the Child taken Abroad

6.7 On adoption of the child by the foreign parent according to the law of his/her country, it is presumed that subject to the laws of the land the child would acquire the same status as a natural born child within wedlok with the same rights of inheritance and suggestion and the same nationality as the foreign parent adopting the child.

6.8 Where the child is not legally adopted by the adoptive parents of the receiving State within two years from the date of order of the Court in India appointing the adoptive parents as guardians either on account of disruption in the family or on account of the adoptive parents failing to get adjusted to the behaviour of the child or otherwise, the foreign agency which has processed the adoption of the child in the receiving State should immediately withdraw the child from the adoptive parents and keep the child in its custody and care and find out new adoptive parents for placement of the child in adoption as soon as possible. The foreign agency shall give an undertaking to this effect to the Court processing the case in India.

6.9 All enlisted foreign agencies shall send a copy of their annual report to CARA every year.

6.10 The foreign agency shall with reference to every child placed by it send follow-up reports through India's Diplomatic Mission abroad with photographs of the child on a quarterly basis for the first two years and on a half yearly basis for the next three years to CARA and to the Court that awarded the guardianship in India and to the Indian placement agency concerned. The foreign enlisted agency shall send a photoalbum of the children alongwith their adoptive parent to CARA once in a year.

6.11 The enlisted foreign agency will forward a copy of the legal adoption order of the appropriate authority in that country as soon as it is made to the Central Adoption Resource Agency, the Court which awarded the guardianship and to the Indian agency concerned.

6.12 Even after the adoption is legalised the enlisted foreign agency should maintain contact with the adoptive family in keeping with the need of privacy of the adoptive family and provide support and counselling services, if necessary and safeguard the interest of the child till such time as he/she attains majority.

6.13 The enlisted foreign agency should help the Indian Diplomatic Mission in its country to arrange get-togethers of adopted children of Indian original and their adoptive families for exposing them to the culture of India. These get-togethers may be organised at the time of national occassions like 15th August, 14th November, 2nd October and 26th January etc. CARA may on some occasions participants in these get-together in order to know the feedback on progress of the adoption child.

6.14 The enlisted foreign agencies cannot employ their representatives in India for any kind of activities relating to inter-country adoption.

CHAPTER VII: VOLUNTARY COORDINATING AGENCIES (VCA)

7.1 There shall be a centralised agency, namely, voluntary coordinating agency (VCA) in the State or even in a large city where there are several recognised placement and child welfare agencies. The principal functions of VCA shall be as follows:

(a) It shall actively promote Indian adoption and formulate, develop and execute programmes and active for generating awareness in this regard;

(b) It shall ensure that the priority laid down by the Supreme Court on placement adoption within the country or with Indian abroad is adhered to. All recognised social child welfare agencies, Juvenile Welfare Boards and Government homes within the country, desirous of placing children in adoption placement shall furnish lists of children legally free for adoption to the concerned VCA and also to CARA;

(c) It shall maintain a register of all prospective adoptive parents;

(d) It shall maintain a register or all available children who are legally free for adoption;

(e) It shall coordinate the work of all its member agencies and other child welfare institutions in the field of Indian adoption. Where Indian adoption is difficult within its area of operation it shall coordinate with other VCAs in the State and in the country;

(f) Where Indian placement is not materialised, it shall issue a no-objection certificate within a period of two months from the date of receipt of application for 'No objection' in the VCAs to the recognised placement agency so as to enable the child to be placed in inter-country adoption;

(g) In the case of a child requiring immediate medical or surgical assistance, the VCA may waive the supported waiting period on production of medical certificate as provided in paragraph 4.24 above and issue a no-objection certificate at the earliest.

(h) It shall call a meeting of member agencies at least once every quarter;

(i) In cases where these guidances are not being followed by any recognised placement agency, the concerned VCA will bring it or the notice of CARA with substantive evidence for taking appropriate action.

7.2 The VCA shall be registered under the Societies Registration Act and will comply with all the rules laid down under the Act and also these guidelines.

7.3 Every VCA shall have, on its staff, at least two professionally trained social workers.

7.4 Every VCA shall have to seek recognition from CARA by means of an application which shall be routed through the State Government and the State Government shall offer its comments on such application within a period of 30 days from the date of receipt of such application and if no such comments are forthcoming within the period of 30 days, it shall be presumed that the State Government has no objection.

7.5 All the recognised placement agencies (whether doing only in-country and inter-country adoptions, would be enlisted to become members of the VCA and those child welfare agencies which are not placing children adoption but are merely running homes for children it would also be eligible to be members of VCA. The final decision in case of the later would rest with the executive committee of the VCA. If any agency is derecognised by CARA on account of malpractice of any other valid reason or any child welfare agency is delicensed by the State Government, then it shall cease to be a member of VCA and it shall not be eligible for membership of VCA unless it is once again recognised or licensed.

7.6 The recognised placement agencies would have the right to vote for electing the executive committee of the VCA. The child welfare agencies would not enjoy any voting right. The VCA should be an independent periodical body with a democratic structure. The Chairman should not be connected with either in-country or inter-country placements.

Structure of VCA

7.7 There shall be an executive committee for managing the day-to-day affairs of VCA. The executive committee shall consist of not less than 3 members and not more than one-third members of the VCA.

Executive Committee of VCA

7.8 The executive committee of VCA shall comprise:

(a) The Chairman of VCA.

(b) A representative of the State Government of the level of the Deputy Director (Welfare) Social Welfare or above.

(c) One Senior representative of each scrutinising agency working in the jurisdiction of the concerned VCA.

(d) One representative from the agencies exclusively doing Indian adoption.

(e) Three representatives of the recognised placement agencies out of these at leasts two shall be from those placement agencies, which have placed at least 50 per cent children within the country during last three years to be elected by the recognised placement agencies which are members of VCA. The terms of office of the members of the executive committee of items (c) and (d) shall be two years and they shall not be eligible for re-appointment for the next succeeding period of 2 years.

The executive committee of VCA may appoint staff to carry out the day-to-day functions of the VCA. Such paid staff would be accountable in the executive committee.

7.9 The no-objection certificate issued by the VCA would be signed and issued by two persons but Chairperson and Member Secretary both of whom will not be connected with adoption activities whether in-country or inter-country. No recognised placement agency shall process the application for inter-country adoption before obtaining the no-objection certificate save in the case of exceptional and for exempted categories referred to above at these guidelines.

The Following are the Broad Procedure to be Followed by the VCA

7.10 (a) All member agencies must submit a list of children and prospective adoptive parents on a monthly basis to the VCA.

(b) When an agency wishes to place a child in foreign adoption it must check with the VCA to ascertain whether there is any Indian parent willing to take the child in adoption.

(c) The period of 30 days provided for in the Supreme Court jugdment for trying to place a child with Indian parents has been found to be inadequate and this should be extended to 60 days from the date when VCA assistance is sought to locate an Indian family. This procedure may be adopted during the period of 5 weeks within such CARA is required to give a final clearance.

(d) The time frame for VCA to find a placement in India will be 60 days as provided in clause (c) above and only after that, an inter-country placement may be processed.

(e) If these differences between the placement agency and VCA in regard to the clearance of a child for inter-country adoption, the placement agency concerned may refer the cases to CARA. In such cases CARA will decide whether to give the clearance of the child or not. The decision of CARA shall be final.

Criteria for Recognition

7.11 In order to be recognised as VCA, an agency must fulfil the following criteria:

(i) It should be a society registered under the Societies Registration Act, 1860.

(ii) The agency must be recommended by the State Government concerned for recognition by CARA.

(iii) The agency should run on a non-commercial and non-profitable basis.

(iv) Its office-bearers at item (d) and (e) in paragraph 7.8 shall be from recognised placement agencies which have given children in in-country adoption to the extent of 50 per cent or more of the total number of children given in the adoption in a year after excluding handicapped children, siblings and children above 6 years of age.

(v) All the office-bearers should be Indian nationals. The initial recognition of VCA shall be for a period of 3 yeas.

Renewal of Recognition

7.12 A VCA which seeks renewal of recognition should apply to CARA through the State Government for renewal of recognition six months prior to the date of expiry of the previous recognition. The following would be the main criteria for renewal of recognition:

(i) Satisfactory performance in the promotion of in-country adoption.

(ii) Timely submission of reports and returns as may be specified by CARA.

Withdrawal of Recognition

7.13 Recognition of a VCA may be withdrawn by CARA on receipt of a report from the State Government regarding unsatisfactory performance, after giving the VCA an opportunity to explain its position. The VCAs should play positive role in bringing greater coordination among all the placement agencies working in the area of their operation. Any malpractice, if proved, would immediately invite action in the shape of derecognition. Delay and non-compliance in the submission of reports/returns asked for by the State Government or CARA may also be a ground for withdrawal of recognition.

7. 14 VCA should conduct the quarterly meetings attended by all the members entitled and eligible to attend the meetings and discuss all matters relating to adoption. The minutes of the meetings should be sent to CARA by the concerned VCA.

Finance of VCA

7.15 The Government of India in the Ministry of Welfare would give grant-in-aid to VCA upto 90% of the cost as per prescribed norms.

Existing VCAs

7.16 The existing VCAs shall stand superseded as soon as VCAs are constituted in accordance with these guidelines for the area of operation of the existing VCAs.

7.17 If in any area there is only one recognised placement agency, it shall be entitled to become a member of VCA operating in the adjacent area.

CHAPTER VIII: SCRUTINIZING AGENCY

8.1 It is open to the Court looking into the matter of appointment of guardian under the Guardians and Wards Act, 1890 in exercise of its powers under Section II to appoint any independent, reputed Social or Child Welfare Agency, as a Security Agency for scrutinising an application from prospective adoptive parents for adoption of a child. The agency must be a body of experts in the field of child care and welfare, not itself involved in any manner in the placement of children in adoption. At present there are two scrutinising agencies, namely, Indian Council for Social Welfare and Indian Council of Child Welfare being appointed by the Court. The Court may be requested to appoint any other eligible child or social welfare agency as scrutinising agency which preferably meets the eligibility criteria as laid down by CARA.

Procedure for Recognition

8.2 CARA shall maintain a panel of agencies which according to it can satisfactorily perform the functions of a scrutinising agency. The procedure to be adopted for recognition of an agency as scrutinising agency other than Indian Council of Child Welfare (ICCW) and Indian Council of Social Welfare (ICSW) will be as follows:

(i) The agency should apply to CARA for recognition as a scrutinising agency.

(ii) The agency should fulfil all the criteria laid down by CARA for recognition as scrutinising agency.

(iii) CARA may seek such information as may be necessary from the scrutinising agency regarding its bonafiders and performance on the basis of such report issue a recognition certificate.

(iv) A scrutinising agency would be recognised initially for a period of three years, renewable as per the procedure given in these guidelines.

Criteria for Recognition

8.3 (i) The agency should be an independent, reputed social child welfare agency.

(ii) The agency must be a body of experts in the field of child care and welfare.

(iii) The agency should not be involved in the placement of children in adoption.

(iv) It should be a society registered under the Societies Registration Act, 1960.

(v) All the office-bearers should be Indian nationals.

(vi) The agency should run on a non-commercial and non-profitable basis.

Renewal of Recognition

8.3 (i) Every recognised scrutinising agency should apply for renewal of recognition, 6 months, prior to the date of expiry of the previous recognition. If the performance of the scrutinising agency has been found satisfactory and there are no adverse reports from any court or the State Government concerned and also if any reports or returns asked for by CARA are submitted by it regularly without delay recognition may be renewed from time to time but each time only for a period of 3 years.

Saving Clause

8.4 Any scrutinising agency may be de-recognised by CARA at any time following reports of malpractice from any State Government or any Court, after giving the agency an opportunity to place its case before CARA.

Functioning of Scrutinising Agency

8.5 It shall be incumbent upon every scrutinising agency to perform the following functions:

(1) To scrutinise the following documents:
  (i) Application for guardianship/adoption made on behalf of the prospective adoptive foreign parents.
  (ii) Home study report.
  (iii) Child study report.
  (iv) Any other documents/certificate attached with the application.

(2) To ensure that the application or copy of the application, as the case may be, has been duly forwarded by a foreign agency to CARA.

(3) To ensure that before a child is placed in guardianship with a foreign adoptive parents, a non-objection certificate has been obtained from the concerned VCA.

(4) To satisfy itself that the child in question is legally free for adoption.

(5) To see the child in person and to check that the information given to prospective, adoptive parents regarding the child is correct. In case of any change in the medical/physical status of the child, the scrutinising agency should ensure that the information of the change is given to the prospective adoptive parents and their consent obtained before a final order is passed by the court concerned.

(6) To satisfy itself that the prospective adoptive parents/guardians are fit persons for adopting the child in question.

(7) To ensure that the adoption would be in the best interest of the child.

(8) To assist the court in ascertaining whether the child has been voluntarily surrendered by the biological parents.

(9) To ensure and satisfy itself that no one, including Indian as well as foreign agencies concerned are making any profit out of the adoption in question.

(10) To verify, in case of older children, the child's own views regarding the adoption. This may be reported to CARA immediately.

(11) To ascertain, as far as possible, as to what are the laws regarding adoption of foreign children in the clearly of the prospective adoptive parents and there is a responsible assurance that the child would be adopted within the minimum possible period but in any case within a period not exceeding two years.

(12) To ensure that all the precautionary measures are taken before the handicapped, sibling, older age and other special needs children are placed to a family who are really interested to such children.

8.6 The Scrutinising Agency will submit a report to CARA since every six months of all the cases it has scrutinised.

8.7 In case of any difference between Scrutiny Agency and placement agency in regard to placing of a child or matching and the child with the prospective adoptive parents or any other related issues, the scrutiny agency may refer it to CARA for consideration. The decision of CARA on such case shall be final.

Scrutinising Charges

8.8 Whenever an Indian parent make an application for appointing himself or herself as guardians of a child or a Hindu parent applies for permission to adopt a child and, if the case is referred to it by the court, the scrutinising agency may charge such amount of expenses upto Rs. 150 as directed by the court unless a higher amount is awarded by the court.

When a foreign agency makes an application for guardianship, the scrutinising agency may charge from the Indian agency an amount as directed by the Court varying between Rs. 450 to Rs. 500, for actual expenditure incurred and the concerned Indian agency shall have the right to recover such amount from the foreign parents whose application for guardianship it has processed. This amount may exceed Rs. 500 if the court concerned specifically orders the actual increment amount to be paid for the specific work done.

CHAPTER IX: MISCELLANEOUS

Violation of Guidelines

9.1 If it come to the notice of any State Government or any of India's Diplomatic Missions abroad or CARA that a recognised Indian agency or enlisted foreign agency is not observing all or any of the provisions of these guidelines or is otherwise functioning in a manner which is not in the interests of children generally, it shall inform CARA immediately with details and CARA may, at its discretion suspend or withdraw recognition for such enlisted agency and/or take any other such action as may be deemed necessary.

9.2 It would be desirable for the Government of India to enter into bilateral agreement with countries which are receiving children from India for the purpose of adoption and such bilateral agreements should provide for full coordination between the appropriate authorities of India and the receiving State and also protection and safeguarding of the welfare of the children taken for adoption in the receiving State.

9.3 Apprehensions have been expressed that unscrupulous elements arrange illegal transfer of babies to adoptive parents at the time of their birth in some hospitals, nursing homes, maternity homes in the country. Such transfer of babies taking place without observing the appropriate norms and procedure is illegal and thus it is not at all in the interest of the child. If any such complaints are brought to the notice of CARA, it shall cause an enquiry to be done and take up the matter with the appropriate authorities of the Central or State Government including the Medical Council of India.

Amendments to Guidelines

9.4 The Ministry of Welfare, Government of India reserves to itself the power, at its discretion to make such amendments, additions, deletions or alterations in these guidelines as are deemed necessary from time to time.

ANNEXURE A

List of documents required from foreign adoptive parents and Social or Child Welfare Agency enlisted by Government of India for consideration of an inter-country application of Indian Child.

(a) Home Study report of the foreign adoptive parents prepared by a professional worker as per Annexure "A".
(b) Recent photographs of the adoptive family.
(c) Marriage certificate of foreign adoptive parents.
(d) Declaration concerning health of adoptive parents.
(e) Certificate of medical fitness of adoptive parents duly certified by a medical Doctor.
(f) Declaration regarding financial status of foreign adoptive parents alongwith supporting documents including employers certificate, where applicable.
(g) Employment certificate, if applicable, of foreign adoptive parents.
(h) Income Tax Assessment order of foreign adoptive parents.
(i) Bank reference.
(j) Particulars of the properties owned by the foreigners adoptive parents.
(k) Declaration from foreign adoptive parents stating willingness to be appointed guardian of the child.
(l) Undertaking from the social or child welfare enlisted agency sponsoring the foreigner to the effect than child would be legally adopted by the foreign adoptive parents according to the law of the country within a period not exceeding two years from the time of arrival of the child and as soon as the adoption is effected. Social or child welfare enlisted will send three certified copies of adoption order each to the social or child welfare agency in India through which the application for guardianship is processed for filling in the Court and one copy of Central Adoption Resources Agency, Ministry of Welfare.
(m) Undertaking from the foreign adoptive parents that adopted child would be provided necessary education and up-bringing according to the status of adoptive parents.
(n) Undertaking from the social and child welfare enlisted agency that report relating to progress of the child alongwith his/her recent photograph would be sent quarterly during last two years and half yearly for the next three years in the prescribed proforma through India's Diplomatic Mission abroad.
(o) Power of Attorney from foreign adoptive parents in favour of officer of the social or child welfare agency in India which will be required to process the case and such Power of Attorney should authorised the Attorney to handle the case on behalf of the foreigner in case the foreigner is not in a position to come to India.
(p) Certificate from the enlisted social or child welfare agency

sponsoring application of the foreigner to the effect that adoptive parents are permitted to adopt a child according to the law of their country.

(q) Undertaking from the social or child welfare enlisted agency to the effect that in case of disruption of the family of the foreigner before legal adoption has been effected, it will take care of the child and find a suitable alternative placement for the child with the approval of Central Adoption Resource Agency. After seeking the necessary approval from CARA it will report alternative placement to the concerned court handing guardianship proceedings in the foreign country. And such information shall be passed on by the court to the Central Adoption Resource Agency.

(r) Undertaking from the social or child welfare enlisted agency that it will reimburse all expenses to the concerned Indian social or child welfare agency as fixed by competent court towards maintenance of the child and processing charge fees.

Important Instructions

(1) The home study report should broadly including information in regard to the various matters set out in Annexure "A" though it need not strictly adhere to the requirements of the Annexure that it should also contain an assessment by the social welfare agency as to whether the foreigner wishing to take a child in adoption is fit and suitable and has the capacity to parent a child coming from a different racial and cultural millieu and whether the child will be able to fit into the environment of the adoptive family and the community in which it lives.

(2) All the above certificates, declaration documents must accompany the application of the foreigner for taking a child in adoption should be duly notarised by a Notary Public whose signature should be duly attested either by an officer of the Ministry of External Affairs or Justice or Social Welfare of the country of the foreigner or by a officer of the Indian Embassy or High Commissions of Consulate in that country.

ANNEXURE B

Procedure for Regulating Inter-Country Adoption

Non-Resident Indians	*Prospective Foreign Adoptive Parents*
1	*2*

Column 2 (Prospective Foreign Adoptive Parents)

To contact

Foreign Enlisted Agency
- To prepare the Home Study Report.
- To complete all the documents.
- To submit the documents to
- Certificate Copies

CARA
- To see whether the foreign agency is enlisted
- To see whether the Indian Placement agency is recognised
- To examine all the documents and ensure that all are in order
- Issue of No-Objective Certificate to the placement agency

Column 1 (Non-Resident Indians)

Original Application and documents

Indian Recognised Placement Agency
- To register the Parents with the Agency
- To contact concerned VCA for clearance certificate

VCA
- To explore the possibilities for the placement of the child within the country
- Issuance of clearance certificate to placement agency

Indian Recognised Placement Agency
- To match of the child with the foreign prospective adoptive parents
- To obtain the approval of the foreign adoptive parents on the proposed child

Enlisted Foreign Agency
- Communicate the approval of the foreign adopting

parents to the placement agency.

Indian Recognised Placement Agency

- Ensure the efforts made by the recognised placement agency in placing the child with Indian family and to that effect VCA clearance is there
- Processing the case in the competent court

Indian Court

- To get the documents scrutinising by the Scrutinising Agency
- To award of the guardianship of the child in favour of the foreign prospective adoptive parents.

Indian Recognised Placement Agency

- To submit a copy of the court order to CARA
- To arrange passport of the child
- To hand over the child to prospective foreign parents or the escorts or to the representative of foreign enlisted agency.

Foreign Enlisted Agency

- To take the child to their country
- To hand over the child to the concerned adoptive parents
- To take up the case of the child for legal adoption
- To watch the progress of the child
- To submit a copy of the order of the legal adoption and progress report to CARA, concerned Indian recognised agency and concerned Indian Court.
- Child finally gets integrated with the adoptive family.

SUBJECT INDEX

by the same author

LEGACY
DOUBLE ENTRY

The Caring Game

During a pleasant evening out with his girlfriend in a trendy bar in Edinburgh, John Leith meets a stunning young student, Dee, who is there to seek news of her missing flatmate. When he tries to help her, he tangles with others who are also searching for the missing girl and especially for something she has in her possession. These are violent, ruthless men who resent his interference and a confrontation is inevitable, with painful results for Leith. From that time on, he is committed to finding out who is behind the organization, and when a murder is discovered in one of the city's beauty spots, he knows that the faceless man must be drawn out into the open.

MARGARET McKINLAY

The Caring Game

THE CRIME CLUB
An Imprint of HarperCollins *Publishers*

First published in Great Britain in 1993
by The Crime Club, an imprint of
HarperCollins Publishers, 77–85 Fulham Palace Road,
Hammersmith, London W6 8JB

9 8 7 6 5 4 3 2 1

A catalogue record for this book is
available from the British Library

ISBN 0 00 232488 1

Photoset in Linotron Baskerville by
Rowland Phototypesetting Ltd
Bury St Edmunds, Suffolk
Printed and bound in Great Britain by
HarperCollins Book Manufacturing, Glasgow

With thanks to Ian, Adam and
Zen Shin Kan Dojo, the experts

For my Mother, Kathleen Collins

PROLOGUE

It was a warm, sunny day, crazy weather for mid-October. The unseasonal weather had brought out more Saturday shoppers than usual and the wide pavement outside the Princes Street shops was filled with a slow-moving mass of bodies. The road too was filled with cars and queues of buses, with frustrated drivers sweating in the heat. The only peaceful spots were in the gardens on the other side of the street, or in the square beside the National Gallery where a lone piper played to a group of tourists. Apart from the weather it seemed to be a normal Saturday afternoon in Edinburgh, but . . .

Only those in close proximity saw the fight begin and those few were trapped as spectators, unable to escape the crush and held too by a ghoulish fascination.

Three men were involved and one of them was the victim. His attackers viciously tugged at his clothes until he was reduced to underpants and socks, and then they drew long wooden batons that resembled polished mahogany from the waistbands of their trousers and began to beat him. For the length of a whole block, the crowds came to a standstill in the log-jam of bodies. Women gasped in horror, some children cried and one man moved to intervene but was jabbed so hard in the ribs that he fell back. No one else went to the victim's aid.

He tried to protect himself and took some blows on his arms, but strangely he made no protest, just whimpered like a whipped dog as each blow landed. It was as if he knew why he was being punished. The sounds of the blows on his body were flat thuds and they left red weals as each man took his turn, smiling as he relentlessly followed the victim's pathetic attempts to escape the blows. After a few steps he slid down a shop front, leaving bloodstains on the plate glass of the window as he fell. Blood ran from cuts on the bridge of his nose, his cheekbones and elbows, but when he began to sob as he lay on the pavement, there was a sudden concerted movement from the crowd, as if the watchers were coming out of a trance. They'd seen enough, perhaps had realized that this was real and not the same as impersonal television fiction.

The attackers sensed the mood but didn't appear concerned. They wiped their batons clean, slid them down inside the trousers of their smart suits which they had been careful to protect from the splashes of blood. There was no getaway car parked at the kerb, they simply walked arrogantly into the crowd which parted to let them through and were soon lost among those who had not witnessed the fight. No tearaways these, not yobbos, but men who could pass as ordinary businessmen in their middle thirties.

Someone went to pick up the man's clothes and drape them over him, and a shop worker came out to say she'd phoned for the police and an ambulance. In a little while the man was in a hospital bed and just another statistic in police records. The traffic flowed, the shop tills rang up record takings and the blood on the pavement dried and then disappeared under the tramp of many feet.

CHAPTER 1

Inside the largest office of the Sentinel Security Agency a couple of men were sweating over reports as John Leith passed through on his way to see Tollis, their boss. Weekends were just like any other day in the security business and most of the men were out and about on various jobs.

In Tollis's room the vertical blinds were almost closed and moving slightly in the breeze. Sunshine leaked through them and made dappled patterns on the opposite wall, while the big man sat hunched over his desk with his shirt sleeves rolled up. A mug of coffee steamed at his elbow and a cigarette burned in an ashtray. John sat down and draped his jacket over the back of another chair.

'What the hell are you doing here?' Tollis asked, pleased as well as surprised. 'I thought Clare wasn't leaving until tomorrow?'

'She isn't, she's gone to have her hair done. We're eating out tonight.'

The room was cool and quite gloomy. Tollis sat with his back to the outer wall with his hands clasped behind his head, his face in shadow. He always made a point of mentioning Clare Aitken but John knew that the boss of the Sentinel Agency had never really believed in their relationship. Divorced himself, Tollis was still a believer in marriage, commitment and having children. He couldn't accept that two people could sleep together when it suited them, especially when Clare now lived and worked in London and only came home occasionally. To Tollis, that meant Clare put her career before all else, so they had never really hit it off as friends.

'Somewhere special?' Tollis asked.

'Clare fancies Chinese but we'll probably end up at Ludo's afterwards.'

That brought a frown from Tollis. 'A coincidence. Mike's

working there for a few days, against my better judgement. You know what I think about providing bouncers for these places but I didn't have anything better for him to do and he was keen enough.'

'Hardly bouncers in a place like that,' John said. 'They only have a man on the door late on when it gets a bit crowded.'

'Mm,' Tollis said, not convinced. 'They still have to keep undesirables out and to me that means bouncing. Anyway, Mike's not on the door, he's working the bar, on the inside. Seems the manager got a whisper there might be trouble but it could be just that, a rumour.'

'It's the wrong area,' John said, concerned that the evening he'd planned might be spoiled.

Tollis shrugged. 'It can happen anywhere if the thugs decide to move around. Just because the white collar boys prefer a bar doesn't mean it's exempt—more likely these days to attract ruffians. Anyway, they're unlikely to get in.' Tollis didn't seem all that interested in what the low life of the city got up to and John left him to go and collect Clare.

He drove across a crowded Princes Street but the violent assault was already over and to him all seemed normal. He regretted in a way that he and Clare hadn't left the city for the day, gone to the coast to enjoy the unexpected spell of good weather, but she had wanted to stay, to do the things she missed while in London, like going to her own hairdresser.

The narrow street of Stockbridge was packed as usual but he managed to find a parking space right outside the salon. He was early and it hadn't occurred to him how uncomfortable he would feel to return to the street where he'd once lived.

He hadn't been back since he sold his flat and it was impossible to shut out painful memories when all around him were the familiar shops where his wife had bought their food, where she'd pushed their son in his pram. At the end of this very street a drunk driver had killed her . . .

'John?' Clare pulled the car door open and fell into the

passenger seat beside him, newly washed dark hair smelling of shampoo as it swung close to her shoulders. She clutched a pile of parcels in her lap. 'I didn't expect you, would have taken a taxi—I didn't mean to buy so much.'

'That's what you always say,' he said as he took some of the parcels from her and put them on the back seat. Her shopping sprees were a running joke because she still preferred to buy her clothes locally instead of from the London stores. 'Is that the lot or have you more to get?'

'No,' she said. 'Just back to the flat.'

They'd spent the last three days in her flat, but instead of staying for the whole weekend Clare was flying to London on the Sunday because she had work to do before getting to her office on Monday.

'I want to get my packing done before we go out tonight.'

It was the part of her visits that he hated, seeing her going through her wardrobe, choosing what she would take with her, laying everything out on the bed . . . And he acted out his part as the lover who could take her departure without a qualm, while all the time he wondered how she could do this, how much longer she would do this or if London would eventually win her over—in which case she might sell her home in Edinburgh. He never knew for certain when he would see her again, if she would tire of commuting, or if she might meet someone else. And although he took his turn of travelling to London to stay with her, the occasional meetings were not enough. There was no going back to the days when she was just half an hour away at any time of the day, when her office had been so near to Kramer House where he had his own business. There were no easy answers to his questions.

By seven-thirty they were on their way to eat at the restaurant that was close to the Usher Hall.

'I've been looking forward to this all week,' Clare said with a sigh. 'And to Ludo's. It always takes me days to unwind and I want to enjoy this evening.'

He told her what Tollis had said, about Mike working there and the possibility of trouble, but like him, Clare couldn't believe that the fashionable bar would invite rowdies.

'Mike won't be there until later,' he told Clare as they waited for their food to arrive. 'He's doing bar duties but I doubt if he'll start before ten.'

She liked Mike Cairns, the big man who looked like an ex-boxer and who was so quiet in company that often his silence was taken for shyness. John knew otherwise, that Mike was basically a dour man who disliked social occasions and who had a built-in distrust of people in general, which probably came from his years with Sentinel. But with Clare he melted, and with Tollis he had an almost telepathic understanding of the criminal mind.

'Wonder how he'll cope with the other bar staff?' Clare said with a sparkle of humour in her eyes. 'They're mostly kids.'

'We'll soon find out,' John said.

The Chinese restaurant was fairly quiet for a Saturday and they were able to linger over coffee. 'It's going to be at least a fortnight before I can get back here,' she said.

'Maybe I'll come down next time,' John suggested. 'Things are pretty quiet at Kramer's.'

'So the business hasn't fallen apart since your uncle died, and have the old hands taken the new young boss to their bosoms?'

'Hardly,' he said, grinning. 'But I have to wear a suit to work and Val keeps nagging me about getting my hair cut.'

'And Sentinel? Is Tollis still putting tempting cases under your nose?' She hadn't mentioned the subject on this visit and he avoided it if at all possible, knowing how she felt about him taking on Sentinel investigations. But with the Sentinel Agency and Kramer's sharing the same building, and because he often slipped down to the Sentinel floor to escape the boredom of property dealing, it was easy for him to get involved with what Tollis did for a living. On top of all that, Tollis provided the security arrangements for Kramer properties, so they met regularly on purely business matters anyway.

'I thought that by now your own business would be demanding all your time,' she said mildly enough.

'It has,' he said quietly. It was true. He'd been busy setting Kramer's to rights after his uncle's death, creating new directors and putting Val, who had been his uncle's assistant, into the manager's position. Clare knew all that and no doubt she also guessed that it gave him more time to work with Tollis if he chose to, and while it wasn't the investigation work she objected to, but fear of the possible dangers he faced, it was another reason why she and Tollis had never hit it off as friends.

They got to Ludo's just after ten, and he saw that there were only two men on the door, but if the manager expected trouble there might be more later. No one got into Ludo's if they were wearing jeans or trainer shoes, or if they were under twenty-one, although the reasoning behind the rules escaped him.

Mike was already on duty behind the bar and John had to smother a chuckle when he caught sight of him. Mike was wearing the same uniform of white shirt and black bow tie as the other staff but he stood out like a dandelion amongst daisies. The others were young, pretty girls in white blouses and mini skirts, and even the young barmen looked pretty compared to Mike Cairns.

At some time in the past he had suffered a broken nose and his face was marked with the minor scars of other violent encounters. He was large in every dimension, slow-moving, and his large hands looked like spades as he served up drinks.

'The tables are full, let's try to reach the bar,' John said as he shielded Clare's body by moving in front of her through the crush. Some couples were trying to dance, pressed close together and with drinks held high. All were smartly dressed but several looked as if the heat was getting to them. The outer doors were wide open but only a slight breeze of balmy air penetrated the largish bar, which was L-shaped.

The owner had tried to create an olde worlde setting,

installing fake beams and retaining the old stone fireplace that in winter contained a log fire, but now had brass and copper what-nots on the stone hearth. Mock-Victorian mirrors showing old adverts lined the roughly plastered walls and in a recess the shelves held pewter tankards. The furniture was dark heavy wood with red leather seating but it certainly wasn't the décor that made Ludo's so popular, it was its location. Ludo's was central, in a sober and respectable street in which there were the offices of insurance brokers, lawyers and investment agencies and it was used by these offices as their local, where they bought bar lunches and brought clients. And in the evenings the white collar workers came back with their girls, to let their hair down. The rock music was loud, the beat irresistible, and although there was no room to dance, those who were caught up in the beat could at least move hips and shoulders in the crush of bodies. It was the 'in' place of the moment, trendy, and selective in its customers.

Mike was surprised to see them. 'Did Tollis ask you to check up on me?' He didn't look put out, just amused.

It was Clare who answered. 'No. We were out for a meal and I wanted to make a night of it.'

Mike wiped wet marks from the bar counter before getting their drinks and Clare went to the Ladies.

'The boss wasn't all that keen for me to take the job,' he told John. 'But there's been a lot of trouble around town lately and the odd word here and there about something new happening. Some of the men have been talking about it in the office, about whispers they've picked up. You know how we get the drift of things, nothing definite, scares in bars and discos and then it all goes quiet for a bit. Tollis says it's for the police to use their own intelligence and he doesn't supply bouncers, but we have to know who's doing what, don't we?'

It was one of Mike's longer speeches and because of the blaring music John only managed to pick up what he said by leaning closer. He was also able to see Tollis's point of view, despite what Mike said. Sentinel wasn't into the clubland scene. Most of the employees were ex-police or from the Services and unlike a lot of similar agencies, Tollis insisted that his men were highly trained and he only accepted quality contracts. He didn't want the reputation of his business to suffer and he considered Sentinel was above providing stewards for clubs and discos.

'Anyway, he didn't exactly say I couldn't do this in my own time,' Mike said before moving off to serve other customers.

John and Clare remained at the bar, out of the main crush, with John leaning with one shoulder against the side wall. He watched a lone girl fight her way through to the bar.

'I'm looking for Peter, Peter Watson,' she said. 'I think he works here.' She was a stunning girl, tall, in black leather jacket and skin-tight leather pants. Her long hair was pulled straight back from her face into a loose coil at the back of her neck but it was her make-up which made her stand out and also made John wonder how she had got past the doormen. Not exactly a punk in her dress, the dark make-up that ringed her eyes and matched her lipstick and nail polish certainly brought her close to fitting that image.

The young bar girl who wore a gold pendant at her throat giving her name as Susan, shook her head. 'I don't usually do weekends so I don't know him.' She was being pressured by other customers wanting to order, but she went off to ask about the missing Peter Watson. John was only half listening as he watched Mike coping with a large order.

The girl came back and had to shout her reply. 'He might be here tomorrow.' The dark-haired girl started to turn away, disappointed. It was at that moment that a glass came through the air to crash into the bottles at the back of the bar. More followed and pandemonium broke out as everyone tried to dodge the missiles and head for the door. John caught a glimpse of Mike heaving his bulk clear over the bar top and pushing his way towards the far side of the room like a battleship forging through heavy seas. He pulled Clare towards him and put her body behind him.

The girl in black leather was trapped by the pressure of bodies and ended up tight up against his chest as more glass shattered. He saw a thin line of blood trickle from a cut on her temple and splinters glinted in her hair. The music never faltered, but it still failed to drown out the sounds of girls screaming as they were swept along in the rush for the door. The stampede also meant that the doormen couldn't get in.

'Head for the Ladies,' John shouted to Clare. He nodded to the door which was only feet away and she understood. The young bar staff were just as frightened as anyone else and were crouched down behind the bar, but that was where most of the broken glass was falling. Tables had been overturned, a couple of mirrors were broken and John could now see that Mike was struggling with two men on the far side of the room.

He got Clare and the girl into the Ladies' room as a chair crashed into the wall and he turned to see one of the men aim another chair at Mike's head.

'Ah well,' he muttered, picking up a metal bar stool. He pushed through the last of the bar's customers and swung the stool hard at the back of the nearest man's legs. It caught him behind the knees and he toppled over. John slotted the legs of the stool over him and the crossbar went down hard on his chest. It took all his weight to hold the man down. In the meantime Mike had the other one in a wrist lock that must have been very painful because the man was screaming in agony.

'You're breaking my arm,' he yelled.

Mike ignored him and watched the doormen finally burst into the bar. The manager arrived from his office at the same time.

'Throw them out,' he said tersely but Mike was having none of that.

'Phone the police.'

The manager gave a negative shake of his head. 'No fuss. If the police are told they'll be back on a regular visit and that's not good for business.' He shrugged. 'Owner's orders.'

Mike still did not move and his prisoner was now bent almost double.

'It was a put-up job—ask them,' he said. 'They sat there all night as quiet as lambs and the fight was a phoney—they'll be buddies again as soon as they get outside.'

John let his man get up and the doormen moved in on either side of him and took his arms. 'Do you think any of those people will come back?' he asked the manager. 'You've already lost business.'

'He's right,' Mike said with disgust. He let go of the man's wrist but somehow managed to give him a sharp tap on his ankle as he moved away. Both men, one limping and cursing, were escorted to the door. The manager, a young man with the pale complexion of someone who worked nights and slept by day, only looked around wearily.

'You're right, but my job is on the line here and the policy is that we don't get the cops in. Let's see what we can salvage from this mess.'

John left them to it and went to find Clare who was now outside talking to the girl in black leather gear.

'This is Dee Oakley,' she said. 'I suggested we give her a lift home.' John looked at the two men who were disappearing around a corner—as Mike said, now the best of friends—and at the groups of people who were still lingering, talking about the sordid scene in the bar. Some drifted off, no doubt looking for somewhere else to find their entertainment. It was Saturday, after all, and the night was still young.

'How's Mike?'

'He's OK, took a few knocks but I doubt if he noticed. Where do you live, Dee?'

'Marchmont.' She looked shaken and was dabbing at her temple but the cut was no more than a scratch and had already stopped bleeding.

'You have glass in your hair,' he said and they all paused

to shake it clear of their clothing before strolling to the corner. 'Student?' he asked, knowing that Marchmont was popular with students but it was more to take her mind off the incident than out of real curiosity, and she nodded.

The tall girl walked gracefully, hands thrust in the pockets of the short leather jacket, feet in soft black ankle boots.

'Those men,' Clare said. 'They weren't drunk and hardly the type to be brawling.'

Dee turned to listen but said nothing.

'No,' John said. They'd both been dressed smartly and Mike had seemed to be taken completely by surprise when they started fighting. 'Mike thought it was a put-up job.'

'But what would be the point?' Clare wanted to know.

And the manager had had some warning that it might happen, quite apart from the rumours Mike and some of the other Sentinel employees had picked up around town.

Dee got into the back seat of the car and John watched her in the mirror to see if she had got over her fright. As he clipped on his seat-belt he suggested they might go somewhere quiet for a coffee but she didn't look keen.

'Straight home, then?'

'If you don't mind,' she said.

Clare was still thinking about the bar. 'I can't understand it happening in a place like that,' she said, and then as John drove into and along Princes Street she settled further down into her seat to look up at the floodlit Castle above them. After the violent scene they had just witnessed, the main thoroughfare was quiet, with just a few couples strolling along in front of the shops. John turned up Lothian Road and Clare twisted in her seat to ask Dee about the course she was doing.

'A B.Sc in general sciences,' the girl said and soon she and Clare were chatting easily. The traffic was almost at a standstill for the length of Lothian Road with a double line of red tail-lights ahead, because people were spilling out of the theatres that were clustered in the area under the shadow of the Castle. They would be heading for their parked cars in the surrounding side streets or looking for late suppers in the many restaurants that did a brisk business at that time of night. The night was balmy so the theatre-goers loitered in the paved area in front of the domed Usher Hall, mingled on the crowded pavements with those leaving the Lyceum and the newly completed Traverse. Long evening skirts brushed against legs in jeans and showed whether the wearers had been in the grand circle or up in the gods. John inched the car forward as the lights changed, half listening to the two women talking, half thinking of the fight in Ludo's.

By the time they reached Marchmont it was as if Clare and Dee had known each other for a long time. 'Nice girl,' Clare said as they watched her cross the road and enter a tall block of flats where the light from the close mouth spilled out on to the path. And as John drove off, Clare said she'd had an interesting chat with Dee while they waited in the safety of the Ladies' room.

'She wasn't looking for her boyfriend,' she said. 'In fact she doesn't know this Peter Watson all that well—he's her flatmate's friend. This flatmate has gone off somewhere and taken the rent money with her, which leaves Dee in a fix. She can't afford to pay the money out twice because she's on a tight grant.'

'Mm,' John said, not all that interested in the finances of students. Clare gave him a sharp look. 'She's left nearly all her clothes behind.'

'Who?'

'The flatmate. Dee has been away for a few days staying with friends and then comes back to find the place all neat and tidy but no Alison.'

'And no rent.'

'That's right. And from what she said I gathered that she can't ask her family to help out. Her mother works and her father's dead.'

'You should work for Tollis if you can get all that out of her in a few minutes.'

Clare turned away and he knew the signs of temper

simmering. 'All right, what do you expect me to say? I'm sorry, but that's how people behave. The friend has probably spent the rent.'

'She's a nice girl. That make-up put you off but it's just what girls do, to be different.'

'I wasn't put off by her make-up. I quite liked it, but it's not our business, is it?'

Clare glanced over at him. 'I think she's really worried about her flatmate, so I told her about Tollis being able to trace people.'

'Tollis doesn't work for nothing.'

'I know,' Clare sighed. 'But if she phones . . .'

'She won't. She'll borrow from her mates and when her friend comes back she'll give her hell.'

In another part of the city, Chief Inspector Robert Jamieson was reading a report on the incident in Princes Street that afternoon but there wasn't much to it. No witnesses apart from those in the shop had come forward and he only had the hospital report to go on. Multiple bruising, some superficial cuts that required stitches, shock but no head injuries to speak of. Whoever had beaten the man had known what they were doing and they'd made a good job of it. They'd been careful to inflict maximum pain without actually doing serious damage.

Professional, then. They were inflicting punishment but the beating would also serve another purpose. When word got around, as it surely would in the circles in which they operated, others would take the message to heart . . . Which was what? It all depended on what the victim had been up to.

The injured man's identity was not yet known because according to the report his face was so badly swollen that even a close relative would not know him. He had declined—or was unable—to make a statement. Probably he couldn't face it and might never cooperate. Jamieson slipped the single sheet of paper into a card file where it would likely remain the only bit of evidence he would have that anything at all had taken place—until the man decided if he would talk or not. Probably not, the policeman thought with a sigh. Fear of another beating would be enough to keep him quiet and also the man would know that if his attackers were apprehended, it was more than likely that they would quickly be out on bail.

Jamieson wondered if there was a drugs connection. Or unpaid debts. Or if the man had foolishly touched up someone's woman. He might never find out. It happened. It didn't particularly bother him nor did he feel any great sympathy for the man in the hospital bed.

But when villains beat up someone in public view, especially in front of shoppers and their kids on a Saturday afternoon, that was a different matter. It showed total unconcern for arrest and punishment. It showed what they thought of the police force of his city. They might as well have stood outside his office window and given him a two-fingered salute. And that made Jamieson very angry indeed.

CHAPTER 2

Clare's flight left at eight so they were up early and she was quiet as she closed the door of the flat, as if her thoughts had flown ahead of her, to the leave-taking at the airport. It had been the same when they made love the night before, begun with laughter and becoming intense, because it had to last . . .

There was a nip in the air and she shivered. 'I really hate travelling,' she said. She pulled her wool jacket closer as he opened the car doors and he wondered if the travelling would eventually get to her, or if she would meet some nice civil servant who worked regular hours and didn't get caught up in detective work. But when they kissed goodbye at Turnhouse she clung to him and he remembered again the love-making of the night. It had been the same as always, with her need matching his own but with an added something that was elusive at the time. Later, he'd lain awake and wondered if Clare hadn't used it as a reassurance—that things could go on as they were. He watched her disappear through the departure gate and at the last moment she turned and waved as if this was the last thing she really wanted to do. 'Bloody hell,' he muttered, confused.

Church bells were starting to ring and the sun was breaking through by the time he got back to Kramer House where he had a small flat on the top floor. It was a base he used during the week and sometimes even at weekends but if his son was coming home from school they went to Elmwood, the house on the coast where his housekeeper tried her best to make it a home.

He left the car at the rear of the building and walked quickly back to the main entrance where the security man in his small office was nearing the end of his shift.

'Do you know if Tollis is in?'

'He's not, but I've a number where he can be reached—he shouldn't be long, though.'

John climbed the stairs, passing the half-glazed door with the gold logo of the Sentinel Agency and on up to his own suite of offices which was the headquarters of his inherited business, Kramer Property. Up more stairs led him to the flat and it was stuffy because he hadn't been in it for days. He threw open a window before carrying his case into the bedroom and then stood looking around at the difference between this small flat and Clare's home. These were bachelor quarters, bare of comfort, purely functional and a convenient base, but sometimes he was too close to the job. If he wasn't careful he'd end up like Tollis, rarely leaving the building at all.

He hadn't had time to shave earlier so he did it now, seeing a lean face with dark eyes, some of the summer's tan remaining, a touch of silver in the dark hair over his ears. He was only thirty-three but he would be white before he was forty, he thought, and would he still be seeing Clare off at Turnhouse Airport?

'Shit!' He pulled on shorts and a top and left the building to go for a run and hopefully shake himself out of the mood that always descended after he saw Clare off. He headed down the High Street with an easy loping stride in the direction of Holyrood Park, an escape route from the city that meant he could pretend he was in open country within minutes. The old volcano of Arthur's Seat was the attraction and Hunter's Bog in particular, which lay at the foot of the Crags. From there the city was invisible and there was the feeling of space that he needed. By the time he reached it, the slog of the run would have cleared away all thoughts of Clare already nearing the end of the flight that was taking her away yet again.

The run did its job and he took the stairs up to the flat three at a time, wondering if Tollis was back yet. He had a shower and just as he was reaching for a towel the phone rang in the other room.

'Mr Leith? It's Dee Oakley.'

He tucked the phone under his chin and then wrapped the towel around him. 'Yes, Dee?'

'Sorry to bother you but Ali's mother has turned up here and I don't know how to help her. I haven't a clue where she's gone.'

'Ali is your flatmate.'

'Yes. Alison Baxter.'

'Well, has her mother tried all her friends—that Peter you were talking about?' He used a corner of the towel to rub his hair as Dee relayed the question to Mrs Baxter.

'She's like me, doesn't know who to ask and it seems that Alison has been gone for a week—I didn't know that. I told her what Clare said, about your friend knowing how to trace people and I think she'd like to talk to him.'

'Oh. Well, I don't know if he's around at the moment. Give me her address and phone number and I'll pass a message on, but she does realize that his charges could work out pretty steep?'

Dee dictated the details and said that Mrs Baxter was so worried that she had to talk to someone. 'And I'm no help at all. We didn't have the same friends, you see.'

'Well, tell her she might not hear from him today.'

'OK,' she sighed.

'Sorry,' John said. 'But if she's that worried she should talk to the police.'

'I think she already has.'

He hung up and went to get dressed, already running late in picking up his son and a friend from their boarding-school. When he found that Clare was not staying the whole weekend he'd rashly promised to take the boys out for the day, lunch followed by a visit to the Zoo, weather permitting. They were waiting on the doorstep when he arrived, dressed in weekend uniform of blue anoraks and grey shorts. Sammy in particular was excited to be invited out because his father was in the diplomatic service, stationed abroad, and he only saw his parents in the long summer vacation.

They ate in a burger place and then headed for the Zoo, which was busy because of the sunshine, and for the next couple of hours John was like all the other fathers, buying ice-creams, peering at sleeping reptiles, or looking over the new penguin enclosure. Not quite like the other fathers, perhaps, because he was only a part-time parent.

A couple of times David slipped his hand into John's and the gesture was enough to startle him. He had a lot to learn about being a father, especially the things like playing with his son, sharing interests, in the way that came naturally to other fathers. He'd so nearly lost the right that it took his breath away when his son ran to him, swung on his arm and no longer treated him like a visiting uncle. That was how it had been when David lived with his aunt but he would never allow it to happen again.

There was time for a visit to a park, a half-hour of kicking a ball about and then the boys had to go back for tea.

'Remember we're going to Grandfather's on Tuesday,' David said. 'And you have to bring his present.'

'I won't forget,' John promised as he dropped them off at school. As if he could forget, he thought with a grimace. Every visit to his father-in-law was a date ringed in red in his diary, like dental appointments. He drove up the Bridges to the High Street and wondered if Tollis was in. He still had to pass on Dee's message and maybe get some action for Mrs Baxter's sake.

The large outer office was in its usual state of chaos and desks looked as if they'd been abandoned after a fire alarm, with papers, half-empty coffee cups and newspapers littering their surfaces. Several of the men were in, with more plastic coffee mugs lining their desks, either still in use or stuffed with empty crisp packets. The Sentinel Agency was in danger of becoming a slum.

Tollis was bent over his desk, looking as if he'd gone without sleep for a long stint, which he probably had. His room too had files sprouting from over-stuffed cabinets and a general air of neglect that came from too much work and too few hours in which to get through it.

'It looks like the *Marie Celeste* out there and a refuse dump for files in here—I thought you were putting all this stuff on computer?' John shifted files from a chair and tried to sort them into some sort of order.

'We did, but machines don't save time—they gobble up information that is gone forever as far as I know. Much better with paper and I know where everything is,' Tollis retorted. 'Paper doesn't vanish if there's a power failure. You can stuff your computers.' He stretched and ended up with his hands behind his neck as if to ease the stiffness. 'Have you eaten?'

They went in search of food, to a little place down one of the nearby closes and Tollis as usual wasn't ready for conversation until the last plate was empty. John often thought that Tollis didn't care what he ate as long as it tasted of garlic and came from an Italian menu.

'I suppose Mike has told you what happened at the bar?'

Tollis lit a cigarette and spooned sugar into his coffee. 'Yes. Sounded pretty typical except that it was on the wrong side of town. If these people won't report such things to the police we'll never get rid of the roughnecks, so serves them right.'

John knew when a subject was closed. 'There's something else. We met a young girl there who told us her friend was missing and now her mother has asked for your help—or at least to see you and get some advice.'

Tollis considered that as he sipped his coffee and he added more sugar before commenting. 'You've had experience of that sort of thing so you know the difficulties. The only cases we have real success with come from inquiries from banks or lawyers and we can solve them with a few phone calls. They're usually bad debts or missing witnesses and the like. The real missing people, the ones who just take off into the blue, are a different matter altogether. It's a costly exercise and beyond the pockets of most people.' He shrugged. 'That's how it is.'

More or less what John had expected him to say.

'Has she been to the police?' Tollis asked.

'I think so.'

'There's not much they can do either unless it's a real emergency, like a young child or someone who is vulnerable because of illness, diabetics for example. If it's just someone who wants to disappear . . . If you have spare time on your hands, why don't you see her? You could tape the interview and I'll listen to it when I can.'

John thought of the staff meeting scheduled for the next morning and knew he couldn't duck it, knew also that it would drag on till lunch-time because some of the managers liked to double-check every point raised. An interview with Mrs Baxter would come as light relief after that.

'OK. I'll ring her tonight and arrange something.'

'Try to meet her in her own home. She'll be more relaxed and you'll be able to suss out the girl's background better. But don't commit us to anything.'

*

They parted company on the Sentinel floor, with Tollis yawning and hoping to catch up on some sleep on the folding bunk in his back room, but for John it was too early to think of bed. He went up to the flat where the window was still wide open and looked down on the occasional taxi or car going up towards the Castle or down the hill in the direction of the Royal Palace at the bottom. He had attended the Garden Party there only a few months previously, with Janet, his housekeeper, as his partner and he'd enjoyed the occasion mainly because Janet had been so thrilled about it all. In an outfit bought for the big day, she'd ended up with cramped toes from standing on tiptoe to see the Queen and her main concern was that she'd made holes in the Royal lawn with her high heels. The food, set out in marquees, had been good, the weather had been kind, and Janet had laughed at the top-hatted brigade who smelled distinctly of mothballs. Afterwards the streets had been closed to traffic and they'd walked from the Palace back to Kramer House among a stream of other guests and dignitaries, their finery slightly wrinkled.

He sniffed the dry air that carried the dust of a parched city mingled with traffic fumes before shutting the window and drawing the curtains, then reached for the phone to dial Mrs Baxter's number.

He arranged to call on her the following afternoon. She didn't ask why he and not Tollis was going to see her but in her anxiety she was probably glad that someone was taking an interest. There was no mistaking the relief in her voice anyway.

'The police don't seem to be doing much at all,' she said.

Only because they couldn't, he thought as he hung up. Where would they begin to look? Probably at Ludo's, as Dee Oakley had done, since Peter Watson was more likely to know where the girl had gone. On impulse he reached for the phone again and called Ian Lambert, a lawyer friend who also used Ludo's for his lunch breaks.

'I'm at a loose end—do you fancy meeting for a drink?'

'Business or pleasure?'

'Bit of both,' John said. They arranged to meet at Ludo's in half an hour.

Ian was there before him in the downstairs bar and had already drunk half of his beer. 'I was beginning to feel lonely,' he said, looking around at the few customers. 'I've never known it this quiet at the weekend.'

'There was some trouble last night and word must have got around,' John said before going to the bar for his own drink. A different barmaid served him and after she put his drink in front of him she leaned her freckled arms on the bar. More freckles dusted her nose and he guessed that she was only just old enough to work there. She looked bored and ready to chat.

'You got everything cleaned up, then,' he said, taking a sip from his glass. 'It was a mess in here last night.'

She straightened up. 'Boss doesn't want us to talk about it, but I think they worked most of the night. It was all surface stuff, though, broken glass mostly.'

Further along the bar a man had been reading a Sunday newspaper and listening to the conversation at the same time. Now he raised a finger for a refill and the girl went to serve him. John went back to join Ian, who was grinning.

'She's too young for you,' he said.

A young barman with longish fair hair tied back in a ponytail was taking his time clearing tables and talking to a couple near the door. He and the girl seemed to be the only ones on duty and there was no sign of Mike. Probably the manager had suspected there would be a lack of customers and had cut back on staff for the evening. Glancing around, John saw that there were only seven people drinking and the music was very muted.

'Are you on a job for Tollis?' Ian said suddenly. 'Why all the interest?'

'I'm just curious,' John said.

'Come off it. You're a devious bastard, but I suppose if that's all you want to tell me . . .'

He sipped from his pint, an amiable young man who was

built like a rugby player and had ambitions to get to the top of his profession. Now he was staring around him as if expecting the yobbos to start hurling beer glasses again.

'If you want to be useful stop behaving like a bloodhound, and no, I'm not expecting more trouble tonight. Clare and I met a girl here last night who was looking for her flatmate's boyfriend. I just wondered if he might be working the bar.'

'Is that him?' Ian asked, jerking his head at the pony-tailed barman, a sickly looking young man who had little energy for his job.

'I don't know. I was going to ask the barmaid when that customer asked for a refill. I'll ask him when he comes a bit closer.' The barman collected empty glasses from the next table and John leaned towards him. 'Peter Watson?'

The man looked sullenly back at him. 'Yes.' His eyes darted to Ian and back to John.

'Have you time to talk? I think you know Alison Baxter.'

The man was nervous now, flicking his eyes towards the bar.

'What about her?' He wiped the table, eyes down.

'She's missing and her mother's anxious.' He was convinced that it was not news to Peter Watson, but he wasn't to get an immediate answer because the barman swung away.

'Not now,' he said. 'I can't stand around or I'll lose my job.'

Ian swung around in his seat to stare openly as Watson went back to the bar and John sighed and thought that subtlety should be a requirement in the training of lawyers. He dragged Ian's attention back by talking about his favourite subject.

'I hear your team is on a winning streak,' he said and that got Ian sidetracked. And as they talked, John watched the comings and goings of the customers. No one, except the man with the newspaper, stayed very long and he wasn't surprised. The Sunday drinkers were looking for fun on the last evening before going back to work on Monday and they weren't going to get it that night in Ludo's.

He saw the wan-looking manager emerge from his office at the back of the bar to take a head count of the customers and then pause to speak to the solitary drinker at the bar who had folded his newspaper now and was draining his glass, standing as if about to leave as well and John got a better look at him. Around fifty, he was stocky in an expensive suit, wearing gold-rimmed glasses and sporting a short, neatly trimmed beard that was flecked with grey.

'I said I'm getting engaged—where were you?' Ian had the sheepish grin of a confirmed bachelor who was surprised to find himself looking forward to marriage. 'You'll get an invite to the stag party.'

He began to talk about his fiancée, Heather, who was going into practice as a GP and they were looking for a house. That led on to the stagnant state of the housing market and how it was affecting Kramer's.

Suddenly raised voices made them both turn towards the bar where the bearded customer was now steering the young manager towards his office, with a hand firmly clutching his elbow.

'Dissatisfied with the beer, do you think?' Ian murmured. 'Something is bothering him and he's an aggressive little sod.'

'Fancy a refill?' John said, picking up their empty glasses and without waiting for an answer he moved through the tables to the bar. But the door to the office was already closing and Watson had tactfully turned up the volume of the music to cover the altercation. He could hear nothing of the quarrel that was going on behind the closed door except for angry tones. The girl came to serve him.

'What was all that about?' he asked but she shrugged.

'Don't know. He was pleasant enough to me. Vince can handle it.'

Watson had stayed at the other end of the bar and John moved towards him. 'About Alison. Have you any idea where she has gone?' He spoke quietly. The barman had got over his initial nervousness but now he looked stubborn.

'Why ask me? I don't know where she is and she's got me into enough trouble.'

'What does that mean? What kind of trouble?'

'Who are you anyway? I don't have to tell you my business,' and he moved away to chat to the girl.

Ian was curious and amused. 'What the hell's going on? All that looked a bit ugly for a minute—the bearded one was definitely hustling the manager,' he said. 'And what's with you and the barman?'

John ignored the reference to Watson. 'Maybe he's from the brewery and the manager has been fiddling the takings,' John said. 'It happens.'

Ian looked deflated. 'I thought I was going to witness you detecting—do you still get tempted by Tollis's sort of work?'

'To be honest I was bored tonight. Clare went back to London this morning. Now, when am I going to see some of my properties moving?'

They talked business for another half an hour and John watched Watson and waited for the angry customer to emerge from the manager's office. And when he did, it was not an amicable parting. The manager was tight-lipped while the bearded man was stony-faced and walking purposefully towards the exit.

'What now?' Ian asked. 'Do we follow him?'

He never knew what made him agree to satisfy Ian's request. He'd only been mildly curious about the argument between the bearded man and the manager, mainly because it came right after the trouble the previous evening. But the evening was still young and he only faced going back to an empty flat . . . 'Why not?' he said. He could come back later and have another go at Watson.

The bearded man seemed to have no transport of his own because he hailed a passing taxi which took off around a corner. By thc time John had negotiated it they were two taxis ahead and Ian started to chuckle.

'What now, Sherlock?'

They were in luck when one cab pulled into the kerb and a woman got out. The other taxi skirted the Meadows and dropped its passenger outside another bar.

'He's on a pub crawl, or in search of better booze, do you think?' Ian muttered.

'Haven't a clue,' John said as they waited. 'This place isn't in the same class as Ludo's—I don't know it.' But he did recognize the man on the door. He was one of the men who had been fighting in Ludo's the previous evening, and suddenly what had started out as a game began to have a different meaning. 'That man who is smoking, the one without a tie, could you take a good look at him—so that you'd know him again.'

Ian too now sensed that things were becoming serious. 'OK, I'd know him—who is he?'

John explained about the fight and Mike's involvement. 'Mike might like to know how to find him again if necessary.' Then the bearded man reappeared, without his newspaper but clutching a large brown envelope instead.

'Do we follow him?' Ian asked.

'Might as well,' John said although he was more interested in the fact that the trouble-maker seemed to be employed at a rival bar as doorman. It was not easy to follow a man who was on foot and John had to let him get some way ahead before driving after him.

'You'll be in trouble if he ducks down a close,' Ian said as a fine drizzle hit the windscreen. 'And it's too quiet around here, he's going to spot us.'

But the man was walking at a smart pace, head down against the rain and in a hurry to get somewhere. He never once glanced over his shoulder.

'He is on a pub crawl,' Ian said, peering through the windscreen as the man ducked into another bar. John parked directly across from it and once more they settled down to wait.

'Don't want to be a nuisance,' Ian said after a while. 'But those two pints are weighing heavily on my bladder.'

John was feeling some of the same discomfort and he

made a note to ask what Tollis's men did when on a long surveillance job. He could hear music coming from the bar which had a steady stream of customers and there were again two men on the door. After half an hour John decided to call it a night.

'Let's go. We're not serving any purpose here,' he said, swinging the car back around the way they had come. 'And if we sit here any longer they're going to begin to wonder what we're up to.'

'We must do this again some time,' Ian said with a grin. 'Tollis has often found missing witnesses for us, but I never imagined what was involved.'

John dropped him back where he'd parked his car and then went back inside Ludo's to have another go at Peter Watson.

'He's gone,' said a disgruntled barmaid who had been left to cope on her own. 'He just put on his jacket and walked out.'

And John drove back to Kramer House, not sure what he'd achieved except that he'd filled up a few hours that would otherwise have been very boring.

CHAPTER 3

He bumped into Mike the following afternoon when he was about to leave for the interview with Mrs Baxter.

'Any idea where Tollis is?'

'He was called out to look into some pilfering.'

'I didn't see you in Ludo's last night.'

'Oh, I did a short stint late on but it was as quiet as a tomb and we closed early. Maybe that's what those two were aiming for—to frighten off the customers,' Mike said cryptically. 'And Vince will be hoping it will all blow over.'

'He had a row with a customer when I was there,' John said, leaving out the bit about tailing the man afterwards until he'd had a chance to tell Tollis about it. 'I suppose you'll be on another job now.'

Mike grunted. 'I still have a bad feeling about that fight, so maybe I'll drop in.'

'Do me a favour—find out what you can about Peter Watson who works there part-time.'

There was no point in reminding him that Tollis wouldn't like it, that he frowned on employees doing their own thing, because once Mike got his heels dug in there was no shifting him. There was something vaguely odd about the fight at Ludo's but as he drove to see Mrs Baxter, he thought that Mike was probably over-reacting to rumours.

Mrs Baxter was probably in her late forties and she looked anxious. She was slim, dressed in a plain blue jumper with a single row of pearls at the neck and a straight tweed skirt, but she hadn't put on any make-up that day. She also looked as if she wasn't sleeping well.

Her home was fussy, with ornaments on every surface, lacy curtains, piles of cushions, and it was spotlessly clean. It was the sort of home that was dusted every day whether it needed it or not, the home of a woman who had little to occupy her except housework.

'I'd like to record the details so that a colleague can hear it later,' John said and she had no objection to that. 'Tell me about your daughter—when did she actually go missing?'

'A week ago—Friday or Saturday, I can't be sure.' She sat sideways on the edge of the settee, facing him and she didn't know what to do with her hands.

'Age?'

'Twenty-two.' Her voice wavered.

'Mrs Baxter, would you like to make some coffee or tea?' Tollis had once said that the domestic act often helped to put people at ease. That talking in the kitchen while doing some normal routine was relaxing and right now Mrs Baxter was not relaxed at all.

'Yes, of course.' She had misunderstood him and thought she was failing as a hostess, but he followed her to the kitchen anyway. It was as cluttered as the sitting-room, with sets of flowery containers, crocheted cosies and loops of net curtains. He sat on a stool beside a fridge decorated with dozens of magnetic flowers stuck to its door.

'Does she always tell you her plans—could she have gone off to friends?'

Mrs Baxter shook her head. 'No, she doesn't always tell me. Alison has had her own flat for three years so of course I don't know everything she does but we had an arrangement to meet on Saturday of that week.' She drew a deep breath and looked blankly at the window, reliving the day. 'We were going shopping and usually she picks me up in her car. We do that sometimes, go for coffee or lunch. When she didn't come I began to worry in case she'd had an accident. She didn't answer the phone.'

She was getting more agitated as she spoke, as if remembering the events was bringing it all back too clearly. John got up and lifted the tray she had prepared and carried it to the sitting-room where he poured tea into delicate china cups.

'Did you go to her flat?'

'Later. I kept phoning at first, trying to get her flatmate, or Peter, but I think he goes to a football match on Saturdays. I don't know him, but Alison mentioned that he often did that. In the end I tried phoning the hospitals but it is so difficult to make people understand. They said I should call the police.'

'And did you?'

'Not right away. It seemed such a final thing to do. I kept putting it off. Alison would have been upset if I made a fuss about nothing and I tried to believe that it was all just a mix-up, that I'd got the wrong day . . . only I was certain really that I hadn't made a mistake. So I went to the flat because I suddenly thought she might be ill, or had a fall. I panicked really because there I was dithering about and all the time she might have been lying unconscious.' She began to cry. 'I suppose all mothers would be the same, thinking the worst. Only it turned out much worse than I ever imagined, didn't it?'

She went to fetch a box of tissues that was packed inside a frilled cover and after she'd dried her eyes she tore the tissue to shreds with nervous fingers.

'I have a spare set of keys to the flat, but she wasn't there.'

John handed her the untouched cup of tea and she sipped it.

'Thank you, you're very kind.' She studied him as if seeing him properly for the first time. 'Very young too, for this sort of job.' And he wasn't sure if she meant 'too young'.

'The flat was very clean, as if she'd gone to a lot of trouble to tidy it before she left.'

'Was that unusual?'

'She was hopeless with housework although the other girl, Dee, was good about cleaning. Not that I thought she was the right person for Alison to be sharing with, mind you . . . but it worked out all right. Later I discovered that Dee was away and she didn't clean up either.' She paused, as if gearing herself up to tell him the worst part of all.

'There was a note,' she said. 'I don't believe a word of it although it was certainly in her own handwriting. It said that she was sorry, but she was leaving in a hurry and didn't have time to phone to explain. There was something about her affairs all being settled . . . Those aren't the exact words, but it was . . . was almost like a suicide note. Which is nonsense because she has everything to live for.'

'Do you have the note?'

'The police took it,' she said flatly.

'What reaction did you get from them?'

'They did seem concerned at first,' she admitted. 'And they were very nice.' She had calmed down now that she'd told him about the note and seemed in a dull state of mind, weary after a week of worry. 'They said she wouldn't harm herself—but how could they know that?'

'They must have had good reason. They get lots of reports of missing people who all turn up eventually and they can't look for them all. Alison can't have seemed like a priority . . . girls don't tell their mothers everything.'

He put a fresh tape into the small recorder and set it going again.

'I'd like some personal details, about her car and her job.'

She rose and fetched a piece of paper and a photograph. 'I thought you'd want that so I wrote them down—the snap was taken during the summer. She works in a dress shop.'

And he got a lot more, about friends, an uncle who seemed to be her only relative, and places Alison had visited and might go back to.

'Does she see much of her uncle? Would she confide in him?'

Mrs Baxter shook her head at once. 'He's my husband's brother—we haven't kept in touch since my husband died.' She looked defeated, as if she could no longer reason why her daughter should behave like she had

John got the uncle's address and phone number anyway and then looked at the snap. Alison Baxter was a blonde with some of her mother's features. A confident-looking girl who didn't seem to have a care in the world.

'What about savings?'

And for the first time the woman looked reluctant to answer. 'The police asked that so I went to her bank. She took out all her savings, quite a lot really. I didn't know she earned that much . . .'

And that was why the police were convinced that she didn't intend suicide. People who were about to end it all didn't usually take a large sum of money with them.

'What about credit cards? When she runs out of money we might be able to trace her if she buys on credit. If that pinpoints where she is, we could see if she's looking for work in another dress shop—it's a long shot, though.'

'But that sounds as if it will take a long time,' Mrs Baxter cried.

'I'm afraid there isn't any quick way if you've already

checked with all the people she knows. She might still be on the move, you see, and where would we start? There isn't any point in putting a man on it yet. Not until there's something to go on.'

'But I've already waited a week, worried out of my mind.' She was looking at him with a pleading expression, hoping for a crumb of comfort and he had none to give her. He felt anger building up towards the girl who was making her mother suffer.

'Can't Dee tell you anything?'

'They weren't really friends. I think Alison took someone in originally to help pay the rent but they didn't get on well. Mr Leith, you must know what makes people do this?'

There were all sorts of reasons why people walked away from apparently happy lives, but none of them would be a comfort to her so he didn't list them. It was often through desperation of some sort associated with a job or debts. Others had been known to leave to punish those they left behind, to make them suffer in some way.

'There's no way for us to know what triggered this off in Alison's case.'

'So you can't go and look for her?'

He hesitated because Tollis had stipulated that he shouldn't promise any definite action by Sentinel. 'I could speak to her flatmate and Peter Watson. There may be something they didn't want to tell you.'

She reached into a bag and brought out a set of keys. 'You can look at the flat as well,' she said.

He slipped them into his pocket. 'Do you have Peter's address?'

'No, just his phone number. I don't know him, just that he works for a car company, delivering cars around the country.'

'Well, I should be able to find him,' John said, knowing that Ludo's would probably have an address for someone who worked there part-time, and he would also be in the phone book. 'There's something else that I should say. If Alison just wanted to leave and intends to stay away we wouldn't be able to tell you where she is without her permission. We could only act as intermediaries.'

A spasm of pain flitted across her face. 'I don't believe Alison would do that but if she did, I wouldn't object as long as she was happy. The main thing that worries me is that my daughter didn't go willingly. You read of such things in the paper, and someone might have forced her to go away . . . but the police don't seem to be thinking along those lines.'

He played the tape back to Tollis later. 'A nasty one,' Tollis said.

'It was the worst thing I've ever had to listen to,' John said, remembering how he'd left Mrs Baxter still in tears.

Tollis nodded. 'The girl must know what she's doing to her mother but you were right to warn her that there's nothing we can do for the moment.' He looked pensive. 'Strange, that suggestion that the girl might not have gone willingly—it's not the first thing that normally comes to mind, is it?'

John disagreed. 'These days, yes. I think that woman has begun facing up to the worst scenario, but the girl emptied her bank account and that sounds like a well planned thing to me.'

Tollis was nodding. 'Wonder how much cash she had? And a car—she had to keep that on the road as well as pay her share of the rent, and she wouldn't earn much in a dress shop.'

That had occurred to John. 'And the thing that bothered me most was the tidy flat. Why take the time to clean the place before she left, especially when she hates housework?'

'That's a thing, isn't it?' Tollis admitted. 'And it ties in with what her mother was afraid of, that someone forced the girl to leave and whoever took her cleaned up the evidence afterwards . . . but don't let's start thinking along those lines.' He shifted in his chair, shaking his head. 'The police will have done that anyway.'

'It wouldn't hurt to talk to Dee Oakley and the boyfriend, though,' John said.

'I can't spare anyone, or justify the expense yet,' Tollis pointed out.

'But . . .'

'Christ, how I hate your "buts". They always mean trouble,' Tollis said.

'Speaking of trouble, there's something else,' John said, pretending not to see the look of pained anticipation in Tollis's eyes.

'I was in Ludo's last night with Ian Lambert and there was a row between the manager and a customer.' He described how the row had continued in the manager's office and saw that Tollis was mildly interested. 'We followed the man after he left and he went on a sort of pub crawl.' He ignored the sudden look of puzzlement in Tollis's eyes and hurried on. 'At one of the bars I saw one of the men who started all that bother in Ludo's on Saturday—he was working as a doorman.'

'That figures,' Tollis said, as if it was no surprise to him at all. 'Where did your man end up?'

John explained about the two pints that he and Ian had drunk and the urgent need to find a toilet, and Tollis burst out laughing.

'You'll have to remember to always carry an emergency supply of food—and a suitable container,' he said, still chuckling.

And it was only later that he realized that Tollis had not explained his lack of surprise to find that the man who tried to wreck Ludo's was a doorman elsewhere.

Clare phoned that evening and he told her about his interview with Mrs Baxter.

'Poor woman—are you going on with it?'

'There's not much we can do. The police will have spoken to the boyfriend and probably to Dee as well by now.'

But Mrs Baxter's distress had got to him and the keys to the flat were still jingling in his pocket. He also had another long, boring evening ahead of him. In the end he drove to Marchmont, not sure what he would do when he got there. It all depended on whether or not Dee was at home or if she would let him look around if she was there. And Mrs Baxter's view of her own daughter was biased, to say the least—Dee might know another side of the girl's character. He might also be able to find out more about Peter Watson.

The flat too would tell him a lot about the missing girl, her taste in clothes, music, what made her tick as a person, perhaps even why she'd left so suddenly. If Alison Baxter was in trouble Dee must have had an inkling of it, but most of all he wanted to be certain that the girl had not had suicide in her mind when she left.

It was a short drive on quiet roads to where the two girls lived, in a close of eight apartments. Students tended to congregate in the area because it was close to the university and the accommodation had large rooms, ideal for cramming in as many as possible to split the cost of living. Two girls sharing one of these largish flats would have plenty of space but high expenses, and he already knew how tight money was for Dee.

The flat he was going to was on the second floor in a newly refurbished block. The outer stonework had been cleaned and the close had been painted a quiet grey. The steps leading upwards were now covered in a grey mock-marble resin and the new lighting was a vast improvement on the old-style dingy gloom.

Both girls had their names on the front door but when he rang the bell there was no answer although he was sure he could hear music playing inside the flat. He rang again and waited a long time before inserting the key in the lock but the door swung open, taking the key and his hand with it. Dee looked angry.

'Mrs Baxter gave me the keys so I could look around,' he said.

'And you were just going to walk in?' She stood tall against the light coming from the room behind her and without the leather jacket she looked almost scrawny in tight jeans. The light gave her loose black hair a navy blue sheen that almost matched the make-up on her eyes, lips and her washed-out vest top.

'You should have phoned first,' she said quietly. 'I don't open the door at night.' But she stood aside so he could go in.

'Sorry, but I came on impulse.' He followed her into a living-room that had books scattered on the floor but the room was unlike any student accommodation he'd been in before because it was nicely furnished, and orderly. To placate a still angry Dee, he sat down and hoped she would do the same, but she stood with her weight on one hip, studying him just as Mrs Baxter had done. He couldn't help taking in her shape, with no breasts to speak of and with not much curve around the hips, yet she was definitely an attractive girl.

'So explain. I know you're not a detective—your girlfriend said that was the other one, I forget his name—that you own a property company. Are you our landlord? Because like I said, Ali went off with the rent and I can't pay my share twice.'

'That's not why I'm here. We do rent out properties but we have nothing to do with this building. It's a bit hard to explain, but I help the friend that Clare mentioned, Tollis. He has offices in the same building.'

She chewed her knuckle and he wondered if she knew that the navy blue nail varnish made it seem as if she had a circulation problem.

'OK, I'll buy that. It must be more fun than collecting rent.'

He didn't bother to point out that Kramer's did a lot more than collect rent.

'But why come here? Ali hasn't come back or phoned.'

'It would help if I could look at her room and if you could say what sort of girl she is. It might help us to understand why she went and where she went.'

'You make it sound so simple but I didn't know her all that well. In fact, I was already looking for somewhere else.

Look around if you want. Her room is the biggest one, second on the right along the hall.' She was off-hand, not interested in helping and that told him a lot too.

As soon as he left the room, the music started up again as if Dee was defiantly pretending he wasn't there. And it made his task easier because it would drown out the sound of him going through drawers and wardrobes, a distasteful task as far as he was concerned.

When he pushed open the door of the large bedroom he saw at once that Alison Baxter was her mother's daughter, with the same taste for frills and flounces. They were everywhere, on the curtains, the duvet, pillows and around the dressing-table. It was a little girl's room, with soft toys on the bed, on shelves, and there was rose-sprigged paper on the walls. A collection of china-faced dolls lined the window-ledge and the dressing-table was littered with make-up and framed photographs. He opened a wardrobe and then frowned when he saw that there seemed to be a very few empty hangers. The clothes had quality labels, no shoddy gear for Alison, but why hadn't she taken them with her? A girl who owned so much expensive clothing would be fussy about what she wore and if she had time to clean the flat, she must have had time to pack.

He looked below the clothes, in the boxes that held shoes, and then on the shelves above. Nothing of interest there, so he turned to the dressing-table and felt below the froth of underwear. No diaries hidden away but there was an address book which he slipped into his pocket. In the small bedside table he found a half-empty pack of contraceptive pills and stood looking at them for some time before replacing them.

He looked under the bed, puzzled by the lack of books, magazines, the normal paper clutter that a girl might have in her bedroom. Then behind the dressing-table he spotted a crumpled piece of paper jammed against the skirting and he put that in his pocket to examine later. In the living-room Dee had put on Axl Rose singing 'Sweet Child of Mine' and at the same time the doorbell rang.

John switched off the light and moved along the hall as Dee once more opened the front door. 'Now what . . .' she was saying as she was slammed backwards as two men burst in. John froze, five feet from the other three.

The stockier of the two men stood in front of Dee and the other man turned to face John as if surprised to find that the girl was not alone. He had alert, suspicious eyes, taking in John's jeans and sweatshirt, and he didn't like having to look up to someone taller than himself. He was cocky too, showing instant dislike, and was probably the more dangerous of the two.

'No hassle,' he said with a smooth smile, holding out flat, spread hands. 'We just came to collect something the girl left behind.'

'Then you should have asked instead of pushing your way in,' John said. The man didn't like that but he was in control of himself and turned to Dee, still smiling.

'Where's your friend's room?'

'Along there,' Dee said, pointing to the door that John had left open. 'What are you taking?'

'None of your concern, honey.' He had to pass close to John and he didn't like that either. 'Step aside, pal,' he said.

John stayed where he was. 'Alison's mother is worried about her. If you know where she is . . .'

'Don't get difficult.' The man pushed by and before he went into Alison's room he pulled a pair of gloves from his pocket and slipped them on. They were thin surgical gloves that fitted like a second skin and John knew the man was a professional who knew what he was about. The bedroom door closed behind him and then they waited while he pulled the room apart. They could hear drawers being opened and slammed shut and John turned to find Dee staring at him wide-eyed with fright. He tried to convey an unspoken message that she should stay calm.

The stocky man who was standing close to her was dressed in a cheap suit, and a grubby shirt without a tie. Even at five feet away John could smell whisky on his breath and he could also read the man's thoughts as he stared insolently at Dee. She was aware of it too and her body was rigid.

If he reached out to touch her . . . John planned his moves and picked the beer belly as his first target. How far he'd get with the other one was a different matter because he looked the type to favour carrying a weapon, a knife more than likely.

The search of the bedroom was not going well, judging by the cursing that accompanied the sounds of furniture being moved around. Then all went quiet and the man emerged with a scowl on his face.

'I'll just take a look at the rest of this place,' he said. 'Tam, you take the living-room and make a good bloody job of it.'

'What are we looking for?' Tam said.

'Oh, forget it! Just make sure these two stay put.'

'No. We're going to the kitchen to make coffee,' John said. He moved purposefully towards Dee, ignoring both men, and led her to the end of the passage.

Dee protested when she saw the younger man going into her bedroom. 'There's nothing belonging to Ali in there.'

'The sooner they look the sooner they'll be gone,' he told her firmly and the younger man laughed.

'You've got the idea, mate.'

Tam tailed along behind them and he sat on a chair close to the door. He wasn't quite as stupid as he appeared, because when John tried to find out what they were looking for, he just grinned. His eyes followed Dee, making her nervous, and all the time they were all aware of the sounds of the other man searching. John wondered uneasily what would happen if the search was fruitless.

Half an hour passed before the other man joined them. He looked hot and empty-handed as he began to open the yellow-fronted units. At first he peered behind dishes but when he was confronted with packets and tins of food, he lost patience and scooped the whole lot out on to the floor. Some packets burst open and beans and lentils crunched under his feet as he moved to the next cupboard. He got more and more angry, slamming the fridge door, kicking a pail out of his way.

'Nothing, bloody nothing,' he said at last, red-faced. He stood, hands flat on a worktop and stared out of the window as if wondering what to do next. Then he whirled around and pointed a finger at Dee.

'You. Did she give you anything to keep for her?'

Dee shook her head but said nothing.

The man's eyes fixed on John, moved on, and he began to pour scorn on the seated Tam. Much younger and fitter than the seated man, he moved fast and pulled him up by his lapels.

'Fancy the girl, dae ye, Tam?' He sneered as he too cast his eyes over Dee's body. 'Sitting on your backside, taking it easy. Silly bugger, do you expect me to wait around while you have fun? Did you see to the phone? Naw, ye bloody didn't, lazy sod—well, do it now.' He shouted the order, pushed the fat man away and Tam jumped to obey.

'Sorry, darling, no offence like, but I fancy birds with a bit more flesh on the bone.' He swung round and with his head on one side he eyed John. 'We were told she'd be on her own—so who are you?' His eyes were sharply suspicious again.

'Dee and I are going out,' John said calmly. 'You almost missed us.' It was clear that the man was uneasy about having an unexpected witness. He'd had orders to fetch something from the flat and been told that there would only be one girl present. No one had mentioned finding a man with Dee and now he wasn't sure what to do about it. John could see the indecision in his eyes but he suddenly shrugged and turned to look for his partner.

'Tam, what the hell's keeping you?' They all heard the sound of Tam destroying the phone fitting before he reappeared. 'Let's go—you two stay put!' The door slammed behind them and John glanced at Dee who was frozen against the wall. He went quickly into the living-room and tried to look down on the street below but the men had left their transport elsewhere and were now walking towards the corner.

'Pack your things—I'll be back in a minute,' he said to a pale Dee. He took the stairs at a run and raced to the corner but the men had already gone.

CHAPTER 4

Dee was in her room when he got back to the flat, trying to sort out her belongings which had been tossed around the room when it was searched. An open suitcase on the floor was full of books and music cassettes, but she was angrily stuffing her clothes into a holdall.

'I don't have much,' she said quietly. 'And now my things feel dirty. I'll have to wash it all before I can wear any of it.'

He leaned on the door frame while he waited and he could tell from her jerky movements that she had been badly scared. 'Well, you're right, I can't stay here now,' she said. 'Who were they? What have they got to do with Ali?'

'I was hoping you could tell me,' he said. 'That you might know what they were looking for.'

'I don't know anything,' she said with stiff lips, going back to her packing. 'You were the one who searched her room.'

'I didn't know what to look for and anyway, I'm not very good at it,' he said. And he hadn't thought it necessary to move the furniture around.

When Dee saw that he was smiling, some of the tension went out of her body. 'Thanks anyway. If you hadn't been here . . .' She bit her lip as she pushed a pair of jeans into the bag and then pulled at the zip.

'What sort of girl is Alison?'

'You saw her room. She was spoilt and she expected everyone else to treat her the same way. And she was selfish—she took the food money as well as the rent.' Dee lifted the bag from the bed and John bent for the suitcase. 'She hated cleaning so I said I'd do that if she did the shopping, only half the time she didn't even do that.'

'Why put up with her then?'

She leaned the bag on the bed and sighed. 'Look, I studied in the evenings, mostly in my room. We were both out all day so we didn't see much of each other and most nights Ali went out as well. I'd already decided that it wasn't going to work out and I was looking for somewhere else—that's why I was away last week, bunking in with friends. I'd given Ali the rent for the rest of this term so I was staying until then. Now can we go?'

'Where?' he asked as he preceded her to the door.

'Back to my friends, I suppose, although I can't stay there for long. I'll manage, and luckily I travel light.'

They reached the front door and Dee dropped her keys on the carpet before they stepped outside. 'That's it then, I won't be back,' she said. She had draped her leather jacket around her shoulders and her long hair was again caught up loosely at the back of her neck, held there by a purple elasticated ribbon. She gripped the holdall with both hands on the straps as they went downstairs to his car and under one arm she had a small plant.

He knew he couldn't just dump her on friends who would then have to feed her as well as make space for her and he could sense that she hated the thought of relying on others. Pride was in every movement the girl made, but for now she had no choice but go begging and she didn't like it one bit. There was also the fact that once she got deposited in student-land she would move around until she managed to find more permanent digs and he would lose track of her. He didn't want that, not until the mystery of Alison Baxter's disappearance was settled. So when they were both in the car and had belted up, he made a suggestion that made sense to him.

'I have somewhere you could stay for a bit.'

She reacted as if he'd touched her, flinching away. 'I don't sleep around,' she said angrily.

'I wasn't suggesting you did,' he said, pulling away from the kerb. 'I have a house complete with a housekeeper called Janet who is quite likely to stuff you with food and ask a lot of questions, but she won't see you without somewhere to sleep.' He grinned at her. 'Janet would make you very welcome and if it bothers you, you could always help with the chores.'

She went quiet and he let her think it over, but when he looked at her he saw that tears were running down her cheeks, smearing the mascara into dark puddles. 'I was scared of those men,' she said, still shocked but angry as well. 'I can't believe Ali would get involved with people like that.'

But she obviously was, which Dee had already worked out for herself.

'What about it—do I take you to my house? I stay in town during the week but we could work out some means of getting you back and forth for your classes.'

She dried her eyes with the back of her hand and nodded. 'OK. But you're not at all as you seem, John Leith.'

'So others keep telling me,' he said, but at the same time he was wondering how Janet would react when they arrived at Elmwood.

'A housekeeper—no wife?' Dee said after a bit.

'She was killed in an accident.' There was no need to tell her the details of the drunk driver, although he could speak about it now without a stab of pain in his gut. 'My son survived and he's nearly eight. He used to live with my sister but now he goes to boarding school here in town—I'll be bringing him to Elmwood tomorrow night so you'll meet him.'

'I like boys—I've got two brothers,' she said. And that was all the background she gave him, but maybe one day she would trust him enough to tell him more. He wondered too if she had told him all she knew about Alison Baxter, but further questioning could wait a while longer.

'How far is it?'

'Not much further. We're a bit cut off from civilization.' He turned into the narrow road and asked if she was hungry, but she gave a low gurgling chuckle.

'Just a bit scared of meeting your Janet,' she said.

And she looked nervous, was still jumpy after the business at the flat but she had guts. He thought Janet and Dee would probably get along just fine, after the initial shock.

'Is that it?' The headlights lit up the house which stood on a slight rise and had views of the surrounding countryside. The grounds, unseen now because it was too dark, were bordered by trees inside a boundary wall. Where once there had been vegetable plots and a small orchard, his uncle, Rees Kramer, had planted lawns and shrubberies. It was all easily cared for by the visiting gardener and John had no plans to change what he had inherited. Elmwood was no mansion but a spacious family home, built solidly to withstand the winds that swept in from the Forth, the only property on a road that led eventually to a farm track. By daylight, Dee would see only rolling country, fields and hedgerows.

'Yes, this is my Elmwood,' he said as he pulled up outside the front door. 'The nearest neighbour is half a mile away and the village is beyond that. My uncle liked his privacy.'

'Does he still live here?' She sounded alarmed that she might have an uncle as well as a housekeeper to contend with.

'No, he died. Are you a country lover?'

'Don't know,' she said, looking up at the house as he went to get her baggage from the boot.

'Sorry I didn't phone to let you know we were coming,' he told a surprised Janet. 'This is Dee and she's temporarily homeless. I said we could put her up for a bit.'

They were in the bright, almost circular hallway, off which several doors led to other rooms, and a wide carpeted staircase led to the upper floor. The hall was lined with light wood panelling and a vase of flowers was reflected in a mirror, the whole effect being one of welcome. Janet didn't let him down either. She smiled and reached for their jackets.

'She can have your old room—and I expect you'd like some supper.' She went off in the direction of the kitchen.

'She's nice,' Dee said, relieved.

'Most people think so. I'm going to have a drink, do you want anything?'

'Don't drink, smoke or take drugs,' she said lightly as she followed him.

'Did Alison?'

She stumbled over the answer, as if he'd taken her by surprise. 'She worked in a bar . . . so I suppose she did take a drink.' Then she felt the need to elaborate. 'She got a part-time job, like Peter, but she didn't stick it for long.'

John poured himself a small scotch. 'Where was that?'

'It would be an up-market place, knowing Ali, but they don't know her at Ludo's.'

'Did you see much of Peter at the flat?'

She had slipped off the ankle boots and was curled up in the wing chair with her arms around her knees. 'He wasn't really a boyfriend, you know—maybe Ali let him think he was. She used people.'

Bit by bit he was getting a better picture of the girl. He remembered the used packet of contraceptive pills. 'Any other male friends?'

'Might have been. Not at the flat, but she stayed away all night a few times.'

It was becoming clear that Mrs Baxter didn't know her daughter well either.

He was almost ignored at the supper table and he marvelled at the chemistry that drew some women together. Dee and Janet were still chatting as he went off to phone Clare.

'Just to let you know that Dee is staying at Elmwood for a bit, until she gets her finances sorted out.' There was no point in telling Clare about the intruders at the flat.

'What a good solution. How did Janet take it?'

They filled ten minutes with small talk. He could hear

her music playing in the background and imagined her bathed and ready for an early night. 'Miss you,' she said before hanging up. Thoughtfully, he went to watch the end of the news on TV.

Janet put her head around the door later and announced that Dee had gone to bed. 'That girl has had a bad fright. I hope you can sort it out.'

He heard her go upstairs to her own room, knowing that she had no prejudices, never made snap judgements. Dee would be happy enough if she decided to stay for a while. He was slouched in a chair, watching a late film when the phone rang.

'John? I hoped I'd find you there.' Tollis had to raise his voice to compete with a babble in the background. 'I'm at the Royal. Mike went back to that bloody bar and got himself clobbered. He's OK, just been x-rayed and no doubt he'll give you the details tomorrow . . . but knowing how it is with you and Mike, I thought you'd want to know.'

'Will I come back tonight?'

'No need. He's going to be fine. The police are involved now—waiting here for a statement from him.'

John hung up, knowing that Tollis was furious but understanding the reason for the phone call. After Mike's son was killed while working for Sentinel, Mike had adopted John as a sort of son-substitute and it wasn't always a comfortable position to be in, with Mike looming like a shadow at unexpected moments. With his battered face and social awkwardness, Mike was a strange sort of guardian angel, but an odd affinity had grown between them all the same. Not like a real blood tie, but it was enough to make John very angry now.

'Dammit, Mike,' he muttered. The man was gentle, more likely to frighten villains with his size than ever needing to use his fists, so if someone had managed to get close enough to hurt him, it must have been from behind.

As he lay in bed later, he almost wished that Tollis had not phoned because his mind was going like a grasshopper over all the events of the past few days. And Mike's instincts about something new happening in the town couldn't be ignored—surely Tollis could see that now?

He woke early next morning and slipped out of bed quietly. Dressed in his tracksuit, he saw that there was a light in the kitchen and found Dee drinking coffee. She was dressed in jeans and baggy sweatshirt, and her face was clean of make-up.

'Sorry, did I wake you?' she asked. 'I didn't sleep very well.'

'I usually go for a run before Janet gets breakfast. Like to come along?'

She lifted a foot and showed him a grubby trainer shoe. 'I run in the Meadows when I can.'

It was a fresh morning, still dark, with a dampness in the air that felt almost like a light rain. They jogged to the end of the drive and then John swung left under the trees where leaves lay in golden heaps.

'Watch your step, the leaves are slippery. This path goes all the way round and we haven't time to go far.'

The path was narrow in places and he took the lead but the girl had no trouble with the pace and kept right on his heels. He could hear her breathing easily, her long stride almost matching his own. When the path widened she ran alongside him. She had tied her hair back but strands broke loose to lie on her shoulders and occasionally she brushed them back from her face. She made no mention of the events of the evening before, so he didn't either. Maybe she'd be more open with Janet when he wasn't around. They did two circuits before more lights went on at the back of the house and they headed back to shower before they ate.

'I'm leaving for town right after breakfast—do you want a lift?'

Dee shook her head. 'No classes today so I'll just hang around here.' He paused at the top of the stairs. 'I'm going to talk to Peter Watson, to try to get this mess cleared up.'

'Good. Maybe he'll know where Ali is and things can get back to normal.'

He was back downstairs before her and as he reached for bacon, he told Janet that she would have company that day. 'See if she'll tell you anything about herself, and about Alison.'

'You're asking me to pry?' Janet was a small slim figure in her blue dressing gown, short greying hair neatly permed into all-over curls.

'Yes, if you can.'

She made tea and brought the pot to the table. 'She's an intelligent girl. She'll guess what I'm up to—and I'm sure she'll tell you everything in her own time.'

'We might not have much time,' he said.

'You think the other girl is in trouble?'

He took the cup she held out. 'Maybe. She's not exactly as her mother described her, I'm sure of that.'

Janet nodded. After years of keeping house for his uncle, she was used to mysteries and the violence that could crop up in the lives of ordinary people. 'I'll do what I can then.'

Dee joined them with her hair wet and her skin glowing. She looked about seventeen without the make-up, and Janet already had her motherly expression on by the time he was ready to leave.

'Shiela is arriving this morning and she'll expect to see you,' Janet reminded him. Turning to Dee she explained, 'My sister. She has a shop in Inverness and one of these days I'm going to help her with it.'

John draped an arm around her shoulders. 'You've been saying that for months—and I didn't forget. I'll be here this evening with David.'

'You took the girl to Elmwood?' Tollis paused with his coffee half way to his mouth.

'I couldn't leave her in that flat—those two might have come back and I didn't want to lose track of her.' He described the men, especially the one who had done most of the talking. 'He looked dangerous, and unpredictable. I think he was thrown by finding me there and wasn't sure what to do.'

'So he'll have gone back to whoever was issuing the orders and told them you were there—did he ask your name? Or get any reference to Kramer's?'

'No. He accepted I was there to take Dee out. He wasn't the type to make on the spot decisions and in the end we were lucky. I think the girl knows that too. I'm not sure how they would have treated her if she'd been on her own. That's why I had to get her away, in case they were told to go back.'

'And you've no idea what they were looking for?'

'No idea. How's Mike?'

'Fine, silly bugger. I told him to stay home and rest his brain today. He knows I'm mad, but now the police are involved so that's the end of Sentinel being dragged in the dirt. One of the customers phoned them, apparently.' He was still angry, maybe because Mike had disregarded one of the main rules of discipline, that no one acted without orders. John changed the subject.

'I'd like to listen to the tapes again, the ones I made with Mrs Baxter.'

They listened to it together and as John thought, the woman made little reference to Peter Watson except that he might work for a car transporting firm, and his phone number. He got the man's address from the directory. Tollis, peering over his shoulder as he copied it down, looked dubious.

'That's a pretty rough area.'

'I'm collecting David from school and it's on my way. I don't want to give this Watson warning that I'm coming because he isn't keen to talk, so I won't phone, but the chances are that he'll be at work anyway.'

'Where are you off to with David?'

'It's his grandfather's birthday and we're invited to tea.'

'Best of luck,' Tollis said, knowing how things were between John and Albert Gumley, his father-in-law. The old man had once been a godfather-like figure in the city's criminal scene but now he was incapacitated by emphysema. An unpleasant character when he was well, illness had turned him into a bitter recluse and he liked nothing better than to needle the son-in-law he detested.

'It's OK when David is there,' John said with a shrug. 'And I don't let him get to me any more. Sometimes I think the old bastard looks forward to me coming, as if a touch of venom brightens his day. Garek thinks so too.'

'You have conversations with Garek now—he expresses opinions?'

'He's almost friendly. He says Gumley perks up after a visit.' He laughed. 'Some people enjoy chess games, Gumley and I play verbal ones instead.'

'Who's winning?' Tollis asked, amused.

'We're about even and he knows it—that makes him try all the harder.

'Sounds like fun.'

But as John drove towards Peter Watson's house later that day, he knew that it wasn't fun at all. On Gumley's part at least it was deadly serious and based on jealousy. Jealousy that he wasn't responsible for David's schooling or his future. The boy was the old man's heir, a product, once removed—according to Gumley—of his sperm, a possession kept just beyond his reach. He wanted to groom his grandson and John was denying him the right. Instead, the old man had to be content with visits controlled by his son-in-law and it caused a frustration bordering on paranoia. Illness had taken away so much of the power he'd once had and only a few loyal followers remained, living in his home, which had always struck John as a weird set up. No doubt criminals, like everyone else, reached retirement age, but did they gather in the dark evenings to reminisce about the good times? Somehow he didn't think so. Gumley was not the type to have any fond memories.

He was under no illusions so far as the old man was concerned. If Gumley could manage it, the game they played at each visit would not be confined to words, it would be physical. Even now, it was only David who kept the fragile peace between the two of them, because the old man wouldn't risk being distanced from the little boy.

It was chilling to see the old man's frustration and he knew that there were times when Gumley yearned to retaliate with more than words. Garek, nurse and companion, watched and controlled the meetings like a safety valve, allowing the old man his venomous pleasures but ready to step in and damp things down if necessary. And David was the oil on the surface of the old man's anger, although he was too young to sense the emotions that swept over his head. One day he might ask questions, if Gumley lived long enough. In the meantime the visits went on, as agreed long before, and Gumley resented that each one was a concession when he thought they should be a right.

The damp morning had developed into a wet day but there were breaks in the clouds that obscured the upper slopes of the Pentlands, with a watery sun breaking through. It was still dismally wet though when he got to the area where Peter Watson lived. He was unfamiliar with this part of Edinburgh and he had to circle around before he found the right street. It wasn't the sort of area to leave a car unattended either and he was glad he'd taken one of the Kramer cars from the pool instead of his own Granada. He parked behind a Telecom van and got out to walk to the block where Watson lived. And all around were the signs of a depressed housing scheme. Gardens were neglected and litter had blown into wire fences and been trapped there. The close he entered was in the same shabby state, with spray-can graffiti on the walls, chipped paintwork and a smell of urine.

He checked the door numbers and began to climb the concrete steps leading upwards. On the second landing he had to pass through a group of youths who looked him over and he knew he was out of place in his office suit. They moved reluctantly to let him through, muttered and laughed after he was above them and he wondered if they intended trouble when he went down again. One of them peered up the stairwell as he knocked on Peter Watson's door.

'He's no' in, mister,' he shouted. The rest sniggered and hooted. 'He's away out wi' his squash racket in his wee bag.' More laughter. And they were probably telling the truth because no one came to the door. He went back down the stairs slowly but the boys caused no trouble. They were keeping in out of the rain, sharing jokes and cigarettes, or so he thought until one of them followed him outside. It was the one who had told him Watson was out, a boy of fifteen or so who had acne on his thin unhealthy face and lank hair.

'Need another address, mister?'

John paused but the boy kept his distance, smirking. 'For Peter Watson? I thought you said he was playing squash?'

The boy hesitated and then became bolder. 'For what else he carries,' he said knowingly. He waited for an answer and when he didn't get it he repeated himself. 'Another place to get what you want.'

'What would that be?' John asked, moving on and knowing very well what was on offer. The boy was skipping along beside him in sideways steps but when John stopped he backed away. There was doubt in his eyes now and he looked poised for flight.

'You a cop?' He didn't wait for an answer and ran off. When he was a safe distance away he turned and grinned, then ran off around the corner. John heard him hooting with laughter and the sound bounced back off the tall buildings. He walked down the depressing street to his car and climbed in, glad to drive away in the direction of David's school, wondering how many other people knocked on Watson's door and how many were re-directed by the young messengers. There was no doubt in his mind now that Watson was a supplier of drugs and that meant the missing girl might have become involved in it too, which might also explain the search of her flat. What had started as a simple inquiry to help a distressed mother was beginning to look much more sinister.

*

David was excited about getting time off school in the middle of the week. 'Did you remember Grandfather's present?'

John nodded to the back seat where the flat parcel lay and his son was satisfied. 'Do you think he'll like it?'

It was an enlarged print that David had taken of his dog, Sheba, and John had had it framed before wrapping it in gift paper as his son had instructed, but he wasn't sure how Gumley would react to the gift. Gumley disliked pets and dogs in particular but allowed David to leave Sheba at his home during term time. With any other grandfather, it would be a measure of his regard for the boy but as far as Gumley was concerned there was a more cynical reason. Gumley kept the dog only because it was another enticement for the boy to visit more often.

'I'm sure he'll hang it where he can see it all the time,' John murmured. 'If you suggest it.' He smiled. The game had already begun. The rain had stopped as the car swung through the open gates and up the gravelled driveway. The gravel ran right up to the walls of the house and as Tollis had pointed out, it was a sensible measure for security, so that intruders would be easily spotted. Gumley even had lights that came on after dark if anyone approached his property, but who in their right mind would want to intrude on him?

David was already slipping out of his seat belt, scrambling on to his knees to reach into the back seat for the present, and then he was off and running. John, who felt none of his son's eagerness, got out more slowly and met Garek waiting at the door with his usual formal welcome and a nod of his bald head.

'Good afternoon, Mr Leith.'

'How are the Harleys?' The motorbikes were a shared enthusiasm ever since Garek revealed his collection of Harley Davidson bikes. Garek thawed when the subject was mentioned but he looked regretful. 'Soon they will be laid up for winter.'

John was interested. 'What does that involve?' They walked along the hall and felt the first blast of the heat that Gumley needed because of his delicate health. John knew that the sitting-room would be worse; it was unbearable at times but he thought it very apt that Gumley's home should be as hot as hell.

'Nothing much. I take out the batteries and charge them up every month or so and the exposed metal is oiled. You have not yet bought one of your own?'

'I've had a look in Alvin's.' Garek would know what that meant; looking over the array of gleaming machines, running hands over soft leather, trying to decide which to choose. 'It's not something to rush.'

Garek nodded, understanding. 'Did you see the parade this year?'

'Mm,' John said. Two thousand motorbikes from all over the world had stopped traffic through the city for over two hours, had paraded in formation to delighted crowds. 'Mostly Japanese machines though, weren't they? A good sprinkling of Goldwings.'

They had paused at the door of the sitting-room to discuss the only interest they had in common, apart from the welfare of one small boy, and Gumley didn't like it. John could see the old man's head turned to watch them and his hooded eyes were full of spite. As usual he was sitting close to the fire and David was nearby in his uniform of grey pullover, shirt and shorts, socks slipping downwards. His dark hair was neatly combed for a change and his skin had the healthy glow of a boy who loved sport. He was sturdy, growing fast and was already taller than average for his age.

Gumley was trying to open his present but his fingers had no strength so he passed it over to his grandson. The old man's chest heaved as he sucked in air and although his expression showed no pleasure, his eyes watched intently as David removed the wrapping paper and held out the framed photograph of his beloved dog. John held his breath, waiting for a caustic comment from Gumley but the old man merely nodded.

'It is an excellent piece of work considering you only have a simple camera. I will buy you a much better one for your birthday.' And he looked over the boy's head with a glitter of malice in his eyes, knowing that the camera that David already had was a present from his father the year before. It was childish, not up to Gumley's usual standard and John felt like laughing.

'Dad says you'll hang it where you can see it,' David said in all innocence and Gumley's eyes swivelled back to where John stood with his hands in his pockets.

'Of course. Your father knows my tastes so well,' he said. He passed the picture to Garek. 'See where the boy wants it hung,' he said.

David picked the spot and then was anxious to see his dog.

'Come,' Garek said. 'Sheba is at the back of the house.'

David shed his pullover, dropped it on a chair and followed the tall man out of the room leaving John alone with Gumley, who ignored him. The old man fiddled with the blanket that covered his knees, dwarfed by the large-winged chair, his shoulders rounded by his illness. He reminded John of a garden gnome that had slipped inside the house after the weather had stripped away its paintwork.

'The boy grows fast,' Gumley said without turning round.

'Trish was tall and I'm six-two,' John pointed out.

'Meaning he inherits nothing from me,' Gumley muttered sourly. Which was true. It was a relief that David looked nothing like his grandfather who, although he had shrunk in recent years, had never been more than average build.

Gumley wouldn't let it go. 'What do appearances matter? There are other qualities that are more subtle that he will get from me and who knows how they will affect his future? The boy will have ambition—which he will certainly not get from you. I hear you have made changes already in the business left you by your uncle, that you let others make your decisions for Kramer Property.' Speaking exhausted him and his chest heaved as his inefficient lungs demanded oxygen, but that never stopped him taunting.

And, thought John, Gumley still kept tabs on him. He knew what his father-in-law was trying to do, so with a sigh he played along. 'The business is doing very well, as no doubt you know. Kramer's is stable and you won't have the pleasure of seeing me go under, I'm afraid.' He walked over to stand by the window to avoid looking at Gumley and heard the old man grunt.

'We'll see, John Leith. You have all the smart alec confidence of youth. Thirty-three. What do you know of business?'

'I'm in an honest one, old man. I don't break the law to make a profit.'

'Honest!' Gumley laughed, which was no more than a rattle of phlegm. 'No business is honest and you're naïve to think it is. It won't guarantee you success, as you will find out,' Gumley said, as if he needed to have the last word.

Garek came back carrying a hammer and proceeded to position the picture with Gumley looking on. It ended up not quite in Gumley's direct line of vision but close enough to satisfy David. Gumley gave it a sour glance, nodded and then stared into the fire as if he had withdrawn from further conversation.

'You will be staying for tea?' Garek asked, and John agreed that they would.

'What's David up to?'

'In the back garden with the dog.' Garek was stiffly formal as if he sensed that there had been words between the other two in his absence.

'I'd like a word—outside,' John said.

They went out of the back door and strolled along the border of a vegetable plot in an area surrounded by a high beech hedge. 'That must be a devil to trim. I haven't seen this side of the house before.'

'A couple of the men have developed an interest in gardening. There is little else to occupy them.'

John knew that some of Gumley's old hands had stuck by him and that there were no females in the house, but he rarely saw any of them on his visits. The house was always quiet except for an occasional sound of a radio in a distant room and if there was a TV he'd seen no sign of it. It was no wonder that the men had taken to gardening as a hobby, and that Garek had his Harley Davidson motorbikes.

They reached the end of the path, stepping over puddles, and turned into a grassed area where David, with muddy knees, was throwing a stick for the Labrador to fetch. The dog almost knocked the boy over in its excitement, romping around him and its barking mingled with the boy's laughter.

Garek was waiting patiently for John to open the conversation, walking with hands clasped at his back but not with any obvious pleasure. His body was stiffly upright, as if walking outdoors or taking any time off for relaxation was unnatural to him.

'Do you still hear what's happening in town?'

Garek paused and turned to watch David, but didn't answer and, John knew there was no point in being anything other than direct with a man like Garek, so he plunged right in. 'There has been some trouble at a bar, the sort of drinking place which attracts a good class of customer and the last place where you'd expect trouble with rowdies. It's happened more than once now and Mike Cairns says there's a new element in town, that there's something brewing. The manager of the bar half expected trouble and was looking for extra doormen.'

Garck said, still staring down at the path, 'How did the manager know what might happen?'

'Mike didn't say, just that word gets around.'

Garek seemed to understand. 'Word is *meant* to get

around. It is like the weather forecast—you are told there will be a storm and everyone buys an umbrella.'

'That's a bit deep for me,' John admitted.

'Tollis will understand,' Garek said with certainty. 'If you are in the business of providing stewards, business improves if your men are in demand. So you create the need. It is the rule of trade, no?'

'But that would mean a firm could create the demand, but not necessarily benefit. There are a lot of security firms in town.'

Garek sighed, as if such innocence was beyond understanding. 'You make sure that the bar employs your men. It is part of one of the oldest rackets, extortion, protection. I will describe a possible way,' Garek said patiently. 'A man will come to the manager and suggest to him—pleasantly—that he should employ his men to protect the premises. Not from any trouble, but just to keep out the riff-raff and only to let the nice people in, who wear suits and buy cocktails. All places that sell drinks want to encourage smart people who have money to spend, yes?' Garek's strange precise speech made the words all the more sinister.

'Of course.' John had already recognized the storyline as it applied to Ludo's but he wanted to hear all of it from Garek.

Garek smiled. It was a slow happening when the bald man smiled. His lips took their time in stretching to reveal surprisingly good teeth but John felt a coldness in the small of his back every time it happened. He was very glad that Garek was reasonably friendly.

'The manager will refuse because he already has good men, but they will discuss this for some time. If he still refuses . . . do you know what the next step is?'

'I can guess.'

'The man, who may be polite, will leave; no threats, no bad feelings, but by coincidence, a little while later there is trouble in the bar. Maybe nothing too serious, but customers are scared and business is not so good. The manager wishes that he had not turned down the offer.'

'And he gets the chance to change his mind.'

'Of course. And in time he *will* sack his own men and take on the new ones, but they will cost a great deal more. However, they are good at the job and the customers are happy. The manager almost believes that he was not blackmailed, that it was his choice all along.'

'You can't blame him, can you?'

'He never had a choice. That is why it succeeds and the people who apply this pressure make a great deal of money. They charge a lot but the manager gets used to it, and anyway, what can he do? Extortion is a nasty business.'

'What if he doesn't play ball? What happens when he digs in his heels and keeps saying no? After all, he has to account somehow for the increased overheads.'

Garek stopped his pacing and turned to face him. 'Then he is brave but stupid. How will he protect his premises—by looking for other men who will only refuse to work there because they know what will happen? How will he protect himself and his family, his staff? He cannot win, Mr Leith, and it will escalate until he is forced to submit or get out of the business. I promise you, this is very dangerous and the men behind it do not care. They are violent, ruthless men who enjoy the work.'

'But they could charge so much that the business goes broke.'

'Only if they are greedy. There is a fine line to walk, to take enough but not too much. And why should they care if they milk a business dry? There are many more places of entertainment and they can put pressure on the new owners of bars or discos which they have already ruined in the past.'

As they walked back to the house the accountant in John wondered how the extra wages were put through the books. And how far would these people go to persuade a manager that they meant what they said?

'And you think this is what is happening now, in Edinburgh? Who's behind it?'

Garek shrugged as if he had no interest in the protection

rackets. Maybe he thought that the crime was suited to the lower orders, the hooligans, and therefore beneath him. John had never tried to find out just what Gumley and Garek had been involved in but knowing the two, it would be more sophisticated than extortion. Garek looked to where David was now sitting on the grass with his arms around his dog's neck and spoke absently.

'The men behind it stay hidden and you will only ever see the front men. Usually they hire men with criminal records, who have experience of a sort. Such men are around in plenty and they are paid for doing what they enjoy anyway. They use violence, fists, weapons, it makes no difference—it is high on the list of qualifications for the work.' He spoke casually, as if it was a simple fact of life. 'And now I must prepare tea. We have a birthday cake, I believe, but no candles.'

Was that a touch of humour? John wasn't sure.

Tea was not formal, but served from a trolley in the sitting-room with Garek as waiter and had been prepared with a small boy's appetite in mind. The adults ate little but David made sure that his grandfather had a slice of the cake. The old man took it and then looked with distaste at the crumbs that fell on his lap and around his feet. John had a mental image of Garek, sent to fetch dustpan and brush, to clear it up after they'd gone. Gumley, an invalid, would make a fastidious and complaining patient but Garek never showed any resentment and not for the first time, John wondered why the man put up with a master who never said a simple 'thank you'.

He was relieved when it was time to go. David said goodbye to Gumley by slipping an arm carefully around his shoulders. 'And you did like your present?'

The old man nodded. 'Come again soon. Tell your father to bring you and we will have another tea for your birthday.'

Garek had another warning for John as they stood outside. 'Don't let curiosity involve you in the protection business. Those who run it call it "the caring game" but it is a sick joke—the opposite is the truth. It is a steamroller that cannot be halted once the target is chosen.'

'Not if the men behind it are caught—the police must know it is happening.'

Garek didn't look optimistic. 'They will operate under a legitimate front and who is going to stand up and complain to the police?'

And as he drove away he could still see Garek standing on the steps of the house in his white shirt, black trousers and waistcoat. He had such a bleak expression that he looked like a harbinger of doom.

CHAPTER 5

David had permission from his school to stay at Elmwood overnight and that evening Dee took him outside to play, giving John the chance to ask Janet how the girl had been during the day.

'Did she say anything about Alison?'

Janet's sister, Shiela, who had arrived, was listening and already knew the story behind Dee's visit. 'She's been busy, doing her washing and sorting out her room all afternoon,' she said. 'She had a fright and I think she's trying to put it out of her mind. Whatever the other girl is mixed up in, I don't think Dee knows much about it.'

John watched from the window as Dee and David kicked a ball around on the flat grass area down by the trees and their laughter floated back to him. The ground was soft after the rain and both slipped several times and ended up with patches of mud on their clothes. Summertime was officially over and it was almost dark but that didn't seem to matter to them. He was glad he'd brought David if it was helping Dee to forget the men who had searched the flat, but he still had to find out why they'd done it.

He went into the study to phone Tollis. 'Garek has been

putting me into the picture about the protection rackets—I suppose that had already occurred to you?'

Tollis seemed reluctant to discuss it. 'It has. I hear what the men are saying in the office—why do you think I wanted Mike to stay out of it? You can never pin this thing down, and it's best left to the police.' And that was all he would say about it.

John did a mental shrug because there was no changing Tollis's mind once it was made up. 'Peter Watson is into drugs,' he said and he got an 'Ah' from Tollis. 'He also works part-time in Ludo's. I need to speak to him but so far I've had no luck. If necessary I'll go back to Ludo's and corner him. Thought you should know.'

'Mike says that after last night they'll have to stay shut for a bit. They wrecked the place this time. I take it you think your missing girl knew about the drugs?'

'It's looking very like it. Why the search of the flat? Makes me wonder if her mother's fears may come true.'

'The flat that was left so tidy,' Tollis muttered. 'Are you discovering what sort of girl she is?'

'I'm making progress on that.'

'Let me know how it goes—we'll chat first thing in the morning.'

John phoned Alison's uncle next and got a cool female who said Mr Baxter was entertaining guests and could she take a message.

'I was hoping to ask him about his niece, Alison.'

'In what connection?'

'Can I make an appointment to see him?'

There was silence and then he heard paper rustling—pages of a diary?

'Mr Baxter will be lunching at the Westmore Hotel on Thursday. If you leave your name at the bar he could see you for a few minutes, around two.'

'I'll be there.' John hung up and wondered if Baxter had a secretary resident in his home.

David had brought a model aeroplane kit with him and he and Dee spent the rest of the evening putting it together on the kitchen table. John did some paper work, aware that Shiela was looking at him as if she had something on her mind. He was used to one or other of his female relatives raising the old topic of 'isn't it time you got married again?' and that was what he was expecting to hear after his son was safely out of the way in bed, but first he wanted a word with Dee. She was clearing the table of bits of plastic off-cuts from the model and gathering up the books that David had left scattered around.

She had been very quiet since he arrived, but it couldn't be easy for her to be lodging with complete strangers, no matter how friendly they were. Her hair hung in a long pleat from the crown of her head and she had on a faded sweatshirt over jeans. She must have reached the limit of her sparse wardrobe.

'Did the police question you about Alison?'

She nodded. 'Asked who her friends were, what she did in her spare time, where she went—all the things you wanted to know. I told them she was into fitness things, like aerobics and she used sunbeds regularly but I don't know who she went around with. Other girls from the shop, I expect. I think they were going to see Peter after me.' Her arms tightened around the books and he knew she disliked being questioned about Alison, but whether she was protecting the missing girl, or merely sorry to be involved, he wasn't sure. It couldn't have been easy for her to struggle on a grant while sharing a flat with a girl who was short of nothing.

'I went looking for Peter today, at his flat,' he said. 'Some boys thought I was a customer of his, looking for drugs. Did you have any idea he was involved in that?'

She looked shocked at first but then seemed to accept the idea. She sat at the table, still clutching the books. 'I never thought he was Ali's boyfriend. I would have stayed out of the way when he came but Ali made sure that I did anyway. He would come in and they talked in another room and sometimes Ali went out with him soon afterwards but she was too smart to get mixed up in anything like drugs.

She thought too much of her looks and keeping fit, and she even hated anyone smoking.' Dee looked worried now and she was clever enough to work out the consequences for herself. 'If the police find out what Peter was doing . . .'

'That's right, it was only routine before, but they may come back and ask you some more questions,' John said quietly. 'You say Alison would never take drugs, but would she be willing to sell them to others?' He read the answer in her eyes.

'Maybe. I think she would have done anything to make money but it would have to be safe—she's pretty shrewd.'

'I think you'd better plan on staying here until it's all cleared up, at least until Alison is found.'

She wasn't happy about that but in the end she agreed. 'I can borrow a friend's Mini—if you can give me a lift in to town tomorrow?'

It was after Janet and Dee had gone up to bed that John finally persuaded Shiela to say what was on her mind. She was five years older than Janet and had the same Highland accent, with the softened consonants that gave every sentence a polite gentleness.

'Get it off your chest, Shiela,' John said. 'You've been wanting to say something all evening but you may as well know that I have no bride in the offing.' They were on either side of the fireplace where a fire had been lit, John sprawled in an easy chair, Shiela playing patience. Only a couple of small lamps were lit and with the dancing flames of the fire, the room was full of soft light. Shiela put down her cards and smiled.

'That's a pity then, but not what I was thinking. I don't know how to put it—you'll think I'm a crazy old woman.'

'You and Janet are the sanest women I know.'

'You may change your mind,' Shiela said with a chuckle. 'Ah well, where to start? It's not something we speak about in the family as a rule. I get . . . feelings that some say come from having the second sight. My mother was the same and her grandmother. We see things.'

'See things?'

She sighed as if to say 'I warned you.' 'That's right. Many Celtic people have the gift, or curse depending on how you look at it. It's not like fairground fortune telling, we don't use crystal balls and the like and it's nothing like Biblical prophecy either but it is real. I didn't ask for it and believe me, no one outside the family knows about it. Am I making sense, John?'

'Not really, no,' he said, amused as well as intrigued.

'I don't understand it any more than you,' she said. 'So I did some reading on it years ago, hoping, I suppose, to discover that it was just my imagination. Who wants to see into the future?' She was slightly embarrassed but determined to be believed.

'And can you do that?'

'Not often. Mostly it's a spontaneous thing, a flash of vision that I can't control. You know in the old days the Gaels believed that animals had the true gift, and when you think about it, that sounds reasonable. Why do animals raise their hackles, back off for no reason, show the whites of their eyes, or howl in the night? Horses were said to be more instinctive than dogs . . . I think I get the same sort of reaction, a sense of what lies ahead, a feeling of dread or sometimes a more definite feeling when I see events as clearly as if I am watching the television. I wish it didn't happen, believe me.'

He couldn't help but take her seriously. 'Do you see something ahead for me—is that what is bothering you, Shiela?'

'I have had to accept that in my case there is a sort of precognition. That is a gift I don't want but I can't stop it happening.' She spoke firmly but her hands were clenched tight in her lap. 'I felt it today as soon as you arrived and it has something to do with a girl—I can't say if it is Dee.'

'Anything specific?'

'It has already begun and there is danger. There is no way I can describe what I see, except that it's like seeing a tightly rolled ream of paper that has begun to loosen its coils and soon it will lay itself flat. I can't see what is inside it yet but it won't be long before it is open.'

With anyone else he would have listened out of politeness and then put it out of his mind but because he had known the sisters since he was ten years old, he had to at least believe in Shiela's good sense.

'And this thing will happen no matter what?'

'That I don't know. You see what I mean about having no control—it can be tantalizing as well.'

He thought about it long after she had gone up to bed. In his student days, when he'd taken part in late night discussions, all sorts of topics had cropped up and once the talk had been about clairvoyance, visions that were out of sight, through time, out of space. Someone had suggested that everyone had the gift but that it had become buried, either lost or never developed. Parapsychology had become a favourite topic until something else took its place but now it had reared its spectral head again, in his own home.

He found it interesting and one day he might have a longer chat with Shiela about it, but he couldn't go about his business wondering if her prediction might come true. He was far more concerned about Dee, about getting her life back to normal, and he decided it was time he had an informal chat to DCI Jamieson. The policeman was in the serious crime squad and probably knew nothing about the case of the missing Alison Baxter, but if there was a connection with drugs, he would want to know about it.

Dee was ready to leave first the next morning, carrying her books in a shabby canvas bag that hung from a strap on her shoulder. She looked exactly as she had when he first met her, in black leather jacket and tight pants, except that now she looked as if she'd slept well and had good food inside her. She got into the front seat beside John while David played with his now completed model aeroplane in the back.

It had rained all night and the forecast promised more to follow. Cars ahead of them sent up sheets of spray and the wipers had to work at full speed to keep the windscreen clear. Dee didn't seem in the mood to talk so John switched on a tape and the songs of Chris Rea kept them happy as the commuter traffic crawled into town.

He dropped her at the university building. 'You're sure you'll get transport back to Elmwood? Give me a call if you can't.'

'So you can keep an eye on me?'

'Something like that,' he said.

She tapped on the back window and waved to David and then slung her bag on her shoulder and mingled with other students going into the building. He dropped David off at school and was late getting to the office, but Val had things under control.

'The new brochures have arrived so you might like to OK them, and Tollis sent a message to say your policeman friend is dropping in for a chat. He said could you come too if possible. You have time for a leisurely coffee though,' and she placed a cup at his elbow.

He looked through the first of the four new brochures, a glossy design that cost a fortune but hopefully would promote new business. Two were simple folders with smart photographs that set out the work of the chartered surveyors and listed the advice services that the firm offered. One was an information booklet, which gave a brief rundown of the different departments, but the largest brochure went more deeply into the investment and development side, a venture that he hoped to expand. He had written the introduction himself but had refused to have his photograph on the page as his managers suggested. He had not yet been accepted by the city brotherhood who felt that a man of thirty-three had a lot of proving to do, so there was no need to rub their noses in it by putting his picture in the new publicity material. He read each one, and then took them into Val's room.

'You still find all this boring, don't you?' she said as she took them from him.

'Only some of the time. The trouble is that I don't get to meet the people at the other end, the customers.'

'It must be very different to the small business you used to have, I suppose. Your uncle never wanted much contact with people.'

'But Rees liked the business side of things, expansion, competition, planning new ventures—I know it must be done but . . .'

'You're very good at it,' she pointed out.

'That must have surprised a lot of people,' he said drily. 'I'm off. Tollis didn't say *why* Jamieson was coming?'

Val shook her head. She was wearing smart new glasses and had let her fair hair grow into a softer style, and he wondered if she and Tollis were still seeing each other after business hours. He wasn't likely to find out because neither discussed their life outside the office.

'Tollis doesn't know either, just that he was dropping in.'

He found Tollis, Mike and Jamieson in the room normally reserved for interviewing clients. It was decorated in cool greens, had comfortable chairs and a few watercolours on the walls. Jamieson had obviously just arrived and was shaking rain from the brim of his hat.

'Ah, Mr Leith, I was wondering if you would be joining us,' he said as he draped his wet raincoat over a chair and placed his hat on top of it. He was a spare man of close to six feet tall, the shortest man in the room, but who didn't need inches to make his presence felt. His eyes gave away the fact that a sharp and assessing mind lurked behind his pleasant manner.

They sat, Mike close to Tollis, and John took the last chair next to Jamieson who sat sideways on, almost facing him. And it was to John that he spoke first. 'I hear you witnessed that little brawl on Saturday.' It was casual, as if Jamieson was barely interested, but to the other three it was a demonstration—perhaps deliberate—that police intelligence had been at work. 'And there was another one in the same locus. How's the head, Mike?'

Mike looked embarrassed. 'I tried to duck when one of them swiped at me, but I was off-balance and I hit the bar on the way down.'

Jamieson pursed his lips, but they twitched first. 'Same men as the previous time?'

'Three this time, heavier mob.'

'I'd like to hear how it started.'

Mike took time to collect his thoughts. 'The place was pretty empty. I was sitting at the bar talking to one of the staff and the three men came in, swinging clubs, no warning. They didn't say a thing, just set out to do the place and they meant business. The customers and staff all scattered and one of the heavies swung the club in my direction. I didn't see what happened after that but I'm told they didn't hang about. They came in, did what they were there for, and cleared off—it took minutes. And now the bar has had to close down for a bit—but you'll know that.' Mike's large hands were hanging loosely between his legs and he looked relaxed. Tollis had heard it before and said nothing.

'Descriptions?'

Mike was used to this. 'Mid-thirties to forty, the usual heavies, dressed in sweaters and jeans. The kind you can hire anywhere. I'd know them again.'

Jamieson turned to John. 'What do you remember about the other two?'

John had sat in with Tollis's men at a training session on how to describe an attacker, so he knew some of the technique. The trick was to concentrate on a part of the body, a hand perhaps and then work your way up it to the face, picking out details that could not be altered later. Clothing wasn't as important as scars and other features that couldn't be altered.

'They were in the same age group, thirtyish, heavy, both with dark hair. One was probably six feet tall, the other a couple of inches shorter and he had a receding hairline. The taller one had a heavy gold ring with a black stone on his ring finger, left hand—he was the one I tackled so I heard his voice. He had a speech impediment, like a lisp but more nasal. The backs of his hands were hairy and the skin was roughened, dirty nails. He had a small badge in his lapel.'

'What sort of badge—football supporter's club?'

'I think I could draw it,' John said and took the sheet of paper that Tollis passed to him. 'Two letters intertwined, A and L, I think, and a diamond or a star in the upper right hand corner. Green on black.' He gave Jamieson the drawing. 'The other man who was struggling with Mike led with his right hand and he had scratches on his neck, under his ear.'

'It must be the accountant's eye for detail,' Jamieson murmured as he studied the drawing. 'Maybe it takes an accountant to spot the things that the rest of us miss, the intuitive touch. I'll get you to look at some pictures.'

Tollis spoke for the first time. 'He does tend to twitch for no apparent reason. Sometimes I wonder if there is anyone he does trust.'

'Well?' Jamieson asked, eyebrows raised. 'Is there?'

John thought about the days when he'd run his own small accountancy business, when he could read so much from a client's figures, right down to the sort of toilet paper he bought. Often the clients who were outwardly honest and sober citizens were the ones who tried to be evasive, who tried to fiddle their tax or mislay receipts. Long ago he had decided that real honesty didn't exist, that everyone fiddled something.

'Not many,' he said, and Jamieson laughed.

'Well,' he said, standing up and reaching for his coat. 'That was most useful and will do to be going on with.' He turned to Tollis but bent his head to the business of doing up the buttons of his coat. 'You seem to have a lot of competition these days, with security firms opening up all over town.'

Tollis narrowed his eyes as if trying to read beyond the words.

'Business is pretty good all the same,' he said.

'And the challenge no doubt spurs you on,' Jamieson said

as he headed for the door. Still pleasant, smartly dressed, he was a gentleman but a policeman first and last. 'Mr Leith, I'd like a word. I'll wait downstairs if you'd like to fetch your coat. The rain shows no sign of letting up.' He put the drawing that John had given him carefully into his inner pocket. 'Nothing comes to mind from this but we should be able to find out what it means.'

They listened to his feet going down through the outer office and then Tollis was on his feet, fuming. 'Why does he do that? He says just so much but never tells you anything.' He reached for his cigarettes. 'Why is someone of his rank so interested in what happens in a place like Ludo's?'

'He has to keep on top of things,' Mike said slowly, implying that he still thought that Tollis should be interested as well. 'He won't want gangs setting up a new fashion in smashing up the city's bars.'

John waited for Tollis to mention the connection with the protection racket but the big man only looked thoughtful. Then he snapped out of it impatiently. 'You'd better fetch your coat as he said—and try to find out what the hell he really came for.'

Jamieson was standing just inside the front entrance, watching the torrent of rain coming straight down from the heavens. 'I'm parked further down,' he said, before stepping outside. They were both very wet before they'd covered the distance to the car but once inside Jamieson removed his coat and threw it on the back seat and urged John to do the same, which meant there was a long session in store with the Chief Inspector.

'Just a chat,' the policeman said as he drove down the Royal Mile and turned left at the bottom. He didn't say where they were heading and John didn't ask.

'I have some time to spare today,' Jamieson said. 'And I like to drive around and have a bit of a think. Better than sitting at my desk. I'm looking for a house, by the way—it was a mistake to move out of town. Keep your eyes open for a place with a bit of ground. Gardening is something else that relaxes the mind.'

John tried to imagine the policeman in old clothes pottering around with seedlings, planting his veg, and didn't quite manage it. Like Tollis, he was wondering what Jamieson really wanted. They were on the shore road now, driving by the docks and heading for Newhaven. There were a few pedestrians about, dodging into shops, struggling with umbrellas, splashing through puddles. A grey day, nice to be in the car, but to what purpose?

'What are your feelings about the trouble at the bar?' Jamieson asked as he overtook a bus and entered the Granton area. 'We'll stop here for a bit and chew it over,' he said, driving on to the quay at the small yacht harbour. He parked, facing the harbour and switched off the engine. 'Has Tollis voiced any opinions?'

'He doesn't want to know.'

Jamieson seemed to understand that. 'Someone is dirtying his backyard so he's looking the other way. But he'll know what it's all about.'

'Protection? I've heard something about it,' John said.

'Looks very like it,' Jamieson said. 'It's like a disease, someone dabbles in it and before you know it we have an epidemic. They get the scent of easy money and then we have a rush of clones, all doing the same thing.' Jamieson was almost talking to himself, studying the sky and water as if expecting answers from the elements. 'Take a small bar in a run-down area, with customers that are dubious to say the least. The owner pays protection and sees most of his profits going into someone else's pocket. He would have every right to feel disillusioned. You follow? Maybe he asks himself "If they can get away with this, why can't I?" If he has half a brain it's not so difficult to sell up, to go and rent premises, stick a notice on the door that says he's now a security consultant. No licence required. He is now in a business that is far more profitable, providing stewards for discos, bars, and if he's successful, pop concerts and the like. And he probably knows some men with a criminal background from the days he ran his bar. No trouble to recruit them anyway, ready made muscle power. This city has a disease, and it's spreading.'

'And Tollis knows.'

'Uh huh. He keeps his nose clean, avoids the muck and hopes it will all go away, but we need the sort of information his men can bring in. I can't ask him directly but any little scrap will be useful.'

'Is it so scattered then? Or is it organized?'

'The little men are not so important and we know most of them,' Jamieson said scornfully. 'But there is a Mr Big, as they say in the films. Someone who has a very good cover indeed and so far all leads fade out before we get anywhere close to him. He's importing his labour—the sort we are not used to seeing in this city and I'm concerned they may introduce guns. I have limited resources, you see.' He looked across at John as if to make sure he understood what he was talking about.

'I do see,' John said, and Jamieson had one more thing to add.

'We need clues—no action. There has been a lot of violence already and I don't want more. There's no telling how far these people will go but in my experience they are very nasty indeed.'

Which echoed Garek's warning.

'The incident you witnessed might have been the start of the targeting that particular bar. We have spoken to the manager but he isn't saying anything. That's the thing we have to overcome, the fear. In a recent incident there was a fight at a disco and later the manager was beaten up. Word gets around, which is what they have in mind, of course.' Jamieson paused to watch a group of young boys wearing bright orange life jackets who were queuing to clamber aboard a training vessel. 'Now that's a brave bunch—did you ever go sailing? I used to have a dinghy down here.'

A pilot's boat suddenly appeared out on the Forth and edged in to moor alongside the quay. Spume was being whipped from the top of the choppy waves and tarpaulin-covered yachts were bobbing and rolling at their moorings. It was hard to believe that only days before people had strolled in bright sunshine.

'We aren't talking about yobbos who come out of the housing schemes either, you know. The hired hands maybe, but not the men behind them. Some of them have gone to public schools. They know how to organize and they have brain power. Down south they still have the casual problem at football matches and incredible as it seems, they find that people like stockbrokers are the organizers so it isn't confined to this city. And there's also the problem that they can operate these security firms under the cloak of legality. The man we want is clever too, and so far he's managed to stay hidden.' Jamieson's anger boiled over and he waved a hand in disgust.

'But these businesses don't have to be licensed,' John said. 'So what's to stop them?'

'Exactly! They are careful to have some genuine contracts but the sidelines are nothing more than extortion. We can't charge these people just because we can prove they pay higher wages than firms like Sentinel. And Sentinel and the many other firms who trade honestly must come under the same scrutiny—which is why Tollis is justifiably incensed. Our hands are tied until we have proof of what they are up to and that means people must come forward. That brings us back full circle, to the fear.' He sounded bitter. 'So use whatever influence you have to drag Tollis out of his apathy. He's in the same business, after all—get him to put feelers out.'

It was the end of the session and Jamieson reached to switch on the engine. They were half way back to town before John broached his own subject. 'Do you know if they are still looking for that missing girl, Alison Baxter?'

'I can ask,' Jamieson said, obviously still thinking on other lines.

John told him about Peter Watson and the possibility that he was dealing in drugs. That got all Jamieson's attention. 'That makes a difference,' the policeman muttered. 'And where's the other girl now?'

'I took her down to Elmwood. She had no money and nowhere to go.'

'You realize that she could be in danger? Someone might begin to wonder how much Alison Baxter told her—flatmates do share confidences. They might already be looking for her and your home is hardly ideal, all that travelling back and forth—she's exposed.'

'And there's another link although it's a bit tenuous. Peter Watson had a part-time job at Ludo's and Alison also worked in a bar, but I don't know which one.'

Jamieson was silent, concentrating on the road ahead, frowning. 'It wouldn't be the first time that the protection rackets have been linked with the drug scene. Drug dealing goes on in any public place where money changes hands openly, hence the ice-cream wars in Glasgow. Then you have newsagents, discos, pop concerts and of course, bars—the list is endless. It is so easy to pass money openly, looking like an innocent customer. The missing girl may have become involved and then got in over her head, or she was a danger to their operation.'

'You think she could have come to some harm then?' He was remembering Alison's mother's instinctive fears that someone else had cleaned the flat to hide an abduction, or worse. 'Dee hasn't thought all this out yet.'

'Is she clean?'

'I'm as sure as I can be,' John said.

'I'll have to see her and she needs somewhere safer to stay. If drugs are involved in this . . . They'll step on anyone, you or the girl, if you become a danger.'

It wasn't cold in the car but John felt as if a cold draught was blowing on the back of his neck. He had faced threats before but mostly from a single person, and there could be a whole network behind the heavy mob.

'Perhaps Tollis could spare someone to keep an eye on her?' Jamieson said as if he had read John's thoughts. 'Get her back into town. The old maxim of safety in numbers is true. If she is one of a crowd with plenty of students around her and one of Tollis's men as back-up . . . We may be jumping to conclusions but better that than a costly mistake.'

He stopped outside Kramer House. 'I hope your missing girl just took a fancy to travel, especially if she offended someone. I'll phone and let you know when I can see that other girl.'

Tollis was out but John wanted some time on his own to think over what Jamieson had said anyway. He couldn't concentrate on the work that Val had left out for him and instead made notes on all that he knew about Peter Watson and Alison Baxter. He thought about the young barmaid, so confident that Vince, the manager of Ludo's could handle an awkward customer, and he wondered if the young man had discovered yet that a ton of bricks hung over his head like the sword of Damacles. Last of all there was Dee, vulnerable in the extreme. And he couldn't even be certain that she had told him all she knew. It was a bloody awful mess.

CHAPTER 6

It was almost a relief when Val put her head around his door. 'Can I have a word?'

'If you can rustle up some sandwiches and coffee. I've missed out on lunch again.'

She withdrew but was back moments later. 'I've sent one of the boys to the takeaway.'

She sat down and he sighed when he saw her serious expression. 'I don't need problems today, Val,' he said.

'It's more up Sentinel's street but Tollis is out and you need to know anyway. I had a call from the property management division about one of the new blocks in that owner-occupied development.'

He knew enough about his inherited company now to

understand what she was on about. 'We're the factors, right?'

She nodded and explained most of what he already knew. 'The contract is for management and we liaise with a committee formed by the residents, to deal with any problems with the common aspects, like repairs, lifts, gardens and all that sort of thing. We operate the budget raised by fees that the owners pay.'

'Mm. So what's gone wrong?'

'One of the flats has been broken into while the owner was abroad.'

'Don't tell me we cover the security angle as well?' he groaned.

'Not in that development. They have entry phones and the usual individual alarms just like any other private home but most of the residents are elderly, even if some of them are in the millionaire bracket.'

'Oh, it's that one.'

'As a matter of our own prestige, I thought Tollis might look into it. It did happen once before—not at this site though—and we found it was someone already resident in the block. There are also cleaners and we have to trust that the contractor knows his own staff, ditto for gardeners and other tradesmen.'

'As long as it's for prestige and not through any fault of ours.'

'No chance of that. The developers have heard about it though and suggested you might go there yourself, as a good relations exercise?'

The boy arrived with sandwiches and Val went to fetch fresh coffee and while she was gone he wondered why anyone in that income bracket should choose to live in a block of flats, no matter how luxurious they might be. He looked through the plans of the layout and then knew why Samuel Baxter's address had sounded familiar; he lived almost next door.

It turned out to be that sort of afternoon, with more problems to deal with. He had delegated much of the decision-making to the managers but it seemed they had worries to off-load and the buck stopped at him.

It was about 4.30 by the time he reached the café where Dee and her friends congregated after lectures and there was no sign of her in any of the booths. Then he spotted her getting out of an old Mini. It was multi-coloured, with a magenta body, but one wing and a door had been replaced and not yet sprayed. There were also pink daisy-like flowers stencilled on the bonnet.

Christ, he thought, if the mob wanted to find her, they would have no trouble if she drove that car. She didn't see him until she was close to the café.

'Hi. This is Julie—she's going to lend me her car.'

'I'm sorry, Julie, but Dee isn't going to need it after all,' he said.

'But it's all arranged,' Dee protested. 'I do need it.'

'Not any more,' he insisted. 'I'll explain later.'

Julie shrugged her shoulders philosophically as Dee handed back the car keys and went to join her friends inside the café. John took Dee's arm and steered her to his own car. 'We need to talk.'

She didn't say a word until she realized that he was heading for Elmwood. 'Has something happened?'

He repeated what Jamieson had said. 'It's because of the drugs connection, Peter Watson, and the fact that Alison may have been mixed up in it too. There's a chance that those men may come looking for you and they would find you very easily in that car. Jamieson also thinks you are too exposed travelling back and forward to town so I'm going to arrange somewhere else for you to stay.'

She didn't believe him. 'I don't know anything about all that so why should they bother me?' She didn't want him arranging her life either.

'I believe you, but these people won't take risks. As far as they are concerned, Alison and you were sharing a flat, and girls talk, exchange confidences. They won't believe that she didn't tell you all about it.'

'Well, she didn't. What am I supposed to do? Why don't

the police find her, or arrest somebody?' She had turned in her seat so that she was facing him and he could see she was angry, which was good. Better than being paralysed with fright.

'They will, but it will take time and until then I want to make sure you are safe.'

She screwed her eyes closed as if to shut out the frightening picture he was creating. 'I won't miss my lectures,' she said in a softly determined voice. 'I can't afford to fail a year because I'll never get the chance again. My mother works shifts, and I should be helping out with finances now. I have young brothers at school.' There was no self-pity in the words. 'I won't let these people spoil everything.'

'So let's do something about it,' he said.

'How?' It was a sign that she was prepared to listen at least.

'By not advertising yourself in that Mini for one thing. You might as well have held up a banner, saying "here I am."' He laughed. 'Daisies on the bonnet!'

Dee grinned. 'It is pretty eye-catching.'

'I'll sort something out,' he said, and she was quiet for a bit, subdued, and he thought what a rotten position she had landed in. None of it was her fault.

'Why are you doing this?' she asked suddenly. 'Why bother with Alison and me and Peter . . . and all the rest of it?'

He thought about that while a couple of cars overtook them. The rain had become a drizzle and the drive a pleasant one, relaxing after a trying day. 'Pretend I'm like Magnus Magnusson. What I start, I finish,' he said. 'Does that make sense?'

'I suppose so—it's why I'm determined to get my degree.'

'You'll have to put up with a minder,' he pointed out.

She made a face. 'Could you make it someone who won't be too obvious then?'

John had been thinking of Mike for the job. Tollis wouldn't object and he would certainly be reliable, but as for Mike being able to merge into the student scene . . .'

'You'll like him,' he said. 'We'll arrange accommodation in the morning, so pack your things tonight.'

And the best place would be a room in Mike's own home, if he agreed.

He phoned Tollis after supper that evening while the three women were chatting over cups of tea. Tollis was keen to know what Jamieson had said.

'I'll tell you that tomorrow. Right now I need to arrange some protection for Dee and wondered if you can spare Mike.'

'He's here. Ask him yourself.'

John explained the situation and asked if Dee could also have a room in his home for a spell.

'Would I need to sit in the classroom with her?' Mike sounded alarmed.

'No, just see that she gets there.'

'OK.' As usual Mike said only as much as he had to. 'Tollis wants a word.'

'What's it all about, John?'

'It stems from the talk I had with Jamieson and I'll explain tomorrow. It's a bit complicated.'

'So what's new?'

Shiela brought his tea to the study and closed the door behind her. 'Janet and I have been thinking of ways to help Dee, financially I mean, but she's prickly on the subject of money.'

'She won't wear that but I may be able to give her some part-time work when things settle down.'

Shiela looked relieved. 'That would be best. There's no sign of the missing girl then?'

'Not yet. I don't suppose you could help—there have been cases where psychics have helped find missing people in the past.' He had wondered how to broach the subject and now she had given him the opening.

'I know. In fact it has been on my mind but it's not something I've ever tried to do.' She looked uncomfortable.

'It's like having horns, if word got around I'd be treated like a freak.'

'It wouldn't get out of this house,' John assured her. 'Do you know how to go about it?'

She nodded. 'I've read documented cases. There was a gifted woman in Illinois who was part Cherokee Indian. In the 'sixties she helped solve fifteen murders and the police thought enough of her to present her with a plaque, but I have a feeling that it's unusual for police forces to welcome that sort of help in this country.'

'Not all that rare. The police wouldn't actively ask for a psychic's help but they wouldn't necessarily turn down the offer—I have heard about cases in this country and there's even a professor of parapsychology in Edinburgh University. That must prove it's not something to make fun of, that it's not all gobbledegook.'

'I know it's real, but try living with it,' she said with a nervous laugh. 'The power of the mind is untested but so many cases have been recorded—are you really interested?'

He nodded and she sat down opposite him.

'There was a case in Italy where a criminal was condemned to death and he was told that his artery would be opened so that he would bleed to death. They blindfolded him and then pricked his neck with a needle. At the same time they poured a stream of water from a jug and in six minutes his heart stopped beating, because he believed he was bleeding to death. In another case a young man died from mercuric poisoning but at the post-mortem they could find no sign of poison. The chemist had suspected the man was going to commit suicide and had given him common salt.'

'All right, you've convinced me of the power of the mind but it's not the same as foretelling the future or tracing missing people. How did the woman in Illinois trace the killers?'

'She chose a peaceful place and then held on to something belonging to the dead person, but she also found some diplomats who had been kidnapped. I don't know if I can do the same thing.'

He could see that she was struggling between a desire to help and the perhaps unwelcome discovery of her own powers.

'Don't do this unless you can live with it later,' he said and as she gazed steadily back at him, he began to have an inkling of how uncomfortable she was feeling.

'Do you have anything belonging to the missing girl?'

'The keys to her flat, and an address book,' he said quietly.

She nodded. 'Fetch them, but I want to be alone when I try this.'

He did as she asked and then closed the door of the study quietly behind him with a lot of misgivings. They were both dabbling in something they didn't really understand but Shiela was a level-headed woman and he had to trust her judgement.

It was fifteen minutes before she joined him in the sitting-room and he could tell from her expression that she had something to tell him.

'Before I say anything I want you to promise you'll not ask me to do that again,' she said. She was quite calm but there was pain in her eyes. 'I don't know the value of it anyway,' she went on.

'It can stop right now—don't tell me anything if that's what you want,' he said quickly, but Shiela shook her head.

'I got the feeling of turmoil, a life that was very mixed up. Then there was nothing . . . except great coldness, and water. I think the young girl is dead.'

He felt cold too, and full of remorse. 'She hinted at suicide,' he said but Shiela shook her head.

'That feels wrong.' She was standing, gripping the back of a chair but still calm. 'To be honest, I shut most of it out, but in a way I feel better now that I know what it's like. I just don't want to try it again. It's like tapping into God's work and we're not meant to do that.'

'Fair enough. We won't mention it again.'

She nodded, tight lipped at first but then smiling. 'Now I'd like a small scotch if you don't mind.'

'Good, I'll join you,' John said, rising to fetch two glasses.

He took a closer look at the address book after the others had gone to bed but there weren't many entries. Written in a neat, rounded hand, Peter's address was there and also Samuel Baxter's, which was near the 'Millionaire's Close' development, as it had been dubbed in the office. The area was pretty exclusive, of course, with large houses set back from the street and more than one car in the garages. It was the reason why the developers had chosen to build there and why the estate they had taken over had netted a million-plus for its owner. So Baxter must be in a high income bracket to have such an address.

Since his talk with Jamieson, the search for Alison would be hotting up and he decided to pass the address book over to the policeman in case any of the other names proved useful. He snapped it shut and put it with the keys to the flat in his jacket pocket, thinking about what Shiela had said. If she was right, Alison Baxter was dead, but how had it happened? And why? He went to bed knowing from experience that conjecture was pointless. The answers would only come after hours of patient investigation, and they were not always pleasant.

Thursday morning brought a chill dampness, a hint of the approaching November. *Dreich* was the word that said it all. Dee added a black scarf to her leather gear and wound it several times around her neck with the ends tucked inside. She was subdued as he put her bags in the car. Janet and Shiela waved them off.

'I can't see why you live in town when you've got a house like that,' Dee said candidly, swivelling round in her seat to take a last look. 'We had to take a flat when Dad died.'

Why did he put up with the small flat at the top of Kramer House? Why did Tollis sleep on a narrow bunk in the back room of the Sentinel offices? 'It's convenient,' he said, knowing it was an evasive answer.

'Where are we going then?'

'Mike Cairns is going to be looking after you for a bit and he has plenty of room at his place. He's in his fifties, quiet, and gentler than he looks. I won't worry about you if Mike has you in his sight.'

'You're worrying about me now?' She looked over at him with a smile tugging at her mouth.

'As if you were my kid sister,' he said in a mock serious tone.

Mike was apologetic that it was some time since he'd got around to housework but Dee looked relieved. 'Reminds me of home,' she said.

It was time to leave for her first lecture and John drove off at the same time, after reminding Mike that Jamieson would want to talk to Dee quite soon.

In the Sentinel offices, the men were being given their day's assignments. Most of the uniformed men had already left but others, wearing the gold insignia of the agency over their breast pockets, mingled with others dressed in suits, around the drinks machine. The girls who worked with the computers in an adjacent office were just arriving and Tollis was not fully dressed.

'Let me get this sorted out,' Tollis said, moving towards his own office, fielding questions and issuing orders as he went. He ran a tight ship even if he did give the impression of being laid-back and he continued pulling work sheets from the muddle on his desk until the last man knew what he was doing that day.

'Coffee,' he said over his shoulder as he reached for his razor from the top of a filing cabinet and began to shave at a mirror stuck to the wall in the back room. His laundry lay in a heap on the floor, ready for the girl who saw that he had a supply of fresh shirts and underwear. The window behind him was open, letting the cigarette fug out and the cold air in. A polystyrene box on the desk sent out a mouth-watering aroma of hot bacon on rolls.

'So what did you get from Jamieson?' he said as he poured a puddle of aftershave into one large hand, patted it on his chin and then wiped the excess on his cropped hair. He twanged his broad black braces on a crisp white shirt and then reached for the breakfast that never varied with a sigh of pleasure. John, who had seen it all many times before, poured the coffee into two mugs and took his to a chair. Tollis bit into a roll and waved a hand for him to continue.

'In a roundabout way, he wants you and the men to put out feelers about who might be behind the protection game. He says his men are thin on the ground and you are more likely to pick up the whispers.'

Tollis paused and then continued chewing but he didn't look happy. 'It's true, I suppose,' he said, wiping his hands together to get rid of the grease before throwing the carton in the direction of the waste basket. 'They meet men from other companies and rumours fly around about this and that. We already have an idea of who the cowboys are, but they're small operators. He must suspect a more organized outfit is in town.' He looked grim. 'That's bad news for everybody. What about the girl?'

'It's tied in with Alison Baxter, the missing girl. Her supposed boyfriend, Peter Watson, is into drugs, so she could be too. That means her flatmate, Dee, could be in danger. Jamieson thinks it's best to be careful instead of sorry later, so he said she should be looked after and moved to somewhere in town instead of staying at Elmwood.'

'It's an odd job for Mike to take on, and who's paying?'

'I suppose I am,' John said ruefully. 'And they'll get on all right. She was already treating him like a big teddy bear when they set off for the university. He'll drop her off and pick her up later so he'll be free to come back here in between.'

Tollis grunted, then went back to what Jamieson expected of him. 'And the trouble is that there's nothing illegal in what these cowboys are doing—the sooner they bring in a vetting system the better I'll like it.' He stood up and paced up and down with a thunderous expression. 'Of course I knew what was going on but it's a bloody nightmare for the honest firms. And Jamieson has no right to expect me to put my men in danger. I can't afford the time it takes anyway.'

'If only I could see the books of these places they're putting pressure on,' John said under his breath.

'Why? They're not likely to put protection payments through the ledgers.'

'No, but there are ways of looking at the signs behind the figures, like a drop in profit margins, sales falling off, increased insurance claims . . . If a manager of one of these places is in on the deal his lifestyle would change, an expensive car and holidays. But it's not likely that I'll get the chance to see their paperwork.'

Tollis looked interested but not hopeful. 'Even if you could do that the manager is not likely to admit he's getting a cut, and nor are the other poor sods who cooperate through fear.'

'So what about the other side, the men behind the rackets?'

Tollis snorted. 'Their books certainly won't show where the money comes from, mainly because they'll take cash from the takings. And no, I can't do a survey of all the firms in town and see who is living beyond his means!' He stopped pacing and sat on the edge of his desk. 'I'll get the men to keep their ears open, if that's what Jamieson wants.' He jabbed a finger at John. 'And you watch your step!'

After lunch John set off for the plush hotel where he was to meet Sam Baxter and as arranged gave his name to the man behind the bar. He settled down to wait with no preconceived ideas of the sort of man Alison's uncle was. It was not unusual for a man to lose touch with a dead brother's family, but he might have the odd scrap of information that would be useful. The hotel was the sort of place where businessmen could meet useful contacts and several groups drifted into the bar as he waited, greeted familiar faces and paused to tell of their latest moves up the ladder of success. One day he might even be expected to do the same, join the old-boys' network and grow fat on expenses. On the other hand, his uncle had done well enough and he'd shunned anything associated with entertaining.

John watched as a slim man with greying hair—Sam Baxter?—spoke to the barman who pointed John out and as the well-dressed man approached the corner where he sat, John noticed that he too stopped to greet acquaintances politely. His dark suit was conservative but shouted out that it had been hand-stitched with loving care. A slim gold watch showed under an inch of shirt cuff, heavy gold rings adorned his slender manicured fingers and the deference of the other occupants of the bar told John that he should feel honoured to be allowed ten minutes of Baxter's time.

'Mr Leith.' Baxter's fingers were cool, his handshake firm. He had the practised smile that John was getting used to since becoming part of the business scene. 'You now own Kramer Property, I hear.'

The man's adept research left John at a disadvantage since he had no idea what Baxter did and had a feeling that he should have found out before setting up this meeting.

'I never met your uncle but have heard of him, of course. What's this about my niece?'

He must have ordered drinks because two scotches were brought on a silver tray and no money changed hands. Baxter didn't even acknowledge the barman's presence.

'She's missing and your sister-in-law asked me to try to trace her.'

Baxter was puzzled and John had to go through the usual routine of explaining his connection with the Sentinel Agency.

'Interesting—if you can spare the time. Well, I'm afraid I can't help you. To be honest, my brother and I didn't keep in touch and I hardly know his widow. As for the girl, she was quite small the last time I saw her. That was at my brother's funeral.'

And Baxter was not the type to welcome family ties, John guessed. In many ways Baxter was like his uncle, Rees Kramer. All the signs were there, of a man hiding behind a façade that shut out close contact, or perhaps it was the veneer of the successful businessman who was used to keeping a poker face. Whatever, John knew he was wasting his time.

'Then I'm sorry to have troubled you,' he said, reaching for the scotch and taking a sip.

'Not at all, I am interested. She is my niece, after all, and if there is anything I can do . . . Marjorie will be upset and I expect the fees for an investigation must be quite a strain for her. Please send me your account.' It was all quickly said, a promise to fulfil a duty that Baxter would carry out as long as it didn't draw him in too deeply. He leaned forward slightly. 'Tell me, how do you go about the business of tracing people?'

'By asking questions of relatives and friends for a start,' John said.

Baxter settled back, nodding. 'Of course, and in this case I believe I'm the only relative. And have you made any progress?'

There was something belittling in the man's attitude that John didn't like but he'd met it before, from his own managers when he took over Kramers, and every time he visited his father-in-law.

'Yes,' he said evenly. Then he looked beyond Baxter, to a couple of men weaving their way through the small tables. One was the bearded man who had sat at Ludo's bar reading his newspaper, who had argued with the manager. The man he and Ian had followed around several bars.

Baxter was waiting for him to explain further.

'There are some leads still to follow up,' he said, aware that the two men were drawing closer, heading for a table close by. Then Baxter saw them and nodded politely.

'Ken. That was a good round of golf—pity the weather has broken down.' He introduced the man to John. 'Ken Harper, the golf professional at the club I use. Mr Leith of

Kramer Property, although at the moment he is acting as an investigator.' He made it sound comic, that anyone should *want* to be a private investigator.

Harper, an open-faced man with none of the panache of Baxter, looked only vaguely interested but his bearded companion was looking at John with a puzzled expression that said 'Haven't I seen you somewhere before?'

Harper brought him into the group. 'Ron Driver,' he said. 'I'm trying to interest him in the new golf course proposal. Nice to meet you, Mr Leith.' They moved away and Baxter looked at his watch. 'Time,' he said regretfully. 'It rules my life.' He began to get up but first knocked back the scotch in one gulp. He paused, bent forward.

'Remember the account—send it to me.'

Then he was gone, moving through the tables, repeating the polite greetings and John knew he didn't give a damn about his missing niece. As for the account, he would certainly receive that, which would at least bring some joy to Mrs Baxter.

'Christ,' he muttered as he fought the gale that always seemed to funnel through the gully that separated the new and old parts of Edinburgh, battering anyone brave enough to cross North Bridge. Would Driver remember that the last time they met, it had been shoulder to shoulder in Ludo's bar, where he'd been asking questions? Would he also be alarmed now that the word 'investigator' had been fixed on him like a badge? Baxter had introduced him as being 'of Kramer Property' as well, and it wouldn't take the man long to find out that Sentinel was in the same building. John tried to remember what questions he'd asked the barmaid that evening, when Driver was listening. He had mentioned being in the bar when the fight broke out the previous evening—would that bother the man? And Harper was trying to interest Driver in a new golf development, so the man must have money to invest. 'How did he come by that, I wonder?' he muttered.

He rounded the corner knowing that he might soon find out how good Driver's memory was. And Tollis would not be pleased if Sentinel was now involved in open hostilities with a man connected with the protection rackets, which Ron Driver almost certainly was.

CHAPTER 7

Mrs Baxter phoned just after six, when he was about to call it a day, not that he had achieved much that afternoon. He'd been reconsidering Sam Baxter's uncaring attitude about his missing niece, and wondering if perhaps the man was afraid of a scandal or even resented being questioned by an outsider.

He got the distinct feeling that Baxter had only agreed to see him because he owned Kramer Property and if he'd simply been a private investigator he wouldn't have got anywhere near the man. As it turned out, Baxter knew nothing about Alison and probably didn't want to.

When John heard Mrs Baxter's voice, his first thought was that her brother-in-law had got on to her to complain about the investigation, but he was wrong. She didn't know anything about the meeting.

'I wondered if there was any news,' she said. 'The police came back to ask more questions today but they haven't made any progress either.'

'Nor have I, Mrs Baxter.' Poor woman. She'd given her daughter a taste for frills and all the good things in life and she didn't have any idea of the existence the spoiled girl had led.

'Peter phoned too, in a state.'

'Did he mention where he was calling from?'

'No, I assumed he was at home. He's quite in the dark, Mr Leith, and he sounded desperate with worry.'

'Did he?' If Watson was at his flat right now . . . 'When did he call?'

'About an hour ago. It's what made me ring you. Poor lad, I hadn't realized he and Alison were so close.'

'I'll speak to him and I'll get back to you as soon as I know anything,' John promised. He hung up. Watson had said Alison had got him into trouble and now he was desperate to know if there was any news of her. Perhaps his drug dealing friends were putting pressure on him over something that Alison had done—but what? Run off with his stock, or the cash to pay for the last delivery? If only he could be persuaded to name some names . . .

John tried to contact DCI Jamieson but he was not in his office and when he tried Mike's number, he discovered that Jamieson had not yet made an appointment to see Dee. 'How did the escort duty go today?'

'No problems,' Mike said. 'I just saw Dee as far as the door and picked her up afterwards. You sound a bit uptight. Anything happening?'

'Maybe. There's a chance that Peter Watson has surfaced and I'm off to have a chat with him.'

Mike didn't like the sound of that. 'I could tag along. The girl's safe enough here.'

John hesitated. 'You'd better stay put in case Jamieson does turn up. She'll want you there.'

Mike grunted. 'Phone me when you get back and let me know how you got on.'

John went up to his flat and put on an old pair of jeans, trainers and a zipped jacket, all in sombre colours that wouldn't draw attention to him in the area where Watson lived. The Sentinel man on the door knew exactly what car he needed and gave him the keys to a Lada. The body was scruffy and dented because it was one of the cars the men sometimes used in surveillance work. 'And if you have to leave it for any length of time, it's not likely to be nicked,' the man said with a grin.

It was after eight by the time he reached the block of flats where a group of boys were playing football in the street. He hunched his shoulders up around his neck in case any of the youths recognized him; he didn't want to risk them running ahead and warning Watson that he was coming.

There was no need for caution as he climbed the steps

inside the building since most of the lights had been vandalized and he was in darkness. The close was deserted and the shouts from the football game drowned the sound of his footsteps. He rang Peter Watson's doorbell and waited but there was no answer. Maybe he hadn't called Mrs Baxter from the flat at all. Then it occurred to John that Watson might be afraid to come to the door. He crouched down and looked through the letterbox and saw a dim light at the end of the passageway. Once more he rang the bell and this time kept his finger on it.

After a few minutes, the door opened a crack, just far enough for him to see half the man's face.

'What do you want?'

'Just a few minutes of your time,' John said.

Watson mumbled and shook his head. He began to close the door but John stuck his foot forward to prevent him. Angry that Watson was being deliberately obstructive, he was determined to force his way in if need be.

'I have to talk to you,' he said, putting his weight against the stained paintwork of the door and suddenly Watson stepped back and allowed him inside. The first thing he noticed was the smell of stale sweat from the man's body. John was much the taller of the two but Watson was walking in a crouching stumble, as if he was ill. As they neared the faint light coming from the room he also saw that Watson was unshaven, and his clothes were filthy. In fact, he looked as if he hadn't washed or changed his clothes for days and John wondered if he'd been hiding in the flat since the previous Sunday.

'You shouldn't be here,' Watson muttered as he pushed open the door of what turned out to be a living-room. The curtains were drawn and the only light came from an oil lamp. 'The power's been cut off,' Watson explained. The room was dirty, smelled of stale air and Watson's unwashed body. It was very cold. Watson, looking decidedly uneasy, stood near a settee on which there was a heap of bedding. There was something very wrong in the way he was staring at John, who realized too late that the man was terrified.

No sooner had the thought registered than he was aware that they weren't alone in the flat. Two men stepped from another room and as they came forward, Watson edged away to stand by the wall.

'Who are you?' one asked. 'And what do you want with him?' He jerked his head in Watson's direction.

And immediately the young man began to babble an explanation, as if to placate his other visitors. 'He was at the bar the other night too, asking questions about Alison,' he said.

'Was he now?' The man moved closer and the other slipped around to cover the door. 'What else did he want to know?'

'About the fight. He told the barmaid that he'd been there when it happened,' Watson said.

A new voice interrupted as a third man came from the kitchen. 'He was at the girl's flat too,' he said, and as he came closer into the dim light, John recognized the younger intruder who had burst in on him and Dee. This man looked with disgust at a stained chair and he brushed it with a hand before sitting on the edge of it.

'So why come looking for our Peter? You wanted to ask him something maybe?' He smiled, in charge of the situation and a lot more confident than he had been the last time they met when he only had 'Tam' to back him up. Tonight his two companions were big men, tough. They were waiting to see what developed and John had an uncomfortable feeling about what that would be.

'I told you Alison's mother was worried about her,' he said calmly enough. 'Dee said Peter might know where she'd gone, so I came to check it out.'

The man listened, eyes narrowed. 'Check it out? You get around, don't you. Asking questions at the flat, the bar—where else I wonder?'

John shrugged as casually as he could considering his body was stiff with tension. 'Alison's mother came to the flat and spoke to Dee. I was just trying to help.' He could see the other two men on the edge of his vision but he deliberately didn't look at them.

'We still don't know your name, pal.'

'Leith.'

The man turned to the other two. 'Ring any bells?'

Both shook their heads but said nothing. Watson was still half crouched, resting his head against the wall and holding his gut as if he was in pain.

'Got any proof, a wallet?'

John reached inside his jacket and brought it out. Before leaving Kramer House he had removed everything except one credit card and a few notes, more because of the risk of mugging than from foresight of this happening.

'Leith, right enough,' the man said but he wasn't satisfied. 'You dress like a student but you're a bit old aren't you?'

Once more Watson burst out with more information.

'He doesn't always look like that—he wore a suit when he came to the bar and he was with one of the regulars, a lawyer.'

The seated man smiled at that but didn't appreciate the interruption.

'Shut him up—or better still get him away out of here. Graham, you know where he's to be delivered.'

The man called Graham didn't look keen to take Watson anywhere. 'Do your own dirty work, Benson—I'm not paid to be a babysitter.'

That dented Benson's confidence somewhat but after a small hesitation he re-issued the order. 'You'll do as I say or you won't be paid at all.'

Was the hired help resenting Benson's attitude, John wondered, or was Benson angry because the man had given away his name? Whatever, Graham took hold of Watson and pulled him towards the door. Watson whined but put up little resistance as he was led away, and John felt a trickle of sweat run down between his shoulder blades. He knew that no matter what he said, Benson would not be satisfied. He was the type who believed that the truth was never volunteered, and he would enjoy beating the answers from his victims—as had probably already happened to Watson before he arrived—and the seated man would feel cheated if the answers came too easily.

The door closed behind Watson and his escort and the three who were left in the room heard their footsteps reach the front door of the flat. Then it too closed.

'Now maybe we'll find out what else you know,' Benson said. 'Where's the other girl, Dee Oakley? Got her tucked away somewhere have you?'

'Look, what is this? I told you before, Dee's my girl.' John played innocent, but even as he finished speaking he saw that Benson wasn't going to accept his answer.

'Cooky,' the seated man said, flicking his fingers, and John felt a blow from what felt like a club across his shoulder blades. He took a staggering step forward and the man called Cooky drew back his arm again as John continued moving forward to duck the next swing that would have landed higher up. He looked around for a weapon or something to defend himself with but took another numbing blow across his ribs. He felt the skin split and a warm trickle of blood ran down his side. For the moment that was to be all and there was a breathing space while Benson thought out the next move.

'Take your clothes off,' he said, grinning. His right leg was swinging but under the casual pose his body was tense with excitement.

'No,' John said.

That didn't bother the smaller man. 'Cooky here can make you do anything in the end,' he said calmly and Cooky demonstrated how clever he was with the baton. It was on a leather thong around his wrist and as he swung it, it made a whining sound, and sent a wave of disturbed air in John's direction. When it landed on the settee a cloud of dust rose into the already musty air. The boys out in the street were still playing, laughing and shouting and it was a shocking normality compared to what was happening in the flat above them.

'Where's the girl?' Benson was growing impatient and as he moved to stand up John aimed a kick at his groin. His trainers were old, the toecaps softened, but even so the force of the kick and the tenderness of his target, was enough to double the man up. He cursed and groaned as he went down on his knees on the floor.

It became confused after that because Cooky was fast on his feet and the club landed on target more than once. The man's strength was frightening and the thong on his wrist allowed him to drop the club while he used his massive hands to jerk John back from the door. Then, with a flick of his wrist he could jerk the leather strap and swing the club, which resembled a baseball bat, back into his hand. At one point John threw a chair but it missed its target and broke the window. The curtains prevented it going into the street although he heard the glass splinters land in a tinkling sound that was almost musical. Futile, he thought. It might draw attention, but nobody would react to a window breaking, not in that area.

A tackle from Cooky brought him to the floor and he tried to use the settee as a shield, rolling to avoid blows and by now Benson was back on his feet and trying to use them. Both men were shouting, cursing at him and it could only have one ending. They were no longer bothering to ask questions, but were kicking in anger, trying to club him. Furniture was toppled and sometimes the other two got in each other's way but he knew that if he was cornered it would be all over. It soon was when he took a solid blow on the back of his head and passed out cold.

They were gone when he woke up but they had tied his hands behind his back and a loop ran down to cords around his ankles so that his body was bowed. The bonds were tight and there was no way he could reach the knots to release himself. They didn't mean him to escape and probably they intended to come back after they'd reported his presence and received fresh orders. He didn't know how long he had been unconscious but he was cold and he couldn't feel his hands or his feet. How much time did he have?

The boys in the street had gone home to bed and all was quiet. He lifted his shoulders so that his face was no longer in the filthy carpet and then rolled on to his side. He got the fright of his life when he saw two yellowish green eyes looking at him out of the gloom. A cat. It came closer, sniffing delicately at the mouldering crumbs on the floor and then it settled down with its body lying close to his chest. After a little while he felt the heat from its body, it purred as it twitched its mangled ears, the yellow eyes blinked and it went to sleep.

Time passed and a cold draught came through the broken window. He felt something nip at his neck and knew that the mangy cat had fleas. Somehow it was the final degradation, worse than the knowledge that he'd walked right into this like a novice. And he was in pain now, with the tendons of his arms and legs over-stretched, and a nagging ache in his shoulder joints that was getting worse by the minute. The blows he'd taken would no doubt add to his discomfort later but for the moment they were the least of his worries. The thought of rolling around to look for something sharp to cut his bonds was horrendous, but the kitchen wasn't so far away.

'Sorry, puss, but I've got to try,' he told the cat. It was ginger and black, a real moggy, and looked as if it had survived many battles. 'So move I must.'

The cat protested and slunk away into the shadows as he tried the first manœuvre. He missed its warmth but not its fleas. He remembered promising Mike that he would phone to say how he had got on and by now Mike would be concerned but that would be no help. Neither Mike nor Dee knew where Peter Watson lived.

He made small progress and that only came from rocking movements. He was also hampered by the toppled furniture which left little space in the cramped room, but at least his body warmed with the effort. The urgency, created by fear that the two men would come back, made him keep trying but it was exhausting. Sweat ran freely as he gained an inch or two towards the kitchen but every movement put a strain on the cord connecting his wrists to his feet and sent his muscles into cramps. They knotted in agony and he rested, gasping, close to crying out. The cramps eased and he forced himself to move again, worried about the tightness of the bonds that had cut off the circulation in his hands and feet which felt dead.

The night outside was still, with only a light wind ballooning the curtains and sucking them back into the hole in the glass. His ears strained for the sound of a returning car and when one did approach he held his breath. Would it pass by?

It stopped and he heard its door closing and then feet moved along the pavement, the feet of one person. Never had he felt so helpless as he heard the same feet coming up the concrete steps.

The outer door opened, then the door to the room where he was. One of the bully boys came closer and stood looking down at him, grim-faced. It was the one who had left with Peter Watson. All their names were etched into his brain, Benson, Cooky and this one they'd called Graham. No doubt they'd sent him back to finish the job.

'Christ, man,' Graham said at last. He stood there for a moment longer, as if undecided and then walked towards the kitchen. John heard him opening drawers and then he came back with a knife, bent down and cut the cords. The relief was indescribable and the solicitous expression totally unexpected. John lay where he was for a moment as he felt his legs stretch out on the floor and the agonizing bow of his body found relief. It didn't last however, because when he tried to push himself up, his hands refused to work.

'Here,' the man said, reaching down to put his hands under John's armpits.

There was no feeling in his feet and he felt angry that now he was free he couldn't walk out of the bloody flat.

'Where's your motor?' the man asked.

'At the end of the street, but it might as well be on the moon,' John told him.

'Have to be mine then,' Graham said. And he hauled John towards the door.

'Don't shut the cat in,' John muttered and Graham gave an incredulous laugh.

'Don't worry about him. He streaked past as soon as I opened the door. He's a survivor.'

'Makes two of us tonight,' John said as he was almost carried out of the flat and down the stairs with his feet dragging behind him. They made quite a bit of noise but no one came to investigate. Half way down the stairs his rescuer paused to catch his breath and reposition his arms around John's waist, draped one of John's arms across his shoulder. He was panicky and soon hurried onwards.

'They'll kill both of us, mate,' he gasped. 'Don't ever forget what I'm doing for you tonight.'

'Why are you?' John asked.

'Ask me some other time will you? Right now I'm not even sure myself.'

On the pavement, John insisted on trying to stand for himself but his legs seemed to end just below his knees and if Graham hadn't caught him he would have fallen over. In the end the man had to stuff him into the car like a sack, pushing at his legs, tucking his feet in before slamming the car door. And John looked down at his hands which were swollen, the fingers like white sausages. Graham looked too and shook his head.

'You're going to suffer when they come to life,' he said. 'Now let's get the hell out of here—where are we going?'

John thought about the public effort of getting into Kramer House and gave Mike's address. The man nodded, he knew where to go.

'Why then? Why come back?' John asked.

There was no answer for a while and when it did come there were no real details. 'Let's just say I was desperate for a job and when you've got a record you don't get many choices.' He was silent for a bit and then went on. 'I knew what I was getting into but when it got right down to it—tonight was the first time for this sort of thing. They make you prove yourself, see?'

'Who gave you the job?' John had to grind out the words because feeling was beginning to return to his numb limbs and he knew it was only an hint of what was to follow. The man's answer was soft and negative.

'Now that far I won't go. You just forget you ever saw me and all the rest of what happened. Keep out of their way and count yourself lucky.'

'Well, thanks then,' John said and the man nodded. He had been employed because of his record—that much he admitted—and for his size. Now that John could get a good look at him he saw a heavy man in his early forties, the sort who was often propped against bars all over the city. He was big but flabby, poorly dressed and with a dragging at the corners of his mouth that spoke of disillusion with life. A loser who had probably just lost another job.

The car slowed as John pointed out Mike's house and when the car came to a stop Graham looked reluctant to go further. 'I'll get you to the door but I'm not hanging about—all right?'

'Anything you say,' John answered wearily. His feet were still not working and it was another humiliating manœuvre getting him the few yards to Mike's door. Lights came on and shone through the top glass panel and by the time the door was opened, Graham was already heading back to his car, leaving John propped against the stone wall.

Mike, who was still fully dressed, didn't ask questions after that first look. He muttered a lot of swear words as he got John to the bedroom and more as he stripped off his clothes as gently as a mother soothing a hurt child.

'You should have a long hot soak in the bath, but not until those are back to normal.' He nodded at John's hands and feet, and the deep grooves left by the tight cords that had cut into the flesh. 'No scotch either—it would make it worse than it's going to be.' Mike put a quilt over him and then stood looking down at him. 'I can give you a couple of strong painkillers but . . . sorry, you'll just have to suffer it out.' The tablets came with a glass of cold water and after John had swallowed them Mike left him on his own.

There was heat at first, an agonizing burning, and it felt as if the skin was going to burst as blood tried to enter vessels that had been deprived. His hands and feet throbbed with a deep pulsing pain that had him writhing on the bed and it went on and on. The darkness helped and the fact that there was no one to see, which Mike had tactfully realized. Then there was a stabbing that felt like a thousand needles and he almost cried out. Sweat poured from his body and in front of his eyes was the image of Benson's face, grinning. He aimed all his anger at the face.

It seemed hours before the pain eased enough for him to think of leaving the bed. His extremities were still swollen and tender but when he tried to stand there was enough sensation for him to feel the carpet under his feet. He fumbled into the dressing-gown that hung behind the door and hobbled out of the room in search of the coffee he could smell.

'How come Bill Graham brought you home?' Mike asked as they sat in the small kitchen.

'He just turned up.' John explained what had happened from the moment he got to Watson's flat. 'He was told to take Watson away from the flat so he wasn't around when they got a bit active with their feet and a club. Then he came back. Do you know him?'

Mike nodded. 'He was a copper but got thrown out for stealing. Drink was his problem.When he was sent to shops that had been broken into he helped himself to some of the stock—spirits mostly. Tollis gave him a job, on trial, but even then he couldn't resist helping himself to somebody's wallet. Later he did time for the same sort of thing and the last I heard he was bumming around.'

'Ideal employee for anyone needing some muscle then,' John said. 'He told me he was expected to prove himself.'

'Well, he failed again, only this time he'd better be able

to talk himself out of it. His new employers have their own way of dealing with anyone who disobeys orders.'

'He must have some conscience left,' John said. 'He may have saved my life.'

'Huh,' Mike grunted.

They had wakened Dee and she looked scared when she came into the kitchen. 'You've got blood on your face. Did this happen because of me?'

John almost shook his head but decided it might fall off if he did.

'He'll clean up all right,' Mike said. 'He was just in the wrong place at the wrong time.'

She went back to bed, only slightly reassured. John wished he had thought to ask Bill Graham where he'd taken Watson.

'So who were they?' Mike asked, pouring fresh coffee into mugs. He was still fully dressed although it was four in the morning.

'One was called Cooky—his surname may be Cook. Benson was one of the ones who came to the flat the night I brought Dee away. They wanted to know where Dee was. She's not safe while she's in Edinburgh, Mike.'

Mike agreed. 'I've already talked her into going home for the weekend. Her mother lives in Stirling.' He raised his head and looked steadily at John. 'You're not so safe yourself. Benson will go back and report that someone called Leith has been bobbing up all over the place and if they concentrate their minds it won't be long before they find out who you are and where you live.'

And Ron Driver, who was in some sort of supervisory role in the protection rackets, had been told he was a private investigator. Mike's painkillers were still dulling down the pain but they were also making his brain sluggish. He couldn't forget the pony-tailed Watson being led from the flat. 'What will they do to Watson?' he said and Mike shrugged.

'Depends what he's been up to. I wouldn't like to be in his shoes.'

'Do you know where Bill Graham hangs around? He must know a lot more than he was ready to give away.'

'We'll find him. You need some sleep. I'll leave out another couple of pills but don't take them unless you have to.'

He slept until mid-morning and then came instantly awake. He tried a few experimental moves and although his body felt as if someone had jumped on it while wearing hiking boots, it was all quite tolerable. Nothing snapped and fell off, nor did he creak as he slid out of bed. His hands and feet felt tender but now it was the bruises that were making themselves felt. On the bedside table there was a brief note from Mike. 'Taking Dee to her classes, back soon.'

There was a lack of mirrors in the bedroom which was just as well because what he could see of his body was not a pretty sight. Exploring, he found the bathroom and then stood under the shower, letting the needles of hot water act like a massage. When Mike arrived back he was in the kitchen, wrapped in a bath towel.

'I made Dee promise not to leave the building today. She's going to stick with the crowds and eat in the university café. And I collected some things from your flat on the way back,' Mike said, dropping an armful of clothing on a chair. 'Your other stuff can be dumped—did you know you had fleas?'

He moved with familiarity around his kitchen and soon had a pan of bacon and eggs on the go. 'Stiff?' he asked once.

'Not as bad as I expected.'

'Those pills help. They really knock you out and the muscles relax, but don't get over confident,' and he grinned as if he spoke from experience.

'Just work out how we can nail the men who did it, and the others behind them,' John said as they ate. 'I don't intend waiting around while they come looking for me. I'd rather do the hunting, especially for the one called Benson.'

CHAPTER 8

He got dressed and blessed Mike's choice of a tracksuit which was easy to slip into. There was also a short leather jacket, the same one that he'd worn the night the men burst into the flat. In the corner of one pocket was the screwed up piece of paper he'd found behind Alison Baxter's dressing table. He smoothed it out and at first glance it didn't seem important.

'What's that?' Mike said, looking over his shoulder.

'Looks like a receipt for membership of a club, one of those healthy places where they have a swimming pool and a gym.'

'Clan Royal—that's pretty exclusive. They offered Sentinel a company discount but even that worked out at over a hundred quid a man.'

There was no clue to who had paid the full amount on the receipt but at a guess it must have been Alison and it was one more pointer that she was getting far more cash than she earned at the dress shop. He folded the receipt carefully and put it back in his pocket. He and Mike headed for the door, but something about the receipt had registered and he had another look at it.

'Look,' he said, pointing to the scrolled heading that said 'Clan Royal'. Below the elaborate print was a line of smaller print that said 'subsidiary of the Alco Leisure Group'. 'That badge I sketched for Jamieson, the one worn by the man who was in the fight at Ludo's . . . it had the letters A and L on it. Let's stop off in George Street on the way to Kramer House. I want to do a bit of research on these two companies.'

The town centre was busy with the usual Friday shoppers, who were not put off by the heavy skies or the forecast of more bad weather on the way. For the moment the rain was holding off and the city looked fresh and newly-washed after an earlier shower. John couldn't help feeling fortunate to be alive to enjoy it.

They were lucky to find a parking slot almost outside the building that housed the Register of Companies but were not totally successful once they got inside.

'You can look up part of what you want to know on the microfiche that's open to the public,' John was told. 'But the Persons' Index is in another part of the building and you can't get access to that. You'll have to phone in a request to the Search department for the rest of what you want to know.'

Fair enough, he thought, scanning the fiche for Clan Royal and then Alco Leisure. Ron Driver's name came up as a director of both companies along with several others whose names rang no bells. 'We'll note them down anyway, then we'll get back,' he said to Mike.

They split up once inside Kramer House, with Mike going to see if Tollis was in and John taking the lift instead of the stairs because he was feeling fragile. He passed a few of his people in the corridor and got sidelong glances because of the tracksuit. Val too followed him with her eyes but he headed straight for his own room and the telephone. He dialled the number of the building they had just left and asked for the Search Department.

'Can you tell me which companies have a director called Ronald Driver?' There was quite a wait before the answer came and he heard Alco Leisure and Clan Royal, as before, but then came four others, all security firms that had recently been set up.

'Thank you very much,' he said, hanging up. In a way it had been too easy and he remembered Garek's warning that Mr Big would be well hidden, which meant that Driver was probably the front man. The sudden rush of adrenalin faded and he felt his bruises, his stiff muscles, and the fingers and toes that were still reminding him to move with care.

'Are you getting 'flu? You look terrible,' Val said, putting her head around his door. Sympathy was never a strong point with Val, however, and he got the feeling she was more concerned that the company should be kept running smoothly.

'Maybe,' he said. 'I'll be around but not very active for a couple of days.' She withdrew without commenting that she was quite used to his inactivity as far as Kramer's was concerned. He decided to go down to Sentinel and face Tollis who would not be pleased with him either. Maybe the rest of the day would improve.

Before he left his office he went to release a blowfly that had got trapped in the room and was banging its body against the glass of the window. He had a lot of sympathy with it after his experience of the night before, and as he held the window open, the first drops of rain hit his sleeve. They were being made to pay for the spell of good weather.

'I hear you cut it pretty fine last night,' Tollis said drily. 'And Mike tells me it was Bill Graham who got you out.'

'He was for dropping John off and scarpering but he obviously didn't know who's doorbell he was ringing—I knew him even from behind,' Mike said.

Tollis was deep in thought and he lit a cigarette absent-mindedly. A sudden splatter of rain on the window seemed to bring him out of it.

'You know, Bill Graham could be another way into the organization,' he said. 'He's often been spotted around town and some of the men will know his usual haunts.'

'I wouldn't want to put him in danger,' John said, thinking of the man's sweating efforts to get him out of the block of flats. 'I may owe him my life.'

'There's no need to feel sorry for him,' Tollis said. 'He's one slippery customer and he'll squirm his way out of this. He must have known what sort of job he was being asked to do and he may not always be so squeamish. He's an alcoholic and he'll do anything for beer money.'

'All the same,' John insisted. 'He didn't have to come back for me.'

Tollis made an 'if you say so' gesture. 'So we'll have a

word with him on the quiet. He was a policeman once, so maybe there are some things he won't do and some of the training must have stuck. He'll have noted things that could be useful. We have to find out where he took Watson anyway.'

That all sounded very positive to John but Mike added a cloud. 'He can't escape some questioning from his bosses though, can he? By now they know John got out of the flat and they're going to start wondering how he managed that.'

'Bill isn't likely to admit he went back,' Tollis said.

'I hope you're right. Depends on how they put the questions, doesn't it?'

All three of them were silent and Tollis rubbed his hands over his face.

'You have a point. Let's see how it adds up. They got John's name last night when he turned up looking for Watson, and Driver knows he's with Kramer's, thanks to Baxter's introduction—and that he is sometimes an investigator—if they add that up it equals working for Sentinel because of the proximity of our two firms.'

'Driver may not remember where he saw me first, but if he does, he knows I was asking questions in Ludo's *and* that I was there the night before when the fight took place.'

'And Benson knows you were in Alison Baxter's flat, and soon afterwards Dee went out of circulation.' Tollis was shaking his head. 'You really do get about, don't you?'

'Look what came from it though,' John said, handing over the list of companies on which Ron Driver was a director. Tollis studied them and began to smile.

'What next then?—Jamieson should know about this,' Mike put in, but Tollis shook his head.

'It's not going to prove much, is it? It's not a crime to be a director. And Jamieson is bound by the rules of Scottish law. He can't hold anyone more than six hours and once he releases a man he can't bring him back in for questioning on the same inquiry. The police never rely on confessions either, so Jamieson needs hard evidence before he can pull anyone in, but having said that, it's up to him to get it.'

'Couldn't you put some of your own men on to watching Driver then?' John suggested. 'He and Mr Big have got to confer at some point.'

Tollis didn't look keen but they discussed the chances that there would be actual contact between Driver and the man who provided the financial backing and who also reaped the bulk of the rewards.

'If he's so bloody careful, it's more than likely they use the phone,' Tollis said gloomily.

For some reason Mike was grinning. 'We could keep an eye on him openly,' he said. 'Do you remember that case . . . ? Can't remember the name of the bloke but Jamieson said that what we did almost amounted to harassment—not that he seriously objected at the time because it got results.'

Tollis was nodding. 'We sat on his tail for three days and let him see us.' He turned to John. 'Every move he made, we were there too. He got quite ratty.'

'You think that would work with Driver?'

'Mm. This one is different. Driver has some rough friends. What do you think, Mike?'

The two men looked at each other and as if their thoughts were telepathic, both smiled. 'For a day. Let him wake up to us on his doorstep, just to let him know we care,' Mike said. 'It wouldn't work for longer than that but it might make him jumpy. And in the meantime John will have to keep a low profile.'

'Oh, no. I'm the one he knows. He's got my name now so he might as well see me when he opens his curtains in the morning. And you can't do it anyway because you promised to take Dee home to Stirling tomorrow, to keep her out of the way for the weekend.'

It was arranged that Mike would take the late shift, covering Driver—if he could tag on to him on his pub crawl—that evening and John would take over early the next morning.

'No risks though. It may sound like jolly fun to taunt Driver but it isn't a game,' Tollis warned.

John headed back to his office and skimmed the paperwork Val had left out for him. She was carrying most of the load but she wasn't complaining, which convinced him that in promoting her to be overall manager, he had made a good choice. In fact, she was blooming with the added responsibility.

He phoned Garek in the late afternoon and read him the list of companies that Driver was connected with. 'Have you heard of any of them?' He wasn't sure Tollis would approve of sharing confidences with Gumley's man but Garek knew all about the protection rackets and how they worked.

'The health club,' Garek said. 'I know two of the members and could get passes for us as visitors if you are interested. It may serve no purpose—Driver might not be there—but I might see some familiar faces.'

It sounded a bit like jumping into a bear pit but it wasn't all that different to what Mike was proposing to do—show your face, tantalize, taunt the opposition . . . as long as you could draw back to safety in time. A health club couldn't be all that dangerous, with wealthy clients floating around.

'Leave it with me. I will arrange it,' Garek said.

There had been no word from Jamieson, although he'd promised to make an appointment to speak to Dee. When he still hadn't phoned by six, John decided to go up to his flat with the intention of a long soak in a hot bath before going in search of something to eat. In the event, Jamieson was coming up the stairs to the office as John left it.

'I'm off for the weekend,' Jamieson said. 'I thought you might come for a drink and then we could go together to see Miss Oakley.'

'As long as food is included.'

Jamieson had looked at him with narrowed eyes as he walked towards the stairs. 'I've seen people move like that before,' he said. 'How bad is it?'

John pulled up the tracksuit at the waist and the policeman winced when he saw the bruising, as if he too could feel the pain.

'Somewhere quiet then, where we can talk,' Jamieson said. 'And you can tell me what you've been up to now.'

The rain was a steady downpour now and since the policeman had left his car parked at the door, they went in that. He had already eaten so he waited until John finished his meal before pushing for explanations. He listened attentively, without commenting, until John had finished.

'Where is Watson now?'

'We don't know.' He hadn't mentioned that he knew who his rescuer was, nor the plans for harassing Driver. Somehow he couldn't bring himself to name Bill Graham and he didn't think Jamieson would approve of how they planned to put pressure on the man fronting the protection racket.

Jamieson had said little and was thoughtful as they left the restaurant to drive towards Mike's place in Newington to interview Dee. Turning up past the shops on the Bridges he asked if Dee was being looked after. 'She may know nothing but these men won't take chances on that. We could bring them in but there will be others we don't know about yet.'

Before John could answer, the car radio which had been relaying messages to various patrol cars, suddenly produced one for Jamieson himself. He reached for the mike. 'Jamieson here.'

'We've got a body, sir. A young woman in Duddingston Loch.'

'On my way,' Jamieson said. He glanced at John. 'I could drop you off here but it's a filthy night. No time to go back I'm afraid—that's a nature reserve and I don't want them trampling around until I see what's what. You can just sit in the car when we get there.'

Jamieson hadn't really given him a choice because already they were swinging past the Commonwealth Swimming Pool and into the Queens Park, site of the royal palace. He knew the area well because it was where he did his running—not the sort of place to be deposited on a stormy night. To the left of them was the dark mass of Arthur's Seat, topped by two rounded humps that were old volcanic vents, and on its slopes, directly overhead at that moment, were the jagged rock columns of dolerite, known as Samson's Ribs.

The car sent up sheets of spray as it approached Duddingston Loch which was set in a tranquil area that was about to lose that tranquillity by the look of the flashing blue lamps on the cars that were already gathering.

More messages were coming in from other sources and Jamieson was shaking his head. 'Do you know the loch? Whoever this girl is, she wasn't swimming because most of it is too shallow for that.'

'I've only seen it from the viewing area on this side,' John said, as they passed that very spot, a sloping piece of land that ran down to the lochside but which was walled off to restrict visitors from venturing further. Tonight he could see right across the loch to the far side where dark figures were moving around, setting up lights. Some were down near the disturbed, rain-lashed surface of the loch itself.

'The Connel Hide is on that side,' Jamieson muttered. 'And I've taken some good pictures of the birds from there. Heron, mute swans, any number of geese and ducks . . . and now we have this.' He twisted the wheel to park at the tail end of a line of police vehicles and a plain-clothes man, recognizing him, came forward to bend towards the window that Jamieson had lowered.

'A local phoned in to report he thought children had got inside the reserve, sir. When the game warden came to investigate he found the body, thought it was a dead swan at first, trapped in the reeds. She's young, naked and looks as if she's been in there for some time.' The rain had plastered his hair to his head and it ran down his face as Jamieson prepared to join him.

'Sit tight,' the Chief Inspector said to John.

From where he sat, John could see through the open gate to where tall weeds had been flattened in front of a fairly flat stretch of land and his view went beyond that to where figures were still erecting lights. Those already lit were shining on thick reed beds and the trees behind them. Only the lucky men wore waterproofs. The lights also showed the driving rain hitting the water as if someone was tossing pebbles on its surface. More vehicles arrived to fill the side of the road that curved dangerously around a blind corner to the right, where another luckless policeman was in charge of directing on-coming traffic. It looked chaotic but no doubt there was a practised system that everyone knew and followed. No sense of urgency though, no one rushing around. The body had been there for some time, wasn't going anywhere, and it was almost as if the new arrivals were reluctant to visit the actual scene. That he could well understand.

Jamieson was gone for some time. The inside of the car got colder and he hadn't bothered with a jacket. As his flesh chilled, his bruises made themselves felt with a vengeance but it didn't seem to matter, considering what was going on outside. The activity was now concentrated in one area where a group of men were clustered under too few umbrellas close to tapes that pegged out what he supposed was the vicinity of the body. The tapes were easily visible, fluttering under the weight of the torrent.

When the Chief Inspector did return he had three other plain-clothes officers with him, all wet through, who squeezed into the back seat. They looked at John but were not introduced as the conference began.

'No incident room yet,' Jamieson said. 'And the conditions are difficult—see if you can get a temporary awning or something fixed up. I know this place pretty well and the only deep water is over by Hangman's Rock. The girl may have drifted over from there before she got lodged in that channel in the reeds but I doubt it, more likely she went in where she was found. Those channels are man-made, deliberately cut in the reed beds so that some of the birds can reach the edges for nesting, but once she was in there she would be well hidden. It's a wonder she was found at all.'

'We aren't going to be able to do a proper search tonight,' one of the men said and Jamieson nodded.

'But come daylight I want the whole circumference checked for clothing and anything else you can find. The bed of the loch and all the channels will have to be checked over too.'

He paused and looked disapprovingly at one man who had taken cigarettes and a lighter from his pocket, and the man sighed and put them back again.

'It's not going to be easy because the undergrowth is dense—specifically allowed to be that way to provide a habitat for the wildlife. Did the game warden find any kids in here after all?'

'No, they were probably over on the cycle path. The sound carried.'

'Does anyone know if the padlock on the gate had been disturbed?'

The three men looked at each other. 'Not sure about that, sir—I'll ask,' one of them said.

'Right. Now then, this place is open to the public. The North side—the public viewing area—anyone can stop their cars over there, park, picnic or just come to the side of the loch to look around but only in a small area. To get into the Bawsinch side, as this bit is called,' Jamieson waved a hand in the direction where the body had been found, 'you need a key to the gate and anyone can get that from the visitors' centre at the Palace gate. Check to see if they keep records of visitors—who may have seen something. People who come are usually bird-watchers, photographers, or just anyone who wants a bit of peace and quiet.'

The three men in the back looked at each other grimly. 'House to house?' one asked.

'Well there aren't many with a direct view but yes, cover the area and ask about any unusual activity as well as cars seen parked near the gate. She might have had transport to get here, although it's not far to walk.' Jamieson looked troubled. 'I want extreme care taken. This is a special place, right in the centre of the city and I want minimum stress to the permanent residents—the birds I mean, Anderson. No ducks going home for Sunday lunch!'

'Of course, sir, but it won't be easy to avoid disturbing them.'

'I know that,' Jamieson growled. 'Just do your best.'

Anderson spoke up again. 'You think she came here of her own accord?'

It was easy to feel the instant tension in the car as the policeman put into words what they had all been thinking.

'We'll have to wait for the PM report, won't we? She's been in the water for a while so it's hard to spot signs of trauma, but . . .' Jamieson didn't need to say anything further. It was obvious that he didn't think the girl had stripped off her clothes for a fun swim in the Loch when just up the road she could have swum in a modern pool in comfort. 'See if the doctor's ready to speak to me,' he added. 'I don't intend going out in that again unless I have to, even under an awning.'

He stared ahead for some time after the three men had slid out into the rain and slammed the car doors behind them. 'It's at times like this that I envy smokers,' he muttered. 'What God-awful weather—it'll be like a mud bath in there soon.'

Rain drummed on the car roof and John eased the kinks in his spine while Jamieson pulled out a large handkerchief to dry his face and neck. His coat was soaked through and his shoes were caked in mud.

'I suppose you've thought that this could be your missing girl,' he said, as he re-folded the white cotton square and laid it on the dashboard.

'When will you know for sure?' John asked.

'Fairly quickly, but how she died will take a bit longer.'

'You think it's murder, don't you?'

'Oh aye,' Jamieson said, quite positively. 'Of course,

young girls do get the worse for drink and do stupid things, like go for a swim without their clothes, but I don't think that's the case here.'

John felt numb. He would have felt the same no matter who the victim was. There was something very repugnant about a dead girl lying with cold rain falling on her and with so many eyes scrutinizing every inch of her naked body. And if the dead girl was Alison Baxter, Shiela's prediction had been uncannily correct.

'A new experience for you—not that it ever gets easier for those of us who see it all too often. Anyway, there's no point in conjecture until the doctor's had his look and done the post-mortem examination. Even then it will be some time before we get a detailed lab report. As Murdo Mitchell will be telling me yet again just shortly, processing the histological tissue can take a week but we can get started without waiting for that—if the bloody man will allow himself a few intelligent guesses.'

The doctor was clearly visible as he approached because he carried a bright red and yellow golf umbrella which he dropped on the floor of the car. He was a bulky figure in a nylon raincoat over a tweed rust-coloured suit, checked shirt and knitted tie in pale green. On his feet he wore green wellingtons which were very muddy now. He smelled of pipe tobacco, had a ruddy complexion and receding ginger hair, and although he looked comfortably dry, he still complained in a genial way about the weather.

'Even the ducks are sheltering tonight. Why is it, Robert, that suspicious deaths are always discovered on nights like this?'

When he brought out his pipe and proceeded to fill it, John fancied he heard Jamieson grind his teeth but the policeman said nothing, probably knew from experience that he would be wasting his breath. Instead he twisted round to open the window beside him and when he turned back to face the doctor, the rain blew in on his back.

'Who's this young fellow then?' the doctor asked, puffing.

'John Leith. He's not a policeman.' Jamieson didn't give

him time to develop his curiosity. 'What have you got to tell me? How long has she been dead?'

'For some time, can't be accurate.'

Jamieson sighed. 'A guess, Murdo. A week, longer?'

'At least a week, probably longer.'

The car was filling with smoke. It snaked around their heads and was prevented from escaping through the window by the incoming draught.

'And?' Jamieson said impatiently.

'And nothing. Examining a corpse by the light of a torch held by a nervous constable isn't ideal. I think there is an injury to the back of her head.'

'Ah,' breathed the policeman. 'At least that gets us going in the right direction.'

'But it could have happened as she entered the water,' the doctor continued. 'Anyway, you know I'll answer the rest of your questions as soon as I can,' he said agreeably. 'Like was she dead or alive when she entered the water, and did she fall in or was she deposited. Was she drugged or drunk.' The doctor had dropped his bantering tone. 'If she drowned here there may be vegetation in her stomach but you'll have to be patient as regards drink or drugs. The blood volume can be increased by one hundred per cent in cases of drowning and that dilutes anything in the bloodstream. You'll know as soon as I do.'

'Any signs of sexual interference?'

The doctor had bent to pick up his umbrella. 'Can't say yet. Just because she's nude doesn't mean much—your killer could be a clever chappie who knows something about modern forensics. By getting rid of her clothing and dumping her in water—always assuming that there is a killer, of course—he will hope he has got rid of any loose fibres and hair. But we're far cleverer than he can possibly imagine.'

He turned up the collar of the raincoat and plunged out into the night and they watched the bobbing umbrella that was angled against the driving rain.

'He's right,' Jamieson said with a chuckle. 'If anyone can give me a lead it's that man and don't think he meant that about not getting a proper look because of the conditions out there. He knows this is classed as a suspicious death and it won't matter what the weather is doing, Murdo will have done a thorough examination. He's the best but the trouble is that he knows it.'

He seemed to weigh up the advantage of letting in fresh air along with the rain and in the end decided it was better to shut the window.

'We won't achieve much here tonight,' he said briskly. 'The next priority is identification and she's not giving us much help apart from a rather unusual ring that she's wearing. The killer probably couldn't remove it, or he missed it.'

'And after that?'

'Immediately, we'll be going over every inch of this place, a horrendous prospect when you consider the difficulties, and bag and label everything that's found but I doubt if it will prove fruitful. After we know who she is we spread out, speak to friends and anyone who knew her. Find out—hopefully—why she ended up in Duddingston Loch.' He reached for the ignition. 'I'm going to be busy now but I'll drop you off.'

'If it is Alison Baxter,' John said hesitatingly. 'She did hint at suicide in her note.' He had an awful feeling that the body was going to turn out to be the missing girl and that Jamieson was almost hinting it might be.

'That depended on how you read it. The note was neatly written by an intelligent girl, good punctuation, very precisely set out. There was no hint of depression. It wasn't scribbled in panic and I get the feeling that the girl wrote it quite calmly. That means nothing, of course. When a suicide reaches the fatal decision they may well be quite cool about it—it's more my gut reaction. I've seen nothing tonight to make me think otherwise, although I will keep an open mind. However, I'd lay bets that Alison Baxter intended leaving town when she wrote the note, and taking money from her account bears that out. What if . . . let's say someone, the killer, had other ideas and persuaded her to leave the note, then took advantage of it?'

They were on the main street, almost deserted now, and in minutes John would be back at Kramer House. What Jamieson was saying made sense.

'If the loch is shallow it would be pretty difficult to commit suicide anyway,' he said. 'Unless you got drunk first.'

'Certainly! The instinct to survive is very strong. Can you imagine anyone lying down in a foot of water, determined to die? It's ludicrous unless you are drunk and demented. Much easier if you jump off a ship in mid-ocean where changing your mind isn't going to do you much good.' He shook his head. 'This is a murder inquiry as far as I'm concerned but why the killer chose the loch and not the docks is beyond me. He could have weighted the body and we might never have found it.'

'More private?'

'I suppose so,' Jamieson said grudgingly, as if he was not convinced.

He drew up at the entrance to Kramer House and watched as John got out of the car stiffly. 'I suggest a hot bath, Mr Leith, and in future, be more careful.'

CHAPTER 9

'You must know by now what sort of girl she was,' Tollis said sombrely. It was close to midnight and John had told him about the discovery of the girl's body, and the likelihood that it was Alison Baxter. They'd discussed possible reasons for the killing and the undoubted intensive inquiries that Jamieson would now have to make into Alison's background, if she was the victim.

'She was mercenary. At a guess I'd say she somehow discovered that Watson was making money from drugs and she wanted in on it. Somewhere along the line she offended somebody or pushed a bit too hard. She did work in a bar after all and so did he, although I haven't discovered how they first met. We know she was getting cash from somewhere and I think it's all linked: Watson, the protection racket, drugs. Watson is connected to them all.'

'Wonder where he is? None of the men has spotted Graham tonight as far as I know and he's the only one who can tell us where he delivered Watson. God, but I'm knackered. Getting too old for this business.' Tollis yawned and then slumped back in his chair.

'Where's Mike? Did he manage to track Driver down?'

'He should be in soon. He phoned earlier to say he was on Driver's tail.'

'Well at least he'll be dry in the car.'

Tollis snorted. 'The weather is only part of it when you're on surveillance—just wait 'till you have to do a long stint,' he said in the middle of another huge yawn. 'You'll get to hate the sight of the car.'

John dragged his aching body from the chair. 'I'm going to bed if I've to be outside Driver's house in the morning. I want to be there when his newspaper is delivered. They're bound to mention that a body has been found in the loch, so that's one more thing to make him jumpy.'

'You're convinced it's her, aren't you? And that he had something to do with it.'

'Jamieson saw the body and I think he knows it fits Alison's description. If Ron Driver had anything to do with it I want him to feel bloody uncomfortable tomorrow morning.'

'You may have a long wait. It's Saturday and there won't be much coming and going.'

Despite taking one of Mike's painkillers he found it difficult to sleep. His mind played tricks in the small dark hours, letting his body fall into a relaxed state only to pull it back from sleep with macabre thoughts of rain-washed bodies lying in the mud of the reed beds. He'd not seen the body but his drowsy imagination also created a picture of what that body must look like after lying in water for many days.

When he did sleep it was shallow and by six he gave up and went to shower, gritty-eyed.

When they'd originally discussed putting a watch on Driver, Tollis had suggested using the waste ground at the side of a garage, where used cars were parked. It would have been ideal because one more car wouldn't have been noticed, but after Mike's suggestion of 'harassing' Driver, they'd decided to park right outside his gate. That was where John came to a halt just after 6.30 a.m. It had stopped raining during the night, although large puddles remained where the camber of the road was uneven. It was still dark and very quiet.

The house was semi-detached and unremarkable, even modest. It was slightly above street level, with a sloping garden that was packed with shrubs, with some overhanging the retaining wall next to the pavement. Built in a short cul-de-sac, it was in a quiet neighbourhood, respectable. Hardly the area he would expect Driver to choose to live in, but perhaps it was just another facet of the 'front' he had adopted.

The car hadn't had time to warm up and he was glad he'd filled a flask with coffee, since there had been no time for breakfast. By seven he was glad of the diversion of the milk float arriving and he watched young boys run from house to house with crates of milk, but it was after eight before there was anything else to take his attention. It was still fairly dark when an elderly woman left the house next to Driver's with her small Yorkshire terrier and she gave him a sharp look as she approached the car. As she drew alongside, she paused and bent to stare in at him. Then she tapped on the window of the passenger side. He leaned over and wound down the window. She seemed surprised when he wished her a friendly 'Good morning.'

'You shouldn't wait around here, young man,' she said. 'This is a neighbourhood watch area and someone might phone the police.'

She didn't seem to realize she was defeating the purpose of the 'Watch' scheme.

'I'm waiting for Mr Driver,' he said. It was more than he'd expected, the chance to talk to a next-door neighbour, but the woman drew back as soon as he spoke and pulled on the dog's lead.

Leaning across the seat was doing unspeakable things to his bruises, so he slid out of the car and went around the front, smiling to reassure her.

'I'm from a debt collecting agency,' he said, and that did the trick. She brightened with interest. 'Are you? It's what we've all been expecting—such strange men coming and going. And girls, late at night.'

John took a notebook from his pocket and began to write. Behind the old girl was the gate and then steps leading upwards. In the window at the front of the house someone had parted the blinds to watch them and John knew that because the street lamp was directly overhead, he was in full view as well as close enough to be recognized.

'He saw you then?' Tollis said.

'Someone did and the old girl said he lived alone—apart from the girls he brings home late at night but according to her they don't stay more than an hour or two.'

'What else did she have to say?'

'He's only lived there about six months and he rejected the welcoming committee of neighbours. They try to make new residents welcome because it's that sort of place—but Driver was quite rude apparently. Told them to mind their own business and leave him to mind his. So she's been keeping an eye on him—mainly because he throws stones at her Yorky if it gets into his garden. Several unsavoury characters have been in and out—she'll do a better job of surveillance than any of us. Anyway, mission accomplished. He saw me asking questions and writing down the answers. It just might bring things to a head.'

'More likely to bring something down on your head,' Tollis said, gloomily. 'Had his newspaper been delivered before you left?'

'Mm. But he didn't appear and I didn't feel like lingering any longer. Any word from Jamieson?'

Tollis shook his head. 'He'll hardly have had time to get someone to identify the body yet.'

'Hope it doesn't have to be Alison's mother.'

'Mike has gone to Stirling with Dee so he should be back soon, but until then, can you mind the shop? I've got to go out and you'll need to be handy in case Jamieson does phone.'

The waiting around wasn't so tedious because Sentinel men phoned in with messages for the boss and there was a steady trickle of others coming in to write reports or share a coffee. John heard snatches of conversations on the various jobs in progress and more than one man spoke of 'heavies' being imported into town. Most of the talk consisted of rumours, gossip overheard, but it was the way that Sentinel got its information. Tollis didn't ignore any of it although, as he said, it was only human nature to try to outdo the latest story and some of it was exaggerated. However, the men were all well trained and when it came down to written reports, these were factual. Between the rumours and the official reports, Sentinel managed to stay on the ball as far as intelligence went.

Jamieson didn't appear until after 5 p.m. and he looked as if he had a lot of sleep to catch up on. John took him into Tollis's room, made fresh coffee and while it brewed he offered the policeman a scotch.

'Well, maybe a small one.' Jamieson stretched out his legs and made full use of the comfortable chair. There were dried mud stains on his trousers and his coat was creased, as if it had dried on him.

'I can't stop long,' he said wearily. 'But the initial report is in and we're pretty certain now that the body is Alison Baxter because her mother identified the ring. It is an unusual design, part of a set of necklace and bracelet that she bought for the girl's twenty-first birthday and all three have her initials engraved on them. We're looking for the missing pieces of jewellery now but I doubt if they're at the locus—the ring was tight so the killer probably couldn't get it off.'

'Did Mrs Baxter have to see the body?'

'No, no. It wouldn't have served any purpose, not with that degree of decomposition. Dental records and the ring should be enough.' Jamieson took small sips of the whisky, savouring it and then gulped the hot coffee. 'There are more tests to be done but the doctor found haemorrhages in the air spaces of the middle ear which means asphyxia, drowning in this case. The thing is that she didn't drown in the loch.'

That made John sit up.

Jamieson continued. 'There was no vegetation in the stomach, as Murdo expected, and then he found evidence of bath oil and bubble bath solution which she must have inhaled.' Jamieson leaned forward. 'She drowned in her bath—not necessarily in her flat. There are also signs of bruising around the girl's ankles which means the killer could have gone into the bathroom, held her ankles up in the air—which meant her head was kept below the surface of the water. There would undoubtedly have been a struggle but a strong man could easily kill a young woman in this way.'

It was a horrifying picture. 'It also answers another question,' John said soberly. 'If he'd dropped the body in the docks you would have expected to find salt water. The killer tried to be clever but he didn't know you could differentiate between bath water and loch water. To him they were both fresh, so he hoped you'd believe she drowned accidentally in the loch.'

'Exactly. So we know he's cunning but not too clever. And we think she was killed soon after she disappeared—no exact date is possible. So, her mother was right and Alison didn't clean the flat.'

'No. The killer probably arranged that in case there were any clues left behind. We don't know, of course, if she was drowned in her own bath, but the killer may have searched the flat, disturbed it, and then was forced to hide the evidence of that search. The note . . . I still think he made use of that, maybe promised her something nice, an expensive holiday, whatever, so that she would write it. We may never know, but obviously she cooperated and walked into our killer's trap. When she wrote the note she believed she was leaving town, not that she was going to die.' He looked at his watch and grimaced. 'I shouldn't be here. I'll need to talk to Dee soon. It's far more important now.'

'We arranged for her to be out of town. She's at home in Stirling.'

Jamieson chewed his lower lip. 'Can you get her back early tomorrow?'

John nodded. 'I'll fetch her myself. Will you catch the man who killed Alison?'

'We'll do our best, of course, but this young woman was mixed up in a bad scene. If we could discover why she was such a danger to them it might help. Miss Oakley might know—even if she's unaware of knowing. And I don't need to warn you again to be careful yourself.'

He stood up and John thought that he looked not only exhausted but also dispirited. 'If we could have pinned down the men behind the protection rackets sooner, this might not have happened,' he said. 'But the trouble is that by the very nature of the offence, when extortion is working successfully, we don't get to hear about it. It has never been a big problem here and it still isn't. We'll just have to make sure that it never gets a firm hold. Pity the girl had to die first though.'

'Mike says that Ludo's has reopened, with a new manager.'

'That's very likely. We'll find new doormen there too and there won't be any more trouble.'

'The owners are paying up then?'

Jamieson nodded. 'Of course. But if we get the top men all the heavy brigade will disappear into the woodwork. It's like kicking down an anthill, the insects scatter.'

'To rebuild elsewhere.'

'As long as it's not in my city,' Jamieson said dourly. 'But remember that prodding isn't enough, Mr Leith. 'If you interfere with an anthill without thoroughly destroying it, you get bitten. Better to wait until you can demolish the lot.'

'There's another analogy,' John said with a grin. 'Set out a goat to draw out the tiger. I may take Mike along to Ludo's for a drink this evening.'

'Let's hope the goat is fleet of foot then,' Jamieson said. He seemed much older as he walked out of the office and past the men in the outer room all of whom paused to watch him with curiosity.

He phoned Clare before putting his idea to Mike and she sounded breathless as she answered the phone.

'You got me out of the bath. I'm going to a show tonight with some of the girls from the office.'

'Sorry if you're dripping on the carpet.'

'I'm not, I'm lying on the bed wrapped in a big pink towel.' Then there was silence as both thought what would be happening if they were together instead of a phone call apart.

'I'm thinking of taking a few days off soon,' he said. 'Can you manage time off?' A visit with Clare was tempting, if things got sorted out, if the police could get Driver and all the rest behind bars.

'That would be lovely. I'll see. I'll ask . . . I'll make sure I can. When will you come?'

'Maybe next weekend, over to the Wednesday, something like that,' he said quietly, wondering if that was time enough. Jamieson had enough on Benson and the others who had tied him up in the flat, and Driver knew by now that he was being watched and that the net was closing. If they could lean on him some more . . . His own bruises would have faded by next weekend and Clare need never know anything of what had happened.

They talked and planned what they would do and for a little while he was able to forget that later on that evening he would once more be taunting Driver.

*

Mike was all for brazening it out and dropping in at Ludo's. 'But not too early. Later, the bouncers will be looking people over and we *do* want to be looked at, don't we?' His beefy face split into a smile.

'Might as well make an impression,' John said.

'And I've another job first. You can come along if you like but you'll have to stay out of sight. Tollis wants me to look for Bill Graham and he'll run if he spots you.'

Finding Watson had to be the priority so locating Graham was equally vital although the Sentinel men had reported no success so far. It would save a lot of leg work if Graham was persuaded to tell who issued the orders to pick up Watson and where he was at the moment.

'Let's hope his conscience is still niggling and he'll talk,' Mike said. 'The trouble is that we've no address for him. The last I heard he was sleeping in hostels, but I know his favourite watering holes.'

No rain had fallen on the sodden city since morning and the air was cold and clean. John remembered a trip to Manchester the previous spring and the sheer relief of coming back to good drinking water and unpolluted air.

'We'll start down by the docks,' Mike said as they set off. Both were wearing old raincoats from the stock of cast-offs that hung in a cupboard in the Sentinel Agency and underneath they wore the smarter shirt and tie outfits that would get them into Ludo's later.

'My face is known in the places that Graham is likely to be so there shouldn't be any trouble in asking questions,' he went on. 'And it takes time. I have to buy a few drinks.'

It was an understatement. Close to eleven, two hours and four pubs later, he saw Mike come out of a seedy bar looking pleased with himself. Bill Graham came out with him, walking on rubber legs and when he reached the edge of the kerb he leaned over and vomited.

'At least that got rid of some of it,' Mike said with disgust. 'And it won't land in my car.' He pulled off his raincoat as if it was infected, reached behind him to drop it at

Graham's feet and at the same time jerked the drunk man upright. 'Don't foul my car, Bill—do you hear?'

Graham mumbled and seemed to fall asleep. 'It'll be hours before he'll talk with any sense. We'll take him to the office and get someone to keep an eye on him.'

No one had paid any attention to them but it was a relief to leave the dingy street and get back on to the wide road leading back to the town centre. One thing about Edinburgh, John thought, it kept its seedy areas well hidden.

It took both of them and the security man on the door to get Graham up the one flight of stairs to Sentinel and they left him in the washroom.

'Don't let him wander off,' Mike told one of the men who was on duty. 'And if he wakes up, fill him up with liquid. I want him sober when I get back.'

Ludo's was packed when they got there, proving that memories were short. Mike remarked on the new faces behind the bar, so it looked as if there had been a complete change-over of bar staff.

'A fresh start with no one to tell tales,' he muttered before pushing towards the bar. The doormen had let them in without question and after half an hour it looked as if their visit wasn't going to achieve anything. None of the staff gave them a second glance; the change-over had been smooth, the men on the door didn't look like gangsters and the customers were having fun. John could understand what Jamieson had meant—when extortion was successful, there was no way that the police would know it was going on.

'Look,' he said as Ron Driver appeared from a door at the side of the bar. The bearded man looked happy and relaxed, joking with a young barmaid, and then, with the smile still on his lips, he saw both John and Mike. He blinked before he looked past them but the smile had vanished.

'Time to go,' Mike shouted over the music. 'We've done what we came for.'

It wasn't easy to get through the crush to the door and by the time they reached the exit, the doormen had been warned via their walkie-talkie radios. There were three of them with short hair cuts, shirts and ties, and suits that strained over bulky bodies. One had elected himself as spokesman.

'Which one of you is Leith?'

Neither John nor Mike answered and the man shrugged.

'Message. You've earned yourself a tag. Watch it doesn't end up tied to your big toe on a cold slab.'

Mike let out his breath in a cross between a loud grunt and a roar and two of the men stepped backwards. Only the spokesman held his ground and Mike grasped him by the lapel.

'Threats are words, easy to say. Message for Driver. You are about to be redundant. And you three should start looking for other work.' He released the man and moved on. John had been watching the other two, saw them reach automatically for their waistbands but they had no weapons. In their new pseudo-respectability, the orders would be that they would not need them and Ludo's reputation was still fragile. They didn't seem to like the situation one bit.

Mike was still simmering with anger when they got back to Kramer House and it didn't help his temper to find that Bill Graham was not yet fully sober.

'Christ, Mike, why bring me here?' the man groaned, bent double in a chair holding his head. Once he might have looked as fit as the other Sentinel employees but now the muscle had gone to flab and the beer hadn't helped. About ten years younger than Mike, his hair was already quite grey and his skin was an unhealthy colour. Someone had removed his stained coat, made him take a wash and he still had a towel draped over his knees.

Mike handed him another plastic mug of coffee and stood over him while he drank it.

'They'll kill me,' Graham muttered.

'No. We'll make sure no one knows you've been here,' Mike assured him.

'Don't talk drivel—you took me out of the pub, didn't you? Someone will get paid for passing that on.'

Mike seemed unconcerned. 'You'll tell us what you know or I'll dump you on Driver's doorstep.'

That sobered Graham quicker than the coffee. John stood to one side, watching a Mike he didn't know, hearing the threat but like Graham, not sure if he meant it.

Mike pulled up a chair and sat facing the other man. 'We already know about Driver, but who's behind him? Who is really giving the orders?'

'Christ, I don't know that! I've never even been close to Driver.' He looked longingly at Mike's cigarette but wasn't offered one.

'Come off it. You were in the police force for years and you don't forget the training. How are things organized?'

Graham still looked scared. The three of them were in Tollis's room which was fairly large but it was crammed with cabinets, a large desk and a group of chairs around a coffee table. With darkness outside and only a desk lamp lit, it was claustrophobic and on top of that Graham was already terrified and feeling ill.

John spoke from the shadows. 'Alco Leisure,' he said and Graham jerked around to face him.

'That's Driver's pet scheme, his baby.' The words slid out and Graham stared at John. 'You forget easy,' he said bitterly. 'I didn't think you'd help anyone to land me in the shit.'

John felt the gibe but ignored it. 'And Clan Royal?'

Graham looked tired as he nodded. 'And others. I don't understand why he has so much on his plate when the first ones were coining it for him. I don't know the details. I just listen to the others talking. They say he's making big money.'

John stepped closer. 'Who's backing him?'

'Are you kidding?—don't you know how something like this works? You never know who puts up the initial money.

People like us aren't told anything and as long as we get paid we don't ask questions.' He turned to Mike. 'The puzzle is why Driver bothers with the clubs and pubs and the security firms. There's a lot of hassle involved with that lot and a big wage bill, when he doesn't need any of it—must do. He's a rotten little runt really.'

'Where does he operate from—how do you get your orders?'

'Two men act as his deputies when he's not available. Not that I even get to see them, you understand—I'm an extra, to tag along if I'm needed. Those two operate from Alco Leisure's office. They take on the hired help. '

'Where were you supposed to take Peter Watson?' John asked and held his breath because it was crucial that they found the young man.

'I didn't take him anywhere.'

'For Christ's sake!—I heard them tell you to deliver him.'

'OK, so I was supposed to take him back to AL's office, but I had a bad feeling about it. He'd been stupid and he wasn't any use to them any more—I could read the signs. So I dropped him off. I told them he gave me the slip and they swallowed it after a bit.' Graham sounded bitter. 'It's easy when you've got my reputation for being unreliable. They know my background. It's a bit of a joke, but I make use of it when it suits me. After tonight I'm not so sure though. You shouldn't have fetched me out of the bar, Mike—I'm a dead man.'

'Where did you drop him? Did he say he had somewhere to go?' John asked and Graham didn't even raise his head when he answered.

'Near the bus station,' Graham said wearily, past caring. 'He still has a mother somewhere around Alloa, I think—or maybe it was Stirling.'

John felt his hopes sink, and Mike interrupted. 'So now you're everyone's guardian angel? You'd nick your best friend's wallet if you needed a drink.'

'No need to rub it in, Mike. That was a long time ago.

This time I wasn't going to set anyone up. Before he,' he nodded in John's direction, 'turned up at the flat things were already getting nasty. They were asking Watson if his girl had given him something, or where she could have hidden it. He didn't know what they were on about.'

'What sort of thing?'

'They didn't tell him that, only that it was small, something that might be in an envelope. I got the feeling they didn't know what it was either, but had been told to ask.' He suddenly turned ashen. 'I feel sick,' he said.

Mike led him from the room and when he came back he sat down heavily. 'He's not going to be much use. How the hell do we find Watson? There must be hundreds in the phone book, if his mother has a phone.'

'What are you going to do with him? He's probably right about being in danger because we brought him here.'

The muscles in Mike's face had sagged with disappointment and now he leaned forward in the chair, resting his arms on his thighs. 'I have a few contacts out of town who might take him for a bit, but he won't thank me for it. The need for booze will override good sense and he'll forget to be careful. Like all drunks he's plausible. He can talk himself out of most things, like telling them that Watson gave him the slip, but I think you're right, this time that won't work. I'll deliver him, warn him to stay put, but after that it's up to him.'

In fact, he lectured Bill Graham as he helped him into his raincoat and then handed him a full packet of cigarettes and some notes from his own wallet. John walked down to the front entrance with them when they left and collected a note of a phone call that had come in for him.

'It was around ten, I think,' the night man said. 'Just when we changed shifts so I didn't notice it at first.'

He read the message. Garek wanted him to phone back when he got in, but it was too late now. It would have to wait until morning. He went up to his flat, fell into bed and slept like a log until after eight.

At eight-thirty he called Garek.

'I have arranged for us to visit Clan Royal,' Garek told him. 'This evening.'

'I thought you had to be a member.'

'Rules can be got around. You will come as my guest.'

They arranged that Garek would pick him up at Kramer House.

He had a full day ahead of him. First he had to collect Dee from Stirling and when he got back Jamieson might want him to sit in on the interview. He ran down the back stairs to Sentinel to make sure that Mike was available to look after Dee for the rest of the day.

Tollis wasn't happy about the jaunt with Garek. 'Why is he so keen to be helpful all of a sudden? And what if Driver is there with half a dozen men?'

John thought of the formality of Garek's invitation and how it gave no clue to the trouble he'd gone to, to get them into Clan Royal. He wouldn't expect gratitude either. John didn't care about his motives but he couldn't expect Tollis to take the man at face value as he did.

'Clan Royal is a legitimate business, hardly needing Driver's attention and even if he does show up, he can't do much with clients around. As for Garek, maybe he gets bored and likes a bit of excitement,' he said. 'I don't expect anything to come from the visit to Clan Royal but I'll get the feel of the place.'

Tollis wasn't about to let up on Garek. 'How do you know you can trust him? Gumley pulls his strings. You've said yourself, many times, that Gumley would dearly like to see you suffer.'

'Funnily enough I do trust him. I think there's a part of him that Gumley doesn't own.'

'I hope you're right,' Tollis grumbled. 'But between them, they could set you up, so don't forget it.'

CHAPTER 10

Dee's mother lived in a fairly new block of flats in the Cornton area of Stirling. He'd phoned to say he was coming to fetch her but not why and she looked anxious as she opened the door.

'Mum and the boys have gone to church. Do you want a coffee, tea?'

He thought that was a good idea and that it would be better to break the news about Alison now rather than in the car.

The flat was ordinary, a home where young boys dragged in mud on their shoes and the mother had to scrub the carpets to make them last. Threadbare covered the state of the suite in the sitting-room as well, but it was a nice room, clean and welcoming.

'Not like you have at Elmwood, is it?' Dee said, putting down a mug of coffee and a plate of biscuits at his elbow. She was in her usual black gear, but no make-up and the long straight hair was loose on her shoulders. Even in early morning light she was a beautiful girl and he wondered if she had a boyfriend.

'I had to live most of my young life on boats,' John said.

She sat down with both hands around her coffee mug. 'That must have been fun.' She wasn't relaxed and he knew she was waiting to hear why he'd thought it necessary to collect her so early. He put off telling her, waiting for the right moment.

'Not really. I got seasick quite often.' He sipped the coffee which was good, but he could tell that Dee wasn't prepared to wait any longer.

'Something's happened,' she said.

He put down the mug. 'Alison's dead. Her body was found in a loch near Duddingston.'

'Oh, my God,' she whispered. 'I never thought anything

like that . . . she did kill herself after all,' she went on.

'No. The police think she was murdered.' It all sounded brutal but he didn't know any other way of breaking the news. There were no tears but the skin on Dee's face looked taut. 'Chief Inspector Jamieson wants to see you when we get back but that's nothing to worry about. We'll talk in Kramer House and then Mike will take you back to his place.'

She stood up. 'I'll get my things.'

He was worried that she might not have realized that she was now in more danger than ever. As she came back into the room with the familiar bag slung over her shoulder, she was anxious to be gone before her mother and brothers returned.

'She's been asking questions and I've never been able to hide anything from Mum. She'll want to know it all and I won't have her being worried about me on top of everything else.'

They didn't speak for some time on the journey back and John left the girl alone with her thoughts. But they must have been too painful because she came up with a question that surprised him. 'How's Janet?' she asked suddenly.

'Just fine. Now that Shiela is staying for a bit they've gone back to watching ice hockey again.'

'Ice hockey?' Dee tried to smile.

John nodded. 'They're fanatical about Murrayfield Racers. They come home almost hyperventilating after a good game. Especially if there's been a fight or two.'

Dee went quiet after that for a bit. 'How did Alison die—did she drown?'

'Yes, but there are no real details yet. She may have been drugged first.' And maybe she hadn't. Maybe Alison had fought for her life, and that didn't bear thinking about. 'It will all be over soon. The police have a good idea of who to question.'

'Peter?' She was pulling at a long strand of hair, staring straight ahead.

'He's still missing. Probably hiding somewhere near here

at his mother's. I don't suppose you heard him talking about his home? We must talk to him.'

'Only that he lived over a newspaper shop,' Dee said quietly. 'Alison teased him that he was still doing deliveries—I think his mother owned the shop and he worked there when he was at school.'

Adrenalin pumped through him. There might be a lot of newspaper shops but if one was in the name of Watson, they were getting somewhere.

Tollis and Jamieson were in the main office talking to some of the men and the policeman looked rested and relaxed, leaning with one arm on the top of a grey metal cabinet. There was no longer any mud on his clothes and he might have come straight from church; Jamieson seemed the sort of man who attended church regularly. He was still smiling when he greeted Dee with a charm that put her at ease.

'Use the visitors' room,' Tollis murmured, heading back to his own office, leaving John to escort Jamieson and Dee.

'This shouldn't take long, Miss Oakley,' Jamieson said pleasantly. 'I know you've already spoken to Mr Leith, so we'll cover the same ground again if you don't mind. How did you come to be sharing a flat with Alison in the first place?'

'She advertised on the student notice board last term. When I met her she said she was working in a bar as well as the dress shop but needed help to pay the rent.'

'So at that time, before the university summer vacation, she needed cash. When did that change?'

'I didn't move in until after the summer break and I think she already regretted having me there. It was obvious sometimes that I was in the way, so I kept to my own room as much as possible.'

Jamieson nodded. 'So during those two months or so, Alison presumably found another means of paying the rent. And things weren't happy between you.'

'I decided to look for somewhere else but I'd already given her the rent for this term.' Dee was sitting up straight, with no contact between her back and the chair. She had an unconscious elegance and was answering the questions quietly. There was no doubting her honesty.

'Now we come to the visits by Peter Watson. Did you overhear any of their conversations?'

'Not really. Sometimes I was around when he arrived. He didn't seem the sort of boyfriend that would suit Ali. She would have wanted someone who took her to the best places, owned an expensive car—Peter didn't even dress well, so I was curious.' Dee shrugged her shoulders expressively. 'And he was weird.'

'Could he have hurt her? Perhaps lost his temper and got a bit rough?'

Dee was certain that wasn't the case. 'I think he was scared of her. I wondered why he came at all.'

Jamieson paused as if wondering what else the girl could possibly help them with. 'We have to find out why she was killed and that means talking to everyone who knew her. Did she have any other visitors?'

'She could have. I only saw her mother or Peter, but I wasn't always there and Ali went out quite a bit.'

Jamieson leaned back in his chair with a defeated expression. 'Well, it was worth a try.' He got up and John followed him to the door. 'If only there were some papers in the flat, receipts . . . There's no clue even to how and when she bought her car.'

Behind them Dee spoke up. 'I know where she got the car. Her uncle bought it for her as a present.'

Jamieson whirled round. 'Did he now? Are you sure?'

'Oh yes. Ali was always keen to show off. She was dancing around the flat waving the keys.'

'And he never came to the flat?'

'I don't think so, but she went to see him. I got the feeling he was well off and Ali hoped he'd be generous. Maybe he was and that was why she was sorry she gave me a room.'

'That is very helpful, Miss Oakley. A word outside,' he said to John. The policeman closed the door behind them and walked through the main office. 'Samuel Baxter said he couldn't identify the girl's body because he'd had no contact with her since she was quite small.'

'He told me the same thing,' John said.

'I wonder why he lied? Some businessmen avoid publicity like the plague and he's the type to resent scandal in the family.'

'But to lie? He could have asked to be kept out of it, surely?' John said as they reached the main staircase outside Sentinel. Here they paused and John remembered the day he had gone to meet Baxter. 'Driver was there when I met Baxter but they didn't know each other. He was introduced to us by the other man, Ken Harper.'

'Mm,' Jamieson said thoughtfully. 'I'll have another word with Baxter anyway.'

'Have your men done a thorough search of the girl's flat?'

'They have—why do you ask?'

'I heard that Driver was looking for something small enough to fit into an envelope.'

'Who told you that?' Jamieson asked sharply.

John shrugged. 'I'd rather not say. He got me out of trouble and I owe him a favour. He isn't involved.'

Jamieson didn't like that. 'If you say so. We all have sources that we like to keep to ourselves, as long as we have the experience to evaluate what we are told. Your source doesn't know why Driver is so keen to find it?'

'No. But whoever killed Alison cleaned the flat, and that could have been to cover that he'd searched it.'

'So now we're looking for other hiding places. Her mother's house? Her uncle's?' Jamieson spread his hands. 'Or just about anywhere.'

It was lunch-time and John was going through the phone books looking for newsagents called Watson. Some of the Sentinel men had been out for takeaways and the office smelled of pizzas. Dee played about with one of the computers while Tollis watched with interest. 'Do you know about those things?'

'I do computing as part of my course,' she said. One of

the men asked her to help him and she easily found the information he wanted. Soon one or two of the others drifted over and she started to give them all an impromptu lesson. Tollis nodded approvingly. 'That should take her mind off things.' He and John went into the other room. 'How did it go?'

'She didn't know much except that Baxter lied when he said he hadn't seen his niece for years. He bought her car.'

Tollis's eyebrows went up. 'So that's where she was getting her cash.'

'Could be. Makes you think, doesn't it?'

'A mercenary girl who likes nice things has a rich uncle, but is Baxter the type to be generous?' Tollis mused. 'Yes, it certainly opens things up a bit.'

'On the other hand, there's nothing wrong with a man wanting to keep clear of a murder inquiry if his only involvement is because he gave his niece a present. And he's not the type to get mixed up with Driver and his mob,' John said.

Tollis snorted. 'There isn't any "type" in that sense. You don't know the cut-throat world of business and what some people will do to make a buck.'

Which was exactly what Gumley always made a point of rubbing in. 'But I'm learning,' John pointed out. 'Jamieson is going to see Baxter again—and I've discovered a possible address for Watson. I've got time to check it out before I meet with Garek.'

'Leave the girl here then, and take Mike with you. She seems happy enough and I've got an idea she could be useful.'

They went to the outer office and Tollis put his idea to Dee. 'I could do with someone here at weekends who is handy with computers. You could earn yourself a bit of spare cash if you've got the time.'

She looked at John and he shook his head. 'Nothing to do with me—it's Tollis's idea.'

'I'll take the job,' she said firmly.

'Fine. That's just fine, start right away,' Tollis said.

'Mike, John needs you this afternoon and Dee will stay here until you get back.'

'Where are we going?' Mike asked.

'To see if we can find Peter Watson. He may have gone back to stay with his mother and if he's hiding, he's not likely to wander far from home.'

Which turned out to be the case. The newsagent's shop was closed but the family—mother, daughter and Peter—was at home, watching a film on television. Peter Watson was reluctant to come outside to the car, but a refusal would have meant explanations to his mother.

'Just as well,' John told him, 'or I'd have explained why we wanted to speak to you. You're not ducking out of it this time.' He sat beside Watson in the back seat and Mike went in front, turning to face them both.

Watson was resentful and scared. His long fair hair was no longer tied back in a pony-tail but hanging lank on his shoulders. 'How did you find me?' he asked. He spoke to John, with sidelong glances at Mike, fearful of a man he didn't recognize.

'It was easy and if we could, so could others. You were lucky that Bill Graham let you go.'

That frightened him and he looked as if he wanted to escape. 'I don't know anything. I told them that already.'

'That's something we'll decide,' Mike said. 'Did you hear about the body being found in Duddingston Loch? That was Alison Baxter.'

John, sitting beside Watson in the back of the car felt the young man's body jerk and then tremble. He pushed home the point.

'So why did they kill her?'

'Christ, I don't know! She was bound to get into trouble—I told her.'

'Then tell us,' Mike said. 'Right from the beginning.'

'I can't. They'll get me too.' And as Watson began to cry, Mike rolled his eyes in disgust. They waited until the sobbing stopped and then Mike asked the question again.

'What were you up to?'

'I took drugs so I needed money. The only way to get it was to sell the stuff myself. Sometimes I sold it in the bar and Alison found out. She saw me dealing and wanted to know if she could do it too. I told her to forget it.'

'Are you sure? Alison didn't sell the stuff?'

'She would have taken my customers.' Watson was indignant and then seemed to remember who he was talking to. 'She couldn't keep her mouth shut, it would have been dangerous.'

'Where does Ron Driver come into it?' John asked.

'He used to come into the bars where I worked—I moved around, built up a lot of customers in different bars. I think he collects from the manager but you never get to see what goes on—it's just talk with the other bar staff. He goes all over the place. So then Alison got on to that as well.' Watson had got over his fright and now the information flowed. 'She was stupid,' he burst out. 'I told her you can't go against these guys but she wouldn't listen. I don't know if Driver had anything to do with the drugs because you only ever see your own supplier, but she said it was all connected. She was one mad bitch. Greedy. And I got really scared she'd land me in it.'

'Then she disappeared,' Mike said and Watson nodded, agitated again.

'She took all the cash I'd collected. That meant I couldn't pay my supplier and I couldn't get anything for myself. Do you know what they do to people who don't pay up?' He shuddered and dropped his chin on his chest.

'So how are you buying now?' Mike demanded. 'You must still need the stuff yourself.'

Watson didn't seem to want to talk about that but Mike persisted.

'My mother gives me money. She makes me earn it though and it's not enough,' he said bitterly. 'Now she wants me to go to a clinic and get right out of the whole scene.'

'And so she should.' Mike was scathing.

'Do you know who's behind Driver?' John asked. 'Who gives him his orders?'

'I don't know anything!' Watson shouted, his voice breaking to a high-pitched whine. 'I got my stuff delivered to whichever bar I was working in and I only ever saw one man. But Alison knew—she followed him. Don't you understand? She followed the guy and found out where the supplies came from! She used me but she didn't tell me anything—and I didn't want to know.'

John had one more question to ask. 'Did she ever give you anything to keep for her, an envelope?'

'No, she bloody didn't. Benson asked me that and beat me up when I said I didn't know what he was on about. If she had asked me to look after something for her, I wouldn't take it.' Watson put his arms around his thin body and groaned. 'Don't tell anyone where I am. Please don't tell.'

They would have to tell Jamieson.

'Get out,' Mike said. 'And for God's sake, listen to your mother's advice.'

They watched Watson run back to the door that led to the flat over the shop and John got into the front seat and let Mike drive them back to Edinburgh. Neither of them had much to say. 'Stupid little git,' was Mike's total comment.

Dee had been busy while they were away and Tollis's room looked tidier than it had been for a long time, with papers sorted into trays on his desk and files stacked ready to be put back into cabinets.

'She's doing the same thing in my kitchen,' Mike said, grinning. 'I may keep her as a permanent lodger.' The comment had been casual enough but once it was said he seemed to like the idea. 'Well, I've got plenty room.'

He and Dee left soon afterwards. John and Tollis went out to find something to eat and talk over what Watson had been saying.

'He was right about one thing, she did use him,' John said. 'I wonder who she tracked down?

'Driver? It's hard to believe any girl would be so stupid as to do what she did.' Tollis lit a cigarette, the last in the pack. The restaurant was quiet because it was still early. The waiters were bunched in a corner talking amongst themselves, waiting for the evening rush.

'Maybe she tied a little blackmail,' John said. 'She must have been very sure of what she had on him if she did. Which brings us back to the missing envelope. She had no real friends, nowhere to hide it except in the flat, or maybe with her mother.'

'But if it was all that important she would have chosen her hiding place very carefully. She was a scheming girl, let's face it, and it won't be lying around. Also, if she was killed because of it, someone else is going to be desperate to find it too,' Tollis said softly. 'Don't go bumping into him, John. And remember what I said about Garek. He's still Gumley's man.'

Garek came for him at seven-thirty, dressed in a black tracksuit with a bright purple slash on the sleeves and across the chest. He took John's sports bag and put it on the back seat beside his own and as John got into the car, Tollis's warning was still making him feel uncomfortable.

'I think we should use as much of the place as we can,' Garek said, 'including the refreshment area.'

'Tollis doesn't think it will achieve much, unless Driver is there himself.'

'But you wish to be seen—and I will look for familiar faces,' Garek said with one of his slow smiles. 'As well as making sure I am seen. We must be like ladles in a pot of soup tonight, to stir and see what floats to the surface. And it will be a pleasure to work out with professional equipment—my own is modest.'

So Garek worked out in the house in Cramond.

'I have to be fit for Mr Gumley's sake,' Garek explained.

'He must be carried to bed now although he weighs little. And I enjoy the discipline of a regular routine.'

Clan Royal Health Club had once been a large private house and now there was a long extension to the rear, built in the same slightly pink stone as the main building. The grounds were beautifully kept, as was the golf course which ran alongside the estate. John had done some research and knew that to become a member you had to be nominated and then vetted by a selection committee. How then had Garek managed to get them into the place at all? He didn't ask.

'Come, Mr Leith, let us sample Mr Driver's empire,' Garek said and they stepped out on to well-raked gravel. They had parked beside other sleek and expensive cars but Garek's Jag wasn't going to be out of place beside them. They got by the receptionist without any questions being asked but she asked them to sign the register as if it was routine. John wrote his name clearly, the first step in letting Driver know that once more he was turning up where he definitely was not welcome.

They smelled chlorine as soon as they passed through the swing doors but there were only a couple of swimmers using the pool. To one side a man lay on a lounger under the potted palms, a jacuzzi bubbling a few feet away. John followed Garek to the changing rooms and then into the gym. So far they had seen several attendants, one sitting discreetly in each room they passed through, all males dressed in white cotton suits with the crest of the club monogrammed over their breast pockets. None of them had given them a second glance. To hell with Driver, John thought. He might as well enjoy himself.

He and Garek split up after a while and John rounded off the session with a swim. The visit had achieved one thing at least, in easing the soreness of his bruises, but Tollis had been right, he thought as he towelled himself dry in the changing room, in every other way it had been a waste of time. There was no reason for Driver to be at the club and what could he do if he did turn up?

He was dressed, on his own in the changing room, when Garek's thin body appeared in wet swimming trunks, his bald head glistening under the ceiling lights. He reached for one of the thick white towels and wrapped it around his body, sarong style, before sitting on a bench. The changing room, like the whole complex was over-warm but Garek seemed in no hurry to leave.

'The attendants are too young to have been around in my time,' Garek said. He rubbed a loose edge of the towel over his upper body, where the skin was white and as hairless as his head. Yet although he was not a heavy man, he was very fit. 'If nothing else we have been able to use superb facilities,' he said as he got up and went to get dressed.

Garek was still in one of the plush cubicles when the door swung open and Driver came in with two attendants. John could see a third man outside and as the door closed, he stayed there, on guard.

'So it is you,' Driver said, standing between the other two. 'I couldn't believe you'd have the nerve to turn up here. It's about time you learned just who you're dealing with.'

'He's got a friend in here with him,' one of the attendants muttered but Driver made a dismissive gesture, as if he was beyond caring about witnesses.

'I've been asking around and you own a property company, but you like to poke your nose into other things, working for that agency. Fancy yourself as a detective, do you?'

The two large men smirked and one folded his arms across his chest as Driver took a threatening step forward. 'Don't you take bloody warnings? Or are you so fucking stupid you don't understand what happens to nosy sods who interfere where they're not welcome?'

'I got your message,' John said. He was still sitting with his sports bag between his feet and a mental check told him that he had nothing to use as a weapon to defend himself.

He knew that Garek must be listening but the bald man hadn't so far emerged from the cubicle. If he had any sense he wouldn't. But at the same time, John remembered Tollis's warning about Garek with some bitterness. If he had been set up, it would have been so easy for Gumley to phone ahead and this was the result.

'Well, smartass, now you'll find out what happens when you don't back off.' Driver stepped back and made onward motions to the two heavies, who began to move forward with some eagerness. Both looked as if they made full use of the gym, with muscles that bulged, and they moved lightly on their feet. One would have been enough, he thought, as he bent to throw the only thing he had, his sports bag. One man batted it aside with a huge hand.

They were three feet away now and he was preparing for the worst when Garek appeared dressed in his tracksuit and carrying his bag. The two attendants only paused as he placed the bag on the padded bench and then stood with his hands loosely at his sides.

'You should have stayed put,' Driver told Garek. 'But if you want to watch, you'd better stand to one side.' He smiled as he leaned against the tiled wall, arms folded. He looked as if he was ready to enjoy the next few minutes. Garek didn't move, didn't speak or look at John. He looked relaxed, his body loose, with his fingertips lightly touching his thighs.

'Out of the way, old man.' One of the men reached out as if to push Garek aside by grabbing him roughly by the front of his tracksuit, but as his arm came forward, Garek moved. It was over so quickly that John couldn't see how it was done, but the big man ended up on the floor, stunned.

'Christ,' said the other one as he came to a sudden stop, looking as stunned as his partner.

Driver pushed himself away from the wall, alarmed.

'Get him first,' he said urgently.

The man did try to obey. Keeping his eyes on Garek, he reached out sideways and picked up a stool that had metal legs and a top padded with towelling. Using both hands he raised it aloft and then aimed it at Garek's head. As it swung downwards Garek reached up to take hold of his wrist and moved back slightly at the same time. The stool dropped to the tiled floor and somehow the man's arm became twisted up his back. They were unequal in size, certainly in strength, and yet Garek didn't seem to be in any trouble.

'Do not struggle,' Garek warned the man quietly.

'Get off me,' the man shouted, then, as if not believing that the slight frame of Garek could possibly hold him, he grunted and tried to get free. All of them heard crunch of bones breaking and the man screamed as he fell writhing to the floor.

Garek looked down at him and then at Driver. 'His elbow is smashed and his shoulder is dislocated. He will need attention,' he said, almost politely. Then he turned to John. 'Come, Mr Leith.' He pushed the door open and waited for John to follow. The third man was still outside but now he looked undecided. No doubt he had seen what had happened to his friends, through the porthole window in the door.

Driver screamed at him. 'Don't just stand there!' but the man slowly shook his head and made no move to stop them. They were passing the reception desk when Driver caught up with them.

'I don't know what the hell you're playing at or who your fancy friend is,' he muttered, keeping his voice low. 'But you'd better believe no one gets away with what you've just done. No one.' He was almost jumping with anger and his face was an unhealthy purple.

The cold fresh air was reality. It turned sweat to ice, and as John followed Garek across the stretch of gravel, there was more bizarre normality in the arrival of other wealthy customers getting out of their cars, laughing, wearing brightly coloured sweatshirts and carrying sports bags. They slammed their car doors, still chatting, moved towards the building, and all John could think was 'Let's get the hell out of here.' Any moment he expected more of the goons to come tearing out of the building, but Garek calmly turned off the car alarm with an electronic gadget before he slid into the driving seat. They were half a mile down the road before he could ask what Garek had done.

Garek looked straight ahead, frowning slightly. 'I do not like violence,' he said at last and John felt like laughing aloud. Instead he let out a deep breath.

'What the hell was that then?'

Garek explained. 'Aikido. It is non-violent and used only for defence. I did warn him not to struggle—that hold is painful but not dangerous if he had only stayed still. The technical name for it is Shomenuchi Udehishigi.'

'And the first one?'

'Irimi Nage.'

'I didn't mean the name of what you did—I meant how . . . ? They were both much bigger and stronger.'

'That doesn't matter.' Garek looked over at him, a quick glance that was grave and in any other circumstances would have made John hoot with laughter but at that moment he didn't feel any inclination for levity.

'You are reasonably fit so you could learn the same skill. Aikido teaches you to divert your opponent's strength in a circular movement and turn it back on him, therefore his strength becomes yours.'

'You make it sound easy,' John said. It had looked easy, but so did anything if done by an expert.

'Women protect themselves using Aikido. It is the most subtle and graceful of the martial arts—although the techniques can cause extreme pain, they are only used to force submission. Injury is to be avoided if possible. I will teach you, Mr Leith.'

Reaction set in and John went over the scene in his mind, his realization that he was in deep shit as the men displayed their muscles, just before Garek did his sleight of hand with both men. If the man hadn't been there he would have been in deep trouble.

'Why? What made you learn it in the first place?'

'I had need of some skill at one time and the philosophy

behind Aikido appealed to me. Aikido is called the way of harmony. It teaches that there is no separation between body and mind. It influences the mind for the good, creates an inner calm and balance in each day of your life.' He smiled, as if the words meant more to him than he was explaining. Then he spoke quietly. 'I need calm and balance in my daily life, as you know. Mr Gumley is not an easy man to live with. And of course, it keeps me very fit although there is no special training except practice. I have become flexible, shall we say, and that brings coordination and fast reactions—speed and agility are essential of course.'

It explained a lot. Now that John knew about Garek's skill in Aikido, he understood so much more about the man. Garek was not so remote after all, just full of inner calm, with his body at one with his mind, for Christ's sake!

'Maybe, if I get the time . . .' he said.

Garek nodded, still looking straight ahead. 'I am qualified to instruct.'

And John felt himself grinning like an idiot, knowing at the same time that it was all part of the relief mechanism, relief that he wasn't lying in separate pieces on the floor of the changing room. And he wondered if Garek ever let himself relax enough to laugh. That would be something to see.

Garek drove them smoothly back to town, the Jag purring like a contented cat. Then he was spinning the wheel and they were in the Royal Mile, close to Kramer House. 'We have stirred up quite a hornets' nest instead of that pot of soup,' he said with a short out-going breath that might have been a chuckle.

'But we didn't learn all that much.'

The car came to a stop. 'I have been making some inquiries on your behalf but as I warned you, it is difficult to get to the people behind the protection rackets—the caring game as it is called.' Garek's expression was stern. 'One of my men has followed Mr Driver as he goes about his business and I have looked up your Mr Baxter. You did not use the steam room tonight or you would have seen him. He certainly saw you and I think it was he who called up the troops. Someone did because Mr Driver arrived too quickly on the scene.'

John had been about to get out of the car before Garek spoke. 'Baxter was there?'

'Perhaps he is a member. I am saying he was present tonight, but that means nothing in itself. However, Baxter is wealthy but rich men want more, more money and power. Mr Gumley was like that once . . .' Garek said as if it explained everything. 'Baxter could be the one you are looking for, but maybe not.'

And as John went inside Kramer House he remembered that he'd almost believed that Garek had set him up.

CHAPTER 11

Jamieson phoned when he was about to go to bed. 'Just to let you know that our team took Alison Baxter's flat apart. There was nothing there. I spoke to her mother this afternoon and Alison didn't leave anything in her house, or give her anything to look after. Whatever Driver and the rest are looking for, it must be somewhere else.'

'How is her mother?'

'Very upset, of course, but I think she expected the worst. The girl's uncle still denies seeing his niece for years, but he did admit providing finance to buy the car. His explanation is that Alison phoned him and because he didn't particularly want to renew contact with her or her mother, he decided he might be generous for a one-off time. He says he told her that there would be no more presents.'

'If Dee is right, he's lying.'

'Quite possibly. He struck me as being a very self-contained man, unflappable. The type who can lie when it suits him and without blinking. We have absolutely nothing on him and indeed, we don't know if there is anything to be found on Mr Baxter. We all lie at times, for different reasons.'

'Did he say whether Alison specifically asked for a car?'

'He says she was pleading hard times and it sounded like he was being touched for a hand-out. He didn't like that and he almost hung up on her, but had second thoughts. The car was the girl's idea apparently. He had no idea what she spent his cheque on.'

'What about Driver himself?'

There was a pause. 'As bent as you can get. We're having a close look at Mr Driver and we'll get him. As for Benson and the others, if you press charges we'll bring them in for assault but it might be better to leave well alone for the time being. Benson would very likely get bail and we're very aware that in these cases we can put witnesses at risk. Villains do get bail—that's a sore point in the force, but there's nothing we can do about it. The answer is to let him think he's safe in the meantime, the devil you know and all that.'

'Any progress on the murder inquiry?'

Jamieson didn't answer right away and when he did, it was reluctantly.

'Some details can't be released yet. We are making progress.'

In other words, John thought, not being in the force meant that there were questions he shouldn't ask. Understandable, especially since he was not always exactly open with Jamieson.

'Did Baxter say what business he's in?'

'Investments,' Jamieson said drily. 'Which can mean anything.'

Like putting up the money for Clan Royal and all the other companies that Driver was the front man for, and then sitting back and letting the money roll in. Top it up with a little extortion, some profitable dealing in drugs, with others taking the risks.

'If Baxter is the man funding Driver, he's home and dry unless Driver talks.'

'It happens,' Jamieson said mildly. 'We have no way of knowing if Driver will crack under pressure and name names. He could simply be doing it because he enjoys it, or if he's getting a fair slice of the takings he'll accept the risks and take his punishment without implicating anyone else. Usually though, there is some pressure to prevent the front man talking. Some incident in his past, perhaps, that he wouldn't want to come to light. And fear is the lever that controls the anthill from top to bottom.'

'We need an earthquake then, something to make the whole structure shudder.

'Indeed we do. Any suggestions?'

'We have to find what Driver is looking for. Maybe it was the reason why Alison was killed and just maybe it is the one thing that would make Baxter restless in his bed at night.'

'Mm. Good night, Mr Leith. Good hunting.'

He hadn't told Jamieson of his visit to Clan Royal with Garek. it wouldn't serve any purpose and it might mean Garek would be interviewed by the police. There were some dodgy rules about how far you could go when defending yourself and a smashed elbow and dislocated shoulder might be construed as assault.

What could Driver be looking for? And on whose behalf? John sat in the small sitting-room of the flat. His uncle had chosen the furnishings, all in cool colours and the winged chairs were covered in a muted green velvet. Only one small lamp was lit and it was behind him. He settled down to think.

He felt in his gut that Baxter was their man, but the one thing that negated that was the murder of the man's own niece. Baxter couldn't have ordered that. However, the men he employed had few scruples and he only controlled them through Driver, who might have felt the threat most of all if the girl had been as pushy as Watson said. Baxter might not have known anything about the killing until it was done.

So, what would it take for a man like Samuel Baxter to start looking over his shoulder? What sort of man was he? Few facts were known except that he had not kept in touch with his brother's family. He was wealthy but how much—if any—of it had been honestly earned? And there was the added factor that Driver would have reported that someone they both knew as Leith was getting too interested in their operations, and that the police were closing in because of the girl's murder. Surely there would be a lot of disquiet, if not panic?

In Baxter's place, he would have ordered that all operations be put in the 'hold' mode and that nothing was done to excite further investigation, but did Baxter have enough control to do that? It seemed not, when someone like Benson, who lacked subtlety, could be sent to question Watson and to look for Dee. It suggested that despite the attention the protection racket was getting, Baxter was desperate enough to risk detection in order to regain whatever was missing. Something small enough to fit into an envelope, a notebook?

At three in the morning he had discounted several lists; of dates for delivery of drugs, their distribution points, and even the likelihood of Baxter's accounts, but handwritten instructions of some kind remained a possibility. Whatever it was, it had to tie Baxter to some activity and that meant it was irrefutable evidence that would land him in gaol.

As he told Tollis the next morning, 'Baxter's the type who likes to parade his wealth and he feeds on respect from others. I watched him that day we met, the way he acknowledged people like royalty as he walked through the restaurant. He would go to great lengths to preserve his supposedly good reputation as a successful businessman. He might risk anything to stay out of gaol. What else?'

'He may not need reasons,' Tollis said gloomily. 'Anyone standing in his way might be enough—you for example. But aren't you relying too much on guesswork?'

'I don't think so, but I need to get to know him better,

maybe dig into his past. That means speaking to Mrs Baxter, unless you can think of anyone else. She'll know how he got started. Who his early business contacts were, or the names of school friends.'

'How old will he be?'

'Late forties, fifty.'

'That means a lot of digging then. Best of luck.'

A simple phone call to Clan Royal, in the guise of a reporter interested in the health club, got him the information that it had been open for only two years. 'The exact day was August 1st,' the receptionist said.

'I expect it was covered by the press at that time then,' John said.

'Oh yes. A reception with all the local bigwigs. It made the national press as well.'

That meant photographs would have been taken and although Baxter might have stayed anonymously out of the limelight, he wouldn't have been able to resist being there. John phoned the man who had taken the photographs for Kramer's new glossy brochures, knowing that he was a freelance who often sold his work to the papers.

'Yes, I was there,' he said. 'And I'll still have the negatives.'

He promised to send copies around to the office later that day.

'Do you know any of the reporters on the local rags? I'm looking for someone who would write up a piece on the body found in Duddingston Loch last week.

'You want the crime reporter then, Joss Williams. I'll get him to give you a buzz. Er, am I likely to be repaid in kind.'

'What did you have in mind?'

'Publicity shots of any new property developments?'

'You're on.'

The morning dragged, even though Val had plenty of work for him to catch up on. Joss Williams didn't phone until close to lunch-time and he sounded as if he would be tight as far as information went.

'What do you want to know?' he said.

'If you got any background on the family. The girl's father for example.'

'Some,' the reporter said cautiously.

John could understand his reticence since such details would be hard to come by if Mrs Baxter was reluctant to give interviews. 'I just want to know if he was local and went to school here in Edinburgh.'

'Why? What's your interest?' What he meant was: *Is there another story in it for me?*

'No special reason. Someone in the office thinks he knew both of the Baxter brothers at school and is wondering if he should visit Mrs Baxter. He doesn't want to intrude . . .' It sounded weak but all he could think of on the spur of the moment.

'Oh, right.' Williams named both the primary and public schools that the Baxter brothers had attended. 'I didn't go into the family background all that deeply myself, but if you dig up anything interesting . . .' He'd obviously heard the old pal's story before and wasn't convinced.

'I'll call you,' John promised.

The photographs arrived early that evening, in an A4 envelope, delivered by special messenger. Also in the envelope was a copy of the paper that had carried the photographs, and in the write-up some of those present were named. The photographs showed the local dignitaries in the foyer of Clan Royal and the same group standing outside with the building in the background. Baxter was there, not prominent but easily spotted, standing with Ken Harper, the golfer. John made a mental note to speak to the golf pro as soon as possible.

He wasn't looking forward to interviewing Mrs Baxter again but it had to be done. He phoned her just after seven. 'Could I drop in for a few minutes later this evening?'

She had no objections and even sounded pleased. 'My friends have been kind but they don't seem to know how to handle this. They send cards and phone, but I'd like to chat with somebody.'

'In about an hour then,' John said.

It was cold when he stepped outside Kramer House. The sky was clear, with the stars clearly visible and that meant there would be a frost overnight. It was the sort of night when the Edinburgh skyline would be seen from as far away as the Fife coast because of the floodlighting of the Castle and the city's other notable buildings. But it wasn't a night for thinking of scenic wonders, not when the woman he was going to see had a daughter lying in the town's mortuary.

She seemed to have become smaller since he last saw her. Still neatly dressed, there was also a look of suffering in Mrs Baxter's eyes and an uncertainty in the way she moved, as if her own home was no longer familiar to her.

'I've made coffee,' she said as she led him into the fussy room, but tonight, with small lamps and a gas fire lit, it seemed homely and comfortable.

'I'm sorry about Alison,' he said and she held up both hands to stop him saying more.

'You were doing your best. Alison was dead even as we spoke,' she said quietly. She was in control of herself or maybe it was just that she had done all her crying.

He didn't know where to begin or how to get around to her brother-in-law, but she did it for him by talking about Alison's father. 'I'm glad he isn't here at a time like this. He doted on Alison.'

'It's a pity Sam didn't keep in touch. He could have been a help now,' John said, feeling uneasy as he said it, as if he was making use of her grief.

'Sam isn't the sort of man to comfort anyone,' she said. She was suddenly agitated. She looked around the room as if searching for some other subject to discuss and found it in a photograph of Alison. 'I got a new frame for it,' she said.

It wasn't the one she'd given him, but a studio portrait, posed in such a way that no matter where you were in the room, the eyes of the girl would appear to be looking at you. He wasn't sure how much of a comfort that would be to her mother. Poor woman. There was more grief to come, especially if there was a murder trial during which Alison's lifestyle would be made public.

'Mrs Baxter, I need to ask you about Sam,' he said and there was no mistaking the flash of alarm in her eyes. 'If you don't mind.'

'I can't speak about him, not now. Please understand—there was some trouble . . . It was a long time ago and I don't want to remember it.' Her eyes were pleading and there was no doubting her alarm.

And he couldn't bring himself to put pressure on her. Others might, if it became necessary, but for now, Baxter's past was not going to be revealed by her. However, at least he now knew that there was something to be discovered, even if it had to come from another source.

'Forget I asked,' he said. He stayed for nearly an hour, letting her talk and when he left he felt ashamed when she thanked him for being kind enough to call.

'Christ,' he muttered as he got back into his car, hating the dirty business of prying, of the underhand questioning of a woman who had enough to worry about already. For now, there was no way of knowing if her painful memories of the past had anything to do with what Baxter had become, but he had to find out, one way or another. If Baxter had drifted apart from his brother around the time Alison was born, that meant he was going to have to find out about the years when Baxter was, at most, in his mid-twenties. That wasn't going to be easy and it might be a wasted effort in the end.

At lunch-time he went to the Westmore hotel where he'd first met Baxter. The barman knew Sam well. 'He's one of our regulars. Don't know about close friends but your best bet is that bloke in the corner.'

The man who was reading a newspaper, was younger than Baxter but of the same breed. John was getting to recognize those who prospered in the business world. 'Do you know if Sam Baxter is likely to be in today?' John asked as an opener.

The man folded his newspaper. 'You never can say when Sam will pop in. Is it important?'

'I'm hoping to do a profile on him—and a selection of the city's successful businessmen,' John said, sitting down. 'John Leith.' He held out his hand.

'Malcolm Roberts,' the man said. 'Maybe I can help. I've known Sam for around ten years—although he's not easy to get close to.'

'Mm. We've covered that period. I was hoping for the earlier years, how he got started.'

'You need Ben Wallace then. I think they went to school together but they're not exactly buddies now. We all meet occasionally through golf or because of business interests, but not many meet socially. Ben might be useful to you. When will the piece be published?'

'Depends on the editor,' John said, smiling, and thinking how easy it was to lie when the reason was valid.

Ben Wallace owned a building company which seemed to be suffering from the recession but he was willing enough to see John straight away, perhaps because he explained he owned the Kramer Property Company.

'We're pretty much reduced in size at the moment—just ticking over to be honest—but if you've a project coming up I can easily recruit men.'

The state of the company was evident from the lack of activity in the office but Wallace had been honest enough to admit the state of his business. That gave John hopes for the rest of their talk.

'Bad times all around,' he said. 'I'm afraid I'm not here to talk about new projects,' and he saw Wallace's expression change from hope to resignation.

'Ah well, I expect you're feeling the pinch like the rest of us,' he said. 'Fancy a cup of tea?' He shouted to the girl in the outer office to put the kettle on and then settled back in his seat. 'What can I do for you then? I'm curious now.'

He was a smallish man, stocky, with weather-beaten skin and thick greying hair. Most important as far as John was concerned, was the directness in his very pale blue eyes. However, he had been in the front rank in the photographs of those present when Clan Royal was opened, so caution was necessary.

'What do you know about the Clan Royal health club?'

Wallace looked surprised. 'That's the last thing I expected you to ask,' he said. 'We did some of the contract work on the interior. I'm not a member though—not my scene.'

'But you were at the opening.'

'Oh aye. So were sponsors and a lot of other contractors. Did you come here just to ask me that?'

John decided to take the plunge. 'Not exactly. Tell me about Samuel Baxter,' John said.

Wallace's expression became guarded. 'What about him?'

'Malcolm Roberts says you've known him for a long time.'

Wallace became very still and his jawline had tightened. John couldn't yet tell how he was going to react and all he could do was sit there and hope.

'What's the purpose of this then? Need a reference do you? Where's the bloody tea, Julia,' he suddenly shouted.

The girl appeared with tea cups and pot, put them down on the desk and Wallace used the time to size John up.

'You're young to own a company like Kramer's, but I heard Rees Kramer had died and left everything to a nephew—didn't expect you to be so young though. I also heard you were making a go of it.' He poured tea, flicking glances at John as he did so. Behind him the windows were sparkling clean, a large palm plant thrived in a corner of the room and the desk was pin-neat. Wallace might be having a hard time but he wasn't letting things go.

'Word gets around,' Wallace said. 'So your name is getting known—we're in the same business after all. So what's this about Baxter?'

'Did you know him when he was getting started in business?'

'What business? I don't even know what line he's in,' Wallace said evasively. He looked curious and slightly suspicious at the same time.

'Did you?' John persisted.

'Aye. I did. And long before that as well. We went to the same school for a bit,' Wallace growled.

John felt his hopes rising. 'Good,' he said. 'I think you're exactly the man I've been looking for.'

The other man's eyes narrowed. 'Maybe so, but what's the owner of Kramer's doing, asking questions about Sam Baxter? Like I said, is it a reference you're after, because it's damned strange if he needs one.'

They were getting nowhere and John knew Wallace was not going to open up until he did the same thing.

'In a way it is a reference I want, but not the usual kind. I'm digging into his background to find out what I can about him and I'm expecting to find some dirt. Baxter is making a lot of money and I have to find out where it comes from.'

'Well, that's straight enough. Now I get your drift.' Wallace was nodding. 'I can tell you this much. Sam Baxter was a bastard when I knew him and for all I know he still is.' His mouth became a narrow line and John felt like reaching out to shake his hand.

'Tell me more,' he said, grinning.

But Wallace was still not keen to talk about Baxter. 'I don't believe in maligning another man, even someone like him, with things that happened a long time ago. Besides, he pulls a lot of weight in this town. Don't get me wrong, I'm not scared of that, but powerful men can ruin a business and I have my men and their families to think about.'

'I can promise it won't go any further. I'm only looking for pointers and if anything comes of it, your name won't be mentioned.'

Wallace thought about that. 'Aye well, I don't know about pointers that will lead you anywhere. You want records and they don't put everything into school reports. I know they covered it up at the time. One day he was there and the next he was gone.'

'Expelled?'

'More likely his parents were asked to remove him. Private schools don't like statistics that show a pupil was expelled.'

'How old was he then?'

Wallace sighed. 'Sixteen. I heard he moved to a school in Glasgow but only as a day boy.'

John wanted to hear the rest. 'What did he do?'

Wallace grimaced, as if he found the subject distasteful. 'It was a long time ago, laddie. A man shouldn't have to carry mistakes on his back all through his life.'

'But what if he never changed? What if Sam Baxter thinks he got away with whatever he did, and is still doing the same thing—making other people suffer into the bargain?'

Wallace blinked rapidly and shifted his weight in his chair as if the thought of that disturbed him greatly. 'Is that what you're thinking? It would make a difference,' he muttered. 'All right then, but I'm going to break one of my own rules and have a drink. You'll join me?'

John nodded and waited while he fetched a bottle of scotch from the bottom drawer of a filing cabinet and poured some of the spirit into two glasses. Wallace was a moderate man and so were the drinks.

'Baxter was up to mischief when he was younger, long before he was sixteen. Small things, but serious for all that. He couldn't have needed cash but he used to bully the younger boys, took their pocket money. Later on he had a following, a sort of gang, and then he let his cronies do the dirty work for him. I remember he always managed to wriggle out of trouble. He was never on the scene if any of the others were caught.'

Wallace sipped from his glass and John knew he was hearing what he'd expected. 'What about his brother?'

'Oh, Kevin was younger and he was different. You'd

never think they came from the same family, but it was because of Kevin that Sam got expelled in the end. By the time Sam was sixteen he had quite a reputation, sort of king of the walk. Top dog in school, with all sorts of stories being whispered, bullying, gambling—and some of the teachers were rumoured to be involved.

'How the hell no one asked questions sooner, I'll never know. Anyway, Kevin was the quiet one who kept his head down and it must have been hard for him because Sam frightened so many of the rest of us. One day there was a fight, just the two of them. By the time the masters came on the scene Kevin was beaten something awful, but for once Sam couldn't get away with it. The next day he was gone. We never did find out what the fight was about, although there were stories flying around.'

'What sort of stories?'

Wallace shook his head. 'I don't mind telling you what I know, but speculating is a different matter. Kids can exaggerate, can't they? And what good are guesses to you? No, you must ask someone else why Sam and his brother fell out. And don't ask me how Baxter got where he is today, because I don't know that either.'

'Michael Roberts suggested you all played golf together.'

'I'm in business, Mr Leith, and I have to make contacts. I'm in the same golf club, but if I even came within striking distance of Sam Baxter I'd be more likely to hit him than the ball,' Wallace said evenly. He drained his scotch and poured another small measure. 'Are you telling me that Baxter is still like that now?'

'I suspected he might be, but maybe I've underestimated him as well,' John said slowly. 'I was making allowances for him. I thought he might be behind the racket, but with little control of the men under him. Now I wonder.'

Wallace looked bleak. 'Sam had a talent for control. He could get those boys to do anything he asked. If he's still the same, as you say, that's frightening, laddie. He's had all these years to grow harder, and get a lot of experience. I wouldn't stand with my back to him, and that's a fact.'

'I take your point. Thanks, Mr Wallace.' John got up and reached out to shake the other man's hand.

'Call me Ben. And I'm not so sure I've done you a favour, not if you're going after Sam Baxter. Get some of your own mates around you, that's my advice.'

He saw John to the door. 'Some time you'll have to explain how a property man gets mixed up in this sort of business.'

'I have to do a lot of explaining these days. I'm not sure I know how it happens myself.'

CHAPTER 12

Ben Wallace had succeeded in scaring him, and as soon as he got back to Kramer House, he went looking for Mike Cairns. He found him in Sentinel's outer office, talking to one of the other men and looking bored.

'Has there been any trouble as far as Dee's concerned, Mike?'

Mike looked pained. 'I'd have told you if there was. No, she's doing as she's told and staying close to the university buildings. I checked with the office up there and they don't give out details of any student's classes or address. As long as she stays with a crowd and we aren't followed, she's safe enough.' Then he put his head on one side and frowned. 'Why are you asking?'

'Oh, just something I heard. Make sure she really understands the danger and don't let her out at night. I think things are coming to a head.'

'Is there something I should know?'

'Nothing I can tell you yet. Is Tollis in?'

Mike shook his head. 'He's gone out to that development of yours. There's been some more thieving.'

Right next door to where Sam Baxter lived. 'Damn, I forgot about that.'

He went up to his own office and looked at the pile of

work awaiting him. It seemed to belong to another life. He decided to fulfil his promise to Val and join Tollis, and at the same time take a look at Baxter's home.

The residents' committee was understandably upset that such a prestigious development should be suffering break-ins. Most were elderly and had paid a lot to retire to their luxurious homes. Tollis had already poured oil on troubled waters by promising to provide a patrol by the time John got there.

'Not that it's up to us,' Tollis grumbled later. 'But they won't have the police in. You are going to be paying the bill, I may add.'

They sat in Tollis's car and John told him what Ben Wallace had said about Baxter. 'He lives over there and we haven't paid him much attention so far.'

'No. He'll have tight security in that place,' Tollis said slowly.

'We aren't going to get anywhere if we don't push him a bit. He's got Driver and all those men acting as screens—he's not going to put a foot wrong, is he?'

'How do you propose we flush him out? He'll be like a winkle, tight in his shell and with an army of men to call on, spread right across the town.'

John looked at the house that was shielded from prying eyes by a screen of trees. Nothing moved in the grounds and there were no cars parked out front. 'He must come and go . . .'

'We're not trying Mike's game on this man, no open surveillance, and it wouldn't do any good if we did.' Tollis ran a finger under the collar of his shirt. He had dressed for his interview with the residents' committee and he was feeling uncomfortable. 'Jamieson said they didn't find anything in the girl's flat.'

'And Mrs Baxter says Alison left nothing with her, but if it is small, it could be slid under a carpet. I'm going back to look at the flat. I still have the keys.'

'Not on your own,' Tollis said flatly. 'I wouldn't put it

past Ron Driver to have someone watching you, waiting for a chance to nail you. He's a vindictive little bastard and you're becoming an irritation he can't ignore.'

'I'll take someone with me.'

'Not Mike, he's tied up with the girl.' Tollis glanced at his watch and did some arithmetic. 'Hang about and I'll go with you this evening, but Alison could have given this thing—whatever it is—to one of her friends and we may never find out what it is.'

'Jamieson has spoken to all the contacts he's been able to find. She did go around with girls from the shop where she worked but none of them were particular friends. Can you imagine that girl saying "Here, look after this for me"? It's worth a fortune in blackmail if I'm right. I think she was a very clever girl and she'll have chosen a clever hiding place. If it was so damned important what would you do with it? You wouldn't want it out of your sight for long and that means she kept it in that flat!

Mike had left to collect Dee when they got back to Sentinel but he'd left a message for John. 'He was dancing around, waiting for you, but in the end he couldn't wait,' one of the men said, handing him a note. Mike's handwriting was no more than a scrawl, but its message was clear.

'Bill Graham is in hospital and he wants to see you.'

Tollis compressed his lips as he read it. 'Looks as if they caught up with him,' he said. He shrugged. 'He was warned to stay away from town but an alcoholic won't give a damn for his own safety if he needs a drink.'

A nurse showed him to the small side ward where Bill Graham was the only occupant. 'He should be in the main ward really,' the nurse said. 'When he dries out we might have trouble with him.'

'You sound as if you're used to that.'

She nodded. 'But sister knows how to handle them. She keeps a bottle of sherry handy—it does the trick and is better than filling them up with pills. When he's fit enough he'll be offered a psychiatric assessment, if he wants it, that is.'

John looked through the glass portion of the door, at the prone figure in the bed. 'How bad is he?'

'Badly beaten, poor man. If he hadn't been heard groaning in that alleyway he might have died.'

John pushed open the door and as he got nearer the bed he saw that Bill Graham's face was a mass of cuts and bruises. Eyes, nose and mouth were grotesquely swollen and discoloured. Several cuts had been stitched. And as he pulled up a chair beside the bed, he couldn't be sure that the man was awake, or if it was possible for him to open his eyes.

'John Leith, I'm glad you came,' Graham croaked through cracked lips. 'I want you to get the bastards who did this.'

'How did they find you?'

Graham shook his head slightly. 'Doesn't matter now.' His hand moved to grasp John by the wrist. 'Had to tell you that something's being cooked up. They thought I was out, that I couldn't hear, but they mentioned your name a lot.'

'Who?'

'Driver, planning moves with the rest.'

It must have hurt him to talk because the cracks in his swollen lips opened up and blood oozed from them. John reached for a glass of water and placed the straw in Graham's mouth.

'Needs a dash of vodka,' Graham said, trying to smile. He ran his tongue over his lower lip before going on. 'I didn't hear much but Driver was blowing his top. He's really flipped about you.' His grip tightened on John's wrist. 'He wants you taken out, mate. You're a real nuisance as far as he's concerned and he's had orders from the top. Don't think he needs orders, to be honest. He's gone crackers and he'd gladly do the job himself.' The words got slower, as if talking had tired him and he slumped deeper into the pillows. 'Be careful. I wouldn't want what I did for you to be wasted. I'm glad I got you out of there. It's the only thing I've got to be proud of for a long time.'

John stayed for a while although Graham said no more. Everyone was telling him to be careful, but how the hell did you do that when there were men all over the city with anonymous faces, working for Driver? On the other hand, it would be just as hard for them to find him in a city of thousands. That was the positive way to look at it, he told himself. Anything else would make the nightmares come true. There was only one way this could end and that was to prove that Driver and his goons were incapable of carrying out their order to get rid of him. Then—maybe—Baxter would take it on himself. If Ben Wallace was right, Baxter was not too squeamish to do just that. Needle him, aggravate him, draw him out.

'And then we'll have him,' he told the sleeping Bill Graham.

'I still think this is a waste of time,' Tollis said as they set out for Alison Baxter's flat. 'You don't know how thorough the police are—they won't have missed a pin. And we'll look pretty foolish, after Graham's warning, if Driver and Co are there waiting for us,' he complained. But John knew Tollis too well to take him seriously, despite the negative words. Tollis was keyed up, glad to be out of the office and active.

'So let's assume we're being tailed right now. I suppose you did bring the mobile phone?'

'I did, and a few other odds and ends,' Tollis said with a grin.

Marchmont was not all that far away and it was impossible to pick out a tail on such a short drive, especially in traffic. The night was cold and both men wore polo-necked sweaters under their jackets.

'Wonder what we're looking for exactly? Have you given it any thought?'

'I've been dreaming about it,' John told him. 'Identifying it will be a problem.'

Tollis parked around the corner and they walked from there to the mouth of the close. There was no sign of anyone following them.

'Not that it means much—you'd not spot an expert.'

They could see the evidence of the police search as soon as they were inside. 'Look, told you, the carpets have been loosened around the edges so that's one of your theories knocked on the head,' Tollis said.

They split up and John chose Alison's bedroom. He stood in the doorway and let his eyes roam over the furniture. Drawers had been removed and were now stacked on the floor so there was no point in hoping there would be something taped under or behind them. He'd hoped the police might have overlooked Alison's collection of china-faced dolls, thinking the heads were hollow and a good hiding place, but they were laid out on the bed and had obviously been checked. John picked them up one at a time but none of the stitching of their soft bodies had been tampered with.

Where else? The light shade was frilled gingham and had a small teddy hanging from one side. He had to stand on the bed to look at that but it wasn't hiding anything. He found Tollis standing in the sitting-room, looking thoughtful.

'This is good quality stuff. Wonder if the cheque Baxter gave her was enough to buy this lot, or if she put pressure on him more than once. If so, maybe he realized that his niece was going to be a real menace. He might have come to the conclusion that she was a risk he couldn't afford.'

'Watson said she was too pushy—it scared him rigid that she didn't seem to realize who she was dealing with, but the man was her uncle—she must have felt physically safe at least. She comes across as totally insensitive to the danger she was in,' John said.

'And they knew there was always the danger she would blab to her friends. You didn't believe that Baxter would be callous enough to get rid of her, but I'm beginning to think he might have done just that.'

'His own flesh and blood?'

'Most killings are done within the family,' Tollis pointed out bleakly. 'It's a fact of life, unfortunately. Let's get out of here. If the girl hid anything in this flat we're not going to find it. And for all we know, she may have made the whole thing up. The thing we're all looking for might not exist!'

'We aren't being very clever with this, are we?' John said as they drove back to the centre of town.

'Jamieson will come up with something in the murder inquiry—apart from that we just have to wait for someone to make their move.'

'In the meantime Dee is still in danger.'

'I'm not so sure that she is any more. If she'd known anything it would be out by this time and Driver and his mates will know that,' Tollis said thoughtfully. 'Sentinel isn't big enough to beat this sort of organization, not even if I put every man on it. Baxter is too well protected and there won't be any tangible evidence against him—even Jamieson will be resigned to that. The Baxters of this world don't get caught. It's time you realized that there's nothing more you can do . . . without some inside information.' He slowed and pulled into the kerb, then did a U-turn and drove back the way they'd come. He was grinning.

'I've remembered a friend who might know something. Have you ever been to a strip club?'

There were no neon signs to say what sort of place they were entering but the music gave it away. A sign on the door said 'Members only' but Tollis was waved through.

'I'm going to talk to a man called Harry McDade, but he might not talk in front of you. Buy yourself a drink.'

The scotch was expensive but probably he was meant to be so absorbed by what the girl was doing on the stage that he wouldn't notice what he was paying. He watched Tollis disappear through a door at the back of the room and then turned to watch the show. The girl had stripped down to tiny spangled pants that were little more than a G-string by the time that Tollis emerged from the office and she looked as bored as when she started. The music changed tempo as she ran from the stage and another girl took her place. He wondered how they could face it, night after night.

'What did he have to say?' he asked Tollis as soon as they were in the car.

Tollis glanced over his shoulder before pulling out into the traffic and shrugged. 'Baxter no, but Driver is known. Harry's had no trouble because he has muscle of his own. He thinks the same way as I do. If Driver is covering up for someone you aren't going to get near him.' That depressing assessment settled on him like a dark cloud as he went up to his flat. 'The Baxters of this world don't get caught,' Tollis had said and his friend Harry agreed with that. Unless . . . but he stopped the thoughts that were leading him along a very dangerous route and reached for the phone instead. Maybe talking to Clare would lift the gloom.

She talked about the coming weekend which they would spend together and he wondered if flying off to London would feel like a cop-out. He would go anyway, he decided. He would go to London to be with her, no matter what.

'You sound . . . preoccupied,' she said.

'No.' He could hardly tell her that he'd had a sudden memory of Bill Graham's battered face, so he told her about the visit to the strip club and heard her giggling.

Shiela phoned early the next morning and he felt a twinge of guilt that he's not found the time to visit Elmwood. She knew that Alison's body had been found and the circumstances that had proved her prediction correct, but it hadn't seemed to upset her. Rather, it had brought a sort of acceptance of her own powers.

'It has been on my mind to call you,' she said. 'I'm having recurring thoughts that young Dee holds the answer to so much that has happened.'

'You may be right, but we've spoken to her many times and if she does know anything, it has slipped from her memory.'

'Oh well, I had to mention it. Will you be down at the weekend?'

He told her about the trip to London. 'And the school has arranged tickets for a rugby match for the boys so David won't be down either. Next weekend for sure though.'

He spent the morning at his desk, sifting through folders and correspondence which got Val's approval for once. The business was healthy despite his neglect; the staff of Kramer's had job security and he was surprised that he felt an increasing satisfaction with the healthy balance sheets. Still, without the added interest of Sentinel work it might be a different story.

He threw down his pen and thought about the reports that were filtering through via Sentinel's workforce. It seemed that there were still fights breaking out in discos and bars around the city that bore all the hallmarks of Driver and his men. The protection racket was flourishing so, far from playing it cautiously, Ron Driver was pushing ahead with plans to sew up the entertainment venues in the city—what would Jamieson be doing about that? The policeman had to abide by rules . . . but they didn't apply to ordinary citizens, like him . . . And that led him back to the half-formed plan of the night before.

He looked up Ken Harper's number. 'We met when I was with Sam Baxter,' he said and the golf pro listened as he explained that he had spare capital to invest. 'I heard you mention a new golf course.' Harper swallowed the bait and couldn't quite hide his eagerness to meet John for a drink at lunch-time at the Westmore hotel.

When he put the phone down, he knew he was about to take the offensive and that it was a dangerous step. He had a feeling that Harper might have sold his soul to Baxter already for the sake of his new golf course and might be phoning him at that very moment—but that was the point of the exercise after all.

Tollis wouldn't give his approval to the meeting and it would be foolhardy to meet Harper on his own, so he made another phone call, this time to Garek. He told Garek what he proposed to do and there was a pause while Garek digested that.

'I could be there at one p.m.,' he said at last. 'Do I know you?'

'No. I'd be happier if you watched my back.'

'Very well, Mr Leith.' Even now, Garek was strictly formal and John would have laughed if he had been able to dig deep enough for a trace of humour. Instead he felt distinctly apprehensive. He'd be out in the open, not knowing who would turn up besides Harper.

The golf pro was early but John was there before him and on the far side of the lounge bar, Garek was holding a newspaper close to his face. Harper had brought a folder containing survey maps and a projection of the costs of the development, both of which John was used to seeing in connection with Kramer business. He had to admit that the man had been thorough.

'What response are you getting from backers?' Outwardly Harper looked friendly and honest, and John was prepared to give him the benefit of the doubt, until he saw Ron Driver and two burly men enter the room and go to lean against the bar.

'So so,' Harper said. 'Money is tight and no one's keen to speculate but I'm confident we'll have no trouble getting sponsors.' He too had seen Driver and he was nervous.

'And Sam Baxter? Will he be investing?'

Harper nodded. He gathered his paperwork together and slid it untidily back into its folder. 'I think so.'

'At a price? I wonder if it's going to be worth it,' John said softly and saw at once that Harper knew exactly what he meant. 'You'd better go, now that you've set me up. Did you call Baxter as well?'

'I don't know what you mean,' Harper said. There was a sheen of sweat on his face as he pushed back his seat and he almost dropped the folder. As he moved towards the door, Sam Baxter was on his way in and neither man acknowledged the other, nor did Baxter give Driver a glance. He walked purposefully, angrily towards John and when he drew back a chair it scraped noisily on the parquet flooring.

'You got Harper's message then,' John said, lifting his glass to suck the foam from the top of his beer. There was a flash in Baxter's eyes as he realized that he'd in fact come by way of a third hand invitation.

'Very clever. But I've been wanting to talk to you.'

'Ditto.'

They looked at each other, the older man despising the younger but wary at the same time. 'You go first,' John said.

'I'm aware that you're probably wired to record this conversation,' Baxter said evenly.

'Wish I'd thought of that,' John said ruefully, meaning it.

'So I'll say just this. I am a busy man and you are hindering my business. There is no reason for you to dig into my affairs. Sentinel could lose its licence if I complain about what is almost criminal harassment of my friends and associates.' His eyes were challenging and he didn't flinch when John grinned at him.

'You're admitting that Driver is an associate?'

Baxter ignored the question. 'I mean it, Mr Leith. I have powerful friends and your business could suffer as well.'

'Bullshit. Right now I'm toying with the idea of standing up and making a public announcement,' John said. He looked around and saw several of Baxter's business acquaintances. 'It's quite busy in here today, a nice size of audience. Where do you think I should start—with the protection racket or one of your sidelines?'

For an instant there was real alarm in Baxter's eyes. 'Do that and I'll sue you for every penny you have.'

'It wouldn't go down well would it? Think how mud sticks. Sam Baxter, extortionist, drug dealer . . . What would your friends say to that? And there isn't much Driver could do to stop me.'

Baxter said nothing but his eyes looked dead, like black buttons.

'Your empire is crumbling at the edges and soon it's going to slide into oblivion.' He didn't need to put any emphasis on the words because his anger did it for him, but there was still no reaction from Baxter except that blank penetrating stare. 'You and Ron are going to end up in prison for a long time.'

'I don't think so, Mr Leith,' Baxter said with supreme confidence. 'Words are all you have,' he continued flatly, frighteningly.

'I know that,' he admitted quietly. 'But I was there when they pulled Alison out of Duddingston Loch, so I'm going to see you pay. Did you watch her being held up by her ankles in that bath? Did you enjoy seeing her fighting for her life? Is that how you get your kicks, watching your own flesh and blood drown?' He hadn't consciously meant to mention the way Alison had died but instinctively knew that Baxter had indeed witnessed her murder when the other man's mouth opened in shock. And John knew he was raising his voice but didn't care, not even when Baxter glanced around to see if anyone had overheard him. Baxter, jaw clenched with fury, began to get up but John hadn't finished with him yet.

'What did you promise her, Baxter?' Beyond him, John could see Driver watching intently. The man wouldn't have heard what was said but he couldn't miss the fact that Baxter had at last lost his temper. For a second John thought that Baxter was going to lose control and hit him, but instead he turned on his heel and strode towards the exit.

'Ooh.' John let out his breath. It was done. He'd gone much further than he intended and he could only wait and see if it was worth it. Had he angered Baxter enough? The man might cool off later and reason that he'd been deliberately needled and then it would all be wasted.

He watched Driver and the two men go towards the door

but he didn't move until he saw Garek lower his newspaper. They met on the other side of the glass door.

'Now what?' he said to the bald man. 'Do you think they'll be waiting outside?'

'My car is parked at the door,' Garek said.

There was no sign of Baxter but further along the pavement, Driver and the two men were in a black Renault which had pulled up on double yellow lines and a traffic warden was ambling towards it. 'They're going to get a ticket,' John said with satisfaction. The anger he'd felt at Sam Baxter was still simmering at boiling point as he turned to Garek.

'What's Gumley saying about all the free time you're taking?'

Garek headed towards Kramer House. 'It interests him to know what you are doing.'

'You mean he's hoping I'll go too far one day?' he muttered, remembering the murderous look in Baxter's eyes in those last minutes and wondered if he'd already done just that. It didn't help to know that his father-in-law was drooling in hope. Garek hadn't denied it.

'Maybe today you did. You took a gamble,' Garek said drily and John, who was beginning to recognize Garek's humour, suddenly felt the tension leave him. Garek had the ability to take the emotion out of any situation and put it in perspective. The anger was gone and he was able to assess what he'd just done.

'A gamble or a challenge, but will he take it up?' There had been a glitter in Baxter's eyes that had promised revenge. 'I spoke to an old school friend of his who said that Baxter has always had his own way. Maybe this is the first time anyone has stood up to him. He'll want to swat me down.'

'You may be right,' Garek agreed calmly. 'And I presume you intend to give him the chance—that is the next step?'

John nodded, and his stomach seemed to flip over as he explained. 'Tonight I intend going out for a meal and maybe a drink later.'

Garek didn't seem surprised. 'The man is not without intelligence. He may not take the bait.'

The car slid smoothly to a halt outside Kramer House and they discussed it further. Later, John's legs were shaking as he walked inside the building. He was still scared, more so now that he'd set things in motion, but there was also an absolute certainty that he was doing the only thing possible to prove that Tollis could be wrong. The Baxters of this world always had a human failing and Sam's was his ego. It was going to be his undoing.

CHAPTER 13

The afternoon passed swiftly in a jangling of nerves and it was impossible to concentrate on work. Several times he changed his mind about what he was going to do, arguing that he was mad to offer himself as a target, but Jamieson was making slow progress with the murder investigation and might never be able to implicate Baxter in any case. He faced up to the alternative, of having to look over his shoulder for the rest of his life.

'I won't live like that,' he admitted, resigned to his original plan. At seven he showered and dressed with more care than usual. He intended using his own car instead of one of the more anonymous ones from the Kramer pool and he even paused on the steps of the building, standing in a pool of light as he looked up into a clear night sky. It was cold, and sweat cooled rapidly on his body in the short time it took to go around the back of the building to the private parking area. He had half expected Driver's men to be waiting there for him but he slid behind the wheel without incident.

The nerves had quietened now that it was begun and he could see the macabre humour of the situation, because like a condemned man he intended to have a really good meal and he knew exactly where he'd get it. There were no prices on the small à la carte menu displayed in the restaurant's foyer, but the customers who went there were not the sort to quibble.

In the end he couldn't do the meal justice and spent an hour toying with the food and sipping an excellent white wine which was dry and crisp on the palate. He lingered, knowing what was to come, but not when or where and he was in no hurry to find out. It was an unreal feeling which made his skin prickle with sweat.

His car was parked in Charlotte Square and as he walked towards it his footsteps rang out on frosted paving that sparkled like diamond chips. The frost nipped his face and ears, and had the same effect as pinching himself to prove he was not dreaming. He knew it was no dream when two men stepped from the shadows and took hold of his arms above the elbows.

'Don't even try to run,' one warned as a third came up from a basement area, and as John watched him climb the steps to street level, he saw that one of his arms was heavily encased in plaster.

'Remember me, you sod?' the man growled. He was the one Garek had disabled and he looked eager for revenge.

'Save it—you'll get your chance,' one of the captors said.

They put him in the Renault he'd seen earlier at the hotel, one on either side of him in the back and the third got behind the driving wheel. He was glad that he'd not eaten much because it felt as if there was a mass of worms coiling in his stomach.

'You must be off your bloody rocker,' one said. They were all jubilant that it had been so easy to lift him without attracting attention—and he didn't enlighten them.

'Bloody stupid,' said another. 'Christ, Driver is going to enjoy himself tonight.'

John couldn't help a glance behind them, at the empty street, the few pedestrians who had not noticed anything untoward, and one of the men beside him gave a short laugh.

'No use looking back there for help, mate. We're not being followed.'

John wanted to ask if Baxter was going to join them but he kept silent, watching to see where they were taking him. He had half expected it to be AL's offices but soon realized that in fact they were going to Clan Royal. The men were alert, continually watching to see if they'd picked up a tail and couldn't believe their luck when they found they had not.

'You're on your own tonight, Leith,' one said with a hint of excitement in his voice which proved what Garek had said, that these men did what they did for pure pleasure. It didn't make him feel any better, especially since it was all too bloody true—he was on his own.

The car sent up a shower of gravel as it braked hard outside the health club's side entrance and the first thing that he noticed was that most of the building was in darkness.

'Closed for emergency repairs,' one said and they all laughed. 'We don't want customers tonight, do we?'

They were rough when they pulled him from the car and he took several deep breaths of the cold night air before they got him inside. Then it was a long walk along a dark corridor, with a light at the end, and his senses seemed to be working overtime. He saw the cleanliness of the sparkling tiles, smelled the chlorine and expensive body oils that lingered in the air.

The light ahead became dazzling as they got closer to it and he soon saw that it came from a tiled treatment room where spa baths bubbled.

Oh shit, he thought, as the full meaning of what he was doing struck him. After the dark corridor, he was blinded by the light at first as it bounced back off the white tiles, but then he became aware that there were six men present, apart from himself. Three had come in with him, two were muscular attendants in white suits and the sixth was Driver, diminutive compared to everyone else but more menacing that the whole lot put together. There was no sign of Sam

Baxter. Driver came towards him and his captors tightened their grip on his arms.

'You'll beg before we're finished with you and I'm going to enjoy that,' he said. He drew back his arm and for a small man he produced a vicious jab that swung upwards into the soft area under the centre of John's ribs. It forced air from his lungs, and some of the partially digested food and wine came sourly into his throat.

'There's no time for that,' another voice snapped and Baxter came through a door on the right. He moved fast, with short stiff strides, to stand in front of John and he was a frightening sight. The muscles of his face twitched and rippled in a manic display of fury while the rest of his body movements were like an automaton's, jerky, only just under control and even Ron Driver drew back, looking wary.

'You have something that belongs to me. Where is it?' The words came out like bullets and there were bright red blotches on his cheeks, a mottling of the same colour flooded his forehead. The room was silent except for the ragged breathing of the man on John's right and the bubbling splutter of the white spa baths.

John didn't answer, knowing that Baxter wouldn't listen to any denials. The man drew back his right arm and then brought it swinging forward to strike John hard across the face with the flat of his hand. It made his ears ring and sent him staggering but the two men holding him pulled him upright. His cheek went numb and his eyes watered. The back-handed blow followed on, and Baxter's ring tore the flesh of his other cheek.

'You would never dare to say what you did if you hadn't found it,' Baxter screamed.

Blood ran into the corner of John's mouth tasting warm and slightly salty and then dripped down to stain his shirt. He stared back at Baxter and said nothing. It didn't seem possible that anyone's features could change in the way Baxter's were changing. It was as if his skin was mobile, plastic, remoulding into a nightmarish image that reminded him of an old film of Jekyll and Hyde.

Baxter got hold of the front of his jacket and shook him. 'Where is it?'

Driver began to fidget, as if he wanted to intervene but thought better of it. Even the attendants were looking at each other uneasily. Violence was one thing but when it was carried out by a madman, it was something different. It spoiled the fun aspect.

'Is this where Alison died?' John's calm words seemed to shock Baxter into reality. 'Is this where you watched them drown her?' he went on.

Spittle formed a froth on Baxter's lips. 'I didn't need any help to dispose of a slut. She came into my home and stole from me, and then thought she could use it to blackmail me. *Me*! She said she'd bring it with her but the little bitch had hidden it. Where?'

'Do you mean you killed your niece with your own hands?' He couldn't help his mouth curling with disgust and Driver was looking more than dismayed at Baxter's revelations. Baxter let go of his jacket and looked down at his wide spread fingers which were as long and slender as a pianist's.

'She didn't know why I brought her here. She thought I was going to give her a share in everything,' he said, as if puzzled by the stupidity of his niece. 'I said she could open a place of her own, abroad, in the sunshine of the Mediterranean. Rich clients—she wanted it all. She didn't need to bring much, I said, all would be provided.' Baxter smiled gently, and John knew he was witnessing the same smile that had lured Alison to her death.

'She went to take a bath and there she was, in a mass of foam . . . a pretty girl. Then she realized what was really going to happen and she wasn't pretty any more.'

'Sam,' Driver said in a warning tone and Baxter seemed to come out of a trance, become aware that there were too many men listening to his confession. He was coldly calm now.

'I don't believe you have found it,' he said slowly. 'You've had all day and where are the police and your Sentinel friends?' He stepped back, considering. 'Get rid of him,' he said flatly.

Driver was still uneasy. 'Not here, Sam. We can go someplace else . . .'

But Baxter wouldn't listen and stood watching, stoney-faced. John was propelled towards one of the baths by his captors and when he tried to put up a fight his feet slithered on the tiled floor. The two attendants stepped forward, took hold of his feet, and after that resistance was impossible. His head was being pushed down over the churning water, with the smell of minerals rising into his face, when all hell broke out. The heavy swing doors burst open and Garek was the first to appear. Behind him came others, in a flood of blue uniforms.

'Mr Leith, that was too close, far too close,' Jamieson said sternly. Baxter and the others had long since been taken away after the initial scuffle, and policemen were all over the building.

'I didn't see much of what happened,' John said, leaning forward with his elbows on his thighs, feeling the trembling in muscles that seemed to be made of jelly. 'Where's Garek?'

Jamieson pursed his lips. 'Mr Garek slipped away. I'm not sure when—things were confused.'

John was wearing an attendant's white suit because when the police burst in, the top half of his body was under water. A constable had found a first aid kit and had dressed the cut on his cheek.

'Did you hear everything that Baxter said?'

'Aye, we did, but only just. We had a job getting in without anyone hearing us—all that gravel outside and tiles inside. Sorry about the delay.' Jamieson was finding it hard not to laugh. 'You must have thought it had all gone wrong.'

John remembered listening, waiting for some sign that Garek hadn't let him down . . . 'I wouldn't like to go through it again, ever,' he said.

'We did our best to get here as fast as we could. You owe a lot of thanks to Mr Garek. I won't ask how he managed to open the place up before we arrived, but drop a word in his ear that I'm taking it for granted he really has retired. What was that he did when Driver went for him?'

'Aikido. It's a defence form of martial art. Garek says it brings a sense of peace and well-being.'

'Does it now? Didn't look all that peaceful to me. Driver says his back's broken.' They were sitting on a cherry-red settee in the foyer while a team of police began sifting through the office paperwork. Jamieson looked suddenly serious. 'They could have been armed, you know.'

'A quick bullet isn't Baxter's style.' John knew that instinctively and he'd been proved right. 'He's a sadist.'

Jamieson made a face. 'He could still plead innocence, you know. Confessions aren't enough and we still don't know what he was making a fuss about.'

'I think I can help you there. It's odd, a trick of the subconscious if you like, but I've been racking my brain about what this bloody missing object could be and it only came to me when they were about to dunk me in the bath. That's when I realized how stupid I had been.'

'How so?'

Jamieson's men were getting noisy, calling to each other and wheeling filing cabinets out of the smaller rooms so they could work unhindered.

'Let's sit in the car and I'll explain,' John said. It was bitterly cold and he shivered as the frosty air took his breath away, but he knew part of it was the after effects of what had happened, shock, disbelief that it was all over. Jamieson turned on the car heater and then was impatient to hear what he had to say.

'I got to know Alison pretty well these last couple of weeks, although I never met her,' John said. 'I was certain that she would want to keep her little treasure where she could easily get it, or make sure it was safe. That meant it had to be in her flat, but we all ignored the fact that Dee took *her* belongings out of there. I think Alison hid it in

Dee's room.' He didn't add that Shiela, psychic friend, had practically told him that all along, because that would be too much for Jamieson to swallow.

'Shall we go and find out?' Jamieson suggested. He had a driver tonight so he sat beside John in the back of the police car. As it went down the drive, past the immaculate lawns and gardens, John hoped he'd never set eyes on the place again.

Mike and Dee were watching a video in the neat sitting-room where Dee's text books and folders of lecture notes were spread over a coffee table.

'Would you mind if we looked through your things, Miss Oakley?' Jamieson asked after initial explanations had been made. 'Mr Leith thinks Alison may have planted something amongst your belongings.'

'I don't mind, but I think I'd have found it.'

They went into Dee's bedroom and it didn't take long to go through her few possessions carefully.

'Nothing. Looks as if you were wrong after all,' Jamieson said, and sighed in frustration. He turned, on the point of giving up, when Mike called to them from the sitting-room.

'It's in here,' he said, holding up a thick text book. 'I can see something.' He had to fetch slim-nosed pliers to pull the tightly rolled envelope from the binding along the spine of the book. 'It was safe at any rate—it would never have fallen out of there.' He passed the tube of paper to the policeman who unrolled it carefully.

'Now, what have we got? A page torn from a notebook and . . . a photograph. My God!' Jamieson took only a quick look and then made sure that Dee could not see it. He looked shocked, repelled, as he passed it to John, then he studied the paper that had ragged edges, as if it had been torn from a book in a hurry.

'Names and dates, and in the last column, amounts of cash paid, all handwritten. She must have torn out a page hoping he wouldn't notice right away—I hope the notebook still exists, and even—God help me—more photographs like this one. Then we'll have Samuel Baxter.' He raised his head, stared into space and then muttered, 'Do you know what we've got here?'

'I can guess,' John said quietly. He had hoped they'd get something on Baxter and they had, but even so it had turned out to be totally unexpected. Mike was curious and so was Dee but Jamieson wasn't going to share the discovery with anyone yet.

'No discussion of this, Mr Leith,' he warned. He straightened up. 'That silly girl didn't know what she did when she stole from Baxter,' he said sadly.

After a sleepless night, the next day was taken up with statements at police headquarters and John told Tollis later how it had ended. 'Jamieson has just phoned to say they've uncovered all the evidence they need in Baxter's home, including Alison's missing jewellery, so that gets him for her murder. Baxter also kept a diary with dates and names, as well as photographs that date right up to recent weeks. The police are still searching the house.'

'No wonder he was afraid it would all come out,' Tollis said.

'I should have had an inkling when Ben Wallace told me about him bullying the younger boys at school, but it never occurred to me that Baxter abused them in other ways.'

'It's not the sort of thing you grow out of,' Tollis said soberly. 'I hope they put him away for life.' He had been chain smoking as he listened and now he stubbed out a cigarette angrily.

'He's sick,' John said. 'But Jamieson says that Driver is denying complicity in it. He thinks Driver will talk in case he's branded with the same things. Maybe he's telling the truth . . .'

'And maybe he isn't. Baxter would need someone on the streets to bring boys in . . . Christ it makes me sick, but the rats will leave the city now. You know, the air was beginning to smell foul lately.'

*

John went up to his flat that evening with a mind that was full of too many vivid images to let him think of sleeping. The men gripping his arms, forcing his head down towards the bubbling water, Baxter's frantic struggle as he realized that it was all over. He'd fought the police as they tried to get him out of the building and at the same time screamed threats that John would hear in his dreams . . . but according to Jamieson the man had been subdued that day.

But most of John's thoughts were about the dead girl, Alison Baxter. She had seen the same photograph that had sickened an experienced policeman like DCI Robert Jamieson and yet she had used it to blackmail her uncle. Somehow the genes must have got passed on, he thought, and the niece had inherited the ones that made Samuel Baxter what he was: evil.

John looked around the flat that had never seemed more impersonal than it did that night. Then he went into the bedroom and began to throw clothes into a suitcase. If he hurried he would catch the late evening flight to London, to be with Clare.